Beiträge zum
ausländischen öffentlichen Recht und Völkerrecht

Edited by

the Max Planck Society
for the Advancement of Science
represented by Prof. Dr. Armin von Bogdandy
and Prof. Dr. Anne Peters

Volume 323

Matthias Lippold

The Interrelationship of the Sources of Public International Law

Open Access funding provided by Niedersachsen-Konsortium.

The Deutsche Nationalbibliothek lists this publication in the
Deutsche Nationalbibliografie; detailed bibliographic data
are available on the Internet at http://dnb.d-nb.de

a.t.: Göttingen, Univ., Diss., 2020

ISBN   978-3-7560-0234-4 (Print)
        978-3-7489-3757-9 (ePDF)

British Library Cataloguing-in-Publication Data
A catalogue record for this book is available from the British Library.

ISBN   978-3-7560-0234-4 (Print)
        978-3-7489-3757-9 (ePDF)

Library of Congress Cataloging-in-Publication Data
Lippold, Matthias
The Interrelationship of the Sources of Public International Law
Matthias Lippold
843 pp.
Includes bibliographic references and index.

ISBN   978-3-7560-0234-4 (Print)
        978-3-7489-3757-9 (ePDF)

1st Edition 2024

© Matthias Lippold

Published by
Nomos Verlagsgesellschaft mbH & Co. KG
Waldseestraße 3–5 | 76530 Baden-Baden
www.nomos.de

Production of the printed version:
Nomos Verlagsgesellschaft mbH & Co. KG
Waldseestraße 3–5 | 76530 Baden-Baden

ISBN   978-3-7560-0234-4 (Print)
ISBN   978-3-7489-3757-9 (ePDF)
DOI   https://doi.org/10.5771/9783748937579

Online Version
Nomos eLibrary

This work is licensed under the Creative Commons Attribution
4.0 International License.

Preface

This book is a revised and updated version of my doctoral thesis which I defended at the Faculty of Law of the University of Göttingen in October 2020.

I would like to thank my academic teacher and the supervisor of this thesis, Professor Andreas Paulus, former Justice of the Federal Constitutional Court, for his constant support, encouragement and academic guidance. He has influenced my thinking about international law in many ways. He also directed my attention to the topic of this thesis.

I would like to thank Professor Peter-Tobias Stoll for providing the second review and Professor Frank Schorkopf for chairing the oral examination. I am grateful for the insightful comments and suggestions I received in the two written reviews and during the defense of the thesis.

I am also grateful to the whole community at the Göttingen Institute of International and European Law for creating a great atmosphere and an inspiring research environment; in particular, I thank the team of the Institute's library.

Outside Göttingen, I am grateful for stimulating discussions on international legal scholarship with my classmates and professors during my LL.M. year at New York University. I thank Professor Georg Nolte, now Judge at the International Court of Justice, for accepting me as an intern during the sixty-sixth ILC session and for the insights into the work of the ILC. I thank Professor Mads Andenæs for inviting me to participate in workshops in Geneva and Paris dedicated to the sources of international law and in particular general principles of law. I thank the participants of both workshops and the organizers and participants of the 2016 ESIL Research Forum in Istanbul. I am grateful for all the comments, feedback, inspirations and for the exchange of views on international law and its sources.

Professor Armin von Bogdandy and Professor Anne Peters accepted this book into the prestigious *Beiträge zum ausländischen öffentlichen Recht und Völkerrecht* series of the Max Planck Institute for Comparative Public Law and International Law in Heidelberg, for which I am much obliged.

I gratefully acknowledge the financial support received for my doctoral research from the *Studienstiftung des deutschen Volkes*. The *Niedersachsen-Konsortium* generously supported the publication of this book. The doctoral dissertation underlying this book received the Faculty Prize of the Juristische Gesellschaft zu Kassel in the winter term 2020/2021.

Finally, I would like to thank my friends and I would like to thank my family. My deepest gratitude goes to my parents for their patience and their continuous, unconditional and generous support.

Göttingen, September 2023

Contents

List of Abbreviations   19

A. Introduction

Chapter 1: Setting the Scene   25
A. The conceptual framework   26
    I.   The plurality of sources and the architecture of public international law   27
        1. The General Law of Treaties   28
            a. Different codification approaches   29
            b. The rules of treaty interpretation and their relationship with customary international law   32
        2. The law of international responsibility   36
    II.   Traditional approaches to the relationship of sources   41
        1. The relationship between sources   41
        2. The relationship between the norms of different sources   44
        3. The relationship between formal sources and material sources   45
    III.   The Politics as to the sources: Source preferences in the international community   47
        1. Source preferences and the spirit of the time   49
        2. Source preferences and the changed composition of the legal community   50
        3. Source preferences and the substantive expansion and diversification of international law   53
    IV.   The Concept of interrelationship of sources and the scope of this study   56
        1. The interrelationship of sources   56
        2. Benefits of a focus on the interrelationship of sources in international practice   60
        3. Contribution of an analysis of the interrelationship of sources to the doctrine relating to each source   62
            a. Customary international law   62

		b. General principles of law	65
		c. Treaties	70
	V.	Situating the present study	72
		1. The work of the ILC	73
		2. Sociological perspectives: the proliferation of norms and socializing states	78
B.	Structure of this study		86
	I.	Comparative-historical perspectives	86
	II.	Institutional perspectives	90
	III.	Perspectives on different normative contexts	91
	IV.	Doctrinal perspectives: revisiting the doctrine of sources	93

B. Comparative and historical perspectives

Chapter 2: Comparative Perspectives	97
A. Introduction: The interrelationship of sources in comparative legal thought	97
B. Example: The common law and the interrelationship of unwritten and written law	103
I. The Historic discourse of the relationship between the common law and the written law in the United Kingdom	105
1. Different law preferences: William Blackstone and Jeremy Bentham	106
2. John Austin and the will of the sovereign as source of all law	109
3. Subsequent perspectives in UK legal theory: Thomas Holland, H.L.A. Hart and Brian Simpson	111
II. The historic discussion of the relationship between unwritten law and the written law in the United States of America	113
1. Roscoe Pound	115
2. Benjamin Cardozo	117
3. Lon Fuller	118
III. A new interest in the interplay between common law and statutory law in the recent UK jurisprudence	120
1. Common law as human rights law	121
2. Common law in light of human rights	123
3. Concluding Observations	125
C. Example: German law and the interrelationship of sources	126

	I.	The historical school	127
		1. Friedrich Carl von Savigny	128
		2. Georg Friedrich Puchta	129
	II.	The declining relevance of custom	131
		1. Rudolf von Jhering's critique and the codification of civil law	131
		2. Approaches prior to the Basic Law	133
		3. Approaches under the Basic law	137
D.	Characteristics of general principles of law from a comparative historical perspective		138
	I.	General principles in legal theory: an overview	140
	II.	Conceptualizations of legal validity and different degrees of normativity of general principles	144
		1. Reflections on the scholarship of Josef Esser and Hans Kelsen's response	144
		2. Conceptualizations of legal validity and different degrees of normativity of general principles	147
	III.	Assessment: recognizing the multifaceted character of general principles	151
E.	Concluding Observations		154

Chapter 3: Historical Perspectives on article 38 PCIJ Statute   157
A. Introduction   157
B. The positivist climate: the doctrinal interest in treaties and general conceptions of law   157
C. Institutional Background: The Hague Conferences of 1899 and 1907   164
   I. The background of the conferences   165
   II. The provisions on applicable law and the recognition of three sources   166
D. The drafting of article 38   170
   I. Triad of sources in the preparatory work   170
   II. The discussion in the Advisory Committee of Jurists   171
      1. General principles of law   171
      2. The discussion of the interrelationship of sources   174
E. Constructing the Interrelationship in the interwar period   178
   I. The PCIJ   178
   II. The 1930 Codification Conference and the discussion of the sources   182

Contents

    III. The inter-war scholarship on the interrelationship of sources   186
        1. Overview   186
        2. Dionisio Anzilotti   189
        3. Georges Scelle   192
        4. Hans Kelsen   195
            a. Legal-theoretical overview   196
            b. The interrelationship of sources within the *Stufenbau*   198
                aa. Customary international law   199
                bb. Treaties as a product of the international community   200
                cc. General principles of law   202
        5. Alfred Verdross   203
        6. Hersch Lauterpacht   207
F. Concluding Observations   211

Chapter 4: Concluding observations on the comparative and historical perspectives   215

C. **Institutional Perspectives**

Chapter 5: The International Court of Justice   221
A. Introduction   221
B. Third-party intervention and the interrelationship of sources   223
    I. The general regime: Articles 59, 62, 63 and 66 ICJ Statute   224
    II. The Court's practice to interventions under article 62 ICJ Statute: from a restrictive to a more inclusive approach?   226
        1. The development of the restrictive approach   227
        2. Tendencies of a more inclusive approach   229
        3. A paradigm shift? Interventions in matters of customary international law - The *Jurisdictional Immunities* case   231
    III. Evaluation   233
C. Jurisdiction and the interrelationship of sources   235
    I. Jurisdiction clauses and their impact on the interrelationship of sources   236
    II. The application of general international law as general part in relation to a specific rule   240
        1. The uncontroversial cases: validity, interpretation, responsibility   240

		2. A controversial case? Succession to responsibility	242
	III.	The relationship between jurisdictional clauses and "substantive" law	245
		1. The relationship between applicable law and interpretation	247
		a. The *Oil Platforms* case	247
		b. The *Pulp Mills* case and the environmental impact assessment under general international law	249
		2. From deconventionalization to reconventionalization? The prohibition of genocide and the distinctiveness of sources for the purposes of jurisdiction	252
	IV.	Recent Confirmations and Concluding Observations: distinctiveness for jurisdictional purposes	255
D.	The normative environment in the jurisprudence of the ICJ		258
	I.	Varying degrees of generality of customary international law	260
	II.	Interpretative Decisions	266
		1. Default positions, starting points and the normative context	267
		a. The *Asylum* case	268
		b. The *Nottebohm* case and the genuine link requirement	269
		c. The significance of the normative context	274
		2. "Scoping" and tailoring of the legal analysis	275
		3. Shaping the rule by acknowledging an exception	277
	III.	The relationship between customary international law and treaty law	278
		1. The *Morocco* case	279
		2. The *North Sea Continental Shelf* judgment	280
		3. Convergence between the Charter and customary international law into common principles	285
		a. Self-determination	285
		b. The prohibition of the use of force	289
		4. Convergence of functionally equivalent rules in the law of the sea	290
		a. From a focus on the distinctiveness to a convergence of functionally equivalent rules	291
		b. Reasons for convergence: the vagueness of rules and judicial pragmatism informed by the normative environment	294
		c. UNCLOS and its impact on customary international law	300

		d. Concluding observations	303
	IV.	General Principles and the normative environment	305
		1. The rare recourse to municipal law analogies	306
		2. General principles and the international legal order	310
E.	Concluding observations		313

Chapter 6: The International Law Commission 317
A. Introduction 317
    I. Codification and the interrelationship of sources 317
    II. The institutionalization of codification and the difficult distinction between progressive development and codification 319
    III. The significance of the normative environment 325
        1. The "blending of customary international law with the new order established by the United Nations" 325
        2. The early consideration of principles expressed in treaties 327
        3. Reconciling the normative environment and state practice: The recent controversy over immunity of State officials from foreign criminal jurisdiction 330
B. The form of codification and progressive development and its implications 338
    I. The form of the ILC product 339
        1. The form and the risk of "decodification" 340
        2. The question of form and the respective spirit of the time 341
        3. *Codification light* as joint enterprise of several actors 348
    II. The substantive form: the codification choice between openness and closedness 350
    III. Concluding Observations on Form and Substance 353
C. The interrelationship of sources in selected projects 354
    I. The law of treaties 355
        1. The scope of the topic 355
        2. The interrelationship within the law of treaties 359
            a. From intertemporality to a means of interpretation 360
            b. Codification policies on the relationship with other principles and rules of international law 363
    II. Responsibility of States for Internationally Wrongful Acts 364
        1. The work of García-Amador 364
        2. The focus on the rules of responsibility as secondary rules 367
    III. Fragmentation of international law: difficulties arising from the diversification and expansion of international law 368

	IV.	The identification of customary international law	372
		1. The role of normative considerations in the identification of customary international law	373
		a. The scoping of the topic by the Special Rapporteur	373
		b. The adopted draft conclusions	374
		aa. The recognition of normative considerations	374
		bb. The relationship between customary international law and treaties	376
		2. Concluding observations: normative considerations addressed with caution	377
	V.	Peremptory norms of general international law (*Jus cogens*)	378
	VI.	General Principles of Law	384
		1. General Principles of Law in the progressive development and codification	384
		2. The new topic of General Principles of Law	386
		a. Overview of the draft conclusions	386
		b. Comments and reflections on the draft conclusions	388
D.	Concluding Observations		395

Chapter 7: Concluding observations on the institutional perspectives   399

D. Perspectives in different fields of international law

Chapter 8: The European Convention on Human Rights		403
A. Introduction		403
B. The interpretation of the ECHR		406
I.	The European Court's approach to interpretation	408
II.	Relating the European Court's practice to the general rules of interpretation	414
III.	Recourse to other rules and principles of international law for content-determination	418
C. Interpretative decisions in establishing the interrelationship		424
I.	The construction of establishing a relation between the European Convention and other principles and rules of international law	425
	1. Incorporation by proportionality analysis	425
	2. Proportionality analysis and customary international law	426
	a. Two different constructions	426

			b.	The operation of proportionality analysis	429
				aa. The *Al-Adsani* judgment	429
				bb. The *Jones* judgment	430
			c.	Repercussion of the construction: the focus on the individual case	432
			d.	Evaluation	434
		3.	Proportionality analysis and treaty law		436
		4.	Reconciliation on the basis of general principles		438
			a.	The prohibition of arbitrariness and international humanitarian law	438
			b.	Security Council Resolutions	441
	II.	Concluding observations			442
D.	The relationship between the ECHR and the law of international responsibility				443
	I.	"Jurisdiction" and the relationship between article 1 ECHR and general international law			443
	II.	The role of attribution in relation to the ECHR			446
	III.	Two notions of "control" in relation to jurisdiction and to attribution			448
	IV.	A treaty-based functional equivalent to attribution under general international law?			451
	V.	Attribution in the context of international organizations			456
		1.	The development of normative criteria for the delimitation of responsibilities		456
		2.	The United Nations as a special case		458
E.	Concluding Observations				460

Chapter 9: International Criminal Law		463
A.	Introduction	463
B.	The recognition of individual's responsibility for violations of international law	463
	I. From the interwar period to the Military Tribunals in Nuremberg and Tokyo	464
	II. The reception in the UNGA and treatymaking practice of states	469
	III. The road towards an international criminal court	473
C.	The interrelationship of sources and the International Criminal Tribunals	476
	I. The preference for customary international law	476

		1. Customary international law and individual responsibility for war crimes in non-international armed conflicts	477
		2. Source preferences: customary international law and alternative avenues	479
	II.	Interpretative decisions and normative considerations in the identification of customary international law and general principles of law	485
		1. The problem of appreciating practice in armed conflicts	485
		2. General principles as a bridge between customary international law and the normative environment	487
		a. Recognizing the interrelationship and distinctiveness of sources: normative inspirations and functional specificities	487
		b. The risk to disregard the functional specificities	491
		c. The role of domestic Law	493
		3. The significance of the legal craft	497
		a. Default positions	497
		b. The determination of the scope of the rule	499
		aa. An absolute prohibition of civilian reprisals?	499
		bb. The conceptual alternative to an absolute prohibition: regulation by stringent criteria	501
	III.	Preliminary evaluation: the stabilizing effect of normative considerations and their limits	502
D.	The Interrelationship of Sources and the Rome Statute		507
	I.	The legal regime	507
	II.	The interrelationship between the general rules of interpretation and the Rome Statute	515
		1. Article 21 Rome Statute and the general rules of interpretation	515
		2. The crimes of the Rome Statute and customary international law	517
		3. Further development of treaty-based approaches or alignment with customary international law?	522
	III.	A conflict of sources? Between JCE, control theory and indirect perpetratorship	526
		1. The construction of JCE and its three distinct categories	528
		a. Indirect perpetratorship as conceptual alternative	531
		b. Attempts of reconciliation	532

		2. Rome and the move towards a new paradigm	534
		3. Evaluation: institutional and conceptual competition instead of conflict of sources	538
	IV.	(No) Immunities under customary international law	546
		1. The legal regime	547
		2. The *Al-Bashir* case	548
		3. The decision of the ICC Appeals Chamber	551
E.	Concluding Observations		554

Chapter 10: International Investment Law — 557
A. Introduction — 557
B. From the interwar period to the modern investment regime — 558
    I. The historical connection between responsibility and the protection of aliens — 558
    II. The importance of unwritten law — 562
        1. The minimum standard and its contestation — 564
        2. The internationalization of contracts by general principles of law — 571
            a. The emergence of this doctrine in the interwar period — 571
            b. The continuation of this doctrine after the second world war — 574
    III. The development of the modern investment regime after WW II — 577
        1. Failed multilateral attempts — 578
        2. Ongoing contestation in the General Assembly — 578
        3. Preference for BITs — 579
C. The interrelationship of sources in a bilateralist structure and the quest for general law — 582
    I. The relationship between treaty obligations and customary international law — 583
        1. The relationship between functionally equivalent rules — 585
            a. The jurisprudence of investment tribunals — 585
            b. The treatymaking practice of states — 590
        2. Reasons for the preference for convergence — 592
    II. The interrelationship of sources in the scholarly debate — 595
        1. Customary International Law — 595
        2. *Jurisprudence Constante* — 597
        3. Multilateralization *qua* interpretation and the rise of general principles — 599

		4. Examples of tribunals' recourses to principles	600
	III.	Evaluation	604
		1. General principles and the development of the law	604
		2. The promotion of paradigms by recourse to principles	607
		3. A remaining role for customary international law as community mindset?	609
D.	The significance of constructions		610
	I.	Competing constructions	610
		1. Alignment between the BIT and necessity under customary international law	612
		2. Differences between the BIT and necessity under customary international law	613
	II.	Revisiting the distinction between primary and secondary rules	616
		1. The distinction in the law of state responsibility	617
		2. The distinction in the case-law of the ICJ	619
		3. The distinction and the relationship between the general law of treaties and the law of state responsibility	621
	III.	Concluding remarks as to the distinction between primary rules and secondary rules	624
E.	Concluding Observations		625

Chapter 11: Concluding observations on the perspectives   629

E. Doctrinal Perspectives and Conclusions

Chapter 12: Doctrinal perspectives on and discussions of the interrelationship of sources			635
A.	Introduction		635
B.	Shifting research interests in specific sources		635
	I.	The early interest in general principles of law prior to the rise of codification conventions	635
	II.	Different approaches to new norms	639
		1. Roberto Ago's spontaneous law	639
		2. Bin Cheng and Karl Zemanek	642
	III.	Codification studies: the interrelationship between treaties and custom	645
		1. Richard Baxter's paradox	645

		2. Anthony d'Amato and the formation of custom by treaties	648
		3. Hugh Thirlway	649
C.	The interrelationship in a value-laden legal order		651
	I.	The continuing interest in customary international law in light of the *Nicaragua* judgments and skepticism	651
	II.	The interrelationship of sources in the international community	656
D.	Recent legal positivist perspectives		667
	I.	Jörg Kammerhofer	667
	II.	Jean d'Aspremont	672
E.	Concluding Observations		677

Chapter 13: Concluding observations		679
A.	Reflections on the interrelationship of sources	679
	I. The interrelationship of sources as a focus of research	679
	II. Forms of interplay and convergences	681
	III. The institutionalization and the interrelationship	683
	IV. Customary international law	686
	V. Treaties	689
	VI. General principles	691
	VII. The distinctiveness of sources and their interrelations	694
	VIII. The politics in relation to the interrelationship of sources	697
	IX. The interrelationship of sources and general international law	701
B.	Conclusions	704

Bibliography	707
Index	841

List of Abbreviations

AC	Appeals Chamber
AJIL	American Journal of International Law
ARIO	Articles on the Responsibility of International Organizations
ARSIWA	Articles on the Responsibility of States for Internationally Wrongful Acts
ASIL	American Society of International Law
BIT	Bilateral Investment Treaty
BYIL	British Yearbook of International Law
CAT	Convention Against Torture and Other Cruel, Inhuman or Degrading Treatment or Punishment
CETA	Comprehensive Economic and Trade Agreement
CJEU	Court of Justice of the European Union
CPTPP	Comprehensive and Progressive Agreement for Trans-Pacific Partnership
Decl	Declaration
Diss Op	Dissenting Opinion(s)
ECCC	Extraordinary Chambers in the Courts of Cambodia
ECHR	European Convention on Human Rights
ECJ	European Court of Justice
ed(s)	editor(s)
EJIL	European Journal of International Law
EU	European Union
FTA	Free Trade Agreement
GC	Grand Chamber
GoJIL	Goettingen Journal of International Law
IACtHR	Inter-American Court of Human Rights
ICC	International Criminal Court
ICCPR	International Covenant on Civil and Political Rights
ICESCR	International Covenant on Economic, Social and Cultural Rights
ICJ	International Court of Justice
ICJ REP	ICJ Reports

List of Abbreviations

ICSID	International Centre for the Settlement of Disputes
ICTR	International Criminal Tribunal for Rwanda
ICTY	International Criminal Tribunal for the former Yugoslavia
ILA	International Law Association
ILC	International Law Commission
ILC Ybk	Yearbook of the International Law Commission
ILM	International Legal Materials
ILR	International Law Reports
IMT	International Military Tribunal for the Far East
IMT	International Military Tribunal
JICJ	Journal of International Criminal Justice
JIDS	Journal of International Dispute Settlement
Max Planck EiPro	Max Planck Encyclopedia of International Procedural Law
Max Planck EPIL	Max Planck Encyclopedia of Public International Law
NAFTA	North American Free Trade Agreement
NPM	Non-Precluded Measures
NYU JILP	New York Journal of International Law and Politics
para(s)	paragraph(s)
PCIJ	Permanent Court of International Justice
PTC	Pre-Trial Chamber
RdC	Recueil des Cours de l'Académie de Droit International
RGDIP	Revue Générale de Droit International Public
RIAA	Reports of International Arbitral Awards
SCC	Stockholm Chamber of Commerce
SCSL	Special Court Sierra Leone
Sep Op	Separate Opinion(s)
STL	Special Tribunal for Lebanon
TC	Trial Chamber
tr	translator
UDHR	Universal Declaration of Human Rights
UN	United Nations
UNC	Charter of the United Nations
UNCITRAL	United Nations Commission on Trade Law
UNCTAD	United Nations Conference on Trade and Development

UNGA	UN General Assembly
UNSC	UN Security Council
UNSG	UN Secretary-General
UNTS	United Nations Treaty Series
VCLT	Vienna Convention on the Law of Treaties
WTO	World Trade Organisation
ZaoeRV	Zeitschrift fuer auslaendisches Recht und Voelkerrecht
ZOR	Zeitschrift fuer öffentliches Recht

Part A.

Introduction

Chapter 1: Setting the Scene

"Die Entwicklung der internationalen Gemeinschaft zwingt dazu, auch die Quellen des Völkerrechts stets neu zu überdenken und ihre Veränderungen zu diagnostizieren."[1]

Questions about the relationship and interaction of sources of law and of written and unwritten law arise in every legal system. Their answers depend on the respective legal culture, the needs of the legal community and the spirit of the times. The international legal order has known three sources of international law which were set forth in article 38 of the Statute of the Permanent Court of International Justice in 1921[2]: written law in the form of treaties and unwritten law in the form of customary international law and general principles of law. Since then, the international legal order has changed in many ways. The so-called decolonization led to the independence of so-called new states and raised the question of the Western character of the international legal order and its sources of law. The proliferation of courts and tribunals in the field of human rights protection, international criminal law, and investment protection law illustrates the increased institutionalization and substantive diversification of the international legal order. These developments also give rise to the question of whether the international legal order continues to recognize one doctrine of legal sources or whether different doctrines of legal sources are emerging in different areas of international

---

1 Rudolf Bernhardt, 'Ungeschriebenes Völkerrecht' (1976) 37 ZaöRV 50 (The development of the international community requires one to constantly review also the sources of international law and to diagnose changes in the sources, translation by the present author).
2 Protocol of Signature relating to the Statute of the Permanent Court of International Justice provided for by Article 14 of the Covenant of the League of Nations (signed 16 December 1920, entered into force 1 September 1921) 6 LNTS 379. Article 38(1) ICJ Statute includes an additional reference to the function of the Court which is "to decide in accordance with international law such disputes as are submitted to it". Furthermore, the last sentence of article 38 PCIJ Statute according to which "[t]his provision shall not prejudice the power of the Court to decide a case *ex aequo et bono*, if the parties agree thereto" became a separate paragraph. See Alain Pellet and Daniel Müller, 'Article 38' in Andreas Zimmermann and others (eds), *The Statute of the International Court of Justice: a commentary* (Oxford University Press 2019) 832-4.

law. The fact that the sources of international law have recently also been the subject of various studies by the International Law Commission may indicate a need for a reassessment of the normative foundations of the international legal system.

Against this background, the present work focuses on the relationship and the interplay of the sources of international law. The aim of this study is to develop a research perspective that contributes to the understanding of the sources in the present international community and shows that the three sources of international law are not unrelated to each other. Rather, different forms of interaction and balance among the various sources of law can be observed in the international legal order.

For this purpose, this book proceeds as follows: After an introduction and presentation of the conceptual approach and the research interest (chapter 1), the book first approaches its topic from comparative legal historical perspectives (chapters 2-4). The subsequent institutional perspectives (chapters 5-7) focus on the relationship and interplay between the sources of international law in the jurisprudence of the International Court of Justice (chapter 5) and in the work of the International Law Commission (chapter 6). Next, the topic of inquiry is examined in three selected areas (chapters 8-11), namely in the context of the European Convention on Human Rights (chapter 8), international criminal law (chapter 9) and international investment law (chapter 10). The last part is devoted to doctrinal perspectives (chapters 12-13). Based on the analysis so far, the penultimate chapter 12 engages with the scholarship on sources and contextualizes selected explanatory models on the relationship and interplay among sources. The thirteenth chapter offers reflections on the interrelationship of sources and conclusions of this study.

A. *The conceptual framework*

The purpose of this first chapter is to contextualize the present study and to explain the approach adopted in this book. This chapter first illustrates by way of example that several international instruments, the law of treaties and the law of international responsibility recognize the plurality of sources of international law which is also set forth in article 38(1) ICJ Statute (I.). Whilst the dominant view holds that there is no abstract hierarchy between the sources, one can observe so-called informal hierarchies in the sense of preferences for one particular source, sometimes at the expense of the other, in scholarship and case-law (II.-III.). However, this study understands the three sources set forth in article 38(1) ICJ Statute as an interrelated regime and argues that this understanding, together with a focus on legal practice, can make a valuable contribution to the doctrine of sources (IV.). This chapter situates this study in the context of the work of the ILC, in particular its recent conclusions on customary international law and the ongoing project on general principles of law. It draws inspiration from recent legal-sociological scholarship which illustrates the connection between treaties and customary international law and therefore invites doctrinal research to approach the interrelationship of sources (V.). The chapter concludes with an account of this study's structure (B.).

I. The plurality of sources and the architecture of public international law

Article 38(1) ICJ Statute is one of many provisions that refer to a plurality of sources. For instance, the Martens clause, which appears in the preamble to the 1899 Hague Convention (II) with respect to the laws and customs of war on land, stipulates that "in cases not included in the Regulations [...] populations and belligerents remain under the protection and empire of *the principles of international law, as they result from the usages established between civilized nations, from the laws of humanity and the requirements of the public conscience.*"[3] The clause reminds one that a question not addressed or regulated by a specific convention remains subject to unwritten international law. In the preamble of the Charter of the United Nations, "the peoples of the United Nations" pledge to "establish conditions under which justice and respect for the obligations arising from treaties and *other sources of international law* can be maintained", and the Charter "*recognizes*" in article 51 "the *inherent right* of individual or collective self-defence".[4] Several codification conventions contain references to international law outside the convention[5],

---

[3] Convention (II) with Respect to the Laws and Customs of War on Land and its annex: Regulations concerning the Laws and Customs of War on Land (signed 29 July 1899, entered into force 4 September 1900) 32 Stat 1803 (italics added).

[4] Charter of the United Nations (signed 26 June 1945, entered into force 24 October 1945) 1 UNTS 16 (italics added).

[5] United Nations Convention on the Law of the Sea (signed 10 December 1982, entered into force 16 November 1994) 1833 UNTS 3 affirms in its preamble "that matters not regulated by this Convention continue to be governed by the rules and principles of general international law"; both the Vienna Convention on Consular Relations (signed 24 April 1963, entered into force 19 March 1967) 596 UNTS 261 and the

Chapter 1: Setting the Scene

indicating that, unlike in domestic law, codification in public international law did not strive to replace customary law completely.[6] Moreover, the Rome Statute, which was drafted in order to define the crimes in a written form, explicitly acknowledges in article 10 that part 1 of the Rome Statute does not limit or prejudice "in any way existing or developing rules of international law for purposes other than this Statute".[7]

If one takes a look at the infrastructure of public international law, the general law of treaties as reflected in the Vienna Convention on the Law of Treaties[8] and the ARSIWA[9] will deserve special attention. They set forth so-called "rules on rules"[10], guiding international lawyers in relation to treaties and to internationally wrongful acts. Here, the pluralism of sources finds expression as well, albeit to varying degrees.

1. The General Law of Treaties

Several articles of the VCLT recognize and touch on the pluralism of sources and reflect different approaches to the codification and its relationship with other sources.[11]

Vienna Convention on Diplomatic Relations (signed 18 April 1961, entered into force 24 April 1964) 500 UNTS 95 include a similar provision in their respective preamble.

6 Cf. Wolfram Karl, *Vertrag und spätere Praxis im Völkerrecht: zum Einfluß der Praxis auf Inhalt und Bestand völkerrechtlicher Verträge* (Springer 1983) 362 ("Ziel einer Kodifikation ist es ja, Gewohnheitsrecht durch vertragliches Recht zu ersetzen, es zu verdrängen.").

7 Rome Statute of the International Criminal Court (signed 17 July 1998, entered into force 1 July 2002) 2187 UNTS 3.

8 Vienna Convention on the Law of Treaties (signed 23 May 1969, entered into force 27 January 1980) 1155 UNTS 331.

9 *Draft Articles on Responsibility of States for Internationally Wrongful Acts (ARSIWA)* UN Doc A/56/10, Supplement no. 10.

10 On this notion see also Mark E Villiger, *Customary International Law and Treaties* (2nd edn, Kluwer Law International 1997) 292; Mārtiņš Paparinskis, 'Masters and Guardians of International Investment Law: How To Play the Game of Reassertion' in Andreas Kulick (ed), *Reassertion of Control over the Investment Treaty Regime* (Cambridge University Press 2017) 36; Matina Papadaki, 'Compromissory Clauses as the Gatekeepers of the Law to be 'used' in the ICJ and the PCIJ' [2014] JIDS 21-22.

11 See also Jan Klabbers, 'Reluctant Grundnormen: Articles 31(3)(C) and 42 of the Vienna Convention on the Law of Treaties and the Fragmentation of International Law' in Matthew Craven, Malgosia Fitzmaurice, and Maria Vogiatzi (eds), *Time, History and International Law* (Martinus Nijhoff Publishers 2007) 141 ff.

a) Different codification approaches

The preamble affirms that the rules of customary international law will continue to govern questions not regulated by the provisions of the present Convention. With respect to questions of the treaty's validity, termination, denunciation or withdrawal, article 42 VCLT provides that the VCLT or the respective treaty will govern these matters exhaustively.[12] Article 73 VCLT, however, opens the door to other sources to some extent since the Vienna Convention does not prejudice any question relating to succession of states, to international responsibility of a state or to the outbreak of hostilities.[13] Article 53 recognizes the voidness of a treaty which conflicts with a peremptory norm of general international law.

The case of "multi-sourced"[14] obligations is addressed in articles 38 and 43 VCLT. Article 38 VCLT constitutes a saving reservation that reminds its readers of the possibility that a rule contained in a treaty can become binding

---

12 It is therefore questionable whether a general principle of law such as the *exceptio non adimpleti contractus* remains additionally available next to article 60 VCLT which governs the termination and suspension of the operation of a treaty as a consequence of its breach, see on this discussion Bruno Simma, 'Reflections on article 60 of the Vienna convention on the law of treaties and its background in general international law' (1970) 20 Österreichische Zeitschrift für öffentliches Recht 5 ff.; Filippo Fontanelli, 'The Invocation of the Exception of Non-Performance: A Case-Study on the Role and Application of General Principles of International Law of Contractual Origin' (2012) 1(1) Cambridge Journal of International and Comparative Law 119 ff.; James Crawford and Simon Olleson, 'The Exception of Non-performance: Links between the Law of Treaties and the Law of State Responsibility' (2000) 21 Australian Year Book of International Law 55 ff.; Maria Xiouri, 'Problems in the Relationship between the Termination or Suspension of a Treaty on the Ground of Its Material Breach and Countermeasures' (2015) 6 Queen Mary Law Journal 63 ff.; Serena Forlati, 'Reactions to Non-Performance of Treaties in International Law' (2015) 25 Leiden Journal of International Law 759 ff.; cf. *Application of the Interim Accord of 13 September 1995 (The former Yugoslav Republic of Macedonia v. Greece)* (Judgment of 5 December 2011) [2011] ICJ Rep 644 Sep Op Judge Simma 708 para 29 (no longer maintaining his earlier held view, now "join[ing] the ranks of those who regard Article 60 as truly exhaustive", at 705 para 22), Diss Op Judge *ad hoc* Roucounas 745 para 66.
13 The attempt to incorporate the exceptio into the law of international responsibility was not successful, see Crawford and Olleson, 'The Exception of Non-performance: Links between the Law of Treaties and the Law of State Responsibility' 55 ff.
14 The term is borrowed from Tomer Broude and Yuval Shany, 'The International Law and Policy of Multi-sourced equivalent norms' in Tomer Broude and Yuval Shany (eds), *Multi-sourced equivalent norms in international law* (Hart 2011) 1 ff.

on third states as an obligation of customary international law.[15] With respect to multi-sourced obligations, article 43 VCLT clarifies that the

> "invalidity, termination or denunciation of a treaty, the withdrawal of a party from it, or the suspension of its operation, as a result of the application of the present Convention or of the provisions of the treaty, shall not in any way impair the duty of any State to fulfil any obligation embodied in the treaty to which it would be subject under international law independently of the treaty."

A similar *ratio* can be found in guideline 4.4.2. of the ILC's formally non-binding *Guide to Reservations* according to which a reservation to a treaty obligation which also reflects a rule of customary international law "does not *of itself* affect the rights and obligations under that rule".[16] In addition, according to guideline 3.1.5.3, "[t]he fact that a treaty provision reflects a rule of customary international law does not *in itself* constitute an obstacle to the formulation of a reservation to that provision."[17] Earlier, the Human Rights Committee had argued that "provisions in the Covenant that represent customary international law (and a fortiori when they have the character of peremptory norms) may not be the subject of reservations."[18] Without taking a view on the respective merit of each approach, it suffices for the purposes of this chapter to point out that both approaches view the relationship between treaty law and customary international law differently. The consequence of the interpretation of the Human Rights Committee would be that customary international law reinforces the treaty obligations under the ICCPR, and, incidentally, the procedural framework treaty obligations are embedded in, by making reservations to such treaty provisions impermissible. In contrast, the position of the ILC stresses the distinctiveness of treaty law and customary international law. They are distinct in that a reservation to a treaty provision does not concern the bindingness of custom, nor does customary international law of itself render a reservation to a treaty provision reflecting customary international law invalid. For the purposes of determining the permissibility

---

15 Article 38 VCLT reads: "Nothing in articles 34 to 37 precludes a rule set forth in a treaty from becoming binding upon a third State as a customary rule of international law, recognized as such."
16 *Guide to Practice on Reservations to Treaties* ILC Ybk (2011 vol 2 part three) 292 (italics added).
17 ibid 220 (italics added).
18 *General Comment No 24: Issues Relating to Reservations Made upon Ratification or Accession to the Covenant or the Optional Protocols thereto, or in Relation to Declarations under Article 41 of the Covenant* Human Rights Committee CCPR/C/21/Rev.1/Add.6 (4 November 1994) para 8.

of a reservation, the treaty's object and purpose are decisive.[19] This distinctiveness does not mean, however, that there is no interrelation at all: the *Guide to Reservations* acknowledges that "in practice, it is quite likely that a reservation to such rule [of customary international law, M.L.] (especially if it is a peremptory norm) will be incompatible with the object and purpose of the treaty by virtue of the applicable general rules."[20] A similar approach can be found in the recently adopted ILC conclusions on peremptory norms of general international law. According to conclusion 13, "[a] reservation to a treaty provision that reflects a peremptory norm of general international law (*jus cogens*) does not affect the binding nature of that norm, which shall continue to apply as such", furthermore, "[a] reservation cannot exclude or modify the legal effect of a treaty in a manner contrary to a peremptory norm of international law".[21] The adopted commentary stresses the distinctiveness: the legality of the reservation would depend on its compatibility with the treaty's object and purpose, which requires an interpretation of the treaty. At the same time, it is stressed that "a State cannot escape the binding nature of a peremptory norm of general international law (*jus cogens*) by formulating a reservation to a treaty provision *reflecting that norm*"[22] which exists outside the treaty.

---

19 *Guide to Practice on Reservations to Treaties* 199, guideline 3.1.
20 ibid 222. See also 225, where the Commission argued "that the principle stated in guideline 3.1.5.3 applies to reservations to treaty provisions reflecting a customary peremptory norm", while adding that it "considers that States and international organizations should refrain from formulating such reservations and, when they deem it indispensable, should instead formulate reservations to the provisions concerning the treaty regime governing the rules in question." Cf. *Armed Activities on the Territory of the Congo (New Application: 2002) (Democratic Republic of the Congo v. Rwanda)* (Jurisdiction and Admissibility, Judgment) [2006] ICJ Rep 33 paras 69-70 (the Court noted that no *jus cogens* norm existed that required a state to consent to the jurisdiction and that the Court lacked jurisdiction because of a reservation to article IX of the Genocide Convention), and Sep Op Higgins, Kooijmans, Elaraby, Owada and Simma 72 para 29 (arguing that it was "not self-evident that a reservation to Article IX could not be regarded as incompatible with the object and purpose of the Convention").
21 *Report of the International Law Commission: Seventy-third session (18 April–3 June and 4 July–5 August 2022)* UN Doc A/77/10 at 54 (conclusion 13).
22 ibid 55 (last italics added).

Chapter 1: Setting the Scene

b) The rules of treaty interpretation and their relationship with customary international law

The rules of treaty interpretation set forth in articles 31-33 VCLT are of central importance for establishing a relationship between a particular treaty and other sources. Article 31 VCLT sets forth the "general rule of interpretation". The fact that article 31 speaks of "rule" as opposed to "rules" even though it refers to various means of interpretation indicates that all means have to be applied simultaneously in light of each other. Considering all means of interpretation constitutes "the rule of interpretation."[23] Occasionally, one speaks of "general rules of interpretation" when one refers to the whole interpretative regime of articles 31-33 VCLT which the International Court of Justice has considered to reflect customary international law.[24]

According to article 31(3)(c) VCLT, the interpreter shall take account of "any relevant rules of international law applicable in the relations between the parties". Undoubtedly, customary international law and general principles of law, binding all parties to the treaty, are to be taken into account.[25] In addition, the debated view has gained ground that based on this provision an interpreter can take other treaties, or better yet the principles and evaluations expressed therein, into account, even when not all parties to the treaty which

---

23 *ILC Ybk (1966 vol 2)* 219 ("single combined operation").
24 *Question of the Delimitation of the Continental Shelf between Nicaragua and Colombia beyond 200 nautical miles from the Nicaraguan Coast (Nicaragua v. Colombia)* (Preliminary Objections) [2016] ICJ Rep 116 para 33; *Alleged Violations of Sovereign Rights and Maritime Spaces in the Caribbean Sea (Nicaragua v. Colombia)* (Preliminary Objections) [2016] ICJ Rep 18 para 35; Enzo Cannizzaro, 'The law of treaties through the interplay of its different sources' in Christian J Tams and others (eds), *Research handbook on the law of treaties* (Edward Elgar Publishing 2014) 17 ff.
25 *Fragmentation of international law: difficulties arising from diversification and expansion of international law, Report of the Study Group of the International Law Commission, Finalized by Martti Koskenniemi* 13 April 2006 UN Doc A/CN.4/L.682 215; Bruno Simma and Theodor Kill, 'Harmonizing Investment Protection and International Human Rights: First Steps Towards a Methodology' in Christina Binder and others (eds), *International Investment Law for the 21st Century Essays in Honour of Christoph Schreuer* (Oxford University Press 2009) 694-695; Gebhard Bücheler, *Proportionality in investor-state arbitration* (Oxford University Press 2015) 99; Oliver Dörr, 'Article 31. General rule of interpretation' in Oliver Dörr and Kirsten Schmalenbach (eds), *Vienna Convention on the Law of Treaties. A Commentary* (2nd edn, Springer 2018) 606-608.

The conceptual framework

is to be interpreted are parties to the respective treaty to which recourse is made.[26] The scope of the general rule of interpretation and its various means can be important in that it may incentivize interpreters to resort to arguments based on customary international law and general principles of law or to adopt the view that treaty interpretation is flexible enough and that it may be not necessary to work with sources of unwritten international law,[27] as the interpreter has further means of interpretation at her disposal, including, but not limited to, subsequent agreements and subsequent practice on the interpretation of the treaty.[28] The difference between customary international

---

26 On this debate see *Fragmentation of international law: difficulties arising from diversification and expansion of international law, Report of the Study Group of the International Law Commission, Finalized by Martti Koskenniemi* 237-238 para 471, arguing that a restrictive interpretation of article 31(3)(c) VCLT would be contrary to the "legislative ethos behind most of multilateral treaty-making and, presumably, with the intent of most treaty-makers."; see *EC - Measures Affecting the Approval and Marketing of Biotech Products* Panel Report (6 February 2006) WT/DS291/R WT/DS292/R WT/DS293/R para 7.68, concluding that only rules applicable between all parties to a treaty can be taken into account under article 31(3)(c) VCLT, para 7.90 ff. suggesting as alternative to use other international law under article 31(1); see Panos Merkouris, *Article 31(3)(c) vclt and the Principle of Systemic Integration* (Brill Nijhoff 2015) 46 ff., pointing out that the Biotech approach was not representative of other panels' and Appellate Bodies' practice, see for instance *United States - Import Prohibition of Certain Shrimp and Shrimp Products* Appellate Body (12 October 1998) AB-1998-4 para 130 ff. (citing conventions not all WTO parties had ratified); see also Isabelle van Damme, *Treaty interpretation by the WTO Appellate Body* (Oxford University Press 2009) 368 ff.; Margaret A Young, 'The WTO's Use of Relevant Rules of International Law: an Analysis of the Biotech Case' (2007) 56(4) ICLQ 914-921 (arguing with respect to article 31(1) that other international law should be used to illuminate the object and purpose rather than the ordinary meaning); on article 31(1) as alternative to article 31(3)(c) see also Mārtiņš Paparinskis, 'Come Together or Do It My Way: No Systemic Preference' (2014) 108 Proceedings of the American Society of International Law at Its Annual Meeting 246 ff. on treaty interpretation by the WTO Appellate Body.
27 Cf. Jean d'Aspremont, 'International Customary Investment Law: Story of a Paradox' in Eric de Brabandere and Tarcisio Gazzini (eds), *International Investment Law* (Martinus Nijhoff 2012) 42, arguing that the principle of systemic integration "already provides judges with a sweeping power to harmonize without unnecessary and costly inroads into the murky theory of customary investment law."
28 For the ILC conclusions on subsequent agreements and subsequent practice see *Report of the International Law Commission: Seventieth session (30 April-1 June and 2 July-10 August 2018)* UN Doc A/73/10 23 ff.; the phenomenon of evolutive treaty interpretation has been examined by Christian Djeffal, *Static and evolutive treaty*

law and subsequent practice is that customary international law establishes an independent norm, whereas subsequent practice relates to an already existing norm of a treaty and embodies an agreement as to the treaty's interpretation.

While "the general rule" set forth in article 31 VCLT requires that all means are simultaneously applied in light of each other in a "single combined operation"[29], the relative weight of each means cannot be determined in the abstract but can differ in each case. When weighing and balancing the different means in order to interpret the treaty in good faith, the interpreter may also be influenced by extra-legal considerations, such as institutional considerations or legal-political considerations.[30] Within this leeway left to law-applying authorities, it is also a question of judicial policy whether and to what extent courts and tribunals adopt an integrative standpoint by invoking the principle of systemic integration and aiming at a decision in accordance with international law as a whole or opt for self-restraint.[31] Thus, the general rules of treaty interpretation can strengthen arguments based on customary international law and general principles of law or render recourse to them less necessary, they offer different ways to further develop the treaty by way

---

interpretation: a functional reconstruction (Cambridge University Press 2015); Eirik Bjørge, *The evolutionary interpretation of treaties* (Oxford University Press 2014); Julian Arato, 'Treaty Interpretation and Constitutional Transformation: Informal Change in International Organizations' (2013) 38 Yale Journal of International Law 289 ff.; Julian Arato, 'Constitutional Transformation in the ECtHR: Strasbourg's Expansive Recourse to External Rules of International Law' (2012) 37(2) Brooklyn Journal of International Law 349 ff.

29 *ILC Ybk (1966 vol 2)* 219.

30 Joost HB Pauwelyn and Manfred Elsig, 'The Politics of Treaty Interpretation: Variations and Explanations across International Tribunals' in *Interdisciplinary perspectives on international law and international relations: the state of the art* (Cambridge University Press 2013) 445 ff.; Daniel Peat, *Comparative Reasoning in International Courts and Tribunals* (Cambridge University Press 2019) 18-21.

31 See Jochen von Bernstorff, 'Hans Kelsen on Judicial Law-Making by International Courts and Tribunals: a Theory of Global Judicial Imperialism?' (2015) 14(1) The law and practice of international courts and tribunals: a practitioners' journal 50:"Instead of hoping for systemic integration through sectorial jurisprudence, I would thus argue in favour of a practice of systemic self-restraint of sectorial courts and tribunals [...] My main fear thus is the future 'colonization' of the fabric of international law by specific and particularly dynamic sectorial regimes."; see also Adamantia Rachovitsa, 'The Principle of Systemic Integration in Human Rights Law' (2017) 66(3) ICLQ 557 ff., 573-575; cf. generally (without reference to article 31(3)(c)) Philip Alston, 'Resisting the Merger and Acquisition of Human Rights by Trade Law: A Reply to Petersmann' (2002) 13(4) EJIL 815 ff., 836.

of interpretation. Whether a specific path will be taken will depend on the interpretative culture which develops both generally and in specific fields of public international law.

If one understood the rules of interpretation under the VCLT and under custom to be separate and distinct, one could argue, as France did in the *Rhine Chlorides* case,[32] that the general rule of interpretation under customary international law could not be applied "with the same kind of minute and analytical rigour as would be the case if [the Vienna Convention] were itself binding as between the parties."[33] This contention could be supported by a *dictum* of the International Court of Justice in the *Nicaragua* case according to which "[r]ules which are identical in treaty law and in customary international law are also distinguishable by reference to the methods of interpretation and application."[34] Yet, the arbitrators did not adopt in the *Rhine Chlorides* case such an artificial distinction between the rules of interpretation under the VCLT and under customary international law. Instead, it was held that the Vienna rules "must be taken as faithful reflection of the current state of customary law."[35] In a similar way, the ILC in its conclusions on subsequent agreements and subsequent practice did not distinguish between the VCLT and customary international law.[36] This view of the relationship between the

---

32 Richard K Gardiner, *Treaty interpretation* (2nd, Oxford University Press 2015) 44-46.
33 *The Rhine Chlorides Arbitration concerning the Auditing of Accounts* The Netherlands v. France, Award (12 May 2004) PCA Case No 2000-02 para 43 (position of France), unofficial English translation of the PCA.
34 *Military and Paramilitary Activities in and against Nicaragua (Nicaragua v. United States of America)* (Merits) [1986] ICJ Rep 95 para 178; cf. Alexander Orakhelashvili, *The Interpretation of Acts and Rules in Public International Law* (Oxford University Press 2008) 497: "Customary rule should be interpreted independently from its conventional counterpart, according to the rationale it independently possesses. The applicable methods of interpretation have to do with the nature of customary rules." The ICJ emphasized the distinctiveness of the sources for jurisdictional purposes while also acknowledging their interrelationship when it comes to interpretation, see below, p. 258 ff.
35 *The Rhine Chlorides Arbitration concerning the Auditing of Accounts* PCA Case No 2000-02 para 77.
36 *ILC Report 2018* at 19: "Hence, the rules contained in articles 31 and 32 apply as treaty law in relation to those States that are parties to the 1969 Vienna Convention, and as customary international law between all States, including to treaties which were concluded before the entry into force of the Vienna Convention for the States parties concerned."

Chapter 1: Setting the Scene

VCLT and customary international law stresses the entanglement, as opposed to a strict separation, of both sources.

2. The law of international responsibility

The law of international responsibility touches on the pluralism of sources only to a limited extent. Its application is triggered by an internationally wrongful act which will come into existence if conduct is attributable to the state and constitutes a breach of an international obligation of that state (article 2 ARSIWA). It is a general regime composed of secondary rules, as opposed to primary rules in the sense of specific substantive obligations.[37] Article 12 ARSIWA defines a breach as "an act of that State [...] not in conformity with what is required of it by that obligation, regardless of its origin or character." It was decided, as the corresponding commentary reveals, not to use the very term "source" and to speak of "origin", "which has the same meaning, [...] [while] not [being] attended by the doubts and doctrinal debates the term 'source' has provoked."[38]

The following parts of the ARSIWA introduce a certain differentiation, not according to the sources but according to the type of obligations. For instance, if a state's responsibility is engaged by a serious breach of an obligation arising under a peremptory norm of general international law (article 40 ARSIWA), states shall cooperate to bring to an end through lawful means any serious breach (article 41(1) ARSIWA) and shall not recognize

---

37 James Crawford, *State Responsibility: The General Part* (Cambridge University Press 2013) 64: "The source of the distinction between primary and secondary rules within the terminology of state responsibility is unclear. Potential sources include an adaptation of H.L.A. Hart's famous distinction between primary and secondary rules, continental jurisprudence, or simply organic development within the ILC itself." As will be demonstrated in below, the idea to understand the law of responsibility as an abstract, secondary regime was already present, for instance, at the 1930 Codification Conference, see below, p. 559. See also Marko Milanovic, 'Special Rules of Attribution of Conduct in International Law' (2020) 96 International Law Studies 299-300 (arguing that the distinction between primary and secondary rules in the context of the ILC differs from Hart's distinction). Cf. Herbert L Hart, *The concept of law: With a postscript* (2nd edn, Clarendon Press 1994) 92; Nicholas Onuf, *Law-making in the global community* (Carolina Acad Press 1982) 11.
38 *ILC Ybk (2001 vol 2 part 2)* 55 para 3; in contrast, delegates at the 1930 codification conference wanted to define the sources and debates at length about making reference to article 38 PCIJ Statute, see below, p. 182 ff.

as lawful a situation created by a serious breach (article 41(2) ARSIWA).[39] Article 41(3) ARSIWA stipulates that this article is without prejudice "to such further consequences that a breach to which this chapter applies may entail under international law". Peremptory norms of general international law are protected from countermeasures (article 50(1)(d) ARSIWA).[40]

Moreover, the articles on reparation and countermeasures benefit international obligations the violation of which results in injury to a specific state.[41] Article 31(1) ARSIWA sets forth the obligation to make full reparation for the injury caused by the internationally wrongful act and defines injury as "any damage, whether material or moral" (article 31(2) ARSIWA).[42] A state is entitled as an injured state to invoke another state's responsibility if the obligation breached is owed to that state individually (article 42(a) ARSIWA) or to a group of states including that state, or the international community as a whole, and the breach of the obligation specially affects that state or is of such a character as to radically change the position of all the other states to which the obligation is owed with respect to the further performance of the obligation (article 42(b) ARSIWA). An injured state may resort to countermeasures (article 49 ARSIWA) which are also recognized as circumstances precluding the wrongfulness of an otherwise internationally wrongful act (article 22 ARSIWA). Article 48 ARSIWA introduces the concept of a "State other than an injured State". "[I]f (a) the obligation breached is owed to a group of states including that state, and is established for the protection of a collective interest of the group; or (b) the obligation breached is owed to the international

---

39 See now also *ILC Report 2022* at 71, commentary to conclusion 19 on peremptory norms of general international law ("[...] the obligation to cooperate to bring to an end serious breaches of obligations arising under peremptory norms of general international law (*jus cogens*) is now recognized under international law").
40 See now also ibid at 69 (conclusion 18).
41 See also André Nollkaemper, 'Constitutionalization and the Unity of the Law of International Responsibility' (2009) 16 Indiana Journal of Global Legal Studies 555: "Large parts of the law of international responsibility, in particular the articles on reparation and countermeasures, remain rooted in the idea that responsibility is based on a breach of an obligation toward a person who is entitled to the performance of that obligation. Somewhat paradoxically, in light of Articles 1 and 2 of the Articles on State Responsibility (that do not require injury as a condition for responsibility), the principles of reparation make clear that no remedy is provided for breaches of international obligations where no material or moral damage has occurred."
42 The second chapter of the ARSIWA's second part then is concerned with "reparation for injury", see the articles 34, 37(1) and (3), 39 ARSIWA as well as with respect to damage article 36(1) ARSIWA.

Chapter 1: Setting the Scene

community as a whole" (article 48 (1) ARSIWA), a so-called "State other than an injured State" may claim from the responsible state cessation of the internationally wrongful act, assurances and guarantees of non-repetition (article 48(2)(a) ARSIWA) and performance of the obligation of reparation in accordance with the preceding articles, in the interest of the injured state or of the beneficiaries of the obligation breached (article 48(2)(b)).[43] The ARSIWA do not explicitly set forth a right of a non-injured state to resort to so-called collective or community countermeasures in response to an internationally wrongful act on behalf of the international community. According to article 54 ARSIWA, they do not "prejudice the right of any State, entitled under article 48, paragraph 1, to invoke the responsibility of another State, to take lawful measures against that State to ensure cessation of the breach and reparation in the interest of the injured State or of the beneficiaries of the obligation breached." Given the risk of potential abuse and the lack of institutional safeguards against vigilantism, there was no agreement for anything more than this saving reservation.[44]

---

43 Cf. on the debate of a "legal", "normative" injury (*préjudice juridique*) Brigitte Stern, 'The Elements of an Internationally Wrongful Act' in James Crawford, Alain Pellet, and Simon Olleson (eds), *The Law of International Responsibility* (Oxford University Press 2010) 194 ff. (arguing that the ILC adopted a narrower understanding of injury and introduced instead the concept of a "State other than an injured State"); see also Brigitte Stern, 'Et si on utilisait le concept de préjudice juridique?: retour sur une notion délaissée à l'occasion de la fin des travaux de la C. D. I. sur la responsabilité des états' (2001) 47 Annuaire français de droit international 5, 19 ff.; see recently *Application of the Convention on the Prevention and Punishment of the Crime of Genocide* (*The Gambia v. Myanmar*) (Preliminary Objections, Judgment of 22 July 2022) [2022] ICJ Rep 477 Decl Judge ad hoc Kreß paras 10 ff. See now also *ILC Report 2022* at 64 and 68 (conclusion 17(2) on peremptory norms of general international law and the corresponding commentary). The commentary is silent on the question of whether every state is to be regarded as an injured state in the case of a *jus cogens* violation and refers to article 42 and article 48 ARSIWA.

44 Thus, the articles do not fully operationalize what Elihu Root and Philip C. Jessup described as states' general interest in preserving law as such, see Elihu Root, 'The Outlook for International Law' (1915) 9 Proceedings of the American Society of International Law at Its Annual Meeting 9; Philip C Jessup, *A modern law of nations: An introduction* (Archon books, reprint 1968) 2, 12; cf. for an overview of the discussion in the ILC Denis Alland, 'Countermeasures of General Interest' (2002) 13(5) EJIL 1221 ff.; cf. Christian J Tams, *Enforcing Obligations Erga Omnes in International Law* (Cambridge University Press 2005) 249-251, describing article 54 as a compromise and concluding (at 250) that "present-day international law recognises a right of all States, irrespective of individual injury, to take countermeasures in re-

The conceptual framework

One lawful measure can consist, for instance, in resorting to proceedings before the ICJ. After the ICJ had held in the South-West Africa cases that international law would not provide for an *actio popularis*[45], the Court's jurisprudence began to include proceedings concerning *erga omnes partes* obligations.[46] With respect to the prohibition of torture under the CAT and to the prohibition of genocide under the Genocide Convention, the Court held that all parties have "a common interest" in compliance with the respective obligations and "a legal interest in the protection of the rights involved".[47]

---

sponse to large-scale or systemic breaches of obligations *erga omnes.*"; cf. Andreas L Paulus, 'Whether Universal Values can prevail over Bilateralism and Reciprocity' in Antonio Cassese (ed), *Realizing Utopia: The Future of International Law* (Oxford University Press 2012) 101-102, arguing that if countermeasures are permitted in cases of breaches of bilateral obligations, "it is inconceivable to provide a lower threshold of protection to those obligations considered *erga omnes* or even *jus cogens*. Protection against vigilantism should be rather found in the general limitations to countermeasures [...] The weak implementation of community interests also signifies something else: in the last resort, it is the international institutions that have to take up collective concerns."

45 *South West Africa* (*Ethiopia v. South Africa; Liberia v. South Africa*) (Second Phase, Judgment) [1966] ICJ Rep 47 para 88.

46 On *erga omnes* see already *Barcelona Traction, Light and Power Company, Limited* (*Belgium v. Spain*) (Judgment) [1970] ICJ Rep 32 paras 33-34; for examples of *erga omnes partes* cases, see *Questions relating to the Obligation to Prosecute or Extradite* (*Belgium v. Senegal*) (Judgment) [2012] ICJ Rep 450 para 70; *Application of the Convention on the Prevention and Punishment of the Crime of Genocide* (*The Gambia v. Myanmar*) (Order of 23 January 2020) [2020] ICJ Rep 13 para 42; *Application of the Convention on the Prevention and Punishment of the Crime of Genocide* (Preliminary Objections) https://www.icj-cij.org/public/files/case-related/178/178-20220722-JUD-01-00-EN.pdf paras 106-112. Since the Court had no jurisdiction in the proceedings initiated by the Marshall Islands, the Court did not have to address the question of standing in relation to obligations under customary international law in the proceedings involving India and Pakistan which were not, unlike the UK, parties to the Non-Proliferation Treaty, cf. *Obligations concerning Negotiations relating to Cessation of the Nuclear Arms Race and to Nuclear Disarmament* (*Marshall Islands v. India*) (Judgment of 5 October 2016) [2016] ICJ Rep 277 para 56; *Obligations concerning Negotiations relating to Cessation of the Nuclear Arms Race and to Nuclear Disarmament* (*Marshall Islands v. India*) (Judgment of 5 October 2016) [2016] ICJ Rep 573 para 56.

47 *Questions relating to the Obligation to Prosecute or Extradite* [2012] ICJ Rep 422, 449 para 68; see also *Application of the Convention on the Prevention and Punishment of the Crime of Genocide* (Preliminary Objections) https://www.icj-cij.org/public/files/case-related/178/178-20220722-JUD-01-00-EN.pdf para 107.

Thus, proceedings concerning *erga omnes partes* obligations confirm the *ratio* of article 48 ARSIWA according to which so-called non-injured states can concern themselves with violations of international law by other states.[48] It has to be stressed though that the ARSIWA are not concerned with the question of standing before an international court,[49] and that the Court so far has not used the ARSIWA terminology of "non-injured" states in its jurisprudence on *erga omnes* obligations.[50]

According to the recently adopted ILC conclusions on peremptory norms of general international law, norms of *jus cogens* "give rise" to obligations *erga omnes* "in relation to which all States have a legal interest".[51] The ILC relied, *inter alia*, on the ICJ jurisprudence on treaty-based obligations *erga omnes partes*.[52] If this view will be accepted, states can have standing in proceedings before the ICJ in relation to violations of *jus cogens* norms. These proceedings require, however, a jurisdictional basis. If the system of compromissory clauses confines jurisdiction to the application of treaties, the question may arise whether the ICJ's jurisdictional framework is in fact more favourable to treaty obligations than to obligations under customary international law.[53]

---

48 *Obligations concerning Negotiations relating to Cessation of the Nuclear Arms Race and to Nuclear Disarmament* [2016] ICJ Rep 255 Diss Op Crawford 522 para 21.

49 ILC, *Draft Articles on Responsibility of States for Internationally Wrongful Acts (ARSIWA)* 120-121; *Obligations concerning Negotiations relating to Cessation of the Nuclear Arms Race and to Nuclear Disarmament* [2016] ICJ Rep 255, 272-273 para 42 and Diss Op Crawford 522 para 22.

50 Cf. *Application of the Convention on the Prevention and Punishment of the Crime of Genocide* (Preliminary Objections) https://www.icj-cij.org/public/files/case-related/178/178-20220722-JUD-01-00-EN.pdf para 106 and Decl Judge *ad hoc* Kreß paras 7-19.

51 *ILC Report 2022* at 64 (conclusion 17(1)). Note that the UNGA decided that consideration of the conclusions and the commentary adopted by the ILC "shall be continued at the seventy-eighth session of the General Assembly", UNGA Res 77/103 (19 December 2022) UN Doc A/RES/77/103 para 3; see also Sean D Murphy, 'Peremptory Norms of General International Law (Jus Cogens) (Revisited) and Other Topics: The Seventy-Third Session of the International Law Commission' (2023) 117(1) AJIL 95-97.

52 *ILC Report 2022* at 65, 68.

53 See below, p. 236 ff.

II. Traditional approaches to the relationship of sources

The plurality of sources raises the question of their relationship. Different models of relationships between sources are proposed in international legal scholarship.[54] In the following, this section zeroes in on the discussion of the relationship of sources (1.), the relationship between norms of different sources (2.) and the relationship between formal sources and material sources (3.).

1. The relationship between sources

As far as an abstract hierarchy of sources is concerned, one may refer to David Kennedy who has pointed out that "the relative authority of various sources is most often discussed in contrasting treaties and custom. Advocates of all logically available positions exist."[55] Certain scholars regard custom to be the supreme source.[56] Its generality *ratione personae* destines custom to be the common law of a community[57] and it is described to be relevant for the other two sources: the customary rule of *pacta sunt servanda* explains the

---

54 See Yoram Dinstein, 'The interaction between customary international law and treaties' (2006) 322 RdC 383 ff.
55 David Kennedy, 'The Sources of International Law' (1987) 2 American University Journal of International Law & Policy 16 footnote 25; on different views on the relative primacy of treaty law and customary law see now Mario Prost, 'Sources and the Hierarchy of International Law: Source Preferences and Scales' in Samantha Besson and Jean d'Aspremont (eds), *The Oxford Handbook of the Sources of International Law* (Oxford University Press 2017) 640 ff.
56 Petros Vallindas, 'General Principles of Law and the Hierarchy of the Sources of International Law' in *Grundprobleme des internationalen Rechts: Festschrift für Jean Spiropoulos* (Schimmelbusch 1957) 426-427, who lists custom as first source, followed by general principles of law and conventions. His account stress the interplay between the first, as "various customary rules of international law can be evolved into a system, a legal order, only by their implementation through the general principles of law" (at 431).
57 On custom as consensus of the international community: Marcelo G Kohen, 'La pratique et la théorie des sources du droit international' in Société Française pour le Droit International (ed), *La pratique et le droit international: Colloque de Genève* (Pedone 2004) 93-94.

Chapter 1: Setting the Scene

binding force of treaties[58], and it has also been argued that general principles were recognized as a source by customary international law.[59] Others regard treaties to be the dominant source. Treaties enjoy a "procedural primacy"[60] in that lawyers will first and foremost apply a treaty and according to *lex specialis derogat legi generali* a treaty prevails over the more general customary international law.[61] In addition, treaties are regarded in certain ways as superior. There is a higher certainty as to a treaty's ascertainment ("ontological determinacy"[62]), treaties can regulate any substance matter with detailed procedural rules, and treatymaking is a conscious process which allows for participation of domestic parliaments and faces less legitimacy concerns in comparison to customary international law[63] which has been described as unconscious lawmaking.[64] Last but not least, it has also been argued that general principles of law rank the highest and provide for the

---

58 Hans Kelsen, 'Théorie du droit international coutumier' (1939) 1 Revue internationale de la théorie du droit, nouvelle série 258; Hans Kelsen, *Principles of International Law* (Rinehart 1952) 366-367.
59 Cf. Alfred Verdross, *Die Verfassung der Völkerrechtsgemeinschaft* (Springer 1926) 59; on the development of Verdross' thinking as to the relationship between customary international law and general principles of law, see below, p. 204.
60 Prost, 'Sources and the Hierarchy of International Law: Source Preferences and Scales' 648.
61 Cf. Pellet and Müller, 'Article 38' 932 para 274.
62 Prost, 'Sources and the Hierarchy of International Law: Source Preferences and Scales' 648.
63 For a critique of the procedural and democratic legitimacy of custom: James Patrick Kelly, 'The Twilight Of Customary International Law' (2000) 40 Virginia Journal of International Law 452, 457-458, 517-535.
64 Cf. Kelsen, *Principles of International Law (1952)* 308; Gennady M Danilenko, *Law-Making in the International Community* (Martinus Nijhoff Publishers 1993) 78; Antonio Cassese, *International Law* (2nd edn, Oxford University Press 2005) 156; Ago coined the term "spontaneous law", Roberto Ago, 'Science juridique et droit international' (1956) 90 RdC 935 ff. But see David Lefkowitz, 'Sources in Legal-Positivist Theories: Law as Necessarily posited and the Challenge of Customary Law Creation' in Samantha Besson and Jean d'Aspremont (eds), *The Oxford Handbook on Sources of International Law* (Oxford University Press 2017) 338, arguing that "[t]he perception that customary norms are the product of a process that is neither intentional nor directed rests on the assumption that acts of willing or positing norms must be legislative".

first rudimentary norms on the basis of which custom and treaty law can develop.[65]

According to the prevailing view, however, there is no abstract hierarchy between the sources in general.[66] If one linked the concept of *jus cogens* to customary international law[67], one could claim that certain rules of customary international law are superior. According to the ILC draft conclusion 5 on *jus cogens*, which the ILC adopted on second reading, "customary international law is the most common basis for peremptory norms of general international law (jus cogens)", yet "[t]reaty provisions and general principles of law may also serve as bases for peremptory norms of general international law (jus

---

65 On the superior value of general principles in relation to other sources see Alfred Verdross, 'Forbidden Treaties in International Law' (1937) 31 AJIL 575; Alfred Verdross, 'Die allgemeinen Rechtsgrundsätze als Völkerrechtsquelle Zugleich ein Beitrag zum Problem der Grundnorm des positiven Völkerrechts' in Alfred Verdross and Josef Dobretsberger (eds), *Gesellschaft, Staat und Recht: Untersuchungen zur reinen Rechtslehre* (Springer 1931) 361; Gerhard Leibholz, 'Verbot der Willkür und des Ermessensmißbrauches im völkerrechtlichen Verkehr der Staaten' (1929) 1 ZaöRV 88-89, 122-125.
66 Karl Zemanek, 'The Legal Foundations of the International Legal System' (1997) 266 RdC 132; Mark E Villiger, *Customary International Law and Treaties* (Martinus Nijhof Publishers 1985) 35; James Crawford, *Brownlie's principles of public international law* (9th edn, Oxford University Press 2019) 20; Pellet and Müller, 'Article 38' 932-936; *Fragmentation of international law: difficulties arising from diversification and expansion of international law, Report of the Study Group of the International Law Commission, Finalized by Martti Koskenniemi* 47 para 85, 233 para 463, considering an "informal hierarchy" of application of the oftentimes more special treaty but also describing that such treaty will be interpreted against the background of the general law and that legal reasoning thus progresses through concentric circles; article 38 itself does not indicate a strict order of application, see below, p. 90. See also Michael Akehurst, 'Hierarchy of Sources' (1974) 47 BYIL 274-275, 279; but cf. Riccardo Monaco, 'Observations sur la hiérarchie des sources du droit international' in Rudolf Bernhardt (ed), *Völkerrecht als Rechtsordnung, Internationale Gerichtsbarkeit, Menschenrechte: Festschrift für Hermann Mosler* (Springer 1983) 599 ff.
67 Cf. Erika de Wet, 'Sources and the Hierarchy of International Law: The Place of Peremptory Norms and Article 103 of the UN Charter within the Sources of International Law' in Samantha Besson and Jean d'Aspremont (eds), *The Oxford Handbook on the Sources of International Law* (Oxford University Press 2017) 633. If one understands *ius cogens* by its function of non-derogability, it can be based on other sources as well, see Robert Kolb, 'The formal source of Ius Cogens in public international law' (1998) 53(1) ZÖR 69 ff.

cogens)."[68] The draft conclusion is less concerned, however, with an abstract hierarchy of sources rather than with the relative importance of each source for the concept of general international law and peremptory norms of general international law.

2. The relationship between the norms of different sources

The question of the relationship and hierarchy of sources can also be discussed as a question of the relationship and hierarchy of the norms of different sources.

Norms of different sources can be coordinated by *jus cogens* from which no derogation by treaty is permitted (article 53 VCLT), the *lex specialis* maxim, according to which the special law prevails over the general law, the maxim of *lex posterior derogat legi priori*, according to which the later law prevails over the prior law,[69] or by way of accommodation through interpretation as set forth in article 31(3)(c) VCLT (systemic integration).[70]

Furthermore, Dinstein described several modes of interplay between rules of treaties and rules of customary international law. For instance: norms of different sources may complement each other,[71] they may resemble each other while addressing unrelated settings, as the rule of the requirement of exhaustion of local remedies applies both to inter-state disputes based on diplomatic protection and to claims submitted by individuals.[72] Treaties may contain a *renvoi* to customary international law,[73] and subordinate themselves to another treaty or rule of custom by way of a so-called "without-prejudice"

---

68 *Report of the International Law Commission: Seventy-first session (29 April–7 June and 8 July–9 August 2019)* UN Doc A/74/10 at 143; the draft conclusions were adopted on second reading in 2022, *ILC Report 2022* at 10, 30-6. For further analysis see below, p. 378.
69 Hugh W Thirlway, *The sources of international law* (2nd edn, Oxford University Press 2019) 147; Paul Guggenheim, *Lehrbuch des Völkerrechts: unter Berücksichtigung der internationalen und schweizerischen Praxis* (vol 1, Verlag für Recht und Gesellschaft 1948) 51 (on *lex posterior*).
70 Thirlway, *The sources of international law* 152; Campbell McLachlan, 'The Principle of Systemic Integration and Article 31 (3) (c) of the Vienna Convention' (2005) 54 ICLQ 286.
71 Dinstein, 'The interaction between customary international law and treaties' 283-386.
72 ibid 387.
73 ibid 388.

The conceptual framework

provision.[74] A treaty rule may extend the protections offered by a rule of customary international law[75], customary international law may fill in loopholes and provide definitions to treaty concepts.[76] In addition, there can be coexistence in the sense of a complete or partial overlap between treaty and custom in relation to one specific issue, in which custom would not necessarily completely vanish but remain in the background.[77] This book will explore these modes of interplay in specific contexts and consider their implications for the topic of the interrelationship of sources of international law.

3. The relationship between formal sources and material sources

Certain authors distinguish between formal sources and material sources. Formal sources are those processes through which law is generated, the formal source is the "source from which the legal rule derives its validity"[78]. Material sources are said to provide "evidence of the existence of rules"[79], to

---

74 ibid 391.
75 ibid 393.
76 ibid 394.
77 ibid 395-396; see also Rudolf Bernhardt, 'Custom and treaty in the law of the sea' (1987) 205 RdC 271: "[...] treaty law and customary law can coexist and can be applicable side by side in the relations between the same States [...] Only customary norms which are in contradiction to treaties become inapplicable as long as the treaty is valid, and they become applicable again after the treaty has lapsed."
78 Robert Yewdall Jennings and Arthur Watts, *Oppenheim's International Law: Volume 1 Peace* (9th edn, Oxford University Press 2008) 23; see also Thirlway, *The sources of international law* 6; Crawford, *Brownlie's principles of public international law* 18; Robert Kolb, 'Legal History as a Source: From Classical to Modern International Law' in Samantha Besson and Jean d'Aspremont (eds), *The Oxford handbook on the sources of international law* (Oxford University Press 2017) 282; Iain GM Scobbie, 'Legal Theory As a Source of International Law: Institutional Facts and the Identification of International Law' in Samantha Besson and Jean d'Aspremont (eds), *The Oxford Handbook on the Sources of International Law* (Oxford University Press 2017) 507; Gerald Fitzmaurice, 'Some Problems Regarding the Formal Sources of International Law' in *Symbolae Verzijl: présentées au professeur J. H. W.Verzijl à l'occasion de son LXX-ième anniversaire* (La Haye: M Nijhoff 1958) 153-155; Prosper Weil, 'Le droit international en quête de son identité: cours général de droit international public' (1992) 237 RdC 132, arguing that formal sources answer the question of "how" law is formed whereas material sources answer the question of "why" law is formed.
79 Crawford, *Brownlie's principles of public international law* 18-19.

45

denote "the provenance of the substantive content of [the] rule"[80], to "furnish the substantive content of the law or of legal relationships between actors"[81], to encompass "all the elements and facts of life which influence and explain the creation of legal norms: for example, social facts, social values, legal conscience, political beliefs, religious motives"[82].

Writers hold different views as to whether all sources set forth in article 38(1)(a)-(c) ICJ Statute qualify as "formal sources"[83] or whether customary international law[84] and general principles of law[85] do not possess the necessary characteristics in order to be described as "formal" source.

This study, in contrast, is not primarily concerned with the relationship of these two categories and with categorizing each source as a formal source or a material source, which would ultimately depend on one's understanding of the attributes formal and material.[86] Nonetheless, certain aspects of the relationship between formal and material sources will be addressed. One relevant aspect concerns treaty law as a material source of customary international

---

80 Jennings and Watts, *Oppenheim's International Law: Volume 1 Peace* 23.
81 Scobbie, 'Legal Theory As a Source of International Law: Institutional Facts and the Identification of International Law' 507.
82 Kolb, 'Legal History as a Source: From Classical to Modern International Law' 282; Alfred Verdross and Bruno Simma, *Universelles Völkerrecht Theorie und Praxis* (3rd edn, Duncker&Humblot 1984) 321; Pellet and Müller, 'Article 38' 864; Samantha Besson, 'Theorizing the Sources of International Law' in Samantha Besson and John Tasioulas (eds), *The Philosophy of International Law* (Oxford University Press 2010) 170; critical of such understanding Thirlway, *The sources of international law* 7.
83 Affirmative ibid 8 f.; Pellet and Müller, 'Article 38' 864, 941, explicitly describing general principles of law as "a formal source".
84 Cf. Ago, 'Science juridique et droit international' 936-944; Jean d'Aspremont, *Formalism and the Sources of International Law* (Oxford University Press 2011) 119 f. (describing "the impossibility of resorting to formal identification criteria of customary international law"); cf. Kolb, 'Legal History as a Source: From Classical to Modern International Law' 290: "The better view is that the customary process is recognized in international law as a formal source, but that the process itself makes direct reference to the manifold social activities of the subjects of the law whose behaviour customary international law seeks to regulate."
85 Weil, 'Le droit international en quête de son identité: cours général de droit international public' 148-151; Jean d'Aspremont, 'What was not meant to be: General principles of law as a source of international law' in Riccardo Pisillo Mazzeschi and Pasquale de Sena (eds), *Global Justice, Human Rights, and the Modernization of International Law* (Springer 2018) 163 ff.
86 See also Crawford, *Brownlie's principles of public international law* 18-19 (arguing that the distinction between formal and material sources is difficult to maintain).

law. Certainly, a rule set forth in a treaty can enter the body of customary international law. The interplay between treaties and custom is, however, not confined to this process which is also addressed in the recent ILC conclusions on customary international law.[87] This study will also submit that general principles of law should be regarded as a source of international law which, for the present author, does not depend on whether they qualify as a "formal" source.

III. The Politics as to the sources: Source preferences in the international community

Even though there is no formal hierarchy between sources, sources can be subject to "informal hierarchies" established by the preferences of states, adjudicators and scholars.[88]

---

87 See below, p. 377.
88 Prost, 'Sources and the Hierarchy of International Law: Source Preferences and Scales' 642, 645, 656 ("informal hierarchies"); on informal hierarchies see also *Fragmentation of international law: difficulties arising from diversification and expansion of international law, Report of the Study Group of the International Law Commission, Finalized by Martti Koskenniemi* 47 para 85, 233 para 463; cf. David Kennedy, 'When Renewal Repeats: Thinking against the Box' (2000) 32 NYU JILP 352: "Are international norms best built by custom or treaty? International lawyers have worried about this for at least a century, one or the other mode coming in and out of fashion at various points."; see for instance for the relative advantage of treaty obligations *vis-à-vis* the uncertainty surrounding customary international law Andrew T Guzman, *How international law works: a rational choice theory* (Oxford University Press 2008) 207; Oscar Schachter, *International law in theory and practice: general course in public international law* (Martinus Nijhoff Publishers 1991) 66; on the uncertainties of treaty obligations due to broad framing see Bruno Simma, 'A Hard Look at Soft Law' (1988) 82 Proceedings of the American Society of International Law at Its Annual Meeting 378; Louise Doswald-Beck and Sylvain Vité, 'International Humanitarian Law and Human Rights Law' (1993) 33 International Review of the Red Cross 106; on the significance of the precision of legal obligations as to fairness and the willingness to accept sanctions for the obligations' violations, see Thomas M Franck, *Fairness in International Law and Institutions* (Clarendon Press 1995) 31-33; cf. on the doctrine of sources Daniel Thürer and Martin Zobl, 'Are Nuclear Weapons Really Legal?: Thoughts on the Sources of International Law and a Conception of the Law "Imperio rationis" instead of "Ratione imperii"' in Ulrich Fastenrath and others (eds), *From bilateralism to community interest: essays in honour of judge Bruno Simma* (Oxford University Press 2011) 187.

Chapter 1: Setting the Scene

The work of Jean d'Aspremont has raised awareness for the "politics of formal law-ascertainment"[89] and the choices for or against non-formal law ascertainment[90], the choice of the international legal profession as to its sources and the way in which normativity is produced. Taking inspiration from the sources-thesis of Hart[91], d'Aspremont has argued that the sources ultimately rest on a practice of recognition of international lawyers[92], from which it follows that the sources of a legal community are susceptible to change. Hugh Thirlway noted in response to d'Aspremont's focus on the politics of law-ascertainment that a choice as to the sources of international law "has presumably already been made: custom and the general principles of law are generally recognized to constitute sources, and it is difficult to see how international society could back away from that established system."[93] Whereas this can be the conclusion one ultimately arrives at, this conclusion is by far not self-evident and requires reasoning and justification. The sources of law in a legal community are not set in stone but can change over time.[94] In fact, scholars often have had certain preferences as to which source is particularly fit or unfit to respond to the present challenges of the international community in light of new paradigms, of a changed composition of the legal community or of the expansion of international law.[95]

---

89 d'Aspremont, *Formalism and the Sources of International Law* 142.
90 ibid 174 ("[...] recognizing customary international law, general principles of law, oral treaties, and oral promises as a source of international legal rules should stem from a conscious choice, i.e. a choice for non-formal law-ascertainment informed by an awareness of its costs, especially in terms of the normative character of the rules produced thereby").
91 Hart, *The concept of law: With a postscript* chapter VI.
92 Jean d'Aspremont, 'The Politics of Deformalization in International Law' (2011) 3 Goettingen Journal of International Law 503 ff.; Jean d'Aspremont, 'The Idea of 'Rules' in the Sources of International Law' (2014) 84 BYIL 116; d'Aspremont, *Formalism and the Sources of International Law* 195 ff.
93 Hugh W Thirlway, *The Sources of International Law* (Oxford University Press 2014) 209-210.
94 See below Chapter 2, p. 97.
95 Joseph HH Weiler, 'The Geology of International Law - Governance, Democracy and Legitimacy' (2004) 64 ZaöRV 547-562, writing that at the beginning of the 20th century, "one discovers a predominance of bilateral, contractual treaties and a very limited number of multilateral lawmaking treaties. One also discovers, in that earlier part of the century, a very sedate, almost 'magisterial' and backward looking practice of customary law typified by a domestic US case such as The Paquete Habana [...]".

1. Source preferences and the spirit of the time

The spirit of the time and leading paradigms can be important for the shift of source preferences. For instance, after a time when municipal law analogies had used to be rejected as dangerous to the recognition of international law as a legal system in its own right,[96] general principles of law based on private law analogies were later considered of great importance for the development of international law by courts and tribunals in the face of failed codification attempts at the international level.[97] In recent years, general principles of public law have been said to be suitable for balancing individual rights of investors and the regulatory interests of the public in the context of international investment law.[98] Moreover, legal principles occupy a prominent place in scholarly accounts analyzing international law from the perspective of a constitutional paradigm.[99]

Turning to treaties and customary international law, Bruno Simma has argued that treaties more than customary international law would be the "workhorses of community interest".[100] Other scholars have emphasized the openness of the concept of customary international law to the "needs of

---

96 See for instance Otto Nippold, *Der völkerrechtliche Vertrag Seine Stellung im Rechtssystem und seine Bedeutung für das internationale Recht* (1894) 82; Hersch Lauterpacht, 'The mandate under international law in the Covenant of the League of Nations' in Elihu Lauterpacht (ed) (3, Cambridge University Press 1977) vol Hersch Lauterpacht International Law Collected Papers 3. The Law of Peace 57 and 58; on Lauterpacht's study see Martti Koskenniemi, *The Gentle Civilizer of Nations The Rise and Fall of International Law 1870-1960* (Cambridge University Press 2002) 374 ff.
97 Hersch Lauterpacht, *Private Law Analogies* (London, 1927) viii.
98 Stephan W Schill, 'Internationales Investitionsschutzrecht und Vergleichendes Öffentliches Recht: Grundlagen und Methode eines öffentlich-rechtlichen Leitbildes für die Investitionsschiedsgerichtsbarkeit' (2011) 71 ZaöRV 277.
99 Cf. Thomas Kleinlein, *Konstitutionalisierung im Völkerrecht Konstruktion und Elemente einer idealistischen Völkerrechtslehre* (Springer 2012) 633, 636, 647, 642, 644, 648-652, 650-660; Jochen Rauber, *Strukturwandel als Prinzipienwandel: theoretische, dogmatische und methodische Bausteine eines Prinzipienmodells des Völkerrechts und seiner Dynamik* (Springer 2018) 153.
100 Bruno Simma, 'From bilateralism to community interest in international law' (1994) 250 RdC 223; Simma argued that "lawmaking by way of custom is hardly capable of accommodating community interests in a genuine sense", ibid 224, similar Mehrdad Payandeh, *Internationales Gemeinschaftsrecht: zur Herausbildung gemeinschaftsrechtlicher Strukturen im Völkerrecht der Globalisierung* (Springer 2010) 296.

Chapter 1: Setting the Scene

the international community",[101] and stressed custom's function as general law[102] of the international community which sets "the ground rules for the international system by imposing a minimum core of binding obligations on all states [...] [protecting] key substantive and structural interests of the international community".[103]

This book will consider these and similar sources preferences and how they inform the way in which the interrelationship of sources is discussed in specific contexts.

2. Source preferences and the changed composition of the legal community

Changing source preferences may also correspond to changes within the particular legal community which concern, for instance, the emergence of new states and of different political and economic systems within states.

Grigory Tunkin, for instance, argued that "in an age of rapid changes in every sphere of life international treaty is a more suitable means of creating norms of international law than custom [...] In contemporary conditions the principal means of creating norms of international law is a treaty."[104]

---

101 Anja Seibert-Fohr, 'Unity and Diversity in the Formation and Relevance of Customary International Law: Modern Concepts of Customary International law as a Manifestation of a Value-Based International Order' in Andreas Zimmermann and Rainer Hofmann (eds), *Unity and Diversity in International Law* (2006) 257 ff., and Anthea Roberts and Sandesh Sivakumaran, 'Lawmaking by Nonstate Actors: Engaging Armed Groups in the Creation of International Humanitarian Law' (2012) 37(1) Yale Journal of International Law 125. The phrase "needs of the international community" was borrowed from the ICJ, see *Reparation for Injuries Suffered in the Service of the United Nations* (Advisory Opinion) [1949] ICJ Rep 178; on the relationship between community interests and customary international law see recently Samantha Besson, 'Community Interests in the Identification of International Law With a Special Emphasis on Treaty Interpretation and Customary Law Identification' in Eyal Benvenisti and Georg Nolte (eds), *Community Interests across international law* (Oxford University Press 2018) 64-68.
102 Zemanek, 'The Legal Foundations of the International Legal System' 167, proposing that the meaning of custom, if the term proves immutable, should be "the current and regular conduct of States which corresponds to the current consensus of opinion on what the law requires. Or simpler: general international law".
103 Anthea Roberts, 'Who killed Article 38(1)(B)? A Reply to Bradley and Gulati' (2010) 21(1) Duke journal of comparative & international law 173, 176.
104 Grigory Ivanovich Tunkin, 'Co-existence and international law' (1958) 85 RdC 8, 22-23; on multilateral treaties see Grigory Ivanovich Tunkin, 'General International Law

Also, Sir Gerald Fitzmaurice was under the impression that customary international law, which he regarded to be indispensable, was challenged by newly independent states because it was understood as a genuine western concept.[105]

Against the background of the cold war and the competition of different economic systems, Tunkin was also skeptical of general principles of law as derived from municipal legal systems, "there are no normative principles or norms common to two opposing systems of law: socialist and capitalist law"[106]. He predicted "that with the development of international law the 'general principles of law' will more and more lose their ties with national legal systems from which they penetrated into international law and become more and more "general principles of international law"[107].

    Customary Law Only?' (1993) 4 EJIL 534 ff.; on Soviet perspectives to international law see Theodor Schweisfurth, 'Das Völkergewohnheitsrecht - verstärkt im Blickfeld der sowjetischen Völkerrechtslehre' (1987) 30 German Yearbook of International Law 36 ff.; Lauri Mälksoo, 'The History of International Legal Theory in Russia: a Civilized Dialogue in Europe' (2008) 19 EJIL 229 (on Tunkin).

105 Gerald Fitzmaurice, 'The Future of Public International Law and of the International Legal System in the Circumstances of Today' (1975) 5(1) International Relations 746-747; cf. also *North Sea Continental Shelf* (*Federal Republic of Germany/Denmark; Federal Republic of Germany/Netherlands*) (Judgment) [1969] ICJ Rep Diss Op Koretsky 157 (advocating the use of the term general international law, since custom "turns its face to the past while general international law keeps abreast of the times"). Also, Onuma Yasuaki argued that the doctrine of sources displays an "excessive judicial-centrism" together supported by "a (West-centric) domestic model approach in international legal thoughts" and that general international law based on international treaties would be far more legitimate than "an old customary norm which was created on State practice and opinio iuris of a limited number of powerful States", Onuma Yasuaki, 'A Transcivilized Perspective on International Law Questioning Prevalent Cognitive Frameworks in the Emerging Multi-Polar and Multi-Civilizational World of the Twenty-First Century' (2009) 342 RdC 221, 236, 240, 242-243; for a critique of customary international law from a TWAIL perspective see BS Chimni, 'Customary International Law: A Third World Perspective' (2018) 112(1) AJIL 1 ff.

106 Grigory Ivanovich Tunkin, '"General Principles of Law" in International Law' in René Marcic and Hermann Mosler (eds), *Internationale Festschrift für Alfred Verdross zum 80. Geburtstag* (1971) 527.

107 Grigory Ivanovich Tunkin, 'Soviet Theory of Sources of International Law' in Peter Fischer, Heribert Franz Köck, and Alfred Verdross (eds), *Völkerrecht und Rechtsphilosophie International Festschrift für Stephan Verosta zum 70. Geburtstag* (Duncker & Humblot 1980) 77.

Looking back, Abdulqawi Yusuf has argued that African states did not oppose customary international law and general principles of law as such, but rather "the genesis and process of identification" and the content of the norms, which African states began to shape.[108] He also has noted a trend from general principles based on domestic law to general principles based on the UN Charter and expressed in the Friendly Relations Declaration, which were "considered more important by newly independent African States" since these principles "offered a protective shield for their newly acquired sovereignty and granted newly independent States equal status with the major powers on the international legal plane."[109]

It is interesting to note that the Asian-African Legal Consultative Organization (AALCO) has taken an active interest in the recent work of the ILC on customary international law. According to Sienho Yee, the AALCO members' motivating concern was "protecting their sovereignty, which manifests itself in three overarching considerations—the promotion of the quality in decision-making in the identification process, the reliance on only the quality exercise of State functions, and the representativeness of the State practice and *opinio juris* at issue."[110] Also, scholars have pointed out that doctrines relating to customary international law, such as the doctrine according to which the identification of custom requires one to pay particular regard to

---

108 Abdulqawi A Yusuf, 'Pan-Africanism and International Law' (2013) 369 RdC 244 ff., 250-251.
109 ibid 247.
110 Sienho Yee, 'Report on the ILC Project on "Identification of Customary International Law"' (2015) 14(2) Chinese Journal of International Law 375; on the AALCO initiative Rahmat Mohamad, 'Some Reflections on the International Law Commission Topic "Identification of Customary International Law"' (2016) 15(1) Chinese Journal of International Law 41 ff.; Michael Wood, 'The present position within the ILC on the topic 'Identification of customary international law': in partial response to Sienho Yee, Report on the ILC Project on 'Identification of Customary International Law'' (2016) 15(1) Chinese Journal of International Law 3 ff.; Sienho Yee, 'A Reply to Sir Michael Wood's Response to AALCOIEG's Work and My Report on the ILC Project on Identification of Customary International Law' (2016) 15(1) Chinese Journal of International Law 33 ff.; on the Twail perspectives and the ILC-AALCO debate George Rodrigo Bandeira Galindo and César Yip, 'Customary International Law and the Third World: Do Not Step on the Grass' (2017) 16(2) Chinese Journal of International Law 251 ff. For the most recent summary of the AALCO meeting of 2018 see Sienho Yee, 'AALCO Informal Expert Group's Comments on the ILC Project on "Identification of Customary International Law": A Brief Follow-up' (2018) 17(1) Chinese Journal of International Law 187.

the practice of specially affected states can be used by the Global South for advancing their interests *vis-à-vis* Western states.[111] This demonstrates that the changes in the composition of the international community can make a particular source of law subject to both criticism and to strategic engagement and can impact the relative significance of each source.

3. Source preferences and the substantive expansion and diversification of international law

Changing source preferences may also be the result of an expansion of the international legal order itself and the emergence of new fields of international law. The expansion itself is the result of the rise of treaties: between 1946 and 2006 more than 50.000 treaties were registered with the United Nations Secretariat pursuant to Article 102(1) of the UN Charter.[112]

Scholars have expressed different views on the consequences of this expansion for the doctrine of sources. Responding to what they considered to be a too expansive use of customary international law, Bruno Simma and Philip Alston have suggested the consideration of general principles of international law as alternative source of human rights law.[113] With a view to the challenges in human rights law, environmental law, economic development and the transnational prosecution of criminality, Cherif M. Bassiouni has predicted that "it is quite likely that 'General Principles' will become the most important and influential source in this decade", which would have been the 1990s, because "conventional and customary international law have not developed the framework, norms, or rules necessary to regulate these issues, nor is it likely that these two sources of law will catch up with the

---

111 Kevin Jon Heller, 'Specially-Affected States and the Formation of Custom' (2018) 112(2) AJIL 191 ff.; cf. also Jean d'Aspremont, 'A Postmodernization of Customary International Law for the First World?' (2018) 112 AJIL Unbound 295-296. Cf. on specially affected states *North Sea Continental Shelf* [1969] ICJ Rep 3, 42 para 73.

112 Dirk Pulkowski, *The Law and Politics of International Regime Conflict* (Oxford University Press 2014) 35-36, pointing also out that one third of the 6000 multilateral treaties concluded during the 20th century were open to accession by any state.

113 Bruno Simma and Philip Alston, 'The Sources of Human Rights Law: Custom, Jus Cogens, and General Principles' (1988) 12 Australian Yearbook of International Law 84-100, 102-106.

needs of the time."[114] The view that general principles can be more important in certain areas of international law than in others has been expressed, for instance, by Christian Tams, according to whom general principles of law are "a wallflower" in public international law in general but at the same time an important source in international investment law.[115]

In comparison thereto, James Crawford argued that "international law is a customary law system, despite all the treaties".[116] Other scholars have raised the question of whether different forms of customary international law have evolved in different fields of international law.[117] Michael Waibel has reflected on the consequences of the functional differentiation for the profession of general international lawyers: "The 'invisible college' of international lawyers appears to be crumbling before our eyes. A patchwork quilt of specialized international lawyers is taking their place."[118] It has also been argued that the specialization and functional differentiation expresses itself in the fact that specific sub-regimes set up "interface-norms" which "regulate to what extent norms and decisions in one sub-order have effect in another", similar to domestic law which regulates the way in which international law

---

114 Mahmoud Cherif Bassiouni, 'A functional approach to "general principles of international law"' (1990) 11(3) Michigan Journal of International Law 769.
115 Christian J Tams, 'The Sources of International Investment Law: Concluding Thoughts' in Tarcisio Gazzini and Eric de Brabandere (eds), *International Investment Law. The Sources of Rights and Obligations* (Martinus Nijhoff Publishers 2012) 324.
116 James Crawford, 'Change, Order, Change: The Course of International Law General Course on Public International Law' (2013) 365 RdC 49, emphasizing the importance of custom as source of *pacta sunt servanda*; similar Ian Brownlie, 'International Law at the Fiftieth Anniversary of the United Nations, General Course on Public International Law' (1995) 255 RdC 36, customary law "is international law".
117 Robert Kolb, 'Selected problems in the theory of customary international law' [2003] Netherlands international law review 128 (arguing that the common bound of the distinct customs still needs to be shown); Seibert-Fohr, 'Unity and Diversity in the Formation and Relevance of Customary International Law: Modern Concepts of Customary International law as a Manifestation of a Value-Based International Order' 257 ff.; d'Aspremont, 'International Customary Investment Law: Story of a Paradox' (arguing that the general doctrine of sources requires modification in the field of investment law); cf. Daniel Bodansky, 'Customary (and Not So Customary) International Environmental Law' (1995) 3 Indiana Journal of Global Legal Studies 115-116.
118 Michael Waibel, 'Interpretive Communities in International Law' in Andrea Bianchi, Daniel Peat, and Matthew Windsor (eds), *Interpretation in International Law* (Oxford University Press 2015) 165.

applies within the domestic legal order.[119] Going one step further, it even has been argued that legal fragmentation is "merely an ephemeral reflection of a more fundamental, multidimensional fragmentation of global society itself"[120] and that a new form of "global law" would grow "from the social peripheries, not from the political centres of nation states and international institutions"[121]. These views illustrate the challenges for "general law" in a

---

119 Nico Krisch, *Beyond Constitutionalism The Pluralist Structure of Postnational Law* (Oxford University Press 2010) 285 ff.; cf. on "hinge" provisions Andreas L Paulus and Johann Leiss, 'Constitutionalism and the Mechanics of Global Law Transfers' (2018) 9 GoJIL 48-52.

120 Gunther Teubner and Andreas Fischer-Lescano, 'Regime-Collisions: The Vain Search for Legal Unity in the Fragmentation of Global Law' (2004) 25 Michigan Journal of International Law 1004.

121 Gunther Teubner, 'Breaking Frames: The Global Interplay of Legal and Social Systems' (1997) 45(1) American Journal of Comparative Law 164-165; Gunther Teubner, 'Global Bukowina: Legal Pluralism in World Society' in Gunther Teubner (ed), *Global law without a state* (Dartmouth 1997) 3 ff.; public international law scholars are skeptical as to the actual existence of such global law without the state and to the desirability of this development which raises questions of political legitimacy and accountability, cf. Crawford, 'Change, Order, Change: The Course of International Law General Course on Public International Law' 143; for a defense of general international law see also Andreas L Paulus, 'Commentary to Andreas Fischer-Lescano & Gunther Teubner The Legitimacy of International Law and the Role of the State' (2004) 25 Michigan Journal of International Law 1050 (arguing that "in spite of an ever-growing functional differentiation, issue areas are held together by a minimum of common values and decision-making procedures - in other words by general international law which bases its legitimacy on decisions of, ideally democratic, national processes of decision-making."); Andreas L Paulus, 'Fragmentierung und Segmentierung der internationalen Ordnung als Herausforderung prozeduraler Gemeinwohlorientierung' in Hans-Michael Heinig and Jörg Philipp Terhechte (eds), *Postnationale Demokratie, Postdemokratie, Neoetatismus Wandel klassischer Demokratievorstellungen in der Rechtswissenschaft* (Mohr Siebeck 2013) 143 ff.; from a private law perspective, Ralf Michaels speaks of the "mirage of non-state governance" and argues that the true *lex mercatoria* was not exclusively non-state law but consisted of a "continuous competition and interplay between state and non-state institutions [...] transcend[ing] the divide between state and non-state law", Ralf Michaels, 'The True Lex Mercatoria: Law Beyond the State' (2007) 14(2) Indiana Journal of Global Legal Studies 465-466; Ralf Michaels, 'The Mirage of Non-State Governance' [2010] Utah Law Review 43; in a similar sense, Lars Viellechner speaks of "transnationalization" of the law, Lars Viellechner, *Transnationalisierung des Rechts* (Velbrück 2013) 301; on this debate, see also Andreas L Paulus, 'Zusammenspiel der Rechtsquellen aus völkerrechtlicher Perspektive' in *Internationales, nationales und privates Recht: Hybridisierung der Rechtsordnungen?:*

Chapter 1: Setting the Scene

legal order that is more and more shaped by specialized regimes. By examining the relative significance of the three sources and their interrelationship in special fields and contexts, this book will also focus on the interplay and the mutual influence between general international law and more special law.

IV. The Concept of interrelationship of sources and the scope of this study

1. The interrelationship of sources

Each source seems to have its own advocates, and it is not the purpose of this book to champion one particular source. This study pursues a different objective and focuses on the interrelationship of sources. This study prefers the term "interrelationship" over "relationship" since this term denotes more clearly the interplay between the sources and the idea of the present sources as an interrelated system.[122]

Immunität, 33. Tagung der Deutschen Gesellschaft für Internationales Recht (CF Müller 2014) 38 (arguing that there is no "hybrid" law but a hybrid set of facts to which the law is applied).

122 Scholars have used the term "interrelationship" before, see for instance Georg Nolte, 'How to identify customary international law? - On the final outcome of the work of the International Law Commission (2018)' [2019] (37) KFG Working Paper Series 19-20 (interrelationship of sources); Alf Ross, *A Textbook of International Law: General Part, originally published 1947* (2nd edn, The LawBook Exchange 2008) 92 (interrelationship of sources); Thirlway, *The sources of international law* 156 (interrelationship of norms of different sources); Jörg Kammerhofer, 'Uncertainty in the formal Sources of international Law: customary international Law and some of its Problems' (2004) 15(3) EJIL 536 (interrelation of sources); Villiger, *Customary International Law and Treaties* xxvii, 146, 189 (interrelation between and of sources). The term "sources" can be understood differently (cf. Thirlway, *The sources of international law* 6-7). For the purposes of the present study, "sources of international law define the rules of the system: if a candidate rule is attested by one or more of the recognized 'sources' of international law, then it may be accepted as part of international law" (Crawford, *Brownlie's principles of public international law* 18). In this sense, sources "refer to processes by which international legal norms are created, modified and annulled, but also to the *places* where their normative outcomes, i.e. valid international legal norms, may be found" (Besson, 'Theorizing the Sources of International Law' 169-170). Cf. also Robert Kolb, 'Principles as Sources of International Law (With Special Reference to Good Faith)' (2006) 53(1) Netherlands International Law Review 3-4; cf. Maarten Bos, 'The Recognized

The question of the interrelationship between written law and unwritten law and the sources as reflected in article 38(1) ICJ Statute[123] is a contingent one, its answer depends on the preferences and perceived needs of the respective legal community.[124] It concerns the relative significance of each source and the distribution of normativity within the international community.[125] This study is, therefore, not meant to be a commentary to article 38. Article 38

Manifestations of International Law A New Theory of "Sources"' (1977) 20 German Yearbook of International Law 10-13, 15.

123 This study is not primarily concerned with the debate on whether additional sources should be recognized, see on this debate, in particular with respect to unilateral acts and decisions of international organizations Verdross and Simma, *Universelles Völkerrecht Theorie und Praxis* 323-328; Pellet and Müller, 'Article 38' 853-864; Thirlway, *The sources of international law* 24-30. Therefore, this study does not engage with scholarship which develops and proposes normative frameworks in which international organizations exercise "global governance", "public authority" and remain accountable and subject to law, see Benedict Kingsbury, Nico Krisch, and Richard B Stewart, 'The Emergence of Global Administrative Law' (2005) 68(3-4) Law and contemporary problems 20, 29; Benedict Kingsbury, 'The Concept of "Law" in Global Administrative Law' (2009) 20(1) EJIL 26; Armin von Bogdandy, Matthias Goldmann, and Ingo Venzke, 'From Public International Public Law: Translating World Public Opinion into International Public Authority' (2017) 28(1) EJIL 122; Matthias Goldmann, 'Inside Relative Normativity: From Sources to Standard Instruments for the Exercise of International Public Authority' (2008) 9(11) German Law Journal 1869 et ff.; Matthias Goldmann, *Internationale öffentliche Gewalt* (Springer 2015) 383; Philipp Dann and Marie von Engelhardt, 'Legal Approaches to Global Governance and Accountability: Informal Lawmaking, International Public Authority, and Global Administrative Law Compared' in Joost HB Pauwelyn, Ramses Wessel, and Jan Wouters (eds), *Informal International Lawmaking* (Oxford University Press 2012) 106 ff.

124 Cf. Ago, 'Science juridique et droit international' 942-943; cf. also Kammerhofer, 'Uncertainty in the formal Sources of international Law: customary international Law and some of its Problems' 547-551 (on whether the sources of international law are "normatively ordered" (at 549) which he rejects as there are no "rules" governing the relationship of sources).

125 Cf. also Weil, 'Le droit international en quête de son identité: cours général de droit international public' 138-139; Jennings and Watts, *Oppenheim's International Law: Volume 1 Peace* 24; Crawford, *Brownlie's principles of public international law* 20-21; on the concept of the international community see Andreas L Paulus, *Die internationale Gemeinschaft im Völkerrecht: eine Untersuchung zur Entwicklung des Völkerrechts im Zeitalter der Globalisierung* (Beck 2001); Simma, 'From bilateralism to community interest in international law' 217 ff.; Christian Tomuschat, 'Die internationale Gemeinschaft' (1995) 33(1-2) Archiv des Völkerrechts 1 ff.; Hermann Mosler, 'The international society as a legal community' (1974) 140 RdC

Chapter 1: Setting the Scene

is first and foremost a treaty provision relating to the applicable law of the Court.[126] Beyond that it surely is part of international law's cultural heritage and the sources continue to be the basis on which today's international legal order as a whole rests.[127] Yet, Article 38 can be nothing more than a starting point for an analysis of the interrelationship of sources today.[128]

In particular, article 38 does not answer the questions of each source's relative significance in the present international community, of whether courts' and tribunals' institutional framework, shifts in the preferred legal doctrinal technique or the spirit of the time favour one source over the other sources. The legal community may have made different choices as to the

---

1 ff.; Payandeh, *Internationales Gemeinschaftsrecht: zur Herausbildung gemeinschaftsrechtlicher Strukturen im Völkerrecht der Globalisierung*.

126 Pierre-Marie Dupuy, 'La pratique de l'article 38 du Statut de la Cour internationale de Justice dans le cadre des plaidoiries érites et orales' in Office of Legal Affairs (ed), *Collection of Essays by Legal Advisers of States, Legal Advisers of International Organizations and Practitioners in the Field of International Law* (The United Nations 1999) 379; Onuma Yasuaki, *International Law in a Transcivilizational World* (Cambridge University Press 2017) 105-6.

127 Kohen, 'La pratique et la théorie des sources du droit international' 82-83; Christian Tomuschat, 'International law: ensuring the survival of mankind on the eve of a new century: general course on public international law' (1999) 281 RdC 307: "Article 38 belongs to the core substance of the constitution of the international community. If major disputes had to be fought on that issue, the notion of an international legal order would be doomed." For a recent study of the reception of article 38, including the jurisprudence of domestic courts see Diego Mejía-Lemos, 'Custom and the Regulation of 'the Sources of International Law'' in Panos Merkouris, Jörg Kammerhofer, and Noora Arajärvi (eds), *The Theory, Practice, and Interpretation of Customary International Law* (Cambridge University Press 2022) 147.

128 See Weil, 'Le droit international en quête de son identité: cours général de droit international public' 138; Bernhardt, 'Ungeschriebenes Völkerrecht'; Hugh W Thirlway, *International Customary Law and Codification: an examination of the continuing role of custom in the present period of codification of international law* (Leiden: Sijthoff, 1972) 39, 145; it has been argued that a law without sources of law ("Recht ohne Rechtsquellen") will emerge if international law publicists will not detach themselves from article 38(1) of the ICJ Statute, Matthias Ruffert, 'Gedanken zu den Perspektiven der völkerrechtlichen Rechtsquellenlehre' in Matthias Ruffert (ed), *Dynamik und Nachhaltigkeit des öffentlichen Rechts: Festschrift für Meinhard Schröder zum 70. Geburtstag* (Duncker & Humblot 2012) 84; for the term "Recht ohne Rechtsquellen" see Christian Tietje, 'Recht ohne Rechtsquellen? Entstehung und Wandel von Völkerrechtsnormen im Interesse des Schutzes globaler Rechtsgüter im Spannungsverhältnis von Rechtssicherheit und Rechtsdynamik' (2003) 24 Zeitschrift für Rechtssoziologie 27 ff.

relative place given to each source.[129] Continuing to recognize customary international law as one of the sources of international law does not indicate whether customary international law in fact is expansively used as a legal basis for rules and concepts, whether it is used for both primary rules of obligation and secondary rules or whether it is confined to one of the just mentioned categories of rules.[130] Examining the functions and the place of each source in the international community can become important for an evaluation of the sources and their different strengths and weaknesses. For instance, from a practical point of view, uncertainties as to the ascertainment of customary international law and general principles may appear tolerable against the background of their relative significance and the function these sources fulfil. If the lack of normative hierarchy between the sources and the possibility that treaties, customary international law and general principles of law may derogate from each other are accepted, the question will still arise as to whether derogation of a rule in a treaty by customary international law frequently occurs in the present legal community or whether the relationship between sources is characterized more by harmony and convergence than by conflict and rivalry.

For these purposes, it is necessary to analyze international practice when it comes to the interpretation and application of international law.[131] This study will explore the sources of international law in relation to each other and in different contexts.[132] In specific contexts it is possible to examine which one of

---

129 As will be pointed out below, the history of international investment law and the move to bilateral treaties can be seen against the background that it was not possible on the basis of general principles of law and customary international law alone to overcome the political tensions relating to the protection of the rights of aliens, p. 564 ff.
130 On doubts whether the rules of treaty interpretation can be conceptualized as customary international law at all, see for instance Jean d'Aspremont, 'The International Court of Justice, the Whales, and the Blurring of the Lines between Sources and Interpretation' (2016) 27(4) EJIL 1030 footnote 7.
131 For a perspective that distinguishes between sources on the one hand and interpretation on the other hand see Ingo Venzke, *How interpretation makes international law: on semantic change and normative twists* (Oxford University Press 2012) 29 ff.
132 For the view that the interpretation of a legal norm requires consideration of the context in which it operates see Friedrich von Kratochwil, 'How Do Norms Matter?' in Michael Byers (ed), *The role of law in international politics: essays in international relations and international law* (Oxford University Press 2000) 40-41, 68; Michael Byers, *Custom, power and the power of rules: international relations and customary international law* (Cambridge University Press 1999) 149 (shared understandings);

the different possible relationships between sources asserts itself and to what extent this can be explained then by the institutional characteristics of this context. Such a contextualized approach can contribute to the understanding of the sources today.

2. Benefits of a focus on the interrelationship of sources in international practice

James Crawford once submitted in respect of customary international law, which arguably holds true *mutatis mutandis* for general principles of law as well: "But if we focus too much on the generic formulas of customary international law, we overlook how it tends to work in practice."[133]

Each source of international law can be subjected to questions which could raise serious doubts. For the purposes of illustration and exemplification: customary international law has been described as "smiling sphinx in the

---

cf. also Oliver Lepsius, *Relationen: Plädoyer für eine bessere Rechtswissenschaft* (Mohr Siebeck 2016) 22-23 (arguing that norms should be analyzed in relation to each other); Lepsius also suggests that a legal analysis of norms should take account of different institutional contexts, be it the context of the legislature, the context of judicial application and the context of scholarly contemplation, Oliver Lepsius, 'The quest for middle-range theories in German public law' (2014) 12(3) Journal of International Constitutional Law 704-707.

133 Crawford, 'Change, Order, Change: The Course of International Law General Course on Public International Law' 69; see also Eyal Benvenisti, 'Customary International Law as a Judicial Tool for Promoting Efficiency' in Moshe Hirsch and Eyal Benvenisti (eds), *The impact of international law on international cooperation: theoretical perspectives* (Cambridge University Press 2004) 101,103, describing how courts "carefully tailored a specific norm pertaining only to the two litigants", in his view, the doctrine on customary international law does "fail if its role is to provide positive norms based on general and persistent state practice simply because on many important questions there is no such practice". Kolb, 'Selected problems in the theory of customary international law' 147, arguing in relation to customary international law and its relationship to a treaty that "the problem can often easily be solved in a concrete context [...] in a specific context, it will become clear what has to be done."; cf. Thomas M Franck, 'Non-treaty Law-Making: When, Where and How?' in Rüdiger Wolfrum and Volker Röben (eds), *Developments of international law in treaty making* (Springer 2005) 423 (rules of unwritten law need to pass the "but of course"- test).

realm of legal theory"[134], "riddled with paradoxes and contradictions"[135]. When does a normative rule emerge from factual practice, how can a new rule which contravenes an existing one emerge, what is the relationship between the material and the psychological element, between practice and *opinio juris*, can one really ascertain a rule exclusively by induction or deduction, or are rules simply asserted?[136] If general principles of law are understood as municipal law analogies, the question will arise what degree of representativeness as to the selected jurisdictions is necessary.[137] If general principles are understood as broad principles that are inherent in any legal order, they may face the criticism that the content of a particular principle is unclear[138] or that they are a form of "natural law". The concept of the treaties raises the questions of whether a treaty is really a source of law or only a source of obligation that is dependent on another source of law,[139] and whether a truly general or common law is possible at all, given that treaties bind only parties. In addition, even though a treaty may be regarded as having a higher ontological determinacy, other sources of law with their uncertainties may enter the content-determination process. Customary international law as reflected in Article 31(3)(c) VCLT requires the interpreter to take into account any relevant rule of international law applicable in the relations between the parties.[140] The rise of treaties does not indicate whether recourse to unwritten international law remains necessary for the purposes of content-determination or whether such recourse actually takes place at all. It is for

---

134 Kolb, 'Selected problems in the theory of customary international law' 119.
135 Crawford, 'Change, Order, Change: The Course of International Law General Course on Public International Law' 68: for an overview see László Blutman, 'Conceptual Confusion and Methodological Deficiencies: Some Ways that Theories on Customary International Law Fail' (2014) 25(2) EJIL 529 ff.
136 Stefan Talmon, 'Determining Customary International Law: the ICJ's Methodology between Induction, Deduction and Assertion' (2015) 26(2) EJIL 417 ff.; for an overview of these questions cf. Daniel H Joyner, 'Why I Stopped Believing in Customary International Law' (2019) 9(1) Asian Journal of International Law 31 ff.
137 Cf. Neha Jain, 'Comparative International Law at the ICTY: The General Principles Experiment' (2015) 109 AJIL 80 ff.
138 Cf. Weil, 'Le droit international en quête de son identité: cours général de droit international public' 146.
139 Fitzmaurice, 'Some Problems Regarding the Formal Sources of International Law' 153 ff.; on the Fitzmaurice *dictum* see Asif Hameed, 'Some Misunderstandings about Legislation and Law' (2017) 16(3) Chinese Journal of International Law 507-510.
140 The term "rule" encompasses both customary international law and general principles of law, see above, p. 32.

Chapter 1: Setting the Scene

this reason that the approach of this study will focus in several chapters on legal practice. This does not mean, however, that the practice of sources and the theory of sources have to be separated from each other. On the contrary, a study of the interrelationship of sources in different contexts can be insightful for the theory of sources.

3. Contribution of an analysis of the interrelationship of sources to the doctrine relating to each source

This book's perspective on the interrelationship of sources can complement perspectives that focus on one particular source. The focus on the interrelationship of sources can arguably make an important contribution to the doctrine of sources generally and the doctrine relating to each source specifically.

a) Customary international law

This book's perspective, for instance, highlights and illustrates the significance of interpretative decisions and the legal craft[141] in relation to customary international law.

It must be admitted at the outset that certain scholars suggest that customary international law cannot be subject to interpretation: the reason for this would be that the identification of a rule and the determination of the content of said rule fall together, hence "content merges with existence".[142]

---

141 For general treatments of legal craft in international law see Clarence Wilfred Jenks, 'Craftsmanship in International Law' (1956) 50(1) American Journal of International Law 32 ff.

142 Maartens Bos, *A methodology of international law* (North-Holland 1984) 109; see also Jean d'Aspremont, 'Reductionist legal positivism in international law' (2012) 106 Proceedings of the American Society of International Law at Its Annual Meeting 369-370; d'Aspremont, *Formalism and the Sources of International Law* 173-174: Rauber, *Strukturwandel als Prinzipienwandel: theoretische, dogmatische und methodische Bausteine eines Prinzipienmodells des Völkerrechts und seiner Dynamik* 564, 569-570; Rudolf Bernhard, 'Interpretation in International Law' in *Encyclopedia of public international law. East African Community to Italy-United States Air Transport Arbitration (1965): [E - I]* (North-Holland 1995) vol 2 1417 (even though "the content and limits of rules of customary international law often need clarification [...] it is neither usual nor advisable to use the notion of inter-

The conceptual framework

However, it is submitted that the intertwinement of rule identification and content-determination which is characteristic of customary international law and general principles of law does not have to mean that the identification of customary international law does not involve interpretative decisions.[143] Already the observations and comparisons of facts entail normative consid-

---

pretation in connection with the clarification of norms of customary law since the process and maxims are different: the rules of interpretation in international law have been developed for written texts [...]"); Félix Somló, *Juristische Grundlehre* (Meiner 1917) 373; cf. Birgit Schlütter, *Developments in customary international law: theory and the practice of the International Court of Justice and the International ad hoc Criminal Tribunals for Rwanda and Yugoslavia* (Martinus Nijhoff Publishers 2010) 89, but see also at 338 ("one preliminary aspect of any assessment of the formation of a new rule of customary international law should be the careful identification, consideration and interpretation of the applicable law as it stands"); see recently Massimo Lando, 'Identification as the Process to Determine the Content of Customary International Law' (2022) 42(4) Oxford Journal of Legal Studies 1045 ff.

143 As put by Kolb, 'Selected problems in the theory of customary international law' 131: "This work of the interpreter is highly creative and introduces into custom an axiological and subjective bent, which hardly jibes with the usual view that custom is simply the faithful reproduction of state practice. It is not. Custom is a legal and intellectual construct, developed through a complex process of analogical reasoning reducing to an 'artificial' unity a series of unconnected facts and acts"; in this sense also Denis Alland, 'L'interprétation du droit international public' (2012) 362 RdC 83-88; Orakhelashvili, *The Interpretation of Acts and Rules in Public International Law* 497; Matthias Herdegen, 'Interpretation in International Law' [2013] Max Planck EPIL para 61; *North Sea Continental Shelf* [1969] ICJ Rep 3 Diss Op Tanaka 181 (on logical and teleological interpretation); on the importance of normative considerations see also Oscar Schachter, 'International Law in Theory and Practice: general course in public international law' (1982) 178 RdC 96, 334-335 (on necessary value-judgments and the significance of resolutions and statements for custom); Andreas L Paulus, 'International Adjudication' in Samantha Besson and John Tasioulas (eds), *The philosophy of international law* (Oxford University Press 2010) 221-222 (on the role of normative consideration in the process judicial application of international law); Emmanuel Voyiakis, 'Customary International Law and the Place of Normative Considerations' (2010) 55 American Journal of Jurisprudence 163 ff.; Albert Bleckmann, 'Zur Feststellung und Auslegung von Völkergewohnheitsrecht' (1977) 37 ZaöRV 520 ff.; Peter Haggenmacher, 'La doctrine des deux éléments du droit coutumier dans la pratique de la Cour internationale' (1986) 90 RGDIP 119. Cf. also Duncan B Hollis, 'The Existential Function of Interpretation in International Law' in Andrea Bianchi, Daniel Peat, and Matthew Windsor (eds), *Interpretation in International Law* (Oxford University Press 2015) 78 ff., arguing that interpretation is also important for the question of what constitutes customary international law.

Chapter 1: Setting the Scene

erations, as the interpreter has to decide what is comparable, to determine default positions and the level of abstractness of the rule to be identified, to evaluate practice and to eliminate practice which is no longer deemed to be appropriate in the present community.[144] In addition, a rule has to be identified, its scope needs to be determined and interpreted and it has to be concretized, which arguably also involves interpretation, by way of application to the case at hand.[145] It has also been questioned whether one can convincingly treat rules of customary international law and such rules which have been codified in a convention differently, as far as interpretability is concerned.[146]

---

144 Ulrich Fastenrath, 'Relative Normativity in International Law' (1993) 4 EJIL 317-318: "[...] the more concrete a norm will be formulated, the fewer cases may be found to fall under it and the more difficult it will be to identify that norm as a rule of customary law. Conversely, if a higher degree of abstraction is applied, the range of actions encompassed by the rule will grow."; on different degrees of abstraction of a rule see also Bleckmann, 'Zur Feststellung und Auslegung von Völkergewohnheitsrecht' 510; Robert Kolb, *Interprétation et création du droit international. Esquisse d'une herméneutique juridique moderne pour le droit international public* (Bruylant 2006) 228; Orfeas Chasapis Tassinis, 'Customary International Law: Interpretation from Beginning to End' (2020) 31 EJIL 243-244, 249-253; Charles de Visscher, *Problèmes d'interprétation judiciaire en droit international public* (Pedone 1963) 9 (the doctrine of interpretation should not be confined to treaties only); Peter Staubach, 'The Interpretation of Unwritten International Law by Domestic Judges' in Helmut Philipp Aust and Georg Nolte (eds), *The Interpretation of International Law by Domestic Courts: Uniformity, Diversity, Convergence* (Oxford University Press 2016) 120-121 (describing a "hermeneutic circle" by which the recognition of custom requires facts and legal principles to be considered in light of each other).
145 Kolb, *Interprétation et création du droit international. Esquisse d'une herméneutique juridique moderne pour le droit international public* 221. Cf. in a similar way Chasapis Tassinis, 'Customary International Law: Interpretation from Beginning to End' 245-246; Bleckmann, 'Zur Feststellung und Auslegung von Völkergewohnheitsrecht' 522-523 and Klaus Ferdinand Gärditz, 'Ungeschriebenes Völkerrecht durch Systembildung' (2007) 45(1) Archiv des Völkerrechts 22-24, both on the value of past acts of subsumption for the interpretation of custom and the necessity to take account not only of the rule but also of the circumstances to which the rule was applied.
146 Kolb, *Interprétation et création du droit international. Esquisse d'une herméneutique juridique moderne pour le droit international public* 221, 233; cf. also Robert Kolb, 'Is there a subject-matter ontology in interpretation of international legal norms?' in Mads Tønnesson Andenæs and Eirik Bjørge (eds), *A Farewell to Fragmentation Reassertion and Convergence in International Law* (Cambridge University Press 2015) 481-483, 485, while the ascertainment of a rule and the rule's interpretation

Whilst the International Law Commission by and large excluded the questions of interpretation of customary international law and of the interrelationship of sources[147], this study illustrates, for instance, the interpretative decisions made by courts and tribunals in relation to customary international law, the structure of the analysis of customary international law and the significance of normative default positions.[148] Reflections on interpretative decisions in the identification of customary international law may help in explaining why different interpreters or law-applying authorities came to different results when identifying customary international law and in locating the points of disagreement. This can lead to the refinement of criticism and improve the quality of engagement with identifications of customary international law.

b) General principles of law

Before setting out this study's contribution to the doctrine of general principles of law, it is helpful to illustrate the background of the discussion. General principles of law are often portrayed as principles which are based on domestic law analogies, hence which are recognized *in foro domestico*[149] and which can be transposed to the international level.[150] This starting point raises the

---

may tend to merge, he argues that the interpretative regime of the VCLT can be extended *mutatis mutandis* to customary international law; see also Bleckmann, 'Zur Feststellung und Auslegung von Völkergewohnheitsrecht' 526-528 (on grammatical, systemic and teleological interpretation).

147 *ILC Report 2018* at 124 paras 5-6; see below, p. 374.
148 Cf. for the importance on judicial practice Pierre-Marie Dupuy, 'L'unité de l'ordre juridique international: cours général de droit international public' (2002) 279 RdC 167: "C'est ainsi par une interprétation a posteriori que le juge construit largement lui-même la démonstration de l'existence de la règle de droit bien plus qu'il ne la dévoile".
149 Pellet and Müller, 'Article 38' 927-928; for an overview see also Béla Vitanyi, 'La signification de la "généralité" des principes de droit' (1976) 80 RGDIP 48 ff.]; Vladimir-Djuro Degan, 'General Principles of Law (A Source of General International Law)' (1992) 3 Finnish Yearbook of International Law 1 ff.
150 Jules Basdevant, 'Règles générales du droit de la paix' (1936) 58 RdC 501; Pellet and Müller, 'Article 38' 930-391; *International Status of South West Africa* (Advisory Opinion) [1950] ICJ Rep 128, Sep Op McNair 148: "The way in which international law borrows from this source is not by means of importing private law institutions "lock, stock and barrel", ready-made and fully equipped with a set of rules."

Chapter 1: Setting the Scene

question of whether general principles of law can also be inferred from the international legal order or whether general principles of international law[151] fall under article 38(1)(c) ICJ Statute or have to be based on a source referred to in article 38(1)(a) or (b) ICJ Statute.[152]

The purpose of general principles is said to fill gaps and to be a "transitory source"[153] of international law through which new norms arise in customary international law or treaty law. According to Humphrey Waldock, "there is a certain overlap between custom and general principles of national law as sources of rules of international law [...] there will always be a tendency for a general principle of national law recognized in international law to crystallize into customary law."[154] It is also suggested that *rules* of customary international law can be distinguished from general *principles* of law according to a distinction between rules and principles in legal theory[155] or

---

151 Cf. already Ian Brownlie, *Principles of Public International Law* (2nd edn, 1973) 19: "The rubric [general principles of international law] may refer to rules of customary law, to general principles of law as in Article 38(1)(c), or to logical propositions resulting from judicial reasoning on the basis of existing pieces of international law and municipal law analogies. [...] Examples of this type of general principle are the principles of consent, reciprocity, equality of states [...] In many cases, these principles are to be raced to state practice. However, they are primarily abstractions from the mass of rules and have been so long and so generally accepted as to be no longer directly connected with state practice. In a few cases the principle concerned, through useful, is unlikely to appear in ordinary state practice."
152 Pellet and Müller, 'Article 38' 926 footnote 764, remain skeptical and refer to the French text: "Another indication that the general principles of article 38, para. 1 (c) cannot be assimilated to those general principles of international law is to be found in the French text of this provision: by using the preposition 'de' ('principes généraux de droit international') instead of 'du', it shows that said principles are not limited to international law—they are not the principes généraux du droit international." For the discussions of general principles in the ILC, see below, pp. 386 ff.
153 ibid 941; cf. also Samantha Besson, 'General Principles in International Law - Whose Principles?' in *Les principes en droit européen = Principles in European law* (Schulthess 2011) 19 ff., describing how principles can transform moral values into the legal order.
154 Humphrey Waldock, 'General course on public international law' (1962) 106 RdC 62, see also at 63, concluding that the ICJ treats "'the common law' which it is authorized to apply under Article 38 paragraph (b) and (c), very much as a single corpus of law".
155 Cf. Niels Petersen, 'Customary Law Without Custom? Rules, Principles, and the Role of State Practice in International Norm Creation' (2008) 23(2) American University International Law Review 275 ff.

that customary international law emerges in situation dominated by factual reciprocity, whereas the general principles emerge in situations which are characterized by the absence of factual reciprocity.[156]

The ICJ itself rarely referred explicitly to general principles of law[157] and does not distinguish between rules and principles in a legal theoretical sense.[158] As the *Gulf of Maine* Chamber held, "the association of the terms 'rules' and 'principles' is no more than the use of a dual expression to convey one and the same idea, since in this context 'principles' clearly means principles of law, that is, it also includes rules of international law in whose case the use of the term 'principles' may be justified because of their more general and more fundamental character."[159]

This study will delineate the concept of general principles in the second chapter.[160] It will be argued that general principles of law are intrinsically connected to the idea of law and to the process of legal reasoning.[161] Based on this understanding which is informed by comparative historical insights and legal theory, it is possible to reconsider certain controversies discussed in relation to general principles.

Firstly, it is true that, as the recognition requirement in article 38(1)(c) ICJ Statute also indicates, a principle needs to be based on a certain amount of legal practice. Whereas a certain representativeness as to the selection of municipal legal orders is important, one should not, however, overemphasize the requirement of representativeness. Representativeness in municipal legal orders can be important for increasing the persuasiveness of a principle but representativeness alone cannot guarantee that a principle can be transposed

---

156 Cf. Thomas Kleinlein, 'Customary International Law and General Principles Rethinking Their Relationship' in Brian D Lepard (ed), *Reexamining Customary International Law* (Cambridge University Press 2017) 132.
157 Pellet and Müller, 'Article 38' 924 para 254; see below, p. 306.
158 Cf. d'Aspremont, 'What was not meant to be: General principles of law as a source of international law' 169: "[D]espite a number of authors mechanically identifying a use of general principles of law every time one of these Courts has mentioned the words 'general principles', it is commonly contended that general principles have played a very marginal role in the case law and advisory opinions of these two adjudicatory bodies".
159 *Delimitation of the Maritime Boundary in the Gulf of Maine Area (Canada/United States of America)* (Judgment) [1984] ICJ Rep 288-290 para 79.
160 See below, p. 138.
161 See also Georg Schwarzenberger, 'The fundamental principles of international law' (1955) 87 RdC 200-202.

to the international legal order.¹⁶² It is perhaps not realistic to assume that an interpreter will always keep both steps, the search for commonalities in municipal legal orders and the evaluation of the transposability of such principle, apart. Presumably, the interpreter will be primarily concerned with international law for which she will search for inspiration in legal practice. General principles then embody maxims, judicial experience, precepts of common sense and of good practice¹⁶³ which can be of assistance in interpreting international law. As Prosper Weil pointed out, a principle thus ascertained and applied in the context of international law may look different from how it exists in a particular domestic setting.¹⁶⁴

Secondly, the question of whether article 38(3) PCIJ Statute and article 38(1)(c) ICJ Statute refer not only to the general principles of law recognized *in foro domestico* but also to general principles formed within international law is a question of the interpretation of this provision, rather than of the concept of general principles. It is plausible that the view to require principles' manifestation *in foro domestico* was motivated by historical experiences, the failure of the Prize Court due to uncertainties as to the origin of principles, and the less sophisticated international legal structure as such back in 1920.¹⁶⁵ Based on the understanding of general principles proposed in this study, Article 38(1)(c) ICJ Statute, and article 38(3) PCIJ Statute, can be understood as declaratory recognition of the role of principles in the interpretation, application and development of the law and of the view that international law may benefit from the consideration of certain general principles and legal precepts to which recourse is had in municipal legal orders.

Based on the understanding developed in the second chapter, general principles of law can be based on extrapolations from more specific rules both of the international legal order and of municipal legal orders. It is perhaps a particularity of the international legal order and explicable by reference to the recorded debates of the Advisory Committee of Jurists that the use of general principles derived from separate legal orders, namely domestic legal orders, seems to be traditionally more accepted in public international law doctrine by and large than in domestic law, where the use of general

---

162 This point has also been raised in the discussions within the ILC, see *ILC Report 2022* at 311, 315.
163 Basdevant, 'Règles générales du droit de la paix' 502.
164 Weil, 'Le droit international en quête de son identité: cours général de droit international public' 147.
165 Kleinlein, 'Customary International Law and General Principles Rethinking Their Relationship' 136-137; see below Chapter 3.

The conceptual framework

principles derived from the same legal order can be less controversial than the use of principles based on comparative legal research.[166]

General principles need to be balanced against each other and specified in relation to the specific context. Therefore, general principles of law should not be understood in isolation from more specific rules of other sources, as they operate within the confines of legal reasoning and reveal themselves in the interpretation of other rules.[167] In general, a legal reasoning certainly

---

166 The ILC commentary on the provisionally adopted draft conclusion 7 on general principles lists as one reason in favour of general principles that formed within the international legal order that "the international legal system like any other legal system, must be able to generate general principles of law that are intrinsic to it [...] and not have only general principles of law borrowed from other legal systems", *ILC Report 2022* at 322; *Report of the International Law Commission: Seventy-fourth session (24 April–2 June and 3 July–4 August 2023)* UN Doc A/78/10 at 22. On the debate on the use of comparative legal insights for the interpretation of the US constitution see Vicki C Jackson, 'Constitutional Comparisons: Convergence, Resistance, Engagement' (2005) 119(1) Harvard Law Review 109 ff.; Jeremy Waldron, 'Foreign Law and the Modern Ius Gentium' (2005) 119(1) Harvard Law Review 129 ff.; Ernest A Young, 'Foreign Law and the Denomination Problem' (2005) 119(1) Harvard Law Review 148 ff.; Koen Lenaerts and Kathleen Gutman, 'The Comparative Law Method and the European Court of Justice: Echoes across the Atlantic' (2016) 64 American Journal of Comparative Law 841 ff.; see recently on the use of other domestic constitutional courts' decisions Stefan Martini, *Vergleichende Verfassungsrechtsprechung: Praxis, Viabilität und Begründung rechtsvergleichender Argumentation durch Verfassungsgerichte* (Duncker & Humblot 2018) 28 ff.; Peter-Michael Huber and Andreas L Paulus, 'Cooperation of Constitutional Courts in Europe: the Openness of the German Constitution to International, European, and Comparative Constitutional Law' in *Courts and Comparative Law* (Oxford University Press 2015) 292-293.
167 Cf. in a similar sense Olufemi Elias and Chin Lim, ''General Principles of Law', 'Soft' Law and the Identification of International Law' (1997) 28 Netherlands Yearbook of International Law 28. See below, p. 138; this study will therefore focus on the ways in which general principles operate through the legal operator, no compilation of a list of "general principles" is here intended; for such a list see Marija Dordeska, *General principles of law recognized by civilized nations (1922-2018). The evolution of the third source of international law through the jurisprudence of the Permanent Court of International Justice and the International Court of Justice* (Brill Nijhoff 2019) 351 ff. according to whom "it sufficed that the Court referred once to the norm as a 'principle' for it to be considered as a general principle within the meaning of Article 38(1)(c) of the Court's Statute" (at 206) and who excluded only phrases such as "in principle", "of principle", "on this principle" and "as a matter of principle" (at 209).

can derive its persuasiveness from recourse to a general principle of law, but at the same time this specific use of this very general principle as opposed to a competing principle needs to derive its persuasiveness from the legal reasoning.

Therefore, and thirdly, the study will submit that general principles of law should be recognized as a distinct concept without being subsumed under the concept of customary international law. Even though it may be difficult to sharply distinguish between custom and a general principle of law in relation to a norm, in particular when this norm operates on a high level of generality, both remain different and yet interrelated concepts, just as a treaty and a general principle of law remain different concepts when a general principle of law is used in relation to the interpretation and application of a treaty. This does not exclude the possibility that a general principle of customary international law can be both a principle and belong to the realm of customary international law.[168]

c) Treaties

A close look at the identification, interpretation and application of international law reveals that treaties can have different subtle effects and inform

---

168 Cf. also Brian D Lepard, *Customary International Law A New Theory with Practical applications* (Cambridge University Press 2010) 162-168. Lepard argues that his understanding of customary international law with a focus on *opinio juris* "helps to break down an artificial barrier" between customary international law and general principles of law (163), while acknowledging that differences between the two concepts continue to exist, as the concept of general principles "can encompass general principles of national law as well as general principles of international law and general principles of moral law" (164). Principles from each category may, but do not necessarily have to, also qualify as customary international law; in the case of principles of moral law this may be the case "if states have a belief that the principles should be recognized immediately or in the near future as legally authoritative" (165). The normativity of principles differs from having only persuasive authority to binding authority (168). "The character of any principle will depend on its content, which in turn is a function of the views and attitudes of states" (168); cf. also recently *Comment by Mathias Forteau, Summary record of the 3588th meeting, 5 July 2022* UN Doc A/CN.4/SR.3588 (PROV.) 12 ("a principle that had been deduced from customary international law continued to belong to customary international law, just as a principle that had been deduced from treaty law continued to belong to treaty law").

the identification of customary international law. A treaty can set forth a specific rule which constitutes a codification of customary international law, crystallized or gave rise to an equivalent rule of customary international law. In addition, it is submitted that treaties can affirm, concretize or rely on a general principle of international law and can sometimes therefore be relied upon for the interpretation of this principle by the legal operator. The concept of general principles thus bridges treaties and customary international law and can, in the hands of the able legal operator, contribute to the harmonization and coherence[169] of the international legal system. Last but not least, the international legal system is in many ways shaped by treaties. This study examines to what extent the practice in a treaty-based regime changes the relative significance of each source and how the construction of incorporation of other sources into treaty interpretation can affect the further development of (customary) international law. It also analyzes whether and how concepts based on treaty law complement or functionally replace concepts of general international law.

---

169 On the aspect of coherence see Mads Andenæs and Ludovica Chiussi, 'Cohesion, Convergence and Coherence of International Law' in Mads Andenæs and others (eds), *General principles and the coherence of international law* (Brill Nijhoff 2019) 9 ff.

Chapter 1: Setting the Scene

V. Situating the present study

This study is not primarily concerned with one particular source[170], one particular paradigm or context[171]. Rather than addressing the interrelationship of sources incidentally, this study puts the interrelationship of sources at the center of its research focus.[172] This choice is underlined by the conviction

---

170 Géza Herczegh, *General Principles of Law and the International Legal Order* (Kiadó 1969); Pierre-Yves Marro, *Allgemeine Rechtsgrundsätze des Völkerrechts* (Schulthess 2010); Robert Kolb, *La bonne foi en droit international public Contribution à l'étude des principes généraux de droit* (Presses Universitaires de France 2000) 82 ff.; Robert Kolb, *Good Faith in international law* (Hart 2017); Merkouris, *Article 31(3)(c) vclt and the Principle of Systemic Integration* 300, demonstrating that customary international law on the rules of interpretation was interpreted by WTO panels and Appellate Bodies and concluded that systemic interpretation as enshrined in article 31(3)(c) VCLT is apposite also to customary international law; Michael P Scharf, *Customary International Law in Times of Fundamental Change Recognizing Grotian Moments* (Cambridge University Press 2013) 5; Peter G Staubach, *The Rule of Unwritten International Law: Customary Law, General Principles, and World Order* (Routledge 2018) examines the "unwritten international law" as instrument of spontaneous self-organization and focuses in particular on purposive interpretation of custom and on analogical reasoning in relation to general principles. Dordeska, *General principles of law recognized by civilized nations (1922-2018). The evolution of the third source of international law through the jurisprudence of the Permanent Court of International Justice and the International Court of Justice* 206, 209; see recently Imogen Saunders, *General Principles as a Source of International Law* (Hart 2021), focusing on general principles of law in the jurisprudence of international courts and tribunals.
171 On general principles and the constitutionalization of international law see Kleinlein, *Konstitutionalisierung im Völkerrecht Konstruktion und Elemente einer idealistischen Völkerrechtslehre*, see below, p. 662; Rauber, *Strukturwandel als Prinzipienwandel: theoretische, dogmatische und methodische Bausteine eines Prinzipienmodells des Völkerrechts und seiner Dynamik*; see below, p. 663.
172 Certain monographic studies on the relationship between sources by Richard Reeve Baxter, 'Treaties and Customs' (1970) 129 RdC 27 ff., Anthony D'Amato, *The Concept of Custom in International Law* (Cornell University Press 1971), Thirlway, *International Customary Law and Codification: an examination of the continuing role of custom in the present period of codification of international law* and Villiger, *Customary International Law and Treaties* were primarily concerned with the relationship between customary international law and treaties, in particular codification treaties and originated under the impression of the *North Sea Continental Shelf* judgment. For a recent examination of the role of customary international law and the UN Charter with respect to the prohibition of the use of force see Christian Marxsen, *Völkerrechtsordnung und Völkerrechtsbruch* (Mohr Siebeck 2021) 80-149.

that the sources doctrine performs an important integrative function in the international community. The legitimacy of judicial pronouncements rests on the idea that courts apply law enacted by others[173] and on a shared understanding or a general consensus as to the sources of international law. If the doctrine of sources shall not become fragmented into a number of doctrines of sources in different fields of international law, it will be the responsibility of the general international lawyers not to remain on an abstract level, aloof from the specificities and particularities. It will be necessary to study the sources in different normative and institutional contexts and to highlight both similarities and differences.[174]

1. The work of the ILC

The topic of the interrelationship of sources as envisaged here might appear to be an ideal topic for the International Law Commission which, however, has so far not decided to dedicate one project to this topic. During the drafting of the Vienna Convention on the Law of Treaties, certain members, in particular Mustafa Kamil Yasseen, suggested a study of the interrelationship of sources.

---

173 Cf. Nils Jansen, *The Making of Legal Authority: Non-legislative Codifications in Historical and Comparative Perspective* (Oxford University Press 2010) 125-126: "[...] even if the declaratory theory of legal argument and judicial decision making [...] may be denounced as a fiction, this fiction has an important institutional function. It works as a device for controlling the legal profession: it prevents lawyers from taking full control of the legal system and arbitrarily and illegitimately developing the law."; cf. also Jürgen Habermas, *Faktizität und Geltung: Beiträge zur Diskurstheorie des Rechts und des demokratischen Rechtsstaats* (Suhrkamp 1992) 317-319; Ingeborg Maus, 'Die Trennung von Recht und Moral als Begrenzung des Rechts' (1989) 20 Rechtstheorie 199, 208; see also below, p. 592.

174 This study takes account of the critique that the doctrine of sources should consider to a greater extent the characteristics of particular contexts, without adopting, however, the sometimes raised conclusion that there no longer is one unified doctrine of sources of international law, cf. Curtis A Bradley, 'Customary International Law Adjudication as Common Law Adjudication' in Curtis A Bradley (ed), *Custom's future: international law in a changing world* (Cambridge University Press 2016) 34 ff.; Steven Ratner, 'Sources of International Humanitarian Law and International Criminal Law: War/Crimes and the Limits of the Doctrine of Sources' in Samantha Besson and Jean d'Aspremont (eds), *The Oxford Handbook on the Sources of International Law* (Oxford University Press 2017) 912 ff.; Michelle Biddulph and Dwight Newman, 'A Contextualized Account of General Principles of International Law' (2014) 26(2) Pace International Law Review 286 ff.

Yet, the Commission as a whole decided, in the words attributed to Special Rapporteur Waldock "possibly out of timidity but nevertheless wisely, not to go too far into the subject. The codification of the relation between customary law and other sources of law should be left to others."[175] The Study Group's Fragmentation report as finalized by Martti Koskenniemi was primarily concerned with the place of treaties in their normative environment, and its suggestion to conduct a study on "general international law" in the future as well was not followed up by the ILC.[176] The ILC's recent conclusions on customary international law address to a certain extent the value of treaties for customary international law, without addressing the question of the interrelationship in great detail.[177] The conclusions on customary international law are concerned with the "identification" and "determination" of customary international law and "do not address, directly, the processes by which customary international law develops over time".[178] In addition, "no attempt is made to explain the relationship between customary international law and other sources of international law listed in Article 38, paragraph 1, of the Statute of the International Court of Justice".[179] In the context of the ongoing project on general principles of law, the ILC Drafting Committee emphasized that the relationship between customary international law and treaties fell

---

175 *ILC Ybk (1966 vol 1 part 2)* 94 para 103. See also *ILC Ybk (1964 vol 2)* 112: "the relationship between international custom and treaties depended to a large extent on the nature of the particular custom involved and on the provisions of the treaty. The subject would be considered later in connexion with interpretation [...]"; see also *ILC Ybk (1964 vol 1)* 109 paras 44-45 and 112 para 181 and 195 para 54 and *ILC Ybk (1966 vol 1 part 2)* 91 para 73 (Yasseen), ibid 93 para 95 (Tunkin) and 93 para 97 (El-Erian).
176 *Fragmentation of international law: difficulties arising from diversification and expansion of international law, Report of the Study Group of the International Law Commission, Finalized by Martti Koskenniemi* 254-255; on the fragmentation report, see below, p. 368.
177 Cf. also Nolte, 'How to identify customary international law? - On the final outcome of the work of the International Law Commission (2018)' 19-20; Paolo Palchetti, 'The Role of General Principles in Promoting the Development of Customary International Rules' in Mads Andenæs and others (eds), *General Principles and the Coherence of International Law* (Brill Nijhoff 2019) 58-59; see in more detail, below, p. 377.
178 *ILC Report 2018* at 124 para 5. See also UNGA Res 73/203 (20 December 2018) UN Doc A/RES/73/203 para 4: the UNGA "[t]akes note of the conclusions [...] brings them to the attention of States and all who may be called upon to identify customary international law, and encourages their widest possible dissemination."
179 *ILC Report 2018* at 124 para 6.

outside the topic's scope; the relationship between general principles of law and the other sources is currently addressed in a draft conclusion.[180]

Whereas the ILC conclusions on customary international law and on general principles of law pursue an important objective as they may guide courts and tribunals in the process of *identifying* customary international law and general principles of law, they do not capture customary international law and general principles of law in their entirety. Customary international law and general principles of law can emerge gradually and sometimes unconsciously.[181] The (draft) conclusions can to a certain extent rationalize the identification process, but the questions of how customary international law and general principles of law will develop, how much room they will be given in an international legal order that is more and more shaped by treaties cannot be answered in an abstract fashion.

Whilst the present study pursues a research objective outside the scope of the specific topics of the ILC, it relies on the ILC's understanding of customary international law. Accordingly, customary international law is a general practice that is accepted as law (conclusion 2).[182] The ILC defended the so-called two-elements approach against alternative views which regarded

---

180 See *Statement of the Chairman of the Drafting Committee, Mr. Ki Gab Park of 29 July 2022* ⟨https://legal.un.org/ilc/documentation/english/statements/2022_dc_chair_statement_gpl.pdf⟩ accessed 1 February 2023 at 16; on this ILC project see below, p. 386. On the recent second report of the Special Rapporteur, see below, p. 216.

181 Cf. William Michael Reisman, 'Canute Confronts the Tide: States versus Tribunals and the Evolution of the Minimum Standard in Customary International Law' (2015) 30 ICSID Review 619: "Nomo-dynamically, customary international law is a video of an ongoing, informal and unorganized process of consuetudo and desuetudo, of formation, confirmation, transformation and termination of the shared expectations and demands of politically relevant international actors about the right ways of doing things. Nomo-statically, customary international law is one still frame of that video, a snapshot, from one moment, of those expectations and demands that were established in that informal and unorganized process of law formation." See also Monica Hakimi, 'Making Sense of Customary International Law' (2020) 118 Michigan Law Review 1495.

182 For the draft conclusions as adopted by the ILC on second reading see *ILC Report 2018* at 116-112.

either *opinio juris*[183] or practice as central element[184] or which opine that in most cases no separate proof of *opinio juris* is necessary[185] or which argue that both elements are positioned on a sliding scale with each being able to compensate for the weak presence of the other.[186] Against the background of a debate of whether the same two-elements approach may adequately reflect the formation of custom in different areas of international law,[187] the ILC commentary to the adopted draft conclusions attempts to reconcile both views which existed in the Commission. According to the commentary, both elements are needed "in all fields of international law"[188], and the

---

183 Bin Cheng, 'Custom: the future of general state practice in a divided world' in Ronald Saint John MacDonald and Douglas Miller Johnston (eds), *The structure and process of international law: essays in legal philosophy, doctrine, and theory* (1983) 514 ff.; Lepard, *Customary International Law A New Theory with Practical applications.*

184 Kelsen, 'Théorie du droit international coutumier' 266; Kelsen, *Principles of International Law (1952)* 307; Paul Guggenheim, *Traité de droit international public: avec mention de la pratique internationale et suisse* (vol 1, Georg 1953) 47-48; but cf. later Paul Guggenheim, *Traité de droit international public: avec mention de la pratique internationale et suisse* (2nd edn, vol 1, Georg 1967) 107; Hans Kelsen and Robert W Tucker, *Principles of International Law* (2nd edn, Holt, Rinehart, Winston, 1967) 450-451, and vii.

185 Maurice Mendelson, 'The subjective Element in Customary International Law' (1996) 66 BYIL 204; ILA, *Statement of Principles Applicable to the Formation of General Customary International Law* (London, 2000) ⟨https://www.ila-hq.org/en_GB/documents/conference-report-london-2000-2⟩ accessed 1 February 2023 at 30 ff.

186 See Frederic L Kirgis, 'Custom on a Sliding Scale' (1987) 81(1) AJIL 146 ff.

187 Different and contrary positions were held in the commission which decided in 2013 to leave this question open, *Report of the International Law Commission: Sixty-fifth session (6 May-7 June and 8 July-9 August 2013)* UN Doc A/68/10 97; International Law Commission, Sixty-fourth session, Note by Michael Wood, Special Rapporteur, UN Doc A /CN.4/653, para 22: "it is neither helpful nor in accordance with principle, for the purposes of the present topic, to break the law up into separate specialist fields."; he would later maintain that "the better view is" that there would be no different approaches to custom while however conceding that there may "be a difference in application of the two-element approach in different fields", *Second report on identification of customary international law by Michael Wood, Special Rapporteur* 22 May 2014 UN Doc A/CN.4/672 at 12 para. 28, but see also ibid 13 para. 28: "Any other approach risks artificially dividing international law into separate fields, which would run counter to the systemic nature of international law." See also *ILC Ybk (2014 vol 2 part 1)* 173-174 para 28.

188 *ILC Report 2018* at 126 paras 4, 6.

application of the two-elements approach "may well take into account the particular circumstances and context in which an alleged rule has arisen and operates".[189]

The present study will not challenge the ILC in this regard. To the present author, attempts to emphasize one element at the expense of the other, to distinguish between modern and traditional, deductive and inductive, moral and facilitative customs[190] run the risk of becoming too artificial.[191] In the end, the interpreter needs to evaluate whether there is "a general practice accepted as law", which requires her to look at both elements simultaneously and in light of each other.[192] Based on this understanding, the difference becomes smaller between those who are critical of the "two-elements" terminology and who would like to speak of a single[193] element, consisting of a "general

---

189 ibid at 126 para 6.
190 Cf. Anthea Roberts, 'Traditional and Modern Approaches to Customary International Law: A Reconciliation' (2001) 95 AJIL 764, 776, 789.
191 Similar Talmon, 'Determining Customary International Law: the ICJ's Methodology between Induction, Deduction and Assertion' 442 (concluding that induction and deduction "are not two competing or opposing monolithic analytical methods but, in practice, are intermixed"); similar William Thomas Worster, 'The Inductive and Deductive Methods in Customary International Law Analysis: Traditional and Modern Approaches' (2014) 45(2) Georgetown journal of international law 520 (demonstrating that "the actual assessment of custom shows a mixed deductive and inductive process, and that observations on the 'traditional' and 'modern' approaches to the assessment of customary international law overlook the deep way the processes are intermingled"); see furthermore *ILC Report 2018* 126 para 5.
192 Haggenmacher, 'La doctrine des deux éléments du droit coutumier dans la pratique de la Cour internationale' 30: "La coutume présente donc bien un double aspect matériel et subjectif, mais les deux sont en fait inséparables: ils ne s'analysent pas en un a élément ' matériel et un autre, subjectif [...] La coutume internationale est saisie comme un tout indifférencié: à aucun moment on n'a visé à isoler ses composantes [...]"; Brigitte Stern, 'La coutume au coeur du droit international: quelques réflexions' in *Mélanges offerts à Paul Reuter: le droit international: unité et diversité* (Pedone 1981) 482; Marco Sassòli, *Bedeutung einer Kodifikation für das allgemeine Völkerrecht: mit besonderer Betrachtung der Regeln zum Schutze der Zivilbevölkerung vor den Auswirkungen von Feindseligkeiten* (Helbing & Lichtenhahn 1990) 34; Jörg P Müller, *Vertrauensschutz im Völkerrecht* (Carl Heymanns Verlag KG 1971) 84-85; Dupuy, 'L'unité de l'ordre juridique international: cours général de droit international public' 166.
193 Cf. Haggenmacher, 'La doctrine des deux éléments du droit coutumier dans la pratique de la Cour internationale' 31 ("seul 'élément'"); cf. in legal theory on customary law Gerald J Postema, 'Custom, Normative Practice, and the Law' (2012)

practice accepted as law",[194] and those who continue to advocate the two-element approach whilst stressing the interrelationship of both elements.[195]

2. Sociological perspectives: the proliferation of norms and socializing states

This study's focus on the interrelationship of sources has been inspired by specific sociological perspectives on international law, in particular on the proliferation of norms. This section's purpose is not to give an exhaustive account on the relationship between international legal doctrine and interdisciplinary approaches to international law. Nevertheless, it should not go unnoticed that the relationship between the so-called "interdisciplinary turn"[196] in international legal scholarship and conventional international legal doctrine was not always without tension, as part of the literature on com-

---

62 Duke Law Journal 718 ff. (against an additive account and in favour of integration in the sense of an understanding of custom as normative practice).

194 Cf. for a recent critique of the two-elements terminology in this regard Christian J Tams, 'Meta-Custom and the Court: A Study in Judicial Law-Making' (2015) 14 The Law and Practice of International Courts and Tribunals 59; Jean d'Aspremont, 'The Four Lives of Customary International Law' [2019] International Community Law Review 229 ff.; cf. on the development of different understandings of customary international law Bradley, 'Customary International Law Adjudication as Common Law Adjudication' 43-47.

195 *ILC Report 2018* at 125: "Draft conclusion 2 sets out the basic approach, according to which the identification of a rule of customary international law requires an inquiry into two distinct, yet related, questions: whether there is a general practice, and whether such general practice is accepted as law (that is, accompanied by *opinio juris*) [...] A general practice and acceptance of that practice as law (opinio juris) are the two constituent elements of customary international law: together they are the essential conditions for the existence of a rule of customary international law. The identification of such a rule thus involves a careful examination of available evidence to establish their presence in any given case. [...] The test must always be: is there a general practice that is accepted as law?".

196 Cf. Anne-Marie Slaughter, Andrew S Tulumello, and Stepan Wood, 'International Law and International Relations Theory: A New Generation of Interdisciplinary Scholarship' (1998) 92 AJIL 367 ff.; Gregory Shaffer and Tom Ginsburg, 'The empirical turn in international legal scholarship' (2012) 106 AJIL 1 ff.; see also generally on international relations and customary international law Byers, *Custom, power and the power of rules: international relations and customary international law* 21-32, 147-166.

pliance and rational game theory as well as the reactions to it illustrates.[197] While this book adopts a legal doctrinal approach which must ultimately rest on legal doctrinal arguments, it is also true that sociological perspectives on the interplay between the practice of states and the emergence and proliferation of legal norms can offer important insights for a doctrinal study of

---

197 Cf. Jack L Goldsmith and Eric A Posner, *The limits of international law* (Oxford University Press 2005); for a critical overview see Stefan Oeter, 'The legitimacy of customary international law' in Thomas Eger, Stefan Oeter, and Stefan Voigt (eds), *Economic Analysis of International Law: Contributions to the XIIIth Travemünde Symposium on the Economic Analysis of Law (March 29-31, 2012)* (Mohr Siebeck 2014) 1 ff.; Detlev F Vagts, 'International Relations Looks at Customary International Law: A Traditionalist's Defence' (2004) 15(5) EJIL 1031 ff.; Hans-Joachim Cremer, 'Völkerrecht - Alles nur Rhetorik?' (2007) 67 ZaöRV 267 ff.; for a critique of Goldsmith's and Posner's biased, short-term understanding of rationality see Anne van Aaken, 'To Do Away with International Law? Some Limits to 'The Limits of International Law'' (2006) 17(1) EJIL 289 ff.; Jens David Ohlin, *The assault on international law* (Oxford University Press 2015) 89 ff.; see also Benedict Kingsbury, 'The Concept of Compliance As a Function of Competing Conceptions of International Law' (1998) 19 Michigan Journal of International Law 345 ff., describing that there is not one but many concepts of compliance with presuppose and are connected with different understandings of international law; see also Robert Howse and Ruti G Teitel, 'Beyond Compliance: Rethinking Why International Law Matters' (2010) 1 Global Policy 127 ff. On the debate of effects of human rights treaties on compliance see Oona A Hathaway, 'Do Human Rights Treaties Make a Difference?' (2002) 111 Yale Law Journal 1935 ff.; Ryan Goodman and Derek Jinks, 'Measuring the Effects of Human Rights Treaties' (2003) 14 EJIL 171 ff.; Beth A Simmons, *Mobilizing for Human Rights International Law in Domestic Politics* (Cambridge University Press 2009) 159 ff.

Chapter 1: Setting the Scene

international law[198], in particular with respect to customary international law and general principles of law.[199]

Against the background of the selected[200] scholarship on the proliferation of norms it may be suggested that treaty-law, customary international law and general principles are not to be understood as separate tracks and that norms enshrined in treaties may shape states' practices. The following account focuses on explanations of how new norms can assert themselves,

---

198 As eloquently put by Georg Schwarzenberger, 'The Standard of Civilisation in International Law' (1955) 8(1) Current Legal Problems 215: "The international lawyer may realise in a becoming spirit of awareness of the interdependence of all learning that, at this stage, he has to equip himself with new and more congenial tools or at least that he has to accept gratefully the labours of others who, better fitted than he, have done the spade work for him."; Julius Stone, 'Problems Confronting Sociological Enquiries Concerning International Law' (1956) 89 RdC 85, 89 ("Recognition that positive international law requires study not only in itself, but also as determined by and as itself determining facts extraneous to itself, is but a beginning of our problems") and at 92 ("dangers can, I believe, be reduced to proportions which are not fatal to the advancement of knowledge, provided that the inquirer brings them into full consciousness"), and 121-124; Bruno Simma, *Das Reziprozitätselement in der Entstehung des Völkergewohnheitsrechts* (Fink 1970) 21-23 (in favour of pluralism of methods); Bruno Simma, 'Völkerrechtswissenschaft und Lehre von den internationalen Beziehungen: Erste Überlegungen zur Interdependenz zweier Disziplinen' (1972) 23 Zeitschrift für öffentliches Recht 300, 305 (the task of the international legal science should not be confined to cognition and description of positive legal norms); Paulus, *Die internationale Gemeinschaft im Völkerrecht: eine Untersuchung zur Entwicklung des Völkerrechts im Zeitalter der Globalisierung* 6-7 (positive international law cannot be observed without any regard to the surrounding social environment but retains its independence).

199 Cf. for instance the so-called interactional account which is based on inspirations from Lon Fuller and sociological constructivism, Jutta Brunnée and Stephen John Toope, 'International Law and Constructivism: Elements of an Interactional Theory of International Law' (2000) 39 Columbia Journal of Transnational Law 65-66, 68; Jutta Brunnée and Stephen John Toope, 'Interactional international law: an introduction' (2011) 3(2) International Theory 308; Jutta Brunnée and Stephen John Toope, *Legitimacy and legality in international law: an interactional account* (Cambridge University Press 2010) 20 ff.; Jutta Brunnée and Stephen John Toope, 'The Rule of Law in an Agnostic World: the Prohibition on the Use of Force and Humanitarian Exceptions' in Wouter G Werner and others (eds), *The law of international lawyers: reading Martti Koskenniemi* (Cambridge University Press 2017) 142.

200 Cf. for a critique of "unregulated reception" of interdisciplinary perspectives in legal discourse Ferdinand Weber, *Staatsangehörigkeit und Status: Statik und Dynamik politischer Gemeinschaftsbildung* (Mohr Siebeck 2018) 303 ff.

how they operate internally within a state and how they are transmitted on the international level through states, all of which can be relevant to understanding the gradual emergence of customary international law and general principles[201].

Norms, broadly speaking, can contribute to the formation of states' identity, which is not predetermined but informing and informed by structure and context.[202] One of the key insights of the approaches discussed here is the so-called norm cycle as described by Martha Finnemore and Kathryn Sikkink. They distinguish three stages or life-cycles of a norm, namely norm-emergence, norm-cascade, and internalization:

> "The characteristic mechanism of the first stage, norm emergence, is persuasion by norm entrepreneurs. Norm entrepreneurs attempt to convince a critical mass of states (norm leaders) to embrace new norms. The second stage is characterized more by dynamic of imitation as the norm leaders attempt to socialize other states to become followers [...] At the far end of the norm cascade, norm internalization occurs; norms acquire a taken-for-granted quality and are no longer a matter of broad public debate."[203]

---

201 On the emergence of general principles through the process of argumentative self-entrapment see Kleinlein, *Konstitutionalisierung im Völkerrecht Konstruktion und Elemente einer idealistischen Völkerrechtslehre* 268; Kleinlein, 'Customary International Law and General Principles Rethinking Their Relationship' 156-157.

202 On the interrelationship between agent and structure see Alexander Wendt, 'Collective Identity Formation and the International State' (1994) 88(2) American Political Science Review 384 ff.; Alexander Wendt, 'Anarchy is what States Make of it: The Social Construction of Power Politics' (1992) 46(2) International Organization 391 ff.; Alexander Wendt, 'The Agent-Structure Problem in International Relations Theory' (1987) 41(3) International Organization 335 ff.; see also on the "duality of structure" Anthony Giddens, *The constitution of society: outline of the theory of structuration* (Polity Press 1984) 25 ("The constitution of agents and structures are not two independently given sets of phenomena, a dualism, but represent a duality"); John Gerard Ruggie, 'What Makes the World Hang Together? Neo-Utilitarianism and the Social Constructivist Challenge' (1998) 52(4) International Organization 864 ("[...] there is growing empirical evidence that normative factors in addition to states' identities shape their interests, or their behavior, directly [...]."; see also Thomas Risse and Kathryn Sikkink, 'The power of human rights: international norms and domestic change' in Thomas Risse, Stephen C Ropp, and Kathryn Sikkink (eds), *The power of human rights: international norms and domestic change* (Cambridge University Press 1999) 9 ("Norms become relevant and causally consequential during the process by which actors define and refine their collective identities and interests").

203 Martha Finnemore and Kathryn Sikkink, 'International Norm Dynamics and Political Change' (1998) 52(4) International Organization 895 ff.

Chapter 1: Setting the Scene

In order to explain how norms can assert themselves among and within states, Thomas Risse, Stephen C. Ropp and Kathryn Sikkink introduced in *The Power of Human Rights* the idea of a spiral-model with a focus on human rights norms. This model consists of five stages: an initial phase of repression within and by a state is followed by a phase of denial of these repressions and human rights violations after those violations had been brought to the attention of a wider public. Subsequently, the state in question makes tactical concessions in order to alleviate concerns of human rights abuses, these concessions could express themselves in a greater tolerance for mass public demonstrations or in communicating the objective to ratify human rights treaties. In the fourth phase ("prescriptive status"), the state has ratified and implemented human rights treaties, thereby granting human rights norms a prescriptive status. The fifth stage is called "rule-consistent behaviour".[204]

Ryan Goodman and Derek Jinks illustrate in their account the subtle ways in which norms are transmitted and received on the international level and how a general practice can emerge. They argue that three processes influence social behaviour of states can be identified, namely material inducement, persuasion and acculturation:

> "Material inducement refers to the process whereby target actors are influenced to change their behavior by the imposition of material costs or the conferral of material benefits. [...] Persuasion refers to the process whereby target actors are convinced of

---

204 See the contributions in Thomas Risse, Stephen C Ropp, and Kathryn Sikkink (eds), *The power of human rights: international norms and domestic change* (Cambridge University Press 1999); Risse and Sikkink, 'The power of human rights: international norms and domestic change' 4, 15 ff.; Thomas Risse and Stephen C Ropp, 'Introduction and overview' in Thomas Risse, Stephen C Ropp, and Kathryn Sikkink (eds), *The Persistent Power of Human Rights From Commitment to Compliance* (Cambridge University Press 2013) 5 ff. Since the first publication of *The Power of Human Rights* in 1999, backlashes against international norms have given rise to the question of whether the spiral model was too optimistic, Kathryn Sikkink, 'The United States and torture: does the spiral model work?' in Thomas Risse, Stephen C Ropp, and Kathryn Sikkink (eds), *The Continuing Power of Human Rights: From Commitment to Compliance* (Cambridge University Press 2013) 150, 156, 162 (on the backlash in the US during the second Bush administration). In particular, Anja Jetschke and Andrea Liese, 'The power of human rights a decade ater: from euphoria to contestation?' in Thomas Risse, Stephen C Ropp, and Kathryn Sikkink (eds), *The Continuing Power of Human Rights: From Commitment to Compliance* (Cambridge University Press 2013) 33-34, 36 ff. questioned the model's linearity and pointed out how even in later phases human rights norms would compete with other norms, such as norms of national security.

the truth, validity, or appropriateness of a norm, belief, or practice. [...] Acculturation, on the other hand, is the process by which actors adopt the beliefs and behavioral patterns of the surrounding culture, without actively assessing either the merits of those beliefs and behaviors or the material costs and benefits of conforming to them. Cognitive and social pressures drive acculturation [...] Whereas persuasion emphasizes the content of a norm, acculturation emphasizes the relationship of the actor to a reference group or wider cultural environment."[205]

Socialization in the form of acculturation can be observed at the international level, as states tend to mimic other states within the same network as regards economic policies or human rights norms.[206] Goodman and Jinks describe the significance of "regional social influence"[207] and Brian Greenhill supports this "social influence" in his study on the transmission of human rights. Greenhill's research demonstrates a tendency of convergence among states which are connected in the same international organization with respect to the average human rights performance.[208] What matters is not the mandate of the particular IGOs, but the networks concluded by states in IGOs, states' individual human rights record as well as similar cultural backgrounds.[209] Goodman and Jinks suggest that acculturation may mitigate uncertainties of broadly framed obligations and that this prevent what Thomas Franck[210]

---

205 Ryan Goodman and Derek Jinks, *Socializing states: promoting human rights through international law* (Oxford University Press 2013) 22, 26.
206 See ibid 58 ff.; see also Xun Cao, 'Networks as Channels of Policy Diffusion: Explaining Worldwide Changes in Capital Taxation, 1998-2006' (2010) 54 International Studies Quarterly 849 (arguing that networks established through international organization without an economic mandate but a cultural or social mandate can lead to convergence among the member states as to capital taxation rates).
207 Goodman and Jinks, *Socializing states: promoting human rights through international law* 70-71, where Goodman and Jinks summarize with reference to Simmons: "[...] a determining factor for whether a state will ratify a human rights treaty is the ratification practices of other states in its region [...] state practice involving reservations to human rights treaties suggests regional social influence"; Simmons, *Mobilizing for Human Rights International Law in Domestic Politics* 89 ("socially motivated ratification").
208 Brian Greenhill, 'The Company You Keep: International Socialization and the Diffusion of Human Rights Norms' (2010) 54 International Studies Quarterly 127 ff., on the spread of physical integrity rights among states which share membership in international organizations.
209 ibid 143; Brian Greenhill, *Transmitting Rights: International Organizations and the Diffusion of Human Rights Practices* (Oxford University Press 2015) 23 ff., 151 ff.
210 Franck, *Fairness in International Law and Institutions* 79.

once described as "unilateral, self-serving exculpatory interpretations of [...] rules".[211]

These perspectives explain the gradual emergence of norms and describe stages of the process of self-entrapment. They illustrate the different roles that states can play in this regard. In particular, the focus on socialization and acculturation offers a possible explanation of why and how states may support a norm by way of acquiescence. This may be relevant for understanding customary international law as resulting not only from instances of practices but also from acquiescence to these practices which is why it is the product of a legal community as a whole.[212] These perspectives are also interesting with a view to a study of the interrelationship of sources. The idea that norms undertaken by states can shape states' practices may suggest that, for instance, treaty law and the norms expressed therein can inform states' actions and practices and can insofar contribute to customary international law. It may also suggest that this renders contradictions between the sources less likely and forms of convergences and a reconciliation and harmonization of the content of different norms more likely. These perspectives are not only interesting with respect to the character of customary international law as "unconscious lawmaking"[213], but they also give rise to the question of whether states can try to shape the development of customary international law.

Adam Bower's research on lawmaking without great powers, for instance, illustrates that these effects can also be the result of a purposive activity in the sense that states can conclude treaties in order to introduce new ideas to the international legal order and to shape customary international law.[214] The written character of treaty obligations is said to be particularly impactful

---

211 Goodman and Jinks, *Socializing states: promoting human rights through international law* 116-119.
212 Cf. Brigitte Stern, 'Custom at the heart of international law' (Michael Byers and Anne Denise trs (2001) 11 Duke Journal of Comparative & International Law 108, arguing that "the content of the *opinio juris* of each state will depend on its position of power within the international order"; Kolb, 'Selected problems in the theory of customary international law' 136; on acquiescence see now also *ILC Report 2018* at 140 ff., conclusion 10(3).
213 See above, footnote 64.
214 Adam Bower, *Norms without the great powers: international law and changing social standards in world politics* (Oxford University Press 2017) 36, 45-52; his focus lies on the Rome Statute of the International Criminal Court (signed 17 July 1998, entered into force 1 July 2002) 2187 UNTS 3 and the Convention on the Prohibition of the Use, Stockpiling, Production and Transfer of Anti-Personnel Mines and on

"because it creates a structure of repetition for legal language that is key to solidifying social expectations over time."[215] Bower demonstrates with reference to the example of the Ottawa convention on the ban of landmines that third states which had not ratified the Convention remain or become "implicated in the broader complex of values from which a treaty derives"[216] and to which the treaty gives expression. Third states are described to offer *de facto* or rhetorical support to the treaties' core objectives, and even when they argue that the complete ban of landmines would not apply in cases where the state's very survival would be at stake, they indirectly affirm the general prohibition of landmines.[217] Bower concludes that the number of non-ratifications is not necessarily a reliable indicator for the degree of opposition to the substance of a treaty.[218] Brian Greenhill and Michael Strausz even suggest that the internalization of a treaty norm by third states can reduce the likelihood of the treaty receiving further ratifications.[219] These suggestions are particularly interesting when studying and evaluating the relative significance of each source in the present international community: treaties can be used to influence the development of customary international law; in particular, the substance of rules set forth in treaties can become accepted customary international law. At the same time, this process can reduce the likelihood of further ratifications and reduce the ratification pres-

---

their Destruction (signed 18 September 1997, entered into force 1 March 1999) 2056 UNTS 211.
215 Bower, *Norms without the great powers: international law and changing social standards in world politics* 35; for a similar observation in doctrinal scholarship see Georges Abi-Saab, 'Les sources du droit international: essai de déconstruction' in Marcelo G Kohen and Magnus Jesko Langer (eds), *Le développement du droit international: réflexions d'un demi-siècle. Volume I* (Graduate Institute Publications 2013) 75 (arguing that states can by treaties structure the legal environment and shape the expectations of the participants in the international legal system).
216 Bower, *Norms without the great powers: international law and changing social standards in world politics* 27.
217 ibid 91; cf. also the process described as argumentative self-entrapment, Thomas Risse, '"Let's argue!": Communicative Action in World Politics' (2000) 54(1) International Organization 32.
218 Bower, *Norms without the great powers: international law and changing social standards in world politics* 75. But see Baxter, 'Treaties and Customs' 99, 100 ("when time passes and States neglect to become parties to a multilateral instrument, that abstention constitutes a silent rejection of the treaty").
219 Cf. Brian Greenhill and Michael Strausz, 'Explaining Nonratification of the Genocide Convention: A Nested Analysis' (2014) 10 Foreign Policy Analysis 374-375, 381-382, 388-389.

Chapter 1: Setting the Scene

sure, potentially at the expense of procedural frameworks which can only be established by treaties.

Taking inspiration from these perspectives, the following chapters will analyze whether the suggested higher likelihood of convergence and harmonization in fact characterizes the interrelationship of sources in the present international community and how norms and, for instance, adjudicatory structures of courts and tribunals shape the way in which other sources of international law are addressed by different actors.

B. Structure of this study

The present work analyzes the interrelationship of sources in different contexts, in scholarship, judicial settings and codification settings. The chapters will strive to strike a balance between studying each field or context on their respective own terms and highlighting similarities and differences between different contexts.

I. Comparative-historical perspectives

The first part will present comparative legal perspectives on the interrelationship of sources which informed and was informed by the historical background of article 38 PCIJ Statute.

The second chapter "Comparative Perspectives" will delve into the interrelationship of sources in domestic contexts. The chapter focuses on experiences and developments in domestic legal orders which have served as a source of inspiration in public international law.[220] In particular, the chapter will focus on the relationship between written and unwritten law in common law systems and on lack of support for customary international law in German law. In

---

220 See Paul Guggenheim, 'Landesrechtliche Begriffe im Völkerrecht, vor allem im Bereich der internationalen Organisationen' in Walter Schätzel and Hans-Jürgen Schlochauer (eds), *Rechtsfragen der internationalen Organisationen Festschrift für Hans Wehberg zu seinem 70. Geburtstag* (Klostermann 1956) 134, 141, 150; Christian Tomuschat, 'Obligations Arising For States Without Or Against Their Will' [1993] (241) RdC 317-318 generally on communication between national and international law; see also Mendelson, 'The subjective Element in Customary International Law' 178-179 on the usefulness to study "domestic customary law societies, past and present" for the international lawyer.

addition and based on the experiences in municipal legal orders, the chapter addresses the doctrinal background and the development of modern theories of "general principles of law". Article 38(3) PCIJ Statute arguably did not invent general principles, it was inspired by and gave further inspiration to the concept of general principles of law. In identifying this comparative historical background of general principles of law, this chapter seeks to lay the foundations for this work's understanding of general principles in the international legal order. The chosen perspective here is consistent with the view that general principles of law can be found within many legal orders, including, but not limited to, international law.[221]

The third chapter will first illuminate the process leading to article 38 PCIJ Statute. In particular, the chapter will then delve into the drafting of article 38 and demonstrate how the members of the Advisory Committee of Jurists discussed the interrelationship of sources. Subsequently, the chapter will turn to the treatment of sources in the jurisprudence of the PCIJ, in codification settings and in scholarship with a particular focus on the interwar period.

The fourth chapter will offer concluding observations on the two preceding chapters.

Two potential biases that may be seen as inherent in this structure shall be briefly addressed. To begin with, the selection of legal orders and of scholars in these two chapters can be criticized for its Western focus.[222] One could argue that the Western influences on article 38 ICJ Statute were particularly dominant. At the same time, such an argument should not be carried too far. Recent scholarship has demonstrated that, in spite of insufficient participation and representativeness and in spite of the use of international law

---

221 See also Robert Kolb, 'Les maximes juridiques en droit international public: questions historiques et théoriques' (1999) 32(2) Revue belge de droit international 412, 424, 430; Schwarzenberger, 'The fundamental principles of international law' 195: "Experience with any of the systems of municipal law teaches that all of them take for granted a stratification of legal principles. Thus, *prima facie*, it may be assumed that the same is true of international law."
222 For a recent treatment of cultural perspectives see Anthea Roberts, *Is International Law international?* (Oxford University Press 2017). See also Arnulf Becker Lorca, 'Eurocentrism in the History of International Law' in Bardo Fassbender and Anne Peters (eds), *The Oxford Handbook of the History of International Law* (Oxford University Press 2012) 1035, arguing that "writing history always entails the production of a perspective from which to include and interpret relevant material and exclude material that is regarded irrelevant to explain the past. However, there is a problem if a Eurocentric perspective generates a distortion in the historical narrative."

Chapter 1: Setting the Scene

by Western states against non-Western states[223], non-Western states did not reject international law and began to engage with it in furtherance of their own objectives, which has been described as a form of "reinterpretation of rules by non-Western states, supporting their admission into the international community."[224]

The Western focus in the first two chapters will be remedied to a certain extent in the next chapters which focus on institutions the members of which are meant to represent "the main forms of civilization and of the principal legal systems"[225] and on perspectives on the sources of international law also by non-western states and scholars. As to the second potential bias, this study

---

223 Cf. Antony Anghie, *Imperialism, Sovereignty and the Making of International Law* (Cambridge University Press 2005).

224 Arnulf Becker Lorca, 'Universal International Law: Nineteenth-Century Histories of Imposition and Appropriation' (2010) 51(2) Harvard International Law Journal 477; Lorca adds nuance to the narrative of European expansion of international law, see Wilhelm G Grewe, 'Vom europäischen zum universellen Völkerrecht Zur Frage der Revision des europazentrischen Bildes der Völkerrechtsgeschichte' (1982) 42 ZaöRV 449 ff.; on the reception in Russia, see Lauri Mälksoo, *Russian approaches to international law* (Oxford University Press 2015); on the reception in Latin-America see Nina Keller-Kemmerer, *Die Mimikry des Völkerrechts: Andrés Bellos "Principios de Derecho Internacional"* (Nomos 2018) 272-273; on African perspectives see Becker Lorca, 'Eurocentrism in the History of International Law' 1045 with further references. See also Stefan Kroll, *Normgenese durch Re-Interpretation: China und das europäische Völkerrecht im 19. und 20. Jahrhundert* (Nomos 2012) 13 ff., 20, 114, 123 ff., 165 ff.; see also Mohammad Shahabuddin, 'The 'standard of civilization' in international law: Intellectual perspectives from pre-war Japan' (2019) 32 Leiden Journal of International Law 14: "[W]hat appears as a straightforward application of European international law and the standard of civilization in Japan's late-nineteenth century imperial projects was in fact shaped by a long-standing process of Japan's historical engagement with a system of cultural hierarchy in the regional order."

225 Article 9 ICJ Statute; Article 8 ILC Statute. It is here acknowledged that also in these institutions problems of representativeness exist; on the underrepresentation of women in the International Law Commission see Miguel de Serpa Soares, 'Seven Women in Seventy Years: A Roundtable Discussion on Achieving Gender Parity at the International Law Commission' [2018] United Nations Office of Legal Affairs ⟨https://legal.un.org/ola/media/info_from_lc/mss/speeches/MSS_ILC70_gender_side_event-24-May-2018.pdf⟩ accessed 1 February 2023; Anne Peters, 'Völkerrecht im Gender-Fokus' in Andreas Zimmermann, Thomas Griegerich, and Ursula E Heinz (eds), *Gender und Internationales Recht* (Duncker & Humblot 2007) 293 ff.; on the underrepresentation of women at international courts and tribunals see Nienke Grossman, 'Achieving Sex-Representative International Court Benches' (2016) 110 AJIL 83; Leigh Swigarth and Daniel Terris, 'Who are International

assumes that the concept of general principles transcends legal orders insofar as this concept can be found both in domestic legal orders and in international law and that scholarly discussions of this concept both in the domestic and in the international context overlapped timewise. Since the municipal legal orders that will be discussed are Western ones, it could be argued that this concept is a genuine Western concept. Such an interpretation then could be based on the fact that in particular Soviet doctrine as well as several newly independent states had reservations as to this concept. The connection of scholarly debates in (Western) municipal legal orders and the international legal order in particular in the first half of the 20th century may explain part of the skepticism. Yet, it is argued here and will be developed further over the course of this study that general principles of law represent a concept which is intrinsically connected to the idea of law and to the practice of further interpreting, concretizing and developing the law through application. It can here only be submitted, but not without some reason, and be left for future scholarship to show that a close study of the interpretation and application of municipal law in many other states will exemplify that general principles can be observed in these domestic legal orders as well.[226]

Judges?' in Cesare P R Romano, Karen Alter, and Yuval Shany (eds), *The Oxford Handbook of International Adjudication* (Oxford University Press 2013) 624.

226 See Bin Cheng, *General Principles of Law as applied by International Courts and Tribunals* (reprint, Cambridge Grotius Publications Limited 1987) 19, 400-408, listing municipal codes which provide for the application of the general principles of law, equity or natural law. Reference to general principles of law as applicable law for the judge to apply is made, for instance, in the Peruvian Civil Code of 1852, in the Ecuadorian Civil Code of 1860, the Italian Civil Code of 1865, the Argentine Civil Code of 1869, the Guatemalan Civil Code of 1877, the Spanish Civil Code of 1888, the Cuban Civil Code of 1889, the Brazilian Civil Code of 1916, the Thai (Siamese) Civil Code of 1925, the Chinese Civil Code of 1929, and arguing that "the national law of three of the ten members (from Brazil, Italy and Spain) who drafted the Statute of the Permanent Court of International Justice contained this very formula", which was "one of the most usual in codified provisions on the application of law in the municipal sphere". See also Antônio Augusto Cançado Trindade, 'International Law for Humankind: Towards a New Jus Gentium (I)' (2005) 316 RdC 86, arguing that "every legal system" has fundamental principles and general principles of law; Schwarzenberger, 'The fundamental principles of international law' 195; see also Elias and Lim, ''General Principles of Law', 'Soft' Law and the Identification of International Law' 19 ff.

Chapter 1: Setting the Scene

II. Institutional perspectives

The study will then analyze how the interrelationship has been discussed in different contexts. Chapter 4 and chapter 5 are dedicated to two institutional actors, namely the International Court of Justice and the International Law Commission.

The focus on institutions will start with the International Court of Justice which, as the principal judicial organ of the United Nations, bears not the sole but a very significant responsibility for the administration of international law. As article 38 ICJ Statute does not specifically indicate a strict order of application,[227] the Court enjoys a certain liberty[228] as to whether it bases its judgment on general concepts rather than on a special agreement,[229] on a treaty without examining in depth general principles of law and customary international law,[230] or whether it engages into systemic integration.[231] The chapter will analyze whether the institutional framework in which the Court operates shapes the way in which the interrelationship of sources is discussed by the Court. It will be demonstrated that the Court emphasizes the distinctiveness of sources for jurisdictional purposes while at the same time acknowledging the interrelationship when it comes to the interpretation. This chapter will explore the normative considerations and the legal craft em-

---

227 Thirlway, *The sources of international law* 152.
228 Pellet and Müller, 'Article 38' 935: "[...] the Court enjoys (or recognizes itself as enjoying) a large measure of appreciation in the choice of the sources of the rules to be applied in a particular case."; Richard D Kearney, 'Sources of Law and the International Court of Justice' in Leo Gross (ed), *The future of the International Court of Justice* (Oceana-Publ 1976) vol 2 697 ("the absence of priorities among the sources of law in Article 38(1)(a), (b), and (c) has afforded a valuable degree of flexibility in the preparation of judgments.").
229 Cf. for the PCIJ *Legal Status of Eastern Greenland: Denmark v Norway* Judgment of 5 April 1933 [1933] PCIJ Series A/B 53, 23, 45 ff. (on Denmark's title to sovereignty over Greenland based on a continued display of authority), for a critique see Diss OpAnzilotti 76 and 94 whose analysis focused on an agreement reached between Denmark and Norway.
230 Cf. *Right of Passage over Indian Territory (Portugal v. India)* (Judgment of 12 April 1960) [1960] ICJ Rep 43: after having based its judgment on bilateral practice of the parties, the Court "does not consider it necessary to examine whether general international custom or the general principles of law recognized by civilized nations may lead to the same result."
231 *Oil Platforms (Islamic Republic of Iran v. United States of America)* (Judgment) [2003] ICJ Rep 182 para 41.

Structure of this study

ployed by the Court when identifying, interpreting and applying customary international law and the function of general principles as a bridge between custom and treaties.

In contrast, the ILC does not apply the law to a particular set of facts but progressively develops and codifies the law in a general and abstract fashion. The sixth chapter will first explore the implications codification can have on the interrelationship of sources and illustrate that both codification and progressive development of customary international law, which cannot always be clearly separated from each other, call for a normative assessment. It will be demonstrated that early on the ILC searched for inspirations from principles expressed in treaties when codifying and progressively developing international law. The chapter will then explore the implications of the form which the ILC chose for its work and of the trend towards nonbinding forms. Subsequently, this chapter will examine how the interrelationship of sources was approached and addressed in specific projects of the ILC.

The seventh chapter will offer concluding observations on the two preceding chapters.

III. Perspectives on different normative contexts

The next three chapters will explore the interrelationship of sources in certain "fields", namely in the context of the ECHR, of international criminal law and of international investment law.[232] These three fields were selected since they represent different contexts with different conditions.

The chapter on the ECHR examines how the interrelationship of sources manifests itself in a very centralized, treaty-based system, with its own judiciary, the European Court of Human Rights. The chapter will first explore the way in which the European Court interprets the ECHR and takes into account other rules of international law for the purpose of interpreting states' obligations under the ECHR. Subsequently, the chapter will demonstrate how the specific incorporation of these sources by the European Court can shape the development of general international law and how the rationale of human

---

232 For international environmental law see Christina Voigt, *Sustainable Development as a Principle of International Law Resolving Conflicts between Climate Measures and Law* (Martinus Nijhoff Publishers 2009); Christina Voigt, 'The Role of General Principles in International Law and their Relationship to Treaty Law' (2008) 31 Retfærd. Nordisk Juridisk Tidsskrift 3 ff.

Chapter 1: Setting the Scene

rights law and the ECHR can inform and pervade international law. It is submitted that the European Court sets general international law into relation with the object and purpose of the ECHR, which may significantly shape the development of general international law.[233] Last but not least, the analysis of the jurisprudence of a regional human rights court raises questions as to the potential tension between special, regional law and general international law. These tensions are illustrated by "functional equivalents" to concepts of general international law which are based on an interpretation of the ECHR.

International criminal law displays a dynamic development from unwritten law to written law. The ninth chapter will firstly revisit the early discussions of the interrelationship of sources in the context of international criminal law which preceded the establishment of the ICTY. The chapter will, secondly, explore the jurisprudence of the International Criminal Tribunals with a particular focus on how the ICTY approaches the interrelationship of sources. Thirdly, the chapter will turn to the Rome Statute. In this context it will focus on the Rome Statute's main features which concern the interrelationship of sources, on the debate on modes of criminal liability as an example of a potential conflict between treaty law and customary international law and on the role of customary international law in relation to immunities.

International investment law can be characterized as a decentralised system that is based on multiple investment treaties. The tenth chapter will first trace the interrelationship of sources in the modern history of international investment law and highlight in particular the prominent role of customary international law and general principles of law, their contested character and the move towards bilateral investment treaties. The chapter will then demonstrate how this bilateralism in form led to a multilateralism in substance and explore the different doctrinal avenues while evaluating their respective explanatory force for this phenomenon of multilateralism in substance. Last but not least, this chapter will focus on the significance of doctrinal constructions in international investment law, exemplified by the distinction between primary rules and secondary rules. The chapter will critically engage with certain receptions of this distinction in international investment law and

---

233 Cf. on the way in which public international law is perceived through the lenses of a special regime's quasi-judicial body, Ralf Michaels and Joost HB Pauwelyn, 'Conflict of Norms or Conflict of Laws: Different Techniques in the Fragmentation of Public International Law' (2012) 22(3) Duke Journal of Comparative & International Law 349 ff.

argue against an expansive interpretation of this distinction which would place treaties and custom in strictly separated compartments.

The eleventh chapter will offer concluding observations on the two preceding chapters.

IV. Doctrinal perspectives: revisiting the doctrine of sources

The twelfth chapter will, in light of the previous chapters, focus on how scholars approached the topic of the interrelationship of sources differently under the impression of the respective spirit of the time.

The thirteenth chapter will present observations and conclusions which this study draws from the preceding chapters.

Part B.

Comparative and historical perspectives

Chapter 2: Comparative Perspectives

A. *Introduction: The interrelationship of sources in comparative legal thought*

The purpose of this chapter is to illustrate debates on the interrelationship between written and unwritten law from comparative legal perspectives as background for reflections on contemporary developments in public international law. These comparative historical perspectives complement accounts which analyze the sources of international law by way of reference to the discussion of the Committee of Jurists.[1] It is submitted here that article 38 of the Statute of the Permanent Court of Justice should not be understood out of the context of the wider development in municipal and international legal theory for several reasons. While a focus on the discussions in the Committee of Jurists is helpful, one must at the same time acknowledge that these discussions were rather short and focused only on selected issues, such as the avoidance of *non-liquet* situations and the importance to find a formula which would secure the acceptance of the statute by states.[2] Also, experiences in municipal law informed the discussion of sources.[3] The drafts

---

1 See also below, chapter 3.
2 Ole Spiermann, ''Who attempts too much does nothing well': The 1920 Advisory Committee of Jurists and the Statute of the Permanent Court of International Justice' (2003) 73 BYIL 212-218, 230; Jean d'Aspremont, 'The Decay of Modern Customary International Law in Spite of Scholarly Heroism' [2016] The Global Community Yearbook of International Law and Jurisprudence 13-14.
3 Lord Phillimore's critique of the distinction between customary international law and general principles of law mirrored William Blackstone's assimilation of custom and so-called maxims under the notion of "common law", Permanent Court of International Justice – Advisory Committee of Jurists, *Procès-Verbaux of the Proceedings of the Committee, June 16th-July 24th 1920* (Van Langenhuysen Brothers 1920) 295, William Blackstone, *Commentaries on the Laws of England* (vol 1, Oxford, 1765) 68; on this observation see also Kleinlein, 'Customary International Law and General Principles Rethinking Their Relationship' 146; according to Tomuschat, 'Obligations Arising For States Without Or Against Their Will' 290, theories developed by Savigny and Puchta informed the drafting of article 38(1)(b) of the PCIJ Statute; Spiermann, ''Who attempts too much does nothing well': The 1920 Advisory Committee of Jurists and the Statute of the Permanent Court of International Justice' 240 ("While national lawyers may have agreed, broadly speaking, to the scope of international law, their

Chapter 2: Comparative Perspectives

submitted by states prior to the discussions of the Advisory Committee of Jurists already resembled article 38 and its three sources.[4] One cannot ignore the similarities between the teachings of François Gény and article 1 of the Swiss Civil Code, article 7 of the Prize Court Convention and article 38 PCIJ Statute[5] which invite one to read article 38 against the background of developments in both public international law and municipal law.

Studying the interrelationship of sources in the municipal legal context reminds one that the success and the viability of a legal concept depend on the care that concept continues to receive by judicial practice and scholarship (*Rechtspflege* in its literal meaning, in the sense of caring for legal concepts). When a legal concept or institute has ceased to find support, some of its functions will likely be assumed by different legal categories.[6] This phenomenon which applies to the relationship between written and unwritten law finds illustration, for instance, in the works of Raymond Saleilles and François Gény.[7] Both authors are commonly associated with the so-called

---

    conception of the content of international law would almost unavoidably have been coloured by national tendencies and traditions."), 259.

4 See below, p. 170.
5 See below, p. 100 and p. 167.
6 Cf. in the context of US constitutional law Kenji Yoshino, 'The New Equal Protection' (2011) 124 Harvard Law Review 748, noting that due process rights functionally replaced claims under the equal protection doctrine: "Squeezing law is often like squeezing a balloon. The contents do not escape, but erupt in another area [...] The Court's commitment to civil rights has not been pressed out, but rather over to collateral doctrines." Already Louis Henkin, 'Privacy and Autonomy' (1974) 74 Columbia Law Review 1417 coined the term of "constitutional displacement" to describe how the concept of substantive due process in essence was functionally replaced by other doctrines.
7 On the relationship between Gény and Saleilles see Eugène Gaudemet, 'L'œuvre de Saleilles et l'œuvre de Gény en méthodologie juridique et en philosophie du droit' in *Recueil D'Etudes Sur Les Sources Du Droit En L'Honneur De François Gény* (Recueil Sirey 1934) vol 2 5 ff.; Wolfgang Fikentscher, *Methoden des Rechts in Vergleichender Darstellung Frühe und Religiöse Rechte, Romanischer Rechtskreis* (vol 1, Mohr Siebeck 1975) 453 ff.; Edward A Tomlinson, 'Tort Liability in France for the Act of Things: A Study of Judicial Lawmaking' (1988) 48(6) Louisiana Law Review 1307-1310; Stefan Vogenauer, *Die Auslegung von Gesetzen in England und auf dem Kontinent Eine vergleichende Untersuchung der Rechtsprechung und ihrer historischen Grundlagen* (Beiträge zum ausländischen und internationalen Privatrecht 72, vol 1, Mohr Siebeck 2001) 330-336. On Gény see also Jaro Mayda, *Francois Gény and Modern Jurisprudence* (Louisiana State University Press 1978) 5 ff., and Wolfgang Friedmann, *Legal Theory* (5th edn, Stevens & Sons 1967) 328-332; Alf

École scientifique.[8] This school was a response to a rigid statutory positivism (*Gesetzespositivismus*, in the French context represented by the *l'école de l'exégèse*) which postulated that every legal interpretation must stem from the statute as intended by the lawmaker; the statute was the sole source, any pre-revolutionary customary law or jurisprudence was regarded to be dubious.[9] In the second half of the 19th century[10], a new generation of scholars increasingly questioned the premises of the *Ecole de l'exégèse* and its explanatory force for the law applied in practice: the legal outcome in a case could not be regarded fully predetermined by the text of the statute. Saleilles and Gény went into the same direction but on different doctrinal vehicles. Saleilles did not work with customary law as an additional source of law next to the statute.[11] However, he refuted the idea that the interpretation of a statute was confined by the subjective intent of the legislator. Rather, statutes would have to be interpreted in an evolutionary fashion, taking into account new ideas of justice and the social transformation that might even run contrary to the initial subjective intent of the legislator.[12] In contrast, Gény maintained that statutes had to be interpreted according to the subjective intent of the

---

Ross, *Theorie der Rechtsquellen: ein Beitrag zur Theorie des positiven Rechts auf Grundlage dogmenhistorischer Untersuchungen* (Deuticke 1929) 48 ff.

8 Fikentscher, *Methoden des Rechts in Vergleichender Darstellung Frühe und Religiöse Rechte, Romanischer Rechtskreis* 453.

9 Ross, *Theorie der Rechtsquellen: ein Beitrag zur Theorie des positiven Rechts auf Grundlage dogmenhistorischer Untersuchungen* 35, 37, 44; see also Dieter Grimm, *Solidarität als Rechtsprinzip: Die Rechts- und Staatslehre Léon Duguits in ihrer Zeit* (Altenhäum Verlag 1973) 8-26, describing how the revolutionary ideals of individualism and voluntarism together with only restrictive (social) legislation began over the 19th century to favour the establishment. Against the background of statutory petrification, new approaches arose which focused on natural law and on substantive criteria to legal interpretation.

10 As noted by Fikentscher, *Methoden des Rechts in Vergleichender Darstellung Frühe und Religiöse Rechte, Romanischer Rechtskreis* 454, the French discipline was influenced by similar movements in other countries at that time, he referred to Rudolf von Jhering in 1860 and to Oliver Wendell Holmes in 1884.

11 François Gény, *Méthode D'Interprétation et Sources en Droit Privé Positif: Essai Critique* (2nd edn, vol 1, Pichon et Durand_Auzias 1954) xx.

12 See Saleilles' preface to Gény's book ibid xiii ff., in particular xv-xvi. On the importance of external elements for the judge to take into account see Raymond Saleilles, 'L'École historique et droit naturel' (1902) 1 Revue trimestrielle de droit civil 102; see also Ross, *Theorie der Rechtsquellen: ein Beitrag zur Theorie des positiven Rechts auf Grundlage dogmenhistorischer Untersuchungen* 45-46.

legislator[13]; however, statutory law would not be the only source to draw on by a judge, it needed to be supplemented by a set of principles outside and above the statute (*"en dehors et audessus de la loi"*).[14] Gény postulated the existence of customary law[15], albeit not in derogation of statutory law[16], and in addition he stressed the legal relevance of tradition and authorities.[17] Central in Gény's account is the recognition of the creative task to be performed by the judge in the act of interpretation:[18] As the judge did not enjoy the free discretion of a legislator, he had to conduct free scientific research (*"libre recherche scientifique"*) and to apply the scientific method and study customary law and social science.[19]

Both approaches differed conceptually from each other: Gény's approach to statutory interpretation focused on the legislator's subjective intent. At the same time, his broad concept of law included customary law. Saleilles adopted a broader, evolutive approach to statutory interpretation, while not recognizing the need for the existence of other legal sources next to statutory law. In practice, the differences between both approaches were more apparent

---

13 In this sense, his approach was characterized as conservative, Vogenauer, *Die Auslegung von Gesetzen in England und auf dem Kontinent Eine vergleichende Untersuchung der Rechtsprechung und ihrer historischen Grundlagen* 331.

14 François Gény, *Science et technique en droit privé positif: nouvelle contribution à la critique de la méthode juridique* (vol 1, Recueil Sirey 1914) 39.

15 Gény, *Méthode D'Interprétation et Sources en Droit Privé Positif: Essai Critique* No 117 ff. Another author to be mentioned here is Lambert who stressed the importance of customary law as made by the judge and of the so-called "droit comparé, Ross, *Theorie der Rechtsquellen: ein Beitrag zur Theorie des positiven Rechts auf Grundlage dogmenhistorischer Untersuchungen* 45. See in this regard also Mayda, *Francois Gény and Modern Jurisprudence* 14 according to whom Lambert's and Saleilles' ideas of comparative law might have been precursors to substantive supranational law and the general principles of law in article 38.

16 Fikentscher, *Methoden des Rechts in Vergleichender Darstellung Frühe und Religiöse Rechte, Romanischer Rechtskreis* 459; in contrast, both Savigny and Windscheid derived from the equal rank of the written source, statutes, and the unwritten source, customary law, the capacity of customary law to dergoate from statutory law, see Friedrich Carl von Savigny, *System des heutigen Römischen Rechts* (vol 1, Veit 1840) 83, and Bernhard Windscheid, *Lehrbuch des Pandektenrechts* (4th edn, vol 1, Buddeus 1875) 49.

17 Gény, *Méthode D'Interprétation et Sources en Droit Privé Positif: Essai Critique* 238.

18 ibid 207 ff.; Gény's approach inspired Eugen Huber when drafting the Swiss Civil Code; on the relationship between Gény and Huber see Mayda, *Francois Gény and Modern Jurisprudence* 31 ff.

19 For an overview, see Friedmann, *Legal Theory* 329.

than real.[20] Saleilles' approach should become influential in French jurisprudence, whereas Gény's approach was to some extent codified in Article 1 of the Swiss Civil Code of 1907, according to which a judge shall apply the statute, in case of the statute's silence, customary law, in the case of the latter's absence according to the rule which the legislator would be expected to enact, based on an assessment of doctrine and tradition.[21] Not only did this provision later give inspiration to article 38 of the Statute of the Permanent Court of International Justice, Gény's and Saleilles' focus on the "law in action" was taken up by US scholars like Pound and Cardozo and became a source of inspiration for theories on "principles" as legal concepts.[22]

Having in mind the significance of the experiences in municipal legal thought for public international law, this chapter will now focus on the relationship between common law and statutory law as the common law metaphor continued to be invoked in international debates in order to describe the role of customary international law (B.).[23] A comparison of the discussions of

---

20 Vogenauer, *Die Auslegung von Gesetzen in England und auf dem Kontinent Eine vergleichende Untersuchung der Rechtsprechung und ihrer historischen Grundlagen* 336.
21 Article 1 of the Swiss Civil Code of 1907 reads: "Kann dem Gesetz keine Vorschrift entnommen werden, so soll das Gericht nach Gewohnheitsrecht und, wo auch ein solches fehlt, nach der Regel entscheiden, die es als Gesetzgeber aufstellen würde. Es folgt dabei bewährter Lehre und Überlieferung."
22 See below, p. 118. On differences between Article 1 of the Swiss Code and article 38 see Alfred Verdross, 'Les principes généraux de droit comme source du droit des gens' (1932) 37 Institute de Droit International Annuaire 296.
23 See for instance Waldock, 'General course on public international law' 54 ff. (with respect to the relationship between customary international law and the general principles of law), Georg Nolte, 'From Dionisio Anzilotti to Roberto Ago: The Classical International Law of State Responsibility and the Traditional Primacy of a Bilateral Conception of Inter-state Relations' (2002) 13(5) EJIL 1093; cf. Staubach, 'The Interpretation of Unwritten International Law by Domestic Judges' 115 footnote 14 (arguing that a common law methodology might focus more on individual precedents of courts "instead of undertaking a complete survey of the relevant state practice"); Stephan W Schill and Katrine R Tvede, 'Mainstreaming Investment Treaty Jurisprudence The Contribution of Investment Treaty Tribunals to the Consolidation and Development of General International Law' (2015) 14 The Law and Practice of International Courts and Tribunals 97; Andrew T Guzman and Timothy L Meyer, 'International Common Law: The Soft Law of International Tribunals' (2008) 9 Chicago Journal of International Law 515 ff.; Chester Brown, *A Common Law of International Adjudication* (Oxford University Press 2007); it has also been argued that common law should be understood as customary law, Alfred William Brian Simpson, 'Common

the interrelationship in the USA and in the UK demonstrates differences, as UK scholars discussed the relationship in less dynamic terms (B. I.) than their US colleagues (B. II.) who, influenced by continental scholarship on the application of the law, developed a doctrine of legal principles. This doctrine, in turn, informed the discussion in Germany and in the United Kingdom, where, as exemplified by way of reference to the case-law on the Human Rights Act, a new interest in the relationship between common law and written law has emerged. The experiences in municipal law contexts illustrate the significance of institutional support by courts and scholars: whereas the UK Supreme Court has continued to support the concept of common law even instead of solely and exclusively interpreting and applying the Human Rights Act, German legal history shows how a legal concept such as customary law could lose its significance in relation to other techniques such as doctrines of interpretation relating to the written law (C.).

The experiences in domestic legal systems are insightful not only with respect to the relationship between written law and customary law or common law, but also with respect to the doctrine of legal principles. This chapter presents a comparative legal perspective on general principles of law (D.). The concept of "general principles of law" gives expression to the insights that law develops through its interpretation and application, to the systematic character of the law and to the significance of the judicial application and creation of law, for which the concept of general principles is said to provide guidance. The chosen perspective here sides with the view that general principles of law may be found within many legal orders, including, but not limited to, international law.[24] The purpose of this comparative historical

---

Law and Legal Theory' in Alfred William Brian Simpson (ed), *Legal Theory and Legal History: Essays on the Common Law* (The Hambledon Press 1987) 362, 373 ff.; Neil Duxbury, 'Custom as Law in English Law' (2017) 76(2) Cambridge Law Journal 337 ff.; cf. also Philip Sales, 'Rights and Fundamental Rights in English Law' (2016) 75(1) Cambridge Law Journal 99 (suggesting to base common law in the legislative practice).

24 Cf. Kolb, 'Les maximes juridiques en droit international public: questions historiques et théoriques' 412, 424, 430; cf. also Schwarzenberger, 'The fundamental principles of international law' 195: "Experience with any of the systems of municipal law teaches that all of them take for granted a stratification of legal principles. Thus, *prima facie*, it may be assumed that the same is true of international law." See also Matthias Goldmann, 'Sources in the Meta-Theory of International Law: Exploring the Hermeneutics, Authority, and Publicness of International Law' in Samantha Besson and Jean d'Aspremont (eds), *The Oxford Handbook on the Sources of International Law* (Oxford University Press 2017) 456-458 on principles' role for hermeneutics.

perspective is to complement the perspective in international legal scholarship on general principles of law in international law. General principles are more than mere gap-fillers. They are not just an alternative to treaty law and customary international law but interwoven and interrelated with both. While article 38(3) PCIJ Statute could be read as a recognition of the role general principles play in the law, general principles need not be understood solely by way of reference to this provision.[25] Article 38(3) PCIJ Statute did not invent general principles. Rather, it was inspired by and gave further inspiration to this concept. In identifying this comparative legal historical background of general principles, this chapter seeks to lay the foundations for this book's understanding of general principles in the international legal order.

B. Example: The common law and the interrelationship of unwritten and written law

This section turns to the relationship between unwritten common law and written statutory law. As will be described below, the discussion of the relationship in the United Kingdom and in the United States of America differed significantly. Scholars used to portray the relationship between common law and statutory law as static, with different preferences given to each concept according to the respective spirit of the time.[26] Institutional conflicts between the judiciary and the legislature are said to explain the understanding of the relationship between the written branch and the unwritten branch of law as one of two separate compartments,[27] which Jack Beatson named the "'oil and water' approach', a form of legal apartheid"[28]. In contrast to the United States, where the relationship used to be discussed in a more dynamic fashion[29] and a doctrine of legal principles developed on the basis of the interaction

---

25 For the recent ILC project on general principles see below, p. 386.
26 Patrick S Atiyah, 'Common Law and Statute Law' (1985) 48(1) The Modern Law Review 7-8, arguing that it might have been more accepted in the 16th century to rely on statutes for the identification of common law than it was in the 18th century.
27 Josef Esser, *Grundsatz und Norm in der richterlichen Fortbildung des Privatrechts Rechtsvergleichende Beiträge zur Rechtsquellen- und Interpretationslehre* (Mohr Siebeck 1956) 264, 129-130, 229.
28 Jack Beatson, 'Has the Common Law a Future?' (1997) 56(2) The Cambridge Law Journal 308.
29 Harlan F Stone, 'The Common Law in the United States' (1936) 50(1) Harvard Law Review 12 on comparing the US approach and the British "Blackstonian conception"

between written law and unwritten law, it was even argued in relation to the United Kingdom that, because of the strict compartmentalization and because of the slow case-by-case development of common law, the concept of legal principles had no place in UK common law.[30] Over time, the picture of "oil and water" gave way to a more dynamic relationship, under the influence of the reception of the US approaches on the relationship between common law and legislation. Neil MacCormick argued that it would be "false to suppose that there is any essential difference between statute and common law as to the force and function of arguments by analogy and from principle [...] For the Scottish and English legal systems, at least, there does appear to be abundant evidence in favour of the account of principles".[31] The recent experience in the UK with the Human Rights Act demonstrates how the concept of common law thrived under the support of the judiciary and scholars. In particular, the debate on a modification or termination of the Human Rights Act has led to a discussion about common law as basis for constitutional rights.[32]

---

which explain the failure to realise the "ideal of a unified system of judge-made and statute law woven into a seamless whole by the processes of adjudication."

30 Cf. Wolfgang Fikentscher, *Methoden des Rechts in vergleichender Darstellung. Anglo-amerikanischer Rechtskreis* (vol 2, Mohr Siebeck 1975) 83 ("Man darf dabei jedoch nicht aus den Augen verlieren, daß eine andere Rechtsordnung des common law, die englische, methodisch ohne jene Grundsätze, principles, auskommt.").

31 Neil MacCormick, *Legal Reasoning and Legal Theory* (Clarendon Press, Oxford University Press 1978) 194; Rupert Cross, *Precedent in English Law* (Clarendon Press 1961) 167-169: "in England, a legislative innovation is received fully into the body of the law to be reasoned from by analogy in the same way as any other rule of law" (169); see also Beatson, 'Has the Common Law a Future?' 310; Axel Metzger, *Extra legem, intra ius: allgemeine Rechtsgrundsätze im Europäischen Privatrecht* (Mohr Siebeck 2009) 193-200.

32 See below, p. 120; see especially Richard Clayton, 'The empire strikes back: common law rights and the Human Rights Acts' [2015] Public Law 3 ff.; Mark Elliott, 'Beyond the European Convention: Human Rights and the Common Law' (2015) 68 Current Legal Problems 85 ff.; Paul Bowen, 'Does the renaissance of common law rights mean that the Human Rights Act 1998 is now unnecessary?' [2016] (4) European Human Rights Law Review 361 ff.; Alan Bogg, 'Common Law and Statute in the Law of Employment' (2016) 69(1) Current Legal Problems 67 ff.; Eirik Bjørge, 'Common Law Rights: Balancing Domestic and International Exigencies' (2016) 75(2) Cambridge Law Journal 220 ff.

Example: The common law and the interrelationship of unwritten and written law

I. The Historic discourse of the relationship between the common law and the written law in the United Kingdom

Debates on the relationship between statutory laws, or legislation, and common law often reflected the respective spirit of the time.[33] One may briefly recall the early generation of common lawyers around Coke, Davies and Hale.[34] Common law was regarded to be the general law, the general standard ("the common Custome of the Realm"[35]), "nothing else but Reason".[36] Coke distinguished conceptually between customs applying only locally and the law that would apply throughout England, which was called "the common law".[37] Statutes affirmed or supplemented common law, "a statute made in the affirmative, without any negative expressed or implied, does not take away the common law".[38]

In the *Bonham* case of 1610, Coke even argued that "common law will controul Acts of Parliaments, and sometimes adjudge them to be utterly void" in case that an Act of Parliament would be "against common right or reason, or repugnant, or impossible to perform".[39] It has been subject to debate whether Coke envisioned judicial review of parliamentary acts or whether he intended to state the principle to construe acts of parliament in consistence with common law.[40] In any case, common law was in relation to legislation

---

33 See Atiyah, 'Common Law and Statute Law' 7-8, arguing that it might have been more accepted in the 16th century to rely on statutes for the identification of common law than it was in the 18th century.
34 Gerald J Postema, 'Classical Common Law Jurisprudence (Part I)' (2002) 2(2) Oxford University Commonwealth Law Journal 169 ff.; Jeffrey A Pojanowski, 'Reading Statutes in the Common Law Tradition' (2015) 101(5) Virginia Law Review 1377-1378.
35 John Davies, Irish Reports (1674), quoted after Gerald J Postema, *Bentham and the Common Law Tradition* (Clarendon Press 1986) 4; Matthew Hale, *The history of the common law of England ; and, An analysis of the civil part of the law* (6th edn, Henry Butterworth 1820) 5.
36 Edward Coke, *The first part of the Institutes of the laws of England, or, A commentary upon Littleton: not the name of the author only, but of the law itself* (1st American, from the 19th London ed., corr, Robert H Small 1853) Sect 138, 97b.
37 ibid 110b Sect. 165: "but a custome cannot be alleged generally within the kingdome of England; for that is the common law."
38 Edward Coke, *The Second Part of the Institutes of the Laws of England* (1824) 200.
39 *Thomas Bonham v College of Physicians* Court of Common Pleas (1610) 77 Eng. Rep. 638.
40 Gerald J Postema, 'Classical Common Law Jurisprudence (Part II)' (2003) 3(1) Oxford University Commonwealth Law Journal 19; Philip Allott, 'The Courts and

the general law which countered fragmentation tendencies in English law[41] and subjected the monarch to the rule of law.[42]

Matthew Hale pointed to the possibility of innovation by parliamentary legislation. He integrated statutory legislation into common law theory and recalled that past statutes had given rise to common law[43] and that law had always evolved.[44] He listed three "formal constituents [...] of the common law [...]. 1. The common usage, or custom, and practice of the kingdom in such parts thereof as lie in usage or custom; 2. The authority of parliament, introducing such laws; and, 3. The judicial decisions of courts of justice, consonant to one another, in the series and succession of time."[45] Whereas some acts of parliament "are perished and lost" and did not stand the test of time, others became "incorporated with the very common law", the "great substratum".[46]

1. Different law preferences: William Blackstone and Jeremy Bentham

After the glorious revolution in 1688/1689, parliamentary sovereignty conceptually changed the relationship between statutes and common law, and between the legislature and the judiciary, in the work of writers to different

---

Parliament: Who Whom?' (1979) 38(1) Cambridge Law Journal 82-86; David Jenkins, 'From Unwritten to Written: Transformation in the British Common-Law Constitution' (2003) 36 Vanderbilt Journal of Transnational Law 884 ff.

41 According to Holdsworth, Coke's emphasis on common law served to rescue English law from internal fragmentation given the many judicial systems that existed in England, William Holdsworth, 'Sir Edward Coke' (1933) 5 Cambridge Law Journal 334-344; on this point, see already Hale, *The history of the common law of England ; and, An analysis of the civil part of the law* 39.

42 As Coke elaborated: "[H]is Majesty was not learned in the laws of his realm of England, and causes which concern the life, or inheritance, or goods, or fortunes of his subjects, are not to be decided by natural reason, but by the artificial reason and judgment of law [...]", Edward Coke, 'Prohibitions Del Roy' in John Henry Thomas (ed), *The Reports of Sir Edward Coke in Thirteen Parts* (Joseph Butterworth and Son 1826) 282; on the conflicts between Coke and the Crown, see Holdsworth, 'Sir Edward Coke' 334-336; Leo Gross, 'Der Rechtsbegriff des Common Law und das Völkerrecht' (1931) 11 Zeitschrift für öffentliches Recht 358-360.

43 Hale, *The history of the common law of England ; and, An analysis of the civil part of the law* 4.

44 ibid 83 ff.

45 ibid 88.

46 ibid 89, 91.

Example: The common law and the interrelationship of unwritten and written law

degrees.[47] According to William Blackstone, legislative innovations posed a risk to the symmetry of the common law.[48] Blackstone distinguished between written and unwritten law the latter of which would consist of general customs ("common law properly so called") and particular (regional) customs.[49] In the view of Blackstone, common law encompassed both customs and maxims and legal propositions.

> "Some have divided the common law into two principal grounds of foundations; 1. established customs; such as that, where there brothers, the eldest brother shall be heir to the second, in exclusion of the youngest; and, 2. Established rules and maxims: as, 'that the king can do no wrong', 'that no man shall be bound to accuse himself,' and the like. But I take these to be one and the same thing. For the authority of these maxims rests entirely upon general reception; and the only method of proving, that this or that maxim is a rule of the common law, is by showing that it hath been always the custom to observe it."[50]

It was in this Blackstonian tradition that Lord Phillimore during the drafting of article 38 PCIJ Statute criticized the "unjustifiable distinction" between custom and general principles of law, which he described as "maxims of law", in the PCIJ Draft Statute.[51] Blackstone maintained that customs were recognized or "found" as preexisting law by judges. However, since he did not suggest a list of criteria for a general custom to meet,[52] Blackstone *de facto* deprived custom from its extrajudicial and popular character.[53]

---

47 Postema, *Bentham and the Common Law Tradition* 14. See also David Lieberman, *The province of legislation determined: legal theory in eighteenth century Britain* (Cambridge University Press 2002) 219, describing "the relationship between common law and legislation [...] a basic problem for legal theory" in the eighteenth century.
48 Blackstone, *Commentaries on the Laws of England* 10-11.
49 ibid 63-64.
50 ibid 68.
51 Permanent Court of International Justice – Advisory Committee of Jurists, *Procès-Verbaux of the Proceedings of the Committee, June 16th-July 24th 1920* 295, 335; see also Kleinlein, 'Customary International Law and General Principles Rethinking Their Relationship' 146.
52 Particular customs, in order to be binding, would have to meet a list of requirements, such as long usage, in accordance with acts of Parliament, continuation without interruption, uncontentiousness, reasonableness, certainty, consistency, Blackstone, *Commentaries on the Laws of England* 76-79.
53 Ross, *Theorie der Rechtsquellen: ein Beitrag zur Theorie des positiven Rechts auf Grundlage dogmenhistorischer Untersuchungen* 83.

Chapter 2: Comparative Perspectives

A different approach to common law was advocated by Jeremy Bentham.[54] Bentham was an advocate of codification[55], in his view, the common law system produced injustices by its retroactive application of newly made rules under the pretense of their existence in the past.[56] Bentham criticized in relation to common law the "unaccommodatingness of its rules"[57] to time and circumstances: common law was sait to admit "of no temparaments, no compromises, no compositions: none of these qualifications which a legislator would see the necessity of applying".[58]

His assessment of the role of common law in relation to the harsh criminal law legislation throughout the 18th century differed from Blackstone's position: Blackstone stressed the importance of common law in protection individual liberties and rights.[59] For Bentham, however, the legislative shortcomings were rooted in the common law attitude as just described, the unaccommodatingness of common law.[60] Bentham wanted to strengthen the written law and protect it from invalidating effects of some form of natural

---

54 The following lines are concerned with Bentham's contribution to the discussion of the relationship between common law and statutory law. Bentham also coined the term "international law", replacing Blackstone's law of nations. Whereas Bentham's term was narrower than Bentham's in that it focused on inter-state relations only, Bentham advocated also the codification in international law and the establishment of an international court; on the international law legacy of Bentham see Mark Weston Janis, 'Jeremy Bentham and the Fashioning of 'International Law'' (1984) 78 AJIL 405 ff.
55 Jeremy Bentham, *A Comment on The Commentaries and A Fragment on Government* (James Henderson Burns and Herbert LA Hart eds, Athlone Press 1977) 320 ("the Common Law must be digested into Statute. The fictious must be substantiated into real. [...] Whatever is to make Law should be brought to light [...]").
56 Postema, *Bentham and the Common Law Tradition* 208.
57 Jeremy Bentham, *Of Laws in General* (Herbert LA Hart ed, Athlone Press 1970) 194.
58 ibid 184, 192-195, quote on 194-195; see also Bentham, *A Comment on The Commentaries and A Fragment on Government* 43, 119-120; see also Bentham, *Of Laws in General* 153: "Written law then is the law of those who can both speak and write: traditional law of those who can speak but can not write: customary law, of those who neither know how to write, nor how to speak. Written law is the law for civilized nations: traditional law, for barbarians: customary law, for brutes."
59 See for instance Blackstone, *Commentaries on the Laws of England* 114 ff.
60 This has been illustrated in Postema, *Bentham and the Common Law Tradition* 264-266, 274-278.

Example: The common law and the interrelationship of unwritten and written law

law.[61] The other target of his critique next to common law was the judiciary.[62] In Bentham's view, the common law that was actually applied was no custom *in pays*, describing a "regularity in the behaviour of people", but a custom *in foro* which was basically judge-made law as it became legally binding through judgments.[63]

2. John Austin and the will of the sovereign as source of all law

Building on Blackstone's and Bentham's insights regarding the role of the judge in relation to common law, John Austin integrated common law into his system that was based on the will of the sovereign.

Austin distinguished at the beginning of his treatise four types, namely divine law, positive law (both "commands"[64] and "laws properly so called"), "positive morality" (laws properly so called or laws improperly so called) and "laws metaphorical or figurative" (laws improperly so called).[65] According

---

61 Bentham, *A Comment on The Commentaries and A Fragment on Government* 55-56: "Nothing is unlawful that is the clear intent of the Legislature. Nothing can be void: neither on account of opposition to a pretended Law of Nature, nor on any other."
62 On this institutional aspect relating to the separation of powers, see Jeremy Waldron, 'Custom Redeemed by Statute' (1998) 51(1) Current Legal Problems 96, 99-100, 107-108, 112-113.
63 Bentham, *A Comment on The Commentaries and A Fragment on Government* 180-183, and 230, 232; See Bentham 185-191, criticizing Blackstone's equalization of customs and maxims. In Bentham's view, a maxim can be deduced "from Statutes as from the Common law" (191); see also 302-309. See also Postema, *Bentham and the Common Law Tradition* 220-221.
64 John Austin, *The province of jurisprudence determined* (John Murray 1832) 6, 18.
65 ibid vii. For Austin, international law would be "positive morality" (130-133) as it relied only on public opinion. The term "positive" should denote the fact that this morality was made by men. In his view, this positive morality can be part of the "science of jurisprudence". In this light, Lobban submitted that Austin regarded international law as some "kind of law" which in its nature differed from municipal law and that his views were more subtle than the way in which they have been criticized, Michael Lobban, 'English Approaches to International Law in the Nineteenth Century' in Matthew Craven, Malgosia Fitzmaurice, and Maria Vogiatzi (eds), *Time, History and International Law* (Martinus Nijhof Publishers 2007) 79, 83-84, 89. The prevailing view however characterizes Austin as one of the "deniers" of international "law", see Frédéric Mégret, 'International law as law' in James Crawford and Martti Koskenniemi (eds), *The Cambridge Companion to International Law* (Cambridge University Press 2012) 73-74, and Manfred Lachs, *The Teacher in International Law: Teachings and*

to Austin, all positive laws were, directly or indirectly, commands of this sovereign. He therefore distinguished four categories, laws made directly by the sovereign or the supreme legislature, and laws which are not made directly by the supreme but by a subordinate legislature, "although they derive their force from the authority of the sovereign".[66] Furthermore, he distinguished between law established directly, "in the legislative manner [...] in the way of proper legislation" and law "introduced and obtained obliquely [...] in the judicial mode [...] in the way of judicial legislation".[67]

According to this system, law could have different "modes" but only one ultimate "source", the sovereign[68]. Consequently, a custom could become legally binding only through the judge whose authority derived from the sovereign will. Before then, custom would constitute a positive form of morality.[69] Austin disagreed with Blackstone who had regarded custom to be preexisting law which only required to be found by the judge. In contrast to "the grandiloquous talk [...] customary law has nothing of the magnificent or mysterious about it. It is but a species of *judiciary* law, or of law introduced by sovereign or subordinate judges as properly exercising their judicial functions."[70]

Teaching (2nd edn, Martinus Nijhof Publishers 1987) 15. See also the critique of the "narrow conception" of law in John Westlake, *International Law Part I* (2nd edn, Cambridge University Press 1910) 8.

66 John Austin, *Lectures on jurisprudence. Being the sequel to "The province of jurisprudence determined", Vol II* (J Murray 1863) 1, 208.

67 ibid 217.

68 He therefore rejected Bentham's term "judge-made law", ibid 217.

69 Austin, *The province of jurisprudence determined* 29: "Now when customs are turned into legal rules by decisions of subject judges, the legal rules which emerge from the customs are tacit commands of the sovereign legislature." See also Austin, *Lectures on jurisprudence. Being the sequel to "The province of jurisprudence determined", Vol II* 222: "Now a merely *moral*, or merely customary rule, may take the quality of a *legal* rule through direct or judicial legislation." A similar view had already been expressed by Thomas Hobbes: "When long Use obtaineth the authority of Law, it is not the Length of Time that maketh the Authority, but the Will of the Sovereign signified by his silence (for Silence is sometimes an argument of consent); and it is no longer law, than the sovereign shall be silent therein", Thomas Hobbes, *Hobbes's Leviathan: reprinted from the edition of 1651* (Clarendon Press 1909) 204. For a critique, see Hart, *The concept of law: With a postscript* 46-48.

70 Austin, *Lectures on jurisprudence. Being the sequel to "The province of jurisprudence determined", Vol II* 227-229 (quote at 229).

Example: The common law and the interrelationship of unwritten and written law

3. Subsequent perspectives in UK legal theory: Thomas Holland, H.L.A. Hart and Brian Simpson

In the following, authors built on Austin's insights and explored ways to better define judges' role. Thomas Holland suggested that it was not the individual judge who transformed a certain custom into a legal rule but "an express or tacit law of the State" which stipulated conditions a custom must meet in order to constitute law.[71] Whereas the classical common law lawyers had stressed that statutes could not detract anything from common law, it was now required for common law to be in accordance with statutory law and meet certain requirements which include reasonableness, conformity with statute law and consistence with other common law.[72] Statutes, however, would not have to meet such requirements in order to be considered law.[73]

Holland's idea of a tacit law establishing conditions for a custom to meet in order to be legally binding resembles H. L. A. Hart's approach. Hart did not accept that judges, as agents of the sovereign, would turn non-binding customs into binding ones. Hart pointed out that, just as statutes constitute law already prior to their first judicial application, the same must be possible for

---

71 Thomas Erskine Holland, *The elements of jurisprudence* (Clarendon Press 1916) 62, and 59-63. For Holland, this rule of general reception is itself judge-made. In contrast, Kiß submitted that the legal status of customs would not derive from a judge-made law but from statutes, in particular from equity as inherent principle of the written law, Géza Kiß, 'Die Theorie der Rechtsquellen in der englischen und anglo-amerikanischen Literatur' (1913) XXXIX Archiv für Bürgerliches Recht 287 ff., in particular 294. But see Ross, *Theorie der Rechtsquellen: ein Beitrag zur Theorie des positiven Rechts auf Grundlage dogmenhistorischer Untersuchungen* 106-108, and 126, criticizing that the concept of statute law would be deprived from every value by the incorporation of such vague principles.
72 John William Salmond, *Jurisprudence* (4th edn, Stevens 1913) 146-147, 152. Salmond considered this the central difference to German authors such as Savigny and Windscheid. Cf. Savigny, *System des heutigen Römischen Rechts* 83: "Sehen wir endlich auf die Wirksamkeit [des Gewohnheitsrechts] im Verhältnis zu den Gesetzen, so müssen wir diesen Rechtsquellen völlige Gleichheit zuschreiben. Gesetze also können durch neues Gewohnheitsrecht nicht nur ergänzt und modificirt, sondern auch außer Kraft gesetzt werden [...]". See also Windscheid, *Lehrbuch des Pandektenrechts* 49.
73 William Jethro Brown, *The Austinian theory of law: being an edition of lectures I, V, and VI of Austin's "Jurisprudence," and of Austin's "Essay on the uses of the study of jurisprudence"* (Murray 1906) 328-329. Brown attributes the idea that an act of parliament could be void to natural law thinking of the past.

Chapter 2: Comparative Perspectives

customary law.[74] Hart also attacked Austin's argument according to which all law must be derived from the will of the sovereign and suggested a secondary rule of recognition according to which so-called primary rules of obligations can be identified.[75] This secondary rule could, in principle, accommodate common law:

> "In a developed legal system the rules of recognition are of course more complex; instead of identifying rules exclusively by reference to a text or list they do so by reference to some general characteristic possessed by the primary rules. This may be the fact of their having been enacted by a specific body, or their long customary practice, or their relation to judicial decisions."[76]

Whereas Hart, only in a cursory and sketchy fashion[77], attempted to reconcile custom and common law with his idea of law as set of primary and secondary rules, Brian Simpson suggested to understand common law as sort of customary law. Rather than understanding common law as a system of clearly defined rules, Simpson suggested "an alternative idea - the idea that the common law is best understood as a system of customary law, that is, as a body of traditional ideas received within a caste of experts"[78]. According to Simpson, certain propositions of common law were so abstract that they could not be reasonably explained by reference to a regularly observable custom in the sense of a behavioural practice, which is why the view of common law as custom "has today fallen almost wholly out of favour."[79] Yet, he suggested to "conceive of the common law as *a system of customary law*, and to recognize that such system may embrace complex theoretical notions which both serve to explain and justify past practice in the settlement of disputes and the punishment of offences, and provide a guide for future conduct in these matters."[80] This system was said to consist "of a body of practices observed and ideas received by a caste of lawyers, these ideas being used by them as providing guidance in what is conceived to be the rational determination of disputes litigated before them [...]".[81] The existence of such

---

74 Hart, *The concept of law: With a postscript* 44-48; Duxbury, 'Custom as Law in English Law' 339.
75 Hart, *The concept of law: With a postscript* 97, 100.
76 ibid 95.
77 Hart did not consider custom to be "in the modern world a very important 'source'", ibid 45; see Duxbury, 'Custom as Law in English Law' 339.
78 Simpson, 'Common Law and Legal Theory' 362.
79 ibid 374, 375-376.
80 ibid 375-376 (italics added).
81 ibid 376.

Example: The common law and the interrelationship of unwritten and written law

ideas and practices was said to depend on the condition "that they are accepted and acted upon within the legal profession"; in this sense, common law was not authoritatively fixed by language the same way that statutory rules are, rather formulations of the common law only describe and systematize those practices, remain as a description subject to correction and should not be equated with the practices described.[82]

II. The historic discussion of the relationship between unwritten law and the written law in the United States of America

In comparison, the discussion in the US turned much earlier and to a greater extent on the interaction between common law and legislation than the debate in the UK did.[83]

---

82 ibid 376. It has been argued that this insight may be helpful for understanding also customary international law in the international legal order, see Chasapis Tassinis, 'Customary International Law: Interpretation from Beginning to End' 261 ("rules of custom are best conceptualized as 'statements of legal science'"); see also Hakimi, 'Making Sense of Customary International Law' 1517-1519.
83 See Atiyah, 'Common Law and Statute Law' 1, arguing that the question of interaction has received little attention in English scholarship; cf. James McCauley Landis, 'Statutes and the Sources of Law' (1965) 2 Harvard Journal of Legislation 8 ("Historically statutes have never played such a confined role in the development of English law.").

Chapter 2: Comparative Perspectives

The *Erie* judgment[84], in which the US Supreme Court rejected the existence of a federal common law in multi-state jurisdictional disputes and thusly reduced the scope of application of common law, the rise of legal realism, the proliferation of legislation in the New Deal era[85] as well as a growing interest in the interpretation of the constitution arguably shifted the discussion away from the relationship between common law and legislation.[86] However, the early discussion's focus on the *law in action* and the idea to apply statutes "beyond their terms"[87] provided inspiration for modern doctrines on general

---

84 *Erie Railroad Company v Tompkins* SCOTUS 304 U.S. 64, courts could apply state common law; in the follow-up, the judgment's implications for the status of international law in the US legal system was subject to intense debate, as international law had been thought of as federal common law. The first argument was made by Jessup, arguing that Erie did not pronounce on the question of international law. If "applied broadly, it would follow that hereafter a state court's determination of a rule of international law would be a finding regarding the law of the state and would not be reviewed by the Supreme Court of the United States." In his view, "any attempt to extend the doctrine of the Tompkins case to international law should be repudiated by the Supreme Court", Philip C Jessup, 'The Doctrine of Erie Railroad V. Tompkins Applied to International Law' (1939) 33(4) AJIL 742, 743; decades later, Curtis Bradley and Jack Goldsmith argued that customary international law should not be understood as federal common law as it was by what they called the "modern" position, Curtis A Bradley and Jack L Goldsmith, 'Customary International Law as Federal Common Law: A Critique of the Modern Position' (1997) 110(4) Harvard Law Review 817, 852 ff.; Curtis A Bradley and Jack L Goldsmith, 'The Current Illegitimacy of International Human Rights Litigation' (1997) 66(2) Fordham Law Review 319 ff.; for a defense of this modern position see Ryan Goodman and Derek P Jinks, 'Filartiga's Firm Footing: International Human Rights And Federal Common Law' (1997) 66(2) Fordham Law Review 463 ff.
85 Ellen Ash Peters, 'Common Law Judging in a Statutory World: An Address' (1982) 43 University of Pittsburgh Law Review 996.
86 Common law remains relevant though at the state level and arguably also at the Federal level, cf. for an overview Caleb Nelson, 'The Legitimacy of (Some) Federal Common Law' (2015) 101(5) Virginia Law Review 1 ff.; Pojanowski, 'Reading Statutes in the Common Law Tradition' 1357 ff.
87 Robert F Williams, 'Statutes as Sources of Law Beyond their Terms in Common-Law Cases' (1982) 50(4) The George Washington Law Review 558 ff., see also 571-573 and 592-593 for examples of interplay between statutes and common law; see also Kent Greenawalt, *Statutory and Common Law Interpretation* (Oxford University Press 2012) 286.

Example: The common law and the interrelationship of unwritten and written law

principles in other domestic legal orders, for instance in the United Kingdom and in Germany, as well as in international legal scholarship.[88]

1. Roscoe Pound

Roscoe Pound suggested four ways in which legislative innovation could relate to the common law and be approached by courts. Firstly, "[courts] might receive [legislative innovation] fully into the body of the law as affording not only a rule to be applied but a principle from which to reason" and regard it as "a more direct expression of the general will" and as superior to judge-made rules on the same subject. They might also, secondly, use legislation as source of inspiration for analogies, "regarding it, however, as of equal or co-ordinate authority in this respect with judge-made rules upon the same general subject". According to the third option, courts might refuse "to receive [legislative innovation] fully into the body of the law" and to reason from it by analogy but at least give the scope of the legislation a liberal interpretation; in contrast, courts might in the fourth scenario interpret the legislation as strictly and narrowly as possible, "holding it down rigidly to those cases which it

---

[88] For a reception of Pound's and Cardozo's scholarship see MacCormick, *Legal Reasoning and Legal Theory* 194; Cross, *Precedent in English Law* 167-169; Fikentscher, *Methoden des Rechts in vergleichender Darstellung. Anglo-amerikanischer Rechtskreis* 211-212, 251-253. US scholarship itself was influenced by European thinkers such as François Gény and Rudolf von Jhering, Benjamin Cardozo, *The Nature of the Judicial Process* (13th edn, Yale University Press 1946) 16 (reference to Gény), 102 (reference to Jhering); on this reception see Jerome Frank, 'Civil Law Influences on the Common Law - Some Reflections on 'Comparative' and 'Contrastive' Law' (1956) 104(7) University of Pennsylvania Law Review 890-893; on differences of principles in common law and civil law jurisdictions see Stone, 'The Common Law in the United States' 6 ("With the common law, unlike the civil law and its Roman law precursor, the formulation of general principles has not preceded decision. In its origin it is the law of the practitioner rather than the philosopher."); but see Esser, *Grundsatz und Norm in der richterlichen Fortbildung des Privatrechts Rechtsvergleichende Beiträge zur Rechtsquellen- und Interpretationslehre* 219 (acknowledging those differences but also noting tendencies of convergence); see also Kolb, 'Les maximes juridiques en droit international public: questions historiques et théoriques' 429. Hersch Lauterpacht referred Roscoe Pound and Benjamin Cardozo who are discussed in this chapter, cf. the index in Hersch Lauterpacht, *The Function of Law in the International Community* (Reprinted with corr., first publ. 1933, Oxford University Press 2012) 461 f.

Chapter 2: Comparative Perspectives

covers expressly."[89] In Pound's view, the last mentioned scenario represented "the orthodox common law attitude towards legislative innovation", whereas he regarded the state of his discipline tending towards the third attitude and he suggested that the legal development would eventually lead to the adoption of the second and the first method in spite of the doubts those methods might face to a common law lawyer.[90]

Since common law became "a custom of judicial decision, not a custom of popular action"[91], it was no longer superior to legislation which became "the more truly democratic form of lawmaking [...] the more direct and accurate expression of the general will."[92] In his view, principles could be extrapolated from legislation.[93] Pound did not reduce law to rules. Rather, he distinguished "laws" from "the law", meaning "the whole body of legal precepts" which "gives them [the laws] life."[94] At the same time, he recognized a difference between rules and principles. Rules, on the one hand, were "precepts attaching a definite detailed legal consequence to a definite, detailed state of facts"[95] and "the bone and sinew of the legal order."[96] Principles, on the other hand, were said to be "the work of lawyers. They organize experience of interpreting and applying rules".[97] They were described as "authoritative starting points for legal reasoning, employed continually and legitimately where cases are not covered or are not fully or obviously covered by rules in the narrower

---

89 Roscoe Pound, 'Common Law and Legislation' (1908) 21(6) Harvard Law Review 385.
90 ibid 385-386, and 400 on a systemic understanding of the relationship between statutory law and common law ("Statute and common law should be construed together, just as statute and statute must be."); see also Landis, 'Statutes and the Sources of Law' 8, 11 ff., originally published 1934 (noting that historically English common law was often preceded by statutes and on necessary modifications to accommodate English common law to US-American realities).
91 Pound, 'Common Law and Legislation' 406.
92 ibid 406. As Cardozo put it, "a legislative policy [...] is itself a source of law, a new generative impulse transmitted to the legal system", *Van Beeck v Sabine Towing Co* SCOTUS 300 U.S. 342 351. Contra: Holland, *The elements of jurisprudence* 76 footnote 2.
93 Pound, 'Common Law and Legislation' 407.
94 Roscoe Pound, *Jurisprudence Part 3. The Nature of Law* (vol 2, West 1959) 104 ff., 106.
95 Roscoe Pound, 'Hierarchy of Sources and Forms in Different Systems of Law' (1933) 7 Tulane Law Review 482.
96 ibid 483.
97 Pound, *Jurisprudence Part 3. The Nature of Law* 126.

sense."[98] Unlike rules, principles "do not attach any definite detailed legal results to any definite, detailed states of facts".[99] The interpreter would have to make a choice between competing principles, "and this choice is seldom authoritatively fixed."[100]

2. Benjamin Cardozo

General principles played a prominent role in Cardozo's work on the judicial process. According to Cardozo, the judge "must first extract from the precedents the underlying principle, the *ratio decidendi*; he must then determine the path or direction along which the principle is move and develop [...]"[101]. The direction could be determined from different perspectives or "methods"[102]: these methods represented considerations which Cardozo considered to be relevant for the ascertainment and the interpretation of general principles. The method of philosophy included reasoning by logical progression or by analogy[103] and emphasized logical consistency of the law. The method of evolution considered the historical development of a principle.[104] The method of tradition referred to custom which may assist in fixing the direction of a principle.[105] The purpose of custom then was "not so much in the creation of new rules, but for the tests and standards that are to determine how established rules shall be applied".[106] Cardozo's method of sociology referred to considerations of social justice and the welfare of the society.[107] All methods were said to be applicable, with the sociological method being "the arbiter between other methods, determining in the last analysis the choice of each, weighing their competing claims, setting bounds to their pre-

---

98 Pound, 'Hierarchy of Sources and Forms in Different Systems of Law' 483.
99 ibid 483.
100 ibid 484.
101 Cardozo, *The Nature of the Judicial Process* 28.
102 ibid 30-31.
103 ibid 49.
104 ibid 51-57.
105 ibid 58.
106 ibid 60, see also 62 ("It is, however, not so much in the making of new rules as in the application of old ones that the creative energy of custom most often manifests itself today").
107 ibid 66-67.

tensions, balancing and moderating and harmonizing them all."[108] Cardozo emphasized the value of uniformity and impartiality as well as consistency of the law and its symmetrical development, all of which, however, had to be balanced against other social interests such as equity or fairness.[109] The judicial task was described as a creative one, as "[t]he law [...] is not found, but made."[110] Unlike the legislator, however, who "is not hampered by any limitations in the appreciation of a general situation"[111], the judge must "base his judicial decision on elements of an objective nature."[112] For this purpose, the judge "is to draw inspiration from consecrated principles" and "exercise a discretion informed by tradition, methodized by analogy, disciplined by system, and subordinated to the 'primordial necessity of order in the social life'."[113]

3. Lon Fuller

Another important perspective on the relationship between written law and unwritten law in US legal theory was developed by Lon L. Fuller. Fuller is well known for his eight criteria of legality: governance by general norms, public ascertainability or public promulgation, in general no retroactivity, clarity of law, non-contradictoriness, the possibility of compliance, constancy of the law over time, congruence between official action and declared rule.[114] Adherence to these eight criteria of legality would produce the internal morality of law as a morality of aspiration, as opposed to a morality of duty.[115]

---

108 Cardozo, *The Nature of the Judicial Process* 98.
109 ibid 112-113.
110 ibid 115.
111 ibid 120.
112 ibid 121.
113 ibid 140-141(quote) with approving reference to François Gény and to the first article of the Swiss Civil Code of 1907, which was said to set "the tone and temper in which the modern judge should set about his task" (140).
114 Lon L Fuller, *The Morality of Law: Revised Edition* (Yale University Press 1969) 46-91; the terminology is in part borrowed from Thomas Schultz, 'The Concept of Law in Transnational Arbitral Legal Orders and some of its Consequences' (2011) 2(1) JIDS 72.
115 Fuller, *The Morality of Law: Revised Edition* 104, 121, and 202-203, for the internal morality as professional commitment of lawyers and object to thrieve to, more than just "good legal craftsmanship" (Herbert LA Hart, 'Book Review of The Morality

Example: The common law and the interrelationship of unwritten and written law

It is, however, Fuller's work on customary law, also termed "implicit law"[116], which Gerald Postema has considered to constitute the "hallmark of Fuller's jurisprudence".[117] Customary law was formed "when a stabilization of interactional expectancies has occurred so that the parties have come to guide their conduct toward one another by these expectancies".[118] Fuller's account stressed the interplay between written law, or law enacted by the lawgiver, and customary law as law emerging between subjects to the law.[119] In Fuller's model, enacted law and customary law are not in a relationship of competition but supplement each other.[120]

Whereas Pound and Cardozo highlighted in their work the role of the judge, Fuller's work pointed to the contributions of the law-subjects. Both in Cardozo's[121] and in Fuller's account[122], the purpose of customary law did not lie in creating new rules but in explaining the meaning of existing rules. The accounts thus envisioned a role of custom which was not in competition to the written law. The horizontal relationship between the written law enacted by the lawmaker and the law's addressees makes Fuller's ideas particularly interesting to the contemporary discussions about the *lex mercatoria*, or

---

of Law by Lon L. Fuller' (1965) 78(6) Harvard Law Review 1285-1286); see also Lon L Fuller, 'Positivism and Fidelity to Law: A Reply to Professor Hart' (1958) 71(4) Harvard Law Review 632.
116 Lon L Fuller, 'Human Interaction and the Law' (1969) 14 The American Journal of Jurisprudence1 ff.
117 Gerald J Postema, 'Implicit Law' (1994) 13(3) Law and Philosophy 364.
118 Fuller, 'Human Interaction and the Law' 9-10.
119 ibid 24 ("the existence of enacted law as an effectively functioning system depends upon the establishment of stable interactional expectancies between lawgiver and subject").
120 ibid 35-36 ("enacted law and the organizational principles implicit in customary law are not simply to be viewed as alternative ways of ordering men's interactions, but rather as often serving to supplement each other by a kind of natural division of labor"); on the congruence between enacted law and social practices in Fuller's work see see Postema, 'Implicit Law' 368, 373-377; cf. Andreas Hadjigeorgiou, 'Beyond Formalism Reviving the Legacy of Sir Henry Maine for Customary International Law' in Panos Merkouris, Jörg Kammerhofer, and Noora Arajärvi (eds), *The Theory, Practice, and Interpretation of Customary International Law* (Cambridge University Press 2022) 186-202 (on the relationship between customary law and written law in the work of Maine).
121 Cardozo, *The Nature of the Judicial Process* 58.
122 Fuller, 'Human Interaction and the Law' 24.

Chapter 2: Comparative Perspectives

nonstate law[123] and his emphasis on the importance of interpretative practices has been referred to in the public international law discourse as well.[124]

III. A new interest in the interplay between common law and statutory law in the recent UK jurisprudence

The portrayal of the English debate has turned so far more on the hierarchy between written and unwritten law and less on the interaction.[125] With the clarification of the primacy of the statutory law, the question of the precise interaction between unwritten law and written law, between common law and statutory law, was seldomly addressed, but it attracted more attention in recent judicial practice. Lord Hoffman commented on the relationship between statutory law and common law in the *Johnson* case, where the question was raised whether the plaintiff had a cause of action under common law, unaffected by the damage cap limitation that applied to the claim under statutory law. He stressed that the "development of the common law by the judges plays a subsidiary role. Their traditional function is to adapt and modernise the common law. But such developments must be consistent with legislative policy as expressed in statutes. The courts may proceed in harmony

---

123 Ralf Michaels, 'A Fuller Concept of Law Beyond the State? Thoughts on Lon Fuller's Contributions to the Jurisprudence of Transnational Dispute Resolution: A Reply to Thomas Schultz' (2011) 2(2) JIDS 421 ff., with further references; Bruce L Benson, 'Customary Law as a Social Contract: International Commercial Law' (1992) 3(1) Constitutional Political Economy 1 ff.; Gregory Shaffer, 'How Business Shapes Law: A Socio-Legal Framework' (2009) 42(1) Connecticut Law Review 150.
124 Brunnée and Toope, *Legitimacy and legality in international law: an interactional account*; Brunnée and Toope, 'International Law and Constructivism: Elements of an Interactional Theory of International Law' 19 ff. For Fuller, international law invites one to qustion the dominant domestic paradigm of vertically imposed law, Fuller, *The Morality of Law: Revised Edition* 237; on this topic, see also Michael Markun, *Law without Sanctions Order in Primitive Societies and the World Community* (Yale University Press 1968) 11, see also 66, 90, 161.
125 Bogg, 'Common Law and Statute in the Law of Employment' 67, according to whom "the interaction between common law and statute has been underexplored"; see already Esser, *Grundsatz und Norm in der richterlichen Fortbildung des Privatrechts Rechtsvergleichende Beiträge zur Rechtsquellen- und Interpretationslehre* 131, 264-265.

with Parliament but there should be no discord."[126] It would not be "a proper exercise of the judicial function"[127] to develop a common law that would circumvent the statutory damage limitation and be "contrary to the evident intention of Parliament".[128]

One cannot say, however, that common law has always a subsidiary role in relation to written law. In particular the relationship between common law and the Human Rights Act was subject to discussions in scholarship. The recent judicial practice in the United Kingdom indicates that the interpretation of common law was informed by statutes and international obligations, while at the same time maintaining common law as a distinct legal concept.

1. Common law as human rights law

Prior to the adoption of the Human Rights Act, the European Convention on Human Rights was not implemented domestically. Courts therefore resorted to common law as legal basis and interpreted this branch of law in light of the ECHR, which was described as "incorporation without incorporation".[129] With the adoption of the Human Rights Act, "the common law did not come to an end"[130], in particular the UK Supreme Court stressed the continuing importance of common law.[131] In *Osborn*, Lord Reed, with whom the other judges agreed, wrote that the constitution of the United Kingdom and the European Convention on Human Rights share common values. Human rights

---

126 *Johnson v Unisys Limited* House of Lords [2001] UKHL 13, Lord Hoffmann para 37.
127 ibid, Lord Hoffmann para 57.
128 ibid, Lord Hoffmann para 58; but see Lord Steyn's dissent, para 23, emphasizing that Parliament did not intend to preclude the principled development of common law. On Lord Hoffmann's approach see Bogg, 'Common Law and Statute in the Law of Employment' 68, identifying three modes of interplay in Hoffmann's opinion: statutes might preempt the development of common law, it might operate as analogical stimulus for common law and common law as fundamental rights.
129 *Watkins v Home Office* House of Lords [2006] UKHL 17, Lord Rodger of Earlsferry, para 64, also arguing: "Now that the Human Rights Act is in place, such heroic efforts are unnecessary".
130 *R (Guardian News and Media Ltd) v City of Westminster Magistrates' Court (Article 19 intervening)* England and Wales Court of Appeal, QB [2013] QB 618 Toulson LJ para 88.
131 Brice Dickson, *Human rights and the United Kingdom Supreme Court* (Oxford University Press 2013) 28 ff.

should be primarily protected through domestic law, through legislation and the common law. Lord Reed acknowledged the importance of the Human Rights Act, while stressing at the same time that the Act "does not however supersede the protection of human rights under the common law or statute [...] Human rights continue to be protected by our domestic law, interpreted and developed in accordance with the Act when appropriate."[132]

In *Kennedy*, Lord Mance, writing for the majority and against a tendency to frame legal questions concerning human rights solely in terms of ECHR rights, explained that "the natural starting point" would be domestic law and in particular common law, "it is certainly not to focus exclusively on the Convention rights, without surveying the wider common law scene."[133] Common law would remain independent, "[i]n some areas, the common law may go further than the Convention, and in some contexts it may also be inspired by the Convention rights and jurisprudence [...] And in time, of course, a synthesis may emerge."[134] He then argued that article 10 ECHR would not contain a positive right of access to information and that such protection was to be looked for instead in the common law.[135] Common law

---

132 *Osborn v The Parole Board, Booth v The Parole Board In the matter of an application of James Clyde Reilly for Judicial Review (Northern Ireland)* UKSC [2013] UKSC 61 Lord Reed in particular para 57. See also para 104 for examples in which the jurisprudence of the EctHR was taken into account for the interpretation of the common law. See also *R (Daly) v Secretary of State for the Home Department* House of Lords [2001] UKHL 26, where the House of Lords decided that common law protects a prisoner's right to confidential privileged legal correspondence. Lord Bingham noted that this common law interpretation corresponds to article 8 ECHR (para 23). Lord Cooke of Thorndorn stressed that "that the common law by itself is being recognised as a sufficient source of the fundamental right to confidential communication" (para 30). See also *Regina v Parole Board ex parte Smith, Regina v Parole Board ex parte West* House of Lords [2005] UKHL 1 para 30 ff., where ECtHR jurisprudence was included in the consideration of what common law would require for a hearing to be regarded as fair. See also on the prohibition of torture as common law *A and others v Secretary of State for the Home Department* House of Lords [2005] UKHL 71 Lord Bingham para 51 ("the English common law has regarded torture and its fruits with abhorrence for over 500 years").
133 *Kennedy v Charity Commission* UKSC [2014] UKSC 20 Lord Mance, para 46.
134 ibid Lord Mance para 46.
135 ibid Lord Mance para 46. See also paras 51-54 on the Wednesbury test and porportionality, and para 94 on the ECHR. But see the dissent by Lord Wilson, paras 188-189, coming to a contrary conclusion on article 10 ECHR by adopting a less narrow interpretation.

Example: The common law and the interrelationship of unwritten and written law

as primarily applicable law continued to be interpreted in light of the HRA and the ECHR.[136]

2. Common law in light of human rights

The ECHR and the HRA have also an impact beyond the interpretation of common law rights. For instance, human rights as enshrined in the ECHR informed the interpretation of established common law concepts such as the doctrine on *ultra vires* and statutory interpretation, according to which an executive practice that infringes human rights will arguably not have been within the scope of the statutory authorization unless the statute is explicit on this point,[137] and the *Wednesbury* doctrine of reasonableness[138].

---

136 The principle to take account of obligations under international law was also stressed in *R (on the application of Faulkner) v Secretary of State for Justice and others* UKSC [2013] UKSC 23 Lord Reed para 29, common law needs to be interpreted and developed "so as to arrive at a result which is in compliance with the UK's international obligations; the starting point being our own legal principles rather than the judgments of an international court."

137 Secondary acts of the executive must remain within the scope of the statutory authorizations. The statute itself has to be interpreted in line with international human rights obligations. An executive practice that infringes human rights will arguably not have been within the scope of the statutory authorization, unless the statute is explicit on this point, see *Regina v The Secretary of State for the Home Department ex Parte Mark Francis Leech)* England and Wales Court of Appeal [1993] EWCA Civ 12; David Feldman, 'Convention Rights and Substantive Ultra Vires' in Christopher Forsyth (ed), *Judicial Review and the Constitution* (Hart Publishing 2000) 253 ff. See also the first judgment delivered by the UK Supreme Court, *Her Majesty's Treasury (Respondent) v Mohammed Jabar Ahmed and others (FC) (Appellants) Her Majesty's Treasury (Respondent) v Mohammed al-Ghabra (FC) (Appellant) R (on the application of Hani El Sayed Sabaei Youssef) (Respondent) v Her Majesty's Treasury (Appellant)* UKSC [2010] UKSC 2, the court decided that an order of Her Majesty's treasury by which the financial assets of the listed individual had been frozen on the grounds of suspected involvement into terrorism, and by which the individual was rendered effectively a prisoner of the state, was an ultra vires act as it was not covered by the very general language of the United Nations Act 1946. See also Elliott, 'Beyond the European Convention: Human Rights and the Common Law' 98: "The HRA thus does not break new conceptual ground when it comes to the protection of rights: it merely utilizes and extends the vires- based technique that was already established at common law."

138 See already Jeffrey Jowell and Anthony Lester, 'Beyond Wednesbury: Substantive Principles of Administrative Law' [1987] Public Law 371-374, 377, 379, the authors

Chapter 2: Comparative Perspectives

Moreover, common law has also continued to constitute a legal basis for infringements of individual rights, as the UK Supreme Court recently maintained with respect to the so-called act of state doctrine. According to this doctrine, certain acts of the Crown were not justiciable and certain tort claims against the Crown by (foreign) citizens were precluded from judicial review.[139] The UK Supreme Court did not follow the Court of Appeals which had argued that it would be for parliament to introduce a procedural bar to claims.[140] Instead, it was argued that in narrow circumstances, a tort claim under foreign law against the Crown might not be enforced by Her Majesty's court based on the Crown act of state doctrine.[141]

---

argued that the reasonableness test should not confine itself to procedural fairness but be committed to human rights and the European Convention. The authors demonstrated that past judgments had already protected for instance the right to property, disguised by the Wednesbury language (at 372).

139 The leading case is *Attorney General v Nissan* House of Lords [1969] UKHL 3, see in particular Lord Wilberforce according to whom the Crown act of state doctrine rests on the "two different conceptions or rules" mentioned in the text. For present discussions see*Rahmatullah v Ministry of Defence and another, Mohammed and others v Ministry of Defence and another* UKSC [2017] UKSC 1 Lady Hale (with whom Lord Wilson and Lord Hughes agree) para 19 ff., Lord Sumption paras 79-81, contra: Lord Mance para 69 (only one principle); on the act of state doctrine, see also Amanda Perreau-Saussine, 'British Acts of State in English Courts' (2008) 78 BYIL 176 ff.

140 *Mohammed (Serdar) v Ministry of Defence, Qasim v Secretary of State for Defence, Rahmatullah v Ministry of Defence, Iraqi Civilians v Ministry of Defence* UK Court of Appeal [2015] EWCA Civ 843 para 364.

141 *Rahmatullah v Ministry of Defence and another, Mohammed and others v Ministry of Defence and another* [2017] UKSC 1 (Lady Hale with whom Lord Wilson and Lord Hughes agree) paras 36-37 on the conditions: "[...] We are left with a very narrow class of acts: in their nature sovereign acts - the sorts of thing that governments properly do; committed abroad; in the conduct of the foreign policy of the state; so closely connected to that policy to be necessary in pursuing it; and at least extending to the conduct of military operations which are themselves lawful in international law"; see also Lord Sumption para 81, raising the question of a further condition, namely whether the Crown act of state doctrine would be applicable only against claims of aliens.

Example: The common law and the interrelationship of unwritten and written law

3. Concluding Observations

The recent judicial practice on the "resurgence"[142] of common law demonstrates that common law is interpreted in light of statutes and international obligations.[143] The success of common law is also the result of efforts by the UK Supreme Court. When parties began to plead almost exclusively on the basis of the HRA without further regard to the common law,[144] the judges of the Supreme Court countered this development by signaling that they continued to understand common law to be the law to be applied in the first place and, if possible, in concordance with the obligations under the ECHR. The judges did not simply regard common law as synonymous and equated with the Human Rights Act, they applied common law "within its own paradigm"[145]. There were reasons related to the UK legal order which may explain the continuing attractiveness of common law: the "proud tradition"[146] of UK constitutionalism and the potential of common law to operate

---

142 See Roger Masterman and Se-shauna Wheatle, 'A common law resurgence in protection?' [2015] (1) European Human Rights Law Review 61 ff.; Bowen, 'Does the renaissance of common law rights mean that the Human Rights Act 1998 is now unnecessary?' 361; see also Brenda Hale, 'UK Constitutionalism on the March? keynote address to the Constitutional and Administrative Law Bar Association Conference 2014' [2015] Judicial Review 201 ff.
143 *Montgomery v Lanarkshire Health Board* UKSC [2015] UKSC 11 Lord Kerr and Lord Reed (with whom Lord Neuberger, Lord Clarke, Lord Wilson and Lord Hodge agree) para 80: "Under the stimulus of the Human Rights Act 1998, the courts have become increasingly conscious of the extent to which the common law reflects fundamental values."
144 For this observation see *Kennedy v Charity Commission* [2014] UKSC 20, Lord Mance para 46: "Since the passing of the Human Rights Act 1998, there has too often been a tendency to see the law in areas touched on by the Convention solely in terms of the Convention rights."; Elliott, 'Beyond the European Convention: Human Rights and the Common Law' 91; Bowen, 'Does the renaissance of common law rights mean that the Human Rights Act 1998 is now unnecessary?' 361-362.
145 See Max Du Plessis and Jolyon Ford, 'Developing the common law progressively - horizontality, the Human Rights Act and the South African experience' [2004] (3) European Human Rights Law Review 312-314 on the need to apply a legal concept such as common law "within its own paradigm".
146 Hale, 'UK Constitutionalism on the March? keynote address to the Constitutional and Administrative Law Bar Association Conference 2014' 201 ff.

Chapter 2: Comparative Perspectives

as domestic counterweight,[147] whilst the opinions differ on whether the idea of judicial review of an act of parliament would be easier to accept, if at all, under the Human Rights Act made by parliament than under the common law.[148] What is important for the purposes of this study is, however, that the treatment of common law in the UK demonstrates that a legal concept, in spite of all the uncertainties from the perspective of legal theory[149], can work if it continued to receive the support of scholars and practitioners.[150] Common law then seems to appear as Simpson described it, "a body of practices observed and ideas received by a caste of lawyers."[151]

C. Example: German law and the interrelationship of sources

The German legal history illustrates how a legal concept such as customary law can lose its support of a legal community in light of functionally equivalent doctrines, such as the role of a standing jurisprudence, the interplay

---

147 Bjørge, 'Common Law Rights: Balancing Domestic and International Exigencies' 234 ff. (pointing to Security Council resolutions which might prevail over the ECHR which would render a domestic counterweight such as common law important).
148 Elliott, 'Beyond the European Convention: Human Rights and the Common Law' 114-115, wondering whether the prospects of "judicial disobedience to statute" are more favourable under the Human Rights Act than under common law; for Bowen, 'Does the renaissance of common law rights mean that the Human Rights Act 1998 is now unnecessary?' 362-365 however, common law would for reasons of parliamentary sovereignty not as strong as the Human Rights Act; expressing also "a note of caution": Clayton, 'The empire strikes back: common law rights and the Human Rights Acts' 4; see also Sales, 'Rights and Fundamental Rights in English Law' 91-92 and 95-96.
149 For an overview of the legal-theoretical difficulties of common law see Simpson, 'Common Law and Legal Theory' 359 ff.; Oliver Lepsius, *Verwaltungsrecht unter dem Common Law: amerikanische Entwicklungen bis zum New Deal* (Mohr Siebeck 1997) 33-36.
150 Cf. Clarence Wilfred Jenks, *The common law of mankind* (Stevens 1958) 104-105, arguing against an unduly rigid and overdogmatic approach to customary international law, since the "future status and effectiveness of established custom depends primarily on certain basic intellectual attitudes."
151 Simpson, 'Common Law and Legal Theory' 376; cf. Sales, 'Rights and Fundamental Rights in English Law' 99, arguing that common law interpretation should not be mere judge-made law but be supported by evidence of a will of a legislature in statutory provisions.

between a written norm and the application of a norm and the doctrine of legal principles all of which made customary law less attractive.[152]

I. The historical school

Both Friedrich Carl von Savigny and Georg Friedrich Puchta are associated with the so-called historical school according to which customary law was the expression of a national spirit (*Volksgeist*), which was the ultimate source of three sources: customary law, enacted law and legal science (*Gewohnheitsrecht, Gesetzesrecht, Juristenrecht*).[153]

Prior to the historical school, there was a tendency to strengthen the written law in form of statutes in relation to custom. As described by Jan Schröder, whilst it was still thought in the 16th century that the consent of the lawmaker was not necessary for a custom to emerge as long as the custom was reasonable and did not contradict natural law or divine law, and had derogatory force in relation to written law,[154] the understanding of law changed in the outset of the 16th century, as law became detached from values

---

152 See in particular Christian Tomuschat, *Verfassungsgewohnheitsrecht? Eine Untersuchung zum Staatsrecht der Bundesrepublik Deutschland* (Heidelberg, 1972) 9; Josef Esser, 'Richterrecht, Gerichtsgebrauch und Gewohnheitsrecht' in Josef Esser (ed), *Festschrift für Fritz von Hippel: zum 70. Geburtstag* (Mohr Siebeck 1967) 118, 122-123, 126; but see on the potential usefulness of the concept of customary law for a judicial jurisprudence Karl Larenz, *Methodenlehre der Rechtswissenschaft* (6th edn, Springer 1991) 356-357, 433; Christian Starck, 'Die Bindung des Richters an Gesetz und Verfassung' (1976) 34 Veröffentlichungen der Vereinigung der Deutschen Staatsrechtslehrer 71.; Bodo Pieroth, *Rückwirkung und Übergangsrecht Verfassungsrechtliche Maßstäbe für intertemporale Gesetzgebung* (Duncker & Humblot 1981) 272-273.
153 Wolfgang Fikentscher, *Methoden des Rechts in Vergleichender Darstellung Mitteleuropäischer Rechtskreis* (vol 3, Mohr Siebeck 1976) 90; see also Paul Guggenheim, 'Contribution à l'histoire des sources du droit des gens' (1958) 94 RdC 52, according to whom Savigny's and Puchta's focus on *opinio juris* was the essential contribution *vis-à-vis* preceding theories.
154 Jan Schröder, *Recht als Wissenschaft: Geschichte der juristischen Methode vom Humanismus bis zur historischen Schule (1500-1850)* (Beck 2001) 14; cf. also Siegfried Brie, *Die Lehre vom Gewohnheitsrecht: eine historisch-dogmatische Untersuchung. Theil 1: Geschichtliche Grundlegung: bis zum Ausgang des Mittelalters* (Marcus 1899) 151-158 on the recognition of the derogatory force of custom in medieval times.

Chapter 2: Comparative Perspectives

or justice and was regarded as the expression of the will of the lawmaker.[155] As a consequence, customary law was brought within this statutory paradigm by being based on a tacit command of the lawmaker.[156] Throughout the 18th century, the derogatory force of custom was questioned or made dependent on the tacit consent of the lawmaker.[157] In contrast to a strong voluntarist understanding of law which depended solely on the will of the lawmaker, the historical school stressed the organic growth of the law through itself, for instance through analogical reasoning which takes account of the "inner consequence" of the legal system.[158] In this context, customary law and the legal craft was given more significance.[159]

1. Friedrich Carl von Savigny

Savigny argued that the seat of all law was the common conscience of the people.[160] It was not custom that *created* this positive law. Rather, custom was "the indicator of positive law and not the basis of its creation".[161] Article 38(2) PCIJ Statute, now article 38(1)(b) ICJ Statute, reflected this understanding[162],

---

155 Schröder, *Recht als Wissenschaft: Geschichte der juristischen Methode vom Humanismus bis zur historischen Schule (1500-1850)* 97-98; Hobbes, *Hobbes's Leviathan: reprinted from the edition of 1651* 203, chapter XXVI.
156 Schröder, *Recht als Wissenschaft: Geschichte der juristischen Methode vom Humanismus bis zur historischen Schule (1500-1850)* 105-107.
157 ibid 112.
158 Savigny, *System des heutigen Römischen Rechts* 290, 292.
159 Schröder, *Recht als Wissenschaft: Geschichte der juristischen Methode vom Humanismus bis zur historischen Schule (1500-1850)* 194.
160 Friedrich Carl von Savigny, *Vom Beruf unsrer Zeit für Gesetzgebung und Rechtswissenschaft* (Mohr und Zimmer 1814) 12; Savigny, *System des heutigen Römischen Rechts* 14.
161 ibid 35: "So ist die Gewohnheit das Kennzeichen des positiven Rechts, nicht dessen Entstehungsgrund."; for the English translation see Christoph Kletzer, 'Custom and Positivity: an Examination of the Philosophic Ground of the Hegel-Savigny Controversy' in Amanda Perreau-Saussine and James Bernard Murphy (eds), *The nature of customary law* (Cambridge University Press 2007) 134, where Kletzner also convincingly argued that the term customary *law* "is not an ontological determination of the law but only an epistemic or heuristic determination"; see also Fikentscher, *Methoden des Rechts in Vergleichender Darstellung Mitteleuropäischer Rechtskreis* 90; similar: Georg Friedrich Puchta, *Das Gewohnheitsrecht. Zweiter Theil* (Palm 1837) 10.
162 Tomuschat, 'Obligations Arising For States Without Or Against Their Will' 290.

when it referred to "custom, as evidence of a general practice accepted as law" as opposed to "a general practice accepted as law, as evidence of international custom"[163]. According to this understanding, the continuation of a certain practice can create law only insofar as it influences the consciousness of the people.[164] Close to customary law in Savigny's conception was the so-called scientific law made by jurists.[165] Legislation, a further source, did not have an only limited or subsidiary role in relation to custom but was equally ranked which implied the mutual derogability between both sources.[166] Even though Savigny had reservations about the codification project, he did not reject codification *per se*, his concern was that legislation should fit within the organic structure of the law.[167]

2. Georg Friedrich Puchta

Whereas Savigny emphasized the organic whole,[168] Puchta focused on a logical structure of law and on a distinction between sources and modes of law.[169]

Puchta's system distinguishes between sources (*Rechtsquellen*) and modes or forms of law (*Gattung*).[170] According to Puchta, the national spirit of a people gave rise to three sources of law each of which is associated with specific modes of law: the direct conscience of a people gave rise to custom, the legislature enacted statutes, and the legal science gave rise to lawyers' law

---

163 See Crawford, 'Change, Order, Change: The Course of International Law General Course on Public International Law' 49; Sienho Yee, 'Arguments for Cleaning Up Article 38 (1) b) and (1) c) of the ICJ Statute' (2007) 4 Romanian Journal of International Law 34.
164 Savigny, *System des heutigen Römischen Rechts* 35-37 (on contingent rules which were not better or worse than alternative rules in order to regulate a certain matter).
165 Friedrich Carl von Savigny, *Pandektenvorlesung 1824/25* (Klostermann 1993) 12, who described the *Juristenrecht* as a new peculiar organ of customary law ("*ein neues eigenthümliches Organ des Gewohnheitsrechts*").
166 ibid 43.
167 ibid 44; cf. Stephan Meder, *Ius non scriptum - Traditionen privater Rechtssetzung* (2nd edn, Mohr Siebeck 2009) 134.
168 Savigny, *Pandektenvorlesung 1824/25* 50-51.
169 Fikentscher, *Methoden des Rechts in Vergleichender Darstellung Mitteleuropäischer Rechtskreis* 92, 703.
170 Cf. recently on a similar distinction Yasuaki, *International Law in a Transcivilizational World* 105, 112.

(*Juristenrecht*).[171] Puchta distinguished custom from the so-called scientific law to a greater extent, he conceded that customary law and lawyers' law were often merged as they share similar features: they do not belong to the written enacted law and they are identified by way of reference to the same evidence, namely the practice of courts.[172] Nevertheless, they were said to derive from different sources, namely the direct conscience of a people and the legal science.[173]

Similar to Savigny, Puchta argued that custom was nothing else than the continuing application of a legal rule, custom's authority derived from the fact that custom was a testimony to the existence of said rule.[174] Custom was the product of a legal community rather than of unconnected, isolated instances of practices. In order to contribute to customary law these acts would have to express a common conscience.[175] In Puchta's view, the mistaken view which regarded custom to be first and foremost practice confused the evidence of custom with the essence of this legal concept.[176] In other words, the *consuetudo*, or practice, is not custom, but the application of custom.[177] Being a product of a legal community and deriving like all law from the national spirit, custom was said to be embedded in a normative environment. Thus, three conditions needed to be met for a rule of custom to exist:[178] there needed to be a practice regarding the rule, this practice must point to a common conscience, or *opinio juris*, in relation to the rule in question. Last but not least, the rule must not be opposed by higher law or certain principles of the existing law which do not permit any derogation or which ensure the maintenance of order in the respective society.[179] Thus, normative considerations, such as divine law, *bona mores* and higher principles of law, were important when one set out to ascertain a rule of customary law.

---

171 Georg Friedrich Puchta, *Das Gewohnheitsrecht. Erster Theil* (Palm 1828) 139-146.
172 ibid 163-164; in relation to custom see 172.
173 ibid 161.
174 Puchta, *Das Gewohnheitsrecht. Zweiter Theil* 10.
175 Puchta, *Das Gewohnheitsrecht. Erster Theil* 167-172.
176 ibid 189.
177 Fikentscher, *Methoden des Rechts in Vergleichender Darstellung Mitteleuropäischer Rechtskreis* 694.
178 Puchta, *Das Gewohnheitsrecht. Zweiter Theil* 32; cf. Fikentscher, *Methoden des Rechts in Vergleichender Darstellung Mitteleuropäischer Rechtskreis* 695, according to whom practice and *opinio juris* must be safeguarded by basic legal rules ("*grundlegende Rechtssätze*").
179 Puchta, *Das Gewohnheitsrecht. Zweiter Theil* 56-59.

Example: German law and the interrelationship of sources

Whereas the lawmaker was free to derogate from a rule of custom which he deemed to be unreasonable, the judge remained bound by this rule.[180] As far as lawyers' law was concerned, it had to fit to the structures of the legal system.[181]

Both Savigny and Puchta recognized that the relative significance of the sources may differ according to the spirit of the time: Savigny recognized the possibility of a shift of preferences, from custom to legislation, but he emphasized the significance of the organic whole.[182] Puchta acknowledged that the relative importance of custom may decrease once a legal community has matured[183], while also accepting the possibility that statutes can give rise to custom.[184]

II. The declining relevance of custom

1. Rudolf von Jhering's critique and the codification of civil law

Rudolf von Jhering was more skeptical towards custom than the just mentioned scholars.[185] In contradistinction to a national spirit, Jhering emphasized that the legal science transcended national boundaries.[186] In his view, any legal order was built on and expressed universal legal ideas. Jhering's major work on the spirit of the Roman law did therefore not focus only on the Roman law, but also on *the law* as such, studied in the context of the Roman law:[187] *"Durch das römische Recht, aber über dasselbe hinaus"*, through the Roman law, but beyond it.[188] Rather than confining his perspective to single rules, Jhering wanted to ascertain by way of abstraction the underlying

---

180 ibid 61.
181 Puchta, *Das Gewohnheitsrecht. Erster Theil* 166.
182 Savigny, *System des heutigen Römischen Rechts* 50-51.
183 Puchta, *Das Gewohnheitsrecht. Erster Theil* 216.
184 ibid 219.
185 Meder, *Ius non scriptum - Traditionen privater Rechtssetzung* 139.
186 Rudolf von Jhering, *Geist des römischen Rechts auf den verschiedenen Stufen seiner Entwicklung Erster Theil* (2nd ed., Breitkopf und Härtel 1866) 10, 15.
187 ibid IX; see also on this aspect Walter Wilhelm, 'Das Recht im römischen Recht' in Franz Wieacker and Christian Wollschläger (eds), *Jherings Erbe* (Vandenhoeck & Ruprecht 1970) 229 ff.
188 Jhering, *Geist des römischen Rechts auf den verschiedenen Stufen seiner Entwicklung Erster Theil* 14; William Seagle, 'Rudolf von Jhering: Or Law as a Means to an End' (1945) 13(1) The University of Chicago Law Review 77.

Chapter 2: Comparative Perspectives

principle.[189] In that, his scholarship was regarded to be a precursor to the doctrine of general principles of law.[190]

According to Jhering, the idea of custom as an expression of a national spirit was an attempt of the historical school, of Savigny and Puchta, to revitalize custom after the rise of statutes in the 18th and 19th century.[191] In his view, however, this glorification of customary law ignored the tremendous progress which law achieved through formal written statutes.[192] As Jhering saw it, customary law was premised on the idea of harmony and unity between the law and the subjective feelings of the people, the life and spirit of the time.[193] No general theory, however, could help distinguishing between customary law and non-binding standards in the community when one had to ascertain a rule in a concrete case.[194] For Jhering, the greater certainty and stability of the written law outweighed a potential loss of flexibility and responsiveness offered by customary law. By separating law from a national feeling or spirit and replacing such inner subjectivity with an external written form, a distinction between law and non-law became possible and law gained a greater autonomy and independence.[195] At the same time, Jhering did not want to endorse a doctrine of black letter law that was divorced from social reality, on the contrary.[196] The doctrine of interpretation plays a crucial rule in mediating between the written law and social realities on the ground, and he acknowledged that the interpretation of written law can change over time.[197]

The codification of civil law which was pursued at the end of the 19th century in Germany steered a road in the middle: according to Section 2 of the first draft of the German Civil Code, rules of customary law were applicable

---

189 Jhering, *Geist des römischen Rechts auf den verschiedenen Stufen seiner Entwicklung Erster Theil* 23.
190 Fikentscher, *Methoden des Rechts in Vergleichender Darstellung Mitteleuropäischer Rechtskreis* 227-230.
191 Rudolf von Jhering, *Geist des römischen Rechts auf den verschiedenen Stufen seiner Entwicklung Zweiter Theil* (3rd ed., Breitkopf und Härtel 1866) 28-29.
192 ibid 31.
193 ibid 31.
194 ibid 34.
195 ibid 36-38.
196 Rudolf von Jhering, *Der Zweck im Recht* (Breitkopf und Härtel 1877); Fikentscher, *Methoden des Rechts in Vergleichender Darstellung Mitteleuropäischer Rechtskreis* 244.
197 Jhering, *Geist des römischen Rechts auf den verschiedenen Stufen seiner Entwicklung Zweiter Theil* 65, see 66 on evolutive interpretation.

Example: German law and the interrelationship of sources

only to the extent that the statute would refer to them.[198] The final draft left this question open and neither excluded nor endorsed custom: its relation to the written law could not be determined by the legislator and would be left to legal theory under consideration of the prevailing consciousness in public life.[199] The drafters of the civil code thought that customary law would remain more important in public law than in civil law governing the relationship between private individuals,[200] and the doctrinal climate might have appeared favourably with the theories of the historical school. Yet, the story of the concept of customary law in the context of German constitutional law is quite different and demonstrates how a concept was very early pushed to the side by other legal techniques which were regarded to better accommodate the *Zeitgeist* and the desire for a particular formalist reasoning.[201]

2. Approaches prior to the Basic Law

The scholarly attention was early on drawn to the written instrument. Paul Laband introduced the idea of the transformation/change of the written document (*Wandlung der deutschen Reichsverfassung*): just as the foundations

---

198 *Entwurf eines bürgerlichen Gesetzbuches für das deutsche Reich: Erste Lesung: ausgearb. durch die von dem Bundesrathe berufene Kommission* (Guttentag 1888) 1 (section 2); Meder, *Ius non scriptum - Traditionen privater Rechtssetzung* 140-146.
199 "Rechtssätze, die sich in der Judikatur unter dem Namen der Analogie, der einschränkenden und ausdehnenden Auslegung, der feststehenden Praxis under dergleichen herausbildeten, seien in Wahrheit nicht als Gewohnheitsrecht, und dieses mit Fug und Recht ein Produkt der fortbildenden Thätigkeit des Richters [...] Wie [sich dieses Recht] zum geschriebenen Gesetzesrechte verhalte, sei eine Frage, die der Macht des Gesetzgebers entrückt sei und nur von der Theorie nach Maßgabe der jeweilig im öffentlichen Leben herrschenden Anschauungen beantwortet werde.", Benno Mugdan, *Die gesammten Materialien zum Bürgerlichen Gesetzbuch für das Deutsche Reich. Einführungsgesetz und Allgemeiner Theil* (vol 1, Decker's Verlag 1899) 570, see also 359-370 on the discussion of custom; Meder, *Ius non scriptum - Traditionen privater Rechtssetzung* 146.
200 Mugdan, *Die gesammten Materialien zum Bürgerlichen Gesetzbuch für das Deutsche Reich. Einführungsgesetz und Allgemeiner Theil* 361.
201 Heinrich Amadeus Wolff, *Ungeschriebenes Verfassungsrecht unter dem Grundgesetz* (Mohr Siebeck 2000) 215; Stefan Korioth, *Integration und Bundesstaat Ein Beitrag zur Staats- und Verfassungslehre Rudolf Smends* (Duncker & Humblot 1990) 50-51, explaining the little interest in customary constitutional law by 19th century scholars in Germany by reference to the codification movement, the praise of a written constitution and an ideal of positivism.

of a house could remain the same after in its inside extensive redecorations and modifications had taken place, the constitutional structure of the *Reich* would look the same from the outside, whereas a glance in the inside would reveal that the substance is not the same as it used to be.[202] This idea of *Wandlung* which Laband considered to be a political phenomenon introduced the possibility of flexibility to the written constitution, thereby dispensing any need for a concept of customary law.[203]

Similarly, Georg Jellinek considered the phenomenon of "*Verfassungswandlung*" (constitutional transformation/change) at the crossroads between law and politics. He contrasted formal change and further development of law (*Rechtssätze*), be it by statutes, customary law or, some might argue, *Juristenrecht* ("*Gesetz, Gewohnheitsrecht, und, wie die einen behaupten, die anderen bestreiten, durch Juristenrecht*") and informal change which he coined "*Verfassungswandlung*".[204] Customary law was then treated only in a cursory fashion in comparison to his focus on change by interpretation.[205] Jellinek stated that the abolishment of statutes would not necessarily entail the termination of the law expressed therein because of customary law, unless customary law and the given statute were intrinsically connected.[206] Like Laband, he rejected the possibility of customary law derogating from the constitution.[207]

Heinrich Triepel's concept of law included not only the written law but also the unwritten law to which the written law was connected.[208] Triepel addressed the role of unwritten law in his essay on the relationship between the competences of the federal state and the written constitution. He accepted the existence of unwritten competences and the implied powers doctrine of US constitutional law.[209] Unlike the US constitution, the German constitution

---

202 Paul Laband, *Die Wandlungen der deutschen Reichsverfassung* (Zahn & Jaensch 1895) 3.
203 See also Georg Meyer and Gerhard Anschütz, *Lehrbuch des Deutschen Staatsrechtes* (6th edn, Duncker & Humblot 1905) 210.
204 Georg Jellinek, *Verfassungsänderung und Verfassungswandlung Eine staatsrechtlich-politische Abhandlung* (Verlag von O Häring 1906) 2-3, 9.
205 ibid 15.
206 ibid 5.
207 ibid 22.
208 Heinrich Triepel, 'Die Kompetenzen des Bundesstaats und die geschriebene Verfassung' in Wilhelm van Calker and others (eds), *Staatsrechtliche Abhandlungen Festgabe für Paul Laband zum fünfzigsten Jahrestage der Doktor-Promotion* (Mohr Siebeck 1908) vol 2 287, 316 and 335.
209 ibid 252, 256 ff., 278.

would be far easier to amend by way of formal amendment or through reinterpretation and reasoning based on analogy which he found difficult to sharply distinguish from each other.[210] While he accepted that unwritten competences could be based on customary law,[211] he did not elaborate on this legal concept and instead based his reasoning on the interpretation of the written document, analogical reasoning and the written text's "spirit" (*Geiste der Verfassung*).[212]

The three preceding approaches rested primarily on the written instrument, the application of which could involve analogical reasoning, progressive interpretation or constitutional transformation. It was Smend who directed the attention of the field to unwritten constitutional law as legal concept in the context of the relationship between the constitutive states and the Federal *Reich*.[213] Just as contracts had to be performed in good faith, the *Reichverfassung* had to be interpreted according to the principles of "*pacta sunt servanda*" and federal friendliness (*bundesfreundliche Gesinnung*). Compliance with these principles (*Grundsätze*) was not just based on political feasibility or determined by federal courtesy and tradition ("*bundesstaatliche Sitte und Herkommen*"), these principles were said to constitute the continuing legal basis and form of the federal relationship ("*dauernde Rechtsgrundlage und Rechtsform des bundesstaatlichen Gesamtverhältnisses*"). As to the relationship between written and unwritten law, he argued that the unwritten law would stand behind the text[214] and that it was not necessarily customary law.[215] Smend argued that a constitutional transformation (*Verfassungswandlung*) which changes the material content of the constitution would not be bound by the requirements regarding the formation of customary law.[216] Smend's approach distinguished itself from Jellinek by stressing the norma-

---

210 ibid 310, 313.
211 ibid 286.
212 ibid 334.
213 Rudolf Smend, 'Ungeschriebenes Verfassungsrecht im monarchischen Bundesstaat' in *Festgabe für Otto Mayer zum siebzigsten Geburtstag* (Mohr Siebeck 1916) 261. Cf. on Smend Gerhard Anschütz, 'Der deutsche Föderalismus in Vergangenheit, Gegenwart und Zukunft' (1924) 1 Veröffentlichungen der Vereinigung der Deutschen Staatsrechtslehrer 13; Peter Häberle, 'Zum Tode von Rudolf Smend' [1975] (41) Neue Juristische Wochenzeitschrift 1875.
214 Smend, 'Ungeschriebenes Verfassungsrecht im monarchischen Bundesstaat' 262.
215 Cf. ibid 255.
216 Rudolf Smend, 'Verfassung und Verfassungsrecht (1928)' in Rudolf Smend (ed), *Staatsrechtliche Abhandlungen und andere Aufsätze* (2nd edn, Duncker & Humblot 1968) 242.

Chapter 2: Comparative Perspectives

tive connection between the concept of *Verfassungswandlung* and the written constitution.[217]

With the fall of the Weimar Republic and the rise of the national socialist dictatorship in 1933, the law was subjected to the so-called "*Führer* command".[218] As expounded by Bernd Rüthers in his study on the "indefinite interpretation" of civil law in National Socialism, statutes' interpretation and application were governed by *völkisch* legal thinking and "concrete order thinking"[219] by which the law should be derived from the concrete order of the *völkisch* community.[220] Rüthers concluded that "[t]he national socialist theory of sources of law did not set forth a clear concept of source of law, nor did it rank the many sources of law-creation", besides the primacy of the proclaimed dictator will.[221]

---

217 Smend, 'Verfassung und Verfassungsrecht (1928)' 188; see also Korioth, *Integration und Bundesstaat Ein Beitrag zur Staats- und Verfassungslehre Rudolf Smends* 57 and 61.
218 Michael Stolleis, *A History of Public Law in Germany 1914-1945* (Oxford University Press 2004) 395; see also on the international law scholarship in Germany at 416: "Two aspects are characteristic for the state of the discipline of international law up to 1939: first, its ineluctable and growing politicization, which threatened its scholarly character at its very core; second, the uncertainty about the methodological foundations, since all previous sources of law—natural law, the universally accepted international customary law, external state law, and the 'basic norm' of the Vienna School—were cast aside. The '*völkisch* idea' proclaimed in its place was a legally useless propaganda slogan, and it was not accepted internationally." On this topic see also Detlev F Vagts, 'International Law in the Third Reich' (1990) 84 American Journal of International Law 661 ff.
219 This translation for "konkretes Ordnungsdenken" was borrowed from Stolleis, *A History of Public Law in Germany 1914-1945* 396.
220 Bernd Rüthers, *Die unbegrenzte Auslegung* (8th edn, Mohr Siebeck 2017) 124.
221 Translation by the present author of ibid 134: "Die nationalsozialistische Rechtsquellentheorie hat weder einen klaren Begriff der Rechtsquelle noch eine Rangfolge der vielen Quellgebiete der Rechtsschöpfung, die in ihr beschrieben wurden, hervorgebracht."; on the subsequent discussions of so-called Radbruch thesis and the debate on the validity of statutory law, natural law and positivism, cf. Gustav Radbruch, 'Gesetzliches Unrecht und übergesetzliches Recht' (1946) 1(5) Süddeutsche Juristenzeitung 105-108; Herbert LA Hart, 'Positivism and the Separation of Law and Morals' (1958) 71(4) Harvard Law Review 616-621; Fuller, 'Positivism and Fidelity to Law: A Reply to Professor Hart' 651 ff; Stanley L Paulson, 'Lon L. Fuller, Gustav Radbruch, and the 'Positivist' Theses' (1994) 13(3) Law and Philosophy 313 ff.

3. Approaches under the Basic law

Since the establishment of the Federal Constitutional Court under the Basic Law, the focus on the interpretation of the constitution was accompanied by the studies on judicial law (*Richterrecht*) and the act of concretization of general rules of the constitution (*Verfassungskonkretisierung*).[222] Christian Tomuschat considered in his *Habilitation* customary constitutional law to be a concept of a bygone age which would no longer fit to the conditions of modern life in the constitutional context.[223] The so-called "*Richterrecht*", the concretization of general rules by judicial application, the subtle normative differentiation between a norm and the practice interpreting the norm, the mutual conditionality between norm and norm-application ("*wechselseitige Bedingtheit von Rechtsnorm und Rechtsanwendung*") would be better suited to introduce flexibility, if needed.[224] Customary law was associated with the risk of petrification, rather than with an element that keeps the law in flux.[225] For Tomuschat, customary law and the constitution would constitute different and distinct sources which would not be capable of forming a symbiotic relationship. Rather, the relationship would be one of competition rivalry and of displacement.[226]

There were proposals for a continuing usefulness of the concept of customary law: scholars pointed out that customary law could operate as limit to judicial law[227], that it could be positioned in a symbiotic relationship with the

---

222 Wolff, *Ungeschriebenes Verfassungsrecht unter dem Grundgesetz* 176-177; Peter Badura, 'Verfassungsänderung, Verfassungswandel, Verfassungsgewohnheitsrecht' in Josef Isensee and Paul Kirchhof (eds), *Handbuch des Staatsrechts der Bundesrepublik Deutschland* (CF Müller 1992) vol VII 62 para 10.

223 Tomuschat, *Verfassungsgewohnheitsrecht? Eine Untersuchung zum Staatsrecht der Bundesrepublik Deutschland* 9: "Die Lehre vom Gewohnheitsrecht, einst Prunkstück der deutschen Rechtswissenschaft, scheint nicht recht in das heutige Verfassungsleben zu passen."

224 ibid 152-153. In this light, Häberle opined that customary law would be only useful if one adopted a narrow understanding of the doctrine of interpretation applied to the written constitution, Peter Häberle, 'Verfassungstheorie ohne Naturrecht' (1974) 99 Archiv des öffentlichen Rechts 443-444 footnote 37.

225 Tomuschat, *Verfassungsgewohnheitsrecht? Eine Untersuchung zum Staatsrecht der Bundesrepublik Deutschland* 151.

226 ibid 51.

227 Pieroth, *Rückwirkung und Übergangsrecht Verfassungsrechtliche Maßstäbe für intertemporale Gesetzgebung* 272-273.

written constitution and be interpreted in relation to the latter.[228] In the end, customary law did not prevail and alternative doctrines that were attached to the interpretation of the written law and the judicial interpretation, application and development of the law asserted themselves successfully.[229] There may be unwritten rules in isolated instances, for instance in German state liability law, provided that those are not derived from or related to written provisions;[230] there is not, as Uwe Kischel has noted, "a general aversion to the concept of customary law, but rather a lack of familiarity (in Germany) — although every lawyer has heard of customary law, almost none would imagine actually using it in practice."[231]

D. Characteristics of general principles of law from a comparative historical perspective

The last part of this chapter is dedicated to the concept of principles of law. No attempt is made to illustrate the role of "principles" in the history of legal thought.[232] Robert Kolb has described how since the antiquity the concept of general principles had served the purpose of systematizing the law and of accumulating legal experiences in the interpretation and application of specific rules in concrete cases; for this purposes, analogies were drawn and

---

228 Brun-Otto Bryde, *Verfassungsentwicklung: Stabilität und Dynamik im Verfassungsrecht der Bundesrepublik Deutschland* (Nomos 1982) 446; Wolff, *Ungeschriebenes Verfassungsrecht unter dem Grundgesetz* 344.
229 The concept of custom has lost support also in administrative law, as scholars turned to role of judges in the development of the law, on this development see Jeong Hoon Park, *Rechtsfindung im Verwaltungsrecht: Grundlegung einer Prinzipientheorie des Verwaltungsrechts als Methode der Verwaltungsrechtsdogmatik* (Duncker & Humblot 1999) 147-184.
230 See Uwe Kischel, *Comparative Law* (Oxford University Press 2019) 368 for the example of the so-called claim for remedy of legal consequences (*Folgenbeseitigungsanspruch*) concerning the rectification of the effects of unlawful state conduct which legal commentators base on analogies to provisions of the civil code, on a general principle of law or customary law.
231 ibid 368.
232 For such overviews see Sigrid Jacoby, *Allgemeine Rechtsgrundsätze Begriffsentwicklung und Funktion in der Europäischen Rechtsgeschichte* (Duncker & Humblot 1996) 23 ff.; Franz Reimer, *Verfassungsprinzipien Ein Normtyp im Grundgesetz* (Duncker & Humblot 2001) 146 ff.; Kolb, 'Les maximes juridiques en droit international public: questions historiques et théoriques' 407 ff.

Characteristics of general principles of law from a comparative historical perspective

common principles were extrapolated from a mass of single cases. This doctrinal effort met a pressing need over the centuries and in particular in light of the structural transformations in the medieval society, the increased mobility of social actors and the increase of transborder commercial relations.[233] By representing the essence of law and legal experience, general principles of law were linked by some to natural law or the *jus gentium*.[234] General principles commended themselves in international disputes, they asserted themselves in national codifications as well as in international arbitration even during the rise of positivism and dualism in the 19th century.[235]

Rather than revisiting this legal history of general principles, this section concentrates on trends relating to the concept of principles in modern legal thinking against the background of experiences described previously in this chapter: the emphasis on the systematic character of the law by Friedrich Carl von Savigny and Friedrich Puchta; Rudolf Jhering's focus on concepts common to different legal systems; the observation by François Gény and Raymond Saleilles that law may undergo a development not necessarily intended by the legislator of statutes; the insights articulated by Roscoe Pound and Benjamin Cardozo that principles perform an important part in the interpretation of the written law; the recent common law history in the UK as a testimony for the interpretation of unwritten law in light of the normative environment; and the recognition of the importance of the judge in concretizing general and abstract rules which would play an important part in later doctrinal works that originated at the beginning of the 20th century.[236]

---

233 Kolb, *La bonne foi en droit international public Contribution à l'étude des principes généraux de droit* 16-17.
234 See for an overview Degan, 'General Principles of Law (A Source of General International Law)' 6 ff.; see also Kolb, 'Les maximes juridiques en droit international public: questions historiques et théoriques' 413 ff., describing that maxims of law were only non-normative proposals resulting from experience whereas general principles of law is a normative concept which fits to the idea of law as a source-based system.
235 Kolb, *La bonne foi en droit international public Contribution à l'étude des principes généraux de droit* 23-24.
236 See Gény, *Méthode D'Interprétation et Sources en Droit Privé Positif: Essai Critique* 78, 147. The above-mentioned authors partially referred to each other, see for instance Cardozo, *The Nature of the Judicial Process* 16 (reference to Gény), 102 (reference to Jhering).

Chapter 2: Comparative Perspectives

The current section will first present an overview of general principles before delving into specific aspects.[237]

I. General principles in legal theory: an overview

General principles can be classified according to different categories and functions, which cannot always be clearly separated from each other[238]: there are general principles of law which are an expression of the integrity of law as force different from mere power, politics or arbitrariness, and an expression of the judicial process, embodying concepts that are necessary for law to perform its function in a society,[239] for instance *pacta sunt servanda*, good faith, abuse of rights, reasonableness and proportionality. Then there are rather technical principles relating to legal logic, such as *lex specialis* or *lex posterior*; additionally, there are general principles expressing the basic evaluations and values which underline specific rules as ascertained

---

237 This section focuses on scholarship about general principles of law and legal principles of a group of authors which includes, without being limited to, international law scholars. The reason for not strictly separating international law scholars and domestic law scholars is that both groups referred to each other and that the concept of general principles can be found both on the domestic and on the international level. The next subsection draws on Matthias Lippold, 'The Interpretation of UN Security Council Resolutions between Regional and General International Law: What Role for General Principles?' in Mads Andenæs and others (eds), *General Principles and the Coherence of International Law* (Brill Nijhoff 2019) 151-153.
238 For similar taxonomies see Esser, *Grundsatz und Norm in der richterlichen Fortbildung des Privatrechts Rechtsvergleichende Beiträge zur Rechtsquellen- und Interpretationslehre* 36-38ff, 73-75, 90-92; Martti Koskenniemi, 'General principles: reflexions on constructivist thinking in international law' (1985) 18 Oikeustiedejurisprudentia 124 f., republished in Martti Koskenniemi, 'General Principles: Reflexions on Constructivist Thinking in International Law' in Martti Koskenniemi (ed), *Sources of International Law* (Routledge 2000) 359-402; Schachter, 'International Law in Theory and Practice: general course in public international law' 75 ff.; Robert Kolb, *Theory of international law* (Hart Publishing 2016) 136-144.
239 Cf. Franz Bydlinski, *Fundamentale Rechtsgrundsätze Zur rechtsethischen Verfassung der Sozietät* (Springer 1988) 128 and 131, according to whom one of the key characteristics of principles is to ensure a minimum content of the positive law.

by induction or extrapolation,[240] and general principles based on analogies from other branches of law or legal orders.

The focus on the distinction between 'rule' and 'principle',[241] *Rechtssatz* and *Rechtsgrundsatz*,[242] *Regel* und *Prinzip*,[243] *regles juridiques* and *principes*,[244] should not obscure the significance of the interrelationship between rules and principles, which to a certain extent arguably relativizes the importance of the debate on whether the difference between rules and principles is one of kind[245] or one of degree.[246] Principles can emerge from and through the interpretation of the law and unfold themselves in respect of their meaning in

---

240 Sometimes, this kind of principle is classified as a descriptive, as opposed to a normative, principle. Since even these descriptive principles can have "normative consequences" in the interpretation of law, the classification should not be overemphasized, see Koskenniemi, 'General principles: reflexions on constructivist thinking in international law' 128.
241 Ronald Dworkin, 'The Model of Rules' (1967) 35(1) University of Chicago Law Review 25: "The difference between legal principles and legal rules is a logical distinction"; Ronald Dworkin, *Taking Rights Seriously* (Harvard Univ Press 1977) 24; cf. for a similar Scandinavian distinction Koskenniemi, 'General principles: reflexions on constructivist thinking in international law' 134-135 with reference to the work of Torsten Eckhoff and Nils Sundby according to whom rules either would or would not apply, whereas 'guidelines' would operate as arguments that have to be weighed; cf. Torstein Eckhoff, 'Guiding Standards in Legal Reasoning' (1976) 29(1) Current Legal Problems 205 ff.
242 Hermann Heller, *Die Souveränität: ein Beitrag zur Theorie des Staats- und Völkerrechts* (de Gruyter 1927) 127.
243 Robert Alexy, *Theorie der Grundrechte* (Nomos-Verl-Ges 1985) 71 ff. Alexy argued that principles are optimisation requirements in the sense that principles require to be realised to the greatest extent possible in a given situation.
244 Jean Boulanger, 'Principes Généraux du Droit et Droit Positif' in *Le Droit Privé Français au Milieu Du XXe Siècle études Offertes à Georges Ripert* (Libr générale de droit et de jurisprudence 1950) vol 1 55.
245 Dworkin, 'The Model of Rules' 25; Alexy, *Theorie der Grundrechte* 75-76; balanced view: Joseph Raz, 'Legal Principles and the Limits of Law' (1971) 81 Yale Law Journal 834-838, who makes a logical distinction which however would not play out in practice.
246 Hart, *The concept of law: With a postscript* 261-262, 265 (contra a sharp distinction between legal principles and legal rules as suggested by Dworkin); MacCormick, *Legal Reasoning and Legal Theory* 155, 232, where he pointed out that rules can be applied by analogy and therefore would not apply in such a rigid fashion as stipulated by Dworkin; Melvin Aron Eisenberg, *The Nature of the Common Law* (Harvard Univ Press 1988) 77 (no logical distinction); Matthias Goldmann, 'Dogmatik als Rationale Rekonstruktion: Versuch einer Metatheorie am Beispiel völkerrechtlicher

relation to and in interaction with other principles, rules and the normative environment.[247] They can emerge from the continuous judicial application of functionally similar legal standards,[248] reflect the *rationes legis*, the basic evaluations and structure of the legal system, even the understandings of justice and ethics of the respective community as expressed in the law.[249]

Given their degree of generality and abstraction as well as their ascertainment by way of extrapolation, principles cannot, in general, be "conclusive in the way which [...] mandatory rules may be"[250] or, to borrow from Lord McNair, generally be applied "lock, stock and barrel".[251] They need to be balanced against other principles, thereby admitting countervailing considerations, and be adapted to the specific context.[252] This process can entail a

---

Prinzipien' (2014) 53(3) Der Staat 376; András Jakab, *European Constitutional Language* (Cambridge University Press 2016) 370 ff.

247 Claus-Wilhelm Canaris, *Systemdenken und Systembegriff in der Jurisprudenz: entwickelt am Beispiel des deutschen Privatrechts* (2nd edn, Duncker & Humblot 1983) 52, 57; cf. also Giorgio Del Vecchio, *Die Grundprinzipien des Rechts* (Rothschild 1923) 18, 22, stressing that rules and principles need to be construed together in harmony by the jurist.

248 Esser, *Grundsatz und Norm in der richterlichen Fortbildung des Privatrechts Rechtsvergleichende Beiträge zur Rechtsquellen- und Interpretationslehre* 100.

249 ibid 134; MacCormick, *Legal Reasoning and Legal Theory* 235-236; Meinhard Hilf and Goetz J Goettsche, 'The Relation of Economic and Non-economic Principles in International Law' in Stefan Griller (ed), *International economic governance and non-economic concerns: new challenges for the international legal order* (Springer 2003) 9-10: principles express "fundamental legal concepts and essential values of any legal system".

250 MacCormick, *Legal Reasoning and Legal Theory* 180; Metzger, *Extra legem, intra ius: allgemeine Rechtsgrundsätze im Europäischen Privatrecht* 52 on induction and the risk of the naturalistic fallacy to derive an ought from an is; on the generality, see also Eisenberg, *The Nature of the Common Law* 77; cf. Robert Alexy, 'Zum Begriff des Rechtsprinzip' (1979) Beiheft 1 Rechtstheorie 79, 81-82, explaining the generality of principles by their character as 'ideal ought' which has not been conditioned yet by factual and normative limitations.

251 *International Status of South West Africa* 128, Sep Op McNair 148; see also Weil, 'Le droit international en quête de son identité: cours général de droit international public' 148, pointing out that even within one municipal legal order the same principles may appear differently in different branches of law.

252 Canaris, *Systemdenken und Systembegriff in der Jurisprudenz: entwickelt am Beispiel des deutschen Privatrechts* 52, 57; in the right institutional setting, for instance in an adversarial adjudicatory context, principles can function like rules in the sense that on their bases cases can be decided, Kolb, 'Principles as Sources of International Law (With Special Reference to Good Faith)' 11-12, referring to *Temple of Preah*

Characteristics of general principles of law from a comparative historical perspective

mutual elucidation: the content of a principle becomes concretized through subprinciples, rules and judgments, and the content of a rule can be determined by reference to principles.[253] By taking recourse to general principles, the interpreter can relate the rule to be applied to its broader normative environment and make a choice between different interpretations of the rule; in this sense, principles constitute reasons[254], they can define argumentative starting points or shift burdens of argumentation.[255] They are not mere gap-fillers[256], they can help in identifying teleological gaps in the first place.[257]

Vihear (Cambodia v. Thailand) (Judgment) [1962] ICJ Rep 23, 26, 32 where the case was decided on the basis of general principles such as acquiescence and estoppel.
253 MacCormick, *Legal Reasoning and Legal Theory* 235-246; cf. Peter Liver, 'Der Begriff der Rechtsquelle' in Schweizerischer Juristenverein (ed), *Rechtsquellenprobleme im schweizerischen Recht* (Stämpfli 1955) 27; Karl Larenz, *Methodenlehre der Rechtswissenschaft* (3rd edn, Springer 1975) 458-463.
254 Gerald Fitzmaurice, 'The General Principles of International Law considered from the standpoint of the rule of law' (1957) 92 RdC 7: "A rule answers the question 'what': a principle in effect answers the question 'why'."
255 Esser, *Grundsatz und Norm in der richterlichen Fortbildung des Privatrechts Rechtsvergleichende Beiträge zur Rechtsquellen- und Interpretationslehre* 52, 82; Ronald Dworkin, *Law's Empire* (Harvard Univ Press 1986) 243 ff., 263: the interpreter should be guided by a a commitment to law's integrity, assuming that law was structured by a 'coherent set of principles' about justice, fairness and due process; Armin von Bogdandy, 'Grundprinzipien' in Armin von Bogdandy and Jürgen Bast (eds), *Europäisches Verfassungsrecht: theoretische und dogmatische Grundzüge* (2nd edn, Springer 2009) 21 (on principles imposing burdens of argumentation).
256 On the gap-filling function see already Cardozo, *The Nature of the Judicial Process* 71.
257 Claus-Wilhelm Canaris, *Die Feststellung von Lücken im Gesetz: eine methodologische Studie über Voraussetzungen und Grenzen der richterlichen Rechtsfortbildung praeter legem* (2nd edn, Duncker und Humblot 1983) 16-17, 32-33, 37-39, 55-56, 93-94; Lauterpacht, *The Function of Law in the International Community* 64-86 (distinguishing between a formal completeness and a material completeness of a legal system); on the potential of general principles to enable critique of the law see Helmut Coing, *Die obersten Grundsätze des Rechts Ein Versuch zur Neugründung des Naturrechts* (Lambert Schneider 1947) 150ff.; Emmanuel Voyiakis, 'Do General Principles Fill 'Gaps' in International Law?' (2009) 14 Austrian Review of International and European Law 246 ff. (critical of principles as mere gap-fillers). But cf. Jörg Kammerhofer, 'Gaps, the Nuclear Weapons Advisory Opinion and the Structure of International Legal Argument between Theory and Practice' (2010) 80 BYIL 355, arguing that "[t]he distinction of the reference point from within *Recht*, yet outside *Gesetz* (positive law) means transcending positive law for an extra-positive value-judgment. The 'demand' is in effect created by legal scholars, who put their

II. Conceptualizations of legal validity and different degrees of normativity of general principles

The answer to the question of whether general principles constitute valid law ultimately also depends on one's concept of law.[258] For the purposes of illustration, the different perspectives are exemplified by way of reference to the work of Josef Esser and Hans Kelsen. Subsequently, this section will focus on different ways of conceptualizing the legal validity of principles and on the different degrees of normativity of principles.

1. Reflections on the scholarship of Josef Esser and Hans Kelsen's response

Josef Esser focused on the positivization of principles. Under the intellectual influence of authors such as François Gény, Roscoe Pound and Benjamin Cardozo who had stressed the "law in action", Josef Esser developed a

---

personal views of what the law should be in place of what the law is (with all its 'imperfections')."
258 Cf. Roberto Ago, 'Positive Law and International Law' (1957) 51 AJIL 698-699, 724 ff., 728-733, arguing that certain prevonceived ideas of positivism equating the latter with voluntarism, and the label of positivism as such, prevent legal science from studying legal norms which were not "laid down" by a source; Metzger, *Extra legem, intra ius: allgemeine Rechtsgrundsätze im Europäischen Privatrecht* 83 ff. (distinguishing between *Setzungspositivismus* und *Anerkennungspositivismus*).

sophisticated account of legal principles.[259] For Esser, as translated by the present author,

> "positive law includes not only rules ready to apply but also the general legal ideas, the *rationes legis*, the basic evaluations and structural principles of one system, but also the principles of legal-ethical character relating to justice of a legal order, insofar as they have asserted themselves within specific legal institutes. Beyond that, they are guides or *principi informatori* for the law-applying authorities just like all maxims or rules of the past as expression of judicial experience."[260]

Esser highlighted that principles which derive from the overall system would not only in hard cases but constantly inform the interpretation and application of rules[261]: the law would not derive from rules, the rules would derive from the *corpus iuris*.[262] This interplay between principles and norms and the

---

259 Esser, *Grundsatz und Norm in der richterlichen Fortbildung des Privatrechts Rechtsvergleichende Beiträge zur Rechtsquellen- und Interpretationslehre*. Esser's account was not translated into English which might have impacted its reception over time. At the time of publication, it received critical acclaim internationally, see Wolfgang Friedmann, 'Review of Grundsatz und Norm in der richterlichen Fortbildung des Privatrechts by Josef Esser' (1957) 57(3) Columbia Law Review 449 ("one of the most significant, enlightened, and scholarly contributions to the comparative study of the judicial process ever made."); Max Rheinstein, 'Book Review Grundsatz und Norm in der richterlichen Fortbildung des Privatrechts: Rechtsvergleichende Beitraege zur Rechtsquellen- und Interpretationslehre (Principle and Norm in the Judicial Development of Private Law: A Comparative Inquiry into the Problems of the Sources of Law and Their Interpretation) by Joseph Esser' (1957) 24(3) The University of Chicago Law Review 606; on the reception of Esser in Spanish and Italian literature see José Antonio Ramos Pascua, 'Die Grundlage rechtlicher Geltung von Prinzipien- eine Gegenüberstellung von Dworkin und Esser' in Giuseppe Orsi and others (eds), *Prinzipien des Rechts* (Lang 1996) 8 ff.; see also Kolb, *Interprétation et création du droit international. Esquisse d'une herméneutique juridique moderne pour le droit international public* 48.

260 Esser, *Grundsatz und Norm in der richterlichen Fortbildung des Privatrechts Rechtsvergleichende Beiträge zur Rechtsquellen- und Interpretationslehre* 134: "[...] positives Recht, wenn auch nicht selbständig fertige Rechtssätze (rules), sind die sog. allgemeinen Rechtsgedanken, die rationes legis, die Wertungsgrundsaätze und Aufbauprinzipien eines Systems, aber auch die rechtsethischen und Gerechtigkeitsprinzipien eines Rechtskreises, außerhalb seines Schulsystems - alle, soweit sie sich in konkreten Ordnungsformen Geltung verschafft haben. Darüber hinaus sind sie guides oder principi informatori für die rechtsbildenden Organe, wie es alle Maximen und Regeln überlieferter Problemlösungen sind, welche richterliche Erfahrung verkörpern."

261 ibid 149, 219, 253, 264, 287.

262 ibid 309, see also on the stabilizing force of legal principles at 300.

contextuality of principles in need of a structure to operate in have the consequence that principles' precise effects depend on the normative and institutional context, and, last but not least, on the legal operator. For, as translated by the present author, "it is not the principles acting but the legal operator. The question of the correct relation cannot be answered on the basis of the legal system alone without investigating the conflicts [which the legal system seeks to address, M.L.]."[263]

Hans Kelsen critically engaged with the writing of Josef Esser in his *post mortem* published treatise on a general theory of norms.[264] There was agreement on some level, namely that the continuous application of law by courts may create norms and that what Esser described as principles may inform the judges' decisionmaking. In Kelsen's view, however, these principles were no legal norms, nor would these principles become law through continuous application by courts. At best, they may resemble the norms created by courts. Kelsen argued that courts can create general, as opposed to individual, norms through through custom based on a constant jurisprudence (*"im Wege einer durch ständige Judikatur der Gerichte konstituierten Gewohnheit"*):[265] By virtue of the principle of *res judicata* (*Rechtskraft*), courts would possess an almost unfettered (*"beinahe unbeschränkte"*) power which, however, they would rarely make use of. This strong position of courts is characteristic of Kelsen's model which will be explained in more detail in the next chapter[266]: a court makes a decision between possible interpretations of a higher norm and then creates a norm, and this decision is determined by the court alone and not by any natural law or binding principles.[267]

---

263 Josef Esser, *Vorverständnis und Methodenwahl in der Rechtsfindung: Rationalitätsgarantien der richterlichen Entscheidungspraxis* (Altenhäum Verlag 1970) 100: "Nicht die Prinzipien agieren, sondern der Rechtsfinder. Die richtige Relation ist nicht ohne Befragung der Konfliktprobleme aus dem System zu entnehmen."
264 Hans Kelsen, *Allgemeine Theorie der Normen* (Manz 1979) 92-99; Hans Kelsen, *General Theory of Norms* (Clarendon Press 1991) 115-122.
265 Kelsen, *Allgemeine Theorie der Normen* 92-93.
266 See below, p. 195.
267 See also Jochen von Bernstorff, 'Specialized Courts and Tribunals as the Guardians of International Law? The Nature and Function of Judicial Interpretation in Kelsen and Schmitt' in Andreas Føllesdal and Geir Ulfstein (eds), *The judicialization of international law: a mixed blessing?* (Oxford University Press 2018) 15 ("The intrusion of the judge's subjective value judgements into decisions of the court should not be glossed over by the seeming objectivity of the theories of interpretation. Instead, Kelsen construed the scientifically uncontrollable factor as an act of law-making of the judge that was authorized by the legal system.") and 16 (on the potential use

2. Conceptualizations of legal validity and different degrees of normativity of general principles

Scholars suggest different bases for the legal validity of general principles. Canaris, for instance, submitted three different grounds of the validity of legal principles[268]: firstly, specific provisions of statutory law from which general principles have been ascertained by way of induction and in which principles have found some, yet incomplete, degree of realization (*unvollkommene Verwirklichung*)[269]; secondly, the very idea of law (*Rechtsidee*), including equality before the law of the prohibition of arbitrariness or the consistency of the legal order. Reasoning on the basis of the idea of law would often start with the "discovery" of the solution to legal problem, proceeds to the formulation of a legal idea (*Rechtsgedanke*) which by reference to examples would be shaped and hardened to a principle.[270] Thirdly, he suggested rational

---

of principles in the lawcreation by courts); as argued by Ewald Wiederin, 'Regel-Prinzip-Norm. Zu einer Kontroverse zwischen Hans Kelsen und Josef Esser' in Stanley L Paulson and Robert Walter (eds), *Untersuchungen zur Reinen Rechtslehre Ergebnisse eines Wiener Rechtstheoretischen Seminars 1985/1986* (Manzsche Verlags- und Universitätsbuchhandlung 1986) 155-156, whilst Esser and Kelsen accepted judicial lawmaking, they differed on the limits and the normative framework of this exercise; see also Iain GM Scobbie, 'The Theorist as Judge: Hersch Lauterpacht's Concept of the International Judicial Function' (1997) 2 EJIL 269; cf. Frederick Schauer, 'Fuller and Kelsen - Fuller on Kelsen' in Matthias Jestaedt, Ralf Poscher, and Jörg Kammerhofer (eds), *Die Reine Rechtslehre auf dem Prüfstand. Hans Kelsen's Pure Theory of Law: Conceptions and Misconceptions* (Franz Steiner Verlag 2020) 309-318, arguing that Fuller's (and later Dworkin's) focus on lawyers and judges can explain different perspectives on the law between Fuller and Kelsen who, in contrast, refrained from explaining of how judges should interpret and apply a rule, see also below, p. 196 (on Kelsen) and p. 210 (on Lauterpacht and Kelsen); cf. also Alexandre Travessoni Gomes Trivisonno, 'Legal Principles, Discretion and Legal Positivism: Does Dworkin's Criticism on Hart also Apply to Kelsen?' (2016) 102 Archiv für Rechts- und Sozialphilosophie 118, 121-125; cf. also Jörg Kammerhofer, 'Positivist Approaches and International Adjudication' [2019] Max Planck EiPro para 2 ("One could almost say that the more a theory is about adjudication, the less likely it is to be positivist").

268 Canaris, *Die Feststellung von Lücken im Gesetz: eine methodologische Studie über Voraussetzungen und Grenzen der richterlichen Rechtsfortbildung praeter legem* 96-100.
269 ibid 96-106.
270 ibid 106-107.

Chapter 2: Comparative Perspectives

considerations (*Natur der Sache*) which could not explain normative validity but which could operate as an interpretative guide, since the legal order could be presumed to adopt a solution which would accommodate practical realities.[271] Canaris stressed that a principle might derive its force from the idea of law (positive justification) but must not be opposed by the positive legal order (negative delimitation).[272] The farther away a principle would be from the positive rules and the closer it would be to the idea of law as such, the higher would be the principle's abstractness and the lesser might be the likelihood of the principle's concrete legal relevance and applicability.[273]

Other scholars focus on the recognition of legal principles in a given legal system for the validity of these principles.[274] In the view of Neil MacCormick, for instance, "if (one) seek(s) to ascertain the principles of a given system, (one) ought to search for those general norms which the functionaries of the system regard as having, on the ground of their generality and positive value, the relevant justificatory and explanatory function in relation to the valid rules of the system."[275]

Two scholars who are often discussed in relation to principles, Ronald Dworkin and Robert Alexy,[276] have focused on the distinction between rules and principles.

---

271 Canaris, *Die Feststellung von Lücken im Gesetz: eine methodologische Studie über Voraussetzungen und Grenzen der richterlichen Rechtsfortbildung praeter legem* 118-121; similarly already Liver, 'Der Begriff der Rechtsquelle' 43.
272 Canaris, *Die Feststellung von Lücken im Gesetz: eine methodologische Studie über Voraussetzungen und Grenzen der richterlichen Rechtsfortbildung praeter legem* 108, 113.
273 ibid 114.
274 See also Metzger, *Extra legem, intra ius: allgemeine Rechtsgrundsätze im Europäischen Privatrecht* 85 ff.; cf. also Ago, 'Positive Law and International Law' 698-699, 724 ff., 728-733.
275 MacCormick, *Legal Reasoning and Legal Theory* 152-153; Hart, *The concept of law: With a postscript* 265-267 (principles could be identified by pedigree in that they have been consistently invoked by courts).
276 See for instance for an approach based on Alexy's doctrine of principles Petersen, 'Customary Law Without Custom? Rules, Principles, and the Role of State Practice in International Norm Creation' 286 ff.; for an approach relying on Dworkin see John Tasioulas, 'In Defense of Relative Normativity: Communitarian Values and the Nicaragua Case' (1996) 16(1) Oxford Journal of Legal Studies 85 ff.; for an approach informed by Dworkin and a Rawlsian reflective equilibrium see Anthea Roberts, 'Traditional and Modern Approaches to Customary International Law: A Reconciliation' (2001) 95 AJIL 774 ff.

Dworkin's doctrine originated in a debate with H.L.A. Hart's positivism.[277] Dworkin stressed in his early work a "logical distinction" between rules and principles. The former apply in an all-or-nothing fashion, whereas a principle "states a reason that argues in one direction, but does not necessitate a particular decision".[278] In contrast to rules, principles were said to have "a dimension of weight or importance".[279] A conflict between principles would be resolved by taking into account the relative weight of each principle; in a conflict between rules, however, only one rule could be a valid rule.[280] Dworkin's later work on interpretivism focuses on the integrity of law.[281] This integrity of law would be both the product of and the inspiration for "comprehensive interpretation of legal practice" which consists of statutes, judgments and principles flowing therefrom.[282] The judge would have to base her judgment not on policy for this is the competence of the legislator, but on principles, guided by a "spirit of integrity" and a commitment to law's integrity from which the judge derives her authority, assuming that law was structured "by a coherent set of principles" about justice, fairness and due

---

277 See on the debate on whether the judge has "discretion" in "positivism" Dworkin, 'The Model of Rules' 17 ff.; cf erview of the debate Johannes Saurer, 'Die Hart-Dworkin-Debatte als Grundlagenkontroverse der angloamerikanischen Rechtsphilosophie: Versuch einer Rekonstruktion nach fürnf Jahrzehnten' (2012) 98 Archiv für Rechts- und Sozialphilosophie 214 ff.; cf. for a comparison of Dworkin and Esser András Jakab, 'Prinzipien' (2006) 37 Rechtstheorie 49-50 and, following Jakab, Kleinlein, *Konstitutionalisierung im Völkerrecht Konstruktion und Elemente einer idealistischen Völkerrechtslehre* 665, both arguing that Dworkin's account is different from Esser's account because principles led to a greater liberty of the judge in Esser's account while principles restricted judicial discretion in Dworkin's account. However, as described above, principles inform in Esser's account the judges' application of law and have insofar a guiding function. The fact that the principles may appear more dynamic in Esser's account than in Dworkin may perhaps be attributed to the difference between civil law, where new institutes and principles arose more frequently than in constitutional law where the principles as such are often derived from the written constitution, cf. Metzger, *Extra legem, intra ius: allgemeine Rechtsgrundsätze im Europäischen Privatrecht* 27 footnote 55.
278 Dworkin, 'The Model of Rules' 25-26.
279 ibid 27.
280 ibid 27.
281 Dworkin, *Law's Empire*.
282 ibid 226 and 245; cf critically Robert Alexy, *Recht, Vernunft, Diskurs: Studien zur Rechtsphilosophie* (Suhrkamp 1995) 88 (the institutionalized juristic system is necessarily incomplete).

Chapter 2: Comparative Perspectives

process.[283] In particular, this interpretative approach would apply generally, not only in "hard" cases, since the very question of whether a case is a hard case is the result, not the starting point, of interpretation.[284]

Robert Alexy defined principles in his dissertation as "normative propositions of high generality".[285] Analyzing the structure of (constitutional) norms in his *Habilitation*, Alexy argued that the theoretical distinction between rules and principles could explain constitutional legal phenomena such as the balancing of constitutional rights or their impact in the interpretation of statutory law.[286] Alexy postulated a so-called strong separation thesis with respect to rules and principles. Whereas rules would be either fulfilled or not fulfilled, principles would be optimization requirements, that is "norms requiring that something be realized to the greatest extent possible, given the legal and factual possibilities".[287] They would represent an "ideal ought".[288] The extent to which this ideal ought could be realized would depend on opposing principles and rules.[289] If a conflict between rules could not be resolved by reading an exception into one rule, conflicts would be resolved

---

283 Dworkin, *Law's Empire* 243, 245, 263.
284 Dworkin's early work suggested the applicability in hard cases, Ronald Dworkin, 'Hard Cases' (1975) 88(6) Harvard Law Review 1057 ff. He clarified his view later, see Dworkin, *Law's Empire* 255-256, 266, 351: distinction would be "just an expository device", 354; see also Neil MacCormick, *Legal Reasoning and Legal Theory* (Clarendon Press, Oxford University Press 1978) 231.
285 Robert Alexy, *Theorie der juristischen Argumentation Die Theorie des rationalen Diskurses als Theorie der juristischen Begründung* (Suhrkamp 1978) 299 footnote 81, 319 (own translation).
286 Alexy, *Theorie der Grundrechte* 71; Robert Alexy, 'Grundrechte als Subjektive Rechte und als Objektive Normen' (1990) 29 Der Staat 54 ff.
287 Robert Alexy, 'Constitutional Rights, Balancing, and Rationality' (2003) 16(2) Ratio Juris 135; cf. for criticism Peter Lerche, 'Die Verfassung als Quelle von Optimierungsgeboten?' in Joachim Burmeister (ed), *Verfassungsstaatlichkeit Festschrift für Klaus Stern zum 65. Geburtstag* (Beck 1997) 202-206; Ralf Poscher, 'Theorie eines Phantoms - Die erfolglose der Prinzipientheorie nach ihrem Gegenstand' (2010) 4 Rechtswissenschaft 356, 367-368, 370-371, against the distinction between rules and principles as matter of legal theory; For an overview of the critique and his proposal to distinguish between rules, relative principles and absolute principles see Karsten Nowrot, *Das Republikprinzip in der Rechtsordnungengemeinschaft* (Mohr Siebeck 2014) 506 ff.
288 Alexy, 'Zum Begriff des Rechtsprinzip' 79-82; Robert Alexy, *A Theory of Constitutional Rights* (Oxford University Press 2002) 82; Alexy, *Theorie der Grundrechte* 75-76.
289 Alexy, *A Theory of Constitutional Rights* 48.

at the level of validity; in contrast, "the solution of the competition between principles consists in establishing a conditional relation of precedence between the principles in light of the circumstances in the case."[290] While a principle could be trumped in a specific case, a rule would not be necessarily trumped if the rule's underlying principle was trumped, as other, so-called formal principles according to which lawfully enacted rules or established practice must be followed might support the rule.[291]

III. Assessment: recognizing the multifaceted character of general principles

The approaches described in this section illustrate the multifaceted character of general principles and their interplay with other principles, rules and the legal system. The concept of general principles of law often is based on the insight that law evolves and that the law in action might be different from the law in the books as originally envisaged. In this sense, theories on general principles may be seen as implying a certain relativisation of the original lawmaker's subjective intent.[292] At the same time, judges were not supposed to enjoy an unbound discretion in further developing the law through its interpretation and application. Nor should the volitive act entailed in judgments be solely determined by the practicalities of the dispute or the interests of the parties. Instead, account should be taken of the basic principles of the legal system.[293] In this light, the approaches centered on principles

---

290 ibid 52.
291 ibid 58.
292 Esser, *Grundsatz und Norm in der richterlichen Fortbildung des Privatrechts Rechtsvergleichende Beiträge zur Rechtsquellen- und Interpretationslehre* 285 (the lawmaker is not the ultimate authority on the scope given to statutes); see also Martin Kriele, *Theorie der Rechtsgewinnung entwickelt am Problem der Verfassungsinterpretation* (Duncker & Humblot 1967) 311-312 (speaking of legislator's prerogative, rather than monopoly, with respect to lawmaking); Friedrich August von der Heydte, 'Glossen zu einer Theorie der allgemeinen Rechtsgrundsätze' (1933) 33(11/12) Die Friedens-Warte 295.
293 Cf. Coing, *Die obersten Grundsätze des Rechts Ein Versuch zur Neugründung des Naturrechts* 131 recognizing that judges are no simple executors of the will of the lawmaker and that their judgment call should be informed by the statutory's idea of justice; Esser, *Grundsatz und Norm in der richterlichen Fortbildung des Privatrechts Rechtsvergleichende Beiträge zur Rechtsquellen- und Interpretationslehre* 300 ff.; cf. Canaris, *Die Feststellung von Lücken im Gesetz: eine methodologische Studie über*

Chapter 2: Comparative Perspectives

adopted a middle road, on the one hand recognizing the development of the law, on the other hand focusing on the values expressed in the legal order that would inform the acts of the legal operator. Based on this understanding principles are not exclusively either restraining or liberating. They represent both legal experience and the law in action.

The overview illustrated that principles can vary as to their degrees of normativity and as to their embeddedness in legal practice. There are fundamental principles such as the principle of good faith, *pacta sunt servanda*, the protection of legitimate expectations, the prohibition of arbitrariness and of abuse of rights, *audiatur et altera pars* and equality of arms, which are regarded to be deeply connected to the idea of law and thus part of any legal system. As reflection of the law in action and because of the interrelationship between principles and also new rules, principles of law and their respective concretizations can change over time.[294] New ideas may arise and start as mere guides for the legal operator where the law to be applied leaves room for interpretation and discretion and over time become embedded into legal practice and harden into a legal principle.[295]

Thus, principles can be of varying degrees of normativity. They can lack any normativity if they have not been positivized and if they have not asserted

---

Voraussetzungen und Grenzen der richterlichen Rechtsfortbildung praeter legem 33, 37-38, 57, 93 ff.; in this light see also Dworkin's emphasis that the judges do not enjoy discretion as lawmakers do and shall subject their judgment to the evaluations of the legal system from which they derive their authority, Dworkin, *Law's Empire* 243 ff.; Eisenberg, *The Nature of the Common Law* 151; cf. also Cardozo, *The Nature of the Judicial Process* 141.

294 Canaris, *Systemdenken und Systembegriff in der Jurisprudenz: entwickelt am Beispiel des deutschen Privatrechts* 60 ff.; Larenz, *Methodenlehre der Rechtswissenschaft* 471.

295 Cf. on different categories of principles Kleinlein, *Konstitutionalisierung im Völkerrecht Konstruktion und Elemente einer idealistischen Völkerrechtslehre* 671 (distinguishing in legal discourse between *Ordnungsprinzipien* as legal science's abstractions of positive law, *Leitprinzipien* as goals or guides set forth in treaties and *Rechtsprinzipien* as general legal norms); Goldmann, 'Dogmatik als Rationale Rekonstruktion: Versuch einer Metatheorie am Beispiel völkerrechtlicher Prinzipien' 394 ff., distinguishing between general principles of law, principles as doctrinal constructions of the legal discourse, non-binding guiding principles, emerging principles and structural principles; for an example of a principle which was originally regarded to be only a political principle but hardened into a legal one, see the development of the right to self-determination below, p. 285.

themselves in legal practice.[296] These varying degrees and the vagueness of principles as well as the wide range of opinions on principles' validity might be worrying from the perspective of legal certainty. An overemphasis and an idealization of unwritten principles can, as put by Matthias Jestaedt, operate as Trojan horse for extra-legal considerations in the guise of a legal concept and go at the detriment of working closely with the more specific, enacted written rule.[297]

It is therefore important neither to overemphasize general principles of law at the expense of the specifically, and ideally democratically legitimized, enacted law, nor to neglect the role they play in the law, including in the

---

296 See also Crawford, 'Change, Order, Change: The Course of International Law General Course on Public International Law' 143, commenting on the discussions of the *lex mercatoria* and referring to the UNIDROIT principles, arguing that the scholarly distillation of principles common in different domestic legal orders "is a pure confection, unrelated to any real source of authority or any existing praxis. It is a law of and for professors, a *Buchrecht* reduced to a single book, based on the assumption that comparative law techniques can distil a true or real underlying common law — a sort of natural law without the benefit of divinity. The assumption is demonstrably untrue."; cf. Rudolf B Schlesinger, 'Research on the General Principles of Law Recognized by Civilized Nations' (1957) 51(4) AJIL 734 ff.; Rudolf B Schlesinger and Pierre Bonassies, *Formation of contracts: a study of the common core of legal systems; conductes under the auspices of the general principles of law project of the Cornell Law School* (vol 1, Oceana-Publ 1968) 41 (concluding that "the areas of agreement are larger than those of disagreement" and that the areas of agreement and disagreement "are intertwined in subtler and more complex ways than had been surmised."); on a critical discussion of the lack of legal validity of such principles see Ralf Michaels, 'Privatautonomie und Privatkodifikation Zu Anwendbarkeit und Geltung allgemeiner Vertragsrechtsprinzipien' (1998) 62 Rabels Zeitschrift für Ausländisches und Internationales Privatrecht 580 ff.
297 Matthias Jestaedt, 'Bundesstaat als Verfassungsprinzip' in *Handbuch des Staatsrechts der Bundesrepublik Deutschland* (CF Müller 2004) vol 2 801, 810-811; for a critique of the understanding of constitutional fundamental rights as principles see Matthias Jestaedt, *Grundrechtsentfaltung im Gesetz* (Mohr Siebeck 1999) 222 (pointing to the multifaceted interplay between constitutional law and ordinary law); his critique is directed against the principles theory as developed by Robert Alexy. Cf. for further critique Lerche, 'Die Verfassung als Quelle von Optimierungsgeboten?' 202-206 (principles doctrine may favour of a constitutionalization of the legal order and does not do justice to different categories of principles); Poscher, 'Theorie eines Phantoms - Die erfolglose der Prinzipientheorie nach ihrem Gegenstand' 356, 367-368, 370-371 (contra a distinction between rules and principles as matter of legal theory); for an overview of the discussion of Robert Alexy's scholarship see Nowrot, *Das Republikprinzip in der Rechtsordnungengemeinschaft* 506 ff.

Chapter 2: Comparative Perspectives

international legal order. A focus on legal practice, which the present study adopts, can shed light on the operation of principles, their interrelationship with and their elucidation by treaties and customary international law in the international legal order and it can also provide a safeguard against the risks of principles being overemphasized.

By operating within the confines of legal argumentation, interpretation and application of other legal rules and principles, principles are, while being shaped by generality and flexibility, still anchored, as Kolb puts it, "in the realm of legal phenomena, with a definable core-meaning and an overlookable system of extensions, which gives to the principles a genetic code able to grant that minimum of certainty without which the law opens up to the arbitrary [...] it appears that 'principles' are neither simple 'rules' nor simple 'vague ideas'."[298]

The persuasiveness of the legal operator's recourse to, and balancing of, principles must be assessed in each individual case and does not depend in an abstract fashion on a principle's legal validity alone. A principle's legal validity does not relieve the legal operator from her responsibility to relate this particular principle to other rules and principles in the specific case. A legal reasoning certainly can derive a certain persuasiveness from recourse to a general principle of law, but the specific use of a general principle as opposed to a competing principle needs to derive its persuasiveness from the legal reasoning. At the same time, it remains possible that new principles emerge and harden into positive law through case law. While courts have an important function in that regard, they should approach the judicial task not with a view to positivizing new principles but with a view to serving the law. In doing the latter, they may accomplish the former.

E. Concluding Observations

This chapter approached the interrelationship of sources, and of written and unwritten law, in comparative legal thought. In particular, it examined the discourse in the UK common law system[299] and contrasted the latter with the discussion in the US at a certain point of history.[300] Whilst the

---

298 Kolb, 'Principles as Sources of International Law (With Special Reference to Good Faith)' 9.
299 See above, p. 105.
300 See above, p. 113.

common law in the UK still enjoys considerable support of scholars and, in particular, the UK Supreme Court and therefore did not vanish with the adoption of the Human Rights Act[301], customary law in Germany lost support to doctrines relating to the interpretation and application of the written law.[302] Subsequently, this chapter addressed general principles of law from legal-theoretical perspectives.[303]

This chapter demonstrated by way of reference to municipal legal orders different ideas of the relationship between written law and unwritten law, from an "oil and water" relationship[304] or a relationship of competition[305] to relationships of convergence and of a dynamic interplay[306], depending on the spirit of the time and the respective preferences of scholars and courts.

Also, this chapter depicted that the function of the unwritten law differed in relation to the written law, it could be the basis for independent rules[307] or indicate the way in which the written law should be applied[308], it could be seen as the practice of the law-subjects or as the product of a caste of lawyers and courts.[309] It is on the basis of these insights that one can evaluate and consider the role of customary international law in the international legal order.

Furthermore, this chapter demonstrated that the idea of the law in action and the interplay between written law and unwritten law informed the doctrine of general principles of law.[310] Whereas certain explanations of principles focus on the distinction between principles and rules, this chapter

---

301 See above, p. 120.
302 See above, p. 126.
303 See above, p. 138.
304 See above, p. 103.
305 See above, p. 137.
306 See above, p. 119.
307 See above, p. 120.
308 See above, p. 119. Recently, Mark D Walters, 'The Unwritten Constitution as a Legal Concept' in David Dyzenhaus and Malcolm Thorburn (eds), *Philosophical Foundations of Constitutional Law* (Oxford University Press 2016) 35 argued in favour of more attention to unwritten constitutional law as "a discourse of reason in which existing rules, even those articulated in writing, are understood to be specific manifestations of a comprehensive body of abstract principles from which other rules may be identified through an interpretive back-and-forth that endeavours to show coherence between law's specific and abstract dimensions and equality between law's various applications".
309 See above, p. 112.
310 See above, p. 138.

Chapter 2: Comparative Perspectives

submitted that general principles of law are connected to legal reasoning and the systematization of the law and should be understood in their interrelationship with other principles, rules and the normative context, taking also into account the role of the legal operator. It will be demonstrated that this can contribute to the understanding of general principles in the international legal order.[311]

---

311 See also below, p. 216, comparing the second report of the ILC Special Rapporteur with this chapter's perspectives on general principles. Cf. also the index in Lauterpacht, *The Function of Law in the International Community* 461 f., referring to Roscoe Pound and Benjamin Cardozo who were discussed in this chapter; cf. Thirlway, *The sources of international law* 107 who refers only to Dworkin as author who demonstrated the existence of legal principles.

Chapter 3: Historical Perspectives on article 38 PCIJ Statute

A. *Introduction*

This chapter approaches the interrelationship of sources in the context of the drafting[1] of article 38 PCIJ Statute. This chapter will first illuminate the doctrinal (B.) and institutional (C.) background of the drafting of article 38 PCIJ Statute. The chapter will then delve into the drafting of article 38 and demonstrate how the members of the Advisory Committee of Jurists discussed the interrelationship of sources (D.). Subsequently, the chapter will turn to the reception of sources set forth in article 38 in the jurisprudence of the PCIJ, in a codification setting and in scholarship with a particular focus on the interwar period (E.).

B. *The positivist climate: the doctrinal interest in treaties and general conceptions of law*

Even prior to the adoption of article 38 PCIJ Statute, a certain triad of sources or forms of international law can be depicted in the work of certain scholars when discussing the distinction and relationship between natural and positive international law.[2] For instance, Christian Wolff distinguished "the voluntary, the stipulative and the customary law of nations (which forms the positive law of nations) from the natural or necessary law of nations"[3]. The voluntary

---

1 See for a detailed treatment Spiermann, ''Who attempts too much does nothing well': The 1920 Advisory Committee of Jurists and the Statute of the Permanent Court of International Justice' 187 ff.
2 The following is not a comprehensive treatment of international legal history. Cf. recently in particular Valentina Vadi, *War and Peace. Alberico Gentili and the Early Modern Law of Nations* (Brill Nijhoff 2020) 108-115, 159-179; Francesca Iurlaro, 'Grotius, Dio Chrysostom and the 'Invention' of Customary ius gentium' (2018) 39 Grotiana 15 ff.
3 Christian von Wolff, *Jus gentium methodo scientificia pertractatum* (vol 2, Clarendon Press 1934) 19 para 26. See also Thomas Kleinlein, 'Christian Wolff. System as an Episode' in Stefan Kadelbach, Thomas Kleinlein, and David Roth-Isigkeit (eds), *System, Order, and International Law: The Early History of International Legal Thought from Machiavelli to Hegel* (Oxford University Press 2017) 230 ff.

law was derived from the necessary law and was "considered to have been laid down by its fictious ruler and so to have proceeded from the will of nations."[4] Stipulations were said to "bind only the nations between whom they are made"[5] and therefore led only to particular law. The customary law of nations "rests upon the tacit consent of nations, or [...] a tacit stipulation, and it is evident that it is not universal, but a particular law, just as was the stipulative law."[6] All forms of positive law rested on a form of consent, namely presumed consent, express consent and tacit consent.[7] Wolff stressed that the stipulative and the customary law "are by no means to be confused with the voluntary law."[8] The true *lex generalis* then was not customary law but the voluntary law and the necessary law.

A similar distinction can be found in the work of Emer de Vattel.[9] Like Wolff, he distinguished between the necessary law and the positive law. The necessary law comprised an immutable law which is "founded on the nature of things, and particularly on the nature of man"[10] and which "is necessary because nations are absolutely bound to observe it"[11]. According to Vattel, "the necessary law is always obligatory on the conscience, a nation ought

---

4 Wolff, *Jus gentium methodo scientificia pertractatum* 18 para 22.
5 ibid 18 para 23.
6 ibid 18-19 para 23.
7 ibid 19 para 25.
8 ibid 19 para 26.
9 See also Degan, 'General Principles of Law (A Source of General International Law)' 19; on inspirations Vattel took from Wolff see Francis S Ruddy, *International law in the enlightenment: the background of Emmerich de Vattel's Le droit des gens* (Oceana-Publ 1975) 77-123; Alexander Orakhelashvili, 'Natural Law and Customary Law' (2008) 68 ZaöRV 72-73; recently: Francesca Iurlaro, 'Vattel's Doctrine of the Customary Law of Nations between Sovereign Interests and the Principles of Natural Law' in Simone Zurbuchen (ed), *The Law of Nations and Natural Law 1625-1800* (Brill 2019) 280-300. A similar approach was advocated by Henry Wheaton, *Elements of International Law: with a Sketch of the History of the Science* (Carey, Lea & Blanchard 1836) 47-48, distinguishing between the natural law and the positive law, consisting of three branches, namely the voluntary law, the conventional law and the customary law of nations. These were derived from the presumed consent, the express consent and the tacit consent. But see William S Dodge, 'Customary international law, Change, and the Constitution' (2018) 106 The Georgetown Law Journal 1573 on Wheaton changing his position in his posthum published edition.
10 Emer de Vattel, *The Law of Nations; or Principles of the Law of Nature, applied to the conduct and affairs of nations and sovereigns* (6th American edition, TJW Johnson 1844) LVIII para 8.
11 ibid LVIII para 7.

never to lose sight of it", but states may demand from other states only compliance with the positive law of nations, which included the voluntary, the conventional and the customary law, "for they all proceed from the will of nations, - the voluntary from their presumed consent, the conventional from an express consent, and the customary from tacit consent".[12]

August Wilhelm Heffter presented three forms of "European international law" which resemble the later triad of sources when he argued that European international law consisted of consensual agreements, abstractions of the essence of commonly used institutions and the concordant practice of nations.[13] At the same time, however, he emphasized that treaties and custom were only individual forms of the formal appearances of international law and that there was also international law which did not require an expressive recognition by states.[14]

The doctrinal scientific climate leading to article 38 became that of voluntarist positivism and legal conceptualism in the work of authors at the end of the 19th century who were committed to positivism and to the enterprise of constructing international law scientifically.[15]

---

12 ibid LXV para 27; on the discussion of the relationship between the necessary and the positive law see Amanda Perreau-Saussine, 'Lauterpacht and Vattel on the Sources of International Law: the Place of Private Law Analogies and General Principles' in Vincent Chetail and Peter Haggenmacher (eds), *Vattel's international law in a XXIst century perspective* (Martinus Nijhoff Publishers 2011) 174. See Andrew Clapham, *Brierly's Law of Nations* (Oxford University Press 2012) 36 ("exaggerated emphasis on the independence of states").
13 August Wilhelm Heffter, *Das Europäische Völkerrecht der Gegenwart auf den bisherigen Grundlagen* (vol 5, first publ. 1844, Schroeder 1867) 16-17.
14 ibid 4-5.
15 Cf. on the construction of positivism Mónica García-Salmones Rovira, *The Project of Positivism in International Law* (Oxford University Press 2013); see for instance Karl Bergbohm, *Jurisprudenz und Rechtsphilosophie: kritische Abhandlungen* (vol 1, Duncker & Humblot 1892) 90 (on general legal concepts); but see also Miloš Vec, 'Sources of International Law in the Nineteenth-Century European Tradition: The Myth of Positivism' in *The Oxford Handbook of the Sources of International Law* (Oxford University Press 2017) 121, pointing out that naturalist thinking was not completely abandoned; see for instance Robert Phillimore, *Commentaries upon international law* (vol 1, T & J W Johnson, Law Booksellers 1854) 86 and 64, listing as sources "1. The Divine law [...] 2. Revealed Will of Good [...] 3. Reason, which govern the application of these principles to particular cases [...] 4. The universal consent of nations, both as expressed (1) by positive compact or treaty, and (2) as implied by usage, custom, and practice."

One example is Georg Jellinek[16], who argued that if a state was capable of binding herself internally, in the context of constitutional law, the state must be able to do so internationally as well.[17] His objective was a "juristic construction" of international law that emphasized the character of international law as *legal* order. Just like domestic law, international law was said to be based on the will of the state;[18] by entering into other relations with states, a state accepted those rules which regulated the objective living conditions of states.[19] The treaty was objective law, as opposed to a bilateral legal relation[20], since it was governed by norms of positive law which states recognized implicitly when they concluded treaties.[21] Jellinek was confident in that this juristic construction of an objective law on treaties would provide guidance for states in international affairs and even permit the "public opinion of the civilised world" to legally evaluate states' conduct.[22] Yet, the regional and cultural scope of this international law thusly constructed was far from being universal and was said to apply only to those states outside Europe which had recognized it.[23]

---

16 Georg Jellinek, *Die rechtliche Natur der Staatenverträge: ein Beitrag zur juristischen Construction des Völkerrechts* (Hölder 1880); on Jellinek see Jochen von Bernstorff, 'Georg Jellinek and the Origins of Liberal Constitutionalism in International Law' (2012) 4(3) Goettingen Journal of International Law 659 ff.

17 Jellinek, *Die rechtliche Natur der Staatenverträge: ein Beitrag zur juristischen Construction des Völkerrechts* 1, 8; von Bernstorff, 'Georg Jellinek and the Origins of Liberal Constitutionalism in International Law' 669 ff.

18 Jellinek, *Die rechtliche Natur der Staatenverträge: ein Beitrag zur juristischen Construction des Völkerrechts* 46.

19 ibid 48-49.

20 Cf. Ernst Meier, *Über den Abschluss von Staatsverträgen* (Duncker & Humblot 1874) 36.

21 Jellinek, *Die rechtliche Natur der Staatenverträge: ein Beitrag zur juristischen Construction des Völkerrechts* 51-52.

22 ibid 65.

23 Cf. Georg Jellinek, 'China und das Völkerrecht' (1900) 5(19) Deutsche Juristen-Zeitung 402-404 where Jellinek wrote on the relationship between international law based on a European culture and China; for a survey of the use of the term civilized nations in this period see Masaharu Yanagihara, 'Significance of the History of the Law of Nations in Europe and East Asia' (2014) 371 RdC 293-316; Jakob Zollmann, ''Civilization(s)' and 'civilized nations' – of history, anthropology, and international law' in Sean P Morris (ed), *Transforming the Politics of International Law: The Advisory Committee of Jurists and the Formation of the World Court in the League of Nations* (Routledge 2021) 11 ff.

Another prominent example is the work of Otto Nippold. Cautioning against a private law analogy to a contract, Nippold argued that a treaty in the international legal order could constitute a source of law and create objective law.[24] The treaty's validity would not derive from external norms but from the will of the states concluding the treaty.[25] As the will of the states could find its expression not only in treaties but also in custom, all positive international law would be traced back to the will of states, and both should be recognized as objective law.[26] Nippold had reservations against domestic law analogies which could jeopardize the independence of the international legal order.[27] He stressed, however, the importance of a general doctrine of law (*allgemeine Rechtslehre*) and general legal concepts (*juristische Grundbegriffe*) which may functionally resemble general principles of law.[28] According to Nippold, private law concepts such as contracts were just like international treaties a sub-category of the category of agreement with respect to which general concepts and principles would apply.[29] The accuracy of general concepts would depend on their accordance with positive law.[30] While the application of such general legal concepts would support the juristic character of international law as law, the special characteristics of the international legal order needed to be taken into account as well.[31] Nippold argued, for instance, that the international treaty would be governed by the general norms which would follow from general concept of treaty.[32] These general norms would also constitute positive norms of the international legal order as they could be based on the will of states when those conclude treaties.[33] At the same time, the treaty in the international legal order would possess special characteristics which distinguish it from contracts and which would give rise to

---

24 Nippold, *Der völkerrechtliche Vertrag Seine Stellung im Rechtssystem und seine Bedeutung für das internationale Recht* 35 ff.
25 ibid 37.
26 ibid 51, 53, 57-58.
27 ibid 80 ff.
28 Cf. also Lauterpacht, 'The mandate under international law in the Covenant of the League of Nations' 51-56.
29 Nippold, *Der völkerrechtliche Vertrag Seine Stellung im Rechtssystem und seine Bedeutung für das internationale Recht* 84-85.
30 ibid 86.
31 ibid 87.
32 See for instance ibid 168, arguing that it was a general principle of contract law applicable to both private law contracts and international treaties that the conclusion of agreements was based on the free will of states instead of on coercion.
33 ibid 88.

particular norms of the international legal order.[34] Nippold concluded that the international legal order therefore possessed its own norms on treaties which would not depend on private law analogies.[35]

Heinrich Triepel made a distinction between *Vertrag* and *Vereinbarung*. The *Vertrag* could only accommodate conflicting interests without producing a common will (*Gemeinwille*).[36] Only a *Vereinbarung* which expressed a common will as opposed to the single wills of the parties could produce objective law (*objektives Recht*).[37] The *Vereinbarung* would apply only *inter partes*, which is why, in his view, there was only particular international law; general law (*allgemeines Recht*) could only be formulated by way of comparison of particular legal rules.[38] A majority rule could only exist to the extent that it had been agreed on.[39] States' *Vereinbarung* could encompass explicitly agreed rules (*Rechtssätze*), as well as those necessary or latent rules (*latente Rechtssätze*) which were implied or required by the agreed rule.[40] States could agree not only expressively on a *Vereinbarung*, but also tacitly through their acts: "An important part of international law has been created in this fashion; it is usually called customary international law."[41] Triepel argued that customary international law could not be produced by the recurrence of similar treaty provisions, as a treaty could only bind parties, unless a priorly agreed rule provides otherwise, in which case, however, it would not be the treaty which creates objective law.[42]

---

34 Nippold, *Der völkerrechtliche Vertrag Seine Stellung im Rechtssystem und seine Bedeutung für das internationale Recht* 89-90, arguing also that those norms would be based on the objective nature of the relationship between states, with reference to Jellinek, and on the will of states.
35 ibid 90, in Nippold's view, those norms did not need to be explicitly laid down, even though he considered their codification in a treaty as possible).
36 Heinrich Triepel, *Völkerrecht und Landesrecht* (Hirschfeld 1899) 46. He borrowed the distinction from Karl Binding, *Die Gründung des norddeutschen Bundes. Ein Beitrag zur Lehre von der Staatenschöpfung* (Duncker & Humblot 1889) 69, 70.
37 Triepel, *Völkerrecht und Landesrecht* 70.
38 ibid 83-84.
39 ibid 83, 87.
40 ibid 94-95; on custom and *Gemeinwille*, see ibid 95 ff.
41 ibid 95; the English translation is borrowed from Raphael M Walden, 'The Subjective Element in the Formation of Customary International Law' (1977) 12 Israel Law Review 349.
42 Triepel, *Völkerrecht und Landesrecht* 98; cf. for an earlier held different position Heinrich Triepel, *Die neuesten Fortschritte auf dem Gebiet des Kriegsrechts* (C L Hirschfeld 1894) 4-5.

The positivist climate: the doctrinal interest in treaties and general conceptions of law

Lassa Oppenheim, in contrast, rejected the conceptualization of custom as treaty.[43] Whereas treaties would require explicit consent, custom could be based on a "common consent" of a majority which could be expressed tacitly.[44] Oppenheim recognized only two sources of international law, namely treaty and custom, and he rejected to regard reason to be a source of law.[45] Even though Oppenheim was sympathetic to the idea of codification, he argued that customary law would remain relevant to a greater extent than in municipal law and retain the capacity to derogate from treaties.[46]

---

43 Lassa Francis Lawrence Oppenheim, 'Zur Lehre vom internationalen Gewohnheitsrecht' (1915) 25 Niemeyers Zeitschrift für internationales Recht 12.
44 Lassa Francis Lawrence Oppenheim, *International Law* (vol 1, Longmans, Green 1905) 15 describing "common consent" as "the express or tacit consent of such an overwhelming majority of the members that those who dissent are of no importance whatever and disappear totally from the view of one who looks for the will of the community as an entity in contradistinction to its single members." On treaties, see ibid 23-24, distinguishing between universal, particular and general international law created by a lawmaking treaty and arguing that "General International Law has a tendency to become universal because such States as hitherto did not consent to it will in future either expressly give their consent or recognise the respective rules tacitly through custom." On common consent see also John Westlake, *Chapters on the Principles of International Law* (University Press 1894) 78: "When one of those rules is invoked against a state, it is not necessary to show that the state in question has assented to the rule either diplomatically or by having acted on it, though it is a strong argument if you can do so. It is enough to show that the general *consensus* of opinion within the limits of European civilisation is in favour of the rule." William Edward Hall, *Treatise on International Law* (4th edn, Clarendon Press 1895) 5 ("general consent"); see also Dodge, 'Customary international law, Change, and the Constitution' 1572-1574; see also Stern, 'Custom at the heart of international law' 95-99, describing a shift of vocabulary from consent to *opinio juris* and explaining that general consent has been argued to entail "the presumption of a universal acceptance" (98).
45 Oppenheim, *International Law* 21 and 22: "[...] there must exist, and can only exist, as many sources of International Law as there are facts through which such a common consent can possibly come into existence. Of such facts there are only two." For a rejection of legal science as a source see also August von Bulmerincq, *Das Völkerrecht oder das internationale Recht* (2nd edn, Mohr 1889) 188, who recognized only treaties and custom as a source; Franz von Holtzendorff, 'Die Quellen des Völkerrechts' in Franz von Holtzendorff (ed), *Handbuch des Völkerrechts. Einleitung in das Völkerrecht* (Habel 1885) vol 1 109-112, rejecting legal science as a source as well, counts to the sources among treaties and custom also domestic statutes insofar as they address and regulate international legal relations.
46 Oppenheim, 'Zur Lehre vom internationalen Gewohnheitsrecht' 10 ("Die Macht des Gewohnheitsrechts ist eine elementare und spottet jeder Eindämmung.").

With the rise of positivism, there was a tendency to construct international law scientifically by rooting its sources or forms of law in the consent of states and to minimize the role of natural law or necessary law also by expanding the scope of general principles of law and customary international law.[47] Customary international law became less regarded as a tacit treaty[48] or another form of special law, and increasingly regarded as general law, in contradistinction to special treaty law.[49]

C. Institutional Background: The Hague Conferences of 1899 and 1907

The Hague Conferences of 1899 and 1907[50] to some extent foreshadowed the triad of sources that would be reflected in article 38 PCIJ Statute. This section will first illustrate the background of these conferences before approaching in particular article 7 of the Prize Court Convention which inspired the later discussions in the Advisory Committee of Jurists when drafting article 38 PCIJ Statute.

---

47 Cf. Lauterpacht, *The Function of Law in the International Community* 7 on the development of the doctrine of non-justiciable disputes. As argued by Perreau-Saussine, 'Lauterpacht and Vattel on the Sources of International Law: the Place of Private Law Analogies and General Principles' 174-175, Vattel was for Lauterpacht "the *wrong kind* of natual lawyer. Vattel draws the line between the voluntary law and the necessary law in the wrong place, treating too much of the 'necessary' law as a matter of conscience *rather than law.*"
48 On the recent debate on the possibility of a state to withdraw itself from custom and the interpretation of Vattel's work see Curtis A Bradley and Mitu Gulati, 'Withdrawing from International Custom' (2010) 120 Yale Law Journal 215 ff.; Edward T Swaine, 'Bespoke Custom' (2010) 21 Duke Journal of Comparative & International Law 208 ff.; Stacey Marlise Gahagan, 'Returning to Vattel: A Gentlement's Agreement for the Twenty-First Century' (2012) 37 North Carolina Journal of International Law 853-873.
49 See also Yasuaki, *International Law in a Transcivilizational World* 152 ff.
50 Betsy Baker, 'Hague Peace Conferences (1899 and 1907)' [2009] Max Planck EPIL para 28; see also David D Caron, 'War and International Adjudication: Reflections on the 1899 Peace Conference' (2000) 84 AJIL 4 ff.; Christian J Tams, 'Die Zweite Haager Konferenz und das Recht der friedlichen Streitbeilegung' (2007) 82 Friedenswarte 119 ff.; Calvin DeArmond Davis, *The United States and the First Hague Peace Conference* (Cornell Univ Press for the American Historical Association 1962).

I. The background of the conferences

These conferences took place against the background of the so-called peace movement[51] and the enthusiasm for arbitration as means to achieve the peaceful settlement of disputes.[52] They gave rise to the hope of the existence of a world federation.[53] Yet, the conferences revealed existing differences between the participating nations. In particular the proposal to establish a mechanism for compulsory arbitration was met with resistance, in particular by Germany.[54]

Recent research draws an ambiguous picture as to the universality of these conferences. Whereas in 1899 only 24 stated had participated in the conference, more countries were invited to the second conference, convened by the Russian Czar in 1907; 44 states participated at a time when 57 states were claiming to be independent states.[55] Opinions differ as to the extent of true representativeness. For Augusto Cançado Trindade, the 1907 conference "marked the beginning of a long journey" towards a new *Jus Gentium*, as "by the end of the Second Hague Peace Conference of 1907 the universalist

---

51 Caron, 'War and International Adjudication: Reflections on the 1899 Peace Conference' 8.
52 ibid 10; Mark W Janis, 'North America: American Exceptionalism in International Law' in Bardo Fassbender and Anne Peters (eds), *The Oxford Handbook of the History of International Law* (Oxford University Press 2012) 535; Tom Bingham, 'The Alabama Claims Arbitration' (2005) 54 ICLQ 1 ff.; Georg Schwarzenberger, *William Ladd: An examination of an American proposal for an international equity tribunal* (2nd edn, London, 1936) 37; Alfred Zimmern, *The League of Nations and the Rule of Law 1918-1935* (Macmillan 1936) 103.
53 Walter Schücking, *Der Staatenverband der Haager Konferenzen* (Duncker & Humblot 1912) 27; William Isaac Hull, *The two Hague conferences and their contributions to international law* (repr. orig. publ. 1908, Kraus 1970) 496 ff.; Thomas Joseph Lawrence, *International Problems and Hague Conferences* (London, 1906) 42 ff.
54 Caron, 'War and International Adjudication: Reflections on the 1899 Peace Conference' 16; see also Shabtai Rosenne, *The World Court: what it is and how it works* (4th edn, Nijhoff 1989) 6-8 on the problem of selection of judges.
55 Vladlen S Vereshchetin, 'Some reflections of a Russian scholar on the legacy of the Second Peace Conference' in Yves Daudet (ed), *Actualité de la Conférence de La Haye de 1907, Deuxième Conférence de la paix/ Topicality of the 1907 Hague Conference, the Second Peace Conference* (Martinus Nijhoff Publishers 2008) 46, also noting that "[r]egrettably, African and some Asian delegates were not invited [...]".

outlook of international law had gained considerable ground."[56] Vladlen Vereshchetin stresses that "the Hague Conferences gave a great impetus for further consolidation and development of universal international law [...]".[57] On the other side of the spectrum, Shinya Murase is more critical: "From the Asian Perspective, the centennial of the Second Hague Conference is not something to be celebrated. At best, it should be simply commemorated."[58] He spoke of a "non-Presence of Asia"[59]: neither China nor Persia participated due to internal struggles, Siam participated but regarded the invitation and its participation as mere symbolic, and Japan participated since it sought international recognition and wanted to block compulsory jurisdiction after a defeat before the PCA.[60] Furthermore, Asian delegations were in part represented by US-American lawyers, with the extent to which states like the US exercised direct or indirect influence over the delegations of other countries being subject to debate.[61]

II. The provisions on applicable law and the recognition of three sources

Even prior to the conferences, arbitral tribunals had referred to maxims of Roman law and principles derived from municipal legal orders[62] for necessity

---

56 Antônio Augusto Cançado Trindade, 'The presence and participation of Latin America at the Second Hague Peace Conference of 1907' in Yves Daudet (ed), *Actualité de la Conférence de La Haye de 1907, Deuxième Conférence de la paix/ Topicality of the 1907 Hague Conference, the Second Peace Conference* (Martinus Nijhoff Publishers 2008) 78, 80, 82. He also emphasized the innovations, allowing individual complaints to the Prize Court, and the progressive developments on the Latin-American Level, consisting for instance in the Permanent Central American Court of Justice (72).
57 Vereshchetin, 'Some reflections of a Russian scholar on the legacy of the Second Peace Conference' 46.
58 Shinya Murase, 'The presence of Asia at the 1907 Hague Conference' in Yves Daudet (ed), *Actualité de la Conférence de La Haye de 1907, Deuxième Conférence de la paix/ Topicality of the 1907 Hague Conference, the Second Peace Conference* (Martinus Nijhoff Publishers 2008) 101.
59 ibid 89.
60 ibid 87-90.
61 ibid 107, 113, on the role of the lawyer Henry W. Denison who advised Japan; for a nuanced assessment of Japan's skeptical attitude towards international adjudication: Yanagihara, 'Significance of the History of the Law of Nations in Europe and East Asia' 416-417.
62 See *Antoine Fabiani Case* France. v. Venezuela (31 July 1905) X RIAA 98 for an invocation of the "principes généraux du droit des gens"; Verdross and Simma,

as defence[63], the obligation to pay interests as implication of the general principle of the responsibility of states and default rule[64], the limitation of this obligation to pay interest to an amount which does not exceed the amount due according to the Roman law principle *ne ultra alterum tantum*[65], the principle of prescription as a general principle of law.[66] Moreover, a draft on procedural regulations for international courts of arbitration prepared by Levin Goldschmidt and adopted by the Institute de Droit International provided that a judge, in the translation of Goldschmidt's commentary by James Brown Scott, "will apply to the international points in dispute the international law existing between the parties by virtue of treaties or custom; in the second place, general international law; to disputed points of another kind, in the matter of public or private law, the national law which appears to be applicable according to the principles of international law".[67]

The documents produced at the conferences confirmed this trend. For instance, the Martens clause referred to the 1899 convention, to "principles of international law, as they result from the usages established between civilized nations, from the laws of humanity, and the dictates of the public

---

Universelles Völkerrecht Theorie und Praxis 380-382; Pellet and Müller, 'Article 38' 923 with further references; Alfred Verdross, 'Les principes généraux du droit dans la jurisprudence Internationale' (1935) 52 RdC 209 ff.; Marro, *Allgemeine Rechtsgrundsätze des Völkerrechts* 44 ff.

63 *Affaire du Neptune* Great Britain v. U.S.A., Gr. Brit.-U.S. Arb. Trib. 1797 Recueil des arbitrages internationaux Tome 1 (de Lapradelle / Politis, Paris 1905) 137 ff.

64 *Russian Indemnities Case* Russia v. Turkey (11 November 1912) XI RIAA, in this case Turkey could not convincingly demonstrate a contrary rule of customary international law.

65 *Yuille Shortridge & Company* Great Britain v. Portugal, (21 October 1861) XXIX RIAA 68 (obligation to pay interests limited to the due amount according to "le droit commun, seul applicable à cette question"; Fabián Omar Raimondo, *General principles of law in the decisions of international criminal courts and tribunals* (Martinus Nijhoff Publishers 2008) 11.

66 *Gentini* Italy v. Venezuela, Award (1 July 1903) X RIAA 551 (claims which originated 30 years ago no longer enforceable because of prescription as a general principle of law).

67 Levin Goldschmidt, 'International arbitral procedure. Original project and report of Mr Goldschmidt, June 20, 1874' in James Brown Scott (ed and tr), *Resolutions of the Institute of International Law* (James Brown Scott tr, Oxford University Press 1916). For the original French text see Levin Goldschmidt, 'Projet de règlement pour tribunaux arbitraux internationaux (session de Genève, 1874)' (1874) 6 Revue de droit international et de législation comparée 445; for a recent summary see Saunders, *General Principles as a Source of International Law* 23 ff.

conscience". Of particular significance in terms of resemblance with article 38 PCIJ Statute was article 7 of the Prize Court Convention which was based on a proposal by Germany and the United Kingdom to establish a Prize court for maritime warfare at the second Hague Conference.[68] Article 7 of that convention provided:

> "If a question of law to be decided is covered by a treaty in force between the belligerent captor and a Power which is itself or whose subject or citizen is a party to the proceedings, the Court is governed by the provisions in the said treaty.
> In the absence of such provisions, the Court shall apply the rules of international law. If no generally recognized rule exists, the Court shall give judgment in accordance with the general principles of justice and equity."

According to Louis Renault's report, this provision was a "solution, bold to be sure but calculated considerably to improve the practice of international law."[69] The Prize Court was "called upon to *create the law* and to take into account other principles than those to which the national prize court whose judgement is appealed from was required to conform."[70] This task should be executed by the judges "with moderation and firmness"[71]. Renault emphasized that the proposed solution was informed by experiences in domestic law:

> "To sum up, the situation created for the new Prize Court will greatly resemble the condition which long existed in the courts of countries where the laws, chiefly customary, were still rudimentary. These courts made law at the same time that they applied it, and their decisions constituted *precedents*, which became an important source of law."[72]

At that time, however, article 7 of the Prize Court Convention, and in particular the reference to general principles of justice, was quite disputed which became one reason why the convention would not be ratified by states other than Nicaragua.[73] The British government attempted to address the uncertain-

---

68 Davis, *The United States and the First Hague Peace Conference* 222-223; Paul Heilborn, 'Les Sources Du Droit International' (1926) 11 RdC 16-17.
69 Louis Renault, 'Report to the Conference from the First Commission on the draft convention relative to the establishment of an International Prize Court' in James Brown Scott (ed) (Clarendon Press Oxford University Press 1917) 769.
70 ibid 769.
71 ibid 769.
72 ibid 769.
73 Manley O Hudson, *The Permanent Court of International Justice 1920-1942: a treatise* (Macmillan 1943) 76; James Brown Scott, 'The Declaration of London of February 26, 1909: a collection of official papers and documents relating to the International Naval Conference held in London, December, 1908 - February, 1909'

ties as to the applicable law and proposed the London naval conference "with the object of arriving at an agreement as to what are generally recognized principles of international law within the meaning of paragraph 2 of article 7 of the Convention, as to those matters wherein the practice of nations has varied, and of then formulating the rules which, in the absence of special treaty provisions applicable to a particular case, the court should observe in dealing with appeals brought before it for decision".[74] The first world war prevented a third Hague Conference. This experience was part of the background against which the discussions in the Advisory Committee of Jurists took place. In particular Elihu Root emphasized that the draft would have to receive the support of states and work in practice in order avoid the fate of article 7 of the Prize Court convention.[75] At the same time, it is noteworthy, as illustrated in the next section, that several drafts submitted by states included a similar reference to general principles.

(1914) 8(2) AJIL 280 (stating that article 7 was "bitterly criticized"); for a positive evaluation see Henry B Brown, 'The Proposed International Prize Court' (1908) 2 AJIL 485. Walther Schücking saw in article 7(2) nothing else than the "recognition of a modern law of nature", the usefulness of which for the task for the judge he deemed to be self-evident given the unready state of international law on naval warfare, Schücking, *Der Staatenverband der Haager Konferenzen* 138. He maintained that the states still possessed the monopoly on international lawmaking, ibid 139-140, 146. In contrast, Franz von Liszt hoped that because of the lawmaking powers of the Prize Court international law would no longer remain dependent on states' recognition, Franz von Liszt, 'Das Wesen des völkerrechtlichen Staatenverbamdes und der internationale Prisenhof' in *Festgabe der Berliner juristischen Fakultät für Otto Gierke zum Doktor-Jubiläum 21. August 1910, Dritter Band Internationales Recht. Strafrecht. Rechtsvergleichung* (Marcus 1910) 42.

74 British Parliamentary Papers 1905, Cd. 4555, cited after Hersch Lauterpacht, 'History of International Law' in Elihu Lauterpacht (ed), *International Law Being also the Collected Papers of Hersch Lauterpacht, Vol. 2, The Law of Peace, Part 1, International Law in General* (Cambridge University Press 1975) 140.

75 Permanent Court of International Justice – Advisory Committee of Jurists, *Procès-Verbaux of the Proceedings of the Committee, June 16th-July 24th 1920* 108, 133, 137, 286-287 (referring to the Prize Court experience which would indicate that states will not submit themselves to non-positive law); de Lapradelle (287, 314), Loder (311-312), Hagerup (317) and Descamps (310) evaluated the experience with article 7 differently. Whereas de Lapradelle and Loder stressed that the Prize Court convention failed because of lack of public support in the United Kingdom and lack of general agreement as to the convention as a whole, Loder and Descamps regarded article 7(2) of said convention as recognition of the importance of principles.

D. The drafting of article 38

I. Triad of sources in the preparatory work

The fact that several proposals on a provision of applicable law resembled the ultimate wording of article 38 suggests a certain agreement on the sources to be applied by the court. The proposal put forward by Denmark, Norway and Sweden referred to agreements, "established rules of international law" and "in default of generally recognised rules, the Court shall base its decision upon the general principles of Law". An alternative version replaced the reference to general principles of law with a provision according to which "the Court will decide according to what, in its opinion, should be the rules of International Law".[76] The plan of the five neutral powers (Netherlands, Switzerland, Denmark, Norway, Sweden) proposed that the Court should apply applicable treaties, and in the absence of such treaty provisions the court should apply the recognized rules of international law, or, should no rules exist, shall enter judgment according to its own opinion of what the rule of international law should be.[77] The German proposal of 1919 stipulated that the court should pass judgments according to "international agreements, international customary law and according to the general principles of law and equity (*allgemeine Grundsätze von Recht und Billigkeit*)".[78]

---

[76] Hudson, *The Permanent Court of International Justice 1920-1942: a treatise* 113, Draft Scheme of a Convention Concerning an International Judicial Organisation Drawn up by the three Committees nominated respectively by the Governments of Denmark, Norway and Sweden, para 27, in Permanent Court of International Justice – Advisory Committee of Jurists, *Documents presented to the Committee relating to existing plans for the establishment of a Permanent Court of International Justice* (1920) ⟨https://www.icj-cij.org/files/permanent-court-of-international-justice/serie_D/D_documents_to_comm_existing_plans.pdf⟩ accessed 1 February 2023 179.

[77] Hudson, *The Permanent Court of International Justice 1920-1942: a treatise* 113; a similar proposal was submitted by the Brazilian Clovis Bevilaqua, Mohammed Shahabuddeen, *Precedent in the world court* (Cambridge University Press 1997) 52.

[78] David Hunter Miller, *The Drafting of the Covenant* (2, orig. published 1928, Vol 2, New York, 1969) 748, 752-753.

II. The discussion in the Advisory Committee of Jurists

The failure of the 1907 Codification Conference to establish an international prize court led to an institutional self-restraint on the part of the Committee of Jurists and to a separation of the codification project from the project of an international court.[79] The committee made a decision to define the sources,[80] it did not follow a suggestion made by de Lapradelle who preferred a brief reference to "law, justice and equity" since he regarded any definition of the law and its sources "interesting but useless".[81] In the following, this section will first focus on the inclusion of the general principles of law. While in relation to this source reference has been made to natural law in scholarship,[82] the arguments in favour of the inclusion of general principles in the Advisory Committee also show that general principles of law were linked to the judicial interpretation and application of law and could therefore be regarded as a concept that applies in relation to, rather than as an alternative to, the other sources. This section will then turn to the discussion of the interrelationship of sources in the committee.[83]

1. General principles of law

In the 13th meeting, Baron Descamps introduced a draft which resembled previously submitted drafts as well as article 38 in its present form. The draft referred to conventional international law, international custom and in the third place to "the rules of international law as recognised by the legal

---

79 Pellet and Müller, 'Article 38' 826 para 16; d'Aspremont, *Formalism and the Sources of International Law* 149, stating that article 38 was not intended to serve as a model for law-ascertainment.
80 Pellet and Müller, 'Article 38' 828 para 23; see Permanent Court of International Justice – Advisory Committee of Jurists, *Procès-Verbaux of the Proceedings of the Committee, June 16th-July 24th 1920* 293 (Root), establishing the actual rules would exceed the committee's mandate.
81 ibid 295.
82 Cf. Cançado Trindade, 'International Law for Humankind: Towards a New Jus Gentium (I)' 157.
83 This study will quote the members of the committee mainly in the official English translation, it shall be acknowledged here, however, that, with the exception of Elihu Root, all members spoke in the French language, Permanent Court of International Justice – Advisory Committee of Jurists, *Procès-Verbaux of the Proceedings of the Committee, June 16th-July 24th 1920* IV.

Chapter 3: Historical Perspectives on article 38 PCIJ Statute

conscience of civilized nations"[84], the draft became subject to a debate within the committee.

Elihu Root did "not understand the exact meaning of clause 3" and raised the question of whether this clause referred "to something which had been recognised but nevertheless had not the character of a definite rule of law".[85] As Root had remarked earlier, "[n]ations will submit to positive law, but will not submit to such principles as have not been developed into positive rules supported by an accord between all States."[86] He expressed doubts on whether states would submit to compulsory jurisdiction of a court "which would apply principles, differently understood in different countries".[87] Loder, however, defended Descamps' proposal, and argued that the third clause referred to "rules which were, however, not yet of the nature of positive law" and that "it was precisely the Court's duty to develop law, to 'ripen' customs and principles universally recognised, and to crystallise them into positive rules."[88] Lord Phillimore supported the mention of customary law next to written law with reference to the "Anglo-Saxon conception of law"[89] and expressed the view that customary international law encompassed both clause 3 and international jurisprudence to which clause 4 referred.[90] In Hagerup's view, principles were necessary to fill the gaps in positive law and "to avoid the possibility of the Court declaring itself incompetent (*non-liquet*) through lack of applicable rules".[91]

In response to the criticism in particular by Root, Baron Descamps explained in a longer speech the significance of a reference to principles of

---

84 Permanent Court of International Justice – Advisory Committee of Jurists, *Procès-Verbaux of the Proceedings of the Committee, June 16th-July 24th 1920* 306: "The following rules are to be applied by the judge in the solution of international disputes; they will be considered by him in the undermentioned order: 1. conventional international law, whether general or special, being rules expressly adopted by the states; 2. international custom, being practice between nations accepted by them as law; 3. the rules of international law as recognised by the legal conscience of civilised nations; 4. international jurisprudence as a means for the application and development of law."
85 ibid 293-294, he also criticized the fourth clause.
86 ibid 287.
87 ibid 308; but see Hagerup at 311, arguing that one should keep the question of compulsory jurisdiction and the question of sources separate.
88 ibid 294.
89 ibid 295.
90 ibid 294.
91 ibid 296, 307-308; see also de Lapradelle at 313; but see Ricci-Busatti, 314, referring to the principle that whatever is not forbidden is allowed.

"objective justice", disregard of which would imply "a misunderstanding of present conditions, of international law, and the duties of a judge."[92] In his view, it "would be a mistake to imagine that nations can be bound only by engagements which they have entered into by mutual consent."[93] Judges had always applied objective justice and it would be "absolutely impossible and supremely odious" to require the judge to "take a course amounting to a refusal of justice" in a situation where a just solution is possible but "no definite convention or custom appeared" (*"sous prétexte qu'on ne trouve pas de convention out de coutume déterminées"*).[94] Rather than leaving the judge "in a state of compulsory blindness", Baron Descamps wanted to allow the judge "to consider the cases that come before him with both eyes open".[95] In his experience "it is impossible to disregard a fundamental principle of justice in the application of law, if this principle clearly indicates certain rules, necessary for the system of international relations, and applicable to the various circumstances arising in international affairs."[96] Justice was an element for progress and "an indispensable complement to the application of law, and as such essential to the judge".[97]

It emerges from the foregoing that Descamps' invocation of "objective justice" was not concerned with an abstract discussion of the value of natural law or positivism, it was primarily concerned with the practical task of the judge, with the interpretation and the application of international law.[98] He called these justice considerations "objective", as they should not be mere subjective considerations of the judge but be rooted in "concurrent authors whose opinions have authority" and "the legal conscience of civilised nations" to which also the Martens clause referred.[99] This may also indicate that he might not have only principles linked to domestic legal systems in mind.[100] He repeated this point in the discussion. The reference to the conception of justice of civilised nations would in fact "impose on the judges a duty which would prevent them from relying too much on their own subjective

---

92 ibid 322.
93 ibid 323.
94 ibid 323.
95 ibid 323.
96 ibid 324.
97 ibid 325.
98 ibid 324.
99 ibid 323-324.
100 This argument has been made by Saunders, *General Principles as a Source of International Law* 40.

opinion"[101], which was also a response to the concerns expressed by Root and Ricci-Busatti, namely that the court must not become a lawmaker.[102] The different views bring to fore the dual nature of legal principles, as on the one hand the legal operator enjoys a certain liberty, on the other hand, legal principles discipline the legal operator's reasoning.

As requested by Hagerup, Root drafted for the 15th meeting a provision which became article 38 and referred to the general principles recognised by civilized nations.[103] Lord Phillimore opposed Ricci-Busatti's proposal to include a reference to principles of equity within the reference the general principles of law as he and Root "had gone as far as they felt they could on the subject of the liberty to give the judge."[104] Phillimore pointed out that general principles "were these which were accepted by all nations *in foro domestico*, such as certain principles of procedure, the principle of good faith, and the principle of res judicata etc." and that they should be understood as "maxims of law".[105]

2. The discussion of the interrelationship of sources

The interrelationship of the sources was discussed only to a certain extent. The original draft prescribed that the sources "will be considered in the undermentioned order" (*"dans l'ordre successif où elles s'imposent à son examen"*). Ricci-Busatti opposed the formula and its implication that the "judge was not authorised to draw upon a certain source, for instance point 3, before having applied conventions and customs".[106] A reference to any order of application did not become part of article 38.

---

101 Permanent Court of International Justice – Advisory Committee of Jurists, *Procès-Verbaux of the Proceedings of the Committee, June 16th-July 24th 1920* 311; see also at 318, where he agreed with Root "that it would be dangerous to allow the judges to apply the law of right and wrong exclusively according to their own personal understanding of it."
102 ibid 314.
103 ibid 344.
104 ibid 333.
105 ibid 335.
106 ibid 337. While Descamps defended the classification as "natural" since a treaty should not be neglected by applying customary law, Ricci-Busatti claimed that the proposed expression "seems to fail to recognise that these various sources may be applied simultaneously" in relation to one another. Hagerup and De Lapradelle considered the phrase *"ordre succesif"* to be superfluous, 338.

Lord Phillimore criticized the distinction between custom and general principles of law introduced by the proposed draft[107] which can be understood against the background of his socialisation in a legal system in which, since Blackstone, maxims of law and customary law had been assimilated within the concept of common law.[108] Also de Lapradelle wondered as to the relationship between the two.[109] This indicated, however, that both Phillimore and de Lapradelle did not reject the existence of norms which the other members associated to the concept of general principles of law, rather, they adopted a broader understanding of customary international law than other members of the Advisory Committee.[110]

Even though the interrelationship of sources was not subject to detailed discussions, it is possible to draw a number of conclusions from the text itself. Article 38 is illuminating as to differences between the sources by referring to "rules *expressly recognized*", "a general practice *accepted* as law" and "general principles of law *recognized* by civilized nations". Thus, the text indicates the different degrees of (individual) state consent. This point is further illustrated by way of a comparison between article 38(1) and article 38(2) PCIJ Statute. Article 38(1) PCIJ Statute referred to rules "expressly

---

107 ibid 295: "International custom, that is, a general practice accepted as law by nations, constitutes in the main international law. Under these conditions clause 3 and 4 either came within the limits of clause or else were additions to this clause", the latter of which he opposed. See also 311: Lord Phillimore "pointed out that points 3 and 4 of the project were included [in custom]". See also 334: The "sources mentioned in point 3 might be included in point 4, because it was through custom that general principles came to be recognised, and on the other hand, custom is formed by the usage followed in various public and formal documents, and from the works of writers who agree upon a certain point."

108 See also Kleinlein, 'Customary International Law and General Principles Rethinking Their Relationship' 146.

109 Permanent Court of International Justice – Advisory Committee of Jurists, *Procès-Verbaux of the Proceedings of the Committee, June 16th-July 24th 1920* 335 ("how were general principles obtained, unless it was from custom. Point 2 and 3 ought to change place. If customary law had already been dealt with, from whence could general principles be derived, unless it were from the reading of judicial decisions and writers?").

110 See also Cheng, *General Principles of Law as applied by International Courts and Tribunals* 11-12, arguing that Baron Descamps' understanding of custom was more restrictive than Phillimore's, since Baron Descamps stressed the importance of the existence of both practice and *opinio juris* and proposed for certain rules which rather could be based on "juridical conscience" the general principles of law.

recognized *by the contesting States*".[111] The original draft of article 38(2) referred to "*la coutume internationale, comme attestation d'une pratique commune des nations, acceptée par elles comme loi*".[112] In Haggenmacher's view, already this draft rejected the idea of custom as tacit agreement or a mere analogy to treaty law, since the term "nations" referred to the international community as a whole, in contradistinction to "the contesting states".[113] His interpretation is supported by the fact that a proposal of Ricci-Busatti was not adopted, which described custom as "common practice among *said* States, accepted by them as law" ("*d'une pratique commune des dits Etats, acceptée par eux comme loi*").[114] The final version also supports Haggenmacher's reading, since article 38(2) PCIJ Statute did not include any reference to states or nations.

Whereas general principles of law which needed to be "recognized" might appear closer to natural law than the other two sources,[115] the reference to general principles of *law*, rather than of equity[116] supports the view that the general principles of law were considered as normative, legal concept.[117] The examples discussed by the committee illustrate that general principles can encompass rather broad legal concepts, such as the principle of good faith, and also quite specific concretizations, such as the principle of *res judicata*. The discussions highlighted that general principles were deemed to be important for the application of international law in order to avoid a

---

111 Italics added.
112 Permanent Court of International Justice – Advisory Committee of Jurists, *Procès-Verbaux of the Proceedings of the Committee, June 16th-July 24th 1920* Annex 306, italics added.
113 Haggenmacher, 'La doctrine des deux éléments du droit coutumier dans la pratique de la Cour internationale' 27-28; see also Pellet and Müller, 'Article 38' 909 para 226, stressing that article 38(1)(b) refers to an acceptance, rather than to the will, of states.
114 Permanent Court of International Justice – Advisory Committee of Jurists, *Procès-Verbaux of the Proceedings of the Committee, June 16th-July 24th 1920* 351 (italics added); Haggenmacher, 'La doctrine des deux éléments du droit coutumier dans la pratique de la Cour internationale' 27.
115 ibid 21, 26.
116 The text of article 38 distinguishes between the sources of law, the subsidiary means for the determination of law and a decision *ex aequo et bono*.
117 See also Pellet and Müller, 'Article 38' 925 para 257; for the view that general principles cannot be rigidly distinguished from the other sources on the basis that general principles would be non-consensual Elias and Lim, ''General Principles of Law', 'Soft' Law and the Identification of International Law' 3 ff., and 35 and 49.

non-liquet. They were intended to foster judicial creativity and preclude a premature conclusion that no definite rule of treaty or custom would govern the situation before the court. At the same time, the recognition-requirement requires the judge not to make simply a subjective determination but to strive for an objective assessment. It must not go unnoticed that right from the beginning the reference to "civilized nations" was controversial and partly regarded unnecessary since, in the words of de Lapradelle, "law implies civilisation".[118] Today, there is wide agreement that the historical connotation of the term which in fact had been used to exclude so-called non-Western states[119] deprived this formulation of any meaning.[120] In the context of the recent ILC project on general principles, it is proposed to use the term "general principles recognized by the community of nations"[121], which is inspired by article 15(2) ICCPR.

---

118 Permanent Court of International Justice – Advisory Committee of Jurists, *Procès-Verbaux of the Proceedings of the Committee, June 16th-July 24th 1920* 335.
119 *North Sea Continental Shelf* [1969] ICJ Rep 3 Sep Op Ammoun 132 ff.; Jochen von Bernstorff, 'The Use of Force in International Law before World War I: On Imperial Ordering and the Ontology of the Nation-State' (2018) 29(1) EJIL 238; Weil, 'Le droit international en quête de son identité: cours général de droit international public' 144.
120 On the "'archaic' requirement" Pellet and Müller, 'Article 38' 927 para 262; Herczegh, *General Principles of Law and the International Legal Order* 39-41; Béla Vitanyi, 'Les Positions Doctrinales Concernant Le Sens de la Notion de "Principes généraux de Droit Reconnus Par Les Nations Civilisées"' (1982) LXXXVI RGDIP 54; on the different meanings of civilisation see Liliana Obregon, 'The Civilized and the Uncivilized' in Bardo Fassbender and Anne Peters (eds), *Oxford Handbook of the History of International Law* (Oxford University Press 2012) 917 ff.; but see Tomuschat, 'Obligations Arising For States Without Or Against Their Will' 318-319, arguing that "the qualification 'civilized' is an essential screening element which permits distinction between States, departing from formalistic reliance on sovereign equality" and which permits to exclude states "whose policies and practices are bent on ethnic cleansing, flat neglect of any humanitarian rules of warfare and massive discrimination on ethnic or religious grounds."; cf. also Hugh W Thirlway, *The law and procedure of the international court of justice: fifty years of jurisprudence* (vol 1, Oxford University Press 2013) 243-244; Antoine Favre, 'Les Principes Généraux Du Droit, Fond Commun Du Droit des Gens' in *Recueil d'études de droit international en hommage à P. Guggenheim* (Faculté de Droit de l'Univ de Genève 1968), 370-371.
121 *ILC Report 2019* at 336, 338; *Report of the International Law Commission: Seventy-third session (18 April–3 June and 4 July–5 August 2022)* UN Doc A/77/10 317 (draft conclusion 7).

Chapter 3: Historical Perspectives on article 38 PCIJ Statute

E. *Constructing the Interrelationship in the interwar period*

Article 38 is said to have led to a consolidation of the language with respect to the sources.[122] At the same time, different source preferences and understandings of the interrelationship were developed during the interwar years. This section will examine how and to what extent the interrelationship of the sources was discussed and constructed subsequent to the adoption of the PCIJ Statute in the jurisprudence of the PCIJ (I.), in the codification setting of the League of Nations (II.) and in international legal scholarship (III.).

I. The PCIJ

The PCIJ did not explicitly comment on the interrelationship between sources.[123] The Permanent Court of International Justice affirmed in the famous *Lotus* case a consensual-positivist construction of international law:

> "International law governs relations between independent States. The rules of law binding upon States therefore emanate from their own free will as expressed in conventions or by usages generally accepted as expressing principles of law and established in order to regulate the relations between these coexisting independent communities or with a view to the achievement of common aims. Restrictions upon the independence of States cannot therefore be presumed."[124]

This *dictum* has given rise to different interpretations today: one interpretation equates the absence of a prohibition with the existence of a permission, in

---

[122] Thomas Skouteris, *The notion of progress in international law discourse* (TMC Asser Press 2010) 93, 98 ff.; see also Max Sørensen, *Les sources du droit international: étude sur la jurisprudence de la Cour Permanente de Justice Internationale* (Munksgaard 1946) 40.

[123] On the sources of international law in the jurisprudence of the PCIJ see Akbar Rasulov, 'The Doctrine of Sources in the Discourse of the Permanent Court of International Justice' in Christian J Tams and Malgosia Fitzmaurice (eds), *Legacies of the Permanent Court of International Justice* (Martinus Nijhoff Publishers 2013) 300 ff.; see also Robert Kolb, 'The Jurisprudence of the Permanent Court of International Justice Between Utilitas Publica and Utilitas Singulorum' (2015) 14 The Law and Practice of International Courts and Tribunals 17 ff.; Ole Spiermann, *International legal argument in the Permanent Court of International Justice: the rise of the international judiciary* (Cambridge University Press 2005).

[124] *The Case of SS Lotus: France v Turkey* Merits [1927] PCIJ Series A No 10, 18.

the sense that what is not prohibited by international law is permitted.¹²⁵ According to a different interpretation, the PCIJ merely stated that what was not prohibited by law, was not prohibited by law - the ensuing factual freedom would not constitute a legal norm.¹²⁶ Reading the *Lotus* judgment as a whole, the argument could also be made that the Court did not decide just on the basis of silence of international law: Turkey, it could be argued, had a reasonable connection to the case of the collision between a Turkish and a French vessel and, according to the Court, the territoriality of criminal law was "not an absolute principle of international law" as "all or nearly all these systems of law extend their action to offences committed outside the territory of the State which adopts them".¹²⁷ In addition, the PCIJ in fact did consider an argument based on a principle of law derived from different conventions

---

125 Cf. *Accordance with international law of the unilateral declaration of independence in respect of Kosovo* (Advisory Opinion) [2010] ICJ Rep 425-426 para 57, the International Court of Justice had been asked by the General Assembly whether Kosovo's unilateral declaration of independence was "in accordance with" international law; according to the Court, the "answer to that question turns on whether or not the applicable international law prohibited the declaration of independence [...] The Court is not required by the question it has been asked to take a position on whether international law conferred a positive entitlement on Kosovo unilaterally to declare its independence."; critical of the Court's approach: ibid Decl Simma pp. 478-479 (the Court "could also have considered the possibility that international law can be neutral or deliberately silent on the international lawfulness of certain acts"); but see Anne Peters, 'Does Kosovo Lie in the Lotus-Land of Freedom?' (2011) 24 Leiden Journal of International Law 99, noting that the Court phrased its answer in terms of a "non-violation" without declaring the declaration to be "in accordance with" international law, cf. *Accordance with international law of the unilateral declaration of independence in respect of Kosovo* [2010] ICJ Rep 403, 453; recently the UK Court of Appeals rejected in the context of international humanitarian law the view that the lack of a prohibition equals a permission: *Mohammed (Serdar) v Ministry of Defence, Qasim v Secretary of State for Defence, Rahmatullah v Ministry of Defence, Iraqi Civilians v Ministry of Defence* [2015] EWCA Civ 843 paras 195 ff.
126 Kammerhofer, 'Gaps, the Nuclear Weapons Advisory Opinion and the Structure of International Legal Argument between Theory and Practice' 343, 357: "If there is no law, there is no law."
127 *The Case of SS Lotus* PCIJ Series A No 10, 19, 20. A different rule is provided in Article 11 of the Convention on the High Seas (signed 29 April 1958, entered into force 30 September 1962) 450 UNTS which accords the criminal jurisdiction to the flag State of the State of which the person concerned is a national; according to Crawford, 'Change, Order, Change: The Course of International Law General Course on Public International Law' 55, this was "a rare case of a treaty overruling a decision by the Court on custom."

which, "whilst [...] permitting the war and police vessels of a State to exercise a more or less extensive control over the merchant vessels of another State", expressly reserved jurisdiction to the flag state.[128] In the end, the Court held that it was "not absolutely certain that this stipulation is to be regarded as expressing a general principle of law rather than as corresponding to the extraordinary jurisdiction which these conventions confer on the state-owned ships of a particular country in respect of ships of another country on the high sea".[129] The rejection, thus, was based on reasons relating to the substance of the treaties, rather than on a categorical rejection of the mere possibility to derive principles from conventions. In this context, the Court indirectly expressed doubts on whether the principle enshrined in these conventions lent itself to general application beyond the specific contexts regulated by said conventions and on whether such principle was applicable to a situation "which concern two ships and consequently the jurisdiction of two different States."[130]

Whatever interpretation one adopts, the *Lotus* judgment, if interpreted as confirmation of strict voluntarism, is not representative of the overall case-law of the PCIJ.[131] One year after *Lotus*, in 1928, the PCIJ declared that "it is a principle of international law, and even a general conception of law, that any breach of an engagement involves an obligation to make reparation."[132] The PCIJ recognized general principles such as the prohibition of abuse of rights and the principle of good faith[133], it considered third states' treaties in the interpretation of the law of neutrality and the construction of provisions of the Treaty of Peace of Versailles relating to the Kiel canal[134],

---

128 *The Case of SS Lotus* PCIJ Series A No 10, 26.
129 ibid PCIJ Series A No 10, 27.
130 ibid 27.
131 See also Kolb, 'The Jurisprudence of the Permanent Court of International Justice Between Utilitas Publica and Utilitas Singulorum' 34, concluding that it would be "mistaken to consider the PCIJ as being the champion of the singular utility rooted in the sovereignty of States, i.e. in the 'Lotus society'. The only judgment, which can be mobilized unreservedly in this direction, is precisely the Lotus case of 1927."
132 *Case Concerning the Factory at Chorzow: Germany v. Poland* Judgment of 13 September 1928 [1928] PCIJ Series A 17, 29.
133 *Certain German Interests in Polish Upper Silesia: Germany v. Poland* Judgment [1926] PCIJ Series A 7, 30.
134 *Wimbledon: UK et al v. Germany* Judgment of 17 August 1923 [1923] PCIJ Series A 01, 15, 25-8.

and it assumed the existence of an international minimum standard.[135] As Lauterpacht demonstrated[136], the interpretation of international treaties was guided by general principles of law, such as the principle according to which no one shall be judge in his own case.[137]

The PCIJ based its decisions in several cases on one source and explored the relation to other sources only to a certain extent. In the *Wimbledon* case, the PCIJ did not accept Germany's argument that article 380 of the Treaty of Versailles, according to which the Kiel canal "shall be maintained free and open to the vessels of commerce and of war of all nations at peace with Germany on terms of entire equality", had to be interpreted restrictively, in light of Germany's rights and obligations under the law of neutrality.[138] In particular, the Court saw no problem of sovereignty as "the right of entering into international engagements is an attribute of State sovereignty".[139] Rather, the Court interpreted the law of neutrality in light of other international agreements on the Suez and Panama Canals which served as "illustrations of the general opinion according to which when an artificial waterway connecting two open seas has been permanently dedicated to the use of the whole word [...] even the passage of a belligerent man-of war does not compromise

---

135 For a treaty-based international minimum standard, see *Certain German Interests in Polish Upper Silesia* PCIJ Series A No 07, 33; see also *Minority Schools in Albania* Advisory Opinion of 6 April 1935 [1935] PCIJ Series A/B 64, 18 ff., distinguishing between equality in law and equality in fact.

136 Hersch Lauterpacht, *The development of international law by the International Court* (Stevens 1958) 158 ff. For a recent analysis of *dicta* associated with general principles in PCIJ decisions and individual opinions see Saunders, *General Principles as a Source of International Law* 52 ff.

137 *Interpretation of Article 3, Paragraph 2, of the Treaty of Lausanne: Advisory Opinion of 21 November 1925* [1925] PCIJ Series B 12, 29 ff.

138 This argument was supported by Judges Schücking, Anzilotti, and Huber, see *Wimbledon* 01 Diss Op Schücking 43 ff.: "The right to take special measures in times of war or neutrality has not been expressly renounced ; nor can such renunciation be inferred [...]"; Joint Diss Op Anzilotti and Huber 39-40.

139 ibid 25. For a critique of the Court's textual approach without establishing a relationship to other rules of international law see Sheila Weinberger, 'The Wimbledon Paradox and the World Court: Confronting inevitable conflicts between conventional and customary international law' (1996) 10 Emroy International Law Review 423 ff.; see also Clemens Feinäugle, 'The Wimbledon' [2013] Max Planck EPIL paras 15-6.

the neutrality of the sovereign State under whose jurisdiction the waters in question lie."[140]

The PCIJ ruled in the *Turkish Lighthouse* case solely on the basis of a treaty and did not find it necessary to consider whether "according to the general rules of international law, the territorial sovereign is entitled, in occupied territory, to grant concessions legally enforceable against the State which subsequently acquires the territories it occupies, [which] was debated at some length between the Parties."[141] In contrast, the PCIJ decided the *Eastern Greenland* case between Denmark and Norway on the basis of the general concept of title to sovereignty over Greenland based on a continued display of authority, instead of, as suggested by Judge Anzilotti, focusing the analysis on an agreement reached between Denmark and Norway.[142] As concluded by Sørensen in his extensive study on the PCIJ's jurisprudence, the wording of article 38 of the Statute neither posed a practical difficulty to the Court, nor was it particularly impactful in the settlement of disputes.[143]

II. The 1930 Codification Conference and the discussion of the sources

Even though the 1930 Conference was no success in general with respect to the codification of the three topics which had been deemed "ripe" for codification, namely the responsibility of states for damage caused in their territory to the person or property of foreigners, the rules concerning nationality and the law relating to territorial waters,[144] it was of legal-political importance as it ultimately indicated support in favour of the triad of sources.

---

140 *The Case of SS Lotus* Series A No 10, 28; see also Lazare Kopelmanas, 'Custom as a Means of the Creation of International Law' (1937) 18 BYIL 136.
141 *Lighthouse Case between France and Greece: France v Greece* Judgment of 17 March 1934 [1934] PCIJ Series A/B 62, 25.
142 *Legal Status of Eastern Greenland* Series A/B No 53, 23, 45 ff. and Diss Op Anzilotti 76 and 94: "It is consequently on the basis of that agreement which, as between the Parties, has precedence over general law, that the dispute ought to have been decided."
143 Sørensen, *Les sources du droit international: étude sur la jurisprudence de la Cour Permanente de Justice Internationale* 250-251.
144 In the following, this section refers to the documents and protocols compiled in Shabtai Rosenne (ed), *League of Nations Conference for the Codification of International Law (1930)* (vol 4, Dobbs Ferry, NY: Oceana 1975).

The sources discussion started in the context of the Basis of Discussion No 2 on the responsibility for injuries committed to aliens with the question whether the draft should speak of "international obligations" or rather refer explicitly to the sources of international law, and if so, to which one. Three camps can be identified in this debate.

One camp sought to avoid defining "international obligations" and thereby any discussion of the sources and substantive obligations. Cavaglieri opposed the Preparatory Committee's suggestion to speak of international obligations "resulting from treaty or otherwise" and expressed sympathy for simply speaking of "international obligations".[145] The phrase "or otherwise" appeared to Cavaglieri as too vague, and he argued that in case that the reference to treaties would be retained one should rather say "resulting from treaties or from recognised principles of international law".[146] The proposal to speak of international obligations reflected the understanding of international responsibility as an objective regime that presupposes an international wrong, regardless of the source. Cavaglieri placed importance on the distinction between substantive obligations and the law of responsibility and emphasized that the content of the obligations "is not ripe for codification".[147]

In contrast, a second camp stressed the need to be as precise as possible with respect to the origin of international obligations. This camp was skeptical towards any references to unwritten international law which needs to be seen against the background of the discussions of the contested international minimum standard and the question of whether equal treatment of aliens sufficed for compliance with this standard.[148] José Gustavo Guerrero from El Salvador[149], who would later became the last president of the PCIJ and the first president of the ICJ, argued that international obligations should be defined as "resulting from treaties and from the provisions of the present Convention".[150] Mr Sipsom from Roumania endorsed this proposal, arguing that custom itself was (in part) uncertain and that the conference should therefore frame rules and state cases which by legal practice or custom are recognised

---

145 ibid 1455; ibid 1459.
146 ibid 1456.
147 ibid 1464.
148 On this discussion see below, p. 564.
149 On Guerrero's role in the context of international responsibility for injuries to aliens see below, p. 566; Alan Nissel, 'The Duality of State Responsibility' (2013) 44(3) Columbia Human Rights Law Review 815 ff.
150 Rosenne, *League of Nations Conference for the Codification of International Law (1930)* 1456.

Chapter 3: Historical Perspectives on article 38 PCIJ Statute

as cases of responsibility of an extra-contractual nature.[151] In response to a British delegate's criticism that Guerrero's proposal would exclude customary international law,[152] Guerrero suggested to add "well-defined international custom" from which international obligations might emerge.[153] The reference to custom should restrictively include only customary international law that was indisputably recognized by the contracting states.[154] According to Guerrero, the codification conference should not focus too much on article 38 PCIJ Statute which was intended to "supply indications and guidance for the Court in reaching its decisions, [...] [whilst in codification] we are in no way concerned with giving guidance, but with laying down the law. The two things are quite different."[155] Sipsom from Roumania added that "[t]he judge's duty is one thing; the legislator's duty is another", as the latter should make and state the law precise terms, while the former would still be able to find reasons not in the written law if inadequate but "but in custom, in general principles, in legal doctrine and in judicial decisions."[156]

---

151 Rosenne, *League of Nations Conference for the Codification of International Law (1930)* 1457.
152 See for instance the British delegate, Mr Becket from Great Britain argued that Guerrero's formulation would exclude and thus miss customary international law. One should not limit oneself to conventions since "there will still remain a considerable amount of customary law which will impose obligations upon States and to which this principle must apply. [...] it is clear, I think, that we cannot limit the obligations to those resulting from international conventions.", ibid 1457.
153 ibid 1461. Sipsom suggested inserting a provision to the effect that obligations "may arise not only from treaties but from customary law which is indisputably established and recognised by all the contracting States" (1464). d'Avilla Lima from Portugal supported Sipsom's idea since in this way "the text would certainly be more definite" (1465).
154 See Mr d'Avilla Lima from Portugal opted for Sipsom's amendment, "custom indisputably recognised by the contracting States" since in this way "the text would certainly be more definite." Buero from Uruguay strongly emphasized that "[f]rom our point of view, customary law in general is inacceptable, particularly as regards international law [...] we know that customs are established through the domination of certain States, and we cannot now recognise those customs that we have not definitely accepted."
155 ibid 1467 (Guerrero); see also Mr Sipsom from Roumania, according to whom there is no international custom recognised by the whole world; a custom might be imposed on states by judges in litigation, 1474.
156 ibid 1475-1476; cf. on a similar distinction between lawmaker and adjudicator recently Onuma Yasuaki, 'The ICJ: An Emperor Without Clothes? International Conflict Resolution, Article 38 of the ICJ Statute and the Sources of International

A commitment to article 38 PCIJ may be said to characterize the position of a third camp. Castberg from Norway argued that one should not "lay down any rule concerning sources of international law other than those mentioned in Article 38".[157] In particular, under this provision rules would arise "not only from treaties and from custom but from 'the general principles of law recognised by civilised nations', from judicial practice and from doctrine."[158]

In the end, the view prevailed that a decision to base the codification on a different understanding of sources might create unnecessary tensions.[159] After a draft committee had proposed a formula which deliberately did not copy article 38 in order to avoid the impression that the final result of the codification conference would in any way impair or impact article 38,[160] several delegates argued that the question of the sources of obligations was already decided by the international community and referred to article 38.[161]

Law' in Nisuke Ando and others (eds), *Liber amicorum Judge Shigeru Oda* (Kluwer Law Internat 2002) vol 1 192 ff.; cf. also Jan Hendrik Willem Verzijl, *International Law in Historical Perspective. General Subjects* (vol 1, AW Sijthoff 1968) 30 (critical of references in codification conventions to "other rules of international law").

157 Rosenne, *League of Nations Conference for the Codification of International Law (1930)* 1464. In a similar sense Dinichert from Switzerland (1458).

158 ibid 1465. According to Politis, a qualification of customary international law to the effect that it must have been accepted by all states was unnecessary since "[b]y its very definition, custom is a rule accepted by all the States" (1466). Abd el Hamid Bdaoui Pacha from Egypt (1466, 1467) and Dinichert from Switzerland (1467) disagreed. As put by Dinichert: "I cannot accept this formal statement that custom has the force of law, only when the principle in question is recognised by all countries without exception."

159 See ibid 1468, Mr Limburg from the Netherlands; Abd el Hamid Bdaoui Pacha from Egypt, 1477.

160 ibid 1472: "The international obligations referred to in the present Convention are those resulting from treaty or customary law which have for their object to ensure for the persons and property of foreigners treatment in conformity with the principles recognised to be essential by the community of nations."

161 ibid 1480 (Dinichert): "Great and small States are now subject to precisely the same law-the one that we hammered out, the on that exists, the one we intend to develop and not to destroy. That is what I wanted to say. It will explain why the Swiss delegation will very regretfully be unable to support any proposal that does not confirm the existing law." Mr Nagaoka from Japan argued that the general principles of law should be included to avoid an *a contrario* conclusion by which general principles of law would be excluded (1481). Also Mr. Erich from Finland regretted that so far general principles of law were not contemplated in detail, since the discussion concerned only treaty and custom. Furthermore, he made the strong claim that other bases of discussions would rely or include general principles of law, for instance

The Chairman's proposal to establish a sub-committee was accepted and the sub-committee reached unanimous agreement on the following formula which emphasized all three sources:

> "The expression 'international obligations' in the present Convention means obligations resulting from treaty, custom or the general principles of law, which are designed to assure to foreigners in respect of their persons and property a treatment in conformity with the rules accepted by the community of nations."[162]

Even though the 1930 Codification Conference was no success according to its own standards as it failed in achieving agreement on general rules, it was of legal-political significance for the triad of sources. The very idea to maintain three sources in international law was neither uncontroversial nor unchallenged. At the same time, this critique could not assert itself, as the sub-committee's formula indicates. That the project of codification may not necessarily lead to the elimination of unwritten international law will become even clearer in the work of the ILC.[163]

III. The inter-war scholarship on the interrelationship of sources

1. Overview

The inter-war years witnessed lively debates on the sources of international law. In particular, article 38(3) PCIJ Statute gave rise to several monographs and articles.[164]

---

if liability was excluded for reasons of (financial) necessity or if the amount of damage was not further defined (1481). Mr Urrutia from Colombia also opted for continuity to the former conferences. Texts such as the Statute should be considered (1481-1482); see also Rosenne, *League of Nations Conference for the Codification of International Law (1930)* 1473, Castberg from Norway, Nagaoka from Japan on the importance of general principles of law for state responsibility.

162 ibid 1535; in other parts of the 1930 codification, the draft article was aligned with article 38 . In the Nationality committee, the Chairman defended the general reference to other sources, also as placeholder allowing to take account of future developments in international law (see 1087).

163 See below, p. 317.

164 Jean Spiropoulos, *Die allgemeinen Rechtsgrundsätze im Völkerrecht: eine Auslegung von Art. 38,3 des Status des ständigen Internationalen Gerichtshofs* (Verlag des Instituts für Internationales Recht an der Univ Kiel 1928); Elfried Härle, *Die allgemeinen Entscheidungsgrundlagen des Ständigen Internationalen Gerichtshofes: eine kritisch-würdigende Untersuchung über Artikel 38 des Gerichtshof-Statuts* (Vahlen

It is difficult to structure the general debate in terms of classifications such as natural law or positivism for several reasons. Authors' nuanced positions often escape a clear classification. Also, there is a risk to attribute a meaning to each concept which would not necessarily correspond to the historical meaning during the inter-war years. If one attempted to construct these categories according to the meaning of that time, one would be surprised of the way these categories were used. For instance, the Greek international lawyer Jean Spiropoulos declared in his German monograph on general principles the "orthodox international law positivism" to be a deadly born child. As he regarded general principles to be legal ideas which, by virtue of their general

---

1933), Pierre Grapin, *Valeur internationale des principes généraux du droit: contribution à l'étude de l'article 38, § 3 du Statut de la Cour permanente de Justice internationale* (Domat-Montchrestien 1934); see furthermore Arrigo Cavaglieri, 'Concetto e caratteri del diritto internazionale generale' (1922) 14 Estratto dalla Rivista di diritto internazionale 289 ff., 479 ff.; Charles de Visscher, 'Contribution à l'étude des sources du droit international' (1933) 14 Revue de Droit International et de Legislation Comparee 395 ff.; Lazare Kopelmanas, 'Essai d'une Théorie des Sources Formelles de Droit International' (1938) 1 Revue de droit international 101 ff.; Rudolf Aladár Métall, 'Skizzen zu einer Systematik der völkerrechtlichen Quellenlehre' (1931) 11 Zeitschrift für öffentliches Recht 416 ff.; Giorgio Balladore Pallieri, *I "principi generali del diritto riconosciuti dalle nazioni civili" nell' art. 38 dello statuto della Corte permanente di giustizia internazionale* (Istituto giuridico della R università 1931); Georges Scelle, 'Essai sur les sources formelles du droit international' in *Recueil d'études sur les sources du droit en l'honneur de François Gény* (Recueil Sirey 1934) vol 3 400 ff.; Kopelmanas, 'Custom as a Means of the Creation of International Law' 127 ff.; Alfred Verdross, *Die Einheit des rechtlichen Weltbildes auf Grundlage der Völkerrechtsverfassung* (Mohr Siebeck 1923); Verdross, 'Die allgemeinen Rechtsgrundsätze als Völkerrechtsquelle Zugleich ein Beitrag zum Problem der Grundnorm des positiven Völkerrechts'; Heydte, 'Glossen zu einer Theorie der allgemeinen Rechtsgrundsätze' 289 ff.; Karl Strupp, *Das Recht des internationalen Richters, nach Billigkeit zu entscheiden* (Noske 1930); Sørensen, *Les sources du droit international: étude sur la jurisprudence de la Cour Permanente de Justice Internationale*; Nicolas Politis, *The new aspects of international law: A Series of Lectures Delivered at Columbia University in July 1926* (Carnegie Endowment for International Peace 1928); Edwin M Borchard, 'The Theory and Sources of International Law' in *Recueil d'études sur les sources du droit en l'honneur de François Gény* (Recueil Sirey 1936) vol 3 328 ff.; Louis Le Fur, 'La coutume et les principes généraux du droit comme sources du droit international public' in *Recueil d'études sur les sources du droit en l'honneur de François Gény* (Recueil Sirey 1934) vol 3 362 ff.; George A Finch, *The Sources of Modern International Law* (Carnegie Endowment for International Peace 1937); John Chipman Gray, *The Nature and Sources of the Law* (2nd edn, The MacMillan Company 1931).

character, can claim general application and can be regarded as integrating part of any legal order, he classified them, as natural law ("*Naturrecht*").[165] He did so in explicit contradistinction to Hersch Lauterpacht and what he regarded to be Lauterpacht's "positivist" approach. Lauterpacht himself, however, is on record for having characterized general principles as "*un coup mortel au positivisme*".[166]

Notwithstanding, it is possible to identify certain strands. There is a group of authors who were closer to voluntarism or placed greater hopes in the prospect of codification. Karl Strupp is one example, maintaining that only treaty and customary international law would be true sources and that more international law should be achieved through codification. Article 38(3) and similar provisions of other arbitration agreements constituted a *lex arbitri* which addressed solely the applicable law of the PCIJ.[167] Other scholars stressed the importance of general principles for the interpretation and application of treaties and customary international law[168] which could be

---

165 Spiropoulos, *Die allgemeinen Rechtsgrundsätze im Völkerrecht: eine Auslegung von Art. 38,3 des Status des ständigen Internationalen Gerichtshofs*, preface, 67, and 9: "Rechtsgedanken [...], die infolge ihres allgemeinen Charakters Allgemeingültigkeit haben und deshalb auch als integrierender Bestandteil einer jeden Rechtsordnung betrachtet werden müssen."; see Walter Küntzel, *Ungeschriebenes Völkerrecht Ein Beitrag zu der Lehre von den Quellen des Völkerrechts* (Gräfe u Unzer 1935) 36 ff. who by and large is in line with Spiropoulos, except for his classification as "natural law"; likewise Härle, *Die allgemeinen Entscheidungsgrundlagen des Ständigen Internationalen Gerichtshofes: eine kritisch-würdigende Untersuchung über Artikel 38 des Gerichtshof-Statuts* 112-116; as Spiropoulos later remarked, ultimately it depends on one's understanding of the terms positivism and natural law, Jean Spiropoulos, *Théorie générale du droit international* (Pichon et Durand-Auzias 1930) 107.
166 Hersch Lauterpacht, 'Règles générales du droit de la paix' (1937) 62(IV) RdC 164; see also Visscher, 'Contribution à l'étude des sources du droit international' 405-406.
167 Strupp, *Das Recht des internationalen Richters, nach Billigkeit zu entscheiden* 85-86. Strupp is ready to admit that certain characteristics of the treaty might belong to general principles of law.
168 Georges Ripert, 'Les règles du droit civil applicables aux rapports internationaux: (contribution à l'étude des principes généraux du droit visés au statut de la Cour permanente de justice internationale)' (1933) 44 RdC 573-575, 577, 579 (principles are a category distinct from custom and from natural law, they must be found in positive legislation); Leibholz, 'Verbot der Willkür und des Ermessensmißbrauches im völkerrechtlichen Verkehr der Staaten' 77 ff.; Visscher, 'Contribution à l'étude des sources du droit international' 406, 412; see also Sørensen, *Les sources du droit international: étude sur la jurisprudence de la Cour Permanente de Justice*

ascertained not only in municipal law but also in international law where principles were implied in treaties and customary international law.[169] If one attempts to systematize the scholarly discussion, several greater streams can be identified, although one must be aware that there are many authors escaping a clear classification. Anzilotti's voluntarism (2.), Scelle's *droit objectif* (3.), Kelsen's positivism (4.), Verdross' doctrine of principles (5.) and Lauterpacht's study of the judicial function (6.) exemplify that different perspectives on the relationship of sources were connected to different perspectives on the law.

2. Dionisio Anzilotti

Dionisio Anzilotti's approach in scholarship and on the bench of the PCIJ is characterized by dualism and voluntarism.[170] As international law and municipal law did not share a common basic norm from which each system derived its legal force, neither system could establish by itself norms valid for the other one or even determining the validity of the other system's rules.[171] Therefore, normative conflicts were precluded:[172] Violations of international

---

Internationale 241; cf. Arrigo Cavaglieri, 'Concetto E Caratteri Del Diritto Internazionale Generale' (1921) 14 Rivista Di Diritto Internazionale 504-505 footnote 3 (on merging customary international law and general principles); Verdross, *Die Verfassung der Völkerrechtsgemeinschaft* 67.

169 Basdevant, 'Règles générales du droit de la paix' 498-503 (on the technique of extrapolation of principles from treaties and custom, principles more as technique than as a source); Frede Castberg, 'La méthodologie du droit international public' (1933) 43 RdC 370-372; Charles Rousseau, *Principes généraux du droit international public. Introduction. Sources* (vol 1, Pedone 1944) 901; Cf. Visscher, 'Contribution à l'étude des sources du droit international' 406-407 (distinguishing general principles of law and general principles of international law by their origin); Kopelmanas, 'Custom as a Means of the Creation of International Law' 136.

170 For an overview see Giorgio Gaja, 'Positivism and Dualism in Dionisio Anzilotti' (1992) 3 EJIL 123 ff.; on Anzilotti's opinions and his references to general principles of law see José Maria Ruda, 'The Opinions of Judge Dionisio Anzilotti at the Permanent Court of International Justice' (1992) 3(1) EJIL 103 ff.

171 Dionisio Anzilotti, *Corso di Diritto Internazionale* (vol 1, Athenaeum 1912) 35; see also Dionisio Anzilotti, *Cours de droit international 1: Introduction, théoriés, générales* (Gilbert Gidel tr, Sirey 1929) 51 ff.

172 Dionisio Anzilotti, *Lehrbuch des Völkerrechts* (Cornelia Bruns and Karl Schmid trs, de Gruyter 1929) 38. The work was translated by Cornelia Bruns and Karl Schmid, the translation was supervised and authorised by Anzilotti.

law by domestic statutes were considered as "facts",[173] and resolved by the rules of international responsibility.[174]

Anzilotti's understanding of sources is characterized by voluntarist positivism. Both treaties and customary international law were rooted in the explicit respectively tacit consent of states, both sources of law were equally ranked, capable of mutual derogation; the relationship between norms (of different sources) was governed by the *lex posterior* principle and the *lex specialis* principle.[175] The only difference between both sources was the function of customary international law as general international law.[176] Furthermore, as he regarded treaties to be rather static and rigid and difficult to formally change, customary international law was said to better meet with its inherent flexibility the needs of the international community.[177]

---

173 See already *Certain German Interests in Polish Upper Silesia* PCIJ Series A No 07, 19: "From the standpoint of International Law and of the Court which is its organ, municipal laws are merely facts which express the will and constitute the activities of States, in the same manner as do legal decisions or administrative measures. The Court is certainly not called upon to interpret the Polish law as such; but there is nothing to prevent the Court's giving judgment on the question whether or not, in applying that law, Poland is acting in conformity with its obligations towards Germany under the Geneva Convention." It would be misleading to assume on this quotation that the PCIJ was not willing to appreciate and interpret domestic law as "law", see for instance *Case Concerning the Payment in Gold of Brazilian Federal Loans Contracted in France: France v The United States of Brazil* Judgment of 12 July 1929 [1929] PCIJ Series A 21, 124-125: "Once the Court has arrived at the conclusion that it is necessary to apply the municipal law of a particular country, there seems no doubt that it must seek to apply it as it would be applied in that country. [...] Of course, the Court will endeavour to make appreciation of the jurisprudence of municipal courts. If this is uncertain or divided, it will rest with the Court to select the interpretation which it considers most in conformity with the law."; Anzilotti, *Cours de droit international 1: Introduction, théoriés, générales* 57; see also Jean d'Aspremont, 'The Permanent Court of International Justice and Domestic Courts: A Variation in Roles' in Christian J Tams and Malgosia Fitzmaurice (eds), *Legacies of the Permanent Court of International Justice* (Martinus Nijhoff Publishers 2013) 226 ff.
174 Anzilotti, *Lehrbuch des Völkerrechts* 42.
175 ibid 48-49; 69-70, 74-76. Anzilotti conceded that by this mutual derogability the relation of sources in international law differed from the relation in municipal law; on mutual derogability, see also Heilborn, 'Les Sources Du Droit International' 29.
176 Anzilotti, *Lehrbuch des Völkerrechts* 65.
177 ibid 60-63.

Anzilotti recognized next to treaty and custom "constructive norms" which, it is submitted, functionally resemble general principles of law.[178] These constituted the "necessary logical premises" and prerequisites without which rules explicitly agreed on by treaty or custom would make no sense. In Anzilotti's view, these structural norms were an essential element of any legal order.[179] Article 38(3) of the PCIJ Statute not only encompassed these constructive norms but also authorized the Court to resort to rules and principles belonging specifically to municipal law for analogical application. Therefore, reasoning by analogy should foster the productivity of the sources and avoid a *non-liquet* situation. In Anzilotti's opinion, however, article 38(3) constituted a deviation from general international law, as far as these analogies were concerned.[180]

Similar to Kelsen, Anzilotti regarded *pacta sunt servanda* as basic norm[181]. At the same time, he accepted the concept of necessary premises of law and, in line with Georges Scelle, he stressed the role of customary international law as a corrective to the allegedly less flexible and more static treaty law. To him, customary international law was more than just the practice of states and fulfilled a constitutional function in the international legal order.[182]

---

178 See also Degan, 'General Principles of Law (A Source of General International Law)' 64; it is noteworthy that the PCIJ within one year held in Lotus that rules must stem from treaty or custom, and in Chrozow, that legal responsibility was a general conception of law, see *The Case of SS Lotus* PCIJ Series A No 10, 18; *Case Concerning the Factory at Chorzow* PCIJ Series A No 17, 29.
179 Anzilotti, *Lehrbuch des Völkerrechts* 49; Anzilotti, *Cours de droit international 1: Introduction, théoriés, générales* 68.
180 Anzilotti, *Lehrbuch des Völkerrechts* 85-87; see also Ernst Rabel, 'Rechtsvergleichung und internationale Rechtsprechung' (1927) 1 Zeitschrift für ausländisches und internationales Privatrecht 18 according to whom general principles of law become law through the judge.
181 Anzilotti, *Lehrbuch des Völkerrechts* 50; Anzilotti, *Cours de droit international 1: Introduction, théoriés, générales* 44 f.
182 As it was pointed out by Gaja, 'Positivism and Dualism in Dionisio Anzilotti' 128 with reference to a note written by Anzilotti, the late Anzilotti suggested to embrace "a broader concept of custom - and perhaps use a different term - in order to accommodate what is true in the so-called necessary and constitutional law of international society."

Chapter 3: Historical Perspectives on article 38 PCIJ Statute

3. Georges Scelle

Georges Scelle's work stood under the intellectual influence of the teachings of French constitutional legal scholar Leon Duguit who regarded the interdependence of human-beings and intersocial solidarity as basis of law.[183] Scelle's legal monism was not confined to the epistemological perspective of legal cognition.[184] Legal monism implied a normative hierarchy according to which higher ranked norms (of international law) prevailed over lower ranked norms (of domestic law) and addressed not only states but also extrastate groups such as international workers or churches.[185] One aspect of his monism was institutional pluralism. In contrast to a hierarchically organized superstate-system, institutions were by and large missing in the interstate system. This observation led to the introduction of the concept of *dedoublement fonctionnel*[186], according to which national officers had a dual function: they were agents of national law when acting in the national order and agents of international law when acting in the international order. Scelle spoke of

---

183 Léon Duguit, *Traité de Droit Constitutionnel La régle du droit: le probléme de l'Etat* (vol 1, Ancienne Libr Fontemoing 1921) 1-110; on Duguit's influence on Scelle see Robert Kolb, 'Politis and Sociological Jurisprudence of Inter-War International Law' (2012) 23(1) EJIL 237; Oliver Diggelmann, *Anfänge der Völkerrechtssoziologie Die Völkerrechtskonzeptionen von Max Huber und Georges Scelle im Vergleich* (Schulthess 2000) 170-173; see generally Lazare Kopelmanas, 'La pensée de Georges Scelle et ses possibilités d'application à quelques problémes récents de droit international' [1961] Journal du Droit International 350 ff.
184 On Kelsen see below, p. 195.
185 Georges Scelle, 'Règles générales du droit de la paix' (1933) 46 RdC 351-352, 360; see also Hubert Thierry, 'The Thoughts of Georges Scelle' (1990) 1 EJIL 200; for a discussion of Scelle by the late Kelsen, published post mortem, see Hans Kelsen, *Auseinandersetzungen zur reinen Rechtslehre: kritische Bemerkungen zu Georges Scelle und Michel Virally* (Kurt Ringhofer and Robert Walter eds, Springer 1987) 26-60, 58.
186 See also Scelle, 'Essai sur les sources formelles du droit international' 410; Georges Scelle, 'Le phénomène juridique du dédoublement fonctionnel' in Walter Schätzel and Hans-Jürgen Schlochauer (eds), *Rechtsfragen der internationalen Organisation: Festschrift für Hans Wehberg zu seinem 70. Geburtstag* (Klostermann 1956); according to Antonio Cassese, 'Remarks on Scelle's Theory of "Role Splitting" (dédoublement fonctionnel) in International Law' (1990) 1 EJIL 213, 215, Scelle himself recognized after the Inter-War years the suprastate society only as an ideal, and the concept of dedoublement fonctionnel only as tool to overcome current deficiencies of the international legal order, a tool that needs itself being overcome.

the fundamental law of *dedoublement fonctionnel*, which indicated that this concept was a normative, rather than an empirical, concept.[187]

Within Scelle's conception, law was subordinated to the social purpose, it was the "outcome of the solidarity created by social needs" and served the general interests of the community.[188] The function of positive law was said to give expression to the *droit objectif* which was preexisting and yet dependent on the historic state of the respective society.[189] Lawmakers' focus on the *droit objectif* should prevent what otherwise could be considered to constitute "arbitrary" lawmaking.[190] According to Scelle, it must be presumed, unless proven otherwise, that positive law coincided with objective law, otherwise positive law would be deprived of binding force.[191]

By postulating the existence of only one legal order, this monist strand regarded general principles of law and customary international law to be closely connected, in fact, general principles of law constituted a general custom, whereas customary international law was a more special custom that was based on the practice at the international level only.[192]

Similar to the work of Anzilotti, treaty and customary international law were of equal validity, each capable of overriding the other.[193] However, it was the overriding capacity of customary international law which assumed an important, if not constitutional function in Scelle's model. Custom required

---

187 Scelle, 'Règles générales du droit de la paix' 357-358, see also at 150 for the view that national courts would act as international agents when applying private international law; but see Kelsen, *Auseinandersetzungen zur reinen Rechtslehre: kritische Bemerkungen zu Georges Scelle und Michel Virally* 42, and 49-59 (criticizing Scelle's understanding of the relationship between the international legal order and the domestic legal order).

188 See Politis, *The new aspects of international law: A Series of Lectures Delivered at Columbia University in July 1926* 3, 15; Scelle, 'Règles générales du droit de la paix' 349-350.

189 ibid 428; see also Visscher, 'Contribution à l'étude des sources du droit international' 402-403.

190 Politis, *The new aspects of international law: A Series of Lectures Delivered at Columbia University in July 1926* 15-16.

191 Scelle, 'Règles générales du droit de la paix' 349.

192 ibid 436-437; Kolb, *La bonne foi en droit international public Contribution à l'étude des principes généraux de droit* 32-33; cf. for a similar view on the relationship Härle, *Die allgemeinen Entscheidungsgrundlagen des Ständigen Internationalen Gerichtshofes: eine kritisch-würdigende Untersuchung über Artikel 38 des Gerichtshof-Statuts* 301, who regards general prinicples as *lex generalis* and customary international law as *lex specialis*.

193 Scelle, 'Règles générales du droit de la paix' 435.

concordant legal acts and a collective consensus, rather than unanimity.[194] The treaty, in contrast, was just a contractual *instrumentum*, a formal act,[195] which had an objective value when complying with objective law and the social need.[196] Customary law and general principles of law such as *rebus sic stantibus* ("*un principe general du droit*") constituted the means for keeping the positive law updated and in accordance with the *droit objectif*.[197] Should rules no longer meet the social needs and necessities, they must be modified or repelled since there could be no permanent contradiction between the *droit objectif* and positive law. As Scelle put it,[198] the legal dynamic must follow the social dynamic, and the positive law must follow the objective law.

Given this role attributed to customary international law and general principles of law, it is not surprising that Scelle had reservations about codification. In his view, codification had a tendency to become too conservative, to call into question existing law, and to lead to a form (treaty) which was fragile, slow, risky and in need of revision from time to time.[199]

Scelle's scholarship approached the interrelationship of sources from the perspective of the *droit objectif*. Its universalist tones and optimism may have overestimated the solidarity and underestimated conflicting interests which law has to reconcile.[200] It assumed law and its sources only as confirmation of social needs, as a harmonious whole. The idea that law will not exert obligatory force when being considered out of touch with what is regarded as social needs is not so different from Fuller's theory mentioned in the

---

194 Scelle, 'Règles générales du droit de la paix' 383, 421, 434.
195 ibid 446.
196 ibid 454 on third-party effects.
197 ibid 476.
198 ibid 477; Scelle, 'Essai sur les sources formelles du droit international' 402.
199 Scelle, 'Règles générales du droit de la paix' 466-467. For a different view of a scholar of the sociological view see Politis, *The new aspects of international law: A Series of Lectures Delivered at Columbia University in July 1926* 70. He rejected both extremes: the establishment of a complete system of codes and the mere confirmation of existing rules "without adding to them anything new". "The middle way is a work both of confirmation and of reshaping. This is the sense in which the codification of international law is generally understood."
200 Cf. Thierry, 'The Thoughts of Georges Scelle' 204-205; see also Kopelmanas, 'Essai d'une Théorie des Sources Formelles de Droit International' 110; Kopelmanas, 'La pensée de Georges Scelle et ses possibilités d'application à quelques problémes récents de droit international' 373; Kolb, 'Politis and Sociological Jurisprudence of Inter-War International Law' 241.

previous chapter,[201] or Ago's theory of spontaneous law which emphasized the significance of the needs felt by a legal community.[202] Yet, a difference that notably exist today in comparison to Scelle's time and which may affect the relationship of sources is a more developed doctrine of treaty interpretation which allows the legal operator to adapt the interpretation of the treaty to changing circumstances without having to take recourse to customary international law.[203]

4. Hans Kelsen

The Vienna school, the pure science of law, developed an approach which attempted to base international law on an objective grounding, thereby divorcing it from the will of states.[204] Being a general theory of law, the pure science of law concerned both domestic law and international law.[205] It postulated a monism which integrated domestic law and international law within one legal theory.[206] With respect to international law, this school aimed at establishing an objective understanding of the concept of customary international law and the concept of treaty law with important repercussions on the interrelationship of sources. The following lines focus on the work of Hans Kelsen, being aware of the fact that Kelsen was only one proponent of the Vienna school the members of which influenced and partly departed from each other by developing different approaches.[207]

---

201 See above, page 118.
202 See below, p. 639.
203 For examples in legal practice in the context of the ECHR and of international investment law, see below, p. 403, and p. 557.
204 Josef L Kunz, 'The "Vienna School" and International Law' (1933) 11 New York University Law Quarterly Review 370 ff.
205 Josef L Kunz, 'Völkerrechtswissenschaft und reine Rechtslehre' (1923) 6(1) Zeitschrift für öffentliches Recht 1 ff.
206 On the systemic character see Georges Abi-Saab, 'Cours général de droit international public' (1987) 207 RdC 108: "Kelsen est peut-être l'auteur qui a plus contribué à asseoir la vision du droit comme système au cours du XXe siècle."
207 It shall be briefly noted that this section focuses not only on Kelsen's scholarship produced in the interwar period but also on his scholarship after the second world war which confirmed, explained or modified earlier held views.

Chapter 3: Historical Perspectives on article 38 PCIJ Statute

a) Legal-theoretical overview

The monism of the Vienna School rejected a voluntaristic model and proposed a norm-focused positivist approach instead. The idea of monism in this context did not imply that international law and municipal law would not constitute different legal systems. Rather, international and municipal law were linked from the epistemological perspective of legal cognition.[208]

Central to Kelsen's account is the so-called *Stufenbau* of the legal order, the chain of delegations or the "gradual concretization of the law"[209], which Kelsen had borrowed from Adolf Julius Merkl[210]. According to this model, the validity of a norm is determined by whether it constitutes a lawful delegation from a higher norm. A domestic statute owes, for instance, its validity to the higher-ranked constitutional norm. Within this chain of delegations, the law becomes concretized and individualized. The court, by applying a general norm to a particular case, creates an individual norm, the validity of which rests on the statute that had been applied. If the statute allows for different interpretations, it is for the court to make a decision and to determine

---

208 Hans Kelsen, *Das Problem der Souveränität und die Theorie des Völkerrechts Beitrag zu einer reinen Rechtslehre* (Mohr Siebeck 1920) 123. This monism did not necessarily suggest the primacy of international law. Kelsen argued that either system, the municipal and the international law, could reasonably claim hierarchy from the perspective of legal cognition and that the decision in favour of one system would not be predetermined by legal logic but would constitute a political value judgment or decision, ibid 314-317. For an overview see Jochen von Bernstorff, *The public international law theory of Hans Kelsen: believing in universal law* (Thomas Dunlap tr, Cambridge University Press 2010) 104 ff. and 246: "In a paradoxical way, Kelsen's formal understanding of legal scholarship, which sought to expel the political from the realm of legal cognition, generated in the choice hypothesis the far-reaching theoretical concession that legal cognition in international law at its basis was also subjective and political in character."

209 Hersch Lauterpacht, 'Kelsen's pure science of law' in Elihu Lauterpacht (ed), *International Law Being the Collected Papers of Hersch Lauterpacht* (Cambridge University Press 1975) vol 2 411.

210 Adolf Merkl, *Die Lehre von der Rechtskraft entwickelt aus dem Rechtsbegriff* (Franz Deuticke 1923) 201-228.

the meaning of the rule for the concrete case.[211] It is against this background that Kelsen said that

> "[c]reation and application of law are only relatively, not absolutely, opposed to each other. In regulating its own creation, law also regulates its own application. By 'source' of law not only the methods of creating law but also the methods of applying law may be understood."[212]

If the court got the law wrong and the individual norm therefore did not constitute a lawful delegation from the higher norm, the consequence would depend on whether the judgment still met the minimum conditions of the legal order in order to be valid and, depending on the appellate procedure, voidable. This rule of the legal order which establishes minimum conditions and maximum conditions is called "error-calculus"[213] ("*Fehlerkalkül*").[214] In reaction to this doctrine of Merkl, Kelsen developed the idea of an alternative authorization according to which courts are authorized by the legal order

---

211 Hans Kelsen, *Reine Rechtslehre Studienausgabe der 1. Auflage 1934* (Matthias Jestaedt ed, Mohr Siebeck 2008) 100-116; cf. also von Bernstorff, 'Specialized Courts and Tribunals as the Guardians of International Law? The Nature and Function of Judicial Interpretation in Kelsen and Schmitt' 11-14; von Bernstorff, 'Hans Kelsen on Judicial Law-Making by International Courts and Tribunals: a Theory of Global Judicial Imperialism?' 36: "hyper-realistic general theory of court decisions as individualized lawmaking"; cf. also Jörg Kammerhofer, 'Taking the Rules of Interpretation Seriously, but Not Literally? A Theoretical Reconstruction of Orthodox Dogma' (2017) 86(2) Nordic Journal of International Law 136-138.

212 Kelsen, *Principles of International Law (1952)* 304; Hans Kelsen, 'Contribution à la théorie du traité international' (1936) 10 Revue internationale de la théorie du droit 254; Kelsen and Tucker, *Principles of International Law (1967)* 437; see also Kelsen, *Reine Rechtslehre Studienausgabe der 1. Auflage 1934* 73 ff.

213 Christoph Kletzer, 'Kelsen's Development of the Fehlerkalkül-Theory' (2005) 18(1) Ratio Juris 48, 50: "A Fehlerkalkül is a rule in the positive law that distinguishes minimum from maximum conditions in relation to the creation of law; it is a positive rule that renders all conditions other than the minimum conditions irrelevant for the creation of law—sometimes simply by declaring them relevant for the destruction of law via appeal."

214 Merkl, *Die Lehre von der Rechtskraft entwickelt aus dem Rechtsbegriff* 277, 291-300, 293: "Fehlerkalkül ist jene positivrechtliche Bestimmung, die es juristisch ermöglicht, dem Staat solche Akte zuzurechnen, die nicht die Summe der anderweitig positivrechtlich aufgestellten Voraussetzungen ihrer Entstehung und damit ihrer Geltung erfüllen, die es erlaubt, solche Akte trotz jenes Mangels als Recht zu erkennen."

Chapter 3: Historical Perspectives on article 38 PCIJ Statute

alternatively to create a norm which either constituted a delegation of a higher norm or met the minimum conditions of the legal order.[215]

b) The interrelationship of sources within the *Stufenbau*

Kelsen integrated the sources of international law into this *Stufenbau*.[216] In Kelsen's words:

> "The law created by international agencies, especially by decisions of international tribunals established by treaties, derives its validity from these treaties, which, in their turn, derive their validity from the norm of customary international law, pacta sunt servanda. The norms of customary international law represent the highest stratum in the hierarchical structure of the international legal order. The basis, that is the reason of validity, of customary international law, is, as pointed out, a fundamental assumption that international custom established by the practice of states is a law-creating fact. It is the norm presupposed by a juristic interpretation of international relations: that states ought to behave according to custom established by the practice of states."[217]

Within this chain, two orders existed, one of validity which was just mentioned, and one of application. Within that latter order, the "particular conventional (or particular customary) law precedes general customary law. If there is no treaty (or particular customary law) referring to the case, rules of general customary law apply."[218] Against the background of this theoretical

---

215 Hans Kelsen, *Reine Rechtslehre* (2, orig. publ. 1969, Verlag Franz Deuticke 1967) 267, 272-273; Kletzer, 'Kelsen's Development of the Fehlerkalkül-Theory' 53; cf. also for the idea that an alternative authorization belongs to a separate normative order Jörg Kammerhofer, *Uncertainty in international law: a Kelsenian perspective* (Routledge 2011) 188-93; Kammerhofer, 'Positivist Approaches and International Adjudication' paras 26-33.
216 Kelsen, *Reine Rechtslehre Studienausgabe der 1. Auflage 1934* 129-130; von Bernstorff, *The public international law theory of Hans Kelsen: believing in universal law* 166.
217 Kelsen, *Principles of International Law (1952)* 366-367; Kelsen and Tucker, *Principles of International Law (1967)* 508; see also Métall, 'Skizzen zu einer Systematik der völkerrechtlichen Quellenlehre' 424, according to whom only custom (and general principles of law) would constitute constitutional sources (*völkerverfassungsrechtunmittelbare Rechtsquellen*) whereas treaties should be regarded as delegation (*volkerverfassungsrechtsmittelbar*).
218 Kelsen, *Principles of International Law (1952)* 305; Kelsen and Tucker, *Principles of International Law (1967)* 438.

construction, three aspects concerning the interrelationship of sources raised by Kelsen shall be discussed briefly: the function of customary international law, the so-called third-party effects of treaties and general principles of law against the background of the formal completeness of the legal order.

aa) Customary international law

Customary international law was the basis on which the validity of treaties rest, it was therefore, as described by von Bernstorff, "not on the same level as international treaty law but was seen as a normative layer above it."[219] Kelsen regarded customary international law as a mode of law-creation, of "unconscious and unintentional lawmaking" and of being a "law-creating fact", also binding on states which had not participated in its creation.[220]

Kelsen used to reject the usefulness of the subjective element *opinio juris*, in the sense of a legal conviction to be bound by an already existing *legal* norm. In Kelsen's view, if one accepted *opinio juris* as necessary element, new customary international law would then only be possible in cases of a legal error in which states wrongly regard themselves to be bound by a non-existing legal norm.[221] In Kelsen's view the judicial practice did not prove the existence of any subjective element.[222] Within Kelsen's theoretical model, courts and tribunals assumed a very important role in creating norms of customary international law.[223] As von Bernstorff has pointed out,[224] there is a circularity in the "hierarchical logic of the law-generating sources" when courts on "the lower law-generating levels" not just apply preexisting customary international law but create the norm of custom which should have authorized courts in the first place. Kelsen's model undoubtedly put courts in a strong lawmaking position. This model faced limitations, though, as the

---

219 von Bernstorff, *The public international law theory of Hans Kelsen: believing in universal law* 166.
220 Kelsen, *Principles of International Law (1952)* 308 (quote) 311.
221 Kelsen, 'Théorie du droit international coutumier' 262.
222 ibid 264.
223 ibid 268; von Bernstorff, *The public international law theory of Hans Kelsen: believing in universal law* 170-172.
224 See von ibid 171: "The hierarchical logic of the law-generating sources becomes circular, however, if the lower law-generating levels become the most important proof of the highest normative level, that is, customary law."

Chapter 3: Historical Perspectives on article 38 PCIJ Statute

hopes for a general centralised system of compulsory judicial settlement did not become reality.[225] Later, Kelsen considered *opinio juris* as an element of customary international law on the basis of which a law-creating custom is distinguished from mere usage.[226]

bb) Treaties as a product of the international community

Owing its validity to general international law, a treaty was an application of general international law and, therefore, an objective product of the international legal community rather than a product only of the contracting states:[227]

> "By concluding a treaty the contracting states apply a norm of customary international law- the rule pacta sunt servanda- and at the same time create a norm of international law, the norm which presents itself as the treaty obligation of one or of all of the contracting parties, and as the treaty right of the other or the others. [...] The term 'norm' designates the objective phenomenon whose subjective reflections are obligation and right. The statement that the treaty has "binding force" means nothing but that the treaty creates a norm establishing obligations and rights of the contracting parties. Thus, the treaty has a law-applying and at the same time a law-creating character."[228]

While Kelsen accepted that, as a general rule, "treaties impose duties and confer rights only upon the contracting states"[229], he also acknowledged the possibility that a treaty may claim to be applied in relation to third states,[230] which Kelsen discussed in relation to article 17(3) of the Covenant of the League of Nations and to article 2(6) UNC.

Article 17(3) of the Covenant addressed conflicts between a member state of the League of Nations and a non-member state. For cases in which a non-

---

225 Cf. also Kelsen and Tucker, *Principles of International Law (1967)* 452.
226 See Kelsen, *Principles of International Law (1952)* 307; Kelsen and Tucker, *Principles of International Law (1967)* 440; see furthermore Josef L Kunz, 'The Nature of Customary International Law' (1953) 47 AJIL 665 on the distinction between practice that is relevant for customary international law and courtesy.
227 Kelsen, 'Contribution à la théorie du traité international' 263-264.
228 Kelsen, *Principles of International Law (1952)* 319; Kelsen and Tucker, *Principles of International Law (1967)* 456.
229 Kelsen, *Principles of International Law (1952)* 346.
230 In Kelsen's view, the legal doctrine stressed the *pacta tertiis* doctrine for political reasons without acknowledging that exceptions can be found in positive law, Kelsen, 'Contribution à la théorie du traité international' 265.

member state refused to accept the invitation by the Council to temporarily accept obligations under the dispute settlement mechanism under the League of Nations and resorted to war against a member state, article 17(3) of the Covenant stipulated that article 16 of the Covenant should apply and that the state's resort to war against one member should be deemed to be an act of war against all members of the League. In Kelsen's view, the Covenant intended to be applicable to third states.[231]

According to article 2(6) UNC, "[t]he organization shall ensure that states which are not Members of the United Nations act in accordance with these Principles so far as may be necessary for the maintenance of international peace and security." In an early comment on the UN Charter, Kelsen expressed the view that article 2(6) UNC "claims to apply" to third states which was "not in conformity with general international law as prevailing at the moment the Charter came into force. [...] Whether the provision of Art. 2, par. 6 will obtain general recognition remains to be seen. If so, the Charter of the United Nations will assume the character of general international law."[232] In his commentary, he noted that the charter would "indirectly" impose obligations upon all states "provided that it may be interpreted to mean that the Organisation is authorized to react against a non-Member state [...] If the Charter attaches a sanction to a certain behaviour of non-Members, it establishes a true obligation of non-Members to observe the contrary behaviour."[233] The Charter therefore "shows the tendency to be the law not only of the United Nations but also of the whole international community" which he regarded to be "revolutionary".[234]

Kelsen's interpretation according to which article 2(6) UNC could have a third-party effect did not prevail, however. Instead, it has been argued that article 2(6) imposes only obligations on Member States to induce third states

---

231 ibid 281-283; see also Hans Kelsen, *Legal Technique in international law: a textual critique of the League Covenant* (Geneva Research Centre 1939) 139-140: article 17(3) of the League of Nations by which sanctions may be imposed on an aggressive third state "constitutes an attempt to introduce a new juridico-political principle into international law".
232 Hans Kelsen, 'Sanctions in International Law under the Charter of the United Nations' (1946) 31 Iowa Law Review 502, adding that the centralisation of procedure under the Charter would be "the most striking difference between the old and the new general international law."
233 Hans Kelsen, *The Law of The United Nations A Critical Analysis of Its Fundamental Problems* (Stevens 1950) 106-107.
234 ibid 109-110.

to comply with rules and principles which are part of binding customary international law.[235] In other words, the concept of customary international law did not make it necessary to extend the treaty to third states; in this sense, it preserved the consensual character of the concept of treaty.

cc) General principles of law

Kelsen had reservations about general principles of law as source and as positive law.[236] Because of the "fundamental principle that what is not legally forbidden to the subjects of the law is legally permitted to them"[237], "gaps in the law" could not explain the need for general principles of law the existence of which he doubted in light of the ideological differences between communist and capitalist countries.[238] Based on this understanding, there are no gaps unless in the sense that judges do not deem the solution they arrived at by applying treaty and custom as satisfactory.[239] Kelsen did, however, recognize the potential of general principles of law in the application of law. The authorization in article 38(3) PCIJ Statute to apply general principles of law would allow the Court "to adapt positive international law to the particular circumstances of a concrete case according to the demands of justice and equity."[240] Based on this reading, article 38(3) PCIJ Statute and article 38(1)(c) ICJ Statute exceptionally empowered the judges to create law by resorting to

---

235 Tomuschat, 'Obligations Arising For States Without Or Against Their Will' 252; Stefan Talmon, 'Article 2 (6)' in Bruno Simma and others (eds), *The Charter of the United Nations A Commentary* (3rd edn, Oxford University Press 2012) vol 1 255-256 paras 4-6.
236 See also above, p. 146.
237 Kelsen, *Principles of International Law (1952)* 306; Hans Kelsen, 'Théorie du droit international public' (1953) 83 RdC 122.
238 Kelsen, *Principles of International Law (1952)* 393; Kelsen, *The Law of The United Nations A Critical Analysis of Its Fundamental Problems* 533.
239 Kelsen, *Principles of International Law (1952)* 305.
240 Hans Kelsen, 'Compulsory Adjudication of International Disputes' (1943) 37 AJIL 406, arguing that "equity is a general principle of law recognized at least by the Anglo-Saxon nations" and that article 38(3) PCIJ Statute thus implies "the power to decide a case *ex aequo et bono*"; but see later *North Sea Continental Shelf* 48 para 88, on the distinction between equitable principles and a decision *ex aequo et bono*, arguing that "it is precisely a rule of law that calls for the application of equitable principles." See also von Bernstorff, 'Specialized Courts and Tribunals as the Guardians of

this "supplementary source", when the judges deemed the solution provided for by custom and treaty law as "politically not satisfactory"[241]. While Kelsen must conclude that article 38(1)(c) of the Statute "evidently presupposes the idea that there are gaps in international law", he nevertheless considered it "doubtful whether the framers of the statute really intended to confer upon the Court such an extraordinary power."[242]

Kelsen's focus on the *formal* completeness of the legal system and his position that courts engage in an act of lawmaking that cannot be further controlled by normative concepts distinguished his approach from the approach adopted by Hersch Lauterpacht who examined the completeness of a legal order not only from a formal but also from a substantive perspective and who developed a different normative framework for the judicial interpretation, application and development of the law.[243]

5. Alfred Verdross

One influential proponent of the general principles of law was Alfred Verdross who very early advocated in favour of the primacy of international law over

---

International Law? The Nature and Function of Judicial Interpretation in Kelsen and Schmitt' 16.
241 Kelsen, *The Law of The United Nations A Critical Analysis of Its Fundamental Problems* 543; Kelsen, *Principles of International Law (1952)* 393.
242 ibid 393.
243 See below p. 210; von Bernstorff, 'Specialized Courts and Tribunals as the Guardians of International Law? The Nature and Function of Judicial Interpretation in Kelsen and Schmitt' 16 footnote 39; Scobbie, 'The Theorist as Judge: Hersch Lauterpacht's Concept of the International Judicial Function' 269.

domestic law.²⁴⁴ Verdross (together with Josef Kunz²⁴⁵) intended to counter the criticism directed at the Vienna school, according to which the Vienna school was a cold science without any historical and cultural basis through his studies of state practice, legal philosophy and the classics of international law²⁴⁶ since he considered a synthesis between philosophy and sociology important for understanding international law.

Verdross differed from Kelsen as to the ultimate *Grundnorm* and proposed the general principles of law as *lex generalis* to the extent that states did not enact a more special rule by way of custom or treaty.²⁴⁷ Originally, however, Verdross based the validity of the source "general principles of

---

244 Verdross, *Die Einheit des rechtlichen Weltbildes auf Grundlage der Völkerrechtsverfassung* 83-84 (positive international law according to which a successor state would continue to be bound by international obligations of its predecessor state can only be explained by the primacy of international law); on the "quarrel over the Wahlhypothese" see instructively von Bernstorff, *The public international law theory of Hans Kelsen: believing in universal law*; Josef L Kunz, 'Alfred Verdross, Die Einheit des rechtlichen Weltbildes auf Grundlage der Völkerrechtsverfassung' (1924) 7 Archiv des öffentlichen Rechts 123; see also on Verdross Bruno Simma, 'The Contribution of Alfred Verdross to the Theory of International Law' (1995) 6 EJIL 37, 42; on the development of Verdross' evolving understanding of the relationship between municipal law and international law see Alfred Verdross, *Die völkerrechtswidrige Kriegshandlung und der Strafanspruch der Staaten* (Hans Robert Engelmann 1920) 42-43; for an overview of his moderate monism see Anke Brodherr, *Alfred Verdross' Theorie des gemäßigten Monismus* (Herbert Utz Verlag 2005) 27-75.
245 Kunz, 'Alfred Verdross, Die Einheit des rechtlichen Weltbildes auf Grundlage der Völkerrechtsverfassung' 121.
246 Verdross, 'Die allgemeinen Rechtsgrundsätze als Völkerrechtsquelle Zugleich ein Beitrag zum Problem der Grundnorm des positiven Völkerrechts' 358; Alfred Verdross and Heribert Franz Köck, 'Natural Law: The Tradition of Universal Reason and Authority' in Ronald Saint John MacDonald and Douglas Miller Johnston (eds), *The structure and process of international law: essays in legal philosophy doctrine and theory* (Martinus Nijhoff Publishers 1983) 42: "it will not be possible to solve the present and acute problems of the international community, especially the problems of maintaining world peace and bringing about the necessary development of the Third World, without having due regard to the principles and norms of natural law to which the long tradition of universal reason and authority refers us."; cf. von Bernstorff, *The public international law theory of Hans Kelsen: believing in universal law* 82-84, 113-116, 251, describing Verdross' approach as "synthesis of natural-law concepts and actual utterances of state representatives".
247 See Verdross, 'Die allgemeinen Rechtsgrundsätze als Völkerrechtsquelle Zugleich ein Beitrag zum Problem der Grundnorm des positiven Völkerrechts' 362; see later also Verdross and Simma, *Universelles Völkerrecht Theorie und Praxis* 59 f.

law" on customary international law,[248] which encompassed a wide variety of formation of norms.[249] Consequently, article 38(3) of the Statute was thought to constitute a codification of customary international law.[250] For Verdross, this customary international law did not require a universal practice of states, it sufficed that a specific rule had asserted itself in the adjudication of several disputes in a way that the rule's application can be expected in future disputes as well as states expressed not opposition to this norm.[251] Subsequently, Verdross renounced this position and reversed it.[252] General principles were understood as distinct source which did not depend on custom or treaty[253] but directed other sources. He regarded treaties to be null and void when they violated the integrity of the juridical order and the ethics of the respective community.[254] Verdross was also convinced that, without the inspiring potential of general principles for the construction and interpretation

---

(speaking of a set of originary norms which states had to presume in order to create international law).

248 Verdross, *Die Verfassung der Völkerrechtsgemeinschaft* 59.
249 ibid 56; Alfred Verdross, 'Entstehungsweisen und Geltungsgrund des universellen völkerrechtlichen Gewohnheitsrechts' (1969) 29 ZaöRV 642 ff.
250 Similar Borchard, 'The Theory and Sources of International Law' 354-355.
251 Verdross, 'Die allgemeinen Rechtsgrundsätze als Völkerrechtsquelle Zugleich ein Beitrag zum Problem der Grundnorm des positiven Völkerrechts' 359.
252 ibid.
253 Article 38(1)(c) of the Statute was to Verdross of declaratory nature, Verdross, 'Les principes généraux du droit dans la jurisprudence Internationale' 199.
254 Verdross, 'Forbidden Treaties in International Law' 575: "[...] each treaty presupposes a number of norms necessary for the very coming into existence of an international treaty. [...] These principles concerning the conditions of the validity of treaties cannot be regarded as having been agreed upon by treaty; they must be regarded as valid independently of the will of the contracting parties [...] [*jus cogens*] consists of the general principle prohibiting states from concluding treaties contra bonos mores. This prohibition, common to the juridical orders of all civilized states, is the consequence of the fact that every juridical order regulates the rational and moral coexistence of the members of a community." For an emphasis on the public order function of general principles of law that could void treaties, see also Louis Le Fur, 'Règles générales du droit de la paix' (1935) 54 RdC 211-213; *Oscar Chinn* Judgment of 12 December 1934 [1934] PCIJ Series A/B 63 Diss Op Schücking 149-150 (on treaty-based *jus cogens* and nullity as legal effect); see also *Rights of Minorities in Upper Silesia (Minority Schools): Germany v. Poland* Judgment of 26 April 1928 [1928] PCIJ Series A 15, 31 on the "intangibility" of certain treaty provisions.

Chapter 3: Historical Perspectives on article 38 PCIJ Statute

of customary international law, the latter would have experienced an infant death.[255]

The function of general principles of law was that of a true *lex generalis*. Verdross did not regard general principles to be only necessary to prevent a *non liquet*, since every dispute could be settled on the basis of custom or treaty in an adjudicatory context.[256] Rather, and more importantly, the legal operator should render a decision in accordance with general principles of law, instead of blindly applying treaty law or customary international law. Yet, in spite of his interest in natural law, Verdross was careful to stress that general principles of law would not be just natural law, as article 38(3) PCIJ Statute referred to a necessary "recognition".[257] To him, they were positive principles in the sense that they could be found in municipal legal orders, principles of general importance which the shared legal conscience of the modern civilized nations considered to be a necessary part.[258] In his 1935 Hague lecture, he distinguished three groups of principles: principles which were directly connected to the idea of law, such as the principle of effective interpretation; principles which were implicit in or presupposed by a specific legal institution, for instance *pacta sunt servanda* with respect to the treaty; and principles which were affirmed in the positive laws of states and which could therefore be presumed to reflect general principles linked to the idea of law. Thus, principles and positive law were connected, as one would have to go through positive law or legal institutes to the general principles.[259]

---

255 Verdross, 'Die allgemeinen Rechtsgrundsätze als Völkerrechtsquelle Zugleich ein Beitrag zum Problem der Grundnorm des positiven Völkerrechts' 361.
256 Similar Guggenheim, *Lehrbuch des Völkerrechts: unter Berücksichtigung der internationalen und schweizerischen Praxis* 140.
257 Being anchored in municipal law, these principles would be positive law, Verdross, 'Les principes généraux de droit comme source du droit des gens' 290.
258 Verdross, 'Die allgemeinen Rechtsgrundsätze als Völkerrechtsquelle Zugleich ein Beitrag zum Problem der Grundnorm des positiven Völkerrechts' 363-364.
259 Verdross, 'Les principes généraux du droit dans la jurisprudence Internationale' 204-206; on derogability see Verdross, 'Die allgemeinen Rechtsgrundsätze als Völkerrechtsquelle Zugleich ein Beitrag zum Problem der Grundnorm des positiven Völkerrechts' 363; Verdross, *Die Verfassung der Völkerrechtsgemeinschaft* 67; Verdross, 'Les principes généraux de droit comme source du droit des gens' 292 (on derogation by way of *lex specialis*).

6. Hersch Lauterpacht

Hersch Lauterpacht's thinking with respect to municipal law analogies evolved over the years of the 1920s. In his Vienna dissertation of 1922, he rejected domestic private law analogies, as they would would "[endanger] the independence of international law and [fail] to recognize its peculiarity [...] [t]he differences between legal systems are disregarded and the fact forgotten that legal institutions must be construed within the context of their own legal systems."[260] A few years later, Lauterpacht reversed his position in his London dissertation on private law analogies (1927), since "the use of private law analogies exercised, in the great majority of cases, a beneficial influence upon the development of international law."[261] Article 38(3) PCIJ Statute would confirm that "there is no need of justification for divorcing international law, a still undeveloped law of co-ordinated entities, from a system of law, equally governing relations of co-ordinated entities, in which the ideals of legal justice and of the sovereignty of law are admittedly realised in a very high degree."[262]

It deserves to be noted that Lauterpacht's "private law" was not necessarily in opposition to "public law" in principle. It seems plausible, as suggested by Perreau-Saussine[263] and Koskenniemi[264], that Lauterpacht, when he wrote both *Private Law Analogies* and *The Function of Law*, was influenced by English skepticism against the French *Droit Administratif*[265] and by the debate on differences between public law and private law in Germany.[266] He

---

260 Lauterpacht, 'The mandate under international law in the Covenant of the League of Nations' 57-58. He accepted recourse to private law concepts where an international treaty, by referring to agreements for purchase, lease or pledges "enriches itself directly [...] from private law" (58-59).
261 Lauterpacht, *Private Law Analogies* viii.
262 ibid 305.
263 Perreau-Saussine, 'Lauterpacht and Vattel on the Sources of International Law: the Place of Private Law Analogies and General Principles' 176-177.
264 Martti Koskenniemi, 'The Function of Law in the International Community: 75 Years After' (2009) 79 BYIL 355-356.
265 Albert Venn Dicey, *Introduction to the study of the law of the constitution* (Macmillan 1915) 189-190.
266 See Hans Kelsen, *Allgemeine Staatslehre* (Springer 1925) 80-91 (rejecting a distinction between private law and public law when it comes to judicial review); critical on a categorical distinction between private law and public law as well: Lauterpacht, 'Kelsen's pure science of law' 412-413; for a historical analysis of the meaning of the terms *ius publicum* and *ius privatum*, see Max Kaser, ',Ius publicum' und

deemed private law analogies in search of "legal thought and legal experience"[267] more fitting to the individualistic structure of international law, but he acknowledged explicitly the possibility to borrow from public law as well.[268] In a sense, his private law had a what could be described as a "public" dimension of subordination: "Both international and private law are composed of external rules of conduct which, once given their formal existence as law, are independent of the will of the parties, and, as such, above the subjects of law."[269]

In his 1927 monography, Lauterpacht understood general principles of law to be a "subsidiary source" which applied when the "primary source" of international law, the "will of states as expressed in treaties, or, failing that, international custom" was silent, in order to prevent a court from declaring itself incompetent or a *non liquet*.[270] In *The Function of Law*, Lauterpacht further developed his view on the prohibition of *non-liquet* and the role of general principles of law. He distinguished between the completeness of the rule of law (in a formal sense) and the completeness of individual branches of

,ius privatum'' (1986) 103(1) Zeitschrift der Savigny-Stiftung für Rechtsgeschichte: Romanistische Abteilung 97 ff., concluding that the term of "ius publicum" was used for the body of law from which ius privatum may not derogate; on the historical development of the separation between public and private law cf. Dieter Grimm, 'Zur politischen Funktion der Trennung von öffentlichem und privatem Recht in Deutschland' in Walter Wilhelm (ed), *Studien zur europäischen Rechtsgeschichte: Helmut Coing zum 28. Februar 1972* (Klostermann 1972) 224.

267 Lauterpacht, *Private Law Analogies* 50-51.
268 ibid 82 footnote 2: "However, it is probable that with the legal development of international organisation and the creation of central authoritative institutions, a body of rules will evolve, which, as regulating the relations between individual States and the authoritative organs of the international community, will closely correspond to public law within the municipal sphere, for instance, to constitutional and administrative law. In fact, there are already now rudiments of international rules of this kind."
269 ibid 82. In later years, he reevaluated this citizen-state analogy and rejected an anthropomorph understanding of the state, Hersch Lauterpacht, 'The Grotian Tradition in International Law' (1946) 23 BYIL 27 ("The analogy - nay, the essential identity - of rules governing the conduct of states and of individuals is not asserted for the reason that states are like individuals; it is due to the fact that states are composed of individual human beings; it results from the fact that behind the mystical, impersonal, and therefore necessarily irresponsible personality of the metaphysical state there are the actual subjects of rights and duties, namely, individual human beings.").
270 Lauterpacht, *Private Law Analogies* 69.

international law in a material or substantive sense.[271] Lauterpacht regarded the completeness of the legal system as "general principle of law"[272], an "*a priori* assumption of every system of law"[273]. Therefore, "[a]s a matter of fundamental legal principle, no express provision of the positive law is necessary in order to impose upon the judge the duty to give a decision, for or against the plaintiff, in every case before him."[274] Thus, there would be a prohibition for courts to declare a *non-liquet*, to declare themselves incompetent, as matter of custom and as a general principle of law.[275] However, Lauterpacht emphasized that the "principle of the formal completeness [...] is not always calculated to yield results satisfactory from the point of view of justice and of the wider purpose of the law."[276] Formal rules such as the Lotus presumption according to which everything what is not prohibited is permitted for states secured "formal justiciability [...] [b]ut at the same time it may make us forget that the necessary aim of any legal system is also material completeness."[277] He asserted that "there do exist gaps in law - material gaps in the teleological sense [...] as distinguished from formal gaps."[278] Therefore, it was a sign of "intellectual inertia or short sightedness" if the judge regarded any silence of international law as having a "negative effect on the claim."[279] The judge must "go behind the formal completeness of the law"[280] and would then recognize that "even a most obviously novel

---

271 Lauterpacht, *The Function of Law in the International Community* 64.
272 ibid 60.
273 ibid 64.
274 ibid 71-72.
275 ibid 65-66; Hersch Lauterpacht, 'Some observations on the prohibition of 'non liquet' and the completeness of the law' in Frederik Mari van Asbeck (ed), *Symbolae Verzijl: présentées au professeur J. H. W. Verzijl à l'occasion de son 70-ième anniversaire* (Nijhoff 1958) 205: general principles of law "added to the reality of the prohibition of *non-liquet* "in two ways: "by making available without limitation the resources of substantive law embodied in the legal experience of civilized mankind - the analogy of all branches of municipal law and, in particular, of private law - it made certain that there would always be at hand, if necessary, a legal rule or principle for the legal solution of any controversy involving sovereign States. Secondly, inasmuch as the principle of the completeness of the legal order is in itself a general principle of law, it became on that account part of the law henceforth to be applied by the Court."
276 Lauterpacht, *The Function of Law in the International Community* 77.
277 ibid 86.
278 ibid 86; ibid 109.
279 ibid 86.
280 ibid 97.

case is typical when we consider that law is originally and ultimately not so much a body of legal rules as a body of legal principles."[281]

Lauterpacht articulated a decidedly interpretative substantive approach to the interrelationship of sources.[282] His writings display an immense trust in the capacity of law to adjudicate disputes and in the capacity of judges to resort to legal creativity to the extent such creativity remains possible within the legal confines, not unlike Roscoe Pound and Benjamim Cardozo to whom Lauterpacht briefly but approvingly referred.[283] For Lauterpacht, judicial legislation amounted "not to a change of the law, but to the fulfilment of its purpose - a consideration which suggests that the border-line between judicial legislation and the application of the existing law may be less rigid than appears at first sight."[284]

Insofar as he recognized the importance of judicial application, Lauterpacht has been described as operating "within a Kelsenite framework"[285], and similar to Kelsen he assumed the completeness of the legal order. But where Kelsen understood this completeness in a formal way, Lauterpacht postulated a substantive unity.[286] Also, where Kelsen's model deliberately refrained from explaining of how judges should interpret a rule and decide between different equally possible interpretations,[287] Lauterpacht emphasized the importance of legal principles for the exercise of the judicial function.[288]

He concluded that the debate as to whether a judge discovers or makes law

---

281 Lauterpacht, *The Function of Law in the International Community* 110.
282 See also Martti Koskenniemi, *From Apology to Utopia: The Structure of International Legal Argument - Reissue With New Epologue* (2nd edn, Cambridge University Press 2007) 53, comparing Lauterpacht and Dworkin.
283 Cf. the index, Lauterpacht, *The Function of Law in the International Community* 461 f. See above, p. 113
284 Lauterpacht, *The development of international law by the International Court* 161.
285 Scobbie, 'The Theorist as Judge: Hersch Lauterpacht's Concept of the International Judicial Function' 269.
286 See von Bernstorff, *The public international law theory of Hans Kelsen: believing in universal law* 259.
287 See above, p. 196: von Bernstorff, 'Specialized Courts and Tribunals as the Guardians of International Law? The Nature and Function of Judicial Interpretation in Kelsen and Schmitt' 15-16.
288 Scobbie, 'The Theorist as Judge: Hersch Lauterpacht's Concept of the International Judicial Function' 269, describing Lauterpacht's account as "legislation within limits"; for a critique see Julius Stone, 'Non Liquet and the Function of Law in the International Community' (1959) 35 BYIL 133-137, arguing that Lauterpacht's postulate of a prohibition of *non-liquet* required Lauterpacht to admit the lawmaking activity of the judge. On the Lauterpacht-Stone debate see Scobbie, 'The Theorist as

"becomes somewhat unreal. It is futile to maintain that in 'making' law the judge is as free of the existing legal materials as is the legislator; he is bound by the existing principles of law; he is bound by them even, to take the extreme case of his giving a decision apparently contra legem, when he finds that the major purpose of the law compels him to have regard to its spirit rather than to the letter and to disregard its express words. On the other hand, it is futile to assume that the process of 'discovery' of the pre-existing law is a mechanical function of human automata. [...] In recognizing this, one need not go to the extreme point of urging a view which makes of the judge a legislator, instead of seeing in him the servant of the existing law."[289]

Like Verdross, Lauterpacht departed from Kelsen's view on the strict distinction between law and morals.[290] Unlike Verdross, Lauterpacht did not take recourse to "foundational religious principles"[291] and stressed instead that both positivism and natural law belong to the phenomenon of law as "positive law has always incorporated and does incorporate ideas of natural law and justice".[292]

F. Concluding Observations

This chapter illustrated the context in which article 38 PCIJ originated and zeroed in on the triad of sources in earlier writers' work, the positivist climate in the 19th century as well as the Hague conferences, in particular article 7 of the Prize Court Convention.[293] Subsequently, this chapter analyzed the discussion within the Advisory Committee of Jurists[294] and it examined the extent to which the interrelationship of sources was addressed in the

---

Judge: Hersch Lauterpacht's Concept of the International Judicial Function' 285-289; von Bernstorff, 'Specialized Courts and Tribunals as the Guardians of International Law? The Nature and Function of Judicial Interpretation in Kelsen and Schmitt' 16 footnote 39; see also above, p. 146.

289 Lauterpacht, *The Function of Law in the International Community* 110-111.
290 See von Bernstorff, *The public international law theory of Hans Kelsen: believing in universal law* 251.
291 On the difference between Verdross and Lauterpacht: ibid 252.
292 Lauterpacht, 'Kelsen's pure science of law' 429, see also at 425 for a reference to article 1 of the Swiss Civil Code and at 429: "There would, on our part, be no difficulty in admitting that natural law thus incorporated has ceased to be an independent system and has become part and parcel of positive law. We do not mind if natural law has served a good cause at the expense of its separate existence."
293 See above, p. 157.
294 See above, p. 170.

Chapter 3: Historical Perspectives on article 38 PCIJ Statute

interwar period by the PCIJ, at the 1930 Codification Conference and in international legal scholarship.[295] The selected scholars' work illustrated how, only a few years after the adoption of article 38 PCIJ Statute, different legal theoretical perspectives on the law translated into different source preferences and interpretations of article 38.[296]

It is noteworthy that the recognition of general principles of law as a source in arbitration jurisprudence and in treaty law occurred at a time when positivism was on the rise.[297] The discussions in the Advisory Committee of Jurists illustrate that the members of the Committee were well aware of the need to propose a draft which would find the acceptance of states. This did not, however, lead to the exclusion of general principles of law which were considered to be important for the PCIJ to fulfil its functions. It is also noteworthy that Baron Descamps emphasized the function of general principles to limit judges' discretion[298] and that later Hans Kelsen's refusal to recognize general principles of law as legal norms can be seen against the background of his emphasis on courts' lawmaking capacity.[299] This indicates that general principles of law were interrelated with treaties and customary international law and that one's attitude towards this source also depends on the extent to which one seeks to impose normative limits on the judicial function.

---

295 See above, p. 178.
296 Cf. also the different evaluations of the chapeau of article 38(1) ICJ Statute, according to which the ICJ's function is to decide "in accordance with international law": Alfred Verdross, 'General International Law and the United Nations Charter' (1954) 30(3) International Affairs 343, interpreting this formula as indication that the general principles of law "form an integral part of general international law"; Hans Kelsen, *On the issue of the continental shelf: two legal opinions* (Springer 1986) 45: "[General principles of law,] in order to be applicable by the International Court of Justice, must be part of existing international law, and they can be part of existing international law only if they are incorporated either by a general convention or by a general custom."; Karol Wolfke, *Custom in present international law* (Zaklad Narodowy im Ossolínskich 1964) 110; for an overview of similar and further views cf. Vitanyi, 'Les Positions Doctrinales Concernant Le Sens de la Notion de "Principes généraux de Droit Reconnus Par Les Nations Civilisées"' 56 ff.
297 See above, p. 157. Cf. on general concepts in the work of Nippold above, p. 160; on Anzilotti's constructive norms see above, p. 190.
298 See above, p. 172.
299 See above, p. 146, p. 202 and p. 210 (on the difference between Lauterpacht and Kelsen in this regard).

Moreover, the text of article 38 subtly recognizes the differences between the sources and justifies a reading according to which customary international law is not an unwritten treaty.[300] Several scholars emphasized the community aspect of customary international law which explained the legal bindingness of treaties and kept the written law up to date. As the following chapters will demonstrate, certain scholars continue to emphasize these functions of customary international law, whereas other scholars suggest that a doctrine of treaty interpretation may suffice for the purpose of keeping the written law up to date.[301]

As far as international institutions were concerned, the interrelationship of sources was arguably not a central topic in the brief jurisprudence of the PCIJ.[302] The desirability of references to customary international law and general principles of law was discussed in the context of the codification conference in 1930.[303] Even though there was no majority for eliminating such reference in the context of obligations of states with respect to aliens, the debate indicated the existence of different regional views.

The fifth chapter and the sixth chapter will study international institutions in greater detail, delve into the jurisprudence of the ICJ[304] and revisit the discussion of the interrelationship of sources in a codification context when addressing the International Law Commission.[305] Also, this study will contextualize the different views at the 1930 Codification Conference by way of reference to the debate on the protection of aliens.[306]

---

300 See above, p. 175.
301 See below, p. 694.
302 See above, p. 178.
303 See above, p. 182.
304 See below, p. 221.
305 See below, p. 343.
306 See below, p. 564.

Chapter 4: Concluding observations on the comparative and historical perspectives

At the end of the part on comparative and historical perspectives on the interrelationship of sources and of written and unwritten law, a few preliminary observations are in order.

The comparative legal perspectives illustrate the shift of source preferences, the relative importance of written and unwritten law and the recalibration of the sources' relationship the outcome of which may depend on the spirit of the time, the legal culture, the institutional support for one source or the other. Moreover, different source preferences can also be the reflection or symptom of a larger political conflict, as the third chapter pointed out with respect to the debate at the 1930 codification conference.[1] The reasons for source preferences thus can be manifold: they can relate to the relative (un)certainty as to written or unwritten law, they do not even have to strictly relate to the specific sources or forms of law but can be an expression of doctrinal or legal-political preferences or resulting from one's own concept of law, as was illustrated, for instance, reference to the examples of Gény, Saleilles, the comparison between Kelsen and Esser, or Kelsen and Lauterpacht. Therefore, the study of the interrelationship of sources should not stop at sources doctrine but examine the legal reasoning and context more broadly.

The preceding two chapters delved, by way of example, into different contexts. The international legal order has, just as municipal legal orders, its own history. It is submitted, though, that the experiences in international law and in municipal are not strictly separated und unrelated. The Blackstonian assimilation of customs and maxims of law within the concept of common law may have informed Lord Phillimore's thinking when he critiqued what appeared to him to be an artificial distinction between customary international law and general principles of law.[2] Moreover, it has been pointed out that the triad of sources already set forth in the Prize Court Convention and the inclusion of general principles of justice and equity were intended to reflect

---

[1] The substance-matter of this debate will be approached below, p. 558.
[2] See above, p. 107, p. 174.

Chapter 4: Concluding observations on the comparative and historical perspectives

experiences made in municipal law with respect to the judicial administration and development of law.[3]

This study, therefore, considers general principles of law in light of the discussion in legal theory and in municipal legal systems. Certainly, one cannot find all aspects discussed in relation to general principles in legal theory[4] in the discussion of the Advisory Committee of Jurists[5]. Nor can it be completely excluded that a different understanding of general principles of law exists in the international legal order. Yet, it is submitted that the experiences both in domestic legal orders and in the international legal orders informed and continue to inform the discussion of general principles of law which are intrinsically connected to legal reasoning and the systematization of the law.

This view finds support to some extent, for example, in the context of the ILC's recent work on general principles of law the focus of which does not lie on legal theory but on the practice of states and the reasoning of courts and tribunals.[6] According to the draft conclusion six as adopted on first reading, "[a] principle common to the various legal systems of the world may be transposed to the international legal system in so far as it is *compatible with that system*."[7] In a similar sense, it has been argued in the second chapter that general principles need to adapt to a normative context and are qualified by other principles and rules.[8] Draft conclusion 7 recognizes the possibility that principles "may be formed within the international legal system" and that it is "necessary to ascertain that the community of nations has recognised the principle as intrinsic to the international legal system."[9] The commentary to draft conclusion 7 provides that the identification of a general principle of law that may have formed within the international legal system starts with an

---

3 See above, p. 168.
4 See above, p. 138.
5 See above, p. 171.
6 On this project, see below, p. 386.
7 *ILC Report 2022* at 308 footnote 1189 (italics added); see now ILC Report 2023 at 20. See also *Second report on general principles of law by Marcelo Vázquez-Bermúdez, Special Rapporteur* 9 April 2020 UN Doc A/CN.4/741 23 para 75 (arguing that a principle derived from domestic legal orders "must be compatible with the fundamental principles of international law" and "capable of existing within the broader framework of international law."
8 See above, p. 142 and p. 147.
9 *ILC Report 2022* at 308 footnote 1189, 317, 322; see now ILC Report 2023 at 22 ff.

Chapter 4: Concluding observations on the comparative and historical perspectives

analysis of "existing rules in the international legal system".[10] In a similar sense, the views presented in the second chapter have argued that new legal principles can emerge within the same legal system, as abstractions of more specific rules and of legal practice.[11]

However, where certain authors discussed in the second chapter emphasized the creative role of the courts in the positivization of principles[12], the ILC conclusions emphasize that courts' decision are subsidiary means for the determination of principles.[13] The creative role of the law-applying authorities was described to a certain extent in the Special Rapporteur's second report. Addressing the identification of principles underlying general rules of conventional and customary international law, the Special Rapporteur argued that "the approach here is essentially deductive"[14]; but in contrast to customary international law, where the deductive approach "can be employed only 'as an aid' in the application of the two-elements approach"[15], the deduction in relation to the ascertainment of general principles is said to be different:

> "This deduction exercise is not an aid to ascertain the existence of a general practice accepted as law, but the main criterion *to establish the existence* of a legal principle that has a general scope and may be applied to a situation not initially envisaged by the rules from which it was derived. Similar considerations may apply to principles inherent in the basic features and fundamental requirements of the international legal system [...]"[16]

---

10 ibid 322; ILC Report 2023 at 23.
11 Cf. above, p. 141. Cf. also *Second report on general principles of law by Marcelo Vázquez-Bermúdez, Special Rapporteur* 38 para 119 (such principle has been recognized by the community of nations if one can ascertain that it "is widely acknowledged in treaties and other international instruments; underlies general rules of conventional or customary international law; or is inherent in the basic features and fundamental requirements of the international legal system."), 47 para 147 ("This principle inspires and finds reflection in various international instruments, and has been often referred to in the case law"), 52 para 165 ("[w]hat matters is the clear acknowledgment through treaties and other international arguments of the existence of a legal principle of general scope of application").
12 See above, p. 144.
13 *ILC Report 2022* at 307 footnote 1189; ILC Report 2023 at 25 ff. See also *Second report on general principles of law by Marcelo Vázquez-Bermúdez, Special Rapporteur* 32 para 97 (decisions as evidence "that a principle common to the principal legal systems of the world is transposed to the international legal system").
14 ibid 52 para 166.
15 ibid 52 para 167.
16 ibid 53 para 168 (italics added).

Chapter 4: Concluding observations on the comparative and historical perspectives

"The main criterion *to establish the existence*" comes very close to acknowledging the creative or, depending on one's understanding of this term, law-making role of courts. The draft conclusions, however, are mainly concerned with the identification of existing general principles of law, rather than with their formation and emergence. Yet, by recognizing the possibility that general principles may form within the international legal system and by emphasizing at the same time that a general principle must be recognized by the community of nations, the draft conclusions can be read as support of the idea of the dual character of general principles, the reconciliation between stability and change, between the accumulation of legal experience and the law in action, between restraining and liberating the judicial function.

Part C.

Institutional Perspectives

Chapter 5: The International Court of Justice

A. Introduction

The purpose of this chapter is to trace the interrelationship of sources as a *motif* in the Court's jurisprudence and to examine whether specific approaches and judicial policies can be identified. Like any other court, the ICJ is at a certain liberty in deciding on which legal concepts it bases its decision or to which legal concepts it gives support, even when those may not be strictly relevant to the particular case.[1] Also, the Court can explore a treaty's relationship to other sources when interpreting and applying that treaty. In *Tehran Hostages*, for instance, the Court noted that "the obligations established by the Vienna Conventions of 1961 and 1962 [...] [are] also obligations under general international law"[2], and in *Diallo* the Court confirmed the convergence of regional human rights instruments.[3] In 2016, the Court held that the Articles 31 to 33 VCLT (and not only Articles 31-32) "reflect rules

---

1 For instance, the Court emphasized the *jus cogens* character of the prohibition of torture, even though this was not strictly decisive for the outcome of the case, unless one adopts the view that standing in an *erga omnes partes* case requires the obligation to be of peremptory character. Cf. *Questions relating to the Obligation to Prosecute or Extradite* [2012] ICJ Rep 422, 457 para 99. Sometimes, the Court decided not to distinguish between legal concepts. For instance, the Court decided that the sovereignty over Pedra Branca was passed from Singapore to Malaysia by way of tacit agreement "or" by way of acquiescence, without making a choice between the two, *Sovereignty over Pedra Branca/Pulau Batu Puteh, Middle Rocks and South Ledge (Malaysia/Singapore)* (Judgment) [2008] ICJ Rep 50 ff. paras 120 ff., crit. Joint Diss Op Simma and Abraham para 3. In a subsequent case, the majority of the Court based its reasoning on a tacit agreement instead of, as a minority suggested, engaging in an interpretation of a written agreement in light of subsequent practice, *Maritime Dispute (Peru v. Chile)* (Judgment) [2014] ICJ Rep 38-39 paras 90-91, Joint Diss Op Xue, Gaja, Bhandari and Judge *ad hoc* Orrego Vicuña, paras 2, 35.
2 *United States Diplomatic and Consular Staff in Tehran (United States of America v. Iran)* (Judgment) [1980] ICJ Rep 31 para 62.
3 *Ahmadou Sadio Diallo (Republic of Guinea v. Democratic Republic of the Congo)* (Merits, Judgment) [2010] ICJ Rep 664 para 68. On the *erga omnes* character of the rights and obligations enshrined in the Genocide Convention see *Armed Activities on the Territory of the Congo (New Application: 2002)* [2006] ICJ Rep 6, 31 para 64 (before concluding that this character does not lead to the Court having jurisdiction).

of customary international law".[4] The way in which the Court approaches the interrelationship of sources of international law is also a question of judicial policy and based on the choices of the Court.[5]

When tracing the interrelationship of sources as a *motif* in the Court's jurisprudence, one must be mindful of the institutional conditions under which the Court operates. This appears particularly pertinent since the question has been raised whether the institutional setting of the Court impacted the Court's take on the interrelationship of sources to the detriment of general international law, customary international law and general principles. For instance, Judge Weeramantry raised the question of whether the adversarial *inter partes* proceedings before the Court can do "justice to rights and obligations of an *erga omnes* character."[6] In a similar fashion, Martti Koskenniemi

---

4 *Question of the Delimitation of the Continental Shelf between Nicaragua and Colombia beyond 200 nautical miles from the Nicaraguan Coast* [2016] ICJ Rep 100, 116 para 33; *Alleged Violations of Sovereign Rights and Maritime Spaces in the Caribbean Sea* [2016] ICJ Rep 3, 19 para 35. After having referred to its jurisprudence, the Court noted that the parties to the case agreed "that these rules are applicable". As far as article 33 VCLT is concerned, the statement was arguably an *obiter dictum*; on the question of whether it would be good legal policy to declarare article 31-33 VCLT to reflect customary international law, see the exchange of views prior to the decision, *Comment by Georg Nolte, Summary record of the 3274th meeting, 22 July 2015* UN Doc A/CN.4/SR.3274 (PROV.) at 8 and *Comment by Judge Ronny Abraham, Summary record of the 3274th meeting, 22 July 2015* UN Doc A/CN.4/SR.3274 (PROV.) at 8-9, also available in *ILC Ybk (2015 vol 1)* 232. See now also *Application of the International Convention for the Suppression of the Financing of Terrorism and of the International Convention on the Elimination of All Forms of Racial Discrimination* (*Ukraine/Russian Federation*) (Preliminary Objections, Judgment) [2019] ICJ Rep 598 para 106; *Application of the Convention on the Prevention and Punishment of the Crime of Genocide* (Preliminary Objections) https://www.icj-cij.org/public/files/case-related/178/178-20220722-JUD-01-00-EN.pdf para 87.

5 See also Pellet and Müller, 'Article 38' 935 ("[...] the Court enjoys (or recognizes itself as enjoying) a large measure of appreciation in the choice of the sources of the rules to be applied in a particular case."); Kearney, 'Sources of Law and the International Court of Justice' 697 ("the absence of priorities among the sources of law in Article 38(1)(a), (b), and (c) has afforded a valuable degree of flexibility in the preparation of judgments.").

6 *Gabčíkovo-Nagymaros Project* (*Hungary/Slovakia*) (Judgment) [1997] ICJ Rep 7, Sep Op Weeramantry, pp. 117-118. For recent obligations *erga omnes inter partes* cases, see *Questions relating to the Obligation to Prosecute or Extradite* [2012] ICJ Rep 422, 449 para 68; *Application of the Convention on the Prevention and Punishment of the Crime of Genocide* [2020] ICJ Rep 3, 17 para 41. Since the Court had no jurisdiction in the proceedings initiated by the Marshall Islands, the Court did not have to address

has argued that the effect of the Court's restrictive policy as to judicial intervention would be "that the Court defines itself unable to pronounce anything on matters of general law."[7] Since the cases that led Koskenniemi to this conclusion were decided prior to the first edition of From Apology to Utopia in 1989, the question deserves to be re-examined in light of the judicial practice which has originated since then (B.). Subsequently, the chapter turns to the question of whether the jurisdictional basis of the Court shapes the way in which the interrelationship of sources is discussed by the Court (C.).[8] It will be demonstrated that the Court emphasizes the distinctiveness of treaty and custom for jurisdictional purposes insofar as the applicable law is concerned, while at the same time acknowledging the interrelationship when it comes to interpretation. This chapter will explore the normative considerations and the legal craft employed by the Court when identifying, interpreting and applying customary international law and the function of general principles as a bridge between custom and treaties (D.). Finally, the chapter will present concluding observations (E.).

B. Third-party intervention and the interrelationship of sources

This section will first explain the general framework in which third-party interventions are embedded. Subsequently, the chapter will explore how the Court approached third-party interventions in particular under article 62 ICJ on interventions to disputes which do not concern multilateral conventions. This section concludes with an evaluation of the intervention system from the perspective of the interrelationship of sources.

---

the question of standing in relation to obligations under customary international law in the proceedings involving India and Pakistan which were not, unlike the UK, parties to the Non-Proliferation Treaty, cf. *Obligations concerning Negotiations relating to Cessation of the Nuclear Arms Race and to Nuclear Disarmament* [2016] ICJ Rep 255, 277 para 56; *Obligations concerning Negotiations relating to Cessation of the Nuclear Arms Race and to Nuclear Disarmament* [2016] ICJ Rep 552, 573 para 56.

7 Koskenniemi, *From Apology to Utopia: The Structure of International Legal Argument - Reissue With New Epologue* 463, footnote 277.
8 Christian J Tams, 'The Continued Relevance of Compromissory Clauses as a Source of ICJ Jurisdiction' in Thomas Griegerich (ed), *A Wiser Century? Judicial Dispute Settlement, Disarmament and the Laws of War 100 Years after the Second Hague Peace Conferenc* (2009) 491, arguing that compromissory clauses favour treaty claims over general international law, with the exception of so-called interstitial norms.

I. The general regime: Articles 59, 62, 63 and 66 ICJ Statute

According to article 59 ICJ Statute, decisions are only binding *inter partes* (*ratione personae*) for the specific dispute (*ratione materiae*). They can serve as subsidiary means for the determination of rules of law (article 38(1)(d) ICJ Statute). If the subject-matter of a dispute concerns third states, the Court will decline to exercise its jurisdiction.[9] Articles 62 and 63 ICJ Statute govern the interventions by other states to existing disputes.[10]

Article 62 stipulates that a state "may submit a request to the Court to be permitted to intervene", "[s]hould a state consider that it has an interest of a legal nature which may be affected by the decision in the case".[11] In contrast, article 63 applies to a dispute concerning a multilateral convention and provides the other parties to the convention with a right to intervene.[12] The letter of article 63 does not require a legal interest; according to the jurisprudence of the Court, a legal interest is presumed to exist in cases where other states are bound by the specific provision of a multilateral convention in question.[13] References by intervening states to principles and rules of

---

9 *Case of the monetary gold removed from Rome in 1943* (*UK v. Albania*) (Preliminary Question) [1954] ICJ Rep 19; on this doctrine, see Tobias Thienel, *Drittstaaten und die Jurisdiktion des Internationalen Gerichtshofs: die Monetary Gold-Doktrin* (Duncker & Humblot 2016) 26 ff.

10 This section focuses on intervention in contentious proceedings, excluding therefore the participation in Advisory Opinion proceedings governed by article 66 of the Statute. As the provision states, international organizations may be admitted to advisory proceedings if the Court decides to do so. The Court in its Kosovo Advisory Opinion even admitted Palestine and Kosovo both of which were not generally recognized states. On article 66, see Andreas L Paulus, 'Article 66' in Andreas Zimmermann and others (eds), *The Statute of the International Court of Justice: a commentary* (3rd edn, Oxford University Press 2019) para 14.

11 Article 62 reads: "1. Should a state consider that it has an interest of a legal nature which may be affected by the decision in the case, it may submit a request to the Court to be permitted to intervene. 2 It shall be for the Court to decide upon this request."

12 Article 63 reads: "1. Whenever the construction of a convention to which states other than those concerned in the case are parties is in question, the Registrar shall notify all such states forthwith. 2. Every state so notified has the right to intervene in the proceedings; but if it uses this right, the construction given by the judgment will be equally binding upon it."

13 *Allegations of Genocide under the Convention on the Prevention and Punishment of the Crime of Genocide* (*Ukraine v. Russian Federation*) (Order of 5 June 2023) (2023) ⟨https://www.icj-cij.org/sites/default/files/case-related/182/182-20230605-ORD-01-00-EN.pdf⟩ accessed 5 June 2023 para 27 and paras 93-97, as decided by

international law outside the multilateral convention will be considered by the Court to the extent that they can be taken into account in the interpretation of the convention according to customary international law as reflected in article 31(3)(c) VCLT.[14]

Since article 63 governs interventions only to multilateral conventions, "the only opportunity provided by the Statute and Rules for a State which is not a party to the proceedings to express its views on an issue of general international law is to intervene under Article 62".[15] As it emerges from the plain wording of both provisions, states parties to a multilateral convention have a *right* to intervene. In contrast, states do not have such right when the situation is governed by article 62. At first sight, the intervention regime leads to a different treatment of conventions and customary international law.[16] The plain wording of article 62, however, does not exclude the possibility of requesting permission to intervene if the Court were to interpret and apply a rule of general international law.[17] Nor does it indicate how the Court should treat a request to intervene. Therefore, a study of the Court's practice is important.[18]

In 1978, the Court revised its Rules on interventions and introduced article 81(2)(c) according to which it is required for the request to intervene to set

---

the Court, a reservation entered by the United States to the compromissory clause of the Genocide Convention led to the result that the presumed interest did not exist in relation to article IX of the Genocide Convention and that the US intervention in the preliminary objections phase was inadmissible.

14 ibid para 84.
15 *Jurisdictional Immunities of the State* (*Germany v. Italy*) (Application for Permission to Intervene, Order of 4 July 2011) [2011] ICJ Rep 494, Decl. Gaja 531 para 1.
16 Doubting the wisdom of such discrimination, Shigeru Oda, 'The International Court of Justice viewed from the Bench (1976-1993)' (1993) 244 RdC 85: "If an interpretation of a multilateral convention given by the Court is necessarily of concern to a State which is a party to that instrument, though not a party to the case, there seems to be no convincing reason why the Court's interpretation of the principles and rules of international law should be of less concern to a State."
17 *Continental Shelf* (*Libyan Arab Jamahiriya/Malta*) (Application to Intervene, Judgment) [1984] ICJ Rep 3, Diss Op Schwebel 144 ff. As noted it was noted in *Territorial and Maritime Dispute* (*Nicaragua v. Colombia*) (Application for Permission to Intervene, Judgment) [2011] ICJ Rep 348 Diss Op Al-Khasawneh 375 para 5, the wording of article 62 is "plainly liberal".
18 As explained by Alina Miron and Christine Chinkin, 'Article 62' in *The Statute of the International Court of Justice: A Commentary* (3rd edn, Oxford University Press 2019) 1688 para 3: "This deliberate choice of the drafters leaves to the Court the cumbersome responsibility of filling in *lacunae* in the Statute."

out "any basis of jurisdiction which is claimed to exist as between the State applying to intervene and the parties to the case."[19] Against the background of the Court's approach to interventions at that time, the article could be understood in the sense that intervening states under article 62 would require a jurisdictional basis, which would have considerably restricted the mechanism under article 62. It is also noteworthy that article 82 of the Rules on interventions under article 63 ICJ Statute does not include a similar jurisdictional requirement. Since 1978, however, the jurisprudence has begun to change and the Court has adopted the distinction between intervention as a party to the proceeding and intervention as a non-party, which would not require a jurisdictional basis.[20] The following lines will trace this development and analyze its implications for the interrelationship of sources.

II. The Court's practice to interventions under article 62 ICJ Statute: from a restrictive to a more inclusive approach?

The Court had more experience with requests based on article 62 than with requests based on article 63.[21]

Most of the cases touching on article 62 of the Statute concerned maritime boundary disputes,[22] but not all cases belong to this field of law as it is demonstrated by the *Jurisdictional Immunities* case, in which Greece suc-

---

19 ICJ, 'Rules of the Court (1978) Adopted on 14 April 1978 and entered into force on 1 July 1978' ⟨https://www.icj-cij.org/en/rules⟩ accessed 1 February 2023.
20 Miron and Chinkin, 'Article 62' 1704 para 44.
21 Cf. *Asylum Case* (*Colombia/Peru*) (Judgment of 20 November 1950) [1950] ICJ Rep 266; *Whaling in the Antarctic* (*Australia v. Japan: New Zealand intervening*) (Judgment) [2014] ICJ Rep 226. Recently, the Court decided that the declarations of intervention under article 63 ICJ Statute submitted by 32 states in the Dispute Relating to the Allegations of Genocide (Ukraine v Russia) were admissible, while the declaration of the USA was inadmissible, *Allegations of Genocide under the Convention on the Prevention and Punishment of the Crime of Genocide* (Order) https://www.icj-cij.org/sites/default/files/case-related/182/182-20230605-ORD-01-00-EN.pdf para 102; see also ICJ, 'Allegations of Genocide under the Convention on the Prevention and Punishment of the Crime of Genocide (Ukraine v. Russian Federation) - Latest Developments' ⟨https://www.icj-cij.org/en/case/182⟩ accessed 1 February 2023.
22 See generally Taslim O Elias, 'The Limits of the Right of Intervention in a Case before the International Court of Justice' in Rudolf Bernhardt (ed), *Völkerrecht als Rechtsordnung Internationale Gerichtsbarkeit Menschenrechte Festschrift für Hermann Mosler* (Springer 1983) 159 ff.; Eduardo Jiménez de Aréchaga, 'Intervention under Article 62 of the Statute of the International Court of Justice' in Rudolf Bernhardt

cessfully intervened,[23] and the *Nuclear Tests* cases, in which the application to intervene by the government of Fiji was found to have lapsed as the cases had become moot.[24]

1. The development of the restrictive approach

In the first series of cases, the Court rejected interventions of third states which had sought to intervene to boundary disputes. In the continental shelf case between Tunisia and Libya, the Court did not regard Malta's interest "in the legal principles and rules for determining the delimitation of the boundaries of its continental shelf"[25] to be sufficient and expressed a disinclination to allow a state like Malta to communicate its views without being bound by the decision in the case.[26]

In a different proceeding concerning the delimitation of the continental shelf between Libya and Malta, Italy requested permission to intervene since it considered that both states' claims to areas of the continental shelf "in the central Mediterranean [...] extend to areas which would be found to appertain to Italy if a delimitation were to be effected between Italy and Libya, and between Italy and Malta, on the basis of international law."[27] By way of

---

(ed), *Völkerrecht als Rechtsordnung, internationale Gerichtsbarkeit, Menschenrechte: Festschrift für Hermann Mosler* (Springer 1983) 453 ff.; Deepak Raju and Blerina Jasari, 'Intervention before the International Court of Justice - A Critical Examination of the Court's Recent Decision in Germany v. Italy' (2013) 6 NUJS Law Review 63; Serena Forlati, *The International Court of Justice An Arbitral Tribunal or a Judicial Body?* (Springer 2014).

23 *Jurisdictional Immunities of the State* [2011] ICJ Rep 494.
24 See *Nuclear Tests Case (Australia v. France)* (Application to Intervene, Order of 12 July 1973) [1973] ICJ Rep 530; *Nuclear Tests Case (New Zealand v. France)* (Application to Intervene, Order of 12 July 1973) [1973] ICJ Rep 324; *Nuclear Tests Case (Australia v. France)* (Judgment) [1974] ICJ Rep 272; *Nuclear Tests Case (New Zealand v. France)* (Judgment) [1974] ICJ Rep 478; *Nuclear Tests Case (Australia v. France)* (Application to Intervene, Order of 20 December 1974) [1974] ICJ Rep 531; *Nuclear Tests Case (New Zealand v. France)* (Order of 20 December 1974, Application by Fiji for Permission to Intervene) [1974] ICJ Rep 536.
25 *Continental Shelf (Tunisia/Libyan Arab Jamahiriya)* (Application to Intervene, Judgment) [1981] ICJ Rep 8-9 para 13.
26 ibid 18-19 paras 32-33.
27 *Continental Shelf (Libya/Malta Application to Intervene)* [1984] ICJ Rep 3, 10-11 para 15.

intervention, specified to geographical coordinates, Italy wanted to protect its sovereign rights of exploitation as recognized by customary international law and the Geneva Convention on the Continental Shelf[28]. Both parties had opposed the intervention, and the Court decided to reject the request. The Court argued that this intervention was an attempt to introduce a new dispute[29] and that the function of article 62 ICJ Statute was not to serve as an additional basis for the Court's jurisdiction.[30] The Court stressed that Italy would not suffer from any disadvantages because of its non-participation:[31] the judgment would be binding only on the parties, and the Court would not have to "decide in the absolute" but rather "which of the Parties has produced the more convincing proof of title".[32] At the merit stage, the Court then limited its judgment to an area with respect to which Italy had claimed no interest.[33]

Based on both judgments, the impression could emerge that the intervention system under article 62 was doomed to fail: when a state seeking to intervene framed its interest too broadly, as Malta did, the Court rejected the application, and when the interest was narrowed down as in the case of Italy, the Court suspected the introduction of a new dispute.[34] The strategy of a bilateralization of the dispute expressed itself in several ways: The emphasis on party consent to the jurisdiction of the Court favoured a restrictive judicial

---

28 Convention on the Continental Shelf (signed 29 April 1958, entered into force 10 June 1964) 499 UNTS 311.
29 *Continental Shelf (Libya/Malta Application to Intervene)* [1984] ICJ Rep 3, 20-21 para 32.
30 ibid 22 para 35.
31 ibid 25 para 40, the Court denied that "assuming Italy's non-participation, a legal interest of Italy is en cause, or is likely to be affected by the decision" or that a legal interests of Italy would even "form the very subject-matter of a decision."
32 ibid 26-27 para 43. Interestingly, the Court also stated, citing the decision in the Minquiers and Ecrehos case: "The future judgment will not merely be limited in its effects by Article 59 of the Statute : it will be expressed, upon its face, to be without prejudice to the rights and titles of third States. Under a Special Agreement concerning only the rights of the Parties, 'the Court has to determine which of the Parties has produced the more convincing proof of title'".
33 *Continental Shelf (Libyan Arab Jamahiriya/Malta)* (Judgment) [1985] ICJ Rep 26 para 22.
34 *Continental Shelf (Libya/Malta Application to Intervene)* [1984] ICJ Rep 3 Diss Op Ago 130: "The decision on the present case may well sound the knell of the institution of intervention in international legal proceedings [...]"; cf. on this jurisprudence Miron and Chinkin, 'Article 62' 1710-1711.

policy as to interventions under article 62. In turn, the Court protected third states by stressing the *inter partes* nature of judgments[35] and by excluding areas with respect to which third states could have claims. From the perspective of the dissenting judges, this exercise of judicial self-restraint in order to protect Italy's arguable rights came at the expense of rendering a full and complete decision.[36]

2. Tendencies of a more inclusive approach

A Chamber of the ICJ[37] composed of three judges who had dissented from the Court's restrictive approach in earlier cases and of two judges *ad hoc* granted for the first time permission to intervene under article 62 ICJ Statute.[38] A mere general interest in sovereignty was still not in itself sufficient.[39] In the specific case however, Nicaragua was found to possess a restricted legal interest[40] and thus a legal interest affected by the outcome of the case.[41] In attempting to reconcile the general principle of consent to jurisdiction with the institute of intervention, the Chamber emphasized that its competence "in this matter of intervention is not, like its competence to hear and determine the dispute referred to it, derived from the consent of the parties to the case, but from the consent given by them in becoming parties to the Court's Statute [...]".[42] In its view, there was a difference in kind between intervention and participation as a party.[43] Neither the statute nor the rules would require

---

35 See also *Frontier Dispute (Burkina Faso/Republic of Mali)* (Judgment) [1986] ICJ Rep 576-579 paras 44, 46-49.
36 See *Continental Shelf (Libya/Malta)* [1985] ICJ Rep 13 Diss Op Mosler 116-117, Diss Op Oda 131 para 11 and Diss Op Schwebel 172, 174.
37 According to article 26 ICJ Statute, the Court may form chambers. According to article 27 ICJ Statute, a judgment given by any of the chambers provided for in Articles 26 and 29 shall be considered as rendered by the Court.
38 *Land, Island and Maritime Frontier Dispute (El Salvador/Honduras)* (Application to Intervene, Judgment) [1990] ICJ Rep 116 para 56.
39 ibid 119 para 66.
40 ibid 121-122 paras 72-73, 124 para 76, 126-127 para 82. Nicaragua itself had argued that its interests would concern the subject-matter of the dispute, implying that the Court would have to refuse exercising jurisdiction if it did not grant Nicaragua permission to intervene according to the Monetary Gold principle.
41 ibid 128 para 85.
42 ibid 133 para 96.
43 ibid 133-134 para 97.

a jurisdictional link.[44] The Chamber adopted a proposal which had been suggested earlier by Judge Oda and by Italy, namely to distinguish between intervention as a non-party, where no jurisdictional basis would be necessary, and intervention as a party.[45]

The Court followed the Chamber's more inclusive approach. In a subsequent dispute between Cameroon and Nigeria, the Court even invited states to intervene in the proceedings.[46] Subsequent judgments since then, however, have fallen short of explicitly renouncing the earlier restrictive jurisprudence. The Court has continued to affirm that the interest in legal principles or the "wish of a State to forestall interpretations by the Court [...] is simply too remote for the purposes of Article 62."[47] Furthermore, the bilateralization strategy was continuously pursued: as third states were protected by the *inter partes* effect of article 59 of the Statute, Costa Rica's request to intervene was rejected by a narrow majority of 9:7.[48] The dissenting judges continued to speak in favour of a less restrictive approach to article 62, pointing out that such an approach was not excluded by the wording of article 62.[49] Diminishing the difference between articles 62 and 63[50] would put treaty obligations and obligations under customary international law on equal footing, as far as

---

44 *Land, Island and Maritime Frontier Dispute* 135 para 100.
45 *Continental Shelf (Tunisia/Libya, Application to Intervene)* [1981] ICJ Rep 3 Sep Op Oda 30-31.
46 *Land and Maritime Boundary between Cameroon and Nigeria (Cameroon/Nigeria)* (Preliminary Objections, Judgment) [1998] ICJ Rep 324 paras 115-116; Equatorial Guinea successfully requested permission to intervene, restricting the scope of its intervention, see *Land and Maritime Boundary between Cameroon and Nigeria (Cameroon/Nigeria: Equatorial Guinea intervening)* (Order of 21 October 1999) [1999] ICJ Rep 1029.
47 *Sovereignty over Pulau Ligitan and Pulau Sipadan (Indonesia/Malaysia)* (Application for Permission to Intervene, Judgment) [2001] ICJ Rep 603-604 para 83.
48 *Territorial and Maritime Dispute* [2011] ICJ Rep 348, 363 para 51, 368 para 67, 369 para 71, 471-372 paras 85-86.
49 ibid Decl Al-Khasawneh para 5.
50 ibid Diss Op Abraham, para 4; see also ibid Diss Op Al-Khasawneh, paras 10-14; Joint Diss Op Cançado Trindade and Yusuf, paras 6, 24, 28 (all on rejecting the solution based on article 59 ICJ Statute), and para 27 for the importance of article 62 in times of multilateralization of international relations; Diss Op Donoghue, para 6; Judge *ad hoc* Gaja suggested to establish a new procedural mechanism for interventions, ibid Decl Gaja 417-418.

the institution of intervention is concerned.[51] So far, however, the Court has continued to emphasize the difference between articles 62 and 63.[52]

3. A paradigm shift? Interventions in matters of customary international law - The *Jurisdictional Immunities* case

The question of judicial interventions is raised not only in the context of maritime boundary delimitations but also in the context of general international law. The success of such interventions varied. When New Zealand requested an examination of the situation addressed in the *Nuclear Tests* judgment of 20 December 1974[53], the Australian government and the governments of Samoa, Solomon Islands, the Marshall Islands and the Federal State of Micronesia filed applications to intervene.[54] The governments argued that they had a legal interest with respect to the *erga omnes* rights claimed by New Zealand, for instance a right that no nuclear tests that could give rise to radioactive fallout would be conducted and a right to the preservation from unjustified artificial radioactive contamination of the environment.[55] The

---

51 In this sense *Continental Shelf (Libya/Malta Application to Intervene)* [1984] ICJ Rep 3 Diss Op Oda 104-105.
52 *Territorial and Maritime Dispute (Nicaragua v. Colombia)* (Application for Permission to Intervene, Judgment) [2011] ICJ Rep 433-434 para 35, see also 434-435 para 38 reference to Pulau litigation for that the legal interest can aim not only at the dispositif but also at the reasoning; for a different view: ibid Diss Op Abraham para 2. See also paras 12-13 for arguing, contrary to the Court, in favour of a right to intervene under article 62; Diss Op Donoghue, para 2, see also para 50: in case of doubts, states should be allowed to intervene as a non-party. She also suggested to establish a new mechanism, paras 58-59.
53 See *Nuclear Tests Case* [1974] ICJ Rep 457, 477 para 63.
54 See *Request for an Examination of the Situation in Accordance with Paragraph 63 of the Court's Judgment of 20 December 1974 in the Nuclear Tests (New Zealand v France) Case*) (*New Zealand v. France*) (Order of 22 September 1995) [1995] ICJ Rep 288 Diss Op Koroma 379-380, regretting that the intervening states were not granted the opportunity to present their views. Whereas Australia relied solely on article 62, the governments of Samoa, Solomon Islands, the Marshall Islands and the Federal State of Micronesia relied on both article 62 and article 63.
55 All applications can be found here: ICJ, 'Request for an Examination of the Situation in Accordance with Paragraph 63 of the Court's Judgment of 20 December 1974 in the Nuclear Tests (New Zealand v. France) Case - Intervention' ⟨https://www.icj-cij.org/en/case/97/intervention⟩ accessed 1 February 2023.

Court dismissed New Zealand's request and, therefore, also the applications to intervene.[56]

A successful intervention to a dispute on customary international law can be found in the *Jurisdictional Immunities* case. The Court permitted Greece to intervene to the proceedings between Germany and Italy which concerned, inter alia, the enforcement of Greek judgments in Italy rendered against Germany in violation of Germany's state immunity.[57] Greece modified over the course of the proceeding its application. First, it seemed as if the intervention was motivated by "Germany's purported recognition of its international responsibility *vis-à-vis* Greece".[58] Greece no longer relied on this ground in the written proceedings and rather focused on Germany's third claim according to which Italy violated Germany's immunity by declaring Greek judgments against Germany enforceable. Even though Greece wished to inform the Court of "Greece's approach to the issues of State immunity, and to developments in that regard in recent years", Greece argued that this would only be an illustration of the context, as the interest concerned the Greek judgments.[59] The Court decided in favour of the Greek application: The Court "might find it necessary to consider the decisions of Greek courts" and "this is sufficient to indicate that Greece has an interest of a legal nature which may be affected by the judgment in the main proceedings".[60]

Judge Cançado Trindade welcomed Greece's intervention not only because of Greece's interest in the enforcement of Greek judgments:

> "Unlike land and maritime delimitation cases, or other cases concerning predominantly bilateralized issues, the present case is of interest to third States — such as Greece — other than the two contending parties before the Court. The subject-matter is closely related to the evolution of international law itself in our times, being of relevance, ultimately, to all States, to the international community as a whole, and,

---

56 *Request for an Examination of the Situation in Accordance with Paragraph 63 of the Court's Judgment of 20 December 1974 in the Nuclear Tests (New Zealand v France) Case)* [1995] ICJ Rep 288, 307 para 68.
57 *Jurisdictional Immunities of the State* [2011] ICJ Rep 494, on the aspect of intervention: Forlati, *The International Court of Justice An Arbitral Tribunal or a Judicial Body?* 200-201.
58 *Jurisdictional Immunities of the State* [2011] ICJ Rep 494, 499 para 16.
59 ibid paras 17-18.
60 ibid 501-502 para 25, 503 para 32. ibid Diss Op Gaja, according to whom Italy was under no legal obligation to enforce Greek judgments which is why the question of a breach of international law would be a concern to Italy and Germany alone.

in my perception, pointing towards an evolution into a true universal international law."[61]

Greece interpreted the scope of the intervention broadly in the oral proceedings, commenting on the dispute's history, the municipal judgments, general questions of state immunity and state responsibility as well as on an individual right to compensation for violations of international humanitarian law.[62] Neither the Court in its judgment nor individual judges commented on the scope of intervention.[63] Whether this order by which Greece was permitted to intervene as a non-party will, in hindsight, constitute a case-law shifting precedent for disputes on customary international law remains to be seen.

III. Evaluation

As has been demonstrated above, the intervention system, as interpreted by the Court, differentiates between sources in that parties to a multilateral treaty have a right to intervene and their legal interest is presumed because they are bound by the multilateral treaty which will be interpreted by the Court. In contrast, interested states are granted permission to intervene under article 62 of the Statute only in narrow circumstances.

The Court's restrictive policy can be explained by reference to the jurisdictional structure. The lack of a comprehensive compulsory jurisdiction can cause the concern that states would be deterred from submitting disputes to the Court by the possibility that third states could join the dispute by way of intervention.[64] The Court protected third states in the merits by compartmen-

---

61 ibid Sep Op Cançado Trindade para 58. In a similar sense: Christine Chinkin, 'Article 62' in *The Statute of the International Court of Justice: A Commentary* (2nd edn, Oxford University Press 2012) 1546, 1558, 1569.
62 See in particular *Public sitting held on Wednesday 14 September 2011, at 10 am, at the Peace Palace, Verbatim Record* 14 September 2011 CR 2011/19 paras 50-120; but cf. Miron and Chinkin, 'Article 62' 1708 para 54, according to whom "Greece changed tack during the oral hearings, in order to concentrate on how the application of the general rules might affect its legal obligations."
63 Solely Koroma pointed in his separate opinion to the individual compensation argument, cf. *Jurisdictional Immunities of the State (Germany v. Italy: Greece intervening)* (Judgment) [2012] ICJ Rep 99 Sep Op Koroma 159 para 8.
64 In the end, however, it is convincing to say that, when it comes to ruling on applications to intervene, "opposition of the parties to a case is, though very important, no more than one element to be taken into account by the Court.", *Land, Island and Maritime Frontier Dispute* [1990] ICJ Rep 92, 133 para 96.

talizing and bilateralizing the dispute;[65] it excluded certain geographical areas from further judicial consideration and examined which of the two parties had a better title.[66] In this sense, one can say that the restrictive policy as to judicial interventions under article 62 ICJ Statute may have confined the judicial perspective. Not only does it make interventions to disputes on customary international law more difficult, it also led to judgments which adopted a more bilateral perspective than a perspective on general international law.[67]

Yet, one should not overstate this claim. The next sections will illustrate how the wider normative environment has informed the Court's interpretation of the law and that the Court's jurisprudence contributed to the clarification of the general law. Also, it is hard to predict whether a less restrictive approach to interventions under article 62 would favour a greater willingness on the part of the Court to comment on matters of general international law. Contentious proceedings are, of course, not the only possibility, the advisory opinion procedure may also be considered as procedure in which questions of general international law and of abstract relationships between different fields of law could be discussed.[68] Whether states would use the opportunity to intervene if the Court adopted a less restrictive approach is difficult to evaluate, and one cannot fail to note that interventions under article 63 ICJ Statute have not occurred frequently. It remains to be seen whether the recent interventions by states to the ongoing proceedings between Ukraine and Russia[69] under

---

65 Abi-Saab, 'Cours général de droit international public' 261, speaking of an arbitralisation of the Court after 1966 during the 1970 and 1980s which was reflected in a restrictive policy as to judicial interventions.
66 *Continental Shelf (Libya/Malta)* [1985] ICJ Rep 13, 25 para 21.
67 Cf. Koskenniemi, *From Apology to Utopia: The Structure of International Legal Argument - Reissue With New Epologue* 463 footnote 277.
68 *Legality of the Threat or Use of Nuclear Weapons* (Advisory Opinion) [1996] ICJ Rep 240 para 25 on the relationship between human rights law and international humanitarian law; *Legal Consequences of the Construction of a Wall* (Advisory Opinion) [2004] ICJ Rep 178 para 106. For contentious proceedings see *Armed Activities on the Territory of the Congo (Democratic Republic of the Congo v. Uganda)* (Judgment) [2005] ICJ Rep 242-243 para 216 in which the Court recalled its approach in the Wall-Opinion; *Application of the Convention on the Prevention and Punishment of the Crime of Genocide (Bosnia and Herzegovina v. Serbia and Montenegro)* (Judgment of 3 February 2015) [2015] ICJ Rep para 474, holding that a certain conduct may be "perfectly lawful under one body of legal rules and unlawful under another [...] However, it is not the task of the Court in the context of the counter-claim to rule on the relationship between international humanitarian law and the Genocide Convention."
69 See the references above in Fn. 21.

article 63 of the ICJ Statute will be indicative of a development that will be characterized by a greater interest of states to articulate their views on international law in specific disputes and whether that will influence the future interpretation of article 62. Of course, states have ample ways to let their view on a certain legal question be known to the public and to the Court.[70] While informal *amicus curiae* briefs could reduce the pressure on the intervention system, it appears to be worth considering whether one should not formalize the ways to communicate information to the Court by taking a less restrictive approach to article 62.

C. Jurisdiction and the interrelationship of sources

This section will first lay out the impact of jurisdictional clauses on how the Court addresses the interrelationship of sources (I.). It will then examine how the Court's jurisdiction based on a specific treaty can also encompass general international law in the sense of a "general part" (II.). Subsequently, the section will address the relationship between the jurisdictional clauses and "substantive" international law which does not belong to the just mentioned "general part" (III.). In this context, the section will, in particular, focus on

---

70 Cf. on this topic also Miron and Chinkin, 'Article 62' 1740 para 147; as it has been pointed out, even an unsuccessful application to intervene achieves the objective to inform the Court of one's legal views, see Thomas Cottier, *Equitable Principles of Maritime Boundary Delimitation: The Quest for Distributive Justice in International Law* (Cambridge University Press 2015) 504; *Continental Shelf (Libya/Malta Application to Intervene)* [1984] ICJ Rep 3 Sep Op Nagendra Singh 32 ("The purpose of warning the Court as to the area of Italian concern has indeed been totally fulfilled"); but see also ibid Diss Op Ago 29-30, who criticized "a tendency of the Court [...] to feel convinced that the aims which the procedure of intervention properly so called was intended to achieve, would in fact already be practically attained by the mere holding of the preliminary proceedings on the question of admission of the intervention." Cf. for a recent critique of a "mass intervention strategy" under article 63 *Allegations of Genocide under the Convention on the Prevention and Punishment of the Crime of Genocide* (Order) https://www.icj-cij.org/sites/default/files/case-related/182/182-20230605-ORD-01-00-EN.pdf Decl Gevorgian paras 7, 9; Diss Op Xue para 28 (both on the possibility that such interventions could create political pressure on the Court); on the idea of the establishment of an *amicus curiae* proceeding before the Court see Paolo Palchetti, 'Opening the International Court of Justice to Third States: Intervention and Beyond' (2002) 6 Max Planck Yearbook of United Nations Law 165 ff.

the relationship between applicable law and the doctrine of interpretation and on the way in which the Court addresses the jurisdiction under the Genocide Convention. In its concluding observations, this section will highlight that recent decisions confirm the Court's tendency to emphasize the distinctiveness of sources when it comes to the Court's jurisdiction (IV.).

I. Jurisdiction clauses and their impact on the interrelationship of sources

This subsection concerns the question of whether the Court's jurisdictional regime impacts the way in which the interrelationship of sources is addressed. Article 36 of the Statute governs the question of jurisdiction. According to article 36(1) ICJ Statute, jurisdiction can be based on special agreements or on general treaties providing for dispute settlement and specialized treaties with compromissory clauses.[71] When a state had applied for proceedings against another state without a previous agreement, the latter could consent to the Court's jurisdiction (*forum prorogatum*).[72] According to article 36(2) ICJ Statute, states can submit unilateral declarations by which they recognize the Court's jurisdiction as compulsory in advance.[73] The Court then will have jurisdiction in a dispute between two states which accepted "the same obligations". The declarations can be subject to reservations and withdrawal.[74] Being bound by its Statute, the Court cannot recognize bases of jurisdiction outside article 36; therefore, two states cannot confer on the Court jurisdiction outside the Statute.[75] Concepts such as *jus cogens* or *erga omnes* obligations have so far not altered the consensual equation. The Court rejected the argument that it would automatically have jurisdiction in case of

---

71 For an overview see Peter Tomka, 'The Special Agreement' in *Liber amicorum judge Shigeru Oda* (Kluwer Law International 2002) 553 ff.
72 *Corfu Channel Case (UK v Albania)* (Preliminary Objection) [1948] ICJ Rep 27; *Haya de la Torre Case (Colombia/Peru)* (Judgment of June 13th, 1951) [1951] ICJ Rep 78; *Anglo-Iranian Oil Co (United Kingdom v. Iran)* (Judgment of July 22nd, 1952) [1952] ICJ Rep 114; *Certain Questions of Mutual Assistance in Criminal Matters (Djibouti v. France)* (Judgment) [2008] ICJ Rep 203 para 60.
73 For an overview see ICJ, 'Declarations recognizing the jurisdiction of the Court as compulsory' ⟨https://www.icj-cij.org/en/declarations⟩ accessed 1 February 2023.
74 France withdrew its declaration after the Nuclear Test cases (907 UNTS 129), the United States of America withdrew its declaration after the Nicaragua decision (1408 UNTS 270).
75 Robert Kolb, *The International Court of Justice* (Alan Perry tr, Hart 2013) 297 ff.

an alleged violation of *jus cogens* or *erga omnes* obligations.[76] In particular, the Court held that the *jus cogens* nature of an obligation would not render a reservation to a jurisdictional clause invalid; five judges, however, would have preferred if the Court had examined the admissibility of such reservation with the Genocide Convention's object and purpose.[77]

Both titles of jurisdiction, article 36(1) and article 36(2), are distinct. Failures by one party to meet the procedural obligations under a treaty's compromissory clause do not exclude the Court's jurisdiction under article 36(2).[78] Whereas this was controversial in 1939 when a minority of judges had argued that the more burdensome procedural obligations under a treaty with a compromissory clause would determine jurisdiction under article 36(2) as well,[79] the majority's view was confirmed by subsequent judgments.[80]

Also, reservations attached to a unilateral declaration under article 36(2) ICJ Statute, by virtue of which a specific treaty is excluded from the Court's jurisdiction, do not affect functionally equivalent obligations under customary

---

76 *East Timor (Portugal v. Australia)* (Judgment) [1995] ICJ Rep 102 para 29; *Armed Activities on the Territory of the Congo (New Application: 2002) (Democratic Republic of the Congo v. Rwanda)* (Provisional Measures, Order of 10 July 2002) [2002] ICJ Rep 245 para 71; *Armed Activities on the Territory of the Congo (New Application: 2002)* [2006] ICJ Rep 6, 32 para 64 and 35 para 78.

77 ibid 33 para 69; ibid Joint Separate Opinion by Judges Higgins, Kooijmans, Elaraby, Owada and Simma 65. See also Christian Tomuschat, 'Article 36' in Andreas Zimmermann and others (eds), *The Statute of the International Court of Justice: A Commentary* (3rd edn, Oxford University Press 2019) 733-734, 758-759; Dapo Akande, 'Selection of the International Court of Justice for Contentious and Advisory Proceedings (Including Jurisdiction)' (2016) 7 JIDS 326, arguing that "[...] that the Court's decision in these cases is sufficiently well reasoned that it will not yield easily to alternative analysis."

78 See already *Electricity Company of Sofia and Bulgaria: Belgium v Bulgaria* Judgment of 4 April 1939 Preliminary Objection [1939] PCIJ Series A/B 77, 76.

79 ibid 77 Diss Op Hudson 131 ff., Anzilotti Sep Op 90 as well as Diss Op Urrutia 105 and Diss Op Jonkheer van Eysinga 112.

80 *Land and Maritime Boundary between Cameroon and Nigeria* [1998] ICJ Rep 275, 321-322 para 109, the obligations under UNCLOS would not apply to art. 36(2); *Territorial and Maritime Dispute between Nicaragua and Honduras in the Caribbean Sea (Nicaragua v. Honduras)* (Judgment) [2007] ICJ Rep 702 paras 136-137 (distinct bases of jurisdiction); *Border and Transborder Armed Actions (Nicaragua v. Honduras)* (Jurisdiction and Admissibility, Judgment) [1988] ICJ Rep 88 para 41 (reservation to the declaration under article 36(2) not applicable to the compromissory clause).

international law.[81] In the *Nicaragua* case, the United States of America invoked the *Vandenberg* reservation entered to the 1947 declaration by which the USA accepted the Court's jurisdiction under article 36(2). This reservation excluded disputes "arising under a multilateral treaty, unless (1) all parties to the treaty affected by the decision are also parties to the case before the Court, or (2) the United States of America specially agrees to jurisdiction".[82] The United States contended that this reservation precluded recourse to "general and customary international law" as well,[83] whereas Nicaragua argued that "general international law" had a bearing independent from the Charter, and that any arguments as to the state of the former would not be mere reiterations of the latter.[84] The Court sided with the legal position advanced by Nicaragua:

> "Principles such as those of the non-use of force, non-intervention, respect for the independence and territorial integrity of States, and the freedom of navigation, continue to be binding as part of customary international law, despite the operation of provisions of conventional law in which they have been incorporated."[85]

In particular, the Court did not adopt Judge Schwebel's line of reasoning who would have applied the reservation to customary international law as well insofar as the latter was "essentially the same" as the multilateral treaty obligations.[86] This distinctiveness between sources, however, concerns applicability for jurisdictional purposes. It does not concern the substantive interrelationship between customary international law and other sources in relation to the interpretation and application of norms.[87]

For the purposes of this section, compromissory clauses are of particular interest. On the one hand, they are often intended to confine the dispute which states would like the Court to adjudicate[88], and the Court may be well advised to respect the confinement and not undermine it by an extensive

---

81 Shabtai Rosenne, *The Law and Practice of the International Court 1920-2005* (4th edn, vol 2, Martinus Nijhof Publishers 2006) 648-649.
82 *Military and Paramilitary Activities in and against Nicaragua (Nicaragua v. United States of America)* (Jurisdiction and Admissibility, Judgment) [1984] ICJ Rep 421-422 para 67.
83 ibid 423 para 69.
84 ibid [1984] ICJ Rep 392, 423-424 para 71.
85 ibid 424 para 73.
86 *Military and Paramilitary Activities in and against Nicaragua* [1986] ICJ Rep 14, Diss Op Schwebel 303-306; ibid 392, Diss Op Schwebel 614-616.
87 On this aspect, see in this chapter below, p. 258.
88 On the function of confinement of the dispute by compromissory clauses see William Michael Reisman, 'The Other Shoe Falls: The Future of Article 36 (1) Jurisdiction in the Light of Nicaragua' (1987) 81 AJIL 170 ("presumption of confinement").

interpretation and application of the general rules of interpretation[89] and by considering all international law to be "relevant" for the purposes of article 31(3)(c) VCLT.[90] Disregarding the confinements may lead to a decline of the adoption of new compromissory clauses.[91]

On the other hand, treaties can leave many questions open: they do not set forth, for instance, rules governing the interpretation or the consequences of a breach of the treaty, certain terms in the treaty may explicitly or implicitly invoke or rely on a concept of general international law. Moreover, a treaty is part of the international legal order which is why applicable rules and principles shall be taken into account (article 31(3)(c) VCLT).[92] Parties cannot compartmentalize the law for the administration of which the Court is ultimately responsible according to the maxim *iura novit curia*. As Robert Kolb has argued, compromissory clause in fact "pursue a double aim, that of strengthening a particular treaty by providing a means to better guarantee its proper application (legal security *inter partes*), and that of promoting the rule of law international society in general (legal security *inter omnes*)."[93]

Judicial policy thus is of utmost importance and the way in which the Court reconciles the possible tension between respect for the confinement

---

89 *Oil Platforms* [2003] ICJ Rep 161 Sep Op Buergenthal para 22.
90 As Simma and Kill remarked, "[a]lmost any rule of international law will be 'relevant' when considered with the proper degree of abstraction", Simma and Kill, 'Harmonizing Investment Protection and International Human Rights: First Steps Towards a Methodology' 696.
91 Cf. Akande, 'Selection of the International Court of Justice for Contentious and Advisory Proceedings (Including Jurisdiction)' 324, noting an "appreciable decline in the number of treaties which include compromissory clauses [...] apparently, no treaty with such a clause has been concluded since 2006. This is a worrisome trend [...]". It is open to question whether this decline is a reaction to the jurisprudence of the Court or rather the sign of *Zeitgeist* which is less enthusiastic with respect to judicial settlement of disputes before the Court than it used to be. Recently, Colombia denounced the Treaty of Bogota "specifically because of its compromissory clause", Tomuschat, 'Article 36' 749.
92 Cf. Enzo Cannizzaro and Beatrice Bonafé, 'Fragmenting International Law through Compromissory Clauses? Some Remarks on the Decision of the ICJ in the Oil Platforms Case' (2005) 16(3) EJIL 495: "[...] the mere inclusion in a treaty of a compromissory clause cannot, by itself, have the effect of fragmenting the unity and the coherence of international law."
93 Robert Kolb, 'The Compromissory Clause of the Convention' in Paola Gaeta (ed), *The UN Genocide Convention: A Commentary* (Oxford University Press 2009) 413.

Chapter 5: The International Court of Justice

and recognizing that the treaty is anchored in the international legal order may vary over time and must, therefore, be subject to constant examination.[94]

II. The application of general international law as general part in relation to a specific rule

1. The uncontroversial cases: validity, interpretation, responsibility

According to the Court's jurisprudence, the jurisdiction based on a compromissory clause of a treaty encompasses jurisdiction for general international law on the validity and interpretation of a treaty as well as on the law of international responsibility. One could speak in this regard of a "general part" or of "interstitial norms" or "meta-norms", in other words, rules on rules.[95]

The PCIJ already rejected the view that "jurisdiction to assess the damages and to fix the mode of payment does not, in international law, follow automatically from jurisdiction to establish the fact that a treaty has not been applied".[96] Instead, the PCIJ argued:

> "It is a principle of international law that the breach of an engagement involves an obligation to make reparation in an adequate form. Reparation therefore is the indispensable complement of a failure to apply a convention and there is no necessity for this to be stated in the convention itself. Differences relating to reparations, which

---

94 As Robert Kolb, 'The Scope Ratione Materiae of the Compulsory Jurisdiction of the ICJ' in Paola Gaeta (ed), *The UN Genocide Convention: A Commentary* (Oxford University Press 2009) 454-455 rightly stated principally with respect to the interpretation of compromissory clauses, "[t]he answer given to these questions depends largely on considerations of legal policy, and are thus variable in time."
95 Cf. Tams, 'The Continued Relevance of Compromissory Clauses as a Source of ICJ Jurisdiction' 491: "Of course, interstitially, general international law remains crucial in many cases, including those under compromissory clauses: remedies depend on the customary rules of State responsibility, as do questions of attribution; and treaties may have to be interpreted in the light of general international law. But the number of compromissory clause cases centring on violations of customary international law is very limited indeed."; Papadaki, 'Compromissory Clauses as the Gatekeepers of the Law to be 'used' in the ICJ and the PCIJ' 6, 18 ff., does not use the term of interstitial norms but distinguishes norms stemming from the treaty, meta-norms on the validity and interpretation of the treaty, constructive norms as used by Anzilotti, meaning the logical presuppositions and the necessary logical consequences of norms, such as responsibility, and conflicting norms.
96 *Case Concerning the Factory at Chorzow: Germany v Poland* Judgment of 26 July 1927 [1927] PCIJ Series A 09 Diss Op Ehrlich 38.

may be due by reason of failure to apply a convention, are consequently differences relating to its application."[97]

Since then, the Court has affirmed throughout its case-law that no specific authorization is required to apply the general rules of international law concerning international responsibility, and the Court defended this jurisprudence against challenges. The Court, for instance, did not accept the argument that the jurisdiction based on the compromissory clause of the VCCR did not extend to claims based on diplomatic protection as part of customary international law.[98] In addition to the law of state responsibility, the Court has applied the general rules of interpretation[99] as well as the rules on the validity of a treaty.[100] Against this background, it is rather surprising that the Court referred in the *Nicaragua* case to its additional jurisdictional basis under article 36(2) ICJ Statute when it addressed Nicaragua's submission that the United States had violated customary international law by defeating the object and purpose of the applicable treaty.[101] If one accepts such a rule of customary international law to exist, this rule will concern the application

---

97 ibid 21, see also 22 and 24-25 according to which this interpretation is in line with the object and purpose of the compromissory clause, which is the settlement of disputes.
98 *LaGrand (Germany v. United States of America)* (Judgment) [2001] ICJ Rep 482-484 paras 40-45.
99 *Application of the Convention on the Prevention and Punishment of the Crime of Genocide (Bosnia and Herzegovina v. Serbia and Montenegro)* (Judgment) [2007] ICJ Rep 105 para 149: "The jurisdiction of the Court is founded on Article IX of the Genocide Convention, and the disputes subject to that jurisdiction are those 'relating to the interpretation, application or fulfilment' of the Convention, but it does not follow that the Convention stands alone. In order to determine whether the Respondent breached its obligations under the Convention, as claimed by the Applicant, and, if a breach was committed, to determine its legal consequences, the Court will have recourse not only to the Convention itself, but also to the rules of general international law on treaty interpretation and on responsibility of States for internationally wrongful acts."
100 *Fisheries Jurisdiction (Federal Republic of Germany v. Iceland)* (Jurisdiction of the Court, Judgment) [1973] ICJ Rep 58-59 para 24 on duress, 64-65 paras 40 and 43 on change of circumstances; *Appeal Relating to the Jurisdiction of the ICAO Council (India v. Pakistan)* (Judgment) [1972] ICJ Rep 64-65 para 32 on the validity of a treaty containing a compromissory clause.
101 *Military and Paramilitary Activities in and against Nicaragua* [1986] ICJ Rep 14, 135-136 paras 270-271.

of the treaty which, just like the rules of responsibility, is governed by the compromissory clause.[102]

2. A controversial case? Succession to responsibility

The "general part" of international law is not excluded in situations where jurisdiction is conferred upon the Court according to compromissory clauses. The precise scope of this general part, however, has been subject to debate in the recent judgment of 2015 on the dispute between Croatia and Serbia. The case was based on the compromissory clause of the Genocide Convention and concerned potential violations of the convention starting in 1991.

Prior to 1992 the Socialist Federal Republic of Yugoslavia (SFRY) was a party to the Genocide Convention. From the SFRY the Federal Republic of Yugoslavia (FRY) emerged in 1992 and claimed at the beginning to be the continuator of SFRY.[103] This claim, however, was contested and "not free from legal difficulties".[104] After the Milošević regime had been overthrown, the new FRY (Serbia and Montenegro) was no longer claiming to be the legal continuator of SFRY and applied successfully for membership to the UN and to the Genocide convention. Montenegro declared itself independent, and Serbia claimed to be the legal continuator of FRY (Serbia and Montenegro). As such, Serbia accepted in a case against Croatia that article IX of the Genocide Convention conferred on the Court jurisdiction *ratione temporis* for the time since the FRY had acceded to the Genocide convention; but it

---

102 See also Kolb, 'The Scope Ratione Materiae of the Compulsory Jurisdiction of the ICJ' 462-3.
103 See Vojin Dimitrijević and Marko Milanović, 'The Strange Story of the Bosnian Genocide Case' (2008) 21(1) Leiden Journal of International Law 66 ff.; Marko Milanović, 'Territorial Application of the Convention and State Succession' in *The UN Genocide Convention: a commentary* (Oxford University Press 2009) 473 ff.; Federica Paddeu, 'Ghosts of Genocides Past? State Responsibility for Genocide in the Former Yugoslavia' (2015) 74(2) The Cambridge Law Journal 199.
104 *Application of the Convention on the Prevention and Punishment of the Crime of Genocide* (*Bosnia and Herzegovina v. Serbia and Montenegro*) (Order of 8 April 1993) [1993] ICJ Rep 14 para 18; *Application of the Convention on the Prevention and Punishment of the Crime of Genocide* [2007] ICJ Rep 43, 97-98 paras 130-131; Andreas Zimmermann, 'The International Court of Justice and State Succession to Treaties: Avoiding Principled Answers to Questions of Principle' in Christian J Tams and James Sloan (eds), *The Development of International Law by the International Court of Justice* (Oxford University Press 2013) 56.

challenged Croatia's claim that the Court had jurisdiction for events prior to this date. Croatia, for her part, argued that Serbia was responsible for acts prior to 27 April 1992, when the FRY became a party to the Genocide convention, based on state succession into responsibility of the SFRY.

The Court sided with Croatia on jurisdiction. In contrast to the *Badinter* Commission which once had held that "rules applicable to State succession and State responsibility fell within distinct areas of international law"[105], the ICJ accepted that it had jurisdiction on state succession in principle:

> "[T]he rules on succession that may come into play in the present case fall into the same category as those on treaty interpretation and responsibility of States."[106]

This conclusion was important for jurisdictional purposes. On the merits, however, the Court held that the necessary genocidal intent (*dolus specialis*) for acts committed by the SFRY could not be established.[107] Therefore, the Court did not address the question of whether Serbia had succeeded into the responsibility of SFRY for genocide.

This jurisdictional holding of the Court can be read as support for the view according to which international responsibility is no longer understood as a personal obligation (*actio personalis*) which was incapable of being succeeded into by another state.[108] Since an internationally wrongful act now

---

105 *International Conference on the Former Yugoslavia Arbitration Commission* Opinion No 13 (16 July 1993) 96 ILR 727; see also *Application of the Convention on the Prevention and Punishment of the Crime of Genocide* [2015] ICJ Rep 3, Sep Op Judge ad hoc Kreća para 76: "Responsibility of a State is one thing and succession to responsibility is another. Suffice it to say that, whereas the rules on responsibility are secondary rules, the rules on succession are a part of the corpus of primary norms whose violation entails activation of the rules on responsibility."
106 ibid 56-57 para 115.
107 ibid 128-129 paras 440-442.
108 Cf. for this classical view Max Huber, *Die Staatensuccession. Völkerrechtliche und staatsrechtliche Praxis im XIX. Jahrhundert* (Duncker & Humblot 1898) 100 ff.; Arrigo Cavaglieri, 'Règles générales du droit de la paix' (1929) 26 RdC 374; Michael John Volkovitsch, 'Righting wrongs: toward a new theory of state succession to responsibility for international delicts' (1992) 92(8) Columbia Law Review 2195; *Robert E Brown* U.S. v. U.K, Gr. Brit.-U.S. Arb. Trib. (23 November 1923) VI RIAA 120 ff. and *F H Redward* U.K. v. U.S.A, Gr. Brit.-U.S. Arb. Trib. (10 November 1925) VI RIAA 158 ff.; critical of the historical genesis of the rule of non-succession: Ernst H Feichenfeld, *Public Debts and State Succession* (The MacMillan Company 1931) 20, 423, 424 note 4; Daniel Patrick O'Connell, 'Recent problems of state succession in relation to new states' (1970) 130 RdC 162-165; American Law Institute, *Restatement of the law, The Foreign Relations Law of the United States* (vol 1, 1987)

is understood as a form of objective responsibility divorced from the personal fault or *culpa*[109], the idea of a clean slate rule regarding responsibility is difficult to reconcile with "the stability of international relations governed by law and the very idea of equity and justice."[110]

According to a minority in the Court, however, the Court went too far when it stated the principle that the law of state succession fell into the same category as the law of international responsibility and treaty interpretation: the compromissory clause of the Genocide Convention, the argument goes, did not confer upon the Court jurisdiction for state succession into responsibility.[111] The Court, it was argued, had endorsed a controversial doctrine of state succession into responsibility without serious examination.[112] Furthermore, the dissenting judges argued[113] that the Court's endorsement implied a retroactive application of the Genocide Convention which stood in contrast to the Court's earlier judgment in the *Hissene Habre* case where the Court had rejected the retroactive application of the Convention against Torture.[114]

---

para 209; Wladyslaw Czaplinski, 'State Succession and State Responsibility' (1990) 28 Canadian Yearbook of International Law 339 ff.; Brigitte Stern, 'La succession d'États' (1996) 262 RdC 174.

109 On this development cf. Stern, 'Et si on utilisait le concept de préjudice juridique?: retour sur une notion délaissée à l'occasion de la fin des travaux de la C. D. I. sur la responsabilité des états' 4 ff.

110 Marcelo G Kohen, 'La succession d'Etats en matière de responsabilité internationale State Succession in Matters of State Responsibility' (2016) 76 Yearbook of the Institute of International Law - Tallinn Session 525 para 28; on this topic see also Pavel Šturma, 'State Succession in Respect of International Responsibility' (2016) 48 The George Washington International Law Review 653 ff.; Crawford, *State Responsibility: The General Part* 455; Patrick Dumberry, *State succession to international responsibility* (Martinus Nijhoff 2007) 302; *Report of the International Law Commission: Sixty-ninth session (1 May-2 June and 3 July-4 August 2017)* UN Doc A/72/10 203-210.

111 See *Application of the Convention on the Prevention and Punishment of the Crime of Genocide* [2015] ICJ Rep 3 Sep Op Tomka paras 24-25 and Sep Op Judge *ad hoc* Kreća para 65.

112 ibid Sep Op Owada para 20; see also Sep Op Skotinov para 2; see Decl. of Xue para 23 and Sep Op Judge *ad hoc* Kreća para 65.

113 ibid Decl. of Judge Xue para 21, Sep Op Sebutinde para 13; see also Sep Op Tomka paras 7-9.

114 *Questions relating to the Obligation to Prosecute or Extradite* [2012] ICJ Rep 422, 457 para 100 referring to article 28 VCLT. Even though the Court had jurisdiction under article 36(2) as well, it argued that no dispute as to the prohibition of torture under customary international law existed.

Jurisdiction and the interrelationship of sources

It is argued here, however, that both judgments are not in conflict since the Court did not apply the Genocide Convention retroactively. On the contrary, the Court affirmed the presumption against retroactivity as set forth by article 28 VCLT with respect to the Genocide Convention generally and with respect to its compromissory clause specifically[115], which answered a question the Court had left open in earlier decisions.[116] The jurisdiction for "acts said to have occurred before 27 April 1992"[117] was not based on a retroactive application of a convention but on general international law, namely succession into the responsibility of SFRY. As Robert Kolb has argued, the link to the Genocide convention was so strong that the succession to responsibility was covered by the compromissory clause.[118]

III. The relationship between jurisdictional clauses and "substantive" law

The Court's jurisprudence does not suggest that compromissory clauses direct the Court's focus solely to the respective treaty. In other words, the confinement as to the applicable law does not necessarily correspond to a confinement of the Court's perspective.

---

115 *Application of the Convention on the Prevention and Punishment of the Crime of Genocide* [2015] ICJ Rep 3, 49-51, paras 93-100, referring also to *Questions relating to the Obligation to Prosecute or Extradite* [2012] ICJ Rep 422. The Court rejected to endorse a "general presumption of temporal non-limitation of the titles of the jurisdiction", Kolb, 'The Compromissory Clause of the Convention' 422; Robert Kolb, 'Chronique de la jurisprudence de la cour International de Justice en 2015' (2016) 1(26) Swiss Review of International and European Law 143-144.
116 In earlier cases, the Court "confine[d] itself to the observation hat the Genocide Convention - and in particular Article IX -does not contain any clause the object or effect of which is to limit in such manner the scope of its jurisdiction *ratione temporis*, and nor did the Parties themselves make any reservation to that end", *Application of the Convention on the Prevention and Punishment of the Crime of Genocide (Bosnia and Herzegovina v. Serbia and Montenegro)* (Preliminary Objections, Judgment) [1996] ICJ Rep 617 para 34; see also *Application of the Convention on the Prevention and Punishment of the Crime of Genocide (Croatia v. Serbia)* (Preliminary Objections, Judgment) [2008] ICJ Rep 458 para 123.
117 *Application of the Convention on the Prevention and Punishment of the Crime of Genocide* [2015] ICJ Rep 3, 51 para 101.
118 Kolb, 'Chronique de la jurisprudence de la cour International de Justice en 2015' 140: "Le lien avec le traité est manifestement si fort qu'il serait artificiel d'expulser la question de cette succession du domaine de la clause compromissoire."

The Court emphasized on several occasions that jurisdictional clauses would not constitute a bar to "considering", as opposed to ruling on, events and violations outside the jurisdictional limitations.[119] Furthermore, the Court's willingness to confirm the customary status of a treaty obligation did not seem to depend on whether the Court had jurisdiction under article 36(1)[120] or under article 36(2)[121] of the ICJ Statute.

The terms of the treaty may refer to concepts of customary international law or included in other treaties to which the Court then will refer.[122] This is of particular importance with respect to NPM provisions setting forth a list of measures which are not precluded by the treaty. According to the jurisprudence of the Court, these provisions do not exclude the listed matters from the Court's jurisdiction. They constitute a "defence on the merits", which means that the Court will assess whether this provision is pertinent to the present case and whether a state invoking such a provision can rely on

---

119 *United States Diplomatic and Consular Staff in Tehran* [1980] ICJ Rep 3, 42 para 91: after the Court had found a violation of the Vienna Conventions, the Court considered further human rights violations of the UDHR and the Charter. *Application of the Convention on the Prevention and Punishment of the Crime of Genocide* [2015] ICJ Rep 3, 45 para 85, the Court was not being prevented from "considering [...] whether a violation of international humanitarian law or international human rights law has occurred to the extent that this is relevant for the Court's determination of whether or not there has been a breach of an obligation under the Genocide Convention."

120 *Questions relating to the Obligation to Prosecute or Extradite* [2012] ICJ Rep 422, 457 para 99: "[T]he prohibition of torture is part of customary international law and it has become a peremptory norm (*jus cogens*). That prohibition is grounded in a widespread international practice and on the *opinio juris* of States. It appears in numerous international instruments of universal application [...], and it has been introduced into the domestic law of almost all States; finally, acts of torture are regularly denounced within national and international fora." The Court could have affirmed jurisdiction based on article 36(2) though, but it held that there had been no dispute on customary international law, 445 para 55.

121 *Ahmadou Sadio Diallo (Republic of Guinea v. Democratic Republic of the Congo)* (Compensation, Judgment) [2012] ICJ Rep 671 para 87, where the Court held "that the prohibition of inhuman and degrading treatment is among the rules of general international law which are binding on States in all circumstances, even apart from any treaty commitments."

122 Kolb, 'The Scope Ratione Materiae of the Compulsory Jurisdiction of the ICJ' 456 ("'renvoi'-logic").

it.[123] At the same time, the Court also stressed the distinctiveness of sources and the confinement to the treaty as far as the applicable law is concerned.

This section will first examine how the Court approached the relationship and the difference between applicable law and interpretation; by way of illustration, it will focus on the *Oil Platforms* case and the *Pulp Mills* case (1.). Subsequently, the section will zero in on the Court's interpretation of the Genocide Convention's compromissory clause and the Court's emphasis on the distinction between the convention and customary international law (2.).

1. The relationship between applicable law and interpretation

a) The *Oil Platforms* case

The *Oil Platform* case concerned a dispute between the United States of America and Iran on whether the destruction of Iranian oil platforms violated the freedom of commerce as guaranteed by the 1955 Treaty of Amity, Economic Relations and Consular Rights[124]. The treaty's compromissory clause, article XXI(2), was in conjunction with article 36(1) ICJ Statute the sole jurisdictional basis.

The United States denied a violation of the treaty and relied, *inter alia*, on the treaty's NPM provision; according to article XX(1)(d), the treaty shall not preclude the application of measures "necessary to fulfill the obligations of a High Contracting Party for the maintenance or restoration of international peace and security, or necessary to protect its essential security interests." Iran argued that the treaty should be construed in light of the Charter, custom on the use of force and UNGA resolutions, so that the treaty obliged both

---

123 *Military and Paramilitary Activities in and against Nicaragua* [1986] ICJ Rep 14, 116 para 222; *Certain Iranian Assets (Islamic Republic of Iran v. United States of America)* (Preliminary Objections Judgment of 13 February 2019) [2019] ICJ Rep 25 para 47; *Oil Platforms (Islamic Republic of Iran v. United States of America)* (Preliminary Objections, Judgment) [1996] ICJ Rep 811 para 20; Kolb, 'The Scope Ratione Materiae of the Compulsory Jurisdiction of the ICJ' 460-461.
124 Treaty of Amity, Economic Relations, and Consular Rights between Iran and the United States of America (signed 15 August 1955, entered into force 16 June 1957) 248 UNTS 93.

parties to conduct their relations in a peaceful manner.[125] The Court accepted the existence of a dispute for the purposes of the compromissory clause on the basis of a literal interpretation of the treaty without any reference to other international law or to article 31(3)(c) VCLT.[126] This was different in the final judgment where the Court referred to article 31(3)(c) VCLT in its interpretation of the NPM provision:

> "[The Court] cannot accept that Article XX, paragraph 1 (d), of the 1955 Treaty was intended to operate wholly independently of the relevant rules of international law on the use of force, so as to be capable of being successfully invoked, even in the limited context of a claim for breach of the Treaty, in relation to an unlawful use of force. The *application of the relevant rules of international law* relating to this question thus forms an integral part of the task of interpretation entrusted to the Court by Article XXI, paragraph 2, of the 1955 Treaty [...]. [The Court's jurisdiction] extends where appropriate, to the determination whether action alleged to be justified under that paragraph was or was not an unlawful use of force, by reference to international law applicable to this question, that is to say, the provisions of the Charter of the United Nations and customary international law. The Court would, however, emphasize that its jurisdiction remains limited to that conferred on it by Article XXI, paragraph 2, of the 1955 Treaty. The Court is always conscious that it has jurisdiction only so far as conferred by the consent of the parties."[127]

In the end, the Court reached the conclusion that the actions of the United States did not comply with the law of self-defence and were, therefore, not precluded from the applicability of the treaty pursuant to article XX(1)(d) of the treaty. Having held that the treaty was applicable in principle, the Court concluded that the treaty had not been violated. As there had not existed any commerce between both states in respect of oil produced by those platforms at the time of the attack, the attacks could not have infringed the freedom of commerce in oil as protected by X(1) of the treaty.[128]

The legal construction and the style of legal reasoning when addressing the law of self-defence were controversial on the bench. Eleven individual opinions were attached, only two of which constituted dissenting opinions disagreeing with the ultimate outcome, whereas the others concerned the judicial reasoning in the judgment. Judge Kooijmans noted that it could have

---

125 *Oil Platforms* [1996] ICJ Rep 803, 809 para 13, 812-813 paras 23, 25.
126 ibid 820 para 53. Cf. for the view that article 31(3)(c) VCLT had been rarely applied before Philippe Sands, 'Treaty, Custom and the Cross-fertilization of International Law' (1998) 1(1) Yale Human Rights and Development Journal 96, 101 ff., advocating in favour of a greater use of article 31(3)(c) VCLT.
127 *Oil Platforms* [2003] ICJ Rep 161, 182-183 paras 41-42 (italics added).
128 ibid 207 para 98.

been more economical to have held that the treaty had not been violated, which would have made any discussion of the law of self-defence unnecessary; yet he accepted that the Court was at liberty to make a point in relation to the law of self-defence.[129] Whereas for Judge Simma the Court proceeded too cautiously and even appeared to "attemp[t] to conceal the law of the Charter rather than to emphasize it"[130], several judges criticized the style of legal reasoning and argued that the Court should have focused more on the treaty. They criticized the use in the above-quoted passage of the word "application" since in their opinion the Court did not have jurisdiction to "apply" other rules of international law which could become relevant only incidentally in the interpretation of the treaty.[131] In particular, Judge Higgins criticized the Court for "incorporating the totality of the substantive international law [...] on the use of force" by virtue of article 31 3 (c) of the VCLT into the treaty.[132]

b) The *Pulp Mills* case and the environmental impact assessment under general international law

Against the background of this controversy, the Court stressed in the subsequent *Pulp Mills* case that, while the Court would have recourse to customary rules on treaty interpretation as set forth in article 31 VCLT and therefore take account for the interpretation of the 1975 Statute of the River Uruguay[133] of relevant rules, "whether these are rules of general international law or contained in multilateral conventions to which the two States are parties",

---

129 ibid Sep Op Kooijmans para 31.
130 ibid Sep Op Simma 329 para 8; see also Sep Op Elraby 291, advocating a more detailed assessment of the self-defence problematique.
131 See ibid Sep Op Higgins para 48, Sep Op Kooijmans paras 19-23, Sep Op Buergenthal para 22.
132 ibid Sep Op Higgins para 46. According to Judges Higgins and Owada, there was no complete overlap between the treaty and the law of self-defense under general international law, ibid Sep Op Higgins, Sep Op Owada para 5. For Simma, the *jus cogens* character of the law of self-defence limited the possible interpretations of the treaty, ibid Sep Op Simma para 9: "If these general rules of international law are of a peremptory nature, as they undeniably are in our case, then the principle of interpretation just mentioned turns into a legally insurmountable limit to permissible treaty interpretation."
133 Statute of the River Uruguay (signed 26 February 1975, entered into force 18 September 1976) 1295 UNTS 331.

the jurisdiction "remains confined to disputes concerning the interpretation or application of the Statute."[134] The Court did not use the word "application" with respect to the other rules which are taken into account in the process of interpretation, only the 1975 Statute was applied.[135] Against this jurisdictional background, one may consider the fact that the Court referred to the environmental impact assessment as "a requirement under general international law".[136] The use of the term "general international law" in this context gave rise to debates. Judge Cançado Trindade stressed the importance of general principles of law and criticized the Court for that "diligence and zeal seem to have vanished in respect of general principles of law".[137] In a subsequent judgment, the Court recalled its classification of the obligation to conduct an environmental impact assessment as an obligation under general international law.[138] In an individual opinion, Judge *ad hoc* Dugard pointed to "some debate about the precise meaning attached to this term" and stressed that "'general international law' cannot be equated to general principles of law" which would by and large concern rules of evidence, procedure or defences.[139] For Dugard and for Judge Donoghue, the obligation to conduct

---

134 *Pulp Mills on the River Uruguay* (*Argentina v. Uruguay*) (Judgment) [2010] ICJ Rep 46-47 paras 65-66 (quote).
135 Cf. Papadaki, 'Compromissory Clauses as the Gatekeepers of the Law to be 'used' in the ICJ and the PCIJ' 15-16; cf. on the distinction between applicable law and interpretation Anastasios Gourgourinis, 'The Distinction between Interpretation and Application of Norms in International Adjudication' (2011) 2(1) JIDS 31 ff.
136 *Pulp Mills on the River Uruguay* [2010] ICJ Rep 14, 83 para 204: "In this sense, the obligation to protect and preserve, under Article 41(a) of the Statute, has to be interpreted in accordance with a practice, which in recent years has gained so much acceptance among States that it may now be considered a requirement under general international law to undertake an environmental impact assessment where there was a risk that the proposed industrial activity may have a significant adverse impact in a transboundary context, in particular, on a shared resource."
137 ibid [2010] ICJ Rep 14 Sep Op Cançado Trindade 137 paras 4 and 5.
138 *Certain Activities Carried out by Nicaragua in the Border Area - Construction of a Road in Costa Rica Along The San Juan River* (*Costa Rica v. Nicaragua /Nicaragua v. Costa Rica*) (Judgment) [2015] ICJ Rep 706 para 104.
139 ibid Sep Op Dugard paras 13, 14. He also noted the secondary character of general principles of law, such as responsibility, which presuppose primary obligations. He referred to the PCIJ, cf. *Mavrommatis Palestine Concessions: Greece v. The United Kingdom* Judgment of 30 August 1924 [1924] PCIJ Series A 02, 27.

environmental impact assessments was a rule of customary international law.[140]

Hence, the term of general international law might not have been used as a conceptual alternative or in opposition to customary international law.[141] One possible explanation for the use of the term in *Pulp Mills* might be the jurisdictional context. In light of the jurisdictional discussions in *Oil Platforms*, the Court stressed the jurisdictional limitation in *Pulp Mills* and used the term of "general" international law against the background of the long-standing jurisprudence that "general international law" remains applicable in the context of the interpretation and application of a specific treaty.[142]

---

140 *Certain Activities Carried out by Nicaragua in the Border Area - Construction of a Road in Costa Rica Along The San Juan River* [2015] ICJ Rep 665 Sep Op Judge ad hoc Dugard para 17; ibid Sep Op Donoghue para 2: "[The Court] uses the terms 'general international law' and 'customary international law', apparently without differentiation."

141 The Court's practice as to the use of the term is not very consistent. For an early use in the context of international organizations see *Interpretation of the Agreement of 25 March 1951 between the WHO and Egypt* (Advisory Opinion) [1980] ICJ Rep 95 para 48 on the obligation to negotiate in good faith: "The Court does so the more readily as it considers those obligations to be the very basis of the legal relations between the Organization and Egypt under general international law, under the Constitution of the Organization and under the agreements in force between Egypt and the Organization."; *Accordance with international law of the unilateral declaration of independence in respect of Kosovo* [2010] ICJ Rep 403, 437 para 80 (discussing customary international law in a section on general international law); "general international law" invoked in order to address rules relating to state responsibility, see *Jurisdictional Immunities of the State* [2012] ICJ Rep 99, 153 paras 136-137; *Questions relating to the Obligation to Prosecute or Extradite* [2012] ICJ Rep 422, 461 para 121; the pleading of the parties is not always clear: Senegal denied the violation of "any other rule of conventional law, general international law or customary international law", ibid 12; Michael Wood, 'The International Tribunal for the Law of the Sea and General International Law' (2007) 22 International Journal of Marine and Coastal Law 354, noting "a certain degree of imprecision" of the term; see also Nele Matz-Lück, 'Norm Interpretation across International Regimes: Competences and Legitimacy' in Margaret A Young (ed), *Regime Interaction in International Law Facing Fragmentation* (Cambridge University Press 2012) 206: "[I]t is questionable whether the establishment of a defined category of 'general international law' is beneficial, since it seems impossible to identify the content. Moreover it is unclear how such a category should relate to the sources of international law".

142 See also Tomuschat, 'Article 36' 754 para 60.

2. From deconventionalization to reconventionalization? The prohibition of genocide and the distinctiveness of sources for the purposes of jurisdiction

The jurisprudence based on the compromissory clause of the Genocide Convention illustrates how the Court acknowledged the interrelationship between treaty law and customary international law while emphasizing the distinctiveness of the sources for jurisdictional purposes. Article IX of the convention reads as follows:

> "Disputes between the Contracting Parties relating to the interpretation, application or fulfilment of the present Convention, including those relating to the responsibility of a State for genocide or any of the other acts enumerated in Article 3, shall be submitted to the International Court of Justice at the request of any of the parties to the dispute."[143]

The convention, however, does not set forth in explicit terms a prohibition of genocide applicable in the relations between states, it identifies genocide as a crime and imposes obligations on states parties to prosecute individuals committing this crime.[144]

According to judge Owada[145], the prohibition directed at states was not a conventional obligation and, therefore, could not be the subject of a dispute regarding the application and interpretation of the Convention. He acknowledged that this prohibition was part of general international law but did not belong to the realm of general international law which included the rules on interpretation and state responsibility and which traditionally was encompassed by jurisdiction based on a compromissory clause. However, in his view, the Court had nevertheless jurisdiction with respect to the prohibition of genocide since the jurisdictional clause of article IX Genocide Convention

---

143 Convention on the Prevention and Punishment of the Crime of Genocide (signed 9 December 1948, entered into force 12 January 1951) 78 UNTS 277.
144 See in particular ibid articles I and VI.
145 *Application of the Convention on the Prevention and Punishment of the Crime of Genocide* [2007] ICJ Rep 43 Sep Op Owada para 58 ff., para 73 for his conclusions. He rejected the Court's incorporation-by-implication argument; for a similar critique see Paola Gaeta, 'On What Conditions Can a State Be Held Responsible for Genocide?' (2007) 18(4) EJIL 637 ff., 641-643 on two primary rules regarding the prohibition of genocide; for a positive assessment of the Court's interpretation see Pierre-Marie Dupuy, 'A Crime without Punishment' (2016) 14 JICJ 882.

confers jurisdiction for disputes relating to the responsibility of a State for genocide. Other judges expressed similar views.[146]

The majority of the Court, however, considered this part of the compromissory clause to be an "unusual feature".[147] Instead, the Court argued that the prohibition to commit genocide existed also as an obligation under the treaty.[148] The Court argued that the Court's earlier characterization of the prohibition of genocide as "binding on States, even without any conventional obligation"[149] and as "peremptory norm of international law (jus cogens)"[150] was "significant for the interpretation of the second proposition stated in Article I"[151] and therefore for the conventional obligation not to commit genocide.

In its judgment of 2015, the Court acknowledged that principles of customary international law are enshrined in the convention, but it also stressed that its jurisdiction was confined to the treaty. Referring to the *Nicaragua* case, the Court held:

"Where a treaty states an obligation which also exists under customary international law, the treaty obligation and the customary law obligation remain separate and distinct [...] Accordingly, unless a treaty discloses a different intention, the fact that the treaty embodies a rule of customary international law will not mean that the compromissory clause of the treaty enables disputes regarding the customary law

---

146 *Application of the Convention on the Prevention and Punishment of the Crime of Genocide* [2007] ICJ Rep 43 Sep Op Tomka 41, 45, 56 61, in his view the additional reference in article IX would confer jurisdiction upon the Court for determining the responsibility of states for violations of the prohibitions of genocide. See also Joint Declaration Shi and Koroma paras 1-6, criticizing the Court's incorporation-by-implication argument See also Skotinov pp. 370-372, speaking of an "absolute prohibition of genocide" under general international law" (273).
147 ibid 114 para 169. The Court left this open in an earlier judgment, *Application of the Convention on the Prevention and Punishment of the Crime of Genocide* [1996] ICJ Rep 595, 616 para 32: "The Court would observe that the reference in Article IX to "the responsibility of a State for genocide or for any of the other acts enumerated in Article III", does not exclude any form of State responsibility."
148 *Application of the Convention on the Prevention and Punishment of the Crime of Genocide* [2007] ICJ Rep 43, 113 para 166: "In short, the obligation to prevent genocide necessarily implies the prohibition of the commission of genocide."
149 *Reservations to the Convention on the Prevention and Punishment of the Crime of Genocide* (Advisory Opinion) [1951] ICJ Rep 23.
150 *Armed Activities on the Territory of the Congo (New Application: 2002)* [2006] ICJ Rep 6, 32 para 64.
151 *Application of the Convention on the Prevention and Punishment of the Crime of Genocide* [2007] ICJ Rep 43, 111 para 162.

obligation to be brought before the Court. In the case of Article IX of the Genocide Convention no such intention is discernible [...]"[152]

One could say that a deconventionalization in the sense of an emphasis of the binding character of the Genocide Convention's underlying principles even without any conventional obligation in 1951[153] was followed by a re-conventionalization in the sense of an emphasis of the conventional character of the prohibition of genocide for jurisdictional purposes. Instead of interpreting article IX of the Genocide Convention in a way that would confer jurisdiction on the violation of an obligation under customary international law, the Court developed this obligation as a matter of treaty law. This treaty obligation is informed by the prohibition's status in general international law. For the purposes of jurisdiction, the Court affirmed the distinctiveness of sources while for the purposes of content-determination acknowledging the interrelationship.[154] As far as a State's international responsibility is concerned, claims in this regard "remain confined to the provisions of the treaty concerned and cannot be extended to a parallel customary rule."[155] To this extent, one can say that compromissory clauses favour treaty law or disfavour customary international law.[156]

In the very recent dispute between Ukraine and Russia during the Russian invasion of Ukraine which started on 24 February 2022 the question was raised whether the Genocide Convention entails a right not to be subject to a false claim of genocide and to another state's military operation based on an abuse of the obligation to prevent genocide under article 1 Genocide Con-

---

152 *Application of the Convention on the Prevention and Punishment of the Crime of Genocide* [2015] ICJ Rep 3, 42-43 paras 87-88; see also Anja Seibert-Fohr, 'State Responsibility for Genocide under the Genocide Convention' in Paola Gaeta (ed), *The UN Genocide Convention: A Commentary* (Oxford University Press 2009) 354: "A case challenging the violation of customary international law could not be based on this clause."
153 Cf. *Reservations to the Convention on the Prevention and Punishment of the Crime of Genocide* [1951] ICJ Rep 15, 23.
154 It is possible that the Court will refer in future cases for the interpretation to the conventional obligation again to the development in customary international law, see Kolb, *The International Court of Justice* 436 for the prospect of the development of the concept of genocide through the jurisprudence of the ICC.
155 Tomuschat, 'Article 36' 754 para 60.
156 See also Tams, 'The Continued Relevance of Compromissory Clauses as a Source of ICJ Jurisdiction' 491: "This is yet another consequence of a dispute settlement system dominated by treaty-specific compromissory clauses – put simplistically, such a system favours treaty over custom."

vention. The Court accepted, *prima facie* in an order of provisional measures Ukraine's submissions that there is "a divergence of views as to whether certain acts allegedly committed by Ukraine in the Luhansk and Donetsk regions amount to genocide in violation of its obligations under the Genocide Convention, as well as whether the use of force by the Russian Federation for the stated purpose of preventing and punishing alleged genocide is a measure that can be taken in fulfilment of the obligation to prevent and punish genocide contained in Article I of the Convention."[157] The order is based on a 13:2 majority; two judges, Gevorgian and Xue, dissented, arguing that the Court had no jurisdiction,[158] Judge Bennouna declared that, while he voted in favour of the order because he felt "compelled by the tragic situation", he was not convinced that the Genocide Convention was intended to "to enable a State, such as Ukraine, to seise the Court of a dispute concerning allegations of genocide made against it by another State, such as the Russian Federation, even if those allegations were to serve as a pretext for an unlawful use of force".[159]

IV. Recent Confirmations and Concluding Observations: distinctiveness for jurisdictional purposes

Recent decisions confirm the Court's emphasis on the distinctiveness of sources for jurisdictional purposes. The Court held in *Immunities and Criminal Proceedings* between Equatorial Guinea and France that it had no jurisdiction to entertain Equatorial Guinea's claim that France violated the immunity from foreign criminal jurisdiction of the Vice-President of the Republic of Equatorial Guinea and the immunity of State property of Equatorial

---

157 *Allegations of Genocide under the Convention on the Prevention and Punishment of the Crime of Genocide* (*Ukraine v. Russian Federation*) (Order of 16 March 2022) (2022) ⟨https://www.icj-cij.org/public/files/case-related/182/182-20220316-ORD-01-00-EN.pdf⟩ accessed 1 February 2023 para 45. On this order see Andreas Kulick, 'Provisional Measures after Ukraine v Russia (2022)' (2022) 13(2) JIDS 323 ff., 337 (on the possibility that the order "may incidentally serve the integrity of international legal argument" and preclude future uses of force under humanitarian pretence).
158 *Allegations of Genocide under the Convention on the Prevention and Punishment of the Crime of Genocide* (Order of 16 March 2022) Decl Gevorgian, Decl Xue.
159 ibid Decl Bennouna paras 1-2.

Guinea. The Palermo Convention[160] provides for the Court's jurisdiction for any dispute concerning the interpretation or application of the convention pursuant to article 35. Article 4 of the convention provides that "States Parties shall carry out their obligations under this Convention in a manner consistent with the principles of sovereign equality and territorial integrity of States and that of non-intervention [...]" and that "[n]othing in this Convention entitles a State Party to undertake in the territory of another State the exercise of jurisdiction [...]".[161] Whereas France argued that article 4 only recalls without incorporating the rules of customary international law,[162] Equatorial Guinea expressed the view that respect for the principles of sovereign equality and non-intervention "becomes a treaty obligation for a State party when it is applying the other provisions of the Convention" and that the rules relating to immunity "flow directly from the principles of sovereign equality and non-intervention".[163] The Court held that the reference to sovereign equality did not entail an obligation "to act in a manner consistent with the many rules of international law which protect sovereignty in general, as well as all the qualifications to those rules"[164] and that article 4 could not be interpreted as incorporating the customary international rules on immunities.[165] It is notable that the Court's conclusion related to the customary international law rules on immunity; the Court did not adopt the view that article 4(1) would be only "a without prejudice clause" which would not impose any obligation to act in accordance with the principles referred therein.[166]

In *Certain Iranian Assets* between Iran and the USA, the Court decided that the dispute on the freezing of Iranian assets in the USA, in particular assets of the Iranian national bank Markazi, fell within the Court's jurisdiction under the Treaty of Amity, Economic Relations and Consular Rights. At the

---

160 United Nations Convention against Transnational Organized Crime (signed 15 November 2000, entered into force 25 December 2003) 2225 UNTS.
161 *Immunities and Criminal Proceedings* (*Equatorial Guinea v. France*) (Preliminary Objections, Judgment) [2018] ICJ Rep 318 para 78.
162 ibid 318 para 79, 320 para 87.
163 ibid [2018] ICJ Rep 292, 319 para 83, 318 para 81.
164 ibid 321 para 93.
165 ibid 322 para 96. The decision to uphold France's first preliminary objects was based on eleven votes to four majority. The four judges argued in their joint dissenting opinion in favour of a less restrictive interpretation of article 4 of the convention, see ibid Joint Diss Op Vice-President Xue, Judges Sebutinde and Robinson and Judge *ad hoc* Kateka 340, 341, 346 ff.
166 On this point see ibid Decl Judge Crawford 390, 391.

same time, the Court stressed that its jurisdiction did not extend to violations of sovereign immunity under customary international law. The Court held that the various provisions of the treaty (article IX, article XI(4)) did not incorporate the customary rules on sovereign immunity.[167] The fact that article XI(4) excluded claims of immunity in relation to the specific case of publicly owned and controlled enterprises did not mean that there was a treaty obligation to respect immunities under customary international law in all other cases.[168] Moreover, the freedom of commerce protected by article X of the bilateral treaty between Iran and the USA did not "cover matters that have no connection, or too tenuous a connection, with the commercial relations between the States Parties to the Treaty. In this regard, the Court is not convinced that the violation of the sovereign immunities to which certain State entities are said to be entitled under international law in the exercise of their activities *jure imperii* is capable of impeding freedom of commerce, which by definition concerns activities of a different kind."[169]

In this context, the Court held that the fact that a certain act violated multiple rules of international law did not exclude jurisdiction under one particular treaty, as certain acts "may fall within the ambit of more than one instrument and a dispute relating to those acts may relate to the 'interpretation or application' of more than one treaty or other instrument."[170]

Whereas the Court respects the jurisdictional confinements as to the applicable law,[171] its practice also indicates that the interpretation of a conventional rule that is to be applied may require recourse to other principles and rules

---

167 *Certain Iranian Assets* [2019] ICJ Rep 7, 28 para 58, 30 para 65, 32 para 70, 33 para 74, 34 para 79; the Court made clear that the question of incorporation needs to be answered by an interpretation of the treaty which is confined to a literal interpretation, see 32 para 70, where the Court held that the fact that an article "makes no mention of sovereign immunities, and that it also contains no renvoi to the rules of general international law, does not suffice to exclude the question of immunities from the scope ratione materiae of the provision at issue".
168 ibid para 65.
169 ibid para 79.
170 *Alleged Violations of the 1955 Treaty of Amity, Economic Relations, and Consular Rights (Islamic Republic of Iran v. United States of America)* (Preliminary Objections, Judgment of 3 February 2021) [2021] ICJ Rep 27 para 56 ("To the extent that the measures adopted by the United States following its decision to withdraw from the JCPOA might constitute breaches of certain obligations under the Treaty of Amity, those measures relate to the interpretation or application of that Treaty").
171 *Application of the Convention on the Prevention and Punishment of the Crime of Genocide* [2015] ICJ Rep 3, 48 para 89: "It is not enough that these events may

of international law. The distinctiveness of the sources for jurisdictional purposes should not be equated with the relationship between the sources when it comes to the interpretation and application of international law. This aspect which will be the topic of the next section.

D. The normative environment in the jurisprudence of the ICJ

The purpose of this section is to illustrate the relevance of normative considerations and the normative environment[172] for the interpretation and application of customary international law.[173] The Court often related a rule of international law to its normative environment[174] and took account of "trends" and normative developments in the international legal order.[175] Customary

---

have involved violations of the customary international law regarding genocide; the dispute must concern obligations under the Convention itself."

172 Cf. on this term *Fragmentation of international law: difficulties arising from diversification and expansion of international law, Report of the Study Group of the International Law Commission, Finalized by Martti Koskenniemi* 212 para 423. Cf. Christian J Tams, 'The ICJ as a 'Law-Formative Agency': Summary and Synthesis' in Christian J Tams and James Sloan (eds), *The Development of International Law by the International Court of Justice* (Oxford University Press 2013) 380, the ICJ judgments would operate in a broader normative environment.

173 On general principles, see in this chapter below, p. 305.

174 Cf. *Interpretation of the Agreement of 25 March 1951 between the WHO and Egypt* [1980] ICJ Rep 73, 76 para 10: "But a rule of international law, whether customary or conventional, does not operate in a vacuum; it operates in relation to facts and in the context of a wider framework of legal rules of which it forms only a part." *Legal Consequences for States of the Continued Presence of South Africa in Namibia (South West Africa) notwithstanding Security Council Resolution 276 (1970)* (Advisory Opinion) [1971] ICJ Rep 31 para 53: "[A]n international instrument has to be interpreted and applied within the framework of the entire legal system prevailing at the time of the interpretation."; also, the Court referred in the context of treaty interpretation to third treaties which were close in substance, see *Wimbledon* PCIJ Series A 01 26-28 and the reference to the "general opinion", and *Ahmadou Sadio Diallo* [2010] ICJ Rep 639, 664 para 68 (referring to regional human rights treaties which were "close in substance"); see also *Ahmadou Sadio Diallo* [2012] ICJ Rep 324, 331 para 13 ff. and the references to the European Court of Human Rights, the Inter-American Court of Human Rights, the Iran-United States Claims Tribunal, the Eritrea-Ethiopia Claims Commission, and the United Nations Compensation Commission.

175 *Asylum Case* [1950] ICJ Rep 266, 277, not using the term trend or tendency, but noting that there was too much inconsistency among conventions on asylum and too

international law and general principles of law are not only important as background against which treaties are to be interpreted, customary international law and general principles of law also provide a normative reservoir for general rules and principles which can help the Court in deciding a legal dispute.[176] They ensure the adjudicability of such disputes on the basis of international law, in particular where no treaty is applicable.

In the following, it will be shown that the Court's jurisprudence provides for illustrations of customary norms of varying degrees of generality (I.). Subsequently, the section will focus on the Court's interpretative decisions when it applies customary international law; in particular, it will illustrate the role of default positions and starting points, the Court's "scoping" and tailoring of the legal analysis and the formulation of a rule and of possible exceptions (II.). The section will then examine the Court's jurisprudence on

---

much political expediency in order to speak of "any constant and uniform usage, accepted as law". *Nottebohm Case (second phase)* (*Liechtenstein v. Guatemala*) (Judgment of April 6th, 1955) [1955] ICJ Rep 22, speaking of a tendency in arbitration and scholarship that would support the genuine link theory. *Fisheries Jurisdiction (Federal Republic of Germany v. Iceland)* (Merits, Judgment) [1974] ICJ Rep 191-192 para 44 referring to the 1960 Conference which had failed to adopt a text by one vote. *Continental Shelf (Tunisia/Libya, Application to Intervene)* [1981] ICJ Rep 3, 38 para 24, the Court was authorized by the compromis to take account "recent trends", the Court stressed that it would have done so proprio motu anyway, for it could not ignore negotiations of multilateral conventions possibly embodying or crystallizing a rule of customary law. *Continental Shelf (Tunisia/Libyan Arab Jamahiriya)* (Judgment) [1982] ICJ Rep 48 para 47; *Legality of the Threat or Use of Nuclear Weapons* [1996] ICJ Rep 226, 237 para 18, noting that stating the law can involve noting the law's "general trend". See also *Continental Shelf (Libya/Malta)* [1985] ICJ Rep 13, 29-30 para 27: "It is of course axiomatic that the material of customary international law is to be looked for primarily in the actual practice and *opinio juris* of States, even though multilateral conventions may have an important role to play in recording and defining rules deriving from custom, or indeed in developing them." See also at 33 para 33, where the Court relied on the 1982 Convention to conclude that the continental shelf and the exclusive economic zone "are linked together in modern law".

176 Cf. already in the context of arbitration *Eastern Extension, Australasia and China Telegraph Company, Ltd* Great Britain v. United States (9 November 1923) VI RIAA 114: "International law [...] may not contain, and generally does not contain, express rules decisive of particular cases; but the function of jurisprudence is to resolve the conflict of opposing rights and interests by applying, in default of any specific provisions of law, the corollaries of general principles, and so to find [...] the solution of the problem."

259

the relationship between customary international law and treaty law (III.). This examination will include not only the case-law on the relationship but also illustrations of forms of convergence between the Charter and customary international law and forms of convergence of functionally equivalent rules in the Court's maritime delimitation jurisprudence. Against the background of the previous subsections, the chapter will then zero in on the role of general principles (IV.).

I. Varying degrees of generality of customary international law

Principles and rules of customary international law, terms which the Court used interchangeably,[177] can display a high degree of generality and abstractness and yet remain capable of being applied and concretized by the Court to the individual case.

The Court referred in its *Corfu Channel* judgment to "certain general and well-recognized principles, namely: elementary considerations of humanity, even more exacting in peace than in war; the principle of the freedom of maritime communication; and every State's obligation not to allow knowingly its territory to be used for acts contrary to the rights of other States."[178] The Court concretized these principles and held that Albania's obligations "consisted in notifying, for the benefit of shipping in general, the existence of a minefield in Albanian territorial waters and in warning the approaching British warships of the imminent danger to which the minefield exposed them."[179]

A further example is the *Fisheries jurisdiction* case where the Court argued that, even though "the practice of States does not justify the formulation of any general rule of law"[180] on maritime delimitation, there was still "general international law" available: "It does not at all follow that, in the absence of rules having the technically precise character alleged by the United Kingdom Government, the delimitation undertaken by the Norwegian Government in

---

177 *Delimitation of the Maritime Boundary in the Gulf of Maine Area* [1984] ICJ Rep 246, 288-290 para 79; cf. Weil, 'Le droit international en quête de son identité: cours général de droit international public' 150: "Loin de relever d'une source autonome de droit international, tous ces principes ont en réalité le caractère de règles coutumières."
178 *Corfu Channel Case (UK v Albania)* (Merits) [1949] ICJ Rep 22.
179 ibid 22.
180 *Fisheries (United Kingdom v. Norway)* (Judgment) [1951] ICJ Rep 131.

1935 is not subject to certain principles which make it possible to judge as to its validity under international law."[181] The Court then referred to "certain basic considerations inherent in the nature of the territorial sea, which bring to light certain criteria which, though not entirely precise, can provide courts with an adequate basis for their decisions, which can be adapted to the diverse facts in question."[182]

These general principles and rules can require a focus on the particularities of the case. In the case between Tunisia and Libya the Court held that so-called historic waters and historic bays "continued to be governed by general international law which does not provide for a *single* 'règime' [...] but only for a particular règime for each of the concrete, recognized cases".[183]

In the *North Sea Continental Shelf* cases, the Court began to develop its jurisprudence on delimitation on the basis of "equitable principles" and good faith in order to reach an "equitable result" by applying criteria which in part have found expression in law, in part followed from the particularities of the case.[184]

The principle of good faith can also give rise to basic procedural obligations.[185] In the *Icelandic Fisheries* case, the Court highlighted the obligation

---

181 ibid 132. As was pointed out by individual judges, the Court did not adopt the so-called Lotus-approach, ibid Op Judge Alvarez 152; Diss Op McNair 160; Gerald Fitzmaurice, 'The Law and Procedure of the International Court of Justice, 1951-54: General Principles and Sources of Law' (1953) 30 BYIL 11.
182 *Fisheries* [1951] ICJ Rep 116, 133.
183 *Continental Shelf (Tunisia/Libya)* 74 para 100; see also *Land, Island and Maritime Frontier Dispute (El Salvador/Honduras: Nicaragua Intervening)* (Judgment) [1992] ICJ Rep 351, 592-593, 598-602 on the Gulf of Fonseca as "historic bay" and "closed sea" and the joint sovereignty of the three coastal states based on the succession from the Spanish Crown in 1821 as "logical outcome of the principle of *uti possidetis juris* itself" (at 602 para 405); see also Hugh W Thirlway, *The law and procedure of the international court of justice: fifty years of jurisprudence* (vol 2, Oxford University Press 2013) 1164 f., 1198 f., 1421; Maurice H Mendelson, 'The International Court of Justice and the sources of international law' in Vaughan Lowe and Malgosia Fitzmaurice (eds), *Fifty years of the International Court of Justice Essays in honour of Sir Robert Jennings* (Cambridge University Press 1996) 72.
184 *North Sea Continental Shelf* [1969] ICJ Rep 3, 46-47 para 85. Cf. also the section below, p. 290.
185 Cf. *Gabčíkovo-Nagymaros Project* [1997] ICJ Rep 7, 66 para 109, where "both parties agree that articles 65 to 67 of the Vienna Convention on the Law of Treaties, if not codifying customary law, at least generally reflect customary international law and contain certain procedural principles which are based on an obligation to act in good faith."

to "pay reasonable regard to the interests of other states" when a state exercises its preferential rights of fishing.[186] And in the *Pulp Mills* case, the Court related the "principle of prevention, as a customary rule" to "the due diligence that is required of a State in its territory" with respect to "activities which take place in its territory, or in any area under its jurisdiction".[187] This is an example of how a traditional principle can be interpreted and applied in a contemporary fashion.

However, these examples should not create the impression, which could arise from a reading of the *Gulf of Maine* judgment, that customary international law consisted only of old, very general rules and principles[188] or that there are two strictly separated categories of customary international law, namely "a limited set of norms for ensuring the co-existence and vital co-operation of the members of the international community" and "a set of customary rules whose presence in the *opinio juris* of States can be tested by induction based on the analysis of a sufficiently extensive and convincing practice".[189] Rather, customary international law consists of principles and rules of varying degrees of generality which can interrelate with each other and which should be studied in their interrelationship.[190]

---

186 *Fisheries Jurisdiction* [1974] ICJ Rep 175, 198 para 59.
187 *Pulp Mills on the River Uruguay* [2010] ICJ Rep 14, 55-56 para 101, with reference to *Corfu Channel Case* [1949] ICJ Rep 4, 22 and to *Legality of the Threat or Use of Nuclear Weapons* [1996] ICJ Rep 226, 242 para 29; see also *Certain Activities Carried out by Nicaragua in the Border Area - Construction of a Road in Costa Rica Along The San Juan River* [2015] ICJ Rep 665, 706 para 104; ibid [2015] ICJ Rep 665 Sep Op Donoghue para 3. On procedural obligations under customary international law in the context of international environmental law see Jutta Brunnée, 'International Environmental Law and Community Interests: Procedural Aspects' in Georg Nolte and Eyal Benvenisti (eds), *Community Interests Across International Law* (Oxford University Press 2017) 156-165.
188 According to *Delimitation of the Maritime Boundary in the Gulf of Maine Area* [1984] ICJ Rep 246, 290 para 81, customary international law "can of its nature only provide a few basic legal principles, which lay down guidelines to be followed with a view to an essential objective."
189 ibid 229 para 111: "A body of detailed rules is not to be looked for in customary international law which in fact comprises a limited set of norms for ensuring the co-existence and vital co-operation of the members of the international community, together with a set of customary rules whose presence in the *opinio juris* of States can be tested by induction based on the analysis of a sufficiently extensive and convincing practice, and not by deduction from preconceived ideas."
190 Nolte, 'How to identify customary international law? - On the final outcome of the work of the International Law Commission (2018)' 20, speaking of the "risk

Normative and functional considerations[191] as well as state practice can be relevant in specifying and concretizing these broad rules and principles to the particularities of the case and in interpreting specific rules of customary international law against the background of broader principles and rules. As Rudolf Geiger has argued, the Court's analysis of customary international law would often start with first basic principles which the Court would interpret in light of their respective aims and functions and in light of the specific case before the Court. Based on this interpretation, the Court would arrive at more specific norms.[192]

For instance, in the *Jurisdictional Immunities* case, the Court related the rule of state immunity to its wider normative environment, thereby demonstrating that broad rules and principles can give rise to more specific ones and that the latter are to be considered against the background of the former, just as broad principles have to be viewed together:

"[The rule of state immunity] derives from the principle of sovereign equality of States, which, as Article 2, paragraph 1, of the Charter of the United Nations makes clear, is

---

that customary international law is perceived as only consisting of an assortment of certain specific rules, such as those on immunity or diplomatic protection, which can be simply recognized by looking at practice. Customary international law rather consists of rules on a different level of generality which may influence each other." Furthermore, in *Territorial and Maritime Dispute (Nicaragua v. Colombia)* (Judgment) [2012] ICJ Rep 674 para 139, the Court decided that article 121 UNCLOS as a whole formed part of an "indivisible regime" and as such reflected customary international law. The Court thusly indicated that customary international law consisted not only of separate rules but of rules which can interrelate with each other.

191 In the *Arrest Warrant* case, the Court extended immunities to Foreign ministers because the Foreign Minister assumes functions that are similar to those assumed by the head of the government or the head of state who are protected from personal immunities, the Court also referred to article 7 VCLT which provides that heads of state, heads of governments and foreign ministers are considered as representative of their state, *Arrest Warrant of 11 April 2000 (Democratic Republic of Congo v. Belgium)* (Judgment) [2002] ICJ Rep 21-22 paras 53-54. This is an instance of reasoning by analogy.

192 Rudolf H Geiger, 'Customary International Law in the Jurisprudence of the International Court of Justice: A Critical Appraisal' in Ulrich Fastenrath and others (eds), *From bilateralism to community interest: essays in honour of Judge Bruno Simma* (Oxford University Press 2011) 692-694: "This method of detecting customary international law norms - that is, looking for legal principles and interpreting these principles to find specifying rules suitable for deciding the case, and making use of law-making treaties and resolutions of international organs as guidelines - seems to be the law-finding method which the Court really applies."

one of the fundamental principles of the international legal order. This principle has to be viewed together with the principle that each State possesses sovereignty over its own territory and that there flows from that sovereignty the jurisdiction of the State over events and persons within that territory. Exceptions to the immunity of the State represent a departure from the principle of sovereign equality. Immunity may represent a departure from the principle of territorial sovereignty and the jurisdiction which flows from it."[193]

The Court then examined practice as to whether an exception to immunity had crystallized.[194]

In the *Chagos* opinion, the Court considered that "[b]oth State practice and *opinio juris* at the relevant time confirm the customary law character of the right to territorial integrity of a non-self-governing territory as a *corollary of the right to self-determination.*"[195] Arguably, as the right to self-determination, including respect for territorial integrity, had been firmly anchored in the international legal order, the burden of reasoning with respect to this right's application to the specific case shifted: as the Court noted, "no example has been brought to the attention of the Court in which, following the adoption of resolution 1514(XV), the General Assembly or any other organ of the United Nations has considered as lawful the detachment by the administering Power of part of a non-self-governing territory, for the purpose of maintaining it under its colonial rule."[196] The rule that was then applied appeared to have been the right to self-determination, rather than the right to territorial integrity as corollary,[197] as the Could held hat "any detachment by the administering Power of part of a non-self-governing territory, unless

---

193 *Jurisdictional Immunities of the State* [2012] ICJ Rep 99, 123-124 para 57.
194 ibid 127 ff.
195 *Legal consequences of the Separation of the Chagos Archipelago from Mauritius in 1965* (Advisory Opinion) [2019] ICJ Rep [2019] ICJ Rep 95, 134 para 160 (italics added).
196 ibid 134 para 160; the Court also noted that resolution 1514 (XV) was not met with contestation, ibid 132 para 152.
197 On this aspect see in particular Chasapis Tassinis, 'Customary International Law: Interpretation from Beginning to End' 262-263. He also points out that the Court did not always apply the more general standard, as it applied in the *Jurisdictional Immunities* case the rule of state of immunity, rather than the principle of sovereign equality of states, and in the *Nicaragua* case it applied the principle of non-intervention, rather than the principle of sovereign equality.

based on the freely expressed and genuine will of the people of the territory concerned, is contrary to the right to self-determination."[198]

In the *Nicaragua case* the Court considered the principle of non-intervention to be

> "part and parcel of customary international law [...] Expressions of an *opinio juris* regarding the existence of the principle of non-intervention in customary international law are numerous and not difficult to find [...] The existence in the *opinio juris* of States of the principle of non-intervention is backed by established and substantial practice. It has moreover been presented as corollary of the principle of the sovereign equality of States".[199]

The Court interpreted the principle of non-intervention by way of reference to its *telos*, against the backdrop of state sovereignty and under consideration of the Friendly Relations Declaration: "A prohibited intervention must accordingly be one bearing on matters in which each State is permitted, by the principle of State sovereignty, to decide freely [...] Intervention is wrongful when it uses methods of coercion in regard to such choices, which must remain free ones."[200] The Court then examined whether "state practice justified" this interpretation of this principle.[201] The Court did not, however, search for affirmative practice; rather, it examined whether state practice derogated from this principle by creating a general right to intervention, which the Court concluded was not the case.[202]

This line of reasoning is partly discussed as an illustration of the difficulty of proving a prohibitive rule, to identify "an intangible practice of abstention"[203] and of the importance of *opinio juris*.[204] It is submitted here that the case also indicates the significance of scoping the case and determining the question which needs to be answered by an examination of the practice

---

198 *Legal consequences of the Separation of the Chagos Archipelago from Mauritius in 1965* 134 para 160.
199 *Military and Paramilitary Activities in and against Nicaragua* [1986] ICJ Rep 14, 106 para 202.
200 ibid 108 para 205.
201 ibid 108 para 206.
202 ibid 108-109 paras 206-209.
203 d'Aspremont, 'The Decay of Modern Customary International Law in Spite of Scholarly Heroism' 26.
204 Cf. *ILC Report 2018* at 128: "In particular, where prohibitive rules are concerned, it may sometimes be difficult to find much affirmative State practice (as opposed to inaction); cases involving such rules are more likely to turn on evaluating whether the inaction is accepted as law."

265

of states.[205] As the principle of non-intervention is firmly anchored in the international legal order, the question turned on whether there is a sufficient body of practice derogating from this principle. In other words, the right to intervention was characterized as an exception to the rule, and with the exception came the burden of reasoning.

Furthermore, practice can shed light on the application of a general principle or a general rule of customary international law. In *Burkina Faso v. the Republic of Mali*, the Court addressed the *uti possidetis* principle, which had characterized the decolonialization in Spanish America in the 19th century, and held that "[t]he fact that the new African States have respected the administrative boundaries and frontiers established by the colonial power must be seen not as a mere practice contributing to the gradual emergence of a principle of customary international law, limited in its impact to the African continent as it had previously been to Spanish America, but as the application in Africa of a rule of general scope."[206]

State practice can also limit the scope of an emerging or latent rule, as the *Nuclear Weapons* Advisory Opinion demonstrates. In the view of the Court, the emergence of an absolute prohibition "is hampered by the continuing tensions between the nascent *opinio juris* on the one hand, and the still strong adherence to the practice of deterrence on the other."[207]

II. Interpretative Decisions

The legal craft is particularly relevant in light of the broadness of rules and principles. This section will, by way of example, focus on default positions, starting points and differences in the normative context (1.), on the "scoping" and tailoring of the legal analysis (2.) and on the way in which the Court shapes a rule by acknowledging an exception (3.).

---

205 On legal techniques see also below, p. 266.
206 *Frontier Dispute* [1986] ICJ Rep 554, 565 para 21.
207 *Legality of the Threat or Use of Nuclear Weapons* [1996] ICJ Rep 226, 255 para 73. Hence, the fact that nuclear weapons had not been used since 1945 was, as it was argued by a group of states, "not on account of an existing or nascent custom but merely because circumstances that might justify their use have fortunately not arisen" (254 para 66).

1. Default positions, starting points and the normative context

Presumptions, default positions and starting points are important when identifying customary international law. The ICJ jurisprudence illustrates that territory, for instance, can be a starting point, presumption or an important consideration in legal reasoning[208] which, of course, has to be considered against the background of other legal principles and interests.[209] A famous default position is perhaps the interpretation of the *Lotus* judgment according to which states were free to act unless there was a prohibition.[210] However, it is difficult to resolve a conflict of different sovereignties on the basis of the *Lotus* presumption alone; as Sir Gerald Fitzmaurice argued, the outcome of a case would then "depend largely on the accident of which side was plaintiff and which defendant".[211] Arguably, there is no single static default position; rather, the appropriate default position must be determined in each case anew, normative considerations which shift the burden of reasoning can be of particular importance in this regard.

---

208   Cf. on territorial jurisdiction *Jurisdictional Immunities of the State* [2012] ICJ Rep 99, 124 para 57 (territorial jurisdiction flows from territorial sovereignty); *Asylum Case* [1950] ICJ Rep 266, 275 (territorial sovereignty as default position, a derogation requires a legal basis); *The Case of SS Lotus* PCIJ Series A 10, 18-19 (referring to the exercise of jurisdiction in a state's own territory); *Military and Paramilitary Activities in and against Nicaragua* [1986] ICJ Rep 14, 106 para 202 (on the relationship between territorial sovereignty and non-intervention). See on the role of territorial considerations in the context of maritime delimitation *North Sea Continental Shelf* [1969] ICJ Rep 3, 51 para 96 ("[...] the land dominates the sea"); *Continental Shelf (Tunisia/Libya)* [1982] ICJ Rep 18, 61 para 73; *Maritime Delimitation and Territorial Questions between Qatar and Bahrain (Qatar v. Bahrain)* (Merits, Judgment) [2001] ICJ Rep 97 para 185, on the question of what counts as territory see 102 para 206: "The few existing rules do not justify a general assumption that low-tide elevations are territory in the same sense as islands." See also Geiger, 'Customary International Law in the Jurisprudence of the International Court of Justice: A Critical Appraisal' 688-689.
209   Cf. *Jurisdictional Immunities of the State* 124 para 57 (referring to the sovereign equality of states); cf. *Territorial and Maritime Dispute* [2012] ICJ Rep 624, 690-692 paras 177-180 (on the right to establish a territorial sea of 12 nautical miles).
210   Cf. *The Case of SS Lotus* PCIJ Series A 10, 18.
211   Fitzmaurice, 'The Law and Procedure of the International Court of Justice, 1951-54: General Principles and Sources of Law' 11-13 (quote at 12); see also Martti Koskenniemi, 'The Politics of International Law' (1990) 1 EJIL 18.

Chapter 5: The International Court of Justice

Two very early cases of the Court illustrate the role of interpretative decisions, the normative environment and the overall context[212], namely the *Asylum* case and the *Nottebohm* case. To Josef Kunz, the Court's rather loose treatment of customary international law in relation to the genuine link requirement in *Nottebohm* was difficult to reconcile with the Court's rather stringent conditions in the *Asylum* case.[213] It is argued here that both cases are difficult to compare because of the different normative settings and default positions.

a) The *Asylum* case

In the *Asylum* case, Colombia relied on several conventions as arguments in support of a rule of (regional) customary international law which would have entitled Colombia to grant Víctor Raúl Haya de la Torre political asylum in a Colombian embassy in Peru.[214] The starting point of the Court's legal analysis was the territorial sovereignty of Peru, and this may explain that the burden

---

212 The importance of the "overall context" is addressed in the third ILC conclusion on customary international law, *ILC Report 2018* at 126-129. The first paragraph of the third conclusion reads: "In assessing evidence for the purpose of ascertaining whether there is a general practice and whether that practice is accepted as law (opinio juris), regard must be had to the overall context, the nature of the rule and the particular circumstances in which the evidence in question is to be found".

213 Cf. Josef L Kunz, 'The Nottebohm Judgment (Second Phase)' (1960) 54 AJIL 554, 557, according to whom the Court's identification of the genuine link requirement in customary international law is conflict with the "very stringent conditions which the Court laid down in the Asylum case for the coming into existence of a rule of customary international law."

214 While it could be argued that the *Asylum* case concerns only regional custom and therefore cannot be used for an analysis of general customary international law, it is submitted here that the Court's judgment does not support such a reading. The Court invoked article 38 ICJ Statute in order to explain that a party which relies on a custom needs to substantiate the existence of a rule of customary international law, see *Asylum Case* [1950] ICJ Rep 266, 276-277 and 274 (phrasing Colombia's argument as one based on customary international law); see also Fitzmaurice, 'The General Principles of International Law considered from the standpoint of the rule of law' 106 (the same principles apply to regional and general custom); *Fragmentation of international law: difficulties arising from diversification and expansion of international law, Report of the Study Group of the International Law Commission, Finalized by Martti Koskenniemi* para 214 (pointing out that "the Court treated the

of reasoning was on the legal view advanced by Colombia: according to this argument, customary international law as reflected in the Havana convention of 1928 on asylum[215], to which Peru was not a party,[216] or regional customary international law should have provided for a legal ground for diplomatic asylum. According to the Court, however, such a right to grant political asylum would have been tantamount to a unilateral right of qualification with respect to the grounds of asylum, which would have constituted a significant derogation from territorial sovereignty and, therefore, could not lightly be assumed.[217] The Court also related the Havana convention to the overall context and concluded that the convention, rather than endorsing a right to grant political asylum, intended to constrain abusive practices.[218]

b) The *Nottebohm* case and the genuine link requirement

In *Nottebohm*, the ICJ pronounced itself on the genuine link requirement when it determined under which conditions a state can exercise diplomatic protection on behalf of individuals. The dispute between Liechtenstein and Guatemala concerned the question of whether Liechtenstein could exercise diplomatic protection on behalf of Friedrich Nottebohm. Nottebohm was born in Germany in 1881, went to Guatemala in 1905 and lived there until 1943 and successfully applied for Liechtenstein's citizenship in 1939, thereby losing his German citizenship. Guatemala, which sided with the Allies against Germany, treated Nottebohm as an enemy alien, he was arrested, detained, expelled to the United States and denied readmission, his property was seized without compensation.[219]

Colombian claim as a claim about customary law [...] There was, in other words, no express discussion of 'regionalism' in the judgment").
215 Convention on Asylum (signed 20 February 1928, entered into force 21 May 1929) OAS Official Records, OEA/SerX/I Treaty Series 34.
216 *Asylum Case* [1950] ICJ Rep 266, 274, 275.
217 ibid 274-275, 278.
218 ibid 275, 286.
219 Cf. Liechtenstein's Memorial, summarized in *Nottebohm Case (second phase)* [1955] ICJ Rep 4, 5-6; William Thomas Worster, 'Reining in the Nottebohm Case' [2022] SSRN ⟨https://papers.ssrn.com/sol3/papers.cfm?abstract_id=4148804⟩ accessed 1 February 2023 at 2.

269

The Court held that, while each state was free to enact rules on the grant of its nationality, a state could not claim recognition of its rules by other states

"unless it has acted in conformity with this general aim of making the legal bond of nationality accord with the individual's genuine connection with the State which assumes the defence of its citizens by means of protection as against other States."[220]

In its analysis the Court referred to international arbitrators and domestic courts of third states both of which were said to have given their preference to the "real and effective nationality", and the Court considered that "[t]he same tendency prevails in the writing of publicits and in practice".[221] It would be reflected in article 3(2) of the ICJ Statute according to which "[a] person who for the purposes of membership in the Court could be regarded as a national of more than one state shall be deemed to be a national of the one in which he ordinarily exercises civil and political rights" as well as in those national laws which "make naturalization dependent on conditions indicating the existence of a link".[222] Furthermore, certain states would not exercise diplomatic protection on behalf of naturalized persons who have severed their links.[223] The Court also referred to bilateral nationality treaties between the USA and other States since 1868, the so-called Bancroft Treaties which had been abrogated since 1917.[224] Moreover, the Court found support for the existence of international criteria in Article I of the 1930 Convention relating to the Conflict of Nationality Laws which provided that a national law on nationality "shall be recognised by other States in so far as it is consistent with international conventions, international custom, and the principles of law generally recognised with regard to nationality"; according to article 5, a third state shall recognize in a case of multiple nationalities "either the nationality of the country in which [the individual] is habitually and principally resident, or the nationality of the country with which in the circumstances [the individual] appears to be in fact most closely connected."[225]

---

220 *Nottebohm Case (second phase)* [1955] ICJ Rep 4, 23. See also at 22-23 for a distinction between the conferral of nationality and the exercise of diplomatic protection which the Court considered the case at hand to be concerned with.
221 ibid 22.
222 ibid 22.
223 ibid 22.
224 ibid 22-23.
225 Convention on Certain Questions Relating to the Conflict of Nationality Law (signed 13 April 1930, entered into force 1 July 1937) 179 UNTS; *Nottebohm Case (second phase)* [1955] ICJ Rep 4, 23. See recently Peter Tomka, 'Custom and the International

The Court searched for principles enshrined in the regulation of dual nationality and found a certain effectiveness principle or requirement which it applied to diplomatic protection under customary international law.[226] The general principle of abuse of rights might also have provided some inspiration:[227] Acting for Guatemala, Henri Rolin, while not explicitly advocating in favour of the genuine link requirement as part of customary international law, argued that the grant of naturalization by Liechtenstein without any close relationship constituted an abuse of rights.[228]

Court of Justice' (2013) 12(2) The law and practice of international courts and tribunals 205: "The Court was careful not to rely directly on the Convention, but noted rather that distilling a rule of law from the various indications of practice - in other words, interpreting the regularity of usage as the expression of a general practice *accepted as law* - served to 'explain' why certain States would adopt that rule as binding in a codification convention. In this way, the codification convention served as a tool for interpreting the evidence regarding State practice, which itself was silent as to the reasons motivating the practice."

226 See also Ian Brownlie, 'The Relations of Nationality in Public International Law,' [1963] (39) BYIL 286, 328, 349, 353, 354, 356, 362 (on the application of a general principle); according to Jessup, the ICJ did not "invent" or legislate this principle, see *Barcelona Traction, Light and Power Company, Limited* 3 Sep Op Jessup 186 para 44, pointing out that the principle or requirement of a genuine link had already been established piror to Nottebohm in particular with respect to corporations and constituted a general principle of law. See also Lucius C Caflisch, 'The Protection of Corporate Investments Abroad in the Light of the Barcelona Traction Case' (1971) 31 ZaöRV 177: "Though using different terms, [the formula] expresses the long recognised idea that nationality conferred upon a person in a manifestly abusive manner need not be taken into account internationally". For a different view, see Kunz, 'The Nottebohm Judgment (Second Phase)' 560: "[...] a clear-cut instance of judicial legislation."; Audrey Macklin, 'Is it time to retire Nottebohm?' (2017) 111 AJIL Unbound 493 ff.

227 See on this aspect in particular Robert D Sloane, 'Breaking the Genuine Link: The Contemporary International Legal Regulation of Nationality' (2009) 50(1) Harvard International Law Review 4, 19 ff.

228 *Minutes of the Public Sittings held at the Peace Palace, The Hague, on February 10th to 24th, March 2nd to 8th, and April 6th, 1955, Verbatim Record* 1955 CR 1955/2 413. The principle of abuse of rights also featured prominently in the dissenting opinions of Guggenheim and Read, both of whom rejected its applicability because of the lack of any damage suffered by Liechtenstein, *Nottebohm Case (second phase)* [1955] ICJ Rep 4 Diss Op Read 37 and Diss Op Guggenheim 57; cf. Sloane, 'Breaking the Genuine Link: The Contemporary International Legal Regulation of Nationality' 13 ff.; see also the Court's brief reference to the status of a national of a neutral

The *Nottebohm* decision caused mixed reactions. Proponents like Ian Brownlie argued that "[t]he evidence of practice both before and since Nottebohm, as well as the logical force of other principles of international law, justify the conclusion that the principle of effective nationality is a general principle of international law and should be recognized as such."[229] In Brownlie's view, the Court's "major point is made on the basis of a 'general principle of international law' and not on the basis of a rule which could be classified as a customary rule of the usual sort. [...] Not all the materials support any rule in this way, but there is much material [...] which supports the general principle."[230] Critics of the decision opined that the decision "was wrong then, and may be even more wrong now"[231], arguing that the principle derived from regulations of dual nationality would not fit to situations where individuals possessed only one nationality, the Court's idea of nationality as a bond would be anachronistic and outdated in times of globalization, and that the decision which rendered Nottebohm effectively statelessness for the purpose of diplomatic protection does not align with today's importance of human rights law.[232]

After *Nottebohm*, the genuine link principle could be found in other contexts as well. The subsequent *Flegenheimer* arbitration affirmed the possibility of international judicial review of whether "the right to citizenship was regularly acquired, is in conformity with the very broad rule of effectivity

---

    state, *Nottebohm Case (second phase)* [1955] ICJ Rep 4, 26; on this point see also Brownlie, 'The Relations of Nationality in Public International Law,' 361.

229 ibid 364.

230 ibid 353, see also 314. The dissenting opinions of judge Read and judge *ad hoc* Guggenheim can be read as a critique against deriving principles of general application from bilateral treaties and decisions on cases of dual nationality for the specific case of diplomatic protection on behalf of a naturalized person, see *Nottebohm Case (second phase)* [1955] ICJ Rep 4 Diss Op Read 41-42 and Diss Op Guggenheim 59-60; see also Kunz, 'The Nottebohm Judgment (Second Phase)' 557.

231 Macklin, 'Is it time to retire Nottebohm?' 492.

232 Kunz, 'The Nottebohm Judgment (Second Phase)' 566; JMervyn Jones, 'The Nottebohm Case' (1956) 5 ICLQ 244; Worster, 'Reining in the Nottebohm Case' 3, 5, 9-10; William Thomas Worster, 'Nottebohm and 'Genuine Link': Anatomy of a Jurisprudential Illusion' [2019] Investment Migration Working Papers ⟨https://investmentmigration.org/wp-content/uploads/2020/10/IMC-RP-2019-1-Peter-Spiro.pdf⟩ accessed 1 February 2023; Sloane, 'Breaking the Genuine Link: The Contemporary International Legal Regulation of Nationality' 33 ff.

which dominates the law of nationals".[233] At the same time, the arbitration commission considered it "doubtful that the International Court of Justice intended to establish a rule of general international law in requiring, in the *Nottebohm* Case, that there must exist as effective link between the person and the State in order that the latter may exercise its rights of diplomatic protection in behalf of the former", the Commission stressed the "relative nature" of the decision which would have concerned in particular the opposability of the newly acquired nationality towards Guatemala.[234] Furthermore, article 5 of the 1958 Geneva Convention on the High Seas stipulated that "[t]here must exist a genuine link between the State and the ship [...]".[235] In *Barcelona Traction*, however, the Court rejected an application of this genuine connection requirement. Belgium had instituted proceedings against Spain on behalf of Belgium shareholders in a company incorporated in Canada. On the basis of the reasoning underlying *Nottebohm*, a minority on the bench had doubts as to the Canadian nationality of the corporation because of the lack of a genuine link to the corporation apart from the incorporation.[236] The majority, however, rejected the relevance of the analogy based on the *Nottebohm* judgment[237] and rejected Belgium's standing. Later, the International Law Commission, in its commentary on article 4 of the Articles on Diplomatic

---

233 *Flegenheimer Case* United States of America v. Italy, Italian-United States Conciliation Commission (20 September 1958) XIV RIAA 338 para 25, speaking of "abusive practice of diplomatic protection"; the Commission was presided by Georges Sauser-Hall who had acted in the *Nottebohm* case as counsel on behalf of Liechtenstein. For a critical evaluation see Myres S McDougal, Harold D Lasswell, and Lung-chu Chen, 'Nationality and Human Rights: The Protection of the Individual and External Arenas' (1974) 83 The Yale Law Journal 913 ff.
234 *Flegenheimer Case* XIV RIAA 327, 376.
235 Convention on the High Seas (signed 29 April 1958, entered into force 30 September 1962) 450 UNTS 11.
236 See *Barcelona Traction, Light and Power Company, Limited* [1970] ICJ Rep 3 Sep Op Fitzmaurice 80 para 28 and 81 para 30; Sep Op Jessup 189 para 48 and 205 para 80; Sep Op Gros 281 para 22, 282 para 24; see also Diss Op Riphagen 335 para 3, 347 para 17 ff., who criticized the *renvoi* to municipal law with respect to the corporation and advocated a functional approach similar to Nottebohm. See furthermore on the importance of the development by treaties Nigel S Rodley, 'Corporate Nationality and the Diplomatic Protection of Multinational Enterprises: The Barcelona Traction Case' (1971) 47(1) Indiana Law Journal 86.
237 *Barcelona Traction, Light and Power Company, Limited* [1970] ICJ Rep 3, 42 para 70: "[...] given both the legal and factual aspects of protection in the present case the Court is of the opinion that there can be no analogy with the issues raised or the decision given in that case."

Protection of 2006, argued that the ICJ expounded "only a relative rule according to which a State in Liechtenstein's position was required to show a genuine link between itself and Mr. Nottebohm in order to permit it to claim on his behalf against Guatemala with whom he had extremely close ties", noting also that a strict application of the genuine link requirement "would exclude millions of persons from the benefit of diplomatic protection".[238]

c) The significance of the normative context

The comparison illustrates that the identification of customary international law and, in particular, the genuine link requirement depended significantly on the specific context. Whereas the alleged rule of customary international law in the *Asylum* case would have constituted a derogation from territorial sovereignty, the genuine link requirement in *Nottebohm* concerned a state's unilateral legislation on nationality conferral and the effects that legislation had on other states, in particular on the state of residence of the individual concerned. Two legal policies underlined the *Nottebohm* judgment: to be entitled to claim opposability and thus recognition of the nationality conferral at the international level, one needed a legitimate, effective, genuine link for extending one's laws to a subject or situation; the second policy is the avoidance of international disputes in cases of nationality conferrals.[239] The genuine link requirement would have had different effects in *Barcelona Traction* than in Nottebohm. In *Barcelona Traction*, it would have enabled

---

238 *ILC Ybk (2006 vol 2 part 2)* 30; see also also Crawford, *Brownlie's principles of public international law* 503.

239 Cf. the controversial judgments in the South West Africa cases for a policy of avoidance of disputes before the Court, *South West Africa* [1966] ICJ Rep 6, 47 para 88; on the phenomenon of "passportization", the conferral of nationalities in order to construe a basis for subsequent exercises of diplomatic protection in the context of the conflict between Russia and Georgia, see Heidi Tagliavini, Independent International Fact-Finding Mission on the Conflict in Georgia Vol I (2009) ⟨https://www.mpil.de/files/pdf4/IIFFMCG_Volume_I2.pdf⟩ accessed 1 February 2023 18 para 12, and Heidi Tagliavini, Independent International Fact-Finding Mission on the Conflict in Georgia Vol II (2009) ⟨https://www.mpil.de/files/pdf4/IIFFMCG_Volume_II1.pdf⟩ accessed 1 February 2023 155-179; Kristopher Natoli, 'Weaponizing Nationality: An Analysis of Russia's Passport Policy in Georgia' (2010) 28 Boston University International Law Journal 389 ff.; Serena Forlati, 'Nationality as a human right' in *The Changing Role of Nationality in International Law* (Routledge 2013) 23.

an international dispute before the ICJ, its rejection in result affirmed the Canadian nationality of the company and denied Belgium standing before the Court.[240]

2. "Scoping" and tailoring of the legal analysis

The art of scoping[241], of specifying the scope of the legal question and legal analysis, presents itself not only in advisory proceedings when the Court had to interpret the respective request for an advisory opinion[242] but also in contentious proceedings. One example is the *Jurisdictional Immunities* case, when the Court addressed Italy's argument according to which a state would be "no longer entitled to immunity in respect of acts occasioning death, personal injury or damage to property on the territory of the forum state, even if the act in question was performed *jure imperii*" (so-called territorial tort principle or territorial tort exception).[243] It is illuminating to compare the Court's approach with the approach advocated by Judge *ad hoc* Gaja.

The Court carefully characterized the question it had to answer for its analysis of state immunity:[244] It did not need to clarify whether there was a general territorial tort principle to immunity. Since the case involved the conduct of troops, the Court identified as central question whether there was a territorial tort exception to immunity for the conduct of the foreign military in the course of conducting an armed conflict.[245] In contrast, the dissenting Judge *ad hoc* Gaja took the tort principle as a starting point and

---

240 But see also *Barcelona Traction, Light and Power Company, Limited* 32 paras 33-34 on the importance of the judgment for the *erga omnes* jurisprudence and above, p. 38.
241 See Sienho Yee, 'Article 38 of the ICJ Statute and Applicable Law: Selected Issues in Recent Cases' (2016) 7 JIDS 480, speaking of "scoping" when describing how the ICJ formulated the legal issue that needed to be addressed in the *Jurisdictional Immunities* case.
242 Cf. *Legality of the Threat or Use of Nuclear Weapons* [1996] ICJ Rep 226, 238-239 paras 20-22; *Accordance with international law of the unilateral declaration of independence in respect of Kosovo* [2010] ICJ Rep 403, 423-426 paras 49-56.
243 *Jurisdictional Immunities of the State* [2012] ICJ Rep 99, 126 para 62.
244 On this "scoping" see Yee, 'Article 38 of the ICJ Statute and Applicable Law: Selected Issues in Recent Cases' 480; *Jurisdictional Immunities of the State* Diss Op Judge *ad hoc* Gaja 309 ff.
245 ibid 127-128 para 65.

as the general rule,[246] which arguably shifted the burden of reasoning to the proposed exception for conduct of armed troops.

When examining customary international law on immunity, the Court took also account of conventions and on whether those reflected customary international law. The Court noted that Article 11 of the European Convention on State Immunity[247] set forth a territorial tort principle and that article 31 of this convention qualified this principle by excluding from the scope of the convention "any immunities or privileges enjoyed by a Contracting State in respect of anything done or omitted to be done by, or in relation to, its armed forces when on the territory of another Contracting State." Therefore, the territorial tort principle as set forth in article 11 of the Convention did not have any effect on customary international law in relation to troops during situations of armed conflict.[248] For Judge *ad hoc* Gaja, however, the European Convention as a regional convention with only a limited number of parties was of limited relevance.[249]

The Court then observed that article 12 of the United Nations Convention[250] sets forth the territorial tort principle; yet, based on the ILC commentary to a draft, this provision does not apply to situations involving armed conflicts.[251] Judge *ad hoc* Gaja noted that this view in the ILC commentary was not taken up by the UN convention's text.[252]

With respect to the case-law of domestic courts and the European Court of Human Rights, the Court concluded that "State immunity for *acta jure imperii* continues to extend to civil proceedings for acts occasioning death, personal injury or damage to property committed by the armed forces and other organs of a State in the conduct of armed conflict [...]".[253] Judge *ad hoc* Gaja noted that domestic courts have taken "a variety of approaches".[254]

It is not submitted here that the difference in starting points was necessarily outcome-determinative and that the identification of customary international

---

246 *Jurisdictional Immunities of the State* Diss Op Judge *ad hoc* Gaja, 309-322.
247 European Convention on State Immunity (signed 16 May 1972, entered into force 11 June 1976) 1495 UNTS 181.
248 *Jurisdictional Immunities of the State* [2012] ICJ Rep 99, 129 para 68.
249 ibid Diss Op Judge *ad hoc* Gaja 310 para 2.
250 United Nations Convention on Jurisdictional Immunities of States and Their Property (signed 2 December 2004) UN Doc A/RES/59/38.
251 *Jurisdictional Immunities of the State* 129-130 para 69.
252 ibid Diss Op Judge *ad hoc* Gaja 315.
253 ibid 134-5 para 77.
254 ibid Diss Op Judge *ad hoc* Gaja 318.

law is only a question of phrasing the question. The choice of a default rule can be subject to reevaluation, a judge can modify the default position if said judge finds that practice suggests a different default rule or scope of the question. Yet, in cases of doubt, it can become decisive whether one attempts to ascertain an exception to immunity for armed forces during armed conflicts or whether one attempts to ascertain an exception to the tort exception to immunity.

Another important aspect of tailoring in the legal reasoning in the *Jurisdictional Immunities* case concerned the use of a distinction between substantive rules and rules that are procedural in nature, such as state immunity.[255] On the basis of this distinction, the Court rejected the possibility of a conflict between *jus cogens* operating at the level of substantive rules and state immunity.[256]

3. Shaping the rule by acknowledging an exception

An important interpretative decision concerns the determination of the scope of the rule that is ascertained.

The scope of the prohibition identified by the Court in the *Nuclear Weapons* opinion is characterized by the rule-exception classification. The Court came, based on an interpretation of existing legal rules of international humanitarian law, human rights law and international environmental law, to the conclusion that "the threat or use of nuclear weapons would generally be contrary to the rules of international law applicable in armed conflict, and in particular the principles and rules of humanitarian law".[257] Yet, "[t]he emergence, as lex lata, of a customary rule specifically prohibiting the use of nuclear weapons as such is hampered by the continuing tensions between the nascent *opinio juris* on the one hand, and the still strong adherence to the practice of deterrence on the other hand".[258] The Court was, therefore, unable to affirm an absolute prohibition "under any circumstances", in particular in an "extreme circumstance of self-defence, in which the very survival of a State

---

255 ibid [2012] ICJ Rep 99, 124 para 58; *Arrest Warrant of 11 April 2000* 25 para 60; cf. on this aspect generally Stefan Talmon, 'Jus Cogens after Germany v. Italy: Substantive and Procedural Rules Distinguished' (2012) 25 Leiden Journal of International Law 979 ff.
256 *Jurisdictional Immunities of the State* [2012] ICJ Rep 99, 140 para 93, 141 para 95.
257 *Legality of the Threat or Use of Nuclear Weapons* [1996] ICJ Rep 226, 266.
258 ibid 255 para 73.

would be at stake".[259] In other words, the Court considered both the normative environment, which pointed to a prohibition, and the existing practice of deterrence which could not be reconciled with an absolute prohibition. Rather than rejecting a prohibition in principle, the Court recognized a general prohibition subject to an exception.

In the case of practice which conflicts with a possible rule only occasionally, the Court did not modify the scope of the general rule in the *Nicaragua* case and argued that practice supporting a rule of customary international law does not have to be "in absolutely rigorous conformity with the rule"; it sufficed that states generally complied with the rule and that instances of inconsistent state conduct "have been treated as breaches of that rule" without having challenged the rule's validity.[260]

The ICJ's jurisprudence indicates that the identification of customary international law requires a determination of whether practice contrary to a possible rule modifies that rule's scope in the sense of an exception to the rule, whether it is only a violation of the rule, leaving the validity of the rule itself intact, or whether a rule can no longer be assumed to exist because of contrary practice.

III. The relationship between customary international law and treaty law

The jurisprudence of the Court illustrates that treaties and principles expressed in treaties can be important for the identification and interpretation of customary international law. Not only can one rule set forth in a treaty reflect or give rise to a rule of customary international law, treaties can also express legal evaluations and principles which inform the interpretation of customary international law in subtle ways, leading often to a convergence between functionally equivalent rules in treaties and customary international law. At the same time, the Court's jurisprudence makes also clear that customary international law and treaties are distinct sources.

This section will first review early instances in the Court's jurisprudence where the question of the relationship posed itself, namely the *Morocco* case (1.) and the *North Sea Continental Shelf* judgment (2.) the analysis of

---

259 *Legality of the Threat or Use of Nuclear Weapons* 266.
260 *Military and Paramilitary Activities in and against Nicaragua* [1986] ICJ Rep 14, 98 para 186, noting that this applies in particular when a state "defends its conduct by appealing to exceptions or justifications contained within the rule itself".

which will be informed by the Court's subsequent decisions. Turning from an abstract discussion of the relationship of the sources to the interplay, this section will illustrate forms of convergence, namely convergence between the Charter and customary international law into common principles (3.) and convergence of functionally equivalent rules in the law of the sea (4.).

1. The *Morocco* case

The question of the distinctiveness and the convergence of the sources arose in the *Morocco* case. The case turned on whether the United States was entitled to exercise consular jurisdiction in the French zone of Morocco. The Court found unanimously that the USA was entitled to such exercise based on the treaty with Morocco of September 1936, and, by 10 to 1, that such exercise could also be based on the General Act of Algeciras of April 7 1906. The Court rejected, by a narrow majority of six to five, the US claim according to which rights of consular jurisdiction could be based also on custom.[261] The disagreement concerned the relationship between sources. The dissenting judges emphasized the convergence of customary international law and treaty law. In their view, usage (by which they arguably referred to the Court's expression of "custom and usage") was always an "established source of extraterritorial jurisdiction" and both sources,

> "treaties and usage, in the broad sense of these terms, have contributed to the total result in varying measure. It is not possible, nor is it of any practical interest, at this distance of time, to isolate and assess separately the contribution made by each of these sources. Both were at work supplementing each other."[262]

The majority, however, put a greater emphasis on the distinctiveness, concluding that it could not be established that "the States exercising consular jurisdiction in pursuance of treaty rights enjoyed in addition an independent title thereto based on custom or usage."[263] Therefore, the United States had

---

261 *Rights of Nationals of the United States of America in Morocco* (*France v. United States of America*) (Judgment of August 27th, 1952) [1952] ICJ Rep 212, four of the five issued a dissenting opinion, Hackworth, Badawi, Levi Carneiro and Sir Benegal Rau.
262 ibid [1952] ICJ Rep 176 Diss Op Judges Hackworth, Badawi, Levi Carneiro and Sir Benegal Rau at 220 and 221 ff., where it was argued that the US had always maintained *vis-à-vis* France customary international law as a legal basis and that France acquiesced thereto.
263 ibid 200.

not satisfied the burden to show that the enjoyment of consular jurisdiction was based not only on treaty but on custom.[264] Notably, neither the majority nor the minority supported the French argument according to which "after incorporation [of the usage in a treaty, M.L.] the usages shared the fate of the treaty".[265]

2. The *North Sea Continental Shelf* judgment

The question of the relationship was approached anew and in more detail in the *North Sea Continental Shelf* judgment, where the Court held that the first three articles of the 1958 Convention on the Continental Shelf had been "regarded as reflecting, or as crystallising, received or at least emergent rules of customary international law relative to the continental shelf."[266]

Article 6(2) of the Geneva Convention on the Continental Shelf stipulated that the boundaries between two parties should be determined by the principle of equidistance if no agreement is applicable or no special circumstances advocate for a different solution. Germany was a signatory-state but did not ratify the convention. Denmark and Norway therefore argued, *inter alia*, that Article 6(2) created a customary international law norm which as such would be binding upon Germany.[267] The Court, while considering the passing of a conventional provision "of a fundamentally norm-creating character" "into the general corpus of international law" possible,[268] ultimately rejected that this process, by which a rule of customary international law "has come into being since the Convention, partly because of its own impact, partly on the basis of subsequent State practice"[269], had occurred with respect to article 6.[270] Furthermore, the principle of equidistance was not regarded by the

---

264 *Rights of Nationals of the United States of America in Morocco* 200. For a critique of the Court's terminology with respect to usage, see Bin Cheng, 'Rights of United States Nationals in the French Zone of Morocco' (1953) 2 ICLQ 361.
265 Cf. *Rights of Nationals of the United States of America in Morocco* Diss Op Judges Hackworth, Badawi, Levi Carneiro and Sir Benegal Rau at 220.
266 *North Sea Continental Shelf* [1969] ICJ Rep 3, 39 para 63; Cottier, *Equitable Principles of Maritime Boundary Delimitation: The Quest for Distributive Justice in International Law* 74.
267 *North Sea Continental Shelf* [1969] ICJ Rep 3, 41 para 70.
268 ibid 39-41.
269 ibid 41 para 70.
270 ibid 43.

Court as an *a priori* principle of the law relating to the continental shelf, it was therefore not binding by virtue of logical necessity on Germany.²⁷¹

The Court emphasized the distinct nature of sources while also acknowledging their interrelationship. The Court pointed to three aspects of the interrelationship of sources: a rule embodied in a treaty could constitute a codification of international law; its adoption could crystallize a rule of customary international law; or the substance of a provision could later become a rule of general international law.²⁷² The latter process was said to be "a perfectly possible one and does from time to time occur: it constitutes indeed one of the recognized methods by which new rules of customary international law may be formed. At the same time this result is not lightly to be regarded as having been attained."²⁷³ In the specific case before the Court, this process did not occur but the Court argued that, in principle, "it might be [...] that, even without the passage of any considerable period of time, a very widespread and representative participation in the convention might suffice of itself, provided it included that of States whose interests were specially affected."²⁷⁴

The Court's tailoring in its legal analysis is not immune to criticism. The Court's analysis was narrowly confined to ascertaining whether the equidistance rule had become part of customary international law. Only if this had been the case, it seems, would the Court have proceeded to examine whether

---

271 ibid [1969] ICJ Rep 3, 32 para 46.
272 The term of crystallization was used by Counsel Waldock who argued that the negotiation of the law in the ILC and on the Drafting conference had crystallized this norm as custom: "the emerging customary law, now become more defined, both as to the rights of the coastal State and the applicable regime, crystallized in the adoption of the Continental Shelf Convention by the Conference; and that the numerous signatures and ratifications of the Convention and the other State practice based on the principles set out in the Convention had the effect of consolidating those principles as customary law.", NSCS Verbatim record 1968 242. The term of crystallization had been used earlier, see *The Panevezys-Saldutiskis Railway Case: Estonia v. Lithuania* Merits [1939] PCIJ Series A/B No 76 Diss Op van Eysinga 34-35.
273 *North Sea Continental Shelf* [1969] ICJ Rep 3, 41 para 71; cf. later *Continental Shelf (Tunisia/Libya)* [1982] ICJ Rep 18, 38 para 24: "[The Court] could not ignore any provision of the [Law of the Sea] Draft Convention if it came to the conclusion that the content of such provision is binding upon all members of the international community because it embodies or crystallizes a pre-existing or emergent rule of customary law."
274 *North Sea Continental Shelf* [1969] ICJ Rep 3, 42 para 73.

the special circumstances rule had become part of custom as well.[275] A different approach could have been to regard the equidistance rule together with the special circumstances exception as an "indivisible regime"[276], to borrow a formula the Court used in a later case to indicate that two treaty provisions have to be seen together and jointly reflect customary international law. Commentators take different views on whether a combined equidistance-special circumstances rule could have reflected a general practice accepted as law.[277] The Court, while emphasizing that "there are still rules and principles of law to be applied"[278], held that "certain basic notions [...] have from the beginning reflected the *opinio juris* in the matter of delimitation; those principles being that delimitation must be the object of agreement between the States concerned, and that such agreement must be arrived at in accordance with equitable principles."[279] The equidistance method would be one, but not the only method for this purpose,[280] the parties were asked to take account of "all

---

275 *North Sea Continental Shelf* 46 para 82: "It becomes unnecessary for the Court to determine whether or not the configuration of the German North Sea Coast constitutes a 'special circumstance' for the purposes either of Article 6 of the Geneva Convention or of any rule of customary international law,-since once the use of the equidistance method of delimitation is determined not to be obligatory in any event, it ceases to be legally necessary to prove the existence of special circumstances in order to justify not using that method."
276 cf. *Territorial and Maritime Dispute* [2012] ICJ Rep 624, 674 para 139.
277 See in favour Kolb, *Interprétation et création du droit international. Esquisse d'une herméneutique juridique moderne pour le droit international public* 224; for the contrary view see Cottier, *Equitable Principles of Maritime Boundary Delimitation: The Quest for Distributive Justice in International Law* 360-1 ("[...] the actual use of methods other than equidistance or equidistance-special circumstances in some 40 per cent of the sample treaties examined shows a lack of sufficiently developed state practice to support a customary law character of equidistance [...] This suggests that equidistance rules are not perceived as legal rules, but rather are seen merely as methods of delimitation; methods, moreover, that can be replaced by others where it is advantageous to do so.").
278 *North Sea Continental Shelf* [1969] ICJ Rep 3, 46 para 83.
279 ibid 46 para 85; cf. already United States of America, *Proclamation 2667 of September 28, 1945. Policy of the United States with respect to the natural resources of the subsoil and sea bed of the continental shelf, 10 Fed. Reg. 12.305 (1945)* ("In cases where the continental shelf extends to the shores of another State, or is shared with an adjacent State, the boundary shall be determined by the United States and the state concerned in accordance with equitable principles").
280 *North Sea Continental Shelf* [1969] ICJ Rep 3, 47 para 85.

the relevant circumstances".[281] As will be described below, the Court would later note a convergence between the customary standard of equitable principles and relevant circumstances and the equidistance-special circumstances rule.[282]

Another interesting aspect concerns the Court's approach to evaluating the practice of states. According to the Court, most states referred to by Denmark and the Netherlands were "or shortly became parties to the Geneva Convention, and were therefore presumably, so far as they were concerned, acting actually or potentially in the application of the Convention. From their action no inference could legitimately be drawn as to the existence of a rule of customary international law in favour of the equidistance principle."[283] According to one interpretation of this passage of the *North Sea Continental* judgment, the identification of customary international law *dehors* a treaty would become difficult if not impossible. Based on the interpretation that practice of State parties did not count as practice for customary international law, Richard Baxter considered that "the proof of a consistent pattern of conduct by non-parties becomes more difficult as the number of parties to the instrument increases [...] Hence the paradox that as the number of parties to a treaty increases, it becomes more difficult to demonstrate what is the state of customary international law *dehors* the treaty."[284]

---

281 ibid 47 para 85.
282 *Maritime Delimitation in the Area between Greenland and Jan Mayen (Denmark v. Norway)* (Judgment) [1993] ICJ Rep 62 para 56; cf. earlier *Delimitation of the Continental Shelf between the United Kingdom of Great Britain and Northern Ireland, and the French Republic* Court of Arbitration (Decisions of 30 June 1977 and 14 March 1978) XVIII RIAA 45-8, 57; cf. Cottier, *Equitable Principles of Maritime Boundary Delimitation: The Quest for Distributive Justice in International Law* 405, according to whom the convergence "helped to narrow the opposing views of the parties as to the application of conventional or general international law. Secondly, the Award may also have intended to make a contribution to what the judges considered a false and politicized debate over equidistance versus equity at UNCLOS III."
283 *North Sea Continental Shelf* [1969] ICJ Rep 3, 43-44 para 76.
284 Baxter, 'Treaties and Customs' 64. Jennings would later base his dissenting opinion in the Nicaragua case and his critique of the Court's finding on a rule of customary international law similar to article 2(4) of the Charter on this argument: *Military and Paramilitary Activities in and against Nicaragua* [1986] ICJ Rep 14 Diss Op Jennings 531: "But there are obvious difficulties about extracting even a scintilla of relevant 'practice' on these matters from the behaviours of those few States which are not parties to the Charter; and the behaviours of all the rest, and the *opinio juris*

The implications of this interpretation should not be exaggerated, however. That the identification of customary international law "becomes more difficult" does not necessarily mean that it becomes impossible. Also, Baxter summarized his view in that "[r]ules found in treaties can never be *conclusive* evidence of customary international law",[285] and, indeed, one may consider external, additional elements to mere treaty participation which, however, is one important factor as well.[286] It is doubtful whether the Court really intended to suggest that practice of parties in relation to the treaties would bear no significance at all for the purpose of identifying customary international law. In any case, such a suggestion was not clearly confirmed in the Court's later jurisprudence. In particular in the *Nicaragua* case, the Court argued with a view to the Friendly Relations Declaration that the "effect of consent to the text of such resolutions cannot be understood as merely that of a 'reiteration or elucidation' of the treaty commitment undertaken in the Charter", it could also indicate consent as to the validity of the rule in the resolution and therefore be significant for customary international law.[287] It remains true that treatymaking does not necessarily affect customary international law.[288] However, it is also difficult to establish the presumption that states do not wish to shape customary international law by concluding treaties.[289]

---

which it might otherwise evidence, is surely explained by their being bound by the Charter itself." On this Baxter-paradox, see also Theodor Meron, 'The Continuing Role of Custom in the Formation of International Humanitarian Law' (1996) 90 AJIL 247, see also Crawford, 'Change, Order, Change: The Course of International Law General Course on Public International Law' 90-94.

285 Baxter, 'Treaties and Customs' 99 (italics added).
286 But cf. *North Sea Continental Shelf* [1969] ICJ Rep 3, 43 para 73 (italics added): "[...] a very widespread and representative participation in the convention might suffice *of itself*, provided it included that of States whose interests were specially affected."
287 *Military and Paramilitary Activities in and against Nicaragua* [1986] ICJ Rep 14, 100 para 188.
288 *Ahmadou Sadio Diallo (Republic of Guinea v. Democratic Republic of the Congo)* (Preliminary Objections, Judgment) [2007] ICJ Rep 615 para 90: "[The invocation of agreements] is not sufficient to show that there has been a change in the customary rules of diplomatic protection; it could equally show the contrary."; *Questions relating to the Obligation to Prosecute or Extradite* [2012] ICJ Rep 422 Diss Op Abraham 479 para 37, arguing that no obligation to prosecute torture without any connecting link would exist under customary international law, the 51 states cited by Belgium would act in implementation of the CAT.
289 Cf. also Max Sørensen, 'Principes de droit international public: cours général' (1960) 101 RdC 51, according to whom a consistent practice indicates a presumption of

The so-called Baxter paradox should be understood as a useful reminder that treaties and customary international law are interrelated but distinct concepts which should not be equated.[290]

3. Convergence between the Charter and customary international law into common principles

The purpose of this section is to illustrate the convergence between the Charter and customary international law as it is reflected in the jurisprudence of the Court. Two examples are selected, the right to self-determination and the prohibition of the use of force.

a) Self-determination

One example of convergence concerns the right to self-determination.
After the First World War, the right to self-determination did not find entrance into the Covenant of the League of Nations and was regarded to be more of a political, rather than a legal, principle.[291] This perception changed

---

opinio juris; see Crawford, 'Change, Order, Change: The Course of International Law General Course on Public International Law' 109 para 167: "One possibility [to resolve the Baxter paradox] would be to generate a presumption of *opinio juris* from widespread participation in a treaty, at least in normative terms. Indeed this is effectively what the Eritrea-Ethiopia Claims Commission did as regards the four 1949 Geneva Conventions and its Additional Protocol I."; Tams, 'Meta-Custom and the Court: A Study in Judicial Law-Making' 68.

290 In this sense Crawford, 'Change, Order, Change: The Course of International Law General Course on Public International Law' 107, 112.

291 Malcolm N Shaw, *International Law* (7th edn, Cambridge University Press 2014) 183; Antonio Cassese, *Self-Determination of Peoples. A Legal Reappraisal* (repr., Cambridge University Press 1996) 32-33; Stefan Oeter, 'Self-Determination' in Bruno Simma and others (eds), *The Charter of the United Nations: A Commentary* (3rd edn, Oxford University Press 2013) vol 1 317 para 5; Daniel Thürer and Thomas Burri, 'Self-Determination' [2008] Max Planck EPIL para 4. Even though this text speaks of the "principle" of self-determination, it is not neglected that self-determination consists of different aspects, which is why James Crawford agreed with Cassese that self-determination consists "both of general principles and particular rules", he argued that with regard to neither self-determination nor to

after the Second World War when the right to self-determination received increasing recognition as a legal concept. According to article 1(2) UN Charter, one of the purposes of the UN is to "develop friendly relations among nations based on respect for the principle of equal rights and self-determination of peoples [...]", which is taken up by article 55 UNC. The text of Chapter XI of the UN Charter on non-self-governing territories, however, does not refer to the principle of self-determination as set forth in article 1(2) UNC, but only to self-government (Art. 73(b) UNC).[292] The General Assembly adopted on 14 December 1960 the Declaration on the granting of independence to colonial countries and peoples, which declared that "all peoples have the right to self-determination; by virtue of that right they freely determine their political status and freely pursue their economic, social and cultural development."[293] In 1966 the common article 1 to the ICCPR[294] and the ICESCR[295] of 1966 emphasizes the right of self-determination of all peoples.

The right to self-determination is said to be the product of an interplay of treaty law and customary international law[296] and the jurisprudence of the

---

the law relating to the use of force one can find "a single, self-sufficient norm" James Crawford, 'Book Review' (1996) 90(2) AJIL 331; for a discussion of the norm-type of self-determination see Karen Knop, *Diversity and Self-Determination in International Law* (Cambridge University Press 2002) 29-38.

292 Rosalyn Higgins, *Problems and Process: International Law and How We Use It* (Clarendon Press 1995) 112-113.

293 UNGA Res 1514 (XV) (14 December 1960) UN Doc A/Res/1514(XV) para 2.

294 International Covenant on Civil and Political Rights (signed 16 December 1966, entered into force 23 March 1976) 999 UNTS 171.

295 International Covenant on Economic, Social and Cultural Rights (signed 16 December 1966, entered into force 3 January 1976) 993 UNTS 3.

296 See also Orfeas Chasapis Tassinis and Sarah Nouwen, ''The Consciousness of Duty Done'? British Attitudes towards Self-Determination and the Case of the Sudan' (2019) First View BYIL 50: "Britain was advancing self-determination both as a right under the UN Charter, as well as a right sourced outside the confines of treaty law. International legal scholars have suggested, with respect to the anti-colonial self-determination resolutions, that these two tracks for the establishment of self-determination as a right – that is subsequent practice informing the meaning of the Charter and state practice leading to the formation of a new rule of customary international law – may indeed largely overlap, making it hard neatly to distinguish the two."; Shaw, *International Law* 183: "Practice since 1945 within the UN, both generally as regards the elucidation and standing of the principle and more particularly as regard its perceived application in specific instances, can be seen as having ultimately established the legal standing of the right in international law. This may

ICJ contributed to this convergence as well as to the recognition of the right to self-determination as a *legal*, as opposed to a political, concept.

As the Court held in *East Timor*, the right to self-determination is "one of the essential principles of contemporary international law", has "evolved from the Charter and from United Nations practice has an erga omnes character, is irreproachable. The principle of self-determination of peoples has been recognized [...] in the jurisprudence of the Court."[297] The Court addressed here the principle as customary international law and referred to earlier advisory opinions on the interpretation of this principle as treaty law.[298] Already in these opinions, however, the Court took care to stress the principle's basis both in treaty law and in customary international law.[299]

This principle which was based both on the Charter and customary international law became relevant to the interpretation of Chapter XI of the

---

be achieved either by treaty or by custom or indeed, more controversially, by virtue of constituting a general principle of law. All these routes are relevant [...] The UN Charter is a multilateral treaty which can be interpreted by subsequent practice, while the range of state and organization practice evident within the UN system can lead to the formation of customary international law."; Higgins, *Problems and Process: International Law and How We Use It* 112-113, pointing out that Chapter XI of the UN Charter does not refer to the principle of self-determination, "[b]ut international law does not develop from written words alone"; cf. also Cassese, *Self-Determination of Peoples. A Legal Reappraisal* 67-69; Oeter, 'Self-Determination' 316 para 1.

297 *East Timor* [1995] ICJ Rep 90, 102 para 29.
298 Cf. Niels Petersen, 'The International Court of Justice and the Judicial Politics of Identifying Customary International Law' (2017) 28(2) EJIL 383: "But the decisions the ICJ referred to – the South West Africa and the Western Sahara advisory opinions – dealt with the interpretation of the principle of self-determination governed by treaty instruments, while the court in East Timor referred to the principle of self-determination contained in customary law."
299 See *Legal Consequences for States of the Continued Presence of South Africa in Namibia (South West Africa) notwithstanding Security Council Resolution 276 (1970)* [1971] ICJ Rep 16, 31-32 paras 52-53, where the Court paid regard to the principle's emergence in the "subsequent development of international law [...] as enshrined in the Charter of the United Nations [...]" but it also emphasized that "the Court must take into consideration the changes which have occurred in the supervening half-century, and its interpretation cannot remain unaffected by the subsequent development of law, through the Charter of the United Nations and by way of customary law. [...] In the domain to which the present proceedings relate, the last fifty years, as indicated above, have brought important developments. [...] In this domain, as elsewhere, the *corpus iuris gentium* has been considerably enriched, and this the Court, if it is faithfully to discharge its functions, may not ignore." See also *Western Sahara* (Advisory Opinion) [1975] ICJ Rep 32 para 56.

UN Charter on non-self-governing territories. Even though Chapter XI does not explicitly refer to self-determination, the Court held that the law of self-determination constituted the applicable law in relation to non-self-governing territories.[300]

The Court recapitulated this normative development in its recent advisory opinion on the *Chagos Islands*. According to the Court, the process of decolonialization of Mauritius was not lawfully completed when Mauritius was granted independence in 1968, following the separation of the Chagos Archipelago from Mauritius by the United Kingdom.[301] When addressing the applicable law, the Court argued that the "determination of the applicable law must focus on the period from 1965 to 1968", without excluding, however, "the evolution of the law on self-determination since the adoption of the Charter of the United Nations and of resolution 1514 (XV) of 14 December 1960 entitled 'Declaration on the Granting of Independence to Colonial Countries and Peoples'" since the two elements of customary international law "are consolidated and confirmed gradually over time."[302] The Court affirmed the customary status of the right to self-determination and held that "[b]oth State practice and *opinio juris* at the relevant time confirm the customary law character of the right to integrity of a non-self-governing territory as a corollary of the right to self-determination."[303]

This example illustrates that the identification of customary international law is informed by the whole normative environment, including treaties, a General Assembly resolution which represented "a defining moment in the consolidation of State practice on decolonization [...] although resolution 1514 (XV) is formally a recommendation, it has a declaratory character with

---

300 *Legal Consequences for States of the Continued Presence of South Africa in Namibia (South West Africa) notwithstanding Security Council Resolution 276 (1970)* [1971] ICJ Rep 16, 31 para 52; *Legal consequences of the Separation of the Chagos Archipelago from Mauritius in 1965* [2019] ICJ Rep 95, 134-135 paras 160-161.
301 ibid 101 para 1, 140 para 183.
302 ibid 130 para 142.
303 ibid 134 para 160; see also Ulrich Fastenrath, 'Article 73' in Bruno Simma and others (eds), *The Charter of the United Nations: A Commentary* (3rd edn, Oxford University Press 2013) vol 2 1836 para 13: "The term 'self-government', which was originally intended to mean no more than autonomy within the State organization of the colonial power and only in exceptional cases to also cover independent statehood for the (former) colony [...], should today only be understood as referring to unrestricted self-determination. In line with Art. 31(3) VCLT this follows from the practice of both States and UN organs as well as from the context of the two Human Rights Covenants of 1966 and from the norm concretizing effect of resolutions."

The normative environment in the jurisprudence of the ICJ

regard to the right to self-determination as customary norm"[304] and subsequent resolutions based on the assumption that those confirmed customary international law.

b) The prohibition of the use of force

Another example of convergence concerns the law relating to the use of force. In the *Nicaragua* case, the Court not only affirmed the distinctiveness between customary international law and treaties for jurisdictional purposes,[305] it also stressed the interrelationship.

The Court noted that the Charter did not purport to fully regulate the use of force; not only did it reserve a place for customary international in article 51 UNC, it also continued to rely on customary international law for the definitions of armed attack, self-defence and for the requirement of proportionality with respect to self-defence.[306] According to the Court, the Charter contributed to customary international law which developed "under the influence of the Charter"[307]:

---

304 *Legal consequences of the Separation of the Chagos Archipelago from Mauritius in 1965* [2019] ICJ Rep 95, paras 150, 152; see already *Legality of the Threat or Use of Nuclear Weapons* [1996] ICJ Rep 226, 254-255 para 70: "The Court notes that General Assembly resolutions, even if they are not binding, may sometimes have normative value. They can, in certain circumstances, provide evidence important for establishing the existence of a rule or the emergence of an *opinio juris*. To establish whether this is true of a given General Assembly resolution, it is necessary to look at its content and the conditions of its adoption; it is also necessary to see whether an *opinio juris* exists as to its normative character. Or a series of resolutions may show the gradual evolution of the *opinio juris* required for the establishment of a new rule." See also Tomka, 'Custom and the International Court of Justice' 211, according to whom it is "the attitude of States towards certain United Nations resolutions that is relevant for deriving an *opinio juris*, and not the existence of the resolution itself".
305 *Military and Paramilitary Activities in and against Nicaragua* [1986] ICJ Rep 14, 94-96 paras 177-179.
306 ibid 94 para 176; on proportionality see also *Legality of the Threat or Use of Nuclear Weapons* [1996] ICJ Rep 226, 245 para 41, where the Court held that the above mentioned requirement of proportionality of self-defense as "rule of customary international law [...] applies equally to Article 51 of the Charter".
307 *Military and Paramilitary Activities in and against Nicaragua* [1986] ICJ Rep 14, 96-97 para 181.

"The essential consideration is that both the Charter and the customary international law flow from a common fundamental principle outlawing the use of force in international relations."[308]

Rather than having separate principles of the prohibition of the use of force in custom and treaty law, it is, based on this *dictum*, more convincing to assume that there is one principle which is defined by both customary international law and the Charter together.[309] This does not mean, however, that no differences between both sources would exist.[310]

4. Convergence of functionally equivalent rules in the law of the sea

Another example of the convergence of functionally equivalent rules can be found in the Court's jurisprudence on the law of the sea. Whereas a "legislative" process by treaty started in the 1950s in particular with the conclusion of the Geneva conventions on the law of the sea[311], ultimately leading to the 1982 United Nations Convention on the Law of the Sea, the applicable law in maritime disputes for the Court was for a long time by and large customary international law. The 1958 Geneva Convention on the Continental Shelf was for the first time applicable *ratione personae* in 1984 in a case before

---

308 *Military and Paramilitary Activities in and against Nicaragua* 97 para 181.
309 Abi-Saab, 'Les sources du droit international: essai de déconstruction' 78.
310 See *Military and Paramilitary Activities in and against Nicaragua* [1986] ICJ Rep 14, 94 para 176 (UN Charter does not contain the proportionality requirement or the definition of an armed attack), 95 para 178 (norms retain a separate existence "from the standpoint of applicability"), 97 para 181, 121 para 235 (reporting obligation under article 51 UNC does not apply under customary international law). For a recent treatment of the relationship and an overview of different views see Marxsen, *Völkerrechtsordnung und Völkerrechtsbruch* 134-49.
311 Convention on the Territorial Sea and the Contiguous Zone (signed 29 April 1958, entered into force 10 September 1964) 516 UNTS 205; Convention on the High Seas (signed 29 April 1958, entered into force 30 September 1962) 450 UNTS 11; Convention on the Continental Shelf (signed 29 April 1958, entered into force 10 June 1964) 499 UNTS 311; and Convention on Fishing and Conservation of the Living Resources of the High Seas (signed 29 April 1958, entered into force 20 March 1966) 559 UNTS 205; see for a general overview Vaughan Lowe and Antonios Tzanakopoulos, 'The Development of the Law of the Sea by the International Court of Justice' in Christian J Tams and James Sloan (eds), *The Development of International Law by the International Court of Justice* (Oxford University Press 2013) 178: "[T]he Court's influence on the development of the law of the sea has not been great, and seems to be diminishing."

a Chamber.³¹² The Chamber, however, decided that the convention was not applicable *ratione materiae*, since the parties had requested the Court to draw a single line delimitation including both the continental shelf and the superjacent waters, and that the convention could also not be applied by way of extension.³¹³ The Chamber, therefore, based its decision on the norm that delimitation "must be based on the application of equitable criteria and the use of practical methods capable of ensuring an equitable result."³¹⁴ Before the Court as a whole, the convention was applicable *ratione personae* in 1993³¹⁵. By then, the Court had developed its jurisprudence mainly based on customary international law the identification of which, however, was informed by legal evaluations expressed in the respective conventions.³¹⁶

This section will first recapitulate the Court's jurisprudence and its development from a focus on the distinctiveness to the convergence of functionally equivalent rules in treaty law and customary international law (a)). The section will then point to reasons for this convergence (b)). Lastly, this section will comment on UNCLOS and its impact on customary international law in the Court's jurisprudence (c)).

a) From a focus on the distinctiveness to a convergence of functionally equivalent rules

In *North Sea Continental Shelf*, the Court emphasized the distinctiveness of article 6 of the 1958 Convention on the Continental Shelf and the rules of law based "[o]n a foundation of very general precepts of justice and good faith"³¹⁷, according to which "delimitation must be the object of agreement between the States concerned, and that such agreement must be arrived at in accordance with equitable principles".³¹⁸

---

312 *Delimitation of the Maritime Boundary in the Gulf of Maine Area* [1984] ICJ Rep 246, 291 para 84.
313 ibid 301 para 119, 303 para 124.
314 ibid [1984] ICJ Rep 246, 300 para 113.
315 *Maritime Delimitation in the Area between Greenland and Jan Mayen* [1993] ICJ Rep 38, 52 para 31.
316 The Court spoke of "trends", see *Continental Shelf (Tunisia/Libya)* [1982] ICJ Rep 18, 23 para 3, 38 para 24.
317 *North Sea Continental Shelf* [1969] ICJ Rep 3, 46 para 85.
318 ibid 46 para 85.

Equidistance was applied by the Court as one possible method in the delimitation between opposite coasts. In *Libya v. Malta*, the Court continued to emphasize that international law did not prescribe the use of equidistance [319]; at the same time, it held that the equidistance method could be appropriate in order to achieve an equitable result, provided that all relevant circumstances were examined.[320]

Fifteen years later in *Gulf of Maine*, the Chamber maintained that the equidistance method set forth in article 6 of the Geneva Convention on the Continental Shelf was not a mandatory rule under general international law.[321] Yet, the decision also displayed signs of intertemporal convergence between the two functionally equivalent standards: The 1958 Convention was interpreted and applied in light of the jurisprudence which had been developed under general international law subsequently to the adoption of the convention. As stated by article 6 of the 1958 convention, the delimitation must be determined by an agreement of the states concerned. The Chamber added an additional requirement based on the Court's jurisprudence on equitable principles.

> "To this one might conceivably add - although the 1958 Convention does not mention the idea, so that it entails going a little far in interpreting the text - that a rule which may be regarded as logically underlying the principle just stated is that any agreement or other equivalent solution should involve the application of equitable criteria, namely criteria derived from equity which - whether they be designated 'principles' or 'criteria', the latter term being preferred by the Chamber for reasons of clarity - are not in themselves principles and rules of international law."[322]

This convergence was emphasized even more in the *Jan Mayen* case between Denmark and Norway. Both parties were bound by the Geneva Convention

---

319 *Continental Shelf (Libya/Malta)* [1985] ICJ Rep 13, 38 para 44.
320 ibid 47 paras 62-3, 48 para 65, 56 para 78.
321 *Delimitation of the Maritime Boundary in the Gulf of Maine Area* [1984] ICJ Rep 246, 297 para 107, 302 para 122, where the Chamber held that the "method has rendered undeniable service in many concrete situations", while maintaining that this concept "has not thereby become a rule of general international law, a norm logically flowing from a legally binding principle of customary international law, neither has it been adopted into customary law simply as a method to be given priority or preference." Cf. Robert Kolb, *Case law on equitable maritime delimitation: digest and commentaries = Jurisprudence sur les délimitations maritimes selon l'équité: répertoire et commentaires* (Alan Perry tr, Martinus Nijhof Publishers 2003) 246 (critical of the "anti-equidistance reflex").
322 *Delimitation of the Maritime Boundary in the Gulf of Maine Area* [1984] ICJ Rep 246, 292 para 89.

on the Continental Shelf. According to the definition set forth in article 1, the continental shelf is defined for the purpose of the convention

> "as referring (a) to the seabed and subsoil of the submarine areas adjacent to the coast but outside the area of the territorial sea, to a depth of 200 metres or, beyond that limit, to where the depth of the superjacent waters admits of the exploitation of the natural resources of the said areas; (b) to the seabed and subsoil of similar submarines areas adjacent to the coasts of islands."

In contrast, article 76 UNCLOS, which was not in force yet, provides that the continental shelf

> "comprises the seabed and subsoil of the submarine areas that extend beyond its territorial sea throughout the natural prolongation of its land territory to the outer edge of the continental margin, or to a distance of 200 nautical miles from the baselines from which the breadth of the territorial sea is measured where the outer edge of the continental margin does not extend up to that distance."

As Thirlway pointed out, both parties assumed to be entitled to the greater extent defined by UNCLOS as reflection of customary international law, because "[i]f the areas of continental shelf appertaining to the parties were to be determined according to the criterion of the 1958 Geneva Convention [...] there would be no need for a delimitation, since the shelf of neither coast would extend far enough offshore to encounter the shelf of the other."[323] The Court held that the 1958 convention "governs the continental shelf delimitation to be effected", and it referred only to article 6 on the delimitation and not to the definition in article 1 of the convention.[324] The applicable law for the delimitation of the fishery zone was customary international law.[325]

Moreover, the Court noted in the *Jan Mayen* case a convergence between customary international law and article 6 of the Geneva Convention, and it entertained the idea expressed before by the Anglo-French Court of Arbitration in 1977, namely that "the equidistance-special circumstances rule of the 1958 is, in the light of this 1977 Decision, to be regarded as expressing a general norm based on equitable principles".[326] In particular, the Court argued that taking provisionally the median line between the territorial sea baselines not only followed from the applicable article 6 of the 1958 convention but would also have been appropriate in the case of opposite coasts if the applicable

---

323 Thirlway, *The Sources of International Law* 137-138.
324 *Maritime Delimitation in the Area between Greenland and Jan Mayen* [1993] ICJ Rep 38, 57-8 para 44, 59 para 49.
325 ibid 59 para 47.
326 ibid 58 para 46.

law had been customary international law.[327] Furthermore, when turning to the delimitation of the fishery zones according to customary international law, the Court held that "there is inevitably a tendency towards assimilation between the special circumstances of article 6 of the 1958 Convention and the relevant circumstances under customary international law, and this if only because they both are intended to enable the achievement of an equitable result."[328] In this case, the Court then came to the conclusion that the median line provisionally drawn needed to be adjusted because "the relationship between the length of the relevant coasts and the maritime areas generated by them by application of the equidistance method [...] is so disproportionate that it has been found necessary to take this circumstance into account in order to ensure an equitable solution".[329] The ultimate boundary line had to be "located in such a way that the solution obtained is justified by the special circumstances contemplated by the 1958 Convention on the Continental Shelf, and equitable on the basis of the principles and rules of customary international law."[330]

In a subsequent decision on a dispute between Cameroon and Nigeria, the Court again noted the similarity of the "equitable principles/relevant circumstances method" and the "equidistance/special circumstances method".[331]

b) Reasons for convergence: the vagueness of rules and judicial pragmatism informed by the normative environment

One can point to several factors which favoured this convergence in the ju-

---

327 *Maritime Delimitation in the Area between Greenland and Jan Mayen* 60-1 paras 50-1.
328 ibid 62 para 56, cf. Sep Op Shahabuddeen 148.
329 ibid 67 para 65. Cf. *Land and Maritime Boundary between Cameroon and Nigeria (Cameroon/Nigeria)* (Judgment) [2002] ICJ Rep 448 paras 305-6, where the Court applied the equidistance line for the first without modification, on this point see Cottier, *Equitable Principles of Maritime Boundary Delimitation: The Quest for Distributive Justice in International Law* 318, 351, concluding after a survey of the jurisprudence that "strict equidistance without modification has rarely been adopted by the Courts."
330 *Maritime Delimitation in the Area between Greenland and Jan Mayen* [1993] ICJ Rep 38, 70 para 71.
331 *Land and Maritime Boundary between Cameroon and Nigeria* [2002] ICJ Rep 303, 441 para 288.

risprudence of the Court. The vagueness of both the equitable principles under customary international law and the equidistance-special circumstances rule under treaty law put the Court in a dominant position and favoured a focus on the particularities of the case and the interests of the parties.[332] The jurisprudence was marked by pragmatism, accommodation and reasonableness[333] and informed by the normative environment and developments in treatymaking, which may explain the convergence between treaty-based standards and customary international law.

For instance, in the disputes between Germany and the United Kingdom and Iceland on an extension of Iceland's exclusive fishery zone to 50 nautical miles, the 1958 Convention on the High Sea was not applicable. Yet the Court searched for inspiration from this convention for the solution of this dispute when it interpreted and applied customary international law. The Court held that the Icelandic national regulation constituted "an infringement of the *principle enshrined in Article 2 of the 1958 Geneva Convention on the High Seas* which requires that all States, including coastal States, in exercising their freedom of fishing, pay reasonable regard to the interests of other states."[334] The Court concluded that the fishery rights of different states needed to be reconciled, and this reconciliation was informed by principles articulated in international treaties. For instance, the reconciliation in adjacent waters could not be the same as in the zone within 12 miles because of "the notion of preferential rights as it was recognized at the Geneva Conferences of 1958 and 1960".[335] Furthermore, in the view of the Court, "the former *laissez-faire* treatment of the living resources of the sea in the high seas has been replaced by a recognition of a duty to have due regard to the rights of other States and

---

332 Cf. Massimo Lando, *Maritime Delimitation as a Judicial Process* (Cambridge University Press 2019) 294: "Judicial law-making is justified so long as the applicable law in a given case is sufficiently indeterminate so as not to provide for the manner in which specific rules of international law are practically to be applied." See also Cottier, *Equitable Principles of Maritime Boundary Delimitation: The Quest for Distributive Justice in International Law* 103 on the ICJ's "crucial role in shaping doctrines related to the continental shelf. The ICJ shows the characteristics of an activist, law-making court willing to promote the law."
333 Cf. Koskenniemi, 'General principles: reflexions on constructivist thinking in international law' 141.
334 *Fisheries Jurisdiction (United Kingdom v. Iceland)* (Merits, Judgment) [1974] ICJ Rep 29 para 67; *Fisheries Jurisdiction* [1974] ICJ Rep 175, 198 para 59 (italics added).
335 *Fisheries Jurisdiction* [1974] ICJ Rep 3, 30 para 69; *Fisheries Jurisdiction* [1974] ICJ Rep 175, 199 para 62.

the needs of conservation for the benefit of all."³³⁶ Therefore, all parties to the disputes had with respect to conservation an obligation "to keep under review the fishery resources in the disputed waters and to examine together, in the light of scientific and other available information".³³⁷

The judgments in relation to Iceland demonstrate that the Court took account of the ongoing treatymaking process of states, when it interpreted and applied broad principles and rules of customary international law in the context of the law of the sea. On the one hand, the Court took into consideration the negotiation during the 1960 Conference when it determined the breadth of the territorial sea and the extent of fishery rights after the negotiated convention had failed to be adopted by only one vote.³³⁸ On the other hand, the Court attempted not to interfere with the ongoing legislative process.³³⁹ These cautious judgments were then outstripped by legal-political

---

336 *Fisheries Jurisdiction* [1974] ICJ Rep 3, 31 para 72; *Fisheries Jurisdiction* [1974] ICJ Rep 175, 200 para 64.
337 *Fisheries Jurisdiction* [1974] ICJ Rep 3, 31 para 72; *Fisheries Jurisdiction* [1974] ICJ Rep 175, 200 para 64: an "obligation to keep under review the fishery resources in the disputed waters and to examine together, in the light of scientific and other available information, the measures required for the conservation and development, and equitable exploitation, of those resources, taking into account any international agreement in force between them, such as the North-East Atlantic Fisheries Convention of 24 January as well as such other agreements as may be reached in the matter in the course of further negotiation."
338 *Fisheries Jurisdiction* [1974] ICJ Rep 3, 23 para 52; *Fisheries Jurisdiction* [1974] ICJ Rep 175, 191-192 para 44: "The 1960 Conference failed by one vote to adopt a text governing the two questions of the breadth of the territorial sea and the extent of fishery rights. However, after that Conference the law evolved through the practice of States on the basis of the debates and near-agreements at the Conference."
339 *Fisheries Jurisdiction* [1974] ICJ Rep 3, 23 para 53; *Fisheries Jurisdiction* [1974] ICJ Rep 175, 192 para 45: "The Court is also aware of present endeavours, pursued under the auspices of the United Nations, to achieve in a third Conference on the Law of the Sea the further codification and progressive development of this branch of the law [...] Such a general desire is understandable since the rules of international maritime law have been the product of mutual accommodation, reasonableness and Cooperation. So it was in the past, and so it necessarily is today. In the circumstances, the Court, as a court of law, cannot render judgment sub specie legis ferendae, or anticipate the law before the legislator has laid it down."

developments since both Germany and the UK, as well as other states,[340] began to establish 200-mile fishery zones.[341]

The ongoing legislative process was also important for the criteria to be applied to the delimitation of the continental shelf. In the case between Tunisia and Libya, the Court felt compelled to turn "to the question whether principles and rules of international law applicable to the delimitation may be derived from, or may be affected by, the 'new accepted trends' which have emerged at the Third United Nations Conference on the Law of the Sea."[342]

In a different case between Libya and Malta, the Court stressed that UNCLOS was "of major importance, having been adopted by an overwhelming majority of states".[343] The Court considered it as its "duty [...] to consider in what degree any of its relevant provisions are binding upon the Parties as a rule of customary international law"[344] even if the parties had not referred to UNCLOS.

The Court was not just paying lip service to the ongoing treaty developments as the jurisprudence on the definition of the continental shelf illustrates. Whereas article 1 of the 1958 Continental Shelf Convention defines the continental shelf "to a depth of 200 metres or, beyond that limit, to where the depth of the superjacent waters admits of the exploitation of the natural resources of the said areas", article 76(1) UNCLOS does not take up the criterion of exploitation and referred instead to the natural prolongation of a state's land territory or to a distance of 200 nautical miles from the baselines form which the breadth of the territorial sea is measured. In the dispute between Tunisia and Libya where the applicable law was customary international law, the Court concluded that the concept of the continental shelf had been "modified by this criterion"[345] of the 200 nautical miles and that the 1982 definition

---

340 According to Benvenisti, 'Customary International Law as a Judicial Tool for Promoting Efficiency' 96, "[b]etween 1976 and 1979, about two-thirds of the exclusive economic zones and exclusive fishery zones of up to two hundred miles had been unilaterally created".
341 Peter Tomka, 'Fisheries Jurisdiction Cases (United Kingdom v Iceland; Federal Republic of Germany v Iceland)' [2007] Max Planck EPIL para 16; one decade later, the Court held that the exclusive economic zone became customary international law, *Continental Shelf (Libya/Malta)* [1985] ICJ Rep 13, 33 para 34; Benvenisti, 'Customary International Law as a Judicial Tool for Promoting Efficiency' 96.
342 *Continental Shelf (Tunisia/Libya)* [1982] ICJ Rep 18, 47 para 45.
343 *Continental Shelf (Libya/Malta)* [1985] ICJ Rep 13, 29-30 para 27.
344 ibid 30 para 29.
345 *Continental Shelf (Tunisia/Libya)* [1982] ICJ Rep 18, 48 para 47.

"discards the exploitability test which is an element in the definition of the Geneva Convention of 1958."[346] Since states began to agree on a distance of 200 nautical miles, the ICJ argued in the case between Libya and Malta that "there is no reason to ascribe any role of geological or geophysical factors within that distance either in verifying the legal title of the States concerned or in proceedings to a delimitation" since within a distance of 200 nautical miles the title "depends solely on the distance from the coasts of the claimant States [...] and the geological or geo- morphological characteristics of those areas are completely immaterial."[347]

While the convergence in the long run is a characteristic of the ICJ jurisprudence on maritime delimitation, the jurisprudence was also characterized by different approaches or preferences on maritime delimitation.[348] For instance, it was debated whether the criteria which the Court applied for the purposes of delimitation were only factual criteria, but no law. In the *North Sea Continental Shelf cases*, the Court stressed that "the decision finds its objective justification in considerations lying not outside but within the rules, and in this field it is precisely a rule of law that calls for the application of equitable principles." [349] Years later, the ICJ argued in the dispute between Tunisia and Libya that each dispute "should be considered and judged on its own merits, having regard to its peculiar circumstances; therefore, no attempt should be made here to overconceptualize the application of the principles and rules relating to the continental shelf." [350] The Chamber in the *Gulf of Maine* case

---

346 *Continental Shelf (Tunisia/Libya)* 48 para 47.
347 *Continental Shelf (Libya/Malta)* [1985] ICJ Rep 13, 35 para 39, see also 35-36 para 40, where the Court argued that jurisprudence which ascribed a role to geophysical or geological factors in delimitation "now belongs to the past, in so far as sea-bed areas less than 200 miles from the Coast are concerned." Bjarni Már Magnússon, *The Continental Shelf Beyond 200 Nautical Miles* (Brill Nijhoff 2015) 16-17; for an overview of the development of the law relating to the continental shelf, see Joanna Mossop, *The Continental Shelf Beyond 200 Nautical Miles: Rights and Responsibilities* (Oxford University Press 2016) 52 ff; Kate Purcell, *Geographical Change and the Law of the Sea* (Oxford University Press 2019) 77 ff.; Peter-Tobias Stoll, 'Continental Shelf' [2008] Max Planck EPIL para 2 ff.
348 See on the debate between equidistance and equitable principles Cottier, *Equitable Principles of Maritime Boundary Delimitation: The Quest for Distributive Justice in International Law* 378-389, 603 ff., submitting that "the controversy between the equidistance and equitable principles schools reflect nothing short of fundamental divergences in jurisprudence and approach to law" (at 389).
349 *North Sea Continental Shelf* [1969] ICJ Rep 3, 48 para 88.
350 *Continental Shelf (Tunisia/Libya)* [1982] ICJ Rep 18, 92 para 132.

emphasized that customary international law "cannot also be expected to specify the equitable criteria to be applied or the practical, often technical, methods to be used for attaining that objective - which remain simply criteria and methods"[351], and argued that "neither the Court's own jurisprudence nor 'any trend in favour thereof discernible in international customary law' would determine methods and criteria."[352] According to Robert Kolb, even though law oscillates between normative and factual dimensions, the Chamber overemphasized the particularities and facts at the expense of the law[353] and implied a "normative poverty of general international law."[354] In a subsequent case between Libya and Malta, the Court as a whole emphasized the values of "consistency and a degree of predictability; even though [justice] looks with particularity to the peculiar circumstances of an instant case, it also looks beyond it to principles of more general application".[355] The Court spoke of the "normative character of equitable principles applied as a part of general international law".[356]

Other decisions of the Court also suggest that the use of these criteria when applying the very general rule of customary international law on maritime delimitation were related to, and inspired by, the wider normative environment. With respect to the process of delimitation, the Court rejected to apply criteria which were "totally unrelated to the underlying intention of the applicable rules of international law"[357] and which would not have received any recognition by law, such as landmass or pure economic considerations[358]; also, the Court made clear that security and defence interests would not generally favour the use of the equidistance method, and that the principle of equality of states would "not imply an equality of extent of shelf, whatever

---

351 *Delimitation of the Maritime Boundary in the Gulf of Maine Area* [1984] ICJ Rep 246, 298 para 110.
352 ibid 313 para 159, 162-163.
353 Kolb, *Case law on equitable maritime delimitation: digest and commentaries = Jurisprudence sur les délimitations maritimes selon l'équité: répertoire et commentaires* 253.
354 ibid 250.
355 *Continental Shelf (Libya/Malta)* [1985] ICJ Rep 13, 39 para 45.
356 ibid [1985] ICJ Rep 13, 39 para 46.
357 ibid 41 para 50.
358 See already *Continental Shelf (Tunisia/Libya)* [1982] ICJ Rep 18, 77 para 107: "A country might be poor today and become rich tomorrow as a result of an event such as the discovery of a valuable economic resource."

the circumstances of the area".[359] The Court stressed that it "may only take into account those that are pertinent to the institutions of the continental shelf as it has developed within the law, and to the application of equitable principles to its delimitation."[360]

c) UNCLOS and its impact on customary international law

In recent years, UNCLOS[361] became more important in proceedings before the Court. UNCLOS does not establish a genuinely new legal regime of delimitation. It refers in several provisions to international law: according to article 74, "[t]he delimitation of the exclusive economic zone [...] shall be effected by agreement on the basis of international law, as referred to in Article 38 [ICJ Statute]". The same principle applies to the delimitation of the continental shelf according to article 83 UNCLOS.[362]

In the jurisprudence of the Court, large parts of UNCLOS were regarded to reflect customary international law. In the case between Qatar and Bahrain, the Court treated several provisions of existing maritime conventions as reflections of customary international law.[363]

---

359 *Continental Shelf (Libya/Malta)* [1985] ICJ Rep 13, 42 para 51, 43 para 54; on security interests see *Maritime Delimitation in the Black Sea (Romania/Ukraine)* (Judgment) [2009] ICJ Rep 128 para 204 ("[...] the legitimate security considerations of the Parties may play a role in determining the final delimitation line [...] The provisional equidistance line determined by the Court fully respects the legitimate security interests of either Party."); cf. also Cottier, *Equitable Principles of Maritime Boundary Delimitation: The Quest for Distributive Justice in International Law* 537-8, 590-3 (arguing that "security does not amount to an inherent element which should be the subject of a prime principle. Instead, it is an aspect of a factual nature, which has to be considered, as the case may be, as a relevant circumstance in order to achieve an equitable solution responding to the needs of acceptability.").
360 *Continental Shelf (Libya/Malta)* [1985] ICJ Rep 13, 40 para 48. For a list of equitable standards see Cottier, *Equitable Principles of Maritime Boundary Delimitation: The Quest for Distributive Justice in International Law* 525 ff.
361 United Nations Convention on the Law of the Sea (signed 10 December 1982, entered into force 16 November 1994) 1833 UNTS 3.
362 Cf. Lando, *Maritime Delimitation as a Judicial Process* 294 (judicial lawmaking as "consequences of the vagueness of Articles 74 and 83 UNCLOS").
363 *Maritime Delimitation and Territorial Questions between Qatar and Bahrain* [2001] ICJ Rep 40, 94 para 167 (both parties agreed that "most of the provisions of the 1982 Convention which are relevant for the present case reflect customary law."),

Moreover, the Court continued to hold customary international law relevant where UNCLOS was applicable. In a case between Nicaragua and Honduras, UNCLOS was the applicable law "together", as the Court stressed, with state practice and the principles and rules of customary law.[364]

Interestingly, UNCLOS as a treaty may even be relevant when the applicable law in a legal dispute was customary international law, in particular insofar as claims on a continental shelf beyond 200 nautical miles were concerned. In a dispute between Nicaragua and Colombia on the law relating to the zone beyond 200 nautical miles, the applicable law was customary international law, since Colombia had not ratified UNCLOS. Nicaragua submitted that article 76 UNCLOS as a whole constituted custom, whereas according to Colombia only article 76(1) UNCLOS reflected customary international law. Article 76 UNCLOS prescribes a procedure for establishing the outer edge of the continental margin which includes recommendations by the Commission on the Limits of the Continental Shelf on the basis of which the coastal state shall establish the limits of the continental shelf (article 76(8) UNCLOS).[365] The Court solely noted that article 76(1) "forms part of customary international law", on which the parties had agreed before, and did not decide on the customary status of the other paragraphs.[366] Even though customary international law was the applicable law, the Court did not ignore the legal

---

94 para 176 (article 15 UNCLOS "is virtually identical to Article 12, paragraph 1, of the 1958 Convention on the Territorial Sea and the Contiguous Zone, as is to be regarded as having a customary character."), 100 para 201 (the Court held that article 11 of the 1958 Convention on the Territorial Sea which resembles article 11 UNCLOS reflect custom); 102 para 208: based on an analysis of article 4 of the 1958 Convention on the Territorial Sea and of article 7 paragraph 4 of the UNCLOS, the Court declined that low-tide elevations are territory in the same sense as islands. Custom was also relevant in relation to the concept of a single maritime boundary line which according to the Court "does not stem from multilateral treaty law but from State practice", ibid 93 para 173.

364 *Territorial and Maritime Dispute between Nicaragua and Honduras in the Caribbean Sea* [2007] ICJ Rep 659, 738-740 paras 261-266. The Court referred here to its earlier *dictum* in the case between Qatar and Bahrain which demonstrates that the sources were not regarded as being placed in competition to each other, rather, they complement each other.

365 For an overview see Ted L McDorman, 'The Continental Shelf' in Donald R Rothwell and others (eds), *The Oxford Handbook on the Law of the Sea* (Oxford University Press 2015) 190-198.

366 *Territorial and Maritime Dispute* [2012] ICJ Rep 624, 666 para 118; cf. Naomi Burke, 'Nicaragua v Colombia at the ICJ: Better the Devil You Don't?' (2013) 2(2) Cambridge Journal of International and Comparative Law 317-318.

obligations incumbent on Nicaragua under UNCLOS and placed considerable significance on them. The Court recalled that "any claim of continental shelf rights beyond 200 miles [by a State party to UNCLOS] must be in accordance with Article 76 of UNCLOS and reviewed by the Commission on the Limits of the Continental Shelf established thereunder".[367] Recalling UNCLOS' preamble according to which UNCOS intends to establish "a legal order for the seas and oceans which will facilitate international communication, and will promote the peaceful uses of the seas and oceans, the equitable and efficient utilization of their resources", the Court argued that "[g]iven the object and purpose of UNCLOS [...] the fact that Colombia is not a party thereto would not relieve Nicaragua of its obligations under Article 76 of that Convention."[368] The Court then observed that Nicaragua by its own admission "falls short of meeting the requirements"[369], and stated that Nicaragua "has not established that it has a continental margin that extends far enough to overlap with Colombia's 200-nautical-mile entitlement to the continental shelf, measured from Colombia's mainland coast".[370] In the end, the Court could not uphold Nicaragua's claim.[371] In a subsequent case between Nicaragua and Colombia, the Court did not find Nicaragua in violation of its treaty obligations, which is why it did not need to discuss whether a third state like Colombia could invoke another state's failure to honour its treaty commitments.[372]

---

367 *Territorial and Maritime Dispute* [2012] ICJ Rep 624, 668-669 para 126; see already *Territorial and Maritime Dispute between Nicaragua and Honduras in the Caribbean Sea (Nicaragua v. Honduras)* (Judgment) [2007] ICJ Rep 759 para 319. Cf. in a different context *Military and Paramilitary Activities in and against Nicaragua* [1986] ICJ Rep 14, 121 para 235: the Court noted in a case where it had to apply customary international law that the United States did not comply with the obligation to report to the Security Council under article 51 UNC. The failure to report did not amount to a breach of customary international law, but the Court observed that " this conduct of the United States hardly conforms with the latter's avowed conviction that it was acting in the context of collective self-defence [...]").
368 *Territorial and Maritime Dispute* [2012] ICJ Rep 624, 669 para 126; critical ibid Decl of Judge *ad hoc* Mensah paras 6-8; ibid Decl of Judge *ad hoc* Cot paras 18-19.
369 ibid 669 para 127.
370 ibid para 129.
371 See ibid 670 para 131, 719 para 251; cf. for the subsequent dispute on whether the formula implies a substantial decision to which *res judicata* applies: *Question of the Delimitation of the Continental Shelf between Nicaragua and Colombia beyond 200 nautical miles from the Nicaraguan Coast* [2016] ICJ Rep 100, 129 para 74.
372 For a brief discussion see ibid Sep Op Owada para 35.

The recent jurisprudence confirms the tendency in the Court's earlier jurisprudence to stress the alignment between UNCLOS and customary international law and the convergence of the sources. In April 2022, the Court considered that multiple provisions of UNCLOS reflected customary international law, namely the rights and duties in the exclusive economic zone of coastal states and other states in articles 56, 58, 61, 62 and 73 UNCLOS.[373] Customary international law was said to be also reflected "in Articles 88 to 115 of UNCLOS" which apply to the exclusive economic zone.[374] The Court also decided that the 24-nautical-mile limit in article 33 UNCLOS and the prescribed grounds of control (customs, fiscal, immigration or sanitary laws and regulations) that may be exercised by the coastal state reflected customary international law which had been called into question by Colombia.[375] In particular, the Court pointed out that security matters were deliberated not included to article 24 of the 1958 Convention, the precursor to article 33 UNCLOS and that Colombia could not establish that "customary rules on the contiguous zone have evolved since the adoption of UNCLOS".[376]

d) Concluding observations

To sum up, sources remain separate and distinct for jurisdictional purposes, but the Court does not regard treaties and custom as strictly separated and impenetrable compartments when it comes to content-determination. The Court even considered in the just mentioned case the obligation of one party under UNCLOS, even though the applicable law between both parties was customary international law. This illustrates that the Court does not simply collect and examine state practice and *opinio juris*, it understands customary international law as part of one normative system which treaties, in particular widely ratified treaties such as UNCLOS, are part of as well. The context

---

373 *Alleged Violations of Sovereign Rights and Maritime Spaces in the Caribbean Sea (Nicaragua v. Colombia)* (Judgment of 21 April 2022) (2022) ⟨https://www.icj-cij.org/public/files/case-related/155/155-20220421-JUD-01-00-EN.pdf⟩ accessed 1 February 2023 paras 57, 94, 100.
374 ibid para 62.
375 Colombia had established by Presidential Decree 1946 of 2013 an "integral contiguous zone" beyond 24 nautical miles, ibid paras 145-55.
376 ibid (Judgment) https://www.icj-cij.org/public/files/case-related/155/155-20220421-JUD-01-00-EN.pdf para 154.

of maritime delimitation is an example where customary international law provide for very broad, general principles and rules which are interlinked with general principles such as the principle of good faith.[377] At the same time, it is noteworthy that some of the treaty-based rules of the 1958 Geneva Convention or UNCLOS were not particularly more specific than their respective counterpart in customary international law. This decision of states opens up considerable room for the Court to specify these general principles in particular cases by employing a methodology which focuses on the relevant circumstances of the particular case and takes account of the earlier jurisprudence.[378] Over time, the Court developed a methodology as to the delimitation. Most notably, the ICJ held in the dispute between Romania and the Ukraine, that "the Court proceeds in defined stages"[379], at the first stage it draws a provisional equidistance line between the adjacent coasts, at the second stage it considers whether factors called for the adjustment of the provisional line and at the third stage it will confirm that "no great disproportionality of maritime areas is evident".[380] The Court's methodology raises further questions,[381] but these debates cannot be fully addressed here.

---

[377] As Cottier noted, "Customary law and general principles of law, as much as the general principles of international law, often overlap and are mutually supportive in the establishment of the legitimacy of a normative concept." See Cottier, *Equitable Principles of Maritime Boundary Delimitation: The Quest for Distributive Justice in International Law* 428, with reference to Clarence Wilfred Jenks, *The Prospects of International Adjudication* (Stevens 1964) 264 ("Custom as a basis of legal obligation neither can be nor should be rigidly separated from general principles of law, equity, public policy and practical convenience.").

[378] Cf. Malcolm Evans, 'Relevant Circumstances' in Alex G Oude Elferink, Tore Henriksen, and Signe Veierud Busch (eds), *Maritime Boundary Delimitation: The Case Law* (Cambridge University Press 2018) 261 ("recourse to relevant circumstances within the delimitation process represents a principle of customary law").

[379] *Maritime Delimitation in the Black Sea* [2009] ICJ Rep 61, 101 para 115.

[380] ibid 101, 103 para 122.

[381] Cf. on the proportionality jurisprudence see Yoshifumi Tanaka, 'The Disproportionality Test in the Law of Maritime Delimitation' in Alex G Oude Elferink, Tore Henriksen, and Signe Veierud Busch (eds) (Cambridge University Press 2018) 302, 313-4 (considering it arguable "that the disproportionality test can be regarded as an operationalization of the equitable principles that require to resulting in an equitable result", while expressing doubts as to "whether the disproportionality test developed through the jurisprudence is adequately objective and scientific as a norm of international law"); in favour of the role of disproportionality: Lando, *Maritime Delimitation as a Judicial Process* 246 ff. Cf. on the applicable law also Donald McRae, 'The Applicable Law' in Alex G Oude Elferink, Tore Henriksen, and Signe

They are the consequence of the room given by States' choice in favour of general principles and rules and of leaving the delimitation process to a significant extent to the Court. At the same time, it should not be overlooked that the Court responded to the contention of states, that treaties concluded by states informed the Court's reasoning and that states implemented the Court's decisions. As stated by Massimo Lando, maritime delimitation "should be better conceived as having been determined by the continuous interaction between states and international tribunals."[382]

IV. General Principles and the normative environment

General principles of law are said to perform an important function in relation to procedural law[383] and the Court referred to general principles, such as *res judicata*[384], equality of the parties before a court or tribunal[385] or elementary

---

Veierud Busch (eds), *Maritime Boundary Delimitation: The Case Law* (Cambridge University Press 2018) 107 ("the applicable law today consists of a requirement to utilize a particular methodology and to engage in a particular process of assessment within that methodology in order to delimit a boundary").

382 Lando, *Maritime Delimitation as a Judicial Process* 322, see also 317 ("Both the formulation of the two-stage approach, and the separation of disproportionality from other relevant circumstances resulting in the formulation of the three-stage approach, built upon the contentions of states.").

383 See the overview in Giorgio Gaja, 'General Principles in the Jurisprudence of the ICJ' in Mads Andenæs and others (eds), *General principles and the coherence of international law* (Brill Nijhoff 2019) 36-39; on the notion of "general principles of procedural law" see *Land, Island and Maritime Frontier Dispute* [1990] ICJ Rep 92, 136 para 102; *Difference Relating to Immunity from Legal Process of a Special Rapporteur of the Commission on Human Rights* (Advisory Opinion) [1999] ICJ Rep 88 para 63.

384 *Effect of Awards of Compensation Made by the United Nations Administrative Tribunal* (Advisory Opinion of July 13th, 1954) [1954] ICJ Rep 53; *Question of the Delimitation of the Continental Shelf between Nicaragua and Colombia beyond 200 nautical miles from the Nicaraguan Coast* [2016] ICJ Rep 100, 125 para 58.

385 *Application for Review of Judgment No 158 of the United Nations Administrative Tribunal* (Advisory Opinion) [1973] ICJ Rep 181 para 36, see also 177 para 29 ("principles governing the judicial process"); *Application for Review of Judgment No 273 of the United Nations Administrative Tribunal* (Advisory Opinion) [1982] ICJ Rep 338 para 29.

fairness[386]. Against the background of the previous sections, this section will reflect on the general principles, which are more often derived from and related to the international, as opposed to the domestic, legal order and which often function as a bridge between customary international law and treaties.

1. The rare recourse to municipal law analogies

The Court hardly invokes general principles of law in the sense of municipal law analogies. According to Giorgio Gaja, the prospect of engaging in comparative legal analysis and making a choice between municipal legal orders may explain Court's reluctance to invoke general principles of law.[387] It is also true, however, that the omission to mention general principles of law explicitly in judgments may not necessarily allow for the conclusion that such general principles did not play a role for the judges' interpretation of the law,[388] in particular since, according to article 9 of the ICJ Statute, the judges on the Court are meant to represent the main forms of civilization and of the principal legal systems of the world. The references to general principles of law in individual opinions suggest that general principles played a role in the legal reasoning,[389] even though the Court was reluctant to base

---

386 "It is an established rule of law that the plea of error cannot be allowed as an element vitiating consent if the party advancing it contributed by its conduct to the error, or could have avoided it, or if the circumstances were such as to put that party on notice of a possible error.", *Temple of Preah Vihear* [1962] ICJ Rep 6, 26.
387 Giorgio Gaja, 'General Principles of Law' [2013] Max Planck EPIL para 16.
388 Michael Bothe, 'Die Bedeutung der Rechtsvergleichung in der Praxis internationaler Gerichte' (1976) 36 ZaöRV 287.
389 Examples; several judges invoked general principles of law in different contexts, see for instance *Pulp Mills on the River Uruguay* [2010] ICJ Rep 14 Sep Op Cancado Trindade; *Right of Passage over Indian Territory* [1960] ICJ Rep 6 Diss Op Ferndandes; *Oil Platforms* [2003] ICJ Rep 161 Sep Op Simma; *Gabčíkovo-Nagymaros Project* [1997] ICJ Rep 7 Sep Op Weeramantry; see generally Marcelo G Kohen, 'Les principes généaux du droit international de l'eau à la lumière de la jurisprudence récente de la Cour Internationale de Justice' in *L'eau en droit international: Colloque d'Orléans* (Pedone 2011) 91 ff.; Pierre d'Argent, 'Les principes généraux à la Cour internationale de Justice' in Samantha Besson, Pascal Pichonnaz, and Marie-Louise Gächter-Alge (eds), *Les principes en droit européen* (Schulthess 2011) 107 ff.; Bettina Rentsch, 'Konstitutionalisierung durch allgemeine Rechtsgrundsätze des Völkerrechts? - Zur Rolle des völkerrechtlichen Gutglaubensgrundsatzes für die Integration einer internationalen Werteordnung in das Völkerrecht' in Bardo

The normative environment in the jurisprudence of the ICJ

a decision on them.³⁹⁰ Furthermore, it has been argued that the process of judicial reasoning applied to a treaty provision or customary international law and, for instance, teleological reasoning or logical deductions provided the Court with ample instruments to fill gaps or preclude any gap, which may have reduced the need to resort to general principles as additional gap filler.³⁹¹

The Court's treatment of municipal law analogies did not incentivize parties to the proceedings to invoke general principles of law thusly ascertained. One early example is the *Indian Passage* case.³⁹² Portugal's territory in the Indian Peninsula encompassed two enclaves, Dadra and Nagar-Aveli, and littoral territory, Daman.³⁹³ The case turned on whether Portugal had *vis-à-vis* India a right of passage. Portugal relied not only on an old treaty of 1799 and on decrees of 1783 and 1785 but also on customary international law and general principles of law. For this purpose, Portugal had commissioned an extensive study compiled by the renowned comparative law scholar Max Rheinstein.³⁹⁴ The Court concluded that "there existed during the British and post-British periods a constant and uniform practice allowing free passage between Daman and the enclaves [...] that practice was accepted as law by the Parties and has given rise to a right and a correlative obligation."³⁹⁵ The Court then did not consider it necessary to examine "whether general international custom or the general principles of law recognized by civilized nations [on which Portugal had also relied] may lead to the same result."³⁹⁶

Fassbender and Angelika Siehr (eds), *Suprastaatliche Konstitutionalisierung: Perspektiven auf die Legitimität, Kohärenz und Effektivität des Völkerrechts* (Nomos 2012) 101 ff.; Saunders, *General Principles as a Source of International Law* 91 ff.

390 For an exception, see *Temple of Preah Vihear* [1962] ICJ Rep 6, 23, 26, 32, where the case was decided on the basis of general principles such as acquiescence and estoppel; on this case see Kolb, 'Principles as Sources of International Law (With Special Reference to Good Faith)' 11-12.

391 Mendelson, 'The International Court of Justice and the sources of international law' 80-81.

392 *Right of Passage over Indian Territory* [1960] ICJ Rep 6.

393 ibid 27.

394 Reference to this study is made by judge Wellington Koo, see ibid [1960] ICJ Rep 6 Sep Op Wellington Koo 66 para 26.

395 ibid 40. According to this practice, passage of armed forces, police and arms was not encompassed from the right of passage and required a formal request, ibid 31-43.

396 ibid 43. In a similar fashion, the Court based its decision in the Nuclear Test cases on an unilateral act of France declaring not to conduct such tests, without addressing the compliance of such tests with the applicable rules of international law, *Nuclear*

Chapter 5: The International Court of Justice

The policy behind this choice of the Court was a preference for a *lex specialis* approach that focused on "a practice clearly established between two States which was accepted by the Parties".[397] The Court's decision did not address the relationship of this established *lex specialis* to the *lex generalis*[398] and did not honour Portugal's effort to utilize general principles of law based on comparative law.

In the joined *South West Africa* cases, the Court held that Ethiopia and Libera had no standing in the proceedings against South Africa. The Court did not recognize an

> "'*actio popularis*', or right resident in any member of a community to take legal action in vindication of a public interest. But although a right of this kind may be known to certain municipal systems of law, it is not known to international law as it stands at present: nor is the Court able to regard it as imported by the 'general principles of law' referred to in Article 38, paragraph 1 (c), of its Statute."[399]

The joint *North Sea Continental Shelf* cases are an example of the rejection of a general principle based on the view that it could not be transposed to the international level; instead the Court based its decision on a different, more general one. The Federal Republic of Germany argued that the delimitation of the continental shelf should take into account Germany's "claim for a

---

Tests Case [1973] ICJ Rep 324, 472-477; *Nuclear Tests Case* [1974] ICJ Rep 253, 267-272; Thirlway, *The law and procedure of the international court of justice: fifty years of jurisprudence* vol 1 at 130-131; in the *Gabčikovo-Nagymaros* case the Court could base its decision on the interpretation of a bilateral treaty in force and did not find it necessary whether the proposed principle of "approximate application" was "a principle of international law or a general principle of law", *Gabčikovo-Nagymaros Project* [1997] ICJ Rep 7, 53 para 76. In the dispute between Tunisia and Libya, Malta justified its application to intervene with arguments based on comparative law. The Court did not address these arguments when it rejected the application, Thirlway, *The law and procedure of the international court of justice: fifty years of jurisprudence* 245-246.

397 *Right of Passage over Indian Territory* [1960] ICJ Rep 6, 44.
398 See for a treatment of this question in individual opinions ibid Sep Op Wellington Koo (the Court's result would fly in the face of the Charter); Diss Op Ferndandes para 29 pointing to the possibility of general rules from which no derogation would be possible, he distinguished general principles of law as analogies from municipal law and certain "fundamental principles inherent in the very fabric of international law" (para 33).
399 *South West Africa* [1966] ICJ Rep 6, 47 para 88; judge Tanaka argued in his dissenting opinion that "the legal norm of non-discrimination or non-separation denying the practice of apartheid can be recognized as a principle enunciated in the said provision", ibid Diss Op Tanaka 294-300 (quote on 294).

just and equitable share" which Germany advanced as a general principle of law.[400] The Court held, however, that the doctrine of just and equitable share could not be transposed to the international legal level:

> "[T]he doctrine of the just and equitable share appears to be wholly at variance with what the Court entertains no doubt is the most fundamental of all the rules of law relating to the continental shelf, enshrined in Article 2 of the 1958 Geneva Convention, though quite independent of it - namely that the rights of the coastal State in respect of the area of continental shelf that constitutes a natural prolongation of its land territory into and under the sea exist *ipso facto* and *ab initio*, by virtue of its sovereignty over the land, and as an extension of it in an exercise of sovereign rights for the purpose of exploring the seabed and exploiting its natural resources."[401]

The Court then based its judgment on more abstract principles; the equitable principles on which a delimitation were based were regarded as principles of law and reflected "very general precepts of justice and good faith".[402]

Against this background, it is not surprising that states rarely plead general principles of law derived from municipal legal orders. A recent example is the litigation strategy in the case between Timor-Leste and Australia. The case turned on the confidentiality of communications between legal counsel and client and could have invited the parties to conduct comparative legal research to examine a general principle of law. Instead, Sir Michael Wood, acting as counsel for Timor-Leste, focused mainly on the confidentiality as a general principle of international law and its recognition in several

---

400 *North Sea Continental Shelf* [1969] ICJ Rep 3, 21 para 17.
401 ibid 22 para 19.
402 ibid 46 para 58; see in particular ibid Sep Op Ammoun 139 ff., who conducted an impressive survey of common law, Muslim law, Soviet law, Hindu law and the law of countries in Africa and Asia in order to demonstrate that equity was a general principle of law; see also Thirlway, *The law and procedure of the international court of justice: fifty years of jurisprudence* vol 1 at 241 f., who speaks of an "eclipse of general principle by conflicting principle of international law"; another example for the special character of the international legal order can be found in *Certain Expenses of the United Nations (Article 17, paragraph 2, of the Charter)* (Advisory Opinion) [1962] ICJ Rep 168, where the Court argued that "[b]oth national and international law contemplate cases in which the body corporate or politic may be bound, as to third parties, by an ultra vires act of an agent."In contrast to domestic legal systems however, the United Nations lacked a "procedure for determining the validity of even a legislative or governmental act [...] Therefore, each organ must, in the first place at least, determine its own jurisdiction."

branches of international law.[403] Similarly, Australia examined the scope of this general principle in international law.[404] In light of these arguments, it is no surprise that the Court noted that "this claimed right might be derived from the principle of the sovereign equality of States, which is one of the fundamental principles of the international legal order and is reflected in Article 2, paragraph 1, of the Charter of the United Nations", whereas Judge Greenwood expressed his doubts as to whether principle would not be better regarded as a general principle of law.[405]

2. General principles and the international legal order

Very general and abstract principles can be operationalized through the interplay with particular rules. They bridge the different sources and enable legal ideas expressed in treaties to pervade customary international law. As the Court's jurisprudence demonstrates, treaties can rely on a principle of general international law and then be relied upon by the Court for the purpose of interpreting this principle. Treaties can confirm existing, older principles or contribute to the emergence of new principles.

For instance, the Court held that the object of the Genocide Convention is to "confirm and endorse the most elementary principles of morality."[406] In the *Nicaragua* judgment, the Court argued that the "Geneva Conventions are in some respects a development, and in other respects no more than an expression of such principles".[407] Moreover, the rules set forth in common article 3 of the Geneva Conventions "constitute a minimum yardstick [...] and they are rules which, in the Court's opinion, reflect what the Court

---

403 *Public sitting held on Monday 20 January 2014, at 10 am, at the Peace Palace, Verbatim Record* 20 January 2014 CR 2014/1 paras 19 ff., paras 31-38 for international case-law that would support the classification as general principles of law.
404 *Public sitting held on Tuesday 21 January 2014, at 10 am, at the Peace Palace, Verbatim Record* 21 January 2014 CR 2014/2 para 15.
405 *Questions relating to the Seizure and Detention of Certain Documents and Data (Timor-Leste v. Australia)* (Provisional Measures, Order of 3 March 2014) [2014] ICJ Rep 153 para 27, and Diss Op Greenwood para 12.
406 *Reservations to the Convention on the Prevention and Punishment of the Crime of Genocide* [1951] ICJ Rep 15, 23.
407 *Military and Paramilitary Activities in and against Nicaragua* [1986] ICJ Rep 14, 113 para 218. By "such principles", the Court referred to the earlier mentioned "fundamental general principles of humanitarian law".

in 1949 called 'elementary considerations of humanity'."[408] Considering that the applicable law was customary international law in this context, the conventions were used in order to elucidate a general principle such as elementary considerations of humanity[409] which was then used in order to interpret and apply customary international law.

In the *Nuclear Weapons* advisory opinion, the Court argued that many states ratified the Hague and Geneva Conventions "because a great many rules of humanitarian law applicable in armed conflict are so fundamental to the respect of the human person and 'elementary considerations of humanity'" [...] Further these fundamental rules are to be observed by all States whether or not they have ratified the conventions that contain them, because they constitute intransgressible principles of international customary law."[410]

In addition to the just mentioned examples, where treaties specified already existing general principles of international law, the *Gabčikovo-Nagymaros* case and the *Nuclear Weapons* opinion illustrate how new ideas and emerging norms contributed to the operationalization of broad general principles and rules of customary international law.

In the *Gabčikovo-Nagymaros* case, the Court noted in an *obiter dictum* that the interpretation and application of customary international law on necessity which is now reflected in article 25 ARSIWA and was then reflected in draft article 33 should take account of new international obligations. According to draft article 33, a state could rely on necessity if "the act was the only means of safeguarding an essential interest of the State against a grave and imminent peril" and "the act did not seriously impair an essential interest of the State towards which the obligation existed". For the determination of

---

408 ibid 114 para 218.
409 Cf. Ian Brownlie, *Principles of public international law* (3rd edn, Clarendon Press 1979) 29: "[c]onsiderations of humanity may depend on the subjective appreciation of the judge, but, more objectively, they may be related to human values already protected by positive legal principles which, taken together, reveal certain criteria of public policy [...]".
410 *Legality of the Threat or Use of Nuclear Weapons* [1969] ICJ Rep 226, 257 para 79. It remains a subject of speculation whether the Court used this phrase of "intransgressible principles of international customary law" to indicate the customary nature of the general prinicples of humanitarian law or whether this phrase was intended to compensate for the lack of treatment of jus cogens, cf. ibid 258 para 83 ("no need for the Court to pronounce on this matter"); cf. Claus Kreß, 'The International Court of Justice and the Law of Armed Conflicts' in Christian J Tams and James Sloan (eds), *The Development of International Law by the International Court of Justice* (Oxford University Press 2013) 266, 282.

what qualifies as an "essential interest of the State", the Court referred to contemporary international law, in particular international environmental law. The Court had "no difficulty in acknowledging that the concerns expressed by Hungary for its natural environment in the region affected by the Gabčikovo-Nagymaros Project related to an 'essential interest' of that State [...]".[411] The Court later added, as guiding posts for the further negotiations of the parties (which have not been concluded yet), that "new environmental norms" are to be taken into account, as "[t]he awareness of the vulnerability of the environment and the recognition that environmental risks have to be assessed on a continuous basis have become much stronger in the years since the Treaty's conclusion".[412] This case can be read as confirmation for the applicability *mutatis mutandis* of a *dictum* which the Court expressed with respect to international instruments, according to which those are "to be interpreted and applied within the framework of the entire legal system prevailing at the time of the interpretation."[413]

In *Nuclear Weapons*, the Court affirmed the "existence of the *general* obligation of States to ensure that activities within their jurisdiction and control respect the environment of other States or of areas beyond national control" as "part of the corpus of international law relating to the environment."[414]

---

411 *Gabčíkovo-Nagymaros Project* [1997] ICJ Rep 7, 41 para 53. The idea of ecological necessity was not completely new: See with reference to the ILC discussions on article 33 and the state practice discussed there Andrea K Bjorklund, 'Emergency Exceptions: State of Necessity and Force Majeure' in Peter Muchlinski, Frederico Ortino, and Christoph Schreuer (eds), *The Oxford handbook of international investment law* (Oxford University Press 2008) 474 ff.; Robert D Sloane, 'On the Use and Abuse of Necessity in the Law of State Responsibility' (2012) 106 AJIL 466 ff. In the end, however, the necessity argument could not convince the Court, 42 para 54.
412 *Gabčíkovo-Nagymaros Project* [1997] ICJ Rep 7, 67-68 para 112.
413 *Legal Consequences for States of the Continued Presence of South Africa in Namibia (South West Africa) notwithstanding Security Council Resolution 276 (1970)* [1971] ICJ Rep 16, 31 para 53: "Moreover, an international instrument has to be interpreted and applied within the framework of the entire legal system prevailing at the time of the interpretation." Cf. also *Legal consequences of the Separation of the Chagos Archipelago from Mauritius in 1965* ibid [2019] ICJ Rep 95, 130 para 142; see above p. 288.
414 *Legality of the Threat or Use of Nuclear Weapons* [1996] ICJ Rep 226, 241-242 para 29 (italics added), cf. 242 para 30, where the Court then spoke of "treaties in question", and 242 para 31, where the Court "notes *furthermore*" (italics added) that articles 35, paragraph 3, and 55 of Additional Protocol I to be "powerful constraints for all the States having subscribed to these provisions". The Court did not say that these provisions reflected customary international law. Arguably, the *dictum* in para

The Court then concluded that "[s]tates must take environmental considerations into account when assessing what is necessary and proportionate in the pursuit of legitimate military objectives. Respect for the environment is one of the elements that go to assessing whether an action is in conformity with the principles of necessity and proportionality."[415] Assuming that the principles of necessity and proportionality in the context of the pursuit of legitimate military objectives are part of customary international law, the *Nuclear Weapons* advisory opinion illustrates that principles and rules of customary international law are to be applied under consideration of the international legal order as a whole that exists at the time of application.

E. Concluding observations

Complementing scholarly perspectives which focus on the materials used by the Court when identifying customary international law[416] or distinguish between inductive and deductive approaches to and assertions of customary international law[417], this chapter traced the interrelationship of sources as a *motif* in the ICJ jurisprudence. It began by examining the procedural framework in which the ICJ operates and zeroed in, in particular, on the intervention system[418] and the Court's jurisdiction[419]. Subsequently, it analyzed the importance of normative considerations[420] when identifying customary international law by highlighting the varying levels of generality of principles and rules of customary international law[421] and the Court's

---

31 does not qualify para 30 in the sense that the consideration of "respect for the environment" does apply only to states parties to the additional protocol.
415 ibid 242 para 30.
416 Cf. Petersen, 'The International Court of Justice and the Judicial Politics of Identifying Customary International Law' 357 ff., 368-369.
417 Talmon, 'Determining Customary International Law: the ICJ's Methodology between Induction, Deduction and Assertion' 434. As Talmon demonstrated, deductive and inductive approaches do not necessarily correspond to a distinction between traditional and modern customary international law, 429-434. Cf. on the mix of deduction and induction in legal reasoning Worster, 'The Inductive and Deductive Methods in Customary International Law Analysis: Traditional and Modern Approaches' 520.
418 See above, p. 224.
419 See above, p. 236.
420 See above, p. 258.
421 See above, p. 260.

Chapter 5: The International Court of Justice

interpretative decisions[422]. Moreover, the relationship between customary international law and treaty law in the Court's jurisprudence was analyzed[423], and convergences into common principles[424] or of functionally equivalent rules[425] could be identified. The chapter then considered the importance of general principles in the Court's jurisprudence.[426]

This chapter highlighted that the institutional setting in which the Court operates is not necessarily neutral towards the sources. The intervention regime which, as applied by the Court, restricted the participation of third states in disputes on customary international law, may have favoured to a certain extent a bilateralist approach of the Court to the law. Moreover, the jurisdictional regime in relation to compromissory clauses will arguably lead to claims based on treaty law instead of customary international law. This chapter also demonstrated that the way in which the intervention regime[427] and the jurisdiction regime are applied is also an expression of the judicial policy of the Court. In particular when it comes to jurisdiction based on compromissory clauses, the Court has to strike a delicate balance between respecting jurisdictional limitations and respecting the general rule of interpretation as set forth in article 31 VCLT.[428] This chapter demonstrated how the Court respected jurisdictional limitations by interpreting its jurisdiction as confined to the particular treaty and so-called rules on rules, as far as applicable law is concerned.

However, the emphasis on the distinctiveness of sources for jurisdictional purposes is different from the interrelationship of sources when it comes to interpretation.[429] This chapter's focus on the significance of the normative environment, in particular in relation to the unwritten international law, illustrated that customary international law should not be understood as just a set of separate rules, but as a set of rules and principles which interrelate with each other.[430] Acknowledging both the distinctiveness of sources as far as applicable law is concerned and the interrelationship of sources when it comes to interpretation can be regarded as a reconciliation of state consent

---

422 See above, p. 266.
423 See above, p. 278.
424 See above, p. 285.
425 See above, p. 290.
426 See above, p. 310.
427 See above, p. 233.
428 See above, p. 245.
429 See above, p. 258.
430 See above, p. 262.

on the one hand and the rule of law in the international community on the other hand. The Court was careful to take account of developments in treaty-making and principles expressed in treaties, when identifying and applying customary international law, and of relevant customary international law when interpreting and applying treaties. Therefore, a convergence between the sources and between functionally equivalent rules could be observed and principles expressed in treaties informed the identification of customary international law.

Chapter 6: The International Law Commission

A. Introduction

This chapter analyzes the work of the ILC and to what extent codification choices of the ILC can explain that, in contrast to experiences in municipal law, codification in the context of public international law did not tend to drive out customary international law. The chapter will first explore the implications codification can have on the interrelationship of sources and illustrate that both codification and progressive development, which cannot always be clearly separated, call for a normative assessment (I.). It will be demonstrated that, early on, the ILC searched for inspiration in principles expressed in treaties when codifying and progressively developing international law. The chapter will then explore the implications of the form which the ILC chose for its work and of the trend from a binding to a non-binding form (II.). Subsequently, this chapter will examine how the interrelationship of sources was approached and addressed in specific projects, for which the work on the general law of treaties, on the law of state responsibility, on the fragmentation of international law, on customary international law, on *jus cogens* and on general principles of law were selected (III.).

I. Codification and the interrelationship of sources

Codification has repercussions on the interrelationship of sources and has been rightfully described as an "activity which is intimately concerned with the sources of the law."[1] In 1905, upon reflection of the codification movement, Lassa Oppenheim expressed his sympathy for codification in awareness of its implications for other sources: "It cannot be denied that codification always interferes with the growth of customary law, although the assertion is not justified that codification does cut off such growth."[2] Since then, concerns

---

1 Robert Yewdall Jennings, 'The Progressive Development of International Law and Its Codification' (1947) 24 BYIL 303.
2 Oppenheim, *International Law* 39, 41. For precursors in Latin-America see Antônio Augusto Cançado Trindade, 'The Contribution of Latin American Legal Doctrine to the Progressive Development of International Law' (2014) 376 RdC 53-56. For an overview

Chapter 6: The International Law Commission

have been expressed that the work of codification would endanger the "superiority of customary over treaty law within the international community"[3], would have "the effect of arresting change and flux in the state of customary international law"[4] and would "have a freezing effect on the customary law even for states non-parties to [the treaty]"[5]. Even though similar concerns continue to be expressed today,[6] by and large codification is regarded to have been beneficial for customary international law.[7] It has even been argued that the very purpose of progressive development and codification is very much about influencing customary international law, rather than replacing it.[8]

---

of the history of codification in international legal thought Shabtai Rosenne, 'The International Law Commission, 1949-59' (1960) 36 BYIL 106-109; James Crawford, 'The Progressive Development of International Law: History, Theory and Practice' in Denis Alland and others (eds), *Unity and Diversity of International Law. Essays in Honour of Pierre-Marie Dupuy* (Martinus Nijhoff Publishers 2014) 4-6.

3   Krystyna Marek, 'Thoughts on Codification' (1971) 29 ZaöRV 497: "To sum up, failure to safeguard - or inadequate safeguarding of - the customary nature of the codified rules might lead directly to the absence of all legal links among States, in other words, to the liquidation of all international legal order."

4   Richard R Baxter, 'Multilateral Treaties as Evidence of Customary International Law' (1965) 41 BYIL 299.

5   Thirlway, *International Customary Law and Codification: an examination of the continuing role of custom in the present period of codification of international law* 126. Furthermore, against the background of the negative codification experiences made at the Codification Conference 1930 (or generally throughout the 1920s), Hurst was skeptical regarding the possibility to codify international law, see Cecil Hurst, 'A Plea for the Codification of International Law on New Lines' (1946) 32 Transactions of the Grotius Society 139.

6   Cf. Timothy L Meyer, 'Codifying Custom' (2012) 160 University of Pennsylvania Law Review 1001, 1021, 1046 ff.

7   Arthur Watts, 'Codification and Progressive Development of International Law' [2006] Max Planck EPIL para 44.

8   Vladimir-Djuro Degan, *Sources of International Law* (Martinus Nijhoff Publishers 1997) 203 (on codification conventions); for his earlier view that codification could go at the expense of customary international law and general principles of law, the so-called "sources impartfaites", see Vladimir-Djuro Degan, *L' interprétation des accords en droit international* (Nijhoff 1963) 14; Roberto Ago, 'Nouvelles reflexions sur la codification du droit international' (1988) 92 RGDIP 573-576.

II. The institutionalization of codification and the difficult distinction between progressive development and codification

Codification and its repercussions on the relationship of sources were not discussed during the drafting of article 38 of the PCIJ Statute. The Advisory Committee of Jurists only adopted a resolution by which it recommended to call a new interstate conference for the codification of international law.[9] The codification conferences organized by the League of Nations failed to meet the expectations.[10] There was no agreement on substance and on the question of whether the codification conferences should be about a restatement of already binding customary international law or whether conferences should attempt to make exclusively new law in the sense of legislation.[11]

These historical experiences informed the establishment of the International Law Commission after the Second World War. According to article 13(1)(a) UNC, the General Assembly shall initiate studies and make recommendations for the purposes of promoting international co-operation in the political field and encouraging the progressive development of international law and its codification. As put by Rosenne, article 13 UNC "stresses the political intent of the organized international community in what had hitherto been commonly regarded as little more than the special preserve of lawyers."[12]

The UN General Assembly firstly appointed by UNGA resolution 94(1) of 11 December 1946 a "Committee on the Progressive Development of International Law and its Codification", with Professor Leslie Brierly acting as the committee's Special Rapporteur.[13] By resolution 174 (II) of 21 November

---

9 1920 Advisory Committee of Jurists Annexes, 747-748.
10 Ian Sinclair, *The International Law Commission* (Cambridge, 1987) 4; Charles de Visscher, 'Stages in the Codification of International Law' in Wolfgang Friedmann, Louis Henkin, and Oliver Lissitzyn (eds), *Transnational law in a changing society: essays in honor of Philip C. Jessup* (Columbia University Press 1972) 19-21; James Leslie Brierly, 'The Future of Codification' (1931) 12 BYIL 1 ff.; Crawford, 'The Progressive Development of International Law: History, Theory and Practice' 8-9.
11 Cf. Brierly, 'The Future of Codification' 1 ff., in particular 3-4, 7-8; Manley O Hudson, 'The Prospect for Future Codification' (1932) 26 AJIL 137 ff.; Jennings, 'The Progressive Development of International Law and Its Codification' 301-310.
12 Rosenne, 'The International Law Commission, 1949-59' 111.
13 UNGA Res 94 (I) (11 December 1946) UN Doc A/RES/94(I); *Survey of International Law in Relation to the Work of Codification of the International Law Commission: Preparatory work within the purview of article 18, paragraph 1, of the International*

1947[14], the General Assembly decided to establish the International Law Commission as subsidiary organ, rather than many specialized organs for different fields of international law.[15] As article 8 of the ILC Statute indicates, the ILC is intended to represent "the main forms of civilization and of the principal legal systems of the world".[16]

The ILC Statute sharply distinguishes between progressive development and codification[17] and suggests different formats for each. According to article 15 of the ILC Statute, "the expression 'progressive development of international law' is used for convenience as meaning the preparation of draft conventions on subjects which have not yet been regulated by international law or in regard to which the law has not yet been sufficiently developed in the practice of States." Codification is understood as "the more precise formulation and systematization of rules of international law in fields where there already had been extensive state practice, precedent and doctrine" (article 15 ILC Statute), here the ILC Statute envisions the use of draft articles that would be submitted to the General Assembly (article 20 ILC Statute).

Yet, from the very beginning, it was clear that this distinction, while being important for the sake of analytical clarity, can be challenging to make in practice. It has been pointed out that codification was not a simple recording of existing law, but an exercise in which old practices were evaluated and

---

Law Commission Memorandum submitted by the Secretary-General (10 February 1949) A/CN.4/1/Rev.1 3.
14 UNGA Res 174 (II) (21 November 1947) UN Doc A/RES/174(II).
15 General Assembly resolution 174 (II) of 21 November 1947; Herbert Whittaker Briggs, *The international Law Commission* (Cornell University Press 1965) 3 ff.; 'Report of the Committee on the Progressive Development of International Law and its Codification on the Methods for Encouraging the Progressive Development of International Law and its Eventual Codification, UN Doc. A/AC.10/51, 17 June 1947' (1947) 41 Supplement AJIL 18.
16 The Statute was annexed to UNGA Res 174 (II) (21 November 1947) UN Doc A/RES/174(II).
17 For a detailed drafting history see Crawford, 'The Progressive Development of International Law: History, Theory and Practice' 11-15: on the discussion within the ILC see *ILC Ybk (1951 vol 2)* 137-139. According to Crawford, 'The Progressive Development of International Law: History, Theory and Practice' 22, the emphasis on this distinction "was the compromised product of the confrontation between Western and Eastern blocs current at the time."

dismissed, when they had been regarded unbeneficial for the further course of the law.[18]

As argued by James Leslie Brierly, in his capacity as Special Rapporteur of the Committee on the Progressive Development of International Law and its Codification of 12 May - 17 June 1947, codification would involve not only the decision to deselect certain practices, but also the filling of gaps:

> "As soon as you set out to do this, you discover that the existing law often uncertain, and that for one reason or another there are gaps in it which are not covered. [...] Hence, the codifier, if he is competent for his work, will make suggestions of his own; where the rule is uncertain, he will suggest which is the better view; where a gap exists, he will suggest how it can best be filled. If he makes it clear what he is doing, tabulates the existing authorities, fairly examines the arguments pro and con, he will be doing his work properly. But it is true that in this aspect of his work he will be suggesting legislation - he will be working on the *lex ferenda*, not the *lex lata* - he will be extending the law and not merely stating the law that already exists."[19]

In this sense, Robert Yewdall Jennings suggested that "codification, properly conceived, is itself a method for the progressive development of the law."[20]

---

18 Cf. Carl Ludwig von Bar, 'Grundlage und Kodifikation des Völkerrechts' (1912) 6(1) Archiv für Rechts- und Wirtschaftsphilosophie 158 ("Jede [...] völkerrechtliche Norm, jedes völkerrechtliche Verhalten muss der Prüfung unterworfen sein, ob bei allgemeiner Anwendung, Beobachtung, die gedeihliche Existenz und Fortentwicklung der Menschheit nicht nur möglich, sondern wahrscheinlich ist [...]"); cf. PJ Baker, 'The Codification of International Law' (1924) 5 BYIL 44 ("[Codification] is to improve the form of the law by getting rid of apparent ambiguities or conflicts, by bringing customary law and statutory law together into one coherent and consistent whole [...]"); Hersch Lauterpacht, 'Codification and Development of International Law' (1955) 49 AJIL 29 ("Even within that very limited field where there is both agreement and considerable practice, the work of codification cannot discard a limine the legislative function of developing and improving the law."); James Crawford, 'Multilateral Rights and Obligations in International Law' (2006) 319 RdC 453 ("'Codifying' the law means stating what it is to be rather than - or at least as much as - stating what it has been."); Fernando Lusa Bordin, 'Reflections of Customary International Law: The Authority of Codification Conventions and ILC Draft Articles in International Law' (2014) 63 ICLQ 554.

19 Cited according to *Survey of International Law in Relation to the Work of Codification of the International Law Commission: Preparatory work within the purview of article 18, paragraph 1, of the International Law Commission* 3 (with reference to A/AC.10/30, pp. 2-3).

20 Jennings, 'The Progressive Development of International Law and Its Codification' 302; cf. on the resulting difficulty to distinguish lex lata and lex ferenda Michel Virally, 'À propos de la "lex ferenda"' in *Mélanges offerts à Paul Reuter: le droit international:*

Several examples of the Commission's own practice illustrate the difficulty of always clearly distinguishing both elements.[21] In 1956, the ILC acknowledged in the context of draft articles concerning the law of the sea that "the Commission has become convinced that, in this domain at any rate, the distinction established in the statute between these two activities can hardly be maintained [...] Although [the Commission] tried at first to specify which articles fell into one and which into the other category, the Commission has had to abandon the attempt, as several do not wholly belong to either."[22] In the context of the work on state responsibility the Commission noted that "the relative importance of progressive development and of the codification of accepted principles cannot be settled according to any pre-established plan. It must emerge in practical form from the pragmatic solutions adopted to the various problems."[23] In 1996, the Commission even concluded that "[t]he distinction between codification and progressive development is difficult if not impossible to draw in practice; the Commission has proceeded on the basis of a composite idea of codification and progressive development. Distinctions drawn in its statute between the two processes have proved unworkable and could be eliminated in any review of the statute [...]".[24]

However, the distinction between codification and progressive development cannot, and should not, be neglected altogether.[25] The ILC itself continues to make the distinction[26] and also the International Court of Justice demonstrated that it could examine whether a certain rule, such as article

---

unité et diversité (Pedone 1981) 521-523; Philippe Manin, 'Le juge international et la règle générale' [1976] RGDIP 35.
21 Rosenne, 'The International Law Commission, 1949-59' 142 ("[...] the formal differentiation established in the Statute has been blurred [...]").
22 *ILC Ybk (1956 vol 2)* 255-256.
23 *ILC Ybk (1974 vol 2 part 1)* 276 para 122.
24 *ILC Ybk (1996 vol 2 part 2)* 84.
25 See also Bordin, 'Reflections of Customary International Law: The Authority of Codification Conventions and ILC Draft Articles in International Law' 556.
26 *ILC Ybk (2001 vol 2 part 2)* 114, 127 (draft articles on state responsibility); *ILC Ybk (2006 vol 2 part 2)* 36, 48, 83 (draft articles on diplomatic protection); *Report of the International Law Commission: Sixty-sixth session (5 May–6 June and 7 July–8 August 2014)* UN Doc A/69/10 17-18, 76 (draft articles on expulsion of aliens); Bordin, 'Reflections of Customary International Law: The Authority of Codification Conventions and ILC Draft Articles in International Law' 556; see recently Nikolaos Voulgaris, 'The International Law Commission and Politics: Taking the Science Out of International Law's Progressive Development' (2022) 33(3) EJIL 761 ff., 783.

6 Geneva Convention on the Continental Shelf[27], could be regarded as a codification of already binding customary international law.[28] In particular, it can be argued that with the rise of non-binding instruments as an outcome of the work of the ILC in specific projects, the importance of classifying the work as codification or as progressive development has increased rather than decreased: States had not the opportunity to decide on the rules in the context of a treaty conference, and courts, when resorting to ILC materials, should be informed of whether these materials reflect existing international law.[29]

Whether a specific project of the ILC is rather about the progressive development or about codification can change over the course of this project. Whilst the League of Nations Committee of Experts for the Progressive Codification of International Law had determined which topics were sufficiently "ripe" for codification,[30] codification conferences revealed a high level of disagreement. In 1955, Hersch Lauterpacht pointed to "the absence of agreed law"[31] and noted that "there is very little to codify if by that term is meant no more than giving, in the language of Article 15 of the Statute of the International Law Commission, precision and systematic order to rules of international law in fields 'where there already has been extensive State

---

27 Convention on the Continental Shelf (signed 29 April 1958, entered into force 10 June 1964) 499 UNTS 311.
28 *North Sea Continental Shelf* 33 para 49, 34 para 50, the Court concluded that article 6 did not constitute a codification of already binding customary international law.
29 As Nolte (*Comment by Georg Nolte, Summary record of the 3365th meeting, 30 May 2017* UN Doc A/CN.4/SR.3365 (PROV.) 3) opined, "[when the Commission prepared treaties], it did not make a great difference whether a proposed rule reflected existing customary law or would be new law. The negotiating States would, after all, decide what to include in a treaty and whether to accept the treaty. However, in the context of the current topic, the Commission did not seem to be elaborating a treaty. Any views it expressed on existing law might be used by national and international courts, which needed to know what the existing law was. The Commission therefore needed to be transparent about whether it was stating existing law or proposing new law."
30 League of Nations Committee of Experts for the Progressive Codification of International Law, 'Report to the Council of the League of Nations on the Questions which appear ripe for international regulation' C.196.M.70.1927.V., printed in (1928) 22 AJIL Supp 4; Jennings, 'The Progressive Development of International Law and Its Codification' 324; Arthur Watts, *The International Law Commission 1949-1998: The Treaties* (vol 1, Oxford University Press 1999) 3; see on the notion of "ripeness" also Julius Stone, 'On the Vocation of the International Law Commission' (1957) 57(1) Columbia Law Review 35-38.
31 Lauterpacht, 'Codification and Development of International Law' 17, 23.

practice, precedent and doctrine.'"³² One purpose of the codification activity can consist very much in bringing about agreement on substance, rather than presupposing such agreement to exist from the very start.³³

The work of the ILC in relation to the law of the sea is an example of growing agreement over the course of a project. The ILC did at the beginning not affirm that the "numerous proclamations", among them the Truman proclamation³⁴, by themselves established custom.³⁵ Over the course of the next years, however, agreement on coastal states' rights regarding the continental shelf began to increase.³⁶

---

32 Lauterpacht, 'Codification and Development of International Law' 17 (referring to the language of article 15 of the ILC Statute.
33 ibid 27; Robert Yewdall Jennings, 'Recent Developments in the International Law Commission: Its Relation to the Sources of International Law' (1964) 13 ICLQ 395, according to whom "the merging of codification into progressive development has meant that the old futile search of the League days for topics 'ripe for codification' has been happily abandoned [...] The simple truth is that there are no topics of international law ripe for codification; they all need working up into something more than a set of vague principles." Certain scholars had reservation about the success of codification against the background of the ideological differences in the cold war: cf. Charles de Visscher, *Theory and reality in public international law* (Percy Ellwood Corbett tr, Princeton University Press 1957) 147; on the skeptical Soviet scholarship after the second world war see Rosenne, 'The International Law Commission, 1949-59' 155-157; Crawford, 'The Progressive Development of International Law: History, Theory and Practice' 16-17.
34 United States of America, *Proclamation 2667 of September 28, 1945. Policy of the United States with respect to the natural resources of the subsoil and sea bed of the continental shelf*, 10 Fed. Reg. 12.305 (1945).
35 *ILC Ybk (1951 vol 2)* 142: "Though numerous proclamations have been issued over the past decade, it can hardly be said that such unilateral action has already established a new customary law. It is sufficient to say that the principle of the continental shelf is based upon general principles of law which serve the present-day needs of the international community." When justifying the Commission's decision to address the law of the sea, Yepes argued that the Truman "Proclamation and those measures could be considered, if not as a veritable customary law in the sense already given to that expression by the Commission, at least as an embryonic customary law. [...] There was, as the Commission had decided, no need at all for the practice to date back a long time. It was sufficient for States to recognize it as constituting law and for it to have aroused no protests from other States.", *ILC Ybk (1950 vol 1)* 216-217.
36 The agreement is expressed, for instance in the adoption of the Convention on the Continental Shelf (signed 29 April 1958, entered into force 10 June 1964) 499 UNTS 311.

Introduction

III. The significance of the normative environment

Once it has been recognized that codification requires the filling of gaps the question arises of how to fill these gaps. Here, legal-political judgment and discretion may play a role; the practice of the Commission indicates that general principles of the international legal order were taken into account as well. This section will first illustrate how the Commission discussed at its very beginning how its work on progressive development and codification would relate to the UN Charter (1.) and that principles expressed in treaties were taken into consideration (2.). The section will finally comment on a recent example, the discussion of immunity before foreign courts, which raised the question of how to reconcile state practice and normative considerations (3.).

1. The "blending of customary international law with the new order established by the United Nations"

It is helpful to look at how the ILC constructed the interrelationship of sources at the beginning of its work, when the Commission's institutional practice began to develop. The question of the relationship between customary international law and the UN Charter arose in the context of the Draft Declaration on Rights and Duties of States.

In 1948, Panama submitted to the UN General Assembly a draft declaration on the rights and duties of states. Article 20 of the Draft Declaration provided that "[i]t is the duty of *every State* to take, in cooperation with other States, the measures prescribed by the competent organs of the Community of States in order to prevent or put down the use of force by a State in its relations with another State, or in the general interests."[37]

After Greece, the United Kingdom and the United States of America had expressed their concerns that the declaration's claim to spell out the duty "of every State" was not compatible with the *pacta tertiis* rule, according to which only parties to the Charter were bound by the Charter,[38] the International

---

37 Preparatory Study Concerning A Draft Declaration on the rights and Duties of States (Memorandum submitted by the Secretary-General) (15 December 1948) UN Doc A/CN.4/2 at 38 (italics added).
38 See Talmon, 'Article 2 (6)' 260 para 22.

Chapter 6: The International Law Commission

Law Commission took the issue under consideration.[39] In the context of the plenary discussion Alfrado argued that

> "the Commission should find a text which would indicate the blending of customary international law with the new order established by the United Nations through its Charter, the Universal Declaration of Human Rights etc."[40]

Other members were reluctant to declare the Charter to constitute already general international law. Brierly, for instance, opposed a suggestion to that effect since the Charter "did not constitute all the common law of nations"[41]. The Commission eventually agreed on the preamble according to which "it is [...] desirable to formulate certain basic rights and duties of States *in the light of new developments of international law and in harmony with the Charter of the United Nations*".[42]

This legal-political compromise through which the Commission attempted to accommodate the normative ambition of the UN Charter with the traditional sources doctrine would go at the expense of legal clarity, Hans Kelsen argued in a critical note. In particular, Kelsen considered the phrase "In the light of new developments of international law and in harmony with the Charter of the United Nations" to be "highly ambiguous"[43]:

> "If the 'new developments' did not lead to a new general international law, the rights and duties established by the old and still existing law cannot be formulated 'in the light' of these new developments; and if the new developments lead to a new general international law, the rights and duties must be formulated in accordance with the new law, not merely 'in the light' of the developments. If the Charter does constitute general international law, [...] [the formulation of the rights and duties]

---

39 *ILC Ybk* (1949) 161.
40 ibid 159. Kerno, Assistant Secretary-General, observed that "general international law included primarily customary international law, but it also included conventional law, of which the United Nations Charter formed an important part." (135-136): "The Charter set forth a body of international law which had been accepted by 59 States and all other States in the world had indicated their willingness to abide by it, with the exception of traditionally neutral Switzerland and of Franco Spain which was precluded from admission to membership in the United Nations in consequence of resolutions of the General Assembly. The Principles of the Charter were certainly as broadly accepted as those of customary international law." His concern was that the draft declaration did not reflect the special position of the Charter.
41 ibid 159.
42 ibid 159, and UNGA Res 375 (IV) (6 December 1949) UN Doc A/RES/375(IV), italics added.
43 Hans Kelsen, 'The Draft Declaration on Rights and Duties of States Critical Remarks' (1950) 44 AJIL 263.

must be identical with that in the Charter, and it is not sufficient to formulate them 'in harmony' with the Charter. If, however, the Charter does not constitute general international law, rights and duties of Members of the United Nations which are not established by general international law must not be inserted in the Declaration; and rights and duties of Members which are established by general international law must be formulated in accordance with general international law, not in harmony with the Charter [...]."[44]

Kelsen criticized the Commission for not taking a clear position on the interpretation of article 2(6) and on the question whether the Charter, as a treaty, imposes obligations on non-member states.[45]

In contrast to the categorical alternatives which Hans Kelsen put to his readers, the compromise which the Commission had adopted suggested a more gradual development in which the legal evaluations and principles of the Charter would slowly pervade the corpus of international law. The draft declaration of the rights and duties of states itself was not very influential, as the General Assembly ultimately abandoned the work on this topic.[46] The described gradual development, however, became characteristic of the Commission's work which has been shaped by an effort to consider the legal evaluations and principles of modern international law in the progressive development and codification of customary international law.

2. The early consideration of principles expressed in treaties

Further examples from the beginning illustrate that a "blending" of customary international law with international legal order as a whole and the values expressed therein took place in the Commission's work. The Commission took account of principles in order to fill gaps and exercise its discretion inherent in progressive development and codification, as, for instance, the

---

44 ibid 263.
45 ibid 263: "The texts of Articles 6, 8, 9, 10 and 12 of the Declaration seem to indicate that it presupposes that the Charter establishes general international law. However, other provisions, and especially the fact that the obligations to give the United Nations assistance in its action established by Article 2 (5) of the Charter, is intentionally not formulated as a duty of all states (although under Article 2 (6) of the Charter it could be considered to be an obligation of non-members), allow the contrary assumption." See also chapter 3, p. 200.
46 Sergio Carbone and Lorenzo Schiano di Pepe, 'States, Fundamental Rights and Duties' [2009] Max Planck EPIL para 14.

Chapter 6: The International Law Commission

early work on consular intercourse and immunities and on slave trade in the law of the sea illustrates.

In the context of the work on consular intercourse and immunities, Special Rapporteur Jaroslav Zourek sought to "find formulae which, while representative of customary international law, at the same time would generalize the provisions of the numerous treaties".[47] Reliance solely on custom would "inevitably give an air of incompleteness [...] [Also codifying the principles generally observed by international conventions] would permit the preparation of a much more complete scheme of codification and would have the advantage of generalizing the application of principles derived from an analysis of international conventions".[48] Several members of the Commission agreed with the approach to "deduce principles likely to be accepted by all States by examining international treaties"[49] in order to complete the analysis of customary international law.[50]

An illuminating example of value judgments informed of the normative environment is the slave trade exception to the freedom of the High Seas. Special Rapporteur François was requested by the Commission "to study treaty regulations in this field with a view to deriving therefrom a general principle applicable to all vessels which might engage in slave trade".[51] He then suggested a draft provision according to which a foreign merchant ship must not be boarded unless there was substantive reason to believe that said ship engaged in piracy or unless a treaty provides otherwise.[52] The Commission had a debate on whether there would be also a right to approach a merchant vessel if there was reasonable ground that the ship was engaged in slave trade. Until then, article 3(1) of the 1926 Slavery Convention obliged states "to adopt all appropriate measures with a view to preventing and suppressing the embarkation, disembarkation and transport of slaves *in their territorial waters* and upon all vessels flying their respective flags."[53]

---

47 *ILC Ybk (1956 vol 1)* 249.
48 ibid 250.
49 ibid 250 (Amado).
50 ibid 250 (Spiropolous): "It should not be a codification of existing rules, for there were very few, but rather the deduction of certain rules from the existing conventions." See also Fitzmaurice, 250.
51 *ILC Ybk (1951 vol 1)* 351.
52 *Second Report on the Regime of the High Seas by J P A François, Special Rapporteur* 10 April 1951 UN Doc A/CN.4/42 83 para 43 in *ILC Ybk (1951 vol 2)*.
53 Slavery Convention (signed 25 September 1926, entered into force 9 March 1927) 60 LNTS 254, italics added.

Introduction

The convention thus addressed only the territorial sea, as opposed to the high seas.[54] The debate in the Commission concerned the question of whether this principle should be extended beyond territorial waters, to the effect that slavery would be treated like piracy and therefore justify the boarding of a foreign vessel.[55] Special Rapporteur François argued that "States were not prepared to go nearly so far in the case of the slave trade as in the case of piracy"[56] and that any such right to approach in case of slavery should be limited to a special maritime zone.[57] Manley Hudson, however, was against a restriction to a particular zone and referred to "the many conventions"[58] and to "the several hundred treaties"[59] on slave trade: "In view of the attitude of world opinion to slavery [...] it should be laid down as a principle that the high seas might not be used by vessels of any State for the transport of slaves."[60] Hudson also pointed out that "France, which had been the major objector in the past, now favoured such a provision."[61] Whereas Hudson also referred to the Universal Declaration of Human Rights[62], other members, namely Jean Pierre Adrien François and Jean Spiropoulus argued that the prohibition of slave trade "was one thing, to recognize the right to stop the suspected vessel was another."[63] In the end, the Commission voted in favour of Hudson's proposal,[64] the substance of which can also be found in article 22(1) (b) of the Geneva Convention on the High Seas[65] and article 110(1)(b) UNCLOS[66].

---

54 *ILC Ybk (1951 vol 1)* 352 (Alfaro).
55 Cf. ibid 350 (Cordova).
56 ibid 350.
57 ibid 351.
58 ibid 351.
59 ibid 352.
60 ibid 351, 252 (Sandström).
61 ibid 353; contra François at 351.
62 ibid 353; see also at 352: Kerno, Assistant Secretary-General, referred to the *ad hoc* committee on slavery which was established by the ECOSOC and according to which the principle of the prohibition of slavery "was considerably more far-reaching in its implications than that which inspired the League of Nations to formulate the 1926 Slavery Convention."
63 ibid 353 (quote: François).
64 ibid 354.
65 Convention on the High Seas (signed 29 April 1958, entered into force 30 September 1962) 450 UNTS 11.
66 United Nations Convention on the Law of the Sea (signed 10 December 1982, entered into force 16 November 1994) 1833 UNTS 3.

The discussion indicated that the identification and the codification of customary international law are not confined to recollecting single instances of state practice. Principles expressed in treaties, such as the prohibition of slavery, can inform this process and shift the argumentative burden. In case of a sufficient clear conviction of the international community, the question then turned to whether significant opposition of states would still exist.

3. Reconciling the normative environment and state practice: The recent controversy over immunity of State officials from foreign criminal jurisdiction

The recent discussion in the context of the work on immunity of State officials from foreign criminal jurisdiction illustrates the challenges in evaluating the practice of states and considering the systemic relationship between rules of customary international law on immunity and international crimes, *jus cogens* and the fight against impunity.[67]

The International Law Commission began its work on immunity of State officials from foreign criminal jurisdiction in 2007. It is useful to take the broader context into account. The ICJ addressed different aspects of immunity under customary international law in its recent case-law. In 2002, the ICJ decided in the *Arrest Warrant* case that an acting Minister for Foreign Affairs enjoyed immunity *ratione personae* even when being accused of crimes constituting grave violations of international humanitarian law. The Court pointed out, however, that immunities may not constitute "a bar to criminal prosecution in certain circumstances": immunities do not apply when the individual is tried in his home state, they will not apply in a foreign state if the home state "decides to waive that immunity", they will no longer apply after the person concerned ceased to hold office, at least "in respect of acts committed prior or subsequent to his or her period of office, as well as in respect of acts committed during that period of office in a private capacity".[68] The Court also added that "an incumbent or former Minister for Foreign Affairs may be subject to criminal proceedings before certain

---

67 Cf. *Fifth report on immunity of State officials from foreign criminal jurisdiction, by Concepción Escobar Hernández, Special Rapporteur* 14 June 2016 UN Doc A/CN.4/701 paras 190-217; *ILC Report 2017* at 181.
68 *Arrest Warrant of 11 April 2000* [2002] ICJ Rep 3, 25 para 61.

Introduction

international criminal courts, where they have jurisdiction."[69] In 2008, the ICJ held that functional immunities, or immunity *ratione materiae*, from which functionaries of a state may benefit, belonged to the State[70] and that is for that state to invoke immunity as a challenge to a foreign court's jurisdiction: "The State which seeks to claim immunity for one of its State organs is expected to notify the authorities of the other State concerned."[71] In 2012, the ICJ characterized state immunity as a procedural rule which does not operate on the same level as substantive law. The Court stressed that "the question of whether, and if so, to what extent, immunity might apply in criminal proceedings against an official of the State is not in issue in the present case."[72]

The discussion that took place in 2017 concerned draft article 7 which stipulates the inapplicability of immunity *ratione materiae* in respect to crimes under international law, namely genocide, crimes against humanity, war crimes, the crime of apartheid, torture and enforced disappearance.[73] According to the Special Rapporteur, the draft article uses the phrase "shall not apply" instead of the terms "exception" or "limitation", because "the distinction between limitations and exceptions [...] had been controversial in normative terms."[74] The draft article was controversial within the Commission[75]: it was necessary to have an indicative vote in order to send the draft article to the Drafting Committee. The draft article then was adopted by ma-

---

69 ibid 25 para 61.
70 *Certain Questions of Mutual Assistance in Criminal Matters* [2008] ICJ Rep 177, 242 para 188.
71 ibid 244 para 196.
72 *Jurisdictional Immunities of the State* [2012] ICJ Rep 99, 139 para 91.
73 *ILC Report 2017* at 176; see also *ILC Report 2022* at 228.
74 *Fifth report on immunity of State officials from foreign criminal jurisdiction, by Concepción Escobar Hernández, Special Rapporteur* para 244; Dire Tladi, 'The International Law Commission's Recent Work on Exceptions to Immunity: Charting the Course for a brave new world in international law?' (2019) 32 Leiden Journal of International Law 175; see now *ILC Report 2022* at 237 (the Commission explained that it preferred the phrase "shall not apply" over the phrase "cannot be invoked" because of the "procedural component of that phrase").
75 For an overview of the ILC's work and in particular the voting on draft article 7, see Tladi, 'The International Law Commission's Recent Work on Exceptions to Immunity: Charting the Course for a brave new world in international law?' 170 ff.; Hervé Ascensio and Béatrice I Bonafé, 'L'absence d'immunité des agents de l'Etat en cas de crime international : pourquoi en débattre encore?' (2018) 122 RGDIP 821-824. On draft article 7 see also Curtis A Bradley, 'Introduction to the Symposium on the Present and Future of Foreign Official Immunity' (2018) 112 AJIL Unbound 1

jority, with 21 members voting in favour of the article, whilst eight members voted against, with one member abstaining.[76] The controversy concerned the question of whether article 7 reflected the *lex lata* and could therefore be regarded to be a codification of customary international law or whether it was more of a progressive development or even a proposal for new law.[77] In 2022, the Commission adopted the draft articles and the commentary on first reading, draft article 7 was adopted without a vote; as summarized in the ILC report, several members "stated that the fact that no vote had taken place in 2022 did not mean that either the law of their legal position had in any way changed".[78]

The disagreement over draft article 7 can be explained by different interpretative choices which proponents and critics of the principle expressed in draft article 7 inside and outside the ILC made in relation to the identification of customary international law.[79] For instance, opinions differed on whether and to what extent civil law proceedings should be included when examining the practice of domestic courts[80] and on whether statutes which served the

---

ff. Cf. Rosanne van Alebeek, 'The "International Crime" Exception in the ILC Draft Articles on the Immunity of State Officials from Foreign Criminal Jurisdiction: Two Steps Back?' (2018) 112 AJIL Unbound 27-32, arguing that over the course of the project the consensus in favour of recognizing international crimes limitations to immunity decreased.

76 See Tladi, 'The International Law Commission's Recent Work on Exceptions to Immunity: Charting the Course for a brave new world in international law?' 171. For individual explanations of the votes see *Provisional summary record of the 3378th meeting, 20 July 2017* UN Doc A/CN.4/SR.3378 (PROV.) 9-16.

77 *ILC Report 2017* at 169-170; cf. Tladi, 'The International Law Commission's Recent Work on Exceptions to Immunity: Charting the Course for a brave new world in international law?' 172; 179; Sean D Murphy, 'Immunity Ratione Materiae of State Officials from Foreign Criminal Jurisdiction: Where is the State Practice in Support of Exceptions?' (2018) 112 AJIL Unbound 8 ("Draft Article 7 is not grounded in law, but in policy-making by the Commission."); see now for a summary of the debate *ILC Report 2022* at 231 ff.

78 ibid 189, 230 (quote).

79 On interpretative choices in the selection of cases see the chart in Ingrid Brunk Wuerth, 'Pinochet's Legacy Reassessed' (2012) 106(4) AJIL 746-747; for an overview of many relevant decisions of domestic courts see Rosanne van Alebeek, 'Functional Immunity of State Officials from the Criminal Jurisdiction of Foreign National Courts' in Tom Ruys, Nicolas Angelet, and Luca Ferro (eds), *The Cambridge Handbook of Immunities and International Law* (Cambridge University Press 2019) 509-517.

80 See Tladi, 'The International Law Commission's Recent Work on Exceptions to Immunity: Charting the Course for a brave new world in international law?' 175-7; *Fifth*

Introduction

domestic implementation of the Rome Statute were confined to the Rome Statute or could also be considered for the purpose of identifying customary international law.[81]

Additionally, the recourse to past practice proved to be controversial. To name a few examples for the purposes of illustration: Should the practice of the IMT and other international tribunals be counted or should they be discounted when examining the practice of foreign domestic courts?[82] Are the cases before the military tribunals in Germany or before domestic courts in other jurisdictions after World War II of less relevance because Germany did not invoke immunity or is the very idea that immunities *ratione materiae* must be invoked by a state based on a misreading of the ICJ's *Mutual Assistance in Criminal Matters* case?[83] What is the legal value of the *Blaškić* decision, in which the Appeals Chamber held that "those responsible for such

---

report on immunity of State officials from foreign criminal jurisdiction, by Concepción Escobar Hernández, Special Rapporteur paras 114-121; Comment by Sean Murphy, Summary record of the 3362nd meeting, 23 May 2017 UN Doc A/CN.4/SR.3362 (PROV.) 5; Comment by Roman A Kolodkin, Summary record of the 3361st meeting, 19 May 2017 UN Doc A/CN.4/SR.3361 (PROV.) 7; critical: Quinmin Shen, 'Methodological Flaws in the ILC's Study on Exceptions to Immunity Ratione Materiae of State Officials from Foreign Criminal Jurisidction' (2018) 112 AJIL Unbound 12.

81 Tladi, 'The International Law Commission's Recent Work on Exceptions to Immunity: Charting the Course for a brave new world in international law?' 177.

82 See ibid 182; Wuerth, 'Pinochet's Legacy Reassessed' 741, 763: "The willingness of some states to lift *ratione personae* immunity before certain international criminal tribunals has not extended to foreign national courts. [...] Germany, after its unconditional surrender, was under four-party occupation and in no position to assert immunity."

83 In favour of the invocation-requirement ibid 745-756; but see Claus Kreß, 'Article 98' in Kai Ambos (ed), *The Rome Statute of the International Criminal Court* (4th edn, Beck 2021) para 36, arguing, *inter alia*, that the legitimate interests of the state official "will be more safely protected" if immunity must be observed regardless of invocation and that such requirement would not be supported by a general practice accepted as law, and para 62, arguing that Article II(4)(a) and not the absence of a German claim of immunity led to the irrelevance of official capacity which, according to a reading of the *Nuremberg* Judgment had been understood "to be indistinguishable from the inapplicability of functional immunity"; also skeptical of the invocation requirement: Aziz Epik, 'No Functional Immunity for Crimes under International Law before Foreign Domestic Courts' (2021) 19 JICJ 1273 with reference to *Judgment of 28 January 2021* Bundesgerichtshof 3 StR 564/19; see on the practice of domestic courts also Tladi, 'The International Law Commission's Recent Work on Exceptions to Immunity: Charting the Course for a brave new world in international law?' 183.

333

crimes cannot invoke immunity from national or international jurisdiction even if they perpetrated such crimes while acting in their official capacity"[84], considering that the decision actually concerned only the ability of the ICTY to subpoena state officials,[85] which would make the part of the statement on national jurisdiction an *obiter dictum*? What is the value of the *Pinochet* case where "three of the Opinions specifically raised the *jus cogens* nature of the crime as a basis for the non-applicability of immunity"[86], but which arguably ultimately concerned the CAT and therefore a treaty-based exception to immunity?[87] What is the value of the *Bouterse* case where the Amsterdam Court of Appeal held that a former head of state is not protected by immunity *ratione materiae* in respect of torture and crimes against humanity, considering that the Dutch Supreme Court overturned the result on the basis of lack of jurisdiction without, however, commenting on immunity?[88]

Depending on how one answers these questions, one tends to agree or disagree with the statement that "in 1990 it was long established that functional immunity under CIL is inapplicable to crimes under CIL"[89]. And if one agrees that the recent practice is unclear and may be interpreted as a

---

84 *Prosecutor v Blaskić* ICTY AC Judgement on the Request of the Republic of Croatia for Review of the Decision of Trial Chamber II of 18 July 1997 (29 October 1997) IT-95-14-AR10 para 41.
85 *Comment by Sean Murphy, Summary record of the 3362nd meeting, 23 May 2017* at 5.
86 Tladi, 'The International Law Commission's Recent Work on Exceptions to Immunity: Charting the Course for a brave new world in international law?' 184.
87 For this argument see for instance Shen, 'Methodological Flaws in the ILC's Study on Exceptions to Immunity Ratione Materiae of State Officials from Foreign Criminal Jurisidction' 11.
88 Cf. Liesbeth Zegveld, 'The Bouterse Case' (2001) 32 Netherlands Yearbook of International Law 113: "The decision of the Amsterdam Court of Appeal on this matter was thus left intact."; cf. Tladi, 'The International Law Commission's Recent Work on Exceptions to Immunity: Charting the Course for a brave new world in international law?' 184: "The Court's consideration of whether the laws could be applied retrospectively itself indicates the non-applicability of immunity. [...] What is at issue is whether the Court exercised its jurisdiction, and, in the case of *Bouterse*, it clearly did but found that there were no grounds for prosecution because the law could not be applied retroactively." But see Wuerth, 'Pinochet's Legacy Reassessed' 758.
89 Kreß, 'Article 98' para 65.

trend in favour of[90] or as a countertrend[91] against draft article 7, the question of what constitutes the default position will become more important. In other words: is the default position the continuing availability of immunity[92] (when being invoked?) or is the default position that there is no immunity in respect of crimes? In the latter case, one would have to examine whether the recent practice has sufficiently established a new rule of customary international law recognizing immunity.

If one understands immunity in relation to officials of a state as a procedural rule, direct conflicts with rules of *jus cogens* character which operate on a different level than the procedural rule of immunity will not be likely.[93] Yet, the character as a procedural rule arguably does not completely preclude considerations of substantive nature.[94] The interpreter arguably can factor in normative considerations relating to the *telos*, the rationale and the scope

---

90 *Fifth report on immunity of State officials from foreign criminal jurisdiction, by Concepción Escobar Hernández, Special Rapporteur* paras 121, 179, 188; but see Roger O'Keefe, 'An "International Crime Exception" to the Immunity of State Officials from Foreign Criminal Jurisdiction: Not Currently, not Likely' (2015) 109 AJIL Unbound 167 ff.

91 See *Comment by Sean Murphy, Summary record of the 3362nd meeting, 23 May 2017* at 4: "In fact, some evidence actually seemed to suggest the lack of a trend, for example in recent cases brought before the International Court of Justice and the European Court of Human Rights, or perhaps even a countertrend, as illustrated by a recent narrowing of the scope of some national laws."

92 Cf. Ascensio and Bonafé, 'L'absence d'immunité des agents de l'Etat en cas de crime international : pourquoi en débattre encore?' 825-832 (critical with respect to the rule-exception scheme where immunity would be the rule); Micaela Frulli, 'On the existence of a customary rule granting functional immunity to State officials and its exceptions: back to square one' (2016) 26 Duke Journal of Comparative & International Law 481 ff. (expressing doubts as to the existence of a general rule of immunity), 498: "There is no need to find an exception to a general rule. Instead, existing rules suffice to justify the prosecution of state officials suspected of having committed international crimes."

93 Cf. with respect to state immunity *Jurisdictional Immunities of the State* [2012] ICJ Rep 99, 136 para 82, 140 para 93.

94 *Fifth report on immunity of State officials from foreign criminal jurisdiction, by Concepción Escobar Hernández, Special Rapporteur* 64-65 para 150; Kreß, 'Article 98' para 35; critical towards the classification as a procedural rule and the distinction between substantive and procedural rules Ascensio and Bonafé, 'L'absence d'immunité des agents de l'Etat en cas de crime international : pourquoi en débattre encore?' 833-840.

Chapter 6: The International Law Commission

of the respective rules[95] and other concepts when evaluating the international practice. However, these normative considerations and the evaluation of practice are best considered as being in a dialectical relationship[96] and should not be considered unrelated from each other. For instance, the Special Rapporteur Escobar Hernández, after having concluded that "the commission of international crimes may indeed be considered a limitation or exception to State immunity from foreign criminal jurisdiction based on a norm of international law"[97], offered additional arguments in order to responds to doubts as to the analysis of customary international law. She argued:

> "Whether or not there is a customary norm defining international crimes as limitations or exceptions to immunity, a systemic analysis of the relationship between immunity and international crimes in contemporary international law shows that there are various arguments in favour of such a norm."[98]

The "arguments" to which she referred included the protection of the values of the international community, *jus cogens*, the fight against impunity, access to justice and the right of victims to reparation as well as the obligation to prosecute international crimes.[99] As has been rightly pointed out, however, these conceptual considerations neither were used in order to interpret international practice nor were interpreted under consideration of international practice, they were used as additional arguments or grounds for that immunity *ratione materiae* does not apply in relation to specific crimes.[100] Additional

---

95 Cf. Alebeek, 'Functional Immunity of State Officials from the Criminal Jurisdiction of Foreign National Courts' 501, addressing the scope of immunity: "A limitation to the rule may be established without proof of a widespread and consistent State practice."
96 Cf. Ascensio and Bonafé, 'L'absence d'immunité des agents de l'Etat en cas de crime international : pourquoi en débattre encore?' 828.
97 *Fifth report on immunity of State officials from foreign criminal jurisdiction, by Concepción Escobar Hernández, Special Rapporteur* para 189.
98 ibid para 190.
99 ibid paras 191-217 (concluding that "there are sufficient grounds in contemporary international law to conclude that the commission of international crimes may constitute a limitation or exception to the immunity of State officials from foreign criminal jurisdiction").
100 See Alebeek, 'Functional Immunity of State Officials from the Criminal Jurisdiction of Foreign National Courts' 518; for the view that one must examine practice in order to analyze the balance struck between competing principles see *Comment by Georg Nolte, Summary record of the 3365th meeting, 30 May 2017* at 3: "There was no easy answer but the balance between two fundamental principles must ultimately be determined by the rules of customary international law."

considerations which were raised by members of the Commission, for instance, the possibility of abuse of the draft article by "enabling politically motivated trials" which "could weaken stability in international relations and run counter to the cause of fighting impunity and promoting human rights"[101], should be taken into account as well.[102]

An interesting solution to the problem of reconciling the competing considerations, taking into account the lack of unanimity within the Commission, was a proposal which resembled the *aut dedere aut judicare* obligation under the CAT. The proposal's starting point is a general obligation under customary international law to prosecute international core crimes. The state of the official must waive the immunity from which the official benefit for a proceeding before a foreign domestic court or prosecute itself (*waive or prosecute*).[103] The proposal seeks to overcome the dissent by returning to a more general obligation to prosecute, over which there is more agreement. When it comes to the obligation's implementation, the state of the official concerned would have a choice between either prosecuting or waiving immunity.[104]

The Commission did not take up this proposal when it recently adopted on first reading the draft articles and the corresponding commentary. Instead, both positions are contrasted and spelled out in detail. The commentary on draft article 7 explains the reasons for including this draft, namely "a

---

101 *ILC Report 2017* at 170.
102 Cf. ibid 181 where the commentary to draft article 7 states that the international legal order's "unity and systemic nature cannot be ignored", which is why "legal principles enshrined in such important sectors of contemporary international law as international humanitarian law, international human rights law and international criminal law" should not be overlooked and that "the consideration of crimes to which immunity from foreign criminal jurisdiction does not apply must be careful and balanced, taking into account the need to preserve respect for the principle of the sovereign equality of States".
103 *Comment by Georg Nolte, Summary record of the 3365th meeting, 30 May 2017* 6-7, on the different reactions see ibid 7-8; for a positive reception see Kreß, 'Article 98' para 81 (pointing out that the proposal reflects the *lex lata* in that there is an obligation to prosecute and that the exercise of universal jurisdiction is "governed by the principle of subsidiarity"; Mathias Forteau, 'Immunities and International Crimes before the ILC: Looking for Innovative solutions' (2018) 112 AJIL Unbound 25 ("interesting suggestion"); cf. Ascensio and Bonafé, 'L'absence d'immunité des agents de l'Etat en cas de crime international : pourquoi en débattre encore?' 843-4 (interesting proposal which requires further exploration).
104 Cf. *Questions relating to the Obligation to Prosecute or Extradite* [2012] ICJ Rep 422, 456 para 95 on the relationship between the obligation to prosecute under article 7 CAT and extradition as an option.

discernible trend towards limiting the applicability of immunity from jurisdiction *ratione materiae*" in respect to specific crimes [105] and "the fact that the draft articles [...] are intended to apply within an international legal order whose unity and systemic nature cannot be ignored", which would lead to a balancing which takes into account the principle of sovereign equality of states, accountability, individual criminal responsibility and the end of impunity.[106] In contrast, the minority within the Commission advanced a couple of arguments against the draft article: The draft article could not be based on practice or a trend; the availability of immunity as a procedural could not depend on the gravity of the act in question; the practice of international courts could not be relevant for an analysis of immunity before domestic courts; the draft risked undermining inter-state relations and there would be no impunity if the individual concerned was prosecuted before a court in his or her state, before an international court or before a foreign domestic courts, provided that in the latter case the immunity would have been waived.[107]

The draft articles have now been submitted to the governments for comments and observations.[108] It remains to be seen whether the balance between different considerations as suggested by the ILC in draft article 7 will be accepted in international practice and how the international practice will further develop.

B. The form of codification and progressive development and its implications on the interrelationship of sources

This section discusses the form of the products of the ILC and distinguishes between two aspects. Firstly, it will approach what can be called the external

---

105 *ILC Report 2022* at 232.
106 ibid 234.
107 ibid 235-6.
108 ibid 189; see also Murphy, 'Peremptory Norms of General International Law (Jus Cogens) (Revisited) and Other Topics: The Seventy-Third Session of the International Law Commission' 100-103, referring also to *Judgment of 13 January 2021* French Court of Cassation, Criminal Division Appeal No. 20-80.511 para 25 (custom is said to be against the prosecution of State officials) and the German Bundesgerichtshof *Judgment of 28 January 2021* para 16 ff. (no immunity for lower-ranking foreign officials in relation to war crimes).

form (I.)[109]: This concerns the question of whether the respective work was intended to lead to the conclusion of a convention at a diplomatic conference, to constitute an authoritative code stating what customary international law is or to be used as draft convention open for signatures.[110] Subsequently, this section will turn to the substance of the ILC products and examine to what extent they relate to, reaffirm or build on other international law (II.).

I. The form of the ILC product

This section will first address the risk of "decodification" and how it is associated with the question of the form of the ILC's products (1.). It will then illustrate the importance of the spirit of the time in the discussion of the form of the product (2.) and then engage with the discussion about the ILC's turn to nonbinding instruments, which has been characterized as "codification light", and the role of other actors (3.).

---

109 As summarized by Laurence Boisson de Chazournes, 'The International Law Commission in a Mirror - Firms, Impact and Authority' in The United Nations (ed), *Seventy Years of the International Law Commission* (Brill Nijhoff 2020) 136-8, possible forms of the ILC products include draft conventions, draft articles, draft principles, draft guidelines, reports, model rules, draft declarations, resolutions, conclusions.

110 See David Caron, 'The ILC Articles on State Responsibility: The Paradoxical Relationship Between Form and Authority' (2002) 96 AJIL 857 ff. (describing the increasing influence for the Commission by choosing the "weak" form and thus bypassing the influence which states can exert on a codification conference); Sean D Murphy, 'Codification, Progressive Development, or Scholarly Analysis? The Art of Packaging the ILC's Work Product' in Maurizio Ragazzi (ed), *The Responsibility of International Organizations: Essays in Memory of Sir Ian Brownlie* (Martinus Nijhoff Publishers 2013) 29 ff.; Laurence R Helfer and Timothy L Meyer, 'The Evolution of Codification: A Principal-Agent Theory of the International Law Commission's Influence' in Curtis Bradley (ed), *Custom's Future: International Law in a Changing World* (Cambridge University Press 2016) 305 ff. (looking at political dynamics between the General Assembly and the Commission and its impact on the choice of form); Yejoon Rim, 'Reflections on the Role of the International Law Commission in Consideration of the Final Form of Its Work' (2020) 10 Asian Journal of International Law 23 ff.; Luigi Crema, 'The ILC's New Way of Codifying International Law, the Motives Behind It, and the Interpretive Approach Best Suited to It' in Panos Merkouris, Jörg Kammerhofer, and Noora Arajärvi (eds), *The Theory, Practice, and Interpretation of Customary International Law* (Cambridge University Press 2022) 162 ff.

Chapter 6: The International Law Commission

1. The form and the risk of "decodification"

There are risks and promises inherent in the codification of customary international law. A written codification can be more precise than unwritten rules, it can enhance the law's clarity as well as certainty, it can contain detailed procedural regulations. Then again, it binds only parties.[111] Codification, therefore, is also associated with risks. The omission to include an unwritten rule in a codification can be read as indication that said unwritten rule no longer is or never was a binding rule.[112] Furthermore, the failure of a codification convention to attract a significant number of ratification not only can be detrimental to the rules of the codification convention but can also introduce uncertainty as to the state of unwritten law.

A good example is the failure of the 1930 Conference to reach an agreement on the breadth of the territorial waters. The Commission's early discussions of the breadth of the territorial waters illustrate the uncertainty introduced by this failed codification attempt. The ILC was divided on the state of customary international law before and after the 1930 conference as well as on the implications of the 1930 conference. While certain members argued that the three-mile rule was a rule of custom before the 1930 conference but no longer subsequent to it,[113] other members interpreted the lack of consensus in 1930 as an indication for that the three-mile rule had never been part of customary international law[114] or that the three-mile rule had been and

---

111 Santiago Villalpando, 'Codification Light: A New Trend in the Codification of International Law at the United Nations' (2013) 2 Anuário Brasileiro de Direito Internacional = Brazilian Yearbook of International Law 128: "International codification, in other words, provokes an unsolvable tension in the quest for certainty and universality in the application of law."
112 Jennings, 'The Progressive Development of International Law and Its Codification' 305, on the "concern over the possibility of the application of the maxim *expressio unios exclusio alterius* to a partial codification" during the 1930 Hague Conference.
113 Spiropolous, *ILC Ybk (1952 vol 1)* 162 and *ILC Ybk (1955 vol 1)* 173, (stating that in the 1930s Greece and other states claimed 6 miles). Zourek argued that only a small number of states claim and defend three miles, which was criticized by Fitzmaurice, ibid 174-175. Hudson argued that the 1930 conference did not reject any rule but only took no decision on the territorial waters' breadth, *ILC Ybk (1952 vol 1)* 170.
114 Kozhenikov, ibid 154 and 170, no custom; Cordova, Zourek, 167, Amado 154, 170 (custom to extend territorial sea between three and 12 miles), and Yepes at 154, see also Liang (Secretary to the Commission) 161.

remained custom.[115] In light of this uncertainty, the ILC reached agreement on general rules and principles which left sufficient room for state practice to further develop. The Commission's ultimate compromise recognized a minimum breadth of the territorial sea of three miles and allowed for the recognition of greater breadths "if it is based on customary law"[116], without further defining customary international law. This compromise responded to the lack of agreement on a uniform breadth and, as Fitzmaurice put it, confirmed the three-mile rule "while not excluding the possible validity of individual claims to greater distances."[117] In this way, the possibility of further development of the law of the sea by state practice was reconciled with the idea that states remain subject to the law and that the law provides for certain rules that can offer orientation. Eventually, the law became settled through the negotiations of further conventions.

2. The question of form and the respective spirit of the time

The risk of "decodification"[118], meaning the uncertainty introduced by un-ratified codification conventions, was the reason why very early Jennings suggested that the ILC might consider writing authoritative statements of custom, rather than preparing codification conventions.[119]

---

115 Alfaro, ibid 169, pointing out that of the thirty-two governments represented at that Conference, seventeen had voted in favour of the three-mile limit, and Lauterpacht, 171.
116 The compromise can be found in *ILC Ybk (1956 vol 1)* 162: "1. Save as provided in paragraphs 2 and 3 of this article, the breadth of the territorial sea is three miles. 2. A greater breadth shall be recognized if it is based on customary law. 3. A State may fix the breadth of the territorial sea at a distance exceeding that laid down in paragraphs 1 and 2, but such an extension may not be claimed against States which have not recognized it and have not adopted an equal or greater distance. 4. The breadth of the territorial sea may not exceed 12 miles."
117 Fitzmaurice, *ILC Ybk (1955 vol 1)* 175; see also for the suggestion to focus on the limits until which a state may lawfully claim its territorial waters to be Padilla Nervo (170), Amado (proposing a later adopted resolution 171, 173, 174, adopted in 194) and Salamanca (179-180). The resolution was adopted 7 to 6.
118 Cf. *Third report on State responsibility, by Mr James Crawford, Special Rapporteur* 15 March, 15 June, 10 and 18 July and 4 August 2000 UN Doc A/CN.4/507 and Add. 1–4 in *ILC Ybk (2000 vol 2 part 1)* 52 para 165 ("decodifying effect").
119 Jennings, 'The Progressive Development of International Law and Its Codification' 305-308. He refers (at 305) to the Preparatory Committee of the 1930 Conference

Chapter 6: The International Law Commission

Taking again an example of the early history of the ILC, the question of the form features prominently in the context of the preparation of a convention on diplomatic relations law. The choice for a codification convention was not a foregone conclusion. A convention, it was argued, would unlikely achieve wide-spread ratification, it would either introduce uncertainty as to the law in existence or freeze the status quo and prevent the further development of international practice.[120] Within the ILC, several members of the Commission favoured a convention[121], other members argued that the form would depend on the subject-matter and on whether the substance-matter would tend rather into the direction of a codification or of a progressive development of the law.[122] Adopting such a pragmatic standpoint, Sir Gerald Fitzmaurice supported those of his colleagues who aimed for a convention in the field of diplomatic relations, while also emphasizing that there were more effective means of codification than the negotiation of multilateral treaties at diplomatic conferences.[123] For the topic of the law of treaties, however,

---

which stated: "A particular Government which is prepared to sign some provision or other as a conventional rule might possibly refuse to recognise it as being the expression of existing law, whereas another Government which recognises this provision as existing law may not desire to see it included in a convention, being apprehensive that the authority of the provision will be weakened thereby."

120 *ILC Ybk (1958 vol 2)* 133 (A/CN.4/116) (USA).

121 *ILC Ybk (1958 vol 1)*: Amado and Verdross spoke in favour of a convention (85), Yokota spoke in favour of a convention in spite of the risk of freezing international law (86): "The reasons put forward, particularly the argument that a convention 'would tend to freeze the *status quo*', applied equally well to other branches of international law, and could apply to the law of the sea." According to Zourek, "international conventions had proved to be the only effective way of achieving progress in international law" (87). François pointed out the difficulty of obtaining enough ratifications (88); Tunkin preferred a convention "[w]henever possible" (89); Amado agreed with Tunkin (while "custom was the common law of international relations [...] international law [nevertheless] consisted essentially in written texts (with the force of conventional obligations)" (89).

122 ibid 87: Sandström suggested that the substance of the Commission's work and its categorization as codification or progressive development should be decisive (likewise Hsu, 88); Ago did not think that the commission should always aim at a convention which is prone to non-ratifications and reservations, but would prefer a convention for this case (86).

123 ibid 85: "The method of convening a diplomatic conference was suitable for a subject like the law of the sea in which there were at least two important questions, those of conservation and the continental shelf, which were comparatively new to general international law. In the case of diplomatic intercourse and immunities the position

Fitzmaurice favoured a code over a convention.[124] This may not be surprising, considering Fitzmaurice's appreciation of customary international law: in his view treaties merely constituted sources of obligations rather than sources of law, in contrast to customary international law.[125] His successor Humphrey Waldock and the Commission as a whole adopted the opposite approach, however, and decided that the law of treaties should be codified in a convention; Waldock even made the acceptance of the post as Special Rapporteur dependent on a change back to draft convention articles.[126] This choice for a binding treaty and the decision that questions of interpretation should be addressed shaped the understanding of the nature of the means of treaty interpretation, namely as "rules" and legal norms, as opposed to mere doctrine, legal technique or "technical rules".[127]

The process of decolonization and the emergence of so-called newly independent states favoured the trend towards conventions.[128] Waldock, for instance, argued that "an expository code, however well formulated, [could

---

was completely different; it was a subject with which Governments were eminently familiar and one in which there had been State practice for centuries." Rather than sending to a conference, "[t]he General Assembly could simply recommend it to Member States for signature".

124 *ILC Ybk (1956 vol 1)* 218; and *First report by Sir Gerald Fitzmaurice, Special Rapporteur* 14 March 1956 UN Doc A/CN.4/101 in *ILC Ybk (1956 vol 2)* 106-107.

125 Fitzmaurice, 'Some Problems Regarding the Formal Sources of International Law' 159-160. But cf. Maurice H Mendelson, 'Are Treaties Merely a Source of Obligation?' in William E Butler (ed), *Perestroika and International Law* (1980) 81 ff.

126 See Mark E Villiger, 'The 1969 Vienna Convention on the Law of Treaties: 40 Years After' (2009) 344 RdC 28.

127 *Third Report on the Law of Treaties, by Sir Humphrey Waldock, Special Rapporteur* 3 March, 9 June, 12 June and 7 July 1964 UN Doc A/CN.4/167 and Add.1-3 in *ILC Ybk (1964 vol 2)* 53-55; Verdross, *ILC Ybk (1964 vol 1)* 21, argued that the ILC should "decide whether it recognized the existence of such rules; for it was highly controversial whether the rules established by case-law [...] were general rules of international law or merely technical rules"; see also Djeffal, *Static and evolutive treaty interpretation: a functional reconstruction* 112-114.

128 Arnold Jan Pieter Tammes, 'Codification of International Law in the International Law Commission' (1975) 22(3) Netherlands International Law Review 326: "I think that the reason for which the Commission definitely switched from the code to the convention is still valid, namely, that although any new-comer (including a new State) which enters a society must generally comply with its governing order, the legislative convention provides an opportunity to consider *de novo* the legal heritage of a world of States that was very small indeed." Villalpando, 'Codification Light: A New Trend in the Codification of International Law at the United Nations' 131; Bordin, 'Reflections

not] in the nature of things be so effective as a convention for consolidating the law" and that "the codification of the law of treaties through a multilateral convention would give all the new States the opportunity to participate directly in the formulation of the law if they so wished."[129] Roberto Ago, in hindsight, explained that the change in the social structure of the international community had required codification to go beyond the confines of mere systematization of the law and to aim at the conclusions of conventions which required the consent of newly emerged states.[130]

In spite of this *Zeitgeist* in favour of conventions, the ILC did not lose sight of customary international law.[131] One reason was the disenchantment with the speed of the ratification process. In 1968, Roberto Ago, as a member of the ILC, noted the slow ratification speed of conventions and pointed out that one "reason why ratifications were so tardy was not deliberate opposition, but the complexity of the procedure whereby States established their consent to be bound."[132] Therefore, treaties were said to operate as "agents in the formation of customary international law"[133] and the ILC itself recommended the drafting of convention relating to state-succession precisely because of the potentially positive effect of this endeavour on customary international law.[134] Related to the slow ratification process, customary international law

---

of Customary International Law: The Authority of Codification Conventions and ILC Draft Articles in International Law' 540; Yusuf, 'Pan-Africanism and International Law' 254-5; see on the relationship between the so-called third world and the International Law Commission the new study by Anna Krueger, *Die Bindung der Dritten Welt an das postkoloniale Völkerrecht: die Völkerrechtskommission, das Recht der Verträge und das Recht der Staatennachfolge in der Dekolonialisierung* (Springer 2018).

129 *ILC Ybk (1962 vol 2)* 160 para 17.
130 Roberto Ago, 'Droit des traités à la lumière de la Convention de Vienne' (1971) 134 RdC 306-309; see already *ILC Ybk (1961 vol 1)* 249.
131 The ILC was aware of its own influence: as Humphrey Waldock (ibid 252) emphasized, "[a] draft convention prepared by so large and representative body as the Commission possessed an authority of its own even if the General Assembly decided against submitting it to a conference of plenipotentiaries."
132 *ILC Ybk (1968 vol 1)* 98; see also the memorandum by Roberto Ago "The final stage of codification of international law", *ILC Ybk (1968 vol 2)* 171-178.
133 *ILC Ybk (1970 vol 1)* 167 (Humphrey Waldock); *ILC Ybk (1968 vol 1)* 98 (Mustafa Yasseen): "even if unratified, could be the source of a general custom".
134 See the report of the commission to the General assembly in *ILC Ybk (1974 vol 2 part 1)* 170.

continued to play an important role in international practice.[135] Whereas the Court decided that article 6 of the Geneva Convention on the Continental Shelf did not reflect customary international law in the *North Sea Continental Shelf* cases, the work of the ILC has been referred to as supplementary means in other cases when identifying customary international law.[136]

The other reason was the Commission's decision to prepare non-binding instruments which were not intended to necessarily lead to the negotiation of a treaty. This move to nonbinding instruments might have become politically possible precisely because earlier newly independent states had been in the position, through the negotiations of conventions prepared by the ILC, to take part in the creation of the common international legal order. Also, the ILC early on consulted with regional bodies on the progressive development and codification of international law.[137] Historically, the importance of this consideration at the end of the 1950s and in the 1960s could hardly be overemphasized.

The ARSIWA are perhaps the most important example of nonbinding instruments. In 1974, the ILC decided to favour "draft articles" while leaving open "[t]he final form given to the codification of State responsibility".[138] When the project approached its completion, states[139] and the ILC[140] were divided on whether the project should ultimately result into a convention. Supporters of a binding instrument pointed to the Vienna Convention on the Law of Treaties as role model and emphasized the higher certainty and reliability as compared to customary international law and its inadequacies. Supporters of a non-binding instrument pointed to the difficulty to obtain

---

135 As stated by Villalpando, 'Codification Light: A New Trend in the Codification of International Law at the United Nations' 135, the Court "rarely applied (the VCLT) as such" since at least one party to the proceeding did not ratify the VCLT or since the VCLT was not applicable to earlier treaties according to article 4 VCLT.

136 *ILC Ybk (1972 vol 1)* paras 39-40 (Waldock); *ILC Ybk (1970 vol 1)* 70 (Waldock, arguing that there was no rivalry between the ICJ and the ILC.); Villalpando, 'Codification Light: A New Trend in the Codification of International Law at the United Nations' 135, for an overview of ILC conventions applied as evidence of custom.

137 See Rosenne, 'The International Law Commission, 1949-59' 133-137.

138 *ILC Ybk (1974 vol 2 part 1)* 272-273; see also Villalpando, 'Codification Light: A New Trend in the Codification of International Law at the United Nations' 142-143.

139 *ILC Ybk (2001 vol 2 part 1)* 46-48; *ILC Ybk (1999 vol 2 part 1)* 104; *ILC Ybk (1998 vol 2 part 1)* 93-99.

140 *ILC Ybk (2001 vol 2 part 2)* 24-25; for an overview see Laurence T Pacht, 'The Case for a Convention on State Responsibility' (2014) 83(4) Nordic Journal of International Law 446 ff.

Chapter 6: The International Law Commission

a high number of ratifications and the risk to introduce uncertainty as to the rules of customary international law in case of a failure to obtain a significant number of ratification (so-called "reverse codification").[141] Special Rapporteur James Crawford suggested in his last report "that an Assembly resolution taking note of the text and commending it to Governments may be the simplest and most practical form, in particular if it allows the Assembly to avoid a lengthy and possibly divisive discussion of particular articles."[142] The Commission ultimately

> "reached the understanding that in the first instance, it should recommend to the General Assembly that the Assembly should take note of the draft articles in a resolution and annex the text of the articles to it [...] The recommendation would also propose that, given the importance of the topic, in the second and later stage the Assembly should consider the adoption of a convention on this topic."[143]

A similar course had earlier been adopted with respect to the draft articles on nationality of natural persons: rather than endorsing the conclusion of a convention, the ILC "decided to recommend to the General Assembly the adoption, in the form of a declaration, of the draft articles on nationality of natural persons in relation to the succession of States."[144] Since then, several projects of the ILC resulted into a guide to practice on reservations on treaties, guiding principles on unilateral acts of states, draft conclusions or draft articles.[145]

As demonstrated by Laurence Helfer and Timothy Meyer,[146] there was a significant decline in recommendations of the ILC to the GA to adopt a convention based on the work of the ILC. Helfer and Meyer show that during 1947-1999 the ILC completed 30 projects and recommended 20 conventions

---

141 For a summary of the positions see *Fourth report on State responsibility, by Mr James Crawford, Special Rapporteur* 2 and 3 April 2001 UN Doc A/CN.4/517 and Add. 1 in *ILC Ybk (2001 vol 2 part 1)* 24-25.
142 *Fourth report on State responsibility, by Mr James Crawford, Special Rapporteur* in *ILC Ybk (2001 vol 2 part 1)* 7.
143 *ILC Ybk (2001 vol 2 part 2)* 25. Cf. UNGA Res 56/83 (12 December 2001) UN Doc A/RES/56/83 para 3, where the UNGA took note of the ARSIWA and "commend[ed] them to the attention of Governments without prejudice to the question of their future adoption or other appropriate action". UNGA Res 74/180 (18 December 2019) UN Doc A/RES/74/180 para 1.
144 ILC Ybk (1999 vol 2 part 2) 20.
145 Villalpando, 'Codification Light: A New Trend in the Codification of International Law at the United Nations' 118.
146 Helfer and Meyer, 'The Evolution of Codification: A Principal-Agent Theory of the International Law Commission's Influence' 315-317.

of which 14 conventions were later adopted and entered into force. Within that period, during 1947-1974 most projects (21) were concluded, most conventions recommended (14) and most conventions were adopted and entered into force (12). In contrast, during 2000-2014 the ILC completed 12 projects and recommended the adoption of a convention twice[147]. Similarly, Luigi Crema recently pointed out that, out of 43 concluded topics, 16 topics ended with articles that eventually culminated in a multilateral treaty, 12 topics resulted in articles which have not led to the adoption of a treaty so far, three topics culminated in guidelines or principles, six topics led to studies, two topics (three if one includes the recently adopted *jus cogens* conclusions) resulted in conclusions, and six topics escaped the aforementioned categories.[148]

The last conventions which had been based on the work of the ILC and were adopted are the Rome Statute[149], the 1997 Convention on the Law of the Non-Navigational Uses of International Watercourses which entered into force in 2014[150] and the not yet in force 2004 United Nations Convention on Jurisdictional Immunities of States and their Property[151].[152]

---

147 The authors refer to the topics of the Prevention of transboundary damage from hazardous activities and of Diplomatic Protection, ibid 315 f., cf. *Report of the International Law Commission: Fifty-third session (23 April–1 June and 2 July–10 August 2001)* UN Doc A/56/10 145; *Report of the International Law Commission: Fifty-eighth session (1 May-9 June and 3 July-11 August 2006)* UN Doc A/61/10 24. In addition, at the sixty-sixth session in 2014, the ILC adopted the draft articles on the expulsion of aliens and recommended to the General Assembly "to consider, at a later stage, the elaboration of a convention on the basis of the draft articles", *ILC Report 2014* at 21. In 2016, the ILC recommended to the General Assembly the "elaboration of a convention on the basis of the draft articles on the protection of persons in the event of disasters", *Report of the International Law Commission: Sixty-eighth session (2 May-10 June and 4 July-12 August 2016)* UN Doc A/71/10 at 24. In 2019, the ILC recommended a convention on crimes against humanity, *ILC Report 2019* at 10 para 42.
148 Crema, 'The ILC's New Way of Codifying International Law, the Motives Behind It, and the Interpretive Approach Best Suited to It' 163-5.
149 See also below, 473.
150 Convention on the Law of the Non-Navigational Uses of International Watercourses (signed 21 May 1997, entered into force 17 August 2014) (1997) 36 ILM 700.
151 United Nations Convention on Jurisdictional Immunities of States and Their Property (signed 2 December 2004) UN Doc A/RES/59/38.
152 See also Villalpando, 'Codification Light: A New Trend in the Codification of International Law at the United Nations' 117-118; Bordin, 'Reflections of Customary International Law: The Authority of Codification Conventions and ILC Draft Articles in International Law' 542.

3. *Codification light* as joint enterprise of several actors

The increasing use of nonbinding codifications, such as draft articles or conclusions and the corresponding commentaries, guidelines, principles, studies, has been called "codification light"[153]. This development may be said to correspond *prima facie* to a position of greater authority of the ILC[154] since it bypasses an international conference, which would shift the focus to states representatives;[155] courts, tribunals and adjudicators would be a target audience.[156] At best, this "codification light" comes with the clarity and precision of a written form and with the general application *ratione personae* that is associated with customary international law.[157] To have this effect, however, these nonbinding codifications must be regarded by the relevant actors, courts, the UN and, in particular, the majority of states, to reflect customary international law and not to constitute a quasi-legislative innovation.[158] The ILC is in a central position, but it will not be the only

---

153 Villalpando, 'Codification Light: A New Trend in the Codification of International Law at the United Nations' 117; cf. Crema, 'The ILC's New Way of Codifying International Law, the Motives Behind It, and the Interpretive Approach Best Suited to It' 174 (speaking of a "weakening" of general international law by the ILC).
154 Caron, 'The ILC Articles on State Responsibility: The Paradoxical Relationship Between Form and Authority' 857 ff.
155 Helfer and Meyer, 'The Evolution of Codification: A Principal-Agent Theory of the International Law Commission's Influence' 313 ff. (arguing that the ILC's turn to nonbinding instruments has to be seen against the background of a gridlock in the UNGA which "increases the likelihood of General Assembly inaction"); Caron, 'The ILC Articles on State Responsibility: The Paradoxical Relationship Between Form and Authority' 866: "[I]t is entirely proper for the ILC to consider the endgame of its work product, and to take account of possible dysfunctions in the state system generally or relating to a particular topic." Of course, states can comment on the work of the ILC in the 6th Committee.
156 Crema, 'The ILC's New Way of Codifying International Law, the Motives Behind It, and the Interpretive Approach Best Suited to It' 173, 175-6.
157 Villalpando, 'Codification Light: A New Trend in the Codification of International Law at the United Nations' 150.
158 Crawford, 'The Progressive Development of International Law: History, Theory and Practice' 19-20: "[T]he answer is to be provided via end user interpretation, in other words through the practice of states. The question is whether a proposition put to such users of international law by the Commission is accepted or rejected, and within what time scale. International law, like Schrödinger's cat, cannot exist in the absence of the observer."; Murphy, 'Codification, Progressive Development, or Scholarly Analysis? The Art of Packaging the ILC's Work Product' 32, 40. See also

actor in the process of "staging the authority"[159] of nonbinding documents. The reception of states, for instance in the 6th Committee of the UNGA[160], of courts and tribunals and of academics is also important and can influence the consolidation of customary international law.

To give two examples[161]: After the ILC had adopted the provision on necessity as a circumstance precluding wrongfulness on its first reading,[162] both Hungary and Slovakia agreed before the ICJ that "the existence of a state of necessity must be evaluated in the light of the criteria laid down by the International Law Commission"[163], and the Court agreed as well.[164] In turn, the ILC approvingly referred to the ICJ in order to support the retention on a provision on necessity.[165] In contrast, when the European Court of Human Rights analyzed the development of customary international law of state immunity, the European Court noted that "a working group of the ILC acknowledged the existence of some support for the view that State officials should not be entitled to plead immunity for acts of torture committed in

---

Danae Azaria, ''Codification by Interpretation': The International Law Commission as an Interpreter of International Law' (2020) 31 EJIL 190, speaking of an "offer of interpretation" and convincingly argues that the silence of states "may not be construed outright as acquiescence. However, whenever states fail to engage with the ILC's interpretative offer, international courts and tribunals are likely to rely on the ILC's interpretative pronouncements as a subsidiary means [...]" (200).

159 Bordin, 'Reflections of Customary International Law: The Authority of Codification Conventions and ILC Draft Articles in International Law' 552 ff.

160 For a recent treatment of the ILC's working methods and interactions with governments in the UN see Azaria, ''Codification by Interpretation': The International Law Commission as an Interpreter of International Law' 188-189. See also United Nations, *The Work of the International Law Commission Volume I* (9th edn, 2017) ⟨https://www.un-ilibrary.org/content/books/9789210609203⟩ accessed 1 February 2023 73-87.

161 For further examples, in particular the reception of the work of the ILC in the jurisprudence of investment tribunals see Crema, 'The ILC's New Way of Codifying International Law, the Motives Behind It, and the Interpretive Approach Best Suited to It' 178-80.

162 *ILC Ybk (1980 vol 2 part 2)* 34.

163 *Gabčíkovo-Nagymaros Project* [1997] ICJ Rep 7, 39 para 50.

164 ibid 40-41 paras 51-52.

165 In this sense, see *Second report on State responsibility, by Mr James Crawford, Special Rapporteur* 17 March, 1 and 30 April, 19 July 1999 UN Doc A/CN.4/498 and Add.1-4 in *ILC Ybk (1999 vol 2 part 1)* 74; *ILC Ybk (2001 vol 2 part 2)* 82.

their own territories in either civil or criminal actions".[166] Yet, the European Court did not stop there and concluded on the basis of its evaluation of international practice that the grant of immunity to State officials "reflected generally recognised rules of public international law."[167]

In conclusion, international actors such as states, courts and tribunals engage with nonbinding instruments of the ILC even when those have been at an early stage and have not been formally adopted by the ILC yet. Ideally, they evaluate the intrinsic quality of said instruments as to whether they fairly reflect customary international law.[168] In doing so, they can contribute to the clarification of international law and shape its further development.

II. The substantive form: the codification choice between openness and closedness

Another important aspect concerns the way in which the ILC products would relate to international law and whether they would constitute a closed system in the sense of a complete codification. This question arose first in the discussion of the law on consular relations because of the dense network of bilateral conventions in this field. Special Rapporteur Zourek proposed a draft article

---

166 *Jones and Others v The United Kingdom* App no 34356/06 and 40528/06 (ECtHR, 14 January 2014) para 209, see also para 213, referring to the view of then Special Rapporteur Kolodkin who regarded it as "fairly widespread view that grave crimes under international law could not be considered as acts performed in an official capacity [...] However, the statement did not meet with unanimous agreement in the ILC and further comment on the issue is expected from the new Special Rapporteur [...]".
167 ibid para 215.
168 See also Caron, 'The ILC Articles on State Responsibility: The Paradoxical Relationship Between Form and Authority' 866, 872; Villalpando, 'Codification Light: A New Trend in the Codification of International Law at the United Nations' 153; but see also for a critique of the ECtHR's handling of ILC materials on state immunity Riccardo Pavoni, 'The Myth of the Customary Nature of the United Nations Convention on State Immunity: Does the End Justify the Means?' in Anne van Aaken and Iula Motoc (eds), *ECHR and General International Law* (Oxford University Press 2018) 264 ff., 268-269, Pavoni also speaks of "outsourcing" of the identification of custom to the ILC (at 267), he borrowed the term "outsourcing" in this context from Talmon, 'Determining Customary International Law: the ICJ's Methodology between Induction, Deduction and Assertion' 437.

The form of codification and progressive development and its implications

59[169] according to which the envisioned Convention on Consular Intercourse should affect neither previous conventions nor the parties' ability to conclude future conventions. The provision became subject to debate.[170] By allowing states to conclude future conventions, others argued, the provision might endanger the authority of the draft and prevent the emergence of general international law on this subject.[171] The supporters of the provision pointed to the interests of states in having such a provision, the lack of which risked the convention's acceptance by states; moreover, the convention could serve as a model for bilateral agreements.[172]

The Commission agreed on affirming the applicability of prior conventions,[173] just like previous conventions had done.[174] In relation to future

---

169 Article 59 reads: "Article 59. Relationship between the present articles and previous conventions 1. The provisions contained in the present articles shall in no way affect conventions previously concluded between the Contracting Parties and still in force between them. Where conventions regulating consular intercourse and immunities between the Contracting Parties already exist, these articles shall apply solely to questions not governed by the previous conventions. 2. Acceptance of the present articles shall be no impediment to the conclusion in the future of bilateral conventions concerning consular intercourse and immunities.", *ILC Ybk (1960 vol 2)* 39-40.
170 *ILC Ybk (1961 vol 1)* Edmonds ("one of the most important provisions in the draft", 170), Yasseen ("direct connection with codification of international law", 170).
171 *ILC Ybk (1960 vol 1)* Daftine-Martary (225) doubting the desirability of the provision which would in no way encourage the formation of general international law) Hsu (226, arguing that the purpose of harmonizing consular practice would be defeated by paragraph 2, allowing states to conclude bilateral agreements); Scelle, proposing the article's deletion (227); Sandström (229, arguing that article 59 would weaken the draft); Yasseen desire to secure acceptance of the draft and to safeguard the authority of the draft (237), see also 238 for the view that multilateral conventions should have greater force than treaties.
172 See eg. ibid Special Rapporteur Zourek (agreeing with Tunkin that the instrument might have an unifying influence, emphasizing the interests of states, 225, see also 230, 238, pointing out the need for a multilateral convention in a world of 100 states), Tunkin (emphasizing the interests of states, alluding to the possibility that the convention might nevertheless have a unifying influence, 225), Fitzmaurice (emphasizing the interests of states, 224-225), Erim (227-228) Yokota (224, 229). But see Amado (arguing that the outcome of the codification and progressive development should not be confined to model rules, 228-229).
173 ibid 243. The proposals by Bartoš and François according to which conflicting bilateral conventions should be considered to be abrogated ipso facto, automatically, failed to be supported by a majority (225-226).
174 See Harvard Law School, 'Codification of International Law: Part II: Legal Position and Functions of Consuls' (1932) 26 AJIL. Supplement 369 (article 33); Convention

conventions, Scelle's proposal to preserve the integrity of the draft convention and to safeguard its fundamental principles by declaring it to be *jus cogens*[175] did not find a majority. Instead, the consensus emerged that the draft convention should not draw the states' attention to future conventions, which is why any reference to the future conventions was deleted and mentioned only by implication in the Commentary.[176] The Vienna Convention on Consular Relations contained a provision according to which the Convention should neither affect previous conventions (article 73(1)) nor "preclude States from concluding international agreements confirming or supplementing or extending or amplifying the provisions thereof".[177] Furthermore, several conventions based on ILC drafts affirm in their respective preamble that "that the rules of customary international law should continue to govern questions not expressly regulated by the provisions of the present Convention".[178]

---

    on Consular Agents (signed 20 February 1928, entered into force 3 September 1929) OAS Law and Treaty Series No 34, Article 24; Convention on the High Seas (signed 29 April 1958, entered into force 30 September 1962) 450 UNTS 11, Article 30; Convention on the Territorial Sea and the Contiguous Zone (signed 29 April 1958, entered into force 10 September 1964) 516 UNTS 205, Article 25.

175 See Scelle in *ILC Ybk (1960 vol 1)* 240; see also Yasseen in *ILC Ybk (1961 vol 1)* 170. Bartoš (173) did not think that sovereignty of states would enable them to conclude conventions subsequent to the general convention. But see for instance Pal, who could not follow Scelle in making all parts of the draft imperative (235). François, pointing out the difficulty to determine which parts should be considered *jus cogens* (171).

176 ibid 175; *ILC Ybk (1961 vol 2)* 128. See also *ILC Ybk (1961 vol 1)* 174 (Ago, considering any reference to future conventions dangerous, because, as indicated by Bartoš, it would detract from the aim pursued in the codification of consular law).

177 Vienna Convention on Consular Relations (signed 24 April 1963, entered into force 19 March 1967) 596 UNTS Art. 73.

178 Both the Vienna Convention on Consular Relations, ibid 261, the Vienna Convention on Diplomatic Relations, Vienna Convention on Diplomatic Relations (signed 18 April 1961, entered into force 24 April 1964) 500 UNTS 95, and the Vienna Convention on the Law of Treaties, Vienna Convention on the Law of Treaties (signed 23 May 1969, entered into force 27 January 1980) 1155 UNTS 331, and the United Nations Convention on Jurisdictional Immunities of States and Their Property, United Nations Convention on Jurisdictional Immunities of States and Their Property (signed 2 December 2004) UN Doc A/RES/59/38.

III. Concluding Observations on Form and Substance

Unlike in many domestic law settings, codification in public international law did not drive out customary international law.[179] Experience has taught that customary international law will remain important in the international legal system, even in an age of codification, in particular as long as certain states do not ratify a given convention and as long as the consensual character of a treaty and the *pacta tertiis* principle will be maintained. Furthermore, customary international law may continue to play a role also in the relationship between the parties to conventions, as such conventions often constitute a partial codification that leaves room for customary international law. In addition, the development according to which the work of the ILC would not be intended to lead to a binding treaty and which has been described as "codification light" contributed to the importance customary international law still enjoys in the international legal system.

Probably nothing else like the fact that several provisions of a codification convention, namely the Vienna Convention on the Law of Treaties, have become subject to a re-analysis by the Commission recently[180] demonstrates more clearly that treaties based on the Commission's work are anchored in international life.[181] In this reanalysis no distinction was made between the rules on interpretation of the Vienna Convention on the Law of Treaties and the rules of interpretation under customary international law which are said to be set forth in the Vienna Convention.[182] In its second conclusion on subsequent agreements and subsequent practice and in the corresponding

---

179 Villalpando, 'Codification Light: A New Trend in the Codification of International Law at the United Nations' 119, 128.
180 The Study on "Fragmentation of international law: difficulties arising from the diversification and expansion of international law" concerned article 31(3)(c) VCLT; the Commission analyzed in a separate study the role of subsequent agreements and subsequent practice (art. 31(3)(a) and (b) VCLT) and the provisional application of treaties (art. 25 VCLT). The new *jus cogens* project includes, but is not limited to, an analysis of articles 53 and 64 VCLT. On the interpretation of the VCLT by the ILC see Azaria, ''Codification by Interpretation': The International Law Commission as an Interpreter of International Law' 178-182.
181 As observed by Lachs, "codification stimulates development no less than development calls out for codification", Lachs, *The Teacher in International Law: Teachings and Teaching* 187.
182 Cf. also Azaria, ''Codification by Interpretation': The International Law Commission as an Interpreter of International Law' 180 (in relation to Guide to Practice on Reservations to Treaties).

commentary, the Commission emphasized the multi-sourced character of the rules of interpretation and thereby paid attention to both sources rather than to one at the expense of the other.[183] This is another example of the convergence of customary international law and a convention into general rules and principles. The generality and the focus on rules on rules which characterizes the Commission's work for instance on subsequent agreements and subsequent practice, customary international law, peremptory norms and general principles of law can ensure that the ILC conclusions can be applied in different contexts. Thus, the ILC strenghtens general international international law and a general methodology against the background of the diversification and expansion of international law.[184]

C. The interrelationship of sources in selected projects

A memorandum submitted by the Secretary-General in 1949 expressed the opinion that the codification of the sources of international law had been completed by the adoption of article 38 of the ICJ Statute, and it was regarded to be "doubtful whether any useful purposes would be served by attempts to make it more specific, as, for instance, by defining the conditions of the creation and of the continued validity of international custom or by enumerating, by way of example, some of the general principles of law which article 38 of the Statute recognizes".[185] Nevertheless, it was deemed useful to "assembl[e] the experience of the International Court of Justice and of other international tribunals in the application of the various sources of international law."[186]

---

183 *ILC Report 2018* at 19: "Hence, the rules contained in articles 31 and 32 apply as treaty law in relation to those States that are parties to the 1969 Vienna Convention, and as customary international law between all States, including to treaties which were concluded before the entry into force of the Vienna Convention for the States parties concerned."; see already *ILC Report 2013* at 19. UNGA Res 73/202 (20 December 2018) UN Doc A/RES/73/202 para 4: the UNGA "[t]akes note of the conclusions [...] brings them to the attention of States and all who may be called upon to interpret treaties, and encourages their widest possible dissemination."
184 See also Crema, 'The ILC's New Way of Codifying International Law, the Motives Behind It, and the Interpretive Approach Best Suited to It' 172.
185 *Survey of International Law in Relation to the Work of Codification of the International Law Commission: Preparatory work within the purview of article 18, paragraph 1, of the International Law Commission* 22.
186 ibid 22.

The ILC has approached the sources in several of its projects. It has assembled legal experience and, by doctrinally systematizing international practice, devised so-called "rules on rules" that can guide legal operators. This section analyzes to what extent the interrelationship of sources was addressed in selected topics. This section will first focus on the ILC's work on the law of treaties (I.); in particular, it will demonstrate that the question of the interrelationship was partly excluded from the topic's scope and it will examine the different ways in which the substance of the work related to other sources. Subsequently, the section will examine the question of the interrelationship in the work on the responsibility of states for internationally wrongful acts (II.) and in the so-called fragmentation report (III.). At the end of this section, the recent projects on customary international law (IV.), on *jus cogens* (V.) and on general principles of law (VI.) will be examined.

I. The law of treaties

The relationship between a given codification and unwritten law can be indicative of the preferences of a given legal community. It will be particularly important if the subject of the codification is the general law of treaties, since here the question arises how any written law shall relate to unwritten law. The present section will focus on how the ILC approached the interrelationship of sources when it worked on the general law of treaties. It is divided into two subsections. First, it will be analyzed to what extent the topic of the interrelationship of sources was addressed and discussed in the context of the design of the general regime (1.). Secondly, the section examines the codification approach(es) as to the relation between a treaty and other sources (2.).

1. The scope of the topic

The Commission decided not to address the relationship between treaty law and other sources explicitly beyond a saving reservation in what became article 35 VCLT. An exception concerns the role of other sources in the context of interpretation of treaty obligation, which the next subsection will focus on.

Chapter 6: The International Law Commission

After his predecessors Brierly and Lauterpacht had not examined, in the context of the ILC[187], the interpretation of treaties and the relationship with other sources, Special Rapporteur Sir Gerald Fitzmaurice dedicated no less than 21 articles of his fifth report to the effects of treaties on third states.[188] Fitzmaurice's objective was to explain exceptions to the *pacta tertiis* rule not by "some mystique attached to certain types of treaties", such as their character as "lawmaking treaty" as opposed to a mere contract, but by a general obligation of states not to interfere in the treaty-relations between states.[189] With respect to the interplay between custom and treaties, Fitzmaurice's report set out

> "to describe a process rather than to formulate a rule. Whether the treaty concerned will have the effects stated, must depend on a number of uncertain factors, such as its precise terms, the nature of its subject matter, the circumstances in which it was concluded, the number of States subscribing to it, their importance relative to the subject matter of the treaty, the history of the treaty subsequent to its conclusion, and of the topic to which it relates-and so forth."[190]

---

187 Waldock was the first Special Rapporteur who addressed the rules of interpretation of treaties. His predecessors dealt with this topic in their academic capacity outside of the ILC, see Hersch Lauterpacht, 'L'interprétation des traités' (1950) 43 Annuaire de l'Institut de droit international 366 ff.; Gerald Fitzmaurice, 'The Law and Procedure of the International Court of Justice 1951-4: Treaty Interpretation and Other Treaty Points' (1957) 33 BYIL 210-212.

188 *Fifth report by Sir Gerald Fitzmaurice, Special Rapporteur* 21 March 1960 UN Doc A/CN.4/130 in *ILC Ybk (1960 vol 2)* 69 ff. One important study in this regard on which Fitzmaurice relied was written by Ronald F Roxburgh, *International conventions and third states* (Longman, Green and Co 1917).

189 *Fifth report by Sir Gerald Fitzmaurice, Special Rapporteur* in *ILC Ybk (1960 vol 2)* 98: "To the Special Rapporteur, the considerable lack of enthusiasm evinced over the supposedly inherently 'legislative' effect of some kinds of treaties, is evidence of a certain uneasiness at the idea. Exactly which classes have this effect, and why and how? [...] The Special Rapporteur does not deny that, in the result, they do; but it seems to him preferable to reach this conclusion, not on the esoteric basis of some mystique attaching to certain types of treaties, but simply on that of a general duty for States-which can surely be postulated at this date (and which is a necessary part of the international order if chaos is to be avoided)-to respect, recognize and, in the legal sense, accept, the consequences of lawful and valid international acts entered into between other States, which do not infringe the legal rights of States not parties to them in the legal sense."

190 *Fifth report by Sir Gerald Fitzmaurice, Special Rapporteur* in *ILC Ybk (1960 vol 2)* 94.

Fitzmaurice did not, however, advocate that a treaty can impose obligations on third states against their respective will or without any acquiescence. With respect to "law-making or norm-enunciating treaties", Fitzmaurice argued that these treaties "constitute vehicles whereby such rules or regimes are or become generally mediated so as also to bind States not actually parties to the treaty as such."[191] Yet, he added "[i]n any such case however, it is the rule of customary international law thus evidenced, declared or embodied that binds the third State, not the treaty as such."[192]

His successor as Special Rapporteur, Humphrey Waldock, departed from Fitzmaurice's approach and found a general duty not to interfere in lawful treaties difficult to reconcile with the general idea of treaties as *res inter alios acta*.[193] Waldock significantly shortened the articles and designed an interrelated regime of only four articles on third-party effects,[194] which came close to the present articles 34-38 VCLT. Draft article 61 stated the *pacta tertiis* rule as general rule, draft article 62 addressed the situation in which parties to a treaty intended to create rights or obligations for a third state and in which said third state consented to the respective provisions. Draft article 63 concerned treaties establishing objective regimes. Finally, draft article 64 was a provision similar to what is now article 38 VCLT, a saving reservation which stated that "nothing in articles 61 to 63 is to be understood as precluding principles of law laid down in a treaty from becoming applicable to States not parties thereto in consequence of the formation of an international custom embodying those principles."[195]

The most controversial proposal concerned the suggestion that treaties could create an objective regime over a region or an area with respect to which the states concluding the treaty would possess or assume a special territorial competence.[196] The tension with the *pacta tertiis* principle should

---

191 *Fifth report by Sir Gerald Fitzmaurice, Special Rapporteur* in *ILC Ybk (1960 vol 2)* 80.
192 *Fifth report by Sir Gerald Fitzmaurice, Special Rapporteur* in *ILC Ybk (1960 vol 2)* 80.
193 *ILC Ybk (1964 vol 1)* 28, 32.
194 *Third Report on the Law of Treaties, by Sir Humphrey Waldock, Special Rapporteur* in *ILC Ybk (1964 vol 2)* 17-34.
195 *Third Report on the Law of Treaties, by Sir Humphrey Waldock, Special Rapporteur* in *ILC Ybk (1964 vol 2)* 34.
196 *Third Report on the Law of Treaties, by Sir Humphrey Waldock, Special Rapporteur* in *ILC Ybk (1964 vol 2)* 26: "A treaty establishes an objective regime when it appears from its terms and from the circumstances of its conclusion that the intention of the

be overcome by recourse to tacit assent or recognition of other states.[197] The failure of other states to protest would imply their consent to this regime. In contrast to the draft articles 62 and 63, article 64 was intended to constitute a mere "saving reservation", acknowledging that the content of treaties can become custom without further explaining this process. Since treaties and custom constituted "distinct sources", Waldock did not want to blur the lines between both sources and, therefore, considered such a saving reservation to be sufficient in a convention about treaties.[198]

Waldock's system can be regarded as an attempt to strengthen treaties in relation to custom. Waldock clarified that article 63 on objective regimes was intended "to provide a means for the speedy consolidation of a treaty as part of the international legal order, without having to await the longer process of formation of a customary rule of international law".[199] Article 63 was intended to be "a provision of the law of today".[200] However, the Commission could not agree on this proposal and whether it could be reconciled with the sovereignty of states and the *pacta tertiis* principle.[201]

---

parties is to create in the general interest general obligations and rights relating to a particular region, State, territory, locality, river, waterway, or to a particular area of sea, sea-bed, or air-space; provided that the parties include among their number any State having territorial competence with reference to the subject-matter of the treaty, or that any such State has consented to the provision in question."

197 *Third Report on the Law of Treaties, by Sir Humphrey Waldock, Special Rapporteur* in *ILC Ybk (1964 vol 2)* 32.

198 *Third Report on the Law of Treaties, by Sir Humphrey Waldock, Special Rapporteur* in *ILC Ybk (1964 vol 2)* 27: "Treaty and custom are distinct sources of law, and it seems undesirable to blur the line between them in setting out the legal effects of treaties upon States not parties to them. It is therefore thought preferable in a draft convention on the law of treaties not to include positive provisions regarding the role of custom in expanding the effects of law-making treaties, but merely to note and recognize it in a general reservation. Such a 'saving' reservation is formulated in article 64." See also 34.

199 *ILC Ybk (1964 vol 1)* at 105.

200 ibid 105 (Waldock).

201 See ibid: While Verdross tried to find common ground between article 63 and 64, in that a treaty provision can become general law (106), others emphasized the differences, and Tunkin even regarded objective regimes as an "obsolete practice" (103), Ago argued that an objective treaty did not itself constitute the legal basis but only lays out conditions necessary to enable a situation to come into existence (106). Reuter pointed out that sovereignty of states could be reconciled with rules binding on third states by way of customary law (83). In this sense also eg Jiménez de Aréchaga (101), Briggs (103).

The interrelationship of sources in selected projects

Given the rejection of draft article 63 on objective regimes, the saving reservation on customary international law became more important. Despite three governments doubting the usefulness of such a saving reservation, the Commission decided to retain the respective article precisely as response to the deletion of the article on objective regimes.[202] This is an example of how the (failed) extension of one legal concept, the concept of the treaty, could have perhaps functionally replaced another, namely customary international law, to a certain extent.

If it had been for Mustafa Yasseen, the interaction between treaties and custom might have been studied in more detail in the draft or even in a separate study.[203] Waldock, however, successfully defended his reluctance to analyze the interrelationship of sources beyond a saving reservation. As he put it, the Commission decided, "possibly out of timidity but nevertheless wisely, not to go too far into the subject. The codification of the relation between customary law and other sources of law should be left to others."[204] In his view, "the relationship between international custom and treaties depended to a large extent on the nature of the particular custom involved and on the provisions of the treaty. The subject would be considered later in connexion with interpretation [...]".[205]

2. The interrelationship within the law of treaties

While emphasizing the distinct character of the sources, Waldock also acknowledged that treaties should not be interpreted and applied without any regard to other sources of international law[206]. He first conceived this re-

---

202 Waldock explained that the Commission's "desire to include [...] had been reinforced by the compromise reached over article 60 and the reluctance of some members to drop an article dealing with objective regimes", *ILC Ybk (1966 vol 1 part 2)* at 91, 94; Jiménez de Aréchaga called then-article 62 the survival of the idea of objective regimes (178). See also Jiménez de Aréchaga in *ILC Ybk (1964 vol 1)* 109: "the Commission had decided to drop article 63 on the understanding that its omission would be partly offset by article 64." See also Verdross, 109: "[I]f article 63 disappeared, article 64 would be all the more necessary".
203 ibid 109 paras 44-45 and 112 para 181 and 195 para 54 and *ILC Ybk (1966 vol 1 part 2)* 91 para 73.
204 ibid 94 para 103.
205 *ILC Ybk (1964 vol 1)* 112 para 2.
206 Waldock was the first Special Rapporteur who addressed the rules of interpretation of treaties. His predecessors dealt with this topic in their academic capacity outside

359

lationship under the concept of intertemporality. As explained by Richard Gardiner, "this concept addresses two questions: first, whether the legal significance of facts in a particular situation is to be assessed as at the time of relevant events rather than at the time at which a difference or dispute is being resolved; and, second, what account is to be taken of changes or developments in international law in any intervening period."[207]

a) From intertemporality to a means of interpretation

Waldock's draft of 1964 was inspired by Max Huber's famous *dictum*:

> "[A] juridical fact must be appreciated in the light of the law contemporary with it, and not of the law in force at the time when a dispute in regard to it arises or falls to be settled [...] The same principle which subjects the act creative of a right to the law in force at the time the right arises, demands that the existence of the right, in other words its continued manifestation, shall follow the conditions required by the evolution of law."[208]

Waldock proposed draft article 56 which distinguished between the interpretation and the application of a treaty. According to draft article 56(1), a treaty was to be interpreted in light of the law in force when the treaty was concluded. According to draft article 56(2), the treaty's application was to be governed by the rules of international law in force during application.[209]

Since the distinction between interpretation and application received as much criticism as the characterization of the relationship between different norms as question of intertemporal law,[210] Roberto Ago suggested in his capacity as chairman to postpone the consideration of draft article 56 on intertemporal law.[211]

---

of the ILC, see Lauterpacht, 'L'interprétation des traités' 366 ff.; Fitzmaurice, 'The Law and Procedure of the International Court of Justice 1951-4: Treaty Interpretation and Other Treaty Points' 210-212.
207 Gardiner, *Treaty interpretation* 290.
208 *Island of Palmas Case* Netherlands v. U.S.A. (4 April 1928) II RIAA 845.
209 *Third Report on the Law of Treaties, by Sir Humphrey Waldock, Special Rapporteur* in *ILC Ybk (1964 vol 2)* 8-9. Contrary to what has been suggested by Kontou, the second paragraph was not meant to cover *jus cogens* only, Nancy Kontou, *The Termination and Revision of Treaties in the Light of New Customary International Law* (Clarendon Press 1994) 135.
210 *ILC Ybk (1964 vol 1)* 33-39.
211 ibid 40.

The interrelationship of sources in selected projects

The Commission then discussed both limbs of intertemporal law as means of interpretation in separate provisions.

Waldock's first drafts on interpretation were still based on the idea of intertemporal law. Accordingly, a treaty should be interpreted "in the context of the rules of international law in force at the time of the conclusion of the treaty" (Draft Article 70) while also taking account of "the emergence of any later rule of customary international law affecting the subject-matter of the treaty and binding upon all the parties", subsequent agreements and subsequent practice (Draft Article 73).[212] By using "take account of", Waldock highlighted the openness of the process of interpretation relation to which several aspects would be relevant.[213]

Several members had reservations about an inclusion of subsequent custom as means of interpretation[214]. The draft articles submitted to the General Assembly distinguished with respect to customary international law between interpretation and application. The general rule of interpretation set forth in draft article 69 referred to "general international law in force at the time of [the treaty's] conclusion".[215] Draft article 68(c) on the modification of a treaty stipulated that the operation of a treaty may be modified "[b]y the subsequent emergence of a new rule of customary law relating to matters dealt with in the treaty and binding upon all the parties."[216] In response, four governments

---

212 *Third Report on the Law of Treaties, by Sir Humphrey Waldock, Special Rapporteur* in *ILC Ybk (1964 vol 2)* 52-53.

213 *Third Report on the Law of Treaties, by Sir Humphrey Waldock, Special Rapporteur* in *ILC Ybk (1964 vol 2)* 61: "The term 'take account of' is used rather than 'be subject to' or any similar term because, if the rule is formulated as one of interpretation, it seems better, at any rate in sub-paragraphs (a) and (b), to use words that leave open the results of the interpretation."

214 *ILC Ybk (1964 vol 1)* 279, Tunkin (73 only subsidiary means); Bartoš 280 (not a rule of interpretation); Yasseen 282 should be modified to be confined to jus cogens, Verdross 296 (art. 73 not a provision on interpretation, later custom would raise the question of interpretation not of the treaty but of the later custom); 296 de Luna (later custom a question of modification not of interpretation); but see Rosenne, 296, who saw no difficulty in the draft provision and recommended otherwise to go back to article 56 (2). But see Pal, 206-297 (not a question of interpretation); Chairman Ago 297 (later custom would involve question of interpretation); Yasseen 297 (article does not belong to interpretation with the exception of subsequent practice, contrary to Ago).

215 See *ILC Ybk (1964 vol 2)* 199. Draft article 69(3) referred to subsequent agreements and subsequent practice, without referring to general international law in force at the time of the treaty's application.

216 ibid 198.

Chapter 6: The International Law Commission

suggested to delete any distinction between prior customary international law as means of interpretation and subsequent customary international law as means of modification, since it would be difficult to determine whether a specific rule of customary international law would have to be regarded as existing at the time of the conclusion of the treaty or at the time subsequent thereto.[217]

Waldock, therefore, suggested eliminating the distinction between customary international law in force at the time of the treaty's conclusion and subsequent customary international law and drafted a new article 69 according to which "a treaty shall be interpreted in good faith in accordance with the ordinary meaning to be given to its terms in the light of [...] the rules of international law".[218] The Commission agreed to keep the reference to other international law simple and not to distinguish between both limbs of intertemporality[219]. In addition, reference was made only to other rules,

---

217 *ILC Ybk (1966 vol 2)* 88 Israel (arguing that the reference to contemporary custom as second limb of intertemporal law is not in the proper place and suggesting to move it to article 69); UK (proposing the deletion of paragraph c since it would be difficult to determine the exact point of time when custom has emerged, arguing further that modification requires consent by parties to the treaties); USA (arguing that paragraph c might lead to serious differences of opinion because of differing views as to what constitutes customary law, suggesting therefore the omission of the paragraph, "leaving the principle to be applied under the norms of international law in general rather than as a specific provision in a convention on treaty law"; recognizing that treaties are to be interpreted in accordance with the evolution of international law). Pakistan (arguing that paragraph c should be deleted).

218 ' *Sixth Report on the Law of Treaties, by Sir Humphrey Waldock, Special Rapporteur* 11 March, 25 March, 12 April, 11 May, 17 May, 24 May, 1 June and 14 June 1966 UN Doc A/CN.4/186 and Add.1-7 in *ILC Ybk (1966 vol 2)* 101; compare *Third Report on the Law of Treaties, by Sir Humphrey Waldock, Special Rapporteur* in *ILC Ybk (1964 vol 2)* 52 on draft article 70, where the interpretation should be informed by "the rules of general international law in force at the time of its conclusion".

219 Cf. *ILC Ybk (1966 vol 1 part 2)* 185 de Luna (later custom should be included); 187 Briggs (if temporal law is to be addressed, both limbs need to be included); Castrén 188 (delete temporal limitation); 190 Jiménez de Aréchaga and Tunkin (delete temporal limitation); Reuter 195 (against temporal limitation, because of territorial sea, arguing further that it must be presumed that states do not seek to violate their undertakings); El-Erian, 196 (reference to custom would cover not only rules of interpretation but also substantive rules.

rather than rules of general international law, in order to allow for regional and local customary international law to be taken into account.[220]

b) Codification policies on the relationship with other principles and rules of international law

When it came to interpretation, the ILC emphasized the interrelationship of a treaty with other rules of international law. This focus has been articulated perhaps best by Yasseen, when explaining that "reference to the rules of international law was indispensable [...] it was impossible to understand the treaty except within the whole international legal order of which it formed a part, which it influenced and by which it was influenced. A treaty was an act of will; the parties had reached agreement, but their agreement was not *in vacuo*; it was situated in a legal order."[221]

A different codification policy can be identified in relation to a treaty's termination and denunciation and the withdrawal of a party which can now be found in article 42 VCLT. According to article 42 VCLT, these questions are solely governed by the treaty in question or the Vienna Convention. This provision purported to constitute "a safeguard for the stability of treaties"[222]. Thus, the provision therefore could have had the potential to create a vacuum around the Vienna Convention;[223] however, since the ILC decided to exclude matters of state succession and state responsibility and to pursue only a partial codification,[224] a significant scope of application for customary international law was preserved.

---

220 ibid 188 Castren, Tunkin 190, Amado 191, Yasseen 197; for a reference explicitly to custom see Verdross 191, contra: Amado, 191.
221 ibid 197.
222 *ILC Ybk (1966 vol 2)* 236 on draft article 39 which resembles what is now article 42 VCLT. See also 237 on draft article 40, according to which the invalidity, termination or denunciation of a treaty, the withdrawal of a party to it, or the suspension of its operation shall not in any way impair the duty of any State to fulfil any obligation embodied in the treaty to which it is subject under any other rule of international law.
223 On this topic see Klabbers, 'Reluctant Grundnormen: Articles 31(3)(C) and 42 of the Vienna Convention on the Law of Treaties and the Fragmentation of International Law' 148-156.
224 *ILC Ybk (1966 vol 2)* 176-177, 267-268 on draft article 69 which is now article 73 VCLT; *ILC Ybk (1963 vol 2)* 189 para 14.

II. Responsibility of States for Internationally Wrongful Acts

The codification of the law of state responsibility was among those topics which was considered from the very beginning in a memorandum submitted by the Secretary-General as one possible subject of codification.[225] The ILC included in its first session the topic of state responsibility in its provisional list of 14 topics selected for codification,[226] and the UNGA requested "the International Law Commission, as soon as it considers it advisable, to undertake the codification of the principles of international law governing State responsibility."[227]

1. The work of García-Amador

The first Special Rapporteur, Francisco V. García-Amador, appointed in 1955, followed up on the codification efforts during the League of Nations and approached state responsibility in the context of injuries to aliens.[228] At the same time, he argued that "it is necessary to introduce in the traditional law other changes that might have been determined by the profound transformation undergone by international law"[229] and to focus on the position of the individual as subject of international law.[230] His reports therefore set out to attempt both: laying out both general features of state responsibility and the content of substantive obligations, in particular human rights.[231] However,

---

225 *Survey of International Law in Relation to the Work of Codification of the International Law Commission: Preparatory work within the purview of article 18, paragraph 1, of the International Law Commission* 56.
226 *ILC Ybk (1949)* 281.
227 UNGA Res 799 (VIII) (7 December 1953) UN Doc A/RES/799 (VIII).
228 Nissel, 'The Duality of State Responsibility' 821: "After the Second World War, the United Nations picked up the codification ball from where the League of Nations dropped it."
229 Francisco García-Amador, 'State Responsibility in the Light of the New Trends of International Law' (1955) 49 AJIL 346.
230 ibid 342; *ILC Ybk (1956 vol 1)* 228-229; on the significance of human rights see *International responsibility: report by F V Garcia Amador, Special Rapporteur* 20 January 1956 UN Doc A/CN.4/96 in *ILC Ybk (1956 vol 2)* 201-203; *ILC Ybk (1957 vol 2)* 112-115.
231 *International responsibility: Second report by F V Garcia Amador, Special Rapporteur* 15 February 1957 UN Doc A/CN.4/106 in *ILC Ybk (1957 vol 2)* 113;

The interrelationship of sources in selected projects

García-Amador's reports did not have much of a practical effect in the ILC.[232] This can be explained in part by the Commission's occupation with other topics, such as the law of the sea, and in part by the fact that García-Amador's approach was controversial within the Commission, in particular as far as it concerned questions of substantive obligations of protection of aliens.[233]

At the outset, García-Amador did not distinguish between sources.[234] He clarified that the draft article on international obligations "did not mean the 'sources' to be restricted exclusively to treaties and custom [...] the term 'sources' can be construed so broadly that the narrowest construction that can be envisaged is the one contained in Article 38 of the Statute of the International Court of Justice; that provision has the signal virtue of modifying the narrow positivist idea of sources which used to prevail."[235]

While not distinguishing between sources explicitly, García-Amador designed in his reports a system of responsibility which included not only wrongful acts, consisting of the non-fulfilment of international obligations, but also what he called arbitrary acts[236], where international responsibility would be based not exclusively on the non-fulfilment of an international obligation but "on something different: the absence of a reason or purpose to justify the measure, some irregularity in the procedure, the measure's

---

International responsibility: Third report by F V Garcia Amador, Special Rapporteur 2 January 1958 UN Doc A/CN A/111 in *ILC Ybk (1958 vol 2)* 49.

232 Daniel Müller, 'The Work of García Amador on State Responsibility for Injury Caused to Aliens' in James Crawford and others (eds), *The Law of International Responsibility* (Oxford University Press 2010) 69.

233 Nissel, 'The Duality of State Responsibility' 823-835; Alain Pellet, 'The ILC's Articles on State Responsibility for Internationally Wrongful Acts and Related Texts' in James Crawford and others (eds), *The Law of International Responsibility* (Oxford University Press 2010) 75-76; Müller, 'The Work of García Amador on State Responsibility for Injury Caused to Aliens' 72; Marina Spinedi, 'From one Codification to another: Bilateralism and Multilateralism in the Genesis of the Codification of the Law of Treaties and the Law of State Responsibility' (2002) 13(5) EJIL 1109; on the contested topic of the protection of aliens abroad see below, p. 562.

234 See Draft Article 1 of his second report, *ILC Ybk (1957 vol 2)* 105: "The expression 'international obligations of the State' shall be construed to mean, as specified in the relevant provisions of this draft, the obligations resulting from any of the sources of international law."

235 *International responsibility: Third report by F V Garcia Amador, Special Rapporteur* in *ILC Ybk (1958 vol 2)* at 50.

236 *Fourth Report on State Responsibility by Francisco V Garcia Amador,* 26 February 1959 UN Doc A/CN.4/119 in *ILC Ybk (1959 vol 2)* 7-8 paras 22-25.

discriminatory nature or, according to the circumstances, the amount, the degree of promptness or form of the compensation."[237] The prohibition of abuse of rights which was characterized in his report as a general principle of law or as a principle of international law[238] would "find its widest application in the context 'unregulated matters', that is, matters which 'are essentially within the domestic jurisdiction' of States."[239] When proposing his draft conclusion on abuse of rights, he admitted that "the distinction between cases of non-performance of concrete, exactly defined and specific international obligations and cases of 'abuse of rights' is a times very slight and difficult to establish."[240] The resulting draft conclusion then related the abuse of rights to conventional and general rules of international law, expressing the "understanding that an act or omission of this kind can only engage the responsibility of the State if such act or omission involves a breach of a rule established by treaty or of a rule of general international law stipulating the limitations to which the (legitimate) exercise of the right in question is subject."[241] In case that the Commission would prefer not to dedicate a draft article to abuse of rights, he suggested that it should be made clear that the concept of international obligations included abuse of rights as a general principle of law or a principle of international law.[242] The Commission's subsequent work on state responsibility, however, would not address substantive obligations or abuse of rights as ground for responsibility specifically, and instead focused on the consequences of a violation of international obligations.

---

237 *Fifth State responsibility report by FV Garcia-Amador, Special Rapporteur* 9 February 1960 UN Doc A/CN.4/125 and Corr. 1 in *ILC Ybk (1960 vol 2)* 60 para 78.
238 *Fifth State responsibility report by FV Garcia-Amador, Special Rapporteur* in *ILC Ybk (1960 vol 2)* 66 para 100, see also 58-59.
239 *Fifth State responsibility report by FV Garcia-Amador, Special Rapporteur* in *ILC Ybk (1960 vol 2)* 60 para 77. He referred to the question of expropriation (at 60 para 78) and to nuclear tests within a state's territory or on the high seas (64 para 93) as examples.
240 *Fifth State responsibility report by FV Garcia-Amador, Special Rapporteur* in *ILC Ybk (1960 vol 2)* 66 para 99.
241 *Fifth State responsibility report by FV Garcia-Amador, Special Rapporteur* in *ILC Ybk (1960 vol 2)* 66 para 99.
242 *Fifth State responsibility report by FV Garcia-Amador, Special Rapporteur* in *ILC Ybk (1960 vol 2)* 66 para 100; see also *International responsibility: Second report by F V Garcia Amador, Special Rapporteur* in *ILC Ybk (1957 vol 2)* 105, 107 para 11 (defining international obligations as those resulting from "any of the sources of international law").

The interrelationship of sources in selected projects

2. The focus on the rules of responsibility as secondary rules

In the codification of the law on state responsibility a significant change of method took place in the 1970s under Special Rapporteur Roberto Ago. Instead of treating substantive obligations and violations such as denial of justice as an aspect of the project, Ago suggested to separate primary norms from secondary norms[243]: The latter would constitute the abstract regime of international responsibility which followed from the violation of a so-called primary obligation. Following this approach and confining itself solely to those secondary rules, the ILC emphasized that the source of the obligation would not matter, which expressed itself in the often used formula "treaty, custom or other"[244], later changed into "whatever [the obligation's] origin"[245].

Ago's successor, Wilhelm Riphagen, attempted to introduce a certain nuance to a strict separation between primary and secondary rules. He regarded international law to be modelled "on a variety of interrelated sub-systems, within each of which the so-called 'primary rules' and the so-called 'secondary rules' are closely intertwined - indeed, inseparable."[246] Riphagen contended that the different sources are suited to different types of obligations: whereas obligations of customary international law were often implied by the intercourse of states of "mostly have the function of keeping the States apart, obligations founded on treaties may have quite a different function and may reflect a notion of sharing a common substratum, or at least a notion of organizing a parallel exercise of sovereignty in respect of certain interna-

---

243 According to Dupuy, the separation was recognized already by Anzilotti, see Pierre-Marie Dupuy, 'Dionisio Anzilotti and the Law of International Responsibility of States' (1992) 2 EJIL 143. On this distinction see also below, p. 559.

244 *ILC Ybk (1971 vol 2)* at 346 (Report to the General Assembly): "First, it would be made clear that the source of the international legal obligation which had been violated (customary, treaty or other) did not affect in any way the determination as to whether the violation was an internationally wrongful act."

245 eg *ILC Ybk (1976 vol 1)* 8 (Ago), 236 (Yasseen, criticizing the change which would be less clear than the reference to the formal sources); *ILC Ybk (1980 vol 2 part 2)* at 32. *ILC Ybk (2001 vol 2 part 2)* at 55 para 3 (commentary to article 12 ARSIWA, arguing that the term "origin" is not attended by the doubts and doctrinal debates the term "source" has provoked).

246 *Third report on the content, forms and degrees of international responsibility (part 2 of the draft articles), by Mr Willem Riphagen, Special Rapporteur* 12 and 30 March and 5 May 1982 UN Doc A/CN.4/354 and Add. 1 and 2 in *ILC Ybk (1982 vol 2 part 1)* 28 para 35.

tional situations."[247] Based on his argument that the primary obligation may affect the secondary obligations and that certain types of primary obligations relate to a particular source, Riphagen appeared to have argued in favour of a distinction between sources for the purpose of determining international responsibility. The better view is, however, that Riphagen's focus was on the relationship between primary rules and secondary rules.

His successor, Vincenzo Arangio-Ruiz had reservations about Riphagen's approach on "self-contained regimes".[248] Ultimately, the Commission adopted under Special Rapporteur Crawford, as put by Simma and Pulkowski,[249] "a pragmatic maybe", in effect leaving the question of self-contained regimes and of the relationship between special and general law[250] to the study group of fragmentation. The ARSIWA in their final version do not distinguish between sources for the purposes of international responsibility.[251]

III. Fragmentation of international law: difficulties arising from the diversification and expansion of international law

At the end of the 1990s, international legal scholars began to discuss challenges which originated from the proliferation of international court of tri-

---

247 *Third report on the content, forms and degrees of international responsibility (part 2 of the draft articles), by Mr Willem Riphagen, Special Rapporteur* in *ILC Ybk (1982 vol 2 part 1)* 29 para 46.
248 *Fourth report on State responsibility, by Mr Gaetano Arangio-Ruiz, Special Rapporteur* 12 and 25 May and 1 and 17 June 1992 UN Doc A/CN.4/444 and Add.1-3 in *ILC Ybk (1992 vol 2 part 1)* 37 para 102, 40 para 112. The object and purpose of the treaty and the relationship between special rules on responsibilities and general rules could, in the field of countermeasures, be taken into account by the principle of proportionality, 41 para 116.
249 Bruno Simma and Dirk Pulkowski, 'Of Planets and the Universe: Self-contained Regimes in International Law' (2006) 17 EJIL 493-494.
250 See article 55 ARSIWA on *lex specialis, ILC Ybk (2001 vol 2 part 2)* at 140; cf. Helmut Philipp Aust, 'The Normative Environment for Peace - On the Contribution of the ILC's Articles on State Responsibility' in Georg Nolte (ed), *Peace through International Law The Role of the International Law Commission. A Colloquium at the Occasion of its Sixtieth Anniversary* (Springer 2009) 45 on the relationship between primary and secondary rules.
251 On the distinction according to the type of obligations see also above, p. 36.

bunals and the diversification of public international law.²⁵² The debate was taken up by the International Law Commission which decided to establish a study group in order to study the difficulties arising from the diversification and expansion of international law.²⁵³ Martti Koskenniemi as chairman of the study group finalized a report, accompanied by conclusions of the Study Group. The ILC as a whole took note of the conclusions without, however, adopting the conclusions or the report as its own.²⁵⁴ The report contributed to alleviating "fragmentation anxieties"²⁵⁵ and highlighted the "omnipresence of general law" the assessment of which would remain necessary in order to understand to what extent the *lex specialis* would modify or replace the general law.²⁵⁶

The approach of the report was to seek relationships between "rules and principles (norms) of international law [...] between special and general norms, between prior and subsequent norms, and with rules and principles

---

252 Gilbert Guillaume, 'The Future of International Judicial Institutions' (1995) 44(4) ICLQ 848 ff.; Benedict Kingsbury, 'Is the Proliferation of International Courts and Tribunals a systemic Problem' (1998) 31 NYU JILP 679 ff.; Jonathan I Charney, 'The Impact on the International Legal System of the Growth of International Courts and Tribunals' (1998) 31 NYU JILP 697 ff.; Pierre-Marie Dupuy, 'The Danger of Fragmentation or Unification of the International Legal System and the International Court of Justice' (1998) 31 NYU JILP 791 ff.; Georges Abi-Saab, 'Fragmentation or Unification: Some Concluding Remarks' (1998) 31 NYU JILP 919 ff.; on the fragmentation debate considered from a historical perspective see Anne-Charlotte Martineau, 'The Rhetoric of Fragmentation: Fear and Faith in International Law' (2009) 22(1) Leiden Journal of International Law 1 ff.; see also Crema, 'The ILC's New Way of Codifying International Law, the Motives Behind It, and the Interpretive Approach Best Suited to It' 172 (arguing that "[t]he recent work of the ILC has been dedicated to help international law to find its centre, fighting back these centrifugal phenomena.").
253 Bruno Simma, 'Fragmentation in a Positive Light' (2004) 25(4) Michigan Journal of International Law 847 (on the history of the study group's name and the ultimate positive connotations of the subject-matter by speaking of "difficulties" rather than of "risks").
254 *ILC Report 2006* at 176.
255 Cf. Martti Koskenniemi and Päiv Leino, 'Fragmentation of International Law? Postmodern Anxieties' (2002) 15 Leiden Journal of International Law 553 ff.
256 *Fragmentation of international law: difficulties arising from diversification and expansion of international law, Report of the Study Group of the International Law Commission, Finalized by Martti Koskenniemi* 64 paras 119-120.

Chapter 6: The International Law Commission

with different normative power"[257] through legal reasoning.[258] Legal reasoning was understood as "purposive activity" which "should be seen not merely as a mechanic application of apparently random rules, decisions or behavioural patterns but as the operation of a whole that is directed toward some human objective".[259]

Most statements in the report on the "normative environment (system)"[260] concerned the interpretation of treaties, which is why customary international law and general principles of law were discussed mainly in relation to the interpretation and application of treaty law.[261] The report points out that the written law will not necessarily lead to the extinction of prior customary international law on a given subject.[262] The three sources, treaty, custom and general principles of law, were not ranked in "a general order of priority"[263], even though legal reasoning will often progress through concentric circles "from the treaty text to customary law and general principles of law".[264] The presumptions according to which parties "refer to general principles of international law for all questions which [the treaty] does not itself resolve in express terms or in a different way"[265] and according to which "parties intend not to act inconsistently with generally recognized principles of international law or with previous treaty obligations towards third States"[266]

---

257 *Fragmentation of international law: difficulties arising from diversification and expansion of international law, Report of the Study Group of the International Law Commission, Finalized by Martti Koskenniemi* 206 para 410.
258 ibid 20 paras 27-28.
259 ibid 24 para 35.
260 ibid 208 para 413; on the idea of law as a system and as an aim towards which interpretation strives see also Armin von Bogdandy and Ingo Venzke, 'Zur Herrschaft internationaler Gerichte: Eine Untersuchung internationaler öffentlicher Gewalt und ihrer demokratischen Rechtfertigung' (2010) 70 ZaöRV 44.
261 But see also *Fragmentation of international law: difficulties arising from diversification and expansion of international law, Report of the Study Group of the International Law Commission, Finalized by Martti Koskenniemi* 64 para 120: "No rule, treaty, or custom, however special its subject-matter or limited the number of the States concerned by it, applies in a vacuum."
262 ibid 115 para 224.
263 ibid 166 para 342.
264 ibid 223 para 463.
265 ibid 234 para 465, referring to *Georges Pinson case* France v. United Mexican States (19 October 1928) V RIAA 327 ff.
266 *Fragmentation of international law: difficulties arising from diversification and expansion of international law, Report of the Study Group of the International Law Commission, Finalized by Martti Koskenniemi* 234 para 465.

open "an especially significant (role) for customary international law and general principles of law"[267] as "customary law, general principles of law and general treaty provisions form an interpretative background for specific treaty provisions"[268].

While highlighting the importance of general principles of law and customary international law as part of the normative background against which a treaty is to be interpreted and applied, the report did not examine in detail to what extent this normative environment is important for customary international law and general principles of law. It recommended studying the scope and nature of "general international law" which might include not only custom and general principles of law in the sense of article 38(1)(c), but also "principles of international law proper and [...] analogies from domestic laws, especially principles of the legal process (such as *audiatur et altera pars*)".[269] "Principles of international law proper" were not introduced by the report as a new source of international law, but as an attempt to move from mere form to substance, to take general principles abstracted from the international legal order into account when interpreting international law.[270] As will be demonstrated below, the ILC decided to follow this suggestion in the context of its study on customary international law only to a limited extent. It is too early to tell whether these recommendations will be reflected more prominently in the Commission's work on general principles.

---

267 ibid 235 para 466.
268 ibid 211 para 421.
269 ibid 254; For a critique of this terminology see Anastasios Gourgourinis, 'General/Particular International Law and Primary/Secondary Rules: Unitary Terminology of a Fragmented System' (2011) 22 EJIL 1010, 1016.
270 See already Brownlie, *Principles of Public International Law* 19: "The rubric [general principles of international law] may refer to rules of customary law, to general principles of law as in Article 38(1)(c), or to logical propositions resulting from judicial reasoning on the basis of existing pieces of international law and municipal law analogies. [...] Examples of this type of general principle are the principles of consent, reciprocity, equality of states [...] In many cases, these principles are to be traced to state practice. However, they are primarily abstractions from the mass of rules and have been so long and so generally accepted as to be no longer directly connected with state practice. In a few cases the principle concerned, through useful, is unlikely to appear in ordinary state practice."

IV. The identification of customary international law

This section focuses on the Commission's recent work on the identification of customary international law. In this context, mention must be made of Manley O. Hudson who delivered a working paper on customary international law to the ILC in 1950 in which he suggested "that perhaps the differentiation between customary international law and conventional international law ought not to be too rigidly insisted upon" and that therefore the ILC "may deem it proper to take some account of the availability of the materials of conventional international law in connexion with its consideration of ways and means for making the evidence of customary international law more readily available."[271] In this sense, the ILC later identified custom in a legal environment that became increasingly shaped by treaties. Hudson suggested four elements, namely

> "a) concordant practice by a number of States with reference to a type of situation falling within the domain of international relations; (b) the continuation or repetition of the practice over a considerable period of time; (c) conception that the practice is required by, or consistent with, prevailing international law; (d) general acquiescence in the practice by other States."[272]

In response to his colleagues' questions about the requirement of "lawful practice", he clarified that "a single State could not decide of its own accord that the constituents of a custom were present."[273] The result of the ILC's

---

271 *Article 24 of the Statute of the International Law Commission A Working Paper by Manley O Hudson* 3 March 1950 UN Doc A/CN.4/16 + Add.1 25: "A principle or rule of customary law may be embodied in a bipartite or multipartite agreement so as to have, within the stated limits, conventional force for the States parties to the agreement so long as the agreement is in force; yet it would continue to be binding as a principle or rule of customary law for other States. Indeed, not infrequently conventional formulation by certain States of a practice also followed by other States is relied upon in efforts to establish the existence of a rule of customary law. For present purposes, therefore, the Commission may deem it proper to take some account of the availability of the materials of conventional international law in connexion with its consideration of ways and means for making the evidence of customary international law more readily available."
272 ibid 26.
273 Yepes wondered whether custom would cease to be a source of law if it had to be consistent with international law, *ILC Ybk (1950 vol 1)* 5-6, see also 5 (Hudson, Scelle), against this criterion, see Amado at 275.

preoccupation was a brief treatment of customary international law[274]. In 2011, the ILC decided to reapproach this topic, with Sir Michael Wood as Special Rapporteur.

1. The role of normative considerations in the identification of customary international law

The ILC addressed the interrelationship of sources in the context of its recent work on customary international law only to a limited extent. Even though normative considerations are not completely absent, it is submitted here that the ILC could have given more room to the question of interpretation and the role of normative considerations.

a) The scoping of the topic by the Special Rapporteur

At the beginning of the project, it seemed as if the interrelationship of sources ("merging of sources"[275]) would be given a prominent role.[276] As the ILC report indicated, "[s]everal members agreed with the proposal of the Special Rapporteur to study the relationship between customary international law and general principles of international law and general principles of law."[277] In his second report, however, the Special Rapporteur considered it to be important "as the work on the topic proceeds, to avoid entering into matters relating to other sources of international law, including general principles of law".[278] In response, several members "raised concerns about omitting

---

274 Ways and means for making the evidence of customary international law more readily available, in *ILC Ybk (1950 vol 2)* 367 ff.
275 *Report of the International Law Commission: Sixty-third session (26 April-3 June and 4 July-2 August 2011)* UN Doc A/66/10 Annex A, 306.
276 Cf. *First report on formation and evidence of customary international law by Michael Wood, Special Rapporteur* 17 May 2013 UN Doc A/CN.4/663 16-17 para 36 also available in *ILC Ybk (2013 vol 2 part 1)* 125 (the distinction between custom and general principles of law would be important, but not always clear in case-law and literature); *ILC Report 2013* at 99.
277 ibid 96.
278 *Second report on identification of customary international law by Michael Wood, Special Rapporteur* 5 para 14 also available in *ILC Ybk (2014 vol 2 part 1)* 170.

a detailed examination of the relationship between customary international law and other sources of international law, in particular general principles of law."[279] The Special Rapporteur addressed in his third report the relationship between treaties and custom and noted that general principles of law may crystallize into rules of customary international law, which is why the Special Rapporteur described general principles of law a "transitory source".[280] General principles were excluded from further consideration.[281]

b) The adopted draft conclusions

Against this background, it is not surprising that the present conclusions of the ILC excluded general principles of law and addressed only treaties in a separate conclusion.

aa) The recognition of normative considerations

The present conclusions are concerned with the "identification" and "determination" of customary international law and "do not address, directly, the

---

279 *ILC Report 2013* 243; Statement of the Chairman of the Drafting Committee, Mr. Gilberto Saboia of 7 August 2014 ⟨https://legal.un.org/ilc/sessions/66/pdfs/english/dc_chairman_statement_identification_of_custom.pdf⟩ accessed 1 February 2023 at 3-4.
280 This phrase was coined by Pellet, Alain Pellet, 'Article 38' in Andreas Zimmermann, Karin Oellers-Frahm, and Christian J Tams (eds), *The Statute of the International Court of Justice A Commentary* (2nd edn, Oxford University Press 2012) 848 para 288, 850 para 295.
281 *Third report on identification of customary international law by Michael Wood, Special Rapporteur* 27 March 2015 UN Doc A/CN.4/682 41 para 55 footnote 137 ("a source of law distinct from customary international law, and as such are beyond the scope of the present topic") also available in *ILC Ybk (2015 vol 2 part 1)* 119. On Sir Michael Wood's treatment of general principles see Michael Wood, 'What Is Public International Law? The Need for Clarity about Sources' (2011) 1(2) Asian Journal of International Law 214; Michael Wood, 'Customary international law and general principles of law' (2019) 21(3-4) International Community Law Review 307 ff.

processes by which customary international law develops over time".²⁸² In addition, "no attempt is made to explain the relationship between customary international law and other sources of international law listed in Article 38, paragraph 1, of the Statute of the International Court of Justice".²⁸³

The ILC carefully signalled that the identification of customary international law is more than a mere collection of practice and *opinio juris*, and requires one to be aware of the wider normative framework in which a given rule interacts.

> "The two-element approach does not in fact preclude a measure of deduction as an aid, to be employed with caution, in the application of the two-element approach, in particular when considering possible rules of customary international law that operate against the backdrop of rules framed in more general terms that themselves derive from and reflect a general practice accepted as law, or when concluding that possible rules of international law form part of an 'indivisible regime'."²⁸⁴

In order to illustrate that rules and principles of customary international law interrelate with each other, the ILC referred to the *Pulp Mills* case, where the ICJ related the "principle of prevention, as a customary rule" to "the due diligence that is required of a State in its territory" and with respect to "activities which take place in its territory, or in any area under its jurisdiction"²⁸⁵; the ILC also referred to the *Territorial and Maritime Dispute* case for that rules can be connected to each other and can form together one legal regime.²⁸⁶

Another example of the relevance of normative considerations can be found in conclusion 3 and the corresponding commentary, even though the very term "normative consideration" is not used. Conclusion 3 requires for an assessment of "evidence for the purpose of ascertaining whether there is a general practice and whether that practice is accepted as law" to have regard "to the overall context, the nature of the rule and the particular circumstances in which the evidence in question can be found."²⁸⁷ The commentary to this conclusion calls for contextual assessment that takes account "the subject

---

282 *ILC Report 2018* at 124 para 5.
283 ibid 124 para 6.
284 ibid 126 para 5.
285 *Pulp Mills on the River Uruguay* [2010] ICJ Rep 14, 55-56 para 101, with reference to *Corfu Channel Case* [1949] ICJ Rep 4, 22 and to *Legality of the Threat or Use of Nuclear Weapons* [1996] ICJ Rep 226, 242 para 29.
286 *Territorial and Maritime Dispute* [2012] ICJ Rep 624, 674 para 139, arguing that article 121 UNCLOS as a whole forms part of an indivisible regime.
287 *ILC Report 2018* at 126.

matter that the alleged rule is said to regulate. That implies that in each case any underlying principles of international law that may be applicable to the matter ought to be taken into account".[288] The Commission referred here in particular to the *Jurisdictional Immunities* case where state immunity was "derived from the principle of sovereign equality of States and, in that context, had to be viewed together with the principle that each State possesses sovereignty over its own territory and that there flows from that sovereignty the jurisdiction of the State over events and person within that territory".[289] The commentary points out that the assessment of evidence may also be informed by the "nature of the rule" in the sense that the identification of a prohibitive rule may often require the evaluation of inaction and its acceptance as law rather than of affirmative practice.[290]

bb) The relationship between customary international law and treaties

While not explicitly engaging with general principles of law, the conclusions address the significance of treaties for the identification of customary international law.

Conclusion 11 stipulates:

"1. A rule set forth in a treaty may reflect a rule of customary international law if it is established that the treaty rule:
(a) codified a rule of customary international law existing at the time when the treaty was concluded;
(b) has led to the crystallization of a rule of customary international law that had started to emerge prior to the conclusion of the treaty; or
(c) has given rise to a general practice that is accepted as law (opinio juris), thus generating a new rule of customary international law."
2. The fact that a rule is set forth in a number of treaties may, but does not necessarily, indicate that the treaty rule reflects a rule of customary international law."[291]

---

288 *ILC Report 2018* at 127 para 3.
289 ibid at 127 footnote 682; see also *Jurisdictional Immunities of the State* [2012] ICJ Rep 99, 123-124 para 57; see also *Interpretation of the Agreement of 25 March 1951 between the WHO and Egypt* [1980] ICJ Rep 73, 76 para 10.
290 *ILC Report 2018* at 128 para 4.
291 ibid at 143.

The commentary clarifies that the "use of the term 'rule set forth in a treaty' seeks to indicate that a rule may not necessarily be contained in a single treaty provision, but could be reflected by two or more provisions read together."[292]

With respect to the question of whether States act with *opinio juris* in pursuance of their treaty obligations, the ILC did not endorse a general presumption[293] and merely reminded the readers that the practice of States to a convention "could presumably be attributed to the treaty obligation, rather than to acceptance of the rule in question as binding under customary international law" which is why the practice of non-parties or in relation to non-parties "will have particular value".[294]

2. Concluding observations: normative considerations addressed with caution

The ILC commentary is not completely silent on normative considerations, in particular in respect to relations to other rules of customary international law.[295] The ILC highlighted the relation between a specific concretization, such as state immunity, and a more general rule or principle, such as equality of states, and recognized that rules in a treaty can reflect or give rise to rules of customary international law.

However, treaties and general principles of law are not simply material sources for customary international law but contribute to a normative environment which constantly informs, and is informed by, the identification,

---

[292] ibid at 144 para 4. In the view of the present author, this comes close to an assessment of whether rules of a treaty spell out a principle which can be important for the identification of customary international law.

[293] The Special Rapporteur came close to endorsing a general presumption in his third report: the practice of state parties to a treaty among themselves "is likely to be chiefly motivated by the conventional obligation, and thus is generally less helpful in ascertaining the existence or development of a rule of customary international law", *Third report on identification of customary international law by Michael Wood, Special Rapporteur* 28 para 41 also available in *ILC Ybk (2015 vol 2 part 1)* 113 para 41.

[294] *ILC Report 2018* at 146 para 7.

[295] Cf. already *ILC Ybk (1999 vol 1)* 290 (Tomka): "Moreover, it was difficult to conceive of two customary rules being contradictory, with one requiring a certain type of conduct and the other requiring a different type. By definition, there could not be two customary rules with conflicting content. There could be a conflict between treaty rules, but that would be an issue of the application and applicability of treaties."

interpretation and application of customary international law. If the ILC had adopted a different scope, it could have exemplified the meaning of the reference to "overall context", "nature of the rule" and "particular circumstances". It could have considered the ways in which a rule of customary international law relates to other principles of international law or to general principles of law.²⁹⁶ Taking into account new legal principles spelled out in treaties might be useful in order to interpret a rule of customary international law and its constitutive elements, practice and *opinio juris*. Such normative considerations are potentially relevant when it comes to weighing and evaluating practice. It surely makes a difference as to whether the practice is in conformity with other international obligations. Normative considerations may also be relevant for determining whether silence can be regarded as acquiescence.²⁹⁷ This could have led the ILC to adopt a draft conclusion which involves the interpretation of customary international law and addresses the interrelationship of sources. Such a draft conclusion could have looked similar to article 31(3)(c) VCLT on the interpretation of treaties: "In identifying and interpreting customary international law the normative environment as composed of the general principles of international law should be taken into account."²⁹⁸

V. Peremptory norms of general international law (*Jus cogens*)

Another project that concerns also the interrelationship of sources is the *jus cogens* project under the chairmanship of Dire Tladi.²⁹⁹ From the perspective of the interrelationship of sources, *jus cogens* raises two questions. Firstly,

---

296 As Kolb put it, "pas de texte sans context, pas de norme sans context (environment normative)", Kolb, *Interprétation et création du droit international. Esquisse d'une herméneutique juridique moderne pour le droit international public* 457.
297 Cf. conclusion 10(3), *ILC Report 2018* at 140.
298 A similar draft conclusion was proposed by *Comment by Georg Nolte, Summary record of the 3226th meeting, 17 July 2014* UN Doc A/CN.4/SR.3226 (PROV.) at 6, also available in *ILC Ybk (2014 vol 1)* 131 para 25: "In identifying rules of customary international law, account is to be taken of general principles of international law." Cf. for a similar critique Palchetti, 'The Role of General Principles in Promoting the Development of Customary International Rules' 53-56, 59. See also earlier Andrea Bianchi, 'Human Rights and the Magic of Jus Cogens' (2008) 19(3) EJIL 504.
299 The ILC adopted the draft conclusions and the commentaries on second reading in 2022 and submitted both to the UNGA, *ILC Report 2022* at 10-11.

which source can be the basis of a *jus cogens* norm? Secondly, are the effects of *jus cogens* confined to treaty law or do they extend to customary international law and even general principles of law as well?

The International Law Commission took as a starting point the definition set forth in the articles 53 and 64 VCLT. According to article 53 VCLT, a treaty is void if it conflicts with a peremptory norm of general international law, also article 64 speaks of "a new peremptory norm of general international law", which may invalidate priorly concluded treaties. Article 53 VCLT defines peremptory norm as "a norm accepted and recognized by the international community of States as a whole as a norm from which no derogation is permitted and which can be modified only by a subsequent norm of general international law having the same character." Interestingly, the phrase "accepted and recognized" was the result of the Drafting Committee's decision to add to the word "recognized" the word "accepted" because "it was to be found, together with the word 'recognized', in Article 38 of the Statute of the International Court of Justice."[300]

The Commission agreed with the Special Rapporteur that "[c]ustomary international law *is* the most common basis for peremptory norms of general international law" (conclusion 5(1)) and that "[t]reaty provisions and general principles of law *may* also serve as bases for peremptory norms of general international law" (conclusion 5(2)).[301] With respect to treaties, the commentary suggested that "[t]he role of treaties as an exceptional basis for peremptory norms of general international law (*jus cogens*) may be understood as a consequence of the relationship between treaty rules and customary international law."[302] The commentary stated it was "appropriate to refer to the possibility" that general principles of law serve as a basis and that these "are a part of general international law since they have a general scope of

---

300 *United Nations Conference on the Law of Treaties, First session Vienna, 26 March - 24 May 1968, Official Records* (vol A/CONF.39/11, 1969) 471 para 4; see also *ILC Report 2022* at 35. The ILC considers the "acceptance and recognition" to be one criterion for the identification of peremptory norms of international law, ibid 37.

301 ibid at 12, 30-35 (italics added); see also *Second report on jus cogens by Dire Tladi, Special Rapporteur* 16 March 2017 UN Doc A/CN.4/706 21-31, 46; *ILC Report 2017* 196 (general agreement on customary international law, divergent views with respect to the other sources), 199 (on the view in the debate that a norm of *jus cogens* should be equally present in all three sources).

302 *ILC Report 2022* at 34; *ILC Report 2019* at 163.

application".[303] In conclusion, the ILC conclusions accept all three sources as potential legal bases for peremptory norms of general international law, while at the same time highlighting the role of customary international law and the "scarcity of practice" in relation to treaties and general principles of law as such bases.[304]

The ILC introduced a certain differentiation also with respect to the legal effects. Several scholars argue that *jus cogens* represents the idea of normative hierarchy and thus prevails over and invalidates a contrary rule of custom which is not of a peremptory character.[305] But this approach which focuses on normative hierarchy is not unanimously shared. It has been argued by Robert Kolb that the "jus cogens mechanism centered on derogation (vel non-derogation)"[306] from special law, such as treaties, and is less suited to address collisions of general, "objective" norms.[307] The legal effect of *jus cogens* would not be described as nullity which is the effect applicable to legal acts such as treaties. Rather, a rule of custom will not emerge if a rule to the contrary is of peremptory character; likewise, a rule of custom will no longer be supported by a general practice accepted as law if a rule to the contrary of a peremptory character has emerged.[308] In Kolb's view, conflicts with general principles of law would be "hardly imaginable".[309]

---

303 *ILC Report 2022* at 34-5; *ILC Report 2019* at 161-162, it also acknowledged the existence of the view "that there was insufficient support from either the position of States or international jurisprudence" for general principles of law as legal bases.
304 *ILC Report 2022* at 35.
305 See Kleinlein, *Konstitutionalisierung im Völkerrecht Konstruktion und Elemente einer idealistischen Völkerrechtslehre* 363; Karl Zemanek, 'The Metamorphosis of Jus Cogens: From an Institution of Treaty Law to the Bedrock of the International Legal Order?' in Enzo Cannizzaro (ed), *The Law of Treaties beyond the Vienna Convention* (Oxford University Press 2011) 394-395, but see also 400-405 (critical of merging the concept of *jus cogens* with the concept of constitutional principles); cf. Alexander Orakhelashvili, *Peremptory norms in international law* (Oxford University Press 2008) 340-58.
306 Robert Kolb, *Peremptory international law - jus cogens: a general inventory* (Hart 2015) 67.
307 ibid 67.
308 ibid 69 see also at 66, pointing out that international courts so far have not given precedence to a *jus cogens* norm over customary international law; cf. *Al-Adsani v the United Kingdom [GC]* App no 35763/97 (ECtHR, 21 November 2001) paras 62-67; *Jurisdictional Immunities of the State* [2012] ICJ Rep 99, 140-142 paras 92-96.
309 Kolb, *Peremptory international law - jus cogens: a general inventory* 72.

The ILC conclusions support the view that *jus cogens* had effects not only on treaties (conclusions 10-13) but also on customary international law (conclusion 14).[310] However, whereas a treaty is or becomes void in case of conflict with a norm of jus cogens, the ILC avoided the term "void" in relation to customary international law and instead argued that a rule of customary international law "does not come into existence" (conclusion 14(1)) in case of a conflict with an already existing norm of *jus cogens* or "ceases to exist if and to the extent that it conflicts with a new peremptory norm of general international law" (conclusion 14(2)).[311] The commentary describes conclusion 14(2) as a "separability provision"[312]. This separation principle applies only to an already existing norm of customary international law, as an emerging rule would not have come into existence in the first place in case of a conflict with *jus cogens*. In a similar way, a treaty which at the time of its conclusion conflicts with *jus cogens* "is void in whole, and no separation of the provisions of the treaty is permitted" (conclusion 11(1)); in case of a conflict with a new peremptory norm, a treaty becomes void unless the provision conflicting with *jus cogens* are separable from the treaty and were not an essential basis of the consent of the parties to be bound and if the continued performance of the remainder of the treaty would not be unjust (conclusion 11(2)).[313] Separability is characterized to be an exception in relation to treaties which conflict with new *jus cogens* norms.

These conclusions indicate that the ILC recognized the different *modus operandi* of customary international law as compared to treaty law, even though the ultimate effect of peremptory norms on norms under treaties and customary international law is not different. The ILC does not endorse, however, the view that the lower ranked customary international law can also be important for defining the scope and extent of the peremptoriness[314]. Instead, the ILC emphasized the hierarchical superiority of *jus cogens*;[315] conclusion 14(1) in light of the corresponding commentary suggests that

---

310 *ILC Report 2022* at 13-14, 48 ff.; *ILC Report 2019* at 144-145; *Third report on peremptory norms of general international law (jus cogens) by Dire Tladi, Special Rapporteur* 12 February 2018 UN Doc A/CN.4/714 56-59; *ILC Report 2018* at 232 para 126.
311 *ILC Report 2022* at 55-56 (conclusion 14(1) and (2)).
312 ibid 58.
313 See ibid 51 (conclusion 11(2)). The conclusion echoes article 44(3) VCLT.
314 Cf. on this point Kolb, *Peremptory international law - jus cogens: a general inventory* 73-74.
315 *ILC Report 2022* at 56.

a norm of *jus cogens* can only be modified by a norm having the same character.[316]

The draft conclusions do not address conflicts between *jus cogens* and general principles of law. The Special Rapporteur, even though he did not address such conflicts in his reports, expressed his willingness to engage into this subject which certain members of the Commission were interested in.[317] The Drafting Committee supported the Special Rapporteur's conclusions on the effect of *jus cogens* in relation to customary international law and decided, after a debate on whether general principles of law should be addressed as well, to postpone a decision, taking account of the ongoing project on general principles of law.[318] Based on the understanding of general principles adopted in this study, it is suggested not to mechanically affirm the possibility of a conflict between *jus cogens* and general principles of law only in order to cover all three sources.[319] Since a general principle needs to be balanced against other, sometimes competing principles and be interpreted under consideration of more specific concretizations, an interpreter will unlikely arrive at a situation where a general principle will conflict with a peremptory norm.

Last but not least, the commentary on all legal effects of conflicts between *jus cogens* and treaties, customary international law, unilateral acts of states and obligations created by resolutions, decisions or other acts of international organizations refers to conclusion 20.[320] According to this con-

---

316 *ILC Report 2022* 55 (conclusion 14(1)), 57 f.; *ILC Report 2019* at 183.
317 *ILC Report 2018* at 238 para 163, see also 230 para 115: "Some members supported such non-inclusion on the ground that no conflict could possibly be conceived of in the case of general principles of law."
318 Peremptory Norms of General International Law (Jus Cogens). Statement of the Chair of the Drafting Committee Mr Claudio Grossmann Guiloff of 31 May 2019 (2019) ⟨https://legal.un.org/ilc/documentation/english/statements/2019_dc_chairman_statement_jc.pdf⟩ accessed 1 February 2023 4.
319 See also *Comment by Georg Nolte, Summary record of the 3417th meeting, 2 July 2018* UN Doc A/CN.4/SR.3417 (PROV.) at 12: Nolte did not consider it "necessary to address the consequences of peremptory norms on general principles of law. He could not conceive of a situation in which a general principle of international law could conflict with a norm of jus cogens. If such a situation were to be asserted by a State, the general principle of law would surely be interpreted in a way that would render it consistent with jus cogens." In this sense, see also Kolb, *Peremptory international law - jus cogens: a general inventory* 72, according to whom conflicts with general principles of law would be "hardly imaginable".
320 *ILC Report 2022* at 50, 60, 62, 64.

clusion, "[w]here it appears that there may be a conflict between [...] [*jus cogens*] and another rule of international law, the latter is, as far as possible, to be interpreted and applied so as to be consistent with the former." This conclusion does not distinguish between sources;[321] as the commentary emphasizes, conclusion 20 "does not apply only in relation to treaties, but to the interpretation and application of all other rules of international law."[322]

Furthermore, the commentary on legal effects also refers to conclusion 21.[323] This conclusion recommends a procedure to be followed by a state which invokes a *jus cogens* norm as a ground for the invalidity or termination of another rule of international law, a state shall notify other states concerning its claim "in writing", it should explain which measures are proposed, and depending on whether any state raises an objection within the time frame of three months, except in cases of urgency, the state can take this measure or the states concerned should seek a solution of their dispute through the means indicated in Article 33 UN Charter. Conclusion 21(3) provides that "[i]f no solution is reached within a period of twelve month, and the objecting State offers to submit the matter to the International Court of Justice or to some other procedure entailing binding decisions, the invoking State should not carry out the measure which it has proposed until the dispute is resolved."[324] This conclusion which is modelled after articles 65-67 VCLT on the procedure with respect to the invalidity, termination, withdrawal from or suspension of the operation of a treaty attempts to strike a balance:[325] it cannot impose a legally binding procedure on states which can only be done by treaty. The commentary is very clear on this point, it stresses that articles 65 to 67 VCLT, "in particular the provisions pertaining to the submission to the International Court of Justice of a dispute, cannot be said to reflect customary international law"[326] and that the conclusion "is couched in hortatory terms, to avoid any implications that its content is binding on States."[327] At the same time it seeks to address the risk of unilateral invalidation of rules by way of reference to a conflict between said rules with jus cogens and to avoid the impression that

---

321 ibid 79.
322 ibid 80 and 81 (conclusion 20 refers "to obligations under international law, whether arising under a treaty, customary international law, a general principle of law, a unilateral act or a resolution, decision or other act of an international, organization").
323 ibid 50, 53, 60, 62, 64.
324 ibid 81 (conclusion 21) and 82 on article 65-67 VCLT.
325 ibid 82-3.
326 ibid 82.
327 ibid 83.

Chapter 6: The International Law Commission

the ILC conclusions undermine somehow the procedures established under article 65-7 VCLT.

VI. General Principles of Law

1. General Principles of Law in the progressive development and codification

General principles of law played a role, albeit a limited one, in the work of the ILC. When drafting the Model Rules on Arbitral Procedure, for instance, article 10 on the applicable law copied article 38 of the ICJ-Statute and included a reference to the general principles of law.[328] At the beginning of the work on the continental shelf, the ILC attempted to explicitly base the law on the continental shelfs on general principles of law as opposed to customary international law.[329] Yet, this proposal was not well received. Sweden, for instance, agreed with the ILC in that there would be no customary law, but Sweden found itself "unable to reconcile" this position with the position that the continental shelf would be based on general principles of law.[330]

The record of plenary discussions indicates that members of the Commission did argue on the basis of general principles[331] and resorted to concepts familiar in one's own domestic law. In the discussion on the high sea, for instance, the member El-Khouri referred to Syrian municipal law for "that the owner of a property was the rightful owner of all above it to the summit

---

328 *ILC Ybk (1958 vol 2)* 83 (84), Article 10.
329 "Though numerous proclamations have been issued over the past decade, it can hardly be said that such unilateral action has already established a new customary law. It is sufficient to say that the principle of the continental shelf is based upon general principles of law which serve the present-day needs of the international community." *ILC Ybk (1951 vol 2)* 142.
330 *ILC Ybk (1953 vol 2)* 263: "The Swedish Government is unable to reconcile these two views. Moreover, the Commission gives no particulars of the "general principles of law" to which it refers."
331 *ILC Ybk (1949)* 206: Scelle emphasized, based on his monist understanding, that custom "was actually a repetition by States of acts covered by their municipal law. Before becoming a principle of international law, therefore, any principle was first a general principle of municipal law and at both stages of its development it could be applied by the Court in international matters."; *Fifth State responsibility report by FV Garcia-Amador, Special Rapporteur* in *ILC Ybk (1960 vol 2)* 65 (on abuse of rights).

of the sky and all below it to the bottom of the earth. If the principle were applied to the high seas, which belonged to no man, it must be admitted that both the sky above them and the sea-bed and subsoil below them belonged to no man, but were rather the public property of the entire world."[332]

An interesting debate arose in the context of drafting a provision on fraud in relation to the law of treaties, which is now article 49 VCLT.[333] Whereas the draft article arguably expressed a general principle of law, as the debate progressed, it was realized that the principle's applicability and concrete manifestation would depend on the international legal institutions to which it will be applied, in this case international treaties at the international level where international courts, unlike domestic courts in the domestic setting, have no compulsory jurisdiction.[334] Because of the necessary adaptation, "(i)nternational rules should not be modelled too closely on the internal law of States, seeing that the situations they were designed to regulate must be of a different character."[335] In a similar way, Yasseen required the possibility of the application of a principle in question in the international legal order, and he stressed that "there must be an environment similar to that in which it was applied in internal law."[336] In the context of this discussion, Special Rapporteur Waldock arrived at the conclusion that his draft on fraud followed fairly the concept in fraud in English law which was wider than that commonly accepted in continental legal systems.[337] On the basis of this comparative legal exercise in which the Commission had been engaged during its discussion he concluded that the wide understanding of fraud had no place in the relations between states on the international plane where stability of treaty relations would matter.[338]

---

[332] *ILC Ybk (1956 vol 1)* 137.
[333] Article 49 VCLT reads: "If a State has been induced to conclude a treaty by the fraudulent conduct of another negotiating State, the State may invoke the fraud as invalidating its consent to be bound by the treaty."
[334] *ILC Ybk (1963 vol 1)* 27-38.
[335] ibid 41 (Tunkin).
[336] ibid 42-43 (Yasseen).
[337] ibid 37.
[338] ibid 37: "A narrow definition would at the same time serve to obviate the dangers of abuse whereby States would seek to invoke fraud as a mere pretext to free themselves from obligations deriving from treaties which had proved less advantageous than originally expected. It was also desirable in order to maintain a clear distinction between fraud and other elements vitiating consent, such as coercion."

That general principles of law such as the principle of good faith inspired the progressive development and codification of international law can also be seen in the fact that the ILC included the maxim according to which no one shall take advantage of his or her own wrong in the articles 23(2)(a), 24(2)(a), 25(2)(a) ARSIWA.

2. The new topic of General Principles of Law

The ILC recently decided to include the topic "General Principles of Law" in its programme of work.[339] So far, the Special Rapporteur presented three reports.[340] In 2023, the ILC adopted the draft conclusions and the commentaries on first reading and transmitted the draft conclusions to governments for comments and observations by 1 December 2024.

a) Overview of the draft conclusions

As provisionally adopted[341], draft conclusion 1 denotes the scope of the project's topic, draft conclusion 2 stipulates that "for a general principle to exist, it must be generally recognized by the community of nations."[342] Draft conclusion 3 provides that general principles comprise those "(a) that are derived from national legal systems; (b) that may be formed within the international legal system." Draft conclusion 4 addresses the identification of general principles of law derived from national legal system, calling for

---

339 *ILC Report 2018* at 299 para 363.
340 *First report on general principles of law by Marcelo Vázquez-Bermúdez, Special Rapporteur* 5 April 2019 UN Doc A/CN.4/732; *Second report on general principles of law by Marcelo Vázquez-Bermúdez, Special Rapporteur*; *Third report on general principles of law by Marcelo Vázquez-Bermúdez, Special Rapporteur* 18 April 2022 UN Doc A/CN.4/753.
341 See *ILC Report 2022* at 306-7; *Statement of the Chairman of the Drafting Committee, Mr. Ki Gab Park of 29 July 2022* 18-9; see ILC Report 2023 at 11 ff.
342 The ILC decided to replace the formula "civilized nations" with "community of nations", see *Report of the International Law Commission: Seventy-second session (26 April–4 June and 5 July–6 August 2021)* UN Doc A/76/10 162 ("Draft conclusion 2 employs the term 'community of nations' as a substitute for the term 'civilized nations' found in Article 38, paragraph 1 (c), of the Statute of the International Court of Justice, because the latter term is anachronistic").

the ascertainment of "the existence of a principle common to the various legal systems of the world" and its "transposition to the international legal system". Draft conclusion 5 specifies the determination of the existence of such a general principle, calling for "a comparative analysis of national legal systems" that is "wide and representative" and includes "the different regions of the world" as well as an assessment of "national laws and decisions of national courts, and other relevant materials". According to draft conclusion 6, "[a] principle common to the various legal systems of the world may be transposed to the international legal system in so far as it is compatible with that system."[343] Draft conclusion 7 addresses the identification of general principles of law formed within the international legal system, requiring an ascertainment that the community of nations has recognised the principle as intrinsic to the international legal system.[344] At the same time, the conclusion stipulates that its just summarized first paragraph "is without prejudice to the question of the possible existence of other general principles of law formed within the international legal system." Draft conclusion 8 explains the function of decisions of international and national courts and tribunals as subsidiary means for the determination of such principles. Draft conclusion 9 explains the function of teachings of the most highly qualified publicists as subsidiary means. Draft conclusion 10 describes the functions of general principles. According to this conclusion, "[g]eneral principles of law are mainly resorted to when other rules of international law do not resolve a particular issue in whole or in part" (draft conclusion 10(1)).[345] Furthermore,

---

343 See *Statement of the Chairman of the Drafting Committee, Mr. Ki Gab Park of 29 July 2022* at 6; ILC Report 2023 at 21 (stressing that transposition does not occur in an automatic fashion).

344 This category of general principles was disputed within the drafting committee. The Drafting Committee's Chairman described this conclusion as "a compromise solution" the adoption of which was based "on the understanding that the discussion within the Committee and the differing views among members would be elaborated in the commentary." See ibid at 7, on the different views see also *ILC Report 2022* at 318-9, 323; ILC Report 2023 at 24 f.

345 The Drafting Committee did not take up the Special Rapporteur's formulation of the "gap-filling" role, "as the Committee considered this term to be colloquial and not entirely accurate [...] It was considered important to avoid the misconception that general principles of law played an ancillary role." The term "mainly resorted to" and the qualifier "mainly" "aims to convey the idea that this is the main role played by general principles in practice, while preserving a certain degree of flexibility, since they may play other roles." See *Statement of the Chairman of the Drafting Committee, Mr. Ki Gab Park of 29 July 2022* at 12-3; ILC Report 2023 at 29; cf.

general principles are said to "contribute to the coherence of the international legal system. They may serve, *inter alia*, (a) to interpret and complement other rules of international law; (b) as a basis for primary rights and obligations, as well as a basis for secondary and procedural rules."[346] Draft conclusion 11 addresses the relationship between general principles of law and treaties and customary international law.[347] It provides that general principles "are not in a hierarchical relationship" with the other two sources, that a general principle of law "may exist in parallel with a rule of the same or similar content in a treaty or customary international law" and that any conflict between a general principle "and a rule in a treaty or customary international law is to be resolved by applying the generally accepted techniques of interpretation and conflict resolution in international law."[348]

b) Comments and reflections on the draft conclusions

The project is still ongoing, but several points deserve emphasis: There is no unanimity as to the category of general principles of international law. Both the Special Rapporteur's third report and the Report of the Commission illustrate concerns within the Commission and among states with respect to the second category of general principles.[349] Still, it is noteworthy that despite

---

Third report on general principles of law by Marcelo Vázquez-Bermúdez, Special Rapporteur at 16 ff.

346 Cf. *Statement of the Chairman of the Drafting Committee, Mr. Ki Gab Park of 29 July 2022* 13; ILC Report 2023 at 29 f. ("While rules dervied from other sources of international law also contribute ti the coherence of the international legal system, certain general principles appear to be aimed at performing this function in a more direct manner.").

347 ILC Report 2023 at 33 ff.

348 See ILC Report 2023 at 33; cf. *Third report on general principles of law by Marcelo Vázquez-Bermúdez, Special Rapporteur* 35 ff.

349 ibid 9-10; *ILC Report 2022* at 318-9 ("The existence of this category of general principles of law [...] appears to find support in the jurisprudence of courts and tribunals and teachings. Some members, however, consider that Article 38, paragraph 1 (c), does not encompass a second category of general principles of law, or at least remain sceptical of its existence as an autonomous source of international law."); ILC Report 2023 at 25; see also *Comment by Shinya Murase, Summary record of the 3587th meeting, 4 July 2022* UN Doc A/CN.4/SR.3587 (PROV.) 5 (article 38(1)(c) referred only to "domestic law principles"); *Comment by Huikang Huang, Summary*

the lack of unanimity, general principles formed within the international legal system were included by the Special Rapporteur and the ILC. The commentary to draft conclusion 7 justifies the existence of this category of general principles by way of reference to several arguments: examples in judicial practice in support of this category, "the international legal system, like any other legal system, must be able to generate general principles of law that are intrinsic to it, which may reflect and regulate its basic features, and not have only general principles of law borrowed from other legal systems", the lack of indications in the text of article 38 or in its traveaux préparatoires that would exclude such principles.[350]

When it comes to the methodology, the commentary stresses the similarities between both categories of general principles; both categories require "an inductive analysis of existing norms", furthermore, "the methodology is also deductive" as "the compatibility with the international legal system" in case of general principles of the first category needs to be examined, whereas in the case of general principles of the second category "it must be shown that such principles are intrinsic to the international legal system."[351]

At the same time, the commentary points to concerns expressed in the Commission.[352] Those who remained sceptical expressed, for instance, the "concern that no sufficient State practice, jurisprudence or teachings existed to support fully the existence of the second category" and that the distinction between customary international law and such principles was unclear.[353] It was also argued that "during the drafting of the Statute of the International Court of Justice, the proposal for creation of general principles of law within the international legal system was not accepted".[354] However, the Chilean proposal was based on the motivation to include a reference to "international law", and the rejection of several delegates was motivated by the view "that

---

record of the 3590th meeting, 7 July 2022 UN Doc A/CN.4/SR.3590 (PROV.) at 7; on doubts see *Comment by Mathias Forteau, Summary record of the 3588th meeting, 5 July 2022* at 12; *Comment by Ki-Gab Park, Summary record of the 3588th meeting, 5 July 2022* UN Doc A/CN.4/SR.3588 (PROV.) at 18; *Comment by August Reinisch, Summary record of the 3589th meeting, 6 July 2022* UN Doc A/CN.4/SR.3589 (PROV.) 18.

350 *ILC Report 2022* at 322; ILC Report 2023 at 22 f.
351 ibid at 322; ILC Report 2023 at 23; see also *Third report on general principles of law by Marcelo Vázquez-Bermúdez, Special Rapporteur* at 38.
352 *ILC Report 2022* at 323; ILC Report 2023 at 25.
353 ibid at 323; see now ILC Report 2023 at 25.
354 ibid at 323.

Article 38 had always been regarded as carrying an implicit mandate to apply international law."[355]

When it comes to the subsidiary means for the identification, the functions of general principles and the relationship with other sources, the draft conclusions do not distinguish between the two categories of general principles. It is noteworthy that the Drafting Committee did not follow the Special Rapporteur's emphasis on the "gap-filling" function which the Special Rapporteur considered to be "the essential function" and the "basic role" of general principles.[356] Some of the examples cited by the Special Rapporteur in support of this "gap-filling" function can also be read as examples illustrating that recourse to general principles can help establishing default positions and operate as the general law.[357] In contrast to a strong emphasis on the gap-filling function of general principles, the view has been expressed in the Commission that "general principles of law did not have a monopoly on filling gaps, since treaties and customary international law could also play a similar role" and that the main role of general principles might rather concern "the interpretation and application of existing rules", providing "coherence to the international legal system."[358] In addition, it was argued that a strong focus on the gap-filling function was in tension with the Special Rapporteur's

---

355 *Documents of the United Nations Conference on International Organization, San Francisco, 1945 Vol XIII* (United Nations Information Organizations 1945) 164, the delegate of Chile had proposed the insertion of the phrase "and especially the principles of international law" in article 38(1)(c) ICJ Statute. Cf. on this amendment and the accepted amendment to include a reference to the function of the Court, namely "to decide in accordance with international law", Pellet and Müller, 'Article 38' 833.
356 Cf. *Third report on general principles of law by Marcelo Vázquez-Bermúdez, Special Rapporteur* 15 ff. (quote at 16).
357 Cf. ibid 19, where the Special Rapporteur refers to the *Russian Indemnity* case where the Tribunal held that "the general principle of the responsibility of States implies a special responsibility in the matter of delay in the payment of a monetary debt, *unless* the existence of contrary international custom is established" (italics added). See also ibid 20, reference to *Beagle Channel* case, where "the Court considers it as amounting to an overriding general principle of law that, in the absence of express provision to the contrary, an attribution of territory must *ipso facto* carry with it the waters appurtenant to the territory attributed." See also the reference to the *Proceedings concerning the OSPAR Convention*: "An international tribunal, such as this Tribunal, will also apply customary international law and general principles unless and to the extent that the Parties have created a *lex specialis*."
358 *ILC Report 2022* at 312-3; see also *Comment by August Reinisch, Summary record of the 3589th meeting, 6 July 2022* at 16-17; *Comment by Eduardo Valencia-Ospina*,

assumption of a lack of hierarchy between the sources[359] and that "finding evidence of State recognition of the general principle of law in question would be challenging."[360] In response to the Special Rapporteur's proposal to have one conclusion on the "essential function" of gap-filling and another conclusion on "specific functions" of general principles,[361] several members suggested merging the conclusions on functions and not to distinguish between essential and specific functions, certain members also argued that "the functions listed in the draft conclusion were not specific to general principles of law, but rather functions common to all sources of international law."[362] Against the background of this discussion, the present draft conclusion 10 provides that general principles are "*mainly* resorted to when other rules of international law do not resolve a particular issue in whole or in part"[363] and stresses the role of general principles in interpreting and complementing other rules and as a basis for primary rights and obligations as well as a basis for secondary and procedural rules. Different views were expressed, however, on the question of whether general principles of law could serve as an independent basis for rights and obligations.[364] Certain members were reluctant and regarded general principles to be a subsidiary source[365], other members argued that general principles of law can serve as an independent source, but this particular function should not be "unduly emphasiz[ed] [...] in part because it was not common, and in part because the Commission's work should not encourage attempts to turn to general principles of law

---

Summary record of the 3589th meeting, 6 July 2022 UN Doc A/CN.4/SR.3589 (PROV.) 4-5.

359 *Comment by Sean Murphy, Summary record of the 3587th meeting, 4 July 2022* UN Doc A/CN.4/SR.3587 (PROV.) 8; *Comment by Claudio Grossman Guiloff, Summary record of the 3590th meeting, 7 July 2022* UN Doc A/CN.4/SR.3590 (PROV.) 4.
360 *ILC Report 2022* 310.
361 ibid at 307 footnote 1188.
362 ibid 313.
363 ibid 308 footnote 1189 (italics added); see now ILC Report 2023 at 29, the formula "mainly" indicates that general principles "may be directly resorted to depending on the circumstances".
364 ibid 313.
365 *Comment by Huikang Huang, Summary record of the 3590th meeting, 7 July 2022* at 5; but see now ILC Report 2023 at 29, 31 f., 33, where the commentary stresses that the role of general principles is not necessarily confined to an ancillary role, that "like any other source of international law, general principles of law may give rise to substantive rights and obligations" and that "no hierarchical relationship exists" between the three sources.

to find rights and obligations that did not appear in treaties or arise from customary international law."[366] In particular, the concern was raised that the ILC's work on general principles formed within the international legal system could entail the "risk of dissipating the requirement for State consent to international obligations".[367]

The relationship between the sources is addressed at an abstract level. The present draft conclusion 11 on the relationship between general principles and the other two sources does not take up the Special Rapporteur's suggestion of a separate conclusion according to which "[t]he relationship between general principles of law with rules of the other sources of international law addressing the same subject-matter is governed by the *lex specialis* principle"[368], certain members had expressed reservations against such a focus since the relationship could be governed by other principles as well, such as the *lex posterior* principle.[369] The present draft conclusion 11 now highlights the lack of hierarchy between general principles of law and the other two sources, the parallel existence between a general principle of law and a rule in a treaty or in customary international law and "the generally accepted techniques of interpretation and conflict resolution in international

---

[366] *Comment by Sean Murphy, Summary record of the 3587th meeting, 4 July 2022* at 9 ("While he was not taking the position that general principles of law could never serve as an independent source of rights and obligations, he believed that the Commission should avoid unduly emphasizing such a function, in part because it was not common, and in part because the Commission's work should not encourage attempts to turn to general principles of law to find rights and obligations that did not appear in treaties or arise from customary international law.").

[367] ibid at 7 ("Such a methodology was not likely to resolve existing concerns about the second category, and ran the risk of encouraging decision-makers to identify miscellaneous principles as general principles of law that overwhelmed the other sources of international law, as well as the risk of dissipating the requirement for State consent to international obligations – perhaps even at the risk of unravelling the system of international law."); *Comment by August Reinisch, Summary record of the 3589th meeting, 6 July 2022* at 19; see also *Comment by Claudio Grossman Guiloff, Summary record of the 3590th meeting, 7 July 2022* at 3.

[368] Cf. *ILC Report 2022* 307; *Third report on general principles of law by Marcelo Vázquez-Bermúdez, Special Rapporteur* 35 ff.

[369] Cf. *ILC Report 2022* at 312; see also for reservations *Comment by Mathias Forteau, Summary record of the 3588th meeting, 5 July 2022* at 14; *Comment by Sir Michael Wood, Summary record of the 3588th meeting, 5 July 2022* UN Doc A/CN.4/SR.3588 (PROV.) at 16 (sceptical of sole focus on lex specialis); *Comment by Ki-Gab Park, Summary record of the 3588th meeting, 5 July 2022* at 18; *Comment by August Reinisch, Summary record of the 3589th meeting, 6 July 2022* at 17.

The interrelationship of sources in selected projects

law" which are said to govern potential conflicts between general principles of law and a rule in a treaty or in customary international law. Within the commission, the usefulness of draft conclusion 11 on the relationship between general principles on the one hand and treaties and customary international law on the other hand was debated.[370]

The commentary to draft conclusion 11 now describes the interplay to a certain extent, in that a general principle of law which has been codified in a treaty can continue to inform the interpretation and application of said treaty and that similar considerations apply to customary international law.

The creative role of the law-applying authorities has been described to a certain extent with respect to principles underlying general rules of conventional and customary international law in the Special Rapporteur's second report. According to the Special Rapporteur, "the approach here is essentially deductive"[371]. But in contrast to customary international law, where the deductive approach "can be employed only 'as an aid' in the application of the two-elements approach"[372], the deduction in relation to the ascertainment of general principles is different:

> "This deduction exercise is not an aid to ascertain the existence of a general practice accepted as law, but the main criterion *to establish the existence* of a legal principle that has a general scope and may be applied to a situation not initially envisaged by the rules from which it was derived. Similar considerations may apply to principles inherent in the basic features and fundamental requirements of the international legal system [...]"[373]

The expression of "the main criterion *to establish the existence*" comes very close to acknowledging the creative role of courts but there have not been further elaborations on this expression in the third report or in the commentary on draft conclusion 7. Rather than a focus on the role of law-applying authorities, one can find an emphasis on state consent and of the recogni-

---

370 *ILC Report 2022* at 312 (certain members suggested that "the content of draft conclusion 11 could be dealt with in the commentary and that the discussion on parallel existence was not relevant to the topic since the Commission was not engaged in a general discussion on sources."); see also the scepticism expressed by *Comment by Sir Michael Wood, Summary record of the 3588th meeting, 5 July 2022* at 15; *Comment by Aniruddha Rajput, Summary record of the 3589th meeting, 6 July 2022* UN Doc A/CN.4/SR.3589 (PROV.) at 14; but see now ILC Report 2023 at 34 f.
371 *Second report on general principles of law by Marcelo Vázquez-Bermúdez, Special Rapporteur* 52 para 166.
372 ibid 52 para 167.
373 ibid 53 para 168 (italics added).

tion requirement. The Special Rapporteur proposed that the requirement of recognition "takes place on two levels", as it relates to the acceptance of a principle in domestic legal systems and to the principle's transposition.[374] The commentary stipulates that "recognition is implicit when the compatibility test is fulfilled" and that the recognition of the transposition can be inferred if a principle of the common legal systems is suitable for application within international law.[375]

It remains to be seen how the project will further develop. Since general principles of law are one of the three sources according to article 38(1) ICJ Statute, legal operators and in particular courts need to apply them. The ILC could provide guidance, as it did with respect to customary international law or to the interpretation of treaties in light of subsequent agreements and subsequent practice. The ILC's focus on international practice can lead to a product which will reaffirm and strengthen the acceptability of general principles as a source of international law but its focus may at the same time leave questions unanswered. Not every aspect can be proven by decisions of courts and tribunals which are important evidence in the debates within the ILC.[376] For instance, the ILC draft conclusions and the commentary have

---

374 *Third report on general principles of law by Marcelo Vázquez-Bermúdez, Special Rapporteur* 30; cf. on the different views on the Commission *ILC Report 2022* at 310; *Comment by Sean Murphy, Summary record of the 3587th meeting, 4 July 2022* at 6 ("requirement of recognition was pertinent both to the principle's existence across national legal systems and to the principle's transposition")*Comment by August Reinisch, Summary record of the 3589th meeting, 6 July 2022* at 15 ("He supported the Special Rapporteur's view that transposition was not a formal act, but rather an implicit recognition that a principle was suitable to be applied in the international legal system."); *Comment by Eduardo Valencia-Ospina, Summary record of the 3589th meeting, 6 July 2022* at 3 ("the transposability requirement could not result from the requirement that States must "recognize" a given principle, because the former was passive, whereas the latter was active."); see also *ILC Report 2021* at 163 (commentary to draft conclusion 4: "[the requirement of recognition] is necessary to show that a principle is not only recognized by the community of nations in national legal systems, but that it is also recognized as applicable within the international legal system").
375 See ILC Report 2023 at 22; cf. *ILC Report 2022* at 311.
376 Cf. *Comment by August Reinisch, Summary record of the 3589th meeting, 6 July 2022* at 16 ("[...] any perceived 'proof' in a specific decision should always be treated with caution, since judicial and arbitral decisions might be ambiguous and unclear in terms of the extent to which they relied on classical concepts of general principles of law formed within national legal systems or, indeed, on principles formed within the international legal system.").

so far not addressed in detail the differences between general principles of law and the other sources which relate to the generality and abstractness of many general principles.[377] At the same time, a certain institutional self-restraint does not have to be criticized. Just like customary international law, general principles can evolve unconsciously and, in the words of Wolfgang Friedmann, "remain implicit, insofar as they are assumed rather than spelled out"[378]. If general principles of law constitute a concept that is intrinsic to the idea of law as such, potentially present in any legal order and an expression of the law in action, then a codifier can arguably not authoritatively set in stone which principles exist[379] and how principles operate.[380]

D. Concluding Observations

This chapter examined the interrelationship of sources in the work of the ILC. It began by exploring the implications and repercussions of the codification project on the interrelationship of sources and the place of normative considerations.[381] Subsequently, it analyzed how the form given to an ILC project favoured customary international law.[382] The chapter then delved into selected topics in order to explore the interrelationship of sources as a *motif*.[383]

In particular, this chapter demonstrated that the progressive development and codification of international law entail judgment calls which the ILC has made under consideration of the normative environment and principles

---

377 *Comment by Sean Murphy, Summary record of the 3587th meeting, 4 July 2022* at 8 ("General principles of law were not just another source of law; they advanced more abstract legal concepts than were generally found in treaties or custom. Given their abstract and fundamental nature, general principles of law were arguably lex generalis."); on arguments based on the difference between principles and rules see *Comment by Ki-Gab Park, Summary record of the 3588th meeting, 5 July 2022* at 18-9.
378 Wolfgang Friedmann, 'The Uses of "General Principles" in the Development of International Law' (1963) 57 AJIL 283.
379 For the proposal to focus on a list of general principles see *Comment by Huikang Huang, Summary record of the 3590th meeting, 7 July 2022* at 6.
380 Cf. Esser, *Grundsatz und Norm in der richterlichen Fortbildung des Privatrechts Rechtsvergleichende Beiträge zur Rechtsquellen- und Interpretationslehre* 330.
381 See above, p. 317.
382 See above, p. 340.
383 See above, p. 354.

expressed in the international legal order.[384] The recent discussions in the context of immunity from foreign criminal jurisdiction illustrate the challenges that can arise, both in relation to normative considerations and when interpreting possible forms of evidence of customary international law.[385]

Furthermore, this chapter highlighted by way of example factors which explained that codification in public international law did not lead to the elimination of customary international law. Perhaps counterintuitively, the choice for conventions as form for the product's outcome may have been favourable to customary international law in the long run, since conventions and diplomatic conferences provided all states with the opportunity to take part in shaping, and to become invested in, the international legal order. The decision to include "rules" on interpretation in what became the VCLT implied a scope of application of customary international law as legal basis for these rules when the VCLT was not applicable as the ratification process of codification conventions proved to be tardy.[386] Another reason for the continuing relevance of customary international law is what this chapter referred to as "codification light",[387] meaning the ILC's increased use of nonbinding documents the authority of which rest on their accordance with customary international law. This chapter illustrated that several actors take part in "staging the authority" of a nonbinding codification. For all of these reasons, codification in international law cannot withdraw itself from the international practice and the risk which von Savigny[388] alluded to, namely that an artificial codification is out of touch with the views of a legal community, is minimized in public international law.

A certain policy seems to be to avoid a potential sources bias. The ILC did not distinguish between sources in its work on state responsibility, also because of the focus on secondary rules, or in its analysis of subsequent agreements and subsequent practice after the adoption of the Vienna Convention. In its recent *jus cogens* project, all sources are considered to be potentially relevant, even though a preference is expressed for customary international law as legal basis and differences between the sources as far as legal effects of *jus cogens* are concerned are acknowledged. Last but not

---

384 See above, p. 320.
385 See above, p. 330.
386 See above, p. 344.
387 See above, p. 348.
388 See above, p. 129.

least, the decision to dedicate one project to general principles of law aligns with this approach.

Chapter 7: Concluding observations on the institutional perspectives

The preceding two chapters examined two institutions in greater detail, the International Court of Justice and the International Law Commission. They share commonalities in that they are both organs of the United Nations, the ICJ being a principal organ (articles 7(1), 92 UNC) and the ILC a subsidiary organ of the UNGA (articles 7(2), 22 UNC). Moreover, their mandates are not confined to one field or area of international law; in principle, they can be concerned with all questions of international law, not only incidentally through the lenses of a particular regime. In other aspects, the institutions are different. The ICJ is primarily concerned with the application of the law to a specific set of facts, whereas the ILC examines international law on a more general level. The ICJ has to apply the *lex lata*, whereas the ILC engages in the progressive development and codification of international law and can propose solutions *de lege ferenda*.

The preceding chapters demonstrated that institutions are not necessarily neutral when it comes the interrelationship of sources. In particular, the setting in which the ICJ operates favours to a certain extent conventions over other sources, when it comes to the intervention system or the Court's jurisdiction based on the Statute in conjunction with compromissory clauses. The ICJ was nevertheless willing and able to pronounce itself on questions of general international law, in particular, but not only when parties to the dispute agree on the existence of a rule of customary international law. As general principles of law ascertained in municipal legal orders do no feature prominently in the Court's judgments, states will presumably invoke other concepts or general principles of international law when they make case their case. Turning to the ILC, one could have thought that the establishment of the ILC in order to progressively develop and codify international law would go to the detriment of customary international law and that, therefore, the very establishment of the ILC expressed a preference against one source (customary international law) and benefited treaties. The practice since the ILC's establishment has developed differently, however. The ILC contributed to the acceptability of customary international in the international community, and by studying not only questions of treaty law and customary international law but also general principles of law in a separate project, the ILC avoided

399

Chapter 7: Concluding observations on the institutional perspectives

a sources bias which could have arisen if, for instance, general principles had not been chosen as a separate topic.

In conclusion, both the ICJ and the ILC consider principles expressed in treaties when identifying, for the purposes of judicial application or for the purpose of progressively developing and codifying, customary international law.

Whereas the preceding chapters studied the "generalist" perspective, the next chapters will be concerned with the interrelationship of sources through the lenses of specialized courts and tribunals.

Part D.

Perspectives in different fields of international law

Chapter 8: The European Convention on Human Rights

A. Introduction

This chapter analyzes the interrelationship of sources in a centralized, treaty-based system, the ECHR, with its own judiciary, the European Court of Human Rights. The chapter will first explore the way in which the European Court interprets the ECHR and takes into account other rules of international law when interpreting states' obligations under the ECHR (B.). Subsequently, the chapter will demonstrate how the interpretation and application of customary international law and general principles of law can contribute to the interpretation of the ECHR and how the specific incorporation of these sources by the European Court can further and shape the development of general international law (C.). It is submitted that the European Court did not always just apply general international law "as it stands"[1]; in certain instances, the European Court establishes a relationship between the object and purpose of the ECHR and general international law which can influence the development of the latter.[2] Last but not least, the chapter will point to "functional equivalents" to concepts of general international law which are based on an interpretation of the ECHR (D.).

The purpose of this chapter is not to comprehensively address all questions on the relationship between international human rights law and the sources of international law. Since human rights law consists mainly of widely ratified universal and regional treaties, the debate on whether human rights can be justified as part of customary international law in spite of the existence of a practice of numerous human rights violations[3] has lost, at first sight, a certain

---

1 Cf. *Al-Dulimi and Montana Managment Inc v Switzerland [GC]* App no 5809/08 (ECtHR, 21 June 2016) Diss Op Nußberger 145.
2 Cf. on the way in which public international law is perceived through the lenses of a special regime's quasi-judicial body, Michaels and Pauwelyn, 'Conflict of Norms or Conflict of Laws: Different Techniques in the Fragmentation of Public International Law' 349 ff.
3 For an overview, see Theodor Meron, *Human Rights and Humanitarian Norms as Customary Law* (Clarendon Press 1989); Martti Koskenniemi, 'The Pull of the Mainstream' (1989) 88 Michigan Law Review 1947 ff.; Simma and Alston, 'The Sources of Human Rights Law: Custom, Jus Cogens, and General Principles' 83 ff.; Eckart Klein (ed), *Menschenrechtsschutz durch Gewohnheitsrecht: Kolloquium 26.-28. September 2002*

relevance. Reservations to human rights treaties, which in principle illustrate the continuing importance of customary international law as a source of human rights law, have become subject to an evaluation of the reservation's compatibility with the object and purpose of human rights treaties by treaty bodies,[4] and denunciations of treaty obligations have become subject to review by treaty bodies and were, according to a view expressed by the Human Rights Committee with respect to the ICCPR which does not include a provision on denunciation, impermissible.[5] The extraterritorial applicability of human rights treaties has increasingly received more acceptance, which also reduces to some extent the relevance of the question of whether human

---

Potsdam (Berlin, 2003); Hugh W Thirlway, 'Human Rights in Customary Law: An Attempt to Define Some of the Issues' (2015) 28(3) Leiden Journal of International Law 496 ff.; Brownlie, 'International Law at the Fiftieth Anniversary of the United Nations, General Course on Public International Law' 84, referring to the Third Restatement on Foreign Relations Law and arguing that "literature on human rights tend to neglect the role, or potential role, of customary law"; Georg Schwarzenberger, *The Frontiers of International Law* (Stevens & Sons 1962) 130-145 on British practice to invoke human rights against other governments.

4 Human Rights Committee *General Comment No 24: Issues Relating to Reservations Made upon Ratification or Accession to the Covenant or the Optional Protocols thereto, or in Relation to Declarations under Article 41 of the Covenant*; but see also *Report of the Human Rights Committee* UN Doc A/50/40 (3 October 1995) 130 ff. (observations by the United States of Ameria and by the United Kingdom of Great Britain and Northern Ireland); see Bruno Simma, 'Reservations to human rights treaties: some recent developments' in Alfred Rest and others (eds), *Liber amicorum Professor Ignaz Seidl-Hohenveldern in honour of his 80th birthday* (Kluwer Law International 1998) 659 ff.; Ryan Goodman, 'Human Rights Treaties, Invalid Reservations, and State Consent' (2002) 96(3) AJIL 531 ff.; Alain Pellet and Daniel Müller, 'Reservations to Human Rights Treaties: not an Absolute Evil ...' in Ulrich Fastenrath and others (eds), *From bilateralism to community interest: essays in honour of judge Bruno Simma* (Oxford University Press 2011) 521 ff.; see Akbar Rasulov, 'The Life and Times of the Modern Law of Reservations: the Doctrinal Genealogy of General Comment No. 24' (2009) 14 Austrian review of international and European law 105 ff.

5 *General Comment No 26: Continuity of Obligations* CCPR/C/21/Rev.1/Add.8/Rev.1, 8 December 1997 para 5; cf. Yogesh Tyagi, 'The Denunciation of Human Rights Treaties' (2008) 79 BYIL 86 ff.; see also Eckhart Klein, 'Denunciation of Human Rights Treaties and the Principle of Reciprocity' in Ulrich Fastenrath and others (eds), *From bilateralism to community interest: essays in honour of Judge Bruno Simma* (Oxford University Press 2011) 477 ff, 484-487 (with reference to article 54(b) VCLT for the view that all parties together can terminate a treaty).

Introduction

rights apply as a matter of customary international law outside a state's borders.[6]

Yet, it must be pointed out that the topic of human rights as customary international law or general principles of law has not lost all of its relevance.[7] Still, human rights treaties have not been ratified by all states. In addition, customary international law can be relevant for parties to human

---

6 On the extraterritorial application of human rights treaties see *General Comment No 31: The Nature of the General Legal Obligation Imposed on States Parties to the Covenant* Human Rights Committee CCPR/C/21/Rev.1/Add. 13 (26 May 2004) para 10; *General Comment No 36 on article 6 of the International Covenant on Civil and Political Rights, on the right to life Advanced unedited version* Human Rights Committee CCPR/C/GC/36 (30 October 2018) para 63; *Legal Consequences of the Construction of a Wall* [2004] ICJ Rep 136, 178-180 paras 107-111; *Armed Activities on the Territory of the Congo* [2005] ICJ Rep 168, 242-244 paras 216-217; *Application of the International Convention on the Elimination of All Forms of Racial Discrimination (Georgia v. Russian Federation)* (Provisional Measures, Order of 15 October 2008) [2008] ICJ Rep 386 para 109; see already *Legal Consequences for States of the Continued Presence of South Africa in Namibia (South West Africa) notwithstanding Security Council Resolution 276 (1970)* [1971] ICJ Rep 16, 54 para 118 ("physical control of a territory [...] is the basis of State liability for acts affecting other states"); according to Ralph Wilde, 'Human Rights Beyond Borders at the World Court: The Significance of the International Court of Justice's Jurisprudence on the Extraterritorial Application of International Human Rights Law Treaties' (2013) 12 Chinese Journal of International Law 663, the Namibia opinion constituted a "a ground breaking decision on the extraterritorial application of human rights"; *Al-Skeini and Others v The United Kingdom [GC]* App no 55721/07 (ECtHR, 7 July 2011) paras 130-142; but see now *Georgia v Russia (II) [GC]* App no 38263/08 (ECtHR, 21 January 2021) paras 125-144; *Rights and Guarantees of Children in the context of migration and/or in need of international protection* IACtHR Advisory Opinion (19 August 2014) OC-21/14 para 61; *The Environment and Human Rights (State Obligations in Relation to the Environment in the Context of the Protection and Guarantee of the Rights to Life and to Personal Integrity: Interpretation and Scope of Articles 4(1) and 5(1) of the American Convention on Human Rights* IACtHR Advisory Opinion (15 November 2017) OC-23/18 paras 78-82; Walter Kälin and Jörg Künzli, *The Law of International Human Rights Protection* (2nd edn, Oxford University Press 2019) 14-137; not recognizing the extraterritorial applicability of the ICCPR: US Department of Defense, *Law of War Manual June 2015 (Updated December 2016)* (Washington, D.C., 2016) 24, 758, 1035.

7 See for instance *United Nations Basic Principles and Guidelines on Remedies and Procedures on the Right of Anyone Deprived of Their Liberty to Bring Proceedings Before a Court* Report of the Working Group on Arbitrary Detention (6 July 2015) UN Doc A/HRC/30/37, examining customary human rights law on arbitrary detention. On human rights rights as general principles see Simma and Alston, 'The Sources of Human Rights Law: Custom, Jus Cogens, and General Principles' 82 ff.

405

rights treaties. The Human Rights Committee rejected the permissibility of reservations to precisely those human rights obligations which were also protected under customary international law.[8] Custom remains also relevant for instance when it comes to state succession if one is of the view that a new state, while not being bound by treaty obligations, is at least bound by general international law.[9]

The question which this chapter addresses, however, is not whether human rights can be justified as freestanding customary international law[10] but whether and how international law, including customary international law and general principle of law, informs and is informed by the human rights law, in particular the ECHR.[11]

B. The interpretation of the ECHR

The interpretation of the ECHR is governed by the general rules of interpretation as set forth in the articles 31-33 VCLT.[12]

---

8 Human Rights Committee *General Comment No 26: Continuity of Obligations*.
9 On the debate whether a successor is bound by human rights treaties of the predecessor see Akbar Rasulov, 'Revisiting State Succession to Humanitarian Treaties: Is There a Case for Automaticity?' (2003) 14(1) EJIL 141 ff.; Menno Tjeerd Kamminga, 'State succession in respect of human rights treaties' (1996) 7(4) EJIL 469 ff.; Andreas Zimmermann, *Staatennachfolge in völkerrechtliche Verträge: zugleich ein Beitrag zu den Möglichkeiten und Grenzen völkerrechtlicher Kodifikation* (Springer 2000) 543 ff.
10 Both Meron and Cheng justify the importance of *opinio juri*s (*generalis* as opposed to *conventionalis*) in the field of human rights not only by the subject-matter and its contrafactual character, but by the fact that states decided to conclude human rights treaties: Theodor Meron, 'The Geneva Conventions as Customary Law' (1987) 81 AJIL 367; Cheng, 'Custom: the future of general state practice in a divided world' 532-533; see also Thirlway, 'Human Rights in Customary Law: An Attempt to Define Some of the Issues' 495 ff.
11 Convention for the Protection of Human Rights and Fundamental Freedoms (signed 4 November 1950, entered into force 3 September 1953) 213 UNTS 221; for an overview see Luzius Wildhaber, 'The European Court of Human Rights: The Past, The Present, The Future' (2007) 22 American University International Law Review 521 ff.
12 *Golder v United Kingdom [Plenum]* App no 4451/70 (ECtHR, 21 February 1970) para 29 (referring to the articles 31-33 VCLT as well as to article 5 VCLT prior to the Vienna Convention's entry into force); *Saadi v The United Kingdom [GC]* App no 13229/03 (ECtHR, 29 January 2008) paras 26, 61 ("31-33"); *Mamatkulov and Askarov*

These general rules leave the interpreter a certain "leeway" as to how they will be applied in the specific case[13] - the means of interpretation which form "the general rule of interpretation" according to article 31 VCLT need to be balanced against each other and applied in a "single combined operation".[14] This leeway opens the door to institutional preferences and incentives,[15] and the "normative *Missionsbewusstsein* or 'in-built bias'"[16] of the respective law-applying authority. Moreover, when interpreting the broadly framed rights of the Convention according to the rules of interpretation, it may be necessary to resort to second-order considerations when one has to make a

---

v Turkey [GC] App no 46827/99 and 46951/99 (ECtHR, 7 February 2005) paras 39, 111 (31(3)(c)), 123 (31(1)); *Loizidou v Turkey (Preliminary Objections)[GC]* App no 15318/89 (ECtHR, 23 March 1995) para 73 (31(1), (3)(b)); *Banković against Belgium, the Czech Republic, Denmark, France, Germany, Greece, Hungary, Iceland, Italy, Luxembourg, the Netherlands, Norway, Poland, Portugal, Spain, Turkey and the United Kingdom [GC]* App no 52207/99 (ECtHR, 12 December 2001) paras 56-58 (31(1), (3)(b),(c), (32)); *Hassan v The United Kingdom [GC]* App no 29750/09 (ECtHR, 16 September 2014) paras 100-101 (31(3)); *Al-Adsani v the United Kingdom [GC]* para 55 (31(3)(c)); *Soering v The United Kingdom [Plenum]* App no 14038/88 (ECtHR, 7 July 1989) para 103 (referring to "subsequent practice in national penal policy" without, however, explicitly referring to article 31(3)(b) VCLT); on the interpretation of the ECHR in more than one languages see *Wemhoff v Germany* App no 2122/64 (ECtHR, 27 June 1968) paras 7-8; *Brogan and others v United Kingdom* App no 11209/84; 11234/84; 11266/84; 11386/85 (ECtHR, 29 November 1988) para 59 (33(4)); *Stoll v Switzerland [GC]* App no 69698/01 (ECtHR, 10 December 2007) paras 59-61 (31(3), (4)); cf. William Schabas, 'Interpretation of the Convention' in William Schabas (ed), *The European Convention on Human Rights. A Commentary* (Oxford University Press 2015) 35-36; Georg Nolte, 'Second Report for the ILC Study Group on Treaties over Time. Jurisprudence Under Special Regimes Relating to Subsequent Agreements and Subsequent Practice' in Georg Nolte (ed), *Treaties and Subsequent Practice* (Oxford University Press 2013) 244-245.

13 Djeffal, *Static and evolutive treaty interpretation: a functional reconstruction* 351, 126-127.
14 *ILC Ybk (1966 vol 2)* 219; using this phrase as well: *Golder v United Kingdom [Plenum]* para 30; Djeffal, *Static and evolutive treaty interpretation: a functional reconstruction* 126-127.
15 Pauwelyn and Elsig, 'The Politics of Treaty Interpretation: Variations and Explanations across International Tribunals' 445 ff.
16 Yuval Shany, 'No Longer a Weak Department of Power? Reflections on the Emergence of a New International Judiciary' (2009) 20(1) EJIL 81; the latter phrase goes back to Koskenniemi and Leino, 'Fragmentation of International Law? Postmodern Anxieties' 567, 573; cf. also Peat, *Comparative Reasoning in International Courts and Tribunals* 18-21.

choice between different interpretation results to which one had been led by the general rules of interpretation.

In addition to this leeway inherent in applying the general rules of interpretation, the European Court has choices to make, for instance whether it bases its reasoning on general international law on international responsibility[17] or whether it develops functional equivalents based on an interpretation of the Convention, whether it invokes *jus cogens*[18] or whether it regards this concept as not relevant in the particular case and instead works with a "fundamental component of the European Public Order"[19]. These choices, in part, are just a consequence of the *lex specialis* principle, according to which rules of a special regime prevail *inter partes* over general rules, subject to *jus cogens*. These choices can be examined as to whether the European Court applies and refers to concepts of general international law or develops concepts based on an interpretation of the ECHR that are functionally equivalent and yet to some extent also different contentwise as compared to their counterparts in general international law.[20]

This section will first give an overview of how the European Court of Human Rights approaches the interpretation of the ECHR (I.). The section will then relate the Court's practice to the general rules of interpretation (II.). Subsequently, it will focus on the recourse to other principles and rules of international law for the purposes of interpreting the ECHR (III.).

I. The European Court's approach to interpretation

When it comes to the leeway inherent in applying the general rules of interpretation, the European Court developed a jurisprudence on how to approach the interpretation of the ECHR.

In particular, the European Court understands the ECHR as a "constitutional instrument of the European Public Order".[21] The terms of the ECHR

---

17 See below, p. 443.
18 *Al-Adsani v the United Kingdom [GC]* para 57 (prohibition of torture as jus cogens).
19 *Al-Dulimi and Montana Managment Inc v Switzerland [GC]* paras 136, 145.
20 See below, in particular p. 443.
21 *Loizidou v Turkey (Preliminary Objections)[GC]* paras 75, 93; *Neulinger and Shuruk v Switzerland [GC]* App no 41615/07 (ECtHR, 6 July 2010) para 133 (invoked in order to argue that the ECHR has to be taken into account when implementing the obligations under the Hague Convention on the Civil Aspects of International Child Abduction); *Al-Skeini and Others v The United Kingdom [GC]* para 141 (invoked

The interpretation of the ECHR

are to be interpreted autonomously, meaning independent of the meaning in the respondent state's domestic law.[22] At the same time, the European Court stressed that the Convention "cannot be interpreted in a vacuum".[23] The ECHR is said to be "a living instrument which [...] must be interpreted in the light of present-day conditions".[24]

---

in order to explain the extraterritorial application of the ECHR in order to prevent the existence of a vacuum in legal protection for human rights); in this sense already *Cyprus v Turkey [GC]* App no 25781/94 (ECtHR, 10 May 2001) para 78; *Al-Dulimi and Montana Managment Inc v Switzerland [GC]* para 145 (invoked in order to ensure respect for the principle of the rule of law when implementing Security Council resolutions).

22 *Engel and others v The Netherlands* App no 5100/71; 5101/71; 5102/71; 5354/72; 5370/72 (ECtHR, 8 June 1976) paras 80-88; *Frydlender v France [GC]* App no 30979/96 (ECtHR, 27 June 2000) paras 30-31; *Naït-Liman v Switzerland [GC]* App no 51357/07 (ECtHR, 15 March 2018) para 106; Andrew Legg, *The Margin of Appreciation in International Human Rights Law: Deference and Proportionality* (Oxford University Press 2012) 111 ("hardly surprising that the ECtHR defers very little to the state on such matters"); George Letsas, *A theory of interpretation of the European Convention on Human Rights* (Oxford University Press 2007) 40-57; on this topic see also *Öztürk v Germany [Plenum]* App no 8544/79 (ECtHR, 21 February 2084) Diss Op Judge Matscher.

23 *Hassan v The United Kingdom [GC]* para 77.

24 *Tyrer v The United Kingdom* App no 5856/72 (ECtHR, 25 April 1978) para 31; on the phrase "living instrument" see already Max Sørensen, 'Do the Rights Set forth in the European Convention on Human Rights in 1950 have the Same Significance in 1975? Report presented by Max Sørensen to the Fourth International Colloquy about the European Convention on Human Rights, Rome 5-8 November 1975' in Ellen Sørensen and Max Sørensen (eds), *Max Sørensen: en bibliografi* (Aarhus University Press 1988) 54-55; this rejection of originalism was criticized by Judge Sir Gerald Fitzmaurice: *Golder v United Kingdom [Plenum]* Sep Op Judge Sir Gerald Fitzmaurice paras 2, 24 ("the Court has proceeded on the footing of methods of interpretation that I regard as contrary to sound principle"); *Marckx v Belgium [Plenum]* App no 6833/74 (ECtHR, 13 June 1979) Diss Op Judge Sir Gerald Fitzmaurice; on Fitzmaurice's critique see Gerald Fitzmaurice, 'Some Reflections on the European Convention on Human Rights- and on Human Rights' in Rudolf Bernhardt (ed), *Völkerrecht als Rechtsordnung, internationale Gerichtsbarkeit, Menschenrechte: Festschrift für Hermann Mosler* (Springer 1983) 213-214; Ed Bates, *The Evolution of the European Convention on Human Rights. From Its Inception to the Creation of a Permanent Court of Human Rights* (Oxford University Press 2010) 361-365: "[Fitzmaurice participated] in eleven cases. He dissented in most of them [...]"; Mārtiņš Paparinskis, *The international minimum standard and fair and equitable treatment* (Oxford monographs in international law, Oxford University Press 2013) 150-151.

The jurisprudence of the European Court demonstrates that the interpretation of the European Convention has been informed by developments in the member states' legal order as well as in international fora,[25] and that the Court searches for the existence of a "consensus" within Europe[26] or internationally, for "a growing measure of agreement on the subject on the international level"[27] and "takes into account the international law background to the legal question before it."[28]

The existence of a rule of international law or of a "consensus" can have the effect of reducing the margin of appreciation which states can enjoy when they interpret their obligations under the ECHR and apply their domestic law.[29]

---

25 See *Marckx v Belgium [Plenum]* para 41; *Tyrer v The United Kingdom* para 31; *Demir and Baykara v Turkey [GC]* App no 34503/97 (ECtHR, 18 November 2008) paras 69-86; cf. Humphrey Waldock, 'The Evolution of Human Rights Concepts and the Application of the European Convention on Human Rights' in *Mélanges offerts à Paul Reuter* (Pedone 1981) 535 ff.; Djeffal, *Static and evolutive treaty interpretation: a functional reconstruction* 328-336; on comparative treaty interpretation see Franz Matscher, 'Vertragsauslegung durch Vertragsrechtsvergleichung in der Judikatur internationaler Gerichte, vornehmlich vor den Organen der EMRK' in *Völkerrecht als Rechtsordnung, internationale Gerichtsbarkeit, Menschenrechte: Festschrift für Hermann Mosler* (Springer 1983) 545 ff.; for a recent treatment of the European consensus see Thomas Kleinlein, 'Consensus and Contestability: The ECtHR and the Combined Potential of European Consensus and Procedural Rationality Control' (2017) 28(3) EJIL 871 ff. (discussing the relationship between European consensus and margin of appreciation); on the relationship between the judicial function and political discourses: Björnstjern Baade, *Der Europäische Gerichtshof für Menschenrechte als Diskurswächter: zur Methodik, Legitimität und Rolle des Gerichtshofs im demokratisch-rechtsstaatlichen Entscheidungsprozess* (Springer 2017).

26 See generally on European consensus Ineta Ziemele, 'European Consensus and International Law' in Anne van Aaken and Iulia Motoc (eds), *The European Convention on Human Rights and General International Law* (Oxford University Press 2018) 23; Kleinlein, 'Consensus and Contestability: The ECtHR and the Combined Potential of European Consensus and Procedural Rationality Control' 879, 881. According to Kanstantsin Dzehtsiarou, *European Consensus and the Legitimacy of the European Court of Human Rights* (Cambridge University Press 2015) 36-37, "European consensus is a rebuttable presumption in favour of the solution adopted by a significant majority of the Contracting Parties, which is identified on the basis of comparative analysis of laws and practices of these Parties."

27 *Demir and Baykara v Turkey [GC]* para 77.

28 ibid para 76; *Opuz v Turkey* App no 33401/02 (ECtHR, 9 June 2009) para 184, referring to *Saadi v The United Kingdom [GC]* para 63 (international law background).

29 On the margin of appreciation see generally William Schabas, 'Preamble' in William Schabas (ed), *The European Convention on Human Rights. A Commentary* (Oxford

The relationship between a European consensus and the margin doctrine was stressed in the *Handyside* case. The European Court held that it was "not possible to find in the domestic law of the various Contracting States a uniform European conception of morals" and that "[c]onsequently, Article 10(2) leaves the Contracting States a margin of appreciation."[30]

In the *Naït-Liman* case, the European Court had to decide on whether Switzerland had violated article 6 ECHR by refusing to open its courts to universal civil jurisdiction cases so that the applicant, a Tunisian national who has acquired Swiss nationality, could seek civil redress for acts of torture committed in Tunisia on the order of the then Minister of the Interior of Tunisia.[31] In determining whether the restriction on the applicant's right of access to a court was proportionate, the European Court made the margin of appreciation dependent on whether Switzerland was under an international obligation to provide a *forum* for the claims of the applicant. Since such obligation could be established neither under customary international law nor under the Convention Against Torture,[32] Switzerland enjoyed a wide margin of appreciation, and the European Court solely examined whether the interpretation of Swiss law was arbitrary or manifest unjust.[33]

The European Court can consider the existence of an international consensus to be more important than the lack of an European consensus, as the *Goodwin* case demonstrates where the Court decided that the United Kingdom had "failed to comply with a positive obligation to ensure the right

---

University Press 2015) 78 ff.; the quality of domestic reasoning can also impact the width of the margin that is accorded to a state, see *Animal Defenders International v United Kingdom [GC]* App no 48876/08 (ECtHR, 22 April 2013) paras 108, 114-6; on this procedural dimension see Kleinlein, 'Consensus and Contestability: The ECtHR and the Combined Potential of European Consensus and Procedural Rationality Control' 873 ff.

30 *Handyside v The United Kingdom [Plenum]* App no 5493/72 (ECtHR, 7 December 1976) para 48. But see *A, B and C v Ireland [GC]* App no 25579/05 (ECtHR, 16 December 2010) paras 234-241, holding that an existing consensus in the case at hand "*decisively* narrows the broad margin of appreciation of the State" (italics added). Thus, a European consensus can, but does not necessarily have to determine the outcome or reduces the margin of appreciation.

31 *Naït-Liman v Switzerland [GC]* paras 14-15, cf. para 176; *Naït-Liman v Switzerland* App no 51357/07 (ECtHR, 21 June 2016).

32 *Naït-Liman v Switzerland [GC]* paras 187-188, 201-202 (there was no obligation to exercise universal jurisdiction nor to provide a forum of necessity because of no available other fora).

33 ibid paras 209, 216.

Chapter 8: The European Convention on Human Rights

of [...] a post operative male to female transsexual, to respect for her private life, in particular through the lack of legal recognition given to her gender re-assignment."[34] The European Court had held in earlier cases that "there is at present little common ground between the Contracting States in this area and that, generally speaking, the law appears to be in a transitional stage. Accordingly, this is an area in which the Contracting Parties enjoy a wide margin of appreciation."[35] In *Goodwin*, however, the European Court said that

> "the lack of such a common approach among forty-three Contracting States with widely diverse legal systems and traditions is hardly surprising [...] The Court accordingly attaches less importance to the lack of evidence of a common European approach [...] than to the clear and uncontested evidence of a continuing *international* trend in favour not only of increased social acceptance of transsexuals but of legal recognition of the new sexual identity of post-operative transsexuals."[36]

Similarly, the European Court noted in the *Hirst* case on prisoners' right to vote that "even if no common European approach to the problem can be discerned, this cannot in itself be determinative of the issue."[37] In its section on relevant case-law, the European Court referred to a Canadian Supreme Court judgment and to a judgment of the Constitutional Court of South Africa, both affirming the right of prisoners to vote.[38]

When evaluating the existence of a European or international consensus, the Court considers and refers to treaties, including regional and non-regional human rights treaties[39], specific conventions concluded on a subject

---

34 *Christine Goodwin v the United Kingdom [GC]* App no 28957/95 (ECtHR, 11 July 2002) para 71.
35 *Rees v the United Kingdom [Plenum]* App no 9532/81 (ECtHR, 17 October 1986) para 37; see also *Sheffield and Horsham v the United Kingdom [GC]* App no (31–32/1997/815–816/1018–1019 (ECtHR, 30 July 1998) paras 57-58.
36 *Christine Goodwin v the United Kingdom [GC]* para 85 (italics added).
37 *Hirst v the United Kingdom (no 2) [GC]* App no 74025/01 (ECtHR, 6 October 2005) para 81.
38 ibid paras 35-39; Christopher McCrudden, 'A Common Law of Human Rights?: Transnational Judicial Conversations on Constitutional Rights' (2000) 20(4) Oxford Journal of Legal Studies 392-393.
39 *Soering v The United Kingdom [Plenum]* para 88; *Al-Adsani v the United Kingdom [GC]* para 60.

matter, for instance about legal status of children[40], about social rights[41], biomedicine[42] or environmental law[43]. These conventions were used in order to identify a general consensus in substance, without requiring high numbers of ratifications or even ratification by the party to a dispute.[44]

The European Court elaborated on this approach in the *Demir and Baykara* judgment on the right of civil servants to form unions and enter into collective agreements. It explained that the question of whether the specific respondent state did or did not sign or ratify a convention was not a decisive criterion on the basis of which a distinction between sources of law would be made.[45] It also stressed that it needed to consider "elements of international law other than the Convention, the interpretation of such elements by competent organs, and the practice of European States reflecting their common values."[46] The objective of this examination was to identify "a continuous evolution in the norms and principles applied in international law or in the domestic law of the majority of member States of the Council of Europe and show, in a precise area, that there is common ground in modern societies."[47]

---

40 *Marckx v Belgium [Plenum]* para 20, para 41 and para 42; *Pini and Others v Romania* App no 78028/01 and 78030/01 (ECtHR, 22 June 2004) para 138 and para 139.
41 *Sørensen and Rasmussen v Denmark [GC]* App no 52562/99 and 52620/99 (ECtHR, 11 January 2006) para 37.
42 *Glass v the United Kingdom* App no 61827/00 (ECtHR, 9 March 2004) para 75.
43 *Öneryıldız v Turkey* App no 48939/99 (ECtHR, 30 November 2004) para 59.
44 *Marckx v Belgium [Plenum]* para 20, para 41 and para 42, the court referred to two conventions, which Belgium had not ratified; *Vilho Eskelinen and Others v Finland [GC]* App no 63235/00 (ECtHR, 19 April 2007) para 29 and para 60, reference to the Charter of Fundamental Rights of the EU, not yet ratified; *Glass v the United Kingdom* para 75, shortly referring to the Council of Europe's Convention on Human Rights and Biomedicine, even though the instrument had not been ratified by all CoE states; *Siliadin v France* App no 73316/01 (ECtHR, 26 July 2005) paras 85-87 referring for the interpretation of article 4 ECHR to conventions which were ratified by France, namely the Forced Labour Convention, adopted by the International Labour Organisation, the Supplementary Convention on the Abolition of Slavery, the Slave Trade, and Institutions and Practices Similar to Slavery and the International Convention on the Rights of the Child.
45 *Demir and Baykara v Turkey [GC]* para 78, paras 79-84.
46 ibid para 85.
47 ibid para 86. In the specific case, the Court held that Turkey had violated the right for municipal servants to form trade unions (article 11 ECHR) as Turkey did not sufficiently demonstrate that the absolute prohibition on forming trade unions met a pressing social need (para 120). Also, Turkey violated the right to bargain collectively with employers (article 11 ECHR) by the annulment of a collective agreement (para

II. Relating the European Court's practice to the general rules of interpretation

By and large[48], the European Court's approaches are not in conflict with the general rules of treaty interpretation. In particular, the evolutive interpretation can be traced to article 31.[49] According to article 31(3)(a) and (b), the interpreter shall take into account subsequent agreements and a subsequent practice that entails an agreement on the interpretation of the treaty. Such a subsequent agreement does not need to be binding;[50] even when a subsequent agreement on the interpretation of a given treaty is not shared among all parties to that treaty, it can still be considered in the process of interpretation as supplementary means under article 32 VCLT.[51]

It is true, however, that the European Court does not always demonstrate in its judgments that it had examined whether practices within European states indeed were, as article 31(3)(b) VCLT stipulates, "in the application of" the ECHR,[52] nor did states explicitly state that the application of domestic law was based on an agreement as to the interpretation of the ECHR. The lack of explicit invocation can be overcome, however, by the plausible assumption that the European Court "presumes that the member states, when acting in

---

154). Whilst taking into account conventions not ratified by Turkey, the European Court pointed also to instances of Turkish recognition domestically and internationally of a right of municipal servants to form trade unions and of a right to collectively bargain (paras 123-125, 152).

48 The purpose of this section is not to examine the adherence of each interpretation to the general rules of interpretation.

49 See also Bjørge, *The evolutionary interpretation of treaties* 188-189, concluding "that the evolutionary interpretation is, in common with other types of interpretation, an outcome of the process described in the general rule of interpretation"; see also Baade, *Der Europäische Gerichtshof für Menschenrechte als Diskurswächter: zur Methodik, Legitimität und Rolle des Gerichtshofs im demokratisch-rechtsstaatlichen Entscheidungsprozess* 168.

50 See *ILC Report 2018* at 29, 75 (conclusion 10), 77-78; Gardiner, *Treaty interpretation* 244; Philippe Gautier, 'Non-Binding Agreements' [2006] Max Planck EPIL para 14; d'Aspremont, 'The International Court of Justice, the Whales, and the Blurring of the Lines between Sources and Interpretation' 1036-1037.

51 *ILC Report 2018* at 13 (conclusion 4), 33-36.

52 See also *First report on subsequent agreements and subsequent practice in relation to treaty interpretation by Georg Nolte, Special Rapporteur* 19 March 2013 UN Doc A/CN.4/660 16-17 para 37, also available in *ILC Ybk (2013 vol 2 part 1)* 61 para 37: "[T]he Court has referred to the legislative practice of member States without explicitly mentioning article 31(3)(b) of the Vienna Convention."

a particular way, are conscious of their obligations under the Convention and move in a way which reflects their bona fide understanding of their obligations."[53]

To the extent that the European Court refers to documents of the Council of Europe[54], article 5 VCLT, according to which the VCLT "applies to any treaty which is the constituent instrument of an international organization and to any treaty adopted within an international organization without prejudice to any relevant rules of the organization", might be considered as an additional ground that allows the interpreter to take into account documents of the Council of Europe as such "relevant rules of the organization".[55]

From the perspective of the VCLT, the most problematic references are references to practices of states who are not members of the Council of Europe, since these practices have no connection to the ECHR, and taking account of such practice can raise consent concerns.[56] If these practices gave expression to a rule of customary international law binding on the states parties to the ECHR as well, they would fall within article 31(3)(c)

---

53 Nolte, 'Second Report for the ILC Study Group on Treaties over Time. Jurisprudence Under Special Regimes Relating to Subsequent Agreements and Subsequent Practice' 266; *Second report on subsequent agreements and subsequent practice in relation to the interpretation of treaties by Georg Nolte, Special Rapporteur* 26 March 2014 UN Doc A/CN.4/671 8-9 para 14 also available in *ILC Ybk (2014 vol 2 part 1)* 119 para 14; for a critique see Peat, *Comparative Reasoning in International Courts and Tribunals* 166: "It seems tenuous to suggest that the practice cited by the ECtHR reflects how states parties interpret or apply their obligations under the ECHR, nor is it clear that there is even a more attenuated link between the practice cited and the state's awareness of its obligations under the Convention [...]".
54 On this practice see *Tănase v Moldova [GC]* App no 7/08 (ECtHR, 27 April 2010) para 176.
55 See *Golder v United Kingdom [Plenum]* para 29, referring also to article 5 VCLT.
56 Heike Krieger, 'Positive Verpflichtungen unter der EMRK: Unentbehrliches Element einer gemeineuropäischen Grundrechtsdogmatik, leeres Versprechen oder Grenze der Justiziabilität?' (2014) 74 ZaöRV 207; Arato, 'Constitutional Transformation in the ECtHR: Strasbourg's Expansive Recourse to External Rules of International Law' 357: "Demir [...] represents an assertion of competence to hold the Member States to norms they did not consent to, and cannot strictly control." Cf. also Adamantia Rachovitsa, 'Fragmentation of International Law revisited: Insights, Good Practices, and Lessons to be learned from the Case Law of the European Court of Human Rights' (2015) 28(4) Leiden Journal of International Law 868-871, 879, 881-883.

VCLT. However, it is questionable whether a preexisting rule of customary international law can always explain these references.[57]

It stands to reason that, as Heike Krieger has argued, references to other rules of international law in the sense of article 31(3)(c) VCTL cannot expose the European Court to the potential criticism of ECHR parties to have violated the principle of consent.[58] In this sense, the *Golder* judgment, "undoubtedly one of the most important cases in the history of the ECHR"[59], illustrates how the European Court at an early time based its reasoning on arguments of general international law. The European Court decided that article 6 ECHR[60] protects not only fair proceedings within an existing judicial proceeding but also the right to have a judicial proceeding in the first place.[61] The European Court, with reference to article 31(3)(c), submitted that it would be a general principle of law and expression of the prohibition of denial of justice that a civil claim must be capable of being submitted to a judge.[62]

However, even though a rule of international law in the sense of article 31(3)(c) VCLT certainly carries a particular weight,[63] the European Court is

---

57 See for instance Legg, *The Margin of Appreciation in International Human Rights Law: Deference and Proportionality* 119: "It is arguable that international trends ought to affect the European Convention if they are indicative of the emergence of a customary international norm. But this cannot be the case in Christine Goodwin v UK: the handful of states discussed can hardly be representative of the international community of states. Instead, they share in common the fact that they are liberal democracies."
58 Krieger, 'Positive Verpflichtungen unter der EMRK: Unentbehrliches Element einer gemeineuropäischen Grundrechtsdogmatik, leeres Versprechen oder Grenze der Justiziabilität?' 207-208 (arguing that article 31(3)(c) can exercise a greater legitimatizing effect than the dynamic-evolutive interpretation of the ECHR). A similar discussion can be observed in the context of international investment law where advocates of a continuing role of customary international law use this source for legitimacy reasons, see below, p. 609.
59 Letsas, *A theory of interpretation of the European Convention on Human Rights* 61.
60 According to its wording, "[i]n the determination of his civil rights and obligations or of any criminal charge against him, everyone is entitled to a fair and public hearing within a reasonable time by an independent and impartial tribunal established by law".
61 *Golder v United Kingdom [Plenum]*; this decision was not adopted unanimously, as the dissenting opinions of Fitzmaurice, Verdross and Zekia demonstrated. The dissent was motivated by the concern that expansion of the court's jurisdiction would meet the resistance of the states parties.
62 ibid para 35.
63 For an example of interpreting a positive obligation under the ECHR in light of an applicable treaty see *Rantsev v Cyprus and Russia* App no 25965/04 (ECtHR, 7 June

not prevented from seeking inspiration from the experiences made in other legal orders in relation to similar problems.[64] As Björnstjern Baade has argued, references to other legal orders can constitute reasons, or persuasive authorities, and enhance the rationality of a judicial decision. They can guide the judges when they decide between several possible interpretations and when they concretize general rules by applying them to the individual case.[65] It is then for the European Court not only "to decide which international

---

2010) para 286 (referring to the Article 3(a) of the Palermo Protocol and Article 4(a) of the Anti-Trafficking Convention); Protocol to Prevent, Suppress and Punish Trafficking in Persons, Especially Women and Children, supplementing the United Nations Convention against Transnational Organized Crime (signed 15 November 2000, entered into force 25 December 2003) 2237 UNTS 319; Council of Europe Convention on Action against Trafficking in Human Beings (signed 16 May 2005, entered into force 1 February 2008) CETS 197; *Tănase v Moldova [GC]* para 176 (taking into account "the obligations which Moldova has freely undertaken under the ECN").

64 See Baade, *Der Europäische Gerichtshof für Menschenrechte als Diskurswächter: zur Methodik, Legitimität und Rolle des Gerichtshofs im demokratisch-rechtsstaatlichen Entscheidungsprozess* 225-228; Legg, *The Margin of Appreciation in International Human Rights Law: Deference and Proportionality* 131; McCrudden, 'A Common Law of Human Rights?: Transnational Judicial Conversations on Constitutional Rights' 400 (on the different ways in which use of foreign sources can countribute to the decision of the case: they can constitute primary reasons of an interpretation or just contribute to the reasoning); cf. generally Huber and Paulus, 'Cooperation of Constitutional Courts in Europe: the Openness of the German Constitution to International, European, and Comparative Constitutional Law' 292-293, commenting on the citation of the Supreme Courts of the USA and of Canada by the Federal Constitutional Court: "These citations do not mean, however, that the Federal Constitutional Court would feel itself bound by the decisions of other constitutional courts if its opinion were to deviate from them. Rather, the Court sees it as a matter of professionalism in a highly interwoven international (legal) world not only to be aware of legal concepts and ideas from other countries, but also to confront those concepts and ideas and interrogate them."

65 See Baade, *Der Europäische Gerichtshof für Menschenrechte als Diskurswächter: zur Methodik, Legitimität und Rolle des Gerichtshofs im demokratisch-rechtsstaatlichen Entscheidungsprozess* 227, 293-304; Björnstjern Baade, 'The ECtHR's Role as a Guardian of Discourse: Safeguarding a Decision-Making Process Based on Well-Established Standards, Practical Rationality, and Facts' (2018) 31 Leiden Journal of International Law 346-347 (pointing out that "[c]ontrary to popular belief, the use of all these materials does, in principle, not extend the range of decisions the Court can take but actually restricts its interpretative freedom"). On the Kelsenian perspective according to which the application of law is not completely determined by the norm that is applied see above, p. 196 and below p. 668.

instruments and reports it considers relevant and how much weight to attribute to them"[66], but also to explain the interpretation which it arrived at and for which it considered these instruments to be relevant.

III. Recourse to other rules and principles of international law for content-determination

According to article 32 ECHR, the jurisdiction of the Court extends "to all matters concerning the interpretation and application of the Convention and the protocols thereto".[67]

Incidentally, however, the Court can, for the purposes of interpreting and applying the ECHR, take recourse to other rules of international law which, while not being "applicable law", are to be taken into account according to the general rules of treaty interpretation. Moreover, the European Court will examine a state's interpretation and application of international law if the ECHR is thereby affected. As the European Court held,

> "it is primarily for the national authorities, notably the courts, to interpret and apply domestic law. This also applies where domestic law refers to rules of general interna-

---

66 *Tănase v Moldova [GC]* para 176.
67 A draft prepared by the European Movement had proposed that the envisioned court should apply next to the ECHR "(ii) the general principles of law recognised by civilised nations; (iii) judicial decisions and teaching of the most highly qualified publicist of the various nations as subsidiary means for the determination of rules of law; (iv) international conventions, whether general or particular, establishing rules expressly recognized by any State concerned." The proposal to specifically include the general principles of law was not adopted. According to the report of the Legal Committee of 24 August 1950, the "insertion of a specific clause to this effect was unnecessary" and according to David Maxwell Fyfe of the United Kingdom, Plenary Sitting on 25 August 1950, the Legal Committee "could not contemplate the organs or the machinery doing anything else. If they are going to work they must apply these principles, and it is in that spirit that we have made no suggestion for a specific inclusion." See Council of Europe, 'References to the notion of the "general principles of law recognised by the civilised nations" as contained in the travaux préparatoires of the Convention' [1974] CDH (74) 37 ⟨https://www.echr.coe.int/LibraryDocs/Travaux/ECHRTravaux-PGD-CDH(74)37-BIL1678846.pdf⟩ accessed 1 February 2023; William Schabas, 'Article 32. Jurisdiction of the Court' in William Schabas (ed), *The European Convention on Human Rights. A Commentary* (Oxford University Press 2015) 716, 719.

tional law or international agreements. The Court's role is confined to ascertaining whether the effects of such an interpretation are compatible with the Convention."[68]

This section will highlight three ways in which the interpretation and application can require the European Court to consider international law beyond the ECHR. The text of a provision can refer to other international law as it is, for instance, the case with respect to derogations under article 15 ECHR or the foreseeability of criminal liability under article 7 ECHR. A provision can impose positive obligations which, in effect, favour compliance with other obligations of international law. Moreover, the text of a provision can be "read down" and interpreted restrictively in order to reconcile the provision with other international principles and rules, as demonstrated in the *Hassan* case.

The text of the Convention may refer to other rules and principles of international law. For instance, article 15(1) ECHR provides that a party "may take measures derogating from its obligations under this Convention to the extent strictly required by the exigencies of the situation, *provided that such measures are not inconsistent with its other obligations under*

---

68 *Markovic and Others v Italy [GC]* App no 1398/03 (ECtHR, 14 December 2006) para 108; *Waite and Kennedy v Germany [GC]* App no 26083/94 (ECtHR, 18 February 1999) para 54; *Prince Hans-Adam II of Liechtenstein v Germany [GC]* App no 42527/98 (ECtHR, 12 July 2001) para 50; *Van Anraat v the Netherlands* App no 365389/09 (ECtHR, 10 June 2010) para 79; see also *Slivenko v Latvia [GC]* App no 48321/99 (ECtHR, 9 October 2003) paras 105, 120, stating that "it is for the implementing party to interpret the treaty, and in this respect it is not the Court's task to substitute its own judgment for that of the domestic authorities", but a "treaty cannot serve as a valid basis for depriving the Court of its power to review whether there was an interference with the applicants' rights and freedoms under the Convention".

international law."⁶⁹ Article 15(2) ECHR excludes article 2 ECHR from derogation, "except in respect of deaths resulting from lawful acts of war".⁷⁰

Of particular interest in the context is also article 7 ECHR. Article 7(1) ECHR provides that no one shall be held guilty of any criminal offence on account of any act or omission which did not constitute a criminal offence under national or *international law* at the time when it was committed,⁷¹ whilst article 7(2) ECHR clarifies that article 7(1) ECHR is without prejudice to the trial and punishment of any person for any act or omission which, at the time when it was committed, was criminal according to the general principles of law recognised by civilised nations. The European Court regarded both provisions to be "interlinked and [...] to be interpreted in a concordant man-

---

69 Italics added. One possible obligation in this regards concerns the derogation provision of article 4 ICCPR which requires an "officially proclaimed" derogation, William Schabas, 'Article 15. Derogation in Time of Emergency' in William Schabas (ed), *The European Convention on Human Rights. A Commentary* (Oxford University Press 2015) 600-601. In *Brannigan and McBride v The United Kingdom [Plenum]* App no 14553/89, 14554/89 (ECtHR, 25 May 1993) paras 72-73, the European Court observed that "that it is not its role to seek to define authoritatively the meaning of the terms 'officially proclaimed' in Article 4 of the Covenant. Nevertheless it must examine whether there is any plausible basis for the applicant's argument in this respect. [...] In the Court's view the above statement, which was formal in character and made public the Government's intentions as regards derogation, was well in keeping with the notion of an official proclamation. It therefore considers that there is no basis for the applicants' arguments in this regard."
70 According to a broad reading, "Lawful acts of war" can be interpreted as including not only the *ius in bello* but also the *ius ad bellum*, Schabas, 'Article 15. Derogation in Time of Emergency' 601-602; *Georgia v Russia (II) [GC]* Conc Opinion of Judge Keller paras 15-28. If this interpretation is accepted, the European Court will be competent address the *jus ad bellum*.
71 Italics added. The reference to international law includes international treaties, *Ould Dah v France* App no 13113/03 (ECtHR, 17 March 2009); *Jorgig v Germany* App no 74613/01 (ECtHR, 12 July 2007) paras 100-114 (deciding that German courts did not interpret the scope of the crime of genocide too broadly); Antonio Cassese, 'Balancing the Prosecution of Crimes against Humanity and Non-Retroactivity of Criminal Law' (2006) 4 JICJ 414-415 (article 7(1) includes treaties and customary international law); *Korbely v Hungary [GC]* App no 9174/02 (ECtHR, 19 September 2008) paras 82-83 (deciding that the crime of humanity may no longer have required a nexus to an armed conflict in 1956 but must be part of a widespread systematic attack); but cf. Cassese, 'Balancing the Prosecution of Crimes against Humanity and Non-Retroactivity of Criminal Law' 413, commenting on *Kolk and Kislyiy v Estonia* App no 23052/04, 24018/04 (ECtHR, 17 January 2006).

ner."[72] One entry gate for the Court to examine other rules of international law in the context of an analysis under article 7 ECHR is the question of the foreseeability of the personal criminal liability.

In the *Border Guards* case, the European Court had to examine, *inter alia*, whether a conviction for the murder of people who had sought to escape from the German Democratic Republic (GDR) between 1971 and 1989 based on the law of the GDR was foreseeable, given the GDR's border-policing policy.[73] The Court decided that it was, and argued that the right of life had been protected by the law of the German Democratic Republic and that the border regime was in violation of GDR law and international law.[74] The European Court noted the "preeminence of the right to life in all international instruments on the protection of human rights"[75] and referred to the ICCPR and the UDHR:[76] "The convergence of the above-mentioned instruments is significant: it indicates that the right to life is an inalienable attribute of human beings and forms the supreme value in the hierarchy of human rights".[77] Considering that the crucial period (starting in 1971) predated the Covenant's entry into force in 1976 and the ratification by the GDR in 1973, the implicit assumption seemed to have been, as Grabenwarter has argued out,[78] that general international law or customary international law protected

---

72 *Kononov v Latvia [GC]* App no 36376/04 (ECtHR, 17 May 2010) para 186; *Maktouf and Damjanović v Bosnia and Herzegovina [GC]* App no 2312/08 and 34179/08 (ECtHR, 18 July 2013) para 72 (article 7(2) ECHR is only a contextual clarification of article 7(1) ECHR, "included so as to ensure that there was no doubt about the validity of prosecutions after the Second World War in respect of the crimes committed during that war"); William Schabas, 'Article 7' in William Schabas (ed), *The European Convention on Human Rights. A Commentary* (Oxford University Press 2015) 353-355 (on doubts as to the usefulness of article 7(2) ECHR and the tendency of the European Court not to comment on article 7(2) ECHR and instead addressing article 7(1) only).
73 *Streletz, Kessler and Krenz v Germany [GC]* App no 34044/96, 35532/97 and 44801/98 (ECtHR, 22 March 2001) paras 77-89.
74 ibid paras 102-104.
75 ibid para 85.
76 ibid paras 92-93.
77 ibid para 94.
78 See Grabenwarter's comment in Klein, *Menschenrechtsschutz durch Gewohnheitsrecht: Kolloquium 26.-28. September 2002 Potsdam* 164; on the rare references to customary international law by the European Court see Schabas, 'Interpretation of the Convention' 40; Frédéric Vanneste, *General International Law Before Human Rights Courts - Assessing the Speciality Claim of International Human Rights Law* (Inter-

the right to life as well and that therefore problems of retroactivity were precluded.

Moreover, the question of foreseeability can lead the European Court to examine international criminal law. For instance, in the *Jorgic* case, the question arose whether German courts had interpreted the crime of genocide too broadly by holding it sufficient for the intent to commit genocide to relate to the destruction of a group as a social unit, rather than to the physical destruction of a group in whole or in part. The European Court held that courts and tribunals, including the ICJ and the ICTY, preferred a narrow interpretation according to which the intent must refer to the physical or biological destruction; however, "there had already been several authorities at the material time which had construed the offence of genocide in the same wider way as the German courts."[79] That interpretation "could reasonably be regarded as consistent with the essence of that offence and could reasonably be foreseen by the applicant at the material time."[80]

In the *Kononov* case, the European Court examined, and ultimately affirmed, that "by May 1944 war crimes were defined as acts contrary to the laws and customs of war" and that "States were at least permitted (if not required) to take steps to punish individuals for such crimes".[81]

In the *Anraat* case, the European Court examined the status of the prohibition of chemical weapons under customary international law. The applicant who had supplied to Iraq under Saddam Hussein "quantities in excess of eleven hundred metric tons of the chemical thiodiglycol"[82] was convicted of being an accessory to violations of the laws and customs of war.[83] The applicant questioned the "existence [...], knowability and foreseeability, of

---

sentia 2009) 377-384 and 398-401, reading the *Border Guards* case as an example of the use of general principles of law.
79 *Jorgig v Germany* para 113.
80 ibid para 114.
81 *Kononov v Latvia [GC]* para 213. In the view of the Court, "having regard to the flagrantly unlawful nature of the ill-treatment and killing of the nine villagers in the established circumstances of the operation on 27 May 1944 [...] even the most cursory reflection by the applicant would have indicated that, at the very least, the impugned acts risked being counter to the laws and customs of war as understood at that time and, notably, risked constituting war crimes for which, as commander, he could be held individually and criminally accountable." (para 238).
82 *Van Anraat v the Netherlands* para 3; cf. on this case Marten Zwanenburg and Guido den Dekker, 'Introductory Note to European Court of Human Rights: van Anraat vs. the Netherlands' (2010) 49 ILM 1268-9.
83 *Van Anraat v the Netherlands* para 82.

a rule of customary international law"[84] and submitted that later practice derogated from the 1925 protocol's[85] prohibition of chemical weapons, given "the reality of contemporary warfare".[86] The European Court found "nothing to suggest" that the 1925 Protocol was no longer of binding force, "[i]n fact, the precise opposite is the case."[87] The European Court affirmed the "norm-creating character" of the 1925 Protocol.[88] It observed that in the 1970s many parties withdrew their reservation to the protocol regarding no first use, and that the Biological Weapons Convention[89] which would have been ratified at the beginning of the Iraq war by "a considerable majority of the States then in existence" and continued to be ratified, affirmed the 1925 protocol.[90] Taking into account the instructions by states to their armed forces, the drafting of the Chemical Weapons Convention[91] and resolutions of the General Assembly and the Security Council condemning "the use in that war of chemical weapons"[92], the European Court found that "at the time when the applicant supplied thiodiglycol to the Government of Iraq a norm of customary international law existed prohibiting the use of mustard gas as a weapon of war in an international conflict"[93] and also "against civilian populations within their own territory"[94].

International law can also be relevant for interpreting positive obligations under the ECHR. In turn, positive obligations under the ECHR can strengthen

---

84 ibid para 73.
85 Protocol for the prohibition of the use in war of asphyxiating, poisonous or other gases, and of bacteriological methods of warfare (signed 17 June 1925, entered into force 9 May 1926) 94 LNTS 65.
86 *Van Anraat v the Netherlands* paras 73-74.
87 ibid para 87.
88 ibid para 89.
89 Convention on the prohibition of the development, production and stockpiling of bacteriological (biological) and toxin weapons and on their destruction (signed 10 April 1972, entered into force 26 May 1975) 1015 UNTS 163.
90 "The Court takes these developments as proof not only of State practice consistent with the norm created by the 1925 Protocol but also of opinio iuris", *Van Anraat v the Netherlands* para 90.
91 Convention on the Prohibition of the Development, Production, Stockpiling and Use of Chemical Weapons and on their Destruction (signed 3 September 1992, entered into force 29 April 1997) 1975 UNTS 45.
92 *Van Anraat v the Netherlands* para 91.
93 ibid para 92.
94 Ibid para 94.

compliance with international law protecting or benefitting individuals.⁹⁵ Recently, the European Court decided in the *Hanan* case that the obligations to investigate the deaths in Afghanistan under international humanitarian law and domestic law, together with the retention of the exclusive jurisdiction over its troops by Germany, constituted special features which "trigger[ed] the existence of a jurisdictional link for the purposes of article 1 of the Convention in relation to the procedural obligation to investigate under Article 2."⁹⁶ This led to the result that the European Court could examine the compliance of Germany with article 2 ECHR when conducting investigations that were required under international humanitarian law.

Furthermore, the text can be "read down" and interpreted restrictively in order to accommodate other rules of international law. In the *Hassan* case, which concerned detentions for security reasons in a time when the rules of IHL governing international armed conflicts applied, the European Court did not apply the Third and Fourth Geneva Conventions. It applied article 5 ECHR, interpreted in light of the applicable IHL rules which provided for legal bases of a detention for security reasons.⁹⁷ Since such detentions were not reconcilable with the text of article 5 ECHR, article 5 was "read down" under consideration of its fundamental purpose to protect from arbitrariness and to accommodate the fact that taking of prisoners of war and the detention of civilians were an "accepted feature" in international armed conflicts.⁹⁸ This presupposes, however, that the Geneva Conventions were applicable and that the detention complies with the rules of IHL.⁹⁹

C. Interpretative decisions in establishing the interrelationship

The preceding cases were examples in which the European Convention was more or less "at the receiving end" of trends in public international law. The present section will focus on the ways in which international law can be shaped through the interpretation and application of the European

---

95 See below, p. 436.
96 *Hanan v Germany [GC]* App no 4871/16 (ECtHR, 16 February 2021) para 142.
97 *Hassan v The United Kingdom [GC]* para 106.
98 ibid para 104.
99 ibid para 105; *Georgia v Russia (II) [GC]* para 237.

Interpretative decisions in establishing the interrelationship

Convention.[100] This section will first illustrate the ways in which the European Court establishes a relation between the ECHR and other principles and rules of international law (I.). In particular, it will focus on the incorporation of customary international law and other treaties in a proportionality analysis and on the reconciliation of different obligations on the basis of underlying general principles, such as the prohibition of arbitrariness. At the end, this section will offer concluding observations (II.).

I. The construction of establishing a relation between the European Convention and other principles and rules of international law

1. Incorporation by proportionality analysis

States' actions in pursuance of their obligations under customary international law[101], UNSCR resolutions[102] or other international treaties[103] can constitute a *prima facie* interference with a Convention right and therefore need to be justified. A justification requires that the state pursues a legitimate aim and resorts to means in achieving this aim which do not disproportionately infringe the human right "in such a way or to such an extent that the very essence of the right is impaired."[104]

The European Court establishes a relation between the ECHR and other international law in a proportionality analysis. Proportionality analysis then favours the integration of both norms: The legal operator attempts to reconcile both norms with each other and to strike a pragmatic balance in which each norm is realised to a certain extent in the particular case (*praktische Konkordanz*[105]). Applied to the ECHR, this means that a state cannot confine

---

100 Eirik Bjørge, 'The Contribution of the European Court of Human Rights to General International Law' (2019) 79(4) ZaöRV 783 ("The influences (between the ECHR and general international law) go both ways").
101 *Al-Adsani v the United Kingdom [GC]* para 55 f.; *Jones and Others v The United Kingdom* para 186 f.
102 *Nada v Switzerland [GC]* App no 10593/08 (ECtHR, 12 September 2012) para 167 f.; *Al-Dulimi and Montana Managment Inc v Switzerland [GC]* para 126 f.
103 *Neulinger and Shuruk v Switzerland [GC]* para 99 f.
104 *Al-Adsani v the United Kingdom [GC]* para 53; *Al-Dulimi and Montana Managment Inc v Switzerland [GC]* para 124; *Naït-Liman v Switzerland [GC]* para 114.
105 Anne van Aaken, 'Defragmentation of Public International Law Through Interpretation: A Methodological Proposal' (2009) 16(2) Indiana Journal of Global Legal

itself to apply one rule, for instance article 6 ECHR, without having any regard to other rules of international law, for instance state immunity.[106] Proportionality analysis can be performed at two levels, at the level of the general norms and at the level of the application of general norms to the particular case. Thus, the structure of proportionality analysis leads to an examination of the application of immunity by the domestic court. Customary international law no longer then operates solely between states but is examined in the relationship between a state and an individual, with the state carrying the burden of justification for the interference with the right of the individual.

2. Proportionality analysis and customary international law

The case-law on state immunity sheds light on the promises and limits of proportionality analysis as performed by the European Court when it comes to the reconciliation of different norms.

a) Two different constructions

In contrast to British courts, the approach of which will be illustrated below, the European Court in *Al-Adsani* regarded the scope of article 6 ECHR to be engaged and interpreted article 6 ECHR in light of general international law on state immunity:

> "[M]easures taken by a High Contracting Party which reflect generally recognised rules of public international law on State immunity cannot in principle be regarded as imposing a disproportionate restriction on the right of access to a court as embodied in Article 6 para 1. Just as the right of access to a court is an inherent part of the

---

Studies 501 ff.; on *praktische Konkordanz* see in particular Konrad Hesse, *Grundzüge des Verfassungsrechts der Bundesrepublik Deutschland* (20th edn, Müller 1999) 28.

106 In this sense, see also *Fragmentation of international law: difficulties arising from diversification and expansion of international law, Report of the Study Group of the International Law Commission, Finalized by Martti Koskenniemi* 221 para 438: "It is useful to note that here the Court might have simply brushed aside State immunity as not relevant to the application of the Convention. But it did not do so. The conflict between article 6 and rules of customary international law on State immunity emerged only because the Court decided to integrate article 6 in its normative environment [...]".

fair trial guarantee in that Article, so some restrictions on access must likewise be regarded as inherent, an example being those limitations generally accepted by the community of nations as part of the doctrine of State immunity."[107]

Similarly, the European Court examined in *Jones* the proportionality of the restriction of article 6 ECHR when domestic courts recognized state immunity.[108]

In contrast to the approach adopted by the European Court of Human Rights, it is also possible to understand state immunity under customary international law as excluded from the scope of applicability of article 6 ECHR, precluding, therefore, any interference with the right and any need for a justification analysis. Such a view which separates state immunity and article 6 ECHR has been expressed in the jurisprudence of British courts.[109]

In *Holland v Lampen-Wolfe* before the House of Lord, Lord Millett reconciled the right to a court under article 6 ECHR and state immunity at the level of applicability rather than at the level of a justification: article 6 ECHR would presuppose "that the contracting states have the powers of adjudication [...] (b)ut it does not confer on contracting states adjudicative powers which they do not possess".[110] According to this argument, since the UK was bound by customary international law and the rules of state immunity, it had no legal capacity to exercise jurisdiction in the sense of article 1 ECHR, and article 6 ECHR was, therefore, not engaged.

Other justices later expressed their sympathy with Millet's position, even though one year after *Holland v Lampen-Wolfe*, the European Court published its *Al-Adsani* judgment, refuting the UK government's argument that article

---

107 *Al-Adsani v the United Kingdom [GC]* para 56.
108 *Jones and Others v The United Kingdom* paras 186, 189; see also *McElhinney v Ireland [GC]* App no 31253/96 (ECtHR, 21 November 2001) paras 35, 38.
109 Philippa Webb, 'A Moving Target: The Approach of the Strasbourg Court to Immunity' in Anne van Aaken and Iulia Motoc (eds), *The European Convention on Human Rights and general international law* (Oxford University Press 2018) 256-258; cf. earlier also Georg Nolte, 'Menschenrechtliches ius cogens - Eine Analyse von "Barcelona Traction" und nachfolgender Entwicklungen - Kommentar' in Eckart Klein (ed), *Menschenrechtsschutz durch Gewohnheitsrecht* (Berliner Wissenschafts-Verlag 2003) 144, 146, pointing out that the European Court rather than limiting the scope of applicability of article 6 ECHR, interpreted the scope broadly ("Es wird also keine tatbestandliche Eingrenzung des Schutzberechs des Art. 6 EMRK in Hinblick auf die Staatenimmunität vorgenommen (was durchaus begründbar gewesen wäre), sondern der Schutzbereich wird von vornherein weit gezogen [...]").
110 *Holland v Lampen-Wolfe* House of Lords [2000] UKHL 40, Lord Millett (section on State Immunity and the European Convention).

Chapter 8: The European Convention on Human Rights

6 was not engaged. In *Jones*, Lord Bingham "confess[ed] to some difficulty in accepting" the European Court's position that article 6 ECHR was engaged in cases where a state applies the rules of state immunity.[111] Also Lord Hoffman was "inclined to agree with the view of Lord Millett [...] that there is not even a *prima facie* breach of article 6 if a state fails to make available a jurisdiction which it does not possess."[112] However, the justices did not insist on this point since the difference in construction did not lead to different results. In 2015, the Court of Appeal regarded itself to be

> "faced with conflicting authority. The decision of the House of Lords in Holland v. Lampen-Wolfe that Article 6 is not engaged where the grant of immunity is required by international law is binding on this court. However, the Strasbourg court has consistently held in a lengthy line of authority that Article 6 is engaged in these circumstances."[113]

The Court of Appeal found Lord Millett's reasoning "compelling" but did not consider it necessary to choose among the two approaches, as also according to Strasbourg jurisprudence state immunity constituted a proportionate restriction to article 6 ECHR and therefore did not violate article 6 ECHR. The UK Supreme Court saw no need to choose either.[114]

To summarize the different constructions: whereas the European Court regards the grant of state immunity as *prima facie* interference with the right to access to a court which requires justification, the view adopted by certain

---

111 *Jones v Ministry of Interior Al-Mamlaka Al-Arabiya AS Saudiya (the Kingdom of Saudi Arabia) and others* House of Lords [2006] UKHL 26 Bingham, para 14. He stressed that the UK had no jurisdiction over other states: "I do not understand how a state can be said to deny access to its court if it has no access to give." See also para 28.

112 ibid Hoffman para 64.

113 *Benkharbouche & Janah v Embassy of the Republic of Sudan* England and Wales Court of Appeal, QB [2015] EWCA Civ 33 para 16.

114 *Benkharbouche (Respondent) v Secretary of State for Foreign and Commonwealth Affairs (Appellant) and Secretary of State for Foreign and Commonwealth Affairs and Libya (Appellants) v Janah (Respondent)* UKSC [2017] UKSC 62, Lord Sumption (with whom Lord Neuberger, Lady Hale, Lord Clarke and Lord Wilson agree) para 30: "In my view, there may well come a time when this court has to choose between the view of the House of Lords and that of the European Court of Human Rights on this fundamental question. [...] I would not be willing to decide which of the competing views about the implications of a want of jurisdiction is correct, unless the question actually arose."

British justices held that article 6 ECHR would not have been engaged in the first place.[115]

b) The operation of proportionality analysis

So far, this difference in construction may have looked more apparent than real since, as the European Court stressed, "measures [...] which reflect generally recognised rules of public international law on State immunity cannot *in principle* be regarded as imposing a disproportionate restriction."[116] As will be demonstrated in the next subsection, the European Court refrained from conducting its own balancing between the right to access to a court and state immunity; furthermore, the particularities of each case have not become outcome-determinative yet, but they may play a greater role in future cases.

aa) The *Al-Adsani* judgment

In the *Al-Adsani* case, the applicant had unsuccessfully attempted to obtain compensation for ill-treatment and acts of torture in Kuwait from the State of Kuwait before courts in the United Kingdom. The European Court held that "the grant of sovereign immunity to a State in civil proceedings pursues the legitimate aim of complying with international law to promote comity and good relations between States through the respect of another State's sovereignty."[117] It then assessed "whether the restriction was proportionate to the aim pursued".[118] Since the ECHR had to be interpreted in light of "any relevant rules of international law" according to the principle enshrined in article 31(3)(c) VCLT and therefore "so far as possible [...] in harmony with other rules of which it forms part"[119], it followed "that measures taken by a High Contracting Party which reflect generally recognised rules of public international law on State immunity cannot in principle be regarded as imposing a disproportionate restriction to the right of access to a court."[120]

---

115 See also Andrew Sanger, 'State Immunity and the Right of Access to a Court Under the EU Charter of Fundamental Rights' (2016) 65(1) ICLQ 214, 219, 220.
116 *Al-Adsani v the United Kingdom [GC]* para 56 (italics added).
117 ibid para 54; *Jones and Others v The United Kingdom* para 188.
118 *Al-Adsani v the United Kingdom [GC]* para 55.
119 ibid para 55.
120 ibid para 55; *Jones and Others v The United Kingdom* para 189.

The doctrine of state immunity was regarded as inherent restriction on the right of access to a court.[121]

This conclusion was not altered by the fact that the applicants had sought compensation before British courts because of a violation of the prohibition of torture. The European Court took account of "a growing recognition of the overriding importance of the prohibition of torture"[122] and accepted "that the prohibition of torture has achieved the status of a peremptory norm in international law".[123] Yet, the European Court was "unable to discern in the international instruments, judicial authorities or other materials before it any firm basis for concluding that, as a matter of international law, a State no longer enjoys immunity from civil suit in the courts of another State where acts of torture are alleged."[124]

In conclusion, the European Court did not conduct a free balancing of the peremptory prohibition of torture, the right to access to a court and state immunity.[125] Rather, it considered the interpretation of the immunity doctrine in international practice, namely in international instruments and decisions rendered by judicial authorities.[126]

bb) The *Jones* judgment

The same approach was adopted later in the *Jones* case on the question of liability of Saudi Arabia and its state officials for ill-treatment and acts of torture in Saudi Arabia before courts in the United Kingdom. According to the applicants' submission, the European Court should take the *Jones* case as an opportunity to revisit its approach adopted in *Al-Adsani* where it "had failed to conduct a substantive proportionality assessment, including an assessment of the circumstances and merits of the individual case, and in particular to

---

121 *Al-Adsani v the United Kingdom [GC]* para 56.
122 ibid para 60.
123 ibid para 61.
124 ibid para 61.
125 According to the dissenting judges, the prohibition of torture should have prevailed against state immunity because of the former's character as jus cogens, ibid Joint Diss Op of Judges Rozakis and Caflisch, joined by Judges Wildhaber, Costa, Cabral Barreto and Vajic para 2.
126 See also Magdalena Forowicz, *The Reception of International Law in the European Court of Human Rights* (Oxford University Press 2010) 311 (speaking of a "traditional approach").

consider whether alternative means of redress existed."[127] The Chamber did not relinquish this case to the Grand Chamber. Instead, it examined whether there had been "an evolution in the accepted international standards as regards the existence of a torture exception to the doctrine of State immunity since its earlier judgment in *Al-Adsani*".[128] Here, the European Court relied on the then recent *Jurisdictional Immunities* judgment of the ICJ for that "no *jus cogens* exception to State immunity had yet crystallised."[129] The European Court then examined whether "the grant of immunity *ratione materiae* to the State officials reflected [generally recognised rules of public international law on State immunity]."[130] Based on an analysis of domestic and international decisions the European Court concluded that "State immunity in principle offers individual employees or officers of a foreign State protection in respect of acts undertaken on behalf of the State under the same cloak as protects the State itself."[131] Having established this general rule, the Chamber addressed the question of whether a special rule or an exception existed in relation to acts of torture. Careful not to forestall any ongoing development,[132] the European Court pointed out that "a working group of the ILC acknowledged the existence of some support for the view that State officials should not be entitled to plead immunity for acts of torture", but "there was acknowledged not to be any consensus as yet."[133] There was "little national case-law concerning civil claims lodged against named State officials for *jus cogens* violations"[134] and ultimately, the European Court concluded that in spite of "some emerging support in favour of a special rule or exception [...], the bulk of the authority is [...] to the effect that the State's right to immunity may not be circumvented by suing its servants or agents instead."[135]

---

127 *Jones and Others v The United Kingdom* para 193, and para 195.
128 ibid para 196.
129 ibid para 198. The ICJ had considered the jurisprudence of the ECtHR, *Jurisdictional Immunities of the State* [2012] ICJ Rep 99, 139 para 90.
130 *Jones and Others v The United Kingdom* para 201.
131 ibid para 204.
132 The European Court noted after the presentation of its conclusion that the grant of immunity reflected generally recognised rules of public international law: "However, in light of the developments currently underway in this area of public international law, this is a matter which needs to be kept under review by Contracting States.", ibid para 215.
133 ibid para 209, see also para 212 where the criticism within the ILC was mentioned.
134 ibid para 210.
135 ibid para 213.

Finally, the European Court also took account of the individual case and stressed that the House of Lords judgment had "fully engaged with all of the relevant arguments [...] The findings of the House of Lords were neither manifestly erroneous nor arbitrary, but were based on extensive references to international-law materials and consideration of the applicants' legal arguments."[136]

c) Repercussion of the construction: the focus on the individual case

The case-law on immunities in the context of labour disputes, where the applicant used to work as employee in the embassy of a state on the territory of a third state, demonstrates that proportionality analysis, in particular the burden of justification imposed on states and the focus on the individual case, can have the potential of shaping the further development of customary international law.[137]

The European Court used to pay more deference to customary international law and immunities in the context of labour law disputes involving the personnel of embassies. In *Fogarty*, the European Court stated that

> "there appears to be a trend in international and comparative law towards limiting State immunity in respect of employment-related disputes. However, where the proceedings relate to employment in a foreign mission or embassy, international practice is divided on the question whether State immunity continues to apply and, if it does so apply, whether it covers disputes relating to the contracts of all staff or only more senior members of the mission"[138].

The European Court was "not aware of any trend in international law towards a relaxation of the rule of State immunity as regards issues of recruitment to foreign missions."[139] The European Court's assessment began to change with the UN General Assembly's adoption of the 2004 United Nations Convention

---

136 *Jones and Others v The United Kingdom* para 214, also noting that other domestic courts had found the judgment "highly persuasive"; *Jones House of Lords* [2006] UKHL 26 para 19 (Bingham on distinguishing Jones from Pinochet).
137 For a similar assessment Stephan W Schill, 'Cross-Regime Harmonization through Proportionality Analysis: The Case of International Investment Law, the Law of State Immunity and Human Rights' (2012) 27(1) ICSID Review 115.
138 *Fogarty v The United Kingdom [GC]* App no 37112/97 (ECtHR, 21 November 2001) para 37.
139 ibid paras 34-39.

on Jurisdictional Immunities which was based on a draft of the International Law Commission.[140]

Article 11(1) of this convention stipulates:

> "Unless otherwise agreed between the States concerned, a State cannot invoke immunity from jurisdiction before a court of another State which is otherwise competent in a proceeding which relates to a contract of employment between the State and an individual for work performed or to be performed, in whole or in part, in the territory of that other State."

Article 11(2) provides for exceptions to this general rule, excluding, for instance, employees who perform functions in the exercise of governmental authority. Since the convention is to this date ratified by only 22 states, the question posed itself to what extent its provisions reflect customary international law.[141]

Taking this convention into account, the European Court modified its approach in *Cudak*. Even though the European Court began by distinguishing the *Cudak* situation on "dismissal of a member of the local staff of an embassy" from the *Fogarty* situation on recruitment,[142] the judgment did not stop at this distinction and paid regard to new developments concerning immunity reflected in the adoption of the UN convention.

The European Court examined whether "the impugned restriction to the applicant's right of access was proportionate to the aim pursued."[143] The European Court then noted that "the application of absolute State immunity has, for many years, clearly been eroded"[144] and that Article 11 of the 2004 UN Convention on Jurisdictional Immunities "created a significant exception in matters of State immunity by, in principle, removing from the application of the immunity rule a State's employment contracts with the staff of its diplomatic missions abroad."[145] Furthermore, neither the respondent state nor the state of the embassy concerned, Lithuania, had objected to the wording

---

140 United Nations Convention on Jurisdictional Immunities of States and Their Property (signed 2 December 2004) UN Doc A/RES/59/38; Richard Garnett, 'State and Diplomatic Immunity and Employment Rights: European Law to the Rescue?' (2015) 64 ICLQ 791-795.
141 For a detailed examination, see Pavoni, 'The Myth of the Customary Nature of the United Nations Convention on State Immunity: Does the End Justify the Means?' 264 ff.
142 *Cudak v Lithuania [GC]* App no 15869/02 (ECtHR, 23 March 2010) para 62.
143 ibid para 62.
144 ibid para 64.
145 ibid para 65.

of article 11 of the Convention and to the view that this provision reflected customary international law.[146] In addition, the respondent state had not demonstrated that the exceptions of article 11 of the Convention and as reflection of custom were relevant in the case.[147]

Thus, the case did not turn only on the identification and interpretation of customary international law, it was also important whether the respondent government had met the burden of reasoning and justification. Other cases illustrate that the grant of immunity in labour law disputes may constitute an unjustified violation of article 6 when it was not supported by a convincing reasoning. In the cases *Wallishauser* and *Sabeh El Leil*, the European Court argued that the domestic courts did not sufficiently examine the UN convention on jurisdictional immunities and its relation to customary international law.[148]

d) Evaluation

Proportionality analysis can be used as a tool for promoting harmonization as it provides a framework in which the ECHR can be reconciled with other international law. General international law becomes "part and parcel of the Convention's obligations"[149].

Moreover, it leads to an examination of the reasoning of domestic courts in relation to customary international law under consideration of the object and purpose of the ECHR. In other words, proportionality analysis directs the focus to the individual case and ensures that, as emphasized by the

---

146 *Cudak v Lithuania [GC]* paras 66-67.
147 ibid paras 70-73.
148 *Wallishauser v Austria* App no 156/04 (ECtHR, 17 July 2012) paras 70, 73; *Sabeh El Leil v France [GC]* App no 4869/05 (ECtHR, 29 November 2011) para 62 (French organs did not establish how duties of applicant were linked to sovereign interest of Kuwait), paras 63-64 (French Court of Appeal merely asserted additional responsibilities of applicant without further justification or reasoning), para 65 (Court of Cassation "did not give any more extensive reasoning on this point"), para 66 (both French courts failed to consider article 11 of the 2004 UN convention); see also *Oleynikov v Russia* App no 36703/04 (ECtHR, 14 March 2013) para 70; see also Pavoni, 'The Myth of the Customary Nature of the United Nations Convention on State Immunity: Does the End Justify the Means?' 272.
149 Schill, 'Cross-Regime Harmonization through Proportionality Analysis: The Case of International Investment Law, the Law of State Immunity and Human Rights' 116.

European Court, the ECHR is an instrument of the European public order for the protection of the individual being. It is possible, therefore, that the interpretation and application of states' ECHR obligations can shape the future development of customary international law.

The European Court was reluctant, however, to conduct the balancing between the right to access to a court (article 6 ECHR) and customary international law on state immunity. Instead, it examined the balance struck in international practice, concluding that immunity remains "an inherent restriction" to article 6 and that "measures taken by a High Contracting Party which reflect generally recognised rules of public international law on State immunity cannot in principle be regarded as imposing a disproportionate restriction to the right of access to a court."[150] Since the doctrine of state immunity was based on customary international law, the European Court had to examine international practice, careful not to forestall any ongoing developments.

These cases demonstrate that customary international law no longer operates between states only and that the effects of its application on the ECHR are examined, with the state carrying the burden of justification for any infringement to the right of the individual. The ultimate result of the particular case depends, *inter alia*, on the quality of reasoning of the respondent state. This construction which puts pressure on states may, in the long run, have an effect on the development of customary international law.[151]

One word of caution is needed, though: in cases where the reasoning of domestic courts was regarded insufficient and the infringement of a right under the ECHR was regarded to be not justified, no immunity existed in the view of the European Court. These cases concerned *acta jure gestionis* and labour law disputes. In contrast, in cases where immunity was recognized, the European Court did not hold that the infringement to a right under the

---

150 *Al-Adsani v the United Kingdom [GC]* para 55; *Jones and Others v The United Kingdom* para 189. Cf. *Jurisdictional Immunities of the State* [2012] ICJ Rep 99, 136 paras 82-83, where the ICJ argued that an exception to immunity based on the merits of the case presented "a logical problem" because of the preliminary nature of immunity. The Court then nevertheless examined whether an exception had developed in international practice.

151 Schill, 'Cross-Regime Harmonization through Proportionality Analysis: The Case of International Investment Law, the Law of State Immunity and Human Rights' 115: "[These cases] are an example of the ECtHR actively using human rights law to influence and reduce the scope of State immunity, much like substantive investment treaty obligations could be used to reduce the scope of immunity doctrines."

Chapter 8: The European Convention on Human Rights

ECHR was disproportionate on the basis of lack of reasoning or because of the particularities of the case. Yet, the possibility that the specific circumstances of the individual case may play a greater role is, in principle, implied by proportionality analysis and the focus on the individual case. The jurisprudence on state immunity in labour law disputes demonstrates both this possibility and the way in which cases before the European Court can contribute to a consolidation of a trend restricting immunities.

3. Proportionality analysis and treaty law

This construction of the European Court was used not only for customary international law but also for treaty law.

One example relating to treaty law concerns the Hague Convention on the Civil Aspects of International Child Abduction.[152] The convention provides for the speedy return of an abducted child, subject to the exceptions in article 13. According to this provision, a state is

> "not bound to order the return of the child if the person, institution or other body which opposes its return establishes that a) the person, institution or other body having the care of the person of the child was not actually exercising the custody rights at the time of removal or retention, or had consented to or subsequently acquiesced in the removal or retention; or b) there is a grave risk that his or her return would expose the child to physical or psychological harm or otherwise place the child in an intolerable situation."

The case-law of the European Court illustrates the different aspects of the relationship between article 8 ECHR, the right to respect for private and family life, and the Hague Convention on the Civil Aspects of International Child Abduction.

The European Court can strengthen the compliance with the Hague Convention since delayed enforcement of a return order according to the Hague Convention can violate the positive obligations under article 8 ECHR.[153]

---

152 Convention on the Civil Aspects of International Child Abduction (signed 25 October 1980, entered into force 1 December 1983) 1343 UNTS 89; for an in-depth analysis of the case-law in relation to this convention see Forowicz, *The Reception of International Law in the European Court of Human Rights* 107-148.

153 *Sylvester v Austria* App no 36812/97 and 40104/98 (ECtHR, 24 April 2003) para 72; Lara Walker, 'The Impact of the Hague Abduction Convention on the Rights of the Family in the Case-Law of the European Court of Human Rights and the UN

Yet, return orders can also be challenged as infringements to article 8 ECHR. Then, the question arises "whether a fair balance between the competing interests at stake - those of the child, of the two parents, and of the public order - was struck."[154] The European Convention can therefore require a refined interpretation of obligations under other treaties in order to give expression to "the special character of the Convention as an instrument of European public order (*ordre public*) for the protection of individual human beings"[155].

The proportionality analysis leads to an examination of the particular facts of the case and can cut both ways.

In *Maumousseau and Washington*, the domestic authorities had not violated article 8 ECHR, as they had "conducted an in-depth examination of the entire family situation and of a whole series of factors, in particular of a factual, emotional, psychological, material and medical nature, and made a balanced and reasonable assessment of the respective interests of each person".[156]

In *Neulinger*, the European Court took into account developments "that have occurred since the Federal Court's judgment ordering the child's return".[157] An enforcement of a return order at "a certain time after the child's abduction [...] may undermine, in particular, the pertinence of the Hague Convention in such a situation, it being essentially an instrument of a procedural nature and not a human rights treaty protecting individuals on an objective basis."[158]

This jurisprudence exemplifies how the European Court can introduce human rights rationale and a focus on the individual to an international rule governing the relations between states.[159]

Human Rights Committee: The Danger of Neulinger' (2010) 6(3) Journal of Private International Law 658-659.
154 *Maumousseau and Washington v France* App no 39388/05 (ECtHR, 6 December 2007) para 62.
155 *Neulinger and Shuruk v Switzerland [GC]* para 133.
156 *Maumousseau and Washington v France* para 74.
157 *Neulinger and Shuruk v Switzerland [GC]* para 145.
158 ibid para 145.
159 For a discussion of the implications for the Hague convention see Linda J Silberman, 'The Hague Convention on Child Abduction and Unilateral Relocations by Custodial Parents: A Perspective from the United States and Europe - Abbott, Neulinger, Zarraga' (2011) 63 Oklahoma Law Review 742 (critical), and Walker, 'The Impact of the Hague Abduction Convention on the Rights of the Family in the Case-Law of the European Court of Human Rights and the UN Human Rights Committee: The

Chapter 8: The European Convention on Human Rights

4. Reconciliation on the basis of general principles

Recourse to general principles can help in reconciling different obligations, as the European Court's case-law on international humanitarian law and on Security Council resolutions illustrates. The prohibition of arbitrariness performs a coordination function insofar as it offers a basis for a reconciliation of more specific obligations which offer different levels of protection. It can also provide for a framework in which the European Court can articulate the normative ambitions of the ECHR, and it can constitute a general benchmark for cases where states implement other international obligations, for instance the obligation to carry out decisions of the UNSC under article 25 of the UN Charter, and where more specific obligations are missing.[160]

a) The prohibition of arbitrariness and international humanitarian law

The *Hassan* case on the legality of the deprivation of liberty in an international armed conflict constituted a landmark decision concerning the relationship between the ECHR and international humanitarian law.[161]

Danger of Neulinger' 650, 681 (arguing that undermining the Hague convention was not the intention of the Court).

160 On the latter case see *Naït-Liman v Switzerland [GC]* paras 203, 216 (after having concluded that the actions of Swiss authorities could not be evaluated by a treaty obligation or customary international law, the European Court concluded that the Swiss authorities enjoyed a wide margin of appreciation and then examined the compliance with the prohibition of arbitrariness).

161 *Hassan v The United Kingdom [GC]*; in earlier cases in situations of non-international armed conflicts, the European Court interpreted and applied the ECHR without much modification by international humanitarian law: *Güleç v Turkey* App no 54/1997/838/1044 (ECtHR, 27 July 1998); *Ergi v Turkey* App no 540/1993/435/514 (ECtHR, 28 July 1998); *McCann and Others v United Kingdom [GC]* App no 18984/91 (ECtHR, 27 September 1995); *Özkan et al v Turkey* App no 21689/93 (ECtHR, 6 April 2004); *Isayeva v Russia* App no 57950/00 (ECtHR, 24 February 2005). Occasionally, the European Court framed its judgments in the terminology of international humanitarian law, *Ergi v Turkey* paras 79 ff. ("civilian population", "all feasible precautions in the choice of means and methods of a security operation mounted against an opposing group with a view to avoiding and, in any event, to minimising, incidental loss of civilian life"); *Özkan et al v Turkey* para 297. In 1975, the European Commission "has not found it necessary to examine the question of a breach of Article 5 of the European Convention on Human Rights with regard to

Whereas the rules of international humanitarian law, in particular article 21 of the Third Geneva Convention[162] and articles 42, 78 of the Fourth Geneva Convention[163], do not prohibit detentions and internments of prisoner of wars and of civilians for security reasons, article 5 ECHR explicitly sets forth six lawful grounds of detention which do not include security detentions. Article 5 ECHR is more specific than article 9 ICCPR[164] the wording of which prohibits only "arbitrary deprivation of liberty". Furthermore, whereas articles 5, 43 and 78 of the Fourth Geneva Convention provide for an internment review by a "competent tribunal" which does not have to be a court, article 5(4) ECHR stipulates that individuals must have access to a "court" which shall speedily decides on the lawfulness of the detention.

The European Court accommodated the apparently conflicting provisions with each other by striking a pragmatic balance under consideration of the prohibition of arbitrariness as common denominator.[165] Recourse to this general principle of law enabled the European Court not only to reconcile both rules with each other, it also informed the way in which the European Court articulated the normative ambitions of the ECHR in international armed conflicts by requiring procedural safeguards in order to "protect the individual from arbitrariness".[166]

The European Court took into account that the taking of prisoners of war and the detention of civilians were an "accepted feature" in international armed conflicts.[167] It adopted a restrained interpretation of article 5 ECHR and focused on the article's "fundamental purpose" which would consist in the protection of individuals from arbitrariness.[168] The European Court furthermore relaxed the procedural safeguards of article 5(2) and (4), "in

---

persons accorded the status of prisoners of war", *Cyprus v Turkey* App no 6780/74; 6950/75 (Commission Decision, 10 July 1976) para 313.

162 Geneva Convention, relative to the treatment of prisoners of war (signed 12 August 1949, entered into force 21 October 1950) 75 UNTS 135.

163 Geneva Convention relative to the protection of civilian persons in time of war (signed 12 August 1949, entered into force 21 October 1950) 75 UNTS 287.

164 International Covenant on Civil and Political Rights (signed 16 December 1966, entered into force 23 March 1976) 999 UNTS 171.

165 Rule 99 of the ICRC Customary Law Study (Jean-Marie Henckaerts and Louise Doswald-Beck, *Customary International Humanitarian Law: Rules* (vol 1, Cambridge University Press 2005) 344) reads: "Arbitrary deprivation of liberty is prohibited."

166 *Hassan v The United Kingdom [GC]* para 105.

167 ibid para 104.

168 ibid para 105.

a manner which takes into account the context and the applicable rules of international humanitarian law."[169] Thus, the "competent body" periodically reviewing the detention according to articles 43 and 78 of the Fourth Geneva Convention would not need to be a "court in the sense generally required by Article 5 para 4"[170] since this "might not be practicable in an international armed conflict".[171] However, the competent body should "provide sufficient guarantees of impartiality and fair procedure to protect against arbitrariness. Moreover, the first review should take place shortly after the person is taken into detention, with subsequent reviews at frequent intervals, to ensure that any person who does not fall into one of the categories subject to internment under international humanitarian law is released without undue delay."[172]

To summarize, security detentions in international armed conflicts will be considered lawful under article 5 ECHR if they keep within the fundamental purpose of article 5, the prohibition of arbitrariness. The European Court required not only compliance with the articles of the Geneva Convention but also additionally, as matter of human rights law, that the reviews stipulated in article 78 of the Fourth Geneva Convention provide for sufficient guarantees of impartiality and fair procedure to protect against arbitrariness.[173]

Subsequently, the UK Supreme Court based its interpretation of what is required under article 5 ECHR in a non-international armed conflict where a UN Security Council resolution authorized the use all necessary means on the *Hassan* standard[174] which was developed in the context of an international armed conflict and which itself was based on a combination of several elements: a restrained interpretation of article 5 ECHR under consideration of its fundamental purpose, the prohibition of arbitrariness, articles 43 and 78 of the Fourth Geneva Convention as minimum standard, and human rights law safeguards against arbitrariness (impartiality, fair procedure and the individual's participation therein).[175]

---

169 *Hassan v The United Kingdom [GC]* para 106.
170 ibid para 106.
171 ibid para 106.
172 ibid para 106.
173 ibid 52-54 paras 102-107; for a more detailed analysis see Matthias Lippold, 'Between Humanization and Humanitarization?: Detention in Armed Conflicts and the European Convention on Human Rights' (2016) 76(1) ZaöRV 80 ff.; cf. recently *Georgia v Russia (II) [GC]* para 234-7.
174 See above, p. 438.
175 *Abd Ali Hameed Al-Waheed v Ministry of Defence and Serdar Mohammed v Ministry of Defence* UKSC [2017] UKSC 2; Lippold, 'The Interpretation of UN Security

b) Security Council Resolutions

A different example of the reconciliation of different obligations can be found in the jurisprudence on Security Council resolutions.

According to the European Court, there is a rebuttable presumption that UNSCR resolutions do not intend to authorize human rights violations. This presumption of compatibility does not derive from the European Convention but from the UN Charter's commitment both to peace and security and to human rights. In light of this presumption, the court held that the general authorization to use all necessary means could not have been intended to authorize indefinite detention without charge.[176]

When this presumption was rebutted by the explicit wording of a resolution, the European Court examined whether the resolution was implemented in a proportionate way in the specific case.[177] According to the European Court, "the respondent State could not validly confine itself to relying on the binding nature of Security Council resolutions, but should have persuaded the Court that it had taken – or at least had attempted to take – all possible measures to adapt the sanctions regime to the applicant's individual situation."[178] Therefore, there was no need to examine the hierarchy of obligations under the ECHR and under the Charter.[179] The European Court built on this jurisprudence in *Al-Dulimi* on the legality of Security Council sanctions imposed by Switzerland in pursuance of its obligations under the UN Charter. The European Court rejected the argument that the right to access to a court was part of *jus cogens*.[180] However, it took the view that "[o]ne of the fundamental components of European public order is the principle of the rule of law, and arbitrariness constitutes the negation of that principle".[181]

According to the European Court,

    Council Resolutions between Regional and General International Law: What Role for General Principles?' 149 ff.
176 *Al-Jedda v The United Kingdom [GC]* App no 27021/08 (ECtHR, 7 July 2011) 60 para 102, 61 para 105. in part. 63 para 109: "[...] neither Resolution 1546 nor any other United Nations Security Council resolution explicitly or implicitly required the United Kingdom to place an individual whom its authorities considered to constitute a risk to the security of Iraq in indefinite detention without charge."
177 *Nada v Switzerland [GC]* 54 paras 194 ff. and 59 para 213.
178 ibid 52-53 para 196.
179 ibid 53 para 197.
180 *Al-Dulimi and Montana Managment Inc v Switzerland [GC]* 66 para 136.
181 ibid 69 para 145.

"where a resolution such as that in the present case, namely Resolution 1483, does not contain any clear or explicit wording excluding the possibility of judicial supervision of the measures taken for its implementation, it must always be understood as authorising the courts of the respondent State to exercise sufficient scrutiny so that any arbitrariness can be avoided. By limiting that scrutiny to arbitrariness, the Court takes account of the nature and purpose of the measures provided for by the Resolution in question, in order to strike a fair balance between the necessity of ensuring respect for human rights and the imperatives of the protection of international peace and security."[182]

It was then held that Switzerland had not met this standard since the applicants had no "genuine opportunity to submit appropriate evidence to a court, for examination on the merits, to seek to show that their inclusion on the impugned lists had been arbitrary."[183]

II. Concluding observations

As this section has illustrated, the European Court integrated the ECHR and other obligations under international treaties and customary international law within a proportionality analysis and, therefore, indicated that states have to give regard to the ECHR when they fulfil their further obligations under international law. The reason for not conducting a proportionality analysis in the *Hassan case* and for reconciling instead article 5 ECHR and the provisions of the Geneva Conventions on security detention on the basis of a common principle, the prohibition of arbitrariness, might have been related to the fact that both article 5 ECHR and the relevant provisions of the Geneva Conventions concerned the same subject-matter, the deprivation of liberty. The jurisprudence of the European Court illustrates the important function of the prohibition of arbitrariness not only as common denominator of more specific obligations but also as inspiration for a standard of review when the European Court examined states' compliance with the ECHR in

---

182 *Al-Dulimi and Montana Managment Inc v Switzerland [GC]* 70 para 146.
183 ibid 71 para 151; for a critique see the dissenting opinion of Judge Nußberger, in her view, there was a conflict between the ECHR and the applicable UNSC resolution which is why the Charter obligation to implement the resolution should have prevailed according to article 103 UNC. In addition, she argued that the Swiss authorities had sufficiently conducted an arbitrariness review; the last view is shared by judge Ziemele in her partly dissenting opinion.

the implementation of other obligations under international law, as it was the case in relation to UNSC resolutions.

D. The relationship between the ECHR and the law of international responsibility: The development of functional equivalents

This section examines the relationship between the ECHR and the law of international responsibility. This relationship is complex because the European Court can, on the basis of an interpretation of the ECHR, develop functional equivalents to concepts of general international law which can make recourse to the latter unnecessary. In addition, the ECHR employs notions which, while being similar to notions under general international law, do not necessarily have the same meaning. As will be argued below, this complexity constitutes a particular challenge for future studies of general international law.

The purpose of this section is to highlight the complex relationship between the ECHR and concepts of general international law. The section will first address the relationship between jurisdiction in the context article 1 ECHR and jurisdiction in general international law (I.). Subsequently, this section will discuss the role of attribution in relation to the ECHR (II.) and point to the different notions of "control" in relation to jurisdiction under article 1 ECHR and to attribution under general international law (III.). The section will then raise the question of whether the European Court began to develop treaty-based functional equivalents to attribution under general international law (IV.). Last but not least, the section will engage with the Court's take of attribution analysis in the relationship between states and international organizations (V.).

I. "Jurisdiction" and the relationship between article 1 ECHR and general international law

There are different concepts of jurisdiction in general international law and in the context of the ECHR. According to article 1 ECHR, the parties to the ECHR "shall secure to everyone within their jurisdiction the rights and freedoms defined in Section I of this Convention." Jurisdiction is a central concept of the European Convention as it determines the applicability and the scope of the Convention and can raise questions of the interrelationship with other fields of international law.[184]

In *Banković*, the European Court interpreted this concept in light of the doctrine of "jurisdiction" under general international law and concluded that jurisdiction had to be primarily territorial.[185] As Milanovic has pointed out, however, differences between both concepts of jurisdiction exist:[186] the doctrine of jurisdiction under general international law serves the purpose of determining when a state has the competence to exercise its jurisdiction to prescribe, to adjudicate or to enforce; it delimits jurisdictional spheres between states. Jurisdiction in the sense of article 1 ECHR "is meant to denote solely a sort of factual power that a state exercises over persons or territory."[187] The concept of jurisdiction under general international law is therefore of limited guidance for interpreting the concept of jurisdiction in the sense of article 1 ECHR. Since *Banković*, the European Court has further developed its jurisprudence on the extraterritorial application of the ECHR. The Court held in *Al-Skeini*, that jurisdiction, which is primarily territorial,[188] will be exercised extraterritorially in two situations, namely, if a "state through its agents exercises control and authority over an individual"[189] or if a state "exercises effective control of an area outside that national territory".[190] The latter situation does not require the exercise of "detailed control over the policies and actions of the subordinate local administration", it suffices that the survival of the local administration depends on the Contracting State's

---

184 Cf. *Abd Ali Hameed Al-Waheed v Ministry of Defence and Serdar Mohammed v Ministry of Defence* [2017] UKSC 2 Lord Sumption (with whom Lady Hale agrees) para 48. Cf. now *Georgia v Russia (II) [GC]* para 141, where the Court supports its conclusion against jurisdiction in relation to military operations during the active phase of hostilities with the consideration of "the fact that such situations are predominantly regulated by legal norms other than those of the Convention (specifically, international humanitarian law or the law of armed conflict) [...]".
185 *Banković against Belgium, the Czech Republic, Denmark, France, Germany, Greece, Hungary, Iceland, Italy, Luxembourg, the Netherlands, Norway, Poland, Portugal, Spain, Turkey and the United Kingdom [GC]* paras 59-61.
186 Marko Milanovic, 'From Compromise to Principle: Clarifying the Concept of State Jurisdiction in Human Rights Treaties' (2008) 8(3) Human Rights Law Review 417-436.
187 ibid 417.
188 *Al-Skeini and Others v The United Kingdom [GC]* para 131.
189 ibid para 137.
190 ibid para 138.

"military and other support".¹⁹¹ Criteria such as military, economic and political support for the local subordinate administration may be relevant for determining whether the state has effective control over an area.¹⁹² Both situations require a certain degree of control, as the Court emphasized in its recent judgment in the proceeding between Georgia and Russia. Addressing the question of the Convention's applicability to military operations during the active phase of hostilities, the Court held that "the very reality of armed confrontation and fighting between enemy military forces seeking to establish control over an area in a context of chaos not only means that there is no 'effective control' over an area".¹⁹³ The European Court distinguished the bombing and artillery shelling in the active phase of hostilities from "isolated and specific acts of violence involving an element of proximity", in relation to which the Court had applied the concept of "State agent authority and control".¹⁹⁴ The Court summarized recently its jurisprudence to the effect that the ECHR may apply extraterritorially based on the concept of State agent authority and control in case of physical power and control over the victim or in case of isolated and specific acts of violence involving an element of proximity which may include the beating or shooting by State agents of individuals or the extrajudicial targeted killing of an individual.¹⁹⁵

---

191 ibid para 138. On the survival of a non-state entity by virtue of state support see already *Cyprus v Turkey [GC]* para 77. On the development of the survival-test see Milanovic, 'Special Rules of Attribution of Conduct in International Law' 349-355.
192 *Al-Skeini and Others v The United Kingdom [GC]* para 139.
193 *Georgia v Russia (II) [GC]* para 137. For the view that a certain degree of control is required and that an act of violence alone does not suffice in order to make the ECHR applicable, see *Al-Saadoon and Others v Secretary of State for Defence, and Rahmatullah & ANR v The Secretary of State for Defence* England and Wales Court of Appeal, QB [2016] EWCA Civ 811 paras 69-73; for the contrary view see *Al-Saadoon and Others v Secretary of State for Defence* England and Wales High Court of Justice, QB [2015] EWHC 715 paras 39, 95, 102, 107, arguing that Banković had been *de facto* overruled by the ECtHR. See now *Ukraine and the Netherlands v Russia [GC]* App no 8019/16, 43800/14 and 28525/20 (ECtHR, 25 January 2023) para 571.
194 *Georgia v Russia (II) [GC]* paras 131-132.
195 *Ukraine and the Netherlands v Russia [GC]* paras 568-570; *Carter v Russia* App no 20914/07 (ECtHR, 21 September 2021) paras 125-130, 170.

II. The role of attribution in relation to the ECHR

If one applies article 2 ARSIWA[196] rigidly, the questions of attribution and of jurisdiction will be posed in a successive order[197]: first, one has to establish whether the conduct of an entity is attributable to a state. Second, one must examine whether the state breached an international obligation. As far as an obligation under the ECHR is concerned, one has to determine, first, the applicability of the ECHR and, second, the violation of the ECHR. In principle and for the sake of analytical clarity, the law of state responsibility and the question of jurisdiction according to article 1 ECHR are to be distinguished.[198]

It may be necessary, however, to conduct multiple attribution analyses. If a case concerns the extraterritorial application of the ECHR, the Court will first determine whether a potentially jurisdiction-establishing conduct was attributable to the state before it will approach the question of whether a conduct which might have given rise to a violation of the ECHR could be attributed to the state. This was the case in *Jaloud*: The Court decided that the

---

196 "There is an internationally wrongful act of a State when conduct consisting of an action or omission: (a) is attributable to the State under international law; and (b) constitutes a breach of an international obligation of the State."

197 Marko Milanovic, 'Jurisdiction and Responsibility: Trends in the Jurisprudence of the Strasbourg Court' in Anne van Aaken and Iulia Motoc (eds), *The European Convention on Human Rights and General International Law* (Oxford University Press 2018) 106: "[...] an attribution inquiry actually logically precedes the jurisdiction inquiry when it comes to the conduct which is itself constitutive of jurisdiction"; see also *Jaloud v The Netherlands [GC]* App no 47708/08 (ECtHR, 20 November 2014) paras 151-152.

198 *Catan and others v Moldova and Russia [GC]* App no 43370/04, 8252/05 and 18454/06 (ECtHR, 19 October 2012) para 115; *Jaloud v The Netherlands [GC]* para 154: "[...] the test for establishing the existence of "jurisdiction" under Article 1 of the Convention has never been equated with the test for establishing a State's responsibility for an internationally wrongful act under general international law [...]"; cf. generally Iulia Motoc and Johann Justus Vasel, 'The ECHR and Responsibility of the State: Moving towards Judicial Integration: a View from the Bench' in Anne van Aaken and Iulia Motoc (eds), *The European Convention on Human Rights and general international law* (Oxford University Press 2018) 200 ff.; cf. for a different approach Martin Scheinin, 'Just another word? Jurisdiction in the Roadmaps of State Responsibility and Human Rights' in Malcolm Langford (ed), *Global justice, state duties: the extraterritorial scope of economic, social and cultural rights in international law* (Cambridge University Press 2013) 213-215, questioning the significance of jurisdiction as independent criterion.

Netherlands had violated its positive obligation under article 2 ECHR, as the Netherland's investigation into the circumstances surrounding the applicant's death at a checkpoint in Iraq had failed to satisfy the requirements of article 2 ECHR.[199] The Court first held that the applicant fell under the jurisdiction of the Netherlands, as the "vehicle in which he was a passenger was fired upon while passing through a checkpoint manned by personnel under the command and direct supervision of a Netherlands Royal Army officer".[200] In the next step, the European Court determined that the "alleged acts and omissions of Netherlands military personnel" as to the investigation into the applicant's death was attributable to the Dutch state.[201] The judges Spielmann and Raimondi criticized the majority for their examination of the "non-issue of 'attribution'" and for what they considered to be a conflation of jurisdiction under article 1 and state responsibility under general international law.[202] It is submitted that this critique is ultimately not convincing. The two judges have a point in that there is a difference between the ECHR as so-called primary law and the ARSIWA as so-called secondary law which presupposes a violation of primary law. However, both bodies of law are not unrelated compartments of international law, a distinction between primary rules and secondary rules should, therefore, not be overemphasized at the expense of acknowledging the interrelationship between both.[203] In particular, the rules of attribution apply in relation to the primary rules of the ECHR which is why it is submitted here that the majority's approach is not "conceptually unsound". Yet, the judges' concern as to "confusion in an already difficult area of law" is understandable as the relationship between the ECHR and the doctrine of attribution according to the ARSIWA is not without complexities,

---

199 *Jaloud v The Netherlands [GC]* para 227.
200 ibid para 152.
201 ibid para 155 (the headings in paras 112, 154 can misleadingly suggest that the European Court determines first jurisdction (without attribution) and then attribution); on the two attribution inquiries, see Milanovic, 'Jurisdiction and Responsibility: Trends in the Jurisprudence of the Strasbourg Court' 106-107.
202 *Jaloud v The Netherlands [GC]* 81 ("Efforts to seek to elucidate the former by reference to the latter are conceptually unsound and likely to cause further confusion in an already difficult area of law").
203 See in particular below, p. 610; cf. now *Ukraine and the Netherlands v Russia [GC]* para 551; cf. for a strong emphasis of the integration between between the ECHR and general international law Motoc and Vasel, 'The ECHR and Responsibility of the State: Moving towards Judicial Integration: a View from the Bench' 201 ff.

Chapter 8: The European Convention on Human Rights

and the European Court did not always make a clear distinction between the two interrelated and yet distinct concepts.[204]

III. Two notions of "control" in relation to jurisdiction and to attribution

The use of similar terminology, the notion of *control*, contributes to the complexity of the relationship between jurisdiction and attribution; because of functional differences, both should not be conflated. The *Loizidou* case offers an example in this regard. The case turned on the question (which would later be answered in the positive) whether Turkey violated the Convention when subsequent to the Turkish invasion of Cyprus refugees were prohibited to return to their home by Turkey or by a non-state entity (TRNC) which controlled part of the border. In the preliminary objection decision, the applicant presented a twofold argument, merging treaty interpretation and the interpretation of general international law: the applicant argued that Turkey was responsible on the basis of the general rules of state responsibility and the Convention's obligation to avoid a legal vacuum from emerging: "The principles of the Convention system and the international law of State

---

204 James Crawford and Amelia Keene, 'The Structure of State Responsibility under the European Convention on Human Rights' in Anne van Aaken and Iulia Motoc (eds), *The European Convention on Human Rights and General International Law* (Oxford University Press 2018) 179; Milanovic, 'Special Rules of Attribution of Conduct in International Law' 343-344; on different views in scholarship, cf. Crawford and Keene, 'The Structure of State Responsibility under the European Convention on Human Rights' 178, 190; according to Malcolm Evans, 'State Responsibility and the ECHR' in Malgosia Fitzmaurice and Dan Sarooshi (eds), *Issues of State Responsibility before International Judicial Institutions* (Hart 2004) 159, the ECHR "makes the international principles of State responsibility irrelevant to its operation, so it is not clear why they should be referred to at all." See also at 160 where the author claimed that the ECtHR affirmed responsibility for the conduct of privates by adopting a broader test than the effective control test of the law of international responsibility; see also Scheinin, 'Just another word? Jurisdiction in the Roadmaps of State Responsibility and Human Rights' 213-215, arguing that the notion of jurisdiction in the sense of article 1 ECHR is no independent concept and should be equated with an attribution analysis; Maarten den Heijer and Rick Lawson, 'Extraterritorial Human Rights and the Concept of "Jurisdiction"' in Malcolm Langford (ed), *Global justice, state duties: the extraterritorial scope of economic, social and cultural rights in international law* (Cambridge University Press 2013) 154, suggesting three steps to determine state responsibility in the context of human rights: attribution, breach, and "whether victims of human rights violations are within the 'jurisdiction' of a State".

responsibility thus converge to produce a regime under which Turkey is responsible for controlling events in northern Cyprus."[205]

The European Court distinguished the question of jurisdiction in the sense of article 1 ECHR from the question of state responsibility which belonged to the merits.[206] It held:

> "[...], the responsibility of a Contracting Party may also arise when as a consequence of military action - whether lawful or unlawful - it exercises effective control of an area outside its national territory. The obligation to secure, in such an area, the rights and freedoms set out in the Convention derives from the fact of such control whether it be exercised directly, through its armed forces, or through a subordinate local administration."[207]

Having affirmed jurisdiction, the European Court then stressed in its judgment at the merits stage one year later that the policies and actions of a non-state entity, the so-called Turkish Republic of Northern Cyprus (TRNC), was "imputable" to Turkey: it was not necessary to examine whether Turkey had exercised "detailed control over the policies and actions of the authorities of the 'TRNC'"[208], it sufficed

> "that her army exercises effective overall control over that part of the island. Such control [...] entails her responsibility for the policies and actions of the 'TRNC'. [...] Those affected by such policies or actions therefore come within the "jurisdiction" of Turkey for the purposes of Article 1 of the Convention (art. 1)."[209]

The European Court then concluded that the alleged misconduct "falls within Turkey's 'jurisdiction' within the meaning of Article 1 (art. 1) and is thus imputable to Turkey."[210] The European Court did not examine whether the access was denied by Turkish troops or by the TRNC and whether the conduct of the TRNC could be attributed to Turkey; instead, the European Court based its holding on Turkey's positive obligations that were triggered by Turkey exercising "effective overall control over that part of the island" and thus exercising jurisdiction.[211]

---

205 *Loizidou v Turkey (Preliminary Objections)[GC]* para 57.
206 ibid para 61.
207 ibid para 62.
208 *Loizidou v Turkey (Judgment) [GC]* App no 15318/89 (ECtHR, 18 December 1996) para 56.
209 ibid para 56.
210 ibid para 57.
211 Milanovic, 'From Compromise to Principle: Clarifying the Concept of State Jurisdiction in Human Rights Treaties' 443; Crawford and Keene, 'The Structure of

The European Court used the notion of "control", namely "effective overall control" in order to determine whether Turkey had exercised jurisdiction, and not in order to establish attribution under the law of state responsibility.²¹² Since the control related to a geographic area, it becomes clear that the adjective "overall" was not meant as alternative to the adjective "effective", it rather indicated a geographical point of reference.

Yet, perhaps because the European Court wrote that control "entails [Turkey's] responsibility for the policies and actions of the 'TRNC'", this standard of control was partly (mis)understood²¹³ as attribution test for the purpose of establishing a state's international responsibility. In this sense, the ICTY invoked the *Loizidou* jurisprudence in order to justify a deviation from the effective control standard under general international law for the benefit of a standard based on overall control.²¹⁴ The International Court of Justice rejected this interpretation and held that the overall control test was employed by the ICTY in order to determine the international character of the conflict for the purposes of the Geneva Conventions. According to the Court, the effective control test remained the decisive criterion for the purposes of attribution in the context of state responsibility. The overall control test was considered to be too broad and to undermine the "fundamental principle governing the law of international responsibility: a State is responsible only for its own conduct, that is to say the conduct of persons acting, on whatever basis, on its behalf."²¹⁵ The ICJ judgment can be read in support of a dis-

---

State Responsibility under the European Convention on Human Rights' 193-194 (the Court did not apply the ARSIWA).

212 Cf. also Helmut Philipp Aust, *Complicity and the law of state responsibility* (Cambridge University Press 2011) 408, arguing that the European Court "did not have in mind 'effective control' in the sense of the ICJ's *Nicaragua* case"; cf. Olivier de Frouville, 'Attribution of Conduct to the State: Private Individuals' in James Crawford, Alain Pellet, and Simon Olleson (eds), *The Law of International Responsibility* (Oxford University Press 2010) 269.

213 For a critique of the European Court's terminology see Milanovic, 'Special Rules of Attribution of Conduct in International Law' 350-352.

214 See *Prosecutor v Dusko Tadić* ICTY AC Judgement (15 July 1999) IT-94-1-A paras 120-145; *Military and Paramilitary Activities in and against Nicaragua* [1986] ICJ Rep 14, 64-65 para 115; *Application of the Convention on the Prevention and Punishment of the Crime of Genocide* [2007] ICJ Rep 43, 209-211 paras 402-407; see also Antonio Cassese, 'The Nicaragua and Tadić Tests Revisited in Light of the ICJ Judgment on Genocide in Bosnia' (2007) 18(4) EJIL 649 ff.

215 *Application of the Convention on the Prevention and Punishment of the Crime of Genocide* [2007] ICJ Rep 43, 210 para 406. Years later, one of the authors of the

tinction between attribution under the secondary rules of state responsibility under general international law and attribution based on an interpretation of primary rules of a particular treaty.

This standard for establishing whether a state exercises effective control over an area for the purpose of establishing jurisdiction in the sense of article 1 ECHR is different from criteria which determine effective control over an actor for the purpose of establishing attribution under the general law of international responsibility.[216] The effective control test that is employed in the context of state responsibility under article 8 ARSIWA is more demanding, as the "financing, organizing, training, supplying and equipping" of non-state actors, the selection of targets or the planning of operations does not suffice to affirm effective control over that actor.[217]

IV. A treaty-based functional equivalent to attribution under general international law?

The relationship between the ECHR and the law of state responsibility is complex in particular in light of the Court's jurisprudence on article 1 ECHR and positive obligations. Based on the concept of positive obligations, the European Court can evaluate whether a state violated its obligations under the ECHR by the failure to prevent a third entity from engaging in a certain conduct, without having to address the question of whether the conduct was attributable on the basis of the ARSIWA. In this sense and as will be illustrated below, the concept of positive obligations can be seen as an additional aspect to consider after an attribution according to general international law could

---

Tadic decision, Antonio Cassese, argued that the "only point that perhaps Tadic did not sufficiently clarify relates to Loizidou: there the ECtHR inferred the finding that control over the authorities that had breached the claimant's rights was in fact exercised by Turkey from the fact that Turkey had overall control over the whole area of northern Cyprus [...] Thus, the Court preferred to refer to control over the area (from which it inferred control over the authorities operating there) rather than directly to control over the authorities that had violated Ms. Loizidou's rights." Cassese, 'The Nicaragua and Tadić Tests Revisited in Light of the ICJ Judgment on Genocide in Bosnia' 658 footnote 17.

216 Crawford and Keene, 'The Structure of State Responsibility under the European Convention on Human Rights' 195.
217 *Military and Paramilitary Activities in and against Nicaragua* [1986] ICJ Rep 14, 64 para 115; *Application of the Convention on the Prevention and Punishment of the Crime of Genocide* [2007] ICJ Rep 43, 206-215 paras 396-415.

not be established, or as a functional equivalent that makes an attribution analysis or an analysis of the preconditions of complicity under general international law no longer necessary.[218]

In *Kotov*, an attribution analysis under general international law and the concept of positive obligations were applied in a successive order: The European Court decided that Russia was not responsible for the actions of a private creditors' body under the rules of state responsibility, yet Russia violated its positive obligations, which would have required "at least to set up a minimum legislative framework including a proper forum allowing persons who find themselves in a position such as the applicant's to assert their rights effectively and have them enforced".[219]

In certain cases, positive obligations functionally replaced an attribution analysis under general international law. The case *Costello-Roberts* concerned the use of corporal punishment in so-called independent, or private, schools which had to be registered by the state. The European Court examined solely a violation of positive obligations without any reference to attribution under the law of international responsibility.[220] Similarly, the decision of the case *O'Keeffe* on sexual abuse of a child in a school owned by the Catholic church was based on a violation of positive obligations without addressing attribution under the law of state responsibility.[221]

When it comes to (extra)territorial administrations, the relationship between the European Court's jurisprudence and general international law is difficult to determine. In *Ilaşcu*, the European Court held that the acts of a non-state actor, the so-called Moldavian Republic of Transdniestria (MRT), were "under the effective authority, or at the very least under the decisive influence, of the Russian Federation" and therefore within Russia's jurisdiction for the purposes of article 1 ECHR, while it remained unclear whether the conduct was attributed to Russia or whether Russia's failure to prevent the

---

218 On special rules of attribution of conduct see Milanovic, 'Special Rules of Attribution of Conduct in International Law' 366, arguing that, with reference to the *El-Masri* case, "[a]cquiescence and connivance could, but need not, be conceptualized as a special rule of attribution of conduct in the sense of Article 55 ASR." See also below, p. 454.
219 *Kotov v Russia [GC]* App no 54522/00 (ECtHR, 3 April 2012) paras 107-108, 117.
220 *Costello-Roberts v The United Kingdom* App no 89/1991/341/414 (ECtHR, 23 February 1993) paras 25 ff.
221 *O'Keeffe v Ireland [GC]* App no 35810/09 (ECtHR, 28 January 2014) para 150; see Crawford and Keene, 'The Structure of State Responsibility under the European Convention on Human Rights' 181.

conduct was central.²²² In *Chiragov*, the majority held Armenia responsible on the basis of the latter's positive human rights obligations in relation to the Nagorno-Karabakh Autonomous Oblast (NKAO) over which it exercised jurisdiction.²²³ The European Court held that "Armenia, through its military presence and the provision of military equipment and expertise, has been significantly involved in the Nagorno-Karabakh conflict from an early date" and that "the Armenian armed forces and the 'NKR' are highly integrated".²²⁴ The European Court therefore concluded that "the 'NKR' and its administration survive by virtue of the military, political, financial and other support given to it by Armenia which, consequently, exercises effective control over Nagorno-Karabakh and the surrounding territories, including the district of Lachin."²²⁵ Hence, the Court concluded that Armenia was responsible for human rights violations caused by a non-state actors without an examination of the attribution standard according to the ARSIWA, even though it employed the notion of "effective control".²²⁶ In the parallel case *Sargsyan v.*

---

222 *Ilaşcu and others v Moldavia and Russia [GC]* App no 48787/99 (ECtHR, 8 July 2004) para 392. See Milanovic, 'Special Rules of Attribution of Conduct in International Law' 345-346. Moreover, Moldavia was responsible for failing to comply with its positive obligations under the Convention by letting MRT committing their acts, *Ilaşcu and others v Moldavia and Russia [GC]* paras 330-331; cf. Aust, *Complicity and the law of state responsibility* 411-412 ("[j]urisdiction finds itself decoupled from any understanding of effective control"); see the subsequent case *Catan and others v Moldova and Russia [GC]* paras 148, 150, where Russia was again held responsible, whereas the European Court held that Moldavia had complied with its positive obligations.
223 Cf. *Chiragov and others v Armenia [GC]* App no 132116/05 (ECtHR, 16 June 2015) para 192: "Given that the matters complained of come within the jurisdiction of Armenia [...] the question to be examined is whether Armenia is responsible for a violation of the applicants' rights to their possessions."
224 ibid para 180. "NKR" stands for "Nagorno-Karabakh Republic".
225 ibid para 186.
226 See also Crawford and Keene, 'The Structure of State Responsibility under the European Convention on Human Rights' 195 (noting that the Court undertook only a limited analysis of the control); Milanovic, 'Special Rules of Attribution of Conduct in International Law' 384; see also the different views expressed in individual opinions, *Chiragov and others v Armenia [GC]* Conc Op Motoc 80-85 (arguing that "this judgment represents one of the strongest returns to general international law", at 85); Partly Conc, Partly Diss Op Ziemele 86-91 (arguing that "[u]nlike the particularly scrupulous establishment of the facts normally carried out by the International Court of Justice (ICJ) in cases concerning disputes over territories, jurisdiction and attribution of responsibility, the Court appears to be

Azerbaijan, which concerned the NKAO as well, Azerbaijan was held to be responsible for human rights violations caused by the Nagorno-Karabakh Republic (NKR). Even though Azerbaijan had lost control over parts of its territory, it was under the positive obligation "to re-establish control over the territory in question, as an expression of its jurisdiction, and to measures to ensure respect for the applicant's individual rights."[227]

Recently, in *Russia v. Georgia (II)*, the Court held that Russia had exercised "*'effective control', within the meaning of the Court's case-law*, over South Ossetia, Abkhazia and the 'buffer zone' from 12 August to 10 October 2008 [...] Even after that period, the strong Russian presence and the South Ossetian and Abkhazian authorities' dependency on the Russian Federation, on whom their survival depends [...] indicate that there was continued 'effective control' over South Ossetia and Abkhazia."[228] In *Netherlands and Ukraine v. Russia*, the European Court examined the Russian "effective control over an area" in Ukraine and held that the acts and omissions of the local administrations were attributed to Russia which had Article 1 jurisdiction in relation to the areas concerned.[229]

Functional equivalents can also be observed in relation to complicity under customary international law as reflected in article 16 ARSIWA on aid or assistance in the commission of an internationally wrongful act. The *El-Masri* case is an example: In this case, the applicant was handed over by Macedonia to a CIA rendition team which then transferred him to Afghanistan where he suffered ill-treatment. The European Court argued that Macedonia exercised jurisdiction and "must be regarded as responsible under the Convention for acts performed by foreign officials on its territory *with the acquiescence or connivance* of its authorities."[230] The European Court did not attribute

---

watering down certain evidentiary standards in highly controversial situations", at 87); Diss Op Gyulumyan 106 ff. (referring to different attribution tests, at 108).

227 *Sargsyan v Azerbaijan [GC]* App no 40167/06 (ECtHR, 16 June 2015) para 131.
228 *Georgia v Russia (II) [GC]* para 174 (italics added). Russia was held "responsible" for violations of the ECHR committed by South Ossetian authorities, cf. paras 214, 222, 248, 252, 256, 276, 281, 301.
229 *Ukraine and the Netherlands v Russia [GC]* paras 560 ff., 564, 697 ("the finding that the Russian Federation had effective control over the relevant parts of Donbass controlled by the subordinate separatist administrations or separatist armed groups means that the acts and omissions of the separatists are attributable to the Russian Federation in the same way as the acts and omissions of any subordinate administration engage the responsibility of the territorial State").
230 *El-Masri v the former Yugoslav Republic of Macedonia [GC]* App no 39630/09 (ECtHR, 13 December 2012) para 206 (italics added).

The relationship between the ECHR and the law of international responsibility

the misconduct on the basis of the general rules of attribution, nor did it examine Macedonia's responsibility based on complicity under article 16 ARSIWA.[231] It held, however, that "[t]he respondent state must be considered *directly responsible for the violation of the applicant's rights* under this head, since its agents actively facilitated the treatment and then failed to take any measures that might have been necessary in the circumstances of the case to prevent it from occurring"[232], which can be read as an attribution analysis based on the ECHR, rather than the ARSIWA.[233]

In respect of this jurisprudence, James Crawford and Amelia Keene expressed their "concern [...] that the development of positive obligations may have prevented the Court from asking the logically prior question as to whether the respondent State is directly responsible for the commission of the wrongful acts, rather than for a failure to prevent them only."[234] This can constitute a challenge for assessing the development of concepts of general international law. Interpreters may find less explicit invocations and applications of the rules of state responsibility and thus may be unable to point to the jurisprudence of the European Court unless they will consider to what extent interpretations of concepts of the ECHR can shape and elucidate, to some degree, the content of general international law. Such an analysis may be difficult to conduct when the Court's decisions are unclear as to whether a state is responsible for violations of third entities because it did not prevent these violations or because these violations were attributable to the state.[235]

---

231 Crawford and Keene, 'The Structure of State Responsibility under the European Convention on Human Rights' 188; cf. on functionally similar rules to article 16 ARSIWA in human rights law Aust, *Complicity and the law of state responsibility* 393 ff.
232 *El-Masri v the former Yugoslav Republic of Macedonia [GC]* para 211 (italics added).
233 Cf. Milanovic, 'Special Rules of Attribution of Conduct in International Law' 359-360, 362; Crawford and Keene, 'The Structure of State Responsibility under the European Convention on Human Rights' 189.
234 ibid 183-184.
235 See also Milanovic, 'Special Rules of Attribution of Conduct in International Law' 343-344.

V. Attribution in the context of international organizations

1. The development of normative criteria for the delimitation of responsibilities

The jurisprudence of the European Court is of particular interest for the international responsibility of international organizations and for the remaining responsibility of states. So-called dual, or multiple or concurrent international responsibilities are only briefly addressed in the ARSIWA and the ARIO. Article 47 ARSIWA[236] recognizes the "plurality of responsible States" and provides that, "where several States are responsible for the same internationally wrongful act, the responsibility of each State may be invoked in relation to that act." Likewise, article 48 ARIO[237] addresses the "responsibility of an international organization and one or more States or international organization" and provides that the responsibility of each State or organization bay be invoked in relation to an internationally wrongful act for which multiple international organizations or an international organization and a state are responsible."

The Court's jurisprudence indicates that normative criteria are used for the delimitation of responsibilities between international organizations and states, which can further develop general international law.[238] For instance, in *Bosphorus*, the European Court had to decide whether states can be held accountable for violations of the ECHR when these violations resulted from complying with obligations *vis-à-vis* an international organization, such as the European Community. The European Court used the framework of proportionality analysis in order to reconcile the general interests in international cooperation with the respect for rights of the individual. Through its jurisdiction over State parties the European Court integrated international

---

236 ILC, *Draft Articles on Responsibility of States for Internationally Wrongful Acts (ARSIWA)*.
237 *Draft Articles on the Responsibility of International Organizations (ARIO)* UN Doc A/66/10.
238 Cf. Samantha Besson, 'Concurrent Responsibilities under the European Convention on Human Rights: the Concurrence of Human Rights Jurisdictions, Duties, and Responsibilities' in Anne van Aaken and Iulia Motoc (eds), *The European Convention on Human Rights and general international law* (Oxford University Press 2018) 159-160, arguing that one may "consider concurrent-responsibility law under the ECHR itself as developing the general international law of State responsibility on the very particular and controversial issue of concurrent responsibility".

organizations indirectly into the human rights system by examining the balance struck between the general interest in international cooperation and the interests of the applicant with respect to his property rights.[239] The European Court held that it "would be incompatible with the purpose and object of the Convention" if states could completely be absolved from their obligations under the ECHR.[240] In the view of the Court, states' actions in compliance with legal obligations in international organizations is justified "as long as the relevant organisation is considered to protect fundamental rights, as regards both the substantive guarantees offered and the mechanisms controlling their observance, in a manner which can be considered at least equivalent to that for which the Convention provides."[241] The European Court distinguished the requirement of equivalent protection from "identical" protection in order to accommodate the interests of the international organization concerned, and stressed that the assessment of equivalence continues to be susceptible to review.[242] The equivalence creates a rebuttable presumption that a state did not depart from the ECHR when it complies with legal obligations which it has assumed as a member of an international organization. This general presumption can be rebutted, however, if "in the circumstances of a particular case, it is considered that the protection of Convention rights was manifestly deficient."[243] In particular, the presumption can be rebutted by showing a structural deficit in effective human rights protection beyond the single case.[244]

It is noteworthy that the European Court developed a jurisprudence which did not make an attribution to states solely dependent on effective control. Instead, the European Court's jurisprudence assumes a residual, continuing responsibility of states which will become relevant when the international

---

239 *Bosphorus Hava Yolları Turizm ve Ticaret Anonim Şirketi v Ireland [GC]* App no 45036/98 (ECtHR, 30 June 2005) para 151.
240 ibid para 154; see already *Waite and Kennedy v Germany [GC]* para 67, see also para 68, where the European Court examined "whether the applicants had available to them reasonable alternative means to protect effectively their rights under the Convention"; Cornelia Janik, 'Die EMRK und internationale Organisationen: Ausdehnung und Restriktion der "equivalent protection"-Formel in der neuen Rechtsprechung des EGMR' (2010) 70(1) ZaöRV 127 ff.
241 *Bosphorus Hava Yolları Turizm ve Ticaret Anonim Şirketi v Ireland [GC]* para 156.
242 ibid para 156.
243 ibid para 156.
244 Cf. *Gasparini v Italy and Belgium* App no 10750/03 (ECtHR, 12 May 2009), rejecting a structural deficit of an internal review mechanism ("une lacune structurelle du mécanisme interne").

organization does not provide an equivalent protection of human rights. This way, the European Court avoids a legal vacuum and ensures an equivalent protection of the rights under the ECHR.

2. The United Nations as a special case

So far, the European Court has demonstrated a greater deferral towards the United Nations.

In *Behrami*, the European Court wrongly[245] decided that on the basis of the general rules of attribution conduct and omissions by French and Norwegian troops within a UN peacekeeping mission in Kosovo were attributable solely to the United Nations.[246] It is noteworthy that the European Court did not develop a functionally equivalent standard on the basis of an interpretation of the ECHR in order to establish attribution. In particular, the European Court considered but ultimately rejected to establish attribution based on the equivalent protection doctrine in such case because of the special importance of UN missions under Chapter VII of the UN Charter.[247]

The special importance of the United Nations was reaffirmed when the European Court found that the Netherlands had not violated the ECHR by granting immunity from trial to the United Nations according to article 105 UNC in the *Stichting Mothers of Srebrenica* case.[248] The European Court explicitly distinguished the case involving a dispute with the United Nations concerning a chapter VII mission from the cases belonging to the Bosphorus jurisprudence.[249] The European Court also rejected the argument "that in the absence of an alternative remedy the recognition of immunity

---

[245] Milanovic, 'Special Rules of Attribution of Conduct in International Law' 349. For further critique see Marko Milanović and Tatjana Papć, 'As Bad As It Gets: the European Court of Human Rights's Behrami and Saramati Decision and General International Law' (2009) 58(2) ICLQ 267 ff.; Heike Krieger, 'A Credibility Gap: the Behrami and Saramati Decision of the European Court of Human Rights' (2009) 13(1-2) Journal of international peacekeeping 159 ff.; Caitlin A Bell, 'Reassessing Multiple Attribution: the International Law Commission and the Behrami and Saramati Decision' (2010) 42(2) NYU JILP 501 ff.

[246] *Behrami and Behrami against France and Saramati against France, Germany and Norway [GC]* App no 71412/01 and 78166/01 (ECtHR, 2 May 2007) para 144.

[247] ibid paras 145-152.

[248] *Stichting Mothers of Srebrenica and Others against the Netherlands* App no 65542/12 (ECtHR, 11 June 2013) para 154.

[249] ibid paras 152, 154.

is *ipso facto* constitutive of a violation of the right of access to a court".[250] The ICJ developed a similar interpretation in relation to state immunity under customary international law: state practice would not support that "international law makes the entitlement of a State to immunity dependent upon the existence of effective alternative means of securing redress."[251] At the same time, however, alternative means to remedy violations were available in both cases. In the *Jurisdictional Immunities* case, the ICJ referred to the possibility "of further negotiations"[252]; in the *Stichting Mothers of Srebrenica* case, the European Court could not find that the applicants' claims against the Dutch state would necessarily fail.[253]

So far, the equivalent protection doctrine has been applied to the United Nations once by a chamber of the European Court in the *Al-Dulimi* case. The chamber held in a controversial 4:3 decision on the merits that in cases where the presumption of compatibility was rebutted and no implementation discretion was left, UNSC resolutions would not automatically prevail according to article 103 but only if the UN system provided a system of equivalent human rights protection, which was not said to be the case in the case under review.[254]

The Grand Chamber did not go this far, even though several judges endorsed the application of the equivalent protection doctrine in individual opinions,[255] while one judge spoke in favour of the application of article

---

250 ibid para 164.
251 *Jurisdictional Immunities of the State* [2012] ICJ Rep 99, 143 para 101; see also Lorna McGregor, 'State Immunity and Human Rights: Is There a Future after Germany v. Italy?' (2013) 11(1) JICJ 125 ff.
252 *Jurisdictional Immunities of the State* [2012] ICJ Rep 99, 143-144 paras 102-104; cf. ibid Sep Op Judge Bennouna para 25: "To my mind, if Germany were to close all doors to such settlement — and there is nothing to suggest that it will — then the question of lifting its immunity before foreign courts in respect of those same wrongful acts could legitimately be raised again." On this aspect see McGregor, 'State Immunity and Human Rights: Is There a Future after Germany v. Italy?' 131, 138.
253 *Stichting Mothers of Srebrenica and Others against the Netherlands* para 167.
254 *Al-Dulimi and Montana Management Inc v Switzerland* App no 5809/08 (ECtHR, 26 November 2013) 54-56 paras 114-122, 59 para 135. The decision was controversial because of the fact that the decision on admissibility and the decision on the merits were based on different majorities. In particular, Judge Sajó voted in favour of the inadmissibility of the case. On the merits, he voted, together with three other judges and against three other judges in favour of the applicant.
255 *Al-Dulimi and Montana Managment Inc v Switzerland [GC]*, Conc Op of Judge Pinto de Albuquerque, joined by Judges Hajiyev, Pejchal and Dedov 105 paras 54

103 UNC.[256] Ultimately, the Grand Chamber did not have to decide on this point since it arrived at the conclusion that the wording of the resolution in question did not rebut the presumption of compatibility, in other words, the obligation to freeze assets "without delay" and to "immediately transfer" to the Iraqi Development Fund would not prevent Swiss courts from examining the merits of a claim of the applicant.[257]

E. *Concluding Observations*

This chapter illustrated the dynamic interplay between the ECHR and the normative environment. It began by analyzing how the European Court approached the interpretation of the ECHR and considered other rules of international law when interpreting the ECHR.[258] Subsequently, it explored the European Court's interpretative decisions in establishing the relationship with other sources, with a particular focus on proportionality analysis and the prohibition of arbitrariness.[259] Furthermore, the chapter addressed the relationship between the ECHR and general international law on international responsibility, examining how and whether concepts of general international law were applied or functionally replaced with concepts based on treaty interpretation.[260]

In particular, it was demonstrated that the existence of written law does not make recourse to unwritten international law necessarily dispensable, nor is it necessary, however, to frame recourse to the normative environment within the terminology of customary international law and general principles of law. The examples of a European or an international consensus demonstrate that different doctrinal avenues were available to the European Court for such recourse.[261]

---

ff.; Conc Op of Judge Keller, 131 paras 22-23; see also Conc Op of Judge Kuris 133 para 3 (referring to the opinion of Judge Pinto de Albuquerque). The European Court left this question open, 71 para 149.
256 *Al-Dulimi and Montana Managment Inc v Switzerland [GC]* Diss Op of Judge Nussberger 146.
257 ibid 71 para 149, 72 para 155.
258 See above, p. 406.
259 See above, p. 424.
260 See above, p. 443.
261 See above, p. 408.

The focus on the legal techniques of incorporating other international law may offer one explanation for phenomena that are described with the terms "mainstreaming of human rights"[262] or "humanization"[263] of (general) international law.[264] When the implementation of an international obligation leads to a restriction of a right under the ECHR, the legal technique of proportionality analysis establishes a relation between a human right and, for instance, a rule of customary international law, such as immunity. Thus, the interpreter has to examine the object and purpose of human rights law and of the rule of customary international law. It stands to reason that this perspective, which considers the question as to whether a proportionate relationship between the individual right and customary international law exists, can influence the further development of customary international law. When international law outside the ECHR protects or benefits individuals, the state may have a positive obligation under the ECHR to comply with this rule.[265] The prohibition of arbitrariness can be understood as common denominator of different norms, it can serve as a basis for reconciliation or as a standard for judicial review where no more specific obligations on states existed, where the interpretation of domestic law was concerned or where states implemented UNSC resolutions.

---

262 Arnold N Pronto, '"Human-Rightism" and the Development of General International Law' (2007) 20 Leiden Journal of International Law 753 ff.; on the term "human rightism" see Alain Pellet, '"Human rightism" and international law' [2000] Gilberto Amado Memorial Lecture of 18 July 2000 ⟨https://digitallibrary.un.org/record/430167⟩ accessed 1 August 2022.

263 This notion was coined by Theodor Meron, 'The Humanization of Humanitarian Law' (2000) 94(2) American Journal of International Law 239.

264 Simma and Pulkowski, 'Of Planets and the Universe: Self-contained Regimes in International Law' 528: "There is no return to an international law that puts on an indifferent face to human rights. Human rights can no longer be fenced in an exclusive domaine reservé; once their genie was out of the bottle, human rights necessarily transcended to the realm of general international law.", and citing William Michael Reisman, 'Sovereignty and Human Rights in Contemporary International Law' (1990) 84 AJIL 872: human rights are "more than a piecemeal addition to the traditional corpus of international law" and bring about "changes in virtually every component"; see also Anne Peters, *Beyond Human Rights. The Legal Status of the Individual in International Law* (Cambridge University Press 2016) 7, examining individual rights outside human rights law in other fields of international law.

265 See above, p. 423, p. 436.

Lastly, the chapter illustrates challenges for studying general international law.[266] A specific regime such as the ECHR may develop as a matter of treaty law concepts that functionally replace concepts of general international law. This can be challenging for different reasons. Firstly, the European Court is less likely to pronounce itself on concepts of general international law explicitly, which means that it does not refer to the terminology of general international law. Secondly, the European Court may employ similar notions, such as effective control or effective overall control, which assume a different function and meaning than in general international law. Thirdly, the challenge for future studies will consist in determining whether general international law has further developed in light of principles and evaluations expressed in the case-law of the European Court. To give an example: the European Court can hold member states responsible for human rights violations of private entities when these violations occurred within the state's jurisdiction and the state did not meet its positive obligation to prevent these violations. Technically, this legal construction does not attribute the conduct of non-state actors to the state: the state does not assume responsibility because of the conduct of the non-state actors but because of the failure to prevent it. What is attributed to the state is an omission, instead of an act.[267] From a normative standpoint, the end result is that the state will be responsible for violations of human rights by non-state actors over whom the state did not necessarily have effective control in the sense of the law of state responsibility. It is perfectly possible that both perspectives remain separate and independent from each other, that the European Court's approach remains a reflection of a *lex specialis*, a special regulation that differs from the general rules of attribution. It is also perfectly possible, however, that this special regulation may influence the development of general international law. All that can be done here is point to these possibilities; which one will realize itself must be the subject of a continuous examination.

---

266 See above, p. 443.
267 See also Milanovic, 'Special Rules of Attribution of Conduct in International Law' 315.

Chapter 9: International Criminal Law

A. Introduction

International criminal law displays a dynamic development from unwritten law to written law. This chapter will firstly depict the early discussions of the interrelationship of sources in the context of international criminal law which preceded the establishment of the ICTY (B.). The chapter will secondly explore the jurisprudence of the ICTY and analyze the role given to customary international law, its interpretation and application and its interrelationship with treaties and general principles of law (C.). It will illustrate the use of similar techniques which could be observed in the fifth chapter in relation to the International Court of Justice. Thirdly, the chapter will turn to the Rome Statute (D.). In this context, it will focus on the Rome Statute's main features which concern the interrelationship of sources, on the debate on modes of criminal liability as an example of a potential conflict between treaty law and customary international law and on the role of customary international law on immunities.

B. The recognition of individual's responsibility for violations of international law

This section will give an overview of the recognition of individual responsibility for violations of international law and the relative significance of customary international law and treaties before the further implications on the interrelationship of sources in the context of international criminal law will be discussed (see below, C.) This section will survey the development from the interwar period to the Military Tribunals in Nuremberg and Tokyo (I.), the reception in the UNGA and in the treatymaking practice of states (II.) and the road towards an international criminal court (III.)

I. From the interwar period to the Military Tribunals in Nuremberg and Tokyo

International criminal law is concerned with the responsibility of individuals for violations of international law, in particular international humanitarian law. The landmark decision was rendered by the International Military Tribunal in Nuremberg after the second world war:

> "Crimes against international law are committed by men, not by abstract entities, and only by punishing individuals who commit such crimes can the provisions of international law be enforced."[1]

Already after the first world war, the Treaty of Versailles provided in article 227(2) that a special tribunal should be constituted to try the former German *Kaiser* who was publicly arraigned according to article 227(1) "for a supreme offence against international morality and the sanctity of treaties". By virtue of article 228(1), the "German Government recognises the right of the Allied and Associated Powers to bring before military tribunals persons accused of having committed acts in violation of the laws and customs of war."[2] Article 228(2) obliged the German government to "hand over to the Allied and Associated Powers, or to such one of them as shall so request, all persons accused of having committed an act in violation of the laws and customs of war, who are specified either by name or by the rank, office or employment which they held under the German authorities." However, the tribunal was never established, the trial against the former German *Kaiser* who had fled to the Netherlands was not conducted, the German government did not hand over the 896 persons who should have been prosecuted and the Allied decided to abstain from requesting the extradition; instead, national proceedings took place before the *Reichsgericht* in Leipzig.[3]

---

1 *USA et al v Göring et al* IMT Judgment (1 October 1946) Trial of the Major War Criminals before the International Military Tribunal Vol. 1 (1947) 223.
2 Treaty of Peace with Germany (Treaty of Versailles) (signed 28 June 1919, entered into force 10 January 1920) 225 Parry 188.
3 Kai Ambos, *Treatise on International Criminal Law: Vol. I: Foundations and General Part* (Oxford University Press 2013) 3; Gerhard Werle and Florian Jeßberger, *Principles of International Criminal Law* (4th edn, Oxford University Press 2020) 4-5; on the Leipzig trials see Claus Kreß, 'Versailles-Nuremberg-The Hague : Germany and International Criminal Law' (2006) 40 The international lawyer 16-20; on the legacy of the Versailles treaty for international criminal law see Claus Kreß, 'The Peacemaking Process After the Great War and the Origins of International Criminal Law Stricto Sensu' (2021) 62 German Yearbook of International Law 163 ff.

The Advisory Committee of Jurists recommended to consider the establishment of a High Court of Justice competent to try "crimes constituting a breach of international public order or against the universal law of nations."[4] The Third Committee of the Assembly, however, considered it "useless to establish side by side with the Court of International Justice another Criminal Court" and therefore suggested to set up "a criminal department in the Court".[5] Following up on the Advisory Committee's recommendation, international initiatives endorsed the establishment of such a chamber or section at the PCIJ, for instance the Inter-Parliamentary Union in 1925, the International Law Association in 1926 and the International Congress of Penal Law in the time period between 1926-1928.[6] While the draft statute of 1928 envisioned as applicable substantive law written instruments only,[7] other proposals such as the ILA Draft in its articles 21 and 23[8], and the 1943 Draft Convention for the Creation of an International Criminal Court in its article 27[9] resembled article 38 of the PCIJ Statute and included a reference to customary international law and general principles of law.

Other treaties did not explicitly address individual criminal responsibility as matter of international law. By way of treaties, states imposed obligations on each other to criminalize particular behaviour by way of domestic law. However, neither the Hague Regulations of 1907[10], the Geneva Convention of 1929[11] nor the Briand-Kellog pact[12] stipulated that individuals should be responsible for breaches of these treaties.

During the second world war, however, the UN War Crimes Commission was established in order to collect evidence of the commission of war crimes and crimes against humanity and the London Charter of 1945 led to the

---

4 *Historical Survey of the Question of International Criminal Jurisdiction* Memorandum submitted by the Secretary-General (1949) UN Doc A/CN.4/7Rev.1 at 10.
5 ibid 12. The Assembly failed to adopt the recommendation.
6 For an overview see ibid 12-16.
7 ibid 82-83 (articles 35, 36 of the 1928 Statute, revised in 1946).
8 ibid 65-66.
9 ibid 103.
10 Convention (IV) respecting the Laws and Customs of War on Land and its annex: Regulations concerning the Laws and Customs of War on Land (signed 18 October 1907, entered into force 26 January 1910) 2 AJIL Supp 90.
11 Geneva Convention relative to the protection of civilian persons in time of war (signed 27 July 1929, entered into force 19 June 1931) 118 LNTS 343.
12 Treaty between the United States and other Powers Providing for the Renunciation of War as an Instrument of National Policy (Briand-Kellogg Pact) (signed 27 October 1928, entered into force 25 July 1929) 94 LNTS 57.

Chapter 9: International Criminal Law

establishment of the IMT.[13] Article 6 of the Charter of the International Military Tribunal set forth the "crimes coming within the jurisdiction of the Tribunal for which there shall be individual responsibility", namely crimes against peace, war crimes and crimes against humanity. According to the IMT, the Charter "is not an arbitrary exercise of power on the part of the victorious Nations [...] it is the expression of international law existing at the time of its creation; and to that extent is itself a contribution to international law."[14] The IMT's reasoning was not confined to treaties but extended to other sources. Addressing the argument that neither the Briand Kellog pact nor the 1907 Hague Convention[15] expressly prescribed violations of their respective provisions as crimes, the IMT referred to past practices of military tribunals.[16] In particular, it held:

> "The law of war is to be found not only in treaties, but in the customs and practices of states which gradually obtained universal recognition, and from the general principles of justice applied by jurists and practiced by military courts. This law is not static, but by continual adaptation follows the needs of a changing world. Indeed, in many cases treaties do no more than express and define for more accurate reference the principles of law already existing."[17]

This focus on the normative environment was important for the answer to the question of whether individuals could be responsible for violations of international law. In view of the IMT, the proposition "that international law is concerned with the actions of sovereign States, and provides no punishment for individuals"[18] was said to be contradicted by the list of cases

---

13 Agreement for the Prosecution and Punishment of Major War Criminals of the European Axis, and establishing the Charter of the International Military Tribunal (signed 8 August 1945, entered into force 8 August 1945) 82 UNTS 279; Ambos, *Treatise on International Criminal Law: Vol. I: Foundations and General Part* 4; Werle and Jeßberger, *Principles of International Criminal Law* 6-7.
14 *USA et al v Göring et al* 218.
15 Convention (IV) respecting the Laws and Customs of War on Land and its annex: Regulations concerning the Laws and Customs of War on Land (signed 18 October 1907, entered into force 26 January 1910) 2 AJIL Supp 90.
16 *USA et al v Göring et al* IMT Judgment (1 October 1946) 220-221.
17 ibid 221. Cf. for the dynamic nature also *The United States of America vs Carl Krauch et al (IG Farben), United States Military Tribunal*, Trials of War Criminals Before the Nuremberg Military Tribunals under Control Council Law No 10, Vol VIII (1952), 1038: "As custom is a source of international law, customs and practices may change and find such general acceptance in the community of civilised nations as to alter the substantive content of certain of its principles."
18 *USA et al v Göring et al* IMT Judgment (1 October 1946) 222.

"where individual offenders were charged with offenses against the law of nations, and particularly the laws of war. Many other authorities could be cited, but enough has been said to show that individuals can be punished for violations of international law."[19]

The IMT stressed that the war crimes of the Charter

"were already recognized as War Crimes under international law. They were covered by Articles 46, 50, 52 und 56 of the Hague Convention of 1907, and Articles 2, 3, 4, 46, and 51 of the Geneva Convention of 1929. That *violation of these provisions* constituted crimes for which the guilty individuals were punishable is too well settled to admit of argument."[20]

The quote above could be read as an indication that already the violations of *treaty* provisions entailed the international criminal responsibility of the individual. In the specific case before the tribunal, however, the applicability of the 1907 Hague Convention was in doubt because of the "general participation clause" in Article 2 according to which the Hague Convention does only apply between contracting powers and only if all belligerents are parties to the convention. Ultimately, this clause did not prove decisive since the IMT was of the view that the Hague Convention's rules, which were said to represent "an advance over existing international law at the time of their adoption", were "recognized by all civilized nations, and were regarded as being declaratory of the laws and customs of war which are referred to in Article 6 (b) of the Charter."[21]

---

19 ibid 223.
20 ibid, 253 (italics added).
21 ibid 253-254. With respect to the Geneva Convention of 1929 cf. at 232: The IMT quoted the German Admiral Canaris who had argued that prisoners of war were protected not only under the Geneva Convention of 1929, which was not applicable in the relationship with the U.S.S.R., but also under "the principles of general international law", which the IMT characterized as the correct statement of the legal position; cf. *The German High Command Trial Case No 72, Trial of Wilhelm Leeb and Thirteen Others, United States Military Tribunal*, Trials of War Criminals Before the Nuremberg Military Tribunals under Control Council Law No 10, Vol XI (1950) 535: The essence of the 1907 Hague Convention and the 1929 Geneva Convention was considered to "express accepted usages and customs of war [...] Most of the prohibitions of both the Hague and Geneva Conventions, considered in substance, are clearly an expression of the accepted views of civilized nations and binding upon Germany and the defendants on trial before us in the conduct of the war against Russia."; cf. on the reception *Eritrea-Ethiopia Claims Commission* Eritrea's Claim 17, Partial Award: Prisoners of War (1 July 2003) XXVI RIAA 39 para 39.

Chapter 9: International Criminal Law

The jurisprudence of the military tribunals which operated on the basis of Allied Control Council Law No 10 emphasized that the crimes referred to in Control Law No 10 constituted preexisting law.[22]

Moreover, the Tokyo tribunal found itself in accord with the reasoning delivered by the IMT on individual responsibility[23], it considered the 1907 Hague convention "as good evidence of the customary law of nations, to be considered by the Tribunal along with all other available evidence in determining the customary law to be applied in any given situation"[24] and emphasized, with respect to the Geneva Prisoner of War Convention,

> "that under the customary rules of war, acknowledged by all civilized nations, all prisoners of war and civilian internees must be given humane treatment. [...] A

---

22 *US v List et al, Hostage Case, United States Military Tribunal*, Trials of War Criminals Before the Nuremberg Military Tribunals under Control Council Law No 10, Vol XI (1950) 1239; *United States v Friedrich Flick and others, United States Military Tribunal*, Trials of War Criminals Before the Nuremberg Military Tribunals under Control Council Law No 10, Vol VI (1952) 1189; *Krupp Case (United States of America v Alfried Felix Krupp von Bohlen und Halbach et al), United States Military Tribunal*, Trials of War Criminals Before the Nuremberg Military Tribunals under Control Council Law No 10, Vol IX (1950) 1331; *Justice Case (United States of America v Josef Altstoetter, et al), United States Military Tribunal*, Trials of War Criminals Before the Nuremberg Military Tribunals under Control Council Law No 10, Vol III (1951) 966: "All of the war crimes and many, if not all, of the crimes against humanity as charged in the indictment in the case at bar were, as we shall show, violative of preexisting principles of international law. To the extent to which this true, C. C. Law 10 may be deemed to be a codification rather than original substantive legislation. Insofar as C. C. Law 10 may be thought to go beyond established principles of international law, its authority, of course, rests upon the exercise of the "sovereign legislative power" of the countries to which the German Reich unconditionally surrendered."; *Einsatzgruppen Case (United States of America v Otto Ohlendorf et al), United States Military Tribunal*, Trials of War Criminals Before the Nuremberg Military Tribunals under Control Council Law No 10, Vol IV (1952), 457-458; see also ibid, 459 (Art. 46 of the 1907 Hague Regulation "had become international law binding on all nations"); cf. also Kevin Jon Heller, *The Nuremberg Military Tribunals and the Origins of International Criminal Law* (Oxford University Press 2011) 124: "Most of the tribunals, by contrast, claimed that they applied international law not because the London Charter had been approved by the international community, but because Law No. 10 reflected pre-existing rules of international law, both customary and conventional."

23 *Araki and others ('Tokyo Judgment')* IMTFE, Judgment (12 November 1948) in Neil Boister and Robert Cryer (eds), Documents on the Tokyo International Military Tribunal (Oxford University Press 2008) 81-81 paras 48,438-48,439.

24 ibid 102 para 48,491.

person guilty of such inhumanities cannot escape punishment on the plea that he or his government is not bound by any particular convention. The general principles of the law exist independently of the said conventions. The conventions merely reaffirm the pre-existing law and prescribe detailed provisions for its application."[25]

In conclusion, it is noteworthy that tribunals considered references to international law beyond the written instruments necessary in order to address retroactivity concerns and to overcome limitations of treaty law with respect to the treaty's applicability.

II. The reception in the UNGA and treatymaking practice of states

The UN General Assembly "affirm[ed] the principles of international law recognized by the Charter of the Nürnberg Tribunal and the judgment of the Tribunal".[26] It has been argued that the use of the term "affirm" instead of, as it had been proposed, "confirm" or "reaffirm", indicated "a lack of consensus among United Nations Members as to the binding character of the Nuremberg principles as rules of general international law".[27] There might not have been an agreement on all details, yet it is also noteworthy that the General Assembly established the Committee on the Progressive Development of International Law and its Codification (CPDIL) precisely to codify the Nuremberg principles, a task which then was undertaken upon recommendation of the Committee by the International Law Commission. As Ambos has pointed out, the content of the Nuremberg principles can be summarized in one sentence: "The individual criminal responsibility (Principle I) through participation (VII) with regard to international crimes (VI) is neither opposed by interstate-arranged impunity (II) nor-in principle-by acting in an official capacity (III) nor by grounds of command (IV)."[28]

---

25 ibid 578 para 49,720.
26 UNGA Res 95 (I) (11 December 1946) UN Doc A/RES/95(I).
27 Bin Cheng, *Studies in International Space Law* (Oxford University Press 1997) 141; Kevin Jon Heller, 'What is an international crime? (A Revisionist History)' (2017) 58 Harvard International Law Journal 378-379; but see for the contrary view Kreß, 'Article 98' para 43.
28 Kai Ambos, *Treatise on International Criminal Law: Vol. I: Foundations and General Part* (2nd edn, Oxford University Press 2021) 12.

Chapter 9: International Criminal Law

The formulation of those principles by the ILC was neither adopted, affirmed, nor rejected by the General Assembly.[29]

As far as treatymaking was concerned, states did not conclude a comprehensive criminal code defining the individuals' responsibility under international law immediately after the second world war. The Genocide Convention[30], however, confirms "that genocide, whether committed in time of peace or in time of war, is a crime under international law which they undertake to prevent and to punish" (article I Genocide Convention) and that "[p]ersons charged with genocide or any of the other acts enumerated in article III shall be tried by a competent tribunal of the State in the territory of which the act was committed, or by such international penal tribunal as may have jurisdiction with respect to those Contracting Parties which shall have accepted its jurisdiction" (Art. VI Genocide Convention). The Geneva Conventions of 1949[31] do not refer to the concept of crime and use the for-

---

29 For the discussion in the Sixth Committee where the work of the ILC received a mixed reaction, see *Report of the Sixth Committee* (8 December 1950) UN Doc A/1639, 10: "Numerous representatives also commented on the text of the seven principles formulated by the Commission. A great variety of views were expressed, and opinion was generally too divided to permit conclusions as to the sense of the Committee on the controversial issues."; cf. Baxter, 'Treaties and Customs' 92-6 (speaking of an "unsuccessful attempt to codify the Nuremberg Principles", at 92); Richard R Baxter, 'The Effects of Ill-Conceived Codification and Development of International Law' in Faculté de Droit de l'Université de Genève (ed), *En Hommage à Paul Guggenheim* (Faculté de Droit de l'Université de Genève 1968) 146-166.
30 Convention on the Prevention and Punishment of the Crime of Genocide (signed 9 December 1948, entered into force 12 January 1951) 78 UNTS 277. On the crime of genocide see already UNGA Res 96 (I) (11 December 1946) UN Doc A/RES/96 (I): "Affirms that genocide is a crime under international law which the civilized world condemns, and for the commission of which principals and accomplices whether private individuals, public officials or statesmen, and whether the crime is committed on religious, racial, political or any other grounds - are punishable".
31 Geneva Convention for the amelioration of the condition of the wounded and sick in armed forces in the field (signed 12 August 1949, entered into force 21 October 1950) 75 UNTS 31; Geneva Convention for the amelioration of the condition of the wounded, sick and shipwrecked members of the armed forces at sea (signed 12 August 1949, entered into force 21 October 1950) 75 UNTS 85; Geneva Convention, relative to the treatment of prisoners of war (signed 12 August 1949, entered into force 21 October 1950) 75 UNTS 135; Geneva Convention relative to the protection of civilian persons in time of war (signed 12 August 1949, entered into force 21 October 1950) 75 UNTS 287.

mulation "grave breaches" instead.[32] States are under an obligation "to enact any legislation necessary to provide effective penal sanctions for persons committing, or ordering to be committed, any of the grave breaches of the present Convention" and "to search for persons alleged to have committed, or to have ordered to be committed, such grave breaches, and shall bring such persons, regardless of their nationality, before its own courts" (Art. 49(1), (2) GC I, Art. 50(1), (2) GCII, Art. 129(1), (2) GC III, Art. 146(1), (2) GC IV). The Geneva Conventions emphasize that "the accused persons shall benefit by the safeguards of proper trial and defence" (Art. 49(4) GC I, Art. 50(4) GCII, Art. 129(4) GCIII, Art. 146(4) GC IV).[33] As these obligations are directed towards states, it is controversial whether the grave breaches regime of the Geneva Conventions entails the direct responsibility of the individual under international law.[34] It is noteworthy, however, that article

---

[32] During the negotiations of the Geneva Conventions, the term "grave breaches" was given preference over the term "war crime" which had been suggested by the USSR since "the word 'crimes' had a different meaning in the national laws of different countries and because an act only becomes a crime when this act is made punishable by a penal law." (ICRC, *Commentary on the First Geneva Convention (2016)* (Cambridge University Press 2017) Art. 50 para 2917, referring to *Final Record of the Diplomatic Conference of Geneva of 1949* (vol II-B, Federal Political Department) 116-7); on the relationship between the grave breaches regime and war crimes see Marko Divac Öberg, 'The absorption of grave breaches into war crimes law' (2009) 91 International Review of the Red Cross 163 ff.

[33] During the negotiations of the GCs, it was not possible to agree on defences which is why it was decided that defences 'should be left to the judges who would apply the national laws.', see Fourth Report drawn up by the Special Committee of the Joint Committee of 12 July 1949, in *Final Record of the Diplomatic Conference of Geneva of 1949* 114, at 115: "The word 'crime' instead of 'breach' did not seem to be an improvement, nor could general agreement be reached at this stage regarding the notions of complicity, attempted violation, duress or legitimate defence or plea 'by orders of a superior'. These should be left to the judges who would apply the national laws."

[34] Cf. Bruno Simma and Andreas L Paulus, 'The Responsibility of Individuals for Human Rights Abuses in Internal Conflicts: A Positivist View' (1999) 93 AJIL 310-311 ("These provisions merely refer to the obligation of the parties either to try or to extradite alleged criminals [...] They do not qualify grave breaches as crimes of a truly international character."); cf. ICRC, *Commentary on the First Geneva Convention (2016)* Art. 49 para 2853: "The text of Article 49 establishes the individual criminal responsibility of offenders under international law, but limits it to the person committing the crime and the person who ordered the crime, without mentioning other forms of individual responsibility or available defences."

Chapter 9: International Criminal Law

85(5) of the First Additional Protocol to the Geneva Conventions[35] stipulated that "[w]ithout prejudice to the application of the Conventions and of this Protocol, grave breaches of these instruments shall be regarded as war crimes".[36] The grave breaches regime applies only to international armed conflicts. In contrast, the question of individual responsibility for violations of international humanitarian law in non-international armed conflicts is addressed neither in common article 3 of the Geneva Conventions nor in the Additional Protocol II[37].

Whereas the aforementioned treaties do not address individual criminal responsibility as matter of international law explicitly, article 11(2) of the Universal Declaration of Human Rights[38], article 7(2) ECHR[39] and article 15(2) ICCPR[40] recognize that behaviour can be criminalized under international law.[41]

---

35 Protocol additional to the Geneva Conventions of 12 August 1949, and relating to the protection of victims of international armed conflicts (Protocol I) (signed 8 June 1977, entered into force 7 December 1978) 1125 UNTS 3.

36 Simma and Paulus, 'The Responsibility of Individuals for Human Rights Abuses in Internal Conflicts: A Positivist View' 311; Ambos, *Treatise on International Criminal Law: Vol. I: Foundations and General Part* 14; ICRC, *Commentary on the First Geneva Convention (2016)* Article 49 para 2820; Öberg, 'The absorption of grave breaches into war crimes law' 164 ff.

37 Protocol Additional to the Geneva Conventions of 12 August 1949 and relating to the protection of victims of non-international armed conflicts (Protocol II) (signed 8 June 1977, entered into force 7 December 1978) 1125 UNTS 609.

38 UNGA Res 217 A (III) (10 December 1948) UN Doc A/RES/3/217 A. Article 11(2) reads: "No one shall be held guilty of any penal offence on account of any act or omission which did not constitute a penal offence, under national or international law, at the time when it was committed. Nor shall a heavier penalty be imposed than the one that was applicable at the time the penal offence was committed."

39 Convention for the Protection of Human Rights and Fundamental Freedoms (signed 4 November 1950, entered into force 3 September 1953) 213 UNTS 221. Article 7(2) reads: "This article shall not prejudice the trial and punishment of any person for any act or omission which, at the time when it was committed, was criminal according to the general principles of law recognised by civilised nations."

40 International Covenant on Civil and Political Rights (signed 16 December 1966, entered into force 23 March 1976) 999 UNTS 171. Article 15(2) reads: "Nothing in this article shall prejudice the trial and punishment of any person for any act or omission which, at the time when it was committed, was criminal according to the general principles of law recognized by the community of nations."

41 According to Astrid Reisinger Coracini, '"What is an International Crime?": A Response to Kevin Jon Heller' [2018] Harvard International Law Online Symposium ⟨https://harvardilj.org/wp-content/uploads/sites/15/Coracini-Response.pdf⟩

III. The road towards an international criminal court

In the context of the progressive development and codification of international law, the ILC split up international criminal law into different codification projects and appointed Jean Spiropoulos as special rapporteur for the "Formulation of the Nuremberg Principles and Preparation of a Draft Code of Offenses against the Peace and Security of Mankind", and Ricardo Alfaro as well as Emil Sandstrum as special rapporteur for the "Draft Statute for the Establishment of an International Criminal Court" the work on which was submitted to the General Assembly in 1954.[42]

The General Assembly decided to postpone consideration of the project of an international criminal court until the finalization of the Draft Code,[43] and to postpone consideration of the Draft Code until the Special Committee on the question of defining aggression has submitted its report.[44] The General Assembly agreed on a definition of aggression in 1974[45] and the International Law Commission suggested *proprio motu* to the General Assembly that the Draft Code of Offences against the Peace and Security of Mankind "could be reviewed in the future if the General Assembly so wishes".[46] The General

---

accessed 1 February 2023, at 1, this provides "convincing evidence of direct criminalization" under international law; for the contrary view see Kevin Jon Heller, 'What is an International Crime? (A Revisionist History) A Reply to my Critics' [2018] Harvard International Law Journal Online Symposium ⟨https://harvardilj.org/wp-content/uploads/sites/15/Heller-Reply.pdf⟩ accessed 1 February 2023, at 3-5, arguing, *inter alia* that the reference in this articles could be directed at suppression conventions and do therefore not contradict his argument that international law does not provide for direct responsibility of individuals but for an obligation on states to domestically criminalize violations of international law.

42 See Mahmoud Cherif Bassiouni, 'The History of the Draft Code of Crimes Against the Peace and Security of Mankind' (1993) 27(1-2) Israel Law Review 248-251. According to article 2 of the Statute for the Establishment of an International Criminal Court, "the Court shall apply international law, including international criminal law, and where appropriate, national law" , Report of the 1953 Committee on International Criminal Jurisdiction (August 1953) 23.

43 UNGA Res 898 (IX) (14 December 1954) UN Doc A/RES/898(IX); UNGA Res 1187 (XII) (11 December 1957) UN Doc A/RES/1187(XII).

44 UNGA Res 897 (IX) (4 December 1954) UN Doc A/RES/897(IX); UNGA Res 1186 (XII) (11 December 1957) UN Doc A/RES/1186(XII); Bassiouni, 'The History of the Draft Code of Crimes Against the Peace and Security of Mankind' 257.

45 UNGA Res 3314 (XXIX) (14 December 1974) UN Doc A/RES/3314 (XXIX).

46 *ILC Ybk (1977 vol 2 part 2)* 130 para 111.

Assembly allocated the topic of the draft to the Sixth Committee[47] and requested the Secretary-General to invite states and relevant intergovernmental organizations to submit comments and observations,[48] before it ultimately invited the International Law Commission to resume its work.[49]

In 1991, the ILC adopted on first reading the Draft Code of Crimes against the Peace and Security of Mankind which found a mixed reaction due to the number of crimes which included, for instance, the crimes of aggression, intervention, colonial domination and other forms of alien domination, apartheid and terrorism.[50] The 1992 report of an ILC working group on the question of an international criminal jurisdiction made the case for separating the project of a code and the project of the statute of an international criminal court from each other, in order to make each acceptable for states who had reservation about the respective other project.[51] According to the Working Group, recourse to general international law would be no longer necessary once the crimes have been codified. Thus, the Working Group proposed to confine the jurisdiction of the envisioned court to crimes set forth in treaties.[52]

The Special Rapporteur's draft statute for an international criminal court in 1993, therefore, put a reference to general principles of law and custom in a provision on applicable law in square brackets, not without noting, however, that "no previous draft had gone so far in restricting the law that could be applied by an international criminal court."[53] According to some members, it was too restrictive, but it was also suggested "to directly define what would be regarded as international crimes for the purposes of the statute, rather than

---

47 Report of the 6th Committee, Draft Code of Offences Against the Peace and Security of Mankind (UN Doc A/32/470, December 1977).
48 UNGA Res 35/49 (4 December 1980) UN Doc A/RES/3549.
49 UNGA Res 36/106 (10 December 1981) UN Doc A/RES/36/106.
50 As argued by James Crawford, 'The Work of the International Law Commission' in Antonio Cassese, Paola Gaeta, and John RWD Jones (eds), *The Rome Statute of the International Criminal Court* (Oxford University Press 2002) 24, "the renewed work proved controversial and reaction to it was polarized. Much of the Code's support came from the Group of 77; much of the opposition to it came from the West. But neither group was enthusiastic at this stage about the Code's application by an international criminal court."
51 *ILC Ybk (1992 vol 2 part 2)* 67-68.
52 ibid 66, 71.
53 *Eleventh report on the draft Code of Crimes against the Peace and Security of Mankind, by Mr Doudou Thiam, Special Rapporteur* 25 March 1993 UN Doc A/CN.4/449 in *ILC Ybk (1993 vol 2 part 1)* 115.

deal with such a matter through a provision on applicable law."[54] The working group on a draft statute proposed that the jurisdiction of the envisioned court encompassed, by default, a list of crimes defined by treaties (draft article 22) as well as, optionally, crimes under general international law and crimes under national law.[55] According to a provision on applicable law, the court should apply the draft statute, applicable treaties and the rules and principles of international law as well as, as subsidiary source, any applicable rule of national law.[56]

Yet, the proposal to generally refer to crimes under general international law received criticism in the 6th Committee.[57] The 1994 ILC draft included a provision on crimes within the jurisdiction of the proposed court, which included the crime of genocide, of aggression, of serious violations of the laws and customs applicable in armed conflicts, crimes against humanity and crimes established under or pursuant to treaty provisions listed in the annex.[58] Hence, the draft statute did not "confer jurisdiction by reference to the general category of crimes under international law".[59] According to the provision on applicable law, the envisioned court should apply the draft statute, applicable treaties and the principles and rules of general international law and, to the extent applicable, any rule of national law.[60] The expression "applicable treaties" referred to crimes established under or pursuant to the treaty provisions listed in the Annex according to article 20(e). The ILC stressed that "the expression 'principles and rules' of general international law includes general principles of law [...]"[61]. According to James Crawford, draft article 33 was modelled after article 38 ICJ Statute because "the way in which treaties and rules and principles of international law are applied [under

---

54 *ILC Ybk (1993 vol 2 part 2)* 17 para. 63.
55 ibid 106-109.
56 ibid 111.
57 *ILC Ybk (1994 vol 2 part 2)* 36 para 5; see also Crawford, 'The Work of the International Law Commission' 32.
58 *ILC Ybk (1994 vol 2 part 2)* 38 (draft article 20).
59 ibid 38 para. 3 (draft article 20).
60 ibid 51 (draft article 33).
61 ibid 51 para 2 (draft article 33). The quote continues: "[...] so that the court can legitimately have recourse to the whole corpus of criminal law, whether found in national forums or in international practice, whenever it needs guidance on matters not clearly regulated by treaty."

Article 38] is now fairly understood, and there was little point in seeking to elaborate them in one particular context."[62]

The ILC's procedural approach was different from the Rome Statute which both establishes a court and defines the crimes over which the ICC has jurisdiction. A similarity, however, consists in the fact that both the ILC draft and the Rome Statute confined the jurisdiction to crimes as defined by treaties, not extending to crimes under customary international law. As far as the applicable law beyond crimes is concerned, both refer to unwritten international law.[63] In comparison to article 21 Rome Statute, the ILC draft was close to article 38 ICJ Statute.

C. The interrelationship of sources and the International Criminal Tribunals, in particular the ICTY

This section will focus on the jurisprudence of the international criminal tribunals, with a particular emphasis on the jurisprudence of the ICTY. It will examine the ICTY's source preference for customary international law (I.). Subsequently, it will focus on interpretative decisions and normative considerations in the identification of customary international law and general principles of law (II.). In this context, the section will elaborate on the difficulty to appreciate and evaluate practice in armed conflicts (1.), discuss the role of general principles as a bridge between customary international law and the normative environment and considerations as expressed in treaties (2.) and highlight the significance of the legal craft, for instance in determining default positions or the scope of the rule (3.). In conclusion, this section will reflect on the stabilizing effect of normative considerations and their limits (III.).

I. The preference for customary international law

Looking back, Werle and Jeßberger note that "[o]verall, the situation until the 1990s was paradoxical. On the one hand, the legal basis of international criminal law was largely secure and the law of Nuremberg had been consolidated.

---

62 James Crawford, 'The ILC's Draft Statute for an International Criminal Tribunal' (1994) 88(1) AJIL147-8.
63 See below on p. 509 on article 21 Rome Statute.

On the other hand, the states and the community of nations lacked the will and ability to apply these principles."⁶⁴ This changed with the establishment of the international criminal tribunals for the former Yugoslavia and for Rwanda by the Security Council Resolutions 827 and 955.⁶⁵

1. Customary international law and individual responsibility for war crimes in non-international armed conflicts

Until then, the dominant view had been that war crimes could not be committed in non-international armed conflicts.⁶⁶ This changed with the ICTY Appeals Chamber, when it decided in a landmark decision of 2 October 1995 that

> "[a] State-sovereignty-oriented approach has been gradually supplanted by a human-being-oriented approach [...] It follows that in the area of armed conflict the distinction between interstate wars and civil wars is losing its value as far as human beings are concerned [...] If international law, while of course duly safeguarding the legitimate interests of States, must gradually turn to the protection of human beings, it is only natural that the aforementioned dichotomy should gradually lose its weight."⁶⁷

The Appeals Chamber emphasized that not all rules which govern international armed conflicts would also apply in a mechanical fashion in non-international armed conflicts:

---

64 Werle and Jeßberger, *Principles of International Criminal Law* 14. Cf. also *ILC Ybk (1994 vol 1)* at 8 (Crawford), arguing that since Nuremberg "enormous efforts had been made to delineate international crimes in treaties, whereas the customary law process had been largely bypassed. That created real difficulties of definition for the "additional" crimes under general international law."

65 UNSC Res 827/1993 (25 May 1993) UN Doc S/RES/827(1993); UNSC Res 955/1994 (8 November 1994) UN Doc S/RES/955(1994). The work of both tribunals has been continued by the International Residual Mechanism for Criminal Tribunals, see UNSC Res 1966 (22 December 2010) UN Doc S/RES/1966(2010).

66 Cf. Claus Kreß, 'War Crimes Committed in Non-International Armed Conflict and the Emerging System of International Criminal Justice' (2001) 30 Israel Yearbook on Human Rights 104-5; Yoram Dinstein, *Non-International Armed Conflict in International Law* (Cambridge University Press 2014) 174-177; Yudan Tan, *The Rome Statute as Evidence of Customary International Law* (Brill Nijhoff 2021) 81-2, 102-4.

67 *Prosecutor v Dusko Tadić a/k/a "Dule"* ICTY AC Decision on the Defence Motion for Interlocutory Appeal on Jurisdiction (2 October 1995) IT-94-1-AR72 para 97. On the assimilation thesis see Kreß, 'War Crimes Committed in Non-International Armed Conflict and the Emerging System of International Criminal Justice' 107; Ambos, *Treatise on International Criminal Law: Vol. I: Foundations and General Part* 13.

"[O]nly a number of rules and principles governing international armed conflicts have gradually been extended to apply to internal conflicts; and (ii) this extension has not taken place in the form of a full and mechanical transplant of those rules to internal conflicts; rather, the general essence of those rules, and not the detailed regulation they may contain, has become applicable to internal conflicts."[68]

With respect to the violation of these rules, the Appeals Chamber held that "customary international law imposes criminal liability for serious violations of common Article 3, as supplemented by other general principles and rules on the protection of victims of internal armed conflict, and for breaching certain fundamental principles and rules regarding means and methods of combat in civil strife."[69]

The conclusions of the ICTY Appeals Chamber were confirmed by the ICTR which was established to prosecute persons responsible for serious violations of Article 3 common to the Geneva Conventions of 12 August 1949 for the Protection of War Victims, and of Additional Protocol II committed in the territory of Rwanda and Rwandan citizens responsible for such violations committed in the territory of neighbouring states (cf. Art. 1, Art, 4 ICTR Statute).[70]

This development was also confirmed at the international conference in Rome. As Kreß pointed out, even though skeptical and dissenting voices existed, this "minority has not hindered an overwhelming majority of 120 States to accept (and another 21 States not to object to) the inclusion of a list of war crimes committed in non-international armed conflicts in Article 8(2)(c) and (e) of the ICC Statute."[71]

---

68 *Prosecutor v Dusko Tadić a/k/a "Dule"* IT-94-1-AR72 para 126.
69 ibid para 134.
70 See *Prosecutor v Clément Kayishema and Obed Ruzindana* ICTR TC Judgement (21 May 1999) ICTR-95-1-T para 8; *Prosecutor v Jean-Paul Akayesu* ICTR TC Judgement (2 September 1998) ICTR-96-4-T paras 608 ("It is today clear that the norms of Common Article 3 have acquired the status of customary law in that most States, by their domestic penal codes, have criminalized acts which if committed during internal armed conflict, would constitute violations of Common Article 3"), 612-615, 617 ("The Chamber, therefore, concludes the violation of these norms entails, as a matter of customary international law, individual responsibility for the perpetrator").
71 Kreß, 'War Crimes Committed in Non-International Armed Conflict and the Emerging System of International Criminal Justice' 107; see also Tan, *The Rome Statute as Evidence of Customary International Law* 104-33.

2. Source preferences: customary international law and alternative avenues

As was demonstrated above, the ICTY based the individual responsibility for serious violations of international humanitarian law in non-international armed conflicts on customary international law which became the important source in the jurisprudence of the tribunal, as no applicable treaty explicitly set forth individual responsibility for violations of international humanitarian law. Still, the jurisprudence also demonstrates that different paths were explored and different source preferences were expressed, both in the jurisprudence of the ICTY and in scholarship.

The resolution establishing the ICTY did not set forth the applicable law, which was, however, addressed in the Report of the Secretary-General pursuant to paragraph 2 of Security Council Resolution 808 (1993). According to the Secretary-General, international humanitarian law

> "exists in the form of both conventional law and customary law [...] the application of the principle nullum crimen sine lege requires that the international tribunal *should apply rules of international humanitarian law which are beyond any doubt part of customary law* so that the problem of adherence of some but not all States to specific conventions does not arise. This would appear to be particularly important in the context of an international tribunal prosecuting persons responsible for serious violations of international humanitarian law."[72]

Against this background, it is interesting that the ICTY stated that its jurisdiction was not confined to customary international law. The Appeals Chamber

---

[72] *Report of the Secretary-General Pursuant to Paragraph 2 of Security Council Resolution 808 (1993)* (3 May 1993) UN Doc S/25704, paras 33-34 (italics added); cf. *Report of the Secretary-General Pursuant to Paragraph 5 of Security Council Resolution 955(1994)* (13 February 1995) UN Doc S/1995/134, paras 11-12, noting the non-international character of the armed conflict and stating (in para 12) that "the Security Council has elected to take a more expansive approach to the choice of the applicable law than the one underlying the statute of the Yugoslav Tribunal, and included within the subject-matter jurisdiction of the Rwanda Tribunal international instruments regardless of whether they were considered part of customary international law or whether they have customarily entailed the individual criminal responsibility of the perpetrator of the crime. Article 4 of the statute, accordingly, includes violations of Additional Protocol II, which, as a whole, has not yet been universally recognized as part of customary international law, and for the first time criminalizes common article 3 of the four Geneva Conventions." See generally on the drafting of both statutes Joseph Powderly, *Judges and the Making of International Criminal Law* (Brill Nijhoff 2020) 356.

Chapter 9: International Criminal Law

in *Tadić* set out the approach which was followed by Trial Chambers in subsequent proceedings:[73]

> "[T]he International Tribunal is authorised to apply, in addition to customary international law, any treaty which: (i) was unquestionably binding on the parties at the time of the alleged offence; and (ii) was not in conflict with or derogating from peremptory norms of international law, as are most customary rules of international humanitarian law."[74]

In certain instances, Trial Chambers based their decisions on treaties while leaving the status of customary international law open.[75] For instance, the *Galić* Trial Chamber based the crime against terrorism deliberately on a treaty provision, namely Art. 51(2) of the First Additional Protocol to the Geneva Conventions, while taking no position on the customary status of such crime.[76] The Appeals Chamber, however, whilst rejecting the defendant's submission that the tribunal's jurisdiction *ratione materiae* was limited to customary international law, argued that the Tribunal's jurisprudence demonstrated that

> "the Judges have consistently endeavoured to satisfy themselves that the crimes charged in the indictments before them were crimes under customary international law at the time of their commission and were sufficiently defined under that body of law. This is because in most cases, treaty provisions will only provide for the prohibition of a certain conduct, not for its criminalisation, or the treaty provision

---

73 Robert Kolb, 'The Jurisprudence of the Yugoslav and Rwandan Criminal Tribunals on their Jurisdiction and on International Crimes' (2004) 75 BYIL 272; *Prosecutor v Dragoljub Kunarac, Radomir Kovač and Zoran Vuković* ICTY TC Judgement (22 February 2001) IT-96-23-T & IT-96-23/1-T para 403; *Prosecutor v Dario Kordić, Mario Čerkez* ICTY TC Judgement (26 February 2001) IT-95-14/2-T para 167; *Prosecutor v Radoslav Brđanin* ICTY TC Judgement (1 September 2004) IT-99-36-T para 126; *Prosecutor v Stanišić & Župljanin* ICTY TC Judgement (27 March 2013) IT-08-91-T para 35.
74 *Prosecutor v Dusko Tadić a/k/a "Dule"* IT-94-1-AR72 para 143.
75 *Prosecutor v Blaskić* ICTY TC Judgement (3 March 2000) IT-95-14-T IT-95-14-T para 172-173: "the two parties were bound by the provisions of the two Protocols, whatever their status within customary international law [...] The Defence's argument that Additional Protocol I is not part of customary international law is therefore not relevant."; for a similar position see *Prosecutor v Clément Kayishema and Obed Ruzindana* ICTR-95-1-T paras 156-7: the question of custom could be left open since Rwanda was party to the four Geneva Conventions and the Second Additional Protocol and had enacted all offences enumerated in Article 4 as crimes under Rwandan law.
76 See *Prosecutor v Stanislav Galić* ICTY TC Judgement and Opinion (5 December 2003) IT-98-29-T IT-98-29-T paras 94-138.

itself will not sufficiently define the elements of the prohibition they criminalise and customary international law must be looked at for the definition of those elements."[77]

Since individual responsibility was associated to customary international law, tribunals regarded recourse to customary international to be necessary in order to do justice to the principles of legality and non-retroactivity.[78] Even when the Appeals Chamber in the *Čelebići* case proclaimed the principle of automatic succession to treaties of a humanitarian character, the Chamber did not rely on the humanitarian character alone but on the argument that the Geneva Conventions also reflected customary international law which was binding on a successor state.[79]

---

77 *Prosecutor v Stanislav Galić* ICTY AC Judgement (30 November 2006) IT-98-29-A para 83; for the ICTR see *Prosecutor v Jean-Paul Akayesu* ICTR-96-4-T paras 608-609 (reliance on custom); *Prosecutor v Alfred Musema* ICTR AC Judgement (27 January 2002) ICTR-96-13-A paras 236-242 and *Prosecutor v Georges Anderson Nderubumwe Rutaganda* ICTR TC Judgement (6 December 1999) ICTR-96-3-T para 90 (custom and convention).

78 *Prosecutor v Mitar Vasiljević* ICTY TC Judgement (29 October 1997) IT-98-32-T paras 193-202; *Prosecutor v Dario Kordić, Mario Čerkez* ICTY TC Decision on the Joint Defence Motion to Dismiss the Amended Indictment for Lack of Jurisdiction based on the limited Jurisdictional Reach of Articles 2 and 3 (9 March 1999) IT-95-14/2 para 20; *Prosecutor v Blaskić* ICTY AC Judgement (29 July 2004) IT-95-14-A para 141; *Prosecutor v Milan Milutinović and others* ICTY TC Decision on Ojdanić's Motion Challenging Jurisdiction: Indirect Co-Perpetration (22 March 2006) Case No. IT-05-87-PT para 15; *Prosecutor v Hadžihasanović et al* ICTY AC Decision on Interlocutory Appeal Challenging Jurisdiction in Relation to Command Responsibility (16 July 2003) T-01-47-AR72 para 35; cf. Robert Kolb, 'The Jurisprudence of the Yugoslav and Rwandan Criminal Tribunals on Their Jurisdiction and on International Crimes (2004-2013)' (2014) 84(1) BYIL 149: "[...] the customary-law limb has been considered the primary source. Paradoxically perhaps, when judged by standards of municipal law, the unwritten customary rules were considered to be more in line with the principle *nulla poena sine lege* than the written conventional provisions."; also William Schabas, 'Customary Law or Judge-Made Law: Judicial Creativity at the UN Criminal Tribunals' in José Doria, Hans-Peter Gasser, and Mahmoud Cherif Bassiouni (eds), *The Legal Regime of the ICC: Essays in Honour of Prof. I.P. Blishchenko* (Nijhoff 2009) 94; Theodor Meron, 'The Revival of Customary Humanitarian Law' (2005) 99(4) American Journal of International Law 821; see also *Report of the Secretary-General Pursuant to Paragraph 2 of Security Council Resolution 808 (1993)* para 34.

79 "In light of the object and purpose of the Geneva Conventions, which is to guarantee the protection of certain fundamental values common to mankind in times of armed conflict, and of the customary nature of their provisions, the Appeals Chamber is in no doubt that State succession has no impact on obligations arising out from these

Certain commentators agreed, pointing out that, as Mettraux put it, the aforementioned *Galić* Trial Chamber, when it referred to treaties, mixed up two different aspects, namely illegality and criminality, and since the Geneva Convention were no criminal law statute, recourse to customary international law was necessary.[80] According to Robert Kolb, however, alternatives to the customary law route were available. In particular, treaties such as the Geneva Conventions and the Additional Protocols, bilateral agreements such as the Agreement of 22 May 1992 between the parties to the conflict in Bosnia and Herzegovina and domestic criminal legislation could have proven "similarly productive", and partly were used as a legal basis for crimes without violating the principle of legality.[81] He noted a tendency "that a one-sided approach (focused exclusively on customary law) increasingly gives way to a two-tier approach (navigating between customary and conventional law)",[82] even though he also concluded that customary international law

---

fundamental humanitarian conventions.", *Prosecutor v Zdravko Mucic aka "Pavo", Hazim Delic, Esad Landzo aka "Zenga", Zejnil Delalic* ICTY AC Judgement (20 February 2001) IT-96-21-A paras 111 ff., quote at para 113.

80 Guénaël Mettraux, *International Crimes and the ad hoc Tribunals* (Oxford University Press 2005) 8-11; see also Mohamed Shahabuddeen, *International Criminal Justice at the Yugoslav Tribunal: A Judge's Recollection* (Oxford University Press 2012) 52, 61-63.

81 Kolb, 'The Jurisprudence of the Yugoslav and Rwandan Criminal Tribunals on Their Jurisdiction and on International Crimes (2004-2013)' (2014) 84 BYIL 149; Kolb, 'The Jurisprudence of the Yugoslav and Rwandan Criminal Tribunals on their Jurisdiction and on International Crimes' (2004) 75 BYIL 272; see also Robert Kolb, 'The jurisprudence of the Yugoslav and Rwandan Criminal Tribunals on their jurisdiction and on international crimes' (2000) 71 BYIL 262-263: "The natural tendency of the Tribunals will be to postulate custom wherever possible in order to bypass the jurisdictional obstacle. The practice has already shown that these postulates of custom largely rest on undemonstrated assertions. A real analysis of the elements of custom is in effect unimaginable within the compass of the task of the Tribunals. Weak assertions made in more than one case do not add to the authority the Tribunals may enjoy. Moreover, an excessive blurring and blending of conventional and customary law tends to produce unwelcomed side-effects and to weaken the proper mechanisms of treaty law."; cf. *Prosecutor v Blaskić* IT-95-14-T paras 172-173; *Prosecutor v Stanislav Galić* IT-98-29-T paras 94-138; *Prosecutor v Clément Kayishema and Obed Ruzindana* ICTR-95-1-T paras 156-7.

82 Kolb, 'The Jurisprudence of the Yugoslav and Rwandan Criminal Tribunals on their Jurisdiction and on International Crimes' 273.

became the primary source in the jurisprudence of the ICTY.[83] In Kolb's view, it was not necessary to examine with respect to each prohibition of international humanitarian law whether there was a criminalization under customary international law. Rather, customary international law dispensed

> "with a case-by-case analysis into State practice in the context of a prosecution for a single offense. It establishes a simpler equation: as it is a general conception of law that any breach of engagement involves an obligation to make reparation, so it is a general conception of humanitarian law that any serious breach of an important rule of the laws and customs of war entails criminal responsibility."[84]

Based on this reasoning, treaties could have sufficed as a legal basis, together with the general principle that any serious breach entails criminal responsibility. One reason in favour customary international law, however, might have been the dominant criminalization approach when it comes to war crimes. The criminalization approach to war crimes provides that a war crime is a violation of international humanitarian law which is specifically criminalized under international law[85]. Hence, not every violation of international humanitarian law entails individual responsibility. This approach is not beyond criticism: it is said to be circular as "a violation of IHL is prosecutable as an international war crime only if it has previously been prosecuted as a war crime"[86], the search for a criminalization is very subjective[87] and the outcome is not predictable due to the lack of a consistent methodology and therefore

---

83 Kolb, 'The Jurisprudence of the Yugoslav and Rwandan Criminal Tribunals on Their Jurisdiction and on International Crimes (2004-2013)' 149.
84 Kolb, 'The jurisprudence of the Yugoslav and Rwandan Criminal Tribunals on their jurisdiction and on international crimes' 265.
85 See for instance Georges Abi-Saab, 'The Concept of "War Crimes"' in Sienho Yee and Tieya Wang (eds), *International Law in the Post-Cold War World : Essays in Memory of Li Haopei* (Routledge 2001) 112; Michael Cottier, 'Article 8' in Otto Triffterer and Kai Ambos (eds), *Rome Statute of the International Criminal Court: a commentary* (3rd edn, Beck 2016) 304; cf. Oona A Hathaway and others, 'What is a War Crime?' (2018) 44 Yale Journal of International Law 69 ff. with further references on criminalization.
86 ibid 75.
87 Cf. Theodor Meron, 'Is International Law Moving towards Criminalization?' (1998) 9 EJIL 24: "[W]hether international law creates individual criminal responsibility depends on such considerations as whether the prohibitory norm in question, which may be conventional or customary, is directed to individuals, whether the prohibition is unequivocal in character, the gravity of the act, and the interests of the international community."

does not satisfy the principle of legality.[88] Hathaway *et al.* have recently suggested to focus on whether the breach of international humanitarian law constitutes a serious violation.[89] An abstract definition of war crimes outside a particular treaty may, for instance, guide domestic courts in particular with respect to war crimes which were not included in article 8 Rome Statute.[90]

Whether this focus on severity or seriousness is an improvement over the criminalization approach as far as predictability is concerned, is, however, open to question. Also, the question arises whether the seriousness should be assessed from the perspective of the interpreter or whether the interpreter is required to assess the seriousness from the perspectives of the international community. If interpreters tend to the latter in order to objectivize their evaluation, the difference to the criminalization approach will become smaller. The criminalization approach has the merit that it can explain why not every violation of international humanitarian law entails the individual responsibility and that the responsibility must be rooted in customary international law or in a treaty and not in the application of a general principle by a tribunal. It has to be admitted, though, that the criminalization approach did not preclude tribunals from assuming a very important position anyway.

In any case, the concept of war crime is not necessarily tied to customary international law, it can extend to treaties as well.[91] The Rome Statute sets forth a list of crimes for which individuals can incur criminal responsibility, and, as will be addressed below in more detail[92], one interesting question then concerns the relationship between these offences and customary international law and the question of whether the Rome Statute should be read as a substantive Statute or a procedural Statute which gives jurisdiction over specific crimes that are part of customary international law. In the context of the ICTY, however, customary international law was the dominant source and its identification, interpretation and application were informed by treaties and general principles.

---

88 Hathaway and others, 'What is a War Crime?' 78-81.
89 ibid 86.
90 ibid 96 ff.
91 Henckaerts and Doswald-Beck, *Customary International Humanitarian Law: Rules* 572-573; Robert Cryer, 'Introduction: What is International Criminal Law?' in Robert Cryer, Darryl Robinson, and Sergey Vasiliev (eds), *An Introduction to International Criminal Law and Procedure* (4th edn, Cambridge University Press 2019) 9; Dapo Akande, 'Sources of International Criminal Law' in Antonio Cassese (ed), *The Oxford Companion to International Criminal Justice* (Oxford University Press 2009) 48-49.
92 See below, p. 507.

II. Interpretative decisions and normative considerations in the identification of customary international law and general principles of law

1. The problem of appreciating practice in armed conflicts

When it comes to the identification of customary international law, the *Tadić* Appeals Chamber described the problem clearly. It would be difficult "to pinpoint the actual behaviour of the troops in the field for the purpose of establishing whether they in fact comply with, or disregard, certain standards of behaviour"[93], since

> "access to the theatre of military operations [is] normally refused to independent observers [...] what is worse, often recourse is had to misinformation with a view to misleading the enemy as well as public opinion and foreign Governments."[94]

Therefore, "reliance must primarily be placed on such elements as official pronouncements of States, military manuals and judicial decisions."[95] Such an approach could be criticized for failing to appreciate the real practice on the ground.[96] This description of the problem, however, was not novel and already presented by Marco Sassòli in his work on codification[97] and even earlier by Richard Baxter.[98] Sassòli reasoned that the practice regarding

---

93 *Prosecutor v Dusko Tadić a/k/a "Dule"* IT-94-1-AR72 para 99.
94 ibid para 99.
95 ibid para 99.
96 There was a vivid discussion on whether the ICRC Study on Customary International Law was or was not based on such practice, on the debate on custom interpretation by the ICRC see John B Bellinger and William J Haynes, 'A US government response to the International Committee of the Red Cross study Customary International Humanitarian Law' (2007) 89(866) International Review of the Red Cross 443 ff.; Jean-Marie Henckaerts, 'The ICRC and the Clarification of Customary International Humanitarian Law' in Brian D Lepard (ed), *Reexamining customary international law* (Cambridge University Press 2017) 161 ff.
97 Sassòli, *Bedeutung einer Kodifikation für das allgemeine Völkerrecht: mit besonderer Betrachtung der Regeln zum Schutze der Zivilbevölkerung vor den Auswirkungen von Feindseligkeiten* 232 ff., in particular 233: "[D]as tatsächliche Verhalten der Kriegsführenden [ist] aus mehreren Gründen nur schwer erkennbar. Jeder wirft seinem Gegner schwerste Verletzungen vor, während er von sich absolute Rechtstreue behauptet."
98 Baxter therefore suggested to take account of statements on the law that were made outside of an armed conflict, Baxter, 'Multilateral Treaties as Evidence of Customary International Law' 282-283, in particular 300: "The firm statement by the State of

international armed conflicts was rare, given the prohibition of the use of force, and he expressed reservations about giving particular weight to the practice of states which participate in international armed conflicts as each of such armed conflicts started with a violation of the prohibition of the use of force.[99]

Against this background, normative considerations can exert a stabilizing effect: they can help in balancing out *ad hoc* considerations, ensuring that the law is not only one-sidedly shaped by recent conflicts experiences and thereby contributing to the generality of the law. These normative considerations may be informed by rules and principles of other branches of international law.

Before exploring the ICTY's identification of customary international law further, it should not go unnoticed that the ICTY took account of the normative environment also in its interpretation of treaty law, for instance of article 4 of the Fourth Geneva Convention.[100] Article 4 of the Fourth Geneva Convention requires, for the characterization of individuals as "protected persons", that these individuals possess a nationality different from the nationality of their captors. The question arose whether Bosnian serbs would not be capable of being characterized as protected persons because Bosnia and Herzegovina had granted its nationality to them. The Chamber started with examining the limits of public international law on the conferral of nationalities and concluded that "there may be an insufficient link between the Bosnian Serbs and that State for them to be considered Bosnian nationals by this Trial Chamber in the adjudication of the present case".[101] The Chamber then argued that the Bosnian Serbs "must be considered to have been 'protected persons'"[102], since otherwise they would fall outside the protective

---

    what it considers to be the rule is far better evidence of its position than what can be pieced together from the actions of that country at different times and in a variety of contexts."

99 Sassòli, *Bedeutung einer Kodifikation für das allgemeine Völkerrecht: mit besonderer Betrachtung der Regeln zum Schutze der Zivilbevölkerung vor den Auswirkungen von Feindseligkeiten* 232, see also 233-234 on whether every practice attributable to a state for the purposes of state responsibility should be regarded as state practice which contributes to customary international law.

100 Geneva Convention relative to the protection of civilian persons in time of war (signed 12 August 1949, entered into force 21 October 1950) 75 UNTS 287.

101 *Prosecutor v Zdravko Mucic aka "Pavo", Hazim Delic, Esad Landzo aka "Zenga", Zejnil Delalic* ICTY TC Judgement (26 November 1998) IT-96-21-T para 259.

102 ibid para 259.

The interrelationship of sources and the International Criminal Tribunals

scope of the Geneva Conventions. Additionally, the Chamber argued that this interpretation was "fully in accordance with the development of the human rights doctrine which has been increasing in force since the middle of this century"[103] and which should inform the interpretation of article 4 of the IV Geneva Convention.[104]

2. General principles as a bridge between customary international law and the normative environment

a) Recognizing the interrelationship and distinctiveness of sources: normative inspirations and functional specificities

The ICTY considered general principles extrapolated from other fields of international law in the process of identifying customary international law. The ICTY did not necessarily equate a given treaty provision with customary international law, it considered the legal evaluation and principle to which a particular rule gives expression. Legal evaluations expressed in treaties were considered, rather than being applied "lock, stock and barrel"[105], under consideration of the peculiarities of international humanitarian law and international criminal law. Judge Shahabuddeen summarized this process as follows:

> "It is good jurisprudence that particular provisions of internationally recognised human rights instruments do not apply to the Tribunal lock, stock and barrel; it is superfluous to cite authority. What applies is the substance of the standards – or goals – set by the provisions of those instruments, not the provisions themselves. The supreme goal is fairness; that is sought to be ensured, inter alia, by provisions requiring a right of appeal. However, in certain circumstances, that goal can be satisfied even in the absence of a right of appeal from a conviction or sentence by the Appeals Chamber."[106]

In evaluating the extent of convergence of customary international law in the context of international criminal law with trends expressed in treaties, the tribunal did not lose sight of the distinctiveness of sources and the functional

---

103 ibid para 266.
104 ibid para 259, see also paras 250, 263, 265-266.
105 Cf. *International Status of South West Africa* [1950] ICJ Rep 128 Sep Op McNair 148. See also above, p. 258.
106 *Prosecutor v Stanislav Galić* IT-98-29-A Sep Op Shahabuddeen para 19.

characteristics which international criminal law distinguished from other fields of international law.

The example of the definition of torture illustrates this delicate exercise of acknowledging both the convergence and interplay of customary international law and treaty law and at the same time the distinctiveness of the sources and the functional differences. The *Kunarac* Trial Chamber considered the definition of torture under the Convention Against Torture (CAT). According to article 1 CAT, torture must be "inflicted by or at the instigation of or with the consent or acquiescence of a public official or other person acting *in an official capacity*".[107] The Chamber noted that in light of the "paucity of precedent in the field of international humanitarian law", the Tribunal often took

> "recourse to instruments and practices developed in the field of human rights law. Because of their resemblance, in terms of goals, values and terminology, such recourse is generally a welcome and needed assistance to determine the content of customary international law in the field of humanitarian law. With regard to certain of its aspects, international humanitarian law can be said to have fused with human rights law."[108]

The Trial Chamber then stressed the "specificities"[109] of international humanitarian law and international criminal law. In contrast to human rights law, international humanitarian law and international criminal law regulated not only the conduct of states towards persons but also conduct of individuals.[110] At the same time, the Chamber noted that human rights law was not neutral towards torture inflicted in an unofficial or private capacity as human rights law imposed positive obligations on states to prevent torture in a non-official relationship. The Chamber referred to pronouncements of the European Court of Human Rights and the Human Rights Committee which suggested that article 3 of the ECHR could apply "where the danger emanates from persons [...] who are not public officials"[111] and that the state was under an obligation to protect through legislation everyone "against the acts prohibited by article 7, whether inflicted by people acting in their

---

107 Convention against Torture and Other Cruel, Inhuman or Degrading Treatment or Punishment (signed 10 December 1984, entered into force 26 June 1987) 1465 UNTS 85 (italics added).
108 *Prosecutor v Dragoljub Kunarac, Radomir Kovač and Zoran Vuković* IT-96-23-T & IT-96-23/1-T para 467.
109 ibid para 471.
110 ibid para 470.
111 *HLR v France* App no 24573/94 (ECtHR, 22 April 1997) para 40.

official capacity, outside their official capacity or in a private capacity".[112] The Chamber eventually arrived at a definition of torture which consisted of only three elements, namely

> "the level of severity of the ill-treatment, the deliberate nature of the act and the specific purpose behind the act. The requirement that the state or one of its officials take part in the act is a general requirement of the Convention - not a definitional element of the act of torture - which applies to each and every prohibition contained in the Convention."[113]

In this sense, the Chamber parted with other Trial Chambers which had considered that the definition of the CAT "reflects a consensus which the Trial Chamber considers to be representative of customary international law".[114]

The Appeals Chamber presented a different reasoning on the relationship between article 1 CAT and customary international law.[115] The Appeals Chamber clarified that the conventional definition of torture "reflects customary international law as far as the obligation of States is concerned", and it added that the Trial Chamber was correct in that the definition would not "wholly" reflect customary international law "regarding the crime of torture generally".[116]

This example illustrates that a treaty provision may reflect customary international law to a certain degree, in the sense that there may be customary international law beyond the rules that are expressed in the treaty. In the just stated example, the ICTY considered the different addressees of regulation, namely states in human rights law and states and individuals in international criminal law and international humanitarian law. Against this background, the ICTY considered that the public character of torture was a requirement specific to human rights law but not a general requirement.

---

112 *General Comment No 20: Article 7 (Prohibition of Torture, or Other Cruel, Inhuman or Degrading Treatment or Punishment)* Human Rights Committee E/C.12/GC/20 (10 March 1992) para 2.
113 *Prosecutor v Dragoljub Kunarac, Radomir Kovač and Zoran Vuković* IT-96-23-T & IT-96-23/1-T para 478.
114 *Prosecutor v Zdravko Mucic aka "Pavo", Hazim Delic, Esad Landzo aka "Zenga", Zejnil Delalic* IT-96-21-T para 459; see also *Prosecutor v Anto Furundžija* ICTY TC Judgement (10 December 1998) IT-95-17/1-T paras 160-161; *Prosecutor v Dragoljub Kunarac, Radomir Kovač and Zoran Vuković* IT-96-23-T & IT-96-23/1-T paras 472-473.
115 *Prosecutor v Dragoljub Kunarac, Radomir Kovač and Zoran Vuković* ICTY AC Judgement (12 June 2002) IT-96-23 & IT-96-23/1-A paras 144-146.
116 ibid para 147.

The example of the definition of persecution illustrates both the distinctiveness of customary international law in relation to treaty law and that functional specificities in international criminal law may constitute limits to the reception of principles from other branches of international law or at least require adaptation of those principles.

As to the distinctiveness: in the *Kupreškić* case the Trial Chamber had to examine the scope of persecution as a crime against humanity and whether the crime of persecution requires a link to another crime.[117] Such a connection is required in article 7(1)(h) Rome Statute[118]. However, the Chamber regarded this requirement of a connection as a deviation from customary international law which was held to be less restrictive.[119]

As to the specificities: The Chamber found that neither refugee law nor human rights law provided a definition of persecution, but it also noted that "exposing a person to a risk of persecution in his or her country of origin may constitute a violation of Article 3 of the European Convention on Human Rights."[120] Moreover, according to the Chamber, domestic courts in the context of refugee law "have given persecution a broad definition, and have held that it includes denial of access to employment or education".[121] When evaluating these decisions under consideration of the principle of legality, the Chamber pointed out that

> "[t]he emphasis is more on the state of mind of the person claiming to have been persecuted (or to be vulnerable to persecution) than on the actual finding of whether persecution has occurred or may occur. In addition, the intent of the persecutor is not relevant. The result is that the net of 'persecution' is cast much wider than is legally justified for the purposes of imposing individual criminal responsibility."[122]

---

117 *Prosecutor v Kupreškić et al* ICTY TC Judgement (14 January 2000) IT-95-16-T paras 567, 572.
118 Article 7(1)(h): "Persecution against any identifiable group or collectivity on political, racial, national, ethnic, cultural, religious, gender as defined in paragraph 3, or other grounds that are universally recognised as impermissible under international law, in connection with any act referred to in this paragraph or any crime within the jurisdiction of the Court."
119 ibid paras 578-580; *Prosecutor v Dario Kordić, Mario Čerkez* IT-95-14/2-T para 197; see also Kai Ambos and Steffen Wirth, 'The Current Law of Crimes Against Humanity An analysis of UNTAET Regulation 15/2000' (2002) 13 Criminal Law Forum 71 ff.
120 *Prosecutor v Kupreškić et al* para 588.
121 ibid IT-95-16-T para 588.
122 ibid para 589.

Thus, the Chamber demonstrated that the jurisprudence in other fields of international law needed to be contextualized when determining whether this jurisprudence's principles can be meaningfully employed in international criminal law.

The *Tadić* case offers another example which illustrates that a principle's scope needs to be determined under consideration of functional specificities. The Appeals Chamber was "satisfied that the principle that a tribunal must be established by law [...] is a general principle of law", which could be found in several human rights treaties, but it argued that this principle could not be applied in the same way in which it is applied in municipal settings, as "the legislative, executive and judicial division of powers which is largely followed in most municipal systems does not apply to the international setting".[123] Whereas "established by law" could not mean "established by a proper legislature" in the international context, the Chamber identified two other interpretations, namely the establishment by an organ being capable of rendering binding decisions and the establishment of the court being in conformity with the rule of law. In other words, the Chamber interpreted the principle's text and the *telos* and came to the conclusion also against the background of "the necessary safeguards of a fair trial" that the Tribunal's establishment by the UN Security Council did not violate the general principle.[124]

b) The risk to disregard the functional specificities

The *Tadić* judgment also offers a good example of an arguably insufficient regard to functional differences between an attribution analysis in international humanitarian law and the attribution standard under the law of state responsibility. This led to a debate on whether the attribution of non-state actors to states can be established by an attribution standard based on overall-control, rather than effective control.

The ICTY had to determine whether a non-international armed conflict or an international armed conflict had existed. The ICTY argued that international humanitarian law might provide for "legal criteria for determining when armed forces fighting in an armed conflict which is *prima facie* internal may be regarded as acting on behalf of a foreign Power even if they do not

---

123 *Prosecutor v Dusko Tadić a/k/a "Dule"* IT-94-1-AR72 paras 42-43.
124 ibid paras 44-48, quote at para 47.

formally possess the status of its organs" and that these criteria might differ from the attribution criteria of the law of state responsibility in general international law.[125] However, the Chamber eventually came to the conclusion that, whilst "the Third Geneva Convention, by providing in Article 4 the requirement of 'belonging to a Party to the conflict', implicitly refers to a test of control"[126], the degree of authority or control of a state over non-state actors needed to be specified.[127] For these purposes, the Chamber identified a "need for international humanitarian law to be supplemented by general international law"[128] and conducted an analysis of general international law. The Appeals Chamber did not find the ICJ's reasoning in *Nicaragua* "persuasive"[129] which "would not seem to be consonant with the logic of the law of State responsibility"[130] and which would be "at variance with judicial and State practice"[131]. Here, the Chamber referred to the *Loizidou* decision of the European Court of Human Rights and to the standard of "effective overall control".[132] The Chamber did not, however, sufficiently appreciate that the European Court applied its control standard in order to determine whether Turkey had exercised jurisdiction for the purposes of article 1 ECHR.[133] Also,

---

125 *Prosecutor v Dusko Tadić* IT-94-1-A para 90. The Prosecution had argued that "the international law of State responsibility has no bearing" (para 89). For the view that the ICTY should not have approached the general rules of state responsibility cf. ibid IT-94-1-A Sep Op Shahabuddeen paras 17, 20; Kolb, 'The jurisprudence of the Yugoslav and Rwandan Criminal Tribunals on their jurisdiction and on international crimes' 277.
126 *Prosecutor v Dusko Tadić* IT-94-1-A para 95.
127 ibid para 97.
128 See the heading to ibid para 98, see also para 105: "As stated above, international humanitarian law does not include legal criteria regarding imputability specific to this body of law. Reliance must therefore be had upon the criteria established by general rules on State responsibility."
129 ibid para 115.
130 ibid para 116, paras 117-123 for that the general principle of the law of state responsibility seem to be to prevent that states can outsource their responsibility.
131 ibid para 124.
132 ibid para 128, see also para 137 (on the content of the overall control test), para 145 (the overall control test for the case at hand).
133 *Loizidou v Turkey (Judgment) [GC]* para 56: The crucial passage reads: "It is not necessary to determine whether, as the applicant and the Government of Cyprus have suggested, Turkey actually exercises detailed control over the policies and actions of the authorities of the 'TRNC'. It is obvious from the large number of troops engaged in active duties in northern Cyprus [...] that her army exercises effective overall control over that part of the island. Such control, according to the relevant test and in

the International Court of Justice upheld the effective control standard and confined the overall-control standard to the specific IHL question of whether an armed conflict could be classified as international or non-international.[134]

c) The role of domestic Law

Recourse to domestic law helped in concretizing and applying vague rules to a specific case.[135] Different Trial Chambers have argued that "international courts must draw upon the general concepts and legal institutions common to all the legal systems of the world. This presupposes a process of identification of the common denominators in these legal systems so as to pinpoint the basic notions they share."[136] At the same time, the identification of very specific general principles of law that would operate like an independent rule, such as a defence based on diminished mental responsibility[137] or a defence

---

    the circumstances of the case, entails her responsibility for the policies and actions of the 'TRNC' [...]. Those affected by such policies or actions therefore come within the "jurisdiction" of Turkey for the purposes of Article 1 of the Convention (art. 1). Her obligation to secure to the applicant the rights and freedoms set out in the Convention therefore extends to the northern part of Cyprus." See also above, p. 448.

134 *Application of the Convention on the Prevention and Punishment of the Crime of Genocide* [2007] ICJ Rep 43, 210 para 406. For the consolidation of the case-law on overall control see Kolb, 'The Jurisprudence of the Yugoslav and Rwandan Criminal Tribunals on Their Jurisdiction and on International Crimes (2004-2013)' 140-141.

135 See also Peat, *Comparative Reasoning in International Courts and Tribunals* 179.

136 *Prosecutor v Anto Furundžija* IT-95-17/1-T para 178; similar *Prosecutor v Dragoljub Kunarac, Radomir Kovač and Zoran Vuković* IT-96-23-T & IT-96-23/1-T para 439 ("[...] to consider, from an examination of national systems generally, whether it is possible to identify certain basic principles [...]"); see also *Prosecutor v Kupreškić et al* IT-95-16-T para 677 ("[...] to fill any *lacunae* in the Statute of the International Tribunal and in customary law"). For an comprehensive overview of general principles of law emerging from domestic law in the jurisprudence of international criminal tribunals see Raimondo, *General principles of law in the decisions of international criminal courts and tribunals* 74 ff.

137 *Prosecutor v Zdravko Mucic aka "Pavo", Hazim Delic, Esad Landzo aka "Zenga", Zejnil Delalic* IT-96-21-A 584-590 (rejection as defence, but accepted as a consideration relating to sentencing); see also *Second report on general principles of law by Marcelo Vázquez-Bermúdez, Special Rapporteur* para 36, pointing out that this defence was not recognized in the ICTY Statute.

Chapter 9: International Criminal Law

based on duress[138] proved to be difficult.[139] Recourse to domestic law was used in order to interpret the ICTY Statute[140] or for fundamental questions

---

138 *Prosecutor v Drazen Erdemović* ICTY AC Judgement (7 October 1997) IT-96-22-A paras 17-19 and Joint Sep Op McDonald and Vohrah; see also below, p. 498; *Second report on general principles of law by Marcelo Vázquez-Bermúdez, Special Rapporteur* para 38.
139 A similar observation can arguably be made with respect to the ICC: *Prosecutor v Thomas Lubanga Dyilo* ICC AC Judgment on the Appeal of Mr. Thomas Lubanga Dyilo against the Decision on the Defence Challenge to the Jurisdiction of the Court pursuant to article 19 (2) (a) of the Statute of 3 October 2006 (14 December 2006) ICC-01/04-01/06-772 paras 32-35 (the power to stay proceedings for abuse of process is not general principle of law); *Situation in the Democratic Republic of Congo* ICC AC Judgment on the Prosecutor's Application for Extraordinary Review of Pre-Trial Chamber I's 31 March 2006 Decision Denying Leave to Appeal (13 July 2006) ICC-01/04-168 para 32 (the review of decisions of hierarchically subordinate courts disallowing or not permitting an appeal is not required by a general principle of law); *Prosecutor v Abdallah Banda Abakaer Nourain and Saleh Mohammed Jerbo Jamus* ICC AC Judgement (11 November 2011) ICC-02/05-03/09 OA para 33 (no general principle of law establishing a ban for former prosecutors to join the defence immediately after leaving the prosecution); *Second report on general principles of law by Marcelo Vázquez-Bermúdez, Special Rapporteur* paras 67-68.
140 Cf. on the interpretation of article 10 of the ICTY Statute in light of a general principle of law *Prosecutor v Dusko Tadić* ICTY TC Decision on the Defence Motion on the Principle of non-bis-in-idem (14 November 1995) IT-94-1-T para 9, noting that "[t]he principle of *non-bis-in-idem* appears in some form as part of the internal legal code of many nations [...] This principle has gained a certain international status since it is articulated in Article 14(7) of the (ICCPR) [...] The principle is binding upon this International Tribunal to the extent that it appears in Statute, and in the form that it appears there."; see also *Prosecutor v Dusko Tadić a/k/a "Dule"* ICTY AC Judgement on Allegations of Contempt against Prior Counsel, Milan Vujin (31 January 2000) IT-94-1-A-R77 paras 15-29 (on contempt of court): "It is otherwise of assistance to look to the general principles of law common to the major legal systems of the world, as developed and refined (where applicable) in international jurisprudence." (para 15); *Prosecutor v Zdravko Mucic aka "Pavo", Hazim Delic, Esad Landzo aka "Zenga", Zejnil Delalic* IT-96-21-T paras 402-407, the Chamber considered the principles of *nullum crimen sine lege* and *nulla poena sine lege* in the construction of the provisions of the Tribunal's state and Rules. According to the Chamber, these principles are "well recognized in the world's major criminal justice systems as being fundamental principles of criminality" (para 402) but "[i]t is not certain to what extent they have been admitted as part of international legal practice, separate and apart from the existence of the national legal systems. This is essentially because of the different methods of criminalisation of conduct in national and international criminal justice systems" (para 403); on this case, see in particular

The interrelationship of sources and the International Criminal Tribunals

of criminal law doctrine, such as the need to conduct an analysis of both the objective and subjective elements of a crime[141], the principle of burden of proof that rests with the prosecutor[142], the change of legal qualification of facts by the prosecutor and the power of the Chamber when disagreeing with the prosecutor's legal qualification[143] or the proportionality in relation to sentencing.[144]

In addition, chambers considered domestic legal practice in the interpretation of international law more generally. For instance, when elaborating on the elements of sexual assault, one Trial Chamber started with its finding that the elements had been defined neither in a binding treaty[145] nor in customary international law.[146] The Chamber then examined domestic legal practice and found that "a number of jurisdictions place the emphasis upon absence of the victim's consent rather than highlighting the use of violence or threats by the perpetrator."[147] The Chamber interpreted international jurisprudence to the effect that "when a victim performed an act without giving genuine consent to the same, the necessary implication is that that person had been coerced to do so. Therefore, in this respect, domestic solutions are consonant with the existing international jurisprudence."[148] This example illustrates

---

Raimondo, *General principles of law in the decisions of international criminal courts and tribunals* 105-109; see also *Second report on general principles of law by Marcelo Vázquez-Bermúdez, Special Rapporteur* para 103.

141 *Prosecutor v Zdravko Mucic aka "Pavo", Hazim Delic, Esad Landzo aka "Zenga", Zejnil Delalic* IT-96-21-T para 424.
142 ibid para 599-601.
143 *Prosecutor v Kupreškić et al* IT-95-16-T paras 728 ff.
144 *Prosecutor v Blaskić* IT-95-14-T para 796; but see *Prosecutor v Drazen Erdemović* ICTY TC Sentencing Judgement (22 November 1996) IT-96-22-T para 31: "[...] there is a general principle of law common to all nations whereby the severest penalties apply for crimes against humanity in national legal systems. It thus concludes that there exists in international law a standard according to which a crime against humanity is one of extreme gravity demanding the most severe penalties when no mitigating circumstances are present." The meaning of "severest penalty" is open to question, for a convincing critique see Raimondo, *General principles of law in the decisions of international criminal courts and tribunals* 97-98.
145 See *Prosecutor v Milan Milutinović et al* ICTY TC Judgement (26 February 2009) IT-05-87-T para 196 footnote 354, noting that the Rome Statute's Elements of Crime were "not binding rules, but only auxiliary means of interpretation of the substantive definitions of crimes given in the Rome Statute itself."
146 ibid para 196.
147 ibid para 198.
148 ibid para 198.

Chapter 9: International Criminal Law

that international law and domestic legal practice are considered in light of each other.[149]

In *Popovich*, the Trial Chamber faced the question of whether or not the conspiracy to commit genocide would be a continuous crime to which the accused could join after the conspiracy had been concluded.[150] The Trial Chamber held that the conspiracy to commit genocide was a continuous crime, holding otherwise would be "contrary to the common law position".[151] Both in the USA, in Canada and in the UK individuals would be "capable of joining a conspiracy even after the initial agreement". The Trial Chamber regarded its recourse to such "regional" general principle of law[152] justified by the fact that "the concept of criminal conspiracy incorporated into the Genocide Convention derived from the common law approach and that Article 4(3) of the Statute was adopted directly from the Genocide Convention."[153]

It may be asked whether all these references should be associated with the concept of general principles of law. The judgment of the *Tadić* Appeals Chamber is quite instructive in this regard. Based on an analysis of international and national case-law, it concluded "that the notion of common design as a form of accomplice liability is firmly established in customary international law and in addition is upheld, albeit implicitly, in the Statute of the International Tribunal."[154] The Chamber then explained that its "reference to national legislation and case law only served to show that the notion of common purpose upheld in international criminal law has an *underpinning* in many national systems."[155] For establishing the concept of "common pur-

---

149 Cf. recently Ochi Megumi, 'The New Recipe for a General Principle of Law: Premise Theory to "Fill in the Gaps"' [2022] Asian Journal of International Law 10 ff., arguing that judges consider the 'premises' of the field of international criminal law when identifying a general principle of law and that "the process of recognizing general principles of law is materially affected by the premises on which it will be applied" (at 11).
150 *Prosecutor v Vujadin Popović* ICTY TC Judgement (10 June 2010) IT-05-88-T paras 870-876.
151 ibid para 872.
152 Kolb, 'The Jurisprudence of the Yugoslav and Rwandan Criminal Tribunals on Their Jurisdiction and on International Crimes (2004-2013)' 149.
153 *Prosecutor v Vujadin Popović* IT-05-88-T para 873; cf. article III(b) of the Convention on the Prevention and Punishment of the Crime of Genocide (signed 9 December 1948, entered into force 12 January 1951) 78 UNTS 277 and article 4(3)(b) of the ICTY Statute.
154 *Prosecutor v Dusko Tadić* IT-94-1-A para 220.
155 ibid para 225 (italics added). See also below, p. 530.

pose" as a general principle of law, however, "it would be necessary to show that most, if not all, countries adopt the same notion of common purpose"[156], which in the view of the Chamber was not the case, since German and Italian courts "took the same approach" but "did not rely upon the notion of common purpose or common design, preferring to refer instead to the notion of co-perpetration."[157]

The distinction drawn in this judgment between the use of general principles of law and the use of national legal systems as an additional argument and interpretative aid[158] appears to be grounded in a consensualist justification of general principles according to which it would be necessary, as the Chamber put it, that a given principle is adopted by "most, if not all" states in their domestic legal systems. It is questionable, however, whether the requirement that "most, if not all states" supported a "notion" can ever be met. The differentiation has its merits, however. It points to the varying degrees of conclusiveness which can characterize the result of a comparative law analysis, from a mere "underpinning" in domestic legal practice on the one side of the spectrum to the identification of a well-established general principle of law on the other side of the spectrum.

3. The significance of the legal craft

This section focuses on the legal craft employed by the ICTY. In particular, it highlights the role of default positions (a.) and of the determination of the scope of the rule (b.).

a) Default positions

Perspectives, default positions, starting point of an examination and legal techniques are important for the identification of customary international law. It can make a difference whether one seeks to establish a positive rule or the non-existence of a negative rule. In this context, general principles of law which the interpreter might tacitly resort to can play an important

---

156 ibid para 225.
157 ibid para 201.
158 See also Peat, *Comparative Reasoning in International Courts and Tribunals* 207-208.

Chapter 9: International Criminal Law

role in defining the default position and thusly inspire the identification of customary international law.[159]

The default position itself can be subject to debate, as the example of duress as defense illustrates. In the *Erdemovic* case[160], the Appeals Chamber rejected by majority the existence of duress an excuse to the killing of innocent people, with judges Cassese and Stephen dissenting. The divergent views adopted by the judges and the prosecutor can be explained by different default positions.

According to the prosecutor, a rule of customary international law had emerged not to recognize duress as excuse in international criminal law.[161] Thus, the underlying general rule was the non-availability of duress as a defense, and those who claimed the opposite, the emergence of an exception, had to bear the burden of reasoning. According to Judges McDonald and Vohrah, neither treaty law nor customary international law determined whether duress would be an excuse.[162] A comparative analysis of municipal legal systems would not yield to a consistent rule either, and in reaching this conclusion, regard had been had "to our mandated obligation under the Statute to ensure that international humanitarian law [...] is not in any way undermined."[163] For Judge Cassese, however, there was a "general rule"[164] to recognize duress. On the basis of an analysis of domestic legal systems and of what could be termed a general conception of law, he refuted the argument of the Prosecutor that a contrary rule of customary international law had emerged.[165]

---

159 For the example of a general principle on responsibility for breaches of law Kolb, 'The jurisprudence of the Yugoslav and Rwandan Criminal Tribunals on their jurisdiction and on international crimes' 265. See also Kai Ambos, *Der Allgemeine Teil des Völkerstrafrechts: Ansätze einer Dogmatisierung* (Duncker & Humblot 2002) 42-43 on the role of general principles of law for the purposes of verification or falsification of an emerging norm of custom; on a combination of both see also Simma and Paulus, 'The Responsibility of Individuals for Human Rights Abuses in Internal Conflicts: A Positivist View' 313.
160 *Prosecutor v Drazen Erdemović* IT-96-22-A paras 17-18.
161 ibid Diss Op Cassese para 18.
162 ibid Joint Sep Op McDonald and Vohrah paras 51, 55.
163 ibid Joint Sep Op McDonald and Vohrah paras 55, 88 (quote).
164 ibid paras 11, 41. Article 31(1)(d) Rome Statute recognizes duress as a ground for excluding criminal responsibility.
165 ibid Sep and Diss Op Cassese paras 40, 44, 47: "I contend that the international legal regulation of duress in case of murder, as I have endeavoured to infer it from case-law and practice, is both realistic and flexible. It also takes account of social

The focus on default positions, on the determination of the general rule and the exception thereto, can help to understand and to explain why interpreters come to a different assessment of customary international law and to locate the interpretative disagreement. This can improve the quality of the critical engagement with the specific identification of customary international law.

b) The determination of the scope of the rule

When evaluating international practice in order to identify customary international law, one has to consider different possibilities of how to formulate the rule which describes the practice. The debate on the *Kupreškić* case, for instance, turned on whether the identification of an absolute prohibition of civilian reprisals was justified or whether international practice would be better captured by a rule which imposes very strict conditions on the admissibility of civilian reprisals.

aa) An absolute prohibition of civilian reprisals?

The *Kupreškić* Trial Chamber argued that the protection of civilians and civilian objects against reprisals in article 51(6) and article 52 of the First Additional Protocol to the Geneva Conventions had entered the body of customary international law, even though a number of states, "which include such countries as the U.S., France, India, Indonesia, Israel, Japan, Pakistan and Turkey"[166], were no parties to the First Additional Protocol. According to the Chamber, the lack of "a body of State practice consistently supporting"[167] this rule did not prevent the ascertainment of the customary character of articles 51 and 52 of the First Additional Protocol. In view of the Chamber, the Martens clause[168] "clearly shows that principles of international humanitarian law may emerge through a customary process under the pressure of the

---

expectations more than the rule suggested by the Prosecution and that propounded by the majority."
166 *Prosecutor v Kupreškić et al* IT-95-16-T para 527.
167 ibid para 527.
168 "Until a more complete code of the laws of war has been issued, the High Contracting Parties deem it expedient to declare that, in cases not included in the Regulations adopted by them, the inhabitants and the belligerents remain under the protection and the rule of the principles of the law of nations, as they result from the usages

demands of humanity or the dictates of public conscience, even where State practice is scant or inconsistent."[169]

The Chamber also justified its interpretation by recourse to the normative environment and argued that the reprisal killing of innocent persons "can safely be characterized as a blatant infringement of the most fundamental principles of human rights."[170] The Chamber noted that international humanitarian law underwent a "profound transformation [...] under the pervasive influence of human rights".[171] This development was said to be reflected in article 50 (d) ARSIWA which excludes from lawful countermeasures "conduct derogating from basic human rights".[172] Last but not least, with the rise of international criminal law and the prosecution and punishment of war crimes, the possibility of reprisals would no longer necessary in order to induce compliance with international humanitarian law.[173]

This interpretation of the tribunal remained controversial and some commentators argued that the tribunal overemphasized the importance of *opinio juris* and did not pay appropriate regard to international practice and the function reprisals assume in international humanitarian law as means of enforcement in an extra-judicial setting.[174] According to the UK Military Manual published in 2004, "the court's reasoning is unconvincing and the assertion that there is a prohibition in customary law flies in the face of most of the state practice that exists. The UK does not accept the position as stated in this judgment."[175] The authors of the ICRC Customary International Law Study found it difficult to conclude in light of albeit limited contrary practice that there is either a general prohibition or that there is still a right to such reprisals, and noted "a trend in favour of prohibiting such reprisals".[176]

---

    established among civilized peoples, from the laws of humanity, and the dictates of the public conscience."
169 *Prosecutor v Kupreškić et al* para 527.
170 ibid IT-95-16-T para 529.
171 ibid para 529.
172 ibid para 529.
173 ibid para 530.
174 Michael N Schmitt, *Essays on Law and War at the Fault Lines* (Springer 2012) 111-113.
175 Ministry of Defence, United Kingdom, *The manual of the law of armed conflict* (Oxford University Press 2004) para 16.19.2 footnote 62.
176 Henckaerts and Doswald-Beck, *Customary International Humanitarian Law: Rules* 520-523; cf. also Sandesh Sivakumaran, *The law of non-international armed conflict* (Oxford University Press 2012) 452-453: "[S]uch a position is certainly a desirable one and foolish would be the state that undertakes belligerent reprisals against its own

The interrelationship of sources and the International Criminal Tribunals

bb) The conceptual alternative to an absolute prohibition: regulation by stringent criteria

It is argued here that the Chamber cannot be faulted for having employed normative considerations. The identification of customary international law cannot solely rest on the "collection of data about factual patterns" and empirical observations, which are difficult to make in the context of an armed conflict, it must also include a normative justification.[177] The possibility of errors or questionable assessments in the appreciation of normative considerations when identifying customary international law does not of itself suggest that customary international law is too vague in order to be determined. The Chamber's decision invites one, however, to reflect on the importance of the legal craft when translating a practice into the terms of the rule.

Perhaps the Chamber's judgment would have received less criticism if the Chamber had shaped the scope of the rule of customary international law more narrowly or if it had confined itself to applying the stringent criteria which reprisals "even when considered lawful" must meet: the recourse to reprisals must remain the last resort, there must be special precautions which ensure that the decision to resort to such reprisals will be made at the highest political or military level, there must be a proportionate relationship between the reprisals and the initial violations to which the reprisals respond and recourse to reprisals may not be had any longer than necessary. Last but not least, reprisals remain restricted by elementary considerations of humanity.[178] These criteria were also applied by the *Martić* Trial Chamber which did not elaborate on an absolute prohibition and which concluded that the conditions

---

population in a non-international armed conflict."; Ambos, *Treatise on International Criminal Law: Vol. I: Foundations and General Part* 390-393, according to whom it is questionable "whether the reprisal prohibition contained in AP I is indeed part of customary international law", endorsing however the number of stringent requirement of the *Kupreškic* Trial Chamber (*Prosecutor v Kupreškić et al* IT-95-16-T para 535): last resort, special precautions, proportionality in the sense of non-excessiveness, and regard to elementary considerations of humanity; Powderly, *Judges and the Making of International Criminal Law* 402 ("unabashed instance of customary international law-making").

177 Milan Kuhli and Klaus Günther, 'Judicial Lawmaking, Discourse Theory, and the ICTY on Belligerent Reprisals' in Armin von Bogdandy and Ingo Venzke (eds), *International Judicial Lawmaking* (Springer 2012) 382.
178 See *Prosecutor v Kupreškić et al* IT-95-16-T para 535.

for lawful reprisals had not been met in the specific case.[179] Judges enjoy a particular authority for the application of law to facts and are to a lesser degree exposed to criticism than when they identify by way of *obiter dictum* an absolute prohibition which would have immediate repercussions beyond the case in question. In the end, the continuous application of the criteria may lead to a greater acceptance of the prohibition of civilian reprisals.

Furthermore, it is interesting to compare the *Kupreškic* judgment with the *Nuclear Weapons* advisory opinion of the ICJ. The Chamber gave the Martens clause a prominent place in legal reasoning, whereas the ICJ recognized the significance of the Martens clause[180] without attributing to it a decisive effect on the interpretation of customary international law:[181] Unlike the Chamber, which arrived at an absolute prohibition of civilian reprisals, the International Court of Justice did not affirm an absolute prohibition of the threat and use of nuclear weapons, but a general prohibition which remains subject to the exception of self-defense where the very survival of a state is at stake.

III. Preliminary evaluation: the stabilizing effect of normative considerations and their limits

The Tribunal's practice gave rise to the question of whether international criminal law has developed an understanding of sources of law which would differ from the understanding in "public international law in the classical sense".[182] William Schabas, for instance, has argued that in spite of "efforts

---

179 *Prosecutor v Milan Martić* ICTY TC Judgement (12 June 2007) IT-95-11-T paras 465-468; *Prosecutor v Milan Martić* ICTY AC Judgement (8 October 2008) IT-95-11-A paras 263-267.
180 *Legality of the Threat or Use of Nuclear Weapons* [1996] ICJ Rep 226, 257 para 78, 259 para 84, 260 para 87.
181 See also Kreß, 'The International Court of Justice and the Law of Armed Conflicts' 268, 285; cf. also Antonio Cassese, 'The Martens Clause: half a loaf or simply pie in the sky?' (2000) 11(1) EJIL 214 ("Thus, arguably the Martens Clause *operates within the existing system of international sources* but, in the limited area of humanitarian law, *loosens* the requirements prescribed for *usus*, while at the same time *elevating opinio* (*iuris* or *necessitatis*) to a rank higher than that normally admitted.").
182 Schabas, 'Customary Law or Judge-Made Law: Judicial Creativity at the UN Criminal Tribunals' 100; see also Noora Arajärvi, *The changing nature of customary international law: methods of interpreting the concept of custom in international criminal tribunals* (Routledge 2014) 159 (affirming the existence of general and regime-specific secondary rules of recognition which would derive from the con-

to anchor this normative process in earlier case law [...] overall, customary international law mainly seems to provide a convenient license of judicial law-making, a process similar in many respects to the creation of judge-made rules of the English common law."[183]

This study presents a more cautious assessment. Certainly, the jurisprudence brought to fore the interpretation of customary international law. It became clear that custom is not necessarily always just a general practice accepted as law ready to be simply applied but that it requires, just as written law, interpretation, the legal craft and the specification of general rules to the particular case. Not every specification and concretization must be fully determined by a general practice accepted as law. As the Appeals Chamber held:

> "Where a principle can be shown to have been so established (by reference to practice and opinio juris), it is not an objection to the application of the principle to a specific

---

stituting treaty); see also Ratner, 'Sources of International Humanitarian Law and International Criminal Law: War/Crimes and the Limits of the Doctrine of Sources' 916 ff. (affirmative); skeptical: Jean d'Aspremont, 'Théorie des sources' in Raphael van Steenberghe (ed), *Droit international humanitaire: un régime spécial de droit international?* (Bruylant 2013) 99-101; certain scholars focus on one source, see on customary international law Schlütter, *Developments in customary international law: theory and the practice of the International Court of Justice and the International ad hoc Criminal Tribunals for Rwanda and Yugoslavia*; Arajärvi, *The changing nature of customary international law: methods of interpreting the concept of custom in international criminal tribunals*; Micaela Frulli, 'The Contribution of International Criminal Tribunals to the Development of International Law: The Prominence of opinio juris and the Moralization of Customary Law' (2015) 14 The Law and Practice of International Courts and Tribunals 80 ff.; on general principles see Raimondo, *General principles of law in the decisions of international criminal courts and tribunals*; Jain, 'Comparative International Law at the ICTY: The General Principles Experiment' 486 ff.

183 Schabas, 'Customary Law or Judge-Made Law: Judicial Creativity at the UN Criminal Tribunals' 100; see also Arajärvi, *The changing nature of customary international law: methods of interpreting the concept of custom in international criminal tribunals* 148, proposing as new concept "declarative international law" for "norms that are announced, declared, or desired to form part of international law – but not found in widespread practice or being enforced by states"; the term "declarative international law is borrowed from Hiram E Chodosh, 'Neither Treaty nor Custom: The Emergence of Declarative International Law' (1991) 26 Texas International Law Journal 87 ff.

Chapter 9: International Criminal Law

situation to say that the situation is new if it reasonably falls within the application of the principle."[184]

As Nollkaemper has noted, the jurisprudential distinction between interpretation, application and development of the law can sometimes be rather thin and a difference of degree.[185] Given that the ICTY's jurisprudence constituted a landmark moment for international criminal law after dormant decades, the judicial craft and creativity were very visible in developing the modern case-law.[186] Hence, the relative age of a legal regime is one factor which scholars might want to consider when comparing the identification of customary international law in different contexts. Recourse to general principles of international law helped the Tribunal in identifying customary international law and in guiding the subjective element inherent in any interpretation, application and concretization of the law to a specific set of facts. One can, therefore, say that normative considerations had a stabilizing influence and provided a safeguard against arbitrary interpretations.[187]

The selectivity with respect to the principles and the contestability of legal interpretations are the downside to the tribunal's lengthy judgments and its transparency as to the justification of certain interpretations of customary international law by recourse to general principles. The *Furundžija* case highlights the broad interpretative range that was given to the ICTY in the absence of legally binding written definitions of the different crimes. The Trial Chamber based the definition of rape on a general principle of criminal law common to the major legal systems of the world.[188] Since it was not possible to decide on the basis of this source whether forced oral penetration is a crime as opposed to a sexual assault,[189] the Trial Chamber took recourse to

---

184 *Prosecutor v Milan Milutinović and others* IT-01-47-AR72 para 12.
185 André Nollkaemper, 'Decisions of National Courts as Sources of International Law: An Analysis of the Practice of the ICTY' in Gideon Boas and William Schabas (eds), *International Criminal Law Developments in the Case Law of the ICTY* (Martinus Nijhoff Publishers 2003) 291.
186 Kolb, *Interprétation et création du droit international. Esquisse d'une herméneutique juridique moderne pour le droit international public* 228; Powderly, *Judges and the Making of International Criminal Law* 353.
187 Raimondo, *General principles of law in the decisions of international criminal courts and tribunals* 172; cf. also Kolb, 'Principles as Sources of International Law (With Special Reference to Good Faith)' 9.
188 *Prosecutor v Anto Furundžija* IT-95-17/1-T para 177, para 181; for an overview of the jurisprudence see Peat, *Comparative Reasoning in International Courts and Tribunals* 187 ff.
189 *Prosecutor v Anto Furundžija* para 182.

the concept of human dignity which the Trial Chamber identified as "the basic underpinning and indeed the very *raison d'être* of international humanitarian law and human rights law" and which "has become of such paramount importance as to permeate the whole body of international law".[190] It then arrived at a definition of rape which included forced oral penetration.[191]

The lack of representativeness of the municipal legal systems from which principles would be drawn is discussed as a point of concern.[192] This concern, while being valid in principle, should not be exaggerated, however.[193] Firstly, whether a general principle of law can be applied at the international level depends on its fit to the international legal structures of the context in which it might be applied;[194] and this fit is not necessarily dependent on the principle's representativeness among municipal jurisdiction. Jaye Ellis has related the debate in international criminal law to insights from the discipline of comparative law and cast doubts on the idea that a greater representativeness in the selection of today's diverse municipal legal systems would be simply to achieve or could justify general principles of law on the basis of a voluntarist account.[195] Taking into account legal orders from several "legal families" may be intuitively appealing, yet the view that a meaningful classification according to legal families is possible is not unanimously shared within

---

[190] ibid para 183.
[191] ibid para 185; upheld by *Prosecutor v Anto Furundžija* ICTY AC Judgement (21 July 2000) IT-95-17/1-A para 215; see for a subsequent modification *Prosecutor v Dragoljub Kunarac, Radomir Kovač and Zoran Vuković* IT-96-23-T & IT-96-23/1-T paras 439-453, arguing that domestic law "may disclose 'general concepts and legal institutions' which, if common to a broad spectrum of national legal systems, disclose an international approach to a legal question which may be considered as an appropriate indicator of the international law on the subject" (para 439). The chamber identified as legally protected value not the absence of violence but "sexual autonomy" (para 457).
[192] Raimondo, *General principles of law in the decisions of international criminal courts and tribunals* 179-183.
[193] Cf. also *Second report on general principles of law by Marcelo Vázquez-Bermúdez, Special Rapporteur* para 28, advocating a "pragmatic approach", covering a "wide and representative comparative analyses, covering different legal families and regions of the world" without requiring that a principle must be present in every legal order.
[194] Cf. also Megumi, 'The New Recipe for a General Principle of Law: Premise Theory to "Fill in the Gaps"' 10 ff.; see above, Fn. 149.
[195] Jaye Ellis, 'General Principles and Comparative Law' (2011) 22(4) EJIL 953 ff., 970-971.

comparative law theory,[196] and the possibility to borrow legal principles intrinsically connected to a particular legal culture and to transplant them into another system of law is contested as well.[197] According to Ellis, a more thoroughly applied comparative legal research could have supported some of the tribunal's conclusions in the just mentioned *Furundžija* case.[198] Given the difficulties to ever identify a general principle universally recognized in domestic legal orders, Ellis has suggested to consider the idea that "the validity of a general principle would have to be grounded in the soundness and persuasiveness of legal argumentation rather than in claims about the objective nature of law or implicit state consent".[199]

The contestability of the identification and application of customary international law or general principles of law does not necessarily have to go at the detriment of a judgment's persuasiveness or even legitimacy. If one wanted to reduce the room for judicial creativity, one must resort to treatymaking and negotiate a convention. In fact, this was precisely one objective when drafting the Rome Statute and in particular when drafting an exhaustive list of crimes and the corresponding elements of crimes. The next section will explore the interrelationship of sources in the context of the Rome Statute. As will be demonstrated however, a treaty can reduce, but not necessarily eliminate the need for doctrinal considerations and recourse to customary international law and general principles of law.

---

196 Jain, 'Comparative International Law at the ICTY: The General Principles Experiment' 491; Neha Jain, 'Judicial Lawmaking and General Principles of Law in International Criminal Law' (2016) 57(1) Harvard International Law Journal 133-137; Ugo Mattei, 'Three Patterns of Law: Taxonomy and Change in the World's Legal Systems' (1997) 45 American Journal of Comparative Law 19 ff., advocating a classification according to the relationship between law, politics and tradition.

197 In favour Alan Watson, 'Legal Change: Sources of Law and Legal Culture' (1983) 131 University of Pennsylvania Law Review 1121 ff.; contra Pierre LeGrand, 'The Impossibility of Legal Transplants' (1997) 4 Maastricht Journal of European and Comparative Law 111 ff.; according to Gunther Teubner, 'Legal Irritants: Good Faith in British Law or How Unifying Law Ends up in New Divergences' (1998) 61(1) The Modern Law Review 11 ff., the transplant would cause "irritations" in the legal system into which it was transplanted.

198 Ellis, 'General Principles and Comparative Law' 968, noting a development in municipal legal orders to define this crime from the perspective of the victim.

199 ibid 971 ("An advantage of this approach is its honesty. Rather than asserting the commonality of a general principle without providing evidence in support of this assertion, judges could present the actual line of reasoning that led them to identify a particular principle as useful or relevant.").

D. The Interrelationship of Sources and the Rome Statute

This section will examine the interrelationship of sources and its development in the context of the Rome Statute. This section will first give an overview of those articles of the legal regime which are considered to be of relevance for an examination of the interrelationship of sources (I.). This section will then address the relationship between the general rules of interpretation and the Rome Statute (II.) and discuss the question of a potential conflict between customary international law and the Rome Statute with respect to the modes of liability (III.) The section will then examine how the ICC approached immunities under customary international law (IV.).

I. The legal regime

The Rome Statute was adopted in 1998 and entered into force in 2002.[200] It not only establishes the International Criminal Court but also defines the crimes over which the ICC has jurisdiction. The ICC's jurisdiction extends to crimes committed on the territory of a state party (article 12(2)(a) Rome Statute), even when committed by citizens of non-State parties, crimes which nationals of a state parties were accused of (article 12(2)(b) Rome Statute), crimes on the territory of a non-State party if the non-State party accepted the exercise of the ICC's jurisdiction (article 12(3) Rome Statute) and situations referred by the UN Security Council (article 13(b) Rome Statute).

According to article 5 Rome Statute, the ICC has jurisdiction with respect to the crime of genocide (article 6 Rome Statute), crimes against humanity (article 7 Rome Statute), war crimes (article 8 Rome Statute) and, based on an amendment, the crime of aggression (article 8*bis* Rome Statute). Those articles do not include an opening clause which would give the ICC jurisdiction over further crimes under general international law. The list of crimes can only be, and successfully has been, expanded through amendments.[201]

---

200 Rome Statute of the International Criminal Court (signed 17 July 1998, entered into force 1 July 2002) 2187 UNTS 3.
201 *Assembly of States Parties to the Rome Statute, Amendments to article 8 of the Rome Statute, 6 October 2010* RC/Res.5 (Article 8(2)(e)(xiii), (xiv)); *Assembly of States Parties to the Rome Statute, Amendments to article 8 of the Rome Statute, 14 December 2017* ICC-ASP/16/Res.4 (articles 8(2)(b)(xxvii), (xxviii), (xxix), (e)(xvi), (xvii), (xviii)); *Assembly of States Parties to the Rome Statute, Amendments to article 8 of the Rome Statute, 6 December 2019* ICC-ASP/18/Res.5 (article 8(2)(e)(xix)).

Such amendments will be subject to article 121(5) Rome Statute according to which the Court shall not exercise its jurisdiction regarding a crime covered by an amendment when committed on the territory or by nationals of a State party which did not accept the amendment in question.[202] In relation to the crime of aggression, the exercise of jurisdiction is subject to a special regime laid down in articles 15*bis* and 15*ter*.[203]

The Rome Statute leaves room for the further development of customary international law. Article 10 of the Rome Statute stipulates that "[n]othing in this Part shall be interpreted as limiting or prejudicing in any way existing or developing rules of international law for purposes other than this Statute." This provision's inclusion responded to concerns that the treatification of international criminal law would lower the level of protection under customary international law and preempt the further development of custom.[204] Simi-

---

202 Article 121(5) derogates to this extent from article 12(2)(a), Andreas Zimmermann and Meltem Şener, 'Chemical Weapons and the International Criminal Court' (2014) 108 American Journal of International Law 444; Andreas Zimmermann, 'Amending the Amendment Provisions of the Rome Statute: The Kampala Compromise on the Crime of Aggression and the Law of Treaties' (2012) 10 JICJ 217-219; for a different view see Astrid Reisinger Coracini, ''Amended Most Serious Crimes': A New Category of Core Crimes within the Jurisdiction but out of the Reach of the International Criminal Court?' (2008) 21 Leiden Journal of International Law 718; cf. Claus Kreß and Leonie von Holtzendorff, 'The Kampala Compromise on the Crime of Aggression' (2010) 8 JICJ 1197-1198, 1214-1215. The Assembly of State Parties, when introducing the amendments to article 8, "*confirm[ed]* its understanding that in respect to this amendment the same principle that applies in respect of a State Party which has not accepted the amendment applies also in respect of States that are not parties to the Statute", see *Assembly of States Parties to the Rome Statute, Amendments to article 8 of the Rome Statute, 6 October 2010*; *Assembly of States Parties to the Rome Statute, Amendments to article 8 of the Rome Statute, 14 December 2017*; *Assembly of States Parties to the Rome Statute, Amendments to article 8 of the Rome Statute, 6 December 2019*.
203 Cf. in particular article 15*bis*(2), (4). Cf. Marko Milanovic, 'Aggression and Legality: custom in Kampala' (2012) 10 JICJ 177 ff., see also 183-186 on the question of whether the definition in article 8*bis* reflects custom.
204 Alain Pellet, 'Applicable Law' in Antonio Cassese, Paola Gaeta, and John RWD Jones (eds), *The Rome Statute of the International Criminal Court: A Commentary* (Oxford University Press 2002) vol 2 1083 (on normative regressions); Antonio Cassese, 'The Statute of the International Criminal Court: Some Preliminary Reflections' (1999) 10 EJIL 157, according to whom "the Statute itself seems to postulate the future existence of two possible regimes or *corpora* of international criminal law, one established by the Statue and the other laid down in general international criminal law; cf. Leila Nadya Sadat, 'Custom, Codification and some thoughts about

larly, article 22(3) Rome Statute provides that article 22 on *nullum crimen sine lege* "shall not affect the characterization of any conduct as criminal under international law independently of this Statute." Article 10 and article 22(3) indicate that rules of international criminal law may exist outside the Statute and that the Statute, therefore, allows for the possibility that it might not be wholly reflective of customary international law or freeze the latter's further development. Furthermore, according to article 31 Nr. 3 of the Statute, the ICC may consider a ground for excluding criminal responsibility other than those referred to in the Statute where such a ground is derived from applicable law as set forth in article 21.[205] The Statute thus envisions the possibility to include defenses that have been developed in international law.

Article 21 sets forth the applicable law. It stipulates:

"1. The Court shall apply:
a. In the first place, this Statute, Elements of Crimes and its Rules of Procedure and Evidence;
b. In the second place, where appropriate, applicable treaties and the principles and rules of international law, including the established principles of the international law of armed conflict;
c. Failing that, general principles of law derived by the Court from national laws of legal systems of the world including, as appropriate, the national laws of States that would normally exercise jurisdiction over the crime, provided that those principles are not inconsistent with this Statute and with international law and internationally recognized norms and standards.
2. The Court may apply principles and rules of law as interpreted in its previous decisions.
3. The application and interpretation of law pursuant to this article must be consistent with internationally recognized human rights, and be without any adverse distinction founded on grounds such as gender as defined in article 7, paragraph 3, age, race, colour, language, religion or belief, political or other opinion, national, ethnic or social origin, wealth, birth or other status."

Even though article 21 does not include the term customary international law, its reference to principles and rules of international law has been read

---

the relationship between the two: Article 10 of the ICC Statute' (2000) 49(4) DePaul Law Review 912 (critical of "[h]aving law inside and outside the Statute that differ from each other"); see also Leena Grover, *Interpreting Crimes in the Rome Statute of the International Criminal Court* (Cambridge University Press 2014) 269, pointing out, as one effect of article 10, that article 10 "ensures that States can continue to take positions on the (non-)customary status of certain norms by distinguishing between the Rome regime and general international law".

205 Akande, 'Sources of International Criminal Law' 45, 50.

as a reference to customary international law.²⁰⁶ Commentators explain the lack of an explicit reference with the concern that customary international law may seem to lack sufficient precision in the context of international criminal law²⁰⁷, which is interesting against the background of the history of international criminal law and the role customary international law has played in the jurisprudence of the tribunals.

It is debated whether general principles of law to which article 38(1)(c) ICJ Statute refers are covered by article 21(1)(b) or (c) of the Rome Statute.²⁰⁸ The drafting process took place against the background of the ILC draft which provided that the court shall apply the draft statute, applicable treaties and the rules and principles of international law as well as applicable rules of national law.²⁰⁹ The 1994 ILC commentary clarified that "the expression 'principles and rules' of general international law includes general principles of law [...]"²¹⁰ During the negotiation of the Rome Statute, delegates held different views on whether the new court shall be empowered to directly apply national law.²¹¹ Article 21 represents a compromise in that the ICC may derive general principles from national laws of legal systems of the world, including the laws of the state that would normally exercise jurisdiction over

---

206 Margaret M deGuzman, 'Article 21 Applicable Law' in Kai Ambos (ed), *Rome Statute of the International Criminal Court* (4th edn, CH Beck 2022) 1138-40; William A Schabas, *The International Criminal Court* (2nd edn, Oxford University Press 2016) 522; for a critique of the lack of a specific reference, which was also missing in the ILC drafts, see Pellet, 'Applicable Law' 1067 ff.; Johan Verhoeven, 'Article 21 of the Rome Statute and the ambiguities of applicable law' (2002) 22 Netherlands Yearbook of International Law 12.
207 deGuzman, 'Article 21 Applicable Law' 1138; see also *United Nations Report of the Preparatory Committee on the Establishment of an International Criminal Court, Volume I, Proceedings of the Preparatory Committee during March-April and August 1996* (13 September 1996) UN Doc A/51/22 para 190 ("[D]oubts were expressed by some delegations as to whether customary international law covered the issue of punishment in relation to individuals held responsible for their acts or omissions.").
208 See deGuzman, 'Article 21 Applicable Law' 1131, 1138-44; Schabas, *The International Criminal Court* 514-5, 519 ff.
209 *ILC Ybk (1993 vol 2 part 2)* 111; *ILC Ybk (1994 vol 2 part 2)* 51; see above, p. 473.
210 ibid 51 para 2.
211 *United Nations Report of the Preparatory Committee on the Establishment of an International Criminal Court, Volume I, Proceedings of the Preparatory Committee during March-April and August 1996* paras 187-8.

the crime in question.²¹² Interpreting article 21 Rome Statute in light of the ILC draft, William Schabas has argued that article 21(1)(b) comprises the general principles of law in the sense of article 38(1)(c) ICJ Statute, whereas article 21(1)(c) Rome Statute is concerned with general principles of national criminal law.²¹³ According to Margaret deGuzman, article 21(1)(b) Rome Statute encompasses not only custom and general principles of law, but also principles "even when they are neither derived from national laws nor part of customary international law", such as principles intrinsic to the idea of law, principles valid through all kinds of societies, and principles of justice.²¹⁴ According to a third interpretation, the classification in article 21(1)(a)-(c) Rome Statute corresponds to the classification in article 38(1)(a)-(c) ICJ Statute, in the sense that article 21(1)(b) refers exclusively to customary international law and article 21(1)(c) refers to general principles of law.²¹⁵ The ICC has, in an earlier decision, discussed the existence of a general principle of law with reference to article 21(1)(c) Rome Statute, following, however, the categorization of the prosecutor.²¹⁶ The *Bemba* Trial Chamber held that the principles and rules of international law in the sense of article

---

212 Per Saland, 'International Criminal Law Principles' in Roy S Lee (ed), *The International Criminal Court. The Making of the Rome Statute. Issues, Negotiations, Results* (Kluwer 1999) 214-5.
213 Schabas, *The International Criminal Court* 514-5, 519 ff.; see also Ambos, *Treatise on International Criminal Law: Vol. I: Foundations and General Part* 126-30 (article 21(1)(c) would refer to principles in the comparative law sense); cf. also Vladimir-Djuro Degan, 'On the Sources of International Criminal Law' (2008) 4(1) Chinese Journal of International Law 52-3.
214 deGuzman, 'Article 21 Applicable Law' 1139; deGuzman borrows those categories of principles from Schachter, *International law in theory and practice: general course in public international law* 75.
215 Alain Pellet, 'Revisiting the Sources of Applicable Law before the ICC' in Margaret M deGuzman and Diane Marie Amann (eds), *Arcs of Global Justice: Essays in Honour of William A. Schabas* (Oxford University Press 2018) 239-41; Werle and Jeßberger, *Principles of International Criminal Law* 88; Verhoeven, 'Article 21 of the Rome Statute and the ambiguities of applicable law' 8-9 (discussing and rejecting the interpretation that article 21(1)(b) refers not only to customary international law but to general principles of international law that are different from customary international law); Akande, 'Sources of International Criminal Law' 51-2; Raimondo, *General principles of law in the decisions of international criminal courts and tribunals* 150.
216 *Situation in the Democratic Republic of Congo* para 32; Schabas, *The International Criminal Court* 520 f.; deGuzman, 'Article 21 Applicable Law' 1140.

21(1)(b) "are generally accepted to refer to customary international law", without specifically discussing general principles of law.[217]

In theory, the classification may matter in that article 21(1)(c) authorizes the ICC to take recourse to general principles of law in situations in which the sources referred to in article 21(1)(a) and (b) Rome Statute do not provide for an answer, provided that the general principle in question is not inconsistent with the Statute and international law. In other words, recourse to article 21(1)(c) depends on different conditions than article 21(1)(b). In practice, however, the difference does not seem to matter too much. The ICC seems to stress more the commonality of article 21(1)(b) and (c) when it refers to both provisions as "subsidiary sources" in relation to the Statute.[218] In its earlier case-law, the ICC rejected the Prosecutor's submission that there was a general principle of law or a rule of international law which would have permitted the practice of witness proofing and preparation to the prosecution. The TC noted that the Prosecution did not refer to examples from the Roman-Germanic legal system and pointed to the differences between the procedural framework of the *ad hoc* tribunals and the ICC system.[219]

---

217 *Prosecutor v Jean-Pierre Bemba Gombo* ICC TC III Judgment pursuant to Article 74 of the Statute (21 March 2016) ICC-01/05-01/08-3343 para 71.

218 See for instance *Situation in the State of Palestine* ICC PTC I Decision on the Prosecution request pursuant to article 19(3) for a ruling on the Court's territorial jurisdiction in Palestine (5 February 2021) ICC-01/18-143 para 88 (the ICC PTC held that it was "not necessary to have recourse to subsidiary sources of law under article 21(1)(b) and (c) of the Statute"); on the terminology of "subsidiary sources" see also *Prosecutor v Germain Katanga* ICC TC II Judgment pursuant to Article 74 of the Statute (7 March 2014) ICC-01/04-01/07-3436-tENG paras 39-40; *Prosecutor v Jean-Pierre Bemba Gombo et al* ICC AC Judgment (8 March 2018) ICC-01/05-01/13-2275-Red para 76; see also *Prosecutor v William Samoei Ruto et al* ICC PTC II Decision on the Confirmation of Charges Pursuant to Article 61(7)(a) and (b) of the Rome Statute (23 January 2012) ICC-01/09-01/11-373 para 289 ("[T]he chamber should not resort to applying article 21(1)(b), unless it has found no answer in paragraph (a)").

219 *Prosecutor v Thomas Lubanga Dyilo* ICC-01/04-01/06-772 paras 29, 35 (the Prosecution's argument that witness proofing was a widely accepted practice in international criminal law is considered under article 21(1)(b), whereas the argument that witness proofing is a general principle of law is considered under article 21(1)(c) Rome Statute); *Prosecutor v Thomas Lubanga Dyilo* ICC TC I Decision Regarding the Practices Used to Prepare and Familiarise Witnesses for Giving Testimony at Trial (30 November 2007) ICC-01/04-01/06-1049 para 41 (witness proofing no general principle of law pursuant to Article 21(1)(c) of the Statute), para 44 (considering *ad hoc* tribunals and noting that the procedural issue of witness proofing "would

Article 21(3) reminds the interpreter that an interpretation must be consistent with internationally recognized human rights.[220] It thus not only points to the applicable law but also guides the interpreter in interpreting and applying the law. So far, article 21(3) has been used by the Court to bring in human rights law in the interpretation of the Statute.[221] Another provision relevant to the Statute's interpretation is article 22(2) which stipulates that the definition of a crime shall be strictly construed and shall not be extended by analogy and, in case of doubt, be interpreted in favour of the person being investigated, prosecuted or convicted.[222]

---

not, *ipso facto*,prevent all procedural issues from scrutiny under Article 21(1)(b), the Chamber does not consider the procedural rules and jurisprudence of the *ad hoc* Tribunals to be automatically applicable to the ICC without detailed analysis"); cf. *Prosecutor v Milutinović et al* ICTY TC Decision on Ojdanic motion to prohibit witness proofing (12 December 2006) IT-05-87-T paras 11-7 (explaining why the chamber of the ICTY views the practice of witness proofing differently than the chamber of the ICC; for an overview see Megumi, 'The New Recipe for a General Principle of Law: Premise Theory to "Fill in the Gaps"' 15-6.

220 Pellet termed this the imposition of human rights as "super-legality", Pellet, 'Applicable Law' 1067 ff.; Verhoeven, 'Article 21 of the Rome Statute and the ambiguities of applicable law' 12; on the debate on whether the reference to "internationally recognized human rights" includes regional human rights, see Stephen Bailey, 'Article 21(3) of the Rome Statute: a Plea for Clarity' (2014) 14(3) International Criminal Law Review 513 ff., advocating a non-regional approach; Daniel Sheppard, 'The International Criminal Court and "Internationally Recognized Human Rights": Understanding Article 21 (3) of the Rome Statute' (2010) 10(1) International Criminal Law Review 43 ff., advocating a territorial approach by which human rights treaties regionally applicable to the dispute should inform the interpretation of article 21(3); see also James Crawford, 'The Drafting of the Rome Statute' in Philippe Sands (ed), *From Nuremberg to The Hague: The Future of International Criminal Justice* (Cambridge University Press 2003) 129-133 (on human rights of the accused); on the ICC practice see Emma Irving, 'The other side of the Article 21(3) coin: Human rights in the Rome Statute and the limits of Article 21(3)' (2019) 32 Leiden Journal of International Law 837 ff.

221 Cf. for an overview deGuzman, 'Article 21 Applicable Law' 1146 ff.; see *Prosecutor v Ali Muhammad Ali Abd-Al-Rahman ("Ali Kushayb")* ICC AC Judgment on the appeal of Mr Abd-Al-Rahman against the Pre-Trial Chamber II's "Decision on the Defence 'Exception d'incompétence' (1 November 2021) ICC-02/05-01/20-503 paras 83, 86-7 on the interpretation of the *nullum crimen* principle enshrined in article 22(1) of the Statute in light of article 21(3).

222 On the character as interpretative principle in the context of the Rome Statute see recently Jean d'Aspremont, 'The Two Cultures of International Criminal Law' in

In a formalistic way, article 21 provides for a formal hierarchy of sources and even a legal basis for the court to rely on its previous decisions.[223] This regime is intended to restrict judicial creativity[224], but since these rules are in the hands of the ICC, which can refer to other sources under the general rules of treaty interpretation, the ICC still enjoys ample latitude.[225] It, therefore,

Kevin Jon Heller and others (eds), *Oxford Handbook of International Criminal Law* (Oxford University Press 2020) 419-420.

223 For the view that article 33 of the ILC draft was considered as too vague see *United Nations Report of the Preparatory Committee on the Establishment of an International Criminal Court, Volume I, Proceedings of the Preparatory Committee during March-April and August 1996* para 188. First reactions to article 21 of the Rome Statute were critical, see in particular Pellet, 'Applicable Law' 1057, speaking of a "veritable brainwashing operation led by criminal lawyers", resulting into the idea that general international law would be too vague to satisfy the nullum crimen principle; Pellet, 'Revisiting the Sources of Applicable Law before the ICC' 231; for the position that codification was required see Mahmoud Cherif Bassiouni and Christopher L Blaskesley, 'The Need for an International Criminal Court in the New International World Order' (1992) 25(2) Vanderbilt Journal of Transnational Law 175-176; for critiques of article 21 see also Robert Cryer, 'Royalism and the King: Article 21 of the Rome Statute and the Politics of Sources' (2009) 12(3) New Criminal Law Review: An International and Interdisciplinary Journal 393 ff. (arguing that article 21 would establish hierarchies which would not "comport with general international law" and that the "interrelationship of sources is more complex than article 21's apparently rigid hierarchy implies", 393); Verhoeven, 'Article 21 of the Rome Statute and the ambiguities of applicable law' 11 (stressing that general international law should inform the interpretation of the treaty, even if it was "not strictly applicable"); see also Bruno Simma and Andreas L Paulus, 'Le rôle relatif des différentes sources du droit international pénal: dont les principes généraux de droit' in Hervé Ascensio, Emmanuel Decaux, and Alain Pellet (eds), *Droit international pénal* (Pedone 2000) 55 ff.; see also Schabas, *The International Criminal Court* 526 ("The reference to the Court's case law hardly seems necessary.").

224 See for instance Leena Grover, 'A Call to Arms: Fundamental Dilemmas Confronting the Interpretation of Crimes in the Rome Statute of the International Criminal Court' (2010) 21(3) EJIL 571; Powderly, *Judges and the Making of International Criminal Law* 464; on the drafting of article 21 see deGuzman, 'Article 21 Applicable Law' 1131 f.

225 According to Gilbert Bitti, 'Article 21 and the Hierarchy of Sources of Law before the ICC' in Carsten Stahn (ed), *The law and practice of the International Criminal Court* (Oxford University Press 2015) 443 ff., the ICC was more faithful to the textualism indicated by article 21 of the Rome Statute in 2008 than in 2014. According to Joseph Powderly, 'The Rome Statute and the Attempted Corseting of the Interpretive Judicial Function: Reflections on Sources of Law and Interprative Technique' in Carsten Stahn (ed), *The law and practice of the International Criminal Court* (Oxford

remains important to observe how the court uses this latitude and to what extent its reasoning will be confined to the Rome Statute or will include references to general international law.

II. The interrelationship between the general rules of interpretation and the Rome Statute

1. Article 21 Rome Statute and the general rules of interpretation

The interpretation of the Rome Statute and the just stated provisions is governed by the general rules of treaty interpretation as set forth in articles 31-33 VCLT.[226] The abstract relationship between the general rules of interpretation and the applicable law as set forth in article 21 Rome Statute has been addressed by the *Katanga* Trial Chamber and the *Bemba* Trial Chamber.

The *Katanga* Trial Chamber emphasized that "article 21 of the Statute establishes a hierarchy of the sources of applicable law" and that the Chamber "shall therefore apply the subsidiary sources of law under article 21(1)(b) and 21(1)(c) of the Statute only where it identifies a lacuna in the provisions of the Statute".[227] Turning to the general rules of interpretation, the Chamber rightly noted that article 31 VCLT "sets forth *one* general rule of interpre-

---

University Press 2015) 497 ff., "the Rome Statute's attempted corseting of the creative interpretative freedom of the bench through the inclusion of a set of specific 'disciplining' rules [...] proved to be a failure"; see already Pellet, 'Applicable Law' 1053; see also d'Aspremont, 'The Two Cultures of International Criminal Law' 414 ff.; deGuzman, 'Article 21 Applicable Law' 1133; Cryer, 'Royalism and the King: Article 21 of the Rome Statute and the Politics of Sources' 393.

226 Cf. *Prosecutor v Jean-Pierre Bemba Gombo* ICC-01/05-01/08-3343 paras 75-7 ("the interpretation of the Statute is governed, first and foremost, by the VCLT, specifically Articles 31 and 32"); *Situation in the Democratic Republic of Congo* ICC-01/04-168 para 33; *Prosecutor v Germain Katanga* ICC AC, Judgment on the appeal of Mr. Germain Katanga against the decision of Pre-Trial Chamber I entitled "Decision on the Defence Request Concerning Languages" (27 May 2008) ICC-01/04-01/07-522 para 38; *Prosecutor v Germain Katanga* ICC-01/04-01/07-3436-tENG paras 43-5; *Prosecutor v Thomas Lubanga Dyilo* ICC TC I Judgment pursuant to Article 74 of the Statute (14 March 2012) ICC-01/04-01/06-2842 para 601; cf. *Alleged Violations of Sovereign Rights and Maritime Spaces in the Caribbean Sea* [2016] ICJ Rep 3, 19 para 35 ("Article 31 to 33 of the Convention reflect rules of customary international law", with further references); Schabas, *The International Criminal Court* 517.

227 *Prosecutor v Germain Katanga* ICC-01/04-01/07-3436-tENG para 39.

tation"[228], but it then held that "various ingredients - the ordinary meaning, the context, and the object and purpose-" of only article 31(1) shall "be considered together in good faith" without any hierarchical or chronological order between those ingredients.[229] The means of interpretation set forth in article 31(3)(c) VCLT, however, should be referred to in what seems to be a subsidiary fashion, namely "[w]here the founding texts do not specifically resolve a particular issue",[230] including, for instance, when "the text of the Statute itself refers at times to external sources."[231] For this purpose, the Chamber noted that it might be necessary "to refer to the jurisprudence of the ad hoc tribunals and other courts on the matter."[232] With respect to article 7 on crimes against humanity, the Trial Chamber held that "interpretation of the terms of article 7 of the Statute and, where necessary, the Elements of Crimes, requires that reference be had to the jurisprudence of the ad hoc tribunals insofar as that jurisprudence identifies a pertinent rule of custom, in accordance with article 31(3)(c) of the Vienna Convention. Of note in this connection is that the negotiation of the definition of a crime against humanity was premised on the need to codify existing customary law."[233]

The *Bemba* Trial Chamber explained one year after the *Katanga* Trial Chamber that the jurisprudence of the *ad hoc* tribunals may be relevant not only in the interpretation of the Statute according to customary international law as set forth in article 31(3)(c) VCLT, but also in the context of article 21(1)(b). The Chamber acknowledged that "the boundaries between the two approaches may be fluid" and emphasized "that it must not use the concept of treaty interpretation to replace the applicable law".[234] The Chamber summa-

---

228 *Prosecutor v Germain Katanga* para 44.
229 ibid para 45.
230 ibid para 47. Cf. already Grover, 'A Call to Arms: Fundamental Dilemmas Confronting the Interpretation of Crimes in the Rome Statute of the International Criminal Court' 574-575 on *Prosecutor v Omar Hassan Ahmad Al Bashir* ICC PTC I Decision on the Prosecution's Application for a Warrant of Arrest (4 March 2009) ICC-02/05-01/09-3 para 126.
231 *Prosecutor v Germain Katanga* ICC-01/04-01/07-3436-tENG para 48.
232 ibid paras 47 (quote), 1100.
233 ibid para 1100.
234 *Prosecutor v Jean-Pierre Bemba Gombo* ICC-01/05-01/08-3343 para 79. Cf. for a similar formula *Oil Platforms* [2003] ICJ Rep 161 Sep Op Higgins 225 para 49: "[The ICJ] has rather invoked the concept of treaty interpretation to displace the applicable law."; Grover, 'A Call to Arms: Fundamental Dilemmas Confronting the Interpretation of Crimes in the Rome Statute of the International Criminal Court' 574.

rized that it "applies Article 21 of the Statute, in combination with Articles 31 and 32 of the VCLT [...] in full respect of the limitations provided for in Articles 21(3) and 22(2)."[235]

Both Trial Chambers associated customary international law as means of interpretation or as applicable law with the international criminal tribunals and their potential significance for the interpretation of the Rome Statute. The *Bemba* Trial Chamber is correct in that the rules of interpretation and the applicable law are distinct concepts, which, it is here submitted, are also interrelated ones: article 21(1)(a) determines that the ICC shall apply "[i]n the first place this Statute, Elements of Crimes and its Rules of Procedure and Evidence", and the Statute is to be interpreted according to the general rules of interpretation.[236] However, article 31(3)(c) VCLT and customary international law shall be employed always in the interpretation of a treaty and not only when, to borrow a formula from the *Katanga* Trial Chamber, the "texts do not specifically resolve a particular issue", as the question of whether the text does or does not resolve a particular issue is itself subject to interpretation. Of course, the specific relevance of this means of interpretation may differ from case to case.[237]

2. The crimes of the Rome Statute and customary international law

Whereas the foregoing remarks concerned the abstract relationships between the applicable law, the rules of interpretation and the Rome Statute, the relationship in specific cases will depend on whether the provision in question of the Rome Statute was intended to align with or depart from customary international law.

With respect to crimes, the question has arisen whether the Rome Statute should be read as a procedural Statute which refers to crimes as they exist in customary international law or whether it should be understood as a

---

[235] *Prosecutor v Jean-Pierre Bemba Gombo* ICC-01/05-01/08-3343 para 86.
[236] For an in-depth study see Grover, 'A Call to Arms: Fundamental Dilemmas Confronting the Interpretation of Crimes in the Rome Statute of the International Criminal Court' in particular 573-577 (on a presumption of interpretation consistent with custom); Grover, *Interpreting Crimes in the Rome Statute of the International Criminal Court*; see also Darryl Robinson, 'The Identity Crisis of International Criminal Law' (2008) 21 Leiden Journal of International Law 935.
[237] On the single-combined operation see above, p. 406.

substantive statute which defines for the purposes of the Statute the crimes.[238] The drafters intended to codify war crimes which were considered to be part of customary international law.[239] Commentators, however, hold different views on the extent to which the Rome Statute in fact reflects customary international law.[240]

---

238 Marko Milanović, 'Is the Rome Statute Binding on Individuals? (And Why We Should Care)' (2011) 9 JICJ 27 ff.
239 Darryl Robinson and Herman von Hebel, 'War crimes in internal conflicts: Article 8 of the ICC Statute' (1999) 2 Yearbook of International Humanitarian Law 194 ("Delegations agreed that the definitions of these crimes must be articulated in the Statute and that those definitions must reflect existing customary law", with further references); Kreß, 'War Crimes Committed in Non-International Armed Conflict and the Emerging System of International Criminal Justice' 109 ("States have, in their overwhelming and steadily growing majority solemnly expressed the view that the war crimes list in Article 8(2) (c) and e is based on customary law"). According to Milanović, 'Is the Rome Statute Binding on Individuals? (And Why We Should Care)' 32 footnote 25, states held different views on whether the crimes had to be part of customary international law, with reference to *United Nations Report of the Preparatory Committee on the Establishment of an International Criminal Court, Volume I, Proceedings of the Preparatory Committee during March-April and August 1996* 16: "several delegations" argued that the crimes "should be defined by enumeration of the specific offences rather than by reference to the relevant legal instruments, to provide greater clarity and transparency, to underscore the customary law status of the definitions, *to avoid a lengthy debate on the customary law status* of various instruments, to avoid possible challenges by States that were not parties to the relevant agreements, to avoid the difficulties that might arise if the agreements were subsequently amended and to provide a uniform approach to the definitions of the crimes irrespective of whether they were the subject of a convention [...] *Several delegations held the view that the Statute should codify customary international law and not extend to the progressive development of international law*." (italics added). See also ibid para 59 (on the customary status of the crime of genocide).
240 Several commentators note, in particular with respect to crimes in NIACs, that the Statute remains below CIL, see for instance, Werle and Jeßberger, *Principles of International Criminal Law* 508 para 1342 (the delayed repatriation of prisoners of war which is a grave breach under Article 85(4)(b) Add. Prot. I is not regulated by the Statute), 540 para 1432 (no equivalent to Article 8(2)(b)(ii) for NIACs), 564 para 1504 (the Statute's provisions on forbidden methods and means of warfare in NIACs lag behind CIL), 577 para 1545 (use of weapons are criminalized under CIL to a greater extent than under the Rome Statute); O'Keefe, 'An "International Crime Exception" to the Immunity of State Officials from Foreign Criminal Jurisdiction: Not Currently, not Likely' 121 (Article 8 does not represent the customary position); cf. also Cassese, 'The Statute of the International Criminal Court: Some Preliminary Reflections' 150-152; Robert Cryer, 'Of Custom, Treaties, Scholars and the Gavel:

As far as only parties to the Rome Statute are concerned, the debate on whether the Rome Statute is fully reflective of customary international law might appear to be theoretical, as it could be said that the ICC can just interpret and apply the Statute. In this sense, the *Ntaganda* Trial Chamber explicitly argued that article 8 Rome Statute can be applied regardless of its relationship to customary international law.[241] However, such a treaty-based approach has its limits, in particular when non-State parties are involved and the Court's jurisdiction will be based on the *ad hoc* declaration of a non-party State under Article 12(3) or a referral of a situation by the UNSC according to article 13(b) Rome Statute. The view that in such situations the *nullum crimen* principle will require the ICC to apply article 8 only to the extent

---

The Influence of International Criminal Tribunals on the ICRC Customary Law Study' (2006) 11 Journal of Conflict and Security Law 251 ("the Rome Statute is not to be taken as anything more than a base-level of what customary law is"); Beth van Schaack, 'Mapping War Crimes in Syria' (2016) 92 International Law Studies 295-298; cf. Schabas, *The International Criminal Court* 221 (arguing that Article 8 also recognized new crimes, such as the recruitment of child soldiers and attacks on peacekeepers); for a different view as to the customary prohibition of child recruitment see *Prosecutor v Sam Hinga Norman* SCSL AC Decision on Preliminary Motion Based on Lack of Jurisdiction (Child Recruitment) (31 May 2004) SCSL-2004-14-AR72(E) para 53; cf. also *Decision on the Prosecution Request for a Ruling on Jurisdiction under Article 19(3) of the Statute* PTC I (6 September 2018) ICC-RoC46(3)-01/18-37 para 45 (substantial parts of Articles 7 and 8 constituted "pure codification" elements, whereas "other provisions represent a 'progressive evolution' of custom."). See also Grover, *Interpreting Crimes in the Rome Statute of the International Criminal Court* 302: "On balance [...] [there is support for] the idea that the crimes in the Rome Statute are generally or largely reflective of custom. Departures may be discerned that are progressive and retrogressive relative to custom, and the Statute may not reflect all crimes that exist under customary international law." Cf. Michael Cottier and Matthias Lippold, 'Article 8' in Kai Ambos (ed), *Rome Statute of the International Criminal Court: a commentary* (4th edn, Beck 2021) para 48.

241 *Prosecutor v Bosco Ntaganda, ICC TC VI Second decision on the Defence's challenge to the jurisdiction of the Court in respect of Counts 6 and 9 (4 January 2017)* ICC-01/04-02/06-1707 para 35: "The Chamber observes that the Statute is first and foremost a multilateral treaty which acts as an international criminal code for the parties to it. The crimes included in Articles 6 to 8 of the Statute are an expression of the State Parties' desire to criminalise the behaviour concerned. As such, the conduct criminalised as a war crime generally will, but need not necessarily, have been subject to prior criminalisation pursuant to a treaty or customary rule of international law."

that it corresponds with customary international law[242] can find support in a recent decision of the Appeals Chamber in the *Abd-Al-Rahman* case. In that case, the ICC's jurisdiction was based on a UNSC referral (article 13(b) Rome Statute) and the accused was a national of Sudan which was not a party to the Statute at the time when the crimes allegedly took place. The PTC argued that there was no violation of the *nullum crimen* principle as enshrined in article 22(1) Rome Statute since the case was based on the Statute's "provisions detailing the prohibited conduct, which existed and were in force at the time of all of the events underlying the charges."[243] The defence's argument that in such situations the principles of legality and non-retroactivity required the prior criminalization of the conduct in question by customary international law or by the relevant states "would result in restricting its scope to such an extent as to call into question the very raison d'être of that particular triggering mechanism".[244] In contrast, the Appeals Chamber held that article 22(1) of the statute needed to be interpreted and applied in light of internationally recognized human rights according to article 21(3) Rome Statute.[245] Relying on the concepts of foreseeability and accessibility from the jurisprudence of the ECtHR, the AC argued that the criminalization of conduct by the Statute would not suffice in a situation

---

242 Milanović, 'Is the Rome Statute Binding on Individuals? (And Why We Should Care)' 51; Talita de Souza Dias, 'The Nature of the Rome Statute and the Place of International Law before the International Criminal Court' (2019) 17 JICJ 529-532; Talita de Souza Dias, 'The Retroactive Application of the Rome Statute in Cases of Security Council Referrals and Ad hoc Declarations: An Appraisal of the Existing Solutions to an Under-discussed Problem' (2018) 16 JICJ 87 ff.; Rogier Bartels, 'Legitimacy and ICC Jurisdiction Following Security Council Referrals: Conduct on the Territory of Non-Party States and the Legality Principle' in Nobuo Hayashi and Cecilia M Bailliet (eds), *The Legitimacy of International Criminal Tribunals* (Cambridge University Press 2017) 166; Bruce Broomhall, 'Article 22' in Kai Ambos (ed), *The Rome Statute of the International Criminal Court* (4th edn, Beck 2021) paras 20-1, 34; cf. Alexandre Skander Galand, *UN Security Council Referrals to the International Criminal Court* (Brill Nijhoff 2019) 151; but see William A Schabas, *An Introduction to the International Criminal Court* (6th edn, Cambridge University Press 2020) 62 (arguing that, with the adoption of the Rome Statute, the Statute's application to nationals of non-party States was no longer unforeseeable).
243 *Prosecutor v Ali Muhammad Ali Abd-Al-Rahman ("Ali Kushayb")* ICC PTC II Decision on the Defence 'Exception d'incompétence' (ICC-02/05/01/20-302) (17 May 2021) ICC-02/05-01/20-391 para 40 (quote) and paras 36-42.
244 ibid para 41.
245 *Prosecutor v Ali Muhammad Ali Abd-Al-Rahman ("Ali Kushayb")* ICC-02/05-01/20-503 para 83.

where the crime was committed on the territory of a non-party State. Rather, "a chamber must look beyond the Statute to the criminal laws applicable to the suspect or accused at the time the conduct took place and satisfy itself that a reasonable person could have expected, at that moment in time, to find him or herself faced with the crimes charged."[246] Turning to the specific case, the AC concluded that the accused "was reasonably capable of taking steps to comprehend and comply with his obligations under international law".[247] Here, the Statute became important as evidence of those obligations. The AC noted that the statutory crimes resulted from a concerted codification effort and "were intended to be generally representative of the state of customary international law", which "weighs heavily in favour of the foreseeability of facing prosecutions for crimes within the jurisdiction of this Court, eve in relation to conduct occurring in a State not party to the Statute".[248]

Another example of the limits of a purely treaty-based approach concerns arrest warrants against persons who enjoy, in principle, immunity. This situation is addressed by article 27 Rome Statute which applies, however, only *inter partes*. For non-State parties, customary international law matters. In this context, it has been argued that the introduction of the concept of an international crime to the international legal order led to a modification of immunities[249] to the extent that those immunities may not be compatible with the concept of crime and the idea that the international community exercises a *jus puniendi*.[250] Based on this reading, the customary character of the crimes in question matters because only crimes that are part of customary international law could have led to a modification of immunities under customary international law.[251]

---

246 ibid para 86.
247 ibid para 88.
248 ibid para 89; cf. paras 93-5 for a summary of the view of judge Ibáñez who argued that the Statute "has been public since its adoption" and that Sudan signed the Statute, which is why it would be "unnecessary to engage in a discussion as to whether the crimes within the jurisdiction of the Court existed also as customary international law" (all quotes in para 95).
249 Kreß, 'Article 98' paras 32, 37, 40, 43, 53, 130; Cf. Dapo Akande and Sangeeta Shah, 'Immunities of State Officials, International Crimes, and Foreign Domestic Courts' (2010) 21 EJIL 840 (on the concept of crime in conjunction with the principle of extraterritorial jurisdiction).
250 Kreß, 'Article 98' paras 127-130; on the *ius puniendi* see also Ambos, *Treatise on International Criminal Law: Vol. I: Foundations and General Part* 57-60.
251 Kreß, 'Article 98' para 130. See also below p. 546 ff.

3. Further development of treaty-based approaches or alignment with customary international law?

A different question is whether these crimes, regardless of whether they were originally intended to reflect customary international law, will be interpreted and applied in light of customary international law or whether the ICC will strike a different path. While it is true that articles 6, 7, 8 and 8*bis* provide definitions of the crimes "[f]or the purpose of this Statute", in general, several reasons speak in favour of interpreting the Rome Statute, and in particular the crimes, in accordance with customary international law. First, the drafters did not intend to engage in a legislative exercise. Only crimes recognized under customary international law should be included in the Statute.[252] Second, even though article 10 stipulates that the Statute's second part does not prejudice the development of customary international law, the general rule of treaty interpretation as set forth in article 31 VCLT speaks in favour of interpreting the crimes in the Rome Statute in accordance with customary international law.[253] As has been demonstrated throughout this study, functionally equivalent rules of customary international law and treaty law tend to converge rather than to develop differently (which, of course, remains possible though). Third, if the ICC understands itself not just as a

---

[252] Cottier, 'Article 8' paras 17-26; Kreß, 'War Crimes Committed in Non-International Armed Conflict and the Emerging System of International Criminal Justice' 109; see also Grover, *Interpreting Crimes in the Rome Statute of the International Criminal Court* 270, 301-2 (concluding that "the jurisdiction of the Court, the Rome Statute's articulation of the legality principle and applicable law, the Statute's relationship to existing and developing law, the definitions of crimes including their mental elements and the Elements of Crimes lend support to the idea that the crimes in the Rome Statute are generally or largely reflective of custom. Departures may be discerned that are progressive and retrogressive relative to custom, and the Statute may not reflect all crimes that exist under customary international law"); Tan, *The Rome Statute as Evidence of Customary International Law* 187-8 (on the codification of the crimes against humanity and the alignment of the removal of the nexus requirement with an armed conflict and the recognition of the element of policy); see now also *Prosecutor v Ali Muhammad Ali Abd-Al-Rahman ("Ali Kushayb")* ICC-02/05-01/20-391 para 89.

[253] Grover, 'A Call to Arms: Fundamental Dilemmas Confronting the Interpretation of Crimes in the Rome Statute of the International Criminal Court' 572, 575; cf. on Part 3 of the Statute, the so-called general principles of criminal law and the "paucity of customary international law" Kreß, 'War Crimes Committed in Non-International Armed Conflict and the Emerging System of International Criminal Justice' 142-3.

The Interrelationship of Sources and the Rome Statute

treaty body but as an organ exercising the *jus puniendi* of the international community, a reasoning based only on the Statute without regard to customary international law will have its limits, in particular when non-State parties are concerned.

Moreover, recourse to customary international law will be necessary when interpreting and applying the crimes with respect to, for instance, the definition, temporal and geographical scope of armed conflicts or "the established framework of international law" (article 8(2)(b), (e)).[254] At the same time, one must remain aware of functional specificities, which may, even if rarely, exist between international humanitarian law and international criminal law. For instance, a concept such as direct participation in hostilities may assume a different meaning in IHL than the concept of using children to actively participate in hostilities (article 8(2)(b)(xxvi), (e)(vii)). In the context of IHL, the direct participation in hostilities can lead to the loss of protection of civilians by international humanitarian law, which is why this concept should be interpreted narrowly. In contrast, the crime of using children to actively participate in hostilities primarily concerns the perpetrator who uses children in situations which may render children subject to attacks. The interpretation of this crime should not lead to the result that children are considered no longer protected by international humanitarian law.[255]

Nevertheless, it is possible for the ICC to strike a different path; in fact, certain decisions indicate a preference for a *lex specialis* approach that focuses

---

[254] Cf. on the practice of the ICC Rogier Bartels, 'The Classification of Armed Conflicts by International Criminal Courts and Tribunals' (2020) 20 International Criminal Law Review 595 ff. *Prosecutor v Bosco Ntaganda* ICC AC Judgment on the appeal of Mr Ntaganda against the "Second decision on the Defence's challenge to the jurisdiction of the Court in respect of Counts 6 and 9" (15 June 2017) ICC-01/04-02/06-1962 para 53: "Thus, the specific reference to the "established framework of international law" within article 8 (2) (b) and (e) of the Statute permits recourse to customary and conventional international law regardless of whether any lacuna exists, to ensure an interpretation of article 8 of the Statute that is fully consistent with, in particular, international humanitarian law."; *Prosecutor v Thomas Lubanga Dyilo* ICC AC Judgment (1 December 2014) ICC-01/04-01/06-3121-Red para 322.

[255] See also Andreas Zimmermann and Robin Geiß, 'Article 8(2)(e)(vii)' in Kai Ambos (ed), *The Rome Statute of the International Criminal Court* (4th edn, Beck 2021) para 963; Tilman Rodenhäuser, 'Squaring the Circle? Prosecuting Sexual Violence against Child Soldiers by their 'Own Forces'' (2016) 14 JICJ 179-180; on the *Ntaganda* case and other recent examples of expansive interpretations see also Andreas Zimmermann, 'Internationaler Strafgerichtshof am Scheideweg' [2022] JuristenZeitung 264-5.

on the particularities of the Rome Statute. In February 2021, a Pre-Trial Chamber decided in favour of jurisdiction in relation to a situation referred to the ICC by Palestine. The PTC did refer to customary international law when it interpreted the territoriality principle set forth in article 12(2)(a) Rome Statute, concluding that territorial jurisdiction can encompass acts which partly take place outside a state's territory.[256] The majority then saw no need, however, to examine whether Palestine would be a state under general international law; it sufficed that Palestine was a state party to the Rome Statute. According to the majority of the Chamber, there was no need to resort to general international law, article 31(3)(c) VCLT or article 21(1)(b) Rome Statute.[257]

The *Ntaganda* case is another interesting example. The Trial Chamber argued that "the Statute is first and foremost a multilateral treaty which acts as an international criminal code for the parties to it. [...] [T]he conduct criminalised as a war crime generally will, but need not necessarily, have been subject to prior criminalisation pursuant to a treaty or customary rule of international law."[258] The Appeals Chamber did not explicitly endorse this *dictum*. However, noting that article 8(2) does not refer for all war crimes to the "persons and property protected under the provisions of the relevant Geneva Convention"[259], the Appeals Chamber held that there is neither under

---

256 *Decision Pursuant to Article 15 of the Rome Statute on the Authorisation of an Investigation into the Situation in the People's Republic of Bangladesh/Republic of the Union of Myanmar* ICC PTC III (14 November 2019) ICC-01/19-27 paras 55-62.

257 *Situation in the State of Palestine* ICC-01/18-143 para 88, where the Chamber argued that it could rely on article 21(1) and that "it is not necessary to have recourse to subsidiary sources of law under article 21(1)(b) and (c) of the Statute. Furthermore, the Chamber considers that recourse to article 31(3)(c) of the Vienna Convention on the Law of Treaties (the 'Vienna Convention'), being a rule of interpretation, cannot in any way set aside the hierarchy of sources of law as established by article 21 of the Statute, which is binding on the Chamber." Critical of this approach *Situation in the State of Palestine* ICC PTC I Decision on the Prosecution request pursuant to article 19(3) for a ruling on the Court's territorial jurisdiction in Palestine, Judge Péter Kovács, Partly Dissenting Opinion (5 February 2021) ICC-01/18-143-Anx1 paras 63, 73-74.

258 *Prosecutor v Bosco Ntaganda, ICC TC VI Second decision on the Defence's challenge to the jurisdiction of the Court in respect of Counts 6 and 9 (4 January 2017)* ICC-01/04-02/06-1707 para 35.

259 Compare on the one hand Article 8(2)(a) and (c) and on the other hand Article 8(2)(b) and (e) the latter of which do not refer to the concept of protected persons but to the "established framework of international law".

Article 8 nor under the established framework of international law for each crime, or for the crimes of rape and sexual slavery specifically, a general status requirement according to which only persons with the status of a protected person under the Geneva Conventions could be victims of such war crimes.[260] The Appeals Chamber decided that sexual abuse and rape of child soldiers under fifteen years by other members of the same party to the conflict constituted war crimes and that it was the nexus requirement, rather than a status requirement, on the basis of which ordinary crimes were to be distinguished from war crimes.[261] While the Appeals Chamber did not explicitly endorse the Trial Chamber's formulation of the crimes' treaty nature, the Appeals Chamber's reasoning arguably does not differ substantially from the Trial Chamber's reasoning in this regard. It interpreted and applied first and foremost article 8 Rome Statute before examining in a second step whether international humanitarian law would provide for a status requirement limiting the interpretation and application of article 8 Rome Statute. It could not identify a general status requirement, given that certain rules of international law protect, for instance, a party's own forces.[262] While this reasoning led to the result that child soldiers could be victims of a crime under article 8(2)(e)(vi) Rome Statute, this reasoning's unfortunate side effect is that it

---

260 *Prosecutor v Bosco Ntaganda* ICC-01/04-02/06-1962 paras 46-67; see already *Prosecutor v Bosco Ntaganda, ICC TC VI Second decision on the Defence's challenge to the jurisdiction of the Court in respect of Counts 6 and 9 (4 January 2017)* ICC-01/04-02/06-1707 paras 37-44.
261 *Prosecutor v Bosco Ntaganda* ICC-01/04-02/06-1962 para 68; the decisions have received a mixed reaction: Marco Longobardo, 'The Criminalisation of Intra-party Offences in Light of Some Recent ICC Decisions on Children in Armed Conflict' (2019) 19 International Criminal Law Review 630-2 (positive); for the view that the decision should be interpreted restrictively, confined to the special situation of child soldiers see Luca Poltronieri Rosetti, 'Intra-party sexual crimes against child soldiers as war crimes in Ntaganda. 'Tadic moment' or unwarranted exercise of judicial activism?' [2019] Questions of International Law 65; a different way to arrive at the result of the *Ntaganda* AC on the basis of the common article 3 of the Geneva Conventions would have been to argue that according to a *bona fide* interpretation child soldiers who were recruited in violation of international law remain civilians "*vis-à-vis* those who are responsible for their unlawful recruitment", or, alternatively, that they are to be regarded as hors de combat during the time of the crime and that they are therefore protected by common article 3, see Rodenhäuser, 'Squaring the Circle? Prosecuting Sexual Violence against Child Soldiers by their 'Own Forces" 186 and 191–2.
262 *Prosecutor v Bosco Ntaganda* ICC-01/04-02/06-1962 para 59, referring, *inter alia* to article 12 of the first two Geneva Conventions of 1949.

does not answer the question of whether these child soldiers were in fact protected by common article 3 of the four Geneva Conventions. This side effect could be evaluated more positively if one argued that this reasoning relieved the prosecution from examining whether each possible victim of a crime was in fact protected by common article 3 or whether the victim's specific participation in the hostilities led to a loss of protection. If this had been a concern, this concern could have been dealt with, as convincingly suggested by Rodenhäuser, by a *bona fide* interpretation according to which child soldiers who were recruited in violation of international law remain civilians "*vis-à-vis* those who are responsible for their unlawful recruitment"[263], or, alternatively, that they are to be regarded as *hors de combat* during the time of the crime and that they are therefore protected by common article 3.[264]

The question of whether the ICC favours treaty-based approaches over alignment with customary international law will be explored in more detail in the next section on modes of criminal liability and the relationship between the Rome Statute and customary international law in the context of immunities of head of states.

III. A conflict of sources? Between JCE, control theory and indirect perpetratorship

If one focuses on the interrelationship of sources in the judicial practice, one fascinating example concerns the modes of liability. Whereas the ICTY developed on the basis of an analysis of customary international law the concept of joint criminal enterprise (JCE), the ICC developed its interpretation of article 25 Rome Statute on the basis of the doctrines of indirect perpetratorship and of control theory. The example of modes of criminal liability illustrates that international practice can appear to look like a *Rorschach* blot in the sense that the reading and interpretation of international practice depends on the respective viewer's personal and doctrinal background and training.[265]

---

263 Rodenhäuser, 'Squaring the Circle? Prosecuting Sexual Violence against Child Soldiers by their 'Own Forces'' 186.
264 See ibid 191–2.
265 On this metaphor see Leila Nadya Sadat and Jarrod M Jolly, 'Seven Canons of ICC Treaty Interpretation: Making Sense of Article 25's Rorschach Blot' (2014) 27 Leiden Journal of International Law 755-756; for a detailed account that zeros in on the criminal law specificities all of which cannot be addressed here, see Lachezar Yanev, 'Joint Criminal Enterprise' in Jérôme de Hemptinne, Robert Roth,

The Interrelationship of Sources and the Rome Statute

Early criminal decisions tended to follow the unitarian perpetrator model (*Einheitstätermodell*) according to which no meaningful distinction was made between principals and accessories.[266] This approach took account of the fact that war crimes were mass crimes[267] and that individual criminal responsibility should be extended beyond the soldier on the ground, the direct

---

and Elies van Sliedregt (eds), *Modes of Liability in International Criminal Law* (Cambridge University Press 2019) 120 ff.; Elies van Sliedregt and Lachezar Yanev, 'Co-Perpetration Based on Joint Control over the Crime' in Jérôme de Hemptinne, Roberts Roth, and Elies van Sliedregt (eds), *Modes of Liability in International Criminal Law* (Cambridge University Press 2019) 85 ff.

266 Elies van Sliedregt, 'Perpetration and Participation in Article 25(3)' in Carsten Stahn (ed), *The Law and Practice of the International Criminal Court* (Oxford University Press 2015) 502-503; Ambos, *Treatise on International Criminal Law: Vol. I: Foundations and General Part* 105-108; Werle and Jeßberger, *Principles of International Criminal Law* 235; *Trial of Franz Holstein and Twenty-Three Others* UNWCC Law Reports Vol. VII, 26 32 ("a universally recognised principle of modern penal law that accomplices during or after the fact are responsible in the same manner as actual perpetrators or as instigators"); *Justice Case (United States of America v Josef Altstoetter, et al), United States Military Tribunal*, 1063 ("the person who persuades another to commit murder, the person who furnishes the lethal weapon for the purposes of the commission, and the person who pulls the trigger are all principals or accessories to the crime."); for an overview unitary and differentiated models see Elies van Sliedregt, *Individual criminal responsibility in international law* (Oxford University Press 2012) 65-67.

267 Cf. on the mass crime character *Attorney General v Adolf Eichmann* District Court of Israel, Criminal Case No. 40/61 36 ILR 236-237: "[...] these crimes were mass crimes, not only having regard to the numbers of victims but also in regard to the numbers of those who participated [...] and the extent to which any one of the many criminals were close to or remote from the person who actually killed the victims says nothing as to the measure of his responsibility. On the contrary, the degree of responsibility generally increases as we draw further away from the man who uses the fatal instrument with his own hands and reach the higher levels of command, the 'counsellors', in the language of our law."

perpetrator.[268] The ICTY developed as mode of liability the so-called Joint Criminal Enterprise (JCE).[269]

This section will first give an overview of the construction of JCE and its three distinct categories (1.). Subsequently, it will address the question of whether and to what extent the Rome Statute embraced a different paradigm and a different understanding of the modes of liability (2.). Finally, this section will offer concluding observations and express scepticism as to the idea of a conflict between sources in this context (3.).

1. The construction of JCE and its three distinct categories

Starting from principle of personal culpability as "the foundation of criminal responsibility"[270], the ICTY distilled on the basis of an analysis of customary international law as evidenced by "many post World War II cases"[271], the interpretation of its statute and of the criminal law of several national legal systems[272] "the principle that when two or more persons act together to further a *common criminal purpose*, offences perpetrated by any of them may

---

[268] In favour of a unitarian model James G Stewart, 'The End of Modes of Liability for International Crimes' (2012) 25(1) Leiden Journal of International Law 55-73; but see Gerhard Werle and Boris Burghardt, 'Establishing Degrees of Responsibility: Modes of Participation in Article 25 of the ICC Statute' in Elies van Sliedregt and Sergey Vasiliev (eds), *Pluralism in International Criminal Law* (Oxford University Press 2014) 302-319, defending a differentiation model with reference to article 25 Rome Statute, the case-law of the *ad hoc* tribunals and normative arguments , see also 318: "The question of whether a person holds individual criminal responsibility cannot be answered adequately with a simple 'Yes' or 'No'. The task of criminal law is not limited to defining the scope of criminal responsibility; it includes developing normative criteria for gradation of responsibility."

[269] See generally Ambos, *Treatise on International Criminal Law: Vol. I: Foundations and General Part* 108-112. Early solutions to the question of how to hold leaders responsible for crimes perpetrated by others were the so-called command responsibility of superiors for crimes of subordinate soldiers and the concept of a membership in a criminal organization which may be characterized as a crime rather than a mode of participation, see Heller, *The Nuremberg Military Tribunals and the Origins of International Criminal Law* 262 ff., 290 ff.; Yanev, 'Joint Criminal Enterprise' 129; Sliedregt, *Individual criminal responsibility in international law* 27 ff., 183 ff.; Yoram Dinstein, 'Command Responsibility' [2013] Max Planck EPIL.

[270] *Prosecutor v Dusko Tadić* para 186.

[271] ibid para 195.

[272] ibid para 193.

entail the criminal liability of all the members of the group."[273] Furthermore, "the notion of *common purpose* encompasses three distinct categories of collective criminality."[274]

The first category, JCE I, addresses a situation where "all co-defendants, acting pursuant to a common design, possess the same criminal intention"[275], which can also be described as co-perpetratorship. The second category, JCE II, is "a variant of the first category"[276] and is based on the so-called "concentration camp cases"[277], where "the accused held some position of authority within the hierarchy of the concentration camps [...] they had acted in pursuance of a common design to kill or mistreat prisoners and hence to commit war crimes."[278] JCE III "concerns cases involving a common design to pursue one course of conduct where one of the perpetrators commits an act which, while outside the common design, was nevertheless a natural and foreseeable consequence of the effecting of that common purpose."[279]

---

273 ibid para 195, para 220 (italics added).
274 ibid para 195 (italics added).
275 ibid paras 195, 196.
276 ibid para 203.
277 ibid para 202.
278 ibid para 202.
279 ibid para 204. For a critique in particular of JCE III see Ambos, *Treatise on International Criminal Law: Vol. I: Foundations and General Part* 141; Kai Ambos, 'Amicus Curiae Brief in the Matter of the Co-Prosecutors' Appeal on the Closing Order Against Kaing Guek Eav "Dutch" Dated 8 August 2008' (2009) 20 Criminal Law Forum 353; Mohamed Elewa Badar, ''Just Convict Everyone!'-Joint Perpetration: From Tadić to Stakić and Back Again' (2006) 6 International Criminal Law Review 293; *Interlocutory Decision on the Applicable Law: Terrorism, Conspiracy, Homicide, Perpetration, Cumulative Charging* STL AC (11 February 2011) STL-11-01/I/AC/R176bis paras 248-249 (arguing that convictions under JCE III for special intent crimes like terrorism should not be made); *Decision on the Appeals against the Co-Investigating Judges Order on Joint Criminal Enterprise (JCE)* ECCC (20 May 2010) D97/15/9 para 83 (finding that the materials relied upon by the ICTY did not "constitute a sufficiently firm basis to conclude that JCE III formed part of customary international law"); but see *Prosecutor v Stanišić & Župljanin* ICTY AC Judgeement (30 June 2016) IT-08-91-A para 599 (in favour of JCE III under customary international law); see on this jurisprudence Noora Arajärvi, 'Misinterpreting Customary International Law Corrupt Pedigree or Self-Fulfilling Prophecy?' in Panos Merkouris, Jörg Kammerhofer, and Noora Arajärvi (eds), *The Theory, Practice, and Interpretation of Customary International Law* (Cambridge University Press 2022) 50-1.

The ICTY's analysis of concepts in domestic criminal law is characterized by a certain ambiguity. On the one hand, the ICTY did not stop at terminological differences and instead adopted a functional perspective, examining the principle which underlined the municipal concepts. In this sense, the ICTY noted that post-World War II trials in Italy and Germany "took the same approach to instances of crimes in which two or more persons participated with a different degree of involvement. However, they did not rely upon the notion of common purpose or common design, preferring to refer instead to the notion of co-perpetration."[280] On the other hand, this difference led the ICTY to stress that references to municipal law "only serves to show that the notion of common purpose upheld in international criminal law has an underpinning in many national systems" and not to establish a general principle of law for which "it would be necessary to show that, in any case, the major legal systems of the world take the same approach to this notion."[281]

It is open to question whether an analysis characterized by a higher degree of abstraction could have furnished a general principle which, of course, would have to be further developed and concretized. After all, the ICTY itself recognized before that the German and Italian cases, while having adopted a "different notion", "took the same approach". However, once established, this distinction between the concept of common purpose and the concept of indirect perpetratorship played a significant role in the further development of modes of liability. It began to stand for a debate between common law approaches and continental European approaches.[282] One important question in the context of this competition of schools of thought was whether the accused high-ranking official had to be a member of the very same JCE which the physical perpetrator on the ground was part of, or whether he could used the latter as an instrument for committing crimes.

---

280 *Prosecutor v Dusko Tadić* IT-94-1-A para 201.
281 ibid para 225.
282 For an overview see Marjolein Cupido, 'Pluralism in Theories of Liability: Joint Criminal Enterprise versus Joint Perpetration' in Elies van Sliedregt and Sergey Vasiliev (eds), *Pluralism in International Criminal Law* (Oxford University Press 2014) 129 ("There is a division between scholars who affirm and welcome the ICC's approach and those who critically question the Court's distinctive course"); Sliedregt, *Individual criminal responsibility in international law* 101: "The ICC and the international criminal tribunals rely on concepts of co-perpetration that differ on conspicuous points but also overlap. Generally, there is an unwillingness on either side to uncover similarities and overlap between co-perpetration and JCE, let alone apply each other's case law with regard to these concepts."

a) Indirect perpetratorship as conceptual alternative

The *Stakić* Trial Chamber argued that JCE was

> "only one of several possible interpretations of the term 'commission' under Article 7(1) of the Statute and that other definitions of co-perpetration must equally be taken into account. Furthermore, a more direct reference to 'commission' in its traditional sense should be given priority before considering responsibility under the judicial term 'joint criminal enterprise'."[283]

The Chamber then "prefers to define 'committing' as meaning that the accused participated, *physically or otherwise directly or indirectly*, in the material elements of the crime charged through positive acts or, based on a duty to act, omissions, whether individually or jointly with others."[284] With reference to the work of the German criminal law scholar Claus Roxin, the Chamber argued that co-perpetratorship should be defined by the joint control over the act.[285] The Chamber concluded that

> "the end result of its definition of co-perpetration approaches that of the aforementioned joint criminal enterprise and even overlaps in part. However, the Trial Chamber opines that this definition is closer to what most legal systems understand as 'committing' and avoids the misleading impression that a new crime not foreseen in the Statute of this Tribunal has been introduced through the backdoor."[286]

The Trial Chamber's interpretation of Article 7(1) of the ICTY Statute was not well received by the Appeals Chamber and criticized for departing from a concept which the Appeals Chamber considered to be rooted in customary international law. The Trial Chamber's interpretation was not appealed by any of the parties, but the Appeals Chamber considered this issue to be one of "general importance warranting the scrutiny of the Appeals Chamber *proprio motu*", as the "introduction of new modes of liability into the jurisprudence of the Tribunal may generate uncertainty, if not confusion".[287] The Appeals Chamber concluded that the Trial Chamber

> "erred in conducting its analysis of the responsibility of the Appellant within the framework of 'co-perpetratorship'. This mode of liability, as defined and applied by the Trial Chamber, does not have support in customary international law and in the

---

283 *Prosecutor v Milomir Stakić* ICTY TC Judgement (31 July 2003) IT-97-24-T para 438.
284 ibid para 439 (italics added).
285 ibid para 440.
286 ibid para 441.
287 *Prosecutor v Milomir Stakić* ICTY AC Judgement (22 March 2006) IT-97-24-A para 59.

Chapter 9: International Criminal Law

settled jurisprudence of this Tribunal [...] By way of contrast, joint criminal enterprise is a mode of liability which is 'firmly established in customary international law' and is routinely applied in the Tribunal's jurisprudence."[288]

Also, the *Milutinovic* Trial Chamber acknowledged "the possibility that some species of co-perpetration and indirect perpetration can be found in various legal systems throughout the world", yet "the task before the Trial Chamber is not to determine whether co-perpetration or indirect perpetration are general principles of law. [...] Neither *Stakic* nor the Prosecution has cited any authority that convincingly establishes state practice or *opinio juris* for the *Stakic* definition."[289]

b) Attempts of reconciliation

Judge Iain Bonomy sought to reconcile the different doctrinal approaches. With respect to the questions of whether leaders at the top have to form a joint criminal enterprise with the soldiers on the ground or whether the former can use the latter as an instrument, Bonomy found the jurisprudence of the tribunal inconclusive.[290] He suggested to distinguish between small-scale criminal enterprises, where a JCE between the accused and the principal perpetrator must exist,[291] and large-scale criminal enterprises, where no JCE between the accused and the soldier on the ground as principal perpetrator must exist.[292] Based on the observation that in municipal criminal law systems

---

288 *Prosecutor v Milomir Stakić* para 62.
289 *Prosecutor v Milan Milutinović and others* IT-01-47-AR72 para 39.
290 ibid IT-01-47-AR72 Sep Op Bonomy paras 8, 13.
291 *Prosecutor v Radoslav Brđanin* IT-99-36-T para 344: "in order to hold the Accused criminally responsible for the crimes charged in the Indictment pursuant to the first category of JCE, the Prosecution must, *inter alia*, establish that between the person physically committing a crime and the Accused, there was an understanding or an agreement to commit that particular crime." See also paras 345-353, concluding that there was no evidence to establish the existence of such JCE.
292 In a case concerning a large scale enterprise, the Trial Chamber had held the accused general Krstic responsible for the conduct of footsoldiers without requiring the existence of a JCE or an agreement between them, *Prosecutor v Radislav Krstić* ICTY TC Judgement (2 August 2001) IT-98-33-T paras 607 ff., in part. paras 617-618, para 621, para 636 and para 644, where the Chamber held that while Krstic had not personally perpetrated the crimes, he had "fulfilled a key coordinating role in the implementation of the killing campaign". The Appeals Chamber did not "disturb" (*Prosecutor v Radoslav Brđanin* ICTY AC Judgement (3 April 2007) IT-99-36-A

an accused can be liable for a crime even when he had not committed the *actus reus* by himself as long as he had caused an element in the *actus reus*, Bonomy argued that the further "interpretation and delineation of the contours of JCE" should be informed by this general principle of criminal law.[293]

The *Brdanin* Appeals Chamber found in post WW II precedents confirmation for the view that an accused could be responsible for crimes which had been physically committed by another person, even when the latter had not belonged to the JCE of the accused.[294] In an attempt to consolidate the case-law and to bring indirect perpetratorship under the label of JCE,[295] the Chamber concluded, contrary to the Trial Chamber, that the physical perpetrator of a crime would not have to be a member of the JCE. Instead, members of a JCE can "use" other persons to further the common criminal purpose.[296]

---

para 408.) the Trial Chamber's reasoning, see *Prosecutor v Radislav Krstić* ICTY AC Judgement (19 April 2004) IT-98-33-A paras 134-144.

293 *Prosecutor v Milan Milutinović and others* IT-01-47-AR72 Sep Op Bonomy paras 20-26, 30. He also referred to the ICTR for the observation that many traditional cases could not be categorized clearly within the later-made up schema of JCE. His analysis might also demonstrate that practice accepted as law alone without dogmatic considerations cannot support either JCE or indirect perpetratorship alone.

294 *Prosecutor v Radoslav Brđanin* IT-99-36-A paras 394, 404 410. See also Giulia Bigi, 'Joint Criminal Enterprise in the Jurisprudence of the International Criminal Tribunal for the Former Yugoslavia and the Prosecution of Senior Political and Military Leaders: The Krajišnik Case' (2010) 14 Max Planck Yearbook of United Nations Law 74 ff.

295 Sliedregt, *Individual criminal responsibility in international law* 162-163: "While the *Stakić* Appeals Chamber had ended the life of indirect co-perpetration, the *Brđnin* Appeals Chamber seemed to have somewhat revived it, albeit under the JCE label."

296 *Prosecutor v Radoslav Brđjanin* IT-99-36-A paras 410 ff., in part. para 413: "[...] to hold a member of a JCE responsible for crimes committed by non-members of the enterprise, it has to be shown that the crime can be imputed to one member of the joint criminal enterprise, and that this member – when using a principal perpetrator – acted in accordance with the common plan. The existence of this link is a matter to be assessed on a case-by-case basis." See also paras 420 ff., holding that the JCE-doctrine concerns also large-scale cases and that JCE was not about guilt by association, ibid paras 426, 428.

2. Rome and the move towards a new paradigm

Article 25(3) of the Rome Statute distinguishes between different forms of perpetration (article 25(3)(a) Rome Statute) and different forms of participation (article 25(3)(b)-(d) Rome Statute) which include ordering, soliciting or inducing the commission of a crime (b), facilitating, aiding or abetting or otherwise assisting the commission of a crime (c), or otherwise contributing to the commission of the crime (d).

With respect to perpetration, article 25(3)(a) provides that a crime can be committed "as an individual, jointly with another or through another person, regardless whether that other person is criminally responsible." A significant change took place in the course of the drafting: after an earlier draft had limited the indirect perpetration ("through another person") to an innocent agent, meaning a perpetrator who is not criminally responsible, such limitation was ultimately deleted.[297] This change was significant as it allowed the ICC to develop indirect perpetration by means of an organization even when the direct perpetrator was not an innocent agent.

The 2007 *Lubanga* Pre-Trial Chamber decided to distinguish between principals and accessories according to the criterion of control over the crime which the PTC considered to be applied in "numerous" legal systems and searches for the criminal mastermind.[298] The Chamber ruled out alternative approaches. Given that article 25(3)(a) envisioned indirect perpetration ("through another person"), it was no apposite test to look at who objectively committed the *actus reus*.[299] Furthermore, the Chamber argued that the Statute embodied a subjective approach close to the common purpose doctrine of the ICTY in article 25(3)(d) as "residual form of accessory liabil-

---

[297] Thomas Weigend, 'Indirect Perpetration' in Carsten Stahn (ed), *The law and practice of the International Criminal Court* (Oxford University Press 2015) 542-543. Cf. Sadat and Jolly, 'Seven Canons of ICC Treaty Interpretation: Making Sense of Article 25's Rorschach Blot' 774, arguing that the traveaux would not support a strict principal/accessory distinction; critical as to a hierarchy of blameworthiness *Prosecutor v Thomas Lubanga Dyilo* ICC TC II Judgment pursuant to Article 74 of the Statute, Concurring Opinion of Judge Christine Van den Wyngaert (20 December 2012) ICC-01/04-02/12-4 para 22; *Prosecutor v Thomas Lubanga Dyilo* ICC TC I Judgment pursuant to Article 74 of the Statute, Separate Opinion of Judge Adrian Fulford (14 March 2012) ICC-01/04-01/06-2842 paras 8-9; in this sense also *Prosecutor v Germain Katanga* ICC-01/04-01/07-3436-tENG para 1386.

[298] *Prosecutor v Thomas Lubanga Dyilo* ICC PTC I Decision on the confirmation of charges (7 February 2007) ICC-01/04-01/06-803-tEN paras 328-332.

[299] ibid para 333.

ity" for contributions which fell short of constituting "ordering, soliciting, inducing, aiding, abetting or assisting within the meaning of article 25(3)(b) or article 25(3)(c)".[300] For the Chamber, this demonstrated that the drafters could have adopted, but in fact did not adopt, a subjective common purpose approach in article 25(3)(a) of the Statute.[301] The Chamber emphasized that the letter of article 25(3)(a) of the Rome Statute supports the control over the crime approach for the purposes of this distinction.[302] Thus, the Chamber was primarily concerned with treaty interpretation and did not address customary international law.[303] The Appeals Chamber supported the application of the control over the crime theory as "convincing and adequate" for the interpretation of article 25.[304]

Building on the Chamber's reasoning, the PTC in *Katanga & Chui* argued that indirect perpetration was "recognized by the major legal systems"[305] and by doctrine. The chamber referred in particular to Claus Roxin and his

---

300 ibid para 337.
301 ibid para 335.
302 ibid paras 338, 339; see also *Prosecutor v Germain Katanga and Mathieu Ngudjolo Chui* ICC PTC I Decision on the confirmation of charges (13 October 2008) ICC-01/04-01/07-717 paras 484, 485, declaring the control over crime approach as "leading principle for distinguishing between principals and accessories to a crime", being supported by also a "number of legal systems" and by doctrine.
303 Note that the prosecution submitted "that it is important to take into consideration the fundamental differences between the ad hoc tribunals and the Court, because the latter operates under a Statute which not only sets out modes of criminal liability in great detail, but also deliberately avoids the broader definitions found in, for example, article 7(1) of the ICTY Statute", *Prosecutor v Thomas Lubanga Dyilo* ICC-01/04-01/06-803-tEN para 323.
304 *Prosecutor v Thomas Lubanga Dyilo* ICC-01/04-01/06-3121-Red paras 469-473 (quote in para 469), referring also to *Prosecutor v Germain Katanga* ICC-01/04-01/07-3436-tENG paras 1394-5: "The Chamber is therefore of the view that the 'control over the crime' criterion appears the most consonant with article 25 of the Statute, taken as a whole, and best takes its surrounding context into account, in due consideration of the terms of article 30. To the Chamber, the decisive argument is not recognition of the 'control over the crime' theory in domestic legal systems. [...] Here, the prime consideration of the Chamber is to satisfy itself that the guiding principle allowing effect to be given to the distinction between the perpetrators of and accessories to a crime which, as aforementioned, inheres in article 25(3) of the Statute, enables the body of relevant provisions of this article concerning individual criminal responsibility to take full effect."
305 *Prosecutor v Germain Katanga and Mathieu Ngudjolo Chui* ICC-01/04-01/07-717 para 495.

theory according to which an indirect perpetrator can act through a direct perpetrator if the direct perpetrator is embedded into a hierarchical structure and the indirect perpetrator assumes control over the organization.[306] The PTC presented three arguments in favour of perpetration through control over the organization. It had been incorporated into the statute, because "by specifically regulating the commission of a crime through another responsible person, the Statute targets the category of cases which involves a perpetrator's control over the organization"[307]; it was "increasingly used" in national jurisdictions[308] and was addressed in jurisprudence of "international tribunals".[309] A contrary decision such as the Argentinian Supreme Court's rejection of the control over the organization approach was rejected as not relevant within the framework of the Rome Statute which would expressively provide for indirect perpetratorship.[310] Moreover, contrary judgments of the ICTY were characterized as not apposite as they were said to be concerned with customary international law:

> "However, under article 21(1)(a) of the Statute, the first source of applicable law is the Statute. Principles and rules of international law constitute a secondary source applicable only when the statutory material fails to prescribe a legal solution. Therefore, and since the Rome Statute expressly provides for this specific mode of liability, the question as to whether customary law admits or discards the 'joint commission through another person' is not relevant for this Court. This is a good example of the

---

306 *Prosecutor v Germain Katanga and Mathieu Ngudjolo Chui* paras 496-499 ff.; see also *Prosecutor v Germain Katanga* ICC-01/04-01/07-3436-tENG para 1404; cf. Claus Roxin, 'Straftaten im Rahmen organisatorischer Machtapparate' [1963] (7) Goltdammer's Archiv für Strafrecht 201 ff.; Claus Roxin, *Strafrecht Allgemeiner Teil Band II Besondere Erscheinungsformen der Straftat* (vol 2, Beck 2003) 46-58; on Roxin see also Sliedregt, *Individual criminal responsibility in international law* 81-83; for a critique of the reliance on sources see Chantal Meloni, 'Fragmentation of the Notion of Co-perpetration in International Criminal Law?' in Larissa J van den Herik and Carsten Stahn (eds), *The diversification and fragmentation of international criminal law* (M Nijhoff Publishers 2012) 499.
307 *Prosecutor v Germain Katanga and Mathieu Ngudjolo Chui* ICC-01/04-01/07-717 para 501.
308 ibid ICC-01/04-01/07-717 para 502 footnote 666, referring to judgments delivered by the German Supreme Court, the Federal Appeals Chamber of Argentina (which was later overturned by the Supreme Court), the Supreme Court of Justice of Peru, the Supreme Court of Chile, the Supreme Tribunal of Spain as well as the National Court of Spain.
309 ibid para 500.
310 ibid para 505.

The Interrelationship of Sources and the Rome Statute

need not to transfer the *ad hoc* tribunals' case law mechanically to the system of the Court."[311]

The PTC defined the hierarchical structure[312] and the fact that the execution of crimes would be "secured by almost automatic compliance with orders"[313], which is why "the actual executor of the order is merely fungible individual"[314], as important aspects of such organisational apparatus. According to the Chamber, "[a]n alternative means by which a leader secures automatic compliance via his control of the apparatus may be through intensive, strict, and violent training regimens."[315] In addition, the PTC recognized that co-perpetration can be based on joint control over the crime, meaning two or more persons act in a concerted manner for the purpose of committing a crime through another person.[316]

---

311 ibid para 508. See also Sliedregt and Yanev, 'Co-Perpetration Based on Joint Control over the Crime' 94 (on the focus on the ICC Statute and on the importance of customary international law for the legality principle), 110.

312 *Prosecutor v Germain Katanga and Mathieu Ngudjolo Chui* ICC-01/04-01/07-717 para 512.

313 ibid para 515. See also *Prosecutor v Germain Katanga* ICC-01/04-01/07-3436-tENG para 1408.

314 *Prosecutor v Germain Katanga and Mathieu Ngudjolo Chui* ICC-01/04-01/07-717 para 516, with references to German commentaries on the German criminal code.

315 ibid para 518. See Kai Ambos, 'Article 25' in Kai Ambos (ed), *Rome Statute of the International Criminal Court: a commentary* (4th edn, Beck 2021) para 14 (arguing that these factors "arguably capture better [than the fungibility criterion] the typical lack of institutional autonomy of a direct perpertrator acting in a macro-criminal context given the institutionalist pressure exercised by the criminal system or organization upon him", while acknowledging also "specific *evidentiary challenges* to prove the organizational control".

316 *Prosecutor v Germain Katanga and Mathieu Ngudjolo Chui* ICC-01/04-01/07-717 paras 521-522, para 492; see also Ambos, 'Article 25' para 17 ("indirect co-perpetration ('*mittelbare Mittäterschaft*') which however does not constitute a new (fourth) mode of attribution"). Sliedregt and Yanev, 'Co-Perpetration Based on Joint Control over the Crime' 110-114 (pointing out that the Appeals Chamber "did not have the opportunity to rule on the status of indirect co-perpetration, as Katanga decided not to appeal his conviction."), and 116 ("indirect co-perpetration with control through an OSP cannot be regarded as having the status of customary international law [...] It is a theory that is premised on German law and criminal law theory (Roxin)."); for a critique see *Prosecutor v Thomas Lubanga Dyilo* Concurring Opinion of Judge Christine Van den Wyngaert ICC-01/04-02/12-4 paras 58-64 (new mode of liability); cf. Jens David Ohlin, Elies van Sliedregt, and Thomas Weigend, 'Assessing the Control-Theory' (2013) 26 Leiden Journal of International Law 734-738 ("Van den Wyngaert was right to express caution about this mode of liability

In contrast to this situation, where each of the two defendants had control over a separate organization and was held responsible for crimes committed by the members of the other defendant's organization, the *Blé Goudé* PTC also recognized "a form of joint indirect perpetratorship (*'Mittäterschaft in mittelbarer Täterschaft'*) [...] [where] leaders exercise joint control over one hierarchical organization."[317]

Recently, the Appeals Chamber by majority upheld the Trial Chamber's conviction of Bosco Ntaganda based on indirect co-perpetratorship and thus endorsed this doctrine.[318]

3. Evaluation: institutional and conceptual competition instead of conflict of sources

At first sight, the existence of two standards, JCE on the one hand and control theory or indirect perpetratorship on the other hand, can in the context of this study raise associations to the delimitation of the continental shelf with

---

[...] None of this suggests that an adequate theory of indirect co-perpetration cannot be constructed. However, it cannot be merely assumed, and that theory is certainly not a straightforward application of the bare text of the Statute.").

317 Ambos, 'Article 25' para 17; *Prosecutor v Blé Goudé* ICC PTC Decision on the Confirmation of Charges (11 December 2014) ICC-02/11-02/11-186 paras 136-137, 149.

318 See *Prosecutor v Bosco Ntaganda, ICC TC VI Judgment (8 July 2019)* ICC-01/04-02/06-2359 paras 771-857 and pp. 535-8; *Prosecutor v Bosco Ntaganda, ICC AC Judgment on the appeals of Mr Bosco Ntaganda and the Prosecutor against the decision of Trial Chamber VI of 8 July 2019 entitled 'Judgment' (30 March 2021)* ICC-01/04-02/06-2666-Red paras 879-80, 1170; cf. *Prosecutor v Bosco Ntaganda* ICC AC Judgment on the appeals, Partly Concurring Opinion of Judge Eboe-Osujit (30 March 2021) ICC-01/04-02/06-2666-Anx5 paras 13-102 (arguing against indirect co-perpetratorship and control theory and the need for a distinction between perpetrators and accessories); cf. *Prosecutor v Bosco Ntaganda* ICC AC Judgment on the appeals, Separate Opinion of Judge Howard Morrison (30 March 2021) ICC-01/04-02/06-2666-Anx2 paras 1-42 (expressing concerns regarding the theory of indirect co-perpetration, while subscribing to the conviction based on it); cf. *Prosecutor v Bosco Ntaganda* ICC AC Judgment on the appeals, Separate opinion of Judge Luz Del Carmen Ibáñez Carranza (30 March 2021) ICC-01/04-02/06-2666-Anx3 para 214 (defending the interpretation that article 25(3)(a) of the Statute as encompasses indirect co-perpetration); for an analysis see Marjolein Cupido, 'The Control Theory as Multidimensional Concept. Reflections on the Ntaganda Appeal Judgment' (2022) 20 JICJ 637 ff.

respect to which either the equidistance-special circumstances rule or the equitable principles were applied. Unlike in the maritime field, however, where the development of both concepts was, by and large, in the hand of the same court, namely the ICJ, the two concepts of criminal responsibility are associated with different courts and tribunals. This and the competing schools of thought, which respectively promote one of the two concepts, may explain the perception that both concepts are rivals based on different rationales.[319] Yet, it has been pointed out that both concepts pursue similar objectives and share similar features, for instance in their focus on the systemic character of the criminal enterprise.[320]

The differences between both concepts can be explained by different conceptual approaches, doctrinal preconceptions and different visions of how

---

319 Cf. the overview by Cupido, 'Pluralism in Theories of Liability: Joint Criminal Enterprise versus Joint Perpetration', 128-9 (the doctrine of indirect perpetration is rather objective in that it focuses on the *actus reus*, whereas the doctrine of JCE is rather subjective in that it focuses on the common purpose).

320 Kai Ambos, 'Joint Criminal Enterprise and Command Responsibility' (2007) 5(1) JICJ 183; Kai Ambos, 'Command Responsibility and Organisationsherrschaft: Ways of Attributing International Crimes to the Most Responsible' in Harmen van der Wilt and André Nollkaemper (eds), *System criminality in international law* (Cambridge University Press 2009) 157 ("[...] ultimately, the doctrine of *Organisationsherrschaft* confirms what has been identified as the underlying rationales of JCE and also command responsibility"); Florian Jeßberger and Julia Geneuss, 'On the Application of a Theory of Indirect Perpetration in Al Bashir' (2008) 6 JICJ 868 ("applying the admittedly novel concept of indirect perpetration, it may be argued, as a mere 'functional equivalent' to other, firmly acknowledged modes of liability would not necessarily render the decision incorrect with a view to meeting customary law standard."); see also Cupido, 'Pluralism in Theories of Liability: Joint Criminal Enterprise versus Joint Perpetration' 150-158 ("The alleged objective–subjective dichotomy between these theories of liability is nominal rather than actual and should therefore be banned from the debate on theories of liability" (158); Sliedregt, 'Perpetration and Participation in Article 25(3)' 515-516; Ambos, 'Article 25' para 13 (on traces of the doctrine of control over an organization in post WW II case-law); on this aspect see also Heller, *The Nuremberg Military Tribunals and the Origins of International Criminal Law* 271-2; Robert Charles Clarke, 'Together Again? Customary Law and Control over the Crime' (2015) 26 Criminal Law Forum 458; on the differences see Sliedregt and Yanev, 'Co-Perpetration Based on Joint Control over the Crime' 113 ("JCE requires proof of a *significant* instead of an *essential* contribution [...] JCE liability allows for *dolus eventualis* whereas liability under Article 25(3) of the ICC Statute requires *dolus directus* [...]"); Yanev, 'Joint Criminal Enterprise' 131-2; Lachezar D Yanev, *Theories of Co-Perpetration in International Criminal Law* (Brill Nijhoff 2018) 546.

Chapter 9: International Criminal Law

international criminal law should develop.[321] For instance, if one rejects a substantial distinction between perpetrators and accomplices in the field of international criminal law for sentencing purposes, one can be critical of control theory as means for distinguishing forms of participation.[322] If one reads article 25(3) of the ICC Statute as rejection of the *Einheitstätermodell*[323], and if one is of the view that different labels are appropriate for the purposes of labelling justice, with a view to considering the different forms of participation in sentencing,[324] one may look more favourably at the ICC jurisprudence.

The examples of JCE and indirect perpetratorship illustrate the importance of *Dogmatik*[325], of doctrinal considerations, for both concepts[326] when

---

321 Cf. Jens David Ohlin, 'Co-Perpetration: German Dogmatik or German Invasion?' in Carsten Stahn (ed), *The law and practice of the International Criminal Court* (Oxford University Press 2015) 517, speaking of a "the clash of legal traditions embodied by competing doctrinal paradigms"; see also Mikkel Jarle Christensen and Nabil M Orina, 'The International Criminal Court as a Law Laboratory. Professional Battles of Control and the 'Control of the Crime' Theory' (2022) 20 JICJ 699 ff.

322 Judges Fulford and Van den Wyngaert who in two individual opinions voiced criticism against control theory and indirect perpetratorship both rejected any distinction between perpetrators and accomplices, *Prosecutor v Thomas Lubanga Dyilo* ICC-01/04-01/06-2842 Sep Op Fulford para 11; *Prosecutor v Mathieu Ngudjolo Chui* ICC TC II Judgment pursuant to Article 74 of the Statute (18 December 2012) ICC-01/04-02/12-3-tENG Conc Op Judge Van den Wyngaert paras 24-26; cf. Ohlin, Sliedregt, and Weigend, 'Assessing the Control-Theory' 740 ff.; see recently *Prosecutor v Bosco Ntaganda* paras 29-76; *Prosecutor v Bosco Ntaganda* Sep Op Morrison ICC-01/04-02/06-2666-Anx2 paras 7 ff.

323 Ambos, 'Article 25' para 2: "This approach confirms the general tendency in comparative criminal law to reject a pure unitarian concept of perpetration (*Einheitstätermodell*) and to distinguish, at least on the sentencing level, between different forms of participation."; Yanev, *Theories of Co-Perpetration in International Criminal Law* 539; for a different view see Sadat and Jolly, 'Seven Canons of ICC Treaty Interpretation: Making Sense of Article 25's Rorschach Blot' 774-775.

324 Cf. *Sylvestre Gacumbitsi v The Prosecutor: ICTR* ICTR AC Judgement (7 July 2006) ICTR-2001-64-A Sep Op Schomburg paras 6 ff.; cf. for the possible effects on sentencing Ohlin, Sliedregt, and Weigend, 'Assessing the Control-Theory' 745 footnote 91; Ohlin, 'Co-Perpetration: German Dogmatik or German Invasion?' 530-531.

325 Cf. generally George P Fletcher, 'New Court, Old Dogmatik' (2011) 9 JICJ 179, in particular at 184 on the ICC; Ohlin, 'Co-Perpetration: German Dogmatik or German Invasion?' 517 ff.; Sliedregt, 'Perpetration and Participation in Article 25(3)' 515.

326 As Ohlin, Sliedregt, and Weigend, 'Assessing the Control-Theory' 525, 527 correctly observe, whereas the PTC may have developed "an ICC-specific *Dogmatik*", "any

The Interrelationship of Sources and the Rome Statute

identifying customary international law or interpreting a treaty provision. If the debate focuses only on the question of whether indirect perpetratorship is "customary international law" or a "general principle of law"[327], the debate may not sufficiently take account of the difference between the norm and the legal conceptualization that occurs in the interpretation and application of the norm. In this sense, the *Lubanga* Appeal Chamber rightfully remarked

> "that it is not proposing to apply a particular legal doctrine or theory as a source of law. Rather, it is interpreting and applying article 25(3)(a) of the Statute. In doing so, the Appeals Chamber considers it appropriate to seek guidance from approaches developed in other jurisdictions in order to reach a coherent and persuasive interpretation of the Court's legal text."[328]

It is submitted that similar considerations apply to JCE in that doctrinal perspectives and legal technique were involved in constructing three categories

---

approach will inevitably prejudice either a civil-law or common-law approach to perpetration. If a court adopts JCE, it looks suspiciously like conspiracy or other common law modes of liability. If a court adopts co-perpetration based on the control theory, it looks suspiciously like a civil-law approach to co-perpetration."

327 Cf. Sadat and Jolly, 'Seven Canons of ICC Treaty Interpretation: Making Sense of Article 25's Rorschach Blot' 757, 784; see also Powderly, *Judges and the Making of International Criminal Law* 477 (arguing that "a persuasive argument could perhaps be made that co-perpetration ought to be considered a general principle of law in accordance with Article 21(1)(c). However, the Chamber makes no effort to provide such an insight."), see also 484, arguing that a purely textual understanding of article 25(3)(a) is unpersuasive.

328 *Prosecutor v Thomas Lubanga Dyilo* ICC-01/04-01/06-3121-Red para 470; see also *Prosecutor v Germain Katanga* ICC-01/04-01/07-3436-tENG para 1406: "For the Chamber, this does not mean that the theory of control over the organisation is the one and only legal solution that allows the provisions of article 25(3)(a) concerning commission by an intermediary to be construed. As such, the theory need not be held up as an essential constituent element of commission by an intermediary. As mentioned above, the sole indispensable criterion, in its view, is the indirect perpetrator's exertion, in or other some fashion, including from within an organisation, of control over the crime committed through another person." Critical Yanev, *Theories of Co-Perpetration in International Criminal Law* 553-555 (arguing at 553: "The approach that the ICC Chambers have taken on this matter so far shows a regrettable tendency to purposely seek departure from, rather than cohesion with, the settled international case law"; "[...] it is evident that the ICC's adoption of the joint control approach to co-perpetration liability was a matter of choice and not a decision that is strictly required by the text of Article 25(3)", at 555); see also Tan, *The Rome Statute as Evidence of Customary International Law* 284, 311.

Chapter 9: International Criminal Law

based on an analysis of international and national jurisprudence.[329] Of course, the *Stakić* Appeals Chamber rejected the Trial Chamber's "framework of 'co-perpetratorship'" because joint criminal enterprise "is a mode of liability which is 'firmly established in customary international law'"[330]. However, also the ICTY's conceptualization of the international and domestic practice into three specific categories of JCE was arguably not completely dictated by customary international law and can be seen as a conceptualization which can and must be subject to debate. Apparently, it was possible, as demonstrated by Iain Bonomy or the *Brdanin* Appeals Chamber, to search for ways to reconcile the different concepts. If one acknowledges the degree of doctrinal conceptualization involved in formulating a legal rule on the basis of one's evaluation of a general practice accepted as law, it may be possible to identify common ground and to discuss the substantive merits of each concept from the perspective of international criminal law, rather than from the perspective of a sources discussion.[331] It is, therefore, suggested that the dissent that leads

---

329 Cf. for different perspectives *Prosecutor v Blagoje Simić, ICTY TC Judgement* (17 October 2003) IT-95-9-T Sep and Partly Diss Op Lindholm 314 para 2: "The so-called basic form of joint criminal enterprise does not, in my opinion, have any substance of its own. It is nothing more than a new label affixed to a since long well-known concept or doctrine in most jurisdictions as well as in international criminal law, namely co-perpetration."; *Prosecutor v Blagoje Simić, ICTY AC Judgement* (28 November 2006) IT-95-9-A Diss Op Shahabuddeen 124 para 32 (co-perpetratorship and JCE are different); Diss Op Schomburg 130 para 14: "Since Nuremberg and Tokyo, both national and international criminal law have come to accept, in particular, co-perpetratorship as a form of committing" and 130 para 18: "In my opinion, this approach towards interpreting committing is clearly reconcilable with the Tadić Appeal Judgement, which introduced joint criminal enterprise into ICTY jurisprudence. However, the Tadić Appeal Judgement does not only refer to 'common (criminal) design', but also speaks expressly of 'co-perpetrators'."
330 *Prosecutor v Milomir Stakić* IT-97-24-A para 62, referring to *Prosecutor v Dusko Tadić* IT-94-1-A para 220.
331 See for instance Stefano Manacorda and Chantal Meloni, 'Indirect Perpetration versus Joint Criminal Enterprise. Concurring Approaches in the Practice of International Criminal Law?' (2011) 9 Journal of International Criminal Justice 165-167, arguing that JCE is a label encompassing "a variety of criteria" (165), the doctrine led to "divergent results" (166) and is problematic from the perspective of the principle of culpability (166-167); Ohlin, Sliedregt, and Weigend, 'Assessing the Control-Theory' 735-736 f., expressing reservations about the combination of modes of liability and arguing that an adequate theory of indirect co-perpetration "is certainly not a straightforward application of the bare text of the Statute" and needs to be constructed, also arguing (745) that "control theory does not provide the limitation

to the competing concepts lies at the level of doctrinal conceptualisation rather than in an irresolvable conflict between customary international law and the Rome Statute.

Nevertheless, as the ICTY referred to customary international law and the ICC primarily[332] relied on an interpretation of treaty law, the impression has emerged that one now is left with two different standards associated with customary international and the Rome Statute, if one is not of the view that the interpretation of article 25 Rome Statute had an effect on customary international law.[333] According to Yanev's evaluation, this jurisprudence of the ICC is but another example of a "regrettable tendency to purposely seek departure from, rather than cohesion with, the settled international case law, from Nuremberg to The Hague".[334] However, as stated above, it is doubtful whether all conceptual details of JCE can be equated with customary international law; arguably, customary international law is less precise in relation to modes of liability than it is in relation to crimes.[335] Ultimately,

---

of liability that some expected it to bring." For a focus on the way in which the notion of "control" is applied in case-law, see recently Cupido, 'The Control Theory as Multidimensional Concept. Reflections on the Ntaganda Appeal Judgment' 639 ff.; for ordering liability under article 25(3)(b) Rome Statute as conceptual alternative see Johannes Block, 'Ordering as an Alternative to Indirect Co-Perpetration. Observations on the Ntaganda Case' (2022) 20 JICJ 717 ff.

332 See above, p. 536; but cf. also Clarke, 'Together Again? Customary Law and Control over the Crime' 465: "[...] the Appeals Chamber did hint at a broader international legal pedigree for the principle, linking its preference for control over the crime as a 'normative [criterion] to distinguish co-perpetrators' to JCE doctrine"; cf. *Prosecutor v Thomas Lubanga Dyilo* ICC-01/04-01/06-3121-Red paras 445, 471: "Notably, the notion of joint criminal enterprise developed by the ad hoc tribunals also uses normative criteria to distinguish co-perpetrators from accessories, although it puts the emphasis on a subjective criterion and not on an objective one."

333 Cf. Thomas Weigend, 'Perpetration through an Organization: The Unexpected Career of a German Legal Concept' (2011) 9(1) JICJ 106 ("[...] I would regard the issue as still open. There is certainly nothing to even remotely suggest that the concept of 'perpetration through an organization' is a form of criminal liability recognized as customary international law").

334 See Yanev, *Theories of Co-Perpetration in International Criminal Law* 553-5, quote at 553, see also 564, concluding that "the 'basic' (and by extension the 'systemic') form of jce is rightly regarded by the modern international tribunals as a customary form of co-perpetration responsibility." See also 564-567, concluding that JCE is not part of customary international law.

335 Cf. Kreß, 'War Crimes Committed in Non-International Armed Conflict and the Emerging System of International Criminal Justice' 143, arguing that "[d]ue to the

different criminal law preferences, which had articulated themselves already in the jurisprudence of the ICTY, asserted themselves in the context of the ICC, and control theory was regarded by the majority in the chambers to be a good fit for article 25 Rome Statute.[336]

Whether these "two streams"[337] need to be bridged by a new unified theory which is not attached to one particular legal or Western tradition[338] or whether one will see that only one concept will eventually assert itself in international practice, only time will tell. As far as the emancipation from "domestic" doctrines is concerned, it is likely that the doctrine of control theory will be adapted to the present specificities of international criminal law. This applies arguably also to the doctrinal construct of the perpetrator behind the perpetrator, even though this doctrine is, at least in the German legal system, not a tool for everyday criminality but specifically designed to address situations which international criminal law is concerned with. Having in mind the *Eichmann*[339] process, Claus Roxin developed this doctrinal construct as exception to the innocent agent rule, according to which a perpetrator can

---

paucity of customary international law ICTY and ICTR had to undertake a good deal of comparative legal research with a view to identify and applicable principle of law." He also noted that the drafters of the Rome Statute "did not consider their exercise of drafting general principles of criminal law to be a matter of codifying existing customary law as the did with respect to the definitions of crimes. Rather, they consciously acted as international legislators."

336 For the view that the identification of a principle if informed by the setting in which the principle will be applied see above, Fn. 194.
337 Yanev, *Theories of Co-Perpetration in International Criminal Law* 547.
338 Cf. in this regard James G Stewart, 'Ten Reasons for Adopting a Universal Concept of Participation in Atrocity' in Elies van Sliedregt and Sergey Vasiliev (eds), *Pluralism in International Criminal Law* (Oxford University Press 2014) 334-335; cf. Ohlin, 'Co-Perpetration: German Dogmatik or German Invasion?' 537. Further comparative research may identify functionally equivalent theories in other legal orders, see for the view that the Japanese legal order knows of attribution mechanisms that are similar to indirect co-perpetrationship Philipp Osten, 'Indirect Co-Perpetration and the Control Theory. A Japanese Perspective' (2022) 20 JICJ 689 and 696 ("even though the original doctrine was (and is) not in its entirety the prevailing theory in Japanese case law and scholarship, the control theory as adopted by the ICC jurisprudence and the concepts of perpetration based on this theory [...] were for the most part evaluated by Japanese commentators as adequate theoretical concepts, by and large compatible with the statutory frame- work provided by Article 25(3)").
339 *Attorney General v Adolf Eichmann* District Court of Israel; cf. Kai Ambos, 'Adolf Eichmann' in *The Cambridge Companion to International Criminal Law* (Cambridge University Press 2016) 275 ff.

commit a crime through another person only in cases of innocent agents as opposed to fully responsible perpetrators.[340] In this sense, the power by bureaucracy (*Organisationsherrschaft*) was not intended to be a theoretical concept for German municipal criminal law[341], it was crafted to specifically address situations that fall within the scope of international criminal law.[342]

Being a child of its time and drawing "its lifeblood from the intuitive persuasiveness of holding the leaders of National-Socialist organizations such as the SS responsible as perpetrators of the mass atrocities committed by the members of these organizations"[343], the concept of indirect perpetratorship will need to be adapted to the new challenges, for instance holding key figures

---

340 Roxin, 'Straftaten im Rahmen organisatorischer Machtapparate' 201 ff.; Roxin, *Strafrecht Allgemeiner Teil Band II Besondere Erscheinungsformen der Straftat* 46-58. For an overview see Jeßberger and Geneuss, 'On the Application of a Theory of Indirect Perpetration in Al Bashir' 859-862. The question of how a state leader can be responsible for conduct perpetrated by fully responsible individuals has been approached by Murmann. Murmann proposes to imagine two chains or relations of responsibility. The responsibility of the direct perpetrator would result from the violation in the relation *vis-à-vis* the other individual; the relationship of state leaders would be based on a violation of a state's duty to protect through the use of the state's unique *Verletzungsmacht*; see Uwe Murmann, 'Tatherrschaft durch Weisungsmacht' (1996) 143(1) Goltdammer's Archiv für Strafrecht 276-278; Ambos, 'Command Responsibility and Organisationsherrschaft: Ways of Attributing International Crimes to the Most Responsible' 149.

341 For this reason, it is misleading to argue that the concept would not fit outside the German law context in international criminal law, cf. *Prosecutor v Thomas Lubanga Dyilo* ICC-01/04-01/06-2842 Sep Op Fulford paras 7 ff; *Prosecutor v Mathieu Ngudjolo Chui* Judgment pursuant to Article 74 of the Statute Concurring Opinion of Judge Christine Van den Wyngaert (18 December 2012) ICC-01/04-02/12-4 para 27 ff.

342 Ambos, 'Joint Criminal Enterprise and Command Responsibility' 182.

343 Weigend, 'Perpetration through an Organization: The Unexpected Career of a German Legal Concept' 104; see also Meloni, 'Fragmentation of the Notion of Co-perpetration in International Criminal Law?' 502 (concept perhaps too hierarchical); Manacorda and Meloni, 'Indirect Perpetration versus Joint Criminal Enterprise. Concurring Approaches in the Practice of International Criminal Law?' 171. But see *Prosecutor v Germain Katanga* ICC-01/04-01/07-3436-tENG para 1410: "To the Chamber, this type of structure, proof of whose existence in both a factual and legal sense presents a particular challenge, is not, however, inconsistent with the very varied manifestations of modern-day group criminality wherever it arises. It cannot be reduced solely to bureaucracies akin to those of Third Reich Germany and which lie at the root of the theory."

of a non-state apparatus, as opposed to a state apparatus, accountable.[344] Whilst this doctrine might not lose its German origin, it will have to adapt to the international context and then becomes more and more an international doctrine, just like general principles of law recognized *in foro domestico* will take a shape that aligns with the international legal order and may look different from the shape in domestic settings.[345]

IV. (No) Immunities under customary international law

The question of the relationship between immunities under customary international law and the Rome Statute arose recently in the context of the *Al-Bashir* case[346], which concerned immunity *ratione personae* of a then sitting head of state. If one accepts the *Milošević* indictment[347] and the *Taylor* indictment[348] as precedents for or confirmation of the proposition that im-

---

344 One proposal has already been made by the ICC: the PTC defined the hierarchical structure by the fact that the execution of crimes would be "secured by almost automatic compliance with orders", for instance because of the replaceability of individual soldiers or through "intensive, strict, and violent training regimens", *Prosecutor v Germain Katanga and Mathieu Ngudjolo Chui* ICC-01/04-01/07-717 paras 515, 518.
345 Cf. recently Hernán Darío Orozco López and Natalia Silva Santaularia, 'Reflections on Indirect (Co-)Perpetration through an Organization' (2022) 20 JICJ 666-7.
346 See above, p. 330 for the immunity discussion in the ILC.
347 *Prosecutor v Slobodan Milošević* Decision on Review of Indictment and Application for Consequential Orders, Judge David Hunt (24 May 1999) IT-02-54 para 38; Dapo Akande, 'International Law Immunities and the International Criminal Court' (2004) 98 AJIL 417 footnote 70, arguing that at the time of the indictment, "there was some doubt as to whether the FRY was a member of the United Nations" but "by the time Milošević was handed over to the ICTY in June 2001, the FRY had been admitted to the United Nations (in 2000). In any event, surrender by the FRY would have constituted a waiver of any available immunities." Cf. Kreß, 'Article 98' para 119 ("first judicial precedent for the exercise of jurisdiction by an international criminal tribunal over an incumbent Head of State.").
348 *Prosecutor v Charles Ghankay Taylor* Special Court of Sierra Leone, AC Decision on Immunity from Jurisdiction (31 May 2004) SCSL-2003-01-I paras 51-2: "[T]he principle of state immunity derives from the equality of sovereign states and therefore has no relevance to international criminal tribunals which are not organs of a state but derive their mandate from the international community [...] the principle seems now established that the sovereign equality of states does not prevent a Head of State from being prosecuted before an international criminal tribunal or court." Crit.

The Interrelationship of Sources and the Rome Statute

munity *ratione personae* does not apply before international tribunals where those have jurisdiction,[349] the question may arise whether this proposition holds true also in the horizontal relationship between states when one state is requested by the ICC to arrest a sitting head of state.[350]

This section will first give an overview of the Rome Statute's legal regime concerning immunities (1.). It will then illustrate the different positions on immunities under customary international law by different chambers (2.) and the Appeals Chamber (3.).

1. The legal regime

The ICC's jurisdiction extends to crimes committed on the territory of a state party (article 12(2)(a) Rome Statute), even if committed by citizens of non-State parties, crimes which nationals of a state parties were accused of (article 12(2)(b) Rome Statute), crimes on the territory of a non-State party if the non-State party accepted the exercise of the ICC's jurisdiction (article 12(3) Rome Statute) and situations referred by the UN Security Council (article 13(b) Rome Statute).

Article 27(2) of the Rome Statute stipulates in its second paragraph that a person's immunity under national or international law "shall not bar the Court from exercising its jurisdiction over such a person."

Article 98 of the Statute then stipulates that the ICC may not "proceed with a request for surrender or assistance which would require the requested State to act inconsistently with its obligations under international law with respect

---

Micaela Frulli, 'The Question of Charles Taylor's Immunity' (2004) 2 JICJ 1122-4 (arguing that the judges did not pay sufficient regard to the "treaty nature of the SCSL [...] avoid[ing] explicitly addressing *the question of whether a treaty-based court may remove immunities accruing to incumbent high-ranking third states' officials.*"); Rosanne van Alebeek, *The Immunity of States and Their Officials in International Criminal Law and International Human Rights Law* (Oxford University Press 2008) 290.

349 Cf. *Arrest Warrant of 11 April 2000* [2002] ICJ Rep 3, 25 para 61: "[...] an incumbent or former Minister for Foreign Affairs may be subject to criminal proceedings before certain international criminal courts, where they have jurisdiction. Examples include the International Criminal Tribunal for the former Yugoslavia, and the International Criminal Tribunal for Rwanda, established pursuant to Security Council resolutions under Chapter VII of the United Nations Charter, and the future International Criminal Court created by the 1998 Rome Convention."

350 See also Kreß, 'Article 98' para 97.

to the State or diplomatic immunity" (article 98(1)) or with its obligations under "international agreements pursuant to which the consent of a sending State is required to surrender a person of that State to the Court" (article 98(2)).[351]

2. The *Al-Bashir* case

In 2005, the Security Council referred the situation in Darfur to the ICC and decided "that the Government of Sudan and all other parties to the conflict in Darfur shall cooperate fully with and provide any necessary assistance to the Court and the Prosecutor".[352] It emerges from the resolution's text that Sudan was put into a position analogous to a State party *vis-à-vis* the ICC and that, therefore, head of state immunity did not constitute a bar for the International Criminal Court. Yet, the resolution does not explicitly address the relationship between Sudan and the member states of the Rome regime, which raises the question of whether head of state immunity may apply as a matter of customary international law in the relationship between Sudan and state parties to the Rome Statute.[353]

According to one view, article 27 Rome Statute reflected customary international law, which is why head of states were not entitled to immunity from the jurisdiction of an international criminal court such as the ICC. This view was held by the Pre-Trial Chambers in *Malawi* and in *Chad*.[354] Since

---

351 According to Dapo Akande, whilst article 27 governs the relationship between states parties to the effect immunities under international law constitute a bar neither in the relation to the court, nor in relation to other States parties, article 98(1) concerns the relationship between State parties and non-State parties only, Akande, 'International Law Immunities and the International Criminal Court' 419 ff.; on a recent scholarly treatment of potential treaty conflicts between agreements in the sense of article 98(2) Rome Statute and obligations under the Rome Statute see Surabhi Ranganathan, *Strategically Created Treaty Conflicts and the Politics of International Law* (Cambridge University Press 2014) 212-281.
352 UNSC Res 1593 (31 March 2005) UN Doc S/RES/1593(2005) para 2.
353 For this view see Dire Tladi, 'The Duty on South Africa to Arrest and Surrender President Al-Bashir Under South African and International Law: A Perspective from International Law' (2015) 13(5) JICJ 1035, 1037, 1040; cf. also Paola Gaeta, 'Does President Al Bashir Enjoy Immunity from Arrest?' (2009) 7 JICJ 324, 332.
354 *Prosecutor v Omar Hassan Ahmad Al Bashir* ICC PTC I Decision Pursuant to Article 87(7) of the Rome Statute on the Failure by the Republic of Malawi to Comply with the Cooperation Requests Issued by the Court with Respect to the

"customary international law creates an exception to Head of State immunity when international courts seek a Head of State's arrest for the commission of international crimes", there was "no conflict between Malawi's obligations towards the Court and its obligations under customary international law; therefore, article 98(1) of the Statute does not apply."[355]

In response to the criticism of this approach,[356] the PTC II chose a different reasoning to arrive at the same result of the non-availability of immunity in the specific case: whilst article 27 of the Rome Statute applied only *inter partes*, UNSCR 1593 (2005) "was meant to eliminate any impediment to the proceedings before the Court, including the lifting of immunities [...] Consequently, there also exists no impediment at the horizontal level between the DRC and Sudan [...]."[357] The PTC II considered itself "unable to identify

---

Arrest and Surrender of Omar Hassan Ahmad Al Bashir (13 December 2011) ICC-02/05-01/09-139-Corr paras 36, 43: *Prosecutor v Omar Hassan Ahmad Al Bashir* ICC PTC I Decision pursuant to article 87(7) of the Rome Statute on the refusal of the Republic of Chad to comply with the cooperation requests issued by the Court with respect to the arrest and surrender of Omar Hassan Ahmad Al Bashir (13 December 2011) ICC-02/05-01/09-140-tENG paras 13-14.

355 *Prosecutor v Omar Hassan Ahmad Al Bashir* ICC-02/05-01/09-139-Corr para 43.
356 Cf. for an overview Nerina Boschiero, 'The ICC Judicial Finding on Non-cooperation Against the DRC and No Immunity for Al-Bashir Based on UNSC Resolution 1593' (2015) 13 JICJ 636-639.
357 *Prosecutor v Omar Hassan Ahmad Al Bashir* ICC PTC II Decision on the Cooperation of the Democratic Republic of the Congo Regarding Omar Al Bashir's Arrest and Surrender to the Court (9 April 2014) ICC-02/05-01/09-195 paras 25-29. Cf. for a similar reasoning based on the UNSC resolution Dapo Akande, 'The Legal Nature of Security Council Referrals to the ICC and its Impact on Al Bashir's Immunities' (2009) 7 JICJ 342; Erika de Wet, 'Referrals to the International Criminal Court under Chapter VII of the United Nations Charter and the Immunity of Foreign State Officials' (2018) 112 AJIL Unbound 35-37. See also for the argument that the UNSCR imposes the obligation to waive, rather than waives, the immunity of Al-Bashir (Michiel Blommestijn and Cedric Ryngaert, 'Exploring the Obligations for States to Act upon the ICC's Arrest Warrant for Omar Al-Bashir: A Legal Conflict between the Duty to Arrest and the Customary Status of Head of State Immunity' (2010) 6 Zeitschrift für Internationale Strafrechtsdogmatik 441), and that by virtue of this obligation South Sudan would be precluded from invoking the international responsibility of a State the authorities of which would arrest and transfer Al-Bashir, see (critically) Gaeta, 'Does President Al Bashir Enjoy Immunity from Arrest?' 331, who refers to Conforti's proposal to understand non-binding UNSCR-recommendations as justification for what would otherwise be a breach of international law, Benedetto Conforti, 'Le rôle de l'accord dans le système des Nations Unies' (1974) 142(2) RdC 262-265; Carsten Stahn, *A Critical Introduction*

a rule in customary international law that would exclude immunity for Heads of State when their arrest is sought for international crimes by another State, even when the arrest is sought on behalf of an international court, including, specifically, this Court."[358]

Domestic courts in South Africa were also divided. The African High Court held that the South African government was obliged under the Rome Statute and the Implementation Act to arrest Bashir; with respect to the question of immunity, it referred to the PTC I decision and to article 27.[359] The judgment of the Supreme Court of Appeal of South Africa rejected an exception to head of state immunity and decided to resolve the tension between South Africa's obligation to cooperate under the Rome statute and immunities under customary international law at the level of domestic law rather than international law: The domestic implementation of international obligations put more emphasis on the obligations under the Rome Statute.[360]

---

to International Criminal Law (Cambridge University Press 2019) 257 (finding the chamber's argument problematic, arguing, *inter alia* that a waiver needs to be declared explicitly); on the question of explicitness, see also Manuel J Ventura, 'Escape from Johannesburg?: Sudanese President Al-Bashir Visits South Africa, and the Implicit Removal of Head of State Immunity by the UN Security Council in light of Al-Jedda' (2015) 13(5) JICJ 995 ff.

358 *Prosecutor v Omar Hassan Ahmad Al-Bashir* ICC PTC II Decision under article 87(7) of the Rome Statute on the non-compliance by South Africa with the request by the Court for the arrest and surrender of Omar Al-Bashir (6 July 2017) ICC-02/05-01/09-302 para 68, relying on the Arrest Warrant case.

359 *Southern Africa Litigation Centre v Minister of Justice And Constitutional Development and Others* High Court of South Africa (Gauteng Division, Pretoria) (26 June 2015) (27740/2015) [2015] ZAGPPHC 402 paras 31-32.

360 *The Minister of Justice and Constitutional Development v The Southern African Litigation Centre* Supreme Court of Appeal of South Africa (15 March 2016) (867/15) [2016] ZASCA 17 para 103. As a consequence, South Africa declared to leave the ICC because a membership would compel South Africa to violate customary international law. Yet, the High Court of South Africa decided that both the government's notice of withdrawal from the Rome Statute without prior parliamentary approval was unconstitutional and invalid, *In the matter between Democratic Alliance and Minister of International Relations and Cooperation et al* High Court of South Africa (Gauteng Division, Pretoria) (22 February 2017) Case No 83145/2016 paras 47, 51.

3. The decision of the ICC Appeals Chamber

The ICC Appeals Chamber sided in its recent judgment with the approach adopted by the Pre-Trial Chambers in *Malawi* and in *Chad* and decided that article 27(2) of the Rome Statute "reflects the status of customary international law"[361] in that Mr Al-Bashir was not entitled under customary international law to immunity from arrest and surrender by Jordan at the request of the ICC.[362] This reasoning extended also to "the horizontal relationship between States when a State is requested by an international court to arrest and surrender the Head of State of another State".[363] Consequently, "a State Party cannot refuse to arrest and surrender the Head of State of another State Party on the ground of Head of State immunity."[364]

The judgment of the Appeals Chamber employed some of the techniques that have been illustrated in this book in other contexts: for instance, it examined the *telos* of the immunity rule. The object and purpose of this rule, to give expression to the sovereign equality of states and the principle of *par in parem non habet imperium*, was said to be not applicable before international courts: domestic courts "are essentially an expression of a State's sovereign power, which is necessarily limited by the sovereign power of the other States", whereas "international courts act on behalf of the international community as a whole."[365] The Appeals Chamber used this difference also to define the default position and to argue that "the *onus* is on those who claim that there is such immunity in relation to international courts to establish sufficient State practice and opinio juris."[366]

The decision addressed not only customary international law but also the UN Security Council resolution 1593, and while it did not follow the analysis of customary international law by PTC I, it emphasized that the Pre-Trial Chamber "reached the same conclusion [...] based on its interpretation of the

---

361 *Prosecutor v Omar Hassan Ahmad Al-Bashir* ICC AC Judgment (6 May 2019) ICC-02/05-01/09 OA2 paras 103-113 (quote at para 103).
362 ibid para 117.
363 ibid para 114; see also ibid paras 125-127.
364 ibid para 132.
365 ibid para 115.
366 ibid para 116. For a similar argument see Donald Riznik, *Die Immunität ratione personae des Souveräns* (PL Academic Research 2016) 250.

Statute and bearing in mind Sudan's position under Resolution 1593", which the Appeals Chamber endorsed.[367]

By exploring and pursuing both the "customary law avenue" and the "Security Council avenue"[368], the judgment displays a certain degree of ambiguity. In particular, the relationship between both avenues is unclear. The Chamber held, for instance, that "by ratifying or acceding to the Statute, States Parties have *consented* to the inapplicability of Head of State immunity for the purposes of proceedings before the Court"[369], before it then addressed the effect of Resolution 1593 on Sudan which is no State Party. In this context, it argued that "the legal obligation under Resolution 1593, which imposed upon Sudan the same obligation of cooperation that the Rome Statute imposes upon States Parties, *including with regard to the applicability of article 27(2) of the Statute*, prevailed as *lex specialis* over any immunity that would otherwise exist between Sudan and Jordan."[370]

Against this background and taking into account that the joint concurring opinion characterized its reasoning on the UNSC resolution as "dispositive considerations" on which the decision's "primary focus" was, it has been argued that the Security Council route proved to be decisive as far as the relationship between a State party and a non-State party is concerned.[371] Such a reading finds support in the fact the Joint Concurring Opinion addressed three scenarios in which the difficulty of immunity at the horizontal plane between states could present itself[372]: the first scenario concerned the relationship between States Parties to the Rome Statute. The second scenario focused on the relationship between two UN member states one of which would not be party to the Rome Statute and described a situation "where the Security Council specifically requires the third State to cooperate fully with

---

367 *Prosecutor v Omar Hassan Ahmad Al-Bashir* ICC-02/05-01/09 OA2 para 119 ("this interpretation of the Statute was, as such, correct").
368 On this terminology see *Written observations of Professor Claus Kreß as amicus curiae with the assistance of Ms Erin Pobjie* 2018 June 2018 ICC-02/05-01/09-359 3.
369 *Prosecutor v Omar Hassan Ahmad Al-Bashir* ICC-02/05-01/09 OA2 para 132 (italics added).
370 ibid para 144 (first italics added).
371 See Sarah MH Nouwen, 'Return to Sender: Let the International Court of Justice Justify or Qualify International-Criminal-Court-Exceptionalism Regarding Personal Immunities' (2019) 78(3) Cambridge Law Journal 605-607.
372 *Prosecutor v Omar Hassan Ahmad Al-Bashir* ICC AC Joint Concurring Opinion of Judges Eboe-Osuji, Morrison, Hofmański and Bossa (6 May 2019) ICC-02/05-01/09-397-Anx1-Corr ICC-02/05-01/09-397-Anx1-Corr para 451.

the ICC, pursuant to a Resolution taken under Chapter VII of the UN Charter for purposes of conferring jurisdiction upon the Court through an Article 13(b) referral".[373] The third scenario was a variation of the second scenario in the sense that it concerned two UN member states which did not ratify the Rome Statute but which were addressed by a Security Council resolution. According to the Joint Concurring Opinion, immunity would not constitute a bar in the aforementioned scenarios. However, this list of scenarios did not include the scenario in which jurisdiction is based on the territoriality principle set forth in article 12(2)(a) Rome Statute rather than on a UNSC resolution.[374] It is precisely this scenario where the question of the existence of immunities under customary international law is particularly important.

Then again, however, the Appeals Chamber emphasized the customary law avenue by explicitly stating that "[t]he absence of a rule of customary international law recognising Head of State immunity *vis-à-vis* international courts is relevant [...] also for the horizontal relationship between States [...] no immunities under customary international law operate in such a situation to bar an international court in its exercise of its own jurisdiction."[375]

Whereas the Chamber argued only briefly that "international courts act on behalf of the international community as a whole"[376], the concurring opinion is more elaborative.[377] It held that international courts "exercise jurisdiction on behalf of the *international community*, such as is represented by the aggregation of States who have authorised those international judges"[378] and that the court exercises jurisdiction "on behalf of the international community represented in the membership of the Rome Statute"[379], and that an international tribunal "exercises the jurisdiction of all the concerned sovereigns *inter se*, for their overall benefit."[380]

---

373 ibid para 451.
374 See Kreß, 'Article 98' para 112. Cf. also ICC, 'Q&A Regarding Appeals Chamber's 6 May 2019 Judgment in the Jordan Referral Re Al-Bashir Appeal, ICC-PIOS-Q&A-SUD-02-01/19_Eng' ⟨https://www.icc-cpi.int/itemsDocuments/190515-al-bashir-qa-eng.pdf⟩ accessed 1 February 2023.
375 *Prosecutor v Omar Hassan Ahmad Al-Bashir* ICC-02/05-01/09 OA2 para 114.
376 ibid para 115.
377 *Prosecutor v Omar Hassan Ahmad Al-Bashir* ICC-02/05-01/09-397-Anx1-Corr paras 56-60.
378 ibid para 53.
379 ibid para 53.
380 ibid para 59. Cf. *Reparation for Injuries Suffered in the Service of the United Nations* [1949] ICJ Rep 174, 185: "[...] fifty States, representing the vast majority of the members of the international community, had the power, in conformity with

The answer to the question of whether the idea is accepted that the ICC acts not only on behalf of the parties but on the behalf of the international community of the whole will be important for rebutting the counter-argument to the position of the Appeals Chamber: that immunities under customary international law continue to exist in the relationship with non-state parties since states can derogate from customary international law only *inter se* by treaty and cannot accord the ICC powers which each of the states does not possess. It remains to be seen whether a wide interpretation of this judgment according to which no immunities under customary international law exist when it comes to ICC proceedings, including the enforcement of arrest warrants, or a restrictive interpretation according to which the principles of the judgment find application only in the situation of a UNSC referral will assert itself.[381] A reasoning based on the *jus puniendi* of the international community can also have implications for the applicable law: the crimes which are to be prosecuted would have to be crimes under customary international law, as crimes that exist only under a treaty could not have led to a modification of immunities under customary international law.[382]

E. Concluding Observations

This chapter explored the interrelationship of sources in international criminal law. It began by tracing the interrelationship of sources as a *motif* in stages of the historical development of international criminal law.[383] Subsequently, it zeroed in on the jurisprudence of the international criminal tribunals, particularly the ICTY, and examined the preference for customary international

---

international law, to bring into being an entity possessing objective international personality, and not merely personality recognized by them alone [...]" This *dictum*, however, concerned the question of whether an international organization can have the capacity to bring a claim against a non-State party of that organization.

381 The answer to this question is relevant for the ICC arrest warrant of 17 March 2023 against the Russian President or the establishment of a tribunal to prosecute the crime of aggression against Ukraine, see the collection on Just Security, Just Security, 'U.N. General Assembly and International Criminal Tribunal for the Crime of Aggression Against Ukraine' ⟨https://www.justsecurity.org/tag/u-n-general-assembly-and-international-criminal-tribunal-for-aggression-against-ukraine/⟩ accessed 1 February 2023.

382 For this argument see Kreß, 'Article 98' paras 51-52, paras 126-129. See above, p. 521.

383 See above, p. 464.

law, interpretative decisions, normative considerations and the importance of the legal craft in the identification of customary international law.[384] The chapter then examined shifts in the interrelationship of sources in the context of the Rome Statute, with a focus on the applicable law and its interpretation, the modes of liability and immunity under customary international law.[385]

In contrast to the European Court which, because of the written character of the ECHR, could interpret the ECHR without the need to ascertain it first[386], the ICTY had to do both and its decisions were therefore more likely to face a higher level of criticism. As far as the technique, legal craft and consideration of principles are concerned, the way in which the ICTY identified customary international law is arguably similar to approaches that could be observed in the ICJ jurisprudence.[387] It is submitted that a focus on the techniques can explain the disagreement which may exist with respect to certain interpretations and judgments. As disagreement on the law can be explained, disagreement as such does not have to call into question the credibility and legitimacy of customary international law and general principles of law as sources of international law. The jurisprudence of the ICTY made also a valuable contribution to the doctrine of general principles, as it highlighted the importance to take account of the functional specificities of the respective regime in which a principle from a different branch is to be applied.[388] Paying regard to this normative assessment can complement scholarship which discusses primarily the representativeness (or lack thereof) of the materials relied on when identifying a principle.

The Rome Statute raises the question of the extent to which it shifts the relative significance of the sources over time or leads to a "decline" of one source.[389] The ICC jurisprudence includes examples in which chambers focused more on the particularities of the Rome Statute. The shift in the interrelationship can also reflect a shift in preferred doctrinal concepts or criminal

---

384 See above, p. 476.
385 See above, p. 507.
386 The European Court may need to address the question of whether a reservation is valid, cf. *Belilos v Switzerland [Plenum]* App no 10328/83 (ECtHR, 29 April 1988) paras 89-103.
387 See above, p. 499.
388 See above, p. 487.
389 See above, p. 517; cf. Larissa Jasmijn van den Herik, 'The Decline of Customary International Law as a Source of International Criminal Law' in Curtis A Bradley (ed), *Custom's future: international law in a changing world* (Cambridge University Press 2016) 230ff.

Chapter 9: International Criminal Law

law theory. In this sense, JCE on the one hand and indirect perpetratorship and control theory on the other hand primarily represent different, competing conceptualizations. International practice can look like a *Rorschach* blot in which different viewers see different aspects depending on the respective viewer's personal, or in the context of law, doctrinal background and training.[390] It may be worthwhile for future research on customary international law to distinguish also in other contexts between the practice that was interpreted for a specific rule and the doctrinal conceptualization expressed in the formulation of a rule of customary international law.

At the same time, it was demonstrated that a purely treaty-based reasoning has its limitations as long as not all states are parties to the Rome Statute. It will be important to observe whether the ICC will focus on the treaty and its particularities without engaging with customary international law or whether it will emphasize the interrelationship and regard itself not just as a court based on a treaty but as a court in the service of the international community and engage with customary international law in good faith. It is noteworthy that the ICC in the *Al-Bashir* case was conscious of the implications which a judgment resting exclusively on the interpretation of a Security Council resolution and the Rome Statute can have for the future development of customary international law on immunities.[391] Such a judgment could have been read as an implicit confirmation of the view that a UNSC resolution was necessary as immunity applied in the horizontal relationship between a state party to the Rome Statute and a non-state party. Other courts and tribunals might take from this example to be mindful of the implications a reasoning which is or is not based on custom can have for the future development of customary international law.

---

390 On this metaphor see Sadat and Jolly, 'Seven Canons of ICC Treaty Interpretation: Making Sense of Article 25's Rorschach Blot' 755-756.
391 See above, p. 546. See also *Written observations of Professor Claus Kreß as amicus curiae with the assistance of Ms Erin Pobjie* para 6: "The choice between the two legal avenues before [the Appeals Chamber] has implications that transcend the case in question."

Chapter 10: International Investment Law

A. Introduction

The previous chapters brought to fore different aspects of the interrelationship of sources. The eighth chapter on the European Convention on Human Rights demonstrated how functional equivalents to concepts of general international law were developed as a matter of treaty interpretation and how a relation was established between other rules of public international law and the European Convention through proportionality analysis. The ninth chapter on international criminal law illustrated that customary international law was interpreted in light of general principles of international law under consideration of the functional specificities of international criminal law. Both chapters also revealed the importance of doctrinal constructions and perspectives, be it proportionality analysis or a specific understanding of criminal law doctrine.

This chapter on international investment law supports these observations and adds new perspectives on the interrelationship of sources. This chapter will first trace the interrelationship of sources in the modern history of international investment law and highlight in particular the prominent role of customary international law and general principles of law, their contested character and the move towards bilateral investment treaties (B.). The chapter will then demonstrate how this bilateralism in form led to a multilateralism in substance. It will also explore the different doctrinal avenues while evaluating their respective explanatory force for this phenomenon of multilateralism in substance (C.). Last but not least, this chapter will focus on the significance of doctrinal constructions in international investment law, exemplified by the distinction between primary rules and secondary rules (D.). This chapter will critically engage with the reception of this distinction in international investment law and argue against an expansive interpretation of this distinction which would place treaties and custom into strictly separated compartments.

B. From the interwar period to the modern investment regime

This section will examine different steps in the development from the interwar period to the modern investment regime. It will point to the historical connection between responsibility and the protection of aliens (I.), examine the importance of unwritten law, which expressed itself in the international minimum standards and the doctrine of the internationalization of contracts by general principles of law (II.). Subsequently, it will give an overview of the development of the modern investment regime (III.)

I. The historical connection between responsibility and the protection of aliens

Legal responsibility for breaches of the law is "a general conception of law"[1]. Against this background, it is not surprising that the doctrine of international responsibility and international law relating to the rights of aliens were historically intrinsically connected. Since the way in which states treated "their" citizens was (to a large extent) considered to be a matter for each state to decide on and not subject to strict international legal regulation, the treatment of foreigners belonging to another state was one of the few questions with respect to which questions of international responsibility could become relevant.[2] States were entitled to exercise diplomatic protection and to invoke the international responsibility of another state for injuries to their citizens.[3] Both topics, substantive obligations and the law of international

---

1 *Case Concerning the Factory at Chorzow* PCIJ Series A No 17, 29.
2 Edwin Montefiore Borchard, *The diplomatic protection of citizens abroad* (The Banks law publishing Company 1915) 177-180 and 349: "Each state in the international community is presumed to extend complete protection to the life, liberty and property of all individuals within its jurisdiction. If it fails in this duty toward its own citizens, it is of no international concern. If it fails in this duty toward an alien, responsibility is incurred to the state of which he is a citizen, and international law authorizes the national state to exact reparation for the injury sustained by its citizen." Alexander P Fachiri, 'International Law and the Property of Aliens' (1929) 10 BYIL 32-33; Nolte, 'From Dionisio Anzilotti to Roberto Ago: The Classical International Law of State Responsibility and the Traditional Primacy of a Bilateral Conception of Inter-state Relations' 1088.
3 Vattel, *The Law of Nations; or Principles of the Law of Nature, applied to the conduct and affairs of nations and sovereigns* book II 161 para 71: "Whoever uses a citizen ill, indirectly offends the state, which is bound to protect this citizen; ant the sovereign

responsibility, used to be treated together: the League of Nations codification attempted to clarify the rules of responsibility in the context of the rights of aliens, and substantive obligations, such as the prohibition of denial of justice, were studied from the perspective of international responsibility.[4]

However, State responsibility became increasingly understood as a distinct legal category.[5] The *Harvard Draft on the Responsibility of States for Damage Done in Their Territory to the Person or Property of Foreigners*, whilst being concerned with substantive obligations, such as denial of justice (article 9), began to elaborate on an abstract regime relating to responsibility.[6] Also, several delegates at the 1930 codification conference suggested to separate the rules of responsibility from substantive obligations.[7]

---

of the latter should avenge his wrongs, punish the aggressor, and, if possible, oblige him to make full reparation; since otherwise the citizen would not obtain the great end of the civil association, which is safety."; *Mavrommatis Palestine Concessions* PCIJ Series A No 02, 12; Crawford, *Brownlie's principles of public international law* 591; on the description as fiction see Annemarieke Vermeer-Künzli, 'As If: The Legal Fiction in Diplomatic Protection' (2007) 18(1) EJIL 37 ff.

4 Cf. Robert Ago, 'Le délit international' (1939) 68(2) RdC 467, 468: "Pratiquement, et en d'autres termes, au lieu d'étu- dier directement les droits et les devoirs des Etats dans le droit des gens, la doctrine a étudié ces droits et ces devoirs du point de vue indirect de leur violation, et a ramené en quelque sorte tout lo droit international à la notion de la responsabilité."

5 On the law of responsibility as a distinct, objective regime, see already Triepel, *Völkerrecht und Landesrecht* 324-381; Dionisio Anzilotti, 'La responsabilité internationale des états: à raison des dommages soufferts par des étrangers' (1906) 13 RGDIP 5-29. On Anzilotti's influence see Nolte, 'From Dionisio Anzilotti to Roberto Ago: The Classical International Law of State Responsibility and the Traditional Primacy of a Bilateral Conception of Inter-state Relations' 1087-1088. For a historical overview of this development and of earlier writers who did not consider responsibility to be a distinct legal category see Crawford, *State Responsibility: The General Part* 4-26.

6 'Responsibility of States for Damage done in their Territory to the Person or Property of Foreigners' (1929) 23(2) AJIL. Supplement 133-135; see Briggs in *ILC Ybk (1963 vol 2)* 231; Eric David, 'Primary and Secondary Rules' in James Crawford and others (eds), *The Law of International Responsibility* (Oxford University Press 2010) 28 ff.; on the Harvard Draft see Crawford, *State Responsibility: The General Part* 32-35.

7 For the Finnish delegate Erich the general principles on international responsibility "presuppose a wrong, a fault or culpability on the part of the State [...] it would be advisable to reconsider the question whether the idea of international responsibility should be thus limited to acts or omissions which are incompatible with the international obligations of the State", Rosenne, *League of Nations Conference for the Codification of International Law (1930)* 1444. This view was shared by the German delegation which criticized that the bases "dealt with certain special situations:

Later, in the context of the ILC, the distinction between primary rules of obligations and secondary rules of responsibility asserted itself as codification strategy for the responsibility of states for internationally wrongful acts. After the first ILC Special Rapporteur, Francisco V. García-Amador, had followed the approach adopted earlier during the League of Nations, his successor, Roberto Ago, restarted the project and convinced the other members to focus solely on the secondary rules of international responsibility, without studying the primary obligations.[8]

Until the adoption of this new course, the work of the ILC was characterized by a certain proximity to the Harvard Research Project which culminated into a second draft in 1961.[9] The first Special Rapporteur visited Harvard in order to confer with the directors of the Harvard project.[10] The Secretary to the ILC and Director of the Codification Division, Dr. Yuen-li Liang, spoke of a "collaboration between the United Nations Secretariat and the Harvard Law School in the preliminary work on that topic."[11] Certain members referred to this linkage when they criticized the Special Rapporteur's report. Tunkin argued that some of the problems which characterized both the Harvard

---

acts affecting the rights of persons to whom concessions have been granted [...]", Rosenne, *League of Nations Conference for the Codification of International Law (1930)* 1448 (Richter). The method to deal with content of obligations "is open to serious objection". Furthermore, Politis for Greece emphasized that "[w]e are not called upon to deal here with rules of substance or those obligations the infraction of which constitutes responsibility", ibid 1449. See also Cavaglieri from Italy, 1455, 1464, Cruchaga-Tocornal from Chile, 1476-1477, Abdel Hamid Bdaoui Pacha from Egypt ("'remedial law' as contrasted with 'a substantive law'"), 1477; Basdevant from France, 1478.

8 See above, p. 364.
9 On this relationship see James Crawford and Tom Grant, 'Responsibility of States for Injuries to Foreigners' in John P Grant and JCraig Barker (eds), *The Harvard Research in International Law: Contemporary Analysis and Appraisal* (William S Hein & Company 2007) 90-100, 102-106; Nissel, 'The Duality of State Responsibility' 824, 828-830; Philip Allott, 'State Responsibility and the Unmaking of International Law' (1988) 29(1) Harvard International Law Journal 5-7. On the 1961 draft see Crawford, *State Responsibility: The General Part* 34-35.
10 See *ILC Ybk (1961 vol 1)* 208 (the Special Rapporteur summarizing the criticism); Crawford and Grant, 'Responsibility of States for Injuries to Foreigners' 90 with further references.
11 *ILC Ybk (1959 vol 1)* 147; *ILC Ybk (1956 vol 1)* 228; see also *ILC Ybk (1961 vol 1)* 196, where Professor Louis B. Sohn presented a draft of the Convention on the International Responsibility of States for Injuries to Aliens, prepared by the Harvard Law School.

draft and the Special Rapporteur's report "were closely connected with the existence in the world of two different economic systems."[12] Matine-Daftary criticized that "the Special Rapporteur's draft [...] was based on purely European standards of justice" and suggested that "the Harvard Law School and the Special Rapporteur should endeavour to find a formula which would be more acceptable to all States."[13] With the new exclusive focus on the secondary rules, on the codification of "the whole responsibility and nothing but responsibility"[14], the linkage no longer existed as the Harvard Draft was particularly concerned with substantive obligations.[15]

At that time, Ago's approach was not uncontroversial and it was met with criticism. Robert B. Lillich, for instance, preferred the previous approach and criticized Ago's take as too academic and theoretical which therefore would have left no mark on international practice.[16] In hindsight, however, the reorientation under Ago can be evaluated as a success. Not only did the ILC's efforts result in the ARSIWA. The concentration on secondary rules, on rules on rules rather than on the substance of obligations, became a success formula which was applied in relation to other topics as well, for instance in the context of the ILC's work on subsequent agreements and subsequent practice, customary international law, *jus cogens* and general principles of law.[17] Ago's approach was successful because it allowed the Commission to reapproach the topic of state responsibility without having to engage with the contested subject of obligations of states towards aliens.[18] It was for this reason that García-Amador's approach had been met with resistance.[19] As

---

12 *ILC Ybk (1959 vol 1)* 149.
13 ibid 149; Crawford and Grant, 'Responsibility of States for Injuries to Foreigners' 95-98 with further references.
14 *ILC Ybk (1969 vol 1)* 106 (Ago).
15 Crawford and Grant, 'Responsibility of States for Injuries to Foreigners' 106.
16 Richard B Lillich, 'The Current Status of the Law of State Responsibility for Injuries to Aliens' in Richard B Lillich (ed), *International Law of State Responsibility for Injuries to Aliens* (University Press of Virginia 1983) 19-21; see also *ILC Ybk (1963 vol 2)* 231, where Briggs argued that "Ago's paper somewhat artificially stressed the distinction between the international law of State responsibility and the law relating to the treatment of aliens[...] it was perhaps a little too abstract to form the framework of a draft treaty to be submitted to States."
17 See also chapter 6 on the International Law Commission.
18 Cf. on the codification strategy to focus on "technical" rules as opposed to more political topics, Lauterpacht, 'Codification and Development of International Law' 23-27, 33; cf. Stone, 'On the Vocation of the International Law Commission' 38 ff.
19 Nissel, 'The Duality of State Responsibility' 821 ff.

Martti Koskenniemi put it, "[s]tate responsibility for injuries of Aliens was really an American topic"[20], namely an US and Latin American topic.[21] As will be demonstrated below, the different views in particular between the US and Latin American states could not be overcome by unwritten international law and ultimately let states to conclude bilateral agreements.

II. The importance of unwritten law

In the absence of bilateral or multilateral treaties imposing obligations on states with respect to the treatment of foreign nations,[22] obligations could only exist based on unwritten international law. Here, the prohibition of arbitrariness was an important principle, as it was considered to impose limitations on states in areas which were not regulated by more specific

---

20 Martti Koskenniemi, 'The Ideology of International Adjudication and the 1907 Hague Conference' in Yves Daudet (ed), *Topicality of the 1907 Hague Conference, the Second Peace Conference* (Nijhoff 2008) 149.
21 Kathryn Greenman, 'Aliens in Latin America: Intervention, Arbitration and State Responsibility for Rebels' (2018) 31 Leiden Journal of International Law 624.
22 On the so-called minority protection treaties see *Rights of Minorities in Upper Silesia (Minority Schools)* PCIJ Series A No 15; Gentian Zyberi, 'The International Court of Justice and the Rights of Peoples and Minorities' in Christian J Tams and James Sloan (eds), *The Development of International Law by the International Court of Justice* (Oxford University Press 2013) 329-338.

obligations.[23] It is reflected in the international minimum standard[24], which, according to Elihu Root's famous description, was said to be

> "a standard of justice, very simple, very fundamental, and of such general acceptance by all civilized countries as to form a part of the international law of the world. The condition upon which any country is entitled to measure the justice due from it to an alien by the justice which it accords to its own citizens is that its system of law and administration shall conform to this general standard. If any country's system of law and administration does not conform to that standard, although the people of the country may be content or compelled to live under it, no other country can be compelled to accept it as furnishing a satisfactory measure of treatment to its citizens."[25]

---

23 For an early example prior to the League of Nations see Paul Heilborn, *Das System des Völkerrechts entwickelt aus den völkerrechtlichen Begriffen* (Verlag von Julius Springer 1896) 357-361, in the context of interventions; Nicolas Politis, 'Le problème des limitations de la souveraineté et la théorie de l'abus des droits dans les rapports internationaux' (1925) 6 RdC; Leibholz, 'Verbot der Willkür und des Ermessensmißbrauches im völkerrechtlichen Verkehr der Staaten' 98; Lauterpacht, *The Function of Law in the International Community* 94 ff. and 303 ff. with further references; see also at 306 where Lauterpacht said that the principle "plays a relatively small part in municipal law, not because the law ignores it, but because it has crystallized its typical manifestations in concrete rules and prohibitions"; Hans-Jürgen Schlochauer, 'Die Theorie des abus de droit im Völkerrecht' (1933) 17 Zeitschrift für Völkerrecht 373, 378-379 on the importance of this principle for common areas; see later Alexandre-Charles Kiss, *L' abus de droit en droit international* (Pichon & Durand-Auzias 1953); but see to the contrary Cavaglieri, 'Règles générales du droit de la paix' 543-545, skeptical of the concept which would have not been confirmed by international practice; see also Jean David Roulet, *Le caractère artificiel de la théorie de l'abus de droit en droit international public* (Ed de la Baconnière 1958) 150; later Schwarzenberger, 'The fundamental principles of international law' 309.

24 Leibholz, 'Verbot der Willkür und des Ermessensmißbrauches im völkerrechtlichen Verkehr der Staaten' 98.

25 Elihu Root, 'The Basis of Protection to Citizens Residing Abroad' (1910) 4(3) AJIL 521-522. Cf. Andrew C Blandford, 'The History of Fair and Equitable Treatment before the Second World War' (2017) 32 ICSID Review 289-291, 294-297, 302-303 for a historical overview of the notion "principles of justice and equity" and for the view that the principles of justice in Root's formula were those recognized in domestic laws and explained by way of reference to the US constitution, rather than by customary international law. Cf. Stephan W Schill, *The multilateralization of international investment law* (Cambridge University Press 2009) 26 ("rule and basis for customary international law").

Chapter 10: International Investment Law

This section will zero in on the unwritten law. In particular, it will examine the international minimum standard and its contestation (1.) and the doctrine of the internationalization of contracts by general principles of law (2.).

1. The minimum standard and its contestation

The vagueness and indeterminacy of its description made it difficult to determine the meaning of the international minimum standard in relation to aliens.[26] In particular Latin-American countries adopted the view that international law required nothing more than equal treatment between aliens and nationals according to the laws of the host state.[27] This position can be traced back to Carlos Calvo, the writings of whom were cited by Mexico already in 1873 in a dispute with the United States of America.[28] Calvo himself built on the teachings of Andrés Bello[29] who attempted to reconcile the protection of aliens and the interest of states to regulate. Bello recognized that those countries which treated foreigners with more humanity and liberty have achieved greater wealth than countries which imposed restrictions and

---

26 Edwin Borchard, 'The 'Minimum Standard' of the Treatment of Aliens' (1940) 38(4) Michigan Law Review 458: "[...] the variability of time, place and circumstance make it even less precise than the term 'due process of law' [...] the standard is mild, flexible and variable according to circumstances [...]".
27 League of Nations Committee of Experts for the Progressive Codification of International Law, 'Annex to Questionnaire No. 4. Report of the Sub-Committee. M. Guerrero, Rapporteur, Mr. Wang Chung-Hui' [1927] printed in (1926) 20 AJIL Supp 99; as stated by Schill, the position of equal treatment can be traced back to the writings of Calvo and was supported by several Latin American states and "gained ground due to the successful communist revolution in Russia in 1917", Schill, *The multilateralization of international investment law* 27; on Bello and Calvo as discussed in this paragraph see Santiago Montt, *State Liability in Investment Treaty Arbitration. Global Constitutional and Administrative Law on the BIT Generation* (Hart Publishing 2009) 31 ff.
28 Jan Paulsson, *Denial of Justice in international law* (Cambridge University Press 2005) 21.
29 See Carlos Calvo, *Le droit international théorique et pratique; précédé d'un exposé historique des progrès de la science du droit des gens* (vol 3, A Rousseau 1896) 109-110; Montt, *State Liability in Investment Treaty Arbitration. Global Constitutional and Administrative Law on the BIT Generation* 41; on Bello see Keller-Kemmerer, *Die Mimikry des Völkerrechts: Andrés Bellos "Principios de Derecho Internacional"*.

disadvantages to foreigners.[30] At the same time, he affirmed the equality of states and the principle of non-interference.[31] His interpretation of international law presented a reconciliation of the interests for free trade and sovereignty: by entering a country, foreigners submit themselves to local law and the host state offers protection to foreigners, also by applying the local law to them in a just manner.[32] If the state refuses to hear the foreigner's complaint or even commits a "manifest injustice", the foreigner can turn to his state[33] for diplomatic protection.[34] Similarly, Calvo's starting point was the equality of states.[35] According to foreigners more than equal treatment would be contrary to equality since the responsibility of a government to foreigners could not be greater than its responsibility to its citizens.[36] As argued by Montt and Garcia-Amador, Calvo did not exclude the possibility of diplomatic protection in cases of denial of justice.[37] Calvo's and Bello's teachings led to the development of what became known as the *Calvo* doctrine, according to which foreigners are not entitled to better treatment than

---

30 " Las restricciones y desventajas a que por las leyes de muchos paises estan sujetos los estranjeros, se miran jeneralmente como contrarias al incremento de la poblacion y al adalantamiento de la industria y los paises que han hecho mas progressos en las artes y comercio y se han elevado a un grado mas alto de riqueza y poder son cabalmente aquellos que han tratado con mas humanidad y liberalidad a los estranjeros", Andrés Bello, *Principios De Derecho De Jentes* (Imprenta De La Opinion 1832) 53-54.

31 Keller-Kemmerer, *Die Mimikry des Völkerrechts: Andrés Bellos "Principios de Derecho Internacional"* 253 ff.; on the history of European interference in the 19th century on the basis of diplomatic protection and forcible self-help see Montt, *State Liability in Investment Treaty Arbitration. Global Constitutional and Administrative Law on the BIT Generation* 37.

32 Bello, *Principios De Derecho De Jentes* 54-55.

33 ibid 54: "Si éstos (los Estados) contra derecho rehusaren oir sus quejas, o le hiciesen una injusticia manifiesta, puede entónces interponer la autoridad de su propio soberano."

34 See also the summary in Andrés Bello, *Principios de Derecho Internacional* (2nd edn, Almacen de JM de Rojas 1847) 77.

35 Carlos Calvo, *Derecho Internacional teórico y práctico de Europa y América* (vol 1, D'Amyot/Durand et Pedone-Lauriel 1868) 396-397 para 294.

36 ibid 393 para 294; Calvo, *Le droit international théorique et pratique; précédé d'un exposé historique des progrès de la science du droit des gens* 138 para 1276.

37 Montt, *State Liability in Investment Treaty Arbitration. Global Constitutional and Administrative Law on the BIT Generation* 40-41, emphasizing that ; Francisco García-Amador, *The changing law of international claims* (vol 1, Oceana-Publ 1984) 56.

nationals, and to the *Calvo* clause in contracts where foreigners waive their right to seek diplomatic protection by their state of nationality [38]

The *Calvo* doctrine also informed the famous *Guerrero* report of José Gustavo Guerrero, who later became the last President of the PCIJ and the first president of the ICJ. According to this report, international law had only a minor role to play in the treatment of aliens as long as aliens were accorded equal treatment by the host state.[39] He stressed that the binding force of international law rested on "the consent of all States and not merely the consent of some."[40] He was critical of international tribunals rehearing cases that domestic courts had already decided.[41] He, therefore, proposed a quite narrow scope of the international prohibition of denial of justice: in principle, a "decision of a judicial authority, in accordance with the *lex loci*, that a petition submitted by a foreigner cannot be entertained should not, however, be regarded as a denial of justice."[42] In other words, the state had fulfilled its international obligation as soon as its courts gave *any* decision. In his view, "a judicial decision, whatever it may be, and even if vitiated by error or injustice, does not involve the international responsibility of the State."[43]

Opponents of the *Calvo* doctrine argued that this doctrine was too far-reaching, reduced the scope of international law too significantly and did not sufficiently appreciate the independence of the normative content of international law *vis-à-vis* domestic legal orders.[44] According to the General Claims

---

[38] But see also Montt, *State Liability in Investment Treaty Arbitration. Global Constitutional and Administrative Law on the BIT Generation* 40, 45, arguing that the Calvo doctrine "at least as Andrés Bello originally envisioned it - did not intend to dismantle state responsibility" and that the Calvo clause was based on the investor's consent, see also 48 on the common purpose of the doctrine and the clause "to curb the excesses of diplomatic protection"; on the Calvo doctrine and clause see also Patrick Juillard, 'Calvo Doctrine/Calvo Clause' [2007] Max Planck EPIL paras 3 ff.

[39] League of Nations Committee of Experts for the Progressive Codification of International Law, 'Annex to Questionnaire No. 4. Report of the Sub-Committee. M. Guerrero, Rapporteur, Mr. Wang Chung-Hui' 99.

[40] ibid 92.

[41] ibid 99.

[42] ibid 99.

[43] ibid 104.

[44] Borchard, 'The 'Minimum Standard' of the Treatment of Aliens' 447, 452, 460; Edwin M Borchard, '"Responsibility of States," at the Hague Codification Conference' (1930) 24 AJIL 537; Fachiri, 'International Law and the Property of Aliens' 33; Robert Yewdall Jennings, 'State Contracts in International Law' (1961) 37 BYIL 181: "The

Commission (Mexico and United States)[45], "equality is not the ultimate test of the propriety of the acts of authorities in the light of international law. That test is, broadly speaking, whether aliens are treated in accordance with ordinary standards of civilization."[46] Consequently, foreign citizens might in certain circumstances even receive "broader and more liberal treatment" in comparison to nationals.[47]

Claims Commissions attempted to operationalize the vague international minimum standard by explaining its object and purpose. The most influential definition was developed in the *Neer* case[48] which focused on denial of justice. In the *Neer* case, the United States-Mexico Claims Commission had to decide whether Mexico had violated this standard for failing to investigate and prosecute those responsible for the death of US citizen. The commission decided

> "[first] that the propriety of governmental acts should be put to the test of international standards, and [second] that the treatment of an alien, in order to constitute an international delinquency, should amount to an outrage, to bad faith, to wilful neglect of duty, or to an insufficiency of governmental action so far short of interna-

---

international standard thus means little more in practice than the assertion of the primacy of international over municipal law"; see also Paparinskis, *The international minimum standard and fair and equitable treatment* 42.

45 US – Mexico Claims Convention of 8 September 1923 (signed 8 September 1923, entered into force 19 February 1924) 68 UNTS; On the contributions of the Claims Commissions see recently Jean d'Aspremont, 'The General Claims Commission (Mexico/US) and the Invention of International Responsibility' in Ignacio de la Rasilla and Jorge E Viñuales (eds), *Experiments in International Adjudication* (Cambridge University Press 2019) 161 ff.

46 *Harry Roberts* U.S.A. v. United Mexican States, (2 November 1926) IV RIAA 80; cf. Schill, *The multilateralization of international investment law* 27-28, acknowledging that international tribunals in the inter-war period "did not accept that national treatment independent of a specific minimum standard was sufficient to conform to international law".

47 *George W Hopkins* U.S.A. v. United Mexican States (31 March 1926) IV RIAA 47 para 16.

48 Cf. *William Ralph Clayton, William Richard Clayton, Douglas Clayton, Daniel Clayton and Bilcon of Delaware Inc v Government of Canada: Award on Jurisdiction and Liability (17 March 2015)* UNCITRAL PCA Case No. 2009-04 para 434: "The starting point is generally the *Neer* case."; Muthucumaraswamy Sornarajah, *Resistance and Change in the International Law on Foreign Investment* (Cambridge University Press 2015) 87: "The survival of this standard, as stated in the Neer Claim (1926) decided by the Mexican Claims Commission, into modern times is an indication of the influence of the law that was made in this period."

tional standards that every reasonable and impartial man would readily recognize its insufficiency."[49]

The vagueness of this test may be considered against the background of the fact that the commission attempted to describe arbitrary excess of state power in specific contexts which had not been subject to more specific and detailed regulation by international law, namely a state's obligation to prosecute non-state actors for crimes committed against aliens and a state's criminal legal system.[50]

Subsequently, the *Chattin* commission confined this test to situations of indirect liability of governmental branches which had failed to sufficiently address injuries of an alien committed by citizen of the host state, and the commission argued that direct responsibility of the legislature and the executive did not presuppose any bad faith or other criteria set forth in *Neer*.[51] It is therefore still debated whether the *Neer* test provided for a general rule which focused on arbitrary excess of state power in situations in which more specific obligations were lacking,[52] or whether it was confined to denial of justice, understood as a concept which is different from the international minimum standard.[53]

Be that as it may, it was in any case difficult to conceptualize the protection of more specific, substantive rights such as the right to property within the *Neer* formula.[54] Certain authors regarded the protection of property as

---

49 *L F H Neer and Pauline Neer* U.S.A. v. United Mexican States (15 October 1926) IV RIAA 61-62; on the Neer case and the further development of the standard see *William Ralph Clayton, William Richard Clayton, Douglas Clayton, Daniel Clayton and Bilcon of Delaware Inc v Government of Canada* 126-128.
50 Cf. for this observation also Paparinskis, *The international minimum standard and fair and equitable treatment* 51.
51 *B E Chattin* United States v. United Mexican States (23 July 1927) IV RIAA 285-286.
52 Paparinskis, *The international minimum standard and fair and equitable treatment* 52-53.
53 Jan Paulsson and Georgios Petrochilos, 'Neer-ly Misled?' (2007) 22(2) ICSID Review - Foreign Investment Law Journal 242 ff.; see also Montt, *State Liability in Investment Treaty Arbitration. Global Constitutional and Administrative Law on the BIT Generation* 308, writing against a conflation of the minimum standard and the *Neer* dictum, the latter being concerned with denial of justice only.
54 John Fischer Williams, 'International Law and the Property of Aliens' (1928) 9 BYIL 29: "This is not the language in which all sober men in civilized countries would at the present time describe any and every measure of expropriation [...]"; Paparinskis, *The international minimum standard and fair and equitable treatment* 46 ("the focus of the practice of the 1920s and 1930s as well as earlier law was not on protection

a principle accepted in the international legal order[55] which could also be based on a general principle of law as recognized in Western[56] legal orders.[57] Borchard, for instance, argued that "the international standard is compounded of general principles recognized by the domestic law of practically every

---

of property but on denial of justice.") and 54 ("Neer also made it potentially more complicated to develop more detailed rules that did not fit within the procedural framework.").

55 'Report by Dr. J. C. Witenberg to the Protection of Private Property Committee' [1930] International Law Association's Report of the Thirty-Sixth Conference 317-318 (on respect for acquired rights as part of customary international law to which treaties had contributed); Fred K Nielsen, *American-Turkish Claims Settlement: Under the Agreement of December 24, 1923, and Supplemental Agreements between the United States and Turkey* (Government Printing Office 1937) 22: "There is an abundance of evidence in various forms to show a general recognition of the principle that the confiscation of the property of an alien is violative of international law", see also at 289; Alexander P Fachiri, 'Expropriation and international law' (1925) 6 BYIL 169; Fachiri, 'International Law and the Property of Aliens' 33, 54.

56 Paparinskis, *The international minimum standard and fair and equitable treatment* 60, noting that "the broader practice raised (not unjustifiable) concerns about externalization of peculiar Western conceptions." See for instance Edwin Borchard, 'The Minimum Standard of the Treatment of Aliens' (1939) 33 American Society of International Law Proceedings 53: "But international law has not only been woven from the approved practice if states in their diplomatic intercourse and from the decisions of arbitral tribunals. It is also composed of the uniform practices of the civilized states of the western world who gave birth and nourishment to international law." See also *Norwegian shipowners' claims* Norway v. USA (13 October 1922) I RIAA 332, referring to the Fifth Amendment of the Constitution of the United States of America, adding: "It is common ground that in this respect the public law of the Parties is in complete accord with the international public law of all civilised countries." Frederick Sherwood Dunn, 'International Law and Private Property Rights' (1928) 28 Columbia Law Review 175-176.

57 Borchard, 'The 'Minimum Standard' of the Treatment of Aliens' 449 ("In most states, the elementary private rights of life, liberty and property, within their well-recognized and increasing limitations, are not denied to aliens any more than they are to nationals.") and 459; see also the comment by Fred K. Nielsen, printed in 'Discussion' (1939) 33 American Society of International Law Proceedings 65: "Our great constitutional guarantees stand in the way of confiscation of property, and they also safeguard vital personal rights. I like to think [...] that those constitutional guarantees, with the superstructure of interpretation framed by the courts, exemplify the international standards. And I think that, without any improper or dangerous confusion of domestic law with international law, the principles underlying those provisions may so very usefully be given application in the settlement of international controversies relating to property rights."

civilized country, and it is not to be supposed that any normal state would repudiate it or, if able, fail to observe it."[58] Yet, he also acknowledged that the scope of protection "will have to be determined from case to case. The doctrine of vested rights depends on so many variables that prediction is hazardous."[59] Other scholars were skeptical as to the existence of such protection. Notably, John Fischer Williams argued that "it is a long step to convert a constitutional obligation into a duty of international law"[60] and that "[i]t is an error to exalt domestic arrangements of economic or political expediency, which are relative to particular societies at particular times [...] into fundamental principles of eternal morality which are to be enforceable as part of international law."[61]

The different perspectives on the scope of the international minimum standard and the protection of property were presented in a famous exchange of notes between the USA and the Mexican State in 1938 regarding the question of compensation for the take over of agrarian and oil properties in Mexico by Mexico[62]: US Secretary of State Cordell Hull argued that "the right of prompt and just compensation for expropriated property [...] is a principle to which the Government of the United States and most governments of the world have emphatically subscribed"[63] and that it recognized both the host state's right to regulate for public purposes and respect for "legitimately acquired rights of citizens of other countries".[64] The Mexican Minister of Foreign Affairs argued that "there does not exist in international law any principle universally accepted by countries, nor by writers of treatises on this

---

58 Borchard, 'The Minimum Standard of the Treatment of Aliens' 61.
59 ibid 62-63.
60 Williams, 'International Law and the Property of Aliens' 17.
61 ibid 18, and 20: "It is surely impossible, whatever may be our views as to the relative merits of socialist and individualist, doctrines, to assert that modern civilization requires all states to accept so unreservedly the theories of one side in the great economic dispute."
62 The exchange is printed in Green Haywood Hackworth, *Digest of International Law* (vol III, Department of State 1942) 655-665; see also Montt, *State Liability in Investment Treaty Arbitration. Global Constitutional and Administrative Law on the BIT Generation* 57, arguing that "the *classic* claim-the nineteenth century Calvo Doctrine, whoe aim had not been to erode the rule of law but to terminate forcible self-help through national treatment-was transmuted into a new and *opportunistic* one: expropriation without compensation."
63 Hackworth, *Digest of International Law* 657, see also 658 where the formula "adequate, effective and prompt payment" appears.
64 ibid 657.

subject, that would render obligatory the giving of adequate compensation for expropriation of a general and impersonal character."[65] Hull maintained that the view according to which foreigners "are not entitled to better treatment than nationals of the country, presupposes the maintenance of law and order consistent with principles of international law; that is to say, when aliens are admitted into a country the country is obligated to accord them that degree of protection of life and property consistent with the standards of justice recognized by the law of nations."[66] In summary, the unwritten law could not overcome these fundamental differences.

2. The internationalization of contracts by general principles of law

According to a different construction, the international protection was based on general principles of law and the idea of so-called internationalized or delocalized contracts.

a) The emergence of this doctrine in the interwar period

The doctrine began to emerge with arbitration awards in which the arbitrators did not just apply the local law, meaning the host state's law, to a concession agreement between the host state and aliens, but took recourse to general principles of law and of international law.[67] The contracts were said to have

---

65 ibid 658: "Nevertheless Mexico admits, in obedience to her own laws, that she is indeed under obligation to indemnify in an adequate manner; but the doctrine which she maintains on the subject, which is based on the most authoritative opinions of writers of treatises on international law, is that the time and manner of such payment must be determined by her own laws."
66 ibid 660; see also Alfred Verdross, 'Règles générales du droit international de la paix' (1929) 30 RdC 384, according to whom the general rule of national treatment does not apply if the domestic legal system did not live up to international standards.
67 Joost HB Pauwelyn, 'Rational Design or Accidental Evolution? The Emergence of International Investment Law' in Zachary Douglas, Joost HB Pauwelyn, and Jorge E Viñuales (eds), *The Foundations of International Investment Law* (Oxford University Press 2014) 25, 27; Charles Leben, 'La théorie du contrat d'état et l'évolution du droit international des investissements' (2003) 302 RdC 221-234; Irmgard Marboe and August Reinisch, 'Contracts between States and Foreign Private Law Persons' [2011] Max Planck EPIL para 5 ff.; Alfred Verdross, 'Die Sicherung von ausländischen Privatrechten aus Abkommen zur wirtschaftlichen Entwicklung mit Schiedsklauseln'

become "internationalized"[68] or "delocalized"[69]. According to the doctrine of delocalized or internationalized contracts, the parties of a contract could decide *qua* party autonomy to subject the contract to a foreign legal order or even to public international law. This doctrine differed from the jurisprudence of the PCIJ which held that acquired rights were protected by international law[70], but added in the *Serbian Loans* case that "any contract which is not a contract between States in their capacity as subjects of international law is based on municipal law of some country."[71]

The case which, in hindsight, significantly contributed to the doctrine of internationalized contracts was the *Lena Goldfields* arbitration.[72] In a dispute concerning the concession agreement between the USSR and the British Lena Goldfields company, the arbitrators accepted the company's argument that not only Soviet law but general principles of law in the sense of article 38(3) of the PCIJ Statute formed the applicable law.[73] The USSR lost the

---

(1957) 18 ZaöRV 635 ff.; Patrick Dumberry, 'International Investment Contracts' in Tarcisio Gazzini and Eric de Brabandere (eds), *International Investment Law. The Sources of Rights and Obligations* (Martinus Nijhoff Publishers 2012) 224 ff.; Elisabeth Kjos, *Applicable law in investor-state arbitration: the interplay between national and international law* (Oxford University Press 2013) 214.

68 *Texaco Overseas Petroleum Company and California Asiatic Oil Company v The Government of the Libyan Arab Republic* Jean-Marie Dupuy, Sole Arbitrator, Awards on the Merits (19 January 1977) 53 ILR 446; Francis A Mann, 'The theoretical approach towards the law governing contracts between states and private persons' (1975) 11 Revue belge de droit international 564-565.

69 *Texaco Overseas Petroleum Company and California Asiatic Oil Company v The Government of the Libyan Arab Republic* 53 ILR 420, 445.

70 *Certain German Interests in Polish Upper Silesia* PCIJ Series A No 07, 22.

71 *Case Concerning the Payment of Various Serbian Loans Issued in France: France v Kingdom of the Serbs, Croats, and Slovenes* Judgment of 12 July 1929 [1929] PCIJ Series A 20, 41.

72 VV Veeder, 'The Lena Goldfields Arbitration: The historical roots of three ideas' (1998) 47 ICLQ 772: Lena Goledfield's counsel's "internationalisation of a transnational contract was a gigantic first step for international commercial arbitration, almost equivalent to the caveman's discovery of fire."; Sornarajah, *Resistance and Change in the International Law on Foreign Investment* 95-96 on the genesis of the view of the internationalizations of contracts, also arguing: "it would be inexact to elevate the Lena Goldfields Arbitration as being the forerunner of the internationalization theory. It was an aberration that was seized upon later to make exorbitant claims." See also Andrea Leiter, 'Protecting concessionary rights: General principles and the making of international investment law' (2022) 35 Leiden Journal of International Law 55 ff.

73 Arthur Nussbaum, 'Arbitration between the Lena Goldfields Ltd. and the Soviet Government' (1950) 36(1) Cornell Law Review 42-53 (where the award is printed); on

case and was ruled to compensate the company for the unjust enrichment, a principle which was back then not well known in English law.[74] The concession agreement did not refer to general principles of law or any particular law. As Veeder demonstrated, several reasons may explain the reference to general principles of law: the company likely did not want Soviet law to be the sole applicable law. Furthermore, there was no possible argument to be made for English law as applicable law.[75] Hence, the company appealed to general principles of law and the tribunal accepted this argument.[76] The emerged doctrine of internationalized contracts was based on the concern of Western "lawyers for the protection of foreign investors in developing countries"[77], and certain awards were certainly not free from problematic, if not patronizing[78], formulations with respect to the local law.[79]

---

the difficulty to obtain an official citation see Veeder, 'The Lena Goldfields Arbitration: The historical roots of three ideas' 748 footnote 1.

74 ibid 751; cf. Wolfgang Friedmann, *The Changing Structure of international law* (Stevens 1964) 146 on the arbitrators' use of the principle of unjust enrichment.

75 English law was the *lex loci arbitri* as the award "was an English award made in London", Veeder, 'The Lena Goldfields Arbitration: The historical roots of three ideas' 749.

76 ibid 766-767.

77 Arghyrios Athanasiou Fatouros, 'International Law and the Internationalized Contract' (1980) 74 AJIL 140, who also referred to what he described as "the lack of legal sophistication in many of these countries at that time".

78 Vaughan Lowe, 'The Politics of Law-Making: Are the Method and Character of Norm Creation Changing?' in Michael Byers (ed), *The role of law in international politics: essays in international relations and international law* (Oxford University Press 2000) 208; Paparinskis, *The international minimum standard and fair and equitable treatment* 60.

79 In 1939, the Sheikh of Abu Dhabi concluded a concession agreement with the company Petroleum Development (Trucial Coast) Limited in Abu Dhabi. The ensuing arbitration concerned the question whether the concession to drill for and extract mineral oil in Abu Dhabi includes the right to do so from the subsoil of the seabed subjacent to the territorial sea of Abu Dhabi and in any submarine area lying outside territorial waters. The Umpire came in his award to the conclusion that the dispute could not be settled on the basis of municipal law, *Petroleum Development (Trucial Coast) Ltd v Sheikh of Abu Dhabi* Award of Lord Asquith of Bishopstone (September 1951) 1 ICLQ 247 250-251: "[N]o such law can reasonably be said to exist. The Sheikh administers a purely discretionary justice with the assistance of the Koran; and it would be fanciful to suggest that in this very primitive region there is any settled body of legal principles applicable to the construction of modern commercial instrument [...] Clause 17 of the agreement [...] repels the notion that the municipal law of any country, as such, could be appropriate. The terms of that clause invite, indeed prescribe, the application

Chapter 10: International Investment Law

b) The continuation of this doctrine after the second world war

After the second world war, certain awards were based on this doctrine. In the *Sapphire* arbitration between the National Iranian Oil Company (NIOC), a publicly owned company, and the Sapphire Petroleums Ltd., a Canadian company, the arbitrator, Pierre Calvin, decided the case on the basis of what he considered to constitute general principles of law, instead of Iranian law. Article 38 of the contract provided that the parties undertook to carry out the contract's provisions according to the principles of good faith and good will, and to respect the spirit as well as the letter of the agreement. On the basis of this reference to the principles of good faith and good will and under consideration of the *Lena Goldfields* arbitration and the *Abu Dhabi* arbitration, the arbitrator concluded that "such clause is scarcely compatible with the strict application of the internal law of a particular country. It much more often calls for the application of general principles of law, based upon reason and upon the common practice of civilized countries".[80]

The doctrine was also relevant in the so-called Libyan cases concerning the nationalization of the oil industry.[81] The awards dealt with identical choice of law clauses which were construed in different ways.[82] For instance, in the *Texaco* case, the sole arbitrator Pierre-Marie Dupuy[83] decided that the parties could choose international law as applicable law by virtue of the

of principles rooted in the good sense and common practice of the generality of civilised nations- a sort of 'modern law of nature.' [...] albeit English municipal law is inapplicable as such, some of its rules are in my view so firmly grounded in reason, as to form part of this broad body of jurisprudence-this 'modern law of nature.'"

80 *Sapphire International Petroleums Ltd v National Iranian Oil Company* Pierre Cavin, Sole Arbitrator, Award (15 March 1963) 35 ILR 173; Mārtiņš Paparinskis, 'Sapphire Arbitration' [2010] Max Planck EPIL 11; Georges R Delaume, 'The Proper Law of State Contracts and the Lex Mercatoria: A Reappraisal' (1988) 3(1) ICSID Review - Foreign Investment Law Journal 86-87.

81 Kjos, *Applicable law in investor-state arbitration: the interplay between national and international law* 219.

82 The provision read: "This Concession shall be governed by and interpreted in accordance with the principles of law of Libya common to the principles of international law and in the absence of such common principles then by and in accordance with the general principles of law, including such of those principles as may have been applied by international tribunals."

83 On the role of Dupuy see Antonio Cassese, *Five masters of international law: conversations with R-J Dupuy, E Jiménez de Aréchaga, R Jennings, L Henkin and O Schachter* (Hart 2011) 31-36; Julien Cantegreil, 'The Audacity of the Texaco/Calasiatic Award: René-Jean Dupuy and the Internationalization of Foreign Investment Law' (2011)

principle of party autonomy on which the contract was based.[84] According to Dupuy, it was not the host state's law[85] but international law itself which "empowered the parties to choose the law which was govern their contractual relations."[86] Dupuy argued that the references to general principles of law were "always regarded to be a sufficient criterion for the internationalization of a contract".[87] He also pointed to the existence of an arbitration clause[88] and the nature of concession deeds since those were "not concerned only with an isolated purchase or Performance, but tend to bring to developing countries Investments and technical assistance" and aim at a "close cooperation between the State and the contracting party".[89]

In contrast, the *BP* arbitrator held that the governing law consisted first and foremost of the principles of Libyan law: "[I]n the absence of principles common to the law of Libya and international law, the general principles of law, including such of those principles as may have been applied by international tribunals."[90]

22(2) EJIL 441 ff.; for a critical evaluation see Sornarajah, *Resistance and Change in the International Law on Foreign Investment* 113-115; according to Spiermann, out of the awards on the Libyan nationalization, "it was Texaco v. Libya that was most creative, or incorrect, in applying international law", Ole Spiermann, 'Applicable Law' in Peter T Muchlinski, Federico Ortino, and Christoph Scheuer (eds), *The Oxford Handbook of International Investment Law* (Oxford University Press 2008) 99 footnote 38.

84 *Texaco Overseas Petroleum Company and California Asiatic Oil Company v The Government of the Libyan Arab Republic* 53 ILR 420, 442, 447; see recently Kjos, *Applicable law in investor-state arbitration: the interplay between national and international law* 213.

85 *Texaco Overseas Petroleum Company and California Asiatic Oil Company v The Government of the Libyan Arab Republic* 53 ILR 420, 460.

86 ibid 443, 450 (quote).

87 ibid 453.

88 ibid 454-455.

89 ibid 456; cf. on the significance of these contracts for the foreign policy of the host state: Weil, 'Le droit international en quête de son identité: cours général de droit international public' 96.

90 *BP Exploration Company (Libya) Limited v Government of the Libyan Arab Republic* Lagergreen, Sole Arbitrator, Award (10 October 1973, 1 August 1974) 53 ILR 329; *LIAMCO v The Government of the Libyan Arab Republic* Sobhi Mahmassani, Sole Arbitrator, Award (12 April 1977) 20 ILM 34-37; cf. also *The Government of the State of Kuwait v The American Independent Oil Company* Paul Reuter, Hamed Sultan, Sir Gerald Fitzmaurice, arbitrators, Award (14 March 1982) 21 ILM 100, holding that the applicable law is Kuwaiti law and international law which forms part of Kuwaiti

The doctrine as such remained controversial both as matter of legal doctrine and from the perspective of legal policy.[91] It was based on the idea of both parties standing on equal footing, which is why one party, the state, should not be in a position to unilaterally amend the contractual relationship by changing its municipal legislation.[92] General principles such as *pacta sunt servanda*[93] and good faith motivated the search for a legal system different from municipal law and invited tribunals to engage with comparative law for the purpose of identifying the applicable law and to focus on limits imposed by international law on states' capacity to introduce legislative changes. However, the very idea of internationalization according to which the contract was first and foremost subject to international law was not necessary in order to arrive at a different law than the host state's law. The same result could have been achieved by way of conventional choice of law doctrines which take the host state's legal order as a starting point.[94] According to Oscar Schachter, the term "internationalized contracts" should be understood "in a descriptive sense" for certain types of contracts without implying, however, "that the contracts have been transposed to another 'legal order' or that they have become subject to international law in the same way as a treaty between two

---

    law, the tribunal stressed that "Kuwait law is a highly evolved system"; Animoil thus stands for a tendency to "relocalize" contracts and to take account of developments in local law, see Georges R Delaume, 'The Proper Law of State Contracts Revisited' (1997) 12(1) ICSID Review - Foreign Investment Law Journal 2 ff.

91 Muthucumaraswamy Sornarajah, 'The Myth of International Contract Law' (1981) 15 Journal of World Trade Law 187 ff.; Jean Ho, *State Responsibility for Breaches of Investment Contracts* (Cambridge University Press 2018) 187.

92 *Saudi Arabia v Arabian American Oil Company* Sausser-Hall Referee, Badawi/Hassan, Habachy Arbitrators, Award (23 August 1958) 27 ILR 168; *Texaco Overseas Petroleum Company and California Asiatic Oil Company v The Government of the Libyan Arab Republic* 53 ILR 420, 456.

93 Spiermann, 'Applicable Law' 95: "[...] the principle pacta sunt servanda conveys the basic premise upon which applicable law in this field has been internationalized".

94 Fatouros, 'International Law and the Internationalized Contract' 136; Delaume, 'The Proper Law of State Contracts and the Lex Mercatoria: A Reappraisal' 93; cf. also Francis A Mann, 'State Contracts and State Responsibility' (1960) 54 AJIL 580-581, referring to the role of private international law in order to identify the proper law; he did not reject the doctrine of internationlization completely: "there is no room for the doctrine of the possible 'internationalization' of contracts except in cases in which the parties, judge or arbitrator consciously and specifically refer to or apply public international law as such", Francis A Mann, 'The Proper Law of Contracts Concluded by International Persons' (1959) 35 BYIL 54.

states."[95] Also, the existence of an arbitration clause "can hardly be construed as necessarily a sign of internationalization".[96] At the very least, the doctrine inspired to a certain extent the scholarship on the transnationalization of law[97] and article 42 of the ICSID convention.[98] Today, the international protection of contracts does not depend on the doctrine of internationalized contracts but follows from umbrella clauses and the extension of the protections of fair and equitable treatment provisions to contracts.[99]

III. The development of the modern investment regime after WW II

Because of its vagueness and its political background, the content of the unwritten law on the international minimum standard remained contested, and the awards were difficult to enforce. Already in 1931, Beckett argued that the "protection of its nationals (including companies) would be much easier for the State concerned if the rights of such nationals were defined by elaborate treaties and not allowed to rest on general principles of International Law" which had been formulated "when the economic life of nations was much simpler than it is to-day".[100] As will be demonstrated below, states in fact pursued strategies of "treatification"[101], but they did so for different reasons which also concerned the interrelationship of bilateral treaties and customary international law.

---

95 Schachter, 'International Law in Theory and Practice: general course in public international law' 308-309.
96 Fatouros, 'International Law and the Internationalized Contract' 136.
97 cf. Philip C Jessup, *Transnational Law* (Yale University Press 1956) 81-82, referring to the Abu Dhabi arbitration; Delaume, 'The Proper Law of State Contracts and the Lex Mercatoria: A Reappraisal' 85 footnote 25, referring to the Lena Goldfields arbitration.
98 Weil, 'Le droit international en quête de son identité: cours général de droit international public' 97.
99 On this development see Julian Arato, 'Corporations as Lawmakers' (2015) 56 Harvard International Law Journal 230 Fn. 4, 247 ff.; Campbell McLachlan, Laurence Shore, and Matthew Weiniger, *International Investment Arbitration* (2nd edn, Oxford University Press 2017) 128 ff.; Spiermann, 'Applicable Law' 103 ff.
100 WE Beckett, 'Diplomatic Claims in Respect of Injuries to Companies' (1931) 17 Transactions of the Grotius Society 194.
101 Jeswald W Salacuse, 'The Treatification of International Investment Law' (2007) 13 Law and Busines Review of the Americas 155 ff.

1. Failed multilateral attempts

Early attempts after the second world war to establish a multilateral regime failed. The Havanna Charter[102] was intended to establish an international trade organization with competences both on trade and investment. Because of different interests between capital-importing countries and capital-exporting countries, the Havanna Charter "contained only embryonic rules on foreign investment protection."[103] The so-called cold war as well as the difficulty of obtaining the US Senate's advice and consent necessary for a ratification by the US explained the failure of the Havanna Charter.[104]

The 1967 OECD Draft Convention on the Protection of Foreign Property[105] was inspired by the so-called Abs-Shawcross Draft[106], named after Hermann Abs, then Chairman of Deutsche Bank, and Lord Hartley Shawcross, former British Attorney-General and then Director of the Shell Petroleum Company.[107] Both provided for the fair and equitable treatment standard which can be found in modern bilateral investment treaties. However, the OECD Draft Convention was never opened to signature due to the lack of support by OECD states.[108] According to the OECD, the suggested standard of fair and equitable treatment "conforms in effect to the 'minimum standard' which forms part of customary international law."[109]

2. Ongoing contestation in the General Assembly

The substantive obligations, in particular in relation to expropriation, remained contested. The political disputes continued in the General Assembly.

---

102 Havana Charter for an International Trade Organization (signed 24 March 1984) United Nations Conference on Trade and Employment, Final Act and Related Documents, E/CONF2/78.
103 Schill, *The multilateralization of international investment law* 33.
104 ibid 34.
105 OECD Draft Convention on the Protection of Foreign Property (1967, not open to signature) (1968) 7 ILM 117–143; Rudolf Dolzer and Christoph Schreuer, *Principles of International Investment Law* (Oxford University Press 2012) 8-9.
106 Georg Schwarzenberger, 'The Abs-Shawcross Draft Convention on Investments Abroad; a Critical Commentary' (1960) 9 Journal of Public Law 147 ff.
107 Schill, *The multilateralization of international investment law* 36.
108 ibid 36.
109 OECD Draft Convention on the Protection of Foreign Property (1967, not open to signature) (1968) 7 ILM 117–143 at 120.

In 1962 the General Assembly adopted resolution 1803.[110] According to the resolution, "nationalization, expropriation or requisitioning shall be based on grounds or reasons of public utility, security or the national interest which are recognized as overriding purely individual or private interests both domestic and foreign. In such cases the owner shall be paid appropriate compensation, in accordance with the rules in force in the State taking such measures in the exercise of its sovereignty and in accordance with international law."[111] The resolution represented a compromise and was subject to different readings: whereas supporters of the Hull formula could argue that nationalizations required compensation, opponents could point out that only "appropriate compensation" is required which was less than complete compensation and which recognized the public interest in measures of this kind.[112] In 1974, the General Assembly adopted the Declaration on the Establishment of a New International Economic Order (NIEO).[113] The resolution recognized "the right of nationalization or transfer of ownership to its nationals, this right being an expression of the full permanent sovereignty of the State"[114] without recognizing, however, an obligation to pay compensation.[115]

3. Preference for BITs

It is against this background that one has to consider the turn to bilateral investment agreements. States made a "conscious choice for bilateralism"[116], but were motivated by different reasons.

---

110 UNGA Res 1803 (XVII) (14 December 1962) UN Doc A/RES/1803(XVII).
111 ibid para 4.
112 Giorgio Sacerdoti, 'Bilateral treaties and multilateral instruments on investment protection' (1997) 269 RdC 391; Schill, *The multilateralization of international investment law* 37.
113 UNGA Res 3201 (S-VI) (1 May 1974) UN Doc A/RES/3201(S-VI).
114 ibid para 4 e).
115 Schill, *The multilateralization of international investment law* 37-8; cf. UNGA Res 3281 (XXIX) (12 December 1974) UN Doc A/RES/3281(XXIX), "Charter of Economic Rights and Duties of States", Art. 2(2)(c): "[Each State has the right] to nationalize, expropriate or transfer ownership of foreign property, in which case appropriate compensation should be paid by the State adopting such measures".
116 Paparinskis, *The international minimum standard and fair and equitable treatment* 142; Patrick Juillard, 'L'évolution des sources du droit des investissements' (1994) 250 RdC 78 ff.

Chapter 10: International Investment Law

In response to doubts and the "political controversies illustrated by the shaky foundations of the standards of customary international law with regard to the protection of aliens"[117], capital-exporting states attempted to translate what they considered to be general principles of international law into bilateral agreements.[118] Bilateral treaties were, therefore, a means to "prevent a backsliding of customary international law"[119] and to strengthen and reaffirm the international minimum standard. From the perspective of capital-importing states, however, bilateral treaties made it possible for those states to actively shape international law. As Montt pointed out, it was the "relative success" of the NIEO which made bilateral arrangements attractive both for capital-importing and for capital-exporting states.[120]

Since the first modern BIT has been concluded between the Federal Republic of Germany and Pakistan in 1959[121], as over 2.000 BITs are currently

---

117 Schill, *The multilateralization of international investment law* 27-28, acknowledging that international tribunals in the inter-war period "did not accept that national treatment independent of a specific minimum standard was sufficient to conform to international law," adding: "Nevertheless, [...] political controversies illustrated the shaky foundations of the standards of customary international law with regard to the protection of aliens."
118 Kenneth J Vandevelde, 'U.S. Bilateral Investment Treaties: The Second Wave' (1993) 14(4) Michigan Journal of International Law 625: one purpose of BITs "was to counter the claim made during the 1970s by many developing countries that customary international law no longer required that expropriation be accompanied by prompt, adequate, and effective compensation, if indeed it ever had"; Pauwelyn, 'Rational Design or Accidental Evolution? The Emergence of International Investment Law' 25 ff.; Paparinskis, *The international minimum standard and fair and equitable treatment* 165 and in particular pp. 67, 84 ("Compliance with the international minimum standard has often been imposed as a matter of treaty law"); in the *ELSI* case, the Court did not discuss the relationship between treaty and custom in the context of international investment law, *Elettronica Sicula SpA (ELSI)* (*United States of America v. Italy*) (Judgment of 20 July 1989) [1989] ICJ Rep 5 ff.
119 Pauwelyn, 'Rational Design or Accidental Evolution? The Emergence of International Investment Law' 25-26.
120 Montt, *State Liability in Investment Treaty Arbitration. Global Constitutional and Administrative Law on the BIT Generation* 62-63.
121 Treaty between the Federal Republic of Germany and Pakistan for the Promotion and Protection of Investments (signed 25 November 1959, entered into force 28 April 1962) 457 UNTS 23. As part of the first generation of BITs, the treaty between Germany and Pakistan did not provide for investor-state dispute settlement. For a historical overview see Chester Brown, 'Introduction: The Development and Importance of the Model Bilateral Investment Treaty' in *Commentaries on Selected Model Investment Treaties* (Oxford University Press 2013) 3 ff.

in force.¹²² Several BITs have contained so-called umbrella clauses, by which states agree to honour contractual commitments with foreign investors.¹²³ By virtue of such an umbrella clause, breaches of a contract can be elevated to breaches of the BIT.¹²⁴

The multilateral ICSID Convention establishes the International Centre for the Settlement of Investment Disputes (ICSID)¹²⁵ and offers a procedural framework for the settlement of disputes without providing substantive rules that govern a dispute between a state and foreign investors.¹²⁶ According to article 42(1) of the ICSID convention, the tribunal shall decide a dispute in accordance with such rules of law as agreed by the parties. In the absence of such agreement the tribunal shall apply the law of the Contracting State party to the dispute (including its rules on the conflict of laws) and such rules of international law as may be applicable.¹²⁷ More and more BITs built on the

---

122 Dolzer and Schreuer, *Principles of International Investment Law* 13: "close to 3,000 BITs"; José E Alvarez, 'The Public International Law Regime Governing International Investment' (2009) 344 RdC 214: "some 2,600 BITs and an additional 30 or so regional FTAs". According to UNCTAD, there are 2850 bilateral investment treaties in force, UNCTAD, 'International Investment Agreements Navigator' ⟨https://investmentpolicy.unctad.org/international-investment-agreements⟩ accessed 1 February 2023.

123 Marboe and Reinisch, 'Contracts between States and Foreign Private Law Persons' para 38.

124 On the debate as to the scope of umbrella clauses see ibid para 39.

125 Convention on the settlement of investment disputes between States and nationals of other States (signed 18 March 1965, entered into force 14 October 1966) 575 UNTS 159.

126 Ursula Kriebaum, 'Article 42' in Stephan W Schill (ed), *Schreuer's Commentary on the ICSID Convention* (3rd edn, Cambridge University Press 2022) 802 para 1; Rudolf Dolzer, Ursula Kriebaum, and Christoph Schreuer, *Principles of International Investment Law* (3rd edn, Oxford University Press 2022) 16.

127 It is debated whether parties' choice of domestic law, or any other legal order, excludes the application of international law. The dominant view holds, however, that even when domestic law is chosen by the parties, international law remains applicable to some extent and can exercise a "corrective function" and operate as a limit to the application of the host state's law cf. Kriebaum, 'Article 42' 845 para 159, 847 para 165, 849 para 170, 885-891. This statement holds true, of course, from the perspective of the ICSID convention; from the perspective of the respective domestic constitutional law there may be limits to the application of international law, see on the relationship between German constitutional law and investment law Peter-Tobias Stoll, Till Patrik Holterhus, and Henner Gött, *Investitionsschutz und Verfassung: völkerrechtliche Investitionsschutzverträge aus der Perspektive des deutschen und europäischen Verfassungsrechts* (Mohr Siebeck 2017) 97 ff; Peter-

ICSID system and provided for investor-state dispute settlement.[128] In *AAPL v. Sri Lanka*, an ICSID tribunal[129] accepted for the first time that an investor was entitled to bring a claim against a state based on the provisions of a BIT, rather than based on a contract or arbitration agreement with the state.[130] The most recent trend represents a shift to multilateral, or so-called mega-regional trade agreements which combine trade agreements and investment protection.[131]

C. The interrelationship of sources in a bilateralist structure and the quest for general law

International investment law can appear paradoxical when it comes to the interrelationship of sources of international law. As one observer has pointed out, the very form of bilateral treaties "suggests divergence rather than convergence"[132] at first sight; at the same time, is has been argued that "it would be difficult to imagine a category of treaties that is less of a self-contained regime or more dependent for its life upon nourishment from general international

---

Tobias Stoll, 'International Investment Law and the Rule of Law' (2018) 9 Goettingen Journal of International Law 272-273.

128 Sometimes, these BITs are referred to as second generation, see for instance Pauwelyn, 'Rational Design or Accidental Evolution? The Emergence of International Investment Law' 29-30, 33; Marc Jacob, 'Investmens, Bilateral Treaties' in *Max Planck EPIL* (2014) paras 11, 45. For a different genealogy see Anthea Roberts, 'Investment Treaties: The Reform Matrix' (2018) 112 AJIL Unbound 191, distinguishing "[f]irst-generation treaties from the 1990s and earlier" and "second generation of treaties from the mid-2000s onward [...] that aim at striking a better balance between investor protection and state sovereignty, while retaining investor-state arbitration".

129 *Asian Agricultural Products Ltd v Republic of Sri Lanka* Final Award (27 June 1990) ICSID Case No. ARB/87/3 para 18.

130 On this development see also Jan Paulsson, 'Arbitration Without Privity' (1995) 10(3) ICSID Review - Foreign Investment Law Journal 232 ff.; Pauwelyn, 'Rational Design or Accidental Evolution? The Emergence of International Investment Law' 31: "standing for a private investor to invoke a treaty breach".

131 Eyal Benvenisti, 'Democracy Captured: The Mega-Regional Agreements and the Future of Global Public Law' [2016] (2) IILJ Working Paper 1 ff.; see also below, p. 591.

132 Stephan W Schill, 'System-Building in Investment Treaty Arbitration and Lawmaking' in Armin von Bogdandy and Ingo Venzke (eds), *International judicial lawmaking: on public authority and democratic legitimation in global governance* (Springer 2012) 151.

The interrelationship of sources in a bilateralist structure and the quest for general law

law."[133] In spite of this "treatification"[134], investment lawyers and tribunals continued to turn to customary international law.[135] This section explores the jurisprudence of investment tribunals and reasons for a multilateralization in substance in a system that is shaped, by and large, by bilateralism in form. It will focus on the relationship between treaty obligations under investment treaties and customary international law and point to a convergence of functionally equivalent rules in the jurisprudence of tribunals and in the treatymaking practice of states (I.). It will then survey and comment on the scholarly debate on the interrelationship of sources in the context of international investment law (II.) before it will offer an evaluation (III.).

I. The relationship between treaty obligations and customary international law

The emerging network of bilateral relations has cast doubts on the (continued) relevance of any customary international law.[136] In 1970, the International Court of Justice held that the treatment of foreign investors by host states did not belong to the body of *erga omnes* obligations, stressing that this field would be characterized by "bilateral relations".[137] Therefore, "general arbitral jurisprudence" could be of no help for the identification of the general law, as the decisions "rested upon the terms of the instruments establishing the jurisdiction of the tribunal [...] and determining what rights might enjoy protection" and "therefore cannot give rise to generalization".[138]

---

133 Campbell McLachlan, 'Is There an Evolving Customary International Law on Investment?' (2016) 3(2) ICSID Review 262.
134 Salacuse, 'The Treatification of International Investment Law' 155.
135 d'Aspremont, 'International Customary Investment Law: Story of a Paradox' 5.
136 ibid 5 ff., pointing out that recently the interest in custom increased again; cf. Juillard, 'L'évolution des sources du droit des investissements' 130.
137 *Barcelona Traction, Light and Power Company, Limited* 32 paras 33-34, 46-47 para 89: "[T]he law on the subject has been formed in a period characterized by an intense conflict of systems and interests. It is essentially bilateral relations which have been concerned, relations in which the rights of both the State exercising diplomatic protection and the State in respect of which protection is sought have had to be safeguarded. Here as elsewhere, a body of rules could only have developed with the consent of those concerned."
138 ibid 40 para 63; on the lack of references to investment tribunals in the ICJ jurisprudence see Schill and Tvede, 'Mainstreaming Investment Treaty Jurisprudence The Contribution of Investment Treaty Tribunals to the Consolidation and Development

One decade later, however, in light of the increasing network of bilateral regulations, Francis Mann argued that it was not possible for states to reject the same principle of rule in a multilateral, customary, setting but accept it in a multitude of bilateral settings.[139] Mann's writings epitomize the difficulty of characterizing the relationship between the international minimum standard under customary international law and the obligation to accord fair and equitable treatment to investors under different BITs. He argued that fair and equitable treatment exceeded the international minimum standard and provided for a higher level of protection.[140] At the same time, he acknowledged the functional equivalence of the treaty standard and unwritten law insofar as he regarded the FET obligations as "a confirmation of the obligation to act in good faith, or to refrain from abuse or arbitrariness."[141]

---

of General International Law' 112-118. Cf. now *Obligation to Negotiate Access to the Pacific Ocean* (*Bolivia v. Chile*) (Judgment of 1 October 2018) [2018] ICJ Rep 559 para 162, noting that "references to legitimate expectations may be found in arbitral awards concerning disputes between a foreign investor and the host State that apply treaty clauses providing for fair and equitable treatment. It does not follow from such references that there exists in general international law a principle that would give rise to an obligation on the basis of what could be considered a legitimate expectation."

139 Francis A Mann, 'British treaties for the promotion and protection of investments' (1981) 52 BYIL 249-250: "Is it possible for a State to reject the rule according to which alien property may be expropriated only on certain terms long believed to be required by customary international law, yet to accept it for the purpose of these treaties? [...] The cold print of these treaties is a more reliable source of law than rhetorics in the United Nations." Cf. on the role of legitimate expectations created by treaties on the formation of custom Byers, *Custom, power and the power of rules: international relations and customary international law* 89, 125-126.

140 Mann, 'British treaties for the promotion and protection of investments' 241; for the view that fair and equitable treatment cannot be equated with the international minimum standard or customary international law, in particular against the historical background of the controversy concerning the international minimum standard see Stephen Vasciannie, 'The Fair and Equitable Treatment Standard in International Investment Law and Practice' (1999) 70 BYIL 104-105, 144; Patrick Dumberry, *Fair and Equitable Treatment. Its Interaction wit the Minimum Standard and Its Customary Status* (Brill 2018) 28, 76; on the debate see Dolzer and Schreuer, *Principles of International Investment Law* 130 ff.

141 Francis A Mann, *The legal aspect of money* (4th edn, Clarendon Press 1982) 510; see on this point Chester Brown and Audley Sheppard, 'United Kingdom' in *Commentaries on Selected Model Investment Treaties* (Oxford University Press 2013) 721-722; Ioana Tudor, *The Fair and Equitable Treatment Standard in the International Law of Foreign Investment* (Oxford University Press 2008) 66-67.

The interrelationship of sources in a bilateralist structure and the quest for general law

When it comes to functional equivalence and to functionally equivalent rules (see below 1.), the jurisprudence of investment tribunals (a)) and the treaty-practice of states (b)) can be read as confirmation of a convergence of functionally equivalent rules. One reason for this convergence might have been the view that the general obligations under a particular BIT should not be applied and concretized in an isolated fashion but under consideration of the broader normative environment (2.).

1. The relationship between functionally equivalent rules

a) The jurisprudence of investment tribunals

In international investment arbitration jurisprudence, the interrelationship of sources was discussed with respect to the relationship of the treaty-based concept of fair and equitable treatment and the international minimum standard under customary international law, in particular in the context of NAFTA.[142] Article 1105 NAFTA[143] sets forth the "minimum standard of treatment", according to which "each party shall accord to investments of another Party and to investments of investors of another Party treatment in accordance with international law, including fair and equitable treatment and full protection of security." As the obligation to accord fair and equitable treatment can be found in other investment treaties[144], tribunals assumed a convergence of

---

142 For an overview see Roland Kläger, *'Fair and equitable treatment' in international investment law* (Cambridge University Press 2011) 48 ff.; Marcela Klein Bronfman, 'Fair and Equitable Treatment: An Evolving Standard' (2006) 10 Max Planck Yearbook of United Nations law 608 ff. But see, for instance, *Metalclad Corporation v The United Mexican States* Award (30 August 2008) NAFTA ARB(AF)/97/1 paras 70, 76, 88, where the tribunal did not elaborate on the relationship between the FET provision and customary international law and instead interpreted the provision in light of the obligation to ensure transparency which the tribunal derived from article 102 NAFTA. This award illustrates an interpretative approach to fair and equitable treatment which focuses more on the letter and the spirit of the treaty than on customary international law.
143 North American Free Trade Agreement (signed 17 December 1992, entered into force 1 January 1994) 32 ILM (1993) 289.
144 According to *SD Myers, Inc v Government of Canada* Partial Award (13 November 2000) UNCITRAL/NAFTA (2001) 40 ILM 1408 para 259, the "minimum standard of treatment provision of the NAFTA is similar to clauses contained in BITs" and "is a floor below which treatment of foreign investors must not fall, even if a government

585

Chapter 10: International Investment Law

the treaty-based concept and customary international law also outside the NAFTA context, as will be demonstrated below.

The *Pope & Talbot* case was of crucial importance for this development and the discussion of the relationship between customary international law and treaty law. The tribunal rejected Canada's submission according to which the treaty obligations to accord to investors fair and equitable treatment, full protection and security would have to be read in light of international law which in Canada's view addressed only egregious misconduct. The tribunal went even further and adopted the view that article 1105 NAFTA went beyond customary international law.[145] In response to this award, Canada, Mexico and the USA issued through the NAFTA Free Trade Commission a binding interpretation[146] which went against the tribunal's interpretation of the relationship between article 1105 NAFTA and customary international law and instead synchronized both:

> "1. Article 1105(1) prescribes the customary international law minimum standard of treatment of aliens as the minimum standard of treatment to be afforded to investments of investors of another Party.
> 2. The concepts of "fair and equitable treatment" and "full protection and security" do not require treatment in addition to or beyond that which is required by the customary international law minimum standard of treatment of aliens."[147]

---

were not acting in a discriminatory manner" (para 259). In para 260 the Tribunal referred to the US-Mexican Claims Commission which applied the international minimum standard). According to the tribunal, "a breach of Article 1105 occurs only when it is shown that an investor has been treated in such an unjust or arbitrary manner that the treatment rises to the level that is unacceptable from the international perspective" (para 263).

145 *Pope & Talbot Inc v The Government of Canada* Award on the merits of phase 2 (10 April 2001) UNCITRAL/NAFTA 7 ICSID Reports 102; 122 ILR 352, see paras 109-118.

146 Article 1131(2) NAFTA reads: "An interpretation by the Commission of a provision of this Agreement shall be binding on a Tribunal established under this Section."; see Anthea Roberts, 'Power and Persuasion in Investment Treaty Interpretation: The Dual Role of States' (2010) 104 AJIL 179 ff. on the shared interpretative authority of tribunals and states which can shape the interpretation by subsequent agreements and subsequent practice; on the development of states beginning to reasserting control over the development of international investment law by state-state arbitration see also Andreas Kulick, 'State-State Investment Arbitration as a Means of Reassertion of Control: From Antagonism to Dialogue' in Andreas Kulick (ed), *Reassertion of control over the investment treaty regime* (Cambridge University Press 2017) 128 ff.

147 *Notes of Interpretation of Certain Chapter 11 Provisions* NAFTA Free Trade Commission (31 July 2001) 6 ICSID Rep. 567 sect. B; see now article 14.6(2) Agreement

This interpretation raised the questions of the content of the international minimum standard and of the relevance of the *Neer* formula, which the *Pope & Talbot* tribunal had the opportunity to address at the damages stage. According to the Canadian submission, "the principles of customary international law were frozen in amber at the time of the *Neer* decision".[148] The tribunal rejected "this static conception of customary international law" and referred to "an evolution in customary international law concepts since the 1920's" to which the many investment treaties as form of state practice were said to have contributed.[149]

Other tribunals likewise characterized the relationship between the treaty standard and the standard under customary international law as what could be described as convergence.[150] The *Mondev* tribunal argued that custom has evolved since the *Neer* case[151] and that the widespread proliferation of investment treaties as "a body of concordant practice will necessarily have influenced the content of rules governing the treatment of foreign investment in current international law. It would be surprising if this practice and the vast number of provisions it reflects were to be interpreted as meaning no more than the Neer Tribunal".[152] The *Loewen* tribunal argued that "'fair and equitable treatment' and 'full protection and security' are not free-standing

---

between the United States of America, the United Mexican States, and Canada (signed 30 November 2018, entered into force 1 July 2020) Office of the United States Trade Representative 14-5.

148 *Pope & Talbot Inc v The Government of Canada* Award in respect of damages (31 May 2002) UNCITRAL/NAFTA 7 ICSID Reports 148, 126 ILR 131, at para 57.

149 ibid paras 58, 59, 65; see also José Alvarez, 'A Bit on Custom' (2009) 42 NYU JILP 62-63: "One does not have to agree with every aspect of these extensive enumerations of what apparently FET and CIL now require to acknowledge that even if some of these requisites are now widely expected of governments, general public international law has shifted a great deal indeed since the Neer case recognized only the barest minimum requirements of states. It would appear, based on the available FET arbitral decisions, that today a state need not have taken concrete action in bad faith to be guilty of a violation of that standard—or of the underlying international minimum standard. Today, a state's failure to act, particularly to provide a remedy of a breach of the state's own representations to an investor, could ground a violation of general international law."

150 See *Chemtura Corporation v Canada* Award (2 August 2010) PCA Case No. 2008-01 paras 121, 236; *Merrill & Ring Forestry LP v Canada* Award (31 March 2010) ICSID Case No. UNCT/07/1 paras 210-213.

151 *Mondev International Ltd v United States of America* Award (11 October 2002) ICSID Case No. ARB(AF)/99/2 para 116.

152 ibid para 117.

obligations. They constitute obligations only to the extent that they are recognized by customary international law."[153] The *ADF* tribunal indicated a convergence, or even assimilation, by speaking of "the customary international law standard of treatment embodied in Article 1105(1)".[154] As was aptly summarized by *Waste Management* tribunal:

> "[...] the minimum standard of treatment of fair and equitable treatment is infringed by conduct attributable to the State and harmful to the claimant if the conduct is arbitrary, grossly unfair, unjust or idiosyncratic, is discriminatory and exposes the claimant to sectional or racial prejudice, or involves a lack of due process leading to an outcome which offends judicial propriety".[155]

Against the background of this case-law, the *Glamis* tribunal's approach was an outlier. According to the *Glamis* tribunal, "the fundamentals of the *Neer* standard thus still apply today", a violation of the minimum standard continued to require a sufficiently egregious and shocking act; the determination as to the existence of such act could be made, however, according to present standards since "as an international community, we may be shocked by State actions now that did not offend us previously".[156] The *Glamis* tribunal emphasized the separation between treaty based concepts and customary international law. In its view, arbitral awards could serve "as illustrations of customary international law if they involve an examination of customary international law, as opposed to a treaty-based, or autonomous, interpretation."[157] In contrast, "arbitral decisions that apply an autonomous standard provide no guidance inasmuch as the entire method of reasoning does not bear on an inquiry into custom."[158] However, to make the possibility of consideration of awards dependent on whether those awards explicitly apply customary international law instead of examining the possibility of convergence in sub-

---

153 *Loewen Group, Inc and Raymond L Loewen v United States of America* Award (26 June 2003) ICSID Case No. ARB(AF)/98/3 para 128.
154 *ADF Group Inc v United States of America* Award (9 January 2003) ICSID Case No. ARB (AF)/00/1 para 190.
155 *Waste Management, Inc v United Mexican States ("Number 2")* Award (30 April 2004) ICSID Case No ARB(AF)/00/3 para 98; according to the *Bilcon* tribunal, "formulation of the 'general standard for Article 1105' by the Waste Management Tribunal is particularly influential", *William Ralph Clayton, William Richard Clayton, Douglas Clayton, Daniel Clayton and Bilcon of Delaware Inc v Government of Canada* para 442.
156 *Glamis Gold, Ltd v The United States of America* Award (8 June 2009) UNCITRAL/NAFTA 48 ILM 1038 para 22.
157 ibid para 605.
158 ibid para 608.

stance may overemphasize the distinctiveness of the sources and represent an isolationist understanding of sources. In any case, even though treaties and custom were separated, the tribunal still recognized some value in custom, as custom would provide a minimum standard, "a floor, an absolute bottom, below which conduct is not accepted by the international community".[159] As the *Bilcon* tribunal rightly observed, "NAFTA tribunals have, however, tended to move away from the position more recently expressed in *Glamis*".[160]

Moreover, it is difficult to find support for the *Glamis* tribunal's static understanding of custom outside NAFTA. The *Occidental* tribunal concluded that "*in the instant case* the Treaty standard is not different from that required under international law concerning both the stability and predictability of the legal and business framework of the investment. *To this extent* the Treaty standard can be equated with that under international law as evidenced by the opinions of the various tribunals cited above."[161] Likewise, the *CMS* tribunal held that in the case under review differences between the treaty standard and the international minimum standard were not "relevant *in this case*" since "the Treaty standard of fair and equitable treatment and its connection with the required stability and predictability of the business environment [...] is not different from the international law minimum standard and its evolution under customary law."[162]

The passages quoted above highlight that the relationship between treaty standards and customary international law also depends on the particularities of the case and of the respective treaty standard, which, as also recognized by the *Sempra* tribunal and the *Enron* tribunal, may sometimes "be equated" with the minimum standard and in other cases "be more precise than its customary international law forefathers".[163] Also, the *Saluka* tribunal argued

---

159 ibid para 615.
160 *William Ralph Clayton, William Richard Clayton, Douglas Clayton, Daniel Clayton and Bilcon of Delaware Inc v Government of Canada* para 435; for a critique of *Glamis*, see also Reisman, 'Canute Confronts the Tide: States versus Tribunals and the Evolution of the Minimum Standard in Customary International Law' 630-632.
161 *Occidental Exploration and Production Company v The Republic of Ecuador* Final Award (1 July 2004) UNCITRAL LCIA Case No. UN3467 para 190 (italics added).
162 *CMS Gas Transmission Company v Argentine Republic* Award (12 May 2005) ICSID Case No. ARB/01/8 (italics added) para 284.
163 *Sempra Energy International v Argentine Republic* Award (28 September 2007) ICSID Case No. ARB/02/16 para 302; *Enron Creditors Recovery Corp Ponderosa Assets, LP v Argentine Republic* Award (22 May 2007) ICSID Case No. ARB/01/3 para 258.

that the difference between both standards "may well be more apparent than real" and that apparent differences could often be explained "by the contextual and factual differences" of the respective cases.[164]

b) The treatymaking practice of states

This trend of alignment and convergence is also mirrored in treaty practice. As pointed out by Jean Ho,[165] the UNCTAD World Investment Reports have depicted a tendency of states to equate fair and equitable treatment to the international minimum standard under customary international law.[166] According to UNCTAD, two policy objectives underlined this trend, namely to "preserve the right to regulate in the public interest" and to "avoid overexposure to litigation".[167] As the 2016 UNCTAD World Report illustrates, only two percent of the 1,372 BITs that were concluded between 1962 and 2011 referred to the minimum standard of treatment under customary international

---

164 *Saluka Investments BV v The Czech Republic* Award (17 March 2006) UNCITRAL (1976) PCA Case No. 2001-04 para 291; see also *Azurix Corp v The Argentine Republic* Award (14 July 2006) ICSID Case No. ARB/01/12 para 361 (arguing that the text of article II.2(a) of the BIT between Argentina and the USA according to which investors shall be accorded fair and equitable treatment and shall in no case be accorded treatment less than required by international law "permits to interpret fair and equitable treatment and full protection and security as higher standards than required by international law [...] [but] the Tribunal does not consider that it is of material significance for its application of the standard of fair and equitable treatment to the facts of the case [...] [T]he minimum requirement to satisfy this standard has evolved and the Tribunal considers that its content is substantially similar whether the terms are interpreted in their ordinary meaning").
165 Ho, *State Responsibility for Breaches of Investment Contracts* 115.
166 UNCTAD, *World Investment Report 2015* (2015) ⟨https : / / unctad . org / en / PublicationsLibrary/wir2015_en.pdf⟩ accessed 1 February 2023 113; UNCTAD, *World Investment Report 2016* (2016) ⟨https://unctad.org/en/PublicationsLibrary/wir2016_en.pdf⟩ accessed 1 February 2023 111, 113; UNCTAD, *World Investment Report 2017* (2017) ⟨https://unctad.org/en/PublicationsLibrary/wir2017_en.pdf⟩ accessed 1 February 2023 121; UNCTAD, *World Investment Report 2018* (2018) ⟨https://unctad.org/en/PublicationsLibrary/wir2018_en.pdf⟩ accessed 1 February 2023 97; UNCTAD, *World Investment Report 2019* (2019) ⟨https://unctad.org/en/PublicationsLibrary/wir2019_en.pdf⟩ accessed 1 February 2023 107.
167 UNCTAD, *World Investment Report 2015* at 113.

law in relation to fair and equitable treatment, whereas 35 percent of 40 BITs concluded between 2012 and 2014 referred to customary international law.[168]

The so-called megaregional trade and investment agreements confirm this trend to different degrees. Article 9.6(1) CPTPP[169] stipulates that "[e]ach party shall accord to covered investments treatment in accordance with applicable customary international law principles, including fair and equitable treatment and full protection and security". Article 9.6(2) CPTPP specifies that "paragraph 1 prescribes the customary international law minimum standard of treatment of aliens as the standard of treatment to be afforded to covered investments. The concepts of "fair and equitable treatment" and "full protection and security" do not require treatment in addition to or beyond that which is required by that standard".

Also, article 14.6(1) of the so-called New NAFTA refers to the "minimum standard of treatment [...] in accordance with customary international law, including fair and equitable treatment and full protection of security." Article 14.6(2) confirms that "the concepts of 'fair and equitable treatment' and 'full protection of security' do not require treatment in addition to or beyond that what is required by this standard". In an annex, the parties confirm "their shared understanding that 'customary international law' [...] results from a general and consistent practice of States that they follow from a sense of legal obligation. The customary international law minimum standard of treatment of aliens refers to all customary international law principles that protect the investments of aliens."[170]

In 2011, the European Parliament adopted a resolution in which it "considers that future investment agreements concluded by the EU should be based on [...] fair and equitable treatment, defined on the basis of the level of treatment established by international customary law"[171] It is noteworthy

---

168 UNCTAD, *World Investment Report 2016* at 114.
169 Comprehensive and Progressive Agreement for Trans-Pacific Partnership (signed 18 May 2018, entered into force 30 December 2018) Australian Government Department of Foreign Affairs and Trade.
170 Agreement between the United States of America, the United Mexican States, and Canada (signed 30 November 2018, entered into force 1 July 2020) Office of the United States Trade Representative 14-5, Annex 14-A.
171 European Parliament resolution of 6 April 2011 on the future European international investment policy (first published 2011, 2012/C 296 E/05, 2011) para 19.

that article 8.10 CETA[172] defines breaches of fair and equitable treatment without any explicit recourse to customary international law.[173] CETA also provides that "[a] Tribunal established under this Chapter shall render its decision consistent with this Agreement as interpreted in accordance with the Vienna Convention on the Law of Treaties, and other rules and principles of international law applicable between the Parties".[174]

2. Reasons for the preference for convergence

Tribunals preferred to assume convergence between customary international law and the treaty-based standard when they determined the content of "fair and equitable treatment" rather than applying their "own idiosyncratic standard *in lieu* of the standard laid down in Article 1105(1) [NAFTA]".[175] By referring to international law, tribunals strengthened their interpretations of what they regarded to be fair and equitable. That references to international law can have such a strengthening effect stands to reason since the legitimacy of the adjudicative process rested on the application of preexisting norms that were enacted by others.[176] As stated by the *ADF* tribunal, "any general requirement to accord 'fair and equitable treatment' and 'full protection and

---

172 Comprehensive Economic and Trade Agreement between Canada, of the One Part, and the European Union and Its Member States, of the Other Part (signed 29 February 2016) 60 Official Journal of the European Union (2017) 23.
173 See also Dumberry, *Fair and Equitable Treatment. Its Interaction wit the Minimum Standard and Its Customary Status* 44-45, characterizing the list of article 8.10 as "closed list", since previous drafts' opening formulas ("notably", "non exclusively" or "includes") cannot be found in article 8.10's final text, and arguing (at 44) that "the final list of elements [...] is to a very large extent based on how NAFTA tribunals have interpreted Article 1105 over the last 20 years."
174 Art. X.27(1).
175 *Mondev International Ltd v United States of America* Award (11 October 2002) para 120; on the convergence of both standards see also Campbell McLachlan, 'Investment Treaties and General International Law' (2008) 57(2) ICLQ 394.
176 Montt, *State Liability in Investment Treaty Arbitration. Global Constitutional and Administrative Law on the BIT Generation* 309; see also Jürgen Habermas, *Between Facts and Norms. Contributions to a Discourse Theory of Law and Democracy* (William Rehg tr, 2nd edn, MIT Press 1996) 261-262; Habermas, *Faktizität und Geltung: Beiträge zur Diskurstheorie des Rechts und des demokratischen Rechtsstaats* 317-319; Maus, 'Die Trennung von Recht und Moral als Begrenzung des Rechts' 199, 208; Benvenisti, 'Customary International Law as a Judicial Tool for Promoting Efficiency' 103.

security' must be disciplined by being based upon State practice and judicial or arbitral caselaw or other sources of customary or general international law."[177]

For this reason, tribunals also invoked general principles of law. According to the *Sempra* tribunal, "[t]he principle of good faith is thus relied on as the common guiding beacon that will orient the understanding and interpretation of obligations, just as happens under civil codes".[178] The *Merril Ring* tribunal argued that the principle of good faith and the prohibition of arbitrariness "are not stand-alone obligations under Article 1105(1) or international law, and might not be a part of customary law either, these concepts are to a large extent the expression of general principles of law and hence also a part of international law [...] no tribunal today could be asked to ignore these basic obligations of international law."[179]

Turning from single cases to the jurisprudence of international investment tribunals at large, it can be said that tribunals applied and invoked both customary international law and general principles of law.[180] Furthermore, by and large, the cross-reliance between tribunals was not dependent on whether they applied the same source, treaty or customary international law.[181] These standards, the international minimum standard and fair and equitable treatment, have in common that they are broadly framed, characterized by a high

---

177 *ADF Group Inc v United States of America* Award (9 January 2003) para 184; see also *Loewen Group, Inc and Raymond L Loewen v United States of America* Award (26 June 2003) para 128: the obligation to accord fair and equitable treatment was no free-standing obligation but indicated a renvoi to customary international law.
178 *Sempra Energy International v Argentine Republic* Award (28 September 2007) para 297.
179 *Merrill & Ring Forestry LP v Canada* Award (31 March 2010) para 187.
180 Kriebaum, 'Article 42' 870-877. As examples for customary international law, the commentary lists principles of state responsibility, denial of justice, compensation, the standard of protection in case of an insurrection; as general principles, the commentary refers to good faith, nobody can benefit from his or her own fraud, unjust enrichment, compensation, prohibition of abuse of rights, duty to mitigate damage; Ole Kristian Fauchald, 'The Legal Reasoning of ICSID Tribunals - An Empirical Analysis' (2008) 19(2) EJIL 309-313, 324-326.
181 Stephan W Schill, 'Fair and Equitable Treatment, the Rule of Law, and Comparative Public Law' in Stephan W Schill (ed), *International investment law and comparative public law* (Oxford University Press 2010) 153-154; critical of this development Theodor Kill, 'Don't Cross the Streams: Past and Present Overstatement of Customary International Law in Connection with Conventional Fair and Equitable Treatment Obligations' (2008) 106(5) Michigan Law Review 864 ff.

degree of generality[182] and they are functionally equivalent in that they provide for an *international*, as opposed to a domestic, standard.[183] Tribunals, therefore, were particularly interested in the concretization of one of these standards to particular cases.[184]

To the extent that the *Vivendi* tribunal criticized the "equation" of treaty standards and customary international law, it highlighted that article 3 of the BIT between Argentina and France[185] and its "reference to principles of international law supports a broader reading that invites consideration of a wider range of international law principles than the minimum standard alone"; according to the tribunal, the language of the treaty indicated to consider also "contemporary principles of international law".[186] What is described in this study as a convergence of functionally equivalent standard does not necessarily imply "equation" in the sense of a static relationship. Customary international law and the international minimum standard themselves require interpretation in light of the principles of international law. The linkage between both standards which tribunals' jurisprudence suggested cannot freeze or "restrain the evolution of the FET standard".[187] One may ask whether there is a risk of arbitrariness when tribunals are at liberty to decide when a treaty standard such as fair and equitable treatment is similar to, or goes beyond, customary international law. The possibility of such risk, however,

---

182 Cf. *El Paso Energy International Company v Argentina* Award (31 October 2011) ICSID Case No ARB/03/15 para 335: "[...] the scope and content of the minimum standard of international law is as little defined as the BITs' FET standard [...] The issue is not one of comparing two undefined or weakly defined standards; it is to ascertain the content and define the BIT standard of fair and equitable treatment."
183 ibid para 336, and see also para 337.
184 Cf. *Mondev International Ltd v United States of America* Award (11 October 2002) para 118: "A judgment of what is fair and equitable cannot be reached in the abstract; it must depend on the facts of the particular case."
185 Agreement between the Government of the French Republic and the Government of the Republic of Argentina on the Encouragement and Reciprocal Protection of Investments (signed 3 July 1991, entered into force 3 March 1993) 1728 UNTS 281.
186 *Compana de Aguas del Aconquija SA and Vivendi Universal SA v Argentine Republic* Award (20 August 2007) ICSID Case No. ARB/97/3 202-203 para 7.4.7.
187 Dolzer, Kriebaum, and Schreuer, *Principles of International Investment Law* 203: "The emphasis on linkages between FET and customary international law is unlikely to restrain the evolution of the FET standard. On the contrary, this may have the effect of accelerating the development of customary law through the rapidly expanding practice on FET clauses in treaties."; Schill, 'Fair and Equitable Treatment, the Rule of Law, and Comparative Public Law' 153-155.

cannot be evaluated in the abstract but only in the specific case. In the end, it automatically follows from the bilateral structure of international investment law and the *lex specialis* principle, according to which states may decide to agree on a standard different from customary international law.

II. The interrelationship of sources in the scholarly debate

The conceptual roads taken by scholars towards the interpretation of the BITs and the explanation of the emergence of general law differ. International investment law represents an interesting contextual setting for approaches to the interrelationship of sources.[188] In the following, this section will survey selected approaches which can also inform the discussion of the interrelationship of sources outside international investment law. In particular, this section will focus on arguments concerning customary international law (1.), the *jurisprudence constante* (2.), the multilateralization *qua* interpretation (3.) and general principles with examples of the practice of tribunals for the purposes of illustration (4.)

1. Customary International Law

Certain scholars link the emergence of general law in international investment law in spite of the latter's bilateralist structure to the concept of customary international law.[189] In response to criticism according to which a BIT is *lex specialis* to customary international law and replaces the latter *inter partes*[190], José Alvarez has noted that "conclusions that BITs or FTAs are *lex specialis*, are not 'legislative', or lack common content, present artificially constrained black/white choices that bear little resemblance to the complexities of the interactions between treaty and non-treaty sources of law or the international

---

188 Alvarez, 'The Public International Law Regime Governing International Investment' 357: "[T]he investment regime is an excellent place to re-examine the ways international law now gets made."
189 Andreas F Lowenfeld, 'Investment Agreements and International Law' (2003) 42 Columbia Journal of Transnational Law 129.
190 See Alexander Orakhelashvili, 'The Normative Basis of 'Fair and Equitable Treatment': General International Law on Foreign Investment?' (2008) 46(1) Archiv des Völkerrechts 80.

legal process."¹⁹¹ Commenting on what he considered to be the traditional view, namely that the practice contributing to customary international law must be taken from a sense of legal obligation, Andreas Lowenfeld suggested "that perhaps the traditional definition of customary law is wrong, or at least in this area, incomplete."¹⁹² Mārtiņš Paparinskis has argued that the phenomenon of cross-reliance can only be justified by the general rule of interpretation as set forth in article 31 VCLT if one assumes the existence of a rule of customary international law to which the FET provisions in BITs gives expression.¹⁹³ In a similar sense, Campbell McLachlan has argued that customary international law can "constrain the unfettered discretion of the adventurist arbitrator by reference to the constraints of a wider body of law."¹⁹⁴

In the end, however, the relationship between an obligation of a given BIT and customary international law has to be determined by an analysis of the respective BIT.¹⁹⁵ This may explain why the preference for customary international law as explanatory model for the emergence of general law is not unanimously shared. Patrick Dumberry, for instance, concluded in his studies that the practice of FET provisions in BIT was not sufficiently uniform in order to qualify for the characterization of customary international law.¹⁹⁶ In

---

191 Alvarez, 'The Public International Law Regime Governing International Investment' 333; Alvarez, 'A Bit on Custom' 30-31.
192 Lowenfeld, 'Investment Agreements and International Law' 129, 130. See also on this topic Steffen Hindelang, 'Bilateral Investment Treaties, Custom and a Healthy Investment Climate: the Question of Whether Bits Influence Customary International Law Revisited' (2004) 5(5) The journal of world investment & trade; Alvarez, 'A Bit on Custom'; Tudor, *The Fair and Equitable Treatment Standard in the International Law of Foreign Investment* 54-83 (FET emerged as a rule of customary international law "in a different manner compared to the classical theory of custom formation"); Stephen M Schwebel, 'The Influence of Bilateral Investment Treaties on Customary International Law' (2004) 98 Proceedings of the American Society of International Law at Its Annual Meeting 27-30; Christoph Schreuer, 'Investment Arbitration - A Voyage of Discovery' (2005) 5(2) Transnational Dispute Management 73 ff.
193 Paparinskis, *The international minimum standard and fair and equitable treatment* 95, 154; see also Alvarez, 'A Bit on Custom' 76.
194 McLachlan, 'Is There an Evolving Customary International Law on Investment?' 258.
195 Dolzer and Schreuer, *Principles of International Investment Law* 135.
196 Patrick Dumberry, 'Has the Fair and Equitable Treatment Standard Become a Rule of Customary International Law?' (2017) 8 JIDS 155 ff.; Patrick Dumberry, 'Are BITs Representing the "New" Customary International Law in International Investment Law?' (2009) 28(4) Penn State International Law Review 675 ff.; Patrick Dumb-

his view, customary international law would remain important as applicable law in the absence of a treaty or when the treaty incorporates and refers to custom, as gap filler and as answer to the questions left open by treaties and as legal basis for the general rules of responsibility and interpretation.[197] Dumberry's analysis is primarily concerned with references to the notion of "fair and equitable treatment" and emphasizes the particularities of each BIT[198], whereas the above-mentioned tribunals and scholars focused more on the functional equivalence of the different standards. Other scholars are reluctant with respect to customary international law as well and suggest alternative approaches to explain the harmonization and convergence of standards in international investment law, which range from a focus on the jurisprudence of tribunals to the use of the concept of principles.

2. Jurisprudence Constante

One conceptual alternative to customary international law may be seen in the so-called *jurisprudence constante*, or standing jurisprudence.[199] According to Andrea Bjorklund, "[t]he informal and dispersed regime of investment treaty arbitrations is not well suited to developing a system of formal precedent. Eventually, however, an accretion of decisions will likely develop a *jurisprudence constante* - a 'persisting jurisprudence' that secures 'unification and stability of judicial activity'."[200] While admitting that the lack of a hierarchical court system in international investment arbitration makes the *jurisprudence constante* analogy an imperfect one, she values that this anal-

---

erry, *The Formation and Identification of Rules of Customary International Law in International Investment Law* (Cambridge University Press 2016) 151, 189.
197 ibid 352.
198 For a summary of Dumberry's analysis see Dumberry, *Fair and Equitable Treatment. Its Interaction wit the Minimum Standard and Its Customary Status* 71-77.
199 Andrea K Bjorklund, 'Investment Treaty Arbitral Decisions as "Jurisprudence Constante"' in Colin B Picker (ed), *International economic law: the state and future of the discipline* (Hart 2008)265 ff.; Ho, *State Responsibility for Breaches of Investment Contracts* 72 ff.; James Crawford, 'Similarity of Issues in Disputes Arising under the Same or Similarly Drafted Investment Treaties' in Emmanuel Gaillard and Yas Banifatemi (eds), *Precedent in International Arbitration* (Juris Publishing 2007) 102-103; Gabrielle Kaufmann-Kohler, 'Arbitral Precedent: Dream, Necessity or Excuse' (2007) 23(3) Arbitration International 357 ff.
200 Bjorklund, 'Investment Treaty Arbitral Decisions as "Jurisprudence Constante"' 265.

ogy "preserves the primacy of the code provision as a source of law (while recognising) the evolution of code-based law through interpretation."[201]

Awards surely play an important role in the systematization of international law:[202] In spite of not being formally binding except for the parties, a precedent is said to "shif[t] the burden of argumentation by demanding a reasoned justification for departing from precedent"[203], tribunals consider the awards of other tribunals when faced with similar problems to the extent they are persuaded of the quality of the reasoning in the other awards.[204] Arbitral awards are particularly important in international investment law because of the vague substantive standards, by virtue of which states as masters of the treaties leave arbitral tribunals "with ample interpretative choices about how to concretize the content of investment treaty obligations and what concrete obligations to derive from – or to read into – them."[205] Jean d'Aspremont has even argued that because of concepts like *jurisprudence constante* and the general rules of interpretation there would no longer be any need for recourse to customary international law.[206] In his view, *jurisprudence constante* is "a

---

201 Bjorklund, 'Investment Treaty Arbitral Decisions as "Jurisprudence Constante"' 273; but see Ho, *State Responsibility for Breaches of Investment Contracts* 79, who rejects this analogy because of the lack of centralisation while agreeing that arbitral awards "converge on the content of international law".
202 See also Schill, 'System-Building in Investment Treaty Arbitration and Lawmaking' 165 ff.
203 ibid 162 with further references; *Saipem SpA v The People's Republic of Bangladesh* Decision on Jurisdiction and Recommendation on Provisional Measures (21 March 2007) ICSID Case No. ARB/05/07 para 167.
204 Ho, *State Responsibility for Breaches of Investment Contracts* 80; cf. Jan Paulsson, 'International Arbitration and the Generation of Legal Norms: Treaty Arbitration and International Law' (2006) 3(5) Transnational Dispute Management 1, 4: "In practice, it will also doubtless turn out to be subject to the same Darwinian reality: the unfit (awards) will perish."
205 Schill, 'System-Building in Investment Treaty Arbitration and Lawmaking' 151: "The vagueness of the substantive standards that are applied as a yardstick for the international responsibility of host States are the root cause for the significant law-making activities arbitral tribunals engage in. This law-making activity is a consequence of the position that was envisaged for them by States."
206 d'Aspremont, 'International Customary Investment Law: Story of a Paradox' 42: "[...] the principle of systemic integration enshrined in article 31.3(c) of the Vienna Convention on the Law of Treaties already provides judges with a sweeping power to harmonize without unnecessary and costly inroads into the murky theory of customary investment law."

The interrelationship of sources in a bilateralist structure and the quest for general law

self-explanatory and selfsufficient phenomenon" which "does not need to be 'authorized' or 'validated' by any secondary rule".[207]

The constant jurisprudence can be seen as a phenomenon of factual convergence of different standards; it is not, however, concerned with the emergence of general law on a normative level.

3. Multilateralization *qua* interpretation and the rise of general principles

Stephan Schill's multilateralization thesis offers a different model for understanding the formation of general law outside the concept of customary international law.[208] Schill has demonstrated that investment tribunals did not apply a particular BIT as a treaty isolated from other BITs and that the tribunals' interpretations were informed by each other and in particular by BITs and Arbitral Awards concerning third states.[209] He has traced the normative convergence in international investment law in part to the states parties and their use of MFN provisions in BITs and to the tribunals[210]. Tribunals both presupposed, and contributed to, the existence of an international investment law system.[211] In particular, a common multilateralist mindset between arbitrators and teleological approaches to interpretation resulted in normative convergence in international investment law.[212] The result was said to be

---

207 ibid 45-46, also arguing that the multilateral character in the sense of a multilateralization of the investment law system provides for a sufficient basis.
208 Stephan W Schill, 'General Principles of Law and International Investment Law' in Tarcisio Gazzini and Eric de Brabandere (eds), *International investment law: the sources of rights and obligations* (Martinus Nijhoff Publishers 2012) 151 ("multilateral in nature, even though it has taken the form of bilateral treaties").
209 On cross treaty interpretation see Schill, *The multilateralization of international investment law* 295 ff., 359; cf. also Mārtiņš Paparinskis, 'Sources of Law and Arbitral Interpretations of "Pari Materia" Investment Protection Rules' in Ole Kristian Fauchald and André Nollkaemper (eds), *The practice of international and national courts and the (de-)fragmentation of international law* (Hart 2012) 87 ff.
210 Schill, *The multilateralization of international investment law* 312, 314.
211 ibid 294.
212 ibid 312, 314; see also the commitment of the Saipem tribunal to contribute to consolidation: "[The tribunal] believes that, subject to the specifics of a given treaty and of the circumstances of the actual case, it has a duty to seek to contribute to the harmonious development of investment law and thereby to meet the legitimate expectations of the community of States and investors towards certainty of the rule of law", *Saipem SpA v The People's Republic of Bangladesh* para 67.

"a system that behaves and functions according to multilateral rationales and does not, despite the existence of innumerable bilateral investment relationships, dissolve into infinite fragmentation."[213] The shift of authority from states to tribunals connected with this development resulted from states' choices for vague substantive standards.[214]

Schill has argued that the process of multilateralization by investment tribunals can raise legitimacy concerns with respect to the restrictions on states' capacity to regulate in the public interest; in his view, a multilateral system cannot, in terms of legitimacy, rest on the discourse between tribunals alone and instead needs to be linked to the sources of international law.[215] Therefore, "general principles of law may be the best explanation to link the multilateralization of international investment law".[216] General principles would also allow tribunals to "bypass debates about the content of customary international law and about the relationship between treaty and custom and to implement what were formerly firm grounds under customary international law as part of general principles."[217]

4. Examples of tribunals' recourses to principles

The *Continental* tribunal illustrates that interpreters may prefer to take recourse to principles that reveal themselves in other areas of international law instead of relying solely on customary international law. The Continental

---

213 Schill, *The multilateralization of international investment law* 361.
214 Schill, 'System-Building in Investment Treaty Arbitration and Lawmaking' 151; see also Schill, *The multilateralization of international investment law* 355: "Far from constituting merely a subsidiary source of international law, precedent in these cases assumes the function of a primary source of international law."
215 Stephan W Schill, 'From Sources to Discourse: Investment Treaty Jurisprudence as the New Custom?' [2016] BIICL 16th Investment Treaty Forum Public Conference ⟨https://www.biicl.org/files/5630_stephan_schill.pdf.⟩ accessed 1 February 2023 15-16.
216 Schill, 'General Principles of Law and International Investment Law' 135; see also Schill, 'From Sources to Discourse: Investment Treaty Jurisprudence as the New Custom?' 16: "Methodologically, general principles may the be only doctrinally viable and convincing way to justify the multilateralization of international investment law through the discourse of investment treaty tribunals."
217 Schill, 'General Principles of Law and International Investment Law' 134-135. See also Juillard, 'L'évolution des sources du droit des investissements' 130-132.

The interrelationship of sources in a bilateralist structure and the quest for general law

tribunal had to interpret a NPM provision (Art. XI[218]) according to which the treaty "shall not preclude the application by either Party of measures necessary for the maintenance of public order, the fulfillment of its obligations with respect to the maintenance or restoration of international peace or security, or the Protection of its own essential security interests". This article raised the question of how to interpret the term "necessary". Unlike other tribunals, the Continental tribunal did not take recourse to necessity under customary international law as reflected in article 25 ARSIWA. Instead, the tribunal argued that similar provisions in so-called treaties of friendship, commerce, and navigation [219] and in particular Art. XX GATT[220] would be more helpful for illuminating the meaning of Article XI BIT than custom: "[...] the Tribunal finds it more appropriate to refer to the GATT and WTO case law which has extensively dealt with the concept and requirements of necessity in the context of economic measures derogating to the obligations contained in GATT, rather than to refer to the requirement of necessity under customary international law."[221] In its interpretation of whether the alleged conduct was necessary, the tribunal employed a proportionality test.[222]

This example illustrates how general principles can operate: inspirations are sought in other fields of law in order to solve a specific problem, in this case, the interpretation of the term "necessary". Arguably, the interpreter does not look, firstly, at various legal systems in order to ascertain a general principle of law and then, secondly, applies this principle by adapting it to the particular normative context. Presumably, both operations run almost simultaneously, the examination may shift between the provision to be interpreted and the legal materials from which a general principle may be identified. The classification as a general principle of law does not necessarily indicate that it can be "applied" without further regard to the normative environment. Whether, for instance, proportionality analysis fits international investment

---

218 Treaty between the United States of America and the Argentine Republic concerning the reciprocal encouragement and protection of investment (signed 14 November 1991, entered into force 20 October 1994) (1992) 31 ILM 124.
219 *Continental Casuality Company v Argentine Republic* Award (5 September 2008) ICSID Case No. ARB/03/9 para 176 ff.
220 General Agreement on Tariffs and Trade (signed 30 October 1947, entered into force 1 January 1948) 55 UNTS 187.
221 *Continental Casuality Company v Argentine Republic, Award* Award (5 September 2008) para 192.
222 ibid para 227, 232.

law depends on the respective provisions of the BIT, "on the normative setting"[223] as well as on the institutional setting.[224]

The jurisprudence of investment tribunals offers several examples of borrowing principles from other fields of international law[225]: the tribunal in *S.D. Myers* searched for inspirations from WTO jurisprudence on "like products" in order to interpret the investment treaty obligation to treat foreigners no less favourably than nationals in "like circumstances".[226] Tribunals searched for inspirations in the jurisprudence of the European Court of Human Rights in order to interpret the obligation to accord fair and equal treatment[227], took re-

---

223 Bücheler, *Proportionality in investor-state arbitration* 62: "First, proportionality is sufficiently prevalent on the domestic level to pass the first step of identifying a general principle of law-a comparative analysis of domestic legal systems. Second, this alone tells us very little about when adjudicators should apply proportionality at the international level. All depends on the relevant normative setting." Also, the legal-political vision of the future development of one's regime may be an aspect to consider, see below, p. 606; on proportionality analysis as means to accommodate public interests and to balance conflicting interests see Andreas Kulick, *Global public interest in international investment law* (Cambridge University Press 2012) 168 ff.

224 Cf. Georg Nolte, 'Thin or Thick? The Principle of Proportionality and International Humanitarian Law' (2010) 4(2) Law & Ethics of Human Rights 246, 251, according to whom a choice between a thin and a thick proportionality analysis should be made depending on the respective normative as well as institutional setting: "The more the enforcement of a legal rule can typically rely on institutions and a shared vision of the common interest, the more it makes sense that the institution concerned directly evaluates the interests at stake".

225 Anthea Roberts, 'Clash and Paradigms: Actors and Analogies Shaping The Investment Treaty System' (2013) 107 AJIL 51-52.

226 *SD Myers, Inc v Government of Canada* Partial Award (13 November 2000) paras 243-251; contra *Methanex Corporation v United States of America* Final Award of the Tribunal on Jurisdiction and Merits (3 August 2005) UNCITRAL/NAFTA, 44 ILM 1345 Part IV paras 29-35; on this topic see Robert Howse and Efraim Chalamish, 'The Use and Abuse of WTO Law in Investor-State Arbitration: A Reply to Jürgen Kurtz' (2009) 20(4) EJIL 1087 ff.; Jürgen Kurtz, 'The Use and Abuse of WTO Law in Investor-State Arbitration: Competition and its Discontents' (2009) 20(3) EJIL 749 ff.

227 *Mondev International Ltd v United States of America* Award (11 October 2002) para 144; cf. José E Alvarez, 'The Use (and Misuse) of European Human Rights Law in Investor-State Dispute Settlement' in Franco Ferrari (ed), *The impact of EU law on international commercial arbitration* (JurisNet 2017) 519 ff.; on the relationship of human rights law and international investment law see Pierre-Marie Dupuy, 'Unification Rather than Fragmentation of International Law? The Case of International

course to domestic public law, European human rights law, European Union law and public international law in order to interpret the meaning of the protection of "legitimate expectations".[228] In *Tecmed*, the tribunal referred to the Iran-US-Claims tribunal, the European Court of Human Rights and the Inter-American Court of Human Rights in order to define an indirect *de facto* expropriation.[229]

The acceptance of analogies cannot be determined in the abstract but must be assessed in the individual case. In *Occidental* the annulment committee argued that the tribunal "has convincingly explained that the principle of proportionality between intensity and scope of the illicit activity, and severity of the sanction is a general principle of punitive and tort law, both under Ecuadorian and under international law", for which the tribunal had referred to case-law of the WTO Dispute Settlement Body, the European Court of Justice and European Court of Human Rights.[230] Analogies are not always

---

Investment Law and Human Rights Law' in Pierre-Marie Dupuy, Ernst-Ulrich Petersmann, and Francesco Francioni (eds), *Human Rights in International Investment Law and Arbitration* (Oxford University Press 2009) 61 (arguing that both belong to the same legal order); Bruno Simma, 'Foreign Investment Arbitration: A Place For Human Rights?' (2011) 60(3) ICLQ 573; Simma and Kill, 'Harmonizing Investment Protection and International Human Rights: First Steps Towards a Methodology' 691-706 on article 31(3)(c) VCLT and its harmonizing potential.

228 *Total SA v The Argentine Republic* Decision on Liability (27 December 2010) ICSID Case No ARB/04/01 paras 128-134.

229 *Técnicas Medioambientales Tecmed, SA v The United Mexican States* Award (29 May 2003) ICSID Case No. ARB(AF)/00/2 116, 122: "[The tribunal] will consider, in order to determine if they are to be characterized as expropriatory, whether such actions or measures are proportional to the public interest presumably protected thereby and to the protection legally granted to investments, taking into account that the significance of such impact has a key role upon deciding the proportionality." It also referred to *James v United Kingdom [Plenum]* App no 8793/79 (ECtHR, 21 February 1986), in order to illustrate the vulnerability of foreigners in the domestic democratic process; *Azurix Corp v The Argentine Republic* Award (14 July 2006) paras 311-312: The ECHR case law to which *Tecmed* referred "provide useful guidance for purposes of determining whether regulatory actions would be expropriatory and give rise to compensation"; but see *Fireman's Fund Insurance Company v The United Mexican States* Award (17 July 2006) ICSID Case No. ARB(AF)/02/1 para 176 Fn. 161: "[...] it may be questioned whether (the ECHR) is a viable source of interpreting Article 1110 of the NAFTA".

230 See *Occidental Petroleum Corporation and Occidental Exploration and Production Company v The Republic of Ecuador* Decision on Annulment of the Award (2 November 2015) ICSID Case No. ARB/06/11 para 324, 350.

accepted. The *Siemens* tribunal rejected to adopt the margin of appreciation doctrine of the European Court of Human Rights[231] and the *Pezold* tribunal emphasized that "due caution should be exercised in importing concepts from other legal regimes (in this case European human rights law) without a solid basis for doing so."[232]

III. Evaluation

1. General principles and the development of the law

It has been questioned whether the system-building efforts of investment tribunals described above, meaning the reference to other awards rendered on the basis of different BITs between third states or the search for analogies in other fields of international law, can be justified by "the general rule" of interpretation which is set forth in article 31 VCLT and which does not authorize the interpreter to take into account third-party agreements.[233] Moreover, according to Daniel Peat, tribunals took recourse to domestic public law without claiming to apply a general principle of law.[234] Anthea Roberts has argued with respect to analogies borrowed from other fields of international law that such "principles and cases are not necessarily 'relevant rules of international law applicable in the relations between the parties' (in the sense

---

231 *Siemens AG v The Argentine Republic, Award (17 January 2007)* ICSID Case No. ARB/02/8 para 354, the tribunal "observes that Article I of the First Protocol to the European Convention on Human Rights permits a margin of appreciation not found in customary international law or the Treaty."; *Quasar de Valors SICAV SA v Russian Federation* Award (20 July 2012) SCC No. 24/2007 para 158.
232 *Bernhard von Pezold and Others v Republic of Zimbabwe* Award (28 July 2015) ICSID Case No. ARB/10/15 para 465; on the reception of the doctrine of the margin of appreciation see also Julian Arato, 'The Margin of Appreciation in International Investment Law' (2013) 54(2) Virginia Journal of International Law 1 ff.; cf. on ECHR references as "extraneous" to the investment arbitration without any link to the investment *ST-AD GmbH v Republic of Bulgaria* Award on Jurisdiction (18 July 2013) PCA Case No. 2011-06 para 260.
233 Andrew D Mitchell and James Munro, 'Someone Else's Deal: Interpreting International Investment Agreements in the Light of Third-Party Agreements' (2017) 28(3) EJIL 695 (taking into account third-party agreements erroneous application of the customary rules of treaty interpretation).
234 Daniel Peat, 'International Investment Law and the Public Law Analogy: The Fallacies of the General Principles Method' (2018) 9 JIDS 662, 677.

The interrelationship of sources in a bilateralist structure and the quest for general law

of article 31(3)(c) VCLT), even when they originate in public international law."[235] José Alvarez has questioned arbitrators' creative recourse to principles embodied in regional treaties such as the European Convention on Human Rights. Boundary crossings would entail the risk to get the unfamiliar borrowed law wrong, to transform the treaty in a way unintended by its makers, and to opt for a regional treaty without justifying the choice or without searching for general law. Tribunals' practice to cite the ECHR and the jurisprudence of the ECtHR might not even be the expression of a commitment to further the cause of human rights but of an attempt to increase the arbitrators' likeliness for reappointment in subsequent proceedings. Interpretation, however, should not be determined by regional law but be based on general law.[236]

These critical observations caution against an unreflected and overhasty use of analogies or "general principles"; at the same time, it certainly is possible and plausible to seek guidance from the practice in specific legal regimes in which interpreters face similar challenges. This process can contribute to the gradual crystallization of a general principle.[237] Principles can appear attractive in the context of international investment law because of their auxiliary character; since in most cases a tribunal will have a treaty to apply, concepts are needed which help in interpreting the treaty. General principles which are based on the experiences in other legal fields can both offer guidance as to how to interpret the substantive obligations and provide for very technical solutions concerning questions of damages or procedure. Therefore, principles in this sense continue to play an important role even

---

235 Roberts, 'Clash and Paradigms: Actors and Analogies Shaping The Investment Treaty System' 52: "When invoking such analogies, participants are often not claiming that these principles and cases are applicable in the relations between the parties or cross-apply to the investment treaty system as a matter of law. Rather, they are often arguing or simply assuming that textual or functional similarities between these fields make it instructive to draw comparisons when resolving difficult issues. Some of these analogies might fit within the ambit of Article 31(3)(c), but the use of analogical reasoning extends well beyond this."
236 José Alvarez, ''Beware: Boundary Crossings'- A Critical Appraisal of Public Law Approaches to International Investment Law' (2016) 17 The Journal of World Investment & Trade 191 ff., 199-203, 220 ff.; Alvarez, 'The Use (and Misuse) of European Human Rights Law in Investor-State Dispute Settlement' 519 ff.: José E Alvarez, 'The Use (and Misuse) of European Human Rights Law in Investor-State Dispute Settlement' [2016] SSRN ⟨https://papers.ssrn.com/sol3/papers.cfm?abstract_id=2875089⟩ accessed 1 February 2023 49-50, 96.
237 See also above, p. 138, on different perspectives on general principles of law.

when more specific obligations under treaties or customary international law exist.[238]

General principles, however, not only embody legal experience but also represent the law in action. They can emerge through judicial practice. Therefore, the question of whether a certain principle is already a general principle of law which could be considered under article 31(3)(c) VCLT is misleading insofar as it implies that only preexisting principles of law may legitimately inform a judicial reasoning. Within the confines of legal reasoning based on the general rules of interpretation, tribunals can seek inspiration from nonbinding materials, provided that the use of this inspiration is disciplined by legal methodology which is applied to the interpretation of the binding rule.[239] It is not uncommon that a general legal idea in the sense of a nonbinding principle can support the result of an interpretation of the written law according to legal methodology, and over the course of several judgments such principle can harden into a legal principle.

While principles can be employed only within the confines of legal reasoning, principles can have a transformative effect. The interpreter can relate the rule to be interpreted and applied to a broader normative environment and seek guidance from the practice in specific legal regimes in which interpreters face similar challenges. As described by Alec Stone Sweet and Giacinto Della Cananea, "[g]eneral principles are unwritten, doctrinal constructions, institutionalized as case law"[240], and by developing general principles of law judges "become architects of their own legal systems, in relation to other systems."[241]

---

238 See also Tams, 'The Sources of International Investment Law: Concluding Thoughts' 324-325: "If we look at the general sources debate, general principles are 'wallflowers' existing on the margins of international legal argument – occasionally useful to fill gaps, but typically side-lined by legally relevant conduct of a genuinely international character. A quick glance at the current academic debate is sufficient to show that international investment law – again – is different."; but cf. Moshe Hirsch, 'Sources of International Investment Law' in Andrea K Bjorklund and August Reinisch (eds), *International investment law and soft law* (Edward Elgar Publishing 2012) 9 ff., 13 (speaking of a reservoir of legal rules that may fill gaps).
239 On a similar discussion in the context of the ECHR see above, p. 416; on the Kelsenian perspective according to which the application of law is not completely determined by the norm that is applied see above, p. 196 and below p. 668.
240 Alec Stone Sweet and Giacinto Della Cananea, 'Proportionality, General Principles of Law, and Investor-State Arbitration: a Response to José Alvarez' (2014) 46(3) NYU JILP 912-913.
241 ibid 913.

The interrelationship of sources in a bilateralist structure and the quest for general law

The subjectivity involved here which, it should not be forgotten, is always to some extent inherent in applying abstract law to particular cases, can be tamed to a certain extent by a commitment to "a more rigorous methodology" with respect to the comparative legal exercise.[242] Whereas representativeness can be important for the persuasiveness of a given principle, it should not be overestimated, as the normative setting to which the principle is to be applied as well as the underlying vision with respect to this normative setting are important as well. Neither can subjectivity and selectivity be entirely excluded, nor can a methodology release the legal operator from her or his responsibility to reflect on her or his necessary value judgment and to "make a searching enquiry into the values that we want the investment regime to uphold".[243]

2. The promotion of paradigms by recourse to principles

It is submitted that the discussion in international investment law about the significance of paradigms can be seen as an important contribution to international legal doctrine more generally. As Anthea Roberts has explained, behind the choice of analogies and principles on the microlevel for the interpretation of a specific treaty term, one can find a "clash of paradigms" on the macrolevel, meaning "competing conceptualizations of the investment treaty system as a subfield within public international law, as a species of international arbitration, or as a form of internationalized judicial review".[244] Such paradigms are "not inevitably outcome-determinative" but "promote different visions of the investment treaty system, which, in turn, tend to privilege different actors and goals."[245] Gus van Harten, for instance, distinguished a

---

242 Schill, 'General Principles of Law and International Investment Law' 139, 145 ff.; Stephan W Schill, 'International Investment Law and Comparative Public Law - an Introduction' in Stephan W Schill (ed), *International investment law and comparative public law* (Oxford University Press 2010) 27 ff., 37.
243 Peat, 'International Investment Law and the Public Law Analogy: The Fallacies of the General Principles Method' 678.
244 Roberts, 'Clash and Paradigms: Actors and Analogies Shaping The Investment Treaty System' 47.
245 ibid 74.

commercial arbitration analogy[246], a public international law analogy[247], an investor rights approach[248], which focuses on individual rights, and a public law framework[249] which appreciates the regulatory character of disputes and reconciles investors' rights and states' interest to regulate in the public interest.[250] Another example is a "public law paradigm".[251] It focuses on the vertical relationship between a state and an individual and borrows from experiences in other fields of international law which are concerned with the relationship between a state and an individual.[252] Stephan Schill has argued that general principles can provide a public law paradigm which reconciles the rights of individuals and the interests of the public to regulate.[253] Once this paradigm would be established, general principles from several branches could help in defining the general standard and applying it in concrete cases, benefiting from the experiences of others.[254] By linking FET to the rule of law, itself a general principle of (public) law[255], fair and equitable treatment could be concretized to a number of normative requirements, such as the requirements of stability, predictability and consistency of the legal framework, the protection of legitimate expectations, procedural and administrative due process and the prohibition of the denial of justice, the requirements of transparency as well as reasonableness and proportionality.[256]

---

246 Gus van Harten, *Investment Treaty Arbitration and Public Law* (Oxford University Press 2008) 123 ff.
247 ibid 131 ff.
248 ibid 136 ff.
249 ibid 143 ff.
250 Cf. Roberts, 'Clash and Paradigms: Actors and Analogies Shaping The Investment Treaty System' 66; Montt, *State Liability in Investment Treaty Arbitration. Global Constitutional and Administrative Law on the BIT Generation* 7-8; on the accommodation of public interests see Kulick, *Global public interest in international investment law*.
251 See on this topic also Roberts, 'Clash and Paradigms: Actors and Analogies Shaping The Investment Treaty System' 64-65; Alvarez, ''Beware: Boundary Crossings'- A Critical Appraisal of Public Law Approaches to International Investment Law' 181-191.
252 Roberts, 'Clash and Paradigms: Actors and Analogies Shaping The Investment Treaty System' 69.
253 Schill, 'General Principles of Law and International Investment Law' 162.
254 ibid 180.
255 ibid 164.
256 ibid 165 with further references.

The interrelationship of sources in a bilateralist structure and the quest for general law

General principles of law as well as paradigms and underlying visions must be reflected on. They cannot be imposed on a legal reasoning, however, they must emerge from and through the interpretation of the binding law. A legal reasoning can therefore derive persuasiveness from recourse to a principle no more than the specific recourse to the principle derives its persuasiveness from the legal reasoning.

3. A remaining role for customary international law as community mindset?

It is interesting that customary international law seems to be regarded by some to be more important as a mindset of the legal operators that entails a commitment to, and the conscience to be part of, a wider legal community, rather than as applicable law.[257] It is said to provide for a common bound which is said to be the normative justification for cross-reliance, cross-fertilization and a de-facto *jurisprudence constante* in spite of institutional decentralization.[258] Customary international law can offer normative support in a decentralized system for understanding functionally equivalent rules as an expression of a general rule or principle. It is not excluded that the jurisprudence based on investment treaties informed by general principles of international law will furnish the growth of customary international law. In this sense, Campbell McLachlan has convincingly regarded the relationship between treaty and custom as symbiotic and noted a "convergence [...] between treaty practice and custom (with respect to FET and IMS), in which the modern understanding of the content of the customary right is being elaborated primarily through the treaty jurisprudence."[259] Where regulation by way of customary international law falls short, for instance in matters of fair procedure or decision-making processes, general principles of international

---

[257] Cf. Jorge E Viñuales, 'Sources of International Investment Law: Conceptual Foundations of Unruly Practices' in Samantha Besson and Jean d'Aspremont (eds), *The Oxford Handbook of the Sources of International Law* (Oxford University Press 2017) 1029, arguing that one should not underestimate the value of "deeply rooted shared understandings". He refers to a commitment to sources in the context of international investment law which would include customary international law as well.

[258] Cf. Paparinskis, *The international minimum standard and fair and equitable treatment* 95, 154; Alvarez, 'A Bit on Custom' 76.

[259] McLachlan, 'Investment Treaties and General International Law' 394.

law such as human rights law can gain importance.[260] Yet, as demonstrated above, conceptual alternatives to customary international law and to general principles of law are available which would view the convergence as a mere factual phenomenon.[261] Also, the "principles" tribunals apply could be regarded not to be law but only considerations which influence the tribunals in the concretization of the law.[262] From such a perspective, customary international law might not be necessary to consider other tribunals' decisions rendered under different BITs. This demonstrates that one's understanding of the interrelationship is interlinked with one's view of the scope of law that exists in the field of international investment law. Which view will prevail will be indicative not only of the relative significance of each source but also of doctrinal preferences and of the scope given to (general) law within, and in the long run potentially also beyond, the field of international investment law.

D. *The significance of constructions: The distinction between primary rules and secondary rules revisited*

At the end of this chapter, this section focuses on the distinction between primary and secondary rules and the use of this doctrinal construction in the jurisprudence of investment tribunals with respect to the relationship between customary international law on necessity and a treaty's NPM provision (I.). This section will revisit the distinction between primary and secondary rules (II.). It will caution against an understanding of the distinction between primary and secondary rules which would imply that both sources, treaties and custom, are sealed in separated compartments of international law (III.).

I. Competing constructions

The discussion about the relationship between necessity under customary international law as reflected in article 25 ARSIWA and a treaty-based NPM

---

260 McLachlan, 'Investment Treaties and General International Law' 394-400.
261 Cf. Jörg Kammerhofer, *International investment law and legal theory: expropriation and the fragmentation of sources* (Cambridge University Press 2021) 141 f.
262 Cf. for such an argument in the late Hans Kelsen's General Theory of Norms above, p. 146.

provision in the context of the litigation between Argentina and foreign investors illustrates the significance of doctrinal constructions with respect to the interrelationship of sources.

Article XI of the applicable BIT between the USA and Argentina[263] stipulates:

> "This Treaty shall not preclude the application by either Party of measures necessary for the maintenance of public order, the fulfillment of its obligations with respect to the maintenance or restoration of international peace or security, or the protection of its own essential security interests."

Article 25 ARSIWA[264] imposed more burdensome requirements:

> "1. Necessity may not be invoked by a State as a ground for precluding the wrongfulness of an act not in conformity with an international obligation of that State unless the act:
> (a) is the only way for the State to safeguard an essential interest against a grave and imminent peril; and
> (b) does not seriously impair an essential interest of the State or States towards which the obligation exists, or of the international community as a whole.
> 2. In any case, necessity may not be invoked by a State as a ground for precluding wrongfulness if:
> (a) the international obligation in question excludes the possibility of invoking necessity; or
> (b) the State has contributed to the situation of necessity."

This section focuses on the different doctrinal construction employed by tribunals and on its repercussions on the interrelationship of sources.[265]

---

263 Treaty between the United States of America and the Argentine Republic concerning the reciprocal encouragement and protection of investment (signed 14 November 1991, entered into force 20 October 1994) (1992) 31 ILM 124.

264 ILC, *Draft Articles on Responsibility of States for Internationally Wrongful Acts (ARSIWA)*.

265 As the EDFI tribunal would later summarize the development, "eight other tribunals have rejected Argentina's necessity defense under ILC Article 25", whereas "two tribunals that upheld a necessity defense by Argentina invoked Article XI of the Argentina-U.S. BIT", *EDFI International SA, SAUR International SA and LEON Participaciones Argentinas SA v Argentine Republic* Award (11 June 2012) ICSID Case No. ARB/03/23 para 1181. The applicable Argentina-France BIT did not contain a NPM provision, the tribunal ruled that the conditions of article 25 ARSIWA were not met; the Annulment Committee accepted this decision, *EDFI International SA, SAUR International SA and LEON Participaciones Argentinas SA v Argentine Republic* Decision (5 February 2016) ICSID Case No. ARB/03/23 para 319. For an overview of the different constructions see also Jürgen Kurtz, 'Delineating Primary and Secondary Rules on Necessity at International Law' in *Multi-sourced equivalent*

1. Alignment between the BIT and necessity under customary international law

According to one view, the relationship can be described as convergence or confluence: as the BIT does not stipulate how to interpret "necessary", the interpreter shall have recourse to customary international law on necessity.[266]

In this sense, the *Enron* tribunal firstly concluded that Argentina had not met the requirements of customary international law on necessity and then it argued that customary international law informed and determined the interpretation of what is necessary under article XI BIT. "The Treaty thus becomes inseparable from the customary law standard insofar as the conditions for the operation of state of necessity are concerned."[267] The same approach to the relationship between article XI BIT and custom was taken by the *Sempra* tribunal.[268]

---

norms in international law (Hart 2011) 246; Bücheler, *Proportionality in investor-state arbitration* 217-218.

266 José Enrique Alvarez and Kathryn Khamsi, 'The Argentine Crisis and Foreign Investors: a Glimpse into the Heart of the Investment Regime' (2009) 2008-2009 Yearbook on international investment law & policy 379 ff.; José Alvarez and Tegan Brink, 'Revisiting the Necessity Defense' [2010] Yearbook International Investment Law & Policy 319 ff.; Francisco Orrego Vicuña, 'Softening Necessity' in Mahnoush H Arsanjani and others (eds), *Looking to the Future Essays on International Law in Honor of W. Michael Reisman* (Martinus Nijhoff Publishers 2010) 741 ff.; Rudolf Dolzer, 'Emergency Clauses in Investment Treaties: Four Versions' in Mahnoush H Arsanjani and others (eds), *Looking to the future: essays on international law in honor of W. Michael Reisman* (Martinus Nijhoff Publishers 2011) 705.

267 *Enron Creditors Recovery Corp Ponderosa Assets, LP v Argentine Republic* Award (22 May 2007) paras 313, 333, 334 (quote).

268 *Sempra Energy International v Argentine Republic* Award (28 September 2007) paras 376 ff.; for a defense of this approach which he had taken as member of the tribunal see Orrego Vicuña, 'Softening Necessity' 741 ff.; on the basis of this article, Peter Tomka upheld the challenge against Orrego Vicuña as an arbitrator in an UNCITRAL proceeding as by this article the latter would have prejudged the interpretation of the essential security provision, *CC/Devas and the Republic of India* Decision on the Respondent's challenge to the Hon. Marc Lalonde as Presiding Arbitrator and Prof. Francisco Orrego Vicuña as Co-Arbitrator (30 September 2013) PCA Case No 2013-09; for a convincing defense of academic freedom also of arbitrators: Stephan W Schill, 'Editorial' (2014) 15(1-2) Journal of World Investment & Trade 1 ff.

Similarly, the *CMS* tribunal first decided that Argentina did not satisfy the requirements of customary international law on necessity.[269] Subsequently, the tribunal turned to the question of whether the BIT excluded necessity[270], a question, which the tribunal did not clearly answer, it confined itself only to stating that it "must examine whether the state of necessity or emergency meets the conditions laid down by customary international law and the treaty provisions".[271] The *LG&E* tribunal arrived at the opposite result. It concluded that Argentina could invoke article XI BIT and was therefore "excused under Article XI from liability for any breaches of the treaty between 1 December 2001 and 26 April 2003."[272] It then argued that its interpretation of the treaty finds additional support in customary international law, where Argentina could rely on necessity as well.[273]

2. Differences between the BIT and necessity under customary international law

The annulment committees focused on the differences between article XI of the treaty and customary international law on necessity and on the difference between primary rules and secondary rules and between *lex specialis* and *lex generalis*.[274]

---

269 *CMS Gas Transmission Company v Argentine Republic, Award* Award (12 May 2005) paras 315-331.
270 ibid para 353.
271 ibid para 374.
272 *LG&E Energy Corp, et al v Argentine Republic* Decision on Liability (3 October 2006) ICSID Case No. ARB/02/1 paras 206, 229.
273 ibid paras 245-246, 257-262.
274 Cf. also Stone Sweet and Della Cananea, 'Proportionality, General Principles of Law, and Investor-State Arbitration: a Response to José Alvarez' 926-932; Jürgen Kurtz, 'Adjudicating the Exceptional at International Investment Law: Security, Public Order and Financial Crisis' (2010) 59(2) ICLQ 344; Kurtz, 'Delineating Primary and Secondary Rules on Necessity at International Law' 246, identifying three possible models of relationship between both norms, namely "primary-secondary applications", which he favours, a hard *lex specialis* relationship as contract out of customary necessity, which he finds plausible, and a weak *lex specialis* relationship "with the customary plea continuing to have residual effect"; Bücheler, *Proportionality in investor-state arbitration* 217-218, 231 (rejecting to equate both norms); Christina Binder, *Die Grenzen der Vertragstreue im Völkerrecht* (Springer 2013) 643-646, 651-653.

The *CMS* Annulment Committee argued that article XI BIT was a "threshold requirement: if it applies, the substantive obligations under the Treaty will not apply. By contrast, article 25 was an excuse which was only relevant once it has been decided that there has otherwise been a breach of those substantive obligations."[275] According to the Committee, the tribunal committed one manifest error of law by failing to appreciate the substantive differences between article XI BIT and article 25 and another error of law by failing to clarify the relationship between both rules.[276] If necessity under customary international law even precluded a *prima facie* breach of the BIT, it would have to be characterized as a primary rule and article XI BIT would then have to be applied as *lex specialis*.[277] If necessity concerned the issue of responsibility and thus presupposed a breach, an interpreter must first examine whether article XI BIT rendered the BIT inapplicable.[278] The Annulment Committee noted that the tribunal committed a manifest error of law by having considered the question of whether compensation was due only with a view to article 27 ARSIWA, without assessing whether the BIT constituted a *lex specialis*. In view of the Committee, article XI BIT "if and for so long as it applied, excluded the operation of the substantive provisions of the BIT."[279]

The *Sempra* Annulment Committee annulled the award for the failure of the tribunal to apply the applicable law in the form of article XI BIT.[280] According to the Annulment Committee, "Article 25 does not offer a guide to interpretation of the terms used in Article XI. The most that can be said is that certain words or expressions are the same or similar."[281] Additionally, and "[m]ore importantly"[282], the Committee stressed the differences between article XI BIT as primary law regarding the applicability of the BIT

---

275 *CMS Gas Transmission Company v Argentine Republic* Decision of the Ad Hoc Committee on the Application for Annulment of the Argentine Republic (25 September 2007) ICSID Case No. ARB/01/8 para 129.
276 ibid paras 130, 132.
277 ibid para 133.
278 ibid para 134; the award was not annulled on the basis of these errors since there had not been a manifest access of powers, para 136.
279 ibid para 146.
280 *Sempra Energy International v Argentine Republic* Decision on the Argentine Republic's Application for Annulment of the Award (29 June 2010) ICSID Case No. ARB/02/16 para 159.
281 ibid para 199.
282 ibid para 200.

and necessity under customary international law; both provisions "therefore deal with quite different situations."[283] For the Committee, it did not follow from the characterization of necessity as set forth in article 25 ARSIWA as customary international law "that it must be interpreted and applied in exactly the same way in all circumstances [...]"[284]. In short, the tribunal was criticized for having "adopted Article 25 of the ILC Articles as the primary law to be applied, rather than Article XI of the BIT, and in so doing made a fundamental error in identifying and applying the applicable law."[285]

The *Enron* Annulment Committee annulled the award for the failure of the tribunal to interpret and apply all preconditions of article 25 ARSIWA[286] and criticized the tribunal for the lack of a determination as to whether article XI BIT excluded any recourse to article 25 ARSIWA.[287] The defect of the tribunal's treatment of customary international law affected the tribunals conclusion on article XI BIT which relied on the interpretation of custom as well.[288] In view of the Enron Annulment Committee, it would not be for the committee to "reach its own conclusions" on the interrelationship between Article XI BIT and customary international law.[289]

The *Continental* tribunal adopted a nuanced position that can be read as a reconciliation. In line with the approach adopted by the Annulment Committee in *CMS*, the *Continental* tribunal argued that article XI BIT and customary international law on necessity operate on different levels: Measures covered by article XI BIT would lie outside the scope of the substantive provisions of the BIT,[290] whereas necessity as a circumstance precluding wrongfulness presupposed a breach of the treaty.[291] Nevertheless, the tribunal also recognized "a link between the two types of regulation" as both "intend to provide flexibility in the application of international obligations" and would lead to the same result: "condoning conduct that would otherwise be unlawful

---

283 ibid para 200.
284 ibid para 202.
285 ibid para 208.
286 *Enron Creditors Recovery Corp Ponderosa Assets, LP v Argentine Republic* Decision on the Application for Annulment of the Argentine Republic (30 July 2010) ICSID Case No. ARB/01/3 para 393.
287 ibid para 394.
288 ibid para 405.
289 ibid para 405.
290 *Continental Casuality Company v Argentine Republic, Award* Award (5 September 2008) para 164.
291 ibid para 166.

and thus removing the responsibility of the State."[292] It acknowledged that "[t]hese connections may be relevant as to the interpretation of the bilateral provision in Art XI"[293]. Thus, an interpretative relationship is not *a priori* precluded. In the specific case, however, the tribunal decided to take recourse to proportionality analysis in order to interpret the term "necessary", rather than to customary international law on necessity.[294]

II. Revisiting the distinction between primary and secondary rules

In particular the *CMS* Annulment Committee and the *Sempra* Committee referred to the distinction between primary and secondary rules.[295] Based on one reading of these decisions, article XI of the BIT between Argentina and the USA excludes certain matters from the scope of application of the treaty or determines the applicability of the BIT, whereas article 25 ARSIWA presupposes both the applicability and a breach of the treaty. Against the background of this jurisprudence, it has been argued that "[a]n adjudicator that characterizes the treaty exception as a 'primary', norm cannot simply draw on the ILC Articles as guidance in an interpretative task."[296] Also, it has been suggested that the classification as primary or secondary rule should determine the appropriateness of analogies based on municipal law or the UNIDROIT principles: "When the [UNIDROIT] Principles can be relied on, tribunals must ensure that they are drawing appropriate comparisons, using the Principles' secondary rules only to interpret the secondary rules of

---

292 *Continental Casuality Company v Argentine Republic, Award* Award (5 September 2008) para 168. The tribunal noted that this link existed also when article XI BIT was viewed as "specific bilateral regulation of necessity for purposes of the BIT (thus a kind of *lex specialis*)" which then presupposes a breach.
293 ibid para 168; see also *Continental Casuality Company v Argentine Republic* Decision on the Application for Annulment of the Argentine Republic (16 September 2011) ICSID Case No. ARB/03/9 paras 128-131.
294 *Continental Casuality Company v Argentine Republic, Award* Award (5 September 2008) paras 227, 232.
295 Cf. *CMS Gas Transmission Company v Argentine Republic* Decision on Annulment (25 September 2007) para 134. *Sempra Energy International v Argentine Republic* Decision on Annulment (29 June 2010) para 115.
296 Kurtz, 'Delineating Primary and Secondary Rules on Necessity at International Law' 253.

international law, rather than differently-structured primary rules."[297] Based on these interpretations, a meaningful interaction between NPM provisions and customary international law on necessity may become difficult, if not impossible, for reasons relating not necessarily to the particular treaty in question but to a specific understanding of the distinction between primary rules and secondary rules. Both sources, treaties and customary international law, might then be placed in different compartments. In contrast, it will be argued here that one should not read too much into the distinction between primary and secondary rules as far as the interrelationship of sources is concerned.

1. The distinction in the law of state responsibility

Distinguishing between primary and secondary rules was a convenient way for the ILC to divorce the codification of state responsibility from questions of the content of international legal obligations.[298] However, the *Dogmatik* of the ARSIWA and the often-stressed distinction between primary and secondary rules is a more roughly than gracefully built construction and should, therefore, not be exaggerated. For instance, it can indeed be said that the rules of attribution "relate to the application of primary rules", as "an action or omission can [n]ever constitute a violation of a primary rule of international law if it is not attributable to said state according to Articles 4-11".[299] The use of the term secondary remains justified here in that the rules of attribution

---

297 Jarrod Hepburn, 'The Unidroit Principles of International Commercial Contracts and Investment Treaty Arbitration: A Limited Relationship' (2015) 64(4) ICLQ 908, see also 925-926, 928.
298 See the working paper prepared by Ago, *ILC Ybk (1963 vol 2)* 253 ("[...] the consideration of the contents of the various rules of substance should not be an object in itself in the study of responsibility, and that the contents of these rules should be taken into account only to illustrate the consequences which may arise from an infringement of the rules.");Federica Paddeu, *Justification and Excuse in International Law* (Cambridge University Press 2018) 40; on the institutional background of the sub-committee see Nissel, 'The Duality of State Responsibility' 835 ff.; David, 'Primary and Secondary Rules' 29.
299 Ulf Linderfalk, 'State Responsibility and the Primary-Secondary Rules Terminology - the Role of Language for an Understanding of the International Legal System' (2009) 78(1) Nordic Journal of International Law 62. In a similar sense Jure Vidmar, 'Some Observations on Wrongfulness, Responsibility and Defences in International Law' (2016) 63 Netherlands International Law Review 351.

govern attribution solely for the purpose of establishing responsibility; for other purposes, for instance for determining the international character of an armed conflict, other rules of attribution exist.[300] Also, it has been argued that article 16 on aid or assistance in the commission of an internationally wrongful act "does not neatly fit the 'primary'/'secondary' dichotomy"[301], and can be regarded as a primary rule on which the responsibility of the accomplice is based.

Certain circumstances precluding wrongfulness, such as consent (article 20 ARSIWA), relate to the *breach of an international obligation* (Art. 2(b) ARSIWA), the primary rule directly, and constitute "a ground doing completely away with any connotation of breach"[302], whereas other circumstances, such as necessity (article 25 ARSIWA), relate to the *internationally wrongful act* (Art. 1 ARSIWA) and operate as justification or exculpation.[303] It is not argued here that the circumstances precluding wrongfulness should

---

300 Cf. Tomuschat, 'International law: ensuring the survival of mankind on the eve of a new century: general course on public international law' 276, analyzing positive obligations in specific treaty regimes and concluding: "The examples show that with regard to imputability primary and secondary rules are intimately connected."

301 Aust, *Complicity and the law of state responsibility* 6; Georg Nolte and Helmut Philipp Aust, 'Equivocal Helpers - Complicit States, Mixed Messages and International Law' (2009) 58 International and Comparative Law Quarterly 8 ("[...] questionable whether a strict distinction between primary and secondary rules can always be drawn").

302 Tomuschat, 'International law: ensuring the survival of mankind on the eve of a new century: general course on public international law' 286, 288.

303 It is debated whether the characterization as justification or as exculpation or excuse is more appropriate. On the distinction between justification and excuse see Bjorklund, 'Emergency Exceptions: State of Necessity and Force Majeure' 511 ff.; Vaughan Lowe, 'Precluding Wrongfulness or Responsibility: A Plea for Excuses' (1999) 10 EJIL 406 ("The distinction between the two is the very stuff of classical tragedy. No dramatist, no novelist would confuse them. No philosopher or theologian would conflate them. Yet the distinction practically disappears in the Draft Articles"); *Second report on State responsibility, by Mr James Crawford, Special Rapporteur* 60 paras 230-231, 76 para 307 also available in *ILC Ybk (1999 vol 2 part 1)* 60, 76; the ILC commentary takes a pragmatic approach: "They do not annul or terminate the obligation; rather they provide a justification or excuse for non-performance while the circumstance in question subsists" (*ILC Ybk (2001 vol 2 part 2)* 71 para 2); see now the recent study Paddeu, *Justification and Excuse in International Law* 23-97 (endorsing such distinction); skeptical of the usefulness of this distinction in international law Robert Kolb, *The International Law of State Responsibility* (Edward Elgar Publishing 2017) 110.

not be considered as secondary rules. Their characterization as secondary rules remains appropriate: These rules "do not annul or terminate the obligation; rather they provide a justification or excuse for nonperformance while the circumstance in question subsists".[304] As they leave the primary rule itself untouched, they can be regarded as secondary rules.[305] As the just stated examples demonstrate, however, the distance between single circumstances precluding wrongfulness and the primary obligation and the way of interaction differ, which speaks against a rigid understanding of the distinction between primary and secondary rules.

2. The distinction in the case-law of the ICJ

Moreover, the case-law of the ICJ does not justify a rigid distinction, it is in this regard inconclusive. In the *Oil Platform* case[306], the Court addressed the question of whether US conduct, which Iran had argued would constitute a breach of the bilateral treaty, could be regarded as lawful exercise of the right of self-defense. The right of self-defense can be seen as operating on both levels.[307] It justifies, or precludes, a breach of article 2(4) UNC as a primary rule under article 51 UNC and customary international law. In addition, self-defense is recognized as a circumstance precluding wrongfulness in article 21 ARSIWA.[308] According to the bilateral treaty's NPM provision, in particular article XX(1)(d), the treaty shall not preclude the application of measures which are "necessary to fulfil the obligations of a High Contracting Party for the maintenance or restoration of international peace and security, or necessary to protect its essential security interests."[309] The Court interpreted

---

304 *ILC Ybk (2001 vol 2 part 2)* 71 para 2; see also *Gabčíkovo-Nagymaros Project* 63 para 101.
305 See also Kolb, *The International Law of State Responsibility* 113, 117.
306 *Oil Platforms* [2003] ICJ Rep 161 ff.; see also Federica I Paddeu, 'Self-Defence as a Circumstance Precluding Wrongfulness: Understanding Article 21 of the Articles on State Responsibility' [2015] BYIL 37 ff.
307 ibid 16, 37.
308 Cf. *Legal Consequences of the Construction of a Wall* [2004] ICJ Rep 136, 194-195 paras 138-140, where the Court addressed self-defense subsequent to an examination of necessity, which suggests that self-defense was considered as secondary rule.
309 Treaty of Amity, Economic Relations, and Consular Rights between Iran and the United States of America (signed 15 August 1955, entered into force 16 June 1957) 248 UNTS 93.

Chapter 10: International Investment Law

the treaty's NPM provision in light of the law of self-defense and decided that the USA could not rely on the justification of self-defense and that therefore the applicability of the treaty was not precluded.[310] The Court then arrived at the conclusion that the conduct of the USA did not amount to a breach of the treaty.[311]

This judgment allows for different interpretations and is not conclusive as to the abstract relationship between primary and secondary rules. According to one interpretation of this judgment, the Court's choice to treat the NPM provision as a starting point indicates that the NPM provision governed the applicability of the treaty, which would be in line with the interpretation by the *Sempra* Annullment Committee of the BIT's NPM provision. According to the *Sempra* Annullment Committee, however, the BIT's NPM provision governed the applicability of the treaty, whereas necessity was a secondary rule, both provisions "therefore deal with quite different situations."[312] In contrast, the ICJ interpreted the NPM provision of the treaty between Iran and the USA in light of self-defence. This suggests then either that self-defense was used as primary rule under article 51 UNC or that the distinction between primary and secondary rules did not constitute a bar to interpreting one in light of the other.

According to a different interpretation, the Court's order of reasoning was chosen in order to do justice to both parties and exhaustively address the parties' submissions. This interpretation finds support in the judgment. The Court acknowledged that it had addressed the interpretation of the NPM provision after the determination of a breach of the respective treaty in the *Nicaragua* case[313], but the Court considered itself free "to select the ground upon which it will base its judgment".[314] Since the original dispute of the parties was focused on the law of self-defense, the Court decided to examine this question at the beginning.[315]

---

310 *Oil Platforms* [2003] ICJ Rep 161, 199 para 78.
311 ibid 208 para 100.
312 *Sempra Energy International v Argentine Republic* Decision on Annulment (29 June 2010) para 200.
313 cf. *Military and Paramilitary Activities in and against Nicaragua* [1986] ICJ Rep 14, 140-141 para 280.
314 *Oil Platforms* [2003] ICJ Rep 161, 180 para 37, citing *Application of the Convention of 1902 Governing the Guardianship of Infants* (*Netherlands v. Sweden*) (Judgment) [1958] ICJ Rep 62.
315 *Oil Platforms* [2003] ICJ Rep 161, 180-181 paras 37-38.

In a subsequent case, the Court followed the characterization in the *Nicaragua* judgment and stated that the NPM provision "do[es] not restrict its jurisdiction but merely afford[s] the Parties a defence on the merits."[316] The characterization as a "defence" could be understood as implying that the NPM provision is a *lex specialis* defence to the circumstances precluding wrongfulness as set forth in the ARSIWA. Based on this interpretation, when the Court interpreted the NPM provision in light of self-defence, two conclusions could be drawn, depending on whether one characterizes self-defence as primary rule or a secondary rule. In the latter case, the Court did not regard itself prevented by the distinction between primary and secondary rules from interpreting the NPM provision as *lex specialis* in light of self-defence in general international law. In the former case, no conclusion as to the distinction between primary rules and secondary rules could be drawn. In any case, the ICJ aforementioned decisions do not suggest to attach too much significance to the abstract distinction between primary and secondary norms.

3. The distinction and the relationship between the general law of treaties and the law of state responsibility

It has also been argued that the distinction between primary and secondary rules corresponds "*grosso modo*" with the distinction between the general law of treaties and the general law of responsibility.[317]

Judge Bruno Simma argued in his separate opinion in the *Accord* case that

"[i]n the language of the ILC, by now generally accepted and adopted in the literature, the Vienna Convention is designed to provide an exhaustive restatement of the 'primary rules' on treaty breach but does not touch upon matters of State responsibility, regulated by 'secondary rules' as codified and progressively developed in the ILC's 2001 Articles. In other words, Article 60 has nothing to do with State responsibility, and State responsibility has nothing to do with the maxim *inadimplenti non est adimplendum* or the *exceptio non adimpleti contractus*."[318]

---

316 *Certain Iranian Assets* [2019] ICJ Rep 7, 20 para 47; see already *Military and Paramilitary Activities in and against Nicaragua* [1986] ICJ Rep 14, 116 para 222; *Oil Platforms* [1986] ICJ Rep 803, 811 para 20.
317 Binder, *Die Grenzen der Vertragstreue im Völkerrecht* 487.
318 *Application of the Interim Accord of 13 September 1995* [2011] ICJ Rep 644 Sep Op Judge Simma para 20.

To begin with, it is necessary to consider the context of the case. The *Accord* case concerned the question of whether Greece could "justify" the non-compliance with Article 11(1) of the Interim 1995 Accord signed by the former Yugoslav Republic of Macedonia and Greece. Greece relied on countermeasures, the material breach provision of Article 60 VCLT, according to which a material breach of a treaty by one party entitles the other party to suspend the operation of a treaty in whole or in part, and on the *exceptio non adimpleti contractus*. According to this doctrine, one party to a treaty may "withhold the execution of its own obligations which are reciprocal those not performed by the other [party]".[319]

For any of these arguments to succeed, it would have been necessary to demonstrate that the Former Yugoslavic Republic of Macedonia had violated the Interim 1995 Accord, which, however, could not be established. The Court, therefore, did not see any need to engage with the questions of validity and of the preconditions of the *exceptio non adimpleti contractus*: since Greece "failed to establish that the conditions which it has itself asserted would be necessary for the application of the exceptio have been satisfied in this case", the Court considered it unnecessary "to determine whether that doctrine forms part of contemporary international law".[320]

The question of whether the *exceptio* remains applicable next to article 60 VCLT has been controversial. Anzilotti, for instance, called the *exceptio non adimpleti contractus* a general principle of law.[321] It is said to be rooted in the reciprocal nature of treaties[322] and was not codified by the VCLT as a general principle which states could resort to without further conditions. Instead, article 60 VCLT requires a manifest breach for a termination or suspension of a treaty.[323] Article 73 VCLT stipulates that the VCLT is without prejudice to

---

319 *Application of the Interim Accord of 13 September 1995* 680 para 115.
320 ibid [2011] ICJ Rep 644, 691 para 161.
321 For an invocation of this doctrine as general principle of law see *Diversion of Water from the Meuse: Netherlands v. Belgium* Merits [1937] PCIJ Series A/B 70 Diss Op Anzilotti 50: "As regards the first point, I am convinced that the principle underlying this submission (inadempleti non est adimpletum) is so just, so equitable, so universally recognized, that it must be applied in international relations also. In any case, it is one of these "general principles of law recognized by civilized nations" which the Court applies in virtue of Article 38 of its Statute."
322 See on this topic Simma, 'Reflections on article 60 of the Vienna convention on the law of treaties and its background in general international law' 5-83.
323 Art. 60 VCLT is strengthened by Art. 42(2) VCLT according to which the termination of a treaty, its denunciation or the withdrawal of a party, may take place only as a result of the application of the provisions of the treaty or of the VCLT.

the law of international responsibility which is relevant for treaty breaches. It is generally acknowledged that both fields of law, the general law of treaties and the general law of state responsibility, are relevant to treaty breaches.[324] Whereas article 60 VCLT and the *exceptio* are based on the logic of reciprocity in order to "address a contractual imbalance"[325], countermeasures in the law of responsibility serve the purpose of reinforcing the breached obligation.[326] Special Rapporteur James Crawford attempted to reintroduce the *exceptio* in the context of the ARSIWA, but his suggested draft article 30*bis* on reciprocal countermeasures did not find the support of the ILC.[327]

In the *Accord* case, Simma refuted his earlier held view[328] and argued that it was no longer be advisable to argue that there was a place for the *exceptio* next to article 60 of the Vienna Convention as far as the law relating to treaties is concerned. Otherwise, the procedural obligations and the material breach requirement of article 60 would be undermined.[329] Against this background,

---

324 For an overview see Shabtai Rosenne, *Breach of Treaty* (Cambridge University Press 1985); Xiouri, 'Problems in the Relationship between the Termination or Suspension of a Treaty on the Ground of Its Material Breach and Countermeasures' 70.
325 Christian J Tams, 'Regulating Treaty Breaches' in Michael J Bowman and Dino Kritsiotis (eds), *Conceptual and Contextual Perspectives on the Modern Law of Treaties* (Cambridge University Press 2018) 23.
326 ibid. *ILC Ybk (2001 vol 2 part 2)* 129 para 6.
327 See Crawford and Olleson, 'The Exception of Non-performance: Links between the Law of Treaties and the Law of State Responsibility' on the treatment of the exceptio by the Commission in different working projects; see also Forlati, 'Reactions to Non-Performance of Treaties in International Law' 766; see also *ILC Ybk (2001 vol 2 part 2)* 72 para 9: "[...] the exception of non-performance (exceptio inadimpleti contractus) is best seen as a specific feature of certain mutual or synallagmatic obligations and not a circumstance precluding wrongfulness".
328 Simma, 'Reflections on article 60 of the Vienna convention on the law of treaties and its background in general international law' 5 ff.
329 *Application of the Interim Accord of 13 September 1995* [2011] ICJ Rep 644 Sep Op Simma 704 para 21, 705 para 22; for a different view see Diss Op Roucounas 745 para 66 with reference to the separate *dictum* in Nicaragua; see also Thirlway, *The Sources of International Law* 101: "[...] in fact Article 60 of the Convention preserves and enacts the essence of the principle[...]"; cf. on this debate Fontanelli, 'The Invocation of the Exception of Non-Performance: A Case-Study on the Role and Application of General Principles of International Law of Contractual Origin' 119 ff.; Xiouri, 'Problems in the Relationship between the Termination or Suspension of a Treaty on the Ground of Its Material Breach and Countermeasures' 75; Forlati, 'Reactions to Non-Performance of Treaties in International Law' 770: the exceptio would play only a limited role.

Simma's statement cited above highlighted the difference between the treaty regime and the responsibility regime with respect to treaty breaches, with locating the *exceptio non adimpleti contractus* within the treaty regime.[330] It was arguably less about an examination of the abstract distinction between primary and secondary rules.

III. Concluding remarks as to the distinction between primary rules and secondary rules

It is submitted here that the distinction between primary and secondary rules may be a useful heuristic device as it points to differences between rules on the one hand, and rules on rules on the other hand. Yet, the distinction between primary and secondary rules should not be overemphasized[331] and should not be understood as indicating "that in international law legal rules fall into separate and detached compartments".[332]

It is therefore not excluded that the practice on NPM provisions can, in the long run, shape the interpretation of article 25 ARSIWA. Whereas this possibility exists in principle, this effect should not be lightly assumed: NPM provisions are tailormade for the respective treaty regime whereas necessity under customary international law applies, in principle,[333] to all international

---

330 *Application of the Interim Accord of 13 September 1995* [2011] ICJ Rep 644 Sep Op Simma para 20: "Article 60 has nothing to do with State responsibility, and State responsibility has nothing to do with the maxim inadimplenti non est adimplendum or the exceptio non adimpleti contractus."

331 As depicted by Nolte and Aust, 'Equivocal Helpers - Complicit States, Mixed Messages and International Law' 8 footnote 30, Roberto Ago himself responded to the question of whether the draft article on complicity would not leap the barrier between primary and rules with the remark that "in his opinion the Commission should not hesitate to leap that barrier whenever necessary", *ILC Ybk (1978 vol 1)* 240 para 27.

332 Linderfalk, 'State Responsibility and the Primary-Secondary Rules Terminology - the Role of Language for an Understanding of the International Legal System' 72, who criticized for this reason the distinction and proposed to "stop using it." See also Orakhelashvili, *Peremptory norms in international law* 80: "The UN International Law Commission singled out 'primary' and 'secondary' norms in terms of the law of State responsibility, but it did so for descriptive purposes only, without attributing to this distinction any inherent impact on the character of relevant norms and the rights and obligations arising therefrom"; Milanovic, 'Special Rules of Attribution of Conduct in International Law' 299-301.

333 The Court did not exclude the possibility that the necessity defense applied even to violations of human rights law and humanitarian law, *Legal Consequences of the*

obligations which are situated in very different normative and institutional settings.[334]

While it is true that the general law of treaties and the general rules of state responsibility have different legal histories, they have in common their characteristic as "rules on rules".[335]

E. Concluding Observations

This chapter explored the interrelationship of sources in the context of international investment law. It began by focusing on the transition from the interwar period to the modern international investment regime.[336] Subsequently, it analyzed the interrelationship of sources and international lawyers' quest for general law in the bilateralist structure of international investment law.[337] The chapter then turned to the significance of doctrinal constructions by considering certain interpretations of the distinction between primary rules

---

Construction of a Wall [2004] ICJ Rep 136, 194-195 paras 140-142. Art. 26 ARSIWA excludes obligations arising under a peremptory norm of general international law from the chapter on circumstances precluding wrongfulness.

334 Bücheler therefore convincingly argues against reading proportionality analysis into article 25 ARSIWA, Bücheler, *Proportionality in investor-state arbitration* 281-288.

335 According to the ILC fragmentation study as finalized by Martti Koskenniemi, "even single (primary) rules that lay down individual rights and obligations presuppose the existence of (secondary) rules that provide for the powers of legislative agencies to enact, modify and terminate such rules and for the competence of law-applying bodies to interpret and apply them.", *Fragmentation of international law: difficulties arising from diversification and expansion of international law, Report of the Study Group of the International Law Commission, Finalized by Martti Koskenniemi* 20 para 27; see also André Nollkaemper, 'The Power of Secondary Rules to connect the International and National Legal Orders' in Tomer Broude and Yuval Shany (eds), *Multi-sourced equivalent norms in international law* (Oxford University Press 2011) 47-48: "Secondary rules include rules of interpretation, rules of change and rules of responsibility". Cf. *ILC Ybk (2001 vol 2 part 2)* 31 para 4 (a), where it says in the commentary to the ARSIWA that "it is not the function of the articles to specify the content of the obligations laid down by particular primary rules, or their interpretation." One does not have to read this passage as endorsement of a categorical distinction between rules of responsibility and rules of interpretation.

336 See above, p. 558.

337 See above, p. 582.

Chapter 10: International Investment Law

and secondary rules which were developed in relation to the jurisprudence of international investment tribunals.[338]

In particular, this chapter picked up a debate between Latin American states and Western states, in particular between Mexico and the United States of America, which was already addressed in the context of the codification conference of 1930[339] and which was further explored in this chapter. The substance matter of this debate did not solely concern customary international law as such but the rules which were based on customary international law.[340] Whilst the modern history of international investment law bears witness to the creative potential of custom and general principles of law[341], it also illustrates the limited capacity of unwritten law to alleviate and to overcome political contestation, which ultimately explained the move to treaties which, however, was underlined by different motives of capital-importing and capital-exporting states.[342]

The chapter demonstrated that even in a system shaped by bilateralism in form a multilateralism in substance can emerge. States assumed a convergence between their treatymaking and customary international law which may also served the purpose of restricting the extent to which investment tribunals would limit states' capacity to regulate.[343] Moreover, tribunals assumed a convergence between the different treaty standards on fair and equitable treatment and the international minimum standard. This allowed them to buttress their reasoning as to which conduct would violate the obligation to accord fair and equitable treatment, based on the assumption that references to customary international law and general principles of law could enhance the persuasiveness and legitimacy of the respective awards.[344]

This chapter identified different doctrinal proposals in scholarship to explain this multilateralism in substance which can be discussed in other fields of international law as well: from customary international law[345] to a strong focus on the judicial concretization and the technique of treaty interpretation,[346] to the recommendation of general principles of law as guide for this

---

338 See above, p. 610.
339 See above, p. 182.
340 See above, p. 564.
341 See above, p. 571.
342 See above, p. 579.
343 See above, p. 590.
344 See above, p. 592.
345 See above, p. 595.
346 See above, p. 597.

process[347]. Which proposal will assert itself and become dominant will also depend on the future legal-political development of international investment law, for instance on the degree of specificity in which states phrase substantive standards in investment law, on the shift of authority between investment tribunals and states and perhaps even on whether disputes will occur in an investor-state or in a state-state adjudicatory setting.[348]

The variety of perspectives illustrates what this study depicted in the context of the jurisprudence of the European Court of Human Rights[349], namely that reference to other sources of international law are but one possibility to interpret a rule and relate it to its normative environment, whilst the doctrine of interpretation which allows for the consideration of a consensus below the threshold of a legal norm or the developments of functional equivalents can perform a similar function. Furthermore, the debate in international investment law on the appropriateness of a given rule or principle from a

---

347 See above, p. 599.
348 On using state-state arbitration as means of control see Anthea Roberts, 'State-to-State Investment Treaty Arbitration: A Hybrid Theory of Interdependent Rights and Shared Interpretive Authority' (2014) 55(1) Harvard Journal of International Law 28 ff., arguing that states will plead the law in a different way than investors who are not likewise committed to public interests, which can influence the interpretation of the law by tribunals; see also Kulick, 'State-State Investment Arbitration as a Means of Reassertion of Control: From Antagonism to Dialogue' 128 ff.; on the debate on whether a state can bring a claim based on diplomatic protection if the individual concerned pursues enforcement, see *Preliminary Report on Diplomatic Protection by Mr Mohamed Bennouna, Special Rapporteur* 4 February 1998 UN Doc A/CN.4/484 in *ILC Ybk (1998 vol 2 part 1)* 315 para 40: "[W]here the right of the individual is recognized directly under international law (the bilateral agreements referred to above), and the individual himself can enforce this right at the international level, the "fiction" no longer has any reason for being."; but see *contra First report on diplomatic protection, by Mr John R Dugard, Special Rapporteur* 7 March and 20 April 2000 UN Doc A/CN.4/506 and Add. 1 in *ILC Ybk (2000 vol 2 part 1)* at 213; see also Mārtiņš Paparinskis, 'Investment Arbitration and the Law of Countermeasures' (2008) 79 BYIL 280 ff.; Chittharanjan Felix Amerasinghe, *Diplomatic Protection* (Oxford University Press 2008) 341; on article 27 of the ICSID convention which limits a state's recourse to diplomatic protection "in respect of a dispute which one of its nationals and another Contracting State shall have consented to submit or shall have submitted to arbitration under this Convention" see Loretta Malintoppi, 'Article 27' in Stephan W Schill (ed), *Schreuer's Commentary on the ICSID Convention* (3rd edn, Cambridge University Press 2022) 633 ff., 638 f. on the position of non-contracting states.
349 See above, p. 408.

Chapter 10: International Investment Law

different branch or source shifts the attention to the legal operator's vision for the further development of the legal field.[350] It indicates that discussions of the appropriateness of legal principles should not be confined to the principle's representativeness, or lack thereof, and must consider and reflect on the principle's fit to the normative environment in which it is to be applied. Legal operators can in this sense become architects[351], not only in the relationship to other fields of law but also in relation to their own field. The concept of principles can appear particularly attractive to investment lawyers because of the auxiliary nature of principles in relation to treaty law. At the same time, customary international law may remain relevant as well.[352] It may then, however, assume a different function than it did in the jurisprudence of the ICTY or in parts of the jurisprudence of the ICJ. It will not perform the function of applicable law, but of an interpretative means that indicates how the written law is applied in the community.[353]

Yet, whether customary international law has a future at the level of primary rules or only of secondary rules[354] remains to be seen. This chapter critically engaged with the interpretation according to which primary rules and secondary rules need to be kept strictly separated. It was submitted that this doctrinal construction should not be overemphasized as a model for the interrelationship of sources.[355] What this debate in any case shows, however, is that the place of customary international law is subject to an ongoing discussion.

---

350 See above, p. 607.
351 Cf. Stone Sweet and Della Cananea, 'Proportionality, General Principles of Law, and Investor-State Arbitration: a Response to José Alvarez' 913. But see also above on the importance to remain within the structure of legal reasoning, p. 154, p. 416, p. 606.
352 See above, p. 609.
353 Cf. p 119.
354 Cf. above, p. 610.
355 See below, p. 616.

Chapter 11: Concluding observations on the perspectives in different fields of international law

The preceding chapters addressed very different fields of international law. This chapter will start with a couple of observations on the comparison of these fields, followed by observations relating this part to the other parts of this study.

A first observation concerns the importance of principles of international law. Both the ICTY and investor-state tribunals attempted to identify principles of the international legal order which would assist them in applying the respective applicable law. Whereas the ICTY was concerned with the identification of customary international law, investor-state tribunals interpreted and applied bilateral treaties. General principles were equally relevant for the content-determination which also demonstrates that they cannot be reduced to gap-filling when no rule of a treaty or of customary international law exists. One similarity between both contexts may be seen in the fact that tribunals' recourse to other treaties in order to search for inspiration and principles is a consequence of states' decisions to set up these tribunals without defining the law to be applied in great detail. These decisions left ample room for tribunals for interpreting and applying the law. The way in which the tribunals approached this task is very much in alignment with the description of the *modus operandi* of general principles in the second chapter. However, in particular the discussion in the context of international investment law on the paradigms which are promoted by and which are implicit in the recourse of principles highlights an important aspect. Even if one requires courts to apply only principles already recognized by the community of nations, there may remain room left for courts and tribunals, and paradigms or other second-order considerations that inform the choices should be discussed.

The role of customary international law varied in the contexts of the preceding chapters. It played a particularly dominant role in the jurisprudence of the ICTY and its role seemed to have decreased to some extent under the Rome Statute. Yet, the chapter also demonstrated that even then customary international law can remain important as long as the Rome Statute is not universally ratified and as long as the ICC has the ambition to be not just a treaty body but an international court which enforces the *ius puniendi* of the international community. A community aspect can be found in the

Chapter 11: Concluding observations on the perspectives

defenses of customary international law submitted by scholars in the context of international investment law as well. According to such reading, it is customary international law which is concretized and implicitly relied on by BITs and which provides for the normative justification for cross-reliance of tribunals when they interpret bilateral treaties.

Yet, it has also been demonstrated that not all agree with this reading. ICC Chambers have demonstrated a tendency in favour of a *lex specialis* approach that focuses on the treaty, rather than on general international law. In international investment law, certain scholars doubted the appropriateness of customary international law as source of primary obligations. As it will be demonstrated in the twelfth chapter, other scholars doubt the appropriateness of customary international law as source of secondary obligations.

This brings one to the politics as to the sources and to source preferences. The discussions are similar to discussions that have been referred to in the second chapter and the third chapter of this study. Source preferences can be an expression of a preference for a specific style of legal reasoning and for a specific legal culture. Source preferences can also be the result of different institutional reasons. For instance, the ICTY could have adopted a reasoning which would have been based less on customary international law when it comes to the individual criminal responsibility for violations of international law. Resorting to customary international law would not have been necessary if the ICTY had decided to base the individual responsibility on a general principle of law according to which every serious violation of international entails the individual responsibility. Whether such argument would have found acceptance is difficult to say in hindsight. In any case, customary international law was closer to state consent than a deductive reasoning based on principles on a level of high generality. In international investment law tribunals arguably referred to other, external sources in order to objectivize their conclusion as to what constitutes fair and equitable treatment. The example of the ICC demonstrates that distancing oneself from customary international law may be the result of one's support for a different theory of criminal liability. At the same time, it is noteworthy that the ICC Appeals Chamber in *Al-Bashir* did not confine its reasoning on the immunity of a sitting head of state to the applicable UNSC resolution and instead presented a reasoning which focuses on customary international law, mindful of the judgment's implications for the development of customary international law. Future scholarship may examine how and for which reasons courts and tribunals approach the interrelationship of sources in different contexts.

Chapter 11: Concluding observations on the perspectives

The chapter on the ECHR appears to be different at first sight in that the ECHR is a regional treaty. One central element regarding the interrelationship of sources, therefore, concerns the relationship between regional law and general law. Yet, this relationship may ultimately be not so different from the relationship between *lex specialis* and *lex generalis*, at least from the perspective of public international law.[1] The chapter demonstrated that the European Court engaged with other sources of international law when interpreting and applying the ECHR, partly because of a *renvoi* of the ECHR for instance in article 7(2) ECHR, partly because the European Court examined the effects of states' application of international law on individual rights under the ECHR. Positive obligations under the ECHR can strengthen states' compliance with other international law.[2] At the same time, the chapter depicted how the ambition of the ECHR as an instrument of the European public order was articulated when addressing other sources of international law. The ECHR not only is shaped by general international law, it can also contribute to shaping general international law. In the future, it will be particularly challenging to assess to what extent functional equivalents based on an interpretation of the ECHR have contributed to the development of general international law.

On a more abstract level, the preceding chapters show the intertwinement of the several branches of international law. Different interpreters introduce different perspectives when they consider international law from the standpoint of their respective field and when they identify and address customary international law. They engage with other fields, the European Court approaches international criminal law, the ICTY considers the jurisprudence on the ECHR as do investor-state tribunals. All are, to varying degrees, also concerned with general international law. Treaties not just depart from customary international law, but rely on and partly contribute to it as well.

This intertwinement is not without challenges for international lawyers. International lawyers who seek to study the development of the general law will have to go into specific fields and try to disentangle the general from the specific in the interpretation and application of special law and identify to what extent interpretative choices and decisions lend themselves to generalization or are primarily concerned with particular problems of the

---

1 *Fragmentation of international law: difficulties arising from diversification and expansion of international law, Report of the Study Group of the International Law Commission, Finalized by Martti Koskenniemi* 109 para 212.
2 See above, p. 423.

631

Chapter 11: Concluding observations on the perspectives

respective field of international law. At the same time, specialists should be aware of the international legal foundations of their particular order and, when engaging with other international law, do so in good faith, considering external international law not only from the perspective of their respective regime but in its own right.

Part E.
Doctrinal Perspectives and Conclusions

Chapter 12: Doctrinal perspectives on and discussions of the interrelationship of sources

A. Introduction

This section focuses on different trends in the discussion of the interrelationship of sources which illustrate the contingency of the sources discourse and its reflection of contemporary challenges. The chapter will first address the early interest in general principles (B. I.). Subsequently, the chapter will illustrate how scholars developed different approaches to new norms (B. II.) that were discussed in relation to UN General Assembly Resolutions. The enter into force of several codification conventions that had been prepared by the ILC as well as the *North Sea Continental Shelf* judgment of the International Court of Justice shifted the discussion to the relationship between customary international law and treaty law (B. III.). The interest in customary international law which was increased by the Nicaragua judgments of the International Court of Justice inspired both refinements in the discussion of the relationship between treaty and custom and critique which emphasized the merit of treaty law and of general principles of law (C.). While approaches during the 1990s and early 2000s discussed the sources against the background of community interests, so-called postmodern positivist approaches have subsequently emerged which place less emphasis on value-based approaches and more emphasis on methodological self-restraint and on the written law (D.).

B. Shifting research interests in specific sources

I. The early interest in general principles of law prior to the rise of codification conventions

One standard work of reference on general principles originated in the 1950s and was written by Bin Cheng who situated the concept of general principles within the discussions of the judicial interpretation and application of the law

Chapter 12: Doctrinal perspectives on and discussions of the interrelationship of sources

and of the law in action, or in his words, "living law".[1] His cognitive, scholarly interest was directed at the identification of principles in the judgments and decisions of international courts and tribunals by way of induction. Accordingly, he identified four principles which he deemed to be a necessary component of any legal order, namely the principle of self-preservation, the principle of good faith, the principle of responsibility and the principles governing judicial proceedings, from all of which sub-principles could be derived in judicial practice.[2] Cheng discussed the relationship between rules and principles and argued that principles could be understood as "bases of positive rules of law. The latter are the practical formulation of the principles and, for reasons of expediency, may vary and depart, to a greater or lesser extent, from the principle from which they spring."[3] Therefore, the first step in identifying a general principle was "a process of induction from the positive law of any single system".[4] Cheng stressed that this process must examine the positive law's *ratio legis*.[5] The relationship between general principles and other sources of international law was briefly addressed: forming the bases of positive rules and governing the interpretation of other rules, general principles were said to be of "superior value", but rules in derogation of general principles were said to remain binding.[6]

Other scholars stressed the potential of general principles for emerging fields which were not traditionally govern by public international law. Against the background of the *Abu Dhabi* arbitration[7], Arnold Duncan McNair "sub-

---

1 Cheng, *General Principles of Law as applied by International Courts and Tribunals* 16-17.
2 ibid 29 ff., 105 ff., 163 ff., 257 ff., 390.
3 ibid 376.
4 ibid 376.
5 ibid 376-377.
6 ibid 393. He discussed this question after pointing out that general principles can be modified, and stressed that the possibility of derogation will not likely occur very often. The interrelationship was not discussed in great detail cf. Elihu Lauterpacht, 'Review of Books General Principles of Law as Applied by International Courts and Tribunals' (1953) XXX BYIL 545, arguing that the title of Cheng's study would be misleading and that Cheng would depart from the term by not distinguishing between general principles of law and general principles of international law; for a similar critique see Friedmann, 'The Uses of "General Principles" in the Development of International Law' 286 footnote 21.
7 *Petroleum Development (Trucial Coast) Ltd v Sheikh of Abu Dhabi* 1 ICLQ 247, 250-251; see generally Rudolf Dolzer, 'Abu Dhabi Oil Arbitration' [2006] Max Planck EPIL para 8; on the doctrine of internationalized contracts see above, p. 571.

mitted that the legal system appropriate to the type of contract under consideration is not public international law but shares with public international law a common source of recruitment and inspiration, namely, 'the general principles of law recognized by civilized nations'."[8] Francis Mann, however, was skeptical and stressed that general principles of law would not constitute a legal system of their own, "unless they are equiparated to public international law."[9] According to Jenks, the emergence of newly independent states and the cultural diversity would not necessarily detrimental to general law, customary international law or general principles as long as this new development would be taken into account in the identification of those sources.[10]

Wolfgang Friedmann also stressed the significance of general principles for the further development of new branches of international law.[11] He did not expect "a flood of international arbitral or judicial decisions spelling out these principles" as general principles "are and will remain implicit insofar as they are assumed rather than spelled out in international transactions and agreements."[12] He distinguished between general principles of interpretation and of approach, general principles as minimum standards of procedural fairness, and substantive principles.[13] As the distinction between public and

---

8 Arnold Duncan McNair, 'The General Principles of Law Recognized by Civilized Nations' (1957) 33 BYIL 6, see also 19.
9 Mann, 'The Proper Law of Contracts Concluded by International Persons' 44-45; cf. on this debate also Clarence Wilfred Jenks, *The Proper Law of International Organizations* (Stevens & Sons 1962) 152-154.
10 Jenks, *The common law of mankind* 104 ff., see also 120 where Jenks proposed nine general principles which he partially justified by reference to diverse municipal legal orders, namely, the principle of sovereignty being subject to law, the principle of *audiatur et altera pars* and the independence of the judiciary, the principle of self-defence being subject to proportionality, the principle of *pacta sunt servanda*, the principle of respect of acquired rights, the principle of consultation prior to action affecting the interests of others, the principle of liability for unlawful harm to one's neighbour, the principle of respect for human rights, including equality before the law, and the principle that international law is a body of living principles; see also Friedmann, *The Changing Structure of international law* 297-340 on a discussion of universality in light of different legal families and political ideologies.
11 See for instance ibid 190; Wolfgang Friedmann, 'General Course in Public International Law' (1969) 127 RdC 149.
12 Friedmann, 'The Uses of "General Principles" in the Development of International Law' 283.
13 ibid 283, 287, 297. He distinguished general principles from natural law which would only be a "camouflage of the real problem", Friedmann, *The Changing Structure of international law* 77.

Chapter 12: Doctrinal perspectives on and discussions of the interrelationship of sources

private law would lose significance in municipal law, international lawyers should not confine comparative legal research to private law only, they should rather extend it to public law.[14] In contrast, customary international law was said to be "too clumsy" and too "slow to accommodate the evolution of international law in our time", it was said to represent an "unsuitable vehicle for international welfare and cooperative international law", where specific and technical rules were necessary.[15] Friedmann acknowledged that customary international law might form "much easier and faster"[16] and emphasized the "constant interaction between custom-which in contemporary conditions may sometimes be formed with astonishing rapidity-and treaty law."[17] In his view, however, "in the area of the international law of co-operation, it is only by treaty or other international agreements that progress can be achieved".[18] To Friedmann, the formation of customary international law in the law of the sea with respect to the continental shelf or the extension of the territorial sea

---

14 On general principles of administrative law see also Jenks, *The Proper Law of International Organizations* 59-62.
15 Friedmann, *The Changing Structure of international law* 121-122.
16 Friedmann, 'General Course in Public International Law' 132, with reference to transportation and communication. As he noted, the Brierly treatise (edited by Waldock) stated that the customary rule of sovereignty over air developed rather quickly at the beginning of the 20th century, compare James Leslie Brierly, *The law of nations: an introduction to the international law of peace* (6th, ed. by Humphrey Waldock, Clarendon Press 1963) 62: "The growth of a new custom is always a slow process, and the character of international society makes it particularly slow in the international sphere. The progress of the law therefore has come to be more and more bound up with that of the law-making treaty. But it is possible even today for new customs to develop and to win acceptance as law when the need is sufficiently clear and urgent. A striking recent illustration of this is the rapid development of the principle of sovereignty over the air." See also at 218, stating that the doctrine of territorial air space was adopted in the Paris Convention on Air navigation in 1919 and reaffirmed in the Chicago Convention of 1944. As a consequence of this doctrine, "only by virtue of a treaty could one state enjoy rights in the air space of another [...]".
17 Friedmann, 'General Course in Public International Law' 134.
18 ibid 136: "[...] in the area of the international law of co-operation, it is only by treaty or other international agreements that progress can be achieved. The objectives of international welfare organisation require specific regulation, which cannot be achieved by the slow-moving and some- what imprecise methods of custom. It is not possible to agree on fishery conservation measures, or on the stabilisation of prices of commodities, or on international minimum wage standards, other than by specific agreements, which formulate precise standards and obligations."

only represented "a retrograde development" which consolidated "extensions of national sovereignty at the expense of international freedoms".[19]

The early interest in general principles of law of the scholars depicted in this chapter can be seen against the background of the slow progress of success of the International Law Commission in the progressive development and the codification of customary international law.[20] However, when codification conventions were adopted and the ICJ addressed the question of the relationship between conventions and customary international law, the scholarly interest in sources shifted to customary international law.

II. Different approaches to new norms

The emergence of new norms became another subject-matter which was discussed in the doctrine of sources. Roberto Ago proposed the concept of spontaneous law (1.), Bin Cheng and Karl Zemanek approached the question of the normative value of UNGA resolutions from the perspective of customary international law and general principles of law respectively (2.).

1. Roberto Ago's spontaneous law

Roberto Ago's writings on the emergence of spontaneous norms as object of legal research[21] was primarily concerned with legal theory and a critique of voluntaristic positivism, which is noteworthy given its strong roots in the thinking of Italian international lawyers.[22] Spontaneous norms, he claimed, emerged in the general, as opposed to unanimous, conscience of a legal

---

19 Wolfgang Friedmann, 'The North Sea Continental Shelf Cases- A Critique' (1970) 64 AJIL 233 (quote), 239-240.
20 Cf. Lauterpacht, 'Codification and Development of International Law' 17, who spoke of "the absence of agreed law"; for a treatment of custom see Kunz, 'The Nature of Customary International Law' 662 ff.
21 In this aspect his work bore a certain similarity with Cheng's focus on the living law, see above, p. 636.
22 For this observation, see Pierre-Marie Dupuy, 'Communauté Internationale et Disparités de Développement Cours général de droit international public' (1979) 165 RdC 29; but see also Verdross, 'Entstehungsweisen und Geltungsgrund des universellen völkerrechtlichen Gewohnheitsrechts' 640 (noting that already Anzilotti had emphasized the spontaneous character of customary international law); Anzilotti, *Lehrbuch des Völkerrechts* 60-63; for a contextualization within Italian legal scholarship see

community.²³ Because of their unwritten and spontaneous nature, they could not be controlled or predicted by formal law-ascertainment mechanisms and procedures.²⁴ Those norms could only be observed by way of inductions of their manifestations in social life which would be the task of legal science.²⁵ From the perspective of legal methodology, Ago's theory can be read as critique against a legal science which excludes an examination of the empirical reality.²⁶ According to Ago's account, the relation between formally enacted law and spontaneous law could not be determined in the abstract but only under consideration of the particular historical circumstances and the preference of the respective legal society.²⁷

Ago's focus on "law in force" in addition to the law explicitly laid down²⁸ is exposed to the critique that the existence of a common social conscience is unproven, and that speculation thereof should not replace consideration of procedures through which law originates and by which a norm might legitimately receive its legally binding character.²⁹ Also, Ago's theory has been criticized for elevating the legal science improperly to the actual source of this spontaneous law and for blurring the line between law and non-law.³⁰ Furthermore, the objections can be raised that the spontaneous law could be characterized as customary international law which would belong to positive international law and which would be created through elements prescribed by international law, namely a general practice which is accepted as law.³¹ Even

---

Antonello Tancredi, 'The (Immediate) Post-World War II Period' in Giulio Bartolini (ed), *A History of International Law in Italy* (Oxford University Press 2020) 168 ff.
23 Ago, 'Science juridique et droit international' 932.
24 Ago, 'Positive Law and International Law' 729, 732; Ago, 'Science juridique et droit international' 940, 942, 944.
25 ibid 932; on the inductive method in relation to unwritten law see also Ago, 'Positive Law and International Law' 723, 728-9.
26 Tancredi, 'The (Immediate) Post-World War II Period' 179.
27 Ago, 'Science juridique et droit international' 942-943.
28 See Ago, 'Positive Law and International Law' 698-699, 724 ff., 728-733.
29 Herbert Günther, *Zur Entstehung von Völkergewohnheitsrecht* (Duncker & Humblot 1970) 93-95.
30 Tancredi, 'The (Immediate) Post-World War II Period' 180-1; Josef L Kunz, 'Roberto Ago's Theory of a "Spontaneous" International Law' (1958) 52(1) American Journal of International Law 90-1.
31 In this sense ibid 88-90.

though customary international law may emerge or be made unconsciously[32], the creation of customary international law can also, as described by Mendelson, "emerg[e] as the result of careful calculation on the part of its instigators and is thus far from spontaneous".[33] Moreover, it can be argued that Ago's account juxtaposed enacted law that has been explicitly laid down on the one hand and what Ago characterized as spontaneous law on the other hand. This invites the criticism that it is questionable whether the development of the law is best described by a separate category of spontaneous law rather than by a focus on the interpretation and application of the enacted law.[34]

With other scholars discussed in this study, for instance Roscoe Pound[35], Benjamin Cardozo[36], Josef Esser[37] and Lon Fuller[38], Ago shared the idea that law could not be fully understood by way of reference to formal sources only without taking account of the actual legal practice within a given community.[39] It is certainly true that understanding customary international law only as "spontaneous law" is problematic from the perspective of judicial application. In fact, international legal scholarship and the recently adopted conclusions of the ILC[40] can provide important guidance and contribute to a certain formalization of the evidence of customary international law by highlighting the role of the two elements and explaining which materials may be relied upon in order to ascertain the existence of a general practice accepted as law.[41] Without this guidance, a rationality control of the identification, interpretation and application of customary international law would

---

32 Cf. for the view of custom as unconscious lawmaking ibid 88; Kelsen, *Principles of International Law (1952)* 308; Danilenko, *Law-Making in the International Community* 78; Cassese, *International Law* 156.
33 Mendelson, 'The subjective Element in Customary International Law' 179.
34 See in this sense also Kunz, 'Roberto Ago's Theory of a "Spontaneous" International Law' 88 ("But the 'whole law in force' consists also of individual concrete norms, created by judicial and administrative decisions [...]").
35 See above, p. 115.
36 See above, p. 117.
37 See above, p. 144.
38 See above, p. 118.
39 Cf. Carlo Focarelli, 'The Concept of International Law: The Italian Perspective' in Peter Hilpold (ed), *European International Law Traditions* (Springer 2021) 105 (highlighting the "social attunement" of Ago's theory).
40 See above, p. 372.
41 On the two elements, see above, p. 75; see also Bos, *A methodology of international law* 224; d'Aspremont, 'The Decay of Modern Customary International Law in Spite of Scholarly Heroism' 25 ("formal programme of evidence").

be difficult and customary international law might not fulfil its legitimizing function. Having said this, one should also, however, avoid the other extreme. A formalization of customary international law will be possible only to a certain extent.[42] In the end, the emergence unwritten law, of customary international law and general principles of law, is similar to a path which emerges as one walks it.[43] Roberto Ago's scholarship is an important reminder of this characteristic of unwritten law.[44]

2. Bin Cheng and Karl Zemanek

The rise of "parliamentary diplomacy"[45], the exchange of views on legal matters within the United Nations and in particular the General Assembly, the proliferation of resolutions gave rise to debates as to the legal value of formally nonbinding General Assembly resolutions and on how and whether the doctrine of sources could take account of these development.[46]

---

42 For a positive assessment of Ago's theory see Pierre-Marie Dupuy, 'Théorie des sources et coutume en droit international contemporain' in Manuel Rama-Montaldo (ed), *El derecho internacional en un mundo en transformacion: liber amicorum en homenaje al profesor Eduardo Jiménez de Aréchaga* (Fundación de Cultura Universitaria 1994) vol 1, 63; cf. also on the formal character of custom recently Kolb, 'Legal History as a Source: From Classical to Modern International Law' 290: "The better view is that the customary process is recognized in international law as a formal source, but that the process itself makes direct reference to the manifold social activities of the subjects of the law whose behaviour customary international law seeks to regulate."

43 Wolfke, *Custom in present international law* 62.

44 See also Mendelson, 'The subjective Element in Customary International Law' 179 ("Ago's description does serve to remind us that, in trying to fit wild custom into the formalistic clothing of 'civilized' lawmaking, we may deform its nature.").

45 Philip C Jessup, 'Parliamentary diplomacy: an examination of the legal quality of the rules of procedure of organs of the United Nations' (1956) 89 RdC 181 ff.

46 Eg Obed Y Asamoah, *The Legal Significance of the Declaration of the General Assembly of the United Nations* (Martinus Nijhoff 1966) 46 ff. (resolutions as state practice) and 61-62 on whether they could indicate general principles of law; Taslim Olawe Elias, 'Modern Sources of International Law' in Wolfgang Friedmann, Louis Henkin, and Oliver Lissitzyn (eds), *Transnational law in a changing society: essays in honor of Philip C. Jessup* (Columbia University Press 1972) 34 ff.; Krzysztof Jan Skubiszewski, 'A New Source of the Law of Nations: Resolutions of International Organizations' in *Recueil d'études de droit international en hommage à Paul Guggenheim* (Faculté de Droit de l'Univ de Genève 1968) 508 ff.; Christoph Schreuer, 'Recommendations

Commenting on UNGA resolutions on Outer Space Bin Cheng considered the idea of "instant customary international law" which in his view, however, had not emerged in the specific context as states held too diverging views on the content and bindingness of the resolutions 1721A[47] and 1962[48].[49] Cheng argued that a *opinio juris generalis* would be the single constitutive element of custom while practice would be important evidence to identify and interpret the *opinio juris generalis*.[50] He later preferred the term "*general international law* [...] because *consuetudo* is now clearly shown not to be a requisite".[51]

Karl Zemanek adopted a different perspective on the development of the law of outer space in the very same year when Cheng published his article on instant custom. Zemanek did not look at this development through the lenses of customary law, but through the concept of "general principles".[52] In his view, the value of the resolutions would not be adequately captured by way of reference to the resolution's lack of binding force. He suggested that article 38(1)(c) ICJ Statute could be interpreted as referring not only to principles recognized in municipal laws but also to those principles at the international plane.[53] The votes in favour of the resolutions would imply the recognition of the resolutions' underlying principles by the states, which "would appear to make a strong case for suggesting that these principles

---

and the Traditional Sources of International Law' (1977) 20 German Yearbook of International Law; Friedmann, 'General Course in Public International Law' 142: "apart from the traditional sources of law-making, custom and treaty, we must look to other sources of international law."; critical Baxter, 'Multilateral Treaties as Evidence of Customary International Law' 71.

47 UNGA Res 1721 (XVI) A (20 December 1961) UN Doc A/RES/1721(XVI)A-E.
48 UNGA Res 1962 (XVIII) (13 December 1963) UN Doc A/RES/1962(XVIII).
49 As Mendelson stated, it is often not remembered when discussing Cheng's article that Cheng concluded that no instant custom had emerged, Maurice H Mendelson, 'The Formation of Customary International Law' (1998) 272 RdC 371.
50 Bin Cheng, 'United Nations Resolutions on Outer Space: 'Instant' International Customary Law?' (1965) 5 Indian Journal of International Law 36-37, 42, 45-48.
51 Cheng, 'Custom: the future of general state practice in a divided world' 548; see also the often quoted remark of Robert Yewdall Jennings, 'What is International Law and How Do We Tell It When We See It ?' (1981) 37 Schweizerisches Jahrbuch für internationales Recht 5: " [...] most of what we perversely persist in calling customary international law is not only not customary law: it does not even faintly resemble a customary law."
52 Karl Zemanek, 'The United Nations and the Law of Outer Space' (1965) 19 The Year Book of World Affairs 207 ff.
53 ibid 208.

Chapter 12: Doctrinal perspectives on and discussions of the interrelationship of sources

should be treated as General Principles of Law Recognised by Civilized Nations."[54] Yet, principles would not replace customary international law (or treaty obligations) but require the latter: "[P]rinciples are not norms directly applicable. They are abstractions, to be implemented by norms of contractual or customary international law, or by a judgment in a given case"; rather than regulating states' behaviour in outer space, principles are said to "trace the lines along which the law of outer space, whether contractual or customary, is to develop. It is here that their real importance is found".[55]

The articles written by Cheng and Zemanek demonstrate that the very same phenomenon can be discussed under different sources concepts. Cheng's discussion of "instant custom" may have become particularly famous, and be it only because it is usually approached with skepticism; while custom can emerge rapidly, part of the legitimizing function of custom rest on the fact that it offers general rules which had been applied before and on the insight that "what is done repeatedly by a large number of States cannot be fundamentally detrimental to anyone's interests."[56] Zemanek's article opened the concept of general principles up to developments at the international plane and stressed principles' guiding function for the development of treaty law and customary international law.

---

54 Zemanek, 'The United Nations and the Law of Outer Space' 209.
55 ibid 210 (pointing also out that "the development of a divergent evolution of customary rules "would [...] either indicate a change in the general legal conscience, or be evidence to the effect that such a conscience never existed"). Simma later argued that Zemanek failed to consider general principles of law as basis for international responsibility in the context of environmental protection after Zemanek had rejected the existence of a rule of customary international law, Bruno Simma, 'Die Erzeugung ungeschriebenen Völkerrechts: Allgemeine Verunsicherung- klärende Beiträge Karl Zemaneks' in Konrad Ginther and others (eds), *Völkerrecht zwischen normativem Anspruch und politischer Realität: Festschrift für Karl Zemanek zum 65. Geburtstag* (Duncker & Humblot 1994) 112-113, see Karl Zemanek, 'State Responsibility and Liability' in Winfried Lang, Hanspeter Neuhold, and Karl Zemanek (eds), *Environmental Protection and International Law* (Graham & Trotman 1991) 187 ff. It can be argued though that Zemanek's work can be read as suggesting that principles would not directly regulate or apply in the same direct manner in which customary international law and treaty law would apply.
56 Tomuschat, 'International law: ensuring the survival of mankind on the eve of a new century: general course on public international law' 331.

III. Codification studies: the interrelationship between treaties and custom

Against the background of the codification conventions in the 1960s, the discourse on the interrelationship of sources shifted to the relationship between treaties and custom. The question arose whether codification would leave any room for customary international law[57] and whether treaties could be regarded as proper state practice.[58] This section focuses on the work of Richard Baxter, Anthony d'Amato and Hugh Thirlway.

1. Richard Baxter's paradox

Prior to the 1969 *North Sea Continental Shelf* judgment, Baxter commented on the topic of the relationship between treaties and custom. He argued with reference to the judicial practice also of the ICJ that treaties could be evidence of customary international law and even of general principles of law.[59] In his view, treaties could have effects beyond codifying customary international law, they would break "down the barriers of strict State sovereignty", indicating "that the matter is becoming one of international concern and is gradually ceasing to be a question within the domestic jurisdiction of States."[60] Codification conventions could impact the further development of customary international law and arrest the latter's "change and flux".[61] Furthermore, treaties as evidence might have the advantage of "speak[ing] with one voice as of one time", while other evidences of state practice might be "ambiguous and inconsistent" and render reconciliation necessary.[62] Baxter seemed to be also sympathetic to the view that the "adhesion of the great majority of the

---

57 Tammes, 'Codification of International Law in the International Law Commission' 325-326: conventions "tend to drive out customary international law"; see also Karl, *Vertrag und spätere Praxis im Völkerrecht: zum Einfluß der Praxis auf Inhalt und Bestand völkerrechtlicher Verträge* 362.
58 Cf. Wolfke, *Custom in present international law* 70 (rejecting treaties as practice).
59 Baxter, 'Multilateral Treaties as Evidence of Customary International Law' 298. On the role of bilateral treaties see ibid 275-6; Baxter, 'Treaties and Customs' 75 ff.
60 Baxter, 'Multilateral Treaties as Evidence of Customary International Law' 276.
61 ibid 299 ("The clear formulation of rules in a codification treaty and the assent of a substantial number of States may have the effect of arresting change and flux in the state of customary international law. Although the treaty 'photographs' the state of the law as at the time of its entry into force a to individual States, it continues, so long as States remain parties to it, to speak in terms of the present.").
62 ibid 300.

important States of the world to [humanitarian treaties] [...] may act in such a way as to impose the standards of the treaty on non-parties."[63]

He returned to this subject a few years later under the impression of the *North Sea Continental Shelf* judgment.[64] He maintained that treaty ratification can count as state practice.[65] Based on his interpretation of the *North Sea Continental Shelf* judgment he stated what later would be called the Baxter-paradox:

> "It is only fair to observe that the proof of a consistent pattern of conduct by non-parties becomes more difficult as the number of parties to the instrument increases. The number of participants in the process of creating customary law may become so small that the evidence of their practice will be minimal or altogether lacking. Hence the paradox that as the number of parties to a treaty increases, it becomes more difficult to demonstrate what is the state of customary international law dehors the treaty."[66]

In other words, international treaties constituted "an agreed starting point- an attractive force to which non-party practice will be drawn like iron filings to a magnet"[67], but once the treaty becomes successful and increasingly ratified, customary international law would be difficult to prove. Baxter acknowledged that the substance of widely ratified treaties can become "general international law".[68]

If one evaluates Baxter's statements, one can say in hindsight that the so-called Baxter-paradox did not assert itself in practice[69], the paradox remained

---

63 If, he added, one accepts some form of legislation in international law, Baxter, 'Multilateral Treaties as Evidence of Customary International Law' 300, see also at 286, where he argued that such view could be supported by the fact that humanitarian conventions were often build on past conventions. He conceded, however, that the distinction between humanitarian treaties and other treaties was one "which might be made but which is not yet reflected in State practice or in other sources of the positive law."

64 His analysis was informed by the judgment, at the same time he was critical of parts of it, in particular of the requirement of the "fundamental norm-making character", Baxter, 'Treaties and Customs' 62.

65 ibid 55-56: "If 30 States are parties to the treaty, the decision-maker, legal adviser, or scholar must give to the treaty the same weight that would be accorded to 30 simultaneous, contemporary, and identical declarations by those 30 States of their understanding of customary law."

66 ibid 64.
67 ibid 73.
68 ibid 103.
69 Kolb, 'Selected problems in the theory of customary international law' 146.

a theoretical one. States may conclude conventions with the very objective to change customary international law and may act not soley in pursuance of treaty in pursuance of treaty obligation with *opinio juris conventionalis*.[70] The ICJ jurisprudence illustrates that there may be a covergence of sources in the sense that treaty and custom can converge into common principles, for instance the prohibition of the use of force or the right to self-determination.[71] The dynamic relationship between treaties and custom makes it difficult to draw conclusions from the practice of states. In certain instances, it may indeed be argued that "when time passes and States neglect to become parties to a multilateral instrument, that abstention constitutes a silent rejection of the treaty".[72] It is, however, equally possible that states, while supporting the substance of the treaty, disagreed with procedural rules or that states are convinced that the content of the convention has become binding as customary international law.[73]

The so-called Baxter-paradox is important in that it reminds one of the distinctiveness of conventions and customary international law and cautions against an equation of the two without demonstrating a certain level of acceptance of the rule set forth in the convention outside the group of states parties. Moreover, it should be borne in mind that the described paradox was an interpretation of the *North Sea Continental Shelf* judgment and that it, therefore, should be interpreted restrictively, taking the ICJ jurisprudence as a whole into account.

---

70 See Crawford, 'Change, Order, Change: The Course of International Law General Course on Public International Law' 109: "One possibility [to resolve the Baxter paradox] would be to generate a presumption of *opinio juris* from widespread participation in a treaty, at least in normative terms. Indeed this is effectively what the Eritrea-Ethiopia Claims Commission did as regards the four 1949 Geneva Conventions and its Additional Protocol I."
71 See above, p. 285.
72 Baxter, 'Treaties and Customs' 99, 100.
73 Cf. Greenhill and Strausz, 'Explaining Nonratification of the Genocide Convention: A Nested Analysis' 74-375, 381-382.

2. Anthony d'Amato and the formation of custom by treaties

In Anthony d'Amato's view, treaties and customary international law were not isolated from each other.[74] While binding only parties, treaties could constitute state practice relevant for customary international law.

> "Not only do [treaties] carve out law for the immediate parties, but they also have a profound impact upon general customary international law [...] generalizable provisions in bilateral and multilateral treaties generate customary rules of law binding upon all states. [...] The claim made here is not that treaties bind nonparties, but that generalizable provisions in treaties give rise to rules of customary international law binding on all states."[75]

Parties to a treaty could not control the contribution the treaty might make to customary international law as this would depend on the other treaties concluded by different states and the reactions and expectations of the international community.[76] Customary international law, one might describe his view, emerges from the entirety of acts of states in the system.[77] Illustrative in this regard is his critique of the 1986 *Nicaragua* judgment, where he criticized that the Court misunderstood the interaction of treaties and custom.

---

74 D'Amato, *The Concept of Custom in International Law* 149; Anthony D'Amato, 'Treaties As a Source of General Rules of International Law' (1962) 3 Harvard International Law Journal 10-11; Anthony D'Amato, 'Trashing Customary International Law' (1987) 81 AJIL 102 ff. His studies are not primarily concerned with general principles of law which are described as municipal law analogies and associated with "the possibility of systemic dysfunction" when being applied at the international level, Anthony D'Amato, 'Groundwork for International Law' (2014) 108 AJIL 672: "[A] rule that has its origin in the domestic law of many states [...] cannot automatically be lifted up to the plane of international law without risking the possibility of systemic dysfunction." Anthony d'Amato, 'International Law as an Autopoietic System' in Rüdiger Wolfrum and Volker Röben (eds), *Developments of International Law in Treaty Making* (Springer 2005) 393-394 (general principles would play a role in international procedural law).
75 D'Amato, *The Concept of Custom in International Law* 104, 107.
76 ibid 151. Yet, the parties' intent as to whether a provision shall be regarded generalizable should be given weight, at 110.
77 D'Amato, 'Groundwork for International Law' 667-668: "[C]ustomary international law is not a collection of discrete rules or statutes; rather, its norms are generalizations made from observations of state practice and, in particular, from the resolution of conflicting claims within that practice. Because every act of a state is "connected" to every other act—that is, it has ramifications for other state behaviors (Axiom 1)—the network of customary law is an analog (not a digital) network that fills the plenum of international transactions."

In his view, the Court took a "unidimensional approach"[78] to this interplay by simply equating article 2(4) UNC with customary international law without appreciating the entirety of acts, in particular subsequent practice to article 2(4) UNC and contrary practice, all of which led d'Amato to arrive at a conclusion which differed from the Court's outcome.

While one does not have to agree with d'Amato's critique of the judgment, the idea to understand customary international law by reference to states' treaty obligations can explain how the rise of multilateral human rights treaties began to enrich and pervade custom.[79] It also points to the fact that the emergence of customary international law is to some extent unconscious lawmaking. However, to argue that all treaties that contain generalizable provisions contribute to customary international law without making any gradual distinction as to the respective weight or adding any nuance goes too far.[80] Understanding customary international law solely as equilibrium of different practices can risk reducing law to what states do and undervaluing law's normative aspiration and the significance of the legal craft and normative considerations in the identification, interpretation and application of customary international law. Even the observation of what states do requires a perspective, a default position on the basis of which the observation is made.

3. Hugh Thirlway

Hugh Thirlway discussed in his first monograph the future of customary international law in the age of codification conventions. He used to be skeptical of whether the customary process of action and reaction, claim and counterclaim between states could contribute to the emergence of norms which protect the human rights of a state's citizen, and he suggested that the only way to regulate these relationships internationally would consist in the

---

78 D'Amato, 'Trashing Customary International Law' 105.
79 On this topic see Anthony D'Amato, 'Human Rights as Part of Customary International Law: A Plea for Change of Paradigms' (1995) 25(1) Georgia journal of international and comparative law 92 ff.
80 See also the critique by Tomuschat, 'Obligations Arising For States Without Or Against Their Will' 268; Thirlway, *International Customary Law and Codification: an examination of the continuing role of custom in the present period of codification of international law* 81-84, taking issue with the unqualified manner of d'Amato's propositions according to which the process described would always take place.

Chapter 12: Doctrinal perspectives on and discussions of the interrelationship of sources

conclusion of treaties.[81] Nevertheless, in his view, custom would continue to play a role as source of international law.[82] It might, as an independent source, apply *secundum legem* and govern legal relationship which were not covered by a treaty *ratione personae* or *ratione materiae* or in cases of a treaty's *renvoi* to custom.[83] Custom might fill the gaps and provide for the rules of interpretation, and it might even operate *contra legem* and derogate from the treaty.[84]

Thirlway questioned convincingly the underlying idea of the Baxter's paradox, namely that a state, as Thirlway put it, "which becomes a party to the treaty withdraws itself from the body of States which can contribute, by suitable acts, to the formation of customary law on the matter covered by the treaty".[85] In his view, the practice of parties to a treaty should not be counted twice, namely when states ratify a treaty and when they implement a treaty, since "the content of the rule is fixed" by the treaty.[86] The notion of a "fixed content" points to the fact that states have made deliberate decisions when negotiating and concluding the treaty. However, the dynamic element of interpretative practice and the way in which newly emerged rules of international law can inform the interpretation of the treaty according to the general rules of interpretation should not be disregarded.[87] Any consideration

---

81 Thirlway, *International Customary Law and Codification: an examination of the continuing role of custom in the present period of codification of international law* 7-8, 10, arguing that the Nottebohm judgment would indicate that "the whole trend of customary law is opposed" to a development in which states would invoke the responsibility of other states with respect to the latter's treatment of nationals; he later raised the question of the impact of human rights treaties on customary international law, see Thirlway, 'Human Rights in Customary Law: An Attempt to Define Some of the Issues' 495 ff.
82 Thirlway, *International Customary Law and Codification: an examination of the continuing role of custom in the present period of codification of international law* 145.
83 ibid 95.
84 ibid 131-133, applying the teaching of Thomas Aquinas, Thirlway concluded: "Thus, when custom praeter legem begins, as a result of social development, so to encroach on the existing law's domain as to verge on the contra legem, it can nonetheless be regarded, in the light of social development, as still only praeter legem, and as tacit lawmaking so as to effect a repeal."
85 ibid 90, 91; Thirlway, *The Sources of International Law* 131.
86 Thirlway, *International Customary Law and Codification: an examination of the continuing role of custom in the present period of codification of international law* 91.
87 The effects which run both way in this interrelationship were depicted in the context of the ECHR, see above, p. 403.

of the treaty as evidence of customary international law should, therefore, not stop at the letter of the treaty and instead include an assessment of states' practice in the application of the treaty, in particular when this practice expresses an agreement as to the interpretation of the treaty according to article 31(3)(b) and article 32 VCLT.

C. The interrelationship in a value-laden legal order

I. The continuing interest in customary international law in light of the *Nicaragua* judgments and skepticism

In his *Habilitation* published in 1985, Mark E. Villiger made a case in favour of the continuing significance of customary international law in a legal community which had been increasingly shaped by treaties. He noted several references in codification conventions to customary international law which would be a testimony to the importance of custom and the support of this source by states.[88] In particular, Villiger stressed that customary international law and treaties may interact in different ways, they could influence each other, nonidentical rules could modify each other, identical rules could "parallel each other and assist in their mutual interpretation and ascertainment"; at the same time, treaties and customary international law would retain their independence and individuality as sources.[89] He predicted that "customary law will continue to serve as a modern source of law".[90]

The *Nicaragua* judgments of the ICJ[91] directed the attention of many scholars to customary international law. New approaches to custom were

---

88 Villiger, *Customary International Law and Treaties* 290; see also Ignaz Seidl-Hohenveldern, 'Review of Customary International Law and Treaties' (1987) 38 Österreichische Zeitschrift für Öffentliches Recht und Völkerrecht 218 (arguing that the *Nicaragua* decision confirmed Villiger's treatment of the relationship between customary international law and treaties).
89 Villiger, *Customary International Law and Treaties* 295-296.
90 ibid 296-297.
91 *Military and Paramilitary Activities in and against Nicaragua* [1984] ICJ Rep 392, 424-425 para 73, 442 para 113; *Military and Paramilitary Activities in and against Nicaragua* [1986] ICJ Rep 14, 27 para 34, 93 ff.; also, the Court stressed in the Tehran Hostage case that the obligations under review were not just "contractual [...] but also obligations under general international law", *United States Diplomatic and Consular Staff in Tehran* 31 para 62.

suggested which focused on the interplay and the "sliding scale" between both elements.[92] Scholars discussed the significance of customary international law as general law in a value-laden legal order of an international community.[93] Commenting on the *Nicaragua* case, Theodor Meron expressed doubts on whether article 1 and article 3 of the Geneva Conventions were codifications of existing law.[94] He noted that the Court's method in the *Nicaragua* case "cannot but influence future consideration of customary law in various fields of international law, including the Geneva Conventions."[95] In particular, Meron pointed to the possibility that states may conclude treaties in order to articulate norms and values which differ from the actual practice of states.[96] According to the Baxter-paradox mentioned above, it should be "virtually impossible" to prove the customary character of a widely ratified convention such as the Geneva Conventions.[97] Meron recognized that the *Nicaragua* judgment pointed into a different direction and justified a restrictive reading of the *North Sea Continental Shelf* judgment.[98] Meron argued that customary international law in other fields such as human rights law "may have an impact on the transformation of parallel norms of the Geneva Conventions (those with an identical content) into customary norms."[99] In his view, practice in the observance of a treaty can, when accompanied by *opinio*

---

92 Kirgis, 'Custom on a Sliding Scale' 146 ff.; Tasioulas, 'In Defense of Relative Normativity: Communitarian Values and the Nicaragua Case' 85 ff.
93 Hilary CM Charlesworth, 'Customary International Law and the Nicaragua Case' (1984) 11 Australian Yearbook of International Law 30-31, concluding that the ICJ attempted to reconcile the consensualist Westphalian system with idealistic communal orders for instance by regarding GA resolutions as evidence for both practice and opinio juris; in her view, the Court did not achieve a satisfactory accommodation as it emphasized verbal, idealistic practice, over real and failed to announce a new concept of custom, rather than paying lip-service to the two-elements-model; see for a communitarian perspective Tasioulas, 'In Defense of Relative Normativity: Communitarian Values and the Nicaragua Case'.
94 Meron, 'The Geneva Conventions as Customary Law' 353, 356-357.
95 ibid 361-362.
96 ibid 363.
97 Baxter, 'Treaties and Customs' 96.
98 Meron, 'The Geneva Conventions as Customary Law' 365-367; the tension between interpretations of both judgments as to the interrelationship of sources was recognized also by other commentators, see for instance Charlesworth, 'Customary International Law and the Nicaragua Case' 27; Thirlway, *The law and procedure of the international court of justice: fifty years of jurisprudence* 134; Mendelson, 'The International Court of Justice and the sources of international law' 77-78.
99 Meron, 'The Geneva Conventions as Customary Law' 368.

juris, facilitate "the gradual metamorphosis of those conventional norms into customary law".[100] In his article, Meron paved the way for the international criminal tribunals and their interpretations of customary international law in light of other norms of international law.[101]

Other scholars had their reservations with respect to customary international law. Commenting partly prior to the *Nicaragua* decisions, Prosper Weil pointed to the risk that the weight given to customary international law in scholarship went at the expense of the technicalities and precision of treaty law.[102] According to Weil, the traditional theory of custom was mainly consensualist and a "subtle interplay between tacit intention and nonopposability", preserving and ensuring the "delicate, indeed precarious, equilibrium between two opposing concerns", namely rendering the participation of each state in custom unnecessary while permitting each state to opt out of the formation of a specific rule.[103] From Weil's perspective, the practice on which rules of customary international law were said to rest became less and less general and increasingly focused on "specially affected states", whereas the normative effects of custom, in particular when called general international law, would increase and tantamount to universality.[104] He considered these developments to be dangerous for the sovereign equality of states in a time when the "international society (has been) rendered more diverse than ever by the emergence of a hundred new states" and where international law, in order to perform its function, would be required to be

---

100 ibid 368; see later Meron, 'The Continuing Role of Custom in the Formation of International Humanitarian Law' 247; similar Cheng, 'Custom: the future of general state practice in a divided world' 533.
101 Cf. Meron, 'The Geneva Conventions as Customary Law' 356, 361-369. Cf. also Mendelson, 'The Formation of Customary International Law' 322 ff., on the "of its own impact" theory of treaties creating custom.
102 Weil, 'Le droit international en quête de son identité: cours général de droit international public' 186, noting that the customary counterpart to a provision such as article 76 UNCLOS would necessarily contain less institutional and technical rules; Prosper Weil, 'Towards Relative Normativity in International Law' (1983) 77 AJIL 439.
103 ibid 433.
104 ibid 436: "[...] the generality of practice has been reduced to a minimum requirement, the generality of the normative effects of customary international law has been undergoing the reverse process of constant expansion."; see also Weil, 'Le droit international en quête de son identité: cours général de droit international public' 186 ff.

Chapter 12: Doctrinal perspectives on and discussions of the interrelationship of sources

"neutral".[105] Weil's scholarship cautioned against an expansive recourse to customary international law.

Writing also against an expansive understanding of customary international law, Bruno Simma and Philip Alston considered general principles as a source in particular for human rights law. The article can be read as critique of modern approaches to customary international law in particular in the context of US-American scholarship, the Third Restatement and the use of customary international law in the Alien Tort Statute litigation.[106] In their view, customary international law was in an identity crisis which would express itself in the decreasing importance of material, hard, inter-state practice, as well as in a merging of practice and *opinio juris*.[107] "[I]nstead of further manipulating the established concept of customary law based on an effective requirement of concrete practice", they suggested to consider the concept of general principles of law to explain the "the legal force of universally recognized human rights".[108] In their view, customary international law traditionally emerged from constant interactions between states, whereas the performance of most human rights obligations "lacks this element of interaction proper".[109] General principles of law, however, could emerge

---

105 Weil, 'Towards Relative Normativity in International Law' 419, 420, 441; Weil, 'Le droit international en quête de son identité: cours général de droit international public' 189; cf. later in a similar sense Yasuaki, 'A Transcivilized Perspective on International Law Questioning Prevalent Cognitive Frameworks in the Emerging Multi-Polar and Multi-Civilizational World of the Twenty-First Century' 236-237.

106 See Schachter, 'International Law in Theory and Practice: general course in public international law' 75 ff.; 334 ff.; American Law Institute, *Restatement of the law, The Foreign Relations Law of the United States*; for a response to the critique expressed by Simma and Alston see Richard B Lillich, 'The Growing Importance of Customary International Human Rights Law' (1996) 25(1-2) Georgia Journal of International and Comparative Law 1 ff.; cf. Simma, 'From bilateralism to community interest in international law' 289 footnote 194.

107 Simma and Alston, 'The Sources of Human Rights Law: Custom, Jus Cogens, and General Principles' 88, 96; cf. for a similar assessment Godefridus Josephus Henricus van Hoof, *Rethinking the sources of international law* (Kluwer Law and Taxation Publ 1983) 107-108; cf. Jonathan I Charney, 'Universal International Law' (1993) 87 AJIL 536-538, 543 ff.

108 Simma and Alston, 'The Sources of Human Rights Law: Custom, Jus Cogens, and General Principles' 98.

109 ibid 99-100, also arguing that without this element of interaction, *opinio juris* would become the only relevant element in order to distinguish customary rules operating purely domestically and internationally concordant domestic behaviour, which

The interrelationship in a value-laden legal order

not only *in foro domestico*, but also in an international setting.[110] Basing general principles of law on international materials such as UN resolutions and declarations would ensure that "the recourse to general principles suggested here remains grounded in a consensualist conception of international law", without equating the materials with State practice.[111] The article was an important contribution to a debate which often excessively focused on customary international law. It advanced a new understanding of general principles in response to what the authors considered to be an expanding understanding of customary international law.

"would overstretch the limits of even the most lenient, or "progressive", theory of customary law."

110 ibid 102 (arguing that the reference to principles *in foro domestico* stressed the importance to validate general principles without excluding such validation based on materials at the international level).

111 ibid 105; the article's critique of custom is in line with Simma's other scholarship on this topic, see on the "identity crisis" of custom Bruno Simma, 'Editorial' (1992) 3 EJIL 215 and Simma, 'Die Erzeugung ungeschriebenen Völkerrechts: Allgemeine Verunsicherung- klärende Beiträge Karl Zemaneks' 98 ff.; but cf. Simma and Paulus, 'The Responsibility of Individuals for Human Rights Abuses in Internal Conflicts: A Positivist View' 307-308, 313, where the authors stress the combination of custom and general principles. For skepticism of the Simma/Alston thesis to turn to general principles in cases where there is neither custom nor treaty, see Paulus, 'Zusammenspiel der Rechtsquellen aus völkerrechtlicher Perspektive' 94, 98 (debate). Turning to Philip Alston, Alston had a few years prior to the Australian yearbook article pleaded in favour of a "quality control" with respect to the recognition of rights in fora of the UN, see Philip Alston, 'Conjuring Up New Human Rights: A Proposal For Quality Control' (1984) 87 AJIL 607 ff.. However, he was also critical of reducing detailed written obligations to a set of "principles" in the context of the international labour organization, see with respect to this "turn to principles" Philip Alston, ''Core Labour Standards' and the Transformation of the International Labour Rights Regime' (2003) 15(3) EJIL 457 ff.; Bianchi, 'Human Rights and the Magic of Jus Cogens' 493, arguing that "[a]lthough this approach to the source of human rights law was presented by Alston and Simma as 'grounded in a consensualist conception of international law', their final reference to Henkin's stance on general principles common to legal systems as reflecting 'natural law principles that underlie international law' reintroduces the same ambiguity about the origin of the sources of human rights that the authors had probably set out to dispel." The present author would not concur that this last page undermined the consensualist construction, as Simma and Alston just left the question open, whether human rights (not general principles) really have to depend on a positivist, consensualist construction; cf. on this topic, to whom both authors also referred, Koskenniemi, 'The Pull of the Mainstream' 4 ff.

Chapter 12: Doctrinal perspectives on and discussions of the interrelationship of sources

II. The interrelationship of sources in the international community

The scholarship on the international community demonstrates how the same overarching paradigm can lead to different source preferences and to different evaluations as to whether the traditional three sources set forth in the 1920 PCIJ Statute can operate in an international legal order which has embraced community interests expressed, for instance, in the protection of human rights or the environment.

Christian Tomuschat's Hague courses show how the three classical sources can be reconciled with the idea of the constitution of the international community.[112] Tomuschat distinguished different classes of customary international law: the constitutional foundations which included the principle of the sovereign equality of states and common values of mankind; rules which flow from those constitutional foundations, such as the prohibition of the use of force and basic principles of environment which derive from the fact of coexistence of states, and for instance the humanitarian law of warfare and the protection of human life and physical integrity, freedom from torture and slavery.[113] Also, the concept of *jus cogens* was said to "evolve from the common value fund cherished by all nations" and considered as "proof of the existence of an international community grounded on axiomatic premises other than State sovereignty".[114] The last class of rules consists of so-called contingent rules, which emerged in the practice of states.[115] In this account, customary international law is strongly linked to the idea of a legal community from which a single state could not simply withdraw itself.[116] Furthermore, Tomuschat considered that in emergency situations it might be

---

112 On Hague lectures on the international community: Mosler, 'The international society as a legal community' 1 ff.; Simma, 'From bilateralism to community interest in international law' 217 ff.; Robert Kolb, 'German Legal Scholarship as reflected in Hague Academy Courses on Public International Law' (2007) 50 German Yearbook of International Law 201 ff., on the "international community-oriented school of thought" (206) and its objective to "ensure a proper survival of mankind and create a more just world oder" (210).
113 Tomuschat, 'Obligations Arising For States Without Or Against Their Will' 291-304 (these basic human rights "need no additional confirmation through practice and *opinio juris* on the one hand, or through treaty, on the other", at 303); see also Koskenniemi, 'The Pull of the Mainstream' 1946-1947.
114 Tomuschat, 'Obligations Arising For States Without Or Against Their Will' 307.
115 ibid 308.
116 ibid; see also Tomuschat, 'International law: ensuring the survival of mankind on the eve of a new century: general course on public international law' 331 ("What is

"legitimate to derive binding rules from the basic principles upheld by the international community".[117]

The other two sources find their place as well in this conception. Tomuschat stressed the potential of general principles of law in particular for human rights law which would be concerned with the relationship between a state and individuals both at the domestic and at the international level.[118] As developments in domestic legal orders could permeate the international legal order through general principles of law, general principles of law would be different from the idea of immutable natural law.[119] General principles of law and customary international law could be distinguished according to their formation: "Whereas custom crystallizes in a bottom-up process, general principles permeate the legal order from top down."[120] General principles would be more abstract and could not be identified purely by empirical methods or as distinct patterns of behaviour.[121] Tomuschat noted the importance of the legal craft and the constructive efforts to be employed in order to recognize general principles in the law; at the same time, he stressed that recourse to general principles should not be used in order to fill any gaps "according to the arbitrary discretion of the lawyer" and should therefore be handled "with great care".[122] Treaties would constitute a means to protect basic interests of the international community and give expression to, refine and articulate already existing broad principles "which on their part are constituent elements of the international legal order."[123] A certain overlap of sources could not be excluded, in particular in the field of human rights: "Customary law, general principles recognized by civilized nations

---

done repeatedly by a large number of States cannot be fundamentally detrimental to anyone's interests.").
117 Tomuschat, 'Obligations Arising For States Without Or Against Their Will' 309 (with reference to the Nuremberg and Tokyo trials).
118 ibid 315, 321.
119 ibid 317-318, see also 320, where he argues that general principles of international law such as acquiescence or effectiveness "can be considered abstractions from treaty law and customary law in their entirety [...] [these rules], although not immutable, could only be changed in a slow-going process [...]"; Tomuschat, 'International law: ensuring the survival of mankind on the eve of a new century: general course on public international law' 335-337.
120 Tomuschat, 'Obligations Arising For States Without Or Against Their Will' 322.
121 ibid 322.
122 ibid 322.
123 ibid 269, see also 270-271, see also 273 (on treaties "remain[ing] essentially an instrument of self-commitment"), see also 268.

and general principles of international law form an intricate network of principles and rules the substance of which is identical while their legal validity is derived from different basic concepts."[124]

Other scholars' work on the international community displayed partly a stronger source preference or a focus on the legal personality of the international community and on normative concepts outside the three classical sources set forth in article 38. Bruno Simma followed in his Hague lecture on community interests Wolfgang Friedmann and expressed a preference for treaties and general principles over customary international law. In his view, "law-making by way of custom is hardly capable of accommodating community interest in a genuine sense."[125] Customary law would consist of rules "regulating and limiting a sort of "grab race" [...] as international customary law is a natural companion of bilateralism, the multilateral treaty is an indispensable tool for fostering community interests."[126] The notion of "community interest on a bilateralist grounding" may indicate that the title "From Bilateralism to Community Interests" describes a development without suggesting a complete replacement of the former with the latter.[127]

Andreas Paulus argues in *Die Internationale Gemeinschaft* that the international community to which articles 53 VCLT refers is a community of states, and states are said to still remain the decisive actor in international law, also when it comes to lawmaking.[128] At the same time, the international community has acquired the status of a subject of international law.[129] In particular, the introduction of the concept of *jus cogens* is said to point to the development of a law which authorizes the international community to create substantive norms that protect community values.[130] In order to recognize a norm as peremptory, the international community would not require the

---

124 Tomuschat, 'International law: ensuring the survival of mankind on the eve of a new century: general course on public international law' 334.
125 Simma, 'From bilateralism to community interest in international law' 324.
126 ibid 324; customary international law would be important in his account for instance when it comes to state succession, at 357. General principles of law and elementary considerations are invoked for elaborating the legal limits of the UNSC resolutions, at 277.
127 See ibid 248; for this point see Paulus, *Die internationale Gemeinschaft im Völkerrecht: eine Untersuchung zur Entwicklung des Völkerrechts im Zeitalter der Globalisierung* 431.
128 ibid 228-229, 248-249, 444.
129 ibid 329 ff., 446.
130 ibid 362, 423.

consent of all states but the consent of a vast majority as well as the absence of the rejection by a group of states.[131] This law can be enforced through international institutions, where international organizations such as the United Nations exist and can act, and through states.[132] The international legal order continues to be characterized by the coexistence of and tension between bilateralist structures and state interests on the one hand and community interests, values and law on the other hand.[133]

Mehrdad Payandeh derives from the legal personality of the international community arguments in favour of the existence of a concept of "international community law" which goes beyond the traditional sources set forth in article 38 and *jus cogens*.[134] In his view, this "international community law" constitutes a source of international law.[135] In particular, he argues that normative developments which he describes as forms of a non-consensual lawmaking[136] cannot be reconciled with the traditional sources if one does not manipulate the consensual character of treaties, the emergence of custom through the practice of states and the subsidiary role of general principles in filling gaps.[137] A norm of "international community law" requires an openness in the sense that all states must have had the opportunity to influence the norm's formation which can be articulated in particular in resolutions of the General Assembly or international treaty conferences and must be adopted by the international community as a whole (*opinio juris communis*, expressed by a representative majority).[138] This community is said to be composed primarily by states and also by international organizations.[139] Furthermore, a norm of "international community law" must be based on a community

---

131 ibid 348, 360-361, 424 and 444.
132 See ibid 424 on bilateralization as an expression of a weak institutionalization of the international community).
133 ibid 427-431.
134 Payandeh, *Internationales Gemeinschaftsrecht: zur Herausbildung gemeinschaftsrechtlicher Strukturen im Völkerrecht der Globalisierung* 439 ff.
135 ibid 447 ff.
136 ibid 453 and 532-533 (referring to the adoption of treaty drafts by consensus, treaties creating an international regime, the law of state succession into treaties, acquiescence as mere legal fiction weakening the consent element in the doctrine on customary international law, the margin of appreciation when it comes to the application of general principles).
137 ibid 449-453 (also rejecting arguments based on secondary law of international organizations or on *jus cogens*).
138 ibid 454-6.
139 ibid 456-459.

interest, which is to be distinguished from mere states interests, it must also serve values and interests of human beings and come into existence not as some form of natural law but through the recognition by the international community.[140]

Other scholars have offered ways to include the developments of the international legal order into the methodology of specific sources. One example concerns the question of how to identify custom under consideration of the values of the legal order. Anthea Robert's work on customary international law exemplifies an interpretative approach to custom.[141] Combining Dworkin's interpretivism and Rawl's idea of a reflective equilibrium, she suggests that the interpreter would first have to apply a threshold of *fit* to determine whether there were eligible interpretations which would make sense out of the raw material, practice, analyzed. If several interpretations were arguable, the interpreter would have to reflect on each interpretation on the basis of *substance*, which consists of "procedural and substantive normative considerations about whether the content of custom is substantively moral and whether it is derived by a legitimate process".[142] In her view, practice was the dominant part of the fit-stage, whereas *opinio juris* was the dominant part of the substance stage. She positions both stages within a reflective equilibrium and considers each in light of the other.[143] Since she understands under morals "commonly held subjective values about right and wrong that have been adopted by a representative majority of states in treaties and declarations"[144], her approach calls upon the interpreter to

---

140 Payandeh, *Internationales Gemeinschaftsrecht: zur Herausbildung gemeinschaftsrechtlicher Strukturen im Völkerrecht der Globalisierung* 459-460.
141 See already Stein's comment in Antonio Cassese and Joseph HH Weiler (eds), *Change and Stability in International Law-Making* (de Gruyter 1988) 13, who predicted that "the style of reasoning and argument about general international law is going to change from empirical or inductive to principally *interpretative*. We are going to look at texts and what was said about texts, we are going to be analyzing the rules of general international law in much the same way as we analyzed rules that are binding as a matter of treaty law." Cf. for a critical examination of interpretation Başak Çali, 'On Interpretivism and International Law' (2009) 20(3) EJIL 805 ff.
142 Roberts, 'Traditional and Modern Approaches to Customary International Law: A Reconciliation' 778.
143 ibid 779.
144 ibid 778; crit. of requiring morality's recognition in treaties or resolutions adopted by states John Tasioulas, 'Custom, Jus Cogens, and Human Rights' in Curtis A Bradley (ed), *Custom's future: international law in a changing world* (Cambridge University Press 2016) 95 ff.

reflect on how an alleged rule of custom would relate to the normative environment and which principle such rule would further. Even though her distinctions between traditional and modern custom, facilitative custom with "no strong substantive considerations"[145] and moral custom appear a little bit too clear-cut[146], her interpretative approach adds valuable nuance to other approaches to customary international law by highlighting the importance of interpretation and establishing a relation between custom and the values and principles expressed in treaties and resolutions. In her view as expressed in a different article, custom's function is said to be about "protecting key structural and substantive norms in order to best serve the interests of the international community."[147]

As illustrated in the last chapters, doctrinal and normative considerations are of great importance when interpreting customary international law and normative judgment calls can be informed by value judgments expressed in the normative environment. The challenge for an interpreter will not only lie in recognizing her own responsibility but also in exercising this responsibility with care and taking account of international practice. As demonstrated in relation to the ECHR, the European Court was careful not to interpret state immunity under customary international law in a way that would not have been reflected in the actual practice of states.[148] In this sense, the reflection on substance, while remaining the individual responsibility of the interpreter, should be an assessment made under consideration of the views of other interpreters and of the balance between competing principles struck in international practice.

Other scholars put a greater emphasis on general principles than on customary international law. These accounts are based on a constitutional understanding that emphasizes human rights, rule of law and separation of power, democracy or other "goals" such as environmental protection.[149] Next to the

---

145 Roberts, 'Traditional and Modern Approaches to Customary International Law: A Reconciliation' 789.
146 For a critique of the traditional-modern juxtaposition Talmon, 'Determining Customary International Law: the ICJ's Methodology between Induction, Deduction and Assertion' 429-434; see also above, p. 77.
147 Roberts, 'Who killed Article 38(1)(B)? A Reply to Bradley and Gulati' 174.
148 On the careful use of proportionality analysis see above, p. 425.
149 Cf. generally Stefan Kadelbach and Thomas Kleinlein, 'International Law: a Constitution for Mankind?: an Attempt at a Re-appraisal with an Analysis of Constitutional Principles' (2007) 50 German Yearbook of International Law 303 ff.; Niels Petersen, *Demokratie als teleologisches Prinzip: zur Legitimität von Staatsgewalt*

article written by Simma and Alston, the work of Robert Alexy proved to be a source of inspiration for several approaches three of which shall be briefly described.

Niels Petersen agrees with the thesis advanced by Simma and Alston insofar as it suggests a categorical distinction between custom and general principles. However, whereas the distinction in the article written by Simma and Alston was made according to the kind of practice, inter-state or "intrastate"/international practice, Petersen argues that the distinction is a matter of legal theory and corresponds to the distinction between rules and principles according to Robert Alexy.[150] According to Petersen, principles in the Alexian sense as optimization requirements cannot be conceptualized as custom and are not in need of practice, they rest on article 38(1)(c) of the ICJ Statute.[151]

Thomas Kleinlein distinguishes custom and general principles of international law by the "distinction between situations dominated by factual reciprocity (which justify customary norms) and situations where such fac-

---

im Völkerrecht (Springer 2009); Thomas Kleinlein, 'Between Myths and Norms: Constructivist Constitutionalism and the Potential of Constitutional Principles in International Law' (2012) 81 Nordic Journal of International Law 79 ff.; Anusceh Farahat, *Progressive Inklusion* (Springer 2014) 280, 337, 340, 341, 344, 347, 350, 355, 363 (reconstruction migration law as competition between the principle of static attribution and the principle of progressive inclusion). Farahat's study demonstrates the critical potential of general principles and their legal-political dimension; cf. also Andreas L Paulus, 'The International Legal System as a Constitution' in Jeffrey L Dunhoff and Joel P Trachtman (eds), *Ruling the world?: constitutionalism, international law, and global governance* (Cambridge University Press 2009) 87 ff. on constitutionalization from form to substance through principles; on differences between community perspectives and constitutional perspectives see also Jochen Rauber, 'On Communitarian and Constitutional Approaches to International Law' (2013) 26 Leiden Journal of International Law 212-217.

150 See above, p. 150.
151 Niels Petersen, 'Der Wandel des ungeschriebenen Völkerrechts im Zuge der Konstitutionalisierung' (2008) 46(4) Archiv des Völkerrechts 507-508, 520; Petersen, *Demokratie als teleologisches Prinzip: zur Legitimität von Staatsgewalt im Völkerrecht* 92 ff.; Petersen, 'Customary Law Without Custom? Rules, Principles, and the Role of State Practice in International Norm Creation' 284; for another application of the Alexian model of principles see Jasper Finke, 'Sovereign Immunity: Rule, Comity or Something Else?' (2010) 21(4) EJIL 853 ff.

tual reciprocity is absent (which justify general principles)."[152] Examining the constitutionalization in international law, Kleinlein argues that neither the concept of customary international law nor the concept of treaties can satisfactorily explain the emergence of norms that form an objective, universal legal order with norms protecting human rights and global goods and provide for standards of good governance.[153] General principles of law are then proposed as source in the sense of article 38(1)(c) ICJ Statute and as a norm type in the sense of Alexy's theory in order to provide for norms on the exercise of public authority.[154] These emerging norms of unwritten international law are said to bind states without their consent and be capable of emerging both from domestic legal orders and within the international legal order.[155] In particular, these principles on human rights, democracy and rule of law can emerge within a discourse on norms and through states' argumentative self-entrapment, for instance the verbal commitment to human rights, and affect states' identity and self-conception.[156] It is for the legal operator to determine whether the degree of entrapment suffices to give rise to a legal norm and meet Thomas Franck's "but of course"- test of intuitive plausibility[157], and to reconstruct the emerging understandings reflected in political discourses.[158]

Similar to Thomas Kleinlein, Jochen Rauber links the so-called constitutionalization of international law to the concept of general principles, which

---

152 Kleinlein, 'Customary International Law and General Principles Rethinking Their Relationship' 132; Kleinlein, *Konstitutionalisierung im Völkerrecht Konstruktion und Elemente einer idealistischen Völkerrechtslehre* 507 f., 619, 682, 698 f.
153 Kleinlein, 'Customary International Law and General Principles Rethinking Their Relationship' 711-712, see also 403-508 (on the role of reciprocity in relation to customary international law), 496-499 (on the uncertainty that comes when deducing norms from the constitution of the international community), 430-473 (on the lack of a generalizable theory on third-party effects of treaties).
154 ibid 704.
155 ibid 633, 704.
156 Kleinlein, *Konstitutionalisierung im Völkerrecht Konstruktion und Elemente einer idealistischen Völkerrechtslehre* 636 ff., 714-715. See also above, first chapter.
157 Franck, 'Non-treaty Law-Making: When, Where and How?' 423.
158 Kleinlein, *Konstitutionalisierung im Völkerrecht Konstruktion und Elemente einer idealistischen Völkerrechtslehre* 648-652; see also Kleinlein, 'Customary International Law and General Principles Rethinking Their Relationship' 153-157.

Chapter 12: Doctrinal perspectives on and discussions of the interrelationship of sources

he understands, similar to Niels Petersen, in the sense of Alexian principles.[159] In his view, the development of international law is marked by four trends: contentualisation, in the sense that international law is concerned not only with state interests but also with community interests, hierarchization, in the sense that international law recognizes normative priorities such as *jus cogens* norms or Article 103 UNC, privatisation, in the sense that certain non-state-actors are said to enjoy legal personality, and objectivisation, in the sense that the voluntarist basis of international law is partially challenged, when it comes to *jus cogens* norms or the treatment of reservation to treaties.[160] These deveopments are said to be indicative of a change of the foundational principles of international law to which a principle of humanity, a principle of environmental protection and a principle of legal protection belong.[161] The principles' legal validity is traced to article article 38(1)(c) ICJ Statute, they inform the interpretation of rules of treaty law, they can be drawn on *praeter legem* in cases not covered by specific rules and, in certain circumstances, they can justify a development of the law *contra legem*, overriding a specific rule.[162] Customary international law has only little place in this constitutionalist account.[163] It is said to be not open to interpretation, as only practice and *opinio juris*, but not the customary norm, could be interpreted, with the consequence that there would be no room for legal principles to exert their influence.[164] Certain examples that are commonly associated with customary international law and could indicate that customary international law can be subject to interpretation are divorced from this source. For instance, when commenting on necessity as set forth in article 25 ARSIWA and earlier in draft article 33 in the *Gabčikovo-Nagymaros* case, the Court is said to have treated the necessity defence as if it was a treaty rule.[165] Furthermore, it is argued that the Court's jurisprudence on diplomatic protection in case of human rights violations should be better understood as direct recourse to the

---

159 Rauber, *Strukturwandel als Prinzipienwandel: theoretische, dogmatische und methodische Bausteine eines Prinzipienmodells des Völkerrechts und seiner Dynamik* 153.
160 ibid 26-113, 862.
161 ibid 361 ff., 861, 864.
162 ibid 207-210, 491-652, 864-865.
163 See ibid 245-249, 275-278, 564-570.
164 ibid 570, 701-702, 865.
165 ibid 658.

principle of legal protection that filled a gap which existed with respect to individual rights.[166]

As result of the diverse composition of the international community, certain traditional concepts of public international law have been challenged.[167] Often, it was not the doctrine of sources as such but specific norms of treaty law, customary international law or general principles of law which have been opposed by so-called newly independent states.[168] However, the criticism as to the genesis of old rules could also relate to specific sources. One example in this regard was the work of Onuma Yasuaki. He argued that many rules of customary international law "were characterized as international law by a small number of Western Great Powers" and were based "on the limited practice and opinio juris of a small number of the Western Great Powers"; as this practice was often formulated by "leading international lawyers of these Western nations", Yasuaki submitted that "[t]he intellectual/ideational power of the Western powers [...] dominated the process of the creation of 'customary' international law".[169] In his view, the reliance on multilateral treaties and UNGA resolutions "is far more transparent" than the reliance on the traditional concept of customary international law.[170] He therefore suggested that the concept of "general international law" should no longer be linked to the concept of customary international law[171] and that "a norm provided in the multinational treaties with an overwhelming majority of State parties enjoys a far higher degree of global legitimacy than an old 'customary' norm".[172] At the same time, Yasuaki acknowledged that the lack of legitimacy of customary international was "not regarded as a serious problem"[173], and one reason for the persistence of the concept of customary international law

---

166 ibid 701-708.
167 See also above, p. 50.
168 See Yusuf, 'Pan-Africanism and International Law' 243-8.
169 Yasuaki, 'A Transcivilized Perspective on International Law Questioning Prevalent Cognitive Frameworks in the Emerging Multi-Polar and Multi-Civilizational World of the Twenty-First Century' 169-170.
170 ibid 171.
171 ibid 221.
172 ibid 249. See for a similar focus on resolutions Chimni, 'Customary International Law: A Third World Perspective' 42.
173 Yasuaki, 'A Transcivilized Perspective on International Law Questioning Prevalent Cognitive Frameworks in the Emerging Multi-Polar and Multi-Civilizational World of the Twenty-First Century' 242.

Chapter 12: Doctrinal perspectives on and discussions of the interrelationship of sources

was suspected to be the apparent lack of universality of treaties which visibly manifested itself in states that are not parties.[174]

In summary, the perspectives laid out here demonstrate that trends towards a value-laden order did not leave sources doctrine unaffected. Scholars drew different consequences from this trend and developed responses to the substantive changes; some scholars reconciled all three sources set forth in article 38 with the new developments, other scholars focused on concepts such as *jus cogens* and the legal personality of the international community or focused on the methodology of a specific source, be it, for instance, a more interpretative approach to customary international law or a re-discovery of general principles of law.

Value-based approaches to the doctrine of sources are not uncontroversial, however. The doctrine of sources is important because it explains which norms are binding on states. In order for states to accept the bindingness, some form of consent, which can exist at different levels of specificity in relation to the three sources, is important. A doctrine that is deeply embedded in a specific narrative, a specific interpretation of the developments of the international legal order or specific legal-theoretical assumptions and premises may encounter difficulties in finding broad acceptance and remaining capable of accommodating a wide variety of views, interests and counter-trends.[175]

While this study adopts a different approach in comparison to the perspectives described here which does not rely on the persuasiveness of a certain narrative, these perspectives can still be valuable for reading and interpreting practice and the development of law. It remains to be seen whether the developments of the international community will give rise to new source preferences and recalibrations in the relative importance of each source. As of today, it seems that the doctrine of sources provides for enough flexibility and room to accommodate diverse interests and perspectives.

---

174 Yasuaki, 'A Transcivilized Perspective on International Law Questioning Prevalent Cognitive Frameworks in the Emerging Multi-Polar and Multi-Civilizational World of the Twenty-First Century' 242-3.

175 See also Heike Krieger, 'Verfassung im Völkerrecht - Konstitutionelle Elemente jenseits des Staates?' in *Verfassung als Ordnungskonzept. Referate und Diskussionen auf der Tagung der Vereinigung der Deutschen Staatsrechtslehrer in Speyer vom 7. bis zum 10. Oktober 2015* (de Gruyter 2016) vol 75 449 (pointing to counter-trends such as a greater emphasis of state sovereignty, the rise of unilateral actions and tendencies of counter-trend to the legalization of international affairs), 470.

D. Recent legal positivist perspectives

At the end, this section will zero in on selected recent legal positivist perspectives. In particular, it will comment on and engage with the critique in the works of Jörg Kammerhofer and Jean d'Aspremont. This section's approach is, it must be stressed, selective, it is confined to specific points both authors have made in relation to the sources, their interrelationship and the unwritten international law.

I. Jörg Kammerhofer

From Kammerhofer's neo-Kelsenian perspective, norms cannot relate with each other unless by way of authorization and derogation.[176] As far as the "inter-source relationship" is concerned, he does not endorse a *Stufenbau* on the top of which customary international law would provide the authorization to conclude treaties, since customary international law, as understood by Kammerhofer, could "only have such content that can be classified as accumulated factual behaviour [...] A content that refers to other norms cannot be reflected as factual pattern."[177] Consequently, norms which authorize the creation of other norms or which derogate from norms could not be created by way of customary international law.[178] In his view, the sources are not normatively connected,[179] and each treaty is said to be "its own normative

---

176 "Norms can relate to other norms only if they take the functions of 'authorisation' and 'derogation'. [...] There cannot be a breach of a norm by a norm. A norm, for example, claims to derogate from another norm. Where that is validly possible, the other norm simply disappears, loses its validity ('existence'). [...] If a claim to derogate is not valid – as would manifestly be the case between two different and unconnected normative orders- nothing would happen to the purportedly derogated norm. It would still be valid. [...] There cannot be a divergence between claim and observance in the case of derogation since the ideal is confronted by another ideal.", Kammerhofer, *Uncertainty in international law: a Kelsenian perspective* 143.
177 ibid 73.
178 ibid 74, 156; Jörg Kammerhofer, 'The Pure Theory's Structural Analysis of the Law' in Samantha Besson and Jean d'Aspremont (eds), *Oxford Handbook on the Sources of International Law* (Oxford University Press 2017) 356.
179 See Kammerhofer, *Uncertainty in international law: a Kelsenian perspective* 156 ("The 'default solution" is that the two sources [treaty and customary international law, M.L.] are not normatively connected"); cf. on the ideas that either each source has its own *Grundnorm* or that all sources have a common *Grundnorm* Kammer-

island".¹⁸⁰ With respect to general principles of law, Kammerhofer has expressed "grave theoretical doubts as to the very possibility of this source as positive international law", since it would be unclear how "scientific abstractions from diverse legal systems in any shape be willed as part of international law".¹⁸¹

From Kammerhofer's legal-theoretical perspective, a normative connection between a treaty and customary international law and general principles of law cannot be based on the interpretative means enshrined in article 31(3)(c) VCLT which, according to the prevailing view, requires the interpreter to take into account a treaty's normative environment. According to Kammerhofer, however, the rules of interpretation appear to have a different effect than commonly assumed. He distinguishes interpretation as a hermeneutic process from the concretization of law through its application.¹⁸² Relying on Kelsen, he emphasizes that "[n]orms do not necessarily have *one right meaning* and interpretation is the cognition of the frame, rather than of the 'correct meaning' [...] In short: the norm is the frame, not one of the pos-

---

hofer, 'The Pure Theory's Structural Analysis of the Law' 358-60, concluding (at 360): "However, it is still the better argument that neither stratagem can work to unite international law absent a positive legal connection [...] the presumption of a *Grundnorm* cannot create a connection where positive norms do not."

180 Kammerhofer, *Uncertainty in international law: a Kelsenian perspective* 156.
181 ibid 157; on whether the requirement of recognition relates to the recognition in domestic legal orders or whether it could be construed as act of will that a principle applies in the international legal order see Jörg Kammerhofer, 'The Pure Theory of Law and Its "Modern" Positivism: International Legal Uses for Scholarship' (2012) 106 Proceedings of the American Society of International Law at Its Annual Meeting 367; see in more detail Jörg Kammerhofer, 'Die Reine Rechtslehre und die allgemeinen Rechtsprinzipien des Völkerrechts' in Nikitas Aliprantis and Thomas Olechowski (eds), *Hans Kelsen: die Aktualität eines großen Rechtswissenschafters und Soziologen des 20. Jahrhunderts: Ergebnisse einer internationalen Tagung an der Akademie von Athen am 12. April 2013 aus Anlass von Kelsens 40. Todestag* (Manzsche Verlags- und Universitätsbuchhandlung 2014) 33, arguing that recognition in the end may relate to the domestic legal orders; see Giorgio Gaja, 'The Protection of General Interests in the International Community' (2012) 364 RdC 35, arguing that the "category of "general principles of law" also includes principles of international law that have been "recognized" by States, although they may not be regarded as customary principles."
182 Jörg Kammerhofer, 'Systemic Integration, Legal Theory and the International Law Commission' (2010) 19 Finnish Yearbook of International Law 2008 165, 167; Kammerhofer, 'Taking the Rules of Interpretation Seriously, but Not Literally? A Theoretical Reconstruction of Orthodox Dogma' 129 ff.

Recent legal positivist perspectives

sible meanings."[183] Legal scholars can only identify the frame, whereas it is for the body which is authorized by the general norm, for instance a court, to create an individual norm.[184] Against the background of this legal-theoretical understanding, the general rules of treaty interpretation are not about "interpretation properly speaking"; rather, they modify the norm's frame as filter of the cognition and, therefore, unlike interpretation in a hermeneutic sense, modify the norm which is to be interpreted.[185] Such a modification could not take place if the VCLT did not apply to the interpretation of a treaty. Customary international law, as understood by Kammerhofer, could not provide for a rule such as article 31(3)(c) VCLT: Being based on behavioural regularities, customary international law could not relate to other norms and the incorporation of other norms.[186] If article 31(3)(c) VCLT applied to a treaty, though, it would not establish a normative connection between the treaty and a rule of customary international law:[187] the incorporation of a rule

---

183 Kammerhofer, 'Systemic Integration, Legal Theory and the International Law Commission' 166.
184 ibid 166-167.
185 ibid 172-173 (arguing that such modification would be theoretically possible even though it could not be based on the intention of the drafters of the VCLT); Kammerhofer, 'Taking the Rules of Interpretation Seriously, but Not Literally? A Theoretical Reconstruction of Orthodox Dogma' 142 ff.; Kammerhofer, *International investment law and legal theory: expropriation and the fragmentation of sources* 79 ff.
186 Kammerhofer, 'Systemic Integration, Legal Theory and the International Law Commission' 163-165, 174. Kammerhofer, *Uncertainty in international law: a Kelsenian perspective* 155: "It is doubtful that customary law is capable of 'referring' to other norms at all [...] Because customary law is based on behavioural regularities (customs), customary law can only have such content which can be reflected as behavioural pattern; these patterns are required to form state practice. This 'real world' behaviour, e.g. the passage of a ship through straits, or the signing of a piece of paper cannot refer to the ideal or normative content of such action. The specific ideal significance is not part of the behavioural pattern, hence is not part of state practice and thus cannot form part of the content of a customary norm." Kammerhofer, 'Taking the Rules of Interpretation Seriously, but Not Literally? A Theoretical Reconstruction of Orthodox Dogma' 128-129; Kammerhofer, *International investment law and legal theory: expropriation and the fragmentation of sources* 72 ff., 77 ("Customary law does not 'exist' as words, as language. On that view, the customary rules of interpretation by definition cannot be identical to Articles 31-3 VCLT because they cannot have a content that is made up of words. Customary international law is wordless; only our (scholarly or judicial) *reconstruction* of its content is, can be and has to be.").
187 Kammerhofer, 'Systemic Integration, Legal Theory and the International Law Commission' 172: "By incorporating norms 'X' to 'Z', norm 'A' creates a number of

of customary international law by a treaty would lead to treaty norm with an identical content. Alternatively, if a treaty term is assumed to have the same content as a norm of customary international law, "the treaty norm does not incorporate the customary norm as norm; only the attributed meanings are duplicated."[188] Therefore, the "*renvoi* [...] is to meanings, not norms";[189] in his view, tribunals only claimed to be inspired by other treaties and customary international law in order "to observe legal strictures while in fact constructing meaning not from law but from the opinions of professional jurists."[190] The doctrine of systemic integration is said to be "a scholarly attempt to create *unity* in international law where none exists, to alleviate conflict where positive law provides no remedy"[191], and, as this doctrine is not about interpretation properly speaking, the cognition of existing legal norms, it is said to be "yet another - methodologically unsound - tool appropriating law-making status" to scholars.[192] Kammerhofer's scholarship can be understood as a

---

substantially identical norms. Contrary to popular opinion, X to Z are now not normatively linked to A, because they cannot be. This is because the incorporated norms may very well belong to a different legal order [...] In legal terms: A now contains copies of X, Y and Z and the original X to Z are not impinged, even though A only says so in linguistic short form." See also Kammerhofer, *International investment law and legal theory: expropriation and the fragmentation of sources* 182 ("Norm-structurally, incorporation is the taking on board by the target treaty of the normative content of customary law. Incorporation clauses are a shorthand form of law-creation; in this manner, norms with the same content as the customary norm are created in the referring treaty.").

188 ibid 130.
189 ibid 132 ("On the interpreter's perspective, systemic integration is not an incorporation of customary *norms* into the treaty but a method of reasoning by the interpreter which provides a concretization of content/meaning [...] In orthodox parlance, when interpreters are 'taking other rules into account', they are importing not target *norms* but *meanings*. The *renvoi*, such as it is, is to meanings, not norms, norm-content or norm-texts.").
190 ibid 134.
191 Kammerhofer, 'Systemic Integration, Legal Theory and the International Law Commission' 178; see recently Kammerhofer, *International investment law and legal theory: expropriation and the fragmentation of sources* 141 f.
192 Jörg Kammerhofer, 'Law-making by Scholarship? The Dark Side of 21st Century International Legal Methodology' in James Crawford and Sarah Nouwen (eds), *Select Proceedings of the European Society of International Law, Volume 3, 2010* (Hart 2012) 124: "In this sense, this strain of scholarship takes away the competence of the organs to decide and turns 'political' decisions over to scholarship on the basis of the erroneous view that scholarship is somehow better equipped to make this

plea for a self-restrained understanding of scholarship that resists the "pull to engage in effort at (interstitial and subconscious) lawmaking" and focuses more on the cognition of the frame of possible meanings of a norm.[193]

Kammerhofer's account adds an important critical perspective on the interrelationship of sources and its construction by scholars and can facilitate legal-political critique.[194] The focus on positive norms can remind one that certain doctrines and a certain jurisprudence which have been developed in relation to positive norms are not by themselves law but doctrinal constructions which can be questioned.[195] Not every factual convergence does imply a normative convergence in the sense that this convergence has become binding law.[196]

> choice than those whom the law authorises to make them." See also at 118, referring to Jan Wouters and Cedric Ryngaert, 'Impact on the Process of the Formation of Customary International Law' in Menno Tjeerd Kamminga and Martin Scheinin (eds), *The Impact of Human Rights Law on General International Law* (Oxford University Press 2009) 127: "Clearly, doctrinal rigour is not of the utmost importance [...] treaty practice, custom and general principles are liberally combined so as to achieve the desired result: increased promotion and protection of human rights."; Jörg Kammerhofer, 'Lawmaking by Scholars' in Catherine Brölmann and Yannick Radi (eds), *Research handbook on the theory and practice of international lawmaking* (Edward Elgar Publishing 2016) 305 ff. See also Jörg Kammerhofer, 'Scratching an itch is not a treatment. Instrumentalist non-theory contra normativist Konsequenz and the Problem of systemic integration' in Georg Nolte and Peter Hilpold (eds), *Auslandsinvestitionen-Entwicklung großer Kodifikationen -Fragmentierung des Völkerrechts-Status des Kosovo Beiträge zum 31. Österreichischen Völkerrechtstag 2006 in München* (Peter Lang 2008) 166 ff.. Cf. on the positive law status of argumentative devices such as lex specialis, lex posterior, lex superior Kammerhofer, *Uncertainty in international law: a Kelsenian perspective* 146-194.

193 Kammerhofer, *International investment law and legal theory: expropriation and the fragmentation of sources* at 8, 10.

194 For an application to the debate on an expansive reading of self-defence under customary international law see for instance Jörg Kammerhofer, 'The Resilience of the Restrictive Rules on Self-Defence' in Marc Weller (ed), *The Oxford handbook of the use of force in international law* (Oxford University Press 2015) 627.

195 Cf. more generally Kammerhofer, *Uncertainty in international law: a Kelsenian perspective* 261 on questioning existing dogmas and one's responsibility to chose one's dogmas.

196 See recently Kammerhofer, *International investment law and legal theory: expropriation and the fragmentation of sources* 142 ("Coherent interpretative outcomes may exist [...] Yet a factual coherence of behaviour is at the basis of such outcomes, not legal norms of great specificity [...] It is submitted that interpretation achieves less than is commonly assumed [...] It can be *factually* important [...]").

Yet, the positions of Kammerhofer need not be adopted uncritically. One can argue, for instance, that customary international law in its entirety is not best captured by the description of behavioural regularities since it consists of norms of different levels of generality. If the customary law process continues to be accepted it cannot be excluded that, at a certain point, factual convergence may create expectations that can favour the emergence of normative convergence. Article 31(3)(c) VCLT may be said to establish a normative connection to other principles and rules of international law. If one does not endorse the view that courts make or create law, it may also matter that courts refer not just to mere "meanings" but to meanings of law.[197] Customary international law and general principles of law may perform an important legitimizing function in this regard.

Kammerhofer's critique invites one to consider the question of how much international law exists. If one follows Kammerhofer's approach and accepts his understanding of customary international law, namely as mere behavioural regularities on which architectural rules such as the rules of interpretation cannot be based, then the scope of application of customary international law may be significantly reduced. The question will then arise how a general international law remains possible. Given his deviation from Kelsen's organization of the sources within one *Stufenbau*, the community aspect appears to assume a more important role in Kelsen's system than in Kammerhofer's, since it was arguably this *Stufenbau* which explained in Kelsen's account the objective character of treaties as a product of a legal community.[198] Depending on one's viewpoint this restraint can be criticized or welcomed, as it either prevents international law from fulfilling an integrative function in the international community or it refrains from attributing to international law a function which it may be able to fulfil only to a limited extent.

II. Jean d'Aspremont

The objective of d'Aspremont's monograph *Formalism* is said to "make the case for the preservation of formalism in the theory of the sources of international law for the sake of the ascertainment of international legal rules

---

197 Cf. on different understandings of the normative framework of the normative process between Lauterpacht and Kelsen above, p. 210.
198 Cf. von Bernstorff, *The public international law theory of Hans Kelsen: believing in universal law* 173-176.

and the necessity to draw a line between law and non-law."[199] His scholarship can be read as response to tendencies of deformalization in legal scholarship which seek to pursue a strategy of expansion of international law or the field of international legal research.[200] In the following, this section will highlight a few general features of his scholarship which are relevant to the interrelationship of sources.

One important aspect is the understanding of sources as "communitarian constraints". It is proposed to understand sources not as "rules" or "rules on rules" but as communitarian constraints which are a product of the social practice of a legal community, the actors of which include, but are not necessarily limited to, states.[201] This social account of sources is said to be "dynamic as its rules of recognition fluctuate and change along with the practice of law-ascertainment by international law-applying authorities".[202] It can therefore explain changes within a legal community as to the community's recognized sources. It divorces the doctrine of sources from article 38 of the ICJ Statute[203] as "formal repository"[204] and enables "disagreement, conflict and dissent about the criteria of law-identification"[205].

---

199 d'Aspremont, *Formalism and the Sources of International Law* 5; cf. for a longer assessment of his work Matthias Lippold, 'Reflections on Custom Critique and on Functional Equivalents in the Work of Jean d'Aspremont' (2019) 21(3-4) International Community Law Review 257 ff.
200 d'Aspremont, *Formalism and the Sources of International Law* 133-134 and Jean d'Aspremont, 'Softness in International Law: A Self-Serving Quest for New Legal Materials' (2008) 19(5) EJIL 1075 ff.; d'Aspremont, *Formalism and the Sources of International Law* 119 ff.; see also in more detail d'Aspremont, 'The Politics of Deformalization in International Law' 503 ff.; Jean d'Aspremont, 'Expansionism and the Sources of International Human Rights Law' (2016) 46 Israel Yearbook on Human rights 223 ff.
201 d'Aspremont, 'The Idea of 'Rules' in the Sources of International Law' 104 ff., 113-115.
202 ibid 116.
203 d'Aspremont, *Formalism and the Sources of International Law* 149: "providing a model for law-ascertainment has never been the function of article 38 [...] article 38 of the ICJ Statute has been misguidedly elevated into the overarching paradigm of all sources doctrines in international law".
204 According to d'Aspremont, international lawyers tend to associate doctrines to a source as formal repository of this doctrine, Jean d'Aspremont, *International Law as a Belief System* (Cambridge University Press 2018) 39 ff.
205 d'Aspremont, 'The Idea of 'Rules' in the Sources of International Law' 124, 130; Jean d'Aspremont, *Epistemic forces in international law: foundational doctrines and*

One implication of questioning the ruleness is that certain doctrines no longer need to be understood as "rules" and as part of customary international law. Background assumptions, definitions and so-called rules on rules would not constitute proper rules as they do not set forth a clear prohibition or permission.[206] Like Kammerhofer, d'Aspremont doubts whether the so-called rules on interpretation can be based on an orthodox understanding of customary international law, if custom is understood as a process of behavioral generation of legal normativity.[207]

One central aspect of d'Aspremont's analysis is a strongly advocated distinction between ascertainment and content-determination.[208] Whereas law-ascertainment leads to a binary result, i.e. law or non-law, content-determination aims at meaning and at a standard of conduct.[209] This distinction can be regarded as an expression of scholarly self-restraint since "formalism is not envisaged here as a means to describe and delineate the whole phenomenon of law, and in particular, to determine the content of international legal rules."[210] This distinction has several consequences in d'Aspremont's scholarship. For instance, different processes of interpretation with different

---

techniques of international legal argumentation (Edward Elgar Publishing 2015) 220.

206 Cf. d'Aspremont, 'The International Court of Justice, the Whales, and the Blurring of the Lines between Sources and Interpretation' 1030 footnote 7, where he refers to an interpretation of the *North Sea Continental Shelf* judgment which in his view embodied an "elementary 'Continental Shelf' test whereby any potential standard is required to be of a 'fundamentally norm-creating character such as could be regarded as forming the basis of a general rule of law' to ever generate customary law." d'Aspremont, 'The Decay of Modern Customary International Law in Spite of Scholarly Heroism' 19; d'Aspremont, 'International Customary Investment Law: Story of a Paradox' 33-34.

207 d'Aspremont, 'The International Court of Justice, the Whales, and the Blurring of the Lines between Sources and Interpretation' 1030 footnote 7; Jean d'Aspremont, 'Sources in Legal-Formalist Theories: The Poor Vehicle of Legal Forms' in Samantha Besson and Jean d'Aspremont (eds), *The Oxford Handbook of the Sources of International Law* (Oxford University Press 2017) 376.

208 d'Aspremont, *Formalism and the Sources of International Law* 157 ff.

209 d'Aspremont, *Epistemic forces in international law: foundational doctrines and techniques of international legal argumentation* 213.

210 d'Aspremont, *Formalism and the Sources of International Law* 14, 161, 218; d'Aspremont, 'Reductionist legal positivism in international law' 368: "[...] positivism should be stripped of all the straw men that are commonly attached to it: voluntarism, state-centrism, rigid and static theories of sources, theories of interpretation and techniques of content determination, etc.".

Recent legal positivist perspectives

constraints apply to ascertainment and to content-determination[211], and actors, such as scholars, courts and activist, enjoy different relative authority in relation to ascertainment and content-determination.[212] He acknowledges that such a distinction cannot be maintained with respect to customary international law and general principles of law as rigidly as it can be maintained with respect to written law, which is "why legal positivism should emancipate itself from the current theory of sources."[213] His scholarship is a reminder for that "customary international law, general principles of law, oral treaties, and oral promises as a source of international legal rules should stem from a conscious choice, i.e. a choice for non- formal law-ascertainment informed by an awareness of its costs, especially in terms of the normative character of the rules produced thereby."[214] His scholarship invites one to reflect on and evaluate those choices of a legal community as to its sources of law and to approach the topic not solely at an abstract level but also in different contexts or fields of international law in which a different understanding of sources might have emerged.[215]

D'Aspremont is transparent about his choices: he does not regard general principles of law to be a valid source of law but only a means for the interpretation of international law.[216] Also, he calls into question the normative character of broadly framed, general rules of customary international law at the level of primary obligations. Customary international law standards such as the international minimum standard are said to be "dangerously indeterminate, at least as long as they have not been certified by a law-applying

---

211 d'Aspremont, *Epistemic forces in international law: foundational doctrines and techniques of international legal argumentation* 201.
212 ibid 213.
213 d'Aspremont, 'Reductionist legal positivism in international law' 369-370; see also d'Aspremont, *Formalism and the Sources of International Law* 173-174 (arguing that for customary international law, general principles of law, or other "rules in international law which are ascertained short of any written instrument [...] the law-ascertainment criteria are practice, *opinio juris*, convergence of domestic traditions, or orally expressed intent. None of them is a formal identification criterion."
214 ibid 174.
215 d'Aspremont, 'Théorie des sources' 98 ff. (on whether sector-specific secondary rules have emerged in international humanitarian law); d'Aspremont, 'The Two Cultures of International Criminal Law' 400 ff. (on a change from a culture of law-ascertainment of customary international law to a culture of interpretation of the Rome Statute).
216 d'Aspremont, 'What was not meant to be: General principles of law as a source of international law' 163 ff.

675

Chapter 12: Doctrinal perspectives on and discussions of the interrelationship of sources

authority"[217], and they "do not provide for clear standards of behavior and suffer from strong normative weakness."[218] Customary rules are said to "fall short of generating any change in the behaviour of its addressees"[219] and to impair the legitimacy of adjudicatory powers of courts and tribunals.[220]

His critique can, of course, be subjected to criticism as well.[221] Whilst it is not argued here that one should not distinguish between ascertainment and content-determination at all, it is submitted here that, if one is to evaluate the present system of sources, one should not stop at ascertainment. If one excludes content-determination, one will not take into account that similar problems which d'Aspremont discussed in relation to customary international law may exist in the context of content-determination of treaty obligations. Whereas a treaty rule usually comes with a higher certainty as to its validity than custom, the problems of vagueness can occur nevertheless at the level of content-determination, as a broad treaty standard such as the obligation to accord "fair and equitable treatment" illustrates.[222] Moreover, by excluding content-determination, the analysis does not evaluate to what extent the uncertainties that undoubtedly exist with respect to customary international law are mitigated by the administration of the law by law-applying authorities.

It is submitted here that the idea of customary international law as a common law of a legal community beyond specific regimes which ensures, in the words of d'Aspremont, "a minimum content of law" and "a minimal relevance of law"[223], should not be lightly discarded. Whereas a certain institutionalization of customary international law by way of judicial application is helpful,[224] it is arguably also the case that customary international law exercises an important compensatory function precisely with respect to the

---

217 d'Aspremont, *Formalism and the Sources of International Law* 164.
218 d'Aspremont, 'International Customary Investment Law: Story of a Paradox' 33-34.
219 ibid 36.
220 ibid 40.
221 Lippold, 'Reflections on Custom Critique and on Functional Equivalents in the Work of Jean d'Aspremont' 269-270.
222 Alvarez, 'The Public International Law Regime Governing International Investment' 354 ff.
223 d'Aspremont, 'The Decay of Modern Customary International Law in Spite of Scholarly Heroism' 20, 29.
224 Cf. d'Aspremont, *Formalism and the Sources of International Law* 170, arguing that such institutionalization is necessary for the preservation of the normative character of custom.

decentralized structure of the international legal order.[225] It is the general law in a legal community and states can, based, for instance, on past concretizations of customary international law by courts and based on the ILC conclusions on the identification of customary international law, evaluate how their future behaviour will be judged. At the same time, courts do not have to carry the burden of a lawmaker for their particular case. It is submitted here that the criteria on the identification of customary international law constrain legal operators' reasoning and allow for a rationality control of the decisions.[226] Still, d'Aspremont's perspectives are challenging and thought-provoking; in particular the questioning of the character of sources and certain doctrines as rules might become one of the focal points of the debates to come on how much unwritten international law will be needed and will continue to exist.

E. Concluding Observations

This chapter identified stages in scholarly discussions on the interrelationship of sources. It illustrated shifting research interests in specific sources[227], described different perspectives on the interrelationship of sources in a value-laden international legal order[228] and addressed recent skepticism as to unwritten international law[229].

Furthermore, this chapter contextualized the selected scholarly approaches by relating these to the decisions or developments to which these scholars responded. It is possible to see the early interest in general principles of law[230] against the background of the slow progress of success of the International Law Commission in the codification of customary international law and the submission of drafts for codification conventions. However, with the rise of such conventions and the ICJ commenting on the relationship between

---

225 Lippold, 'Reflections on Custom Critique and on Functional Equivalents in the Work of Jean d'Aspremont' 280.
226 See also Andreas Føllesdal, 'The Significance of State Consent for the Legitimate Authority of Customary International Law' in Panos Merkouris, Jörg Kammerhofer, and Noora Arajärvi (eds), *The Theory, Practice, and Interpretation of Customary International Law* (Cambridge University Press 2022) 128-31 (on the importance of limits to judicial discretion in the identification of customary international law).
227 See above, p. 635.
228 See above, p. 651.
229 See above, p. 667.
230 See above, p. 635.

Chapter 12: Doctrinal perspectives on and discussions of the interrelationship of sources

treaty law and customary international law, doctrinal research concerning the relationship of sources focused mainly on this aspect.[231] This chapter demonstrated that the questions of the interrelationship of sources and of the relative place accorded to each source in a legal community can be indicative of the respective legal culture's preferences for formalist or informal, conscious or unconscious lawmaking. Even though the ILC's recent conclusions[232] help to rationalize the identification of customary international law, rationalization can take place only to a certain degree. In the end, the emergence of customary international law is similar to a path which emerges as one walks it.

Finally, this chapter's selectivity has to be acknowledged; many other scholars could have been mentioned as well. The scholars discussed in this chapter were selected partly because their work illustrated different stages in engagement with the interrelationship of sources, and partly because they illustrated different emphases and perspectives against the background of which one can evaluate the future developments of the international community.

---

231 See above, p. 645.
232 See above, p. 372.

Chapter 13: Concluding observations

A. *Reflections on the interrelationship of sources*

This chapter will present final observations and conclusions of a research perspectives on the interrelationship of the sources.

I. The interrelationship of sources as a focus of research

The interrelationship of sources, which denotes the relationship between the sources and their interplay, is a topic that is relevant in any legal order. The present study is primarily concerned with the interrelationship of sources in the international legal order, but it also takes inspiration from comparative legal perspectives.

As illustrated throughout this study, source preferences can be the result of a specific understanding of the law, they can be indicative of the spirit of the time, the legal culture and the doctrinal and legal theoretical preferences of the respective legal community.[1] A recalibration in the relative significance of each source can be a deliberate choice or nothing more than an incidental consequence of certain doctrinal preferences that favour, for instance, the development of the written law by interpretation or the development of functional equivalents to concepts of the unwritten law. For instance, arguments in favour of a rigid distinction between primary rules and secondary rules[2] and in favour of understanding the primary purpose of customary international law as source of secondary rules of interpretation and responsibility can lead to the result that customary international law may be arrested in a separate compartment without meaningful relationships to the developments at the level of the primary rules. According to a different view, customary international law should be understood primarily as a source of primary obligations.[3] In the end, and as result of these diverging views,

---

1 On comparative legal perspectives see above, pp. 97 ff.
2 See above, p. 610.
3 On skepticism of whether rules on rules, such as the rules of responsibility or of treaty interpretation can be conceptualized as custom see d'Aspremont, 'The International Court of Justice, the Whales, and the Blurring of the Lines between Sources and

Chapter 13: Concluding observations

custom might be relevant for neither primary nor secondary rules. Customary international law then might not be needed for so-called rules on rules which could be understood instead as canons, doctrinal propositions or doctrine or *Dogmatik*[4], and it might not be needed at the level of primary obligations because of the proliferation of treaties and the development of functional equivalents to concepts of customary international law based on doctrine or treaty interpretation. Continuing to recognize custom's relevance as a source both of primary rules and of secondary rules, however, can ensure that international lawyers will not lose their familiarity with customary international law, as domestic lawyers did in certain domestic legal systems,[5] and can continue to practice the identification of customary international law and thereby to reinforce the methodology of identification.[6]

Moreover, the scope of law in a legal community can have repercussions on the interrelationship of sources. To give an example: once it was decided that what became the VCLT should address questions of interpretation and that the "rules" of treaty interpretation were to be understood as legal rules that wourd be incorporated in a treaty, the question of the rules' status as customary international law had to arise.[7] In contrast, if the "rules" of interpretation had been understood as mere methods, canons, doctrine or *Dogmatik*, then there would have been no need to argue that the rules are part of customary international law in cases where one party to a dispute is no party to the VCLT. One's understanding of the interrelationship of sources can also concern the scope of law in a legal community. This scope can depend on whether, for instance, one understands convergences of jurisprudence as a mere factual

---

    Interpretation' 1030 footnote 7; Kammerhofer, 'Taking the Rules of Interpretation Seriously, but Not Literally? A Theoretical Reconstruction of Orthodox Dogma' 128-129.

4 Cf. for a treatment of *Dogmatik* or "foundational doctrines" d'Aspremont, *Epistemic forces in international law: foundational doctrines and techniques of international legal argumentation*; Dana Burchardt, 'Book review of Jean d'Aspremont, International Law as a Belief System' (2018) 29 EJIL 1145 (on the equivalence of foundational doctrine and *Dogmatik*).

5 See above, p. 131.

6 On the legal regime governing identification ("*Identifikationsrecht*"), see Christian J Tams, 'Die Identifikation des Völkergewohnheitsrechts' in *Freiheit und Regulierung in der Cyberwelt - Rechtsidentifikation zwischen Quelle und Gericht, Deutsche Gesellschaft für Internationales Recht Zweijahrestagung 34. 2015 Gießen* (CF Müller 2016) 323 ff; *ILC Report 2018* at 122 ff.

7 Cf. above, p. 343.

phenomenon or as an indication of the existence of an underlying general rule.[8]

For these reasons, it is important to contextualize sources discussions by taking into account also the institutional context in which courts and tribunals interact and the challenges to which scholars respond and which inform the debate. Law is a common enterprise of the legislator, courts, scholars and addressees, and discourses within and on law should be brought together rather than being kept separated.

II. Forms of interplay and convergences

What then can be said about the interrelationship of sources in the international legal order based on the previous chapters?

One conclusion of this study is that treaties, customary international law and general principles of law are not unrelated sources and forms of law. Rather, this study suggests that the sources should be understood as an interrelated system in which the relationship between sources can be characterized more often as one of convergence[9] than as one of competition or rivalry.[10] By and large, it is more likely to observe a convergence of functionally equivalent rules of different sources, a convergence of treaty and custom into one common principle and an accommodation contentwise by way of interpretation (principle of systemic integration). In addition, general international law provides for principles and rules for the interpretation, the coordination between different obligations (*lex specialis*, *lex posterior*, *ius cogens*) and for the consequences of a breach of an international obligation and the invocation of international responsibility. This general part[11] applies in relation to a specific rule, subject to derogation within the limits of *jus cogens*.

---

8 Cf. on the debate in international investment law above, p. 595.
9 For an emphasis on the interplay see also Eduardo Jiménez de Aréchaga, 'International law in the past third of a century' (1978) 159 RdC 13; Grigory Ivanovich Tunkin, 'Is General International Law Customary International Law only?' (1993) 4 EJIL 536; Sands, 'Treaty, Custom and the Cross-fertilization of International Law' 85.
10 On competition and rivalry as description of the relationship between written law and customary law in the German legal system see above, p. 137; on the water-oil approach that was used in order to describe the discussion of the relationship between common law and statutory law in the UK, see chapter 2, p. 103.
11 See above, p. 240.

Chapter 13: Concluding observations

To specify these observations: One form of convergence occurs when functionally equivalent rules based on different sources are interpreted and applied in light of each other and each other's concretizations. Examples of the convergence of functionally equivalent rules of different sources are, for instance, the convergence between the equidistance-special circumstances rule of article 6 of the Geneva Convention on the Continental Shelf and customary international law in the jurisprudence of the ICJ.[12] Such convergence can also be observed when the law is in the hands not of one court or tribunal but of multiple tribunals, as the example of the convergence between the international minimum standard and the fair and equitable treatment standard in international investment law illustrates.[13]

The right to self-determination as well as the prohibition of the use of force and the right of self-defence are in the ICJ jurisprudence examples of the convergence of treaty and custom into one common principle.[14] The Court regarded the right to self-determination as a product of the UN Charter and customary international law. Furthermore, the ICJ argued in the *Nicaragua* case that customary international law developed under the influence of the Charter, and the Court added in the *Nuclear Weapons* opinion that self-defence under article 51 UNC, just like self-defence under customary international law, is subject to the requirements of necessity and proportionality, both of which are not laid down in article 51 UNC explicitly.

The general rules of interpretation as reflected in articles 31-33 VCLT are another example of convergence. When the ILC conducted its study on the how courts and tribunals considered the subsequent agreements and subsequent practice in the interpretation of a treaty, the ILC did not distinguish as to whether the courts and tribunals interpreted and applied article 31 (3) (a), (b) VCLT or the functionally equivalent in customary international law. The recently adopted draft conclusions on subsequent agreements and subsequent practice do not make such distinction either.[15]

Some of these observations are reminiscent of the principle of systemic integration and the fragmentation report of the ILC Study Group which was primarily concerned with the interpretation and application of treaties against the background of the normative environment.[16] Based on the afore-

---

12 See above, p. 290.
13 See above, p. 586.
14 See above, p. 285.
15 See above, p. 353; *ILC Report 2018* at 19.
16 See also above, p. 368.

mentioned chapters it is submitted that the same considerations apply *mutatis mutandis* also for customary international law and general principles which together with treaties form part of an interrelated system.[17] While the emergence of a conflict between treaty law and customary international law or general principles of law cannot be categorically excluded, it is not very likely that developments in customary international law and in the context of (in particular widely ratified) conventions will occur in isolation from each other.

III. The institutionalization and the interrelationship

The so-called institutionalization of international law manifests itself in the proliferation of courts and tribunals, international organizations, general codification institutions like the ILC or regional codification institutions. Considering that there are also domestic courts[18], multiple non-state organizations such as the International Law Association, the Institute du Droit International, the International Committee of the Red Cross, one cannot but find that there is a large "community of interpreters"[19]. The institutionalization is an important condition which affects the interrelationship of sources and their development. It has been pointed out that the introduction of general

---

17 See now *ILC Report 2022* at 80: the commentary to conclusion 20 on the interpretation and application cosistent with norms of *jus cogens* indicates that this conclusion, while constituting "a concrete application" of article 31(3)(c) VCLT, applies not only to rules under a treaty but "to all other rules" as well, see also above, p. 382; but cf. also for a different view Orakhelashvili, *The Interpretation of Acts and Rules in Public International Law* 497: "Customary rule should be interpreted independently from its conventional counterpart, according to the rationale it independently possesses. The applicable methods of interpretation have to do with the nature of customary rules."
18 For recent treatments of the identification of customary international law by domestic courts cf. Odile Ammann, *Domestic Courts and the Interpretation of International Law* (2nd edn, Brill Nijhoff 2019) 283 ff.; Cedric MJ Ryngaert and Duco W Hora Siccama, 'Ascertaining Customary International Law: An Inquiry into the Methods Used by Domestic Courts' (2018) 65 Netherlands International Law Review 1 ff. Staubach, 'The Interpretation of Unwritten International Law by Domestic Judges' 113 ff.
19 Cf. Georg Nolte, 'Faktizität und Subjektivität im Völkerrecht Anmerkungen zu Jochen Froweins "Das de facto-Regime im Völkerrecht" im Licht aktueller Entwicklungen' (2015) 75 ZaöRV 730; cf. Peter Häberle, 'Die offene Gesellschaft der Verfassungsinterpreten' (1975) 30 Juristenzeitung 297.

principles of law was linked to the establishment of international courts and tribunals and their practice of taking recourse to such principles.[20] Moreover, as Georges Abi-Saab has put it, customary international law is no longer a wild flower, it has become more of a greenhouse plant, as the diversity of the international community has, perhaps paradoxically, led to a certain centralisation of the customary process and its concentration within the UN system.[21]

This development may give rise to the question of whether customary international law results less from unfiltered state practice and more from a discourse between different actors, including states, courts and tribunals, the organs of the United Nations and certain non-state actors and institutions, resembling "a body of practices observed and ideas received by a caste of lawyers, these ideas being used by them as providing guidance in what is conceived to be the rational determination of disputes litigated before them", similar to the UK common law.[22] The question then is whether one should distinguish in international law between a custom *in foro* and a custom *in pays*.[23] However, the judicial identification, interpretation and application of customary international law is still based on the disciplining idea that one applies law enacted by others. One should, therefore, not confuse the question of who is involved in the interpretation of international law with the question of what is to be interpreted, which remains in the context of customary international law the practice of states (and certain international organizations).[24] The fact that several actors are involved here can produce

---

20 See above, chapter 3, p. 166 ff.
21 Georges Abi-Saab, 'La coutume dans tous ses états ou le dilemme du développement du droit international général dans un monde éclaté' in Marcelo G Kohen and Magnus Jesko Langer (eds), *Le développement du droit international: réflexions d'un demi-siècle* (Presses Universitaires de France 2013) vol 1 88, Abi-Saab argued that, contrary to the famous description of Pierre-Marie Dupuy, the traditional custom, which Dupuy called the wise custom, was truly wild, whereas what Dupuy called the "wild custom" which originated in the context of the UN under the influence of UNGA resolutions was the truly wise, commissioned custom; see Pierre-Marie Dupuy, 'Coutume sage et coutume sauvage' in *Mélanges offerts à Charles Rousseau: la communauté internationale* (Pedone 1974) 75 ff.
22 For the quote see Simpson, 'Common Law and Legal Theory' 376; see above, p. 112; similar Benvenisti, 'Customary International Law as a Judicial Tool for Promoting Efficiency' 85 ff.
23 See above, p. 107.
24 The ILC Conclusion 4(1) on customary international law refers for the requirement of practice "primarily to the practice of states", Conclusion 4(2) acknowledges that

positive effects: interpretations are evaluated as to their merits, leading to the kind of consensus in the sense of general agreement on which customary international law crucially depends.[25]

For this joint interpretative exercise to produce positive effects, agreement as to the criteria on the basis of which one identifies customary international law is necessary. The International Law Commission made an important contribution in this regard when adopting the draft conclusions on the identification of customary international law. By setting forth criteria as well as forms of evidence of a general practice accepted as law, the conclusions can support a certain rationalization of the identification process. The outcome of such process can be evaluated and criticized by others as to its persuasiveness against the background of the ILC conclusions. In this sense, the conclusions and the support they received in the General Assembly[26] express the understanding that customary international law is not simply judge-made law. The draft conclusions on general principles of law can have a similar effect. The draft conclusions' focus on the identification and the emphasis on the element of recognition also express the understanding that general principles of law are not just judge-made law and exist and can be identified outside the judicial context.[27]

At the same time, as both sets of conclusions are concerned with the identification, they are not intended to comprehensively address all aspects relating to these sources, such as the formation or interpretation of custom and general principles of law. This study's conclusions for the understanding of each source are spelt out in more detail below, together with other aspects of the interrelationship for which the institutionalization of international law is an important condition.

"[i]n certain cases, the practice of international organizations also contributes to the formation, or expression, of rules of customary international law."; *ILC Report 2018* at 130. Note also that according to conclusion 6 verbal practice, while being recognized for instance in the case of diplomatic protest, is only one form of practice which also includes physical practice, ibid 133. See Nolte, 'How to identify customary international law? - On the final outcome of the work of the International Law Commission (2018)' 15-16 on the proximity between verbal practice and inaction, and stressing: "Verbal practice can thus be practice where verbal action is part of the formation and expression of the rule, but not just a statement about it."

25 See also above, p. 348.
26 UNGA Res 73/203 (20 December 2018) UN Doc A/RES/73/203 para 4.
27 See also *ILC Report 2022* at 309, where the Special Rapporteur argues that the work on general principles of law as a source of international law is not limited to the judicial perspective.

IV. Customary international law

With a view to better understanding customary international law, the present study submits that it is helpful to reflect, in addition to the criteria set forth in the ILC draft conclusions, on the interpretative decisions, the doctrinal and normative considerations which inform the identification of customary international law.

This study presented several examples that can be found in international legal practice. For instance, the interpretation or evaluation of a practice and the formulation of a rule depend on the observer's doctrinal preconceived understanding (*Vorverständnis*). To give an example, if one observes a general practice according to which individuals are tried before international tribunals for international crimes which were committed by the individuals' subordinates, one can arrive at different conclusions: The practice can indicate that international criminal law does not distinguish between perpetrators and accomplices in the sense of a unitarian perpetratorship model. The practice can also indicate, however, that, while a differentiation between perpetrators and accomplices is to be made, an attribution based on a common purpose or common plan or control over the crime can be established.[28]

One's perspective on international practice also depends on the question that needs to be answered or on the hypothesis that needs to be verified or falsified.[29] One's default position can be important if one wants to ascertain a rule or an exception to the rule. To take the *Jurisdictional Immunities* case[30] as an example: it can matter whether one proceeds on the basis of state immunity as a general rule and examines whether practice supports an exception to this rule for torts committed by troops during an armed conflict. This was the perspective of the ICJ. Alternatively, one could, as it is possible to read the opinion of Judge *ad hoc* Gaja, proceed on the basis of a tort exception to immunity as a general rule and examine whether practice supports an exception to this tort exception for conduct of troops in armed conflicts. The choice of the default position is important as it shifts the burden of reasoning and of justification to the exception.

---

28 See above, p. 526.
29 See also recently Katie A Johnston, 'The Nature and Context of Rules of and the Identification of Customary Inernational Law' (2021) 32(4) EJIL 1168 (arguing that the way in which the two elements are evaluated may depend on whether one examines a permissive or prohibitive rule), 1174.
30 See above, p. 275.

Moreover, those who identify customary international law can employ different techniques in relation to conflicting practice. If the outweighing part of international practice supports the existence of a rule, the examples of practice that cannot be reconciled with the rule can be regarded as a violation of this rule which does not challenge the rule's validity, as it was done by the ICJ in the *Nicaragua* judgment.[31] These examples of practice were not used in order to shape the scope of the rule differently in an attempt to make the rule reflecting the practice as a whole. Conflicting practice or a conflict between *opinio juris* and certain practices can also lead one to define the scope of a rule by acknowledging an exception. In this sense, the ICJ could not identify an absolute prohibition of the use and threat of use of nuclear weapons; the *Nuclear Weapons* advisory opinion can be read to the effect that there is a general prohibition of the use and threat of use of nuclear weapons, which is subject to a possible exception of extreme circumstance of self-defence in relation to which the Court could not conclude that the prohibition would also apply.[32] Alternatively, one could, following the *Kupreškić* Trial Chamber, either emphasize normative considerations and thusly arrive at an absolute prohibition of reprisals against civilians or, following the approach adopted by the *Martić* Chamber, hold that such reprisals must not violate a stringent set of criteria, while leaving the question of the abstract legality open.[33]

It has been demonstrated that customary international law can be understood as a body of law in the sense of a normative system which contains principles and rules of varying degrees of generality, rather than as a set of unrelated rules.[34] The ICJ stressed, for instance, the interrelation between the principle of non-intervention and the equality of states. It characterized immunity as consequence of the equality of states and limitation to the territorial jurisdiction of states. In *Chagos*, the ICJ emphasized the relationship between the right to self-determination and respect for territorial integrity. Moreover, an interpreter will consider whether general principles expressed in international law or domestic law as well as past concretizations of customary international law or functionally equivalent rules can assist her in identifying, concretizing and applying customary international law in a given case. In order to identify customary international law, a systematic under-

---

31 See above, p. 277.
32 See above, p. 277.
33 See above, p. 499.
34 See above, p. 262, p. 374.

standing of the international legal order is required, and this understanding must not be confined to customary international law, it must extend to treaties and general principles of law as well.[35]

Based on the previous chapters, it is submitted that customary international law can be subject to interpretation and that the interpreter has to consider the *telos* of the respective rule, the way in which this rule relates to customary rules of higher or lower levels of generality, and relevant general principles of law, including those expressed in the international legal order. Courts can, to a certain extent, shape the development of customary international through considerations of general principles of law when concretizing customary international law to a particular case. Principles play an important role, but they need to be employed with great care under consideration of the institutional and normative context and structural principles of the international legal order, such as sovereign equality of states and the protection of human rights.[36] In the end, customary international law, while it may protect rights and interests of a minority against the majority in specific cases, remains the law of a majority and has to reflect the distribution of power within a legal community without, however, giving up its prescriptive and normative

---

35 Cf. *Jurisdictional Immunities of the State* 139 para 90, where the ICJ considered the jurisprudence of the European Court of Human Rights when analyzing customary international law. The European Court examined customary international law from the perspective of the ECHR, see above, 425.

36 See also Simma and Pulkowski, 'Of Planets and the Universe: Self-contained Regimes in International Law' 498-499, arguing that international law "certainly possesses the basic characteristics to partake in a specifically legal discourse" and yet caution against "analogizing strong conceptions of legal systems developed in a domestic context" and to remain aware of structural differences and in particular the importance of sovereignty of states as one "major constitutional principle"; see also Paulus, 'The International Legal System as a Constitution' 72: "[...] the transfer of domestic constitutional principles to international law is fraught with difficulty, in particular because international law must always take into account at least two levels of analysis: the interstate level of classical international law and the interindividual level of world citizens at large."

character.[37] It must remain rooted in practice expressing the convictions of states and their citizenry in order to be acceptable and legitimate.[38]

Certainly, the conclusions advanced here will not make the recourse to customary international law, its identification and application easier, as it is submitted to consider in this process general principles of law, treaties and different interpretative decisions. However, reflection of these considerations, which otherwise may be tacitly employed or remain implicit, can improve both the quality of the identification process and the critique rendered against the outcome. The critique can be delivered with a higher degree of precision than it is at times, when it remains on a rather general level, confined to the discussion of the abstract relationship of the two elements of customary international law.

V. Treaties

The importance of treaties does not need to be stressed. International organizations, courts and tribunals are established on the basis of treaties. When interpreting and applying the treaty, the general rules of treaty interpretation as reflected in articles 31-33 VCLT direct the interpreters to the normative environment in which the treaty is situated. At first sight, a treaty's compromissory clause that authorizes a court or tribunal to interpret and apply the treaty may imply a confinement in that the authorization does not extend to the application of other sources or the whole of international law. The interpretation and application of the treaty may, however, be informed by customary international law and general principles of law. In this sense, a treaty can indirectly strengthen the rule of law in the international community

---

37 Cf. Philip Allott, 'Language, Method and the Nature of International Law' (1971) 45 BYIL 132 for the view that short-term circumstances which he associated with treatymaking may average out during customary international law's emergence over a period of time; for a similar point see Føllesdal, 'The Significance of State Consent for the Legitimate Authority of Customary International Law' 127 (arguing against instant custom because of the risk of domination). See recently Hadjigeorgiou, 'Beyond Formalism Reviving the Legacy of Sir Henry Maine for Customary International Law' 189-90.
38 Cf. Andreas L Paulus and Matthias Lippold, 'Customary Law in the Postmodern World (Dis)Order' (2018) 112 AJIL Unbound 312.

and contribute to the development of general international law.[39] A "treatification"[40] of the international legal order does not have to go at the expense of the unwritten law, customary international law and general principles of law. A codification convention may, to take up Baxter's famous description, arrest the "change and flux in the state of customary international law" and "photograp[h] the state of the law"[41]. At the same time, the ILC project on subsequent agreements and subsequent practice[42] illustrates that codification conventions such as the VCLT together with customary international law can become subject to a re-analysis. The extent to which unwritten international law remains relevant depends, of course, on the actors in the international legal system. For instance, the respective law-applying authorities can refer to general principles of law and customary international law or focus on the *lex specialis* character of the treaty which can reduce, even though, arguably, not completely[43], the need to work with other sources. This study demonstrated, for instance in the context of the European Court of Human Rights, that functional equivalents to concepts of general international law can be developed on the basis of treaty law.[44]

Last but not least, rules in a treaty can be a codification, contribute to the crystallization or give rise to new rules of customary international law.[45] As both sources are distinct, a treaty may not simply be equated with customary international law. Whether rules in a treaty have become to reflect customary international law must remain the subject of an analysis on the basis of the methodology relating to customary international law.[46] A treaty may also give expression to principles of a potentially general scope which are suited

---

39 See in particular the section on compromissory clauses above, p. 239; Kolb, 'The Compromissory Clause of the Convention' 413. See in particular the jurisprudence on the European Court of Human Rights above, p. 425.
40 Cf. Salacuse, 'The Treatification of International Investment Law' 155 ff.; Patrick Dumberry, 'A few observations on the remaining fundamental importance of customary rules in the age of treatification in international investment law' (2016) 35(1) ASA bulletin = Schweizerische Vereinigung für Schiedsgerichtsbarkeit 41 ff.
41 Baxter, 'Multilateral Treaties as Evidence of Customary International Law' 299.
42 See above, p. 353.
43 Cf. Bruno Simma, 'Self-contained regimes' (1985) 16 Netherlands Yearbook of International Law 112 ff.
44 See above, p. 446; on the politics of the interrelationship, see below, p. 697.
45 See above, p. 280, p. 376.
46 See also above, p. 376.

to guide and inform the identification of customary international law more generally.[47]

VI. General principles

The approach adopted in this book proposes, informed by comparative historical analysis and legal theory, to understand general principles of law in their interrelation with treaties and customary international law, rather than as conceptual alternative at the expense of customary international law.

Principles can be ascertained inductively and extrapolated from more specific rules, they can also be necessary premises or implied as necessary consequences of more specific rules. The content of general principles can be concretized by more specific rules of treaty law and customary international law or the practice of states. It is necessary that the principle, in order to qualify as a general principle of law, is recognized by the community of nations. The *modus operandi* of general principles formed within the international legal system is similar to the *modus operandi* of general principles of law that are identified in the municipal legal orders[48] or to the *modus operandi* of legal principles discussed in legal theory. It is here submitted that article 38(1)(c) ICJ Statute can be read as declaratory recognition of the role general principles of law play in the interpretation and application of law.

General principles of law perform very different functions. They constitute the necessary elements, premises and precepts that enables a legal order to fulfil its function in a society. General principles of law are an expression of the integrity of law, different from mere power, politics or arbitrariness, of the inner rationality (*Eigengesetzlichkeit*) of law. General principles may thusly derive from the very idea of law (*pacta sunt servanda*; legal responsibility as consequence of a violation); they may express a certain respect towards the other governed by law, which expresses itself in principles concerning the *inter partes* relations, such as principles of fairness in the judicial process, abuse of rights, of no one should be benefit from his own wrongdoing, *audiatur et altera pars* etc. These principles may be regarded as important, admittedly, rudimentary recognition by law of the respect every human being is entitled to. In addition, they give expression to legal evaluations and "value

---

47 See for instance the jurisprudence of the ICTY above, p. 487.
48 See *ILC Report 2022* at 322 (commentary to draft conclusion 7); ILC Report 2023 at 23.

Chapter 13: Concluding observations

judgments"[49] which manifest themselves in particular rules and the legal order and which may guide and inform the interpreter's interpretation of other rules.[50] Structural principles of the international legal order, such as sovereign equality of states and the protection of human rights, may also compete in certain circumstances and call for a reconciliation for the specific case by the legal operator through the interpretation and application of more specific rules.[51] The idea of principles as mere gap-fillers is misleading as the very identification of a gap entails a normative judgment which can be informed by way of reference to principles of the legal system.[52]

Recourse to general principles can, together with customary international law, give meaning to broadly framed treaty obligations[53] or to obligations under customary international law[54] by, inter alia, establishing a relation to the judicial and legal experiences and normative developments in municipal law or in other fields of international law.[55] The use of general principles can help in clarifying the normative concept or framework of a rule, to operationalize the application of a rule through, for instance, proportionality analysis.[56] In addition, general principles can help in coordinating specific obligations

---

49 German language makes a distinction between *Wert* and *Wertung*, as the latter is something made, whereas the origin of the former remains hidden. The english term *value* arguably encompasses both and is overinclusive. Therefore, Simma and Pulkowski, 'Of Planets and the Universe: Self-contained Regimes in International Law' 498 suggest the term "value judgment" as translation of *Wertung*. On the problematic use of the terms *Wert* see Ulrich Fastenrath, 'Subsidiarität im Völkerrecht' in Peter Blickle, Thomas O Hüglin, and Dieter Wyduckel (eds), *Subsidiarität als rechtliches und politisches Ordnungsprinzip in Kirche, Staat und Gesellschaft: Genese, Geltungsgrundlagen und Pespektiven an der Schwelle des dritten Jahrtausends* (Duncker & Humblot 2002) 493 footnote 88.
50 See also Schwarzenberger, 'The fundamental principles of international law' 224-225, describing how principles can cease to be mere abstraction from binding rules and can become normatively superior for future rules.
51 Cf. also Paulus, 'The International Legal System as a Constitution' 86, pointing out that a constitution "cannot solve the value conflicts of the founding principles of a legal order but may provide mechanisms for how to balance them [...]".
52 See above, p. 142; cf. Lauterpacht, *The Function of Law in the International Community* 64-86 (distinguishing between a formal completeness and a material completeness of a legal system).
53 See above on in the interpretation of FET in light of general principles of international law, p. 586.
54 See above, p. 487.
55 See for instance the doctrine of indirect perpetratorship above, p. 534.
56 See above, p. 425.

by providing a framework and a common ground for reconciliation.[57] A general principle such as the prohibition of arbitrariness can also provide an appropriate standard of review when one has to interpret other law.[58] Last but not least, the recourse to principle can help in defining default positions which the distributes the burden of reasoning.[59]

Whether general principles of law can be characterized as "source" depends on the meaning attached to this term and on the functions assigned to this concept. Jean d'Aspremont, for instance, has argued that general principles of law do not constitute a source of law and that they should be regarded solely as "mode of interpretation" that can be helpful for content-determination.[60] In addition, if one associates the concept of a source of law with a unidirectional movement by which the law "flows" from its "source", one may call the characterization of general principles as a source into question, as principles emerge from an interpretation of the law and unfold themselves as to their respective meaning in relation to, and in interaction with, other principles, rules and the respective normative context. Yet, the description of just an interpretative tool undervalues both principles' importance as necessary premises of the legal system as such, for instance *pacta sunt servanda*, good faith, abuse of rights, and the role they play in establishing an understanding of specific obligations. As general principles of law offer ideas and legal inspirations for general norms' interpretation, for their concretization and

---

57 See above, p. 438.
58 See above on the prohibition of arbitrariness as standard of review when more specific obligations under the ECHR do not exist, p. 410, or when the European Court evaluates states' compliance with the ECHR in the implementation of UNSC resolutions, p. 441; cf. on good faith review Dapo Akande and Sope Williams, 'International adjudication on national security issues: what role for the WTO?' (2003) 43(2) Virginia Journal of International Law 407 ff. on good faith review; see also Stephan W Schill and Robyn Briese, '"If the State Considers": Self-Judging Clauses in International Dispute Settlement' (2009) 13 Max Planck Yearbook of International Law 61 ff.; *Certain Questions of Mutual Assistance in Criminal Matters* 229 para 145, and Decl Keith 278-279 paras 4-5.
59 Cf. on default positions above, p. 266, p. 497, p. 551.
60 d'Aspremont, 'What was not meant to be: General principles of law as a source of international law' 179; similar already Weil, 'Le droit international en quête de son identité: cours général de droit international public' 148-149, 151 (general principles of law were only a material source and no formal source); cf. also *ILC Report 2022* at 310 ("Several members agreed that general principles of law were a primary and independent source, while others expressed doubts").

development, it is appropriate to rank general principles of law on one level with treaty and custom as a source of international law.[61]

VII. The distinctiveness of sources and their interrelations

Understanding the sources of international law as an interrelated system presupposes the distinctiveness of the sources which includes differences as to the identification process and the sources' *modus operandi*.[62]

Article 38 ICJ Statute and its counterpart in the PCIJ Statute already subtly emphasize differences in their respective text with respect to way in which consent is described.[63] Different sources can assume similar functions but have different strengths and weaknesses. The treaty recommends itself in particular for detailed, technical regulations, it can crystallize and specify pre-existing understandings[64] and introduce new ideas, principles and values to the international legal order which can contribute to shaping the identities of relevant actors.[65] Even though rules of customary international law can operate on the same level as rules of treaty law, customary international law constitutes a different normative sphere.[66] It is a general practice accepted as law which can include treaties, and treaties can be assessed as to whether they express trends in the international community.[67] Customary international law is linked to the idea of one legal community, it expresses a specific community mindset in which general law serves as foundation. In this sense, certain advocates of customary international law seem to regard this concept

---

61 Kolb, 'Principles as Sources of International Law (With Special Reference to Good Faith)' 9 (describing general principles as "norm source").
62 Cf. in a similar sense Bos, 'The Recognized Manifestations of International Law A New Theory of "Sources"' 73-76 on "mutual independence" and "coherence between the recognized manifestations of international law" (at 76).
63 See above, p. 213.
64 Jutta Brunnée, 'The Sources of International Environmental Law: Interactional Law' in Samantha Besson and Jean d'Aspremont (eds), *Oxford Handbook on the Sources of International Law* (Oxford University Press 2017) 966.
65 See above, p. 81.
66 Cf. von Bernstorff, *The public international law theory of Hans Kelsen: believing in universal law* 166 ("a normative layer above", when describing customary international law in the work of Hans Kelsen).
67 On custom as consensus of the international community see Kohen, 'La pratique et la théorie des sources du droit international' 93-94; Philip Allott, 'The Concept of International Law' (1999) 10 EJIL 38-42.

to be important as mindset of the legal operators that entails a commitment to, and the professional conscience to be part of, a community that goes beyond a specific treaty in question.[68] General principles of law can be more abstract than rules of customary international law, yet they can also be very precise in case of procedural principles such as *res judicata*. They can operate as inspirations and as reasons in a subtle way: they operate within normative structures[69] and yet, they can have a transformative or norm-creating potential[70]. They can help in defining default or starting positions and are therefore also relevant for the identification of customary international law which not only includes inductive analysis but also deductive elements. Whether general principles are part of the law, part of the *corpus iuris*, may depend on the degree of positivization they have received. It might not always be possible to clearly distinguish between a rule of customary international law of high generality and a general principle of law, and this study subscribes to the view that there is no necessary logical or categorical

---

68 See above in the context of international investment law, p. 609; for the view that the crimes set forth in the Rome Statute needed to be interpreted in accordance with customary international law if the international community's *ius puniendi* is to be enforced, and for the implications of this view on immunities, see above, p. 521, p. 554; as was pointed out in the second chapter, the function of the unwritten law in relation to the written law can differ, it could be the basis for independent rules, p. 120, or indicate the way in which the written law should be applied, p. 119. Recently, Walters, 'The Unwritten Constitution as a Legal Concept' 35 argued in favour of more attention to unwritten constitutional law as "a discourse of reason in which existing rules, even those articulated in writing, are understood to be specific manifestations of a comprehensive body of abstract principles from which other rules may be identified through an interpretive back-and-forth that endeavours to show coherence between law's specific and abstract dimensions and equality between law's various applications".

69 As noted by Mosler, 'The international society as a legal community' 89: "But generally, principles require implementation by rules." In the right institutional setting, for instance in an adversarial adjudicatory context, principles can function like rules in the sense that on their bases cases can be decided, Kolb, 'Principles as Sources of International Law (With Special Reference to Good Faith)' 11-12, referring to *Temple of Preah Vihear* 23, 26, 32 where the case was decided on the basis of general principles such as acquiescence and estoppel.

70 Cf. Schwarzenberger, 'The fundamental principles of international law' 224, pointing out that certain principles like sovereignty "may have ceased to be mere abstractions of binding rules. Potentially, they become overriding rules form which [...] other binding rules may legitimately be derived."

distinction between a rule and a principle.[71] Nevertheless, it is also submitted that customary international law and general principles of law are distinct concepts. In general, norms of customary international law will be more specific as to their preconditions and legal consequences since they have been hardened by practice. They may also represent a concretization or a reconciliation of different principles. At the same time and just like rules in a treaty, rules of customary international law can be the expression of a more general principle or give rise to new principles.

The distinctiveness of the sources implies that general principles of law and the other sources can, as suggested by the ILC, exist in parallel.[72] The relationship between different norms will be governed by the well-established conflict rules *lex specialis* and *lex posterior* and by interpretation in the sense of systemic integration.[73] This distinctiveness relates to the applicability and does not exclude an interplay as far as content-determination is concerned.[74]

Based on this study's understanding of sources as an interrelated system, it is not possible to understand customary international law without general principles, nor the latter without the former and the specific structures shaped in particular by treaties. General principles of law as understood here do not replace customary international law, they often depend on specific norms based on treaties or custom. Therefore, it may be misleading to think of general principles as an option which makes it possible, for instance, to circumvent the requirements of customary international law.[75] In addition to the ILC draft conclusions on general principles of law which focus on the identification of general principles,[76] it is submitted that the specific context in which the principle is to be applied is particularly relevant when searching

---

71 See for instance the example very broad principles and rules in the context of maritime delimitation, pp. 290 ff. See also above, chapter 2.
72 *ILC Report 2022* at 308 Fn. 1189, 312, 316; ILC Report 2023 at 33 f.
73 See on the work of the ILC Study Group above, p. 368.
74 For an illustration in the ICJ jurisprudence see above, pp. 258 ff.
75 See also recently Xuan Shao, 'What We Talk about When We Talk about General Principles of Law' (2021) 20 Chinese Journal of International Law 223, 244, 249, 253.
76 On the two-step methodology for general principles of law that are derived from national legal systems and transposed to the international legal system "in so far as they are compatible with that system", see *ILC Report 2022* at 308 Fn. 1189 (draft conclusion 6); on the general principles which formed within the international legal system with respect to which "it is necessary to ascertain that the community of nations has recognized the principle as intrinsic to the international legal system", see ibid at 308 Fn. 1189 (draft conclusion 7(1)); see now ILC Report 2023 at 20 ff.

Reflections on the interrelationship of sources

for a general principle of law. The identification of a general principle does not take place within a vacuum. Arguably, the specific context informs the identification of a general principle of law. A principle that may be a fit for one specific context may not necessarily be an appropriate fit in other contexts. It is, therefore, submitted that a certain context-sensitivity should be preserved with respect to general principles of law and that an analysis should also focus on the interrelation between a general principle and the specific normative and institutional context.[77] General principles remain important in the judicial setting and outside of it when one approaches and interprets the law as a court would interpret it. The fact that principles may be balanced and interpreted differently and that reasonable minds may disagree on the identification of a particular rule of customary international law may explain the contestability of an interpretation of the law. However, mere contestability alone does not necessarily impede the authority and persuasiveness of the law and its sources.

VIII. The politics in relation to the interrelationship of sources

This study demonstrated that legal operators may address the interrelationship of sources in different ways and for different reasons.[78] Certain courts and tribunals, rather than applying just their respective treaty and remaining confined to their field of law, considered other sources and searched for inspirations in other areas of international law.[79] Investment tribunals, for instance, referred to the international minimum standard and other BITs in order to objectivize what they considered to be fair and equitable.[80] This is understandable as the genuine judicial legitimacy rests on the idea that courts apply law enacted by others.[81] The ICTY's recourse to customary interna-

---

77 See also above, p. 505 and recently Megumi, 'The New Recipe for a General Principle of Law: Premise Theory to "Fill in the Gaps"' 10 ff.
78 On source preferences see already above, p. 679.
79 On "the spirit of systemic harmonization" as "new posture of international courts and tribunals" see Anne Peters, 'The refinement of international law: From fragmentation to regime interaction and politicization' (2017) 15(3) International Journal of Constitutional Law 671 ff.
80 See above, p. 592.
81 Cf. Jansen, *The Making of Legal Authority: Non-legislative Codifications in Historical and Comparative Perspective* 125-126; Habermas, *Between Facts and Norms. Contributions to a Discourse Theory of Law and Democracy* 261-262; Habermas, *Fak-*

tional law can be explained in a similar sense when it based the individual responsibility for violations of international law in non-international armed conflicts on customary international law.[82] Certain ICC chambers, however, emphasized in certain situations that, first and foremost, they would have to apply a treaty and used this argument in order to distance themselves from customary international law as identified by the ICTY.[83] As demonstrated above, the ICC jurisprudence raises the question of whether the ICC can and should rely solely on the Rome Statute or focus on the alignment of the Statute and customary international law.[84] Another interesting example for a study of the interrelationship of sources is the case-law of the European Court of Human Rights. The European Court partly establishes relations between the ECHR and customary international law, and partly develops functional equivalents to concepts of customary international law.[85] These examples illustrate that courts and tribunals can make different choices as to the calibration of the interrelationship of sources. These choices can also be indicative of how a particular community or regime regards its relationship with the wider international community. A research perspective on the interrelationship of sources will continue to review these developments.

There are, furthermore, not only conscious engagements with but also unconscious contributions to the development of the sources and their interrelationship. Throughout the study it could also be observed that courts and tribunals do not always refer to customary international law and general principles of law when they considered other treaties or decisions of other courts and tribunals or domestic law.[86] Drawing analogies from other legal materials does not necessarily have to be considered as prohibited, though. Arguably, within the confines of legal reasoning, courts and tribunals can seek inspiration from nonbinding materials, provided that the use of these inspirations is disciplined by legal methodology which is applied to the interpretation of the binding rule. This process can contribute to the emergence of new general principles and new rules of customary international law, which of course would depend on the states' reactions to these decisions. Courts and

---

tizität und Geltung: Beiträge zur Diskurstheorie des Rechts und des demokratischen Rechtsstaats 317-319; Maus, 'Die Trennung von Recht und Moral als Begrenzung des Rechts' 199, 208.
82 See above, p. 484.
83 See above, p. 536.
84 See above, pp. 517 ff.
85 See above, p. 426, p. 443.
86 See above, p. 408 ff., p. 493 ff., 604 ff.

tribunals apply preexisting law and yet they can contribute to law's further development by concretizing law to a particular case.[87] While courts have an important function in this regard, they should approach the judicial task not with a view to positivizing new principles or contributing to new customary international law, but with a view to serving the law. In doing the latter, they may accomplish the former.[88] If a court invokes the authority of customary international law or a general principle of law, this court's use of such rule or principle will, of course, be judged according to its persuasiveness. Here, the ILC conclusions in their focus on the identification can play an important role. A legal reasoning can derive persuasiveness from recourse to a general principle of law, but this specific use of such general principle as opposed to a competing principle needs to derive its persuasiveness from the legal reasoning.[89]

One consequence of the interrelationship of sources is the constant availability of international law based on customary international law and general principles of law on the basis of which disputes could be adjudicated by a court.[90] This general international law will provide for a general content[91] and its application can also be informed by trends and developments in more advanced treaty regimes. This consequence results from the efforts undertaken by international legal practitioners and scholars alike who continue to cultivate and administer unwritten international law, even though the degree of attention dedicated to each source has differed from time to time.[92] The continuing acceptance of unwritten law, the effort to seriously grapple with

---

87 See also above, p. 118; on the Kelsenian perspective according to which the application of law is not completely determined by the norm that is applied see above, p. 196 and p. 668.
88 See above, p. 154; cf. also Lauterpacht, *The Function of Law in the International Community* 110-111, quoted above, p. 210.
89 See above, p. 154.
90 Cf. already *Eastern Extension, Australasia and China Telegraph Company, Ltd* IV RIAA 114: "International law [...] may not contain, and generally does not contain, express rules decisive of particular cases; but the function of jurisprudence is to resolve the conflict of opposing rights and interests by applying, in default of any specific provisions of law, the corollaries of general principles, and so to find [...] the solution of the problem."
91 On the description of virtues attributed to customary international law, which include for instance to ensure "a minimum content of law" and "a minimal relevance of law", see d'Aspremont, 'The Decay of Modern Customary International Law in Spite of Scholarly Heroism' 20, 29.
92 On different stages in the scholarly discussion see above, p. 635 ff.

the identification of customary international law and general principles of law and to create meaningful relationships between the sources may be seen as unique characteristics of the international legal order in comparison to other legal orders.

At the same time, this development, the cherishing of unwritten law, can be criticized. It can be said to reduce the pressure to ratify treaties and go at the expense of a different international legal order in which lawmaking would be characterized by a higher degree of formalization and rules would be embedded in procedural frameworks established by treaties. The governance through custom can make it at least for certain states an option to abstain from treaties, without risking to end up with no law at all, and to strategically advocate for the recognition of only specific provisions as reflection of customary international law. As Vaughan Lowe has observed with respect to the United Nations Convention on the Law of the Sea, "rights tend to pass into customary international law more easily than obligations".[93] If a state, however, decides not to join a treaty and to remain on the customary law route, it must be aware that customary international law can, in the long run, be shaped by recourse to principles expressed in treaties. States cannot be bound by a treaty against their will, but they cannot withdraw from the rule of law in the international community either.[94]

As long as the international legal order remains by and large structured by decentralised lawmaking, in spite of the unquestionable progress of the institutionalization, customary international law will arguably remain signif-

---

[93] Vaughan Lowe, 'Was it Worth the Effort?' (2012) 27 The International Journal of Marine and Coastal Law 879; see also William Michael Reisman, 'The Cult of Custom in the Late 20th Century' (1987) 17 California Western International Law Journal 134: through custom, "[w]e can stay in the world without the need for a veto and still have our way: We can use custom to get the international law we want without having to undergo the "give" part of the "give-and-take" of the legislative process." See also above, p. 85.

[94] Cf. Andrew T Guzman and Jerome Hsiang, 'Some Ways that Theories on Customary International Law Fail: A Reply to László Blutman' (2014) 25(2) EJIL 554: "As a matter of observation, states rarely accept non-consensual laws or external norms as binding law. Yet it is also undeniable that CIL serves and persists as a fundamental building block of international law." They elaborate on the "non-consensual nature" of customary international law. One could say, however, that customary international law indirectly affirms and strengthens the consensual concept of the treaty. See above, p. 242 ff., on the judgment between Croatia and Serbia, where the ICJ did not endorse the retroactive application of the Genocide convention and instead based its jurisdiction on a concept of customary international law, the succession into responsibility.

icant. Because of the slow speed of ratifications, customary international law and general principles of law have retained their importance in legal practice. Ultimately, however, it is for each international lawyer to evaluate whether the benefits associated with the unwritten law and its sources outweigh their potential shortcomings and difficulties.

IX. The interrelationship of sources and general international law

It is submitted that a focus on the interrelationship of sources can potentially add to one's understanding of the concept of general international law. Even though the term "general international law" is often invoked, there are different ways to understand this term.[95] Paul Reuter distinguished different kinds of generality, generality *ratione personae*, generality as synonym for abstractness, and generality as temporal continuity (*celui de la permanence dans le temps*).[96] According to the ILC Study Group on fragmentation, "'general international law' clearly refers to general customary law as well as 'general principles of law recognized by civilized nations' [...] it might also refer to principles of international law proper and to analogies from domestic law, especially principles of the legal process".[97] In the context of the work on peremptory norms of general international law, the ILC pointed out that "the meaning of general international will always be context-specific" and emphasized for the purpose of the *jus cogens* project the generality *ratione personae*.[98] Conclusion 5 which deals with the bases of peremptory norms

---

95 See critical Wood, 'The International Tribunal for the Law of the Sea and General International Law' 354 ("a certain degree of imprecision"); Matz-Lück, 'Norm Interpretation across International Regimes: Competences and Legitimacy' 206.
96 Paul Reuter, 'Principes de droit international public' (1961) 103 RdC 469; cf. also Métall, 'Skizzen zu einer Systematik der völkerrechtlichen Quellenlehre' 423, distinguishing between *allgemeines Völkerrecht*, which is characterized by generality *ratione personae*, and *generelles Völkerrecht* which is characterized by generality or abstractness as opposed to a concretized rule.
97 *Fragmentation of international law: difficulties arising from diversification and expansion of international law, Report of the Study Group of the International Law Commission, Finalized by Martti Koskenniemi* 254; cf. also Tunkin, 'Is General International Law Customary International Law only?' 541: "general international law now comprises both customary and conventional rules of international law", Tunkin referred to codification conventions and the UN Charter.
98 *ILC Report 2019* at 159; on generality *ratione personae* see also Josef L Kunz, 'General International Law and the Law of International Organizations' (1953) 47(3)

of *general international law* and the corresponding commentary emphasize that customary international law "*is* the most common basis", while also recognizing that "treaty provisions and general principles of law *may* also serve as bases"[99].

It is submitted that the ILC's *jus cogens* conclusion 5 is convincing in that it does not tie the concept of general international law to one particular source.[100] General international law is perhaps best described as a status which certain norms have acquired.[101] As persuasively argued by Georges Abi-Saab, norms of general international law are not defined by their origin but by what they have become and received, namely general acceptance. It is not only by way of customary international law but also by treatymaking that states can structure the legal environment and shape the expectations of the participants in the international legal system.[102] Once a rule or principle has been elevated to the level of general international law, the particular source, or origin, loses relevance, rules and principles from different sources can converge into one normative concept.[103]

General international law is a concept with many characteristics some of which have been just described in the previous paragraphs or illustrated throughout this book. For instance, one important aspect is the function of general international law as a general part which encompasses rules on rules, such as the general rules of interpretation, of responsibility, of validity of legal acts and which will apply in relation to and together with any specific rule.[104] Based on this study, it is, in addition, submitted that general international law may be characterized also by a certain generality *ratione materiae* by which the present author does not mean the abstractness of its rules but rather the rules' reflection of the principles and judgment calls of the international legal

---

AJIL 456; Gionata Piero Buzzini, 'La "généralité" du droit international général: réflexions sur la polysémie d'un concept' (2004) 108 RGDIP 381.

99 *ILC Report 2019* at 158, draft conclusion (italics added), see also 161-163 on the different views on general principles of law and treaty provisions.
100 The ILC adopted on second reading the 23 draft conclusions on the identification and legal consequences of peremptory norms of general international law in 2022, *ILC Report 2022* at 5.
101 Cf in a similar sense Yasuaki, *International Law in a Transcivilizational World* 105, 112, 155, 159.
102 Abi-Saab, 'Les sources du droit international: essai de déconstruction' 75.
103 ibid 78.
104 See above, p. 240 ff. See also Christian Tomuschat, 'What is 'general international law'?' in *Guerra y paz: 1945-2009: obra homenaje al Dr. Santiago Torres Bernárdez* (Universidad del Pais Vasco, Servicio Editorial 2010) 342-344.

order. Arguably, several aspects that have been examined in the context of this study on the interrelationship of sources describe a process of a certain *generalization* of international law.

This book has illustrated the convergence into a common principle, by way of reference to the prohibition of the use of force, the right to self-determination[105] or the general rules of treaty interpretation[106]. Courts and tribunals consider principles and trends expressed in treaties when identifying customary international law, which serves the purpose of keeping customary international law and its application in a given case up to date. By way of interpretation, a relationship between a human rights treaty like the ECHR and immunities under customary international law is established by the European Court which considers both in light of each other.[107] Courts and tribunals from specific branches of international law interpret and apply general international law and seek inspiration in other fields of international law. If international law is interpreted in good faith, driven by the motivation to get the other law right and not to impose one-sidedly one particular regime's rationale on other areas of international law[108], this process can lead to a certain *generalization* of the specific law. In this sense, the specific law's interpretation and application are related to the wider normative environment. This process can also serve the general law which is then interpreted and applied in new contexts. Whether this process in fact occurs or continues to occur must be the object of continuous research.

In order to answer the question of the relative significance of each source, of written and unwritten international law in the international community, a constant examination of the international legal practice in specific areas of the international legal order is necessary. In particular, the challenging task of international legal scholarship committed to general international law will be to examine whether and to what extent concepts of general international law are applied in specific contexts or replaced with functionally equivalent concepts.[109] This scholarship must also identify when normative innovations developed in different treaty contexts have further developed

---

105 See above, p. 285 ff.
106 See above, p. 35 ff.
107 See above, p. 426 ff.
108 Cf. von Bernstorff, 'Specialized Courts and Tribunals as the Guardians of International Law? The Nature and Function of Judicial Interpretation in Kelsen and Schmitt' 23; von Bernstorff, 'Hans Kelsen on Judicial Law-Making by International Courts and Tribunals: a Theory of Global Judicial Imperialism?' 50.
109 See above, p. 462 ff.

Chapter 13: Concluding observations

general international law. It is submitted that general international law should not be understood exclusively in contradistinction to special law, but also as reflection of the international legal order as a whole, including its values as expressed through the interpretation and application of treaties, customary international law and general principles.

B. *Conclusions*

1. The interrelationship of sources, meaning the relationship between the sources and their interplay, is a topic which is relevant in any legal order. The answers to the questions regarding the sources' relationship can be indicative of the spirit of the time, the legal culture and the doctrinal and legal theoretical preferences of the respective legal community.

2. The three formal sources enshrined in article 38(1) ICJ Statute do not stand in isolation from each other. In legal practice and in international law scholarship, different forms of interplay, relative significance and balance can be observed. Conflicts or even rivalries between these sources are more the exception than the rule. By and large, it is more likely to observe a convergence of functionally equivalent rules of different sources, a convergence of treaty and custom into one common principle and an accommodation contentwise by way of interpretation (principle of systemic integration). In addition, general international law provides for principles and rules for interpretation, the coordination between different obligations (*lex specialis*, *lex posterior*, *ius cogens*) and for the consequences of a breach of an international obligation and the invocation of international responsibility. This general part applies in relation to a specific rule, subject to derogation within the limits of jus cogens.

3. The so-called institutionalization of international law is of great significance for the development of the interrelationship of sources. A large "community of interpreters" engages with the sources. The value of the ILC conclusions on customary international law and the ILC project on general principles of law can consist in providing orientation and in particular agreed criteria on the identification of customary international law or general principles of law which can enhance the quality of the work of law-applying authorities.

4. The recently adopted ILC draft conclusions on the identification of customary international law provide helpful guidance and in structuring and rationalizing the identification process. With a view to better understand

customary international law, the present study submits that it is helpful to additionally reflect on the interpretative decisions, the doctrinal and normative considerations which inform the identification of customary international law. In particular, the jurisprudence of the ICJ demonstrates that customary international law does not consist of separated but of interrelated rules and principles.

5. A treaty not only can provide for a rule which codified, crystallized or became a rule of customary international law which is in its content almost identical to the treaty-based rule. A treaty can also give expression to principles of potentially general applicability which are suited to guide and inform the identification of customary international law.

6. General principles can be identified not only in municipal legal orders but also in the international legal order. Article 38(1)(c) ICJ Statute can be read as declaratory recognition of the importance of legal principles in the interpretation and application of law. General principles of law are not mere gap-fillers, their meaning, functions and importance reveal themselves in the interplay with treaties and customary international law.

7. If one analyzes the interrelationship of sources, one must not lose sight of the sources' distinctiveness and differences. Each source of international law is subject to a particular methodology and doctrine. In particular, it may not be easily assumed, but must remain subject of a rigorous demonstration, that the substance of a rule of a treaty is also part of customary international law. In addition, customary international law and general principles of law remain separate and distinct concepts, even though the distinction may be difficult to make from time to time. When taking recourse to general principles, a court must remain aware of its task to apply, and not to make, the law. The identification of customary international law must continue to reflect the balance of power in the international community, without, however, giving up the prescriptive and normative character of customary international law.

8. An important topic for a research perspective on the interrelationship of sources is the way in which law-applying authorities address the interrelationship of sources, express source preferences and contribute to the development of the law. Furthermore, Article 38 with its sources and subsidiary means for the determination of the rules of law is a blueprint for a decentralized organized legal community. Because of the interplay of sources, there is always a minimum law, consisting of customary international law and general principles of law, on the basis of which disputes can be adjudicated. At the same time, there is the risk that the importance of unwritten law can reduce

Chapter 13: Concluding observations

the ratification pressure, which can go at the expense of a more formalized international legal order.

9. It is the task of international legal scholarship committed to general international law to study the interrelationship of sources not only on a very abstract level, but also in specific contexts, to diagnose developments in the balance between the sources, and to make use of these insights for a study of the development of general international law.

Bibliography

Monographs

Alebeek, Rosanne van, *The Immunity of States and Their Officials in International Criminal Law and International Human Rights Law* (Oxford University Press 2008).

Alexy, Robert, *Theorie der juristischen Argumentation Die Theorie des rationalen Diskurses als Theorie der juristischen Begründung* (Suhrkamp 1978).

– *Theorie der Grundrechte* (Nomos-Verl-Ges 1985).

– *Recht, Vernunft, Diskurs: Studien zur Rechtsphilosophie* (Suhrkamp 1995).

– *A Theory of Constitutional Rights* (Oxford University Press 2002).

Ambos, Kai, *Der Allgemeine Teil des Völkerstrafrechts: Ansätze einer Dogmatisierung* (Duncker & Humblot 2002).

– *Treatise on International Criminal Law: Vol. I: Foundations and General Part* (Oxford University Press 2013).

– *Treatise on International Criminal Law: Vol. I: Foundations and General Part* (2nd edn, Oxford University Press 2021).

Amerasinghe, Chittharanjan Felix, *Diplomatic Protection* (Oxford University Press 2008).

American Law Institute, *Restatement of the law, The Foreign Relations Law of the United States* (vol 1, 1987).

Ammann, Odile, *Domestic Courts and the Interpretation of International Law* (2nd edn, Brill Nijhoff 2019).

Anghie, Antony, *Imperialism, Sovereignty and the Making of International Law* (Cambridge University Press 2005).

Anzilotti, Dionisio, *Corso di Diritto Internazionale* (vol 1, Athenaeum 1912).

– *Cours de droit international 1: Introduction, théoriés, générales* (Gidel, Gilbert tr, Sirey 1929).

– *Lehrbuch des Völkerrechts* (Bruns, Cornelia and Schmid, Karl trs, de Gruyter 1929).

Arajärvi, Noora, *The changing nature of customary international law: methods of interpreting the concept of custom in international criminal tribunals* (Routledge 2014).

Asamoah, Obed Y, *The Legal Significance of the Declaration of the General Assembly of the United Nations* (Martinus Nijhoff 1966).

Aust, Helmut Philipp, *Complicity and the law of state responsibility* (Cambridge University Press 2011).

Austin, John, *The province of jurisprudence determined* (John Murray 1832).

– *Lectures on jurisprudence. Being the sequel to "The province of jurisprudence determined", Vol II* (J Murray 1863).

Baade, Björnstjern, *Der Europäische Gerichtshof für Menschenrechte als Diskurswächter: zur Methodik, Legitimität und Rolle des Gerichtshofs im demokratisch-rechtsstaatlichen Entscheidungsprozess* (Springer 2017).

Bates, Ed, *The Evolution of the European Convention on Human Rights. From Its Inception to the Creation of a Permanent Court of Human Rights* (Oxford University Press 2010).

Bello, Andrés, *Principios De Derecho De Jentes* (Imprenta De La Opinion 1832).

– *Principios de Derecho Internacional* (2nd edn, Almacen de JM de Rojas 1847).

Bentham, Jeremy, *Of Laws in General* (Hart, Herbert LA ed, Athlone Press 1970).

– *A Comment on The Commentaries and A Fragment on Government* (Burns, James Henderson and Hart, Herbert LA eds, Athlone Press 1977).

Bergbohm, Karl, *Jurisprudenz und Rechtsphilosophie: kritische Abhandlungen* (vol 1, Duncker & Humblot 1892).

Bernstorff, Jochen von, *The public international law theory of Hans Kelsen: believing in universal law* (Dunlap, Thomas tr, Cambridge University Press 2010).

Binder, Christina, *Die Grenzen der Vertragstreue im Völkerrecht* (Springer 2013).

Binding, Karl, *Die Gründung des norddeutschen Bundes. Ein Beitrag zur Lehre von der Staatenschöpfung* (Duncker & Humblot 1889).

Bjørge, Eirik, *The evolutionary interpretation of treaties* (Oxford University Press 2014).

Blackstone, William, *Commentaries on the Laws of England* (vol 1, Oxford, 1765).

Borchard, Edwin Montefiore, *The diplomatic protection of citizens abroad* (The Banks law publishing Company 1915).

Bos, Maartens, *A methodology of international law* (North-Holland 1984).

Bower, Adam, *Norms without the great powers: international law and changing social standards in world politics* (Oxford University Press 2017).

Brie, Siegfried, *Die Lehre vom Gewohnheitsrecht: eine historisch-dogmatische Untersuchung. Theil 1: Geschichtliche Grundlegung: bis zum Ausgang des Mittelalters* (Marcus 1899).
Brierly, James Leslie, *The law of nations: an introduction to the international law of peace* (6th, ed. by Humphrey Waldock, Clarendon Press 1963).
Briggs, Herbert Whittaker, *The international Law Commission* (Cornell University Press 1965).
Brodherr, Anke, *Alfred Verdross' Theorie des gemäßigten Monismus* (Herbert Utz Verlag 2005).
Brown, Chester, *A Common Law of International Adjudication* (Oxford University Press 2007).
Brown, William Jethro, *The Austinian theory of law: being an edition of lectures I, V, and VI of Austin's "Jurisprudence," and of Austin's "Essay on the uses of the study of jurisprudence"* (Murray 1906).
Brownlie, Ian, *Principles of Public International Law* (2nd edn, 1973).
– *Principles of public international law* (3rd edn, Clarendon Press 1979).
Brunnée, Jutta and Toope, Stephen John, *Legitimacy and legality in international law: an interactional account* (Cambridge University Press 2010).
Bryde, Brun-Otto, *Verfassungsentwicklung: Stabilität und Dynamik im Verfassungsrecht der Bundesrepublik Deutschland* (Nomos 1982).
Bücheler, Gebhard, *Proportionality in investor-state arbitration* (Oxford University Press 2015).
Bulmerincq, August von, *Das Völkerrecht oder das internationale Recht* (2nd edn, Mohr 1889).
Bydlinski, Franz, *Fundamentale Rechtsgrundsätze Zur rechtsethischen Verfassung der Sozietät* (Springer 1988).
Byers, Michael, *Custom, power and the power of rules: international relations and customary international law* (Cambridge University Press 1999).
Calvo, Carlos, *Derecho Internacional teórico y práctico de Europa y América* (vol 1, D'Amyot/Durand et Pedone-Lauriel 1868).
– *Le droit international théorique et pratique; précédé d'un exposé historique des progrès de la science du droit des gens* (vol 3, A Rousseau 1896).
Canaris, Claus-Wilhelm, *Die Feststellung von Lücken im Gesetz: eine methodologische Studie über Voraussetzungen und Grenzen der richterlichen Rechtsfortbildung praeter legem* (2nd edn, Duncker und Humblot 1983).
– *Systemdenken und Systembegriff in der Jurisprudenz: entwickelt am Beispiel des deutschen Privatrechts* (2nd edn, Duncker & Humblot 1983).

Cardozo, Benjamin, *The Nature of the Judicial Process* (13th edn, Yale University Press 1946).
Cassese, Antonio, *Self-Determination of Peoples. A Legal Reappraisal* (repr., Cambridge University Press 1996).
– *International Law* (2nd edn, Oxford University Press 2005).
– *Five masters of international law: conversations with R-J Dupuy, E Jiménez de Aréchaga, R Jennings, L Henkin and O Schachter* (Hart 2011).
Antonio Cassese and Joseph HH Weiler (eds), *Change and Stability in International Law-Making* (de Gruyter 1988).
Cheng, Bin, *General Principles of Law as applied by International Courts and Tribunals* (reprint, Cambridge Grotius Publications Limited 1987).
– *Studies in International Space Law* (Oxford University Press 1997).
Clapham, Andrew, *Brierly's Law of Nations* (Oxford University Press 2012).
Coing, Helmut, *Die obersten Grundsätze des Rechts Ein Versuch zur Neugründung des Naturrechts* (Lambert Schneider 1947).
Coke, Edward, *The Second Part of the Institutes of the Laws of England* (1824).
– *The first part of the Institutes of the laws of England, or, A commentary upon Littleton: not the name of the author only, but of the law itself* (1st American, from the 19th London ed., corr, Robert H Small 1853).
Cottier, Thomas, *Equitable Principles of Maritime Boundary Delimitation: The Quest for Distributive Justice in International Law* (Cambridge University Press 2015).
Crawford, James, *State Responsibility: The General Part* (Cambridge University Press 2013).
– *Brownlie's principles of public international law* (9th edn, Oxford University Press 2019).
Cross, Rupert, *Precedent in English Law* (Clarendon Press 1961).
D'Amato, Anthony, *The Concept of Custom in International Law* (Cornell University Press 1971).
d'Aspremont, Jean, *Formalism and the Sources of International Law* (Oxford University Press 2011).
– *Epistemic forces in international law: foundational doctrines and techniques of international legal argumentation* (Edward Elgar Publishing 2015).
– *International Law as a Belief System* (Cambridge University Press 2018).
Damme, Isabelle van, *Treaty interpretation by the WTO Appellate Body* (Oxford University Press 2009).

Danilenko, Gennady M, *Law-Making in the International Community* (Martinus Nijhoff Publishers 1993).

Davis, Calvin DeArmond, *The United States and the First Hague Peace Conference* (Cornell Univ Press for the American Historical Association 1962).

Degan, Vladimir-Djuro, *L' interprétation des accords en droit international* (Nijhoff 1963).

– *Sources of International Law* (Martinus Nijhoff Publishers 1997).

Del Vecchio, Giorgio, *Die Grundprinzipien des Rechts* (Rothschild 1923).

Dicey, Albert Venn, *Introduction to the study of the law of the constitution* (Macmillan 1915).

Dickson, Brice, *Human rights and the United Kingdom Supreme Court* (Oxford University Press 2013).

Diggelmann, Oliver, *Anfänge der Völkerrechtssoziologie Die Völkerrechtskonzeptionen von Max Huber und Georges Scelle im Vergleich* (Schulthess 2000).

Dinstein, Yoram, *Non-International Armed Conflict in International Law* (Cambridge University Press 2014).

Djeffal, Christian, *Static and evolutive treaty interpretation: a functional reconstruction* (Cambridge University Press 2015).

Dolzer, Rudolf, Kriebaum, Ursula, and Schreuer, Christoph, *Principles of International Investment Law* (3rd edn, Oxford University Press 2022).

Dolzer, Rudolf and Schreuer, Christoph, *Principles of International Investment Law* (Oxford University Press 2012).

Dordeska, Marija, *General principles of law recognized by civilized nations (1922-2018). The evolution of the third source of international law through the jurisprudence of the Permanent Court of International Justice and the International Court of Justice* (Brill Nijhoff 2019).

Duguit, Léon, *Traité de Droit Constitutionnel La régle du droit: le probléme de l'Etat* (vol 1, Ancienne Libr Fontemoing 1921).

Dumberry, Patrick, *State succession to international responsibility* (Martinus Nijhoff 2007).

– *The Formation and Identification of Rules of Customary International Law in International Investment Law* (Cambridge University Press 2016).

– *Fair and Equitable Treatment. Its Interaction wit the Minimum Standard and Its Customary Status* (Brill 2018).

Dworkin, Ronald, *Taking Rights Seriously* (Harvard Univ Press 1977).

– *Law's Empire* (Harvard Univ Press 1986).

Dzehtsiarou, Kanstantsin, *European Consensus and the Legitimacy of the European Court of Human Rights* (Cambridge University Press 2015).

Eisenberg, Melvin Aron, *The Nature of the Common Law* (Harvard Univ Press 1988).

Esser, Josef, *Grundsatz und Norm in der richterlichen Fortbildung des Privatrechts Rechtsvergleichende Beiträge zur Rechtsquellen- und Interpretationslehre* (Mohr Siebeck 1956).

– *Vorverständnis und Methodenwahl in der Rechtsfindung: Rationalitätsgarantien der richterlichen Entscheidungspraxis* (Altenhäum Verlag 1970).

Farahat, Anuscheh, *Progressive Inklusion* (Springer 2014).

Feichenfeld, Ernst H, *Public Debts and State Succession* (The MacMillan Company 1931).

Fikentscher, Wolfgang, *Methoden des Rechts in Vergleichender Darstellung Frühe und Religiöse Rechte, Romanischer Rechtskreis* (vol 1, Mohr Siebeck 1975).

– *Methoden des Rechts in vergleichender Darstellung. Anglo-amerikanischer Rechtskreis* (vol 2, Mohr Siebeck 1975).

– *Methoden des Rechts in Vergleichender Darstellung Mitteleuropäischer Rechtskreis* (vol 3, Mohr Siebeck 1976).

Finch, George A, *The Sources of Modern International Law* (Carnegie Endowment for International Peace 1937).

Forlati, Serena, *The International Court of Justice An Arbitral Tribunal or a Judicial Body?* (Springer 2014).

Forowicz, Magdalena, *The Reception of International Law in the European Court of Human Rights* (Oxford University Press 2010).

Franck, Thomas M, *Fairness in International Law and Institutions* (Clarendon Press 1995).

Friedmann, Wolfgang, *The Changing Structure of international law* (Stevens 1964).

– *Legal Theory* (5th edn, Stevens & Sons 1967).

Fuller, Lon L, *The Morality of Law: Revised Edition* (Yale University Press 1969).

Galand, Alexandre Skander, *UN Security Council Referrals to the International Criminal Court* (Brill Nijhoff 2019).

García-Amador, Francisco, *The changing law of international claims* (vol 1, Oceana-Publ 1984).

García-Salmones Rovira, Mónica, *The Project of Positivism in International Law* (Oxford University Press 2013).

Gardiner, Richard K, *Treaty interpretation* (2nd, Oxford University Press 2015).

Gény, François, *Science et technique en droit privé positif: nouvelle contribution à la critique de la méthode juridique* (vol 1, Recueil Sirey 1914).

– *Méthode D'Interprétation et Sources en Droit Privé Positif: Essai Critique* (2nd edn, vol 1, Pichon et Durand_Auzias 1954).

Giddens, Anthony, *The constitution of society: outline of the theory of structuration* (Polity Press 1984).

Goldmann, Matthias, *Internationale öffentliche Gewalt* (Springer 2015).

Goldsmith, Jack L and Posner, Eric A, *The limits of international law* (Oxford University Press 2005).

Goodman, Ryan and Jinks, Derek, *Socializing states: promoting human rights through international law* (Oxford University Press 2013).

Grapin, Pierre, *Valeur internationale des principes généraux du droit: contribution à l'étude de l'article 38, § 3 du Statut de la Cour permanente de Justice internationale* (Domat-Montchrestien 1934).

Gray, John Chipman, *The Nature and Sources of the Law* (2nd edn, The MacMillan Company 1931).

Greenawalt, Kent, *Statutory and Common Law Interpretation* (Oxford University Press 2012).

Greenhill, Brian, *Transmitting Rights: International Organizations and the Diffusion of Human Rights Practices* (Oxford University Press 2015).

Grimm, Dieter, *Solidarität als Rechtsprinzip: Die Rechts- und Staatslehre Léon Duguits in ihrer Zeit* (Altenhäum Verlag 1973).

Grover, Leena, *Interpreting Crimes in the Rome Statute of the International Criminal Court* (Cambridge University Press 2014).

Guggenheim, Paul, *Lehrbuch des Völkerrechts: unter Berücksichtigung der internationalen und schweizerischen Praxis* (vol 1, Verlag für Recht und Gesellschaft 1948).

– *Traité de droit international public: avec mention de la pratique internationale et suisse* (vol 1, Georg 1953).

– *Traité de droit international public: avec mention de la pratique internationale et suisse* (2nd edn, vol 1, Georg 1967).

Günther, Herbert, *Zur Entstehung von Völkergewohnheitsrecht* (Duncker & Humblot 1970).

Guzman, Andrew T, *How international law works: a rational choice theory* (Oxford University Press 2008).

Habermas, Jürgen, *Faktizität und Geltung: Beiträge zur Diskurstheorie des Rechts und des demokratischen Rechtsstaats* (Suhrkamp 1992).

Habermas, Jürgen, *Between Facts and Norms. Contributions to a Discourse Theory of Law and Democracy* (Rehg, William tr, 2nd edn, MIT Press 1996).

Hackworth, Green Haywood, *Digest of International Law* (vol III, Department of State 1942).

Hale, Matthew, *The history of the common law of England ; and, An analysis of the civil part of the law* (6th edn, Henry Butterworth 1820).

Hall, William Edward, *Treatise on International Law* (4th edn, Clarendon Press 1895).

Härle, Elfried, *Die allgemeinen Entscheidungsgrundlagen des Ständigen Internationalen Gerichtshofes: eine kritisch-würdigende Untersuchung über Artikel 38 des Gerichtshof-Statuts* (Vahlen 1933).

Hart, Herbert L, *The concept of law: With a postscript* (2nd edn, Clarendon Press 1994).

Harten, Gus van, *Investment Treaty Arbitration and Public Law* (Oxford University Press 2008).

Heffter, August Wilhelm, *Das Europäische Völkerrecht der Gegenwart auf den bisherigen Grundlagen* (vol 5, first publ. 1844, Schroeder 1867).

Heilborn, Paul, *Das System des Völkerrechts entwickelt aus den völkerrechtlichen Begriffen* (Verlag von Julius Springer 1896).

Heller, Hermann, *Die Souveränität: ein Beitrag zur Theorie des Staats- und Völkerrechts* (de Gruyter 1927).

Heller, Kevin Jon, *The Nuremberg Military Tribunals and the Origins of International Criminal Law* (Oxford University Press 2011).

Henckaerts, Jean-Marie and Doswald-Beck, Louise, *Customary International Humanitarian Law: Rules* (vol 1, Cambridge University Press 2005).

Herczegh, Géza, *General Principles of Law and the International Legal Order* (Kiadó 1969).

Hesse, Konrad, *Grundzüge des Verfassungsrechts der Bundesrepublik Deutschland* (20th edn, Müller 1999).

Higgins, Rosalyn, *Problems and Process: International Law and How We Use It* (Clarendon Press 1995).

Ho, Jean, *State Responsibility for Breaches of Investment Contracts* (Cambridge University Press 2018).

Hobbes, Thomas, *Hobbes's Leviathan: reprinted from the edition of 1651* (Clarendon Press 1909).

Holland, Thomas Erskine, *The elements of jurisprudence* (Clarendon Press 1916).

Hoof, Godefridus Josephus Henricus van, *Rethinking the sources of international law* (Kluwer Law and Taxation Publ 1983).

Huber, Max, *Die Staatensuccession. Völkerrechtliche und staatsrechtliche Praxis im XIX. Jahrhundert* (Duncker & Humblot 1898).

Hudson, Manley O, *The Permanent Court of International Justice 1920-1942: a treatise* (Macmillan 1943).

Hull, William Isaac, *The two Hague conferences and their contributions to international law* (repr. orig. publ. 1908, Kraus 1970).

ICRC, *Commentary on the First Geneva Convention (2016)* (Cambridge University Press 2017).

Jacoby, Sigrid, *Allgemeine Rechtsgrundsätze Begriffsentwicklung und Funktion in der Europäischen Rechtsgeschichte* (Duncker & Humblot 1996).

Jakab, András, *European Constitutional Language* (Cambridge University Press 2016).

Jansen, Nils, *The Making of Legal Authority: Non-legislative Codifications in Historical and Comparative Perspective* (Oxford University Press 2010).

Jellinek, Georg, *Die rechtliche Natur der Staatenverträge: ein Beitrag zur juristischen Construction des Völkerrechts* (Hölder 1880).

– *Verfassungsänderung und Verfassungswandlung Eine staatsrechtlich-politische Abhandlung* (Verlag von O Häring 1906).

Jenks, Clarence Wilfred, *The common law of mankind* (Stevens 1958).

– *The Proper Law of International Organizations* (Stevens & Sons 1962).

– *The Prospects of International Adjudication* (Stevens 1964).

Jennings, Robert Yewdall and Watts, Arthur, *Oppenheim's International Law: Volume 1 Peace* (9th edn, Oxford University Press 2008).

Jessup, Philip C, *Transnational Law* (Yale University Press 1956).

– *A modern law of nations: An introduction* (Archon books, reprint 1968).

Jestaedt, Matthias, *Grundrechtsentfaltung im Gesetz* (Mohr Siebeck 1999).

Jhering, Rudolf von, *Geist des römischen Rechts auf den verschiedenen Stufen seiner Entwicklung Erster Theil* (2nd ed., Breitkopf und Härtel 1866).

– *Geist des römischen Rechts auf den verschiedenen Stufen seiner Entwicklung Zweiter Theil* (3rd ed., Breitkopf und Härtel 1866).

– *Der Zweck im Recht* (Breitkopf und Härtel 1877).

Kälin, Walter and Künzli, Jörg, *The Law of International Human Rights Protection* (2nd edn, Oxford University Press 2019).

Kammerhofer, Jörg, *Uncertainty in international law: a Kelsenian perspective* (Routledge 2011).

– *International investment law and legal theory: expropriation and the fragmentation of sources* (Cambridge University Press 2021).

Karl, Wolfram, *Vertrag und spätere Praxis im Völkerrecht: zum Einfluß der Praxis auf Inhalt und Bestand völkerrechtlicher Verträge* (Springer 1983).

Keller-Kemmerer, Nina, *Die Mimikry des Völkerrechts: Andrés Bellos "Principios de Derecho Internacional"* (Nomos 2018).

Kelsen, Hans, *Das Problem der Souveränität und die Theorie des Völkerrechts Beitrag zu einer reinen Rechtslehre* (Mohr Siebeck 1920).

– *Allgemeine Staatslehre* (Springer 1925).

– *Legal Technique in international law: a textual critique of the League Covenant* (Geneva Research Centre 1939).

– *The Law of The United Nations A Critical Analysis of Its Fundamental Problems* (Stevens 1950).

– *Principles of International Law* (Rinehart 1952).

– *Reine Rechtslehre* (2, orig. publ. 1969, Verlag Franz Deuticke 1967).

– *Allgemeine Theorie der Normen* (Manz 1979).

– *On the issue of the continental shelf: two legal opinions* (Springer 1986).

– *Auseinandersetzungen zur reinen Rechtslehre: kritische Bemerkungen zu Georges Scelle und Michel Virally* (Ringhofer, Kurt and Walter, Robert eds, Springer 1987).

– *General Theory of Norms* (Clarendon Press 1991).

– *Reine Rechtslehre Studienausgabe der 1. Auflage 1934* (Jestaedt, Matthias ed, Mohr Siebeck 2008).

Kelsen, Hans and Tucker, Robert W, *Principles of International Law* (2nd edn, Holt, Rinehart, Winston, 1967).

Kischel, Uwe, *Comparative Law* (Oxford University Press 2019).

Kiss, Alexandre-Charles, *L' abus de droit en droit international* (Pichon & Durand-Auzias 1953).

Kjos, Elisabeth, *Applicable law in investor-state arbitration: the interplay between national and international law* (Oxford University Press 2013).

Kläger, Roland, *'Fair and equitable treatment' in international investment law* (Cambridge University Press 2011).

Eckart Klein (ed), *Menschenrechtsschutz durch Gewohnheitsrecht: Kolloquium 26.-28. September 2002 Potsdam* (Berlin, 2003).

Kleinlein, Thomas, *Konstitutionalisierung im Völkerrecht Konstruktion und Elemente einer idealistischen Völkerrechtslehre* (Springer 2012).

Knop, Karen, *Diversity and Self-Determination in International Law* (Cambridge University Press 2002).

Kolb, Robert, *La bonne foi en droit international public Contribution à l'étude des principes généraux de droit* (Presses Universitaires de France 2000).

- *Case law on equitable maritime delimitation: digest and commentaries = Jurisprudence sur les délimitations maritimes selon l'équité: répertoire et commentaires* (Perry, Alan tr, Martinus Nijhof Publishers 2003).
- *Interprétation et création du droit international. Esquisse d'une herméneutique juridique moderne pour le droit international public* (Bruylant 2006).
- *The International Court of Justice* (Perry, Alan tr, Hart 2013).
- *Peremptory international law - jus cogens: a general inventory* (Hart 2015).
- *Theory of international law* (Hart Publishing 2016).
- *Good Faith in international law* (Hart 2017).
- *The International Law of State Responsibility* (Edward Elgar Publishing 2017).

Kontou, Nancy, *The Termination and Revision of Treaties in the Light of New Customary International Law* (Clarendon Press 1994).

Korioth, Stefan, *Integration und Bundesstaat Ein Beitrag zur Staats- und Verfassungslehre Rudolf Smends* (Duncker & Humblot 1990).

Koskenniemi, Martti, *The Gentle Civilizer of Nations The Rise and Fall of International Law 1870-1960* (Cambridge University Press 2002).
- *From Apology to Utopia: The Structure of International Legal Argument - Reissue With New Epologue* (2nd edn, Cambridge University Press 2007).

Kriele, Martin, *Theorie der Rechtsgewinnung entwickelt am Problem der Verfassungsinterpretation* (Duncker & Humblot 1967).

Krisch, Nico, *Beyond Constitutionalism The Pluralist Structure of Postnational Law* (Oxford University Press 2010).

Kroll, Stefan, *Normgenese durch Re-Interpretation: China und das europäische Völkerrecht im 19. und 20. Jahrhundert* (Nomos 2012).

Krueger, Anna, *Die Bindung der Dritten Welt an das postkoloniale Völkerrecht: die Völkerrechtskommission, das Recht der Verträge und das Recht der Staatennachfolge in der Dekolonialisierung* (Springer 2018).

Kulick, Andreas, *Global public interest in international investment law* (Cambridge University Press 2012).

Küntzel, Walter, *Ungeschriebenes Völkerrecht Ein Beitrag zu der Lehre von den Quellen des Völkerrechts* (Gräfe u Unzer 1935).

Laband, Paul, *Die Wandlungen der deutschen Reichsverfassung* (Zahn & Jaensch 1895).

Lachs, Manfred, *The Teacher in International Law: Teachings and Teaching* (2nd edn, Martinus Nijhof Publishers 1987).

Lando, Massimo, *Maritime Delimitation as a Judicial Process* (Cambridge University Press 2019).

Larenz, Karl, *Methodenlehre der Rechtswissenschaft* (3rd edn, Springer 1975).
– *Methodenlehre der Rechtswissenschaft* (6th edn, Springer 1991).
Lauterpacht, Hersch, *Private Law Analogies* (London, 1927).
– *The development of international law by the International Court* (Stevens 1958).
– *The Function of Law in the International Community* (Reprinted with corr., first publ. 1933, Oxford University Press 2012).
Lawrence, Thomas Joseph, *International Problems and Hague Conferences* (London, 1906).
Legg, Andrew, *The Margin of Appreciation in International Human Rights Law: Deference and Proportionality* (Oxford University Press 2012).
Lepard, Brian D, *Customary International Law A New Theory with Practical applications* (Cambridge University Press 2010).
Lepsius, Oliver, *Verwaltungsrecht unter dem Common Law: amerikanische Entwicklungen bis zum New Deal* (Mohr Siebeck 1997).
– *Relationen: Plädoyer für eine bessere Rechtswissenschaft* (Mohr Siebeck 2016).
Letsas, George, *A theory of interpretation of the European Convention on Human Rights* (Oxford University Press 2007).
Lieberman, David, *The province of legislation determined: legal theory in eighteenth century Britain* (Cambridge University Press 2002).
MacCormick, Neil, *Legal Reasoning and Legal Theory* (Clarendon Press, Oxford University Press 1978).
– *Legal Reasoning and Legal Theory* (Clarendon Press, Oxford University Press 1978).
Magnússon, Bjarni Már, *The Continental Shelf Beyond 200 Nautical Miles* (Brill Nijhoff 2015).
Mälksoo, Lauri, *Russian approaches to international law* (Oxford University Press 2015).
Mann, Francis A, *The legal aspect of money* (4th edn, Clarendon Press 1982).
Markun, Michael, *Law without Sanctions Order in Primitive Societies and the World Community* (Yale University Press 1968).
Marro, Pierre-Yves, *Allgemeine Rechtsgrundsätze des Völkerrechts* (Schulthess 2010).
Martini, Stefan, *Vergleichende Verfassungsrechtsprechung: Praxis, Viabilität und Begründung rechtsvergleichender Argumentation durch Verfassungsgerichte* (Duncker & Humblot 2018).

Marxsen, Christian, *Völkerrechtsordnung und Völkerrechtsbruch* (Mohr Siebeck 2021).

Mayda, Jaro, *Francois Gény and Modern Jurisprudence* (Louisiana State University Press 1978).

McLachlan, Campbell, Shore, Laurence, and Weiniger, Matthew, *International Investment Arbitration* (2nd edn, Oxford University Press 2017).

Meder, Stephan, *Ius non scriptum - Traditionen privater Rechtssetzung* (2nd edn, Mohr Siebeck 2009).

Meier, Ernst, *Über den Abschluss von Staatsverträgen* (Duncker & Humblot 1874).

Merkl, Adolf, *Die Lehre von der Rechtskraft entwickelt aus dem Rechtsbegriff* (Franz Deuticke 1923).

Merkouris, Panos, *Article 31(3)(c) vclt and the Principle of Systemic Integration* (Brill Nijhoff 2015).

Meron, Theodor, *Human Rights and Humanitarian Norms as Customary Law* (Clarendon Press 1989).

Mettraux, Guénaël, *International Crimes and the ad hoc Tribunals* (Oxford University Press 2005).

Metzger, Axel, *Extra legem, intra ius: allgemeine Rechtsgrundsätze im Europäischen Privatrecht* (Mohr Siebeck 2009).

Meyer, Georg and Anschütz, Gerhard, *Lehrbuch des Deutschen Staatsrechtes* (6th edn, Duncker & Humblot 1905).

Miller, David Hunter, *The Drafting of the Covenant* (2, orig. published 1928, Vol 2, New York, 1969).

Montt, Santiago, *State Liability in Investment Treaty Arbitration. Global Constitutional and Administrative Law on the BIT Generation* (Hart Publishing 2009).

Mossop, Joanna, *The Continental Shelf Beyond 200 Nautical Miles: Rights and Responsibilities* (Oxford University Press 2016).

Mugdan, Benno, *Die gesammten Materialien zum Bürgerlichen Gesetzbuch für das Deutsche Reich. Einführungsgesetz und Allgemeiner Theil* (vol 1, Decker's Verlag 1899).

Müller, Jörg P, *Vertrauensschutz im Völkerrecht* (Carl Heymanns Verlag KG 1971).

Nielsen, Fred K, *American-Turkish Claims Settlement: Under the Agreement of December 24, 1923, and Supplemental Agreements between the United States and Turkey* (Government Printing Office 1937).

Nippold, Otto, *Der völkerrechtliche Vertrag Seine Stellung im Rechtssystem und seine Bedeutung für das internationale Recht* (1894).

Nowrot, Karsten, *Das Republikprinzip in der Rechtsordnungengemeinschaft* (Mohr Siebeck 2014).
Ohlin, Jens David, *The assault on international law* (Oxford University Press 2015).
Onuf, Nicholas, *Law-making in the global community* (Carolina Acad Press 1982).
Oppenheim, Lassa Francis Lawrence, *International Law* (vol 1, Longmans, Green 1905).
Orakhelashvili, Alexander, *Peremptory norms in international law* (Oxford University Press 2008).
– *The Interpretation of Acts and Rules in Public International Law* (Oxford University Press 2008).
Paddeu, Federica, *Justification and Excuse in International Law* (Cambridge University Press 2018).
Pallieri, Giorgio Balladore, *I "principi generali del diritto riconosciuti dalle nazioni civili" nell' art. 38 dello statuto della Corte permanente di giustizia internazionale* (Istituto giuridico della R università 1931).
Paparinskis, Mārtiņš, *The international minimum standard and fair and equitable treatment* (Oxford monographs in international law, Oxford University Press 2013).
Park, Jeong Hoon, *Rechtsfindung im Verwaltungsrecht: Grundlegung einer Prinzipientheorie des Verwaltungsrechts als Methode der Verwaltungsrechtsdogmatik* (Duncker & Humblot 1999).
Paulsson, Jan, *Denial of Justice in international law* (Cambridge University Press 2005).
Paulus, Andreas L, *Die internationale Gemeinschaft im Völkerrecht: eine Untersuchung zur Entwicklung des Völkerrechts im Zeitalter der Globalisierung* (Beck 2001).
Payandeh, Mehrdad, *Internationales Gemeinschaftsrecht: zur Herausbildung gemeinschaftsrechtlicher Strukturen im Völkerrecht der Globalisierung* (Springer 2010).
Peat, Daniel, *Comparative Reasoning in International Courts and Tribunals* (Cambridge University Press 2019).
Peters, Anne, *Beyond Human Rights. The Legal Status of the Individual in International Law* (Cambridge University Press 2016).
Petersen, Niels, *Demokratie als teleologisches Prinzip: zur Legitimität von Staatsgewalt im Völkerrecht* (Springer 2009).
Phillimore, Robert, *Commentaries upon international law* (vol 1, T & J W Johnson, Law Booksellers 1854).

Pieroth, Bodo, *Rückwirkung und Übergangsrecht Verfassungsrechtliche Maßstäbe für intertemporale Gesetzgebung* (Duncker & Humblot 1981).

Politis, Nicolas, *The new aspects of international law: A Series of Lectures Delivered at Columbia University in July 1926* (Carnegie Endowment for International Peace 1928).

Postema, Gerald J, *Bentham and the Common Law Tradition* (Clarendon Press 1986).

Pound, Roscoe, *Jurisprudence Part 3. The Nature of Law* (vol 2, West 1959).

Powderly, Joseph, *Judges and the Making of International Criminal Law* (Brill Nijhoff 2020).

Puchta, Georg Friedrich, *Das Gewohnheitsrecht. Erster Theil* (Palm 1828).

– *Das Gewohnheitsrecht. Zweiter Theil* (Palm 1837).

Pulkowski, Dirk, *The Law and Politics of International Regime Conflict* (Oxford University Press 2014).

Purcell, Kate, *Geographical Change and the Law of the Sea* (Oxford University Press 2019).

Raimondo, Fabián Omar, *General principles of law in the decisions of international criminal courts and tribunals* (Martinus Nijhoff Publishers 2008).

Ranganathan, Surabhi, *Strategically Created Treaty Conflicts and the Politics of International Law* (Cambridge University Press 2014).

Rauber, Jochen, *Strukturwandel als Prinzipienwandel: theoretische, dogmatische und methodische Bausteine eines Prinzipienmodells des Völkerrechts und seiner Dynamik* (Springer 2018).

Reimer, Franz, *Verfassungsprinzipien Ein Normtyp im Grundgesetz* (Duncker & Humblot 2001).

Thomas Risse, Stephen C Ropp, and Kathryn Sikkink (eds), *The power of human rights: international norms and domestic change* (Cambridge University Press 1999).

Riznik, Donald, *Die Immunität ratione personae des Souveräns* (PL Academic Research 2016).

Roberts, Anthea, *Is International Law international?* (Oxford University Press 2017).

Shabtai Rosenne (ed), *League of Nations Conference for the Codification of International Law (1930)* (vol 4, Dobbs Ferry, NY: Oceana 1975).

Rosenne, Shabtai, *Breach of Treaty* (Cambridge University Press 1985).

– *The World Court: what it is and how it works* (4th edn, Nijhoff 1989).

– *The Law and Practice of the International Court 1920-2005* (4th edn, vol 2, Martinus Nijhof Publishers 2006).

Ross, Alf, *Theorie der Rechtsquellen: ein Beitrag zur Theorie des positiven Rechts auf Grundlage dogmenhistorischer Untersuchungen* (Deuticke 1929).
– *A Textbook of International Law: General Part, originally published 1947* (2nd edn, The LawBook Exchange 2008).
Roulet, Jean David, *Le caractère artificiel de la théorie de l'abus de droit en droit international public* (Ed de la Baconnière 1958).
Rousseau, Charles, *Principes généraux du droit international public. Introduction. Sources* (vol 1, Pedone 1944).
Roxburgh, Ronald F, *International conventions and third states* (Longman, Green and Co 1917).
Roxin, Claus, *Strafrecht Allgemeiner Teil Band II Besondere Erscheinungsformen der Straftat* (vol 2, Beck 2003).
Ruddy, Francis S, *International law in the enlightenment: the background of Emmerich de Vattel's Le droit des gens* (Oceana-Publ 1975).
Rüthers, Bernd, *Die unbegrenzte Auslegung* (8th edn, Mohr Siebeck 2017).
Salmond, John William, *Jurisprudence* (4th edn, Stevens 1913).
Sassòli, Marco, *Bedeutung einer Kodifikation für das allgemeine Völkerrecht: mit besonderer Betrachtung der Regeln zum Schutze der Zivilbevölkerung vor den Auswirkungen von Feindseligkeiten* (Helbing & Lichtenhahn 1990).
Saunders, Imogen, *General Principles as a Source of International Law* (Hart 2021).
Savigny, Friedrich Carl von, *System des heutigen Römischen Rechts* (vol 1, Veit 1840).
– *Pandektenvorlesung 1824/25* (Klostermann 1993).
– *Vom Beruf unsrer Zeit für Gesetzgebung und Rechtswissenschaft* (Mohr und Zimmer 1814).
Schabas, William A, *The International Criminal Court* (2nd edn, Oxford University Press 2016).
– *An Introduction to the International Criminal Court* (6th edn, Cambridge University Press 2020).
Schachter, Oscar, *International law in theory and practice: general course in public international law* (Martinus Nijhoff Publishers 1991).
Scharf, Michael P, *Customary International Law in Times of Fundamental Change Recognizing Grotian Moments* (Cambridge University Press 2013).
Schill, Stephan W, *The multilateralization of international investment law* (Cambridge University Press 2009).

Schlesinger, Rudolf B and Bonassies, Pierre, *Formation of contracts: a study of the common core of legal systems; conductes under the auspices of the general principles of law project of the Cornell Law School* (vol 1, Oceana-Publ 1968).

Schlütter, Birgit, *Developments in customary international law: theory and the practice of the International Court of Justice and the International ad hoc Criminal Tribunals for Rwanda and Yugoslavia* (Martinus Nijhoff Publishers 2010).

Schmitt, Michael N, *Essays on Law and War at the Fault Lines* (Springer 2012).

Schröder, Jan, *Recht als Wissenschaft: Geschichte der juristischen Methode vom Humanismus bis zur historischen Schule (1500-1850)* (Beck 2001).

Schücking, Walter, *Der Staatenverband der Haager Konferenzen* (Duncker & Humblot 1912).

Schwarzenberger, Georg, *William Ladd: An examination of an American proposal for an international equity tribunal* (2nd edn, London, 1936).

– *The Frontiers of International Law* (Stevens & Sons 1962).

Shahabuddeen, Mohamed, *International Criminal Justice at the Yugoslav Tribunal: A Judge's Recollection* (Oxford University Press 2012).

Shahabuddeen, Mohammed, *Precedent in the world court* (Cambridge University Press 1997).

Shaw, Malcolm N, *International Law* (7th edn, Cambridge University Press 2014).

Simma, Bruno, *Das Reziprozitätselement in der Entstehung des Völkergewohnheitsrechts* (Fink 1970).

Simmons, Beth A, *Mobilizing for Human Rights International Law in Domestic Politics* (Cambridge University Press 2009).

Sinclair, Ian, *The International Law Commission* (Cambridge, 1987).

Sivakumaran, Sandesh, *The law of non-international armed conflict* (Oxford University Press 2012).

Skouteris, Thomas, *The notion of progress in international law discourse* (TMC Asser Press 2010).

Sliedregt, Elies van, *Individual criminal responsibility in international law* (Oxford University Press 2012).

Somló, Félix, *Juristische Grundlehre* (Meiner 1917).

Sørensen, Max, *Les sources du droit international: étude sur la jurisprudence de la Cour Permanente de Justice Internationale* (Munksgaard 1946).

Sornarajah, Muthucumaraswamy, *Resistance and Change in the International Law on Foreign Investment* (Cambridge University Press 2015).

Spiermann, Ole, *International legal argument in the Permanent Court of International Justice: the rise of the international judiciary* (Cambridge University Press 2005).

Spiropoulos, Jean, *Die allgemeinen Rechtsgrundsätze im Völkerrecht: eine Auslegung von Art. 38,3 des Status des ständigen Internationalen Gerichtshofs* (Verlag des Instituts für Internationales Recht an der Univ Kiel 1928).

– *Théorie générale du droit international* (Pichon et Durand-Auzias 1930).

Stahn, Carsten, *A Critical Introduction to International Criminal Law* (Cambridge University Press 2019).

Staubach, Peter G, *The Rule of Unwritten International Law: Customary Law, General Principles, and World Order* (Routledge 2018).

Stoll, Peter-Tobias, Holterhus, Till Patrik, and Gött, Henner, *Investitionsschutz und Verfassung: völkerrechtliche Investitionsschutzverträge aus der Perspektive des deutschen und europäischen Verfassungsrechts* (Mohr Siebeck 2017).

Stolleis, Michael, *A History of Public Law in Germany 1914-1945* (Oxford University Press 2004).

Strupp, Karl, *Das Recht des internationalen Richters, nach Billigkeit zu entscheiden* (Noske 1930).

Tams, Christian J, *Enforcing Obligations Erga Omnes in International Law* (Cambridge University Press 2005).

Tan, Yudan, *The Rome Statute as Evidence of Customary International Law* (Brill Nijhoff 2021).

Thienel, Tobias, *Drittstaaten und die Jurisdiktion des Internationalen Gerichtshofs: die Monetary Gold-Doktrin* (Duncker & Humblot 2016).

Thirlway, Hugh W, *International Customary Law and Codification: an examination of the continuing role of custom in the present period of codification of international law* (Leiden: Sijthoff, 1972).

– *The law and procedure of the international court of justice: fifty years of jurisprudence* (vol 1, Oxford University Press 2013).

– *The law and procedure of the international court of justice: fifty years of jurisprudence* (vol 2, Oxford University Press 2013).

– *The Sources of International Law* (Oxford University Press 2014).

– *The sources of international law* (2nd edn, Oxford University Press 2019).

Tomuschat, Christian, *Verfassungsgewohnheitsrecht? Eine Untersuchung zum Staatsrecht der Bundesrepublik Deutschland* (Heidelberg, 1972).

Triepel, Heinrich, *Die neuesten Fortschritte auf dem Gebiet des Kriegsrechts* (C L Hirschfeld 1894).

- *Völkerrecht und Landesrecht* (Hirschfeld 1899).
Tudor, Ioana, *The Fair and Equitable Treatment Standard in the International Law of Foreign Investment* (Oxford University Press 2008).
Vadi, Valentina, *War and Peace. Alberico Gentili and the Early Modern Law of Nations* (Brill Nijhoff 2020).
Vanneste, Frédéric, *General International Law Before Human Rights Courts - Assessing the Speciality Claim of International Human Rights Law* (Intersentia 2009).
Vattel, Emer de, *The Law of Nations; or Principles of the Law of Nature, applied to the conduct and affairs of nations and sovereigns* (6th American edition, TJW Johnson 1844).
Venzke, Ingo, *How interpretation makes international law: on semantic change and normative twists* (Oxford University Press 2012).
Verdross, Alfred, *Die völkerrechtswidrige Kriegshandlung und der Strafanspruch der Staaten* (Hans Robert Engelmann 1920).
- *Die Einheit des rechtlichen Weltbildes auf Grundlage der Völkerrechtsverfassung* (Mohr Siebeck 1923).
- *Die Verfassung der Völkerrechtsgemeinschaft* (Springer 1926).
Verdross, Alfred and Simma, Bruno, *Universelles Völkerrecht Theorie und Praxis* (3rd edn, Duncker&Humblot 1984).
Verzijl, Jan Hendrik Willem, *International Law in Historical Perspective. General Subjects* (vol 1, AW Sijthoff 1968).
Viellechner, Lars, *Transnationalisierung des Rechts* (Velbrück 2013).
Villiger, Mark E, *Customary International Law and Treaties* (Martinus Nijhof Publishers 1985).
- *Customary International Law and Treaties* (2nd edn, Kluwer Law International 1997).
Visscher, Charles de, *Theory and reality in public international law* (Corbett, Percy Ellwood tr, Princeton University Press 1957).
- *Problèmes d'interprétation judiciaire en droit international public* (Pedone 1963).
Vogenauer, Stefan, *Die Auslegung von Gesetzen in England und auf dem Kontinent Eine vergleichende Untersuchung der Rechtsprechung und ihrer historischen Grundlagen* (Beiträge zum ausländischen und internationalen Privatrecht 72, vol 1, Mohr Siebeck 2001).
Voigt, Christina, *Sustainable Development as a Principle of International Law Resolving Conflicts between Climate Measures and Law* (Martinus Nijhoff Publishers 2009).

Watts, Arthur, *The International Law Commission 1949-1998: The Treaties* (vol 1, Oxford University Press 1999).

Weber, Ferdinand, *Staatsangehörigkeit und Status: Statik und Dynamik politischer Gemeinschaftsbildung* (Mohr Siebeck 2018).

Werle, Gerhard and Jeßberger, Florian, *Principles of International Criminal Law* (4th edn, Oxford University Press 2020).

Westlake, John, *Chapters on the Principles of International Law* (University Press 1894).

– *International Law Part I* (2nd edn, Cambridge University Press 1910).

Wheaton, Henry, *Elements of International Law: with a Sketch of the History of the Science* (Carey, Lea & Blanchard 1836).

Windscheid, Bernhard, *Lehrbuch des Pandektenrechts* (4th edn, vol 1, Buddeus 1875).

Wolff, Christian von, *Jus gentium methodo scientifica pertractatum* (vol 2, Clarendon Press 1934).

Wolff, Heinrich Amadeus, *Ungeschriebenes Verfassungsrecht unter dem Grundgesetz* (Mohr Siebeck 2000).

Wolfke, Karol, *Custom in present international law* (Zaklad Narodowy im Ossolínskich 1964).

Yanev, Lachezar D, *Theories of Co-Perpetration in International Criminal Law* (Brill Nijhoff 2018).

Yasuaki, Onuma, *International Law in a Transcivilizational World* (Cambridge University Press 2017).

Zimmermann, Andreas, *Staatennachfolge in völkerrechtliche Verträge: zugleich ein Beitrag zu den Möglichkeiten und Grenzen völkerrechtlicher Kodifikation* (Springer 2000).

Zimmern, Alfred, *The League of Nations and the Rule of Law 1918-1935* (Macmillan 1936).

Contributions to edited volumes

Abi-Saab, Georges, 'The Concept of "War Crimes"' in Sienho Yee and Tieya Wang (eds), *International Law in the Post-Cold War World : Essays in Memory of Li Haopei* (Routledge 2001), pp 99–118.

- 'La coutume dans tous ses états ou le dilemme du développement du droit international général dans un monde éclaté', in Marcelo G Kohen and Magnus Jesko Langer (eds), *Le développement du droit international: réflexions d'un demi-siècle* (Presses Universitaires de France 2013) vol 1, pp 81–92.
- 'Les sources du droit international: essai de déconstruction', in Marcelo G Kohen and Magnus Jesko Langer (eds), *Le développement du droit international: réflexions d'un demi-siècle. Volume I* (Graduate Institute Publications 2013), pp 61–80.

Akande, Dapo, 'Sources of International Criminal Law' in Antonio Cassese (ed), *The Oxford Companion to International Criminal Justice* (Oxford University Press 2009), pp 41–53.

Alebeek, Rosanne van, 'Functional Immunity of State Officials from the Criminal Jurisdiction of Foreign National Courts' in Tom Ruys, Nicolas Angelet, and Luca Ferro (eds), *The Cambridge Handbook of Immunities and International Law* (Cambridge University Press 2019), pp 496–524.

Alvarez, José E, 'The Use (and Misuse) of European Human Rights Law in Investor-State Dispute Settlement' in Franco Ferrari (ed), *The impact of EU law on international commercial arbitration* (JurisNet 2017), pp 519–648.

Ambos, Kai, 'Command Responsibility and Organisationsherrschaft: Ways of Attributing International Crimes to the Most Responsible' in Harmen van der Wilt and André Nollkaemper (eds), *System criminality in international law* (Cambridge University Press 2009), pp 127–157.
- 'Adolf Eichmann', in *The Cambridge Companion to International Criminal Law* (Cambridge University Press 2016), pp 275–294.
- 'Article 25', in Kai Ambos (ed), *Rome Statute of the International Criminal Court: a commentary* (4th edn, Beck 2021).

Andenæs, Mads and Chiussi, Ludovica, 'Cohesion, Convergence and Coherence of International Law' in Mads Andenæs and others (eds), *General principles and the coherence of international law* (Brill Nijhoff 2019), pp 9–34.

Arajärvi, Noora, 'Misinterpreting Customary International Law Corrupt Pedigree or Self-Fulfilling Prophecy?' in Panos Merkouris, Jörg Kammerhofer, and Noora Arajärvi (eds), *The Theory, Practice, and Interpretation of Customary International Law* (Cambridge University Press 2022), pp 40–61.

Aust, Helmut Philipp, 'The Normative Environment for Peace - On the Contribution of the ILC's Articles on State Responsibility' in Georg Nolte (ed), *Peace through International Law The Role of the International Law Commission. A Colloquium at the Occasion of its Sixtieth Anniversary* (Springer 2009), pp 13–46.

Badura, Peter, 'Verfassungsänderung, Verfassungswandel, Verfassungsgewohnheitsrecht' in Josef Isensee and Paul Kirchhof (eds), *Handbuch des Staatsrechts der Bundesrepublik Deutschland* (CF Müller 1992) vol VII, pp 57–77.

Bartels, Rogier, 'Legitimacy and ICC Jurisdiction Following Security Council Referrals: Conduct on the Territory of Non-Party States and the Legality Principle' in Nobuo Hayashi and Cecilia M Bailliet (eds), *The Legitimacy of International Criminal Tribunals* (Cambridge University Press 2017), pp 141–178.

Baxter, Richard R, 'The Effects of Ill-Conceived Codification and Development of International Law' in Faculté de Droit de l'Université de Genève (ed), *En Hommage à Paul Guggenheim* (Faculté de Droit de l'Université de Genève 1968), pp 146–166.

Becker Lorca, Arnulf, 'Eurocentrism in the History of International Law' in Bardo Fassbender and Anne Peters (eds), *The Oxford Handbook of the History of International Law* (Oxford University Press 2012), pp 1034–1057.

Benvenisti, Eyal, 'Customary International Law as a Judicial Tool for Promoting Efficiency' in Moshe Hirsch and Eyal Benvenisti (eds), *The impact of international law on international cooperation: theoretical perspectives* (Cambridge University Press 2004), pp 85–116.

Bernhard, Rudolf, 'Interpretation in International Law' in *Encyclopedia of public international law. East African Community to Italy-United States Air Transport Arbitration (1965): [E - I]* (North-Holland 1995) vol 2, pp 1416–1425.

Bernstorff, Jochen von, 'Specialized Courts and Tribunals as the Guardians of International Law? The Nature and Function of Judicial Interpretation in Kelsen and Schmitt' in Andreas Føllesdal and Geir Ulfstein (eds), *The judicialization of international law: a mixed blessing?* (Oxford University Press 2018), pp 9–25.

Besson, Samantha, 'Theorizing the Sources of International Law' in Samantha Besson and John Tasioulas (eds), *The Philosophy of International Law* (Oxford University Press 2010), pp 163–185.

– 'General Principles in International Law - Whose Principles?', in *Les principes en droit européen = Principles in European law* (Schulthess 2011), pp 19–64.

- 'Community Interests in the Identification of International Law With a Special Emphasis on Treaty Interpretation and Customary Law Identification', in Eyal Benvenisti and Georg Nolte (eds), *Community Interests across international law* (Oxford University Press 2018), pp 50–69.
- 'Concurrent Responsibilities under the European Convention on Human Rights: the Concurrence of Human Rights Jurisdictions, Duties, and Responsibilities', in Anne van Aaken and Iulia Motoc (eds), *The European Convention on Human Rights and general international law* (Oxford University Press 2018), pp 155–177.

Bitti, Gilbert, 'Article 21 and the Hierarchy of Sources of Law before the ICC' in Carsten Stahn (ed), *The law and practice of the International Criminal Court* (Oxford University Press 2015), pp 411–443.

Bjorklund, Andrea K, 'Emergency Exceptions: State of Necessity and Force Majeure' in Peter Muchlinski, Frederico Ortino, and Christoph Schreuer (eds), *The Oxford handbook of international investment law* (Oxford University Press 2008), pp 459–523.

- 'Investment Treaty Arbitral Decisions as "Jurisprudence Constante"', in Colin B Picker (ed), *International economic law: the state and future of the discipline* (Hart 2008), pp 265–280.

Bogdandy, Armin von, 'Grundprinzipien' in Armin von Bogdandy and Jürgen Bast (eds), *Europäisches Verfassungsrecht: theoretische und dogmatische Grundzüge* (2nd edn, Springer 2009), pp 13–71.

Boisson de Chazournes, Laurence, 'The International Law Commission in a Mirror - Firms, Impact and Authority' in The United Nations (ed), *Seventy Years of the International Law Commission* (Brill Nijhoff 2020), pp 133–155.

Borchard, Edwin M, 'The Theory and Sources of International Law' in *Recueil d'études sur les sources du droit en l'honneur de François Gény* (Recueil Sirey 1936) vol 3, pp 328–361.

Boulanger, Jean, 'Principes Généraux du Droit et Droit Positif' in *Le Droit Privé Français au Milieu Du XXe Siècle études Offertes à Georges Ripert* (Libr générale de droit et de jurisprudence 1950) vol 1, pp 51–74.

Bradley, Curtis A, 'Customary International Law Adjudication as Common Law Adjudication' in Curtis A Bradley (ed), *Custom's future: international law in a changing world* (Cambridge University Press 2016), pp 34–61.

Broomhall, Bruce, 'Article 22' in Kai Ambos (ed), *The Rome Statute of the International Criminal Court* (4th edn, Beck 2021).

Broude, Tomer and Shany, Yuval, 'The International Law and Policy of Multi-sourced equivalent norms' in Tomer Broude and Yuval Shany (eds), *Multi-sourced equivalent norms in international law* (Hart 2011), pp 1–15.

Brown, Chester, 'Introduction: The Development and Importance of the Model Bilateral Investment Treaty' in *Commentaries on Selected Model Investment Treaties* (Oxford University Press 2013), pp 1–14.

Brown, Chester and Sheppard, Audley, 'United Kingdom' in *Commentaries on Selected Model Investment Treaties* (Oxford University Press 2013), pp 697–754.

Brunnée, Jutta, 'International Environmental Law and Community Interests: Procedural Aspects' in Georg Nolte and Eyal Benvenisti (eds), *Community Interests Across International Law* (Oxford University Press 2017), pp 151–175.

– 'The Sources of International Environmental Law: Interactional Law', in Samantha Besson and Jean d'Aspremont (eds), *Oxford Handbook on the Sources of International Law* (Oxford University Press 2017), pp 960–986.

Brunnée, Jutta and Toope, Stephen John, 'The Rule of Law in an Agnostic World: the Prohibition on the Use of Force and Humanitarian Exceptions' in Wouter G Werner and others (eds), *The law of international lawyers: reading Martti Koskenniemi* (Cambridge University Press 2017), pp 137–166.

Cançado Trindade, Antônio Augusto, 'The presence and participation of Latin America at the Second Hague Peace Conference of 1907' in Yves Daudet (ed), *Actualité de la Conférence de La Haye de 1907, Deuxième Conférence de la paix/ Topicality of the 1907 Hague Conference, the Second Peace Conference* (Martinus Nijhoff Publishers 2008), pp 51–84.

Cannizzaro, Enzo, 'The law of treaties through the interplay of its different sources' in Christian J Tams and others (eds), *Research handbook on the law of treaties* (Edward Elgar Publishing 2014), pp 16–38.

Cheng, Bin, 'Custom: the future of general state practice in a divided world' in Ronald Saint John MacDonald and Douglas Miller Johnston (eds), *The structure and process of international law: essays in legal philosophy, doctrine, and theory* (1983), pp 513–554.

Chinkin, Christine, 'Article 62' in *The Statute of the International Court of Justice: A Commentary* (2nd edn, Oxford University Press 2012), pp 1529–1572.

Coke, Edward, 'Prohibitions Del Roy' in John Henry Thomas (ed), *The Reports of Sir Edward Coke in Thirteen Parts* (Joseph Butterworth and Son 1826).

Cottier, Michael, 'Article 8' in Otto Triffterer and Kai Ambos (eds), *Rome Statute of the International Criminal Court: a commentary* (3rd edn, Beck 2016).

Cottier, Michael and Lippold, Matthias, 'Article 8' in Kai Ambos (ed), *Rome Statute of the International Criminal Court: a commentary* (4th edn, Beck 2021).

Crawford, James, 'The Work of the International Law Commission' in Antonio Cassese, Paola Gaeta, and John RWD Jones (eds), *The Rome Statute of the International Criminal Court* (Oxford University Press 2002), pp 23–34.

– 'The Drafting of the Rome Statute', in Philippe Sands (ed), *From Nuremberg to The Hague: The Future of International Criminal Justice* (Cambridge University Press 2003), pp 109–156.

– 'Similarity of Issues in Disputes Arising under the Same or Similarly Drafted Investment Treaties', in Emmanuel Gaillard and Yas Banifatemi (eds), *Precedent in International Arbitration* (Juris Publishing 2007), pp 97–105.

– 'The Progressive Development of International Law: History, Theory and Practice', in Denis Alland and others (eds), *Unity and Diversity of International Law. Essays in Honour of Pierre-Marie Dupuy* (Martinus Nijhoff Publishers 2014), pp 3–22.

Crawford, James and Grant, Tom, 'Responsibility of States for Injuries to Foreigners' in John P Grant and JCraig Barker (eds), *The Harvard Research in International Law: Contemporary Analysis and Appraisal* (William S Hein & Company 2007), pp 77–26.

Crawford, James and Keene, Amelia, 'The Structure of State Responsibility under the European Convention on Human Rights' in Anne van Aaken and Iulia Motoc (eds), *The European Convention on Human Rights and General International Law* (Oxford University Press 2018), pp 178–198.

Crema, Luigi, 'The ILC's New Way of Codifying International Law, the Motives Behind It, and the Interpretive Approach Best Suited to It' in Panos Merkouris, Jörg Kammerhofer, and Noora Arajärvi (eds), *The Theory, Practice, and Interpretation of Customary International Law* (Cambridge University Press 2022), pp 161–182.

Cryer, Robert, 'Introduction: What is International Criminal Law?' in Robert Cryer, Darryl Robinson, and Sergey Vasiliev (eds), *An Introduction to International Criminal Law and Procedure* (4th edn, Cambridge University Press 2019), pp 3–27.

Cupido, Marjolein, 'Pluralism in Theories of Liability: Joint Criminal Enterprise versus Joint Perpetration' in Elies van Sliedregt and Sergey Vasiliev (eds), *Pluralism in International Criminal Law* (Oxford University Press 2014), pp 128–158.

d'Amato, Anthony, 'International Law as an Autopoietic System' in Rüdiger Wolfrum and Volker Röben (eds), *Developments of International Law in Treaty Making* (Springer 2005), pp 335–399.

d'Argent, Pierre, 'Les principes généraux à la Cour internationale de Justice' in Samantha Besson, Pascal Pichonnaz, and Marie-Louise Gächter-Alge (eds), *Les principes en droit européen* (Schulthess 2011), pp 107–119.

d'Aspremont, Jean, 'International Customary Investment Law: Story of a Paradox' in Eric de Brabandere and Tarcisio Gazzini (eds), *International Investment Law* (Martinus Nijhoff 2012), pp 5–47.

– 'The Permanent Court of International Justice and Domestic Courts: A Variation in Roles', in Christian J Tams and Malgosia Fitzmaurice (eds), *Legacies of the Permanent Court of International Justice* (Martinus Nijhoff Publishers 2013), pp 221–242.

– 'Théorie des sources', in Raphael van Steenberghe (ed), *Droit international humanitaire: un régime spécial de droit international?* (Bruylant 2013), pp 73–101.

– 'Sources in Legal-Formalist Theories: The Poor Vehicle of Legal Forms', in Samantha Besson and Jean d'Aspremont (eds), *The Oxford Handbook of the Sources of International Law* (Oxford University Press 2017), pp 365–383.

– 'What was not meant to be: General principles of law as a source of international law', in Riccardo Pisillo Mazzeschi and Pasquale de Sena (eds), *Global Justice, Human Rights, and the Modernization of International Law* (Springer 2018), pp 163–184.

– 'The General Claims Commission (Mexico/US) and the Invention of International Responsibility', in Ignacio de la Rasilla and Jorge E Viñuales (eds), *Experiments in International Adjudication* (Cambridge University Press 2019), pp 150–168.

– 'The Two Cultures of International Criminal Law', in Kevin Jon Heller and others (eds), *Oxford Handbook of International Criminal Law* (Oxford University Press 2020), pp 400–422.

Dann, Philipp and Engelhardt, Marie von, 'Legal Approaches to Global Governance and Accountability: Informal Lawmaking, International Public Authority, and Global Administrative Law Compared' in Joost HB

Pauwelyn, Ramses Wessel, and Jan Wouters (eds), *Informal International Lawmaking* (Oxford University Press 2012), pp 106–121.

David, Eric, 'Primary and Secondary Rules' in James Crawford and others (eds), *The Law of International Responsibility* (Oxford University Press 2010), pp 27–33.

deGuzman, Margaret M, 'Article 21 Applicable Law' in Kai Ambos (ed), *Rome Statute of the International Criminal Court* (4th edn, CH Beck 2022), pp 1129–1148.

Dolzer, Rudolf, 'Emergency Clauses in Investment Treaties: Four Versions' in Mahnoush H Arsanjani and others (eds), *Looking to the future: essays on international law in honor of W. Michael Reisman* (Martinus Nijhoff Publishers 2011), pp 705–718.

Dörr, Oliver, 'Article 31. General rule of interpretation' in Oliver Dörr and Kirsten Schmalenbach (eds), *Vienna Convention on the Law of Treaties. A Commentary* (2nd edn, Springer 2018).

Dumberry, Patrick, 'International Investment Contracts' in Tarcisio Gazzini and Eric de Brabandere (eds), *International Investment Law. The Sources of Rights and Obligations* (Martinus Nijhoff Publishers 2012), pp 215–243.

Dupuy, Pierre-Marie, 'Coutume sage et coutume sauvage' in *Mélanges offerts à Charles Rousseau: la communauté internationale* (Pedone 1974), pp 75–87.

– 'Théorie des sources et coutume en droit international contemporain', in Manuel Rama-Montaldo (ed), *El derecho internacional en un mundo en transformacion: liber amicorum en homenaje al profesor Eduardo Jiménez de Aréchaga* (Fundación de Cultura Universitaria 1994) vol 1, pp 51–68.

– 'La pratique de l'article 38 du Statut de la Cour internationale de Justice dans le cadre des plaidoiries érites et orales', in Office of Legal Affairs (ed), *Collection of Essays by Legal Advisers of States, Legal Advisers of International Organizations and Practitioners in the Field of International Law* (The United Nations 1999), pp 377–395.

– 'Unification Rather than Fragmentation of International Law? The Case of International Investment Law and Human Rights Law', in Pierre-Marie Dupuy, Ernst-Ulrich Petersmann, and Francesco Francioni (eds), *Human Rights in International Investment Law and Arbitration* (Oxford University Press 2009), pp 45–62.

Elias, Taslim O, 'The Limits of the Right of Intervention in a Case before the International Court of Justice' in Rudolf Bernhardt (ed), *Völkerrecht als*

Rechtsordnung Internationale Gerichtsbarkeit Menschenrechte Festschrift für Hermann Mosler (Springer 1983), pp 159–172.

Elias, Taslim Olawe, 'Modern Sources of International Law' in Wolfgang Friedmann, Louis Henkin, and Oliver Lissitzyn (eds), *Transnational law in a changing society: essays in honor of Philip C. Jessup* (Columbia University Press 1972), pp 34–69.

Esser, Josef, 'Richterrecht, Gerichtsgebrauch und Gewohnheitsrecht' in Josef Esser (ed), *Festschrift für Fritz von Hippel: zum 70. Geburtstag* (Mohr Siebeck 1967), pp 95–130.

Evans, Malcolm, 'State Responsibility and the ECHR' in Malgosia Fitzmaurice and Dan Sarooshi (eds), *Issues of State Responsibility before International Judicial Institutions* (Hart 2004), pp 139–160.

– 'Relevant Circumstances', in Alex G Oude Elferink, Tore Henriksen, and Signe Veierud Busch (eds), *Maritime Boundary Delimitation: The Case Law* (Cambridge University Press 2018), pp 222–261.

Fastenrath, Ulrich, 'Subsidiarität im Völkerrecht' in Peter Blickle, Thomas O Hüglin, and Dieter Wyduckel (eds), *Subsidiarität als rechtliches und politisches Ordnungsprinzip in Kirche, Staat und Gesellschaft: Genese, Geltungsgrundlagen und Pespektiven an der Schwelle des dritten Jahrtausends* (Duncker & Humblot 2002), pp 475–536.

– 'Article 73', in Bruno Simma and others (eds), *The Charter of the United Nations: A Commentary* (3rd edn, Oxford University Press 2013) vol 2, pp 1830–1839.

Favre, Antoine, 'Les Principes Généraux Du Droit, Fond Commun Du Droit des Gens' in *Recueil d'études de droit international en hommage à P. Guggenheim* (Faculté de Droit de l'Univ de Genève 1968), pp 366–390.

Feldman, David, 'Convention Rights and Substantive Ultra Vires' in Christopher Forsyth (ed), *Judicial Review and the Constitution* (Hart Publishing 2000), pp 254–268.

Fitzmaurice, Gerald, 'Some Problems Regarding the Formal Sources of International Law' in *Symbolae Verzijl: présentées au professeur J. H. W.Verzijl à l'occasion de son LXX-ième anniversaire* (La Haye: M Nijhoff 1958), pp 153–176.

– 'Some Reflections on the European Convention on Human Rights- and on Human Rights', in Rudolf Bernhardt (ed), *Völkerrecht als Rechtsordnung, internationale Gerichtsbarkeit, Menschenrechte: Festschrift für Hermann Mosler* (Springer 1983), pp 203–219.

Focarelli, Carlo, 'The Concept of International Law: The Italian Perspective' in Peter Hilpold (ed), *European International Law Traditions* (Springer 2021), pp 97–136.

Føllesdal, Andreas, 'The Significance of State Consent for the Legitimate Authority of Customary International Law' in Panos Merkouris, Jörg Kammerhofer, and Noora Arajärvi (eds), *The Theory, Practice, and Interpretation of Customary International Law* (Cambridge University Press 2022), pp 105–136.

Forlati, Serena, 'Nationality as a human right' in *The Changing Role of Nationality in International Law* (Routledge 2013), pp 18–36.

Franck, Thomas M, 'Non-treaty Law-Making: When, Where and How?' in Rüdiger Wolfrum and Volker Röben (eds), *Developments of international law in treaty making* (Springer 2005), pp 417–437.

Frouville, Olivier de, 'Attribution of Conduct to the State: Private Individuals' in James Crawford, Alain Pellet, and Simon Olleson (eds), *The Law of International Responsibility* (Oxford University Press 2010), pp 257–280.

Gaja, Giorgio, 'General Principles in the Jurisprudence of the ICJ' in Mads Andenæs and others (eds), *General principles and the coherence of international law* (Brill Nijhoff 2019), pp 35–46.

Gaudemet, Eugène, 'L'œuvre de Saleilles et l'œuvre de Gény en méthodologie juridique et en philosophie du droit' in *Recueil D'Etudes Sur Les Sources Du Droit En L'Honneur De François Gény* (Recueil Sirey 1934) vol 2, pp 5–15.

Geiger, Rudolf H, 'Customary International Law in the Jurisprudence of the International Court of Justice: A Critical Appraisal' in Ulrich Fastenrath and others (eds), *From bilateralism to community interest: essays in honour of Judge Bruno Simma* (Oxford University Press 2011), pp 673–694.

Goldmann, Matthias, 'Sources in the Meta-Theory of International Law: Exploring the Hermeneutics, Authority, and Publicness of International Law' in Samantha Besson and Jean d'Aspremont (eds), *The Oxford Handbook on the Sources of International Law* (Oxford University Press 2017), pp 447–468.

Goldschmidt, Levin, 'International arbitral procedure. Original project and report of Mr Goldschmidt, June 20, 1874' in James Brown Scott (ed and tr), *Resolutions of the Institute of International Law* (Scott, James Brown tr, Oxford University Press 1916), pp 205–328.

Grimm, Dieter, 'Zur politischen Funktion der Trennung von öffentlichem und privatem Recht in Deutschland' in Walter Wilhelm (ed), *Studien zur europäischen Rechtsgeschichte: Helmut Coing zum 28. Februar 1972* (Klostermann 1972), pp 224–242.

Guggenheim, Paul, 'Landesrechtliche Begriffe im Völkerrecht, vor allem im Bereich der internationalen Organisationen' in Walter Schätzel and Hans-Jürgen Schlochauer (eds), *Rechtsfragen der internationalen Organisationen Festschrift für Hans Wehberg zu seinem 70. Geburtstag* (Klostermann 1956).

Hadjigeorgiou, Andreas, 'Beyond Formalism Reviving the Legacy of Sir Henry Maine for Customary International Law' in Panos Merkouris, Jörg Kammerhofer, and Noora Arajärvi (eds), *The Theory, Practice, and Interpretation of Customary International Law* (Cambridge University Press 2022), pp 183–202.

Heijer, Maarten den and Lawson, Rick, 'Extraterritorial Human Rights and the Concept of "Jurisdiction"' in Malcolm Langford (ed), *Global justice, state duties: the extraterritorial scope of economic, social and cultural rights in international law* (Cambridge University Press 2013), pp 153–191.

Helfer, Laurence R and Meyer, Timothy L, 'The Evolution of Codification: A Principal-Agent Theory of the International Law Commission's Influence' in Curtis Bradley (ed), *Custom's Future: International Law in a Changing World* (Cambridge University Press 2016), pp 305–332.

Henckaerts, Jean-Marie, 'The ICRC and the Clarification of Customary International Humanitarian Law' in Brian D Lepard (ed), *Reexamining customary international law* (Cambridge University Press 2017), pp 161–188.

Herik, Larissa Jasmijn van den, 'The Decline of Customary International Law as a Source of International Criminal Law' in Curtis A Bradley (ed), *Custom's future: international law in a changing world* (Cambridge University Press 2016), pp 230–252.

Hilf, Meinhard and Goettsche, Goetz J, 'The Relation of Economic and Non-economic Principles in International Law' in Stefan Griller (ed), *International economic governance and non-economic concerns: new challenges for the international legal order* (Springer 2003), pp 5–46.

Hirsch, Moshe, 'Sources of International Investment Law' in Andrea K Bjorklund and August Reinisch (eds), *International investment law and soft law* (Edward Elgar Publishing 2012), pp 9–38.

Hollis, Duncan B, 'The Existential Function of Interpretation in International Law' in Andrea Bianchi, Daniel Peat, and Matthew Windsor (eds), *Inter-*

pretation in International Law (Oxford University Press 2015), pp 78–110.

Holtzendorff, Franz von, 'Die Quellen des Völkerrechts' in Franz von Holtzendorff (ed), *Handbuch des Völkerrechts. Einleitung in das Völkerrecht* (Habel 1885) vol 1, pp 79–155.

Huber, Peter-Michael and Paulus, Andreas L, 'Cooperation of Constitutional Courts in Europe: the Openness of the German Constitution to International, European, and Comparative Constitutional Law' in *Courts and Comparative Law* (Oxford University Press 2015), pp 281–299.

Iurlaro, Francesca, 'Vattel's Doctrine of the Customary Law of Nations between Sovereign Interests and the Principles of Natural Law' in Simone Zurbuchen (ed), *The Law of Nations and Natural Law 1625-1800* (Brill 2019), pp 278–303.

Jacob, Marc, 'Investmens, Bilateral Treaties' in *Max Planck EPIL* (2014).

Janis, Mark W, 'North America: American Exceptionalism in International Law' in Bardo Fassbender and Anne Peters (eds), *The Oxford Handbook of the History of International Law* (Oxford University Press 2012), pp 525–552.

Jestaedt, Matthias, 'Bundesstaat als Verfassungsprinzip' in *Handbuch des Staatsrechts der Bundesrepublik Deutschland* (CF Müller 2004) vol 2, pp 785–842.

Jetschke, Anja and Liese, Andrea, 'The power of human rights a decade ater: from euphoria to contestation?' in Thomas Risse, Stephen C Ropp, and Kathryn Sikkink (eds), *The Continuing Power of Human Rights: From Commitment to Compliance* (Cambridge University Press 2013), pp 26–42.

Jiménez de Aréchaga, Eduardo, 'Intervention under Article 62 of the Statute of the International Court of Justice' in Rudolf Bernhardt (ed), *Völkerrecht als Rechtsordnung, internationale Gerichtsbarkeit, Menschenrechte: Festschrift für Hermann Mosler* (Springer 1983), pp 453–465.

Kammerhofer, Jörg, 'Scratching an itch is not a treatment. Instrumentalist non-theory contra normativist Konsequenz and the Problem of systemic integration' in Georg Nolte and Peter Hilpold (eds), *Auslandsinvestitionen-Entwicklung großer Kodifikationen -Fragmentierung des Völkerrechts-Status des Kosovo Beiträge zum 31. Österreichischen Völkerrechtstag 2006 in München* (Peter Lang 2008), pp 155–184.

– 'Law-making by Scholarship? The Dark Side of 21st Century International Legal Methodology', in James Crawford and Sarah Nouwen (eds), *Select*

Proceedings of the European Society of International Law, Volume 3, 2010 (Hart 2012), pp 115–127.

Kammerhofer, Jörg, 'Die Reine Rechtslehre und die allgemeinen Rechtsprinzipien des Völkerrechts' in Nikitas Aliprantis and Thomas Olechowski (eds), *Hans Kelsen: die Aktualität eines großen Rechtswissenschafters und Soziologen des 20. Jahrhunderts: Ergebnisse einer internationalen Tagung an der Akademie von Athen am 12. April 2013 aus Anlass von Kelsens 40. Todestag* (Manzsche Verlags- und Universitätsbuchhandlung 2014), pp 25–35.

- 'The Resilience of the Restrictive Rules on Self-Defence', in Marc Weller (ed), *The Oxford handbook of the use of force in international law* (Oxford University Press 2015), pp 627–648.
- 'Lawmaking by Scholars', in Catherine Brölmann and Yannick Radi (eds), *Research handbook on the theory and practice of international lawmaking* (Edward Elgar Publishing 2016), pp 305–325.
- 'The Pure Theory's Structural Analysis of the Law', in Samantha Besson and Jean d'Aspremont (eds), *Oxford Handbook on the Sources of International Law* (Oxford University Press 2017), pp 343–362.

Kearney, Richard D, 'Sources of Law and the International Court of Justice' in Leo Gross (ed), *The future of the International Court of Justice* (Oceana-Publ 1976) vol 2, pp 610–726.

Klabbers, Jan, 'Reluctant Grundnormen: Articles 31(3)(C) and 42 of the Vienna Convention on the Law of Treaties and the Fragmentation of International Law' in Matthew Craven, Malgosia Fitzmaurice, and Maria Vogiatzi (eds), *Time, History and International Law* (Martinus Nijhoff Publishers 2007), pp 141–162.

Klein, Eckhart, 'Denunciation of Human Rights Treaties and the Principle of Reciprocity' in Ulrich Fastenrath and others (eds), *From bilateralism to community interest: essays in honour of Judge Bruno Simma* (Oxford University Press 2011), pp 477–487.

Kleinlein, Thomas, 'Christian Wolff. System as an Episode' in Stefan Kadelbach, Thomas Kleinlein, and David Roth-Isigkeit (eds), *System, Order, and International Law: The Early History of International Legal Thought from Machiavelli to Hegel* (Oxford University Press 2017), pp 216–239.

- 'Customary International Law and General Principles Rethinking Their Relationship', in Brian D Lepard (ed), *Reexamining Customary International Law* (Cambridge University Press 2017), pp 131–158.

Kletzer, Christoph, 'Custom and Positivity: an Examination of the Philosophic Ground of the Hegel-Savigny Controversy' in Amanda Perreau-

Saussine and James Bernard Murphy (eds), *The nature of customary law* (Cambridge University Press 2007), pp 125–148.

Kohen, Marcelo G, 'La pratique et la théorie des sources du droit international' in Société Française pour le Droit International (ed), *La pratique et le droit international: Colloque de Genève* (Pedone 2004), pp 81–111.

– 'Les principes généaux du droit international de l'eau à la lumière de la jurisprudence récente de la Cour Internationale de Justice', in *L'eau en droit international: Colloque d'Orléans* (Pedone 2011), pp 91–108.

Kolb, Robert, 'The Compromissory Clause of the Convention' in Paola Gaeta (ed), *The UN Genocide Convention: A Commentary* (Oxford University Press 2009), pp 407–424.

– 'The Scope Ratione Materiae of the Compulsory Jurisdiction of the ICJ', in Paola Gaeta (ed), *The UN Genocide Convention: A Commentary* (Oxford University Press 2009), pp 442–472.

– 'Is there a subject-matter ontology in interpretation of international legal norms?', in Mads Tønnesson Andenæs and Eirik Bjørge (eds), *A Farewell to Fragmentation Reassertion and Convergence in International Law* (Cambridge University Press 2015), pp 473–485.

– 'Legal History as a Source: From Classical to Modern International Law', in Samantha Besson and Jean d'Aspremont (eds), *The Oxford handbook on the sources of international law* (Oxford University Press 2017), pp 279–300.

Koskenniemi, Martti, 'General Principles: Reflexions on Constructivist Thinking in International Law' in Martti Koskenniemi (ed), *Sources of International Law* (Routledge 2000), pp 359–402.

– 'The Ideology of International Adjudication and the 1907 Hague Conference', in Yves Daudet (ed), *Topicality of the 1907 Hague Conference, the Second Peace Conference* (Nijhoff 2008), pp 127–152.

Kratochwil, Friedrich von, 'How Do Norms Matter?' in Michael Byers (ed), *The role of law in international politics: essays in international relations and international law* (Oxford University Press 2000), pp 35–68.

Kreß, Claus, 'The International Court of Justice and the Law of Armed Conflicts' in Christian J Tams and James Sloan (eds), *The Development of International Law by the International Court of Justice* (Oxford University Press 2013), pp 263–298.

– 'Article 98', in Kai Ambos (ed), *The Rome Statute of the International Criminal Court* (4th edn, Beck 2021).

Kriebaum, Ursula, 'Article 42' in Stephan W Schill (ed), *Schreuer's Commentary on the ICSID Convention* (3rd edn, Cambridge University Press 2022), pp 797–905.

Krieger, Heike, 'Verfassung im Völkerrecht - Konstitutionelle Elemente jenseits des Staates?' in *Verfassung als Ordnungskonzept. Referate und Diskussionen auf der Tagung der Vereinigung der Deutschen Staatsrechtslehrer in Speyer vom 7. bis zum 10. Oktober 2015* (de Gruyter 2016) vol 75, pp 439–472.

Kuhli, Milan and Günther, Klaus, 'Judicial Lawmaking, Discourse Theory, and the ICTY on Belligerent Reprisals' in Armin von Bogdandy and Ingo Venzke (eds), *International Judicial Lawmaking* (Springer 2012), pp 365–386.

Kulick, Andreas, 'State-State Investment Arbitration as a Means of Reassertion of Control: From Antagonism to Dialogue' in Andreas Kulick (ed), *Reassertion of control over the investment treaty regime* (Cambridge University Press 2017), pp 128–152.

Kurtz, Jürgen, 'Delineating Primary and Secondary Rules on Necessity at International Law' in *Multi-sourced equivalent norms in international law* (Hart 2011), pp 231–258.

Lauterpacht, Hersch, 'Some observations on the prohibition of 'non liquet' and the completeness of the law' in Frederik Mari van Asbeck (ed), *Symbolae Verzijl: présentées au professeur J. H. W. Verzijl à l'occasion de son 70-ième anniversaire* (Nijhoff 1958), pp 196–221.

– 'History of International Law', in Elihu Lauterpacht (ed), *International Law Being also the Collected Papers of Hersch Lauterpacht, Vol. 2, The Law of Peace, Part 1, International Law in General* (Cambridge University Press 1975), pp 95–172.

– 'Kelsen's pure science of law', in Elihu Lauterpacht (ed), *International Law Being the Collected Papers of Hersch Lauterpacht* (Cambridge University Press 1975) vol 2.

– 'The mandate under international law in the Covenant of the League of Nations', in Elihu Lauterpacht (ed) (3, Cambridge University Press 1977) vol Hersch Lauterpacht International Law Collected Papers 3. The Law of Peace, pp 29–84.

Le Fur, Louis, 'La coutume et les principes généraux du droit comme sources du droit international public' in *Recueil d'études sur les sources du droit en l'honneur de François Gény* (Recueil Sirey 1934) vol 3, pp 362–374.

Lefkowitz, David, 'Sources in Legal-Positivist Theories: Law as Necessarily posited and the Challenge of Customary Law Creation' in Samantha

Besson and Jean d'Aspremont (eds), *The Oxford Handbook on Sources of International Law* (Oxford University Press 2017), pp 323–342.

Lerche, Peter, 'Die Verfassung als Quelle von Optimierungsgeboten?' in Joachim Burmeister (ed), *Verfassungsstaatlichkeit Festschrift für Klaus Stern zum 65. Geburtstag* (Beck 1997), pp 197–209.

Lillich, Richard B, 'The Current Status of the Law of State Responsibility for Injuries to Aliens' in Richard B Lillich (ed), *International Law of State Responsibility for Injuries to Aliens* (University Press of Virginia 1983), pp 1–60.

Lippold, Matthias, 'The Interpretation of UN Security Council Resolutions between Regional and General International Law: What Role for General Principles?' in Mads Andenæs and others (eds), *General Principles and the Coherence of International Law* (Brill Nijhoff 2019), pp 149–176.

Liszt, Franz von, 'Das Wesen des völkerrechtlichen Staatenverbamdes und der internationale Prisenhof' in *Festgabe der Berliner juristischen Fakultät für Otto Gierke zum Doktor-Jubiläum 21. August 1910, Dritter Band Internationales Recht. Strafrecht. Rechtsvergleichung* (Marcus 1910), pp 21–44.

Liver, Peter, 'Der Begriff der Rechtsquelle' in Schweizerischer Juristenverein (ed), *Rechtsquellenprobleme im schweizerischen Recht* (Stämpfli 1955), pp 1–55.

Lobban, Michael, 'English Approaches to International Law in the Nineteenth Century' in Matthew Craven, Malgosia Fitzmaurice, and Maria Vogiatzi (eds), *Time, History and International Law* (Martinus Nijhof Publishers 2007), pp 65–90.

Lowe, Vaughan, 'The Politics of Law-Making: Are the Method and Character of Norm Creation Changing?' in Michael Byers (ed), *The role of law in international politics: essays in international relations and international law* (Oxford University Press 2000), pp 207–226.

Lowe, Vaughan and Tzanakopoulos, Antonios, 'The Development of the Law of the Sea by the International Court of Justice' in Christian J Tams and James Sloan (eds), *The Development of International Law by the International Court of Justice* (Oxford University Press 2013), pp 177–193.

Malintoppi, Loretta, 'Article 27' in Stephan W Schill (ed), *Schreuer's Commentary on the ICSID Convention* (3rd edn, Cambridge University Press 2022), pp 633–654.

Matscher, Franz, 'Vertragsauslegung durch Vertragsrechtsvergleichung in der Judikatur internationaler Gerichte, vornehmlich vor den Organen der

EMRK' in *Völkerrecht als Rechtsordnung, internationale Gerichtsbarkeit, Menschenrechte: Festschrift für Hermann Mosler* (Springer 1983), pp 545–566.

Matz-Lück, Nele, 'Norm Interpretation across International Regimes: Competences and Legitimacy' in Margaret A Young (ed), *Regime Interaction in International Law Facing Fragmentation* (Cambridge University Press 2012), pp 201–234.

McDorman, Ted L, 'The Continental Shelf' in Donald R Rothwell and others (eds), *The Oxford Handbook on the Law of the Sea* (Oxford University Press 2015), pp 181–202.

McRae, Donald, 'The Applicable Law' in Alex G Oude Elferink, Tore Henriksen, and Signe Veierud Busch (eds), *Maritime Boundary Delimitation: The Case Law* (Cambridge University Press 2018), pp 92–116.

Mégret, Frédéric, 'International law as law' in James Crawford and Martti Koskenniemi (eds), *The Cambridge Companion to International Law* (Cambridge University Press 2012), pp 64–91.

Mejía-Lemos, Diego, 'Custom and the Regulation of 'the Sources of International Law'' in Panos Merkouris, Jörg Kammerhofer, and Noora Arajärvi (eds), *The Theory, Practice, and Interpretation of Customary International Law* (Cambridge University Press 2022), pp 137–160.

Meloni, Chantal, 'Fragmentation of the Notion of Co-perpetration in International Criminal Law?' in Larissa J van den Herik and Carsten Stahn (eds), *The diversification and fragmentation of international criminal law* (M Nijhoff Publishers 2012), pp 481–502.

Mendelson, Maurice H, 'Are Treaties Merely a Source of Obligation?' in William E Butler (ed), *Perestroika and International Law* (1980), pp 81–88.

– 'The International Court of Justice and the sources of international law', in Vaughan Lowe and Malgosia Fitzmaurice (eds), *Fifty years of the International Court of Justice Essays in honour of Sir Robert Jennings* (Cambridge University Press 1996), pp 63–89.

Milanovic, Marko, 'Jurisdiction and Responsibility: Trends in the Jurisprudence of the Strasbourg Court' in Anne van Aaken and Iulia Motoc (eds), *The European Convention on Human Rights and General International Law* (Oxford University Press 2018), pp 97–111.

Milanović, Marko, 'Territorial Application of the Convention and State Succession' in *The UN Genocide Convention: a commentary* (Oxford University Press 2009), pp 473–493.

Miron, Alina and Chinkin, Christine, 'Article 62' in *The Statute of the International Court of Justice: A Commentary* (3rd edn, Oxford University Press 2019), pp 1686–1740.

Monaco, Riccardo, 'Observations sur la hiérarchie des sources du droit international' in Rudolf Bernhardt (ed), *Völkerrecht als Rechtsordnung, Internationale Gerichtsbarkeit, Menschenrechte: Festschrift für Hermann Mosler* (Springer 1983), pp 599–615.

Motoc, Iulia and Vasel, Johann Justus, 'The ECHR and Responsibility of the State: Moving towards Judicial Integration: a View from the Bench' in Anne van Aaken and Iulia Motoc (eds), *The European Convention on Human Rights and general international law* (Oxford University Press 2018), pp 199–212.

Müller, Daniel, 'The Work of García Amador on State Responsibility for Injury Caused to Aliens' in James Crawford and others (eds), *The Law of International Responsibility* (Oxford University Press 2010), pp 69–74.

Murase, Shinya, 'The presence of Asia at the 1907 Hague Conference' in Yves Daudet (ed), *Actualité de la Conférence de La Haye de 1907, Deuxième Conférence de la paix/ Topicality of the 1907 Hague Conference, the Second Peace Conference* (Martinus Nijhoff Publishers 2008), pp 85–102.

Murphy, Sean D, 'Codification, Progressive Development, or Scholarly Analysis? The Art of Packaging the ILC's Work Product' in Maurizio Ragazzi (ed), *The Responsibility of International Organizations: Essays in Memory of Sir Ian Brownlie* (Martinus Nijhoff Publishers 2013), pp 29–40.

Nollkaemper, André, 'Decisions of National Courts as Sources of International Law: An Analysis of the Practice of the ICTY' in Gideon Boas and William Schabas (eds), *International Criminal Law Developments in the Case Law of the ICTY* (Martinus Nijhoff Publishers 2003), pp 277–296.

– 'The Power of Secondary Rules to connect the International and National Legal Orders', in Tomer Broude and Yuval Shany (eds), *Multi-sourced equivalent norms in international law* (Oxford University Press 2011), pp 45–67.

Nolte, Georg, 'Menschenrechtliches ius cogens - Eine Analyse von "Barcelona Traction" und nachfolgender Entwicklungen - Kommentar' in Eckart Klein (ed), *Menschenrechtsschutz durch Gewohnheitsrecht* (Berliner Wissenschafts-Verlag 2003), pp 141–146.

– 'Second Report for the ILC Study Group on Treaties over Time. Jurisprudence Under Special Regimes Relating to Subsequent Agreements and Subsequent Practice', in Georg Nolte (ed), *Treaties and Subsequent Practice* (Oxford University Press 2013), pp 210–308.

Obregon, Liliana, 'The Civilized and the Uncivilized' in Bardo Fassbender and Anne Peters (eds), *Oxford Handbook of the History of International Law* (Oxford University Press 2012), pp 917–942.

Oeter, Stefan, 'Self-Determination' in Bruno Simma and others (eds), *The Charter of the United Nations: A Commentary* (3rd edn, Oxford University Press 2013) vol 1, pp 313–334.

– 'The legitimacy of customary international law', in Thomas Eger, Stefan Oeter, and Stefan Voigt (eds), *Economic Analysis of International Law: Contributions to the XIIIth Travemünde Symposium on the Economic Analysis of Law (March 29-31, 2012)* (Mohr Siebeck 2014), pp 1–22.

Ohlin, Jens David, 'Co-Perpetration: German Dogmatik or German Invasion?' in Carsten Stahn (ed), *The law and practice of the International Criminal Court* (Oxford University Press 2015), pp 517–537.

Orrego Vicuña, Francisco, 'Softening Necessity' in Mahnoush H Arsanjani and others (eds), *Looking to the Future Essays on International Law in Honor of W. Michael Reisman* (Martinus Nijhoff Publishers 2010), pp 741–752.

Palchetti, Paolo, 'The Role of General Principles in Promoting the Development of Customary International Rules' in Mads Andenæs and others (eds), *General Principles and the Coherence of International Law* (Brill Nijhoff 2019), pp 47–59.

Paparinskis, Mārtiņš, 'Sources of Law and Arbitral Interpretations of "Pari Materia" Investment Protection Rules' in Ole Kristian Fauchald and André Nollkaemper (eds), *The practice of international and national courts and the (de-)fragmentation of international law* (Hart 2012), pp 87–115.

– 'Masters and Guardians of International Investment Law: How To Play the Game of Reassertion', in Andreas Kulick (ed), *Reassertion of Control over the Investment Treaty Regime* (Cambridge University Press 2017), pp 30–52.

Pascua, José Antonio Ramos, 'Die Grundlage rechtlicher Geltung von Prinzipien- eine Gegenüberstellung von Dworkin und Esser' in Giuseppe Orsi and others (eds), *Prinzipien des Rechts* (Lang 1996), pp 7–33.

Paulus, Andreas L, 'The International Legal System as a Constitution' in Jeffrey L Dunhoff and Joel P Trachtman (eds), *Ruling the world?: constitutionalism, international law, and global governance* (Cambridge University Press 2009), pp 69–109.

- 'International Adjudication', in Samantha Besson and John Tasioulas (eds), *The philosophy of international law* (Oxford University Press 2010), pp 207–224.
- 'Whether Universal Values can prevail over Bilateralism and Reciprocity', in Antonio Cassese (ed), *Realizing Utopia: The Future of International Law* (Oxford University Press 2012), pp 89–104.
- 'Fragmentierung und Segmentierung der internationalen Ordnung als Herausforderung prozeduraler Gemeinwohlorientierung', in Hans-Michael Heinig and Jörg Philipp Terhechte (eds), *Postnationale Demokratie, Postdemokratie, Neoetatismus Wandel klassischer Demokratievorstellungen in der Rechtswissenschaft* (Mohr Siebeck 2013), pp 139–158.
- 'Zusammenspiel der Rechtsquellen aus völkerrechtlicher Perspektive', in *Internationales, nationales und privates Recht: Hybridisierung der Rechtsordnungen?: Immunität, 33. Tagung der Deutschen Gesellschaft für Internationales Recht* (CF Müller 2014), pp 7–47.
- 'Article 66', in Andreas Zimmermann and others (eds), *The Statute of the International Court of Justice: a commentary* (3rd edn, Oxford University Press 2019), pp 1812–1834.

Pauwelyn, Joost HB, 'Rational Design or Accidental Evolution? The Emergence of International Investment Law' in Zachary Douglas, Joost HB Pauwelyn, and Jorge E Viñuales (eds), *The Foundations of International Investment Law* (Oxford University Press 2014), pp 11–43.

Pauwelyn, Joost HB and Elsig, Manfred, 'The Politics of Treaty Interpretation: Variations and Explanations across International Tribunals' in *Interdisciplinary perspectives on international law and international relations: the state of the art* (Cambridge University Press 2013), pp 445–473.

Pavoni, Riccardo, 'The Myth of the Customary Nature of the United Nations Convention on State Immunity: Does the End Justify the Means?' in Anne van Aaken and Iula Motoc (eds), *ECHR and General International Law* (Oxford University Press 2018), pp 264–284.

Pellet, Alain, 'Applicable Law' in Antonio Cassese, Paola Gaeta, and John RWD Jones (eds), *The Rome Statute of the International Criminal Court: A Commentary* (Oxford University Press 2002) vol 2, pp 1051–1084.
- 'The ILC's Articles on State Responsibility for Internationally Wrongful Acts and Related Texts', in James Crawford and others (eds), *The Law of International Responsibility* (Oxford University Press 2010), pp 75–92.
- 'Article 38', in Andreas Zimmermann, Karin Oellers-Frahm, and Christian J Tams (eds), *The Statute of the International Court of Justice A Commentary* (2nd edn, Oxford University Press 2012), pp 731–870.

Pellet, Alain, 'Revisiting the Sources of Applicable Law before the ICC' in Margaret M deGuzman and Diane Marie Amann (eds), *Arcs of Global Justice: Essays in Honour of William A. Schabas* (Oxford University Press 2018), pp 227–256.

Pellet, Alain and Müller, Daniel, 'Reservations to Human Rights Treaties: not an Absolute Evil ...' in Ulrich Fastenrath and others (eds), *From bilateralism to community interest: essays in honour of judge Bruno Simma* (Oxford University Press 2011), pp 521–551.

– 'Article 38', in Andreas Zimmermann and others (eds), *The Statute of the International Court of Justice: a commentary* (Oxford University Press 2019), pp 819–962.

Perreau-Saussine, Amanda, 'Lauterpacht and Vattel on the Sources of International Law: the Place of Private Law Analogies and General Principles' in Vincent Chetail and Peter Haggenmacher (eds), *Vattel's international law in a XXIst century perspective* (Martinus Nijhoff Publishers 2011), pp 167–185.

Peters, Anne, 'Völkerrecht im Gender-Fokus' in Andreas Zimmermann, Thomas Griegerich, and Ursula E Heinz (eds), *Gender und Internationales Recht* (Duncker & Humblot 2007), pp 199–299.

Powderly, Joseph, 'The Rome Statute and the Attempted Corseting of the Interpretive Judicial Function: Reflections on Sources of Law and Interprative Technique' in Carsten Stahn (ed), *The law and practice of the International Criminal Court* (Oxford University Press 2015), pp 444–498.

Prost, Mario, 'Sources and the Hierarchy of International Law: Source Preferences and Scales' in Samantha Besson and Jean d'Aspremont (eds), *The Oxford Handbook of the Sources of International Law* (Oxford University Press 2017), pp 640–659.

Rasulov, Akbar, 'The Doctrine of Sources in the Discourse of the Permanent Court of International Justice' in Christian J Tams and Malgosia Fitzmaurice (eds), *Legacies of the Permanent Court of International Justice* (Martinus Nijhoff Publishers 2013), pp 271–317.

Ratner, Steven, 'Sources of International Humanitarian Law and International Criminal Law: War/Crimes and the Limits of the Doctrine of Sources' in Samantha Besson and Jean d'Aspremont (eds), *The Oxford Handbook on the Sources of International Law* (Oxford University Press 2017), pp 912–938.

Renault, Louis, 'Report to the Conference from the First Commission on the draft convention relative to the establishment of an International Prize

Court' in James Brown Scott (ed) (Clarendon Press Oxford University Press 1917), pp 758–793.

Rentsch, Bettina, 'Konstitutionalisierung durch allgemeine Rechtsgrundsätze des Völkerrechts? - Zur Rolle des völkerrechtlichen Gutglaubensgrundsatzes für die Integration einer internationalen Werteordnung in das Völkerrecht' in Bardo Fassbender and Angelika Siehr (eds), *Suprastaatliche Konstitutionalisierung: Perspektiven auf die Legitimität, Kohärenz und Effektivität des Völkerrechts* (Nomos 2012), pp 101–134.

Risse, Thomas and Ropp, Stephen C, 'Introduction and overview' in Thomas Risse, Stephen C Ropp, and Kathryn Sikkink (eds), *The Persistent Power of Human Rights From Commitment to Compliance* (Cambridge University Press 2013), pp 3–25.

Risse, Thomas and Sikkink, Kathryn, 'The power of human rights: international norms and domestic change' in Thomas Risse, Stephen C Ropp, and Kathryn Sikkink (eds), *The power of human rights: international norms and domestic change* (Cambridge University Press 1999), pp 1–18.

Ruffert, Matthias, 'Gedanken zu den Perspektiven der völkerrechtlichen Rechtsquellenlehre' in Matthias Ruffert (ed), *Dynamik und Nachhaltigkeit des öffentlichen Rechts: Festschrift für Meinhard Schröder zum 70. Geburtstag* (Duncker & Humblot 2012), pp 73–84.

Saland, Per, 'International Criminal Law Principles' in Roy S Lee (ed), *The International Criminal Court. The Making of the Rome Statute. Issues, Negotiations, Results* (Kluwer 1999), pp 189–216.

Scelle, Georges, 'Essai sur les sources formelles du droit international' in *Recueil d'études sur les sources du droit en l'honneur de François Gény* (Recueil Sirey 1934) vol 3, pp 400–430.

– 'Le phénomène juridique du dédoublement fonctionnel', in Walter Schätzel and Hans-Jürgen Schlochauer (eds), *Rechtsfragen der internationalen Organisation: Festschrift für Hans Wehberg zu seinem 70. Geburtstag* (Klostermann 1956), pp 324–342.

Schabas, William, 'Customary Law or Judge-Made Law: Judicial Creativity at the UN Criminal Tribunals' in José Doria, Hans-Peter Gasser, and Mahmoud Cherif Bassiouni (eds), *The Legal Regime of the ICC: Essays in Honour of Prof. I.P. Blishchenko* (Nijhoff 2009), pp 77–101.

– 'Article 15. Derogation in Time of Emergency', in William Schabas (ed), *The European Convention on Human Rights. A Commentary* (Oxford University Press 2015), pp 587–605.

Schabas, William, 'Article 32. Jurisdiction of the Court' in William Schabas (ed), *The European Convention on Human Rights. A Commentary* (Oxford University Press 2015), pp 715–722.
- 'Article 7', in William Schabas (ed), *The European Convention on Human Rights. A Commentary* (Oxford University Press 2015), pp 328–356.
- 'Interpretation of the Convention', in William Schabas (ed), *The European Convention on Human Rights. A Commentary* (Oxford University Press 2015), pp 33–52.
- 'Preamble', in William Schabas (ed), *The European Convention on Human Rights. A Commentary* (Oxford University Press 2015), pp 54–83.

Schauer, Frederick, 'Fuller and Kelsen - Fuller on Kelsen' in Matthias Jestaedt, Ralf Poscher, and Jörg Kammerhofer (eds), *Die Reine Rechtslehre auf dem Prüfstand. Hans Kelsen's Pure Theory of Law: Conceptions and Misconceptions* (Franz Steiner Verlag 2020), pp 309–317.

Scheinin, Martin, 'Just another word? Jurisdiction in the Roadmaps of State Responsibility and Human Rights' in Malcolm Langford (ed), *Global justice, state duties: the extraterritorial scope of economic, social and cultural rights in international law* (Cambridge University Press 2013), pp 212–229.

Schill, Stephan W, 'Fair and Equitable Treatment, the Rule of Law, and Comparative Public Law' in Stephan W Schill (ed), *International investment law and comparative public law* (Oxford University Press 2010), pp 151–182.
- 'International Investment Law and Comparative Public Law - an Introduction', in Stephan W Schill (ed), *International investment law and comparative public law* (Oxford University Press 2010), pp 3–37.
- 'General Principles of Law and International Investment Law', in Tarcisio Gazzini and Eric de Brabandere (eds), *International investment law: the sources of rights and obligations* (Martinus Nijhoff Publishers 2012), pp 133–181.
- 'System-Building in Investment Treaty Arbitration and Lawmaking', in Armin von Bogdandy and Ingo Venzke (eds), *International judicial lawmaking: on public authority and democratic legitimation in global governance* (Springer 2012), pp 133–178.

Scobbie, Iain GM, 'Legal Theory As a Source of International Law: Institutional Facts and the Identification of International Law' in Samantha Besson and Jean d'Aspremont (eds), *The Oxford Handbook on the Sources of International Law* (Oxford University Press 2017), pp 493–512.

Seibert-Fohr, Anja, 'Unity and Diversity in the Formation and Relevance of Customary International Law: Modern Concepts of Customary International law as a Manifestation of a Value-Based International Order' in Andreas Zimmermann and Rainer Hofmann (eds), *Unity and Diversity in International Law* (2006), pp 257–283.
- 'State Responsibility for Genocide under the Genocide Convention', in Paola Gaeta (ed), *The UN Genocide Convention: A Commentary* (Oxford University Press 2009), pp 349–373.

Sikkink, Kathryn, 'The United States and torture: does the spiral model work?' in Thomas Risse, Stephen C Ropp, and Kathryn Sikkink (eds), *The Continuing Power of Human Rights: From Commitment to Compliance* (Cambridge University Press 2013), pp 145–163.

Simma, Bruno, 'Die Erzeugung ungeschriebenen Völkerrechts: Allgemeine Verunsicherung- klärende Beiträge Karl Zemaneks' in Konrad Ginther and others (eds), *Völkerrecht zwischen normativem Anspruch und politischer Realität: Festschrift für Karl Zemanek zum 65. Geburtstag* (Duncker & Humblot 1994), pp 95–114.
- 'Reservations to human rights treaties: some recent developments', in Alfred Rest and others (eds), *Liber amicorum Professor Ignaz Seidl-Hohenveldern in honour of his 80th birthday* (Kluwer Law International 1998), pp 659–682.

Simma, Bruno and Kill, Theodor, 'Harmonizing Investment Protection and International Human Rights: First Steps Towards a Methodology' in Christina Binder and others (eds), *International Investment Law for the 21st Century Essays in Honour of Christoph Schreuer* (Oxford University Press 2009), pp 678–707.

Simma, Bruno and Paulus, Andreas L, 'Le rôle relatif des différentes sources du droit international pénal: dont les principes généraux de droit' in Hervé Ascensio, Emmanuel Decaux, and Alain Pellet (eds), *Droit international pénal* (Pedone 2000), pp 55–69.

Simpson, Alfred William Brian, 'Common Law and Legal Theory' in Alfred William Brian Simpson (ed), *Legal Theory and Legal History: Essays on the Common Law* (The Hambledon Press 1987), pp 359–382.

Skubiszewski, Krzysztof Jan, 'A New Source of the Law of Nations: Resolutions of International Organizations' in *Recueil d'études de droit international en hommage à Paul Guggenheim* (Faculté de Droit de l'Univ de Genève 1968), pp 508–520.

Sliedregt, Elies van, 'Perpetration and Participation in Article 25(3)' in Carsten Stahn (ed), *The Law and Practice of the International Criminal Court* (Oxford University Press 2015), pp 499–516.

Sliedregt, Elies van and Yanev, Lachezar, 'Co-Perpetration Based on Joint Control over the Crime' in Jérôme de Hemptinne, Roberts Roth, and Elies van Sliedregt (eds), *Modes of Liability in International Criminal Law* (Cambridge University Press 2019), pp 85–120.

Smend, Rudolf, 'Ungeschriebenes Verfassungsrecht im monarchischen Bundesstaat' in *Festgabe für Otto Mayer zum siebzigsten Geburtstag* (Mohr Siebeck 1916), pp 246–270.

– 'Verfassung und Verfassungsrecht (1928)', in Rudolf Smend (ed), *Staatsrechtliche Abhandlungen und andere Aufsätze* (2nd edn, Duncker & Humblot 1968), pp 119–276.

Sørensen, Max, 'Do the Rights Set forth in the European Convention on Human Rights in 1950 have the Same Significance in 1975? Report presented by Max Sørensen to the Fourth International Colloquy about the European Convention on Human Rights, Rome 5-8 November 1975' in Ellen Sørensen and Max Sørensen (eds), *Max Sørensen: en bibliografi* (Aarhus University Press 1988), p 23.

Spiermann, Ole, 'Applicable Law' in Peter T Muchlinski, Federico Ortino, and Christoph Scheuer (eds), *The Oxford Handbook of International Investment Law* (Oxford University Press 2008), pp 89–118.

Staubach, Peter, 'The Interpretation of Unwritten International Law by Domestic Judges' in Helmut Philipp Aust and Georg Nolte (eds), *The Interpretation of International Law by Domestic Courts: Uniformity, Diversity, Convergence* (Oxford University Press 2016), pp 113–131.

Stern, Brigitte, 'La coutume au coeur du droit international: quelques réflexions' in *Mélanges offerts à Paul Reuter: le droit international: unité et diversité* (Pedone 1981), pp 479–499.

– 'The Elements of an Internationally Wrongful Act', in James Crawford, Alain Pellet, and Simon Olleson (eds), *The Law of International Responsibility* (Oxford University Press 2010), pp 193–220.

Stewart, James G, 'Ten Reasons for Adopting a Universal Concept of Participation in Atrocity' in Elies van Sliedregt and Sergey Vasiliev (eds), *Pluralism in International Criminal Law* (Oxford University Press 2014), pp 320–341.

Swigarth, Leigh and Terris, Daniel, 'Who are International Judges?' in Cesare P R Romano, Karen Alter, and Yuval Shany (eds), *The Oxford Handbook of International Adjudication* (Oxford University Press 2013), pp 619–638.

Talmon, Stefan, 'Article 2 (6)' in Bruno Simma and others (eds), *The Charter of the United Nations A Commentary* (3rd edn, Oxford University Press 2012) vol 1.

Tams, Christian J, 'The Continued Relevance of Compromissory Clauses as a Source of ICJ Jurisdiction' in Thomas Griegerich (ed), *A Wiser Century? Judicial Dispute Settlement, Disarmament and the Laws of War 100 Years after the Second Hague Peace Conferenc* (2009), pp 461–492.

– 'The Sources of International Investment Law: Concluding Thoughts', in Tarcisio Gazzini and Eric de Brabandere (eds), *International Investment Law. The Sources of Rights and Obligations* (Martinus Nijhoff Publishers 2012), pp 319–332.

– 'The ICJ as a 'Law-Formative Agency': Summary and Synthesis', in Christian J Tams and James Sloan (eds), *The Development of International Law by the International Court of Justice* (Oxford University Press 2013), pp 377–396.

– 'Die Identifikation des Völkergewohnheitsrechts', in *Freiheit und Regulierung in der Cyberwelt - Rechtsidentifikation zwischen Quelle und Gericht, Deutsche Gesellschaft für Internationales Recht Zweijahrestagung 34. 2015 Gießen* (CF Müller 2016), pp 323–372.

– 'Regulating Treaty Breaches', in Michael J Bowman and Dino Kritsiotis (eds), *Conceptual and Contextual Perspectives on the Modern Law of Treaties* (Cambridge University Press 2018), pp 440–467.

Tanaka, Yoshifumi, 'The Disproportionality Test in the Law of Maritime Delimitation' in Alex G Oude Elferink, Tore Henriksen, and Signe Veierud Busch (eds) (Cambridge University Press 2018), pp 291–318.

Tancredi, Antonello, 'The (Immediate) Post-World War II Period' in Giulio Bartolini (ed), *A History of International Law in Italy* (Oxford University Press 2020), pp 168–189.

Tasioulas, John, 'Custom, Jus Cogens, and Human Rights' in Curtis A Bradley (ed), *Custom's future: international law in a changing world* (Cambridge University Press 2016), pp 95–116.

Teubner, Gunther, 'Global Bukowina: Legal Pluralism in World Society' in Gunther Teubner (ed), *Global law without a state* (Dartmouth 1997), pp 3–30.

Thürer, Daniel and Zobl, Martin, 'Are Nuclear Weapons Really Legal?: Thoughts on the Sources of International Law and a Conception of the Law "Imperio rationis" instead of "Ratione imperii"' in Ulrich Fastenrath and others (eds), *From bilateralism to community interest: essays in honour of judge Bruno Simma* (Oxford University Press 2011), pp 184–197.

Tomka, Peter, 'The Special Agreement' in *Liber amicorum judge Shigeru Oda* (Kluwer Law International 2002), pp 553–565.

Tomuschat, Christian, 'What is 'general international law'?' in *Guerra y paz: 1945-2009: obra homenaje al Dr. Santiago Torres Bernárdez* (Universidad del Pais Vasco, Servicio Editorial 2010), pp 329–348.

– 'Article 36', in Andreas Zimmermann and others (eds), *The Statute of the International Court of Justice: A Commentary* (3rd edn, Oxford University Press 2019), pp 712–798.

Triepel, Heinrich, 'Die Kompetenzen des Bundesstaats und die geschriebene Verfassung' in Wilhelm van Calker and others (eds), *Staatsrechtliche Abhandlungen Festgabe für Paul Laband zum fünfzigsten Jahrestage der Doktor-Promotion* (Mohr Siebeck 1908) vol 2, pp 247–335.

Tunkin, Grigory Ivanovich, '"General Principles of Law" in International Law' in René Marcic and Hermann Mosler (eds), *Internationale Festschrift für Alfred Verdross zum 80. Geburtstag* (1971), pp 523–532.

– 'Soviet Theory of Sources of International Law', in Peter Fischer, Heribert Franz Köck, and Alfred Verdross (eds), *Völkerrecht und Rechtsphilosophie International Festschrift für Stephan Verosta zum 70. Geburtstag* (Duncker & Humblot 1980), pp 67–79.

Vallindas, Petros, 'General Principles of Law and the Hierarchy of the Sources of International Law' in *Grundprobleme des internationalen Rechts: Festschrift für Jean Spiropoulos* (Schimmelbusch 1957), pp 425–431.

Vec, Miloš, 'Sources of International Law in the Nineteenth-Century European Tradition: The Myth of Positivism' in *The Oxford Handbook of the Sources of International Law* (Oxford University Press 2017), pp 121–145.

Verdross, Alfred, 'Die allgemeinen Rechtsgrundsätze als Völkerrechtsquelle Zugleich ein Beitrag zum Problem der Grundnorm des positiven Völkerrechts' in Alfred Verdross and Josef Dobretsberger (eds), *Gesellschaft, Staat und Recht: Untersuchungen zur reinen Rechtslehre* (Springer 1931), pp 354–365.

Verdross, Alfred and Köck, Heribert Franz, 'Natural Law: The Tradition of Universal Reason and Authority' in Ronald Saint John MacDonald and Douglas Miller Johnston (eds), *The structure and process of international law: essays in legal philosophy doctrine and theory* (Martinus Nijhoff Publishers 1983), pp 17–50.

Vereshchetin, Vladlen S, 'Some reflections of a Russian scholar on the legacy of the Second Peace Conference' in Yves Daudet (ed), *Actualité de la Conférence de La Haye de 1907, Deuxième Conférence de la paix/ Topicality of the 1907 Hague Conference, the Second Peace Conference* (Martinus Nijhoff Publishers 2008), pp 41–50.

Viñuales, Jorge E, 'Sources of International Investment Law: Conceptual Foundations of Unruly Practices' in Samantha Besson and Jean d'Aspremont (eds), *The Oxford Handbook of the Sources of International Law* (Oxford University Press 2017), pp 1069–1094.

Virally, Michel, 'À propos de la "lex ferenda"' in *Mélanges offerts à Paul Reuter: le droit international: unité et diversité* (Pedone 1981), pp 519–533.

Visscher, Charles de, 'Stages in the Codification of International Law' in Wolfgang Friedmann, Louis Henkin, and Oliver Lissitzyn (eds), *Transnational law in a changing society: essays in honor of Philip C. Jessup* (Columbia University Press 1972), pp 17–33.

Waibel, Michael, 'Interpretive Communities in International Law' in Andrea Bianchi, Daniel Peat, and Matthew Windsor (eds), *Interpretation in International Law* (Oxford University Press 2015), pp 147–165.

Waldock, Humphrey, 'The Evolution of Human Rights Concepts and the Application of the European Convention on Human Rights' in *Mélanges offerts à Paul Reuter* (Pedone 1981), pp 535–547.

Walters, Mark D, 'The Unwritten Constitution as a Legal Concept' in David Dyzenhaus and Malcolm Thorburn (eds), *Philosophical Foundations of Constitutional Law* (Oxford University Press 2016), pp 33–52.

Webb, Philippa, 'A Moving Target: The Approach of the Strasbourg Court to Immunity' in Anne van Aaken and Iulia Motoc (eds), *The European Convention on Human Rights and general international law* (Oxford University Press 2018), pp 251–263.

Weigend, Thomas, 'Indirect Perpetration' in Carsten Stahn (ed), *The law and practice of the International Criminal Court* (Oxford University Press 2015), pp 538–556.

Werle, Gerhard and Burghardt, Boris, 'Establishing Degrees of Responsibility: Modes of Participation in Article 25 of the ICC Statute' in Elies van Sliedregt and Sergey Vasiliev (eds), *Pluralism in International Criminal Law* (Oxford University Press 2014), pp 3019–319.

Wet, Erika de, 'Sources and the Hierarchy of International Law: The Place of Peremptory Norms and Article 103 of the UN Charter within the Sources of International Law' in Samantha Besson and Jean d'Aspremont (eds), *The*

Oxford Handbook on the Sources of International Law (Oxford University Press 2017), pp 625–639.

Wiederin, Ewald, 'Regel-Prinzip-Norm. Zu einer Kontroverse zwischen Hans Kelsen und Josef Esser' in Stanley L Paulson and Robert Walter (eds), *Untersuchungen zur Reinen Rechtslehre Ergebnisse eines Wiener Rechtstheoretischen Seminars 1985/1986* (Manzsche Verlags- und Universitätsbuchhandlung 1986), pp 137–166.

Wilhelm, Walter, 'Das Recht im römischen Recht' in Franz Wieacker and Christian Wollschläger (eds), *Jherings Erbe* (Vandenhoeck & Ruprecht 1970).

Wouters, Jan and Ryngaert, Cedric, 'Impact on the Process of the Formation of Customary International Law' in Menno Tjeerd Kamminga and Martin Scheinin (eds), *The Impact of Human Rights Law on General International Law* (Oxford University Press 2009), pp 111–131.

Yanev, Lachezar, 'Joint Criminal Enterprise' in Jérôme de Hemptinne, Robert Roth, and Elies van Sliedregt (eds), *Modes of Liability in International Criminal Law* (Cambridge University Press 2019), pp 120–170.

Yasuaki, Onuma, 'The ICJ: An Emperor Without Clothes? International Conflict Resolution, Article 38 of the ICJ Statute and the Sources of International Law' in Nisuke Ando and others (eds), *Liber amicorum Judge Shigeru Oda* (Kluwer Law Internat 2002) vol 1, pp 191–212.

Zemanek, Karl, 'State Responsibility and Liability' in Winfried Lang, Hanspeter Neuhold, and Karl Zemanek (eds), *Environmental Protection and International Law* (Graham & Trotman 1991), pp 187–197.

– 'The Metamorphosis of Jus Cogens: From an Institution of Treaty Law to the Bedrock of the International Legal Order?', in Enzo Cannizzaro (ed), *The Law of Treaties beyond the Vienna Convention* (Oxford University Press 2011), pp 381–410.

Ziemele, Ineta, 'European Consensus and International Law' in Anne van Aaken and Iulia Motoc (eds), *The European Convention on Human Rights and General International Law* (Oxford University Press 2018), pp 23–40.

Zimmermann, Andreas, 'The International Court of Justice and State Succession to Treaties: Avoiding Principled Answers to Questions of Principle' in Christian J Tams and James Sloan (eds), *The Development of International Law by the International Court of Justice* (Oxford University Press 2013), pp 53–68.

Zimmermann, Andreas and Geiß, Robin, 'Article 8(2)(e)(vii)' in Kai Ambos (ed), *The Rome Statute of the International Criminal Court* (4th edn, Beck 2021).

Zollmann, Jakob, ''Civilization(s)' and 'civilized nations' – of history, anthropology, and international law' in Sean P Morris (ed), *Transforming the Politics of International Law: The Advisory Committee of Jurists and the Formation of the World Court in the League of Nations* (Routledge 2021), pp 11–33.

Zyberi, Gentian, 'The International Court of Justice and the Rights of Peoples and Minorities' in Christian J Tams and James Sloan (eds), *The Development of International Law by the International Court of Justice* (Oxford University Press 2013), pp 327–352.

Periodicals

Aaken, Anne van, 'To Do Away with International Law? Some Limits to 'The Limits of International Law'' (2006) 17(1) EJIL 289–308.
– 'Defragmentation of Public International Law Through Interpretation: A Methodological Proposal' (2009) 16(2) Indiana Journal of Global Legal Studies 483–512.
Abi-Saab, Georges, 'Cours général de droit international public' (1987) 207 RdC 9–463.
– 'Fragmentation or Unification: Some Concluding Remarks' (1998) 31 NYU JILP 919–933.
Ago, Robert, 'Le délit international' (1939) 68(2) RdC 415–554.
Ago, Roberto, 'Science juridique et droit international' (1956) 90 RdC 851–958.
– 'Positive Law and International Law' (1957) 51 AJIL 691–733.
– 'Droit des traités à la lumière de la Convention de Vienne' (1971) 134 RdC 297–331.
– 'Nouvelles reflexions sur la codification du droit international' (1988) 92 RGDIP 539–576.
Akande, Dapo, 'International Law Immunities and the International Criminal Court' (2004) 98 AJIL 407–433.
– 'The Legal Nature of Security Council Referrals to the ICC and its Impact on Al Bashir's Immunities' (2009) 7 JICJ 333–352.
– 'Selection of the International Court of Justice for Contentious and Advisory Proceedings (Including Jurisdiction)' (2016) 7 JIDS 320–344.
Akande, Dapo and Shah, Sangeeta, 'Immunities of State Officials, International Crimes, and Foreign Domestic Courts' (2010) 21 EJIL 815–852.

Akande, Dapo and Williams, Sope, 'International adjudication on national security issues: what role for the WTO?' (2003) 43(2) Virginia Journal of International Law 365–404.

Akehurst, Michael, 'Hierarchy of Sources' (1974) 47 BYIL 273–285.

Alebeek, Rosanne van, 'The "International Crime" Exception in the ILC Draft Articles on the Immunity of State Officials from Foreign Criminal Jurisdiction: Two Steps Back?' (2018) 112 AJIL Unbound 27–32.

Alexy, Robert, 'Zum Begriff des Rechtsprinzip' (1979) Beiheft 1 Rechtstheorie 59–87.

– 'Grundrechte als Subjektive Rechte und als Objektive Normen' (1990) 29 Der Staat 49–68.

– 'Constitutional Rights, Balancing, and Rationality' (2003) 16(2) Ratio Juris 131–140.

Alland, Denis, 'Countermeasures of General Interest' (2002) 13(5) EJIL 1221–1239.

– 'L'interprétation du droit international public' (2012) 362 RdC 41–394.

Allott, Philip, 'Language, Method and the Nature of International Law' (1971) 45 BYIL 79–135.

– 'The Courts and Parliament: Who Whom?' (1979) 38(1) Cambridge Law Journal 79–117.

– 'State Responsibility and the Unmaking of International Law' (1988) 29(1) Harvard International Law Journal 1–26.

– 'The Concept of International Law' (1999) 10 EJIL 31–50.

Alston, Philip, 'Conjuring Up New Human Rights: A Proposal For Quality Control' (1984) 87 AJIL 607–621.

– 'Resisting the Merger and Acquisition of Human Rights by Trade Law: A Reply to Petersmann' (2002) 13(4) EJIL 815–844.

– ''Core Labour Standards' and the Transformation of the International Labour Rights Regime' (2003) 15(3) EJIL 457–521.

Alvarez, José, 'A Bit on Custom' (2009) 42 NYU JILP 17–80.

– ''Beware: Boundary Crossings'- A Critical Appraisal of Public Law Approaches to International Investment Law' (2016) 17 The Journal of World Investment & Trade 171–228.

Alvarez, José and Brink, Tegan, 'Revisiting the Necessity Defense' [2010] Yearbook International Investment Law & Policy 319–362.

Alvarez, José E, 'The Public International Law Regime Governing International Investment' (2009) 344 RdC 193–541.

- 'The Use (and Misuse) of European Human Rights Law in Investor-State Dispute Settlement' [2016] SSRN ⟨https://papers.ssrn.com/sol3/papers.cfm?abstract_id=2875089⟩ accessed 1 February 2023.
- Alvarez, José Enrique and Khamsi, Kathryn, 'The Argentine Crisis and Foreign Investors: a Glimpse into the Heart of the Investment Regime' (2009) 2008-2009 Yearbook on international investment law & policy 379–478.
- Ambos, Kai, 'Joint Criminal Enterprise and Command Responsibility' (2007) 5(1) JICJ 159–183.
- 'Amicus Curiae Brief in the Matter of the Co-Prosecutors' Appeal on the Closing Order Against Kaing Guek Eav "Dutch" Dated 8 August 2008' (2009) 20 Criminal Law Forum 353–388.
- Ambos, Kai and Wirth, Steffen, 'The Current Law of Crimes Against Humanity An analysis of UNTAET Regulation 15/2000' (2002) 13 Criminal Law Forum 1–90.
- Anschütz, Gerhard, 'Der deutsche Föderalismus in Vergangenheit, Gegenwart und Zukunft' (1924) 1 Veröffentlichungen der Vereinigung der Deutschen Staatsrechtslehrer 11–34.
- Anzilotti, Dionisio, 'La responsabilité internationale des états: à raison des dommages soufferts par des étrangers' (1906) 13 RGDIP 5–29.
- Arato, Julian, 'Constitutional Transformation in the ECtHR: Strasbourg's Expansive Recourse to External Rules of International Law' (2012) 37(2) Brooklyn Journal of International Law 349–387.
- 'The Margin of Appreciation in International Investment Law' (2013) 54(2) Virginia Journal of International Law 1–34.
- 'Treaty Interpretation and Constitutional Transformation: Informal Change in International Organizations' (2013) 38 Yale Journal of International Law 289–357.
- 'Corporations as Lawmakers' (2015) 56 Harvard International Law Journal 229–295.
- Ascensio, Hervé and Bonafé, Béatrice I, 'L'absence d'immunité des agents de l'Etat en cas de crime international : pourquoi en débattre encore?' (2018) 122 RGDIP 821–850.
- Atiyah, Patrick S, 'Common Law and Statute Law' (1985) 48(1) The Modern Law Review 1–28.
- Azaria, Danae, ''Codification by Interpretation': The International Law Commission as an Interpreter of International Law' (2020) 31 EJIL 171–200.
- Baade, Björnstjern, 'The ECtHR's Role as a Guardian of Discourse: Safeguarding a Decision-Making Process Based on Well-Established Stan-

dards, Practical Rationality, and Facts' (2018) 31 Leiden Journal of International Law 335–361.

Badar, Mohamed Elewa, ''Just Convict Everyone!'-Joint Perpetration: From Tadić to Stakić and Back Again' (2006) 6 International Criminal Law Review 293–302.

Bailey, Stephen, 'Article 21(3) of the Rome Statute: a Plea for Clarity' (2014) 14(3) International Criminal Law Review 513–550.

Baker, Betsy, 'Hague Peace Conferences (1899 and 1907)' [2009] Max Planck EPIL.

Baker, PJ, 'The Codification of International Law' (1924) 5 BYIL 38–65.

Bar, Carl Ludwig von, 'Grundlage und Kodifikation des Völkerrechts' (1912) 6(1) Archiv für Rechts- und Wirtschaftsphilosophie 145–158.

Bartels, Rogier, 'The Classification of Armed Conflicts by International Criminal Courts and Tribunals' (2020) 20 International Criminal Law Review 595–668.

Basdevant, Jules, 'Règles générales du droit de la paix' (1936) 58 RdC 471–715.

Bassiouni, Mahmoud Cherif, 'A functional approach to "general principles of international law"' (1990) 11(3) Michigan Journal of International Law 768–818.

– 'The History of the Draft Code of Crimes Against the Peace and Security of Mankind' (1993) 27(1-2) Israel Law Review 247–267.

Bassiouni, Mahmoud Cherif and Blaskesley, Christopher L, 'The Need for an International Criminal Court in the New International World Order' (1992) 25(2) Vanderbilt Journal of Transnational Law 151–182.

Baxter, Richard R, 'Multilateral Treaties as Evidence of Customary International Law' (1965) 41 BYIL 275–300.

Baxter, Richard Reeve, 'Treaties and Customs' (1970) 129 RdC 27–105.

Beatson, Jack, 'Has the Common Law a Future?' (1997) 56(2) The Cambridge Law Journal 291–314.

Beckett, WE, 'Diplomatic Claims in Respect of Injuries to Companies' (1931) 17 Transactions of the Grotius Society.

Bell, Caitlin A, 'Reassessing Multiple Attribution: the International Law Commission and the Behrami and Saramati Decision' (2010) 42(2) NYU JILP 501–548.

Bellinger, John B and Haynes, William J, 'A US government response to the International Committee of the Red Cross study Customary International Humanitarian Law' (2007) 89(866) International Review of the Red Cross 443–471.

Benson, Bruce L, 'Customary Law as a Social Contract: International Commercial Law' (1992) 3(1) Constitutional Political Economy 1–27.

Benvenisti, Eyal, 'Democracy Captured: The Mega-Regional Agreements and the Future of Global Public Law' [2016] (2) IILJ Working Paper 1–23.

Bernhardt, Rudolf, 'Ungeschriebenes Völkerrecht' (1976) 37 ZaöRV 50–76.

– 'Custom and treaty in the law of the sea' (1987) 205 RdC 247–330.

Bernstorff, Jochen von, 'Georg Jellinek and the Origins of Liberal Constitutionalism in International Law' (2012) 4(3) Goettingen Journal of International Law 659–675.

– 'Hans Kelsen on Judicial Law-Making by International Courts and Tribunals: a Theory of Global Judicial Imperialism?' (2015) 14(1) The law and practice of international courts and tribunals: a practitioners' journal 35–50.

– 'The Use of Force in International Law before World War I: On Imperial Ordering and the Ontology of the Nation-State' (2018) 29(1) EJIL 233–260.

Bianchi, Andrea, 'Human Rights and the Magic of Jus Cogens' (2008) 19(3) EJIL 491–508.

Biddulph, Michelle and Newman, Dwight, 'A Contextualized Account of General Principles of International Law' (2014) 26(2) Pace International Law Review 286–344.

Bigi, Giulia, 'Joint Criminal Enterprise in the Jurisprudence of the International Criminal Tribunal for the Former Yugoslavia and the Prosecution of Senior Political and Military Leaders: The Krajišnik Case' (2010) 14 Max Planck Yearbook of United Nations Law 51–83.

Bingham, Tom, 'The Alabama Claims Arbitration' (2005) 54 ICLQ 1–25.

Bjørge, Eirik, 'Common Law Rights: Balancing Domestic and International Exigencies' (2016) 75(2) Cambridge Law Journal 220–243.

– 'The Contribution of the European Court of Human Rights to General International Law' (2019) 79(4) ZaöRV 765–784.

Blandford, Andrew C, 'The History of Fair and Equitable Treatment before the Second World War' (2017) 32 ICSID Review 287–303.

Bleckmann, Albert, 'Zur Feststellung und Auslegung von Völkergewohnheitsrecht' (1977) 37 ZaöRV 504–529.

Block, Johannes, 'Ordering as an Alternative to Indirect Co-Perpetration. Observations on the Ntaganda Case' (2022) 20 JICJ 717–735.

Blommestijn, Michiel and Ryngaert, Cedric, 'Exploring the Obligations for States to Act upon the ICC's Arrest Warrant for Omar Al-Bashir: A Legal Conflict between the Duty to Arrest and the Customary Status of Head of State Immunity' (2010) 6 Zeitschrift für Internationale Strafrechtsdogmatik 428–444.

Blutman, László, 'Conceptual Confusion and Methodological Deficiencies: Some Ways that Theories on Customary International Law Fail' (2014) 25(2) EJIL 529–552.

Bodansky, Daniel, 'Customary (and Not So Customary) International Environmental Law' (1995) 3 Indiana Journal of Global Legal Studies 105–119.

Bogdandy, Armin von, Goldmann, Matthias, and Venzke, Ingo, 'From Public International Public Law: Translating World Public Opinion into International Public Authority' (2017) 28(1) EJIL 115–145.

Bogdandy, Armin von and Venzke, Ingo, 'Zur Herrschaft internationaler Gerichte: Eine Untersuchung internationaler öffentlicher Gewalt und ihrer demokratischen Rechtfertigung' (2010) 70 ZaöRV 1–49.

Bogg, Alan, 'Common Law and Statute in the Law of Employment' (2016) 69(1) Current Legal Problems 67–113.

Borchard, Edwin, 'The Minimum Standard of the Treatment of Aliens' (1939) 33 American Society of International Law Proceedings 51–63.

– 'The 'Minimum Standard' of the Treatment of Aliens' (1940) 38(4) Michigan Law Review 445–461.

Borchard, Edwin M, '"Responsibility of States," at the Hague Codification Conference' (1930) 24 AJIL 517–540.

Bordin, Fernando Lusa, 'Reflections of Customary International Law: The Authority of Codification Conventions and ILC Draft Articles in International Law' (2014) 63 ICLQ 535–567.

Bos, Maarten, 'The Recognized Manifestations of International Law A New Theory of "Sources"' (1977) 20 German Yearbook of International Law 9–76.

Boschiero, Nerina, 'The ICC Judicial Finding on Non-cooperation Against the DRC and No Immunity for Al-Bashir Based on UNSC Resolution 1593' (2015) 13 JICJ 625–653.

Bothe, Michael, 'Die Bedeutung der Rechtsvergleichung in der Praxis internationaler Gerichte' (1976) 36 ZaöRV 280–299.

Bowen, Paul, 'Does the renaissance of common law rights mean that the Human Rights Act 1998 is now unnecessary?' [2016] (4) European Human Rights Law Review 361–277.

Bradley, Curtis A, 'Introduction to the Symposium on the Present and Future of Foreign Official Immunity' (2018) 112 AJIL Unbound 1–3.

Bradley, Curtis A and Goldsmith, Jack L, 'Customary International Law as Federal Common Law: A Critique of the Modern Position' (1997) 110(4) Harvard Law Review 815–876.
- 'The Current Illegitimacy of International Human Rights Litigation' (1997) 66(2) Fordham Law Review 319–369.
Bradley, Curtis A and Gulati, Mitu, 'Withdrawing from International Custom' (2010) 120 Yale Law Journal 202–275.
Brierly, James Leslie, 'The Future of Codification' (1931) 12 BYIL 1–12.
Brown, Henry B, 'The Proposed International Prize Court' (1908) 2 AJIL 476–489.
Brownlie, Ian, 'The Relations of Nationality in Public International Law,' [1963] (39) BYIL 284–264.
- 'International Law at the Fiftieth Anniversary of the United Nations, General Course on Public International Law' (1995) 255 RdC 9–228.
Brunnée, Jutta and Toope, Stephen John, 'International Law and Constructivism: Elements of an Interactional Theory of International Law' (2000) 39 Columbia Journal of Transnational Law 19–74.
- 'Interactional international law: an introduction' (2011) 3(2) International Theory 307–318.
Burchardt, Dana, 'Book review of Jean d'Aspremont, International Law as a Belief System' (2018) 29 EJIL 1440–1447.
Burke, Naomi, 'Nicaragua v Colombia at the ICJ: Better the Devil You Don't?' (2013) 2(2) Cambridge Journal of International and Comparative Law 314–326.
Buzzini, Gionata Piero, 'La "généralité" du droit international général: réflexions sur la polysémie d'un concept' (2004) 108 RGDIP 381–406.
Caflisch, Lucius C, 'The Protection of Corporate Investments Abroad in the Light of the Barcelona Traction Case' (1971) 31 ZaöRV 162–106.
Çali, Başak, 'On Interpretivism and International Law' (2009) 20(3) EJIL 805–822.
Cançado Trindade, Antônio Augusto, 'International Law for Humankind: Towards a New Jus Gentium (I)' (2005) 316 RdC 9–440.
- 'The Contribution of Latin American Legal Doctrine to the Progressive Development of International Law' (2014) 376 RdC 9–92.
Cannizzaro, Enzo and Bonafé, Beatrice, 'Fragmenting International Law through Compromissory Clauses? Some Remarks on the Decision of the ICJ in the Oil Platforms Case' (2005) 16(3) EJIL 481–497.

Cantegreil, Julien, 'The Audacity of the Texaco/Calasiatic Award: René-Jean Dupuy and the Internationalization of Foreign Investment Law' (2011) 22(2) EJIL 441–458.
Cao, Xun, 'Networks as Channels of Policy Diffusion: Explaining Worldwide Changes in Capital Taxation, 1998-2006' (2010) 54 International Studies Quarterly 823–854.
Carbone, Sergio and Schiano di Pepe, Lorenzo, 'States, Fundamental Rights and Duties' [2009] Max Planck EPIL.
Caron, David, 'The ILC Articles on State Responsibility: The Paradoxical Relationship Between Form and Authority' (2002) 96 AJIL 857–873.
Caron, David D, 'War and International Adjudication: Reflections on the 1899 Peace Conference' (2000) 84 AJIL 4–30.
Cassese, Antonio, 'Remarks on Scelle's Theory of "Role Splitting" (dédoublement fonctionnel) in International Law' (1990) 1 EJIL 210–231.
– 'The Statute of the International Criminal Court: Some Preliminary Reflections' (1999) 10 EJIL 144–171.
– 'The Martens Clause: half a loaf or simply pie in the sky?' (2000) 11(1) EJIL 187–216.
– 'Balancing the Prosecution of Crimes against Humanity and Non-Retroactivity of Criminal Law' (2006) 4 JICJ 410–418.
– 'The Nicaragua and Tadić Tests Revisited in Light of the ICJ Judgment on Genocide in Bosnia' (2007) 18(4) EJIL 649–668.
Castberg, Frede, 'La méthodologie du droit international public' (1933) 43 RdC 309–384.
Cavaglieri, Arrigo, 'Concetto E Caratteri Del Diritto Internazionale Generale' (1921) 14 Rivista Di Diritto Internazionale 479–506.
– 'Concetto e caratteri del diritto internazionale generale' (1922) 14 Estratto dalla Rivista di diritto internazionale 289–314, 479–506.
– 'Règles générales du droit de la paix' (1929) 26 RdC 311–585.
Charlesworth, Hilary CM, 'Customary International Law and the Nicaragua Case' (1984) 11 Australian Yearbook of International Law 1–31.
Charney, Jonathan I, 'Universal International Law' (1993) 87 AJIL 529–551.
– 'The Impact on the International Legal System of the Growth of International Courts and Tribunals' (1998) 31 NYU JILP 697–708.
Chasapis Tassinis, Orfeas, 'Customary International Law: Interpretation from Beginning to End' (2020) 31 EJIL 235–267.
Chasapis Tassinis, Orfeas and Nouwen, Sarah, ''The Consciousness of Duty Done'? British Attitudes towards Self-Determination and the Case of the Sudan' (2019) First View BYIL 1–56.

Cheng, Bin, 'Rights of United States Nationals in the French Zone of Morocco' (1953) 2 ICLQ 854–876.
- 'United Nations Resolutions on Outer Space: 'Instant' International Customary Law?' (1965) 5 Indian Journal of International Law 23.
Chimni, BS, 'Customary International Law: A Third World Perspective' (2018) 112(1) AJIL 1–46.
Chodosh, Hiram E, 'Neither Treaty nor Custom: The Emergence of Declarative International Law' (1991) 26 Texas International Law Journal 87–124.
Christensen, Mikkel Jarle and Orina, Nabil M, 'The International Criminal Court as a Law Laboratory. Professional Battles of Control and the 'Control of the Crime' Theory' (2022) 20 JICJ 699–716.
Clarke, Robert Charles, 'Together Again? Customary Law and Control over the Crime' (2015) 26 Criminal Law Forum 457–495.
Clayton, Richard, 'The empire strikes back: common law rights and the Human Rights Acts' [2015] Public Law 3–12.
Conforti, Benedetto, 'Le rôle de l'accord dans le système des Nations Unies' (1974) 142(2) RdC 203–288.
Crawford, James, 'The ILC's Draft Statute for an International Criminal Tribunal' (1994) 88(1) AJIL 140–152.
- 'Book Review' (1996) 90(2) AJIL 331–333.
- 'Multilateral Rights and Obligations in International Law' (2006) 319 RdC 325–482.
- 'Change, Order, Change: The Course of International Law General Course on Public International Law' (2013) 365 RdC 9–389.
Crawford, James and Olleson, Simon, 'The Exception of Non-performance: Links between the Law of Treaties and the Law of State Responsibility' (2000) 21 Australian Year Book of International Law 55–74.
Cremer, Hans-Joachim, 'Völkerrecht - Alles nur Rhetorik?' (2007) 67 ZaöRV 267–296.
Cryer, Robert, 'Of Custom, Treaties, Scholars and the Gavel: The Influence of International Criminal Tribunals on the ICRC Customary Law Study' (2006) 11 Journal of Conflict and Security Law 239–263.
- 'Royalism and the King: Article 21 of the Rome Statute and the Politics of Sources' (2009) 12(3) New Criminal Law Review: An International and Interdisciplinary Journal 390–405.
Cupido, Marjolein, 'The Control Theory as Multidimensional Concept. Reflections on the Ntaganda Appeal Judgment' (2022) 20 JICJ 637–656.

Czaplinski, Wladyslaw, 'State Succession and State Responsibility' (1990) 28 Canadian Yearbook of International Law 339–360.

D'Amato, Anthony, 'Treaties As a Source of General Rules of International Law' (1962) 3 Harvard International Law Journal 1–43.

– 'Trashing Customary International Law' (1987) 81 AJIL 101–105.
– 'Human Rights as Part of Customary International Law: A Plea for Change of Paradigms' (1995) 25(1) Georgia journal of international and comparative law 47–98.
– 'Groundwork for International Law' (2014) 108 AJIL 650–679.

d'Aspremont, Jean, 'Softness in International Law: A Self-Serving Quest for New Legal Materials' (2008) 19(5) EJIL 1075–1093.

– 'The Politics of Deformalization in International Law' (2011) 3 Goettingen Journal of International Law 503–550.
– 'Reductionist legal positivism in international law' (2012) 106 Proceedings of the American Society of International Law at Its Annual Meeting 368–370.
– 'The Idea of 'Rules' in the Sources of International Law' (2014) 84 BYIL 103–130.
– 'Expansionism and the Sources of International Human Rights Law' (2016) 46 Israel Yearbook on Human rights 223–242.
– 'The Decay of Modern Customary International Law in Spite of Scholarly Heroism' [2016] The Global Community Yearbook of International Law and Jurisprudence 9–29.
– 'The International Court of Justice, the Whales, and the Blurring of the Lines between Sources and Interpretation' (2016) 27(4) EJIL 1027–1041.
– 'A Postmodernization of Customary International Law for the First World?' (2018) 112 AJIL Unbound 293–296.
– 'The Four Lives of Customary International Law' [2019] International Community Law Review 229–256.

Degan, Vladimir-Djuro, 'General Principles of Law (A Source of General International Law)' (1992) 3 Finnish Yearbook of International Law 1–102.

– 'On the Sources of International Criminal Law' (2008) 4(1) Chinese Journal of International Law 45–83.

Delaume, Georges R, 'The Proper Law of State Contracts and the Lex Mercatoria: A Reappraisal' (1988) 3(1) ICSID Review - Foreign Investment Law Journal 79–106.

– 'The Proper Law of State Contracts Revisited' (1997) 12(1) ICSID Review - Foreign Investment Law Journal 1–28.

Dimitrijević, Vojin and Milanović, Marko, 'The Strange Story of the Bosnian Genocide Case' (2008) 21(1) Leiden Journal of International Law 65–94.

Dinstein, Yoram, 'The interaction between customary international law and treaties' (2006) 322 RdC 243–428.

– 'Command Responsibility' [2013] Max Planck EPIL.

'Discussion' (1939) 33 American Society of International Law Proceedings 64–74.

Dodge, William S, 'Customary international law, Change, and the Constitution' (2018) 106 The Georgetown Law Journal 1559–1591.

Dolzer, Rudolf, 'Abu Dhabi Oil Arbitration' [2006] Max Planck EPIL.

Doswald-Beck, Louise and Vité, Sylvain, 'International Humanitarian Law and Human Rights Law' (1993) 33 International Review of the Red Cross 94–119.

Du Plessis, Max and Ford, Jolyon, 'Developing the common law progressively - horizontality, the Human Rights Act and the South African experience' [2004] (3) European Human Rights Law Review 286–313.

Dumberry, Patrick, 'Are BITs Representing the "New" Customary International Law in International Investment Law?' (2009) 28(4) Penn State International Law Review 675–702.

– 'A few observations on the remaining fundamental importance of customary rules in the age of treatification in international investment law' (2016) 35(1) ASA bulletin = Schweizerische Vereinigung für Schiedsgerichtsbarkeit 41–61.

– 'Has the Fair and Equitable Treatment Standard Become a Rule of Customary International Law?' (2017) 8 JIDS 155–178.

Dunn, Frederick Sherwood, 'International Law and Private Property Rights' (1928) 28 Columbia Law Review 166–180.

Dupuy, Pierre-Marie, 'Communauté Internationale et Disparités de Développement Cours général de droit international public' (1979) 165 RdC 9–232.

– 'Dionisio Anzilotti and the Law of International Responsibility of States' (1992) 2 EJIL 139–147.

– 'The Danger of Fragmentation or Unification of the International Legal System and the International Court of Justice' (1998) 31 NYU JILP 791–808.

– 'L'unité de l'ordre juridique international: cours général de droit international public' (2002) 279 RdC 9–489.

– 'A Crime without Punishment' (2016) 14 JICJ 879–891.

Duxbury, Neil, 'Custom as Law in English Law' (2017) 76(2) Cambridge Law Journal 337–359.
Dworkin, Ronald, 'The Model of Rules' (1967) 35(1) University of Chicago Law Review 14–46.
– 'Hard Cases' (1975) 88(6) Harvard Law Review 1057–1109.
Eckhoff, Torstein, 'Guiding Standards in Legal Reasoning' (1976) 29(1) Current Legal Problems 205–219.
Elias, Olufemi and Lim, Chin, ''General Principles of Law', 'Soft' Law and the Identification of International Law' (1997) 28 Netherlands Yearbook of International Law 3–49.
Elliott, Mark, 'Beyond the European Convention: Human Rights and the Common Law' (2015) 68 Current Legal Problems 85–117.
Ellis, Jaye, 'General Principles and Comparative Law' (2011) 22(4) EJIL 949–971.
Epik, Aziz, 'No Functional Immunity for Crimes under International Law before Foreign Domestic Courts' (2021) 19 JICJ 1263–1281.
Fachiri, Alexander P, 'Expropriation and international law' (1925) 6 BYIL 159–171.
– 'International Law and the Property of Aliens' (1929) 10 BYIL 32–55.
Fastenrath, Ulrich, 'Relative Normativity in International Law' (1993) 4 EJIL 305–340.
Fatouros, Arghyrios Athanasiou, 'International Law and the Internationalized Contract' (1980) 74 AJIL 134–141.
Fauchald, Ole Kristian, 'The Legal Reasoning of ICSID Tribunals - An Empirical Analysis' (2008) 19(2) EJIL 301–364.
Feinäugle, Clemens, 'The Wimbledon' [2013] Max Planck EPIL.
Finke, Jasper, 'Sovereign Immunity: Rule, Comity or Something Else?' (2010) 21(4) EJIL 853–881.
Finnemore, Martha and Sikkink, Kathryn, 'International Norm Dynamics and Political Change' (1998) 52(4) International Organization 887–917.
Fitzmaurice, Gerald, 'The Law and Procedure of the International Court of Justice, 1951-54: General Principles and Sources of Law' (1953) 30 BYIL 1–70.
– 'The General Principles of International Law considered from the standpoint of the rule of law' (1957) 92 RdC 1–228.
– 'The Law and Procedure of the International Court of Justice 1951-4: Treaty Interpretation and Other Treaty Points' (1957) 33 BYIL 203–293.

- 'The Future of Public International Law and of the International Legal System in the Circumstances of Today' (1975) 5(1) International Relations 743–775.
Fletcher, George P, 'New Court, Old Dogmatik' (2011) 9 JICJ 179–190.
Fontanelli, Filippo, 'The Invocation of the Exception of Non-Performance: A Case-Study on the Role and Application of General Principles of International Law of Contractual Origin' (2012) 1(1) Cambridge Journal of International and Comparative Law 119–136.
Forlati, Serena, 'Reactions to Non-Performance of Treaties in International Law' (2015) 25 Leiden Journal of International Law 759–770.
Forteau, Mathias, 'Immunities and International Crimes before the ILC: Looking for Innovative solutions' (2018) 112 AJIL Unbound 22–26.
Frank, Jerome, 'Civil Law Influences on the Common Law - Some Reflections on 'Comparative' and 'Contrastive' Law' (1956) 104(7) University of Pennsylvania Law Review 887–926.
Friedmann, Wolfgang, 'Review of Grundsatz und Norm in der richterlichen Fortbildung des Privatrechts by Josef Esser' (1957) 57(3) Columbia Law Review 449–451.
- 'The Uses of "General Principles" in the Development of International Law' (1963) 57 AJIL 279–299.
- 'General Course in Public International Law' (1969) 127 RdC 39–246.
- 'The North Sea Continental Shelf Cases- A Critique' (1970) 64 AJIL 229–240.
Frulli, Micaela, 'The Question of Charles Taylor's Immunity' (2004) 2 JICJ 1118–1129.
Frulli, Micaela, 'The Contribution of International Criminal Tribunals to the Development of International Law: The Prominence of opinio juris and the Moralization of Customary Law' (2015) 14 The Law and Practice of International Courts and Tribunals 80–93.
- 'On the existence of a customary rule granting functional immunity to State officials and its exceptions: back to square one' (2016) 26 Duke Journal of Comparative & International Law 479–502.
Fuller, Lon L, 'Positivism and Fidelity to Law: A Reply to Professor Hart' (1958) 71(4) Harvard Law Review 630–672.
- 'Human Interaction and the Law' (1969) 14 The American Journal of Jurisprudence 1–36.
Gaeta, Paola, 'On What Conditions Can a State Be Held Responsible for Genocide?' (2007) 18(4) EJIL 631–648.

Gaeta, Paola, 'Does President Al Bashir Enjoy Immunity from Arrest?' (2009) 7 JICJ 315–332.

Gahagan, Stacey Marlise, 'Returning to Vattel: A Gentlement's Agreement for the Twenty-First Century' (2012) 37 North Carolina Journal of International Law 847–888.

Gaja, Giorgio, 'Positivism and Dualism in Dionisio Anzilotti' (1992) 3 EJIL 123–138.

– 'The Protection of General Interests in the International Community' (2012) 364 RdC 9–186.

– 'General Principles of Law' [2013] Max Planck EPIL.

Galindo, George Rodrigo Bandeira and Yip, César, 'Customary International Law and the Third World: Do Not Step on the Grass' (2017) 16(2) Chinese Journal of International Law 251–270.

García-Amador, Francisco, 'State Responsibility in the Light of the New Trends of International Law' (1955) 49 AJIL 339–346.

Gärditz, Klaus Ferdinand, 'Ungeschriebenes Völkerrecht durch Systembildung' (2007) 45(1) Archiv des Völkerrechts 1–34.

Garnett, Richard, 'State and Diplomatic Immunity and Employment Rights: European Law to the Rescue?' (2015) 64 ICLQ 783–827.

Gautier, Philippe, 'Non-Binding Agreements' [2006] Max Planck EPIL.

Goldmann, Matthias, 'Inside Relative Normativity: From Sources to Standard Instruments for the Exercise of International Public Authority' (2008) 9(11) German Law Journal 1865–1908.

– 'Dogmatik als Rationale Rekonstruktion: Versuch einer Metatheorie am Beispiel völkerrechtlicher Prinzipien' (2014) 53(3) Der Staat 373–399.

Goldschmidt, Levin, 'Projet de réglement pour tribunaux arbitraux internationaux (session de Genève, 1874)' (1874) 6 Revue de droit international et de législation comparée 421–452.

Gomes Trivisonno, Alexandre Travessoni, 'Legal Principles, Discretion and Legal Positivism: Does Dworkin's Criticism on Hart also Apply to Kelsen?' (2016) 102 Archiv für Rechts- und Sozialphilosophie 112–127.

Goodman, Ryan, 'Human Rights Treaties, Invalid Reservations, and State Consent' (2002) 96(3) AJIL 531–560.

Goodman, Ryan and Jinks, Derek, 'Measuring the Effects of Human Rights Treaties' (2003) 14 EJIL 171–183.

Goodman, Ryan and Jinks, Derek P, 'Filartiga's Firm Footing: International Human Rights And Federal Common Law' (1997) 66(2) Fordham Law Review 463–529.

Gourgourinis, Anastasios, 'General/Particular International Law and Primary/Secondary Rules: Unitary Terminology of a Fragmented System' (2011) 22 EJIL 993–1026.
– 'The Distinction between Interpretation and Application of Norms in International Adjudication' (2011) 2(1) JIDS 31–57.
Greenhill, Brian, 'The Company You Keep: International Socialization and the Diffusion of Human Rights Norms' (2010) 54 International Studies Quarterly 127–145.
Greenhill, Brian and Strausz, Michael, 'Explaining Nonratification of the Genocide Convention: A Nested Analysis' (2014) 10 Foreign Policy Analysis 371–391.
Greenman, Kathryn, 'Aliens in Latin America: Intervention, Arbitration and State Responsibility for Rebels' (2018) 31 Leiden Journal of International Law 617–639.
Grewe, Wilhelm G, 'Vom europäischen zum universellen Völkerrecht Zur Frage der Revision des europazentrischen Bildes der Völkerrechtsgeschichte' (1982) 42 ZaöRV 449–479.
Gross, Leo, 'Der Rechtsbegriff des Common Law und das Völkerrecht' (1931) 11 Zeitschrift für öffentliches Recht 353–367.
Grossman, Nienke, 'Achieving Sex-Representative International Court Benches' (2016) 110 AJIL 82–95.
Grover, Leena, 'A Call to Arms: Fundamental Dilemmas Confronting the Interpretation of Crimes in the Rome Statute of the International Criminal Court' (2010) 21(3) EJIL 543–583.
Guggenheim, Paul, 'Contribution à l'histoire des sources du droit des gens' (1958) 94 RdC 1–84.
Guillaume, Gilbert, 'The Future of International Judicial Institutions' (1995) 44(4) ICLQ 848–862.
Guzman, Andrew T and Hsiang, Jerome, 'Some Ways that Theories on Customary International Law Fail: A Reply to László Blutman' (2014) 25(2) EJIL 553–559.
Guzman, Andrew T and Meyer, Timothy L, 'International Common Law: The Soft Law of International Tribunals' (2008) 9 Chicago Journal of International Law 515–535.
Häberle, Peter, 'Verfassungstheorie ohne Naturrecht' (1974) 99 Archiv des öffentlichen Rechts 437–463.
– 'Die offene Gesellschaft der Verfassungsinterpreten' (1975) 30 Juristenzeitung 297–305.

Häberle, Peter, 'Zum Tode von Rudolf Smend' [1975] (41) Neue Juristische Wochenzeitschrift 1874–1875.

Haggenmacher, Peter, 'La doctrine des deux éléments du droit coutumier dans la pratique de la Cour internationale' (1986) 90 RGDIP 5–125.

Hakimi, Monica, 'Making Sense of Customary International Law' (2020) 118 Michigan Law Review 1487–1537.

Hale, Brenda, 'UK Constitutionalism on the March? keynote address to the Constitutional and Administrative Law Bar Association Conference 2014' [2015] Judicial Review 201–208.

Hameed, Asif, 'Some Misunderstandings about Legislation and Law' (2017) 16(3) Chinese Journal of International Law 475–514.

Hart, Herbert LA, 'Positivism and the Separation of Law and Morals' (1958) 71(4) Harvard Law Review 593–629.

– 'Book Review of The Morality of Law by Lon L. Fuller' (1965) 78(6) Harvard Law Review 1281–1296.

Hathaway, Oona A, 'Do Human Rights Treaties Make a Difference?' (2002) 111 Yale Law Journal 1935–2042.

Hathaway, Oona A and others, 'What is a War Crime?' (2018) 44 Yale Journal of International Law 53–113.

Heilborn, Paul, 'Les Sources Du Droit International' (1926) 11 RdC 1–63.

Heller, Kevin Jon, 'What is an international crime? (A Revisionist History)' (2017) 58 Harvard International Law Journal 353–420.

– 'Specially-Affected States and the Formation of Custom' (2018) 112(2) AJIL 191–243.

– 'What is an International Crime? (A Revisionist History) A Reply to my Critics' [2018] Harvard International Law Journal Online Symposium 1–8 ⟨https://harvardilj.org/wp-content/uploads/sites/15/Heller-Reply.pdf⟩ accessed 1 February 2023.

Henkin, Louis, 'Privacy and Autonomy' (1974) 74 Columbia Law Review 1410–1433.

Hepburn, Jarrod, 'The Unidroit Principles of International Commercial Contracts and Investment Treaty Arbitration: A Limited Relationship' (2015) 64(4) ICLQ 905–933.

Herdegen, Matthias, 'Interpretation in International Law' [2013] Max Planck EPIL.

Heydte, Friedrich August von der, 'Glossen zu einer Theorie der allgemeinen Rechtsgrundsätze' (1933) 33(11/12) Die Friedens-Warte 289–300.

Hindelang, Steffen, 'Bilateral Investment Treaties, Custom and a Healthy Investment Climate: the Question of Whether Bits Influence Customary

International Law Revisited' (2004) 5(5) The journal of world investment & trade 789–809.

Holdsworth, William, 'Sir Edward Coke' (1933) 5 Cambridge Law Journal 332–346.

Howse, Robert and Chalamish, Efraim, 'The Use and Abuse of WTO Law in Investor-State Arbitration: A Reply to Jürgen Kurtz' (2009) 20(4) EJIL 1087–1094.

Howse, Robert and Teitel, Ruti G, 'Beyond Compliance: Rethinking Why International Law Matters' (2010) 1 Global Policy 127–136.

Hudson, Manley O, 'The Prospect for Future Codification' (1932) 26 AJIL 137–142.

Hurst, Cecil, 'A Plea for the Codification of International Law on New Lines' (1946) 32 Transactions of the Grotius Society 135–153.

Irving, Emma, 'The other side of the Article 21(3) coin: Human rights in the Rome Statute and the limits of Article 21(3)' (2019) 32 Leiden Journal of International Law 837–850.

Iurlaro, Francesca, 'Grotius, Dio Chrysostom and the 'Invention' of Customary ius gentium' (2018) 39 Grotiana 15–44.

Jackson, Vicki C, 'Constitutional Comparisons: Convergence, Resistance, Engagement' (2005) 119(1) Harvard Law Review 109–128.

Jain, Neha, 'Comparative International Law at the ICTY: The General Principles Experiment' (2015) 109 AJIL 486–497.

– 'Judicial Lawmaking and General Principles of Law in International Criminal Law' (2016) 57(1) Harvard International Law Journal 111–150.

Jakab, András, 'Prinzipien' (2006) 37 Rechtstheorie 49–65.

Janik, Cornelia, 'Die EMRK und internationale Organisationen: Ausdehnung und Restriktion der "equivalent protection"-Formel in der neuen Rechtsprechung des EGMR' (2010) 70(1) ZaöRV 127–179.

Janis, Mark Weston, 'Jeremy Bentham and the Fashioning of 'International Law'' (1984) 78 AJIL 405–418.

Jellinek, Georg, 'China und das Völkerrecht' (1900) 5(19) Deutsche Juristen-Zeitung 401–403.

Jenkins, David, 'From Unwritten to Written: Transformation in the British Common-Law Constitution' (2003) 36 Vanderbilt Journal of Transnational Law 863–960.

Jenks, Clarence Wilfred, 'Craftsmanship in International Law' (1956) 50(1) American Journal of International Law 32–60.

Jennings, Robert Yewdall, 'The Progressive Development of International Law and Its Codification' (1947) 24 BYIL 301–329.

Jennings, Robert Yewdall, 'State Contracts in International Law' (1961) 37 BYIL 156–182.
- 'Recent Developments in the International Law Commission: Its Relation to the Sources of International Law' (1964) 13 ICLQ 385–397.
- 'What is International Law and How Do We Tell It When We See It ?' (1981) 37 Schweizerisches Jahrbuch für internationales Recht 59–91.

Jeßberger, Florian and Geneuss, Julia, 'On the Application of a Theory of Indirect Perpetration in Al Bashir' (2008) 6 JICJ 853–869.

Jessup, Philip C, 'The Doctrine of Erie Railroad V. Tompkins Applied to International Law' (1939) 33(4) AJIL 740–743.
- 'Parliamentary diplomacy: an examination of the legal quality of the rules of procedure of organs of the United Nations' (1956) 89 RdC 181–320.

Jiménez de Aréchaga, Edurardo, 'International law in the past third of a century' (1978) 159 RdC 1–344.

Johnston, Katie A, 'The Nature and Context of Rules of and the Identification of Customary Inernational Law' (2021) 32(4) EJIL 1167–1190.

Jones, JMervyn, 'The Nottebohm Case' (1956) 5 ICLQ 230–244.

Jowell, Jeffrey and Lester, Anthony, 'Beyond Wednesbury: Substantive Principles of Administrative Law' [1987] Public Law 368–382.

Joyner, Daniel H, 'Why I Stopped Believing in Customary International Law' (2019) 9(1) Asian Journal of International Law 31–45.

Juillard, Patrick, 'L'évolution des sources du droit des investissements' (1994) 250 RdC 9–216.
- 'Calvo Doctrine/Calvo Clause' [2007] Max Planck EPIL.

Kadelbach, Stefan and Kleinlein, Thomas, 'International Law: a Constitution for Mankind?: an Attempt at a Re-appraisal with an Analysis of Constitutional Principles' (2007) 50 German Yearbook of International Law 303–347.

Kammerhofer, Jörg, 'Uncertainty in the formal Sources of international Law: customary international Law and some of its Problems' (2004) 15(3) EJIL 523–553.
- 'Gaps, the Nuclear Weapons Advisory Opinion and the Structure of International Legal Argument between Theory and Practice' (2010) 80 BYIL 333–360.
- 'Systemic Integration, Legal Theory and the International Law Commission' (2010) 19 Finnish Yearbook of International Law 2008 175–181.
- 'The Pure Theory of Law and Its "Modern" Positivism: International Legal Uses for Scholarship' (2012) 106 Proceedings of the American Society of International Law at Its Annual Meeting 1–13.

- 'Taking the Rules of Interpretation Seriously, but Not Literally? A Theoretical Reconstruction of Orthodox Dogma' (2017) 86(2) Nordic Journal of International Law 125–150.
- 'Positivist Approaches and International Adjudication' [2019] Max Planck EiPro.

Kamminga, Menno Tjeerd, 'State succession in respect of human rights treaties' (1996) 7(4) EJIL 469–484.

Kaser, Max, ',Ius publicum' und ,ius privatum'' (1986) 103(1) Zeitschrift der Savigny-Stiftung für Rechtsgeschichte: Romanistische Abteilung 1–101.

Kaufmann-Kohler, Gabrielle, 'Arbitral Precedent: Dream, Necessity or Excuse' (2007) 23(3) Arbitration International 357–378.

Kelly, James Patrick, 'The Twilight Of Customary International Law' (2000) 40 Virginia Journal of International Law 449–543.

Kelsen, Hans, 'Contribution à la théorie du traité international' (1936) 10 Revue internationale de la théorie du droit 253–292.
- 'Théorie du droit international coutumier' (1939) 1 Revue internationale de la théorie du droit, nouvelle série 253–274.
- 'Compulsory Adjudication of International Disputes' (1943) 37 AJIL 397–406.
- 'Sanctions in International Law under the Charter of the United Nations' (1946) 31 Iowa Law Review 499–543.
- 'The Draft Declaration on Rights and Duties of States Critical Remarks' (1950) 44 AJIL 259–276.
- 'Théorie du droit international public' (1953) 83 RdC 1–203.

Kennedy, David, 'The Sources of International Law' (1987) 2 American University Journal of International Law & Policy 1–96.
- 'When Renewal Repeats: Thinking against the Box' (2000) 32 NYU JILP 335–500.

Kill, Theodor, 'Don't Cross the Streams: Past and Present Overstatement of Customary International Law in Connection with Conventional Fair and Equitable Treatment Obligations' (2008) 106(5) Michigan Law Review 853–880.

Kingsbury, Benedict, 'Is the Proliferation of International Courts and Tribunals a systemic Problem' (1998) 31 NYU JILP 679–696.
- 'The Concept of Compliance As a Function of Competing Conceptions of International Law' (1998) 19 Michigan Journal of International Law 345–372.
- 'The Concept of "Law" in Global Administrative Law' (2009) 20(1) EJIL 23–57.

Kingsbury, Benedict, Krisch, Nico, and Stewart, Richard B, 'The Emergence of Global Administrative Law' (2005) 68(3-4) Law and contemporary problems 15–61.

Kirgis, Frederic L, 'Custom on a Sliding Scale' (1987) 81(1) AJIL 146–151.

Kiß, Géza, 'Die Theorie der Rechtsquellen in der englischen und anglo-amerikanischen Literatur' (1913) XXXIX Archiv für Bürgerliches Recht 265–297.

Klein Bronfman, Marcela, 'Fair and Equitable Treatment: An Evolving Standard' (2006) 10 Max Planck Yearbook of United Nations law 609–680.

Kleinlein, Thomas, 'Between Myths and Norms: Constructivist Constitutionalism and the Potential of Constitutional Principles in International Law' (2012) 81 Nordic Journal of International Law 79–132.

– 'Consensus and Contestability: The ECtHR and the Combined Potential of European Consensus and Procedural Rationality Control' (2017) 28(3) EJIL 871–893.

Kletzer, Christoph, 'Kelsen's Development of the Fehlerkalkül-Theory' (2005) 18(1) Ratio Juris 46–63.

Kohen, Marcelo G, 'La succession d'Etats en matière de responsabilité internationale State Succession in Matters of State Responsibility' (2016) 76 Yearbook of the Institute of International Law - Tallinn Session 509–719.

Kolb, Robert, 'The formal source of Ius Cogens in public international law' (1998) 53(1) ZÖR 69–105.

– 'Les maximes juridiques en droit international public: questions historiques et théoriques' (1999) 32(2) Revue belge de droit international 407–434.

– 'The jurisprudence of the Yugoslav and Rwandan Criminal Tribunals on their jurisdiction and on international crimes' (2000) 71 BYIL 259–315.

– 'Selected problems in the theory of customary international law' [2003] Netherlands international law review 119–150.

– 'The Jurisprudence of the Yugoslav and Rwandan Criminal Tribunals on their Jurisdiction and on International Crimes' (2004) 75 BYIL 269–335.

– 'Principles as Sources of International Law (With Special Reference to Good Faith)' (2006) 53(1) Netherlands International Law Review 1–36.

– 'German Legal Scholarship as reflected in Hague Academy Courses on Public International Law' (2007) 50 German Yearbook of International Law 201–241.

– 'Politis and Sociological Jurisprudence of Inter-War International Law' (2012) 23(1) EJIL 233–241.

- 'The Jurisprudence of the Yugoslav and Rwandan Criminal Tribunals on Their Jurisdiction and on International Crimes (2004-2013)' (2014) 84(1) BYIL 131–186.
- 'The Jurisprudence of the Permanent Court of International Justice Between Utilitas Publica and Utilitas Singulorum' (2015) 14 The Law and Practice of International Courts and Tribunals 16–34.
- 'Chronique de la jurisprudence de la cour International de Justice en 2015' (2016) 1(26) Swiss Review of International and European Law 125–159.

Kopelmanas, Lazare, 'Custom as a Means of the Creation of International Law' (1937) 18 BYIL 127–151.
- 'Essai d'une Théorie des Sources Formelles de Droit International' (1938) 1 Revue de droit international 101–150.
- 'La pensée de Georges Scelle et ses possibilités d'application à quelques problémes récents de droit international' [1961] Journal du Droit International 350–375.

Koskenniemi, Martti, 'General principles: reflexions on constructivist thinking in international law' (1985) 18 Oikeustiede-jurisprudentia 121–163.
- 'The Pull of the Mainstream' (1989) 88 Michigan Law Review 1946–1962.
- 'The Politics of International Law' (1990) 1 EJIL 4–32.
- 'The Function of Law in the International Community: 75 Years After' (2009) 79 BYIL 353–366.

Koskenniemi, Martti and Leino, Päiv, 'Fragmentation of International Law? Postmodern Anxieties' (2002) 15 Leiden Journal of International Law 553–579.

Kreß, Claus, 'War Crimes Committed in Non-International Armed Conflict and the Emerging System of International Criminal Justice' (2001) 30 Israel Yearbook on Human Rights 103–177.
- 'Versailles-Nuremberg-The Hague : Germany and International Criminal Law' (2006) 40 The international lawyer 15–39.
- 'The Peacemaking Process After the Great War and the Origins of International Criminal Law Stricto Sensu' (2021) 62 German Yearbook of International Law 163–187.

Kreß, Claus and Holtzendorff, Leonie von, 'The Kampala Compromise on the Crime of Aggression' (2010) 8 JICJ 1179–1217.

Krieger, Heike, 'A Credibility Gap: the Behrami and Saramati Decision of the European Court of Human Rights' (2009) 13(1-2) Journal of international peacekeeping 159–180.

Krieger, Heike, 'Positive Verpflichtungen unter der EMRK: Unentbehrliches Element einer gemeineuropäischen Grundrechtsdogmatik, leeres Versprechen oder Grenze der Justiziabilität?' (2014) 74 ZaöRV 187–213.

Kulick, Andreas, 'Provisional Measures after Ukraine v Russia (2022)' (2022) 13(2) JIDS 323–340.

Kunz, Josef L, 'Völkerrechtswissenschaft und reine Rechtslehre' (1923) 6(1) Zeitschrift für öffentliches Recht 1–83.

– 'Alfred Verdross, Die Einheit des rechtlichen Weltbildes auf Grundlage der Völkerrechtsverfassung' (1924) 7 Archiv des öffentlichen Rechts 120–126.

– 'The "Vienna School" and International Law' (1933) 11 New York University Law Quarterly Review 370–421.

– 'General International Law and the Law of International Organizations' (1953) 47(3) AJIL 456–462.

– 'The Nature of Customary International Law' (1953) 47 AJIL 662–669.

– 'Roberto Ago's Theory of a "Spontaneous" International Law' (1958) 52(1) American Journal of International Law 85–91.

– 'The Nottebohm Judgment (Second Phase)' (1960) 54 AJIL 536–571.

Kurtz, Jürgen, 'The Use and Abuse of WTO Law in Investor-State Arbitration: Competition and its Discontents' (2009) 20(3) EJIL 749–771.

– 'Adjudicating the Exceptional at International Investment Law: Security, Public Order and Financial Crisis' (2010) 59(2) ICLQ 325–371.

Landis, James McCauley, 'Statutes and the Sources of Law' (1965) 2 Harvard Journal of Legislation 7–39.

Lando, Massimo, 'Identification as the Process to Determine the Content of Customary International Law' (2022) 42(4) Oxford Journal of Legal Studies 1040–1066.

Lauterpacht, Elihu, 'Review of Books General Principles of Law as Applied by International Courts and Tribunals' (1953) XXX BYIL 544–547.

Lauterpacht, Hersch, 'Règles générales du droit de la paix' (1937) 62(IV) RdC 95–422.

– 'The Grotian Tradition in International Law' (1946) 23 BYIL 1–53.

– 'L'interprétation des traités' (1950) 43 Annuaire de l'Institut de droit international 366–432.

– 'Codification and Development of International Law' (1955) 49 AJIL 16–43.

Le Fur, Louis, 'Règles générales du droit de la paix' (1935) 54 RdC 1–307.

Leben, Charles, 'La théorie du contrat d'état et l'évolution du droit international des investissements' (2003) 302 RdC 197–377.

LeGrand, Pierre, 'The Impossibility of Legal Transplants' (1997) 4 Maastricht Journal of European and Comparative Law 111–124.
Leibholz, Gerhard, 'Verbot der Willkür und des Ermessensmißbrauches im völkerrechtlichen Verkehr der Staaten' (1929) 1 ZaöRV 77–125.
Leiter, Andrea, 'Protecting concessionary rights: General principles and the making of international investment law' (2022) 35 Leiden Journal of International Law 55–69.
Lenaerts, Koen and Gutman, Kathleen, 'The Comparative Law Method and the European Court of Justice: Echoes across the Atlantic' (2016) 64 American Journal of Comparative Law 841–846.
Lepsius, Oliver, 'The quest for middle-range theories in German public law' (2014) 12(3) Journal of International Constitutional Law 692–709.
Lillich, Richard B, 'The Growing Importance of Customary International Human Rights Law' (1996) 25(1-2) Georgia Journal of International and Comparative Law 1–30.
Linderfalk, Ulf, 'State Responsibility and the Primary-Secondary Rules Terminology - the Role of Language for an Understanding of the International Legal System' (2009) 78(1) Nordic Journal of International Law 53–72.
Lippold, Matthias, 'Between Humanization and Humanitarization?: Detention in Armed Conflicts and the European Convention on Human Rights' (2016) 76(1) ZaöRV 53–95.
– 'Reflections on Custom Critique and on Functional Equivalents in the Work of Jean d'Aspremont' (2019) 21(3-4) International Community Law Review 257–282.
Longobardo, Marco, 'The Criminalisation of Intra-party Offences in Light of Some Recent ICC Decisions on Children in Armed Conflict' (2019) 19 International Criminal Law Review 600–634.
Lorca, Arnulf Becker, 'Universal International Law: Nineteenth-Century Histories of Imposition and Appropriation' (2010) 51(2) Harvard International Law Journal 475–552.
Lowe, Vaughan, 'Precluding Wrongfulness or Responsibility: A Plea for Excuses' (1999) 10 EJIL 405–411.
– 'Was it Worth the Effort?' (2012) 27 The International Journal of Marine and Coastal Law 875–881.
Lowenfeld, Andreas F, 'Investment Agreements and International Law' (2003) 42 Columbia Journal of Transnational Law 123–130.
Macklin, Audrey, 'Is it time to retire Nottebohm?' (2017) 111 AJIL Unbound 492–497.

Mälksoo, Lauri, 'The History of International Legal Theory in Russia: a Civilized Dialogue in Europe' (2008) 19 EJIL 211–232.

Manacorda, Stefano and Meloni, Chantal, 'Indirect Perpetration versus Joint Criminal Enterprise. Concurring Approaches in the Practice of International Criminal Law?' (2011) 9 Journal of International Criminal Justice 159–178.

Manin, Philippe, 'Le juge international et la règle générale' [1976] RGDIP 7–54.

Mann, Francis A, 'The Proper Law of Contracts Concluded by International Persons' (1959) 35 BYIL 34–57.

– 'State Contracts and State Responsibility' (1960) 54 AJIL 572–591.

– 'The theoretical approach towards the law governing contracts between states and private persons' (1975) 11 Revue belge de droit international 562–567.

– 'British treaties for the promotion and protection of investments' (1981) 52 BYIL 241–254.

Marboe, Irmgard and Reinisch, August, 'Contracts between States and Foreign Private Law Persons' [2011] Max Planck EPIL.

Marek, Krystyna, 'Thoughts on Codification' (1971) 29 ZaöRV 489–520.

Martineau, Anne-Charlotte, 'The Rhetoric of Fragmentation: Fear and Faith in International Law' (2009) 22(1) Leiden Journal of International Law 1–28.

Masterman, Roger and Wheatle, Se-shauna, 'A common law resurgence in protection?' [2015] (1) European Human Rights Law Review 57–65.

Mattei, Ugo, 'Three Patterns of Law: Taxonomy and Change in the World's Legal Systems' (1997) 45 American Journal of Comparative Law 5–44.

Maus, Ingeborg, 'Die Trennung von Recht und Moral als Begrenzung des Rechts' (1989) 20 Rechtstheorie 191–210.

McCrudden, Christopher, 'A Common Law of Human Rights?: Transnational Judicial Conversations on Constitutional Rights' (2000) 20(4) Oxford Journal of Legal Studies 499–532.

McDougal, Myres S, Lasswell, Harold D, and Chen, Lung-chu, 'Nationality and Human Rights: The Protection of the Individual and External Arenas' (1974) 83 The Yale Law Journal 900–998.

McGregor, Lorna, 'State Immunity and Human Rights: Is There a Future after Germany v. Italy?' (2013) 11(1) JICJ 125–145.

McLachlan, Campbell, 'The Principle of Systemic Integration and Article 31 (3) (c) of the Vienna Convention' (2005) 54 ICLQ 279–320.

- 'Investment Treaties and General International Law' (2008) 57(2) ICLQ 361–401.
- 'Is There an Evolving Customary International Law on Investment?' (2016) 3(2) ICSID Review 257–269.

McNair, Arnold Duncan, 'The General Principles of Law Recognized by Civilized Nations' (1957) 33 BYIL 1–19.

Megumi, Ochi, 'The New Recipe for a General Principle of Law: Premise Theory to "Fill in the Gaps"' [2022] Asian Journal of International Law 1–19.

Mendelson, Maurice, 'The subjective Element in Customary International Law' (1996) 66 BYIL 177–208.

Mendelson, Maurice H, 'The Formation of Customary International Law' (1998) 272 RdC 155–410.

Meron, Theodor, 'The Geneva Conventions as Customary Law' (1987) 81 AJIL 348–370.
- 'The Continuing Role of Custom in the Formation of International Humanitarian Law' (1996) 90 AJIL 238–249.
- 'Is International Law Moving towards Criminalization?' (1998) 9 EJIL 18–31.
- 'The Humanization of Humanitarian Law' (2000) 94(2) American Journal of International Law 239–278.
- 'The Revival of Customary Humanitarian Law' (2005) 99(4) American Journal of International Law 817–834.

Métall, Rudolf Aladár, 'Skizzen zu einer Systematik der völkerrechtlichen Quellenlehre' (1931) 11 Zeitschrift für öffentliches Recht 416–428.

Meyer, Timothy L, 'Codifying Custom' (2012) 160 University of Pennsylvania Law Review 995–1069.

Michaels, Ralf, 'Privatautonomie und Privatkodifikation Zu Anwendbarkeit und Geltung allgemeiner Vertragsrechtsprinzipien' (1998) 62 Rabels Zeitschrift für Ausländisches und Internationales Privatrecht 580–626.
- 'The True Lex Mercatoria: Law Beyond the State' (2007) 14(2) Indiana Journal of Global Legal Studies 447–468.
- 'The Mirage of Non-State Governance' [2010] Utah Law Review 31–45.
- 'A Fuller Concept of Law Beyond the State? Thoughts on Lon Fuller's Contributions to the Jurisprudence of Transnational Dispute Resolution: A Reply to Thomas Schultz' (2011) 2(2) JIDS 417–426.

Michaels, Ralf and Pauwelyn, Joost HB, 'Conflict of Norms or Conflict of Laws: Different Techniques in the Fragmentation of Public International

Law' (2012) 22(3) Duke Journal of Comparative & International Law 349–376.

Milanovic, Marko, 'From Compromise to Principle: Clarifying the Concept of State Jurisdiction in Human Rights Treaties' (2008) 8(3) Human Rights Law Review 411–448.

– 'Aggression and Legality: custom in Kampala' (2012) 10 JICJ 165–187.

– 'Special Rules of Attribution of Conduct in International Law' (2020) 96 International Law Studies 295–393.

Milanović, Marko, 'Is the Rome Statute Binding on Individuals? (And Why We Should Care)' (2011) 9 JICJ 25–52.

Milanović, Marko and Papć, Tatjana, 'As Bad As It Gets: the European Court of Human Rights's Behrami and Saramati Decision and General International Law' (2009) 58(2) ICLQ 267–296.

Mitchell, Andrew D and Munro, James, 'Someone Else's Deal: Interpreting International Investment Agreements in the Light of Third-Party Agreements' (2017) 28(3) EJIL 669–695.

Mohamad, Rahmat, 'Some Reflections on the International Law Commission Topic "Identification of Customary International Law"' (2016) 15(1) Chinese Journal of International Law 41–46.

Mosler, Hermann, 'The international society as a legal community' (1974) 140 RdC 1–320.

Murmann, Uwe, 'Tatherrschaft durch Weisungsmacht' (1996) 143(1) Goltdammer's Archiv für Strafrecht 269–302.

Murphy, Sean D, 'Immunity Ratione Materiae of State Officials from Foreign Criminal Jurisdiction: Where is the State Practice in Support of Exceptions?' (2018) 112 AJIL Unbound 4–8.

– 'Peremptory Norms of General International Law (Jus Cogens) (Revisited) and Other Topics: The Seventy-Third Session of the International Law Commission' (2023) 117(1) AJIL 92–112.

Natoli, Kristopher, 'Weaponizing Nationality: An Analysis of Russia's Passport Policy in Georgia' (2010) 28 Boston University International Law Journal 389–417.

Nelson, Caleb, 'The Legitimacy of (Some) Federal Common Law' (2015) 101(5) Virginia Law Review 1–64.

Nissel, Alan, 'The Duality of State Responsibility' (2013) 44(3) Columbia Human Rights Law Review 793–858.

Nollkaemper, André, 'Constitutionalization and the Unity of the Law of International Responsibility' (2009) 16 Indiana Journal of Global Legal Studies 535–563.

Nolte, Georg, 'From Dionisio Anzilotti to Roberto Ago: The Classical International Law of State Responsibility and the Traditional Primacy of a Bilateral Conception of Inter-state Relations' (2002) 13(5) EJIL 1083–1098.
- 'Thin or Thick? The Principle of Proportionality and International Humanitarian Law' (2010) 4(2) Law & Ethics of Human Rights 244–255.
- 'Faktizität und Subjektivität im Völkerrecht Anmerkungen zu Jochen Froweins "Das de facto-Regime im Völkerrecht" im Licht aktueller Entwicklungen' (2015) 75 ZaöRV 715–732.
- 'How to identify customary international law? - On the final outcome of the work of the International Law Commission (2018)' [2019] (37) KFG Working Paper Series 1–22.

Nolte, Georg and Aust, Helmut Philipp, 'Equivocal Helpers - Complicit States, Mixed Messages and International Law' (2009) 58 International and Comparative Law Quarterly 1–30.

Nouwen, Sarah MH, 'Return to Sender: Let the International Court of Justice Justify or Qualify International-Criminal-Court-Exceptionalism Regarding Personal Immunities' (2019) 78(3) Cambridge Law Journal 596–611.

Nussbaum, Arthur, 'Arbitration between the Lena Goldfields Ltd. and the Soviet Government' (1950) 36(1) Cornell Law Review 31–53.

O'Connell, Daniel Patrick, 'Recent problems of state succession in relation to new states' (1970) 130 RdC 95–206.

O'Keefe, Roger, 'An "International Crime Exception" to the Immunity of State Officials from Foreign Criminal Jurisdiction: Not Currently, not Likely' (2015) 109 AJIL Unbound 167–172.

Öberg, Marko Divac, 'The absorption of grave breaches into war crimes law' (2009) 91 International Review of the Red Cross 163–183.

Oda, Shigeru, 'The International Court of Justice viewed from the Bench (1976-1993)' (1993) 244 RdC 9–190.

Ohlin, Jens David, Sliedregt, Elies van, and Weigend, Thomas, 'Assessing the Control-Theory' (2013) 26 Leiden Journal of International Law 725–746.

Oppenheim, Lassa Francis Lawrence, 'Zur Lehre vom internationalen Gewohnheitsrecht' (1915) 25 Niemeyers Zeitschrift für internationales Recht 1–13.

Orakhelashvili, Alexander, 'Natural Law and Customary Law' (2008) 68 ZaöRV 69–110.

Orakhelashvili, Alexander, 'The Normative Basis of 'Fair and Equitable Treatment': General International Law on Foreign Investment?' (2008) 46(1) Archiv des Völkerrechts 74–105.

Orozco López, Hernán Darío and Silva Santaularia, Natalia, 'Reflections on Indirect (Co-)Perpetration through an Organization' (2022) 20 JICJ 657–676.

Osten, Philipp, 'Indirect Co-Perpetration and the Control Theory. A Japanese Perspective' (2022) 20 JICJ 677–697.

Pacht, Laurence T, 'The Case for a Convention on State Responsibility' (2014) 83(4) Nordic Journal of International Law 439–475.

Paddeu, Federica, 'Ghosts of Genocides Past? State Responsibility for Genocide in the Former Yugoslavia' (2015) 74(2) The Cambridge Law Journal 198–201.

Paddeu, Federica I, 'Self-Defence as a Circumstance Precluding Wrongfulness: Understanding Article 21 of the Articles on State Responsibility' [2015] BYIL 1–43.

Palchetti, Paolo, 'Opening the International Court of Justice to Third States: Intervention and Beyond' (2002) 6 Max Planck Yearbook of United Nations Law 139–181.

Papadaki, Matina, 'Compromissory Clauses as the Gatekeepers of the Law to be 'used' in the ICJ and the PCIJ' [2014] JIDS 1–45.

Paparinskis, Mārtiņš, 'Investment Arbitration and the Law of Countermeasures' (2008) 79 BYIL 264–352.

– 'Sapphire Arbitration' [2010] Max Planck EPIL.

– 'Come Together or Do It My Way: No Systemic Preference' (2014) 108 Proceedings of the American Society of International Law at Its Annual Meeting 246–249.

Paulson, Stanley L, 'Lon L. Fuller, Gustav Radbruch, and the 'Positivist' Theses' (1994) 13(3) Law and Philosophy 313–359.

Paulsson, Jan, 'Arbitration Without Privity' (1995) 10(3) ICSID Review - Foreign Investment Law Journal 232–257.

– 'International Arbitration and the Generation of Legal Norms: Treaty Arbitration and International Law' (2006) 3(5) Transnational Dispute Management 1–13.

Paulsson, Jan and Petrochilos, Georgios, 'Neer-ly Misled?' (2007) 22(2) ICSID Review - Foreign Investment Law Journal 242–257.

Paulus, Andreas L, 'Commentary to Andreas Fischer-Lescano & Gunther Teubner The Legitimacy of International Law and the Role of the State' (2004) 25 Michigan Journal of International Law 1047–1058.

Paulus, Andreas L and Leiss, Johann, 'Constitutionalism and the Mechanics of Global Law Transfers' (2018) 9 GoJIL 35–69.

Paulus, Andreas L and Lippold, Matthias, 'Customary Law in the Postmodern World (Dis)Order' (2018) 112 AJIL Unbound 308–312.

Peat, Daniel, 'International Investment Law and the Public Law Analogy: The Fallacies of the General Principles Method' (2018) 9 JIDS 654–678.

Pellet, Alain, '"Human rightism" and international law' [2000] Gilberto Amado Memorial Lecture of 18 July 2000 ⟨https://digitallibrary.un.org/record/430167⟩ accessed 1 August 2022.

Perreau-Saussine, Amanda, 'British Acts of State in English Courts' (2008) 78 BYIL 176–253.

Peters, Anne, 'Does Kosovo Lie in the Lotus-Land of Freedom?' (2011) 24 Leiden Journal of International Law 95–108.

– 'The refinement of international law: From fragmentation to regime interaction and politicization' (2017) 15(3) International Journal of Constitutional Law 671–704.

Peters, Ellen Ash, 'Common Law Judging in a Statutory World: An Address' (1982) 43 University of Pittsburgh Law Review 995–1011.

Petersen, Niels, 'Customary Law Without Custom? Rules, Principles, and the Role of State Practice in International Norm Creation' (2008) 23(2) American University International Law Review 275–310.

– 'Der Wandel des ungeschriebenen Völkerrechts im Zuge der Konstitutionalisierung' (2008) 46(4) Archiv des Völkerrechts 502–523.

– 'The International Court of Justice and the Judicial Politics of Identifying Customary International Law' (2017) 28(2) EJIL 357–385.

Pojanowski, Jeffrey A, 'Reading Statutes in the Common Law Tradition' (2015) 101(5) Virginia Law Review 1357–1424.

Politis, Nicolas, 'Le problème des limitations de la souveraineté et la théorie de l'abus des droits dans les rapports internationaux' (1925) 6 RdC 1–121.

Poscher, Ralf, 'Theorie eines Phantoms - Die erfolglose der Prinzipientheorie nach ihrem Gegenstand' (2010) 4 Rechtswissenschaft 349–372.

Postema, Gerald J, 'Implicit Law' (1994) 13(3) Law and Philosophy 361–387.

– 'Classical Common Law Jurisprudence (Part I)' (2002) 2(2) Oxford University Commonwealth Law Journal 155–180.

– 'Classical Common Law Jurisprudence (Part II)' (2003) 3(1) Oxford University Commonwealth Law Journal 1–28.

Postema, Gerald J, 'Custom, Normative Practice, and the Law' (2012) 62 Duke Law Journal 707–738.

Pound, Roscoe, 'Common Law and Legislation' (1908) 21(6) Harvard Law Review 383–407.
- 'Hierarchy of Sources and Forms in Different Systems of Law' (1933) 7 Tulane Law Review 475–487.
Pronto, Arnold N, '"Human-Rightism" and the Development of General International Law' (2007) 20 Leiden Journal of International Law 753–765.
Rabel, Ernst, 'Rechtsvergleichung und internationale Rechtsprechung' (1927) 1 Zeitschrift für ausländisches und internationales Privatrecht 5–47.
Rachovitsa, Adamantia, 'Fragmentation of International Law revisited: Insights, Good Practices, and Lessons to be learned from the Case Law of the European Court of Human Rights' (2015) 28(4) Leiden Journal of International Law 863–885.
- 'The Principle of Systemic Integration in Human Rights Law' (2017) 66(3) ICLQ 557–588.
Radbruch, Gustav, 'Gesetzliches Unrecht und übergesetzliches Recht' (1946) 1(5) Süddeutsche Juristenzeitung 105–108.
Raju, Deepak and Jasari, Blerina, 'Intervention before the International Court of Justice - A Critical Examination of the Court's Recent Decision in Germany v. Italy' (2013) 6 NUJS Law Review 63–80.
Rasulov, Akbar, 'Revisiting State Succession to Humanitarian Treaties: Is There a Case for Automaticity?' (2003) 14(1) EJIL 141–170.
- 'The Life and Times of the Modern Law of Reservations: the Doctrinal Genealogy of General Comment No. 24' (2009) 14 Austrian review of international and European law 105–214.
Rauber, Jochen, 'On Communitarian and Constitutional Approaches to International Law' (2013) 26 Leiden Journal of International Law 201–217.
Raz, Joseph, 'Legal Principles and the Limits of Law' (1971) 81 Yale Law Journal 823–854.
Reisinger Coracini, Astrid, '"Amended Most Serious Crimes': A New Category of Core Crimes within the Jurisdiction but out of the Reach of the International Criminal Court?' (2008) 21 Leiden Journal of International Law 699–718.
- '"What is an International Crime?": A Response to Kevin Jon Heller' [2018] Harvard International Law Online Symposium 1–4 ⟨https://harvardilj.org/wp-content/uploads/sites/15/Coracini-Response.pdf⟩ accessed 1 February 2023.

Reisman, William Michael, 'The Cult of Custom in the Late 20th Century' (1987) 17 California Western International Law Journal 133–145.
- 'The Other Shoe Falls: The Future of Article 36 (1) Jurisdiction in the Light of Nicaragua' (1987) 81 AJIL 166–173.
- 'Sovereignty and Human Rights in Contemporary International Law' (1990) 84 AJIL 866–876.
- 'Canute Confronts the Tide: States versus Tribunals and the Evolution of the Minimum Standard in Customary International Law' (2015) 30 ICSID Review 616–634.

'Report by Dr. J. C. Witenberg to the Protection of Private Property Committee' [1930] International Law Association's Report of the Thirty-Sixth Conference 301–362.

'Report of the Committee on the Progressive Development of International Law and its Codification on the Methods for Encouraging the Progressive Development of International Law and its Eventual Codification, UN Doc. A/AC.10/51, 17 June 1947' (1947) 41 Supplement AJIL.

'Responsibility of States for Damage done in their Territory to the Person or Property of Foreigners' (1929) 23(2) AJIL. Supplement 133–218.

Reuter, Paul, 'Principes de droit international public' (1961) 103 RdC 425–656.

Rheinstein, Max, 'Book Review Grundsatz und Norm in der richterlichen Fortbildung des Privatrechts: Rechtsvergleichende Beitraege zur Rechtsquellen- und Interpretationslehre (Principle and Norm in the Judicial Development of Private Law: A Comparative Inquiry into the Problems of the Sources of Law and Their Interpretation) by Joseph Esser' (1957) 24(3) The University of Chicago Law Review 597–606.

Rim, Yejoon, 'Reflections on the Role of the International Law Commission in Consideration of the Final Form of Its Work' (2020) 10 Asian Journal of International Law 23–37.

Ripert, Georges, 'Les règles du droit civil applicables aux rapports internationaux: (contribution à l'étude des principes généraux du droit visés au statut de la Cour permanente de justice internationale)' (1933) 44 RdC 565–664.

Risse, Thomas, '"Let's argue!": Communicative Action in World Politics' (2000) 54(1) International Organization 1–39.

Roberts, Anthea, 'Traditional and Modern Approaches to Customary International Law: A Reconciliation' (2001) 95 AJIL 757–791.
- 'Traditional and Modern Approaches to Customary International Law: A Reconciliation' (2001) 95 AJIL 757–791.

Roberts, Anthea, 'Power and Persuasion in Investment Treaty Interpretation: The Dual Role of States' (2010) 104 AJIL 179–225.
- 'Who killed Article 38(1)(B)? A Reply to Bradley and Gulati' (2010) 21(1) Duke journal of comparative & international law 173–190.
- 'Clash and Paradigms: Actors and Analogies Shaping The Investment Treaty System' (2013) 107 AJIL 45–94.
- 'State-to-State Investment Treaty Arbitration: A Hybrid Theory of Interdependent Rights and Shared Interpretive Authority' (2014) 55(1) Harvard Journal of International Law 1–70.
- 'Investment Treaties: The Reform Matrix' (2018) 112 AJIL Unbound 191–196.
Roberts, Anthea and Sivakumaran, Sandesh, 'Lawmaking by Nonstate Actors: Engaging Armed Groups in the Creation of International Humanitarian Law' (2012) 37(1) Yale Journal of International Law 107–152.
Robinson, Darryl, 'The Identity Crisis of International Criminal Law' (2008) 21 Leiden Journal of International Law 925–963.
Robinson, Darryl and Hebel, Herman von, 'War crimes in internal conflicts: Article 8 of the ICC Statute' (1999) 2 Yearbook of International Humanitarian Law 193–209.
Rodenhäuser, Tilman, 'Squaring the Circle? Prosecuting Sexual Violence against Child Soldiers by their 'Own Forces'' (2016) 14 JICJ 171–193.
Rodley, Nigel S, 'Corporate Nationality and the Diplomatic Protection of Multinational Enterprises: The Barcelona Traction Case' (1971) 47(1) Indiana Law Journal 70–86.
Root, Elihu, 'The Basis of Protection to Citizens Residing Abroad' (1910) 4(3) AJIL 517–528.
- 'The Outlook for International Law' (1915) 9 Proceedings of the American Society of International Law at Its Annual Meeting 2–11.
Rosenne, Shabtai, 'The International Law Commission, 1949-59' (1960) 36 BYIL 104–173.
Rosetti, Luca Poltronieri, 'Intra-party sexual crimes against child soldiers as war crimes in Ntaganda. 'Tadic moment' or unwarranted exercise of judicial activism?' [2019] Questions of International Law 49–68.
Roxin, Claus, 'Straftaten im Rahmen organisatorischer Machtapparate' [1963] (7) Goltdammer's Archiv für Strafrecht 193–207.
Ruda, José Maria, 'The Opinions of Judge Dionisio Anzilotti at the Permanent Court of International Justice' (1992) 3(1) EJIL 100–122.

Ruggie, John Gerard, 'What Makes the World Hang Together? Neo-Utilitarianism and the Social Constructivist Challenge' (1998) 52(4) International Organization 855–885.

Ryngaert, Cedric MJ and Hora Siccama, Duco W, 'Ascertaining Customary International Law: An Inquiry into the Methods Used by Domestic Courts' (2018) 65 Netherlands International Law Review 1–25.

Sacerdoti, Giorgio, 'Bilateral treaties and multilateral instruments on investment protection' (1997) 269 RdC 251–455.

Sadat, Leila Nadya, 'Custom, Codification and some thoughts about the relationship between the two: Article 10 of the ICC Statute' (2000) 49(4) DePaul Law Review 903–923.

Sadat, Leila Nadya and Jolly, Jarrod M, 'Seven Canons of ICC Treaty Interpretation: Making Sense of Article 25's Rorschach Blot' (2014) 27 Leiden Journal of International Law 775–788.

Salacuse, Jeswald W, 'The Treatification of International Investment Law' (2007) 13 Law and Busines Review of the Americas 155–166.

Saleilles, Raymond, 'L'École historique et droit naturel' (1902) 1 Revue trimestrielle de droit civil 80 et seq.

Sales, Philip, 'Rights and Fundamental Rights in English Law' (2016) 75(1) Cambridge Law Journal 86–108.

Sands, Philippe, 'Treaty, Custom and the Cross-fertilization of International Law' (1998) 1(1) Yale Human Rights and Development Journal 85–105.

Sanger, Andrew, 'State Immunity and the Right of Access to a Court Under the EU Charter of Fundamental Rights' (2016) 65(1) ICLQ 213–228.

Saurer, Johannes, 'Die Hart-Dworkin-Debatte als Grundlagenkontroverse der angloamerikanischen Rechtsphilosophie: Versuch einer Rekonstruktion nach fürnf Jahrzehnten' (2012) 98 Archiv für Rechts- und Sozialphilosophie 112–127.

Scelle, Georges, 'Règles générales du droit de la paix' (1933) 46 RdC 327–703.

Schaack, Beth van, 'Mapping War Crimes in Syria' (2016) 92 International Law Studies 282–339.

Schachter, Oscar, 'International Law in Theory and Practice: general course in public international law' (1982) 178 RdC 9–395.

Schill, Stephan W, 'Internationales Investitionsschutzrecht und Vergleichendes Öffentliches Recht: Grundlagen und Methode eines öffentlich-rechtlichen Leitbildes für die Investitionsschiedsgerichtsbarkeit' (2011) 71 ZaöRV 247–289.

Schill, Stephan W, 'Cross-Regime Harmonization through Proportionality Analysis: The Case of International Investment Law, the Law of State Immunity and Human Rights' (2012) 27(1) ICSID Review 87–119.
– 'Editorial' (2014) 15(1-2) Journal of World Investment & Trade 1–11.
– 'From Sources to Discourse: Investment Treaty Jurisprudence as the New Custom?' [2016] BIICL 16th Investment Treaty Forum Public Conference ⟨https://www.biicl.org/files/5630_stephan_schill.pdf.⟩ accessed 1 February 2023.
Schill, Stephan W and Briese, Robyn, '"If the State Considers": Self-Judging Clauses in International Dispute Settlement' (2009) 13 Max Planck Yearbook of International Law 61–140.
Schill, Stephan W and Tvede, Katrine R, 'Mainstreaming Investment Treaty Jurisprudence The Contribution of Investment Treaty Tribunals to the Consolidation and Development of General International Law' (2015) 14 The Law and Practice of International Courts and Tribunals 94–129.
Schlesinger, Rudolf B, 'Research on the General Principles of Law Recognized by Civilized Nations' (1957) 51(4) AJIL 734–753.
Schlochauer, Hans-Jürgen, 'Die Theorie des abus de droit im Völkerrecht' (1933) 17 Zeitschrift für Völkerrecht 373.
School, Harvard Law, 'Codification of International Law: Part II: Legal Position and Functions of Consuls' (1932) 26 AJIL. Supplement 189–450.
Schreuer, Christoph, 'Recommendations and the Traditional Sources of International Law' (1977) 20 German Yearbook of International Law 103–118.
– 'Investment Arbitration - A Voyage of Discovery' (2005) 5(2) Transnational Dispute Management 73–77.
Schultz, Thomas, 'The Concept of Law in Transnational Arbitral Legal Orders and some of its Consequences' (2011) 2(1) JIDS 59–85.
Schwarzenberger, Georg, 'The fundamental principles of international law' (1955) 87 RdC 191–385.
– 'The Standard of Civilisation in International Law' (1955) 8(1) Current Legal Problems 212–234.
– 'The Abs-Shawcross Draft Convention on Investments Abroad; a Critical Commentary' (1960) 9 Journal of Public Law 147–171.
Schwebel, Stephen M, 'The Influence of Bilateral Investment Treaties on Customary International Law' (2004) 98 Proceedings of the American Society of International Law at Its Annual Meeting 27–30.

Schweisfurth, Theodor, 'Das Völkergewohnheitsrecht - verstärkt im Blickfeld der sowjetischen Völkerrechtslehre' (1987) 30 German Yearbook of International Law 36–77.

Scobbie, Iain GM, 'The Theorist as Judge: Hersch Lauterpacht's Concept of the International Judicial Function' (1997) 2 EJIL 264–298.

Scott, James Brown, 'The Declaration of London of February 26, 1909: a collection of official papers and documents relating to the International Naval Conference held in London, December, 1908 - February, 1909' (1914) 8(2) AJIL 274–329.

Seagle, William, 'Rudolf von Jhering: Or Law as a Means to an End' (1945) 13(1) The University of Chicago Law Review 71–89.

Seidl-Hohenveldern, Ignaz, 'Review of Customary International Law and Treaties' (1987) 38 Österreichische Zeitschrift für Öffentliches Recht und Völkerrecht 217–218.

Shaffer, Gregory, 'How Business Shapes Law: A Socio-Legal Framework' (2009) 42(1) Connecticut Law Review 147–183.

Shaffer, Gregory and Ginsburg, Tom, 'The empirical turn in international legal scholarship' (2012) 106 AJIL 1–46.

Shahabuddin, Mohammad, 'The 'standard of civilization' in international law: Intellectual perspectives from pre-war Japan' (2019) 32 Leiden Journal of International Law 13–32.

Shany, Yuval, 'No Longer a Weak Department of Power? Reflections on the Emergence of a New International Judiciary' (2009) 20(1) EJIL 73–91.

Shao, Xuan, 'What We Talk about When We Talk about General Principles of Law' (2021) 20 Chinese Journal of International Law 219–255.

Shen, Quinmin, 'Methodological Flaws in the ILC's Study on Exceptions to Immunity Ratione Materiae of State Officials from Foreign Criminal Jurisidction' (2018) 112 AJIL Unbound 9–15.

Sheppard, Daniel, 'The International Criminal Court and "Internationally Recognized Human Rights": Understanding Article 21 (3) of the Rome Statute' (2010) 10(1) International Criminal Law Review 43–71.

Silberman, Linda J, 'The Hague Convention on Child Abduction and Unilateral Relocations by Custodial Parents: A Perspective from the United States and Europe - Abbott, Neulinger, Zarraga' (2011) 63 Oklahoma Law Review 733–749.

Simma, Bruno, 'Reflections on article 60 of the Vienna convention on the law of treaties and its background in general international law' (1970) 20 Österreichische Zeitschrift für öffentliches Recht 5–83.

Simma, Bruno, 'Völkerrechtswissenschaft und Lehre von den internationalen Beziehungen: Erste Überlegungen zur Interdependenz zweier Disziplinen' (1972) 23 Zeitschrift für öffentliches Recht 293–324.
- 'Self-containted regimes' (1985) 16 Netherlands Yearbook of International Law 112–136.
- 'A Hard Look at Soft Law' (1988) 82 Proceedings of the American Society of International Law at Its Annual Meeting 377–381.
- 'Editorial' (1992) 3 EJIL 215–218.
- 'From bilateralism to community interest in international law' (1994) 250 RdC 217–384.
- 'The Contribution of Alfred Verdross to the Theory of International Law' (1995) 6 EJIL 33–54.
- 'Fragmentation in a Positive Light' (2004) 25(4) Michigan Journal of International Law 845–847.
- 'Foreign Investment Arbitration: A Place For Human Rights?' (2011) 60(3) ICLQ 573–597.
Simma, Bruno and Alston, Philip, 'The Sources of Human Rights Law: Custom, Jus Cogens, and General Principles' (1988) 12 Australian Yearbook of International Law 82–108.
Simma, Bruno and Paulus, Andreas L, 'The Responsibility of Individuals for Human Rights Abuses in Internal Conflicts: A Positivist View' (1999) 93 AJIL 302–316.
Simma, Bruno and Pulkowski, Dirk, 'Of Planets and the Universe: Self-contained Regimes in International Law' (2006) 17 EJIL 483–529.
Slaughter, Anne-Marie, Tulumello, Andrew S, and Wood, Stepan, 'International Law and International Relations Theory: A New Generation of Interdisciplinary Scholarship' (1998) 92 AJIL 367–397.
Sloane, Robert D, 'Breaking the Genuine Link: The Contemporary International Legal Regulation of Nationality' (2009) 50(1) Harvard International Law Review 1–60.
- 'On the Use and Abuse of Necessity in the Law of State Responsibility' (2012) 106 AJIL 447–508.
Sørensen, Max, 'Principes de droit international public: cours général' (1960) 101 RdC 1–254.
Sornarajah, Muthucumaraswamy, 'The Myth of International Contract Law' (1981) 15 Journal of World Trade Law 187–217.
Souza Dias, Talita de, 'The Retroactive Application of the Rome Statute in Cases of Security Council Referrals and Ad hoc Declarations: An

Appraisal of the Existing Solutions to an Under-discussed Problem' (2018) 16 JICJ 65–89.
– 'The Nature of the Rome Statute and the Place of International Law before the International Criminal Court' (2019) 17 JICJ 507–535.

Spiermann, Ole, ''Who attempts too much does nothing well': The 1920 Advisory Committee of Jurists and the Statute of the Permanent Court of International Justice' (2003) 73 BYIL 187–260.

Spinedi, Marina, 'From one Codification to another: Bilateralism and Multilateralism in the Genesis of the Codification of the Law of Treaties and the Law of State Responsibility' (2002) 13(5) EJIL 1099–1125.

Starck, Christian, 'Die Bindung des Richters an Gesetz und Verfassung' (1976) 34 Veröffentlichungen der Vereinigung der Deutschen Staatsrechtslehrer 43–93.

Stern, Brigitte, 'La succession d'États' (1996) 262 RdC 9–437.
– 'Custom at the heart of international law' (Byers, Michael and Denise, Anne trs (2001) 11 Duke Journal of Comparative & International Law 89–108.
– 'Et si on utilisait le concept de préjudice juridique?: retour sur une notion délaissée à l'occasion de la fin des travaux de la C. D. I. sur la responsabilité des états' (2001) 47 Annuaire français de droit international 3–44.

Stewart, James G, 'The End of Modes of Liability for International Crimes' (2012) 25(1) Leiden Journal of International Law 165–219.

Stoll, Peter-Tobias, 'Continental Shelf' [2008] Max Planck EPIL.
– 'International Investment Law and the Rule of Law' (2018) 9 Goettingen Journal of International Law 267–292.

Stone, Harlan F, 'The Common Law in the United States' (1936) 50(1) Harvard Law Review 4–26.

Stone, Julius, 'Problems Confronting Sociological Enquiries Concerning International Law' (1956) 89 RdC 61–175.
– 'On the Vocation of the International Law Commission' (1957) 57(1) Columbia Law Review 16–51.
– 'Non Liquet and the Function of Law in the International Community' (1959) 35 BYIL 124–161.

Stone Sweet, Alec and Della Cananea, Giacinto, 'Proportionality, General Principles of Law, and Investor-State Arbitration: a Response to José Alvarez' (2014) 46(3) NYU JILP 911–954.

Šturma, Pavel, 'State Succession in Respect of International Responsibility' (2016) 48 The George Washington International Law Review 653–678.

Swaine, Edward T, 'Bespoke Custom' (2010) 21 Duke Journal of Comparative & International Law 207–220.
Talmon, Stefan, 'Jus Cogens after Germany v. Italy: Substantive and Procedural Rules Distinguished' (2012) 25 Leiden Journal of International Law 979–1002.
– 'Determining Customary International Law: the ICJ's Methodology between Induction, Deduction and Assertion' (2015) 26(2) EJIL 417–443.
Tammes, Arnold Jan Pieter, 'Codification of International Law in the International Law Commission' (1975) 22(3) Netherlands International Law Review 319–326.
Tams, Christian J, 'Die Zweite Haager Konferenz und das Recht der friedlichen Streitbeilegung' (2007) 82 Friedenswarte 119–138.
– 'Meta-Custom and the Court: A Study in Judicial Law-Making' (2015) 14 The Law and Practice of International Courts and Tribunals 51–79.
Tasioulas, John, 'In Defense of Relative Normativity: Communitarian Values and the Nicaragua Case' (1996) 16(1) Oxford Journal of Legal Studies 85–128.
Teubner, Gunther, 'Breaking Frames: The Global Interplay of Legal and Social Systems' (1997) 45(1) American Journal of Comparative Law 149–169.
– 'Legal Irritants: Good Faith in British Law or How Unifying Law Ends up in New Divergences' (1998) 61(1) The Modern Law Review 11–32.
Teubner, Gunther and Fischer-Lescano, Andreas, 'Regime-Collisions: The Vain Search for Legal Unity in the Fragmentation of Global Law' (2004) 25 Michigan Journal of International Law 999–1046.
Thierry, Hubert, 'The Thoughts of Georges Scelle' (1990) 1 EJIL 139–209.
Thirlway, Hugh W, 'Human Rights in Customary Law: An Attempt to Define Some of the Issues' (2015) 28(3) Leiden Journal of International Law 495–506.
Thürer, Daniel and Burri, Thomas, 'Self-Determination' [2008] Max Planck EPIL.
Tietje, Christian, 'Recht ohne Rechtsquellen? Entstehung und Wandel von Völkerrechtsnormen im Interesse des Schutzes globaler Rechtsgüter im Spannungsverhältnis von Rechtssicherheit und Rechtsdynamik' (2003) 24 Zeitschrift für Rechtssoziologie 27–42.
Tladi, Dire, 'The Duty on South Africa to Arrest and Surrender President Al-Bashir Under South African and International Law: a Perspective from International Law' (2015) 13(5) JICJ 1027–1047.

- 'The International Law Commission's Recent Work on Exceptions to Immunity: Charting the Course for a brave new world in international law?' (2019) 32 Leiden Journal of International Law 169–187.
Tomka, Peter, 'Fisheries Jurisdiction Cases (United Kingdom v Iceland; Federal Republic of Germany v Iceland)' [2007] Max Planck EPIL.
- 'Custom and the International Court of Justice' (2013) 12(2) The law and practice of international courts and tribunals 195–216.
Tomlinson, Edward A, 'Tort Liability in France for the Act of Things: A Study of Judicial Lawmaking' (1988) 48(6) Louisiana Law Review 1299–1367.
Tomuschat, Christian, 'Obligations Arising For States Without Or Against Their Will' [1993] (241) RdC 195–374.
- 'Die internationale Gemeinschaft' (1995) 33(1-2) Archiv des Völkerrechts 1–20.
- 'International law: ensuring the survival of mankind on the eve of a new century: general course on public international law' (1999) 281 RdC 9–438.
Tunkin, Grigory Ivanovich, 'Co-existence and international law' (1958) 85 RdC 1–81.
- 'General International Law Customary Law Only?' (1993) 4 EJIL 534–541.
- 'Is General International Law Customary International Law only?' (1993) 4 EJIL 534–541.
Tyagi, Yogesh, 'The Denunciation of Human Rights Treaties' (2008) 79 BYIL 86–193.
Vagts, Detlev F, 'International Law in the Third Reich' (1990) 84 American Journal of International Law 661–704.
- 'International Relations Looks at Customary International Law: A Traditionalist's Defence' (2004) 15(5) EJIL 1031–1040.
Vandevelde, Kenneth J, 'U.S. Bilateral Investment Treaties: The Second Wave' (1993) 14(4) Michigan Journal of International Law 621–704.
Vasciannie, Stephen, 'The Fair and Equitable Treatment Standard in International Investment Law and Practice' (1999) 70 BYIL 99–164.
Veeder, VV, 'The Lena Goldfields Arbitration: The historical roots of three ideas' (1998) 47 ICLQ 747–792.
Ventura, Manuel J, 'Escape from Johannesburg?: Sudanese President Al-Bashir Visits South Africa, and the Implicit Removal of Head of State Immunity by the UN Security Council in light of Al-Jedda' (2015) 13(5) JICJ 995–1025.

Verdross, Alfred, 'Règles générales du droit international de la paix' (1929) 30 RdC 271–517.
- 'Les principes généraux de droit comme source du droit des gens' (1932) 37 Institute de Droit International Annuaire 283–298.
- 'Les principes généraux du droit dans la jurisprudence Internationale' (1935) 52 RdC 191–251.
- 'Forbidden Treaties in International Law' (1937) 31 AJIL 571–577.
- 'General International Law and the United Nations Charter' (1954) 30(3) International Affairs 342–348.
- 'Die Sicherung von ausländischen Privatrechten aus Abkommen zur wirtschaftlichen Entwicklung mit Schiedsklauseln' (1957) 18 ZaöRV 635–647.
- 'Entstehungsweisen und Geltungsgrund des universellen völkerrechtlichen Gewohnheitsrechts' (1969) 29 ZaöRV 635–653.
Verhoeven, Johan, 'Article 21 of the Rome Statute and the ambiguities of applicable law' (2002) 22 Netherlands Yearbook of International Law 2–22.
Vermeer-Künzli, Annemarieke, 'As If: The Legal Fiction in Diplomatic Protection' (2007) 18(1) EJIL 37–68.
Vidmar, Jure, 'Some Observations on Wrongfulness, Responsibility and Defences in International Law' (2016) 63 Netherlands International Law Review 335–353.
Villalpando, Santiago, 'Codification Light: A New Trend in the Codification of International Law at the United Nations' (2013) 2 Anuário Brasileiro de Direito Internacional = Brazilian Yearbook of International Law 117–155.
Villiger, Mark E, 'The 1969 Vienna Convention on the Law of Treaties: 40 Years After' (2009) 344 RdC 9–192.
Visscher, Charles de, 'Contribution à l'étude des sources du droit international' (1933) 14 Revue de Droit International et de Legislation Comparee 395–420.
Vitanyi, Béla, 'La signification de la "généralité" des principes de droit' (1976) 80 RGDIP 536–545.
- 'Les Positions Doctrinales Concernant Le Sens de la Notion de "Principes généraux de Droit Reconnus Par Les Nations Civilisées"' (1982) LXXXVI RGDIP 48–116.
Voigt, Christina, 'The Role of General Principles in International Law and their Relationship to Treaty Law' (2008) 31 Retfèrd. Nordisk Juridisk Tidsskrift 3–25.

Volkovitsch, Michael John, 'Righting wrongs: toward a new theory of state succession to responsibility for international delicts' (1992) 92(8) Columbia Law Review 2162–2214.

Voulgaris, Nikolaos, 'The International Law Commission and Politics: Taking the Science Out of International Law's Progressive Development' (2022) 33(3) EJIL 761–788.

Voyiakis, Emmanuel, 'Do General Principles Fill 'Gaps' in International Law?' (2009) 14 Austrian Review of International and European Law 239–256.

– 'Customary International Law and the Place of Normative Considerations' (2010) 55 American Journal of Jurisprudence 163–200.

Walden, Raphael M, 'The Subjective Element in the Formation of Customary International Law' (1977) 12 Israel Law Review 344–364.

Waldock, Humphrey, 'General course on public international law' (1962) 106 RdC.

Waldron, Jeremy, 'Custom Redeemed by Statute' (1998) 51(1) Current Legal Problems 93–114.

– 'Foreign Law and the Modern Ius Gentium' (2005) 119(1) Harvard Law Review 129–147.

Walker, Lara, 'The Impact of the Hague Abduction Convention on the Rights of the Family in the Case-Law of the European Court of Human Rights and the UN Human Rights Committee: The Danger of Neulinger' (2010) 6(3) Journal of Private International Law 649–682.

Watson, Alan, 'Legal Change: Sources of Law and Legal Culture' (1983) 131 University of Pennsylvania Law Review 1121–1157.

Watts, Arthur, 'Codification and Progressive Development of International Law' [2006] Max Planck EPIL.

Weigend, Thomas, 'Perpetration through an Organization: The Unexpected Career of a German Legal Concept' (2011) 9(1) JICJ 91–111.

Weil, Prosper, 'Towards Relative Normativity in International Law' (1983) 77 AJIL 413–442.

– 'Le droit international en quête de son identité: cours général de droit international public' (1992) 237 RdC 11–370.

Weiler, Joseph HH, 'The Geology of International Law - Governance, Democracy and Legitimacy' (2004) 64 ZaöRV 547–562.

Weinberger, Sheila, 'The Wimbledon Paradox and the World Court: Confronting inevitable conflicts between conventional and customary international law' (1996) 10 Emroy International Law Review 397–440.

Wendt, Alexander, 'The Agent-Structure Problem in International Relations Theory' (1987) 41(3) International Organization 335–370.
- 'Anarchy is what States Make of it: The Social Construction of Power Politics' (1992) 46(2) International Organization 391–425.
- 'Collective Identity Formation and the International State' (1994) 88(2) American Political Science Review 384–396.

Wet, Erika de, 'Referrals to the International Criminal Court under Chapter VII of the United Nations Charter and the Immunity of Foreign State Officials' (2018) 112 AJIL Unbound 33–37.

Wilde, Ralph, 'Human Rights Beyond Borders at the World Court: The Significance of the International Court of Justice's Jurisprudence on the Extraterritorial Application of International Human Rights Law Treaties' (2013) 12 Chinese Journal of International Law 639–677.

Wildhaber, Luzius, 'The European Court of Human Rights: The Past, The Present, The Future' (2007) 22 American University International Law Review 521–538.

Williams, John Fischer, 'International Law and the Property of Aliens' (1928) 9 BYIL 1–30.

Williams, Robert F, 'Statutes as Sources of Law Beyond their Terms in Common-Law Cases' (1982) 50(4) The George Washington Law Review 554–600.

Wood, Michael, 'The International Tribunal for the Law of the Sea and General International Law' (2007) 22 International Journal of Marine and Coastal Law 351–367.
- 'What Is Public International Law? The Need for Clarity about Sources' (2011) 1(2) Asian Journal of International Law 205–216.
- 'The present position within the ILC on the topic 'Identification of customary international law': in partial response to Sienho Yee, Report on the ILC Project on 'Identification of Customary International Law'' (2016) 15(1) Chinese Journal of International Law 3–15.
- 'Customary international law and general principles of law' (2019) 21(3-4) International Community Law Review 307–324.

Worster, William Thomas, 'The Inductive and Deductive Methods in Customary International Law Analysis: Traditional and Modern Approaches' (2014) 45(2) Georgetown journal of international law 445–521.
- 'Nottebohm and 'Genuine Link': Anatomy of a Jurisprudential Illusion' [2019] Investment Migration Working Papers ⟨https://investmentmigration.org/wp-content/uploads/2020/10/IMC-RP-2019-1-Peter-Spiro.pdf⟩ accessed 1 February 2023.

- 'Reining in the Nottebohm Case' [2022] SSRN ⟨https://papers.ssrn.com/sol3/papers.cfm?abstract_id=4148804⟩ accessed 1 February 2023.
Wuerth, Ingrid Brunk, 'Pinochet's Legacy Reassessed' (2012) 106(4) AJIL 731–768.
Xiouri, Maria, 'Problems in the Relationship between the Termination or Suspension of a Treaty on the Ground of Its Material Breach and Countermeasures' (2015) 6 Queen Mary Law Journal 63–76.
Yanagihara, Masaharu, 'Significance of the History of the Law of Nations in Europe and East Asia' (2014) 371 RdC 273–435.
Yasuaki, Onuma, 'A Transcivilized Perspective on International Law Questioning Prevalent Cognitive Frameworks in the Emerging Multi-Polar and Multi-Civilizational World of the Twenty-First Century' (2009) 342 RdC 77–418.
Yee, Sienho, 'Arguments for Cleaning Up Article 38 (1) b) and (1) c) of the ICJ Statute' (2007) 4 Romanian Journal of International Law 33–51.
- 'Report on the ILC Project on "Identification of Customary International Law"' (2015) 14(2) Chinese Journal of International Law 375–398.
- 'A Reply to Sir Michael Wood's Response to AALCOIEG's Work and My Report on the ILC Project on Identification of Customary International Law' (2016) 15(1) Chinese Journal of International Law 33–40.
- 'Article 38 of the ICJ Statute and Applicable Law: Selected Issues in Recent Cases' (2016) 7 JIDS 472–498.
- 'AALCO Informal Expert Group's Comments on the ILC Project on "Identification of Customary International Law": A Brief Follow-up' (2018) 17(1) Chinese Journal of International Law 187–194.
Yoshino, Kenji, 'The New Equal Protection' (2011) 124 Harvard Law Review 747–803.
Young, Ernest A, 'Foreign Law and the Denomination Problem' (2005) 119(1) Harvard Law Review 148–167.
Young, Margaret A, 'The WTO's Use of Relevant Rules of International Law: an Analysis of the Biotech Case' (2007) 56(4) ICLQ 907–930.
Yusuf, Abdulqawi A, 'Pan-Africanism and International Law' (2013) 369 RdC 161–359.
Zegveld, Liesbeth, 'The Bouterse Case' (2001) 32 Netherlands Yearbook of International Law 97–118.
Zemanek, Karl, 'The United Nations and the Law of Outer Space' (1965) 19 The Year Book of World Affairs 199–222.
- 'The Legal Foundations of the International Legal System' (1997) 266 RdC 9–336.

Zimmermann, Andreas, 'Amending the Amendment Provisions of the Rome Statute: The Kampala Compromise on the Crime of Aggression and the Law of Treaties' (2012) 10 JICJ 209–227.
– 'Internationaler Strafgerichtshof am Scheideweg' [2022] JuristenZeitung 261–266.
Zimmermann, Andreas and Şener, Meltem, 'Chemical Weapons and the International Criminal Court' (2014) 108 American Journal of International Law 436–448.
Zwanenburg, Marten and Dekker, Guido den, 'Introductory Note to European Court of Human Rights: van Anraat vs. the Netherlands' (2010) 49 ILM 1268–1269.

Treaties

Agreement between the Government of the French Republic and the Government of the Republic of Argentina on the Encouragement and Reciprocal Protection of Investments (signed 3 July 1991, entered into force 3 March 1993) 1728 UNTS 281.
Agreement between the United States of America, the United Mexican States, and Canada (signed 30 November 2018, entered into force 1 July 2020) Office of the United States Trade Representative.
Agreement for the Prosecution and Punishment of Major War Criminals of the European Axis, and establishing the Charter of the International Military Tribunal (signed 8 August 1945, entered into force 8 August 1945) 82 UNTS 279.
Charter of the United Nations (signed 26 June 1945, entered into force 24 October 1945) 1 UNTS 16.
Comprehensive and Progressive Agreement for Trans-Pacific Partnership (signed 18 May 2018, entered into force 30 December 2018) Australian Government Department of Foreign Affairs and Trade.
Comprehensive Economic and Trade Agreement between Canada, of the One Part, and the European Union and Its Member States, of the Other Part (signed 29 February 2016) 60 Official Journal of the European Union (2017) 23.
Convention (II) with Respect to the Laws and Customs of War on Land and its annex: Regulations concerning the Laws and Customs of War on Land (signed 29 July 1899, entered into force 4 September 1900) 32 Stat 1803.

Convention (IV) respecting the Laws and Customs of War on Land and its annex: Regulations concerning the Laws and Customs of War on Land (signed 18 October 1907, entered into force 26 January 1910) 2 AJIL Supp 90.

Convention against Torture and Other Cruel, Inhuman or Degrading Treatment or Punishment (signed 10 December 1984, entered into force 26 June 1987) 1465 UNTS 85.

Convention for the Protection of Human Rights and Fundamental Freedoms (signed 4 November 1950, entered into force 3 September 1953) 213 UNTS 221.

Convention on Asylum (signed 20 February 1928, entered into force 21 May 1929) OAS Official Records, OEA/SerX/I Treaty Series 34.

Convention on Certain Questions Relating to the Conflict of Nationality Law (signed 13 April 1930, entered into force 1 July 1937) 179 UNTS 89.

Convention on Consular Agents (signed 20 February 1928, entered into force 3 September 1929) OAS Law and Treaty Series No 34.

Convention on Fishing and Conservation of the Living Resources of the High Seas (signed 29 April 1958, entered into force 20 March 1966) 559 UNTS 205.

Convention on the Civil Aspects of International Child Abduction (signed 25 October 1980, entered into force 1 December 1983) 1343 UNTS 89.

Convention on the Continental Shelf (signed 29 April 1958, entered into force 10 June 1964) 499 UNTS 311.

Convention on the High Seas (signed 29 April 1958, entered into force 30 September 1962) 450 UNTS 11.

Convention on the Law of the Non-Navigational Uses of International Watercourses (signed 21 May 1997, entered into force 17 August 2014) (1997) 36 ILM 700.

Convention on the Prevention and Punishment of the Crime of Genocide (signed 9 December 1948, entered into force 12 January 1951) 78 UNTS 277.

Convention on the prohibition of the development, production and stockpiling of bacteriological (biological) and toxin weapons and on their destruction (signed 10 April 1972, entered into force 26 May 1975) 1015 UNTS 163.

Convention on the Prohibition of the Development, Production, Stockpiling and Use of Chemical Weapons and on their Destruction (signed 3 September 1992, entered into force 29 April 1997) 1975 UNTS 45.

Bibliography

Convention on the Prohibition of the Use, Stockpiling, Production and Transfer of Anti-Personnel Mines and on their Destruction (signed 18 September 1997, entered into force 1 March 1999) 2056 UNTS 211.

Convention on the settlement of investment disputes between States and nationals of other States (signed 18 March 1965, entered into force 14 October 1966) 575 UNTS 159.

Convention on the Territorial Sea and the Contiguous Zone (signed 29 April 1958, entered into force 10 September 1964) 516 UNTS 205.

Council of Europe Convention on Action against Trafficking in Human Beings (signed 16 May 2005, entered into force 1 February 2008) CETS 197.

European Convention on State Immunity (signed 16 May 1972, entered into force 11 June 1976) 1495 UNTS 181.

General Agreement on Tariffs and Trade (signed 30 October 1947, entered into force 1 January 1948) 55 UNTS 187.

Geneva Convention for the amelioration of the condition of the wounded and sick in armed forces in the field (signed 12 August 1949, entered into force 21 October 1950) 75 UNTS 31.

Geneva Convention for the amelioration of the condition of the wounded, sick and shipwrecked members of the armed forces at sea (signed 12 August 1949, entered into force 21 October 1950) 75 UNTS 85.

Geneva Convention relative to the protection of civilian persons in time of war (signed 12 August 1949, entered into force 21 October 1950) 75 UNTS 287.

Geneva Convention relative to the protection of civilian persons in time of war (signed 27 July 1929, entered into force 19 June 1931) 118 LNTS 343.

Geneva Convention, relative to the treatment of prisoners of war (signed 12 August 1949, entered into force 21 October 1950) 75 UNTS 135.

Havana Charter for an International Trade Organization (signed 24 March 1984) United Nations Conference on Trade and Employment, Final Act and Related Documents, E/CONF2/78.

International Covenant on Civil and Political Rights (signed 16 December 1966, entered into force 23 March 1976) 999 UNTS 171.

International Covenant on Economic, Social and Cultural Rights (signed 16 December 1966, entered into force 3 January 1976) 993 UNTS 3.

North American Free Trade Agreement (signed 17 December 1992, entered into force 1 January 1994) 32 ILM (1993) 289.

Protocol Additional to the Geneva Conventions of 12 August 1949 and relating to the protection of victims of non-international armed conflicts

(Protocol II) (signed 8 June 1977, entered into force 7 December 1978) 1125 UNTS 609.

Protocol additional to the Geneva Conventions of 12 August 1949, and relating to the protection of victims of international armed conflicts (Protocol I) (signed 8 June 1977, entered into force 7 December 1978) 1125 UNTS 3.

Protocol for the prohibition of the use in war of asphyxiating, poisonous or other gases, and of bacteriological methods of warfare (signed 17 June 1925, entered into force 9 May 1926) 94 LNTS 65.

Protocol of Signature relating to the Statute of the Permanent Court of International Justice provided for by Article 14 of the Covenant of the League of Nations (signed 16 December 1920, entered into force 1 September 1921) 6 LNTS 379.

Protocol to Prevent, Suppress and Punish Trafficking in Persons, Especially Women and Children, supplementing the United Nations Convention against Transnational Organized Crime (signed 15 November 2000, entered into force 25 December 2003) 2237 UNTS 319.

Rome Statute of the International Criminal Court (signed 17 July 1998, entered into force 1 July 2002) 2187 UNTS 3.

Slavery Convention (signed 25 September 1926, entered into force 9 March 1927) 60 LNTS 254.

Statute of the River Uruguay (signed 26 February 1975, entered into force 18 September 1976) 1295 UNTS 331.

Treaty between the Federal Republic of Germany and Pakistan for the Promotion and Protection of Investments (signed 25 November 1959, entered into force 28 April 1962) 457 UNTS 23.

Treaty between the United States and other Powers Providing for the Renunciation of War as an Instrument of National Policy (Briand-Kellogg Pact) (signed 27 October 1928, entered into force 25 July 1929) 94 LNTS 57.

Treaty between the United States of America and the Argentine Republic concerning the reciprocal encouragement and protection of investment (signed 14 November 1991, entered into force 20 October 1994) (1992) 31 ILM 124.

Treaty of Amity, Economic Relations, and Consular Rights between Iran and the United States of America (signed 15 August 1955, entered into force 16 June 1957) 248 UNTS 93.

Treaty of Peace with Germany (Treaty of Versailles) (signed 28 June 1919, entered into force 10 January 1920) 225 Parry 188.

Bibliography

United Nations Convention against Transnational Organized Crime (signed 15 November 2000, entered into force 25 December 2003) 2225 UNTS 209.
United Nations Convention on Jurisdictional Immunities of States and Their Property (signed 2 December 2004) UN Doc A/RES/59/38.
United Nations Convention on the Law of the Sea (signed 10 December 1982, entered into force 16 November 1994) 1833 UNTS 3.
US – Mexico Claims Convention of 8 September 1923 (signed 8 September 1923, entered into force 19 February 1924) 68 UNTS 459.
Vienna Convention on Consular Relations (signed 24 April 1963, entered into force 19 March 1967) 596 UNTS 261.
Vienna Convention on Diplomatic Relations (signed 18 April 1961, entered into force 24 April 1964) 500 UNTS 95.
Vienna Convention on the Law of Treaties (signed 23 May 1969, entered into force 27 January 1980) 1155 UNTS 331.

Permanent Court of International Justice

Case Concerning the Factory at Chorzow: Germany v Poland Judgment of 26 July 1927 [1927] PCIJ Series A 09.
Case Concerning the Factory at Chorzow: Germany v. Poland Judgment of 13 September 1928 [1928] PCIJ Series A 17.
Case Concerning the Payment in Gold of Brazilian Federal Loans Contracted in France: France v The United States of Brazil Judgment of 12 July 1929 [1929] PCIJ Series A 21.
Case Concerning the Payment of Various Serbian Loans Issued in France: France v Kingdom of the Serbs, Croats, and Slovenes Judgment of 12 July 1929 [1929] PCIJ Series A 20.
Certain German Interests in Polish Upper Silesia: Germany v. Poland Judgment [1926] PCIJ Series A 07.
Diversion of Water from the Meuse: Netherlands v. Belgium Merits [1937] PCIJ Series A/B 70.
Electricity Company of Sofia and Bulgaria: Belgium v Bulgaria Judgment of 4 April 1939 Preliminary Objection [1939] PCIJ Series A/B 77.
Interpretation of Article 3, Paragraph 2, of the Treaty of Lausanne: Advisory Opinion of 21 November 1925 [1925] PCIJ Series B 12.
Legal Status of Eastern Greenland: Denmark v Norway Judgment of 5 April 1933 [1933] PCIJ Series A/B 53.

Lighthouse Case between France and Greece: France v Greece Judgment of 17 March 1934 [1934] PCIJ Series A/B 62.
Mavrommatis Palestine Concessions: Greece v. The United Kingdom Judgment of 30 August 1924 [1924] PCIJ Series A 02.
Minority Schools in Albania Advisory Opinion of 6 April 1935 [1935] PCIJ Series A/B 64.
Oscar Chinn Judgment of 12 December 1934 [1934] PCIJ Series A/B 63.
Rights of Minorities in Upper Silesia (Minority Schools): Germany v. Poland Judgment of 26 April 1928 [1928] PCIJ Series A 15.
The Case of SS Lotus: France v Turkey Merits [1927] PCIJ Series A 10.
The Panevezys-Saldutiskis Railway Case: Estonia v. Lithuania Merits [1939] PCIJ Series A/B No 76.
Wimbledon: UK et al v. Germany Judgment of 17 August 1923 [1923] PCIJ Series A 01.

International Court of Justice

Accordance with international law of the unilateral declaration of independence in respect of Kosovo (Advisory Opinion) [2010] ICJ Rep 403.
Ahmadou Sadio Diallo (Republic of Guinea v. Democratic Republic of the Congo) (Preliminary Objections, Judgment) [2007] ICJ Rep 582.
Ahmadou Sadio Diallo (Republic of Guinea v. Democratic Republic of the Congo) (Merits, Judgment) [2010] ICJ Rep 639.
Ahmadou Sadio Diallo (Republic of Guinea v. Democratic Republic of the Congo) (Compensation, Judgment) [2012] ICJ Rep 324.
Allegations of Genocide under the Convention on the Prevention and Punishment of the Crime of Genocide (Ukraine v. Russian Federation) (Order of 16 March 2022) (2022) ⟨https://www.icj-cij.org/public/files/case-related/182/182-20220316-ORD-01-00-EN.pdf⟩ accessed 1 February 2023.
Allegations of Genocide under the Convention on the Prevention and Punishment of the Crime of Genocide (Ukraine v. Russian Federation) (Order of 5 June 2023) (2023) ⟨https://www.icj-cij.org/sites/default/files/case-related/182/182-20230605-ORD-01-00-EN.pdf⟩ accessed 5 June 2023.
Alleged Violations of Sovereign Rights and Maritime Spaces in the Caribbean Sea (Nicaragua v. Colombia) (Preliminary Objections) [2016] ICJ Rep 3.
Alleged Violations of Sovereign Rights and Maritime Spaces in the Caribbean Sea (Nicaragua v. Colombia) (Judgment of 21 April 2022) (2022) ⟨https:

Bibliography

//www.icj-cij.org/public/files/case-related/155/155-20220421-JUD-01-00-EN.pdf⟩ accessed 1 February 2023.

Alleged Violations of the 1955 Treaty of Amity, Economic Relations, and Consular Rights (*Islamic Republic of Iran v. United States of America*) (Preliminary Objections, Judgment of 3 February 2021) [2021] ICJ Rep 9.

Anglo-Iranian Oil Co (*United Kingdom v. Iran*) (Judgment of July 22nd, 1952) [1952] ICJ Rep 93.

Appeal Relating to the Jurisdiction of the ICAO Council (*India v. Pakistan*) (Judgment) [1972] ICJ Rep 46.

Application for Review of Judgment No 158 of the United Nations Administrative Tribunal (Advisory Opinion) [1973] ICJ Rep 166.

Application for Review of Judgment No 273 of the United Nations Administrative Tribunal (Advisory Opinion) [1982] ICJ Rep 325.

Application of the Convention of 1902 Governing the Guardianship of Infants (*Netherlands v. Sweden*) (Judgment) [1958] ICJ Rep 55.

Application of the Convention on the Prevention and Punishment of the Crime of Genocide (*Bosnia and Herzegovina v. Serbia and Montenegro*) (Order of 8 April 1993) [1993] ICJ Rep 3.

Application of the Convention on the Prevention and Punishment of the Crime of Genocide (*Bosnia and Herzegovina v. Serbia and Montenegro*) (Preliminary Objections, Judgment) [1996] ICJ Rep 595.

Application of the Convention on the Prevention and Punishment of the Crime of Genocide (*Bosnia and Herzegovina v. Serbia and Montenegro*) (Judgment) [2007] ICJ Rep 43.

Application of the Convention on the Prevention and Punishment of the Crime of Genocide (*Croatia v. Serbia*) (Preliminary Objections, Judgment) [2008] ICJ Rep 412.

Application of the Convention on the Prevention and Punishment of the Crime of Genocide (*Bosnia and Herzegovina v. Serbia and Montenegro*) (Judgment of 3 February 2015) [2015] ICJ Rep 3.

Application of the Convention on the Prevention and Punishment of the Crime of Genocide (*The Gambia v. Myanmar*) (Order of 23 January 2020) [2020] ICJ Rep 3.

Application of the Convention on the Prevention and Punishment of the Crime of Genocide (*The Gambia v. Myanmar*) (Preliminary Objections, Judgment of 22 July 2022) [2022] ICJ Rep 477.

Application of the Interim Accord of 13 September 1995 (*The former Yugoslav Republic of Macedonia v. Greece*) (Judgment of 5 December 2011) [2011] ICJ Rep 644.

Application of the International Convention for the Suppression of the Financing of Terrorism and of the International Convention on the Elimination of All Forms of Racial Discrimination (*Ukraine/Russian Federation*) (Preliminary Objections, Judgment) [2019] ICJ Rep 558.

Application of the International Convention on the Elimination of All Forms of Racial Discrimination (*Georgia v. Russian Federation*) (Provisional Measures, Order of 15 October 2008) [2008] ICJ Rep 353.

Armed Activities on the Territory of the Congo (*Democratic Republic of the Congo v. Uganda*) (Judgment) [2005] ICJ Rep 168.

Armed Activities on the Territory of the Congo (New Application: 2002) (*Democratic Republic of the Congo v. Rwanda*) (Provisional Measures, Order of 10 July 2002) [2002] ICJ Rep 219.

Armed Activities on the Territory of the Congo (New Application: 2002) (*Democratic Republic of the Congo v. Rwanda*) (Jurisdiction and Admissibility, Judgment) [2006] ICJ Rep 6.

Arrest Warrant of 11 April 2000 (*Democratic Republic of Congo v. Belgium*) (Judgment) [2002] ICJ Rep 3.

Asylum Case (*Colombia/Peru*) (Judgment of 20 November 1950) [1950] ICJ Rep 266.

Barcelona Traction, Light and Power Company, Limited (*Belgium v. Spain*) (Judgment) [1970] ICJ Rep 3.

Border and Transborder Armed Actions (*Nicaragua v. Honduras*) (Jurisdiction and Admissibility, Judgment) [1988] ICJ Rep 69.

Case of the monetary gold removed from Rome in 1943 (*UK v. Albania*) (Preliminary Question) [1954] ICJ Rep 19.

Certain Activities Carried out by Nicaragua in the Border Area - Construction of a Road in Costa Rica Along The San Juan River (*Costa Rica v. Nicaragua /Nicaragua v. Costa Rica*) (Judgment) [2015] ICJ Rep 665.

Certain Expenses of the United Nations (Article 17, paragraph 2, of the Charter) (Advisory Opinion) [1962] ICJ Rep 151.

Certain Iranian Assets (*Islamic Republic of Iran v. United States of America*) (Preliminary Objections Judgment of 13 February 2019) [2019] ICJ Rep 7.

Certain Questions of Mutual Assistance in Criminal Matters (*Djibouti v. France*) (Judgment) [2008] ICJ Rep 177.

Continental Shelf (*Tunisia/Libyan Arab Jamahiriya*) (Application to Intervene, Judgment) [1981] ICJ Rep 3.

Continental Shelf (*Tunisia/Libyan Arab Jamahiriya*) (Judgment) [1982] ICJ Rep 18.

Continental Shelf (Libyan Arab Jamahiriya/Malta) (Application to Intervene, Judgment) [1984] ICJ Rep 3.
Continental Shelf (Libyan Arab Jamahiriya/Malta) (Judgment) [1985] ICJ Rep 13.
Corfu Channel Case (UK v Albania) (Preliminary Objection) [1948] ICJ Rep 15.
Corfu Channel Case (UK v Albania) (Merits) [1949] ICJ Rep 4.
Delimitation of the Maritime Boundary in the Gulf of Maine Area (Canada/United States of America) (Judgment) [1984] ICJ Rep 246.
Difference Relating to Immunity from Legal Process of a Special Rapporteur of the Commission on Human Rights (Advisory Opinion) [1999] ICJ Rep 62.
East Timor (Portugal v. Australia) (Judgment) [1995] ICJ Rep 90.
Effect of Awards of Compensation Made by the United Nations Administrative Tribunal (Advisory Opinion of July 13th, 1954) [1954] ICJ Rep 47.
Elettronica Sicula SpA (ELSI) (United States of America v. Italy) (Judgment of 20 July 1989) [1989] ICJ Rep 5.
Fisheries (United Kingdom v. Norway) (Judgment) [1951] ICJ Rep 116.
Fisheries Jurisdiction (Federal Republic of Germany v. Iceland) (Jurisdiction of the Court, Judgment) [1973] ICJ Rep 49.
Fisheries Jurisdiction (Federal Republic of Germany v. Iceland) (Merits, Judgment) [1974] ICJ Rep 175.
Fisheries Jurisdiction (United Kingdom v. Iceland) (Merits, Judgment) [1974] ICJ Rep 3.
Frontier Dispute (Burkina Faso/Republic of Mali) (Judgment) [1986] ICJ Rep 554.
Gabčíkovo-Nagymaros Project (Hungary/Slovakia) (Judgment) [1997] ICJ Rep 7.
Haya de la Torre Case (Colombia/Peru) (Judgment of June 13th, 1951) [1951] ICJ Rep 71.
Immunities and Criminal Proceedings (Equatorial Guinea v. France) (Preliminary Objections, Judgment) [2018] ICJ Rep 292.
International Status of South West Africa (Advisory Opinion) [1950] ICJ Rep 128.
Interpretation of the Agreement of 25 March 1951 between the WHO and Egypt (Advisory Opinion) [1980] ICJ Rep 73.
Jurisdictional Immunities of the State (Germany v. Italy) (Application for Permission to Intervene, Order of 4 July 2011) [2011] ICJ Rep 494.

Jurisdictional Immunities of the State (*Germany v. Italy: Greece intervening*) (Judgment) [2012] ICJ Rep 99.
LaGrand (*Germany v. United States of America*) (Judgment) [2001] ICJ Rep 466.
Land and Maritime Boundary between Cameroon and Nigeria (*Cameroon/Nigeria*) (Preliminary Objections, Judgment) [1998] ICJ Rep 275.
Land and Maritime Boundary between Cameroon and Nigeria (*Cameroon/Nigeria: Equatorial Guinea intervening*) (Order of 21 October 1999) [1999] ICJ Rep 1029.
Land and Maritime Boundary between Cameroon and Nigeria (*Cameroon/Nigeria*) (Judgment) [2002] ICJ Rep 303.
Land, Island and Maritime Frontier Dispute (*El Salvador/Honduras*) (Application to Intervene, Judgment) [1990] ICJ Rep 92.
Land, Island and Maritime Frontier Dispute (*El Salvador/Honduras: Nicaragua Intervening*) (Judgment) [1992] ICJ Rep 351.
Legal Consequences for States of the Continued Presence of South Africa in Namibia (South West Africa) notwithstanding Security Council Resolution 276 (1970) (Advisory Opinion) [1971] ICJ Rep 16.
Legal Consequences of the Construction of a Wall (Advisory Opinion) [2004] ICJ Rep 136.
Legal consequences of the Separation of the Chagos Archipelago from Mauritius in 1965 (Advisory Opinion) [2019] ICJ Rep.
Legality of the Threat or Use of Nuclear Weapons (Advisory Opinion) [1996] ICJ Rep 226.
Maritime Delimitation and Territorial Questions between Qatar and Bahrain (*Qatar v. Bahrain*) (Merits, Judgment) [2001] ICJ Rep 40.
Maritime Delimitation in the Area between Greenland and Jan Mayen (*Denmark v. Norway*) (Judgment) [1993] ICJ Rep 38.
Maritime Delimitation in the Black Sea (*Romania/Ukraine*) (Judgment) [2009] ICJ Rep 61.
Maritime Dispute (*Peru v. Chile*) (Judgment) [2014] ICJ Rep 3.
Military and Paramilitary Activities in and against Nicaragua (*Nicaragua v. United States of America*) (Jurisdiction and Admissibility, Judgment) [1984] ICJ Rep 392.
Military and Paramilitary Activities in and against Nicaragua (*Nicaragua v. United States of America*) (Merits) [1986] ICJ Rep 14.
North Sea Continental Shelf (*Federal Republic of Germany/Denmark; Federal Republic of Germany/Netherlands*) (Judgment) [1969] ICJ Rep 3.

Nottebohm Case (second phase) (*Liechtenstein v. Guatemala*) (Judgment of April 6th, 1955) [1955] ICJ Rep 4.
Nuclear Tests Case (*Australia v. France*) (Application to Intervene, Order of 12 July 1973) [1973] ICJ Rep 320.
Nuclear Tests Case (*New Zealand v. France*) (Application to Intervene, Order of 12 July 1973) [1973] ICJ Rep 324.
Nuclear Tests Case (*Australia v. France*) (Judgment) [1974] ICJ Rep 253.
Nuclear Tests Case (*New Zealand v. France*) (Judgment) [1974] ICJ Rep 457.
Nuclear Tests Case (*Australia v. France*) (Application to Intervene, Order of 20 December 1974) [1974] ICJ Rep 530.
Nuclear Tests Case (*New Zealand v. France*) (Order of 20 December 1974, Application by Fiji for Permission to Intervene) [1974] ICJ Rep 535.
Obligation to Negotiate Access to the Pacific Ocean (*Bolivia v. Chile*) (Judgment of 1 October 2018) [2018] ICJ Rep 507.
Obligations concerning Negotiations relating to Cessation of the Nuclear Arms Race and to Nuclear Disarmament (*Marshall Islands v. India*) (Judgment of 5 October 2016) [2016] ICJ Rep 255.
Obligations concerning Negotiations relating to Cessation of the Nuclear Arms Race and to Nuclear Disarmament (*Marshall Islands v. India*) (Judgment of 5 October 2016) [2016] ICJ Rep 552.
Oil Platforms (*Islamic Republic of Iran v. United States of America*) (Preliminary Objections, Judgment) [1996] ICJ Rep 803.
Oil Platforms (*Islamic Republic of Iran v. United States of America*) (Judgment) [2003] ICJ Rep 161.
Pulp Mills on the River Uruguay (*Argentina v. Uruguay*) (Judgment) [2010] ICJ Rep 14.
Question of the Delimitation of the Continental Shelf between Nicaragua and Colombia beyond 200 nautical miles from the Nicaraguan Coast (*Nicaragua v. Colombia*) (Preliminary Objections) [2016] ICJ Rep 100.
Questions relating to the Obligation to Prosecute or Extradite (*Belgium v. Senegal*) (Judgment) [2012] ICJ Rep 422.
Questions relating to the Seizure and Detention of Certain Documents and Data (*Timor-Leste v. Australia*) (Provisional Measures, Order of 3 March 2014) [2014] ICJ Rep 147.
Reparation for Injuries Suffered in the Service of the United Nations (Advisory Opinion) [1949] ICJ Rep 174.
Request for an Examination of the Situation in Accordance with Paragraph 63 of the Court's Judgment of 20 December 1974 in the Nuclear Tests

(New Zealand v France) Case) (*New Zealand v. France*) (Order of 22 September 1995) [1995] ICJ Rep 288.

Reservations to the Convention on the Prevention and Punishment of the Crime of Genocide (Advisory Opinion) [1951] ICJ Rep 15.

Right of Passage over Indian Territory (*Portugal v. India*) (Judgment of 12 April 1960) [1960] ICJ Rep 6.

Rights of Nationals of the United States of America in Morocco (*France v. United States of America*) (Judgment of August 27th, 1952) [1952] ICJ Rep 176.

South West Africa (*Ethiopia v. South Africa; Liberia v. South Africa*) (Second Phase, Judgment) [1966] ICJ Rep 6.

Sovereignty over Pedra Branca/Pulau Batu Puteh, Middle Rocks and South Ledge (*Malaysia/Singapore*) (Judgment) [2008] ICJ Rep 12.

Sovereignty over Pulau Ligitan and Pulau Sipadan (*Indonesia/Malaysia*) (Application for Permission to Intervene, Judgment) [2001] ICJ Rep 575.

Temple of Preah Vihear (*Cambodia v. Thailand*) (Judgment) [1962] ICJ Rep 6.

Territorial and Maritime Dispute (*Nicaragua v. Colombia*) (Application for Permission to Intervene, Judgment) [2011] ICJ Rep 348.

Territorial and Maritime Dispute (*Nicaragua v. Colombia*) (Application for Permission to Intervene, Judgment) [2011] ICJ Rep 420.

Territorial and Maritime Dispute (*Nicaragua v. Colombia*) (Judgment) [2012] ICJ Rep 624.

Territorial and Maritime Dispute between Nicaragua and Honduras in the Caribbean Sea (*Nicaragua v. Honduras*) (Judgment) [2007] ICJ Rep 659.

Territorial and Maritime Dispute between Nicaragua and Honduras in the Caribbean Sea (*Nicaragua v. Honduras*) (Judgment) [2007] ICJ Rep 659.

United States Diplomatic and Consular Staff in Tehran (*United States of America v. Iran*) (Judgment) [1980] ICJ Rep 3.

Western Sahara (Advisory Opinion) [1975] ICJ Rep 12.

Whaling in the Antarctic (*Australia v. Japan: New Zealand intervening*) (Judgment) [2014] ICJ Rep 226.

Public Sittings at the International Court of Justice

Minutes of the Public Sittings held at the Peace Palace, The Hague, on February 10th to 24th, March 2nd to 8th, and April 6th, 1955, Verbatim Record 1955 CR 1955/2.

Bibliography

Public sitting held on Wednesday 14 September 2011, at 10 am, at the Peace Palace, Verbatim Record 14 September 2011 CR 2011/19.
Public sitting held on Monday 20 January 2014, at 10 am, at the Peace Palace, Verbatim Record 20 January 2014 CR 2014/1.
Public sitting held on Tuesday 21 January 2014, at 10 am, at the Peace Palace, Verbatim Record 21 January 2014 CR 2014/2.

European Commission of Human Rights and European Court of Human Rights

A, B and C v Ireland [GC] App no 25579/05 (ECtHR, 16 December 2010).
Al-Adsani v the United Kingdom [GC] App no 35763/97 (ECtHR, 21 November 2001).
Al-Dulimi and Montana Managment Inc v Switzerland App no 5809/08 (ECtHR, 26 November 2013).
Al-Dulimi and Montana Managment Inc v Switzerland [GC] App no 5809/08 (ECtHR, 21 June 2016).
Al-Jedda v The United Kingdom [GC] App no 27021/08 (ECtHR, 7 July 2011).
Siliadin v France App no 73316/01 (ECtHR, 26 July 2005).
Al-Skeini and Others v The United Kingdom [GC] App no 55721/07 (ECtHR, 7 July 2011).
Animal Defenders International v United Kingdom [GC] App no 48876/08 (ECtHR, 22 April 2013).
Banković against Belgium, the Czech Republic, Denmark, France, Germany, Greece, Hungary, Iceland, Italy, Luxembourg, the Netherlands, Norway, Poland, Portugal, Spain, Turkey and the United Kingdom [GC] App no 52207/99 (ECtHR, 12 December 2001).
Behrami and Behrami against France and Saramati against France, Germany and Norway [GC] App no 71412/01 and 78166/01 (ECtHR, 2 May 2007).
Belilos v Switzerland [Plenum] App no 10328/83 (ECtHR, 29 April 1988).
Bosphorus Hava Yolları Turizm ve Ticaret Anonim Şirketi v Ireland [GC] App no 45036/98 (ECtHR, 30 June 2005).
Brannigan and McBride v The United Kingdom [Plenum] App no 14553/89, 14554/89 (ECtHR, 25 May 1993).
Brogan and others v United Kingdom App no 11209/84; 11234/84; 11266/84; 11386/85 (ECtHR, 29 November 1988).

Catan and others v Moldova and Russia [GC] App no 43370/04, 8252/05 and 18454/06 (ECtHR, 19 October 2012).
Carter v Russia App no 20914/07 (ECtHR, 21 September 2021).
Chiragov and others v Armenia [GC] App no 132116/05 (ECtHR, 16 June 2015).
Christine Goodwin v the United Kingdom [GC] App no 28957/95 (ECtHR, 11 July 2002).
Costello-Roberts v The United Kingdom App no 89/1991/341/414 (ECtHR, 23 February 1993).
Cudak v Lithuania [GC] App no 15869/02 (ECtHR, 23 March 2010).
Cyprus v Turkey App no 6780/74; 6950/75 (Commission Decision, 10 July 1976).
Cyprus v Turkey [GC] App no 25781/94 (ECtHR, 10 May 2001).
Demir and Baykara v Turkey [GC] App no 34503/97 (ECtHR, 18 November 2008).
El-Masri v the former Yugoslav Republic of Macedonia [GC] App no 39630/09 (ECtHR, 13 December 2012).
Engel and others v The Netherlands App no 5100/71; 5101/71; 5102/71; 5354/72; 5370/72 (ECtHR, 8 June 1976).
Ergi v Turkey App no 540/1993/435/514 (ECtHR, 28 July 1998).
Fogarty v The United Kingdom [GC] App no 37112/97 (ECtHR, 21 November 2001).
Frydlender v France [GC] App no 30979/96 (ECtHR, 27 June 2000).
Gasparini v Italy and Belgium App no 10750/03 (ECtHR, 12 May 2009).
Georgia v Russia (II) [GC] App no 38263/08 (ECtHR, 21 January 2021).
Glass v the United Kingdom App no 61827/00 (ECtHR, 9 March 2004).
Golder v United Kingdom [Plenum] App no 4451/70 (ECtHR, 21 February 1970).
Güleç v Turkey App no 54/1997/838/1044 (ECtHR, 27 July 1998).
Hanan v Germany [GC] App no 4871/16 (ECtHR, 16 February 2021).
Handyside v The United Kingdom [Plenum] App no 5493/72 (ECtHR, 7 December 1976).
Hassan v The United Kingdom [GC] App no 29750/09 (ECtHR, 16 September 2014).
Hirst v the United Kingdom (no 2) [GC] App no 74025/01 (ECtHR, 6 October 2005).
HLR v France App no 24573/94 (ECtHR, 22 April 1997).
Ilaşcu and others v Moldavia and Russia [GC] App no 48787/99 (ECtHR, 8 July 2004).

Isayeva v Russia App no 57950/00 (ECtHR, 24 February 2005).
Jaloud v The Netherlands [GC] App no 47708/08 (ECtHR, 20 November 2014).
James v United Kingdom [Plenum] App no 8793/79 (ECtHR, 21 February 1986).
Jones and Others v The United Kingdom App no 34356/06 and 40528/06 (ECtHR, 14 January 2014).
Jorgig v Germany App no 74613/01 (ECtHR, 12 July 2007).
Kolk and Kislyiy v Estonia App no 23052/04, 24018/04 (ECtHR, 17 January 2006).
Kononov v Latvia [GC] App no 36376/04 (ECtHR, 17 May 2010).
Korbely v Hungary [GC] App no 9174/02 (ECtHR, 19 September 2008).
Kotov v Russia [GC] App no 54522/00 (ECtHR, 3 April 2012).
Loizidou v Turkey (Preliminary Objections)[GC] App no 15318/89 (ECtHR, 23 March 1995).
Loizidou v Turkey (Judgment) [GC] App no 15318/89 (ECtHR, 18 December 1996).
Maktouf and Damjanović v Bosnia and Herzegovina [GC] App no 2312/08 and 34179/08 (ECtHR, 18 July 2013).
Mamatkulov and Askarov v Turkey [GC] App no 46827/99 and 46951/99 (ECtHR, 7 February 2005).
Maumousseau and Washington v France App no 39388/05 (ECtHR, 6 December 2007).
Marckx v Belgium [Plenum] App no 6833/74 (ECtHR, 13 June 1979).
Markovic and Others v Italy [GC] App no 1398/03 (ECtHR, 14 December 2006).
McCann and Others v United Kingdom [GC] App no 18984/91 (ECtHR, 27 September 1995).
McElhinney v Ireland [GC] App no 31253/96 (ECtHR, 21 November 2001).
Nada v Switzerland [GC] App no 10593/08 (ECtHR, 12 September 2012).
Naït-Liman v Switzerland App no 51357/07 (ECtHR, 21 June 2016).
Naït-Liman v Switzerland [GC] App no 51357/07 (ECtHR, 15 March 2018).
Neulinger and Shuruk v Switzerland [GC] App no 41615/07 (ECtHR, 6 July 2010).
O'Keeffe v Ireland [GC] App no 35810/09 (ECtHR, 28 January 2014).
Oleynikov v Russia App no 36703/04 (ECtHR, 14 March 2013).
Öneryıldız v Turkey App no 48939/99 (ECtHR, 30 November 2004).
Opuz v Turkey App no 33401/02 (ECtHR, 9 June 2009).
Ould Dah v France App no 13113/03 (ECtHR, 17 March 2009).

Özkan et al v Turkey App no 21689/93 (ECtHR, 6 April 2004).
Öztürk v Germany [Plenum] App no 8544/79 (ECtHR, 21 February 2084).
Pini and Others v Romania App no 78028/01 and 78030/01 (ECtHR, 22 June 2004).
Prince Hans-Adam II of Liechtenstein v Germany [GC] App no 42527/98 (ECtHR, 12 July 2001).
Rantsev v Cyprus and Russia App no 25965/04 (ECtHR, 7 June 2010).
Rees v the United Kingdom [Plenum] App no 9532/81 (ECtHR, 17 October 1986).
Saadi v The United Kingdom [GC] App no 13229/03 (ECtHR, 29 January 2008).
Sabeh El Leil v France [GC] App no 4869/05 (ECtHR, 29 November 2011).
Sargsyan v Azerbaijan [GC] App no 40167/06 (ECtHR, 16 June 2015).
Sheffield and Horsham v the United Kingdom [GC] App no (31–32/1997/815–816/1018–1019 (ECtHR, 30 July 1998).
Slivenko v Latvia [GC] App no 48321/99 (ECtHR, 9 October 2003).
Soering v The United Kingdom [Plenum] App no 14038/88 (ECtHR, 7 July 1989).
Sørensen and Rasmussen v Denmark [GC] App no 52562/99 and 52620/99 (ECtHR, 11 January 2006).
Stichting Mothers of Srebrenica and Others against the Netherlands App no 65542/12 (ECtHR, 11 June 2013).
Stoll v Switzerland [GC] App no 69698/01) (ECtHR, 10 December 2007).
Streletz, Kessler and Krenz v Germany [GC] App no 34044/96, 35532/97 and 44801/98 (ECtHR, 22 March 2001).
Sylvester v Austria App no 36812/97 and 40104/98 (ECtHR, 24 April 2003).
Tănase v Moldova [GC] App no 7/08 (ECtHR, 27 April 2010).
Tyrer v The United Kingdom App no 5856/72 (ECtHR, 25 April 1978).
Ukraine and the Netherlands v Russia [GC] App no 8019/16, 43800/14 and 28525/20 (ECtHR, 25 January 2023).
Van Anraat v the Netherlands App no 365389/09 (ECtHR, 10 June 2010).
Vilho Eskelinen and Others v Finland [GC] App no 63235/00 (ECtHR, 19 April 2007).
Waite and Kennedy v Germany [GC] App no 26083/94 (ECtHR, 18 February 1999).
Wallishauser v Austria App no 156/04 (ECtHR, 17 July 2012).
Wemhoff v Germany App no 2122/64 (ECtHR, 27 June 1968).

Bibliography

Inter-American Court of Human Rights

Rights and Guarantees of Children in the context of migration and/or in need of international protection IACtHR Advisory Opinion (19 August 2014) OC-21/14.
The Environment and Human Rights (State Obligations in Relation to the Environment in the Context of the Protection and Guarantee of the Rights to Life and to Personal Integrity: Interpretation and Scope of Articles 4(1) and 5(1) of the American Convention on Human Rights IACtHR Advisory Opinion (15 November 2017) OC-23/18.

International Military Tribunal

USA et al v Göring et al IMT Judgment (1 October 1946) Trial of the Major War Criminals before the International Military Tribunal Vol. 1 (1947).

International Military Tribunal for the Far East (Tokyo)

Araki and others ('Tokyo Judgment') IMTFE, Judgment (12 November 1948) in Neil Boister and Robert Cryer (eds), Documents on the Tokyo International Military Tribunal (Oxford University Press 2008).

US Military Tribunals at Nuremberg

Einsatzgruppen Case (United States of America v Otto Ohlendorf et al), United States Military Tribunal, Trials of War Criminals Before the Nuremberg Military Tribunals under Control Council Law No 10, Vol IV (1952).
Justice Case (United States of America v Josef Altstoetter, et al), United States Military Tribunal, Trials of War Criminals Before the Nuremberg Military Tribunals under Control Council Law No 10, Vol III (1951).
Krupp Case (United States of America v Alfried Felix Krupp von Bohlen und Halbach et al), United States Military Tribunal, Trials of War Criminals Before the Nuremberg Military Tribunals under Control Council Law No 10, Vol IX (1950).
The German High Command Trial Case No 72, Trial of Wilhelm Leeb and Thirteen Others, United States Military Tribunal, Trials of War Criminals

Before the Nuremberg Military Tribunals under Control Council Law No 10, Vol XI (1950).

The United States of America vs Carl Krauch et al (IG Farben), United States Military Tribunal, Trials of War Criminals Before the Nuremberg Military Tribunals under Control Council Law No 10, Vol VIII (1952).

United States v Friedrich Flick and others, United States Military Tribunal, Trials of War Criminals Before the Nuremberg Military Tribunals under Control Council Law No 10, Vol VI (1952).

US v List et al, Hostage Case, United States Military Tribunal, Trials of War Criminals Before the Nuremberg Military Tribunals under Control Council Law No 10, Vol XI (1950).

Trial of Franz Holstein and Twenty-Three Others UNWCC Law Reports Vol. VII, 26.

International Criminal Tribunal for the Former Yugoslavia

Prosecutor v Anto Furundžija ICTY TC Judgement (10 December 1998) IT-95-17/1-T.

Prosecutor v Anto Furundžija ICTY AC Judgement (21 July 2000) IT-95-17/1-A.

Prosecutor v Blagoje Simić, ICTY AC Judgement (28 November 2006) IT-95-9-A.

Prosecutor v Blagoje Simić, ICTY TC Judgement (17 October 2003) IT-95-9-T.

Prosecutor v Blaskić ICTY AC Judgement on the Request of the Republic of Croatia for Review of the Decision of Trial Chamber II of 18 July 1997 (29 October 1997) IT-95-14-AR10.

Prosecutor v Blaskić ICTY TC Judgement (3 March 2000) IT-95-14-T.

Prosecutor v Blaskić ICTY AC Judgement (29 July 2004) IT-95-14-A.

Prosecutor v Dario Kordić, Mario Čerkez ICTY TC Judgement (26 February 2001) IT-95-14/2-T.

Prosecutor v Dario Kordić, Mario Čerkez ICTY TC Decision on the Joint Defence Motion to Dismiss the Amended Indictment for Lack of Jurisdiction based on the limited Jurisdictional Reach of Articles 2 and 3 (9 March 1999) IT-95-14/2.

Prosecutor v Dragoljub Kunarac, Radomir Kovač and Zoran Vuković ICTY TC Judgement (22 February 2001) IT-96-23-T & IT-96-23/1-T.

Prosecutor v Dragoljub Kunarac, Radomir Kovač and Zoran Vuković ICTY AC Judgement (12 June 2002) IT-96-23 & IT-96-23/1-A.

Prosecutor v Drazen Erdemović ICTY AC Judgement (7 October 1997) IT-96-22-A.

Prosecutor v Drazen Erdemović ICTY TC Sentencing Judgement (22 November 1996) IT-96-22-T.

Prosecutor v Dusko Tadić ICTY AC Judgement (15 July 1999) IT-94-1-A.

Prosecutor v Dusko Tadić ICTY TC Decision on the Defence Motion on the Principle of non-bis-in-idem (14 November 1995) IT-94-1-T.

Prosecutor v Dusko Tadić a/k/a "Dule" ICTY AC Decision on the Defence Motion for Interlocutory Appeal on Jurisdiction (2 October 1995) IT-94-1-AR72.

Prosecutor v Dusko Tadić a/k/a "Dule" ICTY AC Judgement on Allegations of Contempt against Prior Counsel, Milan Vujin (31 January 2000) IT-94-1-A-R77.

Prosecutor v Hadžihasanović et al ICTY AC Decision on Interlocutory Appeal Challenging Jurisdiction in Relation to Command Responsibility (16 July 2003) T-01-47-AR72.

Prosecutor v Kupreškić et al ICTY TC Judgement (14 January 2000) IT-95-16-T.

Prosecutor v Milan Martić ICTY TC Judgement (12 June 2007) IT-95-11-T.

Prosecutor v Milan Martić ICTY AC Judgement (8 October 2008) IT-95-11-A.

Prosecutor v Milan Milutinović and others ICTY TC Decision on Ojdanić's Motion Challenging Jurisdiction: Indirect Co-Perpetration (22 March 2006) Case No. IT-05-87-PT.

Prosecutor v Milan Milutinović et al ICTY TC Judgement (26 February 2009) IT-05-87-T.

Prosecutor v Milomir Stakić ICTY TC Judgement (31 July 2003) IT-97-24-T.

Prosecutor v Milomir Stakić ICTY AC Judgement (22 March 2006) IT-97-24-A.

Prosecutor v Milutinović et al ICTY TC Decision on Ojdanic motion to prohibit witness proofing (12 December 2006) IT-05-87-T.

Prosecutor v Mitar Vasiljević ICTY TC Judgement (29 October 1997) IT-98-32-T.

Prosecutor v Radislav Krstić ICTY TC Judgement (2 August 2001) IT-98-33-T.

Prosecutor v Radislav Krstić ICTY AC Judgement (19 April 2004) IT-98-33-A.

Prosecutor v Radoslav Brđanin ICTY TC Judgement (1 September 2004) IT-99-36-T.
Prosecutor v Radoslav Brđanin ICTY AC Judgement (3 April 2007) IT-99-36-A.
Prosecutor v Slobodan Milošević Decision on Review of Indictment and Application for Consequential Orders, Judge David Hunt (24 May 1999) IT-02-54.
Prosecutor v Stanišić & Župljanin ICTY TC Judgement (27 March 2013) IT-08-91-T.
Prosecutor v Stanišić & Župljanin ICTY AC Judgeement (30 June 2016) IT-08-91-A.
Prosecutor v Stanislav Galić ICTY TC Judgement and Opinion (5 December 2003) IT-98-29-T.
Prosecutor v Stanislav Galić ICTY AC Judgement (30 November 2006) IT-98-29-A.
Prosecutor v Vujadin Popović ICTY TC Judgement (10 June 2010) IT-05-88-T.
Prosecutor v Zdravko Mucic aka "Pavo", Hazim Delic, Esad Landzo aka "Zenga", Zejnil Delalic ICTY AC Judgement (20 February 2001) IT-96-21-A.
Prosecutor v Zdravko Mucic aka "Pavo", Hazim Delic, Esad Landzo aka "Zenga", Zejnil Delalic ICTY TC Judgement (26 November 1998) IT-96-21-T.

International Criminal Tribunal for Rwanda

Prosecutor v Alfred Musema ICTR AC Judgement (27 January 2002) ICTR-96-13-A.
Prosecutor v Clément Kayishema and Obed Ruzindana ICTR TC Judgement (21 May 1999) ICTR-95-1-T.
Prosecutor v Georges Anderson Nderubumwe Rutaganda ICTR TC Judgement (6 December 1999) ICTR-96-3-T.
Prosecutor v Jean-Paul Akayesu ICTR TC Judgement (2 September 1998) ICTR-96-4-T.
Sylvestre Gacumbitsi v The Prosecutor: ICTR ICTR AC Judgement (7 July 2006) ICTR-2001-64-A.

Bibliography

ICC and the Assembly of States Parties

Assembly of States Parties to the Rome Statute, Amendments to article 8 of the Rome Statute, 14 December 2017 ICC-ASP/16/Res.4.

Assembly of States Parties to the Rome Statute, Amendments to article 8 of the Rome Statute, 6 December 2019 ICC-ASP/18/Res.5.

Assembly of States Parties to the Rome Statute, Amendments to article 8 of the Rome Statute, 6 October 2010 RC/Res.5.

Decision on the Prosecution Request for a Ruling on Jurisdiction under Article 19(3) of the Statute PTC I (6 September 2018) ICC-RoC46(3)-01/18-37.

Decision Pursuant to Article 15 of the Rome Statute on the Authorisation of an Investigation into the Situation in the People's Republic of Bangladesh/Republic of the Union of Myanmar ICC PTC III (14 November 2019) ICC-01/19-27.

Prosecutor v Abdallah Banda Abakaer Nourain and Saleh Mohammed Jerbo Jamus ICC AC Judgement (11 November 2011) ICC-02/05-03/09 OA.

Prosecutor v Ali Muhammad Ali Abd-Al-Rahman ("Ali Kushayb") ICC AC Judgment on the appeal of Mr Abd-Al-Rahman against the Pre-Trial Chamber II's "Decision on the Defence 'Exception d'incompétence' (1 November 2021) ICC-02/05-01/20-503.

Prosecutor v Ali Muhammad Ali Abd-Al-Rahman ("Ali Kushayb") ICC PTC II Decision on the Defence 'Exception d'incompétence' (ICC-02/05/01/20-302) (17 May 2021) ICC-02/05-01/20-391.

Prosecutor v Blé Goudé ICC PTC Decision on the Confirmation of Charges (11 December 2014) ICC-02/11-02/11-186.

Prosecutor v Bosco Ntaganda ICC AC Judgment on the appeal of Mr Ntaganda against the "Second decision on the Defence's challenge to the jurisdiction of the Court in respect of Counts 6 and 9" (15 June 2017) ICC-01/04-02/06-1962.

Prosecutor v Bosco Ntaganda ICC AC Judgment on the appeals, Partly Concurring Opinion of Judge Eboe-Osujit (30 March 2021) ICC-01/04-02/06-2666-Anx5.

Prosecutor v Bosco Ntaganda ICC AC Judgment on the appeals, Separate Opinion of Judge Howard Morrison (30 March 2021) ICC-01/04-02/06-2666-Anx2.

Prosecutor v Bosco Ntaganda ICC AC Judgment on the appeals, Separate opinion of Judge Luz Del Carmen Ibáñez Carranza (30 March 2021) ICC-01/04-02/06-2666-Anx3.

Prosecutor v Bosco Ntaganda, ICC AC Judgment on the appeals of Mr Bosco Ntaganda and the Prosecutor against the decision of Trial Chamber VI of 8 July 2019 entitled 'Judgment' (30 March 2021) ICC-01/04-02/06-2666-Red.

Prosecutor v Bosco Ntaganda, ICC TC VI Judgment (8 July 2019) ICC-01/04-02/06-2359.

Prosecutor v Bosco Ntaganda, ICC TC VI Second decision on the Defence's challenge to the jurisdiction of the Court in respect of Counts 6 and 9 (4 January 2017) ICC-01/04-02/06-1707.

Prosecutor v Germain Katanga ICC TC II Judgment pursuant to Article 74 of the Statute (7 March 2014) ICC-01/04-01/07-3436-tENG.

Prosecutor v Germain Katanga ICC AC, Judgment on the appeal of Mr. Germain Katanga against the decision of Pre-Trial Chamber I entitled "Decision on the Defence Request Concerning Languages" (27 May 2008) ICC-01/04-01/07-522.

Prosecutor v Germain Katanga and Mathieu Ngudjolo Chui ICC PTC I Decision on the confirmation of charges (13 October 2008) ICC-01/04-01/07-717.

Prosecutor v Jean-Pierre Bemba Gombo ICC TC III Judgment pursuant to Article 74 of the Statute (21 March 2016) ICC-01/05-01/08-3343.

Prosecutor v Jean-Pierre Bemba Gombo et al ICC AC Judgment (8 March 2018) ICC-01/05-01/13-2275-Red.

Prosecutor v Mathieu Ngudjolo Chui ICC TC II Judgment pursuant to Article 74 of the Statute (18 December 2012) ICC-01/04-02/12-3-tENG.

Prosecutor v Mathieu Ngudjolo Chui Judgment pursuant to Article 74 of the Statute Concurring Opinion of Judge Christine Van den Wyngaert (18 December 2012) ICC-01/04-02/12-4.

Prosecutor v Omar Hassan Ahmad Al Bashir ICC PTC I Decision on the Prosecution's Application for a Warrant of Arrest (4 March 2009) ICC-02/05-01/09-3.

Prosecutor v Omar Hassan Ahmad Al Bashir ICC PTC I Decision Pursuant to Article 87(7) of the Rome Statute on the Failure by the Republic of Malawi to Comply with the Cooperation Requests Issued by the Court with Respect to the Arrest and Surrender of Omar Hassan Ahmad Al Bashir (13 December 2011) ICC-02/05-01/09-139-Corr.

Prosecutor v Omar Hassan Ahmad Al Bashir ICC PTC I Decision pursuant to article 87(7) of the Rome Statute on the refusal of the Republic of Chad to comply with the cooperation requests issued by the Court with respect to the arrest and surrender of Omar Hassan Ahmad Al Bashir (13 December 2011) ICC-02/05-01/09-140-tENG.

Prosecutor v Omar Hassan Ahmad Al Bashir ICC PTC II Decision on the Cooperation of the Democratic Republic of the Congo Regarding Omar Al Bashir's Arrest and Surrender to the Court (9 April 2014) ICC-02/05-01/09-195.

Prosecutor v Omar Hassan Ahmad Al-Bashir ICC PTC II Decision under article 87(7) of the Rome Statute on the non-compliance by South Africa with the request by the Court for the arrest and surrender of Omar Al-Bashir (6 July 2017) ICC-02/05-01/09-302.

Prosecutor v Omar Hassan Ahmad Al-Bashir ICC AC Judgment (6 May 2019) ICC-02/05-01/09 OA2.

Prosecutor v Omar Hassan Ahmad Al-Bashir ICC AC Joint Concurring Opinion of Judges Eboe-Osuji, Morrison, Hofmański and Bossa (6 May 2019) ICC-02/05-01/09-397-Anx1-Corr.

Prosecutor v Thomas Lubanga Dyilo ICC AC Judgment on the Appeal of Mr. Thomas Lubanga Dyilo against the Decision on the Defence Challenge to the Jurisdiction of the Court pursuant to article 19 (2) (a) of the Statute of 3 October 2006 (14 December 2006) ICC-01/04-01/06-772.

Prosecutor v Thomas Lubanga Dyilo ICC TC I Decision Regarding the Practices Used to Prepare and Familiarise Witnesses for Giving Testimony at Trial (30 November 2007) ICC-01/04-01/06-1049.

Prosecutor v Thomas Lubanga Dyilo ICC TC I Judgment pursuant to Article 74 of the Statute (14 March 2012) ICC-01/04-01/06-2842.

Prosecutor v Thomas Lubanga Dyilo ICC AC Judgment (1 December 2014) ICC-01/04-01/06-3121-Red.

Prosecutor v Thomas Lubanga Dyilo ICC TC II Judgment pursuant to Article 74 of the Statute, Concurring Opinion of Judge Christine Van den Wyngaert (20 December 2012) ICC-01/04-02/12-4.

Prosecutor v Thomas Lubanga Dyilo ICC TC I Judgment pursuant to Article 74 of the Statute, Separate Opinion of Judge Adrian Fulford (14 March 2012) ICC-01/04-01/06-2842.

Prosecutor v Thomas Lubanga Dyilo ICC PTC I Decision on the confirmation of charges (7 February 2007) ICC-01/04-01/06-803-tEN.

Prosecutor v William Samoei Ruto et al ICC PTC II Decision on the Confirmation of Charges Pursuant to Article 61(7)(a) and (b) of the Rome Statute (23 January 2012) ICC-01/09-01/11-373.

Situation in the Democratic Republic of Congo ICC AC Judgment on the Prosecutor's Application for Extraordinary Review of Pre-Trial Chamber

I's 31 March 2006 Decision Denying Leave to Appeal (13 July 2006) ICC-01/04-168.
Situation in the State of Palestine ICC PTC I Decision on the Prosecution request pursuant to article 19(3) for a ruling on the Court's territorial jurisdiction in Palestine (5 February 2021) ICC-01/18-143.
Situation in the State of Palestine ICC PTC I Decision on the Prosecution request pursuant to article 19(3) for a ruling on the Court's territorial jurisdiction in Palestine, Judge Péter Kovács, Partly Dissenting Opinion (5 February 2021) ICC-01/18-143-Anx1.

Extraordinary Chambers in the Courts of Cambodia

Decision on the Appeals against the Co-Investigating Judges Order on Joint Criminal Enterprise (JCE) ECCC (20 May 2010) D97/15/9.

Special Tribunal for Lebanon

Interlocutory Decision on the Applicable Law: Terrorism, Conspiracy, Homicide, Perpetration, Cumulative Charging STL AC (11 February 2011) STL-11-01/I/AC/R176bis.

Special Court Sierra Leone

Prosecutor v Charles Ghankay Taylor Special Court of Sierra Leone, AC Decision on Immunity from Jurisdiction (31 May 2004) SCSL-2003-01-I.
Prosecutor v Sam Hinga Norman SCSL AC Decision on Preliminary Motion Based on Lack of Jurisdiction (Child Recruitment) (31 May 2004) SCSL-2004-14-AR72(E).

Arbitration (ICSID, NAFTA, SCC, UNCITRAL)

ADF Group Inc v United States of America Award (9 January 2003) ICSID Case No. ARB (AF)/00/1.
Asian Agricultural Products Ltd v Republic of Sri Lanka Final Award (27 June 1990) ICSID Case No. ARB/87/3.

Azurix Corp v The Argentine Republic Award (14 July 2006) ICSID Case No. ARB/01/12.

Bernhard von Pezold and Others v Republic of Zimbabwe Award (28 July 2015) ICSID Case No. ARB/10/15.

CC/Devas and the Republic of India Decision on the Respondent's challenge to the Hon. Marc Lalonde as Presiding Arbitrator and Prof. Francisco Orrego Vicuña as Co-Arbitrator (30 September 2013) PCA Case No 2013-09.

Chemtura Corporation v Canada Award (2 August 2010) PCA Case No. 2008-01.

CMS Gas Transmission Company v Argentine Republic Award (12 May 2005) ICSID Case No. ARB/01/8.

CMS Gas Transmission Company v Argentine Republic Decision of the Ad Hoc Committee on the Application for Annulment of the Argentine Republic (25 September 2007) ICSID Case No. ARB/01/8.

Compana de Aguas del Aconquija SA and Vivendi Universal SA v Argentine Republic Award (20 August 2007) ICSID Case No. ARB/97/3.

Continental Casuality Company v Argentine Republic Award (5 September 2008) ICSID Case No. ARB/03/9.

Continental Casuality Company v Argentine Republic Decision on the Application for Annulment of the Argentine Republic (16 September 2011) ICSID Case No. ARB/03/9.

EDFI International SA, SAUR International SA and LEON Participaciones Argentinas SA v Argentine Republic Award (11 June 2012) ICSID Case No. ARB/03/23.

EDFI International SA, SAUR International SA and LEON Participaciones Argentinas SA v Argentine Republic Decision (5 February 2016) ICSID Case No. ARB/03/23.

El Paso Energy International Company v Argentina Award (31 October 2011) ICSID Case No ARB/03/15.

Enron Creditors Recovery Corp Ponderosa Assets, LP v Argentine Republic Award (22 May 2007) ICSID Case No. ARB/01/3.

Enron Creditors Recovery Corp Ponderosa Assets, LP v Argentine Republic Decision on the Application for Annulment of the Argentine Republic (30 July 2010) ICSID Case No. ARB/01/3.

Fireman's Fund Insurance Company v The United Mexican States Award (17 July 2006) ICSID Case No. ARB(AF)/02/1.

Glamis Gold, Ltd v The United States of America Award (8 June 2009) UNCITRAL/NAFTA 48 ILM 1038.

LG&E Energy Corp, et al v Argentine Republic Decision on Liability (3 October 2006) ICSID Case No. ARB/02/1.

Loewen Group, Inc and Raymond L Loewen v United States of America Award (26 June 2003) ICSID Case No. ARB(AF)/98/3.

Merrill & Ring Forestry LP v Canada Award (31 March 2010) ICSID Case No. UNCT/07/1.

Metalclad Corporation v The United Mexican States Award (30 August 2008) NAFTA ARB(AF)/97/1.

Methanex Corporation v United States of America Final Award of the Tribunal on Jurisdiction and Merits (3 August 2005) UNCITRAL/NAFTA, 44 ILM 1345.

Mondev International Ltd v United States of America Award (11 October 2002) ICSID Case No. ARB(AF)/99/2.

Occidental Exploration and Production Company v The Republic of Ecuador Final Award (1 July 2004) UNCITRAL LCIA Case No. UN3467.

Occidental Petroleum Corporation and Occidental Exploration and Production Company v The Republic of Ecuador Decision on Annulment of the Award (2 November 2015) ICSID Case No. ARB/06/11.

Pope & Talbot Inc v The Government of Canada Award on the merits of phase 2 (10 April 2001) UNCITRAL/NAFTA 7 ICSID Reports 102; 122 ILR 352.

Pope & Talbot Inc v The Government of Canada Award in respect of damages (31 May 2002) UNCITRAL/NAFTA 7 ICSID Reports 148, 126 ILR 131.

Quasar de Valors SICAV SA v Russian Federation Award (20 July 2012) SCC No. 24/2007.

Saipem SpA v The People's Republic of Bangladesh Decision on Jurisdiction and Recommendation on Provisional Measures (21 March 2007) ICSID Case No. ARB/05/07.

Saluka Investments BV v The Czech Republic Award (17 March 2006) UNCITRAL (1976) PCA Case No. 2001-04.

SD Myers, Inc v Government of Canada Partial Award (13 November 2000) UNCITRAL/NAFTA (2001) 40 ILM 1408.

Sempra Energy International v Argentine Republic Award (28 September 2007) ICSID Case No. ARB/02/16.

Sempra Energy International v Argentine Republic Decision on the Argentine Republic's Application for Annulment of the Award (29 June 2010) ICSID Case No. ARB/02/16.

Siemens AG v The Argentine Republic, Award (17 January 2007) ICSID Case No. ARB/02/8.

Bibliography

ST-AD GmbH v Republic of Bulgaria Award on Jurisdiction (18 July 2013) PCA Case No. 2011-06.

Técnicas Medioambientales Tecmed, SA v The United Mexican States Award (29 May 2003) ICSID Case No. ARB(AF)/00/2.

Total SA v The Argentine Republic Decision on Liability (27 December 2010) ICSID Case No ARB/04/01.

Waste Management, Inc v United Mexican States ("Number 2") Award (30 April 2004) ICSID Case No ARB(AF)/00/3.

William Ralph Clayton, William Richard Clayton, Douglas Clayton, Daniel Clayton and Bilcon of Delaware Inc v Government of Canada: Award on Jurisdiction and Liability (17 March 2015) UNCITRAL PCA Case No. 2009-04.

Further arbitration awards

Affaire du Neptune Great Britain v. U.S.A., Gr. Brit.-U.S. Arb. Trib. 1797 Recueil des arbitrages internationaux Tome 1 (de Lapradelle / Politis, Paris 1905) 137.

Antoine Fabiani Case France. v. Venezuela (31 July 1905) X RIAA 83.

B E Chattin United States v. United Mexican States (23 July 1927) IV RIAA 282.

BP Exploration Company (Libya) Limited v Government of the Libyan Arab Republic Lagergreen, Sole Arbitrator, Award (10 October 1973, 1 August 1974) 53 ILR 297.

Delimitation of the Continental Shelf between the United Kingdom of Great Britain and Northern Ireland, and the French Republic Court of Arbitration (Decisions of 30 June 1977 and 14 March 1978) XVIII RIAA 3.

Eastern Extension, Australasia and China Telegraph Company, Ltd Great Britain v. United States (9 November 1923) VI RIAA 112.

Eritrea-Ethiopia Claims Commission Eritrea's Claim 17, Partial Award: Prisoners of War (1 July 2003) XXVI RIAA 23.

F H Redward U.K. v. U.S.A, Gr. Brit.-U.S. Arb. Trib. (10 November 1925) VI RIAA 157.

Flegenheimer Case United States of America v. Italy, Italian-United States Conciliation Commission (20 September 1958) XIV RIAA 327.

Gentini Italy v. Venezuela, Award (1 July 1903) X RIAA 551.

George W Hopkins U.S.A. v. United Mexican States (31 March 1926) IV RIAA 41.

Georges Pinson case France v. United Mexican States (19 October 1928) V RIAA 327.

Harry Roberts U.S.A. v. United Mexican States, (2 November 1926) IV RIAA 77.

International Conference on the Former Yugoslavia Arbitration Commission Opinion No 13 (16 July 1993) 96 ILR 727.

Island of Palmas Case Netherlands v. U.S.A. (4 April 1928) II RIAA 829.

L F H Neer and Pauline Neer U.S.A. v. United Mexican States (15 October 1926) IV RIAA 60.

LIAMCO v The Government of the Libyan Arab Republic Sobhi Mahmassani, Sole Arbitrator, Award (12 April 1977) 20 ILM 1.

Norwegian shipowners' claims Norway v. USA (13 October 1922) I RIAA 307.

Petroleum Development (Trucial Coast) Ltd v Sheikh of Abu Dhabi Award of Lord Asquith of Bishopstone (September 1951) 1 ICLQ 247.

Robert E Brown U.S. v. U.K, Gr. Brit.-U.S. Arb. Trib. (23 November 1923) VI RIAA 120.

Russian Indemnities Case Russia v. Turkey (11 November 1912) XI RIAA 421.

Sapphire International Petroleums Ltd v National Iranian Oil Company Pierre Cavin, Sole Arbitrator, Award (15 March 1963) 35 ILR 136.

Saudi Arabia v Arabian American Oil Company Sausser-Hall Referee, Badawi/Hassan, Habachy Arbitrators, Award (23 August 1958) 27 ILR 117.

Texaco Overseas Petroleum Company and California Asiatic Oil Company v The Government of the Libyan Arab Republic Jean-Marie Dupuy, Sole Arbitrator, Awards on the Merits (19 January 1977) 53 ILR 420.

The Government of the State of Kuwait v The American Independent Oil Company Paul Reuter, Hamed Sultan, Sir Gerald Fitzmaurice, arbitrators, Award (14 March 1982) 21 ILM 976.

The Rhine Chlorides Arbitration concerning the Auditing of Accounts The Netherlands v. France, Award (12 May 2004) PCA Case No 2000-02.

Yuille Shortridge & Company Great Britain v. Portugal, (21 October 1861) XXIX RIAA 57.

Bibliography

GATT/WTO Dispute Settlement Body

EC - Measures Affecting the Approval and Marketing of Biotech Products Panel Report (6 February 2006) WT/DS291/R WT/DS292/R WT/DS293/R.
United States - Import Prohibition of Certain Shrimp and Shrimp Products Appellate Body (12 October 1998) AB-1998-4.

Human Rights Committee

General Comment No 20: Article 7 (Prohibition of Torture, or Other Cruel, Inhuman or Degrading Treatment or Punishment) Human Rights Committee E/C.12/GC/20 (10 March 1992).
General Comment No 24: Issues Relating to Reservations Made upon Ratification or Accession to the Covenant or the Optional Protocols thereto, or in Relation to Declarations under Article 41 of the Covenant Human Rights Committee CCPR/C/21/Rev.1/Add.6 (4 November 1994).
General Comment No 31: The Nature of the General Legal Obligation Imposed on States Parties to the Covenant Human Rights Committee CCPR/C/21/Rev.1/Add. 13 (26 May 2004).
General Comment No 36 on article 6 of the International Covenant on Civil and Political Rights, on the right to life Advanced unedited version Human Rights Committee CCPR/C/GC/36 (30 October 2018).
Report of the Human Rights Committee UN Doc A/50/40 (3 October 1995).

United Nations Materials

Historical Survey of the Question of International Criminal Jurisdiction Memorandum submitted by the Secretary-General (1949) UN Doc A/CN.4/7Rev.1.
Preparatory Study Concerning A Draft Declaration on the rights and Duties of States (Memorandum submitted by the Secretary-General) (15 December 1948) UN Doc A/CN.4/2.
Report of the Secretary-General Pursuant to Paragraph 2 of Security Council Resolution 808 (1993) (3 May 1993) UN Doc S/25704.
Report of the Secretary-General Pursuant to Paragraph 5 of Security Council Resolution 955(1994) (13 February 1995) UN Doc S/1995/134.

Report of the Sixth Committee (8 December 1950) UN Doc A/1639.

Survey of International Law in Relation to the Work of Codification of the International Law Commission: Preparatory work within the purview of article 18, paragraph 1, of the International Law Commission Memorandum submitted by the Secretary-General (10 February 1949) A/CN.4/1/Rev.1.

UNCTAD, *World Investment Report 2015* (2015) ⟨https://unctad.org/en/PublicationsLibrary/wir2015_en.pdf⟩ accessed 1 February 2023.

– *World Investment Report 2016* (2016) ⟨https://unctad.org/en/PublicationsLibrary/wir2016_en.pdf⟩ accessed 1 February 2023.

– *World Investment Report 2017* (2017) ⟨https://unctad.org/en/PublicationsLibrary/wir2017_en.pdf⟩ accessed 1 February 2023.

– *World Investment Report 2018* (2018) ⟨https://unctad.org/en/PublicationsLibrary/wir2018_en.pdf⟩ accessed 1 February 2023.

– *World Investment Report 2019* (2019) ⟨https://unctad.org/en/PublicationsLibrary/wir2019_en.pdf⟩ accessed 1 February 2023.

UNGA Res 94 (I) (11 December 1946) UN Doc A/RES/94(I).

UNGA Res 95 (I) (11 December 1946) UN Doc A/RES/95(I).

UNGA Res 96 (I) (11 December 1946) UN Doc A/RES/96 (I).

UNGA Res 174 (II) (21 November 1947) UN Doc A/RES/174(II).

UNGA Res 217 A (III) (10 December 1948) UN Doc A/RES/3/217 A.

UNGA Res 375 (IV) (6 December 1949) UN Doc A/RES/375(IV).

UNGA Res 799 (VIII) (7 December 1953) UN Doc A/RES/799 (VIII).

UNGA Res 898 (IX) (14 December 1954) UN Doc A/RES/898(IX).

UNGA Res 897 (IX) (4 December 1954) UN Doc A/RES/897(IX).

UNGA Res 1187 (XII) (11 December 1957) UN Doc A/RES/1187(XII).

UNGA Res 1186 (XII) (11 December 1957) UN Doc A/RES/1186(XII).

UNGA Res 1514 (XV) (14 December 1960) UN Doc A/Res/1514(XV).

UNGA Res 1721 (XVI) A (20 December 1961) UN Doc A/RES/1721(XVI)A-E.

UNGA Res 1803 (XVII) (14 December 1962) UN Doc A/RES/1803(XVII).

UNGA Res 1962 (XVIII) (13 December 1963) UN Doc A/RES/1962(XVIII).

UNGA Res 3314 (XXIX) (14 December 1974) UN Doc A/RES/3314 (XXIX).

UNGA Res 3201 (S-VI) (1 May 1974) UN Doc A/RES/3201(S-VI).

UNGA Res 3281 (XXIX) (12 December 1974) UN Doc A/RES/3281(XXIX).

UNGA Res 35/49 (4 December 1980) UN Doc A/RES/3549.

UNGA Res 36/106 (10 December 1981) UN Doc A/RES/36/106.

UNGA Res 56/83 (12 December 2001) UN Doc A/RES/56/83.

UNGA Res 73/203 (20 December 2018) UN Doc A/RES/73/203.

Bibliography

UNGA Res 73/202 (20 December 2018) UN Doc A/RES/73/202.
UNGA Res 74/180 (18 December 2019) UN Doc A/RES/74/180.
UNGA Res 77/103 (19 December 2022) UN Doc A/RES/77/103.
United Nations Basic Principles and Guidelines on Remedies and Procedures on the Right of Anyone Deprived of Their Liberty to Bring Proceedings Before a Court Report of the Working Group on Arbitrary Detention (6 July 2015) UN Doc A/HRC/30/37.
United Nations Conference on the Law of Treaties, First session Vienna, 26 March - 24 May 1968, Official Records (vol A/CONF.39/11, 1969).
United Nations Report of the Preparatory Committee on the Establishment of an International Criminal Court, Volume I, Proceedings of the Preparatory Committee during March-April and August 1996 (13 September 1996) UN Doc A/51/22.
UNSC Res 827/1993 (25 May 1993) UN Doc S/RES/827(1993).
UNSC Res 955/1994 (8 November 1994) UN Doc S/RES/955(1994).
UNSC Res 1593 (31 March 2005) UN Doc S/RES/1593(2005).
UNSC Res 1966 (22 December 2010) UN Doc S/RES/1966(2010).

ILC Materials

Article 24 of the Statute of the International Law Commission A Working Paper by Manley O Hudson 3 March 1950 UN Doc A/CN.4/16 + Add.1 24.
Comment by Georg Nolte, Summary record of the 3226th meeting, 17 July 2014 UN Doc A/CN.4/SR.3226 (PROV.)
Comment by Georg Nolte, Summary record of the 3274th meeting, 22 July 2015 UN Doc A/CN.4/SR.3274 (PROV.)
Comment by Judge Ronny Abraham, Summary record of the 3274th meeting, 22 July 2015 UN Doc A/CN.4/SR.3274 (PROV.)
Comment by Roman A Kolodkin, Summary record of the 3361st meeting, 19 May 2017 UN Doc A/CN.4/SR.3361 (PROV.)
Comment by Sean Murphy, Summary record of the 3362nd meeting, 23 May 2017 UN Doc A/CN.4/SR.3362 (PROV.)
Comment by Georg Nolte, Summary record of the 3365th meeting, 30 May 2017 UN Doc A/CN.4/SR.3365 (PROV.)
Comment by Georg Nolte, Summary record of the 3417th meeting, 2 July 2018 UN Doc A/CN.4/SR.3417 (PROV.)

Comment by Sean Murphy, Summary record of the 3587th meeting, 4 July 2022 UN Doc A/CN.4/SR.3587 (PROV.)
Comment by Shinya Murase, Summary record of the 3587th meeting, 4 July 2022 UN Doc A/CN.4/SR.3587 (PROV.)
Comment by Ki-Gab Park, Summary record of the 3588th meeting, 5 July 2022 UN Doc A/CN.4/SR.3588 (PROV.)
Comment by Mathias Forteau, Summary record of the 3588th meeting, 5 July 2022 UN Doc A/CN.4/SR.3588 (PROV.)
Comment by Sir Michael Wood, Summary record of the 3588th meeting, 5 July 2022 UN Doc A/CN.4/SR.3588 (PROV.)
Comment by Aniruddha Rajput, Summary record of the 3589th meeting, 6 July 2022 UN Doc A/CN.4/SR.3589 (PROV.)
Comment by August Reinisch, Summary record of the 3589th meeting, 6 July 2022 UN Doc A/CN.4/SR.3589 (PROV.)
Comment by Eduardo Valencia-Ospina, Summary record of the 3589th meeting, 6 July 2022 UN Doc A/CN.4/SR.3589 (PROV.)
Comment by Claudio Grossman Guiloff, Summary record of the 3590th meeting, 7 July 2022 UN Doc A/CN.4/SR.3590 (PROV.)
Comment by Huikang Huang, Summary record of the 3590th meeting, 7 July 2022 UN Doc A/CN.4/SR.3590 (PROV.)
Draft Articles on Responsibility of States for Internationally Wrongful Acts (ARSIWA) UN Doc A/56/10, Supplement no. 10.
Draft Articles on the Responsibility of International Organizations (ARIO) UN Doc A/66/10.
Eleventh report on the draft Code of Crimes against the Peace and Security of Mankind, by Mr Doudou Thiam, Special Rapporteur 25 March 1993 UN Doc A/CN.4/449.
Fifth State responsibility report by FV Garcia-Amador, Special Rapporteur 9 February 1960 UN Doc A/CN.4/125 and Corr. 1.
Fifth report by Sir Gerald Fitzmaurice, Special Rapporteur 21 March 1960 UN Doc A/CN.4/130.
Fifth report on immunity of State officials from foreign criminal jurisdiction, by Concepción Escobar Hernández, Special Rapporteur 14 June 2016 UN Doc A/CN.4/701.
First report on diplomatic protection, by Mr John R Dugard, Special Rapporteur 7 March and 20 April 2000 UN Doc A/CN.4/506 and Add. 1.
First report on formation and evidence of customary international law by Michael Wood, Special Rapporteur 17 May 2013 UN Doc A/CN.4/663.

Bibliography

First report on general principles of law by Marcelo Vázquez-Bermúdez, Special Rapporteur 5 April 2019 UN Doc A/CN.4/732.
Fourth Report on State Responsibility by Francisco V Garcia Amador, 26 February 1959 UN Doc A/CN.4/119.
Fourth report on State responsibility, by Mr Gaetano Arangio-Ruiz, Special Rapporteur 12 and 25 May and 1 and 17 June 1992 UN Doc A/CN.4/444 and Add.1-3.
Fourth report on State responsibility, by Mr James Crawford, Special Rapporteur 2 and 3 April 2001 UN Doc A/CN.4/517 and Add. 1.
Fragmentation of international law: difficulties arising from diversification and expansion of international law, Report of the Study Group of the International Law Commission, Finalized by Martti Koskenniemi 13 April 2006 UN Doc A/CN.4/L.682.
First report by Sir Gerald Fitzmaurice, Special Rapporteur 14 March 1956 UN Doc A/CN.4/101.
First report on subsequent agreements and subsequent practice in relation to treaty interpretation by Georg Nolte, Special Rapporteur 19 March 2013 UN Doc A/CN.4/660.
Guide to Practice on Reservations to Treaties ILC Ybk (2011 vol 2 part three).
ILC Ybk (1949).
ILC Ybk (1950 vol 1).
ILC Ybk (1950 vol 2).
ILC Ybk (1951 vol 1).
ILC Ybk (1951 vol 2).
ILC Ybk (1952 vol 1).
ILC Ybk (1955 vol 1).
ILC Ybk (1953 vol 2).
ILC Ybk (1956 vol 1).
ILC Ybk (1956 vol 2).
ILC Ybk (1957 vol 2).
ILC Ybk (1958 vol 1).
ILC Ybk (1958 vol 2).
ILC Ybk (1959 vol 1).
ILC Ybk (1959 vol 2).
ILC Ybk (1960 vol 1).
ILC Ybk (1960 vol 2).
ILC Ybk (1961 vol 1).
ILC Ybk (1961 vol 2).

ILC Ybk (1962 vol 2).
ILC Ybk (1963 vol 1).
ILC Ybk (1963 vol 2).
ILC Ybk (1964 vol 1).
ILC Ybk (1964 vol 2).
ILC Ybk (1966 vol 1 part 2).
ILC Ybk (1966 vol 2).
ILC Ybk (1968 vol 1).
ILC Ybk (1968 vol 2).
ILC Ybk (1969 vol 1).
ILC Ybk (1970 vol 1).
ILC Ybk (1971 vol 2).
ILC Ybk (1972 vol 1).
ILC Ybk (1974 vol 2 part 1).
ILC Ybk (1976 vol 1).
ILC Ybk (1977 vol 2 part 2).
ILC Ybk (1978 vol 1).
ILC Ybk (1980 vol 2 part 2).
ILC Ybk (1982 vol 2 part 1).
ILC Ybk (1992 vol 2 part 1).
ILC Ybk (1992 vol 2 part 2).
ILC Ybk (1993 vol 2 part 1).
ILC Ybk (1993 vol 2 part 2).
ILC Ybk (1994 vol 1).
ILC Ybk (1994 vol 2 part 2).
ILC Ybk (1996 vol 2 part 2).
ILC Ybk (1998 vol 2 part 1).
ILC Ybk (1999 vol 1).
ILC Ybk (1999 vol 2 part 1).
ILC Ybk (2000 vol 2 part 1).
ILC Ybk (2001 vol 2 part 1).
ILC Ybk (2001 vol 2 part 2).
ILC Ybk (2006 vol 2 part 2).
ILC Ybk (2013 vol 2 part 1).
ILC Ybk (2014 vol 1).
ILC Ybk (2014 vol 2 part 1).
ILC Ybk (2015 vol 1).
ILC Ybk (2015 vol 2 part 1).

International responsibility: report by F V Garcia Amador, Special Rapporteur 20 January 1956 UN Doc A/CN.4/96.

International responsibility: Second report by F V Garcia Amador, Special Rapporteur 15 February 1957 UN Doc A/CN.4/106.

International responsibility: Third report by F V Garcia Amador, Special Rapporteur 2 January 1958 UN Doc A/CN A/111.

Peremptory Norms of General International Law (Jus Cogens). Statement of the Chair of the Drafting Committee Mr Claudio Grossmann Guiloff of 31 May 2019 (2019) ⟨https://legal.un.org/ilc/documentation/english/statements/2019_dc_chairman_statement_jc.pdf⟩ accessed 1 February 2023.

Preliminary Report on Diplomatic Protection by Mr Mohamed Bennouna, Special Rapporteur 4 February 1998 UN Doc A/CN.4/484.

Provisional summary record of the 3378th meeting, 20 July 2017 UN Doc A/CN.4/SR.3378 (PROV.)

Report of the International Law Commission: Fifty-third session (23 April–1 June and 2 July–10 August 2001) UN Doc A/56/10.

Report of the International Law Commission: Seventy-third session (18 April–3 June and 4 July–5 August 2022) UN Doc A/77/10.

Report of the International Law Commission: Fifty-eighth session (1 May-9 June and 3 July-11 August 2006) UN Doc A/61/10.

Report of the International Law Commission: Sixty-third session (26 April-3 June and 4 July-2 August 2011) UN Doc A/66/10.

Report of the International Law Commission: Sixty-fifth session (6 May-7 June and 8 July-9 August 2013) UN Doc A/68/10.

Report of the International Law Commission: Sixty-sixth session (5 May–6 June and 7 July–8 August 2014) UN Doc A/69/10.

Report of the International Law Commission: Sixty-eighth session (2 May-10 June and 4 July-12 August 2016) UN Doc A/71/10.

Report of the International Law Commission: Sixty-ninth session (1 May-2 June and 3 July-4 August 2017) UN Doc A/72/10.

Report of the International Law Commission: Seventieth session (30 April-1 June and 2 July-10 August 2018) UN Doc A/73/10.

Report of the International Law Commission: Seventy-first session (29 April–7 June and 8 July–9 August 2019) UN Doc A/74/10.

Report of the International Law Commission: Seventy-second session (26 April–4 June and 5 July–6 August 2021) UN Doc A/76/10.

Report of the International Law Commission: Seventy-third session (18 April–3 June and 4 July–5 August 2022) UN Doc A/77/10.

Report of the International Law Commission: Seventy-fourth session (24 April–2 June and 3 July–4 August 2023) UN Doc A/78/10.

Second Report on the Regime of the High Seas by J P A François, Special Rapporteur 10 April 1951 UN Doc A/CN.4/42.

Second report on State responsibility, by Mr James Crawford, Special Rapporteur 17 March, 1 and 30 April, 19 July 1999 UN Doc A/CN.4/498 and Add.1-4.

Second report on subsequent agreements and subsequent practice in relation to the interpretation of treaties by Georg Nolte, Special Rapporteur 26 March 2014 UN Doc A/CN.4/671.

Second report on identification of customary international law by Michael Wood, Special Rapporteur 22 May 2014 UN Doc A/CN.4/672.

Second report on jus cogens by Dire Tladi, Special Rapporteur 16 March 2017 UN Doc A/CN.4/706.

Second report on general principles of law by Marcelo Vázquez-Bermúdez, Special Rapporteur 9 April 2020 UN Doc A/CN.4/741.

Sixth Report on the Law of Treaties, by Sir Humphrey Waldock, Special Rapporteur 11 March, 25 March, 12 April, 11 May, 17 May, 24 May, 1 June and 14 June 1966 UN Doc A/CN.4/186 and Add.1-7.

Statement of the Chairman of the Drafting Committee, Mr. Gilberto Saboia of 7 August 2014 ⟨https://legal.un.org/ilc/sessions/66/pdfs/english/dc_chairman_statement_identification_of_custom.pdf⟩ accessed 1 February 2023.

Statement of the Chairman of the Drafting Committee, Mr. Ki Gab Park of 29 July 2022 ⟨https://legal.un.org/ilc/documentation/english/statements/2022_dc_chair_statement_gpl.pdf⟩ accessed 1 February 2023.

Third Report on the Law of Treaties, by Sir Humphrey Waldock, Special Rapporteur 3 March, 9 June, 12 June and 7 July 1964 UN Doc A/CN.4/167 and Add.1-3.

Third report on the content, forms and degrees of international responsibility (part 2 of the draft articles), by Mr Willem Riphagen, Special Rapporteur 12 and 30 March and 5 May 1982 UN Doc A/CN.4/354 and Add. 1 and 2.

Third report on State responsibility, by Mr James Crawford, Special Rapporteur 15 March, 15 June, 10 and 18 July and 4 August 2000 UN Doc A/CN.4/507 and Add. 1–4.

Third report on identification of customary international law by Michael Wood, Special Rapporteur 27 March 2015 UN Doc A/CN.4/682.

Third report on peremptory norms of general international law (jus cogens) by Dire Tladi, Special Rapporteur 12 February 2018 UN Doc A/CN.4/714.

Bibliography

Third report on general principles of law by Marcelo Vázquez-Bermúdez, Special Rapporteur 18 April 2022 UN Doc A/CN.4/753.

United Kingdom

A and others v Secretary of State for the Home Department House of Lords [2005] UKHL 71.
Abd Ali Hameed Al-Waheed v Ministry of Defence and Serdar Mohammed v Ministry of Defence UKSC [2017] UKSC 2.
Al-Saadoon and Others v Secretary of State for Defence England and Wales High Court of Justice, QB [2015] EWHC 715.
Al-Saadoon and Others v Secretary of State for Defence, and Rahmatullah & ANR v The Secretary of State for Defence England and Wales Court of Appeal, QB [2016] EWCA Civ 811.
Attorney General v Nissan House of Lords [1969] UKHL 3.
Benkharbouche (Respondent) v Secretary of State for Foreign and Commonwealth Affairs (Appellant) and Secretary of State for Foreign and Commonwealth Affairs and Libya (Appellants) v Janah (Respondent) UKSC [2017] UKSC 62.
Benkharbouche & Janah v Embassy of the Republic of Sudan England and Wales Court of Appeal, QB [2015] EWCA Civ 33.
Her Majesty's Treasury (Respondent) v Mohammed Jabar Ahmed and others (FC) (Appellants) Her Majesty's Treasury (Respondent) v Mohammed al-Ghabra (FC) (Appellant) R (on the application of Hani El Sayed Sabaei Youssef) (Respondent) v Her Majesty's Treasury (Appellant) UKSC [2010] UKSC 2.
Holland v Lampen-Wolfe House of Lords [2000] UKHL 40.
Johnson v Unisys Limited House of Lords [2001] UKHL 13.
Jones v Ministry of Interior Al-Mamlaka Al-Arabiya AS Saudiya (the Kingdom of Saudi Arabia) and others House of Lords [2006] UKHL 26.
Kennedy v Charity Commission UKSC [2014] UKSC 20.
Mohammed (Serdar) v Ministry of Defence, Qasim v Secretary of State for Defence, Rahmatullah v Ministry of Defence, Iraqi Civilians v Ministry of Defence UK Court of Appeal [2015] EWCA Civ 843.
Montgomery v Lanarkshire Health Board UKSC [2015] UKSC 11.
Osborn v The Parole Board, Booth v The Parole Board In the matter of an application of James Clyde Reilly for Judicial Review (Northern Ireland) UKSC [2013] UKSC 61.

R (Daly) v Secretary of State for the Home Department House of Lords [2001] UKHL 26.
R (Guardian News and Media Ltd) v City of Westminster Magistrates' Court (Article 19 intervening) England and Wales Court of Appeal, QB [2013] QB 618.
R (on the application of Faulkner) v Secretary of State for Justice and others UKSC [2013] UKSC 23.
Rahmatullah v Ministry of Defence and another, Mohammed and others v Ministry of Defence and another UKSC [2017] UKSC 1.
Regina v Parole Board ex parte Smith, Regina v Parole Board ex parte West House of Lords [2005] UKHL 1.
Regina v The Secretary of State for the Home Department ex Parte Mark Francis Leech) England and Wales Court of Appeal [1993] EWCA Civ 12.
Thomas Bonham v College of Physicians Court of Common Pleas (1610) 77 Eng. Rep. 638.
Watkins v Home Office House of Lords [2006] UKHL 17.

USA

Erie Railroad Company v Tompkins SCOTUS 304 U.S. 64.
Van Beeck v Sabine Towing Co SCOTUS 300 U.S. 342.

South Africa

In the matter between Democratic Alliance and Minister of International Relations and Cooperation et al High Court of South Africa (Gauteng Division, Pretoria) (22 February 2017) Case No 83145/2016.
Southern Africa Litigation Centre v Minister of Justice And Constitutional Development and Others High Court of South Africa (Gauteng Division, Pretoria) (26 June 2015) (27740/2015) [2015] ZAGPPHC 402.
The Minister of Justice and Constitutional Development v The Southern African Litigation Centre Supreme Court of Appeal of South Africa (15 March 2016) (867/15) [2016] ZASCA 17.

Bibliography

Israel

Attorney General v Adolf Eichmann District Court of Israel, Criminal Case No. 40/61 36 ILR 236-237.

France

Judgment of 13 January 2021 French Court of Cassation, Criminal Division Appeal No. 20-80.511.

Germany

Judgment of 28 January 2021 Bundesgerichtshof 3 StR 564/19.

Websites

ICC, 'Q&A Regarding Appeals Chamber's 6 May 2019 Judgment in the Jordan Referral Re Al-Bashir Appeal, ICC-PIOS-Q&A-SUD-02-01/19_Eng' ⟨https://www.icc-cpi.int/itemsDocuments/190515-al-bashir-qa-eng.pdf⟩ accessed 1 February 2023.

ICJ, 'Allegations of Genocide under the Convention on the Prevention and Punishment of the Crime of Genocide (Ukraine v. Russian Federation) - Latest Developments' ⟨https://www.icj-cij.org/en/case/182⟩ accessed 1 February 2023.

– 'Declarations recognizing the jurisdiction of the Court as compulsory' ⟨https://www.icj-cij.org/en/declarations⟩ accessed 1 February 2023.

– 'Request for an Examination of the Situation in Accordance with Paragraph 63 of the Court's Judgment of 20 December 1974 in the Nuclear Tests (New Zealand v. France) Case - Intervention' ⟨https://www.icj-cij.org/en/case/97/intervention⟩ accessed 1 February 2023.

– 'Rules of the Court (1978) Adopted on 14 April 1978 and entered into force on 1 July 1978' ⟨https://www.icj-cij.org/en/rules⟩ accessed 1 February 2023.

Just Security, 'U.N. General Assembly and International Criminal Tribunal for the Crime of Aggression Against Ukraine' ⟨https://www.justsecurity.

org/tag/u-n-general-assembly-and-international-criminal-tribunal-for-aggression-against-ukraine/⟩ accessed 1 February 2023.

UNCTAD, 'International Investment Agreements Navigator' ⟨https://investmentpolicy.unctad.org/international-investment-agreements⟩ accessed 1 February 2023.

International Factfinding Reports

Tagliavini, Heidi, Independent International Fact-Finding Mission on the Conflict in Georgia Vol I (2009) ⟨https://www.mpil.de/files/pdf4/IIFFMCG_Volume_I2.pdf⟩ accessed 1 February 2023.
– Independent International Fact-Finding Mission on the Conflict in Georgia Vol II (2009) ⟨https://www.mpil.de/files/pdf4/IIFFMCG_Volume_II1.pdf⟩ accessed 1 February 2023.

Amicus Curiae Briefs

Written observations of Professor Claus Kreß as amicus curiae with the assistance of Ms Erin Pobjie 2018 June 2018 ICC-02/05-01/09-359.

Miscellaneous

Council of Europe, 'References to the notion of the "general principles of law recognised by the civilised nations" as contained in the travaux préparatoires of the Convention' [1974] CDH (74) 37 ⟨https://www.echr.coe.int/LibraryDocs/Travaux/ECHRTravaux-PGD-CDH(74)37-BIL1678846.pdf⟩ accessed 1 February 2023.

de Serpa Soares, Miguel, 'Seven Women in Seventy Years: A Roundtable Discussion on Achieving Gender Parity at the International Law Commission' [2018] United Nations Office of Legal Affairs ⟨https://legal.un.org/ola/media/info_from_lc/mss/speeches/MSS_ILC70_gender_side_event-24-May-2018.pdf⟩ accessed 1 February 2023.

Documents of the United Nations Conference on International Organization, San Francisco, 1945 Vol XIII (United Nations Information Organizations 1945).

Entwurf eines bürgerlichen Gesetzbuches für das deutsche Reich: Erste Lesung: ausgearb. durch die von dem Bundesrathe berufene Kommission (Guttentag 1888).

European Parliament resolution of 6 April 2011 on the future European international investment policy (first published 2011, 2012/C 296 E/05, 2011).

Final Record of the Diplomatic Conference of Geneva of 1949 (vol II-B, Federal Political Department).

ILA, *Statement of Principles Applicable to the Formation of General Customary International Law* (London, 2000) ⟨https://www.ila-hq.org/en_GB/documents/conference-report-london-2000-2⟩ accessed 1 February 2023.

League of Nations Committee of Experts for the Progressive Codification of International Law, 'Annex to Questionnaire No. 4. Report of the Sub-Committee. M. Guerrero, Rapporteur, Mr. Wang Chung-Hui' [1927] printed in (1926) 20 AJIL Supp 177–203.

– 'Report to the Council of the League of Nations on the Questions which appear ripe for international regulation' C.196.M.70.1927.V., printed in (1928) 22 AJIL Supp 4.

Ministry of Defence, United Kingdom, *The manual of the law of armed conflict* (Oxford University Press 2004).

Notes of Interpretation of Certain Chapter 11 Provisions NAFTA Free Trade Commission (31 July 2001) 6 ICSID Rep. 567.

OECD Draft Convention on the Protection of Foreign Property (1967, not open to signature) (1968) 7 ILM 117–143.

Permanent Court of International Justice – Advisory Committee of Jurists, *Documents presented to the Committee relating to existing plans for the establishment of a Permanent Court of International Justice* (1920) ⟨https://www.icj-cij.org/files/permanent-court-of-international-justice/serie_D/D_documents_to_comm_existing_plans.pdf⟩ accessed 1 February 2023.

– *Procès-Verbaux of the Proceedings of the Committee, June 16th-July 24th 1920* (Van Langenhuysen Brothers 1920).

United Nations, *The Work of the International Law Commission Volume I* (9th edn, 2017) ⟨https : / / www . un - ilibrary.org/content/books/9789210609203⟩ accessed 1 February 2023.

United States of America, *Proclamation 2667 of September 28, 1945. Policy of the United States with respect to the natural resources of the subsoil and sea bed of the continental shelf, 10 Fed. Reg. 12.305 (1945)*.

US Department of Defense, *Law of War Manual June 2015 (Updated December 2016)* (Washington, D.C., 2016).

Index

Article 38
    Doctrinal Context, 157
    Drafting, 170
        Discussions of the Advisory Committee of Jurists, 171
        Governmental Drafts, 170
    Institutional context
        Hague Conferences, 164
    interrelationship
        Interwar scholarship, 186
    Interwar Discussion
        1930 Codification Conference, 182
        Permanent Court of International Justice, 178

Codification
    1930 Conference, 182
    International Law Commission, 317
Comparative Historical Perspectives
    Common Law, 103
        Recent UK Jurisprudence, 120
        UK History, 105
        US History, 113
    General Principles, 138
        History, 138
        Overview from the perspective of legal theory, 140

German law
    customary law, 126
European Convention on Human Rights
    General International Law
        Attribution, 446, 448, 451
        Attribution, International Organizations, 456
        Attribution, International Organizations, United Nations, 458
        Interpretation, 408, 414
        Jurisdiction, 443
        Prohibition of Arbitrariness, 438
        International Humanitarian Law, 438
        Security Council Resolutions, 441
    Proportionality
        Customary International Law, 426, 429, 432
        Other Treaties, 436

International Court of Justice
    Convergence
        Law of the Sea, 290
        Prohibition of the Use of Force, 289
        Self-determination, 285
    craft
        scoping, 277
    Interrelationship

INDEX

General Principles, 305
General principles based on municipal law, 306
General Principles of the International Legal Order, 310
General Principles of the International Legal Order as bridge between treaties and custom, 310
Relationship between Treaty and Custom, 278, 280
interrelationship
  Judicial Policy, 252
  normative environment, 258
Intervention, 223
  Customary International Law, 231
  General Scheme, 224
  Less restrictive Approach, 229
  Restrictive Approach, 226
Jurisdiction
  General Part, 240
  General Scheme, 235
  Substantive Law, 245
  Succession, 242
International Criminal Law
  ICTY, 476
    Customary International Law, 476, 485, 487, 497, 502, 528
    General Principles, 493, 502, 504, 505
    Indirect Perpetratorship, 531

Joint Criminal Enterprise, 526, 528, 532
Legal Craft, 497
Legal craft, 499, 501
Tadic, 491
Rome Statute
  Al-Bashir, 546
  Article 21, 509
  Article 25, 526, 534
  Control Theory, 534, 538
  Immunity, 546
  Indirect Perpetratorship, 534, 538
  Interrelationship of Sources, 509
International Investment Law
  Bilateral Investment Treaties, 579
  Relationship with Customary International Law, 595
  Relationship with Customary International Law, Convergence, 592
  Relationship with Customary International Law, international minimum standard, 582, 585
  Relationship with Customary International Law, Necessity, 613
  Scholarship, 595
Codification, 182
Distinction between Primary rules and Secondary Rules, 616

General law
  Multilateralization, 599
  History, 558, 562, 577
    Contracts,
      Internationalized,
      Delocalized, 571
    Equal Treatment, 564
    International Minimum
      Standard, 564
    Neer Case, 567
  Multilateralism, 578, 591
International Law Commission,
  317
  codification
    form, 338
    gapfilling, 321
    history, 317
    normative environment,
      325

progressive development,
  320, 321
specific projects, 354
  Customary International
    Law, 372
  Fragmentation, 368
  General Principles of Law,
    384
  Jus Cogens, 378
  The Law of
    Responsibility, 364
  The Law of Treaties, 355

Spontaneous norms, 639

Verfassungsgewohnheitsrecht,
  137
Verfassungswandlung, 134